Computer and Controversy

Value Conflicts and Social Choices

Computerization
· and ·
Controversy

Value Conflicts and Social Choices

Edited by

Charles Dunlop

Department of Philosophy
University of Michigan, Flint

Rob Kling

Department of Information and Computer Science
University of California, Irvine

ACADEMIC PRESS, INC.
Harcourt Brace Jovanovich, Publishers
Boston   San Diego   New York
London   Sydney   Tokyo   Toronto

This book is printed on acid-free paper. ∞

Copyright © 1991 by Academic Press, Inc.
All rights reserved.
No part of this publication may be reproduced or
transmitted in any form or by any means, electronic
or mechanical, including photocopy, recording, or
any information storage and retrieval system, without
permission in writing from the publisher.

Designed by Elizabeth E. Tustian.

ACADEMIC PRESS, INC.
1250 Sixth Avenue, San Diego, CA 92101–4311

United Kingdom Edition published by
ACADEMIC PRESS LIMITED
24–28 Oval Road, London NW1 7DX

Library of Congress Cataloging-in-Publication Data:

Computerization and controversy: value conflicts and social choices/
    edited by Charles Dunlop, Rob Kling.
        p.   cm.
    Includes bibliographical references and index.
    ISBN 0-12-224356-0 (alk. paper: paperback)
    1. Computers and civilization.   I. Dunlop, Charles.   II. Kling,
Rob.
QA76.9.C66C6377   1991
303.48'34—dc20   90-19415
                         CIP

Printed in the United States of America

93 94 MV 9 8 7 6 5 4

To Our Parents
Ralph and Mary Helen Dunlop
Louis and Helen Kling

· Contents ·

vii

P·A·R·T· II
Economic and Organizational Dimensions of Computerization

P·A·R·T· III
Computerization and the Transformation of Work

P·A·R·T· IV
Social Relationships in Electronic Communities

P·A·R·T· V
Social Control and Privacy

P·A·R·T· VI
Security and Reliability

P·A·R·T· VII
Ethical Perspectives and Professional Responsibilities

· Preface ·

Computer systems comprise one of the most distinctive and complex technologies of the late 20th century. In a short span of time, these systems have become ubiquitous. Many of our transactions with organizations are mediated by computer systems, as is reflected in bills, payments, and record-keeping. Commercial jets and advanced weapons systems depend upon sophisticated, computerized navigation systems. Interactive computer systems have become standard equipment in many professions, from the sciences to journalism, and are increasingly appearing in schools at all levels. The meteoric spread of computerization has spawned a large industry that is beginning to rival the automobile industry in importance.

Typically, discussions of rapidly improving computer equipment (and its rapid adoption in organizations and professions) are accompanied by excitement and by high hopes for social and economic improvement. Moreover, the public discussion about computers, as reflected in professional journals and popular media, is generally upbeat. To be sure, there are occasional observations about "computer screwups" that lead to massive billing errors,[1] a blackout of telephone services,[2] or the short-term tragedy of a hapless person who learns when she applies for Social Security that her records show her to be deceased (Kiger, 1987). But situations like these are usually treated as idiosyncratic: amusing for bystanders, they will soon be fixed for those who have been harmed or inconvenienced.

We have produced this book because we see the world of computerization in radically

---

[1] In the Fall of 1989, for example, 41,000 Parisians received letters accusing them of various crimes (murder, prostitution, drug-dealing, etc.) and demanding the payment of a small fine. The addressees should have received letters reminding them of unpaid traffic tickets, but apparently the codes for traffic offenses got mixed up with the codes used for other illegal activities. Officials issued 41,000 letters of apology. (*RISKS FORUM-Digest*, 9 (22); also, *The Guardian*, September 6, 1989.)

[2] A major telephone blackout occurred on January 15, 1990, when a software flaw in AT&T's long-distance switching system caused serious degradation of the company's long-distance service for approximately nine hours. For a popular media account of this event, see the *Newsweek* article, "Can We Trust Our Software" (January 29, 1990, pp. 70–73); more technical discussion may be found in *RISKS FORUM-Digest*, 9 (63, 64, 66, 67).

different terms. We see computer systems not only as powerful technology, but also as a powerful factor in social change. Various groups advance visions of computerization in many settings, from workplaces to the networking of nationwide financial operations. Their visions are designed to serve particular interests and sometimes to restructure parts of society (albeit not always in ways that are anticipated). Since computerization usually requires that social practices be altered (and may even facilitate altering them), it is a subtle but important catalyst for social transformation. While there has been far too much hype about the "computer revolution," it is important to understand how computer systems are becoming a pervasive element of organizations and how they affect the way in which people deal with those organizations. Furthermore, many of the opportunities and dilemmas of computerization are systematically connected, even though the key issues are often separated in writings that emphasize either hope or doom.

In our General Introduction, we will explore various ways in which the spread of the automobile in the United States provides a provocative analogy for understanding computerization. Cars have transformed urban America, enabling us to be a much more mobile nation and to live in larger lifescapes. At the same time, cars congest our cities, dirty our air, kill thousands of people annually, and consume immense amounts of space, fuel and money. To understand the role of automobiles in altering society, we must examine whole transportation systems, not just individual components like this year's hottest high-performance car. While some of the problems engendered by the automobile can be reduced by technological improvements, many others cannot be reduced without a substantial reorganization of cities, suburbs, and the lifestyles of millions of people. Cars and computers are both devices that have been parts of large-scale social changes. Their advantages and disadvantages often show up only in social contexts (the high-performance car can't drive fast in a large city or far in a city with dirt roads and no gas stations; a car may be an advantage in New York's suburbs but a liability in downtown Manhattan). With cars so firmly entrenched in our social fabric, many of the associated social choices are now limited. But in the case of computers and the organizational systems built around them, important social options are *still* open.

We have found that many students, professionals, managers, and laypersons are hungry for honest, probing discussions of the opportunities and problems of computerization. This book introduces some of the major social controversies about the computerization of society. It also highlights some of the key value conflicts and social choices about computerization. It aims at helping readers to recognize some of the social processes that drive and shape computerization and to identify some of its paradoxes and ironies.[3]

Many books and articles about computerization focus on emerging or future tech-

---

[3] One simple irony of the microcomputing industry is that IBM, which has been accused of monopoly practices in the mainframe business, has spawned a dynamic industry of firms that make IBM clones and compatible equipment. It is arguable that microcomputers spread rapidly in the 1980s because of the price drops and technological improvements fostered by this competitive environment. In contrast, the Apple Computer Corporation, which positions itself as the computer company for the rest of use, has a monopoly on the architecture of its microcomputers. Apple has blocked the development and marketing of Mac clones. Another example is the way in which laser printers have become major fixtures in the development of the "paperless office." Deeper ironies come from the way that computers are often portrayed as an instrument of rationality but can be the focus of nonrational management and problematic social practices.

nologies, such as computers that recognize speech, rely on writing tablets rather than keyboards, or pack the power of a Mac II or '486 PC into a pocket-sized notebook (Moravec, 1988). Other writings focus on social practices that depend upon major advances in computing—e.g., a cashless society or one in which children get expert instruction at home through exceptionally high-quality educational software. During the 1990s we expect to see an endless stream of publications that emphasize the potential of 21st-century computer technologies to alter our social worlds. We share a concern with the quality of life, and our interest in novel technologies reaches well past the year 2000. But we expect that most of these books and articles are likely to characterize computerization and social change inaccurately.

For two main reasons, we focus primarily on the present and near future. First, many people do not understand how and why individuals and organizations computerize today. Since computerization involves a great deal of human behavior, future speculations are useless if they cannot account for contemporary behavior except in technological terms (e.g., by claiming that most people won't feel comfortable with computerized systems until they interact with spoken language). This important point is easily obscured by the steady march of technological innovation. For example, an IBM PC clone with a 80286 processor, or an Apple Macintosh II, computes as fast as a large room-sized IBM mainframe of the late 1960s. Today's microcomputers are much cheaper, can fit on a desk, and are used by millions of people for activities that were very rarely carried out on computers in the late 1960s (e.g., text processing, spreadsheets, and computer-assisted graphic design). Widely available desktop computing was a future scenario of the 1970s. Yet, impressive though these technological facts are, they do not provide an immediate route to accurate social analysis. Many visionaries have argued that broad access to desktop computing will empower workers, make organizations more flexible, and make work less deadening for many employees in routine jobs. Other visionaries see the extensive computerization of work as an occasion for imposing rigid assembly-line disciplines in offices — disempowering workers, fragmenting jobs, reducing skill levels, and increasing the number of deadening jobs. These are important yet *conflicting* predictions that are worth understanding. Nevertheless, we would be dismissing many important insights about how information technologies are shaped by their adopters and how they do (and do not) change social practices if we assumed that computerization would not really effect important changes until even more advanced (21st-century) technologies were widely available.

Our second reason for focusing on computerization in the present and near future is that people and organizations *today* are making social choices about how to organize with computerized systems — systems that can alter social life as powerfully as automobiles had altered social life by the 1950s. Our analogy between computers and automobiles will suggest that major social choices are made when a technology, even one that is relatively crude in its early phases, is widely deployed. For example, the legal regulations supporting debit cards give consumers much less protection in cases of theft, loss, or error than do the corresponding regulations for credit cards or checks. Computerization presents many important social choices to be made now, and some of them will restrict our social options in the 21st century.

Because of constraints on length, we have not addressed all the topics that we would like to have covered in this book.[4] To economize on space, we have incorporated some themes, especially those of gender and systems design, into sections with other major themes (e.g., work), instead of providing them with their own special sections. And since many of our topics are interrelated, we have often discussed articles from one section in our introductions to other sections. In our various introductory essays, we have also discussed many books and articles beyond those which we have collected here, our aim being to help link key ideas to a larger literature about the social issues of computerization.

Some of our topics have large literatures; others have small literatures. For example, there are many studies of computerization in the contexts of work, future educational opportunities, and privacy, but there are relatively few studies of the health effects of computing, the risks to the public from unreliable computer systems, or the current roles of instructional computing systems in schools. Moreover, the literatures are diffuse. Key articles are published in the professional journals of computer scientists, philosophers, sociologists, political scientists, educators, lawyers, and managers, as well as in popular magazines.

We have collected articles from diverse sources that might not be readily accessible in many libraries. In addition, we have included several articles that were written especially for this book. While our selections are eclectic, the majority of our articles emphasize social science approaches to understanding computerization, rather than approaches anchored in futures studies, technological forecasting, or fiction.[5] We see computerization as comprising a set of social phenomena, and we believe that the social sciences offer a uniquely important vantage point from which to understand them.

We have tried to select readings that would be intelligible to people without an advanced background in any specific academic discipline, although our introductory essays have often drawn upon, and interpreted, more sophisticated and technical studies. (We have also provided references to such studies for readers who want to pursue specific topics in greater depth.) Our introductions provide definitions of terms that may be unfamiliar but whose meaning is presupposed in a selection. We recommend that you read the footnotes — in both our introductions and our selected articles — because they often contain important supplementary ideas.

---

[4] For example, we have omitted a section on computerization in the military and war, because the topic is well covered in the book edited by Bellin and Chapman (1987). In order to allow adequate space for other topics, we have excised a section on computers in schooling and another on ways in which computer-based systems alter organizational decisions. For simplicity, our book is focused on the United States. Many of the major controversies are also salient in other industrialized countries, although their legal systems, social traditions, and industrial structures alter the details of key social choices. We have virtually ignored controversies of computerization that are pertinent to developing countries (e.g., dependency on complex technologies and first-world suppliers; social stratification and urban–rural economies). And we have not discussed the ways in which computer modeling of complex social phenomena (e.g., population change or economic systems) can have a drastic impact on social policy choices.

[5] Short-stories, plays, and novels can, of course, play an important role in helping us understand the ways in which new technologies can alter social life. For example, George Orwell's novel *1984* helped many people understand how a politically repressive regime could use information technologies to retain power. And it put terms like "Big Brother" and "newspeak" into everyday language. But we have attempted to focus the central debates by staying within a single genre.

In choosing our articles, our aim has been to help articulate different sides of key debates and to stimulate further inquiry. Only a small fraction of authors carefully identify major alternative positions in the controversies about which they take sides. We could have saved ourselves a great deal of labor by "letting the articles speak for themselves." Instead, we have attempted to make the key controversies much more accessible through integrative introductions to each section and through leads to related books and articles. Since the literature on computerization is large and widely scattered, we hope that our suggestions for further reading will help readers find useful lines of inquiry and to discover authors and publications that might otherwise have passed unnoticed.

Each of this book's major sections contains an introduction designed to help frame the debates about a topic. We explain how the section's articles relate to the larger literature about computerization and to each other. We also try briefly to create a social context that amplifies the meanings of the selections. At various points, we comment critically on some of the selections, in order to help readers better understand the key assumptions. We have endeavored to be fair but not bland.

We bring our own point of view to these issues, through both our selection of readings and the content of our introductory essays. We are neither indifferent nor always neutral. We like using certain computer-based systems for our own work, especially for writing, organizing records, and communicating via electronic mail. But we also see that computing has inherent social and political dimensions. Organizing themes, such as individual choice, efficiency, productivity, convenience, and aesthetic preference are inadequate for understanding the opportunities, limitations, and potential social problems of computerization, just as they fail to provide adequate illumination of the role of cars in urban America. Since computing requires resources for its acquisition, development, maintenance, and effective use, it has social implications not just in its consequences, but at every stage (Kling and Scacchi, 1982). The cost and complexity of advanced computing systems tends to give special advantage to already powerful groups in shaping their use and in turning them to further advancement of group interests. However, we do not believe that intentions — whether those of individuals, designers, or managers — are good predictors of large-scale social activity. Collective action, including computerization, develops with some non-obvious types of logic.

This is our view, but other analysts see computerization in different terms. Accordingly, the readings presented here include some positions we support and others with which we strongly differ. Above all, we believe that debates about the *social* issues surrounding computerization have not received due attention. Professionals and managers of all kinds, including computer specialists, often take sides through their actions without adequately comprehending the debates and supporting argumentation. We hope that this book will promote a deeper understanding of computerization's key social dimensions and provide a basis for thoughtful and responsible social choices.

Acknowledgments

Many people helped us think through the ideas in this book, refine our analytical introductions, and identify useful articles. We especially wish to thank Anita Barry, Werner Beuschel, Andrew Clement, Peter Denning, Holly Hildreth, Tom Jewett, Nancy Leveson, Ted Morris, Karen Ruhleder, Leigh Star, Greg Trianosky, Linda Weiner, Karen Wieckert, and Terry Winograd. We appreciate their help in developing a much stronger book. Sari Kalin, our editor at Academic Press, helped immensely with advice, resourcefulness, enthusiasm, and commitment.

References

Bellin, David and Gary Chapman (eds.) (1987). *Computers in Battle: Will They Work?*. Boston: Harcourt, Brace, Jovanovich, Boston, Mass.

Kiger, Patrick J. (1987). "Woman Buried by Bills as Social Security Declares Her Dead," *Orange County Register*. (November 27), pp. 15.

Kling, Rob, and Walt Scacchi (1982). "The Web of Computing: Computer Technology as Social Organization," *Advances in Computers*, Vol. 21. Academic Press, New York, pp. 1–90.

Moravec, Hans (1988). *Mind Children: The Future of Robot and Human Intelligence*. Harvard University Press, Cambridge, Mass.

Introduction

Social Controversies about Computerization

Charles Dunlop • Rob Kling

Digital computer systems have been among the most intriguing and most heralded technologies of the 1970s and 1980s. Not surprisingly, many technologists, scientists, journalists, managers, and other professionals have had a romance with computerization. Computer-based technologies have amplified the abilities of people and organizations in amazing ways. Scientists can model complex phenomena and gather and analyze data on a scale they would have found almost unimaginable fifty years ago. Organizations have developed computerized record systems to track a myriad of details about people (their clients and employees), money (revenue, assets, and payments), things (inventory of all kinds), and the relationships among them. Almost anybody who routinely writes books, articles, or reports is likely to use a microcomputer of some kind or at least have their manuscripts typed into one. In addition, computer systems are one of the few technologies where the power and flexibility of the devices increase and the costs decrease by an order of magnitude every decade.

But computerization has also been the source of problems that get relatively little exposure in the popular press and professional magazines. Some of the problems are pragmatic—the dilemmas of dealing with imperfect computer systems that foul up bills, lose key data, or are just much harder to work with than they should be. These kinds of problems can simply seem like minor irritants; however, they foreshadow social problems of much greater significance.

Consider the economic role of computer-based systems. So much of what we encounter in the press identifies computer-based systems with cost savings, efficiency, and productivity that these consequences of computerization seem almost natural (or, if not natural, still worth acquiring). Some writers have argued that computer-based systems are central to developing a dynamic economy that is competitive internationally, thus essential for economic health and well-being. Yet others have criticized this view, wondering why some organizations that have invested substantial amounts of money in computer systems have not experienced big payoffs. Moreover, some analysts believe that the economic success of computer-based systems can lead to large-scale un-employment in certain industries, with serious consequences for people who do not have (and might not readily obtain) computing skills.

The economic role of computerization is not the only area of controversy. There have been other important debates:

Worklife. Is computerization likely to improve or degrade the quality of jobs for managers, professionals, and clerks? How do different approaches to designing computer systems and their social environments alter the character and quality of jobs? Can computer and telecommunications systems improve the flexibility of work by enabling employed people to work at home part- or full-time?

Class divisions in society. To what extent is our increasingly computerized society fostering an underclass of functionally illiterate and disenfranchised people? What happens as jobs require new skills and using computerized services requires expertise in negotiating complex organizational procedures when things go wrong?

Human safety and critical computer systems. How safe are people who rely on computer systems such as those that help manage air traffic control or calculate radiation treatment plans for cancer patients? Should computer systems designers who work on such systems be licensed, much like the professional engineers who design bridges and elevators in skyscrapers?

Democratization. To what extent do computer and telecommunication systems offer new opportunities to strengthen democracy through on-line voting? To what extent does computerization undermine democratic processes in work and public life because the costs and expertise of large computerization projects may lead to centralized control and domination by groups who can control the selection of equipment and expertise?[1]

Employment. How does computerization alter the structure of labor markets and occupations? What kinds of understanding of computer systems are really critical for people who wish to develop different kinds of careers? Do the skill mixes for computer-oriented work help create a lower class with fewer jobs and more barriers to improving their situations?

Education. To what extent can interesting computer-based programs give students the

---

[1] For some key analyses within these debates, see the special issue of *The Information Society* devoted to a debate of Ted Sterling's argument (1986) that computerization weakens democratic processes. Also see Sackman (1971) and Bjerknes, Ehn, and Kyng (1987) for more sympathetic views; Danziger, Dutton, Kling, and Kraemer (1982) for a critical analysis; and Arterton (1987) for a careful assessment of actual attempts at computer-supported democratic political action. We believe that there is much to be learned by focusing on the different theories of technology and social action that these analysts bring to bear, rather than simply on their conclusions.

intellectual and motivational advantages of one-on-one tutoring in a way that is economically affordable? What drawbacks might there be in the widespread introduction of computers to the curriculum?

Gender biases. Is there any special reason why women are more likely to be found feeding data into computer systems, whereas men are more likely to be in the position of specifying the requirements for, and designing, computer-based systems?

Military security. To what extent do swift hi-tech weapons and complex computerized command and control systems amplify the risk of accidental nuclear war by shortening the response time for people to decide whether a perceived attack is real?

Health. To what extent do computer systems pose health hazards through low level radiation and noise?[2] To what extent do certain computer-related jobs have special health hazards because they require people to work intensively at keyboards for grueling time periods? Is eyestrain an occupational hazard for people—programmers and professionals as well as clerks—who spend long hours at terminals? If there are serious health problems associated with computer equipment or computer-related jobs, should there be tougher regulation of equipment or workplaces to enhance people's health and well-being?

Computer literacy. Must all effectively educated citizens have some special knowledge of computer systems? If so, what kinds of insights and skills are most critical—those that are akin to computer programming or those that are akin to understanding how organizational information systems function?

These controversial issues have not yet been resolved. Specialists sometimes disagree about how to characterize key problems and how best to find solutions. As with many social issues, the way they are framed often reflects the interests of groups with conflicting social concerns (Mauss, 1975). Computer systems seem to have immense benefits—in economic payoffs to business firms, in making many social practices more convenient, and in reducing the tedium in many jobs. At first glance, the problems of computerization can seem small or nonexistent. Sometimes, the magnitude of the problems is still becoming apparent (and public), as in the case of risks from computer systems on which people's lives depend. In contrast, other technologies, such as nuclear power and highly polluting pesticides, are perhaps more *obviously* problematic.

The Automobile Analogy

The current situation with computing has important similarities to that of mechanized transport in the early 20th century. Privately driven cars are the primary means of mechanized personal transport in the United States today. But even though the benefits

---

[2] There are about 30 million video display terminals (VDTs) in the United States (including those on microcomputers). There is a major debate about the extent to which unusual clusters of miscarriages in groups that work with VDTs are a byproduct of the very low-level electrical and magnetic fields that they often radiate. For a partisan but comprehensive account of the debate and the evidence, see Paul Brodeur, "Annals of Radiation, The Hazards of Electromagnetic Field: Part III, Video Display Terminals," *The New Yorker* (June 26, 1989), pp. 39–68.

of individual cars to wealthier individuals seeking flexible transportation or social status were easily visible from the earliest days of motor cars, larger-scale effects of individual car ownership were more difficult to discern. And today, automobiles still offer people in suburban and rural areas immense convenience in traveling to work and shopping, as well as in social relations and leisure.

When motor cars first became popular in the early 20th century, they were viewed as a clean technology. Some of the larger cities had annoying pollution problems from another primary transportation mode—horses—when on rainy days, large pools of horse manure would form on busy street corners and make walking hazardous for pedestrians. Not until the 1960s, when smog visibly dirtied the air of major cities, did we begin to view cars as a major polluting technology.

Since there were few cars in the early 1920s, it was very difficult to predict what impact the automobile would have simply by studying the uses to which automobiles were put or by examining the major forms of social organization. If one had wanted to think ahead about what benefits cars would have and what social dilemmas certain styles of social organization could produce, one would have had to be unusually prescient in the early part of the 20th century. There simply were neither enough cars nor a social system sufficiently saturated with them to foresee the major effects with any clarity. But an analyst who thought that automobiles were simply fun to drive, portending nothing ominous regardless of the scale on which they were to be used, would have been very mistaken.

Some major cities actually began to have smog around 1940, some 40 years after the automobile was developed in the United States. Then, after World War II, a new form of metropolitan organization, in which the urban core was dwarfed by bedroom suburbs, developed on a large scale. These suburbs—which many urban critics decried as bland, lifeless places—were extremely attractive to young families seeking affordable housing and open spaces relatively free of crime and congestion. One person's nightmare can be another's utopia. In fact, as smog became more visible in major cities, the automobile industry worked hard to argue that there was no link between cars and smog.[3] (The tobacco industry's continuing response to the reported links between smoking and lung cancer provides an obvious parallel.) By the time major effects became visible, major investments often were already made—investments that would be difficult to alter, even when troubles were obvious. By the time the smog had become intense enough to render the mountains surrounding Los Angeles invisible on most days, people had already become dependent not just on the car, but on forms of social life built around cars—nuclear families dwelling in suburban tracts with little public transportation and living 10 to 30 miles from work, friends, shops, and other posts of daily life. In addition, metropolitan regions had begun to devote huge resources to motorized transport through the building and renovation of highways, roads, parking lots, and garages and the support of traffic police and traffic courts.[4] It is now almost impossible to restructure these social elements in which the automobile has become a central element.

---

[3] See Krier and Ursin (1977). Other more local interest groups also played key roles in the development of road systems within cities. See, for example, Lupo, Colcord, and Fowler (1971).

[4] According to one estimate, about 40% of the developed land in the city of Los Angeles is devoted to the transportation facilities for cars, trucks, and buses.

Each year between 400 and 500 people die in traffic accidents nationwide on each major holiday weekend in the United States. The signs of car accidents are often highly visible, and the attendant ambulances give us clues to human pain and suffering. Even so, the auto industry has often fought the addition of safety features for cars.[5] Simple slogans like "The automobile is simply a transportation tool" don't help us understand the opportunities, problems, or dependency associated with cars. Car use is also habitual, a way of life in city, suburban, and rural regions. It is institutionalized—taken for granted and hard to alter on a social scale, even when there are big incentives to do so. (For example, policies to reduce urban congestion and smog through mass transit and car pools have had modest success at best.)

The automobile analogy helps us appreciate the way in which the links between a better technology and improvements in social life are often ambiguous. There is no simple way to measure a revolution. Saying that the average American family owns 1.8 cars does little to indicate how community life in the United States today differs from community life 100 years ago. Similarly, counting computers, computer expenditures, computer users, etc., only suggests a measure of social activity. Such numbers indicate little by themselves.

Many social observers and computer scientists have been fascinated by the potential of computing to alter social life profoundly. Technologies such as computing do not "impact" social life like a meteor hitting Earth. Rather, technologies are designed to fit ongoing social patterns. Even when the fit is imperfect, people and organizations often alter their practices to accommodate the advantages and limitations of new technologies. Moreover, one can wander widely through major cities with immense computerized businesses and government agencies and still not see signs, whether helpful or harmful, of computing. Computer systems and their consequences are not readily visible outside the workplaces or homes that use them. As a consequence (and like the automobile in its early days), computing can appear to be a clean and safe technology.

We hope that important technologies like computing can be sufficiently well understood by many social groups early on, so that important decisions about whether, when, and how to utilize computer-based systems will be more socially benign than would otherwise be the case. This book provides an opportunity for readers to learn more about the nuances of computerization. Through it, we hope to expand the range of legitimate discourse about consequent social choices.

The Seductive Equation: Technological Progress = Social Progress

Computing is often labeled a seductive technology or—more accurately—the center-piece of seductive dreams. The seduction comes from being drawn into the belief that vast possibilities for information handling and "enhanced intelligence" are readily accessible at relatively low cost and with little effort. Some of the technological advances of computer systems are quite obvious: in each decade, the power of digital computing hardware increases about tenfold for any given price and physical size. Advances in the power and quality of software have also been steady, but much less dramatic. However,

---

[5] See Ralph Nader's classic *Unsafe at Any Speed*, expanded edition (1982). Grossman, New York.

transforming these technological advances into social advances has not been straightforward. In this book we will examine many of the resulting dilemmas.

Like many others, we are often enchanted by graceful high-performance technologies. We like driving (if not owning!) spirited, luxurious cars. We appreciate fast computers with powerful software and bright colorful displays. We have benefited from computer systems with word processors and spell checkers to support our writing. We have used databases and automated library search systems to trace books and articles, and we frequently communicate via electronic mail. But we also realize that the exercise of our personal preferences for high-performance technologies, raised to a social scale, raises a variety of important social issues.[6]

Some technologists suggest that new computer technologies will address key social problems. Falling prices for computer hardware, the 68040 chip, the next generation of Unix, and a band of smart programmers will solve most of them. The remainder will be solved by the 80786 chip and supercomputers, international networks, better environments for programming languages (e.g., Ada and C++), higher-performance database languages, and some artificial intelligence! Although we are obviously caricaturing this position, we are not fundamentally misstating a view held by many technologists and futurists and popularized by some journalists. Few writers make these claims explicit; rather, they focus attention on new (or "revolutionary") technologies while ignoring key aspects of the social environments in which they are used. For example, some educators have argued for computer-assisted instruction in schools without asking what kinds of equipment most schools can afford. Transportation experts have argued that urban congestion can be reduced through the development and widespread use of smart cars; they place much less emphasis on the training of smarter drivers.

Many scenarios of life in the year 2000 assume that social progress will come *primarily* through technological progress. For example, as we were preparing this introduction, the *Los Angeles Times* published a story about "Life in the Year 1999," which focused on a day in the life of a professional couple who live in a "smart house," one filled with computerized convenience and security devices. However useful these devices may be, they increase the cost of housing and the complexity of daily life when the equipment malfunctions or requires special adjustment. During the last decade, the housing market in Los Angeles became among the most expensive in the country. Many working people today have trouble buying a house, even a "stupid house." And there are tens of thousands of homeless people in greater Los Angeles alone. We are struck by the way in which the news media casually promote images of a technologically rich future while ignoring the way in which some of these technologies add cost, complexity, and new dependencies to daily life. The glossy images also ignore the key social choices about how to computerize and the ways in which different forms of computerization advance different values.[7]

---

[6] Many people and organizations desiring high-performance technologies often have trouble acquiring them because of their cost. And those who are able to appropriate more powerful technologies are likely to widen the gap between themselves and those who lack them.

[7] Kling (1983) examines the character of value conflicts stimulated by computerization. His article is reprinted in Part V of this book.

Many forms of computerization are advanced within an overall framework of industrialization. Our industrial civilization has created the conditions for increasing our general health, physical comfort, and safety. But it has also caused immense environmental pollution in many regions of the country. Increasing use of energy and industrial products leads to more smog, more acid rain, more rapid depletion of the ozone layer, more rapid warming of the planet, etc. It is possible that some solutions can rely on computer technologies. For example, having people telecommute may be more environmentally sound than packing the urban freeways with more commuters driving "smarter" cars on their daily trek from home to work. Unfortunately, it is hard to find balanced accounts that carefully examine the social characters of different packages of social and technological alternatives and the values they each support.

Computerization is often bound up with the symbolic politics of modernism and rationality. Advanced technologies offer the giddy excitement of adventure with the liberating lure of new possibilities that have few associated problems. Talk about new technologies offers a new canvas in which to reshape social relationships so that they better fit the speakers' imaginations. The presence of advanced technologies often serves as a sign that the computer-using person or organization is worthy of admiration and trust. It is easier for casual observers to spot the presence of advanced computer equipment than to understand how the equipment actually alters people's abilities to carry out their day-to-day activities.[8] Yet social revolutions are based on changes in ways of life, not just changes in equipment.

Computer Science Skills Involve More Than Developing Hardware and Software

Computer specialists and management consultants often propose computerized systems that, they argue, will help people and organizations in new ways. These planners often unconsciously engage in oversimplified romantic speculation, even when they prefer to be "hardheaded," "factual," and "only technical." We suggest that utopian inquiry and its anti-utopian opposite (both of which we examine in Section I) are useful ways of exploring future possibilities. Much of the problem with utopian thinking comes when people fail to realize how fanciful some of their assumptions about human behavior and social change may be. Visionaries often focus primarily on desirable changes and assume that what *should* happen *must* happen once a particular technology is introduced.[9] Their assumptions often go well beyond technology as it is traditionally conceived to embody views of human-machine interaction, human motivation, and the behavior of social groups. Thus, a critical investigation of visionary viewpoints requires skills that lie beyond hardware and algorithm design.

Paul Goodman argued that technologists, including computer specialists, were primarily social activists who acted in terms of moral philosophy:

---

[8] For an interesting case study of the way an organization exploited the image of efficient administration through computerization, see Kling (1978).

[9] Or, alternatively, that what should *not* happen will not happen. See our discussion in Section I for examples of both kinds of thinking.

> Whether or not it draws on new scientific research, technology is a branch of moral philosophy, not of science. It aims at prudent goods for the commonweal and to provide efficient means for those goods. . . . As a moral philosopher, a technician should be able to criticize the programs given to him to implement. As a professional in a community of learned professionals, a technologist must have a different kind of training. . . . He should know something of the social sciences, law, the fine arts, and medicine, as well as relevant natural sciences. (Goodman, 1969)[10]

One commonplace view of computer science and engineering is reflected in a recent report by the ACM[11] Task Force on the Core of Computer Science:

> Computer science and Engineering is the systematic study of algorithmic processes—their theory, analysis, design, efficiency, implementation and application—that describe and transform information. The fundamental question underlying all of computing is, What can be (efficiently) automated? . . . The roots of computing extend deeply into mathematics and engineering. Mathematics imparts analysis to the field; engineering imparts design. (Denning, et al., 1989, p. 16)

How different this view is from Goodman's! It makes Goodman sound somewhat utopian in his desire that computer specialists be independent professionals who will exert a critical influence on the shape of the products they are asked to produce. In the traditional view, technologists are often asked to refine the means they use to implement a product, but not to question the ends they serve. Ian Reinecke goes even further in that direction, suggesting that technical communities are impervious to serious critical analysis:

> Those who know most about technology are in many cases the worst equipped to appreciate its implications for the lives of ordinary people. Consumed by technical and corporate objectives that become ends in themselves, they fail to see that their work may very often be contrary to the interests of their fellow citizens. So frenetic is the pace of change that the few querulous voices raised from their own ranks are swept aside. Where the voices are more insistent, they are branded as renegades, as unstable people whose work has somehow unhinged them. (Reinecke, 1984, p. 243)

We do not share Reinecke's wholesale condemnation of technical professionals. In Part VIII we will examine some key ethical issues of computing and the different positions that technical professionals have articulated in the controversies. Moreover, some of the better computer science journals, such as *Communications of the ACM*, publish articles that examine the social aspects of computerization from different vantage points. But Reinecke's criticism is most apt for technologists who remain somewhat self-consciously indifferent to the social complexities of computerization, except to acknowledge the importance of their own special interests. Further, we have observed that a substantial fraction of practicing technologists do not read broadly about the social aspects of computerization but focus their professional reading on technical handbooks, such as the manuals for specific equipment, and on occasional articles in the computer trade press.

---

[10] Excerpted from Albert Teich (ed.), *Technology and the Future*, 5th ed., 1990 (quote from pp. 235–236). Goodman's view has immediate implications for computer science curricula—implications that are still not adequately recognized at many universities. (For two exceptions, see Footnote 12.)

[11] The Association for Computing Machinery (ACM) is the major professional organization for computer scientists in the United States.

Skills in the Social Analysis of Computing

The dominant paradigms in academic computer science do not help technical professionals comprehend the social complexities of computerization, since they focus on computability rather than usability. For example, the recent ACM Task Force on the Core of Computer Science quoted above claims that all the analyses of computer science are mathematical. We find this view much too narrow-minded to be helpful, and in fact it does not withstand much scrutiny. The lines of inquiry where it might hold are those where mathematics can impart all the necessary analysis. But there are whole subfields of computer science—such as artificial intelligence, computer-human interaction, social impact studies, and parts of software—where mathematics cannot impart all the necessary analysis. The social sciences provide a complementary theoretical base for studies of computing that examine or make assumptions about human behavior.

In the classic Turing machine model of computability, there is no significant difference between a modest microcomputer like an Apple Macintosh SE and a supercomputer like a Cray Y-MP. Of course, these two machines differ substantially in their computational speed and memory. But the Mac SE, with software designed to match its graphic interface, is a much more usable computer for many small-scale tasks such as writing memos and papers, graphing datasets of 500 data points, etc. Unfortunately, the computability paradigm doesn't help us understand a Mac's relative advantage over a Cray for tasks where the ease of a person's interacting with software, rather than sheer CPU speed or file size, is the critical issue.

This contrast between Macs and Crays is a small-scale, machine-centered example. More significant examples can be found whenever one is trying to ask questions like: What should be computerized for these particular people? How should computerization proceed? Who should control system specifications, data, etc.? These are usability questions on a social scale. Paradigms that focus on the nature of social interaction provide much better insights for designing computer systems in support of group work than does the computability paradigm (Ehn, 1988; Ehn, 1989 (reprinted in Part III of this book); Kling, 1989; Winograd, 1988).[12]

Mathematical analyses help us learn about the properties of computer systems abstracted from any particular use, such as the potential efficiency of an algorithm or the extent to which computers can completely solve certain problems in principle (e.g., the question of undecidability). As long as a computer scientist doesn't make claims about the value of any kind of computer use, mathematical analyses might be adequate. But the advances in computer interface design that led to the Mac and to graphic user interfaces in general, rested on *psychological* insights rather than mathematical insights. Similarly, advances in programming languages, software development tools, and database systems have come, in part, through analyses of what makes technologies easier for people and organizations to use. While some of these technologies have a mathematical base, their

[12] See our discussion in Part III about the social dimensions of systems design, along with the supporting readings. The computer science programs at a few universities, like the University of California, Irvine, and the Arhus University in Denmark, attempt to integrate serious social analysis into more traditional technical computer science.

fundamental justifications have been psychological and social. Claims about how groups of people should use computers are social and value-laden claims.

For example, suppose a computer scientist argues that organizations should computerize by developing networks of high-performance workstations, with one workstation on every employee's desk. This claim embodies key assumptions about good organizational strategies and implicitly rules out alternatives—such as having a large central computer connected to employees' terminals, with a few microcomputers also available for those who prefer to use micro-oriented software. These two architectures for organizational computing raise important social and political questions: Who will get access to what kinds of information and software? What skill levels will be required to use the systems? How much money should be spent on each worker's computing support? How should resources and status be divided within the organization? Who should control different aspects of computerization projects? And so on. The question here is one of *social* and *political* organization, in addition to *computer* organization. Since engineers and computer scientists often make claims in these arenas, Paul Goodman (1969) argues that "technology is a branch of moral philosophy, not of science. It aims at prudent goods for the commonwealth." Computer scientists are keenly interested in having advanced computer-based systems widely *used*, not just studied as mathematical objects. These hopes and related claims rest on social analyses and theories of social behavior.

Mathematical frames of reference lead analysts to focus on behavior that can be formalized and on so-called optimal arrangements. Social analyses usually help analysts identify the ways in which different participants in a computerization project have different preferences for the way that computing technologies are woven into social arrangements. Participants are most likely to have different preferences when computerization projects are socially complex and a project cuts across key social boundaries identified by characteristics such as roles, occupational identity, reward structures, culture, or ethnicity. We do not see social analyses as a panacea. But they help identify the kinds of opportunities and dilemmas participants will actually experience and respond to in their daily lives.

The education of hundreds of thousands of computer science students has been shaped by the computability perspective. These students typically leave academic computer science programs with some skills in the design and programming of software systems and take courses on data structures and algorithms, in which they learn to appreciate and carry out mathematical analyses of computer performance. But too often they leave the university, essentially ignorant of the ways in which social analyses of computer systems provide comparably important insights into the roles and effectiveness of computing in the world. We believe that many segments of the computing community would understand computerization much better, and be able to play more responsible professional roles, by adopting a more fundamentally social view of computerization. We believe that social analysis is an integral part of computer science and a critical skill for all computer specialists. Computer specialists are often computerizing parts of their own organizations, as well as making claims about the social aspects of computerization for others. They should do so insightfully. Social analyses of computerization examine situations analytically, to understand that assumptions are made about social relationships among key participants, as well as to examine the support arrangement for appropriate technologies and the range of technological options, and how these may restructure social life.

In a larger perspective, computer science as a discipline should be able to comment meaningfully on computerization and policy issues in the social order. Computer specialists and professionals also have a special responsibility to share their insights with their employers, clients, and the public in a pro-social way. Computer science of the 21st century will be strong in areas that rest on the social foundations of computerization as well as in areas that rest on its mathematical and engineering foundations.

Computerization and Social Visions

Often, managers and technical professionals develop computerization projects with relatively simple themes—to enhance the operational efficiency of some organizational practice, to provide a new service, or sometimes just to modernize by using current technologies. Even when the social visions of practitioners are relatively skimpy, computerization projects have important social dimensions, as we will see in the various sections of this book. However, computerization in industrial countries has also been the subject of a large body of popular and professional writing about what computer systems are good for and the character of the problems to which most professionals have been exposed. This exposure often influences implicit assumptions about computerization. To illustrate key assumptions made by people who write about advanced computing technologies, we start our book with alternative visions of computerization in Part I.

References

Arteron, F. Christopher (1987). *Teledemocracy: Can Technology Protect Democracy?* Sage, Newbury Park, Calif.

Bellin, David, and Gary Chapman (eds.)(1987). *Computers in Battle: Will They Work?* Harcourt Brace, Jovanovich, Boston, Mass.

Bjerknes, Gro, Pelle Ehn, and Morten Kyng (eds.)(1987). *Computers and Democracy: A Scandinavian Challenge.* Gower Pub. Co., Brookfield, Vt.

Danziger, James, William Dutton, Rob Kling, and Kenneth Kraemer (1982). *Computers and Politics: High Technology in American Local Government.* Columbia University Press, New York.

Denning, Peter J. (Chairman), Douglas E. Comer, David Gries, Michael C. Mulder, Allen Tucker, A. Joe Turner, and Paul R. Young (1989). "Computing as a Discipline," *CACM.* 32(1), PP. 9–23.

Ehn, Pelle (1988). *Work-Oriented Design of Computer Artifacts.* Arbetslivcentrum, Stockholm.

Ehn, Pelle (1989). "The Art and Science of Designing Computer Artifacts," *Scandinavian Journal of Information Systems,* 1 (August), pp. 21–42. (Reprinted in Part III of this book.)

Goodman, Paul (1969). *The New Reformation.* Random House, New York.

Krier, James, and Edmund Ursin (1977). *Pollution & Policy: A Case Essay on California and Federal Experience with Motor Vehicle Air Pollution, 1940–1975.* University of California Press, Berkeley.

Kling, Rob (1978). "Automated Welfare Client-Tracking and Service Integration: The Political Economy of Computing," *Communications of the ACM.* 21(6), pp. 484–493.

Kling, Rob (1983). "Value Conflicts in the Deployment of Computing Applications: Cases in Developed and Developing Countries." *Telecommunications Policy.* 7(1), pp. 12–34. (Reprinted in Part V of this book.)

Kling, Rob (1989). "Usability vs. Computability," Department of Information and computer Science, University of California, Irvine, Calif.

Kraemer, Kenneth, and John King (1990). "Social Analysis in MIS: The Irvine School, 1970–1990," *Proceedings of the HICSS Conference* Kona, Hawaii, January 1990.

Lupo, Alan, Frank Colcord, and Edmund P. Fowler (1971). *Rites of Way: The Politics of Transportation in Boston and the US City.* Little, Brown, Boston, Mass.

Mauss, Armand L (1975). *Social Problems as Social Movements.* Lippincott, Philadelphia, Pa.

Moravec, Hans (1988). *Mind Children: The Future of Robot and Human Intelligence.* Harvard University Press, Cambridge, Mass.

Mowshowitz, Abbe (1977). *The Conquest of Will: Information Processing in Human Affairs.* Addison-Wesley, Reading, Mass.

Reinecke, Ian (1984). *Electronic Illusions: A Skeptic's View of Our High Tech Future.* Penguin, New York.

Sackman, Harold (1971). *Mass Information Utilities and Social Excellence.* Auerbach, Princeton, N.J.

Sterling, Theodor (1986). "Democracy in an Information Society," *The Information Society.* 4(1/2), pp. 9–48.

Teich, Albert H. (ed.) (1990). *Technology and the Future.* New York, St. Martins Press.

Winograd, Terry (1988). A Language/action Perspective on the Design of Cooperative Work," *Human—Computer Interaction* 3: 1, pp. 3–30. Reprinted in Greif, Irene (ed.), *Computer-Supported Cooperative Work: A Book of Readings.* Morgan-Kaufmann, San Mateo, Calif., pp. 623–653.

Wright, Karen (1990). "Trends in Communications: The Road to the Global Village," *Scientific American.* 262(3), pp. 83–94.

P·A·R·T·I

The Dreams of Technological Utopianism

P · A · R · T · I

Introduction

The Dreams of Technological Utopianism

Charles Dunlop • Rob Kling

Stories About Computerization

In this first chapter, we want to help you better understand the unstated but critical social assumptions underlying the images of computerization that permeate many analyses. Every year thousands of articles and dozens of books comment on the meaning of new computer technologies for people, organizations, and society at large. Much of the literature about computing describes emerging technologies and the ways they expand the limits of the possible. Faster, tinier computers can make it easier for people to access information in a wider variety of places. Larger memories can make more data accessible. Richer display devices, employing pictures as well as text, can make interacting with computers more of a reality for more people. Emerging high-speed networks can connect thousands of systems, providing communication links only dreamed of a decade ago. The remarkable improvement in the capabilities of equipment from one decade to the next generates keen excitement for researchers, developers, and entrepreneurs, as well as for the battalions of journalists who document these events in newspapers and magazines. Yet, although we are frequently told that we're in the midst of a momentous "computer revolution," we're rarely told precisely what that means.

Stores about the powerful information-processing capabilities of computer systems are usually central in accounts of computerization and social change. Some visionaries enchant us with images of the ways that new technologies offer exciting possibilities for manipulating large amounts of information rapidly with little effort—to search for information, to enhance control, to create insights, etc. While acknowledging (and sometimes embracing) the new and interesting technological possibilities, we believe that many analysts pay too little attention to the ways in which computers are used in real-life contexts.

Utopian Storylines

We have selected readings that illustrate the ways in which utopian analyses shape some key discussions about the social role of computerization. Utopian thinkers portray societies whose members live very ideal lives. The first such description appeared in Plato's *Republic*, written some 2,500 years ago. But the name *Utopia* derives from Thomas More, who in 1516 published a story about an ideal society—Utopia—where people lived harmoniously and free of privation. More's fanciful name, which literally meant "nowhere," has been picked up and applied to a whole tradition of writing and thinking about the forms of society that would supposedly make people happiest. There have been hundreds of utopian blueprints. They differ substantially in their details: some have focused on material abundance as the key to human happiness, and others have advanced ideal visions of austerity and simplicity. Some utopian thinkers advocate private property as a central social institution, and alternative visions place a premium on shared property. The utopian's emphasis on ideal forms of society is most easily understood by contrasting Thomas More's ideal society in *Utopia* to Machiavelli's *The Prince*, which was published only three years earlier in 1513. "The two works could hardly have been more different. While *Utopia* is an exploration of how medieval institutions can be developed to create a stable and successful society for almost all of its members, *The Prince* is a lesson in expediency—how an individual can take power and hold onto it. Concerned with power politics, it is a handbook of techniques. . . [and would recommend] whatever violence or cynical deception was necessary to preserve. . . [political] power" (Todd and Wheeler, 1978, p. 35).

The most obvious utopian sources are discourses explicitly identified by their authors as fictional accounts, complete with traditional devices like invented characters and fanciful dialogue. But here we are concerned with discourses about computerization, which their authors present as primarily realistic or factual accounts (and which are catalogued as nonfiction in bookstores and libraries). We will show how some of these discourses are shaped by the conventions of utopian and anti-utopian blueprints.

Among the authors represented in this section, Poppel is closest to the Machiavellian tradition. He does not advocate violence or deception, but he accepts people's well-being in organizations much as he finds them. The Machiavellian theme in Poppel's writing comes from his focus on changing organizations to make them more *efficient* for their modern day rulers—their owners and upper managers—and not necessarily *better* work-places for their employees. In contrast, Feigenbaum and McCorduck explicitly identify with utopian ideals when they close their contribution with this observation: "'Utopian' also means something we have said many times and in many ways that we desire as a human good. . . . [A]ll this . . . corresponds to Adam Smith's vision in *The Wealth of Nations* of a universal opulent society, a condition of plenty that frees the people from dependence and subordination to exercise true independence of spirit in autonomous actions."

Tom Stonier also illustrates the utopian tradition in writing about information technology. His book, *The Wealth of Information*, looks at the ways in which information technologies can transform societies. Stonier concludes with this observation: "To sum up, everyone an aristocrat, everyone a philosopher. A massively expanded education system to provide not only training and information about how to make a living, but also on how to live. In late industrial society, we stopped worrying about food. In late communicative society, we will stop worrying about material resources. And just as the industrial economy eliminated slavery, famine, and pestilence, so will the post-industrial economy eliminate authoritarianism, war, and strife. For the first time in history, the rate at which we will solve problems will exceed the rate at which they will appear. This will leave us to get on with the real business of the next century. To take care of each other. To fathom what it means to be human. To explore intelligence. To move out into space" (Stonier, 1983, p. 214).

Utopian images permeate the literatures about computerization in society. Unfortunately, we have found that many utopian writers distort social situations to fit their preferences (see, for example, the third sentence of Stonier's quote). We are not critical of utopian ideals concerned with a good life for all. The United States was founded on premises that were utopian premises in the 1700s. The Declaration of Independence asserts that "all men are created equal." This stood in significant contrast to the political cultures of the European monarchies of the time, where the rule of the king or queen, along with nobles (most of whom were "elected" by heredity) determined people's fates. Of course, asserting the right to "life, liberty, and the pursuit of happiness" as universal didn't immediately make it so. Until 1865, for example, slaves were legally property and could be bought and sold, told where to live, and broken apart from their families. Women were not allowed to vote until 1919. And even in 1963, Martin Luther King's major speech about a country free of racial discrimination was called "I Have a Dream"—not "An Old Dream Has Now Come True."

Utopian ideals are hard to put into practice. Their advocates often have to fight hard to change social practices to fit their ideals better. The United States broke free of the English Crown through a four-year war. Almost 200 years later, Martin Luther King and others advanced the cause of improved civil rights in the United States through aggressive confrontations: marches, rallies, court injunctions, and sit-ins, as well as through more quiet persuasion. The resulting social changes, which altered the balance of privilege and exploitation, did not come quietly and peacefully.

Although utopian visions often serve important roles in stimulating hope and giving people a positive sense of direction, they can mislead when their architects exaggerate the likelihood of easy and desirable social changes. We are particularly interested in what can be learned from, and how we can be misled by, a particular brand of utopian thought —*technological utopianism*. This line of analysis places the use of some specific technology —computers, nuclear energy, or low-energy, low-impact technologies—as the central enabling element of a utopian vision.[1] Sometimes people will casually refer to exotic technologies, like pocket computers that understand spoken language, as utopian gadgets. Technological utopianism does not refer to a set of technologies. It refers to *analyses* in which the use of specific technologies plays a key role in shaping a utopian social vision. In contrast, technological anti-utopianism examines how certain broad families of technology facilitate a social order that is relentlessly harsh, destructive, and miserable. George Orwell's novel *1984* is representative of this genre.

Technological utopians sometimes recognize that new technologies cause new problems, but these are to be solved with additional technologies. Buckminster Fuller argued that it was difficult and almost pointless to teach people to drive very cautiously and to harass them with rigid laws. Consequently, he argued for safer cars rather than for programs aimed at changing human behavior. Similarly, he thought that automobile pollution would be better eliminated by new fuels and improved engines than by regulations that discourage driving. Technological utopians would usually prefer to see government funds invested in stimulating the development of new technologies than to increase the scale and scope of regulatory bureaucracies.

New Technological Blueprints or Utopian Dreams?

Technologists who characterize new or future technologies often employ utopian imagery when they examine the social meanings or implications of those technologies. In 1945, Vannevar Bush, the former science advisor to President Roosevelt, published a provocative article in the *Atlantic Monthly* called "As We May Think." Bush wrote before there were any working electronic computers, even the room-sized, slow, and computationally limited early computers like EDVAC, ENIAC, and Johnniac. He set forth a vision of a fast, flexible, remotely accessible desk-sized computer, called *memex*, which would allow a researcher to search electronically through vast archives of articles, books, and notes. In Bush's vision,

> Wholly new forms of encyclopedia will appear, ready-made with a mesh of associative trails running through them, ready to be dropped into the memex, and there amplified. The lawyer has at his touch the associated opinions and decisions of his whole experience. The patent attorney has on call millions of issued patents, with familiar trails to every point of his client's interest. The physician, puzzled by a patient's reaction, strikes the trail established in studying an earlier similar case, and runs rapidly through analogous case histories, with side references to the classics for the pertinent anatomy and histology. The chemist, struggling with the synthesis of an organic compound, has all the chemical literature before him in his laboratory, with trails following the analogies of compounds, the side trails to their physical and chemical behavior.

---

[1] See Howard Segal's article on technological utopianism for a description of technological utopianism in the period between 1880 and 1930. The technologies of technological utopians can change from one era to another. But the assumption that a society that adopts the proper technologies will be harmonious and prosperous remains constant. For visions based on low-energy technologies that do relatively little harm to the natural environment, see Dorf and Hunter (1978).

The historian, with a vast chronological account of people, parallels it with a skip trail which stops only at the salient items, and can follow at any time, contemporary trails which lead him all over civilization at a particular epoch. There is a new profession of trail blazers, those who find delight in the task of establishing useful trails through the enormous mass of the common record. The inheritance from the master becomes not only his additions to the world's record, but for his disciples, the entire scaffolding by which they were erected.

Thus science may implement the ways in which man produces, stores, and consults the records of the race. (Reprinted in Greif [1988], p. 32).

Bush continued by describing the ways in which users have the "ability to associate items, gather together the useful clusters of information that showed up during the search, and 'instantly' project any or all of them onto displays for selective review, fast or slow. Presumably, man's spirit should be elevated if he can better review his shady past and analyze more completely and objectively his present problems" (in Greif [1988], p. 34).

Bush envisioned a flexible, compliant research assistant able to fish artfully through vast archives of textual information and gather the useful data embodied in an un-complaining, ever-ready machine.[2] A seductive image indeed! This vision was more remarkable because the image of digital computers that dominated scientific writing at the time—and even dominates scientific thinking in today's talk about supercomputers—concentrated on high-speed calculation of numerical data.

We could have opened with any number of other technological visions—e.g., computer-based instruction to transform education, information systems that would enable managers to control their business enterprises more tightly, electronic democracy through nationwide networks of home terminals, etc. In part, these visions, like Bush's, rest on descriptions of computer-based devices and their information-processing capabili-ties. In Chapter 2, Edward Feigenbaum and Pamela McCorduck speculate about several possible applications of artificial intelligence to medicine, library searches, life at home, and help for the elderly. Feigenbaum and McCorduck speculate in terms similar to Bush's —by describing how these technologies might work under ideal conditions. But they ignore key social conditions under which these technologies would be likely to be used.

A remarkably talented engineer, Douglas Engelbart, was inspired by Vannevar Bush's vision. About 20 years after Bush's article was published, Engelbart assembled a brilliant research team at the Stanford Research Institute, dedicated to building computer systems that embodied Bush's vision. At the time, computer technology had advanced to the point at which room-sized computers could be "time-shared" by dozens of people who could access them through video displays in their offices. Engelbart described his project "to augment human intellect" in these terms:

By "augmenting human intellect" we mean increasing the capability of a man to approach a complex problem situation, gain comprehension to suit his particular needs, and to derive solutions to his problems. Increased capability in this respect is taken to mean a mixture of the following: that comprehension can be gained; that a useful degree of comprehension can be gained more quickly; that better comprehension can be gained where previously the situation was too complex; that solutions can be produced more quickly; that better solutions can be produced; that better solutions could be found where previously the human could

---

[2] In another section of his article, he presaged the invention of charge cards for department stores.

find none. And by "complex situations" we include the professional problems of diplomats, executives, social scientists, life scientists, physical scientists, attorneys, designers—whether the problem exists for twenty minutes or twenty years. We do not speak of isolated clear tricks that help in particular situations. We refer to a way of life in an integrated domain where hunches, cut-and-try, intangibles, and human "feel for the situation" usefully coexist with powerful concepts, streamlined terminology and notation, sophisticated methods, and high powered electronic aids. (Engelbart, 1963)

Engelbart's team designed a novel system that included technologies that began to appear in the marketplace only in the mid-1980s—technologies such as the mouse,[3] hypertext,[4] and context-sensitive help available with function keys.[5] The team was concerned with computer systems that would enhance the performance of groups of people working together. They developed text systems that allowed different group members to have different, individual views of the same body of text. They built an electronic mail system that enabled people to track messages sent about various topics within their group. Today, some of these systems facilitate the functioning of groups by allowing many people to work with common bodies of text, schedules, etc. Appropriately, they are called "groupware."[6] Visions such as Bush's and Engelbart's, from which we have drawn tiny excerpts, serve as an inspiration for many technologists and aficionados of new technologies. But those visions are also flawed in the way they characterize technologies, people, and social life. They emphasize the ways that a technology should work ideally, under conditions where all the participants are highly cooperative and committed to making things work their best. In fact, the field that researches and develops computer

---

[3] A mouse provides an alternative to the keyboard for communicating information to a computer. It is a palm-sized device that rolls on a desktop and moves a cursor on a computer screen. It usually has two or three keys for entering simple commands. It can be used to select various menu options on the screen, mark blocks of text, draw figures, etc.

[4] Hypertext, a concept introduced by Ted Nelson in 1963, allows various text files to be linked conceptually rather than linearly. In this way, people can follow chains of data that are connected in a sequence that interests them, without being locked into the linear ordering of the documents. Nelson's concept appeared some 20 years later as HyperCard on the Macintosh and LinkWay on IBM PCs. The notion is now being extended to *hypermedia*, which would allow the interconnecting of related information in different formats. For example, a biography of J.S. Bach might be linked to a digitalized portrait of him and to digitalized Bach fugues that could be played through the computer's speaker. See Landow (1990) for a description of a hypertext system (Intermedia) used to support liberal arts courses at Brown University in the late 1980s. He describes some concrete examples of the kinds of texts and pictures that Intermedia can make available. It is difficult to communicate in a printed (linear) article the experience of browsing nonlinearly through a complex set of texts and pictures. But Landow's article describes the best aspects of use of Intermedia for college instruction without examining the complexities of students' experiences with the implemented system—including its location in a centralized laboratory, the painfully slow response times of the early versions, and their limited explorations of the system. Thus Landow's article has important elements of technological utopianism while appearing more realistic in approach.

[5] It's worth noting that these technological innovations are most frequently used in single-user systems on microcomputers such as Apple Macintoshes and IBM PCs for prosaic tasks like editing memos and papers. Englebart's team seems to have done little actually to enhance the practical problem-solving abilities of the professionals he described.

[6] See, for example, Robert Johansen, *Groupware* (1988), and the special section in *Byte Magazine* of December 1988.

systems to support group activities is sometimes called "computer supported cooperative work" (CSCW). That is, the work of groups is cooperative by definition. Other kinds of social relationships in work groups, such as those marked by conflict, competition, coercion, and even combat, are implicitly nonexistent. In fact, a great many discussions of computerization in organizations are marked by jargon and by vague, and sometimes questionable, terminology that obscures important social relationships.

Moving Computer Systems from the Laboratory to a Larger World

New technologies and new times beget new labels. Today, terms like *personal productivity software, groupware, hypermedia,* and *strategic information systems* have entered the discourse about emerging computer-based systems. A recent issue of *PC Magazine* devoted a special section to evaluating nine different software packages, designed to facilitate the activities of work groups.[7] The editors of *PC Magazine* coined their own alternative to the term "groupware": *workgroup productivity software.* The reviewer, Frank Derfler Jr., argued that group scheduling or calendaring software was a critical module of "workgroup productivity software," although other modules, such as text processing and electronic mail, are also important to make a more usable system. In fact, *PC Magazine's* editors excluded several interesting packages from their review (packages that are often reviewed in other groupware product reviews) because they lack scheduling modules.[8] Derfler writes

> Scheduling three or more busy people for a meeting along with arranging for a conference room and a slide projector, can be a frustrating and time-consuming task, requiring at least three phone calls. If one person or facility isn't available at the time the other people or facilities are, a whole series of negotiations begins. Mathematicians refer to it as progressive approximation; you (or your secretary making the arrangements) call it frustration. Before the scheduling problem is resolved, the number of people involved and phone calls made may have increased dramatically. . . .
>
> [Local area network] scheduling products simplify this task and often completely remove the frustration. With these packages, one person can access the public calendars of other persons and resources to quickly find out when everyone involved has free time that can be used to hold a meeting or other event. The process doesn't involve any invasion of privacy—the person planning the meeting doesn't see every detail on a personal calendar, just enough to find the free time. . . .
>
> The programs reviewed vary in how they present free time. Some packages . . . display graphs of conflicting and open schedules. . . . Other programs overlay calendar pages, while a few use text explanations to outline the scheduling options.
>
> Scheduling programs also vary in how they confirm proposed events. The simpler

---

[7] Frank Derfler Jr., "Imposing Efficiency: Workgroup Productivity Software," *PC Magazine.* 8: 16 (Sept 26, 1989): 247–269.

[8] For example, about a year earlier, Derfler reviewed a more varied group of 17 groupware software packages for *PC Magazine.* See "Workgroup productivity Boosters," *PC Magazine.* 7: 11 (June 14, 1988): 195–244. See also the December 1988 issue of *Byte Magazine.*

packages assume that if the event fits on the calendar, that the people scheduled to attend will be there. Other programs ask for confirmation, while some go as far as to tie into electronic mail modules for notification. . . .

The best scheduling software is utterly useless if people aren't willing to play the game by keeping their personal calendars current. Obviously, these personal calendars are at the heart of the group scheduling processes—calendars that aren't readily available or easy to use will never be maintained by group participants. With this in mind, it seems imperative that these programs allow you to run the personal calendar module (interactively while running other programs) and make it easy to use.

Derfler describes and critically evaluates some of the features of each program. We find technical reviews like this helpful in teaching us about the strengths and weaknesses of various programs. They also indicate that claims to solve some organizational problem by using some broad class of program like "electronic mail" can overestimate the value of the technologies actually adopted. Moreover, they draw attention to the marked differences that can exist between the best software on the market and the worst when it comes to range of functions, ease of use, and costs.

In his review, Derfler describes the best of these packages as dreams come true for busy professionals and managers. Like Vannevar Bush and Feigenbaum and McCorduck, he describes how these programs can facilitate various group activities, such as scheduling under the *best* of conditions: machines are up and running properly; people have immediate access to the shared system to keep their calendars up to date; people actually keep their calendars up to date. Unfortunately, like many popularizers, Derfler does not explain what social conditions make these packages most effective—or even usable at all.

In a lively article, Jonathan Grudin (1989) examines some of the *social assumptions* that designers and advocates of groupware make about the use of these packages. He argues that the kinds of meeting scheduling programs championed by Derfler work best when their users all have secretaries to help keep their calendars up to date. These packages are especially attractive to managers, who often have secrataries, and who often want to schedule meetings with subordinates. They can be a burden to professionals who do not have secretarial support. They can also burden people who are away from their desks in meetings, or who are out of their offices part of the day, making new commitments that are not reflected in their shared calendars. More deeply, Grudin examines computer applications with a model of organizations in which resources and authority are not equally distributed. He places computer systems in work-worlds characterized by a political economy of effort—some people can generate work for others. The people who generate work may not have to work as hard as the people who have to meet the requirements of others. Grudin's article opens up key questions about the social assumptions that product designers make.

We also want to point out some of the ironies of the special language that authors use in describing computer-based systems. Grudin originally wrote his article for a conference on "computer supported cooperative work" and used the abbreviation CSCW quite freely. Even so, he suggests that some managers might coerce their subordinates into using meeting scheduling systems with the disciplines that the managers prefer. This form of CSCW could be more accurately called "computer supported coercive work."[9] In contrast, Derfler's article in *PC Magazine* is called "Imposing Efficiency." But he never describes why or how efficiency would be *imposed* by anyone involved with the systems he reviews. In discussing meeting scheduling, he observes, "The best scheduling software is utterly useless if people aren't willing to play the game by keeping their personal calendars current." However, as is clear from the comments we quoted above, Derfler immediately moves from this central observation to a technical point: that the scheduling software should be designed so that it can "pop-up" whenever a person is running some other application. That way, if a person schedules a meeting by telephone while involved in something else (like writing a memo), the electronic calendar can still be updated promptly with a minimum of interruption. This is a valid observation. But Derfler never goes beyond the technical issue to examine the social practices of "imposed efficiencies."

It is a mistake to characterize the differences among these authors merely as a contrast between optimistic and pessimistic; these terms vastly oversimplify.[10] Grudin, for example, is pessimistic about the practical usefulness of certain groupware applications. But he may be quite enthusiastic about other kinds of computer-based systems that provide more benefits to a wider range of participants. Labelling someone like Grudin a pessimist and someone like Derfler an optimist trivializes their positions into statements about their moods.

Visions of Computerized Societies

So far, our examples focus on computer-based systems used by relatively small groups. But our key themes, such as the social assumptions underlying various analyses, also apply to accounts in which authors write about computerization at a societal level. Powerful images that link computing and social change have joined the ordinary language we encounter in newspapers, books, and advertisements. They are embedded in terms like *computer revolution, information society, knowledge worker, computer-mediated work, intelligent machine*. These catch phrases have strong metaphorical associations and are often introduced by authors to advance positive, exciting images of computerization.

The new terms are often worked into more common usage by journalists and authors who write for popular audiences. We live in a period of tremendous social change. And sometimes new language can capture emerging social patterns or new kinds of technologies better than our conventional language. At the same time, the way that many authors casually use these terms often reflects important, unexamined and often questionable assumptions. Sometimes the assumptions are clouded, as in the title of Derfler's

---

[9] One could substitute many other meaningful "c-words" for "cooperative" in the name *computer supported cooperative work*: competitive, coordinated, combative, and convivial. Each word gives the label CSCW substantially different connotations. Since the social relations of workplaces are often complex and not readily characterized by one label, all of these c-words may sometimes accurately characterize groupware technologies in use. See Part III for a more detailed discussion of computerization in workplaces.

[10] Utopian writers are not necessarily optimistic and anti-utopians are not necessarily pessimistic. For example, Aldous Huxley wrote an important utopian novel (*Island*) and an even more famous anti-utopian novel (*Brave New World*). A recent biography of the social philosopher Simone Weil is entitled *Utopian Pessimist* (McLellan, 1990).

article, "Imposing Efficiency." To take another example, a recent article about competition in the computer industry in *Fortune*, a popular business magazine, included this sentence: "The industry that has transformed the way that most people work is about to transform the way that most people *want* to work" (italics in original).[11] Does this mean that people who have simply become accustomed to new technologies often won't want to return to older forms: the refrigerator inexorably replaces the ice box, the flush toilet inexorably replaces the outhouse, the computerized word processor and spell checker inexorably replace the typewriter and pen, and so on? Or does it mean something more?

Alvin Toffler's best seller, *The Third Wave*, helped stimulate popular enthusiasm for computerization. Toffler characterized major social transformations in terms of large shifts in the organization of society, driven by technological change. The "second wave" was the shift from agricultural societies to industrial societies. Toffler contrasts industrial ways of organizing societies to new social trends that he links to computer and microelectronic technologies. He is masterful at employing succinct, breathless prose to suggest major social changes. He also invented terminology to help characterize some of these social changes—terms like *second wave, third wave, electronic cottage, infosphere, technosphere, prosumer, intelligent environment*, etc. Many of Toffler's new terms did not become commonly accepted. Even so, they help frame a seductive description of social change.[12] These lines from his chapter "The Intelligent Environment" illustrate this approach:

> Today, as we construct a new infosphere[13] for a Third Wave civilization, we are imparting to the "dead" environment around us, not life, but intelligence. A key to this revolutionary advance is, of course, the computer. . . .
>
> As miniaturization advanced with lightning rapidity, as computer capacity soared and prices per function plunged, small cheap powerful microcomputers began to sprout everywhere. Every branch factory, laboratory, sales office, or engineering department claimed its own. . . . The brainpower of the computer . . . was "distributed." This dispersion of computer intelligence is now moving ahead at high speed. . . .
>
> The dispersal of computers in the home, not to mention their interconnection in ramified networks; represents another advance in the construction of an intelligent environment. Yet even this is not all. The spread of machine intelligence reaches another level altogether with the arrival of microprocessors and microcomputers, those tiny chips of congealed intelligence that are about to become a part, it seems, of nearly all the things we make and use. . . .
>
> What is inescapably clear, however, whatever we choose to believe, is that we are altering our infosphere fundamentally. . . . We are adding a whole new strata of communication to the social system. The emerging Third Wave infosphere makes that of the Second Wave era —dominated by its mass media, the post office, and the telephone—seem hopelessly primitive by contrast. . . .
>
> In all previous societies, the infosphere provided the means for communication between human beings. The Third Wave multiplies these means. But it also provides powerful facilities, for the first time in history, for machine-to-machine communication, and, even more astonishing, for conversation between humans and the intelligent environment around them.

---

[11] Stuart Gannes, "Tremors From the Computer Quake," *Fortune* 118(3), August 1, 1988, pp. 43–60.

[12] Toffler devoted only one paragraph in his chapter to possible problems of computerization.

[13] Toffler defines an infosphere as "communication channels through which individuals and mass messages could be distributed as goods or raw materials" (Toffler, 1980: 35).

When we stand back and look at the larger picture, it becomes clear that the revolution in the infosphere is at least as dramatic as that of the technosphere—in the energy system and the technological base of society. The work of constructing a new civilization is racing forward on many levels at once. (Toffler, 1980: 168–178)

Toffler's breathless enthusiasm can be contagious; but it also stymies critical thought. He illustrates changes in the infosphere with The Source, a large commercial computer-communication and messaging system that has thousands of individual and corporate subscribers. (Today, he could multiply that example with the emergence of competing commercial systems, such as CompuServe, Genie, and Prodigy, as well as tens of thousands of inexpensive computerized bulletin boards that people have set up in hundreds of cities and towns.) However, there have been a myriad of other changes in the information environment in the United States that are not quite so exciting to people who would like to see a more thoughtful culture. For example, television has become a major source of information about world events for many children and adults.[14] Television news, the most popular "factual" kind of television programming, slices stories into salami-thin 30- to 90-second segments.[15] Moreover, there is some evidence that functional illiteracy is rising in the United States (Kozol, 1985). The problems of literacy in the United States are probably not a by-product of television's popularity. But it is hard to take Toffler's optimistic account seriously when a large fraction of the population has trouble understanding key parts of the instruction manuals for automobiles and for commonplace home appliances like television, VCRs, and microwave ovens.

Toffler opens up important questions about the way that information technologies alter the ways that people perceive information, the kinds of information they can get easily, and how they handle the information they get. Yet his account—like many popular accounts —caricatures the answers by using only illustrations that support his generally buoyant theses. And he skillfully sidesteps tough questions while creating excitement (e.g., "the work of constructing a new civilization is racing forward on many levels at once").

Our second selection is by John Sculley, chairman of the board of the Apple Computer Corporation. In an essay titled "A Lesson in History," he argues that print technology catalyzed the Renaissance, which broke the stranglehold of the church and feudal interests on the population of Europe: "The rise of the printing press led with astonishing speed to an explosion of literacy. The result was a new self-esteem for the individual. A wealth of invention. An excitement of the power of wonderful ideas. Today, we are in need of a second Renaissance which, like the first, can also be galvanized by new technology. We are on the verge of creating new tools which, like the press, will empower individuals, unlock worlds of knowledge, and forge a new community of ideas."

Sculley argues that computer systems based on hypermedia, simulation, and artificial intelligence applied to education are the appropriate means for forging this new com-

---

[14] Many children and adults report that they watch television for far more than five hours a day.

[15] The popularity of television news shows seems to hinge more on the visual personalities of the newscasters than on their special insights as news analysts (newscasters read the scripts prepared by news analysts). The films Network and Broadcast News are popular treatments of the way that television news shows serve primarily as an alternative form of entertainment. See Edward Jay Epstein, News from Nowhere: Television and the News (1st ed.), Random House, New York, for an insightful account of television newsmaking.

munity. His article is typical of a genre that tries to excite a positive sense of purpose for developers and users of computer technologies by referring to big historical changes such as the Renaissance or the Industrial Revolution. Such pieces excite hope by linking computerization to positive social ideals anchored in a vastly oversimplified history. It's useful to examine Sculley's historical analysis in some detail to assess its validity. Sculley describes the printing press as leading to "an explosion of literacy." The printing press was invented in Germany in 1450. But the Renaissance first mushroomed in Italy in the 15th century. Although printing helped stimulate literacy, the simple presence of printing presses didn't automatically stimulate a cultural revolution. The *political* conditions of life in Italy—a region that was split into five major politically independent areas and numerous minor ones—facilitated the spread of literacy, new trends in the arts, and the revival of classical learning. By the end of the Renaissance, Italy was not much wealthier than at the beginning. Italy was politically fragmented into numerous political entities before the Renaissance, and the Italian states were even weaker (and financially poorer) afterwards. Even so, cities like Florence were a mecca for artists from all over Europe. In contrast, countries that built international colonial empires—Spain and England— accumulated the most immense wealth in their royal treasuries. Yet Spain was arguably one of the more intellectually repressive countries in 16th-century Europe.

The Renaissance was not simply a forward-looking and exciting intellectual movement. Before the Renaissance, the Roman Catholic Church had a virtual monopoly on the skills of reading and writing. The battles to expand literacy and to place man at the center of the world—Renaissance humanism—were fought by a variety of interests against the power of the Church. And Church officials fought back, with inquisitions, ex- communications, and swords—as well as with talk and ink. One wonders which major contemporary institutions Sculley would like to identify as the modern equivalent of the dominant Roman Catholic Church during the medieval period. We think that Sculley describes an interesting set of technologies in his article. However, we would like to observe how he suggests their importance by casually linking them to an image of printing's having created the Renaissance and, thus, a wealth of ideas and social vitality.[16]

In our third selection, "Making a Computer Revolution," Rob Kling and Suzanne Iacono examine how authors like Toffler who appear to *report* about a "computer revolution" are actually working to *stimulate* a revolution. Sculley is quite overt in his interest in selling many new (Apple) computer systems, to major corporations as well as to colleges and universities. But analysts like Toffler are more subtle advocates. Kling and Iacono identify serious problems with the stories about what "the technologies" can do, what it takes to make them workable, who will benefit and who will lose, how fast different parties will benefit, in what ways different groups will be advantaged and disadvantaged, etc.[17] They see major problems in the way that some analysts portray

---

[16] In short, many extra-technological factors played key roles in promoting the Renaissance, and not all Renaissance developments were salutary. Feigenbaum and McCorduck's analysis of Japanese-American economic competition seems more plausible than Sculley's claim that exciting educational applications will help stimulate an intellectual and economic Renaissance in the U.S.

[17] Avoiding obsolescence and maintaining the state of the art—as a way of life—is very expensive and demands substantial attention.

computerization as a neutral social process that can serve all interests equally well and that places powerful technologies within easy reach of all participants. Sculley's sketch of Renaissance history is comparably simplified and designed to help promote the technologies that his company (Apple) sells. But these oversimplified stories mislead us all about the nature of complex social changes.

Technological Anti-Utopianism

Some important writings about the social changes linked to computerization criticize utopian assumptions. In fact, some authors articulate a comparably dark, anti-utopian view of computerization. Ian Reinecke's book *Electronic Illusions: A Skeptic's View of Our High Tech Future* is one example. Joseph Weizenbaum, in his popular book *Computer Power and Human Reason*, observes

> Our society's growing reliance on computer systems that were initially intended to "help" people make analyses and decisions, but which have long since surpassed the understanding of their users and become indispensable to them is a very serious development. First, decisions are made with the aid of, and sometimes entirely by, computers whose programs no one any longer knows explicitly or understands since no one can know the criteria or rules on which such decisions are based. Second, the rules and criteria that are embedded in such computer systems become immune to change, because, in the absence of detailed understanding of the inner workings of a computer system, any substantial modification of it is very likely to render the whole system inoperable and possibly unrestorable. Such computer systems can therefore only grow. And their growth and the increasing reliance placed on them is then accompanied by an increasing legitimation of their "knowledge base." (Weizenbaum, 1976, pp. 236–237)[18]

Clearly, Weizenbaum is aghast at the very complex computer decision systems that excite Feigenbaum and McCorduck. He criticizes visions of computerized databases that record historical data (like Vannevar Bush's memex, described earlier), because they usually eliminate important information that is too complex or costly to include:

> The computer has thus begun to be an instrument for the destruction of history. For when society legitimates only those "data" that are in one standard format, then history, memory itself, is annihilated. *The New York Times* has already begun to build a "data bank" of current events. Of course, only those data that are easily derivable as by-products of typesetting machines are admissible to the system. As the number of subscribers to this system grows, as they learn to rely more and more upon "all the news that [was once] fit to print,"[19] as the *Times* proudly identifies its editorial policy, how long will it be before what counts as fact is determined by the system, before all other knowledge, all memory, is simply declared illegitimate? Soon a supersystem will be built, based on *The New York Times'* data bank (or

---

[18] Weizenbaum goes on to describe the ways in which computer systems selected bombing targets during the late 1960s American war in Vietnam. Mathematical criteria were used to select which hamlets were friendly enough to escape attack and which were not, which areas had enough Viet Cong to warrant declaration as "free fire zones," and so on. Weizenbaum asserts, probably correctly, that the officers who operated these systems did not understand their calculations. (Weizenbaum, 1976: p. 238.)

[19] The *New York Times's* masthead slogan is "All the news that's fit to print."

one very much like it), from which "historians" will make inferences about what "really" happened, about who is connected to whom, and about the "real" logic of events. (Weizenbaum, 1976, p. 238)

Weizenbaum's observations gain more force when one realizes that journalists often don't simply report "the facts." They tend to rely upon standard kinds of sources, voices of publicly legitimate authority, in framing stories. For example, when a university alters a curriculum, deans and professors are more likely than students to appear in the resulting news story. Gaye Tuchman characterized reporters in search of a story as casting a selective "newsnet" around their favorite kinds of sources. Journalists often don't cast their nets to give equal voice to all kinds of informed parties. While reporters are much more likely to go to "the grass roots" today than they were in the days of Vannevar Bush, each newspaper prints a mix of stories in a style that reflects a relatively stable character. Even if the mastheads were interchanged, one would not confuse the *New York Times* with a small-town weekly newspaper.[20]

Moreover, Weizenbaum speaks with authority about future events ("Soon a super-system will be built"). Without special design, nothing in the database technology itself would be likely to give the user a clue about its real limitations in representing a narrow range of perspectives. We don't worry much about professional historians who have developed strong criteria for verifying events by appeal to a variety of corroborating sources. Nonetheless, the convenience of database technology might make it very tempting for others to rely on it as a primary source, without appreciating its shortcomings. That is the cautionary note that one might draw from Weizenbaum's bitter observations.

But Weizenbaum's argument is primarily polemical. He doesn't discuss any virtues of news databases or any conditions under which they might not have the deleterious consequences he identifies. After all, news databases can substantially assist in useful research as long as they do not become a sole source of information.

In our last selection, Wendell Berry, a poet, farmer, and essayist, explains why he refuses to buy a computer to facilitate his writing. Berry links his opposition to the complexity of computers to the way they would disrupt social relations that he values, and to their connection with an industrial system that he sees as disfiguring the earth. It is important to appreciate that Berry is *not* antitechnology. True, his wife uses a Royal typewriter for transcribing his handwritten manuscripts, and he farms with horses. But although he has adopted a way of life that seems quaintly low-tech in the 1990s, he has just been unusually self-conscious and selective in bringing new technlogies into his life.

Utopian and anti-utopian analysts paint their portraits of computerization with monochromatic brushes: white or black. The anti-utopians' characterization of the tragic possibilities of computerization provide an essential counterbalance to the giddy-headed optimism of the utopian accounts. The romances and tragedies are not all identical. For example, some anti-utopian writings examine the possibilities of computerized systems

---

[20] For a very readable and revealing account about the way that newspapers shape the reports that appear as "news," see Robert Karl Manoff and Michael Schudson (eds.), *Reading the News*. Pantheon Books, New York, 1986.

for coercion, while others emphasize alienation. But both utopian and anti-utopian genres have some important inherent limitations. Utopian and anti-utopian visions are not all equally credible, even though they are all, in part, speculative. Sometimes they have internal contradictions.[21] For example, one can ask of Feigenbaum and McCorduck how they expect people to engage in socially important activities that reap no profit (such as helping people in roadside accidents) when the dominant virtue in their Smithian world is individual greed. At other times, it is simply unclear how a social group can move from where it is to the more utopian social order. Unfortunately, computer specialists, like most scientists and technologists, aren't taught how to assess the social viability of different clusters of social assumptions. Nor are computer specialists taught to understand the dynamics of social change.

Our four selections and numerous quotations introduce some of the controversies about the visions of computerization: To what extent are utopian or anti-utopian visions helpful in understanding the social possibilities of computerization? To what extent is social realism a more interesting and reliable guide to the future than the more utopian or anti-utopian visions?[22] If one doesn't trust the anti-utopian and utopian visions, how does one develop a broad framework for asking questions about *what should be done* —what activities should be computerized, in what way, and with what associated practices?

Beyond Technological Utopianism and Anti-Utopianism

Technological utopian and anti-utopian visions embody extreme assumptions about technology and human behavior. They portray new technologies either as extremely pure and innocent or as hopelessly corrupting. But the simplicity of these storylines gives them great clarity and makes them easy to grasp—to enjoy or abhor—and to use as a source of inspiration or despair. They can echo our dreams or our nightmares. Consequently, they have immense influence in shaping the discussions (and real directions) of computerization.

In the 1990s, there will be a large market for social analyses of computerization stimulated by

- the steady stream of computing innovations;
- the drive by academic computer science departments and federal funding agencies to justify large expenditures on computing research;

---

[21] See, for example, Daniel Bell's critique of Adam Smith's vision in *The Cultural Contradictions of Capitalism* (1976).

[22] Kling (1990) uses the label *social realism* to characterize a genre that uses empirical data to examine computing as it is actually practiced and experienced. Social realists write their articles and books with a tacit label: "I have carefully observed and examined computerization in some key social settings and I will tell you how it *really* is." The most common methods are the critical inquiries of journalism and the social sciences and the techniques of ethnography. But the genre is best characterized by the efforts of authors to communicate their understanding of computerization as it "really works" based on reporting fine-grained empirical detail. Social realism gains its force through gritty observations about the social worlds in which computer systems will be used. Kling's article contrasts the strengths and weaknesses of the utopian genres with social realism in substantial detail.

- justifications for major national computerization programs; and
- articles examining life and technology in the 21st century.

Many social analyses of computing that appear in popular and professional magazines, as well as in newspapers and the trade press, will be strongly influenced by technologically utopian assumptions. Consequently, we believe that sophisticated professionals should be especially aware of the strengths and limitations of this genre of analysis.

In our view, the actual uses and consequences of developing computer systems depend upon the way the world works. Conversely, computerized systems may slowly, but inexorably, change that way—often with unforeseen consequences. A key issue is how to understand the social opportunities and dilemmas of computerization without becoming seduced by the social simplifications of utopian romance or discouraged by anti-utopian nightmares. Both kinds of images are far too simplified. But they do serve to help identify an interesting and important set of social possibilities.

Sources

Berry, Wendell (1990). "Why I Am Not Going to Buy a Computer" from *What Are People For? Essays by Wendell Berry*. North Point Press, San Francisco, Calif.

Feigenbaum, Edward, and Pamela McCorduck (1983). *The Fifth Generation: Artificial Intelligence and Japan's Computer Challenge to the World*. Addison-Wesley, Reading, Massachusetts. Excerpts: Prolog, Experts in Silicon, Section 7 (Speculations in Knowledge Futures), Epilog.

Kling, Rob, and Suzanne Iacono (1990). "Making a Computer Revolution," *Journal of Computing and Society*, 1(1), pp. 43–58.

Sculley, John (1989). "The Relationship Between Business and Higher Education: A Perspective on the Twenty-first Century," *Communications of the ACM*. 32(9)(September), pp. 1056–1061.

References

Bell, Daniel (1976). *The Cultural Contradictions of Capitalism*. Basic Books, New York.

Boguslaw, Robert (1965). *The New Utopians: A Study of System Design and Social Change*. Prentice Hall, Englewood Cliffs, N.J.

Denning, Peter J. (Chairman), Douglas E. Comer, David Gries, Michael C. Mulder, Allen Tucker, A. Joe Turner, and Paul R. Young (1989). "Computing as a Discipline," *Communications of the ACM*. 32(1)(January, pp. 9–23).

Dorf, Richard C, and Yvonne L. Hunter (eds.)(1978). *Appropriate Visions: Technology, the Environment and the Individual*. Boyd and Fraser Publishing Co., San Francisco, Calif.

Engelbart, Douglas (1963). "A Conceptual Framework for the Augmentation of Man's Intellect," in P. Howerman (ed.), *Vistas in Information Handling*, Vol. I, Spartan Books, Washington, D.C., pp. 1–29. Reprinted in Greif (1988).

Goodman, Paul (1970). *The New Reformation: Notes of a Neolithic Conservative*. Random House, New York.

Greif, Irene (ed.)(1988). *Computer-Supported Cooperative Work: A Book of Readings*. Morgan-Kaufmann, San Mateo, California.

Grudin, Jonathan (1989). "Why Groupware Applications Fail: Problems in Design and Evaluation," *Office: Technology and People*. 4(3), pp. 245–264.

Johansen, Robert (1988). *Groupware: Computer Support for Business Teams.* The Free Press, New York.

Kling, Rob (1990). "Reading 'All About' Computerization: Five Common Genres of Social Analysis," in Doug Schuler (ed.), *Directions in Advanced Computer Systems, 1990.* Ablex Pub. Co., Norwood, N.J.

Kozol, Jonathan (1985). *Illiterate America.* Anchor Press/Doubleday, Garden City, N.Y.

Kumar, Krishan (1987). *Utopia and Anti-Utopian in Modern Times.* Basil Blackwell, New York.

Landow, George (1990). "Hypertext and Cooperative Work: The Example of Intermedia," in Jolene Galegher, Robert Kraut, and Carmen Egido (eds.), *Intellectual Teamwork: Social and Technological Foundations of Cooperative Work.* Lawrence Erlbaum Associates, Hillsdale, N.J.

McLellan, David (1990). *Utopian Pessimist: The Life and Thought of Simone Weil.* Poseidon Press, New York.

Reinecke, Ian (1984). *Electronic Illusions: A skeptic's View of Our High Tech Future.* Penguin, New York.

Segal, Howard P. (1986). "The Technological Utopians," in Joseph J. Corn (ed.), *Imagining Tomorrow: History, Technology and the American Future.* The MIT Press, Cambridge, Mass.

Stonier, Tom (1983). *The Wealth of Information: A Profile of the Post-industrial Economy.* Methuen London Ltd, London, England.

Todd, Ian, and Michael Wheeler (1978). *Utopia.* Harmony Books, New York.

Toffler, Alvin (1980). *The Third Wave.* Bantam Books, New York.

Tuchman, Gaye (1978). *Making News: A Study in the Construction of Reality.* The Free Press, New York.

Weizenbaum, Joseph (1976). *Computer Power and Human Reason.* Freeman Pub. Co., San Francisco.

Further Reading

Burnham, David (1983). *The Rise of the Computer State.* Random House, New York.

Daedalus of the New Scientist (1970). "Pure Technology." *Technology Review* (June), pp. 38–45, also reprinted in Alfred Teich (ed.), *Technology and Man's Future* (1st ed.) St. Martin's Press, New York.

Glendinning, Chellis (1990). *When Technology Wounds: The Human Consequences of Progress.* William Morrow, New York.

Kling, Rob, and Suzanne Iacono (1988). "The Mobilization of Support for Computerization: The Role of Computerization Movements," *Social Problems.* 35(3)(June), pp. 226–243.

Kling, Rob, and Suzanne Iacono (1990). "Making the Computer Revolution," *Journal of Computing and Society.* 1(1).

Lyon, David (1988). *The Information Society: Issues and Illusions.* Polity Press, Cambridge, England.

Pfaffenberger, Bryan (1989). "The Social Meaning of the Personal Computer: Or, Why the Personal Computer Revolution Was No Revolution," *Anthropological Quarterly.* 61(1)(January), pp. 39–47.

Simon, Herbert (1977). "What Computers Mean for Man & Society," *Science.* 195(4283)(March 18), pp. 1186–1190.

Webster, Robin (1986). *Information Technology: A Luddite Analysis.* Ablex, Norwood, N.J.

Winner, Langdon (1984). "Mythinformation in the High-Tech Era," *IEEE Spectrum.* 21(6), pp. 90–96.

P·A·R·T· I

1

Excerpts From *The Fifth Generation: Artificial Intelligence and Japan's Computer Challenge to the World*

Edward Feigenbaum • Pamela McCorduck

Prolog

Time magazine's "Man of the Year" for 1982 was not a man at all, but a machine—the computer. The computer revolution has barely begun, but already we see a startling penetration of computers in most forms of work people do, their gadgets and machinery, and their entertainment. The economists tell us that we have become a nation of knowledge workers: more than half of us are engaged in the various forms of knowledge and information processing. The computer is the knowledge worker's tool, as the planting and harvesting machines are to the farmer and the heavy industrial machines are to the manufacturing worker. The ascendancy of the knowledge worker is reflected in the ascendancy of the tool—the computer. It has been a long time since a child of technology has had such a profound effect upon our lives and our society.

Knowledge is power, and the computer is an amplifier of that power. We are now at the dawn of a new computer revolution. *Business Week* featured it as "the second computer age." We view it as the important computer revolution, the transition from

Reprinted by permission of the authors, Edward Feigenbaum and Pamela McCorduck. *The Fifth Generation: Artificial Intelligence and Japan's Computer Challenge to the World*, New American Library, New York, (1985), pp. xv–xvii, pp. 66–70, pp. 94–101, pp. 265–267, pp. 271–276, pp. 288–292. British Commonwealth edition published by Michael Joseph Ltd. © 1983 by Edward Feigenbaum and Pamela McCorduck.

information processing to knowledge processing, from computers that calculate and store data to computers that reason and inform. Artificial intelligence is emerging from the laboratory and is beginning to take its place in human affairs. Professor Allen Newell of Carnegie-Mellon University, a pioneer of artificial intelligence, once wrote that "computer technology offers the possibility of incorporating intelligent behavior in all the nooks and crannies of our world." The nooks and crannies are right now being filled with computers, and the intelligent behavior is following quickly along.

The American computer industry has been innovative, vital, and successful. It is, in a way, the ideal industry. It creates value by transforming the brainpower of the knowledge workers, with little consumption of energy and raw materials. Today we dominate the world's ideas and markets in this most important of all modern technologies. But what about tomorrow?

The Japanese have seen gold on distant hills and have begun to move out. Japanese planners view the computer industry as vital to their nation's economic future and have audaciously made it a national goal to become number one in this industry by the latter half of the 1990s. They aim not only to dominate the traditional forms of the computer industry but to establish a "knowledge industry" in which knowledge will be a salable commodity like food and oil. Knowledge itself is to become the new wealth of nations.

To implement this vision the Japanese have both strategy and tactics. Their strategy is simple and wise: to avoid a head-on confrontation in the marketplace with the currently dominant American firms; instead to look out into the 1990s to find an arena of great economic potential that is currently being overlooked by the more short-sighted and perhaps complacent American firms; to move rapidly now to build major strength in that arena. The tactics are set forth in a major and impressive national plan of the Ministry of International Trade and Industry (MITI) called Fifth Generation Computer Systems. The plan documents a carefully staged 10-year research and development program on Knowledge Information Processing Systems. The implementation began in April 1982 with the formation of the Institute for New Generation Computer Technology (ICOT) and coordinated laboratories of the major Japanese firms in the computer industry.

The Japanese plan is bold and dramatically forward-looking. It is unlikely to be completely successful in the ten-year period. But to view it therefore as "a lot of smoke," as some American industry leaders have done, is a serious mistake. Even partially realized concepts that are superbly engineered can have great economic value, preempt the market, and give the Japanese the dominant position they seek.

We now regret our complacency in other technologies. Who in the 1960s took seriously the Japanese initiative in small cars? Who in 1970 took seriously the Japanese national goal to become number one in consumer electronics in 10 years? (Have you seen an American VCR that isn't Japanese on the inside?) In 1972, when the Japanese had yet to produce their first commercial microelectronic chip but announced their national plans in this vital "made in America" technology, who would have thought that in 10 years they would have half of the world's market for the most advanced memory chips? Are we about to blow it again? The consequences of complacency, of our spirited attention to the near-in at the expense of the long view, will be devastating to the economic health of our most important industry. Even more important than its direct effect on the computing industry, present complacency will have serious economic effects on all industries. Since computing is the technology that drives all other technologies, a second-rate computing industry will also mean impaired industrial design and manufacturing, and enfeebled management and planning. The Japanese could thereby become the dominant industrial power in the world.

We are writing this book because we are worried. But we are also basically optimistic. Americans invented this technology! If only we could focus our efforts, we should have little trouble dominating the second computer age as we dominated the first. We have a two- or three-year lead; that's large in the world of high technology. But we are squandering our lead at the rate of one day per day.

America needs a national plan of action, a kind of space shuttle program for the knowledge systems of the future. In this book we have tried to explain this new knowledge technology, its roots in American and British research, and the Japanese Fifth Generation plan for extending and commercializing it. We have also outlined America's weak, almost nonexistent response to this remarkable Japanese challenge. The stakes are high. In the trade wars, this may be the crucial challenge. Will we rise to it? If not, we may consign our nation to the role of the first great postindustrial agrarian society.

Experts in Silicon

Speculations in Knowledge Futures

If the creation of artificial intelligence is among the most challenging and controversial tasks the human mind has ever put itself to, if the difficulties often seem overwhelming, that has never prevented the field from being surrounded by fantastic predictions for the future. But the truth is that no one knows exactly what surprises are in store for us all. We can only speculate.

The "Mechanical" Doctor

Many kinds of expertise are unevenly distributed in the world. Medicine is a perfect example. That is one reason the U.S. National Institutes of Health have been at the forefront of supporting expert systems research. It isn't just that the natives of Ulan Bator don't have the same access to medical care as the natives of Los Angeles; it's that the natives of Fresno don't have it either, and poor people in Los Angeles aren't as fortunate in their medical attention as well-off people.

If the idea of a machine doctor repels you, consider that not everyone feels that way. Studies in England showed that many humans were much more comfortable (and candid) with an examination by a computer terminal than with a human physician, whom they perceived as somehow disapproving of them. "Mechanical" doctors are in fact systems that move methodically through possibilities, making inferences and drawing conclusions. They often outperform the very experts who have programmed them because of their methodical ways; they don't skip or forget things, get tired or rushed, or fall subject to some of our other human failings. They will be on call at the patient's convenience, not just the physician's. And they can bring medicine to places where none now exists.

The Intelligent Library

One application anybody interested in knowledge will welcome is the intelligent library. Nowadays, a library has information, even knowledge, but you must supply the intelligence. You pick among topics in the card catalog; you browse in the stacks, sorting and choosing; you go to the reference librarian in despair.

The intelligent library, based on knowledge information processing systems, will supply intelligence along with knowledge and information. It will be active, not passive. It will conduct a dialogue with you, inferring from what you tell it what it is you really want. You can ask a question, state a goal, and by asking you questions in turn, it will infer your desires and try to meet them. It will even prompt you with connected topics you hadn't, at that moment, thought of. It will test your hypotheses, verify your hunches, and explain until you really understand.

All this is done by inference: sometimes the library doesn't have the direct answer, but it can reason its way through the information glut and present you with plausible scenarios, explaining at your request its reasons for arriving at those scenarios.

Does the end of libraries as we know them mean the end of books? Probably not for a long time, if ever. We still write (some) letters, even though we have telephones, Telexes, and other forms of sending messages to each other. Books may very well become pieces of art in the distant future; meanwhile, their great advantages of high resolution, portability, and random access (you can riffle through the pages so easily) will have to be met by any system that wants to replace them. One can imagine such solutions: a personal book-size "reading machine" that allows you to slip chips in and go with them where you will, spring hillside or pleasure cruise; that even allows you to flip from written to spoken word if you'd rather hear than see.

The Intelligent Tutor

A leading Western intellectual, realizing that he knew nothing about science, recently cried out that the universe had gone silent on him. That reaction seemed a bit perfervid, but if he can hold out, help is on the way.

There are many topics we know nothing about, but would like to know something about, if it weren't so painful to learn. As it happens, the pain is inflicted in two ways: first, it is difficult to make your mind grasp concepts that are quite alien from those you're used to dealing with; and second, it is a terrible embarrassment for a grownup to keep on admitting that he just doesn't understand. Thus most of us simply close off whole areas of human intellectual achievement because the difficulties overwhelm us. If, however, we had an infinitely patient, intelligent, and nonjudgmental tutor, we might feel different.

"What can you tell me about physics?" you ask your intelligent tutor in a discreet aside. SHALL WE BEGIN WITH THE UNIFIED THEORY? it asks. "Sure," you say, "why not?" Your intelligent tutor may be talking to you; words may be appearing in print on some sort of receiver, but soon pictures will start to appear. Even today, with the help of computer graphics, phenomena that could not be pictured any other way can be realized pictorially: theorems become breathtakingly beautiful visual designs, their regularity and elegance presented in a visual—and visceral—way that rewrites the old Chinese adage to say that a picture is worth ten thousand terms.

With the intelligent tutor, the experience of knowledge will be available at any level you want, from general, undetailed introduction for the novice to detailed instruction in specialities only an expert might want. When the first explanation of a concept fails to penetrate, the intelligent tutor (either because you have told it so explicitly, or because it has determined that fact for itself by testing you slyly) will try rephrasing the concept, using analogies, pictures, mathematical terms—whatever is necessary to make you understand. If you don't understand even then, it will tactfully tell you what you can indeed absorb, and neither of you need worry about what you cannot.

Knowledge Simulators: "Games" for Teaching

If such tutors are available for adults—and the Japanese count on them to continue the process of lifelong learning for their ever more elderly population—what might education for children look like?

One answer came from a recent symposium devoted to video games. That might seem like an odd forum in which to ponder the educational possibilities of the intelligent computer, but learning was the main theme of nearly all of the speakers.

Several speakers who are working on the frontiers, well beyond the relatively simple shoot-'em-ups in present-day arcades, reminded their scholarly audience that video games are in their infancy in every sense of the term. But even at this primitive stage, it is easy to imagine the kinds of games that are possible in the future, once much higher degrees of computer speed and memory are available, coupled with highly sophisticated graphics capabilities and reasoning power. Perhaps the most important property these future games will have is that although they'll be fun, for that's in the nature of games, they'll teach—painlessly and naturally.

Already certain special groups have such "games" specially designed for them. Pilots learning to fly the latest commercial jet do not take one out for a spin the first time at the controls. Instead, they have $10 million toys called simulators that give them as precisely as possible the feeling of flying the craft they will eventually fly for real.

We have peculiar and mainly pejorative associations with the idea of games—surely they can't be serious, and they have little to do with the business of functioning in an adult world. But of course games have everything to do with that. Scientists often describe what they do as a glorious game, and so do securities analysts (the phrase is "to play the stock market," after all). Some games designers argue persuasively that even today, at the admittedly primitive level where video games have arrived, they can stimulate the intellect and teach various skills and facts as well as anything yet devised. A current game called "Time Zone" pushes the player backward into history, allowing him to participate in the assassination of Julius Caesar (but not to prevent it), to persuade Benjamin Franklin face to face to sign the Declaration of Independence (but not to succeed at that), and so forth. Present-day games even have time constraints—in "Detective," evidence will disappear if the player doesn't reason his way to it quickly enough, and once gone, it's gone for the duration of the game. The player must use his wits to compensate. Does such a game teach reasoning skills, or is it simply fun?

If all this is how children might someday learn, what is to become of classrooms? In the very long run, they may meet the same fate as other precomputing organizations, which is to say, having outlived their usefulness, they will simply wither away and die.

But for the foreseeable future, classrooms of some sort will surely exist, if only because the most exuberant games, or simulations, or fantasies, or whatever name we have for those activities by then, will require installations of a size and expense that most families won't want to undertake for themselves. Moreover, children need the company of other children, and the new classrooms will be one place where they'll get it.

Will human teachers disappear? Probably not. But children will learn in a much more independent fashion than they do now, having control over what they learn and when they learn it. Will children be equipped to make those decisions wisely? Only if the learning games they are presented with are designed to impart wisdom. Artificial Intelligence (AI) researchers have long hoped that by discovering how to design an intelligent computer program, they will shed some light on the human learning process —at the moment, after all, we do nothing but spray words at our pupils and hope some of them stick. One of the great challenges educators and cognitive psychologists face in the next few years is to design games that teach the skills necessary for participation in a new world. Perhaps their first task is to identify those skills.

The Intelligent Newspaper

Some people think current events are fascinating. Some people think they are so ephemeral that any time spent on them is time squandered. Your intelligent newspaper will know the way you feel and behave accordingly.

It will know because you will have trained it yourself. In a none-too-arduous process, you will have informed your intelligent newsgathering system about the topics that are of special interest to you. Editorial decisions will be made by you, and your system will be able to act upon them thereafter. It will have hundreds, perhaps thousands, of competing news sources to choose from, and it will understand (because you have told it) which news sources you trust most, which dissenting opinions you wish to be exposed to, and when not to bother you at all.

You could let your intelligent system infer your interests indirectly by watching you as you browse. What makes you laugh? It will remember and gather bits of fantasia to amuse you. What makes you steam? It may gather information about that, too, and then give you names of groups that are organized for or against that particular outrage. What's going on in the neighborhood? You'll be happy to know the crime rate is down over this time last year (or unhappy to know it's up); that Mr. and Mrs. Morton in the next block have just had a baby girl named Joanna and thank everybody for their interest. You can even program in some randomness: surprise me every now and then, you can say to your intelligent newsgatherer, and your trivia file will grow apace.

KIPS at Home

Although expert systems will probably be developed for businesses first, home applications will probably not be far behind. Home video games and computers are simply precursors of much more sophisticated systems that might offer advice on everything from nutrition and tax computation to exercise and legal questions. An electronic, interactive Dr. Spock might assist parents even more effectively than the printed Dr. Spock has for decades.

Expert systems might advise on any number of other tasks: talking you through the job of fixing a leaky toilet—not the model toilet that appears in the fix-it books but is always just different enough from yours to be almost useless, but your toilet—step by step. Or your automobile, or your home computer. How about the gardening coach you can carry through the vegetable patch, discussing proper fertilizers, weather patterns, pest control, and the pleasures of dirt under your fingernails? How about an intelligent dictionary or, better, an intelligent encyclopedia? All yours, all solving problems you want to solve at the moment, and not some abstract, generalized problem that might or might not have bearing on your situation.

All very unexceptional, McCorduck thinks, just the sort of predictions that have been floating around the field for years, firmly grounded in what certainly, in principle, can be done and probably will be. She has other desires and is therefore gratified to read that one purpose of the Japanese Fifth Generation is to alleviate the problems of aging. She exults. For years she's been nagging for, promoting, advocating the geriatric robot. She'd all but lost hope, watching her friends in AI create intelligent physician-machines, intelligent geologist-machines, even intelligent military-spy-machines, but never anything down-home useful. Time is getting on. The geriatric robot might soon be a matter of immediate personal concern.

The geriatric robot is wonderful. It isn't hanging about in the hopes of inheriting your money—nor of course will it slip you a little something to speed the inevitable. It isn't hanging about because it can't find work elsewhere. It's there because it's yours. It doesn't just bathe you and feed you and wheel you out into the sun when you crave fresh air and a change of scene, though of course it does all those things. The very best thing about the geriatric robot is that it *listens*. "Tell me again," it says, "about how wonderful/dreadful your children are to you. Tell me again that fascinating tale of the coup of '63. Tell me again . . ." And it means it. It never gets tired of hearing those stories, just as you never get tired of telling them. It knows your favorites, and those are its favorites too. Never mind that this all ought to be done by human caretakers, humans grow bored, get greedy, want variety. It's part of our charm.

McCorduck felt a slight jolt a few years ago when she heard Yale's Roger Schank muse in a lecture that he didn't believe a machine could be considered intelligent *until* it got bored, but he reassured her later that the art of programming was already refined to the point that a never-bored robot could be fashioned.

Now here were the Japanese, those clever people, claiming their Fifth Generation would alleviate the problems of an aging society. She read the reports eagerly: lifetime education system; medical care information; other rubbishy pieties. She flung down the proceedings in disgust. She is reconciled that she may have to turn AI from spectator to participant sport and whip one up herself before it's too late.

Epilog, or It Is Hard to Predict, Especially the Future

Alternatives for America

The Japanese have announced that in ten years they will produce knowledge information processors. Several options are open to Americans, but few of them offer truly palatable alternatives to undertaking our own version. Let us examine them.

1. We can maintain the status quo. We can continue doing a lot of short-term (shortsighted, in view of many), research and development, spurred by nothing but immediate market considerations. We can penalize the farsighted by removing them from power, industrial *or* political, every time the bottom line fails to give us instant gratification. We can embrace antitrust as infallible revelation and litigate ourselves into national collapse. Uncoordinated planning, investments in the frivolous, and lack of investment in the serious might still allow us to muddle through. Somehow.

2. We can form industrial consortiums to meet the Japanese challenge and as citizens insist that the Justice Department take a reasonable stance regarding joint industrial R&D. This might take an act of Congress. Americans, however, have little experience with such joint ventures.

3. We could enter a major joint venture with the Japanese. Their Fifth Generation proposal gives a lot of lip service to international cooperation. They might not have really meant it, but we could give their lip service a test. There is also the possibility that as the end of various phases of the project approach, the Japanese might find themselves falling short of their targets—either technologically or financially—and would welcome American collaboration. The United States and Japan would complement each other, and the joint venture could be powerful internationally.

4. As a variation on the third plan, we know that the economic value of KIPS (the so-called value added) is primarily in their software, or their knowledge, and we have a proven record as specialists in great software ideas. We could forget about producing the machines and produce only the software instead, styling ourselves after the razor blade company that gave away razors because profits were in the blades. Chips are cheap, and we've seen competition drive profits out of many segments of the computer hardware business. Let's make software instead. In software, capital investment can be low and profits huge.

5. We can form a national laboratory for the promotion of knowledge technology. It might be a mega-institute, like Los Alamos, embracing all forms of knowledge technology. Or it might be a smaller multiple-university-run laboratory (such as Brookhaven and Fermilab in physics). Or it might have one university as the prime contractor (like the Stanford Linear Accelerator Center). Whatever form it takes, the national laboratory must be newly created. Institutions have a natural lifecycle, being most energetic and creative when new and unbureaucratic. We cannot look to the existing national laboratories for the kind of innovations a knowledge technology laboratory must produce, freighted as they are with tradition, stodginess, and bureaucracy. Those three horsemen of the intellectual apocalypse will eventually come to the new laboratory, but while it is still new, it has at least a fighting chance to achieve brilliance.

6. We can prepare to become the first great agrarian postindustrial society. We are blessed with huge tracts of fertile, arable land. Progress in our agrosciences and in automation applied to agriculture has always been impressive. We absolutely shine in growing things. As General Motors and General Electric decline, we can organize General Agriculture to maintain our balance of trade.

As Americans, we are not without alternatives, however unpalatable the reality of some of them may be. Our own first choice, a center for knowledge technology, follows.

The National Center for Knowledge Technology

The United States is not Japan. The U.S. Commerce Department is not the Ministry of International Trade and Industry, and the Pentagon should not be, even by default. Nearly everyone in the information processing industry agrees that some sort of cooperative effort is necessary to ensure well-educated researchers, fruitful research, and an end to the frittering away of resources in short-term get-rich schemes that benefit the very few. We do *not* have unlimited resources of any kind—not unlimited talent, money, or time—and other nations are moving off into a future where we must follow whether we like it or not, but where we could lead if we wanted.

Though there have been several different attempts by industrial groups to pool certain resources, good intentions have been frustrated by a deeply ingrained tradition of commercial competition (legally reinforced by means of strict antitrust laws), by the lack of any suitable framework in which to carry out cooperation, and by the lack of widely shared national goals.

One eminent scientist has quite seriously suggested that all who are concerned about the Japanese Fifth Generation should put all their energy into persuading our own great national resource, IBM, to take on the task of competing with the Japanese project—that IBM is our best hope. Though the idea has its beguiling aspects (not to mention its bizarre ones), it seems a bit fanciful. Moreover, it would give to one firm an exclusive command over a technology that many firms ought to share, as the Japanese themselves have recognized.

Let us make another proposal. The United States should form a national center for knowledge technology. By "knowledge technology" we mean computing certainly, but we also mean other related forms of knowledge distribution, such as libraries, for which there are important technological needs and exciting opportunities. This idea of a national center of knowledge technology isn't original with us; industrialists, educators, and government officials have all suggested variations on such a plan.

An alternative form of the plan would be a national center for information processing technology, conceived recently by a senior government science administrator. It would cut more deeply into the world of technology but less broadly across the world of knowledge systems. This center would not compete with industry. On the contrary, it would play an ARPA-like role, supporting the kind of basic research no single firm or even group of firms can afford to risk. Like ARPA, it would fund and coordinate high-risk projects through their early research stages until industries could take the results into the development stage. Its responsibilities would be long-term results, not short-term profits. Thus its funds might come from all who would stand to gain from such a center, in both the public and the private sectors. To be effective, funding has to be generous; the amount to vary depending on how widely or narrowly knowledge technology is construed.

If it is narrowly construed, a pilot project something like the Japanese Fifth Generation might be undertaken—we certainly believe the United States owes it to itself to continue the research it pioneered, to develop it, and to reap its obvious benefits. But if the center is broadly construed, it would embrace research in an enormous complex of information and knowledge technologies, from telecommunications to publishing, from new computer designs to new curriculum designs for our schools. Eventually it must assign priorities to national research and take the difficult step of setting standards flexible enough for new technology to be accommodated, yet stern enough to avoid the wasteful incompatibilities we have seen, for example, in video discs and computer software.

Though funds must come first from the government, this should not be a government agency. The civil service salary structure cannot cope with the need, and the civil service machinery is too ponderous to allow the center to work with the speed and suppleness it must have. Indeed, it should probably be staffed by people on temporary loan from firms, research laboratories, universities, and other talent pools.

The difficulties are obvious. How are intellectual property rights to be properly assigned and rewarded? Common law has a long tradition of dealing with real property, but its dealings with intellectual property have been uninspired. We have already talked about the dearth of qualified scientists and engineers in AI and the rest of computer science, and such a center would drain talent from universities and other research laboratories. But this is a problem, like the problems of intellectual property rights, that our society will have to face anyway. The establishment of a center might in fact help in the solution. How is technology to be transferred effectively from the laboratory to industry? How is a high level of innovation to be maintained? There are other, equally serious problems. But what real choice do we have?

The center we propose would be an expression and institutional embodiment of national will, much as the Kennedy and Manned Spacecraft Centers of NASA have been. There has never been an organization like it in the United States. Projects of this magnitude (and there are few enough) have been government- or military-controlled as, for example, the space program was. But then there has never in our history, or in the history of the world, come such a sudden and profoundly exciting opportunity: the convergence of many disparate social functions such as publishing, manufacturing, health care and other professional services, education, entertainment, and newsgathering, to name a few, waiting to be fused into a set of very much more powerful technologies that will allow those functions to thrive with more efficiency, accuracy, and effectiveness for everyone.

We have the opportunity at this moment to do a new version of Diderot's *Encyclopedia*, a gathering up of all knowledge—not just the academic kind, but the informal, experiential, heuristic kind—to be fused, amplified, and distributed, all at orders of magnitude difference in cost, speed, volume, and *usefulness* over what we have now. A book in a library may have important information, but if your library happens not to have that volume, or the volume is crumbling to dust because most books in the last fifty years were printed on acidic papers that self-destruct, the knowledge is lost. If knowledge is buried in a Niagara of information, it is lost to the overburdened human who cannot take the time, or does not have the fortitude, to interpret Niagaras of information.

What faces us, if you like, is the Louisiana Purchase in the manifest destiny of computing. The initial cost seems high, and the skeptics are already having fun. But to the visionaires the investment promises multiple dividends, not the least being a revitalization of the national will, and the pleasures of becoming, once more, the country of "why not?"

Knowledge in our world right now is a cat's cradle of threads which even the most skillful human being cannot grasp in two hands as he or she goes about daily work. The

Japanese believe they can weave those confusing, fragile, and all too easily dropped threads into a garment that will shelter, nurture, decorate, and empower the human intellect. They're also convinced that for national survival, they must.

So can Americans. And for national survival, perhaps we must, too. National security is a multidimensional state of affairs that depends on healthy, productive industry, agriculture, education, commerce, and government, all thriving on the rapid creation, diffusion, and utilization of knowledge.

Should our knowledge technology goals continue to be set only by the military, certain compromises must occur. First, such research might become strategic, subject to government regulation, which would mean an end to the rapid and free exchange of ideas that has so enriched the early work in AI, knowledge systems, and computing in general. Second, research might eventually be skewed primarily toward military objectives. Military and civilian goals can be harmonious, but they are different.

If, of course, Americans can only bear the burden of financial support in the name of national defense, we can call it national defense. We built the interstate highway system in the name of national defense, and with the same justification we educated a generation of college students in everything from Asian art to zoology. In a national center for knowledge technology, we are suggesting no more than insurance in a world where other nations have already perceived the centrality of knowledge to their self-interest and are acting upon it.

The Strategic Computing Program

Well, so we wrote in the first edition of this book, and it must have caused some smiles around the Pentagon, for plans had been forming since 1982, first for a major push in supercomputers, and then for a major push in artificial intelligence, under the auspices of DARPA. In the opinion of DARPA insiders we would later speak to, the announcement of the Fifth Generation had simply helped to sharpen what were a series of good ideas in their formative stages.

One of the first hints that something new might be emerging from DARPA came during a pleasant summer lunch with Lynn Conway and her colleague, Mark Stefik, just after the first edition of this book had been published. Conway wanted to know why we hadn't taken the idea embedded in "A Network of Minds" and applied it to our Center for Knowledge Technology. Why were we so taken with a bricks-and-mortar center, when the lesson of the network adventure was that an electronic center (a virtual center, as computer jargon would put it) was now not only possible, but really more sensible, at least for as large and heterogeneous a country as the United States?

Just hadn't though of it, we frankly confessed.

Such an electronic center for research in knowledge technology is an important part of a plan called "Strategic Computing: New Generation Computing Technology, A Strategic Plan for Its Development and Application to Critical Problems in Defense" that emerged in October 1983 from DARPA.

The plan's major objectives are comprehensive and ambitious: its ultimate aim is to provide a broad base of machine intelligence technology for application to critical defense problems, *and* to create a strong industrial capacity to support national security requirements. (This might be the first time that any official document of the Defense Department has explicitly proposed to create a technology to strengthen the industrial sector and by extension, to strengthen the national economy.)

The plan itself is a skillful (and characteristically American) blend of the concrete and the abstract. Three specific and ambitious military applications have been chosen because they focus and stimulate the creation of the technology, and then provide a ready laboratory to show whether the technology actually works. They are: first, autonomous vehicles, such as unmanned aircraft, submersibles, and land vehicles; second, expert associates for pilots in the cockpit; and third, large-scale battle management systems. These three particular projects are expected to lead to spinoffs that will benefit both national security and the economy.

As the report points out, computing already plays an essential role in defense, but old-style computers are awkward and inflexible, and limited in their adaptability to unanticipated circumstances. DARPA envisions a new (but pointedly not "fifth") generation of computers that can transcend today's computers by a quantum jump. The new generation will be driven by expert systems, and equipped with sensory and communications devices that allow them to hear, talk, see and act on information and data they receive, or develop themselves.

In this, DARPA is only planning to exploit in a grand and coordinated manner a lot of scattered research that the agency itself has largely underwritten in the past two decades, research that has yielded a number of advances, but all in separate areas of artificial intelligence, computer science, and microelectronics. The agency's planners see the opportunity for the joint development of these advances to produce highly intelligent machines.

The three specific projects provide different, though sometimes overlapping and sometimes complementary opportunities for research. The autonomous vehicle, for example, whether for land, air or sea, would be a true robot that can see and sense, and respond specifically to general instructions or goals. Thus such a land vehicle might be capable of planning a route toward some destination from data it knows about the terrain it will move over, and will then be able to rearrange that route based on information from its sensors as it moves along resolving ambiguities between sensed and pre-stored data: checking on itself as it moves by comparing its route to anticipated landmarks, just as a human traveler might. The computer, of course, can occupy no more than 6 to 15 cubic feet in such a vehicle, can weigh no more than 500 pounds, and should consume less than 1 kw of power. As the DARPA plan points out, these requirements will mean at least one to four orders of magnitude reduction in weight, space, and power over today's computing systems. For other kinds of space, air and sea vehicles, the requirements would be even more stringent, including the ability to operate in high radiation. DARPA's 10-year goal is a robotic reconnaissance tank that can navigate 80 miles from one destination to another at an average of 40 miles per hour, computing all the while. Here, then, are goals of miniaturization, robustness, and intelligent functions, such as reasoning and understanding, on an unprecedented scale.

In combat, a pilot is nearly overwhelmed by the information that floods into the cockpit, and yet he must base life-and-death decisions on his own quick grasp of the situation. Thus the second specific project proposed by the DARPA program is a pilot's associate to help him in the air as well as on the ground, not replacing but complementing him, by taking over lower-level chores and performing special functions so that he can focus on tactical and strategic objectives. In its simplest form, the personal associate does routine tasks, and, when so instructed, initiates actions on its own. In its advanced form, the personal associate performs a set of tasks that are difficult or altogether impossible for the pilot, such as the early detection and diagnosis of an impending malfunction. It's an associate he can talk to and receive answers from in natural language or graphics, and it will be personal to a specific pilot, trained by him to respond in certain ways and perform particular functions that he considers important. Here again are miniaturization and robustness in hardware, combined with goals for processing among complex, integrated knowledge-based systems that must be a hundred times faster than current systems; there must also be unambiguous voice communication in extremely noisy surroundings.

Finally, battle management in modern warfare means decision making under uncertainty. There are open and hidden problems, solutions with various consequences, and conflicting goals. When decisions are made, they must be monitored, and may have to be adjusted as circumstances evolve. Individual intelligent systems address some of these problems, but no single system addresses them all. The battle management system envisioned by DARPA would be the complete assistant. It would be capable of comprehending uncertain data to produce forecasts of likely events. It could draw on previous human and machine experience to suggest potential courses of action, evaluating them and explaining rationales for them. At this point, it could develop a plan for implementing the option selected by the human commanders, disseminate the plan to those concerned, and report progress to the decision maker during the execution phase. All this would take place in natural language between humans and machine. This project includes the much more subtle goals of natural language communication more so, say, than the pilot's associate (which could function with a small command vocabulary based on recognition rather than understanding). Other goals include new and particularly hardy devices for sensing and signal processing, and of course highly sophisticated decision support systems based on the fusion of data and knowledge from many sources.

In summary, the DARPA plan calls for integrated intelligent functions of vision, speech recognition and production, natural language understanding, and expert systems technology to be realized with newly designed software and hardware. In addition, the development of microelectronics technology to support all these must be fostered in a multitude of locations.

Although the research DARPA supports during this project is intended to meet the goals of the three military applications, the resulting technology will be generic, stretching across the spectrum of computing from hardware and other devices through software design and implementation. Signal processing (which is the interpretation of data from a sensor) and symbolic processing (which deals with nonnumeric objects, their relationships, and the ability to infer or deduce new information with the aid of programs that reason) will also be pushed far ahead. The program will put strong emphasis on accelerating and exploiting the miniaturization of microelectronics by dramatically reducing the usual delays between basic research innovations in fabrication and packaging technology and their subsequent exploitation by designers.

Silicon will continue to be the mainstay of the program because of its maturity and accessibility to all researchers. The processors' power consumption will be reduced as computational power is increased. But, to meet the ultimate demands of the plan, a new fabrication technology will be developed to yield devices that are an order of magnitude smaller than those produced today.

The agency expects to manage the activities of a large number of people and groups in universities, research institutes and industry across the United States. To do so, the initial focus (and funds) will concentrate on the "bricks and mortar" of an electronic research center, in other words, the means to coordinate and disseminate technology not only among the participants, but across U.S. industry. Thus, a major part of the budget during the first years will be devoted to upgrading the computing and communications equipment of the participants. (The Strategic Computing Plan's total budget is $50 million in 1984, $95 million in 1985, and $150 million in 1986, leading to costs of approximately $600 million over the first five years of the program.) This high initial investment in computing and communications equipment will also magnify the effect of the most critical resource: trained people. For DARPA, too, notes how few qualified people there are in these fields.

DARPA's Strategic Computing Plan is surely the right plan at the right time. But managers at DARPA expect to undertake a task of management and coordination that is not only staggering in its complexity but unprecedented in its decentralization. Popular futurists assure us that decentralization is the wave of the future, and it is probably true, but DARPA is riding just ahead of the wave. It is a dangerous and heady place to be, as any surfer can attest. The thrills are exceptional, but the wipeouts can be catastrophic.

A key part of the project depends on rapid prototyping and rapid transfer of technology from research laboratories into the firms. But American research laboratories, particularly in the universities, have long enjoyed the luxury of producing experimental devices that need not answer to real-world requirements; they may be astonished to have to try. American firms, on the other hand, are mainly accustomed to evolutionary changes; the revolutionary changes required by the Fifth Generation may be more than cautious American managers are ready to cope with. A habit of looking only at short-term profits as opposed to long-term endurance might be hard for American industrialists to break.

Moreover, the Strategic Computing Program differs from the Japanese Fifth Generation Plan in that although it embraces many of the same goals, in its brash American way it also embraces goals the Japanese have prudently assigned to other national projects, such as the National Superspeed Computing Project and the National Robotics Project. The singular focus of the Fifth Generation Project is therefore somewhat diffused among a number of projects in the Strategic Computing Program.

On the other hand, the concrete objectives of the American plan—the three testbeds —may, after all, focus research just as effectively as the Japanese manage to by organizational means.

Finally, some Americans might be uneasy about depending solely on the Defense Department—however visionary its planners, and however reluctant Americans are to spend money, except in the name of national defense—to provide them with important new knowledge technology. As we have already pointed out, knowledge technology goals, set only by the military, could entail compromises that this democracy might eventually find intolerable. Others were thinking that way too, particularly the group of industrialists who had gathered together in Orlando, Florida, in February 1983 to form the research consortium called the Microelectronics and Computer Technology Corporation.

An American Industrial Response

As soon as the appointment of former Admiral Bobby Ray Inman as president and chief executive officer of the Microelectronics and Computer Technology Corporation (MCC) was announced, changes in that organization began to take place. His appointment not only brought new firms in at once; it continued to attract additional firms. The total number by the end of 1983 was 14, and included Advanced Micro Devices, Allied, Control Data, Digital Equipment, Harris, Honeywell, Martin-Marietta, Mostek, Motorola, National Semiconductor, NCR, RCA, Rockwell and Sperry. The MCC's by-laws make it a for-profit corporation, with a maximum of 30 shareholder companies. It will deliver product-independent technology, the patents of which will belong to MCC, but which the shareholder companies can license and turn into products. Those shareholder companies that support the initial research have a three-year lead in licensing; after that, anybody, including foreign firms, can be licensed. The corporation eventually expects to employ between 400 and 600 people, with a budget that will climb from $50 million a year to $100 million a year.

MCC requires a relatively modest initiation fee of $250,000 for a firm to become a member (and there is a further requirement, that member firms be at least 51% U.S.-owned), but the real expenses for shareholder firms come in the programs they elect to support, expenses that could run as high as ten million dollars a year if a firm decides to participate in all major programs. The three-year advantage shareholder firms have in licensing gives them an incentive to support as many programs as they can afford. As in the Japanese Fifth Generation project, each participant in a program is expected to supply one individual as a technical liaison, who will be resident at MCC, but who will return regularly to his or her sponsoring firm to report information.

Before Inman's arrival, a research agenda had already been put together by preliminary task forces, which included the four major areas mentioned earlier, namely: microelectronics packaging, CAD/CAM, software productivity, and advanced computer architectures (this last is an eight- to ten-year program, originally called Alpha-Omega, meant to focus on architectures for human interfaces with machines, knowledge-based systems, data base systems, and parallel processing, in other words, an American Fifth Generation).

Once he became its president, Inman had the task of finding a site for MCC; hiring the scientists and managers who would guide the projects; managing a collaboration among the shareholder firms; persuading them that the results would not come soon, but would be worth waiting for; and maintaining a friendly relationship with the federal government, especially the Justice Department. None of these would be easy; several were daunting.

The site selection consumed some six months, with a newly sensitized set of American states and cities eager to take advantage of the benefits that were perceived to flow from a high-tech industrial presence. Fifty-seven cities in 27 states vied to be chosen, including such obvious sites as Minneapolis, the home of Control Data and Honeywell; Atlanta; the Research Triangle in North Carolina; San Diego; Silicon Valley; the Boston-Cambridge area; and Pittsburgh.

The winner was Austin, Texas. This was due not to the fact that it was Bobby Inman's home town, but instead to exemplary cooperation—"on a scale not seen since World War II in the United States," Inman would say later—among three segments of the community, namely, state and local government, academics, and the private sector.

In MCC's assessment, each segment in Austin wanted to attract the new corporation for its own purposes, yet could cooperate with the others to make sure that the goal was accomplished. This was extremely important, because Inman and MCC detected only hopes and promises at some of the other sites they considered, with a locality making promises that its state government might not honor, or vice versa. Inman himself feared that, in some cases, the enthusiasm for MCC would disappear with the election of a new governor or mayor. Since MCC would produce no research results in the short term, it needed a long-term commitment on the part of its host.

In Texas, however, legislators had already been asking what would happen to their state when the oil ran out, exhibiting a foresight rare among elected representatives. By the mid-1970s, the Texas legislature was enacting laws that would make Texas a more hospitable place for high-technology corporations. It was almost as if Texas were preparing itself for something like the MCC: the state's commitment preceded its opportunities, and once the opportunity came, it was ready. A fair amount of trading took place between the state and the city of Austin. The University of Texas pledged itself ready to pour more resources into its already respected computer science department and pledged to cooperate with Texas A & M, where the latter school had specialized expertise the university did not—a crucial point for MCC, because it needed to be somewhere where young talent would be coming out to join the consortium five years down the road. The private sector, in the form of the public-spirited wealthy, simply got out checkbooks to make sure that MCC was supplied with important extras, such as mortgage money for MCC employees that was slightly below the market rates, and a job-placement bureau for their spouses. It was all a form of enlightened self-interest, because everybody expects that MCC will create a ripple effect, which is to say it will help create the broad base of high technology that Austin and the state of Texas seek.

"Austin is a good place to work for many reasons," Inman would say in the temporary offices that housed MCC in late 1983. "But maybe the most important reason is that Austin still has a can-do attitude, and that's infectious. It's also essential for an effort like ours." He is a slender, soft-spoken man, articulate and quick, who retains just a touch of the sailor's walk. And though he laughs readily, almost impishly at times, there is ever present the sense of will and discipline that one would cross at one's peril.

Inman's next task was hiring. MCC's planning documents show a deep concern with quality appointments, not only for purposes of good research, but also for attracting researchers from outside the participating firms. Inman sought people who were capable both of conducting long-term, quality scientific research, and of managing that research. "Those two qualities don't often come in the same person," he explained, "and so the obvious answer—and the strategy I've used in the past—is to assemble teams of people who had one or the other and could work together."

He discovered, perhaps not surprisingly, that although there was a good supply of management talent, there was a somewhat scarcer supply of scientific talent, and the timetable he had originally hoped for, that research would be underway at MCC by late 1983, had to be adjusted. Research for most of the programs began in February 1984, and the remainder was underway by late April 1984. Talent already aboard has been preparing detailed roadmaps for the research to be undertaken. Almost Japanese-style, bonuses of up to 50% of a researcher's salary will eventually be rewarded for scientific achievements (not profits). "I'm choosing people for the long term, and I'm being very choosy," he said.

Among the first persons he chose was MCC's chief scientist, John Pinkston. Inman sees his own great strength as a manager of collaborative efforts, where he has had much experience, whether the collaborations were among various government agencies or the different armed services. But he readily admitted his own lack of technical expertise. "So my job was to find a technical person I could treat as an alter ego, somebody I could trust absolutely, to be my chief scientist. For that, I went back to my own past, and I expect that raised a lot of eyebrows."

It had not raised eyebrows so much as it puzzled the computer science community; having done all his work on secret projects, Pinkston was an unknown. But Pinkston had been in the government for seventeen years, where he was in charge of the production of "some very high-level, complex machines for government classified purposes, which the public will not know about for many, many years to come. He has deep technical knowledge, a great intellectual curiosity, and is greatly excited to be doing this."

One of Inman's first challenges, in managing a rather obstreperous collaboration of independent firms that had no experience of cooperation with each other, centered on the Alpha-Omega program, the part of MCC's research most closely resembling the Japanese Fifth Generation. Since it accounts for about half of MCC's commitment to research, there was big trouble. A number of the shareholder firms expressed great uneasiness about a single leader for Alpha-Omega, as called for in the original plan put together by Gordon Bell and his task force. The firms were concerned that a single leader for such a crucial project might bias the research, push the project in one particular aspect—for example, knowledge-based systems, or parallel processing—at the expense of the other parts of the program. This, in turn, might benefit the products of one supporting firm but not the products of another. Inman decided that these fears were reasonable, and committed to manage the Alpha-Omega effort as four independent programs, each to be headed by a separate but equal chief. At the end of 1983, chiefs for three of the positions, data base management, human interface, and parallel processing, had been found, but the knowledge-ased systems slot remained open.

Also by the end of 1983, the detailed scientific plans were still being worked out. When complete, these would not be disclosed in any detail. "I used to guard the nation's secrets, and now I guard proprietary secrets. However, we're trying to plan in such a way that we won't built up a bureaucracy." Again, Japanese-style, MCC hopes to identify inter-mediate technology spinoffs and deliver them to the participating firms. In spite of this, the planning documents acknowledge the problems of efficient technology transfer, including doing it in such a way that no participant has a special advantage over another. This problem will be solved in part by the technical liaison officers each firm appoints.

Is there a chance that some cooperation can be worked out between MCC and the Strategic Computing Program, inasmuch as some of its goals are similar? MCC made an early policy decision to avoid becoming a government contractor, especially in its early years. But Inman notes that if the Strategic Computing Program demonstrates that certain of its goals are exactly congruent with the goals already set by the MCC, then he has been empowered to pursue such a contract sometime in the future.

One of the persistent problems MCC faces is scrutiny by the Justice Department for violating antitrust laws. MCC reportedly spent half a million dollars in its first year and a half on legal fees alone, but at the end of 1983, Inman was confident that the Justice Department would raise no objections to the work MCC proposed. However, he expected that lack of objection to be very specific to MCC, not the clear signal that other parts of American industry were hoping for in their own efforts to collaborate on research and development.

And the baby consortium is already subject to criticism. Outside computer scientists are disturbed (perhaps correctly) by the breakup of Alpha-Omega, because they worry that its goals cannot be reached without the most intimate cooperation among the four segments, each drawing from and helping, not rivaling, the other. Moreover, if Inman waits for just the right people to fill his top positions, he draws criticism for not moving the MCC forward quickly enough, thus delaying even further the American response to the Japanese challenge. (Of course, if he settled for second-rate people, he would be severely criticized for that.) Finally, scientists who are used to working in an open environment, with the free and easy exchange of ideas, predict that the MCC's intentions to make its walls impermeable for proprietary reasons will act as a two-way barrier, preventing the cross-fertilization from the outside that makes basic research flower.

Yet MCC is an optimistic organization with an optimistic and accomplished leader, and it has found a home in an American boom town. Austin is an appealing blend of the Old South and the Old West (though decidedly not the Old Southwest). If its chalky Hill Country brought generations of early farmers to grief, and if it now struggles with all the late-twentieth-century difficulties, such as preservation vs. development, the best way to cope with the homeless, or with fierce complaints from minority groups, the town's natural beauty and its energetic atmosphere ("its can-do attitude," in Inman's phrase) are still apparent to any visitor.

There are more ways an organization as fragile and unprecedented as MCC can go wrong than there are paths to its success. The shortage of first-rate trained scientists and engineers is an international problem, but MCC must also coordinate among fractious firms who have spent corporate lifetimes in savage competition with each other, and convince their technologists and managers alike that long-range research goals are worth pursuing with patience, even for firms that must show profits every relentless quarter. MCC could somehow succeed at all that and still find itself under attack from well-meaning but legalistic adversaries, who believe antitrust laws are a secular equivalent of the Decalogue.

Nearly everybody agrees that if MCC can succeed at all, it has its best chance because of the unique combination of intelligence, tact, persuasive powers, varied experience, and will, possessed by the remarkable Bobby Inman.

It Is Hard to Predict, Especially the Future

The title above is taken from a wise aphorism attributed to the physicist Niels Bohr, and a little examination of matters adds to its obvious persuasiveness.

If, just after it got under way in Jericho in about 6500 B.C., we had asked a prophet of the agricultural revolution what she expected its effects to be, she might have been able to reply confidently that human beings would no longer need to depend on chance for their food—the chance of gathering, the chance of the hunt. With truly astonishing insight, she might also have predicted that surplus food would allow the formation of specialties in labor. But that this, in turn, would lead to the rise of the cities, international trade, or the peanut as an ingredient in shampoo, ink, and linoleum is unlikely to have occurred to her.

With deep insight into the human spirit, she might have been able to predict that a folklore would grow up surrounding cultivation, but she could not have specifically named Persephone, Johnny Appleseed, the death of the Fisher King, or even laetrile.

She would probably have found the idea hilarious that some human beings, with access to unlimited calories, would develop body fat that was socially repugnant, unhealthy, and in some cases even life-threatening, because nature had genetically selected us for survival in a feast-or-famine world.

In other words, if we humans are luckily endowed with the imagination to create revolutions, we nevertheless can hardly anticipate their long-term effects.

This book is concerned with an aspect of the so-called information revolution, the mass production of machine intelligence soon to come. In some sense *revolution* hardly seems the apt term at all: perhaps *evolution* is a better word to describe the history of knowledge in the human race. As we now theorize that the evolution of organisms takes place—slow change, punctuated by quick and radical change, followed by slow or even no change for a long time again—so it is with the evolution of knowledge and its various technologies.

Spoken language between humans was a major step in the transfer of knowledge (and some anthropologists link it with the establishment of the nuclear family), but that, once established, prevailed for a very long time, perhaps 50 million years. Then humans began to draw pictures that stood for the objects that surrounded and concerned them. This kind of pictorial communication was a magnificent achievement, for it meant that information could be preserved beyond mortal human lifetimes and fallible human memory, although the awkwardness of pictographs ensured that writing would remain the specialty of an honored and valuable few.

A modern-day speaker of, say, English, can in time-machine style taste the awkwardness and ambiguities of this stage of the evolution of Indo-European languages by trying to find her way around central Tokyo when she neither speaks nor reads Japanese. Of course she is supplied with a map. But the streets, when they are named at all, are spelled on her map in Roman letters. They appear in Kanji on the street signs. Unless she is very clever about making that conversion (and most casual tourists are not), she must rely on little pictographs scattered about her map that represent well-known buildings. Finding oneself, then, is a matter of matching the building one is standing before with a picture on a small map. But the scales are greatly different. The pictures are somewhat stylized. A great deal of guessing and hoping goes on. Mistakes ensue. Misunderstandings occur with regularity. Subtlety of thought is out of the question.

Around 1000 B.C., the Phoenicians, in their brisk, no-nonsense way, cut through the difficulties of pictographs and produced one of the most influential versions of that abstraction called the alphabet. What inspired them was trade—pictographs slowed down the business of business intolerably. They surely had no conscious intention of fomenting revolution; they simply wanted to make profits. Aside from the fact that they were Mediterraneans, it seems lost to us now precisely who first got the bright idea to have one mark or letter correspond to one sound, therefore streamlining writing most wonderfully and, not incidentally, allowing written words to appear for concepts that didn't lend themselves to being pictured. It was a potent device and was eventually to accelerate the recording and diffusion of knowledge dramatically. Moreover, it also changed the way we think.

Then came another lull in the evolution of knowledge technology. There were small changes, of course. Both Greeks and Romans added letters to the Phoenician alphabet, and paper and vellum caught on as scribes realized those could, for all practical purposes, be made as permanent as stone, with the advantages of portability. Books replaced scrolls. So it went: nothing spectacular, but a slow and steady change by small accretions of differences.

Then came Gutenberg and what we now call the Gutenberg Revolution. In fact, first the Koreans and then the Chinese had developed movable type by the 13th century, but they hadn't been much interested in exporting the idea. Traders who traveled the Silk Route were quick to appreciate the advantages of movable type and the printing press, but the idea seems not to have got beyond the Middle East, where it was squelched for theological reasons.

In any event, Gutenberg's invention was a great success (though not for the poor man himself, who died in debt), and in the space of 50 years nearly 10 million books were distributed in a Europe that, until then, had boasted only scores of thousands of manuscripts. It was an astonishing proliferation under any circumstances, but given the crude means of transport, it was nearly a miracle. We do not know whether Johannes Gutenberg had any idea of the revolution he began; surely his wildest dreams couldn't have pictured products as diverse as the *Physician's Desk Reference Manual*, James Joyce's *Ulysses*, and the *National Enquirer* in the hands of anyone with money to pay for them (and not much money at that). Or perhaps he might have. Arcane information, poetry, and gossip have been staples for the human mind as long as we have records. What Gutenberg surely would have missed—putting him now in the position of prophet— would have been the effects of our old friend, order of magnitude. It bears repeating that from fewer than 100,000 volumes, Europe went in 50 years to acquire nearly 10 million volumes, thanks to Gutenberg's new technology. With that acquisition would come the rapid spread of literacy, then knowledge, and then the profound social effects of both (we know that thousands learned to read solely to get at Tom Paine's radical politics), leading to new governments called democratic republics, which replaced divine right with majority rule by vote, and similar unanticipated changes.

Nearly everybody understands that the development of the computer has begun another spurt of fast revolutionary change in the processing of information, but most of the prophecies have been gadget-centered. These are all quite wonderful, from electronic mail to hand-held expert systems that a barefoot doctor can take into the remotest village in Henan province and thereby supply the most advanced medicine the world has to offer to one of the poorest provinces in one of the poorest countries on earth.

We read predictions that our newspapers and magazines, which up to now we have had to buy in full editions, either delivered to us by human carriers or at a newsstand, will arrive on our home terminals, and, more important, we can pick and choose what we read out of them; we needn't be burdened with the whole thing. The same will be true of books, which will not be bound objects on a shelf, but unbound (in the largest sense: open to update, comment, revision, and change as necessary) pieces of knowledge called on only when needed, stored cheaply, and accessible to anybody, anywhere, any time. (And, yes, our home terminal will allow us to have hard copy to read in the bathtub if that's our heart's desire.)

All these are wonderful indeed and can't come soon enough. They promise enormous savings in energy, in paper, in time. They promise enormous intellectual leverage: fingertip access not to tons of information, but to well-selected, well-designed knowledge. They also promise—or threaten—severe, if temporary dislocations in certain industries and many jobs. We can prepare for those changes in a sensible and compassionate way, or we can construct patchwork defenses that in the end will leave us worse off to certain historical inevitabilities than we need be. This book, of course, is an unambiguous plea for rational planning and preparation, but we are well aware that others hold different views.

We stand, however, before a singularity, an event so unprecedented that predictions are almost silly, since predictions, by their very nature, are extrapolations from things as we know them, and the singularity called reasoning machines will change things from how we know them in vastly unpredictable ways. "The appearance on earth of a nonhuman entity with intelligence approaching or exceeding mankind's would rank with the most significant events in human history," *Fortune* magazine declared in a recent series of articles on thinking machines. "While human beings can't possibly imagine the full consequences, the effects on technology, science, economics, warfare—indeed, on the whole intellectual and sociological development of mankind—would undoubtedly be momentous."

We are no different from our fellow human beings. We can't possibly imagine the full consequences of the widespread use of KIPS either. If hundreds of thousands learned to read so that Tom Paine's pamphlets might persuade them that they had justification for revolting against monarchies as a form of government, who can say how universal access to machine intelligence—faster, deeper, better than human intelligence—will change science, economics, and warfare, and the whole intellectual and sociological development of mankind?

Shadows and Light

No profound change in human fortunes has ever been completely benign. Even the agricultural revolution had some unintended side effects, though few people would wish to return to hunting and gathering, with all that those imply. Much more recently, the widespread distribution of medicine has overtaken our abilities or our will to control world population, but both ethics and compassion tell us that rather than withdrawing medicine, we should prevent overpopulating the globe instead. The great increase in knowledge—by orders of magnitude, as we have tiresomely pointed out in this book—is unlikely to be different. Surely some people will believe they were better off in the good old days.

Automatic creation of knowledge has unpredictable effects. When a machine can use up all the knowledge we have given it, and use it systematically in ways that we cannot, and can make inferences more deeply than we can (because it is not limited, as we are, by our evolutionary legacy of about four items that we can attend to simultaneously), what will happen? We do not know. We may forget how to do things. Though it was drilled mercilessly into us in secondary schools, very few adults today remember how to take square roots. Hand-held calculators do the job beautifully; why burden ourselves and our minds?

We do not know whether, even given the same heuristics that humans use, a system that can think faster and deeper will necessarily think down the same avenues that humans do. If it should go elsewhere, we do not know what lies at the end of such different avenues.

We do not know whether new knowledge can be discovered by a machine (though we suspect it can and have early intimations of it). If so, we do not know what the implications of such new knowledge might be.

We do not know whether such a knowledge network, worldwide as the Japanese envisage or only nationwide, will offer unprecedented opportunities for mischief on the part of governments or of outlaws. In transitional times, such as these now are, we are all accustomed to our fellow humans abrogating their personal responsibilities by blaming it on the computer. Will those possibilities grow more menacing? Will legal systems be devised that can cope with them, even as such systems must cope with intellectual property rights, problems of privacy, and other unpredictable problems? Will fail-safe systems be devised to protect us from the immense amounts of power that are about to be placed in our hands?

We do not know how to imbue humans with the critical intelligence to evaluate the knowledge they are exposed to. The problem is already a difficult one for readers of the written word. We do not know whether the ability to interrogate a reasoning machine, to make it explain itself, will help with this problem or exacerbate it.

For humans who do not value knowledge, we do not know what a world, deeply steeped in knowledge, will seem like. There have been suggestions that the enormously rich recreational possibilities of KIPS will either sedate or stimulate that disenfranchised group that now scorns knowledge. Knowledge as narcotic isn't especially attractive to us, but the other possibility, KIPS as a stimulant toward knowing more, is a hopeful one. Since KIPS are planned to be as easy to use as a telephone or TV, it might be heartening to remember that in the United States the number of television sets grew from 6,000 to 15.5 million in a matter of five years. We might wish KIPS such success.

Not long ago, Feigenbaum was at the San Jose airport, ready to board a plane. An antique craft came wheeling by, a beautiful biplane that had been one of Trans World Airlines' first passenger planes. It struck him that this was where knowledge engineering and expert systems were right now; that they were struggling to transform themselves from a potentially powerful technological novelty into an integrated part of human life.

Airplanes are still not perfect. Sometimes they're late; sometimes they crash catastrophic-ally. But they are ours, and we could hardly imagine life without them. Symbolic inference machines are at the same stage as the Trans World plane that Feigenbaum watched: an elegant promise of things to come.

But we must return to a somber present. In this book we have described a technology that promises to change our lives the way few technologies have: reasoning machines are, as we have said, not just the second computer revolution, but the important one. If the details of the technology itself are complicated, the issues that surround it can be understood by nearly everyone. A superiority in knowledge technology provides whoever holds it with the power to resolve shades of gray into black and white— provides in brief, an unequivocal advantage—whether we are speaking of personal power, national economics, or warfare.

The Japanese understand this perfectly. They have already begun to translate that understanding into the new technology that will give them unequivocal advantage over the rest of the world, perhaps by the middle of the next decade. Other nations recognize the soundness of the Japanese strategy—and, of course, its inevitability. In response to the farsighted Japanese, ambitious national plans are being drawn up in many places. But the United States, which ought to lead in such plans, has, until very recently, trailed along in disarrayed and diffuse indecision.

We have resisted calling this a crisis for the United States. We could pursue a dark thought, imagining artificial intelligence technology to slip away out of our control, which would ultimately have severe effects on our general industry, our standard of living, and our national defense.

We prefer instead to regard this Japanese challenge as an opportunity for the United States to revitalize itself, to join the Japanese and other nations in the world in the exhilarating adventure of moving the Empire of Reason, as historian Henry Steele Commager could once, with justification, call the United States, decisively into the Age of Reasoning Machines.

In the end, we have no choice. We can decide *when* we shall participate, not *if*. The question of when begets how.

To the first question of when, we urge that it be at once. To the second question of how, we urge only that whatever plan is chosen, it embody what the American revolutionary generation possessed in abundance and ought to be ours once more: optimism, energy, authority, pragmatism, candor, audacity, and a taste for succeeding.

At the beginning of this book, we asserted that knowledge is power. We meant it not only in the vulgar sense, that one sleek, smart missile can clobber tons of dumb battleship, though that is demonstrably true, or even that a scientific instrument with built-in intelligence can outperform its dumb cousin that costs much more money, though that too is true. Most applications we've described, or we anticipate, have been material ones. For one thing, they're easiest to describe. For another, those are what Westerners are most comfortable with.

But there's a further dimension to a society dominated by knowledge that we should like to address, a nonmaterial dimension. The Japanese, having a very long history of putting material things in their place, which is an important place but clearly subordinate to and often in the service of nonmaterial concerns, are better at sensing the spiritual change the knowledge society might bring. A book by Yoneji Masuda, *The Information Society as Post-Industrial Society*, has some provocative things to say about the future.

Masuda makes a dense, detailed, and finally plausible case that our knowledge-rich future will coax us away from a preoccupation with material concerns and toward a preoccupation with the nonmaterial. He sees this taking the form of the freedom for each of us to set individual goals of self-realization and then perhaps a worldwide religious renaissance, characterized not by a belief in a supernatural god, but rather by awe and humility in the presence of the collective human spirit and its wisdom, humanity living in a symbiotic tranquillity with the planet we have found ourselves upon, regulated by a new set of global ethics.

It is decidedly *not* an otherworldly religious spirit, which makes it different from religious passions of the past. On the contrary, it is sharply focused on this world, with humans having a serious, direct, and continuous say in all matters that affect their lives. But those exercises will be characterized less by the "me first" attitude that has often prevailed in human affairs, and more by a spirit of mutual assistance toward shared goals.

It sounds utopian. And *utopian* often means hopelessly idealistic, beyond human reach. Surely, we can argue, Masuda's prophecies are unduly shaped by living as he does in a prosperous, homogeneous society where the seeds of such a way of life are already planted and sprouting. But *utopian* also means something we have said many times and in many ways that we deeply desire as a human good. Indeed, Masuda reminds us that all this corresponds to Adam Smith's vision in *The Wealth of Nations* of a universal opulent society, a condition of plenty that frees the people from dependence and subordination to exercise true independence of spirit in autonomous actions. What Masuda is saying is that soon the technology will be in place to permit such a society to exist all over the globe.

The reasoning animal has, perhaps inevitably, fashioned the reasoning machine. With all the risks apparent in such an audacious, some say reckless, embarkation onto sacred ground, we have gone ahead anyway, holding tenaciously to what the wise in every culture at every time have taught: the shadows, however dark and menacing, must not deter us from reaching the light.

P · A · R · T · I

2

The Relationship Between Business and Higher Education: A Perspective on the 21st Century

John Sculley

We are privileged to live during an extraordinary time. It is the turning of an era. The world is in passage from the industrial age to the information age. This is a time of profound changes, in which the key economic resources in the world will no longer be capital, labor, and raw materials, but rather knowledge, individual innovators, and information.

Technologies which are emerging today will give us the ability to explore, convey, and create knowledge as never before. This has enormous implications for us as individuals, as well as for our institutions. Our colleges and universities will take on especially heavy responsibilities as we make this transition.

We have an opportunity that is given only to few generations in history. I believe that if we respond with our best creative energies, we can unleash a new Renaissance of discovery and learning.

In our global economy, we are moving from a hierarchical order to one of inter-dependence. Not long ago the United States stood unchallenged at the top of the world's economic hierarchy. Drawing on the consuming power of an affluent population, this country built a strong industrial base. Our manufacturing companies added value to natural resources through technological know-how. Economies of scale favored the development of large, highly structured institutions.

"The Relationship Between Business and Higher Education: A Perspective on the Twenty-First Century," by J. Sculley, Communications of the ACM, Association for Computing Machinery, Inc. **32** (9), Sept. 1989, pp. 1056–1061.

Today, however, we are not at the top of a pyramid, but rather one node along a network. Our once exclusive know-how is available in many newly industrialized nations, such as Korea, Taiwan, Singapore, Mexico, and Brazil. What is at risk, as the United States loses economic primacy, is not simply our own standard of living, but also the health of the world economy. The global economic system functions like a biological ecosystem. An unbalance in one sector can affect the whole.

A good analogy can be found in the shrinking rain forests of Brazil. Eighty percent of the world's oxygen comes from the Brazilian rain forest. Yet we lose every year, through the cutting of trees and the clearing of land, a land mass the size of the state of Nebraska. If we keep doing that long enough, the decreasing amount of oxygen in the atmosphere will alter the entire ecosystem of the planet.

The United States participates in the world economy not simply as a producer, but also as a marketplace. If our population loses the ability to afford our own products, it also will not afford Japanese automobiles, electronics from the Pacific Rim countries, and so forth. And that would have a tremendous impact on the macroeconomic ecosystem of the world.

Yet it is clear that as a nation, we are living beyond our means. We are no longer creating enough value to sustain our lifestyle, we are falling deeper into debt. There is a compelling need to find new ways to continue to create value in the world.

I believe that in order to do that our businesses and universities must be designed to foster innovation. Yet innovation has never come through bureaucracy and hierarchy. It has always come from individuals.

There is a dangerous timelag built into even the most successful institutions. They are created at one time in response to some particular opportunity in a given historical context. And then as the context shifts, the institution finds itself carrying excess baggage that is no longer useful.

How will the organizations designed to thrive in the 19th and early 20th centuries learn to contribute to the 21st? Only by reinventing themselves through refocusing on *individuals.*

The key strength of 21st-century organizations will be not their size or structure, but their ability to simultaneously unleash and coordinate the creative contributions of many individuals. Unleashing and coordinating may sound like contradictory actions—and in older models they would be—but we must develop new patterns of organization that promote alignment and collaboration while avoiding rigidity and stagnation.

A Lifetime of Learning

Communication in the new organization will be more fluid, action more spontaneous. Think of the speed and agility of basketball versus the massed force of football. Think of a jazz combo trading solos, versus a marching bank in lock step. The individuals who will succeed as contributors in these new organizations also need to change. In fact, change will be the one constant in their careers.

Over-specialization and a limited perspective can be a dead-end trap. Students today cannot count on finding one smooth career path because jobs that exist today will change radically (by the millions) tomorrow. Individuals will need to have tremendous flexibility to be able to move from one company to another, or from one industry to another. Those who are best prepared to do that will be the most successful.

We used to talk of "taking a position with the firm." Those are revealing words: *position* and *firm* belong to a static model of rigid hierarchy. If you are only going to take one position, you can get by on only one point of view. In the information age, however, a diverse educational experience will be the critical foundation for success. What tomorrow's student will need is not just mastery of subject matter, but mastery of *learning*. Education will be not simply a prelude to a career, but a lifelong endeavor.

Let me list some of the requirements of this new paradigm for lifelong learning:

- It should require rigorous mastery of subject matter under expert guidance.
- It should hone the conceptual skills that wrest meaning from data.
- It should promote a healthy skepticism that tests reality against multiple points of view.
- It should nourish individual creativity and encourage exploration.
- It should support collaboration.
- It should reward clear communication.
- It should provoke a journey of discovery.
- And above all it should be energized by the opportunity to contribute to the total of what we know and what we can do.

Higher education has traditionally defined itself in terms of two missions: instruction and research. In the past, these have been seen as very different activities. Research, which is primarily the domain of faculty and graduate students, is the process whereby we increase the world's store of knowledge. Instruction, which involves all students, is the process whereby we transfer some subset of that knowledge to *individuals.*

But, as we have seen, it is no longer enough simply to transfer knowledge to students. It is not as though we can give young people a ration of knowledge that they can draw on throughout their careers. Instead, we need to give them *access* to the unbounded world of knowledge. That means we must prepare all students, not just professional scholars, to embark on a lifetime of learning and discovery. Which means that our students will not simply be passively absorbing subject matter . . . but be more like researchers actively exploring their environment.

To work in research is to recognize that knowledge does not reside privately in individual minds, or text books, or journals, or libraries, or laboratories, or databases. Knowledge resides in a complex web that encompasses all of these. To work in research is to recognize that knowledge is not static. Everyone in the research community shares the responsibility to test our knowledge and to enlarge it.

The challenge for higher education will be to find ways of bringing to the process of instruction the passion for discovery that drives research. Students today should master the skills and tools of research as part of their basic education. To give our students this mastery, we must create a learning environment in which research and instruction are integrated.

I believe we all can make important contributions to that process. If we succeed we will have found new ways of empowering individuals—not in isolation from each other, but with pathways for rich communication and effective collaboration.

A Lesson in History

The transformation I am calling for—shifting focus from the institution to the individual —has a close parallel in history. In medieval Europe people were subservient to the institutions of the church and feudal hierarchies.

Then came the Renaissance, which redefined the individual as the epicenter of intellectual activity. It did more than change people's perspective of the world, it literally invented perspective. The medieval painter depicted great religious events with the most important figures appearing the largest. Composition reflected ideology. Then drawing styles changed. The Renaissance artist drew figures and buildings in perspective, the way they appeared to an individual observer. For the first time, point-of-view came into the world.

The many forces which converged to bring about the Renaissance galvanized around one key technology: printing. The rise of printing led with astonishing speed to an explosion of literacy. The result was a new self-esteem for the individual. A wealth of invention.

An excitement of the power of wonderful ideas. Today, we are in need of a second Renaissance, which like the first can also be galvanized by technology.

We are on the verge of creating new tools which, like the press, will empower individuals, unlock worlds of knowledge, and forge a new community of ideas. These core technologies and the tools they support will help create a new environment of lifetime learning.

We believe the tools that show the most promise for the new learning environment build on three core technologies: hypermedia, simulation, and artificial intelligence. Each of these technologies alone can enrich the educational process. Each gains additional strength when learners can share resources over networks. And when these technologies are fully integrated with each other, they will fuel a 21st-century Renaissance—an outpouring of new learning and achievement.

Technological Tools

Hypermedia is a new word for many of us. Yet this term and its definition will become increasingly important the more we rely on personal computers to store, manage and retrieve information.

In broad terms, hypermedia is the delivery of information in forms that go beyond traditional list management and database report methods. More specifically, it means that you do not have to follow a predetermined organization for information. Instead you can make instant choices about where to go next. What this means for instruction and research is that content is not bound by particular choices of organization. Instead content and organization become complementary tools that act on each other to deepen our understanding of the world around us.

Hypermedia lets us use a type of cross-reference that can be used to span courses that present related material, like physiology or microbiology. It gives us the capability to explore deeper, linking one idea with another as the student or researcher pursues his own personal learning path.

In a sense, hypermedia is nothing new at all. A researcher using a card catalog and reference materials traditionally had the opportunity to pursue ideas according to insight and interest. Hypermedia does not change that process, it merely *accelerates* it.

It's a natural way of working, but until recently, personal computers were too limited to address it. Today, however, desktop computers can have more information on line than the largest mainframe managed 10 years ago. We are coming to expect high-capacity magnetic hard disks, optical media such as CD-ROM, and high-speed networks as standard in our installations.

Once we have experienced hypermedia, established methods of finding related pieces of information seem cumbersome. Hypermedia can also be seen as a new form of publishing. There are now readily available tools that enable faculty in any discipline to create richly branching presentations. The major obstacles still to be cleared are not technological, but social and economic. We have not yet devised licensing procedures for the electronic formats of the textbook or journal abstracts.

We must all work together to address such issues as copyright and royalties, and access and security in the information age. Just as hypermedia offers a new paradigm for exploring vast amounts of information, the second core technology, simulation, pushes the boundaries of experimentation. Simulation takes us beyond the "what" to the "how and why." We move from a static picture to dynamic visualization—from limited experience to diverse, multiple experiences.

The excitement in educational simulations today comes from generalized programs which allow professors and students to design their own simulations in particular disciplines, simulations that permit virtually all dynamic phenomena to be modeled and visualized.

Just as the spreadsheet allowed us to ask "what if" questions about financial calculations, this new class of software allows those "what if" questions to act on a dynamic graphic system, whether in physics, chemistry, electronics, or economics.

Another new application of simulation is in the humanities and social sciences, not normally what you would think of as computer-intensive disciplines. At Stanford University, a toolkit built on HyperCard has been designed in deference to a traditionally nonprogramming group: the humanities and social sciences faculty. (See box.)

Using this toolkit, called ALIAS, professors or students in anthropology, history, or sociology can model a culture or period of history by entering their data into the toolkit. ALIAS will in turn create a HyperCard stack that allows students to play the role of an individual of that culture. It is an approach that combines simulation and hypermedia.

In fact, this very simulation has been developed by Stanford Professor Harumi Befu. It's called SHOGAI, which means *life course*. To Professor Befu, SHOGAI means a new territory for his anthropology students; one in which they can explore the richness of Japan's people, its customs, and events, by assuming the roles of characters profiled in the simulation (see accompanying story).

Using this simulation, students can make some critical decisions about school, social activities and work that will collectively dictate the character's niche in Japanese society.

The point is to understand how and why the choices they make for him will determine the career opportunities he will have and the social status he can achieve. As different choices are made, different results will unfold.

Simulation and hypermedia tools exist today. As they come into more widespread use we will find two things happening. First, authors and publishers will continue to enrich our libraries of linked subject matter. And second, developers will continue to make the underlying tools more powerful. We will have full, three-dimensional motion graphics, and stunning images on CD-ROM. But perhaps the most spectacular advance will not be in the presentation level, but will lie deeper in the programming.

Sooner Than We Think

Just a short way into the future, we will see artificial intelligence (AI) emerge as a core technology. Combined with our core technologies, AI will boost simulations and hypermedia to new levels of realism and usefulness. For example, we will move from building molecules into two- and three-dimensional space, to building the environment in which they combined—where each molecule understands the structure and behavior of the other.

Stanford Courseware Puts World at Students' Fingertips

The Courseware Authoring Tools (CAT) Project at Stanford University is chartered with providing an environment in which faculty members can develop instructional software. Many of the programs are built upon Apple's authoring environment, HyperCard, and all are designed exclusively for the Macintosh II.

The tools created at Stanford to date fall under three rubrics: social science, multimedia and engineering/physical science. One authoring environment—ALIAS—is at the core of some of the more imaginative programs for cultural, social and historical simulations.

By entering data about a certain period of history, ALIAS allows students to play the role of an individual of that culture and time. Students have a choice of simulating such periods as the evolution of French Impressionism; the politics of 16th Century Italy; or life in present-day Japan. Simulations are represented via a series of events that can be as simple as a single historical incident or as complex as an entire era. ALIAS allows four kinds of events:

- One-time events, such as Columbus landing in the New World;
- Cyclical events, such as fall harvest;
- Opportunities, such as trying out for a baseball team;
- Complex events, such as applying for college.

Students can classify events to distinguish, for example, the political from economic situations. They can also determine which event types to include when the simulation begins.

Using the simulation capabilities of ALIAS, one Stanford professor has designed a software program that teaches students about the factors that impinge on the life of a Japanese individual. Harumi Befu, a professor of anthropology, has created an ALIAS-based, role-playing courseware program called SHOGAI that explores the Japanese culture through the simulated life of a 59-year-old Japanese shop owner named Yoshitada Yamada and his 30-year-old daughter, Yoichi.

As Yoshitada, students must make decisions that will enable him to survive a childhood in the midst of World War II, to pursue an academic path in postwar Japan, to reconcile his personal preferences with the dictates of an arranged marriage, and to follow a career within the confines of his education

Another important contribution of AI will be intelligent agents that can learn a user's preferences and search strategies. These agents will transform the nature of academic computing. Agents will be sent to prowl among remote databases and bring back the specific information and citations that the user requires.

These future systems are not that far away. Soon, faculty and students will be using systems that enable them to drive through libraries, museums, databases or institutional archives. These tools will not just take you to the doorstep of these great resources, as sophisticated computers do now; they will invite you deep inside its secrets, interpreting and explaining—converting vast quantities of information into personalized and understandable knowledge.

In a (previous) keynote address, Dr. Herb Simon, professor of computer science and psychology at Carnegie Mellon, reminded, "We think of revolutions as being sudden events, producing far reaching changes in a very short period of time. But the revolution launched by the steam engine took, by any reasonable account, 150 years." Changes in computing have been like a whirlwind in the last 40 years. But I think we have only begun to see what innovation and creativity can produce in this industry.

The personal computer could become as galvanizing as the printing press in stimulating change in the world, in creating an environment for innovation and new ideas. Let us remember that the printing press never wrote a single book. Authors write books. So,

---

and social status. Later, as daughter Yoichi, students make life decisions that focus on a cultural balance in higher education opportunities between Japan and the U.S.

In addition to personal decisions, students are taught to recognize the importance of key people in an individual's life, cultural norms, and historical accidents. The journey is accentuated by a colorful palette of graphics, text, video images, and music to embellish these actions and to impart a distinctly Japanese aura to the simulation.

HardTimes:ALIAS:Alias Demo

Welcome to SHOGAI. You're playing the role of Yoichi Yamada, a Japanese born in 1930.

Your father, Yoshitada Yamada, owns a clothing retail shop. Your mother, Sada Yamada, is a housewife. You live in Senba, Osaka, and have one brother seven years older than you.

Tokyo

Osaka

Hiroshima

Begin

Sculley Envisions Life by 2001 P.C.

By the turn of the century, John Sculley predicts personal computers will house the type of technology and interface design that will seem like descendants of today's UNIX and Macintosh systems. He calls this futuristic PC the *Knowledge Navigator* and has described in several recent speeches the five key technologies crucial to its success.

The first feature is advanced communications technology that can link processors and databases around the world, thus providing better vehicles and broader information pathways. Secondly, real-time, 3-D color animations will become commonplace as users rely more on graphic simulations. Such capabilities will allow scientists to visualize complex numerical models with the same ease with which they now graph a column on a spreadsheet.

Improved database technology—element number three—is the key to creating intuitive and responsive information systems. One approach that Sculley claims shows great promise involves mapping and storing information into object-oriented structures.

Fourth is hypermedia, which will give future PC users more intuitive ways of navigating through enormous collections of information: combining text, graphics, sound, and motion. Rounding out the essentials is artificial intelligence technology—critical to the future vision of personal computing. AI will allow future users to create agents that can recognize and anticipate strategies and preferences as well as increase productivity.

---

too, with the new technologies that I have described. This will only be achieved if we work together—universities, corporations and government—and if we recognize the role of the creative individual within these organizations.

We all have a role in making this vision of the future a reality. The technologies I have talked about are only platforms that represent opportunities and possibilities. They are, however, the tallest of platforms, the richest of opportunities, and the broadest of possibilities that I know of.

They will allow us to set loose an avalanche of personal creativity and achievement. Once we have thousands of ideas to harvest, we may have the chance once again to create a second Renaissance, perhaps every bit as important as the first, in the early part of the next century. It would represent a rebirth and revival of learning and culture unleashed by new technologies. It would bridge the gaps between the arts and sciences. And it would signify the emergence of an integrated environment for instruction and research.

It is an exhilarating time to live. I cannot think of any other time in history in which such profound change has gripped each decade. It is destined to be an eventful journey to the 21st century. And there is no place that journey will be more exciting than in higher education.

3

Making a "Computer Revolution"

Rob Kling • Suzanne Iacono

Introduction

During the last twenty years journalists and academics have produced a flood of books and articles about a "computer revolution." Sometimes they use related concepts like *computer age, wired nation, network nation, information age,* and *information society.* These concepts each have different nuances, and emphasize different aspects of information processing, telecommunications, and computerization. But they are used similarly—to signal the reader that major social transformations driven by information technologies have taken place or are in progress. We will argue that these authors develop world views based on uncritical acceptance of these concepts to legitimize the social changes they wish to advocate.

We recently analyzed books and articles that focus on these concepts. We wanted to better understand how authors have been talking about a "computer revolution": how they explain what it is, where it is happening, who is making it happen, and what it means. While many of these studies are insightful, for the most part they accept a "computer revolution" as social fact rather than as a point of departure for carefully investigating the links between computerization and social change. We will examine the rhetorical strategies and key social concepts of the specific writings by three of these authors later in this article. We have found that many authors use concepts like "computer revolution" and its cousins quite casually and uncritically. We were not surprised to find that some

"Making a 'Computer Revolution'," by Robert Kling and Suzanne Iacono, from *The Journal of Computing and Society,* **1**(1): 69–84.

authors, especially journalists, use these terms casually. But we were surprised that we found few analytical investigations of these terms.[1]

There is a smaller critical literature written by people such as Langdon Winner (1984) and Joseph Weizenbaum (1979), which disparages some of the hype in the more enthusiastic accounts of an emerging computer revolution. They correctly point out that the concept *computer revolution* has been used very casually, often as a marketing device. They also argue that the concept *computer revolution* is nothing more than marketing hype, and that most computerization efforts have more problems than virtues, on balance. As a consequence, Weizenbaum and Winner bind together their critiques of "computer revolution" as hype with a pessimistic assessment of social changes attributable, in part, to computerization. We want to advance the discussion of social repercussions of computerization beyond this polarized "love it" or "hate it" debate.

In this article, we will examine some of the assumptions that undergird discussions of a "computer revolution." The questions about whether or when there will be a computer revolution open an interesting problem: what social choices can shape computerization and what are the consequences of different strategies of computerization for different groups? What social changes can be meaningfully attributed to computerization? Have the social changes attributable to computerization been substantial enough to transform social life in any important area? We will not answer these questions definitively here.[2] But we will shed some light on the forms that meaningful answers can take.

We have found that authors who use the lexicon of "computer revolution" most enthusiastically create a discourse that avoids answering these important questions in adequate detail. Rather, they seem to stimulate their audiences to help make a "computer revolution" by actively using computer-based systems wherever possible—by tele-commuting to work, by using advanced forms of computerized banking systems, and by encouraging their children's schools to adopt instructional computing.

Revolution by Reputation?

Revolutions are radical breaks with an existing order: political revolutions, social revolutions, technological revolutions, and intellectual revolutions all identify specific battles and changes. Most revolutions don't just happen; they are made by identifiable revolutionaries fighting a set of established adversaries.

Early in our reading, we turned to I. Bernard Cohen's *Revolution in Science* to help deepen our insight into revolutionary movements. Cohen observes that the concept *scientific revolution* conveys no sense of continuity and permanence. Rather, "It implies a

---

[1] For analytical scholarly treatments of concepts related to *computer revolution*, like *information society*, see the recent books by Finlay (1987) and Lyon (1988).

[2] During the last 15 years we have conducted systematic studies of computerization in diverse organizations: banks (Kling, 1978b; Kling, 1983), engineering firms (Kling and Scacchi, 1982), insurance companies (Kling and Scacchi, 1982), manufacturing firms (Kling and Iacono, 1984), public agencies (Kling, 1978a), and schools (Kling, 1983; Kling, 1986). We have also been participant observers of several computerization efforts at our home university. The reader can see these articles for our best answers.

break in continuity, the establishment of a new orde56r that has severed its links with the past, a sharply defined plane of cleavage between what is old and familiar and what is new and different" (p. 6). He also argues that scientific and political revolutions are similar in their creating a new order, but differ in the time frame of the goals that political and scientific revolutionaries advocate.

Cohen identifies scientific revolutions by using a set of carefully drawn reputational and consensual criteria: the extent to which participating scientists and other commentators claimed that a scientific advance was "revolutionary." And by similar, but much less careful historiography, he makes this spectacular observation about "a computer revolution": "as I was writing this chapter, a glance at a single shelf in my study showed almost a dozen books on computers had 'revolution' in the title. Who would deny that there has been a computer revolution?" (pp. 21–22).

We recently examined a large index of the books held in the University of California libraries for similar titles. We found 37 books about computers with "revolution" in the title published since 1962, and 20 additional books about information processing with "revolution" in the title. In addition, dozens of articles have been published in popular, professional, and scholarly outlets with similar titles and thematic concerns. Most of these publications accept the lexicon of "computer revolutions" as a useful and acceptable category; only a few authors dissent. But we disagree with Cohen that the existence of such a large literature automatically proves that there has been a "computer revolution" as a set of radical social transformations in computerized social settings. The publication of 50 or 100 books about a topic suggests that it will invite readers and sales; but it doesn't ensure that some of the authors can characterize it in a meaningful way. In the next section we will examine several typical writings to better understand the kinds of changes some key authors identify as signalling a *computer revolution.*

What Kind of Revolution?

Authors who write about a "computer revolution" often use a vocabulary of somewhat distinct, but loosely interchangeable concepts: computer revolution, information technology revolution, computer age, information society, and so on. For simplicity, we will refer to this collection of concepts by the single term *computer revolution.*[3] Most of the books and articles are generally enthusiastic in characterizing a new stage of social development, and only a few analyses are either cautious or critical. But the contrast between "optimistic" and "pessimistic" orientations is not our major concern. Instead, we aim to understand the nature of computerization and what social changes are really attributable to it rather than to other changes in the social order.

Many authors who write about computer revolutions hold what we call "the computer

---

[3] These concepts are quite different in detail. Analysts who focus on an "information society" use measures of the amount of formal information exchange, size of the workforce that specializes in information handling, etc. Only a small fraction of these measures are directly tied to computerization. However, it is common for these authors to examine the social changes that they attribute to computerization in the same way as the computer revolutionaries that we discuss here. See, for example, Daniel Bell's (1980) "A Framework for the Information Society."

revolutionary thesis": there is a social revolution in the making that is driven by advances in information technologies. Unfortunately, most analysts who support this thesis do not characterize carefully the kind of revolution they are writing about or describe explicit indicators. When they are explicit, they refer to two different kinds of phenomena: (a) a technological revolution in the power, flexibility, cost and size of computer equipment; or (b) the large scale usage of equipment that permeates social life and is the basis of a special social transformation.

For example, in *High-Tech Society: The Story of the Information Technology Revolution*, Tom Forester reports his interest in a "technological revolution, which is bringing about major changes in the way we live and work" (p. 1).[4]

Viewing the revolution as *technological* is a conservative and defensible approach. But it is not the kind of approach that sparked the organizing question for the special issue of the *Journal of Computing and Society*, "Has there been a computer revolution?" If a computer revolution is viewed as a technological revolution, then almost anybody would agree that computer and telecommunications equipment has become much more powerful, flexible, cheaper per unit computation, smaller per unit computation, and so on, during the last 30 years. Acknowledging this technological revolution does not automatically answer the question implicit in Forester's claim: what kinds of social changes have occurred as a by-product of the technological changes in the nature of computer and telecommunications technologies?

Edward Yourdon suggests a more expansive sense of computer revolution in *Nations at Risk: The Impact of The Computer Revolutions*:

> I will argue that almost every manufactured product and every service-oriented business in most countries now relies on computers as a vital component. Today, there are more computers on earth than people. . . . Computers now represent such a pervasive force in our lives that there is no realistic way to avoid them. . . . A few Stone Age primitives in remote jungles . . . can afford to ignore computers. A few die-hard Luddites . . . will persist in living out their lives without the benefits of computers. . . . Today, virtually everyone is a user of computer systems (pp. 2–7).

In his first chapter, Yourdon lists nine examples in which computer systems have become (or might become) widespread—such as estimating 250,000 automated teller machines in use by 1986. He also observes that "by 1986, every American citizen over the age of five will have access to a general purpose programmable computer" (p. 5). Yourdon typifies those analysts who characterize a computer revolution by the sheer pervasiveness of computer technologies in organizations and everyday life. Writers like Yourdon assume that widespread computer use must necessitate major, primarily beneficial, changes in social life. However, it would be inaccurate to label books like Forester's and Yourdon's "blindly optimistic" since they identify some problems that inhibit computer use, such as gender biases, or that could result from computerization dominated by some specific interest group like "big business" or "government." Unfortunately, accounts like Yourdon's shape the discourse about computerization and social life in America by stripping computerization out of important social contexts.

---

[4] Forester uses the concept *high-tech* interchangeably with information technology; and he ignores biotechnologies without comment.

Our third example is slightly different. In a recent essay, "Why I believe There is a Revolution Underway in Higher Education," Richard Cyert, President of Carnegie-Mellon University, starts as follows:

> My definition of a revolution is a new way of achieving bold objectives. I would emphasize that our objective in universities is to graduate educated men and women. Our aim is to educate the men and women in our organizations. To do this, we now have a new tool and new ways of achieving our objectives. This is a revolution. It is not a time for cautious optimism, or for any kind of caution; it is a time for recognizing what we want to do and for bold action. . . .
>
> I see this revolution as consisting of two parts, and it is important for both parts to be recognized. The first part is the construction of a new kind of computer system for our universities based on the personal computer. The second part is using the personal work-station in education. (Cyert, 1987, p. 15)

Cyert develops the rest of his paper by examining several examples of new instructional software.

These three examples illustrate the variety of ways in which authors who advance the computer revolutionary thesis write about it as a social fact. Many, like Forester, write about social changes that are taking place "out there." They position themselves as interested, but impartial, bystanders who report the nature of the battles from the sidelines. A few, like Yourdon and Cyert, explicitly advocate specific kinds of computer use such as instructional computing, electronic mail, etc.

Most of these authors use the concept *computer revolution* rhetorically to characterize a social process which they want every listener or reader to help expedite. Cyert implies that other university faculty should immediately develop or adopt the kind of high-performance instructional software that he has supported at his university—without reflection or caution. Yourdon's book is much more wide ranging than Cyert's article; he suggests that readers should telecommute from home and push for computer use in almost every institutional setting in which they participate. For example, in a section devoted to examining people's work at home, Yourdon suggests that readers whose employers won't allow them to telecommute should seriously consider changing jobs.[5]

These authors don't simply advance and examine theses of computer revolution; they beg the central question about the place of computerization in a larger social universe, the varieties of computerization strategies, and specific changes in social relations. They act as "computer revolutionaries" by inspiring others to participate in the social changes they describe by developing or acquiring and using computer equipment.[6]

---

[5] Both authors of this article work at home with computer support a substantial fraction of our time. We "telecommute" and also pass manuscripts and notes to each other with an electronic mail system. As much as we like working at home part of the time, we believe that there are many other more critical aspects of worklife —interesting content, good relations with colleagues, fair pay, professional challenge, appropriate levels of autonomy, schedules that match one's lifestyle, etc. In our own empirical studies of computerization and work, we have found that few organizations, other than research organizations, allow a significant fraction of their workers to telecommute. We believe that many organizations should allow some of their staff to telecommute. But we find Yourdon's recommendation peculiarly technocentric since it ignores other key aspects of worklife.

[6] In "The Mobilization of Support for Computerization" (1988), we examine how computer revolutionaries use their analyses to help drum up support for computerization.

Creating Confidence Through Rhetoric

The future hasn't yet happened; yet computer revolutionaries are quite confident in describing an emerging revolution. They develop legitimacy and authority for their claims through a variety of rhetorical devices and simplifying conceptualizations that merit our attention. We will suggest one rhetorical device, which we label "curt confidence," here, and examine key aspects of their conceptual approach in the next section.

Cyert (1987), for example, masterfully employs a curt, explicit single-minded call for action: "It is not a time for cautious optimism, or for any kind of caution; it is a time for recognizing what we want to do and for bold action" (p. 15). This preamble to his article works to delegitimize questions about the links between well designed instructional computing systems and serious educational outcomes. Ironically, Cyert's aggressive confidence also undermines the kind of reflective inquiry that many university faculty hope to nurture in their students. Cyert is unusually explicit in setting a tone of unequivocal confidence in the lines of action he proposes and confidence in the social and technical assumptions on which they rest.

Authors like Forester (1987) and Yourdon (1986) use the more common strategies that computer revolutionaries employ when they boldly assert their key assumptions and characterizations rather than carefully examining them. Unlike Bernard Cohen, they do not suggest that there are different possible conceptions of a "computer revolution," ambiguities in identifying whether a revolution is emerging and what computer revolutions might mean to participants. While curt confidence might be driven by editorially imposed space limits in articles, it is much more like to reflect the author's preferences in book-length manuscripts like those we are discussing here. Curt confidence, as a device, helps give a book a bouncy "page-turner" tempo. But it undermines the kinds of critical reflection that would give us deep insights into the social transformations that underly a potential "computer revolution."

Every argument and analysis, including our own, uses some kind of rhetorical style and associated devices to enlighten or convince readers. The rhetorical devices used by computer revolutionaries undermine a serious inquiry into the nature of the very social relationships that they claim are being transformed. But the limitations we have found in these analyses are not simply rhetorical. They are also conceptual, as we shall now see.

Constructing a Simplified, More Certain Social World

In addition to communicating exhilarating opportunities and even troublesome problems of computerization through a buoyant terse rhetoric, computer revolutionaries advance their ideas through implicit social concepts that help them structure a more certain social world. We will examine two key concepts here: *isolation* and *denial of implementation details.*

Isolation is a conceptual approach in which the author extracts the central topic from a rich social background and ignores key social contingencies. For example, most writers who extol instructional computing in grade schools or universities as part of their computer revolution ignore many of the conditions that make schooling (un)interesting for students: pedagogical issues like meaningful curricula, well developed courses, engaged instructors, effective assignments, a good balance between structuring and flexibility in a course, uncongested facilities. They also ignore the questions of social milieu: for example, what makes intellectual life, in any form, attractive and engaging to students in a college where fraternities and football dominate campus life?

Every author isolates his or her chosen topic from a complex universe of possible topics. The extent of isolation is the critical conceptual choice. Computer revolutionaries characteristically isolate computerization from most of the surrounding social milieu that could weaken the credibility of their curtly confident storylines. We will discuss two institutional settings that authors often discuss: instructional computing and "privacy/information disclosure practices in financial services."

Instructional Computing and Schooling

Computer revolutionaries isolate people's interactions with computer-based settings to a few primary acts: programming new systems or directly using a computer-based system. They usually ignore related and critical activities, such as the efforts made by innovators to obtain resources for new systems; the confusions of various managers, professionals and workers who are skeptical or are not predisposed to them; learning to use systems; finding space to locate them and time to use them; handling repairs; etc. Forester, Yourdon, and Cyert usually focus on the technological aspects of instructional computing rather than upon these everyday life patterns. Cyert, for example, describes several programs, in these terms:

> We have a program in electrical engineering called the "Transient Wave Program." It is an educational program that "uses interactive computer graphics to provide students with animations of voltage and current wave forms as they propagate on a transmission line with reflections at both ends." This is an example of a program which gives the student a better notion of what is happening through the use of graphics. (p. 20)

And he concludes his published talk with these comments: "I cite these programs simply to give you some notion why I am enthusiastic and why I feel that there is a real revolution under way in higher education. I believe that we have a fantastic opportunity with the technology we now have and that the only limitation is our own intelligence" (p. 21).

In these short passages Cyert isolates the use of instructional programs, like the transient wave program, from any specific experiences that students have in learning about wave propagation or in taking a course about antenna design in which the program might be used. Cyert never explains what precisely is specially novel about this program in contrast with other instructional software, a style that is common for computer revolutionaries. But more seriously, he structures his discourse so that faculty, students, labs, schedules, places, workloads, specific assignments and their contingencies, etc. are all absent. They are left for the reader to fill them in as if the conditions of instructional computer use are necessarily "optimal," or at least very good for all participants.

Forester's account of instructional computing in grade schools relies upon different kinds of details: the number of computers of different kinds acquired by schools in the U.S. and Britain, and the amount of funds spent for instructional computing in national programs. But his account similarly isolates these signifiers of computer use from the concrete experiences of students and teachers in specific settings. Yourdon's account of instructional computing in grade schools is similarly abstracted from any concrete account of teaching practices or students' experiences in classrooms with computer access. Unlike Cyert, both Forester and Yourdon identify some "problems" of instructional computing in schools—such as shortages of good software and "poor planning." They tend to ignore other important changes in schooling—such as growing class sizes and the declining skills of entry-level teachers in many public schools. But they write about these problems in a way that is so abstracted from the operations of any specific school that they give us no meaningful sense of the actual ways that schools and schooling are being transformed—if at all.

Without any special information about relationships between students, faculty and curricula, it is most likely that social relationships are not being substantially altered in some common way by new instructional technologies at Carnegie Mellon University, or elsewhere. In most schools—at all levels—teachers/professors control the curriculum and organization of courses—including schedules and resources. Students find ways to fit themselves into these structures set up for them. In most respects, the social relations between teachers and students in classrooms or courses with access to computer systems are not fundamentally different than those without such equipment.[7]

There are many ways to computerize. The adoption of computer equipment is just one element of computerization strategy. And different strategies can have different consequences, in the very same social setting. Accounts of a "computer revolution" that deny implementation details ignore these crucial points. For example, university faculty might computerize courses by acquiring or developing software for microcomputers, which are commonly owned by students; or they may set up specialized laboratories where the equipment will be available for all. If they set up laboratories, there are many choices in how tightly scheduled the students will be, such as allowing students to come at their discretion or regimenting students into preassigned time slots to make more efficient use of limited equipment. There are many choices about how to staff labs with assistants by varying their skill levels, hours of availability, and relationships to students. There are many ways to integrate the use of a computer program into a course—from making it available as a discretionary additional resource to requiring that students use it in a narrow time band for specific activities. Last, faculty can organize out-of-classroom activities, such as instructional computer use, in many ways. Some reward structures value individual efforts and penalize group efforts as "cheating"; other reward structures tolerate or even reward collaborative work.

In the course of observing instructional computing use at the University of California at Irvine, we have seen courses computerize quite differently and with different consequences. For example, undergraduate students sometimes resented highly regimented laboratories in required courses. But discretionary "open labs" were also troublesome when they weren't staffed with knowledgeable teaching assistants. Since some of the open labs were available 24 hours a day, some students who worked at 3 A.M. would

---

[7] Here we exempt special demonstration projects where relations between students and teachers are more convivial than the norm (Kling, 1986).

collaborate on assignments with tight deadlines—a behavior that their faculty viewed as cheating. In these circumstances the potential euphoria of students exploring novel intellectual work devolved into frustrating conflicts between students and faculty. Overall, many students at Irvine have found instructional labs of educational value, and sometimes interesting. But the experiences vary in ways that hinge on the social organization of their academic work at least as much as they depend upon the intellectual novelty of the instructional equipment they use.

We have focused on instructional computing because it is an interesting domain and one addressed by three authors whom we have examined in detail here. Computer revolutionaries usually use these conceptual elements—isolation and denying implementation details—to help advance their stories of computerization in all domains. These conceptual gaps "delete" many key social elements from their stories of social change and computerization. As a consequence, they become technologically deterministic because they ignore key social influences that shape computerization and the consequences of different computerization strategies.[8]

Social relations can change as a by-product of computerization. But major social changes are not a *necessary* outcome of computerization projects, and social changes that do occur are often contingent on a set of social factors that can vary from one social setting to another.[9] The computer revolutionaries usually ignore these contingencies in their writing.

Information Brokers in Insurance and Finance

Instructional computing has not yet revolutionized the social organization of schooling in any meaningful sense. And we do not see substantial changes from computerization likely in the near future because computer-based systems have been adopted in ways that fit pre-existing relationships between students and teachers, curricular arrangements, etc.

If we focused exclusively upon instructional computing, one might mistakenly conclude that we believe that computerization is inconsequential. We do not believe that either. In fact computerization has been one element of a substantial set of social transformations in some areas of North American life. We will briefly discuss one area where we believe that social relationships are being significantly restructured and where computerization plays a substantial role in the restructuring.

---

[8] There is a socially richer conceptual approach that frames more accurate accounts of the implementation and consequences of computerization within single organizations—"web models" (Kling and Scacchi, 1982; Kling, 1987). Analyses that use web models take account of the social context of computerization and the infrastructure that supports computer-aided activities. There is good evidence that web models help make better social predictions than the undersocialized concepts that computer revolutionaries prefer.

[9] There is a substantial body of careful empirical research that helps document these claims in a number of institutional areas (Kling, 1980; Kling, 1987). Unfortunately, there are few well-documented studies of computerization in schools. Most of the better quality studies examine office automation and work, computerized models in public policy making, and the operations of private firms. Even so, the studies generalize in important ways to instructional computing and schooling.

Scholars, journalists, and policy makers who have examined institutionalized record-keeping in banking, insurance, and policing have observed substantial transformations (Burnham, 1983; Laudon, 1986). The details differ from one institutional setting to another. But generally, the large organizations in each of these institutional arenas have helped to develop (or subsidize) a set of "national information systems" that help them locate and learn about individuals.

In some cases, such as credit reporting and the insurance industry, important data are collected and sold by third-party data brokers such as Medical Information Inc. and TRW CreditData.[10] The demand for these firms' services, and their subsequent influence in acting as data brokers for millions of Americans, has increased for three different kinds of reasons: (1) people have become substantially more mobile since World War II; (2) the banking and insurance industries are dominated by a few dozen firms that dominate national and large regional markets; and (3) individuals have slowly lost significant legal rights to control organizational records about themselves. While the data brokers are substantial computer users, and their corporate clients often interact with them through computer systems, computer use alone is not responsible for their existence and style of operation.

Individuals don't experience the third-party data brokers' presence until "things go wrong." But a person who is "mysteriously" denied insurance or credit from firm after firm can find it hard to learn why (see Burnham, 1983). When they believe that their records are inaccurate, it may be difficult to learn about and correct them. The relationship between insurance companies and financial firms on one hand and individual clients on the other is much more distant than 30 years ago. It is often mediated by networks of branch offices and computer-based information systems to support operations, and by distant relationships with the data brokers.

But the structure of institutional arrangements in banking, insurance, and credit has changed so much since 1970 that they exemplify areas where it is likely that computerization plays a substantial role in facilitating major social changes. Larger firms increasingly dominate national and regional markets, and firms of all size depend upon third-party data brokers to help assess eligibility of clients. The shifts in information handling to assess eligibility for services has shifted control away from individuals to the service-providing firms. When organizations like the Privacy Protection Study Commission have recommended new legislation to reestablish individuals' abilities to learn about, correct, and control their own records, they have been fought hard by the insurance and banking industry—among others.

We do not have the kind of detailed information about people's interactions with service firms like banks and insurance companies, over time, to demonstrate definitively that social relationships have to be radically transformed through specific strategies of computerization. So this argument is tentative. But we sketch it here for three reasons:

1. to indicate that transformed social relationships may be tied to computerization in one institutional sphere (e.g., financial services), even when there may be a few significant changes in another sphere (e.g., schooling);

---

[10] The data brokers' clients are financial companies and insurance companies.

2. to suggest that computerization becomes important as part of a complex of other social changes rather than as an isolated agent; and
3. to suggest that the changes in social relationships that are supported by computerization may reinforce the power of already powerful groups.

Conclusions

We have briefly examined the structure of arguments about "computer revolutions" through a relatively close reading of three typical texts, by Cyert, Forester, and Yourdon. These authors use an "undersocialized" conceptual scheme that isolates computer use from key elements of social life and ignores the details of computerization strategies. They employ a rhetorical strategy of curt confidence to communicate their viewpoint and to help inspire readers to trust in a "computer revolution" made by acquiring and using computer equipment under commonplace social conditions.

It is too facile simply to label writers like Yourdon and Forester as "optimistic." Rather, it is important to appreciate the theoretical perspectives that structure their accounts and the rhetorical devices that amplify their credence. These work together to enthrall us with stories in which the development and presence of computer systems is a dominant theme and the social relationships and social life into which computerization is woven are truly subordinate (Kling, 1983). Roland Barthes characterized stories like these as "myths," in these terms: "Myth does not deny things, on the contrary its function is to talk about them; simply, it purifies them, it makes them innocent, it gives them natural and external justification, it gives them clarity which is not that of an explanation, but that of a statement of fact" (Barthes, 1972: 143). Barthes does not refer to simple falsehoods, like the story of Santa Claus, as a "myth." He lables the scripts that structure discussions by sanctifying and purifying certain groups or objects as myths. He identifies myths by focusing not on a certain kind of topic, but rather on a certain style of narrative. For example, discussions of the U.S. presidency, the working class, or computerization, may be more or less mythological depending upon how much the subjects are treated as exclusively pure, innocent, powerful, and good. In our view, it is comparably mythological to treat subjects as exclusively corrupt, immoral, powerful, and bad as do some of the dystopian thinkers (Weizenbaum, 1976; Winner, 1984). And it is usually a kind of shallow play of mythical forms to force some subject, such as computerization, to be either basically pure or basically corrupt, either basically innocent or basically immoral, and so on. This kind of polar assessment of value is also stripped out of the particular contexts in which people live with computer-based systems (or other social objects). These mythologized assessments also gloss many people's ambivalence and complex relationships with the diverse social shifts that accompany computerization.

The "myths" of computer revolutionary discussions purify new computer technologies and their use by simplifying the social conditions that make them attractive to some participants, and the complexities and sluggishness of institutional change. Computerization is a complex set of social practices, not just the use of a computer system. Different computerization strategies may better serve different social interests and have different social consequences. The limits to computerization may be set by a powerful array of institutionalized social practices. Computer revolutionaries usually ignore these important aspects of computerization because they compromise the innocence, power, and purity of new technologies and their advocates.

Computerization has transformed social life in only a few arenas. These transformations depend upon a complex set of conditions. These conditions include both the "ecology of interests" in a given social setting or institutional arena, as well as new possibilities for restructuring social activities with new technologies. Computer-based ways of work and new services sometimes overturn specific practices, but they do not readily overturn key social relations—such as patterns of power and the division of labor between sexes.

We believe that the questions that underlie the claims of computer revolutionaries are interesting and important. But we haven't found good answers framed in the rhetoric of "computer revolution." The best answers come from a kind of close empirical observation that opens up the real possibilities, limitations, paradoxes, and ironies of computerization situated in very real social settings.

Acknowledgments

Lisa Dowdy helped us conduct some of the research that supports this article. Mark Poster helped us better understand strategies of theoretical interpretation.

References

Attewell, Paul and James Rule (1984). "Computing and Organizations: What We Know and What We Don't Know." *Communications of the ACM*, (December) 27(12): 1184–1192.

Barthes, Roland (1972). *Mythologies*. New York.

Bell, Daniel (1980). "A Framework for the Information Society." in Tom Forester (ed.), *The Microelectronics Revolution*. MIT Press, Cambridge, Ma.

Burnham, David (1983). *The Rise of the Computer State*. Random House, New York.

Cohen, I. Bernard (1985). *Revolution in Science*. Cambridge, Ma. Harvard University Press.

Cyert, Richard (1987). "Why I Believe There Is a Revolution Underway in Higher Education." in *Campus of the Future: Conference on Information Resources*. Online Computer Library Center, Dublin, Ohio.

Dizard, Wilson (1982). *The Coming Information Age*. Longman's, New York.

Finlay, Marike (1987). *Powermatics: A discursive Critique of New Communications Technology*. Routledge and Keegan Paul, London.

Forester, Tom (1987). *High-Tec Society: The Story of the Information Technology Revolution*. MIT Press, Cambridge, Ma.

Iacono, Suzanne, and Kling, Rob (1987). "Changing Office Technologies and Transformations of Clerical Work: A Historical Perspective," pp. 53–75 in Robert Kraut (ed.), *Technology and the Transformation of White Collar Work*. Lawrence Erlbaum, New Jersey.

Kling, Rob (1978). "Automated Welfare Client-tracking and Service Integration: the Political Economy of Computing." *Communications of the ACM*, 21(6), 484–493.

Kling, Rob (1980). "Computer Abuse and Computer Crime as Organizational Activities." *Computers and Law Journal*, 2(2), 403–427.

Kling, Rob (1983). "Value Conflict in the Deployment of Computing Applications: Cases in Developed and Developing Countries." *Telecommunications Policy*, (March), 12–34.

Kling, Rob (1986). "The New Wave of Academic Computing in Colleges and Universities." *Outlook*, (Spring/Summer) 19(1&2), 8–14.

Kling, Rob (1987). "Defining the Boundaries of Computing Across Complex Organizations." in Richard Boland and Rudy Hirschheim (eds.), *Critical Issues in Information Systems*. John Wiley, London.

Kling, Rob, and Iacono, Suzanne (1984). "The Control of Information Systems Development After Implementation." *Communications of the ACM*, (December) 27(12), 1218–1226.

Kling, Rob, and Iacono, Suzanne (1988). "The Mobilization of Support for Computerization: The Role of Computerization movements." *Social Problems* 35(3), 236–243,

Kling, Rob, and Scacchi, Walt (1982). "The Web of Computing: Computer Technology as Social Organization," in Advances in Computers, 21, New York. Academic Press.

Laudon, Kenneth C. 1886. *Dossier Society: Value Choices in the Design of National Information Systems*. New York: Columbia University Press.

Laurie, Peter 1981 *The Micro Revolution: Living with Computers*. New York: Universe Books.

Lyon, David 1988 *The Information Society: Issues and Illusions*. Cambridge, England: Polity Press.

Naisbitt, John 1984. *Megatrends*. New York: Warner Books.

Papert, Seymour 1980. *Mindstorms; Children, Computers and Powerful Ideas*. New York: Basic Books.

Rosenberg, Richard S. 1986. *Computers and the Information Society*. New York: John Wiley & Sons.

Stoner, Tom 1983. *The Wealth of Information, A Profile of the Post-Industrial Economy*. London: Methuen London Ltd.

Strassmann, Paul 1985. *Information Payoff: The Transformation of Work in the Electronic Age*. New York: Free Press.

Toffler, Alvin 1980. *The Third Wave*. New York: William Morrow.

Weizenbaum, Joseph 1979. "Once more: the Computer Revolution" Michael Dertouzos and Joel Moses (eds.). *The Computer Age: A Twenty Year View*. Cambridge, Ma: MIT Press.

Winner, Langdon 1984. "Mythinformation in the High-tech Era." *IEEE Spectrum*, 21 (6) 90–96.

Yourdon, Edward 1986. *Nations at Risk: The Impact of the Computer Revolution*. New York. Yourdon Press.

4

Why I Am Not Going to Buy a Computer

Wendell Berry

Like almost everybody else, I am hooked to the energy corporations, which I do not admire. I hope to become less hooked to them. In my work, I try to be as little hooked to them as possible. As a farmer, I do almost all of my work with horses. As a writer, I work with a pencil or a pen and a piece of paper.

My wife types my work on a Royal standard typewriter bought new in 1956 and as good now as it was then. As she types, she sees things that are wrong and marks them with small checks in the margins. She is my best critic because she is the one most familiar with my habitual errors and weaknesses. She also understands, sometimes better than I do, what *ought* to be said. We have, I think, a literary cottage industry that works well and pleasantly. I do not see anything wrong with it.

A number of people, by now, have told me that I could greatly improve things by buying a computer. My answer is that I am not going to do it. I have several reasons, and they are good ones.

The first is the one I mentioned in the beginning. I would hate to think that my work as a writer could not be done without a direct dependence on strip-mined coal. How could I write conscientiously against the rape of nature if I were, in the act of writing, implicated in the rape? For the same reason, it matters to me that my writing is done in the daytime, without electric light.

I do not admire the computer manufacturers a great deal more than I admire energy industries. I have seen their advertisements, attempting to seduce struggling or failing farmers into the belief that they can solve their problems by buying yet another piece

---

of expensive equipment. I am familiar with their propaganda campaigns that have put computers into public schools in need of books. That computers are expected to become as common as TV sets in "the future" does not impress me or matter to me. I do not own a TV set. I do not see that computers are bringing us one step nearer to anything that does matter to me: peace, economic justice, ecological health, political honesty, family and community stability, good work.

What would a computer cost me? More money, for one thing, than I can afford, and more than I wish to pay to people whom I do not admire. But the cost would not be just monetary. It is well understood that technological innovation always requires the discarding of the "old model"—the "old model" in this case being not just our old Royal standard, but my wife, my critic, my closest reader, my fellow worker. Thus (and I think this is typical of present-day technological innovation), what would be superseded would be not only something, but somebody. In order to be technologically up to date as a writer, I would have to sacrifice an association that I am dependent upon and that I treasure.

My final and perhaps my best reason for not owning a computer is that I do not wish to fool myself. I disbelieve, and therefore strongly resent, the assertion that I or anybody else could write better or more easily with a computer than with a pencil. I do not see why I should not be as scientific about this as the next fellow: when somebody has used a computer to write work that is demonstrably better than Dante's, and when this better is demonstrably attributable to the use of a computer, then I will speak of computers with a more respectful tone of voice, though I still will not buy one.

To make myself as plain as I can, I should give my standards for technological innovation in my own work. They are as follows:

1. The new tool should be cheaper than the one it replaces.
2. It should be at least as small in scale as the one it replaces.
3. It should do work that is clearly and demonstrably better than the one it replaces.
4. It should use less energy than the one it replaces.
5. If possible, it should use some form of solar energy, such as that of the body.
6. It should be repairable by a person of ordinary intelligence, provided that he or she has the necessary tools.
7. It should be purchasable and repairable as near to home as possible.
8. It should come from a small, privately owned shop or store that will take it back for maintenance and repair.
9. It should not replace or disrupt anything good that already exists, and this includes family and community relationships.

1987

After the foregoing essay, first published in the *New England Review and Bread Loaf Quarterly*, was reprinted in *Harper's*, the *Harper's* editors published the following letters in response and permitted me a reply.

W.B.

Letters

Wendell Berry provides writers enslaved by the computer with a handy alternative: Wife —a low-tech energy-saving device. Drop a pile of handwritten notes on Wife and you get back a finished manuscript, edited while it was typed. What computer can do that? Wife meets all of Berry's uncompromising standards for technological innovation: she's cheap, repairable near home, and good for the family structure. Best of all, Wife is politically correct because she breaks a writer's "direct dependence on strip-mined coal."

History teaches us that Wife can also be used to beat rugs and wash clothes by hand, thus eliminating the need for the vacuum cleaner and washing machine, two more nasty machines that threaten the act of writing.

Gordon Inkeles
Miranda, Calif.

I have no quarrel with Berry because he prefers to write with pencil and paper; that is his choice. But he implies that I and others are somehow impure because we choose to write on a computer. I do not admire the energy corporations, either. Their shortcoming is not that they produce electricity but how they go about it. They are poorly managed because they are blind to long-term consequences. To solve this problem, wouldn't it make more sense to correct the precise error they are making rather than simply ignore their product? I would be happy to join Berry in a protest against strip mining, but I intend to keep plugging this computer into the wall with a clear conscience.

James Rhoads
Battle Creek, Mich.

I enjoyed reading Berry's declaration of intent never to buy a personal computer in the same way that I enjoy reading about the belief systems of unfamiliar tribal cultures. I tried to imagine a tool that would meet Berry's criteria for superiority to his old manual typewriter. The clear winner is the quill pen. It is cheaper, smaller, more energy-efficient, human-powered, easily repaired, and non-disruptive of existing relationships.

Berry also requires that this tool must be "clearly and demonstrably better" than the one it replaces. But surely we all recognize by now that "better" is in the mind of the beholder. To the quill pen aficionado, the benefits obtained from elegant calligraphy might well outweigh all others.

I have no particular desire to see Berry use a word processor; if he doesn't like computers, that's fine with me. However, I do object to his portrayal of this reluctance as a moral virtue. Many of us have found that computers can be an invaluable tool in the fight to protect our environment. In addition to helping me write, my personal computer gives me access to up-to-the-minute reports on the workings of the EPA and the nuclear industry. I participate in electronic bulletin boards on which environmental activists discuss strategy and warn each other about urgent legislative issues. Perhaps Berry feels that the Sierra Club should eschew modern printing technology, which is highly wasteful of energy, in favor of having its members hand-copy the club's magazines and other mailings each month?

Nathaniel S. Borenstein
Pittsburgh, Pa.

The value of a computer to a writer is that it is a tool not for generating ideas but for typing and editing words. It is cheaper than a secretary (or a wife!) and arguably more fuel-efficient. And it enables spouses who are not inclined to provide free labor more time to concentrate on *their* own work.

We should support alternatives both to coal-generated electricity and to IBM-style technocracy. But I am reluctant to entertain alternatives that presuppose the traditional subservience of one class to another. Let the PCs come and the wives and servants go seek more meaningful work.

Toby Koosman
Knoxville, Tenn.

Berry asks how he could write conscientiously against the rape of nature if in the act of writing on a computer he was implicated in the rape. I find it ironic that a writer who sees the underlying connectedness of things would allow his diatribe against computers to be published in a magazine that carries ads for the National Rural Electric Cooperative Association, Marlboro, Phillips Petroleum, McDonnell Douglas, and yes, even Smith-Corona. If Berry rests confortably at night, he must be using sleeping pills.

Bradley C. Johnson
Grand Forks, N.D.

Wendel Berry Replies:

The foregoing letters surprised me with the intensity of the feelings they expressed. According to the writers' testimony, there is nothing wrong with their computers; they are utterly satisfied with them and all that they stand for. My correspondents are certain that I am wrong and that I am, moreover, on the losing side, a side already relegated to the dustbin of history. And yet they grow huffy and condescending over my tiny dissent. What are they so anxious about?

I can only conclude that I have scratched the skin of a technological fundamentalism that, like other fundamentalisms, wishes to monopolize a whole society and, therefore, cannot tolerate the smallest difference of opinion. At the slightest hint of a threat to their complacency, they repeat, like a chorus of toads, the notes sounded by their leaders in industry. The past was gloomy, drudgery-ridden, servile, meaningless, and slow. The present, thanks only to purchasable products, is meaningful, bright, lively, centralized, and fast. The future, thanks only to more purchasable products, is going to be even better. Thus consumers become salesmen, and the world is made safer for corporations.

I am also surprised by the meanness with which two of these writers refer to my wife.

In order to imply that I am a tyrant, they suggest by both direct statement and innuendo that she is subservient, characterless, and stupid—a mere "device" easily forced to provide meaningless "free labor." I understand that it is impossible to make an adequate public defense of one's private life, and so I will only point that that there are a number of kinder possibilities that my critics have disdained to imagine: that my wife may do this work because she wants to and likes to; that she may find some use and some meaning in it; that she may not work for nothing. These gentlemen obviously think themselves feminists of the most correct and principled sort, and yet they do not hesitate to stereotype and insult, on the basis of one fact, a woman they do not know. They are audacious and irresponsible gossips.

In his letter, Bradley C. Johnson rushes past the possibility of sense in what I said in my essay by implying that I am or ought to be a fanatic. That I am a person of this century and am implicated in many practices that I regret is fully acknowledged at the beginning of my essay. I did not say that I proposed to end forthwith all my involvement in harmful technology, for I do not know how to do that. I said merely that I want to limit such involvement, and to a certain extent I do know how to do that. If some technology does damage to the world—as two of the above letters seem to agree that it does—then why is it not reasonable, and indeed moral, to try to limit one's use of that technology? *Of course,* I think that I am right to do this.

I would not think so, obviously, if I agreed with Nathaniel S. Borenstein that " 'better' is in the mind of the beholder." But if he truly believes this, I do not see why he bothers with his personal computer's "up-to-the-minute reports on the workings of the EPA and the nuclear industry" or why he wishes to be warned about "urgent legislative issues." According to his system, the "better" in a bureaucratic, industrial, or legislative mind is as good as the "better" in his. His mind apparently is being subverted by an objective standard of some sort, and he had better look out.

Borenstein does not say what he does after his computer has drummed him awake. I assume from his letter that he must send donations to conservation organizations and letters to officials. Like James Rhoads, at any rate, he has a clear conscience. But this is what is wrong with the conservation movement. It has a clear conscience. The guilty are always other people, and the wrong is always somewhere else. That is why Borenstein finds his "electronic bulletin board" so handy. To the conservation movement, it is only production that causes environmental degradation; the consumption that supports the production is rarely acknowledged to be at fault. The ideal of the run-of-the-mill conservationist is to impose restraints upon production without limiting consumption or burdening the consciences of consumers.

But virtually all of our consumption now is extravagant, and virtually all of it consumes the world. It is not beside the point that most electrical power comes from strip-mined coal. The history of the exploitation of the Appalachian coal fields is long, and it is available to readers. I do not see how anyone can read it and plug in any appliance with a clear conscience. If Rhoads can do so, that does not mean that his conscience is clear; it means that his conscience is not working.

To the extent that we consume, in our present circumstances, we are guilty. To the extent that we guilty consumers are conservationists, we are absurd. But what can we do? Must we go on writing letters to politicians and donating to conservation organizations until the majority of our fellow citizens agree with us? Or can we do something directly to solve our share of the problem?

I am a conservationist. I believe wholeheartedly in putting pressure on the politicians and in maintaining the conservation organizations. But I wrote my little essay partly in distrust of centralization. I don't think that the government and the conservation organizations alone will ever make us a conserving society. Why do I need a centralized computer system to alert me to environmental crises? That I live every hour of every day in an environmental crisis I know from all my senses. Why then is not my first duty to reduce, so far as I can, my own consumption?

Finally, it seems to me that none of my correspondents recognizes the innovativeness of my essay. If the use of a computer is a new idea, then a newer idea is not to use one.

P·A·R·T· II

Economic and Organizational Dimensions of Computerization

P·A·R·T · II

Introduction

Economic and Organizational Dimensions of Computerization

Charles Dunlop • Rob Kling

Introduction

This chapter examines several economic aspects of computerization: the ways in which computer systems support new services and alter competition between organizations and the extent to which computerization alters the productivity of organizations and changes their costs.[1] We also examine how organizational processes, bureaucratization, and fights over power influence the way that organizations computerize.

It is quite difficult to find adequate measures of institutional efficiency and productivity. Organizations sometimes have had substantial difficulty demonstrating concrete economic payoffs from computerization, because they changed their business as they computerized. In such cases, quantitative reports of changing costs don't shed much light on the new activities supported by computers. Moreover, it is an important social choice to organize society so as to maximize efficiency and profit—rather than according to other values, such as plentiful jobs, good working conditions, or reliable service to customers. The decisions to computerize are never *merely* economic.[2]

New Services and Business Competition

Business writers, managers, and technologists often argue that computerized information systems are essential if modern businesses are to compete nationally and internationally.

In fact, some have argued that information technology and related skills are "the new wealth of nations."[3] The specific arguments vary and focus on different aspects of organizational life. Some focus on the way that computer systems help firms develop new services, and others emphasize the ways that computerized systems might enhance workers' productivity.

Banks, for example, compete on the interest they offer for savings and the amount they charge for loans. If computer systems lowered administrative costs, banks would be able to offer more favorable interest rates and thus attract more business. But banks also compete on the kinds of services they offer, including notaries, branch locations, banking hours, networks of automated teller machines, and variety of kinds of accounts. So administrative cost savings, instead of being passed on to customers, may be used to support expanded banking services.

In our first selection, "Getting the Electronics Just Right," Barnaby Feder examines computerization at Wells Fargo, a major California bank. Feder's story concisely describes several different computerization efforts, some aimed at providing new services and others aimed at improving internal efficiencies. Feder's account is one of the rare concise portraits of many different computerized information systems in a firm. Because of its brevity, it is necessarily highly simplified. Like many business writers, Feder stresses how a firm succeeded in developing innovative computer systems and new services. Usually such innovation is costly even when things go well. But innovation is fraught with risks, and costs can escalate when things go wrong. And even very expensive projects developed by highly qualified professionals can fail to meet their designers' expectations: in extreme cases they may be aborted. Our second selection, by Douglas Frantz, examines how another major bank, the Bank of America, spent $60 million to get a $20 million computer system to work properly for trust management—and then abandoned the whole project. Bank of America's experience is not unique. Many computerization projects lie between these two—they ultimate work in some way, but they take longer to implement, cost more, and are much more disruptive than their advocates had hoped. Since managers and professionals are usually embarrassed when their computerization projects do not go smoothly and according to schedule, few of the professional articles about computerization accurately portray the dynamics of computerization in real organizations.[4]

The main controversies about the role of computer systems in supporting new services concern the extent to which these services are an economically effective way of drawing new customers, retaining old ones, and improving the economy generally. At the same time, computer-based services are not just conveniences. Their widespread deployment restructures industries as well as relations between people and organizations.

---

[1] We have decided not to examine in this book how computerization changes employment within the economy. See the following sources, listed under Further Reading, for an introduction to the key debates: Brooks (1983); Cyert and Mowery (1987); Forester (1987, Chapter 9); Hartman, Kraut and Tilly (1986); Kling and Turner (1991); McLaughlin (1983); and Menzies (1982).

[2] Kling (1983) examines the character of value conflicts stimulated by computerization. Part of his article is reprinted in Part V.

[3] See, for example, the selection by Feigenbaum and McCorduck (1983) in Part I, and Opel (1987).

[4] See Kling and Iacono (1984), Markus (1984), and Office of Technology Assessment (1986) for cases of problematic information systems implementations.

Computerization and Productivity

Many analysts have argued that organizations could effectively increase the productivity of white-collar workers through careful "office automation." There is almost a routine litany about the benefits of computerization; decreasing costs or increasing productivity are often taken for granted. For example, here is a brief sample news item from a computer science journal:

> Chrysler Corporation's new computerized car design system promises to accelerate the development of cars by thirty percent, saving the automotive giant millions of dollars in car costs. The $200,000 system was developed by the Evans and Sutherland Company of Salt Lake City.[5]

Brief items like this appear frequently in newspapers and magazines. That they are often printed without comment—as statements of fact—indicates the way in which the link between computerization and cost savings is often taken for granted. One might imagine some alternative news clips:

> Chrysler Corporation's new air conditioning system in its design center promises to accelerate the development of cars by thirty percent, saving the automotive giant millions of dollars in car costs.

> Chrysler Corporation's new practice of having designers feel free to look at the ceiling when they let their minds wander promises to accelerate the development of cars by thirty percent, saving the automotive giant millions of dollars in car costs.

These story lines could have plausible rationales. Staring at the ceiling could free up the imagination of designers; better air conditioning might improve their ability to concentrate during Detroit's hot, humid summer days. But stories like these are less likely to appear without some special explanation! The theme of computerization's direct economic value has already become a cultural stereotype in the United States. Like many stereotypes, it is based on some important insights. But like all stereotypes, it alters those insights and goes well beyond them.

Sometimes these stereotypes concerning the economics of computerization actually work against managers and their staffs. Some computer-based systems have enabled organizations to reduce the amount of direct labor required for certain everyday activities —such as calculating and printing routine bills. However, many computer applications improve the quality of the work done, rather than reduce the number of people who work in a specific office. And this result won't readily appear in cost-accounting. For example, some computerized accounting systems provide more detailed, timely, and accurate information about expenditures than do their manual counterparts or simpler computerized precursors. Use of these systems can sometimes help managers and professionals to manage their funds better. But they may also require as many accounting clerks as the simpler systems do for the entering and organization of data. Higher level managers in organizations have sometimes balked at investing in the more sophisticated kinds of applications, refusing to approve proposals for new computer systems without

---

[5] *Communications of the ACM*, Vol. 32, No. 9 (September, 1989).

associated staff reductions. In any event, their approval or disapproval illustrates how managers view many computer systems in direct economic terms—money spent or saved, and revenues generated.

Concerns with economic costs and payoffs might appear rather narrow and very concrete in contrast to the richer array of social values that we examine elsewhere in this book. Even so, there is a substantial debate about why organizations adopt the computer-based system that they select (and why they do not adopt others). One routine claim about computer-based technologies is that they decrease costs and raise productivity: it is remarkably difficult to find careful cost/productivity studies of computerization.[6] One key point that is usually ignored is the way in which the burden for increasing productivity with computer systems usually falls on the poorest-paid workers in an organization. A clerk who is paid $20,000 per year must increase her productivity five times as much as a $100,000 a year executive to get a comparable return on a $10,000 computer investment. Over a three-year period, the clerk must increase her effectiveness (or productivity) by 15% a year (6 hours a week equivalent), while the executive need improve only by 3% a year to break even on the investment. Computerization is one strategy among many that organizations can turn to in order to reduce costs or improve revenues and service. Other common strategies include improving the structure of the organization: reallocating responsibility, reducing the levels of hierarchy,[7] reducing the amount of internal review and paperwork, etc.[8] Computerization often seems most effective when it is coupled with a sensible reform program, rather than simply as a freestanding effort "to modernize."

Our third selection, "Great Expectations: PCs and Productivity" by economist Martin Neal Baily, raises questions about cost effectiveness of many computer applications. Baily keeps his eye on the overall productivity of the U.S. economy, as measured by economists (Baily and Gordon, 1988). He notes that overall productivity growth in the U.S. economy has been very sluggish in the 1980s. While the aggregate statistics about productivity mask large variations among different firms, and even within particular firms, Baily wonders why the nation's major investment in computing technologies has not shown up in national-level data.

Baily notes that computer systems often do things better than their manual equivalents. Computerized word-processing systems make it easier than ever to revise a manuscript 40 times, and financial analysts find it increasingly simple to break their data into finer slices and report them more frequently. But Baily notes that it is usually hard to place an

---

[6] See for example, King and Schrems (1978) for an assessment of key techniques of cost-benefit analyses.

[7] See, for example, Hymowitz (1990).

[8] For example, Smith and Alexander (1988) report that the Xerox Corporation required about 180 reviews and signatures for a new photocopier to reach the market in the late 1970s. In the 1980s the firm was restructured to streamline the reviews, with significant improvements in the speed of releasing more competitive products. Certain kinds of computerization projects could seem helpful but actually simply reinforce problematic organizational practices. For example, an organization that requires many signatures for product reviews might seem to "need" a computerized database system to help track the status of a product in the maze of reviews and approvals. A simpler review process might be of much greater value. See Campbell, Campbell and Associates (1988) for a high quality comprehensive review of the research about productivity in organizations.

economic value on more polished manuscripts and refined reporting.[53] He also questions the role of certain applications in altering productivity within firms or within an industry. He points out that systems that help a firm attract its competitor's customers may be great for the firm, but it doesn't raise overall economic productivity. As Baily asks at one point, somewhat rhetorically, "If this stuff is so good, why do we have the same number of secretaries?"

From 1982 to 1984 there was a boom in the purchase of microcomputers, with annual sales rising about 15% a year. However, the sale of microcomputers slowed a bit, and there was a relative slump around 1985, when sales were increasing "only" by 7–10% a year. Computer sales rose and fell during the 1980s. These figures notwithstanding, we believe that a revolution should be identified by substantial transformations in social relationships and practices, not by the sale of some goods. Rule and Attewell are quite careful in trying to identify those kinds of computer uses that really transform the operations of an organization, rather than those that are just minor enhancements or computerized versions of manual procedures. Nevertheless, many analysts do use sales as a clue to the dynamics of a revolution based on goods.

In our fourth selection, Lynn Salerno uses declining computer sales in the mid-1980s as an indicator that computer-based systems were not paying off according to managers' expectations. She examines some of the reasons for the slump in computer sales during that period. Salerno is an editor of the *Harvard Business Review* and has edited a book of articles about the advantages of computerization.[54] Consequently, she was quite aware of the potential efficiencies that computerization offered to businesses.

Salerno identifies a set of problems that made managers cautious about buying computer-based systems in the mid-1980s. These are different from factors which might impede the effective use of computer-based systems in organizations. She focuses on equipment sales and purchases, not on ways that managers might have to substantially alter their organization's practices and social relations.[55] Salerno claims that upper managers do not understand what computer-based systems could do for their firms. Consequently, they have difficulty in assessing the wisdom of making expensive investments in systems, training, etc. At one point she observes, "[Computer systems] might seem to help the managers, if we knew what their jobs were." This is a rather surprising comment coming from the editor of the *Harvard Business Review*. There is some truth to it, despite an interesting research literature about the nature of managerial work, which Salerno seems to ignore.[56]

There are over 7,000,000 managers in the United States, and their jobs vary considerably. The people who manage the development of a new software product for a major computer firm, the work group that enters data concerning benefits paid by an insurance

---

[9] Sometimes it is also hard to place a precise cost on these products. Moreover, although multiple revisions and fine-grained reporting are even *encouraged* by the availability of new technology (e.g., word processors), the returns may be of diminishing economic and aesthetic value. For example, does a revision from Draft # 40 really represent time well spent?

[10] *Computer Briefing: Using the Trends for Better Managerial Decisions.* New York: Wiley (1986).

[11] See Jewett and Kling (1990) and Chapter 4 of Levering (1988) for case studies that examine the way that effective computerization entails changes in the organization of work and pay, not just in information systems.

[12] See, for example Mintzberg (1973), Golembiewski et al. (1978), and Kotter (1982).

company, and a family-owned pizza shop have very different jobs. Even so, managers spend substantial time communicating—in brief conversations, in longer meetings, in phone calls, in writing, and today with electronic mail.[13] But they often want many different kinds of information to facilitate these conversations: facts about the status of projects, projections of future demands, and resources. They also value "soft information" —about emerging trends, emerging problems in their organization, etc. This observation has led some observers to appreciate the limits of many of today's information systems, since they organize and communicate structured information about operations within an organization. They are much less useful, and often useless, for spotting trends in the firm's environment—among clients, competitors, regulators, and other organizations.[14]

Managers frequently pass on "soft information"—encouragement, demands, rewards, political support, etc. Different kinds of computer-based systems might help with these different tasks.[15] But there may also be a technological gap between the kinds of computer systems that vendors can sell today and the preferences of managers and other professionals. Salerno doesn't pay much attention to this gap. Nevertheless, one should be aware that organization-wide systems have usually provided very structured information, such as inventories, accounting data, and client lists. When Salerno wrote, the vast majority of microcomputers supported word processing and spreadsheets, although there are a large number of applications potentially available.

Salerno frequently faults computer vendors for exaggerating the benefits of computer systems and understating the efforts that people must invest to obtain important value. It is easy to fault vendors, and not just vendors of *computer* technology. A good deal of mass advertising in the United States simplifies complex products to make them seem immensely appealing—often on grounds of excitement, status, and sex appeal. Computer systems are often sold with images of efficiency, ease of use, and "futureness," even though there is often a major gap between the marketing images and practical realities.

The vast majority of articles and books about computerization and work are written as if computer systems were highly reliable and graceful instruments. The few systematic exceptions to this rule appear in some of the software reviews written in popular publications such as *PC World, Mac World, PC Magazine,* and *Byte Magazine,* which sometimes identify clumsy features in commercial microcomputer software. But these reviews are exceptional and are most likely to be read by computer specialists and

---

[13] Mintzberg's (1973) study of the informational roles of managers is still a standard reference, even though he focused on the presidents of small companies.

[14] Laudon and Laudon (1988: 53–55) identify a class of information systems, "executive support systems," which should help managers scan outward for information about competitors, markets, suppliers, etc. However, few such systems have been built. Like many buzzwords in the computing world, different authors give the term different meanings. For example Rockart and DeLong (1988) characterize "executive support systems" by the *managerial level of the user* ("chief executive officer or member of senior management reporting directly to him or her") rather than by the kind of data included. These differences are not merely semantic. For example, if one adopts Laudon and Laudon's rich conception of executive support systems, major problems arise in trying to identify appropriate data. In contrast, if these systems are defined by their primary users, better systems can be characterized by faster computers that manage data more flexibly and present it with richer graphics and summaries (see for example, Paller and Laska, 1990).

[15] When this information is passed on through electronic conferencing and electronic mail, an organization's interactions may alter appreciably. See Part IV of this book for discussion and analysis of this topic.

computer buffs. And the names of some software packages, such as WordPerfect, Perfect Writer, Sidekick, and Ready!, suggest graceful, refined tools that help only as needed.

It's common knowledge that programs can have bugs, or that people may have trouble transferring data between two different kinds of computers. But these problems are usually viewed as rare anomalies. For example, when we were editing the introductions to this book, we found that WordPerfect 5.0 originally printed the footnotes with varying amounts of space between them, even though we believed they should receive identical spacing.[16] Or, suppose that you write a report at home on a computerized word processor and take the file to your office for printing. If the system configurations in both locations are comparable, you naturally expect the report at work to print exactly as you formatted it at home; any differences appear to be anamolous.[17] The folk wisdom about computing is framed in a series of assumptions about the normal operation of equipment, one of which is that reports formatted on one microcomputer will print "properly" on another compatible computer that runs the same version of the software. The conventional wisdom of the computing world also has some general "escape clauses,"—like Murphy's Law.[18] And the vision of computing advanced in many popular and professional sources is of a set of technologies that are easily usable, highly reliable, and relatively seamless.

In "The Integration of Computing and Routine Work," Les Gasser (1986) examines the way in which anomalies are common in the daily use of computing systems. Anomalies can go much farther than system bugs. For example, the *Wall Street Journal* recently reported that the State of Massachusetts billed the city of Princeton, Massachusetts, one cent in interest after it paid a bill for 10-cent underpayment of taxes. Each of these transactions cost 25 cents in postage, as well as several dollars in staff time and computing resources. The reporter viewed the situation as anomalous because one would not expect organizations routinely to invest many dollars in attempting to collect a few cents.[19] However, the computer program was probably working as it was designed—to compute interest on *all* underpayments and produce accurate bills for interest due to the State of Massachusetts.

---

[16] We resolved the anomaly when we found that the footnotes ended with differing numbers of carriage returns.

[17] The report might print differently because of differences in the ways that the word processors are configured, e.g., with different margin or font settings. In this case the anomaly is intelligible, even if it takes some time and fiddling to locate the problem. On the other hand, if the report prints in some weird format, such as printing the top half of the page in a bold font, or placing footer lines in the middle of the page, the source of the problem may be much less clear and even harder to track down. Our point is that, contrary to much advertising and reporting, problems in *ordinary* uses of computer systems can consume large amounts of time and patience.

[18] Murphy's Law is sometimes stated as "If something can go wrong, it will." There are addenda, such as "Murphy was an optimist." There is also Hoffman's Law: "Computer tasks will take twice as long as you expect, even when you take Hoffman's Law into account." These elements of folk wisdom communicate the imperfection of complex technologies and the difficulties that people have of taking many factors into account when planning complex tasks. Of course, if Murphy's Law were really a law, this book would never have been published.

[19] While some organizations routinely sent out bills for $0.00 when they first computerized in the 1960s and 1970s, one might expect that all major organizations would have cleared up these economic inefficiencies by 1990. The situation was especially farcical because the state was facing an $800 million budget dificit. See Tracy (1990.)

Gasser views computer use as a *social* rather than an individual act. He discusses computerized information systems that are developed, used, maintained, and repaired by teams of people—people who pass beliefs to their co-workers about what the systems are good for, how to use them, and their limits or problems on the jobs. In addition, the individuals in Gasser's study depend upon other groups in their organization for key resources like data, training, and equipment fixes. Some of the anomalies occur because of the interactions among these busy groups, which are not organized like firemen to race to each other's aid at a moment's notice. Gasser argues that anomalies are widespread. The anomalies of computing can sometimes be reduced by improved equipment, but they cannot be eliminated.[20] Gasser's argument sheds some light on the question of why computerization may not enhance productivity as readily as many analysts expect. It also sheds light on why some jobs become more complex with computerization: computer users sometimes have to account for anomalies and work around them.[21]

Why Organizations Computerize

In our fifth selection, "What Do Computers Do?," James Rule and Paul Attewell examine the role of computer-based systems as instruments of organizational rationality. In particular, they build on the analysis of social theorists like Daniel Bell and Herbert Simon, who argue that computer-based systems provide fundamentally new opportunities for managers to choose courses of action based on a more careful and explicit assessment of alternatives. There is an important ingredient in utopian thinking that hopes to replace politics—with its emphasis on the power of some selected groups—with greater rationality for all, through the application of science to management. Rule and Attewell list the range of common business applications (see Table 2 in II-5). They argue that managers have adopted computer applications that help them use simple data—such as averages and totals of activity broken down into regular time intervals or other groupings—to better manage their affairs. They also question Bell's argument that managers use computer systems to advance their theoretical understanding of a firm's behavior.

Rule and Attewell's views are important and merit considerable thought. For example, the authors use their list of common applications, which is dominated by payroll, billing, accounting, and word processing, to argue that computerization is not "bringing about a fundamentally new agenda of organizational action."[22] Moreover, they argue, computerization has been a relatively rational process, since the listed applications make good business sense. It is interesting to view Wells Fargo's computerization efforts in light of Rule and Attewell's list of applications: many novel applications would fit on their list.

Lists like Rule and Attewell's help to remind us that organizations continue to do many

---

[20] New equipment has to be integrated carefully into existing equipment configurations to reduce the chance of anomalies occurring. Otherwise, some of the improved features of different details of the new computing equipment may be unexpectedly incompatible with older equipment.

[21] Authors such as Rule and Attewell, Gasser, Iacono and Kling differ from Giuliano, Mowshowitz, and Perrolle by examining the actual use of computer systems and work practices in use in real social settings.

[22] Kraemer and Kling (1985) employ similar lists of computer applications to argue that managers use computerized systems to tighten their control over organizational activities.

routine things when they computerize. But, as Baily suggests, it is difficult to assess the rationality of computer systems without knowing their costs. "Driving to work" is a rational activity for people who live miles from their workplaces. Still, one can't endorse every possible car purchase as rational, even when the car's major uses are the routine events of everyday life. After all, one could commute to work in a new Ferrari sports car or a five-year-old Ford sedan. Moreover, even the central choices of everyday routines are often influenced by considerations of status and trendiness: e.g., the cars one drives, the clothes and watches one wears, and the furniture and computers one uses for work.

According to analysts like Rule and Attewell, computer systems are powerful technologies that managers can effectively use to transform their organizations into more efficient and competitive entities. Rule and Attewell make an interesting argument that computer applications capable of manipulating data in new ways, or automatically applying relatively complex decision rules, are more likely to transform organizations than are applications that just print and store data (e.g., word processing, electronic mail, and billing). This is a provocative line of argument. But in Part V we will examine the ways that electronic communication can significantly restructure social relationships. There are significant controversies about the extent to which one needs specially sophisticated computer technologies to radically reshape social relationships at work.

Models of Organizational Behavior

Studies of computerization often make critical *implicit* assumptions about the way that organizations behave. It is interesting to contrast the analyses by Feder and Rule and Attewell to that by Salerno. The former accounts portray organizations as tightly managed entities, in which major purchases such as computer systems fit narrowly defined organizational purposes very well. In Salerno's analysis, however, managers and professionals have frequently made mistakes by purchasing computer systems that fail to meet their expectations. Salerno's organizations reflect some gaps between what specific managers and professionals have done and what they should do. But when Salerno has to find fault, she points her finger *outside* the computer-using organization—at over-zealous computer salesmen—rather than at systematic practices *within* the organization. In Salerno's account, managers would make good choices for their overall organizations if they only knew which choices were best.

In contrast, Baily and Frantz portray organizations as having internal structures that influence their choices. Baily refers to "staff infection" in which staff groups take on record-keeping and analytical responsibilities in complex organizations. In so doing, they keep staff support decisions—such as how to design buildings and schedule repairs—away from line managers who are closer to customers or workers. Frantz's sketch of trust operations in the Bank of America is the most complex of our selections. He portrays that bank as one in which different managers were either supportive or cautious about computerization projects, in which authority was fragmented, and in which different groups relied on the same staff to carry out incompatible activities.

In our sixth selection, Rob Kling examines the social assumptions that undergird many analyses of computing in organizations. He contrasts two very broad sets of assumptions:

systems rationalism—in which organizational goals are clear, resources are ample, and participants are generally very cooperative; and

segmented institutionalism—in which goals may be ambiguous and resources inadequate and problematic and groups may seriously conflict within and between organizations.

These different sets of assumptions lead analysts to have very different expectations of the roles of computer-based systems in organizations. Systems rationalists (e.g., Salerno) do not always see computerization in rosy terms, although they often do (e.g., Feder). Since segmented institutionalists see large organizations as having multiple and conflicting goals and as incapable of perfectly meeting any goal in a sustained way, they view computerization as much more problematic, even when it works well. While our key selection from the segmented institutionalist perspective, Frantz's story about the Bank of America, examines an information system that failed, other analyses from this perspective have examined how political action is critical for the *success* of systems.[23]

Kling's essay is a small excerpt from a much larger article in which he examines the way that these alternative views of organizations have influenced studies of computerization.[24] During the 1970s and 1980s, a group of scholars including Bill Dutton, Suzanne Iacono, John King, Rob Kling, Kenneth Kraemer, Kenneth Laudon, and Lynne Markus produced a series of detailed studies that examined how the political coalitions within organizations shaped decisions to computerize and the consequences of computerization. These scholars focused on large organizations, with hundreds or thousands of employees. They found that these large organizations were frequently segmented into coalitions that held conflicting views of which goals the organization should emphasize and which strategies would best achieve them. Although the computer projects favored by specific coalitions often had important elements of economic rationality, they could help to strengthen the power of their champions as well. In fact, systems champions often exaggerated what was known about the economic value or necessity of specific projects. From this perspective, computerization entails organizational changes that do not benefit all participants. For example, in some research universities, the scientists have acquired relatively powerful "number crunchers," while instructional computing labs are relatively impoverished. Students and faculty do not necessarily benefit comparably when a university invests several million dollars in new academic computer systems. "Computer power" comes in part from the organized action of social systems rather than simply from "faster" computers with larger memories and greater communications capacity.

Those analysts who examine computerization from a systems rationalist perspective view computerization in very different terms from those holding a segmented institutionalist perspective. It is relatively rare that analysts of these differing persuasions debate each other. The controversies are much more implicit in the diverse stories about computerization. Newspapers and professional journals are most likely to publish systems rationalist accounts, while the segmented institutionalist accounts are most likely to

---

[23]See, for example, Kling and Iacono (1984), Markus (1984), and Kraemer, Dickhoven, Tierney and King (1987).

[24] See Kling (1987) and the collection by Boland and Hirschheim (1987) for a more recent review of some of the studies that treat computerization as a phenomenon embedded within organizations. Also see the article by Mouritzen and Bjorn-Anderson in Section III.

appear in a small number of scholarly journals and books. Although this is a critical controversy, the debate is quiet.

Segmented institutionalists hold that behavior within organizations is really crucial for understanding the role of computerization in shaping organizations. In fact, some analyses within this approach examine computerized systems as forms of organization rather than as easily separable entities (Kling, 1987; Kling and Iacono, 1989). In our final selection, Kenneth Kraemer examines the extent to which computerized information systems have changed organizations in the 1970s and 1980s. Identifying several key claims about the ways that computerization is supposed to transform organizations, Kraemer claims that analysts who argue that computerized systems will change organizations "have the whole equation backwards. Technology is not the driver; it is rarely even the catalyst; at most it is supportive of reform efforts decided on other grounds." Kraemer goes on to identify some of the political and managerial considerations that shape reform efforts. In his view, organizations shape computing arrangements much more than computing shapes (and reshapes) organizations. Kraemer contradicts the large number of writers who argue that "computer revolutions" are transforming organizations, but his is a more conceptually oriented way than Salerno's. He raises the debate about computerization transforming organizations to higher ground by including the behavior of organizations as an essential element of an analysis of the consequences of computerization.[69] His article stimulates us to wonder what mix of technologies and organizational practices will significantly alter organizations. And these arguments hinge on good theories of organizational change as well as on an understanding of the ways that new technologies can transform and represent information.

Sources

Baily, Martin Neal. "Great Expectations: PCs and Productivity," *PC Computing* 2(4)(April 1989), pp. 137–141.

Feder, Barnaby J. "Getting the Electronics Just Right," *New York Times Business Section*, Sunday, June 4, 1989, pp. 1–8.

Frantz, Douglas. "B of A's Plans for Computer Don't Add Up," *Los Angeles Times* Sunday, February 8, 1988.

Kling, Rob. "Social Analyses of Computing: Theoretical Orientations in Recent Empirical Research," *Computing Surveys* 12(1), pp. 61–110.

Kraemer, Kenneth. "Strategic Computing and Administrative Reform."

Rule, James and Paul Attewell. "What Do Computers Do?" *Social Problems* 36(3)(June 1989), pp. 225–241.

Salerno, Lynn. "What Happened to the Computer Revolution?" *Harvard Business Review* 85(6)(Nov/Dec 1985), pp. 129–138.

---

[25] It is useful to contrast Kraemer's characterization of organizational behavior with that of Rule and Attewell. Kraemer's argument has a precedent in Kenneth Laudon's pathbreaking book, *Computers and Bureaucratic Reform*. Lynne Markus and Dan Robey (1988) have written an important theoretical article that examines the different ways that analysts attribute causality to computer systems in arguments about organizational change.

References

Baily, Martin Neal, and Robert J. Gordon (1988). "The Productivity Slowdown, Measurement Issues, and the Explosion of Computer Power," *Brookings Papers on Economic Activity*. 2, pp. 347–431.

Campbell, John P., Richard J. Campbell and Associates (eds.)(1988). *Productivity in Organizations: New Perspectives From Industrial and Organizational Psychology*. Jossey-Bass, San Francisco.

Feigenbaum, Edward, and Pamela McCorduck (1983). *The Fifth Generation: Artificial Intelligence and Japan's Computer Challenge to the World*. Addison-Wesley, Reading, Massachusetts.

Gasser, Les (1986). "The Integration of Computing and Routine Work," *ACM Transactions on Office Information Systems*, 4(3)(July), pp. 205–225.

Golembiewski, Robert T., Frank Gibson, Gerald Miller (eds.)(1978). *Managerial Behavior and Organization Demands: Management as a Linking of Levels of Interaction*. 2nd ed. F.E. Peacock Publishers, Itasca, Ill.

Hymowitz, Carol (1990). "When Firms Cut Out Middle Managers, Those At The Top and Bottom Often Suffer," *Wall Street Journal* (Thursday April 5), pp. B1, B4.

Jewett, Tom, and Rob Kling (1990). "The Work Group Manager's Role in Developing Computing Infrastructure," *Proceedings of the ACM Conference on Office Information Systems*. Boston, Mass.

King, J.L., and E.S. Schrems (1978). "Cost-Benefit Analysis in Information Systems Development and Operation," *Computing Surveys* (March), pp. 19–34.

Kling, Rob, and Suzanne Iacono (1984). "The Control of Information Systems Development After Implementation," *Communications of the ACM* 27(12)(December), pp. 1218–1226.

Kling, Rob, and Suzanne Iacono (1989). "The Institutional Character of Computerized Information Systems," *Office: Technology and People*. 5(1), pp. 7–28.

Kotter, John P. (1982). *The General Managers*. Free Press, New York.

Kraemer, Kenneth L., and Rob Kling (1985). "The Political Character of Computerization in Service Organizations: Citizen's Interests or Bureaucratic Control," *Computers and the Social Sciences*. 1(2)(April–June), pp. 77–89.

Kraemer, Kenneth L., Siegfried Dickhoven, Susan Fallows Tierney, and John Leslie King (1987). *Datawars: The Politics of Federal Policymaking*. Columbia University Press, New York.

Laudon, Kenneth C. (1974). *Computers and Bureaucratic Reform*. John Wiley, New York.

Laudon, Kenneth C., and Jane Laudon (1988). *Management Information Systems: A Contemporary Perspective*. Macmillan, New York.

Levering, Robert (1988). *A Great Place to Work: What Makes Some Employers So Good (and Most So Bad)*. Random House, New York.

Markus, Lynne, and Dan Robey (1988). "Information Technology and Organizational Change: Causal Structure in Theory and Research," *Managements Sciences*. 34(5), pp. 583–598.

Mintzberg, Henry (1973). *The Nature of Managerial Work*. Prentice Hall, Englewood Cliffs, N.J.

Opel, John (1987). "Technology and the New Wealth of Nations," *Society*. 24(6)(Oct./Nov.), pp. 51–54.

Paller, Alan, and Richard Lasker (1990). "Special Report on Executive Information Systems: What Users Want Today," *Personal Computing*. 14(4)(April 27), pp. 72–74.

Rockart, John F., and David W. DeLong (1988). *Executive Support Systems*. Dow Jones Irwin, Homewood, Ill.

Smith, Douglas K., and Robert C. Alexander (1988). *Fumbling the Future: How Xerox Invented, Then Ignored, The First Personal Computer*. William Morrow, New York.

Further Reading

Boland, Richard and Rudi Hirschheim (eds.)(1987). *Critical Issues in Information Systems*. John Wiley, London.

96 Charles Dunlop · Rob Kling

Brooks, Harvey (1983). "Technology, Competition and Employment," *Annals of the American Political Science Association.* 470 (November).

Cyert, Richard M., and David C. Mowery (eds.)(1987). *Technology and Employment: Innovation and Growth in the U.S. Economy.* National Academy Press, Washington, D.C.

Forester, Tom (1987). *High-Tech Society: The Story of the Information Technology Revolution.* MIT Press, Cambridge, Mass.

Hartman, Heidi I., Robert E. Kraut, and Louise A. Tilly (eds.)(1986). *Computer Chips and Paper Clips: Technology and Women's Employment.* National Academy Press, Washington, D.C.

Hirschheim, Rudi (1985). *Office Automation: A Social and Organizational Perspective.* John Wiley, New York.

King, J.L. (1982). "Organizational Cost Considerations in Computing Decentralization," in Goldberg, R., and H. Lorin (eds.), *The Economics of Information Processing,* Volume 2. John Wiley and Sons, New York.

King, J.L. (1983). "Centralized vs. Decentralized Computing: Organizational Considerations and Management Options," *ACM Computing Surveys.* December.

King, J.L., and K.L. Kraemer (1981). "Cost as a Social Impact of Telecommunications and Other Information Technologies," in M. Moss, *Telecommunications and Productivity.* Addison-Wesley, New York.

Kling, Rob (1980). "Social Analyses of Computing: Theoretical Orientations in Recent Empirical Research," *Computing Surveys.* 12(1), pp. 61–110.

Kling, Rob (1984). "Postscript 1988 to 'Social Analyses of Computing: Theoretical Orientations in Recent Empirical Research'" in Pylyshyn, Zenon, and Liam Bannon (eds.), *Perspectives on the Computer Revolution,* 2nd ed. Ablex Publishing Co., Norwood, N.J., pp. 504–518.

Kling, Rob (1983). "Value Conflicts in the Deployment of Computing Applications: Cases in Developed and Developing Countries," *Telecommunications Policy.* 7(1)(March), pp. 12–34.

Kling, Rob (1987). "Defining the Boundaries of Computing Across Complex Organizations," in Boland, Richard, and Rudy Hirschheim (eds.), *Critical Issues in Information Systems.* John Wiley, London.

Kling, Rob, and Walt Scacchi (1982). "The Web of Computing: Computer Technology as Social Organization," *Advances in Computers,* 21. Academic Press, New York.

Kling, Rob, and Clark Turner (1991). "The Structure of Orange County's Information Labor Force," in Kling, Rob, Spencer Olin, and Mark Poster (eds.), *Post-Suburban California.* University of California Press, Los Angeles, CA.

Kraut, R., S. Dumais, and S. Koch (1989). "Computerization, Productivity, and Quality of Work-Life," *Communications of the ACM,* 32(2)(February), pp. 220–238.

Kraemer, Kenneth L., and John L. King (1986). "Computing in Public Organizations," *Public Administration Review,* 46 (November), pp. 488–496.

Markus, Lynne (1984). *Systems in Organizations: Bugs and Features.* Pitman Publishing Co., Boston.

McLaughlin, Doris (1983). "Electronics and the Future of Work: The Impact on Pink and White Collar Workers," *Annals of the American Political Science Association.* 470 (November).

Menzies, Heather (1981). *Women and the Chip: Case Studies of the Effects of Informatics on Employment in Canada.* Institute for Research on Public Policy, Montreal.

Nora, Allain, and Simon Minc (1974). *The Computerization of Society.* MIT Press, Cambridge, Mass.

Office of Technology Assessment (1986). *The Social Security Administration and Information Technology.* U.S. Government Printing Office, Washington, D.C.

Perrolle, Judith A. (1987). "The Information Economy: From Manufacturing to Knowledge Production," Chapter 6 of *Computers and Social Change: Information, Property and Power.* Wadsworth Pub. Co., Belmont, Ca.

Walsham, G., Veronica Symons, and Tim Waema (1988). "Information Systems as Social Systems: Implications for Developing Countries," *Information Technology for Development.* 3(3).

P·A·R·T · II

1

Getting the Electronics Just Right

Barnaby J. Feder

Carl E. Reichardt, the chairman and chief executive of Wells Fargo & Company, doesn't have a personal computer in his office. And he is quite happy to use secretaries, phones and meetings to communicate with underlings.

But that doesn't mean that Wells Fargo, the nation's 11th-biggest bank, is falling behind in an electronic age. An early backer of the telegraph, stage coaches, and the Pony Express to move information and wealth in the 19th century, the company is a case study of the effective use of information systems in carving out a strategic advantage over rivals.

In recent years, Wells Fargo has generally stayed away from the riskier frontiers like home banking by computer and artificial intelligence systems that try to mimic human thinking. But it has been among the largest investors in such bread-and-butter items as automated teller machines and basic computer systems. And it has succeeded in using the technology to pare operating costs, absorb acquisitions efficiently and offer customers new services.

"I am much more interested in reliability than being on the leading edge," said Mr. Reichardt. "There's nothing worse than selling technology-driven services that do not work."

Wells's legacy has proved valuable at a time when businesses prosper or founder depending on how deftly they exploit the rapid advances in computers and telecommunications. No single industry reflects the full sweep of the information technology revolution in America, but big banks are in the forefront.

Financial institutions account for 35 percent of information technology purchases in the United States, though they employ only 5 percent of workers, according to studies by

McKinsey & Company, the New York consultants. Spending by commercial banks alone approached $12 billion last year.

So far, all this spending has led mainly to better and cheaper services for customers rather than to higher profits for banks. Since most major banks can afford the technology's basic building blocks, just as major airlines can buy the newest jets, banks have been spending hundreds of millions of dollars to stay even with rivals. And because banking suffers from overcapacity, only those using the technology effectively prosper in the meantime.

"Wells is a leading-edge example of the transition to the third stage of the revolution in banking," said Thomas Steiner, a McKinsey partner. In the first stage, Mr. Steiner said, "computers are used in functions like accounting, which means fewer back-office people and fewer errors." The second stage brings information systems that perform transactions, "which means that customers see the results faster, everyone gets more information, and the growth in the number of tellers is blunted," he said. "And in the third stage, customers —starting with big business customers—use computers connected to the bank to do more of the work. That leads to increasingly tough price competition among banks offering various services and eventually to big staff reductions."

Already, 50,000 jobs have disappeared from banking since 1986, when employment peaked at 1.5 million, according to McKinsey, which expects the decline to continue (despite projections by the Labor Department that bank jobs will grow through 1999).

Such layoffs are just part of the transformation that has accompanied the electronic revolution at Wells and other banks. "I remember one senior executive saying, 'I'm just a dumb banker; I don't understand technology,'" said Jack Hancock, chief architect of Wells's information technology strategy until his retirement from banking two years ago. "I told him if he didn't understand information technology, he couldn't be a good banker. He's no longer with the bank."

The new technology has also upset traditional notions of which jobs are best done at headquarters and which at branches and has changed how information is shared. At the same time, relationships with customers and suppliers have been altered.

The big challenge has been to harness the changes to the bank's business strategy. Wells concentrates on consumers and small- to medium-sized businesses in California. It also is a major lender for construction and leveraged buyouts. Now, a growing proportion of its dealings involve selling information about money and money management instead of taking deposits and making loans.

At Wells, various departments are in different stages of the information revolution. What follows are snapshots of how the technology has affected some aspects of the bank's structure and style.

Branches Shed Bookkeeping

The painstaking bookkeeping and decision-making once performed at Wells's 455 retail branches—processing loans, verifying signatures on checks, balancing accounts—is now electronically centralized. As a result, the number of branch workers has declined.

Officers at the branches, meanwhile, are freer to concentrate on generating new business and are being given much more freedom to do so. "We have been able to reduce 2,000 pages of rules for operating branches to a 115-page booklet," said William F. Zuendt, the vice chairman who oversees the bank's retail, or consumer, operations.

"I don't think I would have stayed in banking if we hadn't made these changes," said Barbara Crist, who joined Wells 22 years ago as a teller and now manages the street-level branch at Wells Fargo headquarters in the financial district here. "We spend more time on business now and it's more exciting."

The computer backbone of the bank's branches throughout California is the Wells Electronic Banking System, or WEBS. The product of separate systems that Wells and the Crocker Bank were developing when Wells acquired its California rival from Britain's Midland Bank in 1986, WEBS plugs branch employees into the centralized records and processing systems.

With video-screen records of a client's banking activity, the staff can handle 100 transactions—everything from answering questions about safety-deposit boxes to opening accounts—without paperwork. "In the old days, we did a lot of bookkeeping," Ms. Crist said. "You would call other branches for balances just to cash a check."

WEBS—in conjunction with Wells's automated teller system—allows the branches to handle many more customers with fewer full-time employees. (Part-time workers are hired on the basis of computer projections of when they will be needed to limit customer waiting times to five minutes.) Ms. Crist's branch is down from 134 employees to 54.

With all this, Wells has cut the fixed costs at branches—a saving that allowed the bank to move quickly when it decided to extend banking hours to 6 P.M. on weekdays and to open on Saturdays. The bank says that the leanness of its operations also made it tough for competitors to match its moves.

The 24-Hour Customer

"The relationship with the customer has changed completely," said Elizabeth A. Evans, senior vice president in charge of information services for retail banking and corporate systems planning. "A customer can deal with us anytime, almost anywhere."

The most familiar source of this freedom is the automated teller machine. Wells has 1,246 A.T.M.'s, one of the highest figures per branch in the country. And it has linked them to the Star and Plus systems so that its customers have access to 25,000 machines at other banks nationwide. About 1.3 million Wells customers use A.T.M. cards, the equivalent of 71 percent of the bank's checking accounts—the highest percentage for any bank in the country.

WEBS, meanwhile, has been linked with modern telecommunications to make another Wells service—24-hour telephone banking—a success. A Northern Telecom switch automatically distributes calls to balance the load between five sites. The night shift employs students, housewives and people seeking second jobs—a whole new group of low-wage workers the industry was largely unable to tap in its 9-to-3 days. Some two million callers a month request everything from C.D. rates to stopping a cheque.

For corporate customers, Wells offers a system that allows corporate treasurers to see exactly when money moves in and out of their bank accounts and to initiate transactions without ever talking to a banker. And accounts are updated as soon as a transaction occurs —so-called real-time banking.

This corporate equivalent of home banking has major customers like the Chevron Corporation—which 10 years ago typically had $125 million on deposit on a given day —reinvesting cash so quickly that its average daily balance is only $1 million.

Some corporate customers can communicate automatically with the bank's computer system. The Hilton Hotel Corporation's computers contact Wells's computers and those at other major banks, starting in the middle of the night, to find out how much is in the company's accounts. Then, when Richard H. Chambers, Hilton's assistant treasurer, arrives at his Beverly Hills office in the morning, a job that used to take a flurry of phone calls is already done.

The hot new development for corporate customers is electronic data interchange—a system that allows businesses to bill one another and make payments electronically. Wells is now involved in a pilot experiment with Citibank, Philadelphia National Bank, and Chevron, Shell Oil, and Amoco to settle accounts for an oil field Chevron operates in partnership with the other two oil companies.

"I learned to play golf when I started in this business 20 years ago," said David Kvederis, executive vice present in Wells's wholesale services group, commenting on how bankers court business. "Today it is far more valuable to get their PC's to interact with your computers."

Wells's Integrated Office Support System, the commercial bank's equivalent of WEBS, offers a range of computer services to account officers. It helps bankers dream up everything from new lending arrangements to potential mergers and acquisitions. "What used to take a day—studying things in a deal like cash flow and the sensitivity of the figures to changes in interest rates—can be done in 15 minutes," said Michael R. James, head of Wells's commercial banking office in Palo Alto, Calif. "We can use that information as a marketing tool, particularly when approaching small companies that have never been able to do that kind of thing."

Some of Wells's information technology even blurs the lines between the bank and its customers. Wells's cash management service for the Catholic Diocese of Santa Rosa, Calif., automatically pools funds from 200 schools, churches, retirement homes and clubs into an account that Msgr. Thomas Keys, the diocese's financial officer, manages via his Compaq portable computer.

"It allows me to use a program I wrote that tracks the deposits, withdrawals and average daily balances of the different entities and generates a monthly interest check for them," said Monsignor Keys. "We pay Wells a fee of $3,500 to $5,000 a month, and the diocese gets the float. They are a conduit and we have become the bank."

Just-in-Time Suppliers

Electronic ordering and record-keeping has centralized purchasing at Wells so much that the bank now deals with only seven major office-supply vendors instead of 150 and writes only a handful of checks to pay their bills instead of thousands. And now the vendors are mostly those willing to ship what is needed when it is needed, thus allowing the bank to eliminate the practice of maintaining a six-month supply of materials, worth up to $1 million, in an Oakland warehouse.

"It's more of a mutual partnership," said Susan Bosco, a manager who oversees the ordering of 2,000 different forms and 5,000 office-supply items for Wells. Her purchasing staff has been cut from 40 employees to 10. As with other significant staff cuts at Wells, some got other work at the bank. Others were laid off with an offer of severance pay and job placement services.

Management by E-Mail

Electronic mail has been breaking down barriers by encouraging senior executives to exchange information with a far larger and more diverse group of employees.

No one has a better view of such changes than Ms. Evans, who gets her first look at the coming day when she sits down to breakfast in her home in suburban San Mateo, thanks to an E-mail system that she can phone into from her personal computer.

Her E-mail directory routinely includes status reports from night-shift employees who run data and telecommunications centers under her supervision. She might also find suggestions from colleagues for proposed meetings or requests for comments on their ideas. There may also be notes from subordinates about spending decisions they have made or want to make. "There are lots of simple, quick questions that occur to people at odd hours," said Ms. Evans. "Instead of jotting them down on a piece of paper that gets lost, they send them out on E-mail."

Ms. Evans deals with some matters immediately, often by sending an electronic reply. The ability to get a jump on the workday at home, or to extend it there, helps her juggle responsibilities at the bank with the life she shares with her husband and 4-year-old son. "A lot of us use the system to be able to spend more time with family," she said.

Currently, the 6,600 Wells employees on the E-mail system send 15,000 to 20,000 messages daily. "It's more informal than a written memo and less intrusive than a phone call," said Shirley Moore, an information systems manager. "That means you're more likely to communicate and include more people in the loop." Ms. Moore added: "The informality is well suited for developing business proposals. You feel freer to contact people who have information, no matter where they are on the corporate ladder, and you're more likely to get a timely response."

The spreading use of E-mail also has secretaries doing less typing and more administrative work. According to Mr. Zuendt, it also allows executives to get a much better view of the variety of jobs in the bank, which makes it easier for up-and-coming managers to move to new assignments.

It is also making life more difficult in some respects for Andy Anderson, who heads a staff of historians at Wells. "E-mail doesn't leave the kind of paper trail that would have existed prior to the 1980s to show how a project developed," he said. "We have had to do more things like oral interviews to document recent subjects, such as how the Crocker merger was accomplished."

That does not mean Mr. Anderson is opposed to the information technology revolution. Computerized data bases help his department support Wells's legal department and its advertising campaigns, which often feature the company's history. Besides, if it weren't for the computers, he said, scheduling the road shows of the bank's historic stagecoaches would be a real headache.

P·A·R·T · II

2

B of A's Plans for Computer Don't Add Up

Douglas Frantz

In May, 1986, Bank of America was so confident about the impending success of its pioneering new computer system for trust accounts that dozens of the bank's most important corporate clients were invited to a lavish two-day demonstration at the Santa Barbara Biltmore Hotel.

Holes were cut in the hotel roof to ventilate the rooms full of computers, and color monitors were in place to show off the bells and whistles of what B of A officials touted as the industry's most sophisticated technology for handling trust accounts.

The party's $75,000 tab was minor to officials anticipating the lucrative new business that the system seemed sure to generate when it went on line within the next few weeks.

End of Good Times

"There never has been a meeting that went as well as this from a point of view of inspiring the customers," said Clyde R. Claus, a 30-year veteran of banking, who organized the session as the executive in charge of B of A's trust department. "People were trembling with excitement."

The bash at the Biltmore was the last thing that went right.

Last month, Bank of America acknowledged that it was abandoning the $20-million computer system after wasting another $60 million trying to make it work. The bank will no longer handle processing for its trust division, and the biggest accounts were given to a Boston bank. Top executives, including Claus, have lost their jobs already and an undisclosed number of layoffs are in the works.

If the episode involved only a handful of ruined careers and the millions lost in pursuit of a too-fancy computer system, it would merit an embarrassing but forgettable footnote in Bank of America's legendary history.

But the story is more important than a simple footnote because it opens a rare window on what author Martin Mayer has dubbed "a decade of decline" at the San Francisco bank, an unprecedented span in which its fortunes plunged from a $643-million profit in 1980 to a $955-million loss in 1987 and the bank fell from largest in the world to No. 29.

Deeper Questions

Further, the total abandonment of a computer system after five years of development and nearly a year of false starts raises questions about the bank's ability to overcome its technological inadequacy in an era when money is often nothing more than a blip on a computer screen.

A spokesman said last week that Bank of America officials would not respond to questions from The Times about the episode.

"Since last year, we have acknowledged that operational problems existed in our institutional trust business and our energies have been directed toward resolving them as quickly as possible," the spokesman said in a prepared statement. "We are not interested in fixing blame. . . . We do not believe that it is productive to rehash the situation."

The widely publicized difficulties surrounding the trust computer problems obscure the fact that the Bank of America was once a technological leader, developing the first big commercial computer in the 1950s and inventing the magnetic ink that allows machines to read the codes on checks.

By the late 1970s, however, under the leadership of A.W. Clausen, the bank was skimping on the spending required to keep up with technological advances. Instead, the money went into greater profits. By the time Clausen relinquished the helm of the parent company, BankAmerica, to Samuel H. Armacost in 1981, the bank had fallen far behind in the computer race.

Armacost launched a $4-billion spending program to push B of A back to the technological forefront. The phrase he liked was "leapfrogging into the 1990s," and one area that he chose to emphasize was the trust department.

Financial Role

Trust departments serve as custodians and managers of investments for individuals, corporations, unions and government agencies. Investments can be real estate, cash, stocks and bonds. Accounts run from a few thousand to billions of dollars for big pension funds. Banks collect fees for their services, and the amounts can be substantial.

In return, trust departments must provide customers with extensive records and statements to explain their actions and balance the accounts. The reporting is similar to balancing a checkbook for thousands of customers with enormously varied demands.

For instance, a $300-million pension fund might cover six affiliates within the company. The affiliates would share the services of an investment manager, whose trading would be reported to the bank as trustee. The bank must allocate each purchase or sale to the proper affiliate account, keep track of dividends and provide the customer with an ongoing accounting and monthly statements.

Throw in the management of an office building or two and a picture emerges of the complexity of trust accounting.

Developing a computer system that puts all of this information on the computer screens of customers in a microsecond is enormously complex, and it is vital to be competitive.

Traditionally, the field has been dominated by a handful of big Eastern banks, such as Bankers Trust in New York and State Street Bank & Trust in Boston. Although it was the largest trust bank on the West Coast, B of A in the late 1970s was small by comparison, and it was mired in a 1960s-vintage accounting and reporting system.

An effort to update the system ended in a $6-million failure in 1981 after the company's computer engineers worked for more than a year without developing a usable system. So Armacost turned to Claus, who had spent 20 years with New York's Marine Midland Bank before arriving at B of A in 1977.

Gets Ultimatum

Soon after Claus was named executive vice present in charge of the trust department in 1982, Armacost called him to his office on the 40th floor of the bank's granite tower in downtown San Francisco to discuss the trust department's problems.

"Fix it or close it," Armacost ordered Claus.

Claus soon found that abandoning the business would damage client relationships. Many customers who relied on the bank for trust business as a convenience maintained far larger corporate accounts there. He was equally reluctant to return to the in-house technicians who had produced the stillborn system a year before.

So, Claus and two key executives in data processing, Nicholas Caputo and Thomas Anderson, embarked on a search to find an outside vendor to help develop the new system.

In true Bank of America style, the plan was grand: Create a system to surpass Bankers Trust and State Street and turn B of A into a national power in trust business.

In the fall of 1982, the trust industry held its annual convention in Atlanta. Caputo and Anderson attended, and so did Steven M. Katz, a pioneer in creating software for bank trust departments.

Katz, the computer expert, and Alfred P. West Jr., a marketing specialist, had formed a company called SEI Corp. outside Philadelphia in Wayne, Pa. They had parlayed concepts in Katz's MBA thesis into a software system used by about 300 small banks in the 1970s.

Katz left in a dispute and, in June, 1980, he founded a rival company, Premier Systems, across the street from SEI in Wayne. Insiders referred to the pavement between the companies as "the DMZ."

Katz was in Atlanta trying to drum up business. Caputo knew Katz and invited him to meet with the B of A officials at the Hyatt Regency Hotel. By the accounts of people who were there, it was a stormy beginning.

Basis of System

Bank of America's existing system was based on IBM computers, and the bank officials wanted to stick with the familiar hardware. Katz insisted on using Prime Computer, an IBM rival with which he had a long relationship.

There also was a clash on delivery time. According to one participant, Katz boasted that he could put together a system by 1983, and Anderson argued that the promise was ridiculously optimistic. The argument ended the meeting—but did not doom the partnership.

During the next six months, Bank of America and Katz brought together a consortium of banks that agreed to advance Premier money to develop a new, cutting-edge system for trust reporting and accounting.

The other banks, all smaller than B of A, were Seattle–First National Bank (which would later be purchased by BankAmerica), United Virginia Bank (now Crestar), and Philadelphia National Bank. The three smaller banks were using SEI's system.

Nearly a year was spent on additional research before Claus took the proposal to the bank's management committee and got the go-ahead to fund the project in March, 1984.

A contract was signed with Premier to provide a system called MasterNet. While the trust business was by far the biggest task, the contract also called for the bank's technicians to develop eight smaller systems to augment it under the MasterNet umbrella.

While it was not a deadline, the goal was to have the new system, called TrustPlus, in operation by Dec. 31, 1984.

What followed was a textbook structure for designing a computer system.

A committee was formed of representatives from each B of A department that would use the system, and they met monthly to discuss their requirements. Data-processing experts from the four banks gathered for a week each month in Pennsylvania to review progress and discuss their needs with the Premier designers.

"The bank seemed to be doing it right," a B of A executive involved in the project said. "The risks were shared with other banks. A proven vendor was hired. And all areas of the bank were involved."

Some of the bank data-processing experts found Katz difficult to deal with occasionally, particularly when they offered views on technical aspects of the project. "Don't give us the solutions. Just tell us the problems," Katz often said.

Katz declined to answer questions for this article, saying: "It's our policy not to talk about individual customer relationships."

When the ambitious Dec. 31, 1984, goal passed without a system, no one was concerned. There was progress, and those involved were excited about the unfolding system and undaunted by the size of the task.

The immense size of what they confronted is contained in two minor statistics: B of A devoted 20 man-years to testing the software system and its 3.5 million lines of code; 13,000 hours of training, including rigorous testing, were provided to the staff that would run the system.

After 1985 passed without a working system, some team members detected subtle pressures from corporate brass to come up with a return on the bank's investment, which was approaching $20 million. Customers who had been promised the best system in the world were also concerned.

"Major clients were anxious to get the system and we were real late," one executive who was involved said. "Some of these people were threatening to leave the bank."

Claus, the only person connected with the program who would speak for attribution, denied that he had been pressured over costs or timing. He said Thomas A. Cooper, then the president of B of A, told him in 1986: "You're not getting any pressure from me to do it unless you're ready."

That spring, Claus decided the system was about ready. Some smaller parts of MasterNet were already working smoothly in other parts of the bank. Test runs for the trust system had not been perfect, but the technicians thought most bugs could be worked out soon. A demonstration run in Wayne had been successful.

Divergent Opinions

So invitations were mailed for the bash at the Biltmore. Although Claus genuinely thought that the system was about ready, others viewed the party as a means of appeasing anxious customers by giving them a taste.

The taste was good.

"It was a very well-staged function and it really did show the capabilities of a system that had great appeal to us and others attending," said Derek Rowlett, administrator of the $350-million pension fund of the Directors Guild of America.

The plan was to first bring in the institutional trust customers. Although their accounts were larger, totaling assets of $38 billion, there were only 800 of them. The consumer division, with 8,000 smaller accounts, would be converted later.

But the promise that the bank would soon convert the institutional customers to MasterNet was unfulfilled. Technical bugs kept popping up and the system would not work efficiently enough to handle the conversion.

"There were all kinds of problems," a former bank official said. "You could be sitting at a terminal and it would take too long to get a response, too long for the screen to pop up. Other times, the whole system crashed."

The delays put additional pressure on bank employees, many of whom were also operating the old system and working double shifts and weekends to try to get the new system operating, too.

"It was an especially heavy burden on the people involved," one executive who worked on the conversion said.

Late in 1986, Claus received an anonymous letter from someone familiar with the system who warned against a "rush to convert" and told Claus, who was not a computer expert, that people had "pulled the wool" over his eyes.

Memo to Staff

Claus responded with a memo to the staff assuring them that there would be no conversion before it was time.

The three chief components of the system—trust department, systems engineering and the bank's securities clearance operation—had reported to Claus at the start of the project, which gave him the authority to ensure full cooperation.

By 1986, his authority had been restricted. The systems group and the securities staff had been given their own bosses who did not report directly to Claus. It made obtaining cooperation, particularly from the securities group in Los Angeles, difficult as the pressure to perform increased in 1986.

These pressures, whether spoken or not, were felt by many involved in the project. The bank had reported severe losses in 1986 and efforts were being made throughout the giant company to cut back. Some of the bank's most profitable businesses were sold and 9,600 jobs were cut.

One who lost his job was Armacost, and with him went his vision of 1990s technology. Clausen was brought back from retirement to run the bank again, and his perception of computers was not enhanced when he reviewed the trust troubles.

The economic cutbacks and Clausen's reaction made it difficult to justify the continued expense of staffing two trust systems when one was mired in costly troubles.

For several months in late 1986 and early 1987, however, tests of TrustPlus had been running with only a few bugs. "There were still bugs, but the users felt they could run with it and work out the bugs as we went along," one former executive said.

A conversion date was set: March 2, 1987.

Just as the data-processing staff was rushing to complete work for the conversion, half of the 16-member contingent was pulled off the assignment.

Trust Business Sale

In its push to raise money to offset its losses, B of A had sold its consumer trust business to Wells Fargo for $100 million. B of A was rushing to close the deal by March 31, 1987, so the proceeds could be booked in the first quarter. So, half the data-processing staff was switched to help transfer the accounts to the Wells Fargo system, which was based on SEI software.

On Saturday, Feb. 28, and Sunday, March 1, the remaining staff worked almost nonstop to complete the switch of the institutional trust accounts, which had begun a week before. They pulled it off on that Monday—and it lasted until Saturday, March 7.

That was the day the first of the 24 disk-drive units on the Prime computers blew up, causing the loss of a portion of the database and signaling the beginning of the end. Workers spent a discouraging weekend retrieving data from a backup unit. It was past midnight each night before they left the offices.

Over the next month, at least 14 more of the disk drives blew up. None had malfunctioned in the previous months of tests.

It turned out that the units were part of a faulty batch manufactured by Control Data

Corp., a Minneapolis computer firm. But by the time the cause was discovered, delays had mounted and other difficulties had arisen. Taken individually, none would have caused the ensuing disaster. Together, they doomed the system.

"When the stuff hit the fan in the springtime, there was a series of really statistically impossible little disasters that became one big one," Claus said.

At the precise time the technical team was struggling with these setbacks in April, the bank decided to move the staff from San Francisco to its data-processing headquarters across the bay in Concord, 30 miles away, in another money-saving effort.

For many who had been working under great stress for months, the move became the focus for their frustration. Several key people quit and morale sank as many who remained grumbled.

The difficulties were not restricted to San Francisco. The securities clearing operation on the 18th floor of the BankAmerica building in Los Angeles was thrown into disarray by the computer woes and its own unrelated problems.

Securities clearing is critical to a trust operation. It involves reconciling thousands of stock and bond trades daily. At the end of the day, the accounts must balance—each purchase and sale recorded in the proper account and matched to the records from the brokers who actually execute the trades. Stocks, or their equivalent, must be delivered and money accepted.

One of the intended functions of TrustPlus was to both reconcile this activity and ensure that transactions were credited to the proper accounts. When it did not work, the securities group had to rely on records from the outside brokers to settle transactions. The practice, called "blind settling," is abhorrent to any well-run operation.

The computer problems confirmed the suspicions of the securities people in Los Angeles, many of whom had never thought that TrustPlus would work. But its defenders maintain that the securities operation had unrelated problems that contributed to its difficulties.

The securities people had become reluctant to participate in the design process. When the problems erupted in the spring, Claus no longer had authority over the division, and many thought he was unable to force its cooperation. An outside consultant later told bank employees that some securities work was destroyed and some was simply stuck away in drawers during the critical weeks after the ill-fated conversion.

And some in Los Angeles were less inclined to put up with the demands of the collapsing computer system because in March the bank had announced plans to move the operation to San Francisco, which meant many Loss Angeles workers would lose their jobs. Reaction was so strong against the move that the bank put it on hold three months later, but nearly 40 people had left by them.

Whatever the complex causes, dozens of highly paid "temporary" workers were brought into the securities group in Los Angeles to straighten out the reconciliation mess at an enormous cost.

In the ensuing months, there were conflicts between the bank staff and the "temps" from Ernst & Whinney and Touche Ross, and there were turf battles among the consulting firms as they jockeyed for the millions of dollars that B of A was paying in an attempt to fix the problem.

The bank's first public acknowledgement of the problems came in a one-line notice in the earnings report it issued in July, 1987. It said $25 million was being placed in a reserve to cover anticipated losses from problems with MasterNet.

Bank officials assured reporters and clients that the problems would be resolved. But within weeks the bank was quietly seeking a buyer for the entire institutional trust department. The effort was unsuccessful because, an official at a rival bank said, there was not much to buy.

Clausen also ordered an in-house investigation of the debacle, which many staff members viewed as little more than a witch hunt. The result was a "one-copy" report that went only to Clausen. In October, Claus and Louis Mertes, the executive in charge of systems engineering, resigned.

Claus acknowledged that he was leaving over the MasterNet problems and took responsibility for them. Mertes, who had been at the bank only two years, has not spoken publicly about his departure.

Another surprise came in January when the bank announced that an additional $35 million would be reserved to "correct problems" with the system, bringing the total spent on fixing the $20-million system to $60 million.

Period of Decline

By then, the institutional customers were leaving. The number of accounts had dropped from about 800 to around 700, and assets under management had declined to $34 billion from $38 billion.

What the bank did not say was that the decision had been made to abandon the system. But over the next few days, it was disclosed that the bank was shifting 95% of its trust business to Seattle-First National Bank, now a BankAmerica affiliate, which uses an IBM-based system from SEI.

The remaining accounts, deemed too complex for the Seattle bank, were given to State Street Bank in Boston, one of the industry leaders that Bank of America had set out to overtake nearly six years and $80 million ago.

Even the decision to crop the embarrassing program is not immune to criticism, which was summarized by Claus last week.

"A lot of people lay down on the floor and spilled blood over this system, and why they abandoned it now I cannot understand," he said. "A guy called me this morning out of the blue and said that 95% of it was working very well."

P·A·R·T· II

3

Great Expectations: PCs and Productivity

Martin Neil Baily

In recent years, U.S. companies have installed billions of dollars' worth of computer and PC technology, which has changed the way Americans conduct business and propelled an unprecedented boom in the computer industry.

At the same time, though, growth of productivity has declined and the U.S. economy has become less competitive. Computers have yet to prove their benefit in the worldwide race to boost productivity.

Nevertheless, America's commitment to computers and PCs continues to grow. Investment in computers jumped an average of 24 percent a year in the 1980s, while investment in other types of business equipment actually declined. And PCs are becoming an increasingly important factor within this exploding market. Today's PCs pack more power than the mainframes of just a few years ago, and they're found just about everywhere: on the desks of executives, managers, secretaries, and technicians and on the laps of peripatetic salespeople, attorneys, and engineers.

Many people hoped and expected that the rapid growth in computer hardware would help fuel overall economic performance. But in fact, the nation's economic performance has been mixed during the computer boom. The good news is that inflation has been tamed and that U.S. living standards have improved. The bad news is that productivity growth has slowed, the national debt has ballooned, and the country has turned a huge foreign trade surplus into an even bigger trade deficit.

The two sides of this picture are related, of course. Much of the increase in living

By Martin Baily. Professor of Economics and Public Policy, University of Maryland, reprinted from *PC Computing* **2** (4) Apr. 1989, pp. 137–141.

standards came about because we bought more goods such as autos, tanks, and VCRs than we could produce, and we borrowed from foreigners to pay the bills.

Why haven't computers helped improve productivity, and why aren't PCs making a bigger impact today? Well, they may be helping more than we know. A great deal of the improvement due to computer use has come in service industries, where productivity is notoriously difficult to measure. Another point to consider is that managers don't always use PCs to the best effect. Sometimes companies concentrate on using them to steal business from competitors, not to raise overall productivity.

Maybe we're expecting too much: computers and PCs cannot address all our productivity problems. It's unrealistic to expect them to compensate for collapsing infrastructures and poor work habits.

The Slowdown

To understand the role PCs play in productivity, it's helpful to look at the history of American productivity since World War II. After the war, the United States assumed clear leadership of the world economy. We had escaped the devastation that ravaged Europe and Asia; our factories were intact and operating at top capacity. Even more important, U.S. companies could exploit new technologies developed during the war, testing their potential in civilian markets. The Great Depression of the 1930s, which had held back the development of new ideas, was finally laid to rest. It's no surprise that the 1950s and 1960s saw unusually rapid growth in productivity.

The first signs of a slowdown came in the late 1960s, as growth in mining and construction began to ease off. A virtual collapse in productivity growth followed in 1973. The problem spread from blue-collar, goods-producing industries like manufacturing to white-collar service industries like retail and wholesale trade.

Slow productivity growth in the 1970s can be explained by the exhaustion of postwar growth opportunities, the energy crisis, and the onset of economic disruptions such as inflation and recession.

After about 1979, however, the nation's continuing productivity woes become more difficult to explain away. Certain sectors of the economy have recovered, but others remain mired in extended slumps. The recovery has been strangely concentrated in the goods-producing sector, where output per hour has grown an average of 3% a year since 1979. During the same period, the service sector has seen almost no improvement in productivity.

Computers and PCs have played an odd and rather troubling role in the recovery of manufacturing. The biggest contributor to productivity growth has been the manufacture of computer equipment. On the other hand, computers have been used heavily in service industries, where the productivity problem is now concentrated. Apparently we are getting better at making computers, but we still don't really know what to do with them once they're built.

Measurement Problems

Part of the dilemma may lie in the way we measure productivity. The standard measure is output per hour of work. The number of hours worked in the economy is not that hard to count, so the hardest task in assessing productivity is measuring real output—the value of the goods and services produced in a year, adjusted for inflation.

Inflation can be a sticking point. Although government statistical agencies collect precise data on the dollar value of production, in many cases it is hard to know how much of a yearly increase in value is due to inflation. Calculating the effect of inflation on tangible items such as cars and houses is difficult enough, but measuring its effect on the output of many service industries is nearly impossible.

In the medical care industry, for example, the consumer price index overstates inflation and understates real output and productivity. The measuring process has not captured many of the tremendous technological advances in medical care, such as new drugs and new monitoring instruments.

The situation is even worse in banking and financial services, one of the hottest areas of the economy in recent years. The Department of Commerce doesn't even calculate a price index for financial services; it merely assumes that real output is always proportional to the number of hours worked. This approach categorically ignores any productivity increases in the entire banking sector. All the investments that these industries have made in computerizing their operations, from installing bigger and faster mainframes to building networks of automatic teller machines around the country to buying thousands of PCs, do not show up at all in any official measures of productivity.

Many other service industries encounter similar problems. PCs have had a dramatic effect on transportation industries, particularly the airline industry. It's hard to imagine the sheer volume of today's air travel market without computerized reservation systems linking mainframes, PCs, and terminals around the world. The value of these systems is clear. United Airlines recently sold 50 percent of its voting interests in the Covia Corporation, developer and marketer of its Apollo system—generally considered second best to American's Sabre reservation system—for $499 million. But standard measures do a poor job of capturing the productivity improvements they bring.

In "Measurement Issues, the Productivity Slowdown, and the Explosion of Computer Power," a study published this year by the Brookings Institution, Robert Gordon of Northwestern University and I looked at these and many other examples of poor measurement of productivity data. We concluded that the contribution of the computer is indeed being understated, but that the errors in measurement didn't account for the overall slowdown or the puzzle of the weakened service sector.

Independent sources of data for some industries find more improvement in efficiency than the standard numbers do, but still do not show the kind of growth one would expect. A study of productivity in banking, for example, found that output per hour grew about 2 percent a year in the 1980s, after growing at less than 0.5 percent a year from 1973 to 1979. That's an improvement, but only a small one.

Getting the Worst Out of Your PC

One problem is that companies are not properly using their computers and PCs to boost productivity.

It's not hard to find PC applications that don't contribute anything to productivity. And PC vendors are little help: one expert at a large full-line computer company was asked about the productivity benefits of his company's machines. Instead of answering, he turned to the PC on his desk and spoke in great detail about the calendar he kept on it.

Keeping a calendar on a computer is handy, but a $4.95 pocket calendar may do just as well. Thousands of PCs spend most of their time performing such marginal tasks, and thousands more never even get switched on. Instead of serving as a tool to do real work, many a PC has been reduced to a high-tech status symbol.

And even when companies attempt to use PCs for substantive work, the benefits are often arguable. An executive at a large chemical company says that PC-based word processing lets his company put reports through as many as 40 preliminary drafts. But he's not at all sure that the extra drafts have resulted in better reports or better decision making. Such doubts have led companies to question their levels of spending for word processing hardware and software. "If this stuff is so good," they ask, "why do we still have the same number of secretaries?"

Similar problems can arise when the people who decide what computer equipment to buy do not understand how it will be used. In "Remedies for the Bureaucratic Mentality in Private Industry," published in 1985 by the *SAM Advanced Management Journal,* management consultant David Vondle argues that this results from a process he calls "staff infection." As companies grow and become more complex, staff groups begin to take over responsibility for keeping records, managing personnel, and so on. Staff infection keeps support decisions away from line managers, the people in direct contact with customers and/or workers. The line managers may know exactly what the company needs, but they have to plead with the staff groups for support.

The staff groups tend to make hardware and software buying decisions based on their secondhand imaginings of what the company needs, not on the real needs of the line managers. Afraid to dilute their authority, data processing departments often resist using PCs and cling to inefficient mainframes.

Paper Pushing, Not Productivity

Offices and service industries often struggle with these problems more than factories do.

When offices are automated, managers will often resist dismissing employees and simply increase the flow of paper their departments produce, arguing that all the new reports are helping the company. They have an incentive to do this because companies often dispense salary and position according to the number of workers a manager supervises. True efficiency can mean career suicide.

In manufacturing operations, on the other hand, the bottom line is often easier to read, forcing companies to be more productive. The U.S. textile industry, for example, has installed innovative equipment that spins and weaves fabrics many times faster than previous models could. When the new machinery came in, plant managers had no choice but to cut back drastically on the labor required to produce a yard of cloth. Thus they kept their industry afloat in the face of stiff foreign competition.

Stories like the above are rare when one talks about PCs and productivity. Instead, most companies tell horror stories about their computer operations. And while anecdotes don't prove anything, they do suggest a general problem.

The revolution in computer hardware has lowered the *cost* of information. The price of a million calculations has fallen again and again. But the *value* of information remains very difficult to assess. Maybe company reports really are better after 40 drafts, or at least after 5 or 10. No one wants to go back to the old days when entire documents had to be retyped every time a single word was changed, but where do you draw the line?

I don't know, and neither do most company managers. When a department is computerized with no cut in personnel, the manager can rationalize the increased costs by telling the boss about all the new statistics he can produce. Maybe the new information is vital; maybe it isn't. We haven't yet figured out how to value and assimilate the mountains of information computers lay at our feet.

Nor have we learned how to tell which information is worthless. A learning process always involves a good deal of trial and error. When a company cannot even decide whether or not its approach has paid off, it is going to have trouble improving that approach.

PCs have changed the nature of the services many industries provide. No wonder companies and government statistical agencies have trouble evaluating the changes and incorporating them into measures of productivity.

It takes time for productivity to improve in response to a new technology. In fact, it often gets worse before it gets better. The learning process can be surprisingly long. According to a study by Professor Kim Clark and colleagues at the Harvard Business School, the newest and most up-to-date factories are often not the most productive ones.

Every time a company introduces a new production process, its employees must move along a learning curve before they can make the new technology pay off. PCs are hardly new, but the service sector is still learning how to use them effectively.

In some applications, the hardware has outstripped the software. The financial services sector, for example, has had difficulty developing software to fit the operating procedures of individual banks. Interstate banking regulations have allowed thousands of small banks to stay in business. Because each of these banks has developed its own operating procedures, standard software packages are useless.

And the companies that write custom software for banks have had their own problems. Frank Reilly, a Washington, D.C., consultant to the banking industry, says the companies that have written packages for Washington-area banks have had trouble remaining solvent. After they finish the programming, a seemingly endless series of bugs continues to soak up money, raising the overall cost of development to the point where it becomes prohibitive.

Profit Taking

Mistakes can keep PCs from raising productivity, but even when individual companies do everything right, overall industry productivity may not rise. That's because companies may use PCs to enhance their own profits at the expense of their competitors, adding nothing to the output of the economy.

Competition is the life force of a market economy. Adam Smith's capitalist theory postulates that the invisible hand of competition guides the economy for the betterment of all, even though each person is motivated by a desire for individual profit. But sometimes the invisible hand misses the mark. Markets do not operate in all areas, and the lack of a market can distort the economy by burying costs in areas where the producers are not liable. There is no market in clean air, for example, so the invisible hand encourages factories and car owners to spew out air pollution. The polluters do not incur the cost of cleaning up the mess they make.

Sometimes companies see ways to make a profit, not by increasing the value of goods and services they produce, but by taking away profit from someone else. In this kind of zero-sum game, one person's gain equals another's loss: the totals remain the same, but the distribution changes. Companies fight over who gets the slices of the pie, rather than working to increase the size of the pie.

Computers have greatly increased the scope of these zero-sum redistributive activities. According to a data-processing manager at a large Hartford, Connecticut–based insurance company, it's clear why PCs have not raised productivity in the insurance industry. His company uses its computers to create demographic profiles of potential customers and employs computer-aided telemarketing to steal customers away from its rivals. These marketers are not looking for new insurance customers to expand their own business; they are merely trying to get existing customers to switch their policies.

What's the Solution?

The mystifying reasons behind the PC's failure to boost productivity significantly are tied to the nature of what computers do.

Computers analyze and process information. Dazzling technological advances allow them to do this much more easily and cheaply than they did just a few years ago. As information processing got less expensive, companies began to do more of it. But the temptation to do too much can be overwhelming. If it's so easy, why not provide more graphs, more tables, more three-color charts, and more desktop-published glossy reports and brochures?

David Vondle suggests that companies should assign values to their information flows and use these values to assess the performance of white-collar departments. What is it really worth to process shipping invoices in a day instead of a week? What real benefits come from knowing a breakdown of sales by city for each month?

These questions go right to the heart of the problem, but the answers are not at all clear. What do you use to calculate the value of the knowledge?

Using the results of the valuations can be even harder. Any attempt to monitor the activities of white-collar employees can be expected to run into stiff—and possibly legitimate—opposition from most employees and many managers.

So, are PCs helping or hurting productivity?

The move to PCs has obviously encouraged some wasted expenditures, but as PC prices continue to decline, the scope of that waste will decline as well. At least the cost of PC paperweights for status-hungry executives is less than it was.

On the plus side, PCs can free line managers from the tyranny of staff departments and encourage companies to apply the technology to bottom-line activities such as lowering production costs, serving customers, and cutting inventory. In this context, the PC learning process speeds up as line personnel quickly find out which approaches work and which do not. Accountability follows naturally.

For the improvements to spread to the big picture, senior executives as well as line managers must learn to understand computers. Today, the people making decisions about PC investments often have little knowledge of the technology. Conversely, those who recommend the technology often do not fully understand the company's overall strategy or the general needs of its employees and customers. Companies must invest in computer training for senior executives so that they can understand the PC's strengths and weaknesses in pursuing the company's goals.

Research has a role to play, too. The United States remains the world leader in pure science, resting on a still unmatched scientific establishment. Unfortunately, we have not always done so well when it comes to applying science for commercial goals.

We need research aimed at developing organizational innovations to improve the efficiency of white-collar activities, particularly using PCs more effectively. It would make sense to poll different companies' experiences with PCs, and to try to isolate the factors that lead some organizations to do well while others struggle. We also need to work on developing basic models of how information flows and contributes to an organization's output.

Concern over how well PCs have paid back the enormous investment in them is legitimate. But most of the problems are symptoms of the learning process, which, though it can seem agonizingly slow, is proceeding.

American companies are wrestling PC technology to the ground and learning how to shape it to fit real-world needs. Once the current problems are licked, PCs have the potential to make a major contribution to productivity in the future.

P·A·R·T·II

4

What Happened to the Computer Revolution?

Lynn M. Salerno

Home computer sales are slumping, computer makers continue to fail or to withdraw their models, and both the factory and the office of the future remain over the horizon. Only a few years ago, the specter of the automated workplace—office and factory—caused workers to shudder and social planners to draw up scenarios for retraining and reemploying the newly displaced labor force. As late as last year, no respectable prognosticator, when asked to estimate the fate of a new computer-based product or industry, would come up with a sales figure of less than a billion dollars. This year, caution is rampant. Is the computer revolution slowing down?

Automating the office does present some obvious difficulties, not the least being the amorphousness of the concept. But the automated factory would seem to be more definable and thus more attainable. Still, for all the good press that robots have received, these tireless workers have not moved *en masse* into the factory.

Despite the pictures in glossy ads, a glance inside most offices reveals that the "automated" office of today contains only word processors and perhaps a versatile photocopier. In some companies, a self-correcting typewriter represents the state of the art. Personnel costs continue to climb and machines keep getting cheaper. We now have the equipment to automate the basic office functions: word processors, electronic file cabinets, electronic mail, even high-speed laser printers. For the factory, we have increasingly capable robots, numerically controlled tools, and CAD/CAM in its various manifestations. Then what accounts for the backward state of our offices and plants?

In what follows, I will examine the uneven progress of the computer revolution by

Reprinted by permission of *Harvard Business Review*. "Whatever Happened to the Computer Revolution?" by L. Salerno, **63** (6) Nov./Dec. 1985, pp. 129–138.

pointing out some of the problems that have stalled the forward march of computers as well as the potential difficulties that all managers ought to be aware of. I will evaluate both the progress and the promise for the major arenas in which the revolution is taking place—or is stalled for the time being: office automation, telecommunications, and artificial intelligence. I will also discuss problems that come with the electronic era, such as weakening data integrity, since they pose a significant threat as companies move further into the information age.

Without Desks or Workers

One of the greatest roadblocks to the steady march of computers into the workplace has been the difficulty in measuring results. Finding a yardstick for the benefits of automation is especially troublesome in the office. Vendors would have their corporate customers believe that the addition of their latest electronic wonders will accomplish miracles: not only will we have paperless offices but we won't even need desks (except to hold up or contain our computer consoles).

Researchers and corporate advocates of the office of the future have usually tried to show an increase in productivity through study of the most repetitive, most routine office tasks—in other words, where office work most resembles factory work. In fact, these are the areas where office automation has found the greatest favor. The world processor makes a more efficient worker out of the most sluggish typist, and the ability to make any number of corrections without doing the letter or report over saves both boss and secretary a lot of time.

Electronic spreadsheets, the computerized scratch pads that started with VisiCalc in 1978, have caught on in many companies. They have made some managers' jobs easier and have opened new worlds to others not trained in statistical methods who would have otherwise found the testing of assumptions a much too difficult task. Packaged software, often costing only a few hundred dollars, now lightens accounting and other record-keeping chores and is a special boon to smaller companies. Packages even exist for setting up and maintaining a company's data base.[1] So most companies welcome automation to some degree.

Whether computers can alter the manager's job is a harder question. Although a more efficient support staff increases the efficiency of managers, how they do their job remains the same. Efforts to convince executives to move into the electronic office have met flat resistance. And vendors' claims for the accomplishments of so-called decision support systems have attracted little executive attention—with a few rule-proving exceptions.[2]

It might be easier to help managers do their job if we knew what their job was. Or so various vendors and researchers have reasoned. The goal has proved elusive, although the studies have produced some interesting speculation. Paul Strassmann, a long-time

---

[1] James Martin and Carma McClure, "Buying Software off the Rack," *Harvard Business Review* November–December 1983, p. 32.

[2] See John F. Rockart, "Chief Executives Define Their Own Data Needs," *Harvard Business Review* March–April 1979, p. 81.

observer of information systems, makes a gloomy assessment of executives' receptivity to computers:

> I suspect that the formality of written messages accounts much more for the executives' reluctance to use the keyboard than their presumed lack of typing skills. The written medium seems to suit much more the quantitatively oriented, analytic, well-organized person who usually ends up in a staff position.
>
> The traditional senior executive usually prefers to use informal personal conversations and meetings to receive information. Except in unique situations, it is unlikely that a personal electronic workstation could be of much benefit to a person who is conditioned to a face-to-face approach. The executive will certainly not attempt to read a voluminous report on a visual display screen: that is just too inconvenient compared with a portable, bound report printed on paper. Office automation for the executive is to be avoided as a leading application except for terse messages or for the receipt of urgent communications at the executive's home.[3]

Despite such assessments, serious research continues into information needs—not just those of the executive but also of employees throughout the organization. When we learn more about how the company uses information, the power of computers may reach all levels. In the meantime, both the top executive and all managers can benefit from the faster access computers give to facts and figures.

In automating the factory, the benefits of planning and of knowing how machines will improve a process seem obvious. Yet this kind of foresight has so far been rare. Though the goal for the factory of the future must be the workerless workplace, as in the office, the implementers of automation give insufficient attention to the substrate for the electronic overlay—that is, to what the combination of man and machine actually does. In one case, for example, milling robots were installed without any provision for the extra-rapid piling up of metal filings, which soon fouled the machine. Such miscalculations can make Charlie Chaplin's out-of-control, crazy factory of *Modern Times* seem prophetic.

Even when executives carefully plan these installations, the benefits of factory automation in any particular case are often hard to measure, and given the environment that the hard-pressed manufacturing manager now faces, an emphasis on quantifiable results is not surprising.[4]

The Dusty Machine

Vendors who moan at the sight of the computers gathering dust on their shelves must be wondering what impedes the journey toward the electronic future. Considering all the available computer-based enhancements, it is hard to see how office automation and the factory of the future got derailed—or at least why they failed to make their mark in most workplaces.

Besides the difficulty already mentioned of measuring the results, other factors more

---

[3] Paul Strassmann, *Information Payoff: The Transformation of Work in the Electronic Age* (New York: Free Press, 1985), p. 45.

[4] Wickham Skinner explores these economic factors in *Manufacturing: The Formidable Competitive Weapon* (New York: John Wiley, 1985).

directly related to the computer itself stand in the way. Among these are lack of knowledge at top levels about what these machines can do or, more properly, should be able to do; the inadequate standards for both hardware and software; and vendors' excesses in promoting their products. As for the first of these barriers, though executives owe it to themselves and to their companies to master some of the computer basics, it is also true that the fast-changing technology, plus the other two stumbling blocks, remove some of their responsibility for keeping up with the computer revolution.

The inability of some machines to use the software of other machines is just one of the messy problems that crop up when managers try to draw up a coherent plan for automation. When they decide to link the company's microcomputers, or the machines on the factory floor, managers encounter another instance of computer unfriendliness: their software can't bridge the gap between computers that otherwise aren't on speaking terms. Several technically different connections exist. Faced with hard choices among them, many executives are forced to depend on the vendor for advice. Though many of these do their best to help the customer make a good decision, others will sell as much equipment as the floor will hold and the buyer will accept. Pushed by a desire to be "with it," and afraid to be left behind by the competition, the hapless manager often falls into line.

Sometimes the results are catastrophic. Small companies have gone bankrupt when computerization prevented them from keeping up with their accounts; other, larger institutions have had to go to court when consultants hired to put a system together could never link up the parts even after months of trying. Still other companies, seeing their employees buy micros, or themselves acquiring the small computers piecemeal, have discovered when they tried to link them up that the costs of software, peripheral equipment, and maintenance double or triple the cost of the original investment.

Ties That Bind

Another lagging wonder of the electronic age is telecommunications. In some ways telecommunications is the hallmark of the information era. In its linkage of computers, it magnifies their effects, and the speed with which it transmits data and information has already had an enormous influence on how we do business. Still, at the company level, the push-button phone is often the state of the art. The advantage of networking micros, minicomputers, and mainframes are obvious to many managers. Such linkages within a company, called local area networks (LANs), can avoid duplication of machines, effort, and data. They can also provide a pathway for electronic mail. When a message bypasses a secretary and goes directly to the recipient's screen, less confusion results, no message is lost, and everyone saves time.

In the factory, telecommunications holds even greater promise than in the office. By joining its machine tools, robots, and/or programmable controllers, a manufacturer can measurably improve productivity. Several giant corporations, among them General Electric and IBM, have entered this market as suppliers.

The banking industry has recognized the potential of telecommunications technology from the early days, when it leased telephone lines for funds settlement. One of its latest uses of the technology is in automated teller machines (ATMs). ATMs have great advantages for banks, since they cost half as much as a human teller. Large companies such as Sears, Roebuck are using their own expertise and have installed facilities to build new businesses by supplying telecommunications services to others.

Considering the votes of confidence such investments imply, one would expect telecommunications to be a profitable market. In most segments, however, it is not. Teleconferencing, which many thought would revolutionize business communications, has almost slipped from public notice, and AT&T has closed the specially equipped meeting rooms that it rented for such use. Another telemarvel much heralded by feature writers is the electronic library or data base represented by services like Lockheed's Dialog, Mead's Nexis and Lexis, and Bibliographic Retrieval Service (BRS). More than 2,000 of these companies exist, and their offerings range from full texts of many periodicals to a key-word search of the *Encyclopaedia Britannica.* In spite of their apparent usefulness, most are making slim profits, if any.

Videotex is the American name for various home information retrieval services already well known in Britain and on the Continent (not to mention Japan). In the United States it is a product in ceaseless search for a market. Though it requires only a keypad of some sort and a screen, such as television, most Americans hardly know what the name means. They are most likely to encounter Videotex in airports or shopping malls, where it advertises motels or special events. So much for the glowing descriptions of home shopping from a cornucopia of goods and services displayed on our handy TV screens.

As with office automation, telecommunications has suffered from overenthusiastic vendor and media attention. The technology is capable of wondrous feats. But the problems of fitting it into the real world are prodigious. Again like office automation, telecommunications lacks industry standards and compatible equipment. The computers and other equipment to be joined in a network cannot simply be plugged into each other, and often they can't use the same software. Though software exists to bridge these gaps, it may cost thousands of dollars.

In addition, telecommunications presents daunting technical problems for managers. In setting up a network in the first place, a buyer must choose the medium for linking machines (coaxial cable, for example, or optical fiber), and that choice determines the kind of transmission (baseband or broadband). If that sounds technical, it is, and the arrangement or topology of the net presents another option. Small wonder that some executives hesitate to jump on the telecommunications bandwagon.

Beyond Company Walls

While some companies hang back, others make full use of telecommunications technology, thus gaining an edge over their competitors. By establishing electronic links with other companies, these innovative organizations literally tie up a sale—and ensure a continuing relationship. American Hospital Supply represents one increasingly familiar type of these interorganizational systems. It links itself to hospitals through the terminals and software it supplies. Thus it facilitates ordering and, naturally, makes switching suppliers an uncomfortable choice.

Growing also are intraorganizational links, the electronic ties that larger companies especially need to ensure efficient operation of their branches or divisions. Such networks, however, constitute both strategic weapons and security risks. In Europe, where use of telecommunications is more advanced than in the United States, U.S. corporations are discovering that legal barriers have been erected to restrict the easy flow of information across national borders. Though the countries responsible for these laws claim that their aim is to protect the privacy of personal data, U.S. companies see the restrictions as attempts to block competition. And foreign governments are not the only threat to disruption of intracorporate links. In 1982, when the U.S. government decided to penalize Dresser Industries for supplying compressors for the Trans-Siberian pipeline—a project forbidden to American vendors—it forced the company to cut its communication lifeline to its French subsidiary. At least one company cancelled a large order with Dresser-France because it recognized that company's vital need for the corporate data base.

As their strategic and competitive advantages become clearer, communications nets of all kinds will spread, and as the technology advances, more and more companies will make use of telecommunications with all its advantages and drawbacks.

A Great Leap Forward?

Artificial intelligence (AI) is another glamorous area of computer technology that sometimes raises unrealistic expectations. It is not a new field, at least not in terms of the computer revolution. Attempts to make a thinking machine, or at least an automaton with the abilities usually associated with humans, go back to antiquity.[5] Even present-day research aimed at giving computers intelligence began almost 30 years ago. A chief reason for the renewed interest in AI is the development of so-called expert systems, which have practical applications for business. These programs draw on data bases of information in narrow fields and, using a collection of well-defined rules, permit the computer to give the kind of answer that a person well versed in the field would supply.

Among such intelligent programs are MYCIN, which uses hundreds of rules about the diagnosis and treatment of infections to help doctors choose the appropriate therapy, and HELP, which combines diagnostic assistance with billing for a hospital. HELP does not come cheap, however, it costs around $2 million. Other AI applications include mineral exploration, computer design, and diagnosis of equipment failure.

Now that these kinds of AI programs have proved themselves in everyday use, why don't we see an explosion into every area? First, behind the true expert system there really is an expert. The knowledge engineers who develop these systems must work closely with the expert to formulate the rules that make up the AI program. Few experts are eager to devote themselves to making a machine smarter, and the knowledge engineers are in equally short supply. Add to this the need of AI programs for a special language and an expensive machine, and the slow growth of this promising field is not surprising.

Not content with developing such practical aids as expert systems, researchers have been trying to make computers more like humans in their understanding. They want the

---

[5] For a good historical account, see Jasia Reichardt, *Robotics, Fact, Fiction, and Prediction* (New York: Penguin Books, 1978).

machine to respond to "natural language" commands, such as "Find me all customers with incomes over $25,000." Unfortunately for us, computers have very literal "minds." The ambiguities of syntax and variations in word meaning that any language contains will easily confound them. Take the word *fly*, for example. It can be a verb or a noun; it can have a literal meaning and any one of several figurative meanings. The context also can be confusing. The computer would have great difficulty, for example, deciding how to interpret a sentence like "Mary flew to the ringing phone."

If we could make the computer less doggedly literal, users with no knowledge of programs or programming could have easy access to the information that is stored in company data bases. For example, high-level executives and other managers without the time or patience to learn computing would certainly benefit.

Robotics, one branch of artificial intelligence, was touted a few years ago as the harbinger of the factory of the future. Although some large U.S. manufacturers have invested seriously, if not massively, in robotics, most of these machines still serve only as spot welders or spray painters or do other messy or dangerous jobs. Their senses are still rudimentary, and in comparison with the well-known and highly mobile movie robots, they move, if at all, like Frankenstein's monster.

It appears that their voices will develop before their brains. This is an unfortunate sequence, perhaps, but many practical uses exist for a computer that can speak. A "hearing" computer that responds to voice commands has even more applications. Although the technology to implant these talents in the computer is improving constantly, robotics makers have not seen great increases in their profits.

Many are unable to find jobs for the tireless workers they produce. Among the causes for this high unemployment rate is their cost, which ranges from about $10,000 to more than $150,000 for one machine. The price does not include setting the robot up and debugging it, which can double the original cost. In addition, ensuring the smooth running of these machines, especially if they are part of a system, can be a frustrating task, as anyone who has dealt with even much simpler computers can imagine.

CAD/CAM, a technology related to AI, has found limited acceptance in larger companies. As in the case of office automation, the tools exist to move U.S. corporations toward the factory of the future and to make them more competitive in world markets. The reasons for the failure of American companies to make full use of this computer-based technology are complex, but among them is a corresponding failure on the part of managers to see the automated factory, including robots and CAD/CAM, as a new competitive weapon that requires new managerial techniques and new planning directions. As with office automation, the automation of the factory must amount to more than simply replacing human workers with machines.

The high unemployment rate of robots and the failure to install other computer-based tools for automating the factory are also partly explained by the expense involved. Further, labor problems and the operational changes that automation inevitably entails make all but the largest companies hesitate in the face of such a drastic changeover. Although General Electric, Ford, and General Motors have bought into robotics manufacturers—and thus into their advancing technology—other companies that made early and heavy investments in robotics now find their costly equipment outdated.

Considering that modernization has been slow in coming to U.S. factories even where the more conventional equipment and practices are concerned, it is not surprising that automation has been slow to take hold. As has happened in the office, the groundwork for automation has been neglected, and the enthusiasm of computer advocates has paved the way for some ill-considered and inadequate installations. Again as in the office, managers have not considered both the direct and indirect effects of computerization.

If the results are not all we've been led to expect, still the money continues to pour into AI research of all kinds, and more than 200 AI companies exist, most of them developers of expert systems. Already programs labeled as expert systems have multiplied in the marketplace, but many of these do not merit the name. A true expert system is based on the knowledge of an expert, can modify its program in response to experience, and can tell the user the reasons for the answers it gives. Of course, the other programs that trade on the AI name can be useful, but they are far less powerful than the real thing and are often merely practitioners' checklists compiled into a computer program.

Because it has the potential to produce the thinking machine at last, AI will remain a glamorous, closely watched field. And because we want to keep up with the Japanese, who have announced their plans for a "fifth-generation" machine, U.S. companies and universities will pursue their efforts to make computers more intelligent. Further, the military has seen the possibilities in various unmanned vehicles as well as other devices with sensors to gather strategic information. So AI research will continue to have adequate funding, and the results will sooner or later sift down to the real world in the form of smarter, more mobile, more dexterous, and more keen-sighted robots.

The Trojan Computer

We have seen thus far that the computer revolution has moved more slowly in some areas than the prognosticators, especially the vendors, expected. And, as sometimes happens with new technologies, in which only a few users are expert, computers have brought with them unforeseen, and sometimes undesirable, effects. If managers fail to recognize and guard against these threats to efficient and profitable operations, they may find themselves worse off in the automated office or factory of the future than they were before. They need not anguish over lost chances, but they should see the current slowdown as a hiatus in which they can enlarge their awareness and make their computer future more secure.

While a company wrestles with the socialization of the maverick computer, it may be neglecting equally serious problems, among them aging applications and lack of data integrity. Already many companies have made the disturbing discovery that maintenance accounts for well over half the computer budget. Aging programs compound this problem. Often the workhorse programs of an operation become obsolete or have been patched by a succession of programmers to the point where they fail to function.[6] An organization may find that applications that are 10 or more years old are harmful to its health.

---

[6] See Martin D.J. Buss, "Penny Wise Approach to Data Processing," *Harvard Business Review* July–August 1981, p. 111, and F. Warren McFarlan and James L. McKenney, *Corporate Information Systems Management* (Homewood, Ill.: Richard D. Irwin, 1983), p. 23.

Locking the Store

With the introduction of computers have come new opportunities for white-collar crime and the multiplication of false or misleading data. Some managers have already experienced the practical consequences of undisciplined data—whether criminally or innocently produced—but others take a head-in-the-sand approach.

It is difficult to estimate the magnitude of business losses from computer-based theft, but it appears to represent about 1% of all crimes against the corporation, which cost some $40 billion a year. Although money losses are not always great, some reach into the millions for a single misdeed. Equally disturbing are the increasing breaches in privacy and security, such as the break-in to TRW last year. This was the second time that outsiders had gained access to TRW's system, which holds the credit histories of 90 million people. A few years ago, thieves managed to obtain the good credit records of some people in the file and sell them to others with poor ratings.

Such depredations may not have slowed the computer revolution, but they have given the computer a negative aspect in many eyes. They also create a new problem for managers. In the prehistory of business computing, most large companies had a mainframe computer locked away from heat, dust, and prying eyes. Executives rarely encountered either the machine or its byproducts, which they usually considered too arcane for their attention.

Now the situation has almost completely turned around. Almost every manager has some acquaintance with computers, and in some companies the micro sits on every desk. Unfortunately, however, the picture remains the same in one respect: many executives still see computers—and their attendant security problems—as essentially technical concerns. This notion has left companies without any overall security plan and has made them fair game for the most common type of computer criminal—the insider.

Often the wrongdoer is a trusted employee and the one most knowledgeable about the corporate system. Some thefts come about because the perpetrator designed and installed the system; others are possible because an outsider knows that person. Still others have their basis in a grudge against the company. In one of the largest scams, those responsible belonged to two of these categories. Harold R. Smith knew Benjamin Lewis, a disgruntled employee of Wells Fargo Bank who was in a position to cover up a scheme that brought the perpetrators more than $20 million before they were caught.

Larger companies especially, as they join their divisions through telecommunications systems and use the services of the public networks, unlock their doors to another type of computer malefactor. The TRW theft was an unauthorized entry via public network, and many break-ins, like the widely publicized teenager romps through the Los Alamos and Sloan-Kettering computer systems, have been carried out this way. These public networks are caught in a dilemma—they want to make their services easy to use because their popularity depends on simple access, but the furor over recent security breaches makes some kind of barrier seem necessary.

The growing use of electronic links between a company and its suppliers, and within transportation companies to keep track of cargoes and the movement of trains and trucks, makes disruption of operations in addition to theft more possible. Inside the company and out, as more people become computer-literate and gain access to computers, the pool from which wrongdoers might spring increases, as does the need for more lifeguards and perhaps better-marked boundaries.

Painful though it may be, top executives will have to open their eyes to security problems. Perhaps if they recognize that the issues have more to do with people than with technology, they will find the job easier.[7] At the least, companies need an overall security plan and a designated worrier who will see that the plan is implemented. The single most important aspect of the plan is security consciousness, which applies from the CEO down to the parking lot attendant.

Information à la Carte

When corporate data were safely stored within the bastion of the data-processing department, few outsiders dared even enter those air-conditioned, high-tech halls. Now that micros and minis have sprouted outside that central fortress, the data it once contained have also moved beyond its walls.

This broader accessibility of information has had salutary effects, bringing more supervisors and executives into close touch with daily operations and giving them better data for decision making. On the other hand, especially if a company's computers are networked, the possibilities for the spread of false and misleading data have grown. Because telecommunications magnifies the effects of the machines it connects, an error on a microcomputer can reach all parts of the organization with which that machine shares data. If the micro has a link to the mainframe, that faulty piece of information can become part of the corporate data base. So, although networking makes the duplication of data less likely, it also weakens their integrity.

When the company's important information resided in the mainframe, safety and integrity of data were carefully guarded. Now micro users often store vital data on their floppy disks, to take home or to another job. Even when they don't generate the information themselves as part of their work, with a little entrepreneurial spirit they can get it from other parts of the system.[8]

Future Imperfect

If the road to the automated workplace has so far been unexpectedly bumpy, what can we expect for the future? Despite the slump in computer popularity, we have gone too far down this particular highway to turn back. Computers will continue to multiply in their various forms.

The office of the future will eventually arrive, and the new, fully computerized workplace is likely to change the way we work. When telecommunications has become cheaper and almost universal, the boss may be the only business traveler. As computers finally become truly user friendly, so that middle managers can do most of their own

---

[7] For some guidelines, see Martin D.J. Buss and Lynn M. Salerno, "Common Sense and Computer Security," *Harvard Business Review* March–April 1984, p. 112.

[8] For a description of how such a scheme can work, see William Atkins, "Jesse James at the Terminal," *Harvard Business Review* July–August 1985, p. 82.

secretarial chores aided by their efficient electronic calendar, date book, and message center, only the boss may have a secretary.

The computer could further flatten the hierarchy in the automated office by taking over some of the middle manager's chores. Even now, computers can monitor the productivity and whereabouts of workers, check spelling and syntax of letters and reports, and do a certain amount of research via the corporate data base or outside information retrieval services. Since managers can do little if anything to stay the eventual arrival of automation, they may as well look on the bright side.

Although they may lose their secretaries, managers stand to gain from better access to facts they need and from electronic record-keeping. Teleconferences may make up for the loss of a travel budget. Though fewer middle managers may remain, those who are left should be more valuable as improved computers bring them greater efficiency. In addition, the boundary between work and home will probably become less rigid, since telecommunications and ever smaller computers will permit a movable workplace. As an alternative to working in the city or in an electronic cottage, satellite work centers may prove feasible.

In the factory of the future, not only will the ranks of workers be thinned but the layers of management will also shrink. Some futurists see only the top and bottom echelons remaining. According to this scenario, the top will have improved access to information and the bottom will have only the boring task of tending the relentless machine. Though this discouraging scene may be far in the future, its likelihood makes quality-of-worklife planning vital.

If automation can make work arrangements more flexible, it also can introduce rigidity. Workers who once enjoyed some discretion about how they did their jobs now find themselves limited by procedures designed to answer the demands of the computer. And the machine can do more than specify workers' tasks; it can measure how fast they do them. Ford and AT&T are among the companies that monitor workers. Some companies claim that their employees enjoy such measurements and that they make a game of competing with the machine or their co-workers. It is not hard to see, however, that this kind of machine supervision can have a regimenting effect that will eventually bring complaints and result in less productive workers.

Now that U.S. unions are on the defensive, introduction of computers and robots may meet with less opposition than earlier. Even so, unions have not tackled the automation issue head-on, asking instead for retraining, relocation, early retirement, and replacement of workers by attrition.

In the United Kingdom, some companies have used the greenfield approach, whereby automation takes place at an isolated facility so that other workers will not learn of it prematurely. Elsewhere in Britain and in the United States, many companies have decided to alert workers well in advance. In some notably successful cases, the companies adjusted the pay to compensate for the less attractive features of automation and made efforts to upgrade jobs or otherwise improve working conditions. The French government takes another tack. It hires civil servants with "different" attitudes from those of entrenched workers and makes use of nonconformists in each department to form the nucleus of a new information age bureaucracy.

In offices where computers have come in one by one, managers face the opposite situation—many employees want to hasten automation. The problem now lies in making their personal computers part of the corporate team. Some corporations use the former data-processing department—now often called information systems—as a missionary to bring the untutored natives into the fold. Others have created information centers where users can come for help. The aim in most cases is to encourage standards of common programs, techniques, and security.

However they manage the task, all companies with more than a few micros—and factories with isolated machines as well—will have to plan toward a corporate network. Only when all the machines are linked to each other and then to the outside world can managers make full use of the power of automation.

Computers—for Better or Worse

Besides opening the door to unexpected and rising costs, computers and their appurtenances bring with them formidable threats to the security and integrity of data, as we have seen. In addition, ill-considered investments in new technology, whether software or hardware, can place an electronic strait jacket on the organization, especially when the application involves a fundamental operation such as billing or a large data base. And this is even more true of factory processes.

Despite the management challenges that computers pose, companies that have entered the electronic age have discovered advantages they will never give up. In some of these organizations, computers are central to the daily operations; in others, they have brought a new edge to corporate weapons. Thus, like it or not, laggard companies will have to learn gradually to live with computers if they want to say in the competition. Such companies would do well to examine the problems that others have encountered and to resist the blandishments of the overeager vendor. By plunging in, they risk more than they gain.

In the meantime, while some companies order computers by the hundreds and others virtually ignore them, it may appear that we are not in the midst of a computer revolution. It may even appear that because of the many-faceted problems computers bring with them, the revolution will never be fully realized.

In a technical sense, however, it has already arrived. The technological advances have come so fast, however, that most companies have had little opportunity to evaluate one machine or one model before its more powerful replacement came on the market. The makers of these wonders have had to keep up the pace or go under in a sea of innovation. The result has been an often frustrating mismatch between expectations and performance. Both users and vendors have suffered because of this gap—the users because they couldn't get what they wanted, and the vendors because users didn't want what they had.

The overenthusiastic vendors and other boosters of automation and the computer age are hoist with their own petard. In trying to sell computers, literally or figuratively, they have made the task of mastering them look too easy and the attainable rewards appear too great. Now buyers are wary, and many products remain on the shelf. Perhaps it has become clear that the public has some idea of what it needs and wants, even when dazzling electronics are involved.

We may be ready for a more realistic future in which computers become a comfortable part of our working lives. If this is to come about, we need to consider more carefully than we have so far what we want from the office of the future, the automated factory, and the other familiar watchwords of the electronic age. We need to examine and learn from the short history of that age. If we do, we'll see that the pace of the revolution has been uneven, and usually slower than predicted. That is good news—it means that we have time to make the best of it.

Is This Happening?

Top staff people may follow their problems from firm to firm much more closely than they do now, so that ideas about executive turnover and compensation may change along with ideas about tying people down with pension plans. Higher turnover at this level may prove advantageous to companies, for innovators can burn out fast. We may see more brain picking of the kind which is now supposedly characteristic of Madison Avenue. At this creating and innovating level, all the current work on organization and communication in research groups may find its payoff.

Besides innovators and creators, new top-management bodies will need programmers who will focus on the internal organization itself. These will be the operations researchers, mathematical programmers, computer experts, and the like. It is not clear where these kinds of people are being located on organization charts today, but our guess is that the programmer will find a place close to the top. He will probably remain relatively free to innovate and carry out his own applied research on what and how to program (although he may eventually settle into using some stable repertory of techniques as has the industrial engineer).

Innovators and programmers will need to be supplemented by "committors." Committors are people who take on the role of approving or vetoing decisions. They will commit the organization's resources to a particular course of action—the course chosen from some alternative provided by innovators and programmers. The current notion that managers ought to be "coordinators" should flower in the 1980s, but at the top rather than the middle; and the people to be coordinated will be top staff groups.

From Harold J. Leavitt and Thomas L. Whisler, "Management in the 1980s," *Harvard Business Review* November–December 1958, p. 41.

P·A·R·T· II

5

What Do Computers Do?

James Rule • Paul Attewell

In the iconography of our times, the computer is indisputably a central symbol. No other technology, perhaps no other object of any kind is so widely implicated in the emergence of the world of the future. Science and technology are assumed to play a central role in this transformation, and nothing more dramatically epitomizes the social potency of science and technology than computing.

Perhaps for these reasons, computing has become a kind of projective device for social scientists and other social critics. Often enough, each analyst foresees in the social world to come the consummation of whatever trends he or she finds most heartening or most deplorable in the world as it is. And computing is often pictured as the agency by which these fondest hopes or deepest fears are to be realized. Thus for some observers (Kahn 1974), computing promises diffusion of informational riches leading to material prosperity; for others (Lowi 1977, Smith 1980, Cruise O'Brien 1983), similar computerization processes threaten to foster manipulation of the information-poor by the information-rich. Or, while some (Giuliano 1982—see Chapter III-1 of this volume) have seen in computing the prospect for enhancement of job content and enrichment of work, others (Braverman 1974) have seen in these same changes the prospect of oppression and degradation on the job. Some observers (Freeman, Clark, and Soete 1982) have seen in computing the promise of new sources of employment, while others (Hines and Searle 1979) have identified the computer as a potent destroyer of jobs, especially for groups already facing high unemployment. On other fronts some observers (Hiltz and Turoff 1978) have seen in computing the potential for more responsive government, while others (Shils 1975, Rule *et al.* 1980, Laudon 1986) have found in the growth of government computing dangers of excessive surveillance and concentration of power.

"What do Computers Do?" by James Rule and Paul Attewell, *Social Problems*, University of California Press, **36** (3), June 1989, pp. 225–241.

The Rationality of Adoption

No less disputed is the role of computing in promoting rational organizational practice. Does computerization, as a manifestation of science and technology in human affairs, indeed alter the nature of organizational practice? Do such alterations amount to rationalization in the Weberian—or any other—sense of that rich and ambiguous term? If not, what account can we give of the reasons for and results of the now pervasive trend toward computerization of organizational life?

These questions are not simply responses to the shock of recent social change; they have a long pedigree in sociological thought. For Saint Simon (1859) and Comete (1912), scientific thinking and technological practice were the pre-eminent vehicles for rationalization of social institutions. Both saw the growth of science as undermining the vestiges of feudalism; both held that engineers and other members of occupations involving technological practice would lead the way in creating more rational social arrangements. And both held an idea that now seems quaint at best, the conviction that growth of scientific thinking would eventually bring the end of all forms of irrationality in human affairs, banishing conflict from social life while shifting practical questions of human relations from the domain of politics to that of administration.

Today, few if any social scientists would expect the formal rationality embodied in scientific thinking to guarantee substantive rationality in setting the ultimate directions for human action (but see Stinchcombe 1986). Many analysts, however, have pictured scientific practice in general and information technologies in particular as potent agencies of formal rationality in human affairs. That is, they have seen information technologies as helping make organizations more predictable, more closely coordinated, more efficient, and responsive to managerial control.

Consider Daniel Bell's well-known account of the critical role of knowledge in post-industrial society. Computing, it appears, is the technology that most readily lends itself to realizing the central role of knowledge in the world-to-be:

> The chain of multiple calculations that can readily be made, the multivariate analyses that keep track of the detailed interactions of many variables, the simultaneous solution of several hundred equations—these feats which are the foundation of comprehensive numeracy—are possible only with a tool of intellectual *technology*, the computer.
>
> What is distinctive about the new intellectual technology is its effort to define rational action and to identify the means of achieving it. All situations involve constraints (costs, for example) and contrasting alternatives. And all action takes place under condition of certainty, risk, or uncertainty. . . . In all these situations, the desirable action is a strategy that leads to the optimal or "best" solution. . . . Rationality can be defined as judging, between two alternatives, which one is capable of yielding that preferred outcome (Bell 1973: 30–31).

Bell is not the only commentator to see in information technologies far-reaching forces that are fundamentally reshaping social relations in the world's "advanced" societies. In *The Control Revolution*, James Beniger (1986) depicts a broad trend toward the speeding-up of social processes, their aggregation in larger units, and their subjection to closer cybernetic control. Computing is just one of the more recent manifestations of this long-term trend.

For Bell and Beniger, as for many another analyst of today's "advanced" societies, the special capabilities of computing drive basic social change. The forms of knowing afforded by computing offer managers attractive opportunities to pursue interests long implicit in their day-to-day practice. If this view is correct, it should be easy to point to instances where computing and related technologies enable organizations to attain long-standing ends.

To most observers, such analyses no doubt appear virtually self-evident. Computing is perceived as cost-effective, efficient, and profitable; and the quest for cost-effectiveness supposedly drives innovation in modern formal organizations. But for another tradition in the analysis of scientific and technological change, the case is not so clear. In this view, technological innovation is not so much a response to human needs as a generator of such needs. Technologies, in other words, create the mind-set that makes their adoption at first appealing, then indispensable.

The most influential exponent of this view is Jacques Ellul. For Ellul (1964), the very notion of organizational "rationality" is a sham. Technologies, and the social practices in which they are embedded, create the "needs" to which the only admissible response is more rationalization and further technological innovation. Far from being superior solutions to long-standing problems, technological innovations are like viruses that insinuate themselves into living systems by getting those systems to perpetuate the invading agent.

In the words of Ellul's well-known American interpreter Langdon Winner, technology is *autonomous*, growing by its own logic rather than in response to any objective requirements. Winner (1977: 246) writes,

> Megatechnical systems do not all sit idly by while the whims of public taste move toward some specifically desired product or service. Instead they have numerous means available to bring about that most fortunate of circumstances in which the social need and what the system is best able to produce coincide in a perfect one-to-one match. . . . "Roughly speaking," Ellul observes, "the problem is to modify human needs in accordance with the requirements of planning."

Such arguments obviously fly in the face of what everyone "knows" about the reasons for adoption of new technologies: that these innovations represent objectively better ways of doing things, that they serve enduring needs more easily or more fully than the earlier alternatives. Yet the literature on technology readily yields examples that appear to fit Ellul's model. For instance, the willingness of consumers to purchase and, apparently, consume rationalized foods like supermarket tomatoes—the only apparent virtue of which is that they are easier for organizations to produce and distribute than tasty, old-fashioned tomatoes (Whiteside 1977).

While many readers no doubt find it hard to entertain accounts that explain the adoption of new information technologies in terms that might be applied to that of hula hoops or pet rocks, some sophisticated observers have taken virtually such a position. For example, Kling and Iacono (1988: 240) have characterized the essential impetus behind the growth of computing as computerization movements:

> During the last 20 years, CMs [computerization movements] have helped set the stage on which the computer industry expanded. As this industry expands, vendor organizations (like IBM) also become powerful participants in persuading people to automate. Some computer

vendors and their trade associations can be powerful participants in specific decisions about equipment purchased by a particular company. . . . But vendor actions alone cannot account for the widespread mobilization of computing in the United States. They feed and participate in it; they have not driven it. Part of the drive is economic, and part is ideological. The ideological flames have been fanned as much by CM advocates as by marketing specialists from the computer industry. Popular writers like Alvin Toffler and John Naisbitt and academics like Daniel Bell have stimulated enthusiasm for the general computerization movement and provided organizing rationales (e.g., transition to a new "information society") for unbounded computerization. Much of the enthusiasm to computerize is a by-product of this writing and other ideological themes advanced by CMs.

Perhaps collective behavior is a more exact sociological term for what Kling and Iacono have in mind here than social movement. They are describing dissemination of a diffuse mystique in which computing is defined as positive and progressive. The origins of this mystique would seem to lie in the interactive processes of participants in computer culture more than in any objective assessment of the capabilities of computerized versus non-computerized ways of doing things.

There is yet a third variant among interpretations of the causes of computer innovation as nonrational. In this view, the needs alleged to justify computerization are in fact a Trojan Horse for quite different purposes. Specific interest groups insist on creating or enlarging computer capabilities, knowing that such requests for enhanced "efficiency" are unlikely to be resisted. The real reason for the changes being sought, however, may have nothing particular to do with needs for information technology *per se*. Thus, Laudon (1974) reports that computerization efforts in many local governments were, in effect, attempts of one bureaucratic agency—often the police—to dominate others by placing themselves in control of a single, centralized data-management facility. Similar political or interest-group dynamics are reported by Keen (1981), Kling and Iacono (1984), King and Kraemer (1985), Laudon (1986), and Markus (1983).

The contrast between all three versions of such analyses and those in the tradition of Comte and Saint Simon is fundamental. On the one hand, computerization is a force for broad rationalization of social practice, responding to enduring needs for more cost-effective, more responsive, more "rational" practices. On the other, computerization is a response to interests quite different from those it is ostensibly instituted to serve, either interests generated by the technology itself or ones concealed by the pervasive mystique of that technology. Both views have had a number of well-informed exponents.

The New York Study

Seeking to illuminate these and related questions about the role of computing in organizations, we have carried out a survey of some 184 private sector establishments in and near New York City. A number of studies have examined the role of computing in samples of specific types of organizations, for example, local governments (King and Kraemer 1985), insurance companies (Baran 1987), banks (Ernst 1982), or manufacturing firms (Blau *et al.* 1976). We wanted to survey a more heterogeneous array of organizations, ones whose assimilation of computing would display its full range of functions in private sector firms.

Table 1. Distribution of 184 Private Sector Establishments in New York City Area, by Industry Sector

Industry Sector	
Discrete Manufacturing	11.4%
Process Manufacturing	12.5
Durable Wholesale	9.2
Nondurable Wholesale	10.9
Construction	6.5
Transport/Communictions/Utilities	10.3
Finance/Real Estate/Insurance	8.2
Retail .	12.0
Services	14.2
Other	4.9
Total	100.1%

Lists were obtained from a market research firm of all private sector firm locations that had in-house computing. These lists were stratified by area (Manhattan, two outer boroughs of New York City, and two suburban counties); numbers employed at the given site; ten major industrial categories; and extent of computerization within the firm. From an original statistical sample of 200, interviews were completed at 160 sites for a response rate of 80%. These interviews were supplemented with an additional 24 interviews of computerized businesses chosen by random sampling from business telephone directories. Table 1 shows the distribution of the sample.

As Table 1 shows, these sampling efforts yielded a wide variety of computerized private sector organizations. These included both the familiar computerized factories, banks, and insurance companies studied elsewhere and computerized restaurants, veterinary clinics, a gynecological practice, and a number of other less predictable but nonetheless authentically computerized private sector organizations.

Thirty-eight percent of the 184 firms were located in Manhattan, 32% in Brooklyn and Queens, and 30% were in the Nassau/Suffolk area. The workforces of the firms ranged in size from 1 to 1011 employees, with a mean of just over 100 and a median of 57 (sd = 134.6). Strictly speaking, the units of analysis here were not firms but sites. Of the sampled units, 55% were single-location firms, 31% were headquarters of firms with additional branches elsewhere, and 14% were branches, divisions, or franchises. The interview dealt mainly with computing use at the one selected site, although we collected information about terminals connected to computers elsewhere and about networked computers. While we often refer to our cases as firms, a minority were not complete firms.

Standardized interviews were carried out by two full-time interviewers, both with advanced graduate training in sociology, between autumn 1985 and spring 1987. Interviews covered a wide range of issues on the role and effects of computing, including historical data on the inception and growth of computing within the firm. Informants were managers who designated themselves as knowledgeable about computing at the site, and it was not uncommon for our interviewer to gather information from more than one respondent, especially at the larger sites. Some parts of the interview involved fixed-choice questions, while others required more discursive, probing questioning from the interviewers. Interviews lasted from a minimum of about an hour to marathons of many hours, often spread over several visits; the length of interviews was highly correlated with size of the establishment.

We used two measures for the extent of computing in any firm. One measure is the number of distinct activities accomplished by computer or by computerized machinery within a firm. We first developed a checklist of 46 activities that we knew could in principle be accomplished by computer. These varied from accounts receivable to computerized typesetting. In practice, no firm had computerized all activities listed. The sample ranged from 1 to 29 activities computerized, with a mean of 9.

An alternative measure of extent of computer use took into account the fact that many computerized activities were linked with others in a package or *application*. Thus, in some firms, for example, order entry, preparing an invoice, generating a "pick slip" for employees in the warehouse who would ship the item, and updating the customer's account to reflect the amount owed for the order were all accomplished in a single, integrated series of operations, using a single data base and a single software package. To reflect this synergistic quality of computer work, we grouped computerized activities into applications, where the activities could be seen as interdependent in terms of software and data bases. The range in our sample of applications, thus defined, was from 1 to 7 with a mean of 2.7.

What Computers Do

What do computers do? What kinds of activities are most likely to be implemented by computers in ordinary businesses like these? Are these tasks as various as the firms themselves, or do most firms acquire computers to do highly standardized things? What does the profile of such activities imply about the kind of differences in organizational practice, if any, emerging from computerization?

Table 2 summarizes the frequencies of computerized activities as reported in our interviews in descending order of frequency; activities reported computerized in fewer than 10% of the sites in our study are omitted from this table. One simple conclusion is clear in these data: the purposes most commonly served by the new technology are standard business purposes, practices that we would expect to have been long established within these firms before computing became available. (The "other" category in the table includes a heterogeneous group of activities that we could not anticipate when we created this list.)

From this evidence alone, one would hardly conclude that computing is bringing about a fundamentally new agenda of organizational action in these firms. Nor, in this representative selection of firms, do we note many instances of the sweeping and comprehensive "informatization" of corporate action recorded by Zuboff (1988). The computer work systems she studied apparently linked most members of large corporate staffs in single systems of electronic interaction. The primary pattern here, in firms ranging greatly in size, is computerization by gradual conversion of discrete, delimited practices long carried

Table 2. Firms Reporting Computerization, by Type of Activity (N = 184)

Payroll	74%
Invoices/Billing	68
Accounts receivable	66
Accounts Payable	54
Word processing	53
Order Entry	49
General Ledger	48
Financial statements	40
Mailing lists and labels	37
Customer service	37
Inventory Control	36
Sales Analysis	34
Records and Filing	33
Financial Forecasting	30
Sales Commissions	27
Credit Checking	26
Networking	19
Cost Accounting	17
"Other"	17
Purchase Order Processing	16
Job Costing	15
Shipping/Receiving	12
Investments	11
Fixed Assets	10

out by conventional techniques rather than abrupt imposition of fundamentally new organizational agenda.

But we can look more deeply into this issue. Are computerized activities indeed simply old activities performed by new means? Or do firms computerize in order to undertake qualitatively new lines of action? The pilot studies leading up to the main interviews reported here uncovered a number of computing applications that simply had no analog in the precomputerized environment. Indeed, the very founding of some firms is predicated on computing—for example, firms whose work consists of doing computerized payrolls or credit reports for other firms. If such patterns proved to be the norm, computing would be a revolutionary force indeed, with each computerized firm essentially undertaking new kinds of activities from what it undertook in precomputing days.

The interview sought various information on the circumstances under which each application (in the sense of a "bundle" of computerized activities, as defined above) was instated, its intended purposes, and its current role in the work of the firm. We coded each application in terms of whether the purposes it served were qualitatively new to the firm with computerization or whether the computerized application represented some form of conversion of activities previously carried out with prior technologies. As Table 3 shows, the overwhelming majority of these applications are the result of direct conversion from

Table 3. Computerized Applications as New Or Pre-
Existing Tasks

Direct conversion from non-computerized operation	85%
New activity since computing	6
Mix of earlier and new activity	9
Total	100%
	(488)

conventional to computer technologies; they were new ways of performing long-standing activities rather than fundamental revisions of organizational agenda.

But what about the rationality of computerization? Does it bring more efficient, cost-effective ways of accomplishing those ends, as analysis in the tradition of Comte and Saint Simon might suggest? Or does computerization of these activities result from some vague fad or mystique or from some other consideration far removed from the objective superiority of computing as a means of getting the work of the firm accomplished?

While the data were too ambiguous for judgment in some cases, most interviews afforded enough information for coding on these points. For example, consider an application used by Exurban Transit, a family-owned bus company with 35 employees located in a resort area well outside New York City. This firm specializes in transporting city dwellers back and forth to summer recreation spots—as many as three hundred in a single day. Riders are picked up and dropped off by advance reservation at points of their own choice so that the firm has complicated routing plans to make each day. One of its computer applications is devoted to routing.

Planning routes and preparing passenger lists for drivers used to take as much as half the working time of all managerial and clerical persons in this small firm at peak business periods. All of this work is now handled on a single microcomputer, using custom programmed software. In the interviewer's words, "Using the name of the [passenger], the points of origin and destination, cost of ticket and time of departure, the [person responsible for routing] can generate plans for as many vans as needed on any particular day. The computer will figure out how many vans are needed, which people go with vans leaving from point X and which people need to be with a van going to point Z. It will even handle . . . cancellations and . . . keep track of people who bounce checks on the company, should they ever call again for a reservation." As a result, handling reservations and routing is now the equivalent of a full-time job for one person only, a drastic reduction from the time required under conventional technology.

We had little hesitation in coding cases like these as prima facie rational. In other cases, it was easy to draw the opposite conclusion. The following application is from a firm we can call Minimarkets, a small chain of Manhattan grocery stores. The head office in this establishment employed 10 persons at the time of this interview and reported annual revenues of between $11 and $12 million from all its locations. According to the vice president, no one had originally felt the need for a computer. But everyone was getting one, prices were coming down, and the vendor made it sound like they could use one. Once the computer was acquired, the head office attempted to use it to computerize a master list of prices to be charged at each store in the chain. When wholesale costs change, the new costs are fed into the computer, and the computer calculates the new retail price according to a fixed markup. Each week, new lists are prepared for each branch manager.

By the report of the vice president of the firm, the system hasn't really proved very efficient. For example, most prices in the firm are rounded to a 5 or a 9 in the last digit, but a wholesale rise of one cent can cause the rounded price to jump, for example, from a 5 to a 9. The vice president often chooses to override these computerized decisions manually. Thus most of the work done by computer has to be reviewed and corrected before being put into effect. In this and several other ways, the system has not really saved anyone much time. At the time of the interview, the firm was attempting to acquire new software in hopes that further applications would be more successful than this one.

But acquisition decisions dominated by such computer mystique were rare, at least so far as our data suggest. Seventy-six percent of the applications reported by our informants were classified as prima facie rational, as against 5% that appeared clearly nonrational and 19% that could not be classified. In addition, when we asked whether the original decision to computerize appeared to make sense in retrospect, respondents answered affirmatively for some 89% of the applications.

To be sure, more intense immersion in the workings of each firm and each computer application might have yielded different conclusions in some of these cases. Ideally, an investigation of the rationality of computerization would involve detailed ethnographic observation of each firm before, during, and after computer adoption, coupled, perhaps, with accountants' audits of operations at each stage. By contrast, interviewers in our study asked in detail what had been done before each application went on line, what the application had been intended to do, and what had in fact ensued from its introduction. Where possible, these queries were supplemented by actual observation of workplaces where applications were in use. Still, these queries and observations conveyed a predominant picture of relatively hard-headed, instrumental rationality in computerization. At a minimum, our research gives little support to an Ellulian model of technological dissemination in the majority of applications we studied.

This provisional conclusion, however, does not lead us to doubt findings of other researchers to the opposite effect. We see the business planners whose thinking is the focus of our study as a cost-conscious, profit-oriented group; we see these qualities as dominating their decisions to incorporate new information technologies in their firms. Yet it should hardly be surprising that, in the government bureaucracies studied by Laudon (1974, 1986), for example, computing often appeared as a means to some other, strictly political end. In short, we see no reason to think of computing as "of a piece," such that it unfolds under the same auspices in all institutional settings.

Implications for Social Change

The view we are presenting offers some striking reflections on the prophecies of Comte, Saint Simon, and their modern followers. On one hand, computing in our firms does appear as part of a broad press for increased efficiency or, at least, profitability. On the other, the picture we have painted is hardly revolutionary. From the data presented so far, one might conclude that computing offers these firms "more of the same" in relation to their earlier activities rather than qualitative change.

Such a skeptical conclusion is unwarranted, we believe. A deeper look at the notion of computerization suggests that that very concept has to be disaggregated to understand the differences such innovations make in the functioning of organizations. A key dimension of difference among the applications has to do with the form of information processing that they entail. Consider contrasting applications from a single firm, which we will call Suburban Plastics. At the time of our interview, this company had annual revenues of about $30 million and a staff of about 90. It manufactures plastics in bulk for sale to other manufacturers who make such things as auto parts and roller-skate wheels.

Suburban Plastics is highly computerized; we coded seven distinct applications. One involves quality control. The various plastics manufactured by this firm are produced in batches, the characteristics of which are governed by the various raw materials and production conditions used in each batch. The firm must monitor each batch while it is in process and adjust proportions of ingredients and other conditions appropriately.

Such monitoring used to be done manually, by technicians who would draw small samples of material, administer certain analyses, perform hand calculations, and steer the process accordingly. Now such analyses are computerized. According to our informant, the computer "keeps better control of the product because the computer program gives consistent solutions to the same problem. Before computers, each lab tech would plot a graph and decided what should be added and how much [of each ingredient] was required to bring that item to spec. Now they don't really have that much discretion."

Some tests of this kind were simply not performed in this firm before computerization. They were possible in principle, but they were considered too time-consuming. Now these sophisticated analyses are done routinely. Management is looking forward to computerizing these tests entirely, thus removing all direct human control.

Now consider another computer application from this same firm. Customers and staff of the firm often need to check characteristics of batches of plastic well after production is complete. To this end, data on each batch are stored in a word processor in terms of such specifications as acidity, viscosity, and brittleness. When requested, such information is printed out.

Neither of these applications is a more authentic example of computerization than the other. Both have many counterparts among the applications in our sample. But applications of these two kinds have quite different effects on the firms in which they are found. Such differences relate particularly to the extent to which the application *transforms* the information involved. In application B, the data entered in the computer record are not transformed at all, from the standpoint of the people who "consume" it. What is printed out for the use of staff and customers is essentially what was recorded; the data might as well be stored manually for any change it undergoes. By contrast, the transformative character of application A is unmistakable. Information is fed into this application not in order to be preserved, but in order to be transformed.

The repercussions of more transformative applications warrant special attention. By effectively creating information that would not otherwise exist or that could only be produced at much greater cost, the more transformative applications afford bases for new and different forms of action. We classified all the applications under one of the following rubrics:

Non-Transformative: Applications whose role is simply to store information, to reproduce it in its original form, or to move it from one location to another. Examples: Most word processing, production of mailing labels, simple billing.

Moderately Transformative: Applications that entail basic arithmetic operations on data stored in them but no inferential thinking. Examples: Most inventory control programs, order entry, accounts payable and receivable, and other simple accounting programs.

Highly Transformative: Applications that involve application of decision rules more complex than simple arithmetic. Examples: Programs for tax preparation, bid preparation, computer controlled design and manufacturing, most forms of sales and market analysis.

The effects of non-transformative applications need be by no means negligible. But they are different in kind from the others. For example, several firms in the sample prepared contracts using word-processing programs that enabled them to insert or delete various standard clauses, thus rather quickly creating long documents that would otherwise have to be typed entirely by hand. The effects of such innovation on the job experience of clerical staff and on the levels of staffing required for this function are considerable. But they do not entail any qualitative change in the performance of the organization; contracts still get produced in the same form as before.

By contrast, even applications we label as moderately transformative may reshape the way managers think about and control their organizations. One common application of computing is for inventory control of raw materials, finished goods, or some other form of supplies.

A striking example is a system custom-designed by the young manager of a liquor store determined to streamline his work. University Spirits, located in Manhattan, has a staff of ten; we coded its complex computerized monitoring of stock as a single application. Every bottle delivered to the store from its suppliers is entered in the computerized inventory and marked with a code number. When a customer takes one or more of the bottles to the counter, the clerk taps the code number into a console, along with the quantity being purchased and the amount of money being tendered. The computer generates the price, adds tax, and computes the change, displaying all these operations on a display. Inventory is electronically reduced by the amount sold.

Clearly no drastic transformation of data takes place in the procedures described here; the computer is simply keeping a extensive set of tallies. Yet the manager has adapted this tallying system to create some ingenious intellectual tools that qualitatively change his grasp on his firm. The inventory control system tracks not only the presence of bottles within the shop, but also the location of the bottles—specifically, whether the bottle is upstairs on display or downstairs in storage. The same system responds to customers' requests for a particular item by displaying whether the item is in stock and, if so, in what quantity and where in the store it is located. Another feature of the system provides information on the items sold by each of the salespeople who call; for each salesperson, the computer prints the names of all items available from him or her and how much of each item is in stock.

As described thus far, we would count this application as moderately transformative. Yet one additional feature arguably constitutes inclusion of a decision rule and hence led

Table 4. Computer Applications by Degree of Transformativity[a]

Non-transformative	23%
Moderately transformative	47
Highly transformative	30
Total	100%
	(502)

[a]Total of applications in Table 4 is slightly higher than that in Table 3 because Table 4 is based on a recoding using a narrower definition of the concept "application."

to our rating it as highly transformative: the system is programmed to create "need to order" reports that automatically print out instructions to order more of any item that falls below a specified minimum.

Even without this simple feature, however, the mere condensation and summation of information embodied in the application make a difference in the way this business is managed. These features, by the manager's own intent, enable him to transcend the particularities of discrete data and instead gain access to broad patterns of events and realities. The result is that the manager can conceptualize his work more broadly and more readily control whole categories of processes, rather than reacting to events on a piecemeal basis.

Principles at work in this application are ubiquitous among the more transformative applications in our sample. They are evident across the widest array of firm sizes and industrial categories. We note such parallels, for example, in a computerized fast food restaurant, where a single application keeps track of stock, calculates the cost of orders, and prints out change owed to customers; or in a computerized veterinary clinic, where drugs are maintained in the same sort of comprehensive inventory system. In all these cases, ordinary transactions by staff leave electronic records that, when properly compiled, provide management with a broader view of the over-all processes of the firm than would otherwise be possible. Such changes appear to be what Zuboff (1988: 331) has in mind when she writes that computerization makes work more "transparent." Table 4 shows the distribution of the three levels of transformation among the applications.

We had assumed that the more highly transformative applications would be concentrated among firms of particular types, for example, among those that were larger or more associated with "high technology" in some form. These expectations were almost entirely overturned. Staff size at the site, age of firm, length of time that the site had been computerized, and industrial sector had no notable value in predicting how transformative the typical application maintained within a site would be.

Nor is recourse to more transformative applications here a function of time. Many analysts (Noland 1973, 1977, 1979, Laudon and Laudon 1987: 7–11, King and Kraemer 1985: 182–88) have posited "natural history" theories of computing. Many differences nothwithstanding, all these theories suggest predictable patterns of change in the scope and forms of computing within specific types of organizations over time. In formulating this study, we took as axiomatic a version of such a theory, namely that computing applications would grow more transformative over time. Yet our quantitative analyses indicated that this was not the case. Within firms, first applications are not significantly less transformative than later ones. Nor is the absolute age of applications significantly associated with how transformative they are. In these firms, then, entry into the world of computerized operation and extension of those operations to new computer applications takes place at all levels of socio-technical sophistication.

And yet, we have little doubt that the use of computing in our firms is a seductive process. That is, the acquisition of the first computer and the development of the first applications often lead managers and other staff to experiment with computerization ideas that would never have been entertained had the equipment not been on hand. The interview contained a question as follows: "Has the existence of the computing capability in this application led to a search for new ways of using this capability?" Answers were affirmative for 44% of the applications, negative for 53%, and "don't know" for 3%.

Is There an "Information Society" in the Making?

While the more transformative applications of computing are not becoming more common among all computing applications, they are certainly becoming more common in the absolute sense as the total extent of computing among American firms continues to grow. We stress that we are speaking here of *all* firms, not just those with special associations with science or technology.

How can we characterize the effects of the more transformative applications on the functioning of firms? How will businesses like those in this sample and organizations of other kinds be altered by an increase of computerized processes? Do these developments indeed promise to produce "Information society," as has often been alleged?

Among living sociologists, Daniel Bell has put forward the most influential views of the future of the world's "advanced" societies and the role of information processes within that world. Our findings are largely consistent with Bell's characterization of the role of information in "post-modern society." He refers to processes like our more transformative applications as "intellectual technology," that is,

> methods [that] seek to substitute an algorithm (i.e., decision rules) for intuitive judgments. These algorithms may be embodied in an automatic machine or a computer program, or a set of instructions based on some statistical or mathematical formula, and represents a "'formalization" of judgments and their routine application to many varied situations. To the extent that intellectual technology is becoming predominant in the management of organizations and enterprises, one can say that it is as central a feature of postindustrial society as machine technology is in industrial society. (Bell 1979: 166–67)

Less closely borne out in our sample, however, are Bell's assertions on the association between such information processes and science per se. For Bell (1973: 26) sees computing as the conduit by which scientific thought, in the strict sense, makes itself felt in everyday social practice:

> What is true of technology and economics is true, albeit differentially, of all modes of knowledge: the advances in a field become increasingly dependent on the primacy of theoretical work, which codifies what is known and points the way to empirical confirmation. In effect, theoretical knowledge increasingly becomes the strategic resource, the axial

principle, of a society. And the university, research organizations, and intellectual institutions, where theoretical knowledge is codified and enriched, become the axial structures of the emergent society.

The applications of computing adopted by this representative sample of greater New York firms certainly entail the application of abstractions to "illuminate different and varied areas of experience," to use Bell's language (1973: 20). But the kinds of abstractions involved here mostly do not derive from science in any ordinary sense of that term. In this respect, the application developed by Suburban Plastics for analysis of properties of batches of plastic is atypical within this sample. Most of the applications of moderate and high transformativity that we encounter here are not associated with what one would ordinarily bracket as "high-tech" processes. Indeed, applications that could be construed as involving scientific, engineering, or research and development activities were found only in 4.8% of the firms in our sample.

What predominates among the transformative computing applications in this sample is clearly not computerization as a means for applying science or new forms of theory to decision making, but rather as a means for implementing long-standing management interests in control over human processes. These efforts certainly involve abstraction and sometimes also implementation of decision algorithms. But these abstractions and rules are more often vernacular than scientific. They mostly represent managers' own efforts to formalize practical principles such as identification and maximization of the most profitable aspects of business that are abundantly evident, if less effectively pursued, before the computer enters the picture.

Again, the broad themes of applications like those found in manufacturing firms are echoed in the most diverse industrial categories. Consider Dockside Grill, our name for a computerized restaurant employing some 59 persons in a suburban location. Here, too, computerization serves to structure communications and work flow. Waiters and waitresses take orders as usual, then discreetly enter them at computer terminals throughout the establishment. Each order is printed out in the kitchen, and no other communication between waiters and waitresses and kitchen staff is normally permitted. No food is permitted to be prepared or leave the kitchen except as part of a computer-transmitted order. The machine displays to the waiter or waitress what has been ordered for each table, and the computerized order eventually is printed out in the form of a bill. The computer system both controls and streamlines the work of the dining room and kitchen staff. It makes it impossible, for example, for any food to be served that does not appear on the check. It makes it less likely that customers will be served anything other than what they ordered. And, according to the remarks both of dining room and kitchen staff, it obviates disputes between dining room and kitchen as to what really was ordered, disputes endemic in most restaurants.

The new system also affords the possibility (not yet exploited in this establishment) of much closer analysis of sales and productivity. One could program the system to print out productivity ratings for individual waiters and waitresses or to compare sales of various dishes, for example, at various times of the day or week. The system could also, with more difficulty, be linked to inventory of food to help prevent pilferage.

What this application does, like many others in this study, is to provide management with deeper and fuller access to various aspects of how the firm works than would be possible without computing. And "access" here means both *knowledge* of processes that would otherwise be known about only in an approximate and inexact way *and* the potential for control over such processes.

In this restaurant, and often elsewhere, these enhanced powers are used for surveillance and control of staff. Indeed, development of knowledge for purposes of control is a tendency that affects people and things in very similar ways. For example, computerization of communication between dining room staff and the kitchen in this establishment does more than reduce rates of errors and establish responsibility for them. It also obviates collusion between diners and servers in which items are obtained from the kitchen and served but not included on the bill. The waiter or waitress responsible for such "mistakes," we were told, receives handsome tips for his or her trouble.

As in many other areas of work life, management might succeed in informing itself about these unauthorized exchanges without computing if prepared to devote extraordinary time and attention to the matter. But here, as in the inventory control applications developed by University Spirits, computing drastically reduces the time involved and facilitates the thoroughness of the search.

One particularly far-reaching rationalization of work was developed by a woman originally employed as office manager of a firm we call Mercury, a taxicab dispatching company. This firm owns no cabs in its own right. Instead, it acts as a broker between a variety of participating owners of cabs and customers who request taxi service. These range from members of the general public to prosperous Manhattan law firms that pay special rates to the dispatching company for preferential service for their staffs.

The use of computerization developed by this innovative office manager strikes us as particularly ingenious. This firm makes it money by dispatching cabs to the would-be customers who promise the greatest profit. Ordinary members of the public, who pay only the fare for their individual ride, are the least profitable. More profitable are callers from the various subscribing firms, who pay varying monthly rates to Mercury for varying priorities of service. Thus Mercury has great interest in *discriminating* among the constant stream of calls for service.

Previously, the approximately 10 telephone operators/dispatchers on duty would perform these discriminations themselves, answering each call and then deciding how rapidly to dispatch a cab. Now this process is computerized. The computer classifies each incoming call according to its potential profitability: lower priority for calls from the general public and ascending priorities to corporate subscribers according to the fees they pay. "Thus," as our interviewer put it, "on a busy, snowy Monday night, cash customers are told that there are no cars available at all, while 'A' customers get a car in ten minutes."

This same application also affords surveillance and control. The system generates reports for management on the number of calls handled by each operator at each period when she is on duty. Similarly, it records the identity of each cab driver and the particulars of every call that the system forwards to him or her. Since the participating drivers (who pay fees for access to the system) are subject to fines and other discipline for violating various rules, the computer record can figure in adjudication of disputes over such disciplining. These transaction records also serve to help resolve disputes with corporate clients about their accounts.

Note the parallels between this case and Dockside Grill. In both, management uses computing as a way of "reaching" more deeply into the flux of organizational life in order to control practice more fully. The effect is thus to render all sorts of areas of work life more accessible to purposeful and informed decision making by management.

We were also struck by how frequently these transformative applications involved mediating relations between the firm and other organizations in its environment. For Mercury, the taxi dispatching firm, the computer made it possible to monitor more intensely the flow of communication from prospective customers and to respond to such communications with more analytical discrimination than would be possible without the technology. And Mercury is hardly alone in using such techniques to identify the most profitable combinations of customers and services. We see much the same logic in the computerized operations of an otherwise quite different business, Gray Gardens, a nursing home. Here the combinations being effected were between particular patients and the billing possibilities offered by Medicaid.

Computerization in this firm was spurred by direct requirements of an outside institution, in this case, the State of New York. Most patients here are paid through Medicaid, and in 1980 the state adopted billing requirements that could only be fulfilled by computer billing. Specifically, the state required individual billing for each patient under Medicaid, including specification of the exact conditions from which the patient was suffering and the specific treatments that the patient received.

State regulations are arcane and exacting concerning what kinds of care Medicaid patients must receive and what kinds of billing are permitted. This application involves a program that matches the care allocated to patients to what the state will pay for. The firm has further developed this program so as to review applicants for admission to the institution in terms of which ones present the most potentially profitable mixes of illnesses and other needs. Thus, whether or not patients at Gray Gardens get the care they need most, they will at least get the care that is most profitable for the institution to give. The State of New York, for its part, no doubt seeks to enforce administration of the most appropriate care and to avoid paying for care it does not consider itself liable to cover. The tensions and conflicts of interest inherent in this juxtaposition are played out through the computerized exchange of data between the two institutions.

What this highly transformative computer application has done for Gray Gardens is something that we consider basic and important in a broad variety of settings. It has encouraged, if not compelled, decision makers to think in terms of broad patterns of events and processes and to formulate policies to deal with such patterns consistently according to dictates of formal rationality. Again, these transformations appear most often to be dictated by managers' quest for profitability and other long-standing goals rather than any attempt to incorporate "scientific" thinking for its own sake.

Discussion

Does the role of computing in present-day organizations bear any resemblance to the prognostications of Comte and Saint Simon on the role of science and technology in the rationalization of human affairs? Most applications of computing in these typical New York firms, we have shown, involve no qualitative change in the sorts of activities that the companies perform. The majority of the applications surveyed here appear rational in the sense of promising efficiency improvements, but only some of these seem to alter basic decision making in the firms.

Within this subcategory, however, we think the social change ultimately deriving from the more transformative applications is noteworthy. The applications that actually place new, more analytical forms of information in the hands of managers set the stage for far-reaching rationalization of organizational practice. If this sample is any guide, these practices most often do not involve appropriation of principles from natural science. Instead they encourage managers to think more programmatically about how to pursue interests they have long experienced but have been unable to act upon. They do this by effectively extending the range of managerial attention, thus making it possible to formalize and implement policies for phenomena that would otherwise have to be confronted on a piecemeal basis. The effect is to broaden the power of managers to analyze the processes of which their organizations are composed and to intervene in these processes and shape them. Thus the role of purposeful planning and control is extended, and the realm of happenstance is reduced.

There is no reason to imagine, as Comte and Saint Simon did, that the extension of rationality in this sense can resolve fundamental oppositions of interest. Indeed, as in the uses of computing for surveillance, the new information technologies may sharpen such opposition. By directing management attention at hitherto "unrationalized" areas of organizational life where staff have been accustomed to enjoy discretion and by subjecting these areas to more direct control, computing may open new forms of the long-standing struggles between management prerogatives and worker autonomy. And yet, the extension of management monitoring and the resulting attempts at new forms of control to these areas is undoubtedly a manifestation of formal rationalization to organizational practice.

"Know, in order to foresee; in order to control." So might one translate Comte's expression of the essential spirit of science and its role in human affairs. Computing is obviously a much different technology from anything that Comte specifically anticipated. Yet the role of computing in these typical New York firms is hardly inconsistent with what Comte had in mind. Computing, in its more sophisticated forms, encourages managers to rationalize their practices, to see broad patterns in the workings of their firms, and to devise regular policies for dealing with similar eventualities in similar ways. The ability of the computer to assimilate and condense large amounts of discrete data is essential for such changes. In this respect computing offers yet another force on behalf of mastery of a chaotic universe, to put the matter as Comte and Saint Simon might have done, or another step in what Weber (1970: 51) called the "disenchantment of the world."

Acknowledgments

The authors would like to thank the National Science Foundation Programs in Information Science and Sociology (Grant No. IRI-8644358) for the support that made this study possible and Peter Blau and Kenneth Laudon for consulting help at a formative stage of the work. Important suggestions for the development of this article were made by Joseph Eaton, Charles Kadushin, and Michael Schwartz. The interviews on which this article is based were carried out by Kevin Delany and Steve Cohen; their contribution to the work has been immense. Correspondence to: Rule, Department of Sociology, State University of New York, Stoney Brook, NY 11794-4356.

References

Attewell, Paul (1987). "The deskilling controversy." *Work and Occupations* 14: 323–46.

Baran, Barbara (1987). "The technological transformation of white-collar work: a case study of the insurance industry." Pp. 25–62 in Heidi Hartman (ed.), *Computer Chips and Paper Clips*, Vol. 2. National Academy Press, Washington, DC.

Bell, Daniel (1973). *The Coming of Post-Industrial Society.* Basic Books, New York.

Bell, Daniel (1979). "The social framework of the information society." Pp. 163–211 in Michael L. Dertouzos and Joel Moses (eds.), *The Computer Age: A Twenty-Year View.* The MIT Press, Cambridge, MA.

Beniger, James (1986). *The Control Revolution.* Harvard University Press, Cambridge, MA.

Blau, Peter, Cecilia McHugh Falbe, William McKinley, and Phelps K. Tracy (1976). "Technology and organization in manufacturing." *Administrative Science Quarterly* 21: 20–40.

Braverman, Harry (1974) *Labor and Monopoly Capital.* New York: Monthly Review.

Comte, Auguste (1912). *Systeme de Politique Positive*, Paris: Cres.

Cruise O'Brien, Rita ed. (1983). *Information, Economics and Power*, London: Hodder and Stoughton.

Ellul, Jacques (1964). *The Technological Society.* New York: Knopf.

Ernst, M. (1982). "The mechanization of commerce." *Scientific American* 247: 132–47

Freeman, Christopher, John Clark, and Luc Soete (1982). *Unemployment and Technical Innovation: A Study of Long Waves and Economic Development.* London: Francis Pinter.

Giuliano, Vincent (1982). "The mechanization of office work." *Scientific American* 247: 148–65.

Hiltz, Starr Roxanne and Murray Turoff (1978). *The Network Nation.* Reading, MA: Addison-Wesley.

Hines, Colin and Graham Searle (1979). *Automatic Unemployment.* London: Earth Resources Research.

Kahn, Herman (1974). "The future of the corporation." Pp. 95–152 in Herman Kahn (ed.), *The Future of the Corporation.* New York: Mason and Lipscomb.

Keen, Peter (1981). "Information systems and organization change." *Communications of the Association for Computing Machinery* 24: 24–33.

King, John Leslie and Kenneth L. Kraemer (1985). *The Dynamics of Computing.* New York: Columbia University Press.

Kling, Rob (1980). "Social analyses of computing: theoretical orientations in recent empirical research." *Computer Surveys* 12:1.

Kling, Rob and Suzanne Jacono (1984). "The control of information systems: developments after implementation." *Communications of the Association for Computing Machinery* 27: 1218–26.

(1988). "The mobilization of support for computerization: the role of computerization movements." *Social Problems* 35: 226–43.

Laudon, Kenneth (1974). *Computers and Bureaucratic Reform.* New York: Wiley.

(1986). *Dossier Society.* New York: Columbia University Press.

Laudon, Kenneth and Jane Price Laudon (1988). *Management Information Systems: A Contemporary Perspective.* New York: MacMillan.

Lowi, Theodore (1977). "The information revolution, politics, and the prospects for and open society." Pp. 40–61 in Itzhak Galnoor (ed.), *Government Secrecy in Democracies.* New York: Harper and Row.

Markus, M. Lynne (1983). "Power, politics, and MIS implementation." *Communications of the Association for Computing Machinery* 26: 430–44.

Nolan, Richard L. (1973). "Managing the computer resource: a stage hypothesis." *Communications of the ACM* 16: 399–405.

(1977). "Controlling the costs of data services." *Harvard Business Review* 55: 114–24.

(1979). "Managing the crisis in data processing." *Harvard Business Review* 57: 115–26.

Rule, James, Doug McAdam, Linda Stearns, and David Uglow (1980). *The Politics of Privacy*. New York: Elsevier.

Saint Simon, Claude-Henri (1859). *Oeuvres Choisies*, Paris: E. Dentu.

Shaiken, Harley (1984). *Work Transformed*. New York: Holt, Rinehart and Winston.

Shils, Edward (1975). *Center and Periphery*. Chicago: University of Chicago Press.

Smith, Anthony (1980). *The Geopolitics of Information*. New York: Oxford University Press.

Stinchcombe, Arthur (1986). "Reason and Rationalilty." *Sociological Theory* 4:151–66.

Weber, Max (1970). *From Max Weber; Essays in Sociology*. Translated, edited and with an introduction by H.H. Gerth and C. Wright Mills, London: Routledge and Kegan Paul.

Whiteside, Thomas (1977). "A reporter at large (tomatoes)." *The New Yorker* January 24: 36–61.

Winner, Langdon (1977). *Autonomous Technology*. Cambridge, MA: MIT Press.

Zuboff, Shoshana (1988). *In the Age of the Smart Machine*. New York: Basic Books.

P·A·R·T·II

Excerpts From "Social Analyses of Computing: Theoretical Perspectives in Recent Empirical Research"

Rob Kling

Introduction

Almost everyone who has had substantial contact with computer-based systems is impressed by their capacity to store and flexibly manipulate vast amounts of information. The increases in storage and speed of digital computers over both their mechanical precursors and people have led many analysts to view digital computing as a technology with possible social repercussions as potent as those of the automobile and telephone. Speculations about the social repercussions of new computing modalities, from large databases [MICH654], to network information services (LICK78, HILT78], to artificial intelligence [WEIZ76, BODE78], are commonplace. Often there is little choice but to speculate about new technologies since they have not been built and placed in their host social settings. One constructive role of prospective analyses is that of informing affected parties and thus enabling them to make better social and technical choices. Postmortem analyses may be more accurate [KLIN78c, KRAE79b], but they are of substantially lesser utility.

"Social Analysis of Computing: Theoretical Perspectives in Recent Empirical Research," by R. Kling. From *Computing Surveys* **12**(1) (March 1980): 61–110 (excerpt from Section 1, pp. 61–69). Copyright 1980, Association of Computing Machinery, Inc. Reprinted by permission.

Speculative analyses emphasize the capabilities, potential benefits, and potential harm of new technical developments. Consider the case of electronic funds transfer systems. By appreciating the ways in which automated teller machines enable the public to bank at any hour of the day or night, bankers can develop a new set of services. Also by appreciating the ways in which realtime funds transfer systems may be susceptible to "credit blackouts," bankers, technologists, and public alike are alerted to the potential harm of haphazard developments [KLIN78d].

To identify the social impacts of computing one must have, at least implicitly, a theory of the causal powers that computerized systems can exert upon individuals, groups, organizations, institutions, social networks, social worlds, and other social entities. Only the most ardent technical determinist would claim that the consequences of computer use depend exclusively upon the technical characteristics of the mode of computing adopted (e.g., large-scale data systems, point-of-sale terminal networks, "personal" computers). Serious analyses of the consequences of computing consider social and economic characteristics to be important elements in a line of analysis, or "storyline." But what social or economic characteristics should be selected, how are they to be related, and to what are they to be attributed? Shall we start with *social groups* connected by *channels of communication, cooperatively striving* to satisfy *common goals*? Shall we further assume that the social world in which computing is used is relatively well ordered, with participants adopting stable *roles* and acting in accord with stable *norms*? Or shall we start with *social groups, in conflict*, which *manipulate* available *channels of communication* and *messages* to gain more *valued resources* than their competitors? Moreover, shall we assume that *roles* are *fluid*, that lines of action are *situated*, and that *rules* and *norms* may be selectively ignored or renegotiated? In any case, how do *goals* arise among social groups or in organizations, how do they influence the modes of computing adopted and the ways that they are used? Are *goals* to be viewed as the sum of *individual preferences*, reflections of *economic relationships* and *negotiated agreements amongst interested parties*, or as *convenient fictions* retrospectively formulated to make sense of *ambiguous streams of events*?

Any observation or claim about the uses or consequences of new computing technologies (e.g., electronic funds transfer systems, decision support systems) rests on an array of assumptions about these issues, however implicit. For example, if we believe that the social world can be understood as an ecology of cooperating groups, and that conflict is largely a by-product of poor communication, then network information systems may appear as media for reducing intergroup conflict [HILT78]. On the other hand, if we view social worlds as arenas for interaction of groups with overlapping, but often conflicting, interests, then network information systems appear as instruments of both cooperation and conflict [SCH169].

In coming to understand computing technologies, particularly newer ones, it is important to understand which conceptions of social life are likely aids in discerning critical social aspects. Analysts do not select random sets of concepts to examine computing: they cluster useful concepts into coherent bundles which constitute a perspective on social life. Some perspectives are substantially better than others in accurately predicting the future uses and consequences of computing. The choice of core concepts need not simply be a matter of speculation. It is possible to test some of the simpler claims about computing use, and consequently the "goodness" of the perspectives from which they are derived, by examining the development and use of existing systems.

In the United States, there are well over 200,000 digital computers in use [GOTL73, USGO77] and millions of applications developed in thousands of organizations. These applications vary considerably in their technical strategies, and the computer-using organizations vary considerably in characteristics often identified as important, like size and social complexity. Because of this variety, much can be learned from the careful examination of the adoption, development, uses, and consequences of existing computer-based technologies.[1]

This paper selectively examines recent empirical studies of computing in organizations as a way of investigating the appropriateness of different conceptions of social life to understand the use and consequences of computing. Two common and broadly drawn perspectives adopted by social analysts of computing are introduced in the following section. Then we examine how social studies of computing are influenced by these perspectives. Some of these studies focus upon behavior within organizations, such as decision making and worklife. Others focus on social issues such as privacy and social accountability, where empirical studies have shed some light.

•   •   •

Theoretical Perspectives for the Social Analysis of Computing

The literature analyzing the social character and consequences of computer use is fragmented and often bewildering to nonspecialists. The diligent reader who examines the literatures on such topics as computing and personal privacy, or the role of computer-based information systems in organizational decision making, will find a cacophony of voices [KLIN80b]. If he or she reads widely and listens carefully, it is possible to discern distinct choruses. It is difficult to find voices singing precisely the same tune, or even in the same key; but some do sound in relative harmony. To make sense of the singers, and to learn from their songs, the reader must identify the tunes and harmonies of the most notable choruses. These tunes and harmonies are patterned perspectives that provide answers to many of our earlier questions.

Two Theoretical Perspectives

As a first approximation, the collection of analyses about the social character and development of computing can be divided into two major perspectives: *systems rationalism* and *segmented institutionalism* (Table 1). Systems rationalists typically emphasize the positive roles that computerized technologies play in social life. Often, they examine new capabilities of computing technologies (e.g., computer conferencing), or new areas in

---

[1] Many important reasons for this focus on computing in organizations are pragmatic; most computer-based systems have been adopted by organizations. Even computer systems with which the public has direct contact, such as point-of-sale terminals and automated tellers, are administered by organizations. In advanced industrial societies, large organizations play a dominant role in the lives of many, particularly in urban areas. Since many of these organizations use computer-based systems to record transactions with their clients, organizations become a natural focus for certain issues affecting the relations between them and the public [STER79, LENK80c, KRAE80c].

TABLE 1. THEORETICAL PERSPECTIVES ADOPTED BY SOCIAL ANALYSTS OF COMPUTING[a]

	Systems Rationalism				Segmented Institutionalism	
	Rational	Structural	Human Relations	Interactionist	Organizational Politics	Class Politics
Technology	Equipment as instrument	Equipment as instrument	Equipment as instrument/environment	"Package" as milieu	Equipment as instrument	Equipment as instrument
Social setting	Unified organization 1. The user 2. Tasks and goals 3. Consistency and consensus over goals (assumed)	Organizations and formal units (e.g., departments) 1. Formal organizational arrangements 2. Hierarchy of authority, reporting relationships	Small groups and individuals 1. Task groups and their interactions 2. Individual needs 3. Organizational resources and rewards	Situated social actors 1. Differentiated work organizations and their clientele 2. Groups with overlapping and shifting interests 3. Participants in different social worlds	Social actors in positions 1. Individuals/groups and their interests	Social classes in stratified system
Organizing concepts	Rationalization Formal procedures Individual ("personality") differences Intended effects (assumed) Authority Productivity Need Cost benefit Efficiency Task "Better management"	Organizational structure Organizational environment Uncertainty Standard operating procedures Organizations' resources and rewards Uncertainty absorption Rules Authority/power Information flow	Trust Motivation Expectations and rewards Job satisfaction (subjective alienation) Self-esteem Leadership Sense of competence User involvement Group autonomy	Defining situations Labeling events as a social construction Work opportunities/constraints Power Career Legitimacy Social world Social conflict Interaction Role Negotiations Orientation Arenas	Work opportunities/constraints Power Social conflict Legitimacy Elites Coalitions Political resources Bargaining Power reinforcement Gesture	Ownership of means of production Power Social conflict Alienation Deskilling Surplus value
Dynamics of technical diffusion	Economic substitution— "meet a need" Educate users A good technology "sells itself"	Attributes of 1. Innovation 2. Organization 3. Environment	Acceptance through participation in design	Accepted technologies preserve important social meanings of dominant actors	Accepted technologies serve specific interests	Accepted technologies serve dominant class interests
Good technology	Effective in meeting explicit goals or sophisticate' use Efficient Correct	Helps organizations adapt to their environments	Promotes job satisfaction (e.g., enlarges jobs)	Does not destroy social meanings important to lower level participants, public, and underdogs	Serves the interests of all legitimate parties and does not undermine legitimate political process	Does not alienate workers Does not reproduce relations
Workplace ideology	Scientific management	Scientific management	Individual fulfillment through work	Individual fulfillment through evocation of valued social meanings	[Several conflicting ideologies]	Worker's control over production

[a] Adapted from KLING80c; Copyright Academic Press, New York.

which existing computer technologies may be applied. They assume that there is a marked consensus on major social goals relevant to computing use, and often develop a relatively synoptic account of social behavior. Systems rationalists place efficiency, whether economic or organizational, as the predominant value. Moreover, they typically focus on a narrowly bounded world of computer use in which the computer user is a central actor.

In contrast, segmented institutionalists examine the consequences of computerized technologies on many aspects of social life, "legitimate" and "illegitimate." For example, they observe that participants in organizations adopt computing to enhance their personal status or credibility, as well as to improve the technical quality of their decisions or to increase the economic efficiency of specific activities. Rather than assuming a consensus on important goals and values, they assume that intergroup conflict is as likely as cooperation unless the contrary is empirically demonstrated. Segmented institutionalists identify as dominant values the sovereignty of individuals and groups over critical aspects of their lives, the integrity of individuals, and social equity; economic or organizational efficiency is subservient to these values. They typically identify settings of computer use as broad in scope, and are likely to emphasize parties other than the computer user (e.g., clients, regulators, suppliers, competitors, controllers of critical resources).

These two sweeping labels help identify the major choruses and their principal songs.[2] But the voices within each chorus are more diverse and less harmonized than these brief sketches suggest.[3]

Systems rationalists do not sing completely in unison. Analysts who identify with positions as diverse as management science [BUFF79], "the systems approach" [EMER69, CHAR71], and managerial rationalism [KANT77],[4] still share the basic assumptions of systems rationalism.

---

[2] Most analysts adopt a relatively uniform voice from presentation to presentation. Others adopt different perspectives, depending upon the situation they are analyzing. It makes more sense to characterize analyses by the perspectives they embody rather than to pigeonhole analysts. Comments about "analysts" should be understood to apply to the analyses under discussion, not necessarily to other work by the same author.

[3] In a recent review of the literature on the developments, uses, and consequences of computing in organizations, Kling and Scacchi [KLIN80c] identified six major perspectives, which have been simplified here into two, systems rationalism and segmented institutionalism. Their article examines the development and use of computing, not just its consequences, from all six perspectives. In a review of analyses of the social issues raised by computing—within and without organizations—Mowshowitz [MOWS80b] identified eight somewhat different perspectives. Our main aim here is not to define whether there are "really" 2, 4, 6, 8, or 48 major perspectives, but rather to determine which theoretical perspectives provide the greatest insight into the social character of computing.

[4] Managerial rationalism connotes a set of approaches designed to organize and manage efficiently and effectively according to the preferences of high-level managers. Classically, it emphasizes the division of labor according to specialized activity and the existence of logical relationships among various organizational functions [KILL72, SCOT73]. More modern variations on this classical theme, our "structural" and Allison's [ALLI71] "organizational" process, emphasize organizational uncertainties and slack resources as being important contextual conditions in selecting the management strategies. The organizing strategies rely less upon the formal hierarchy of authority, and more extensively upon a variety of "bridging roles" and information systems, to coordinate the diverse activities of internally differentiated organizations [GALB77]. Although sociologists no longer believe that the classical theory provides a credible account of the ways that large organizations are or can be managed, it is still commonly adopted as an analytical posture in the computing literature. For recent examples see KILL72 and especially Table 1 of KERN79.

Both management scientists and managerial rationalists often identify the interests of managers as more legitimate than those of their subordinates. Some managerial rationalists seek to optimize the management of organizations by embedding computing in their operations; others simply emphasize the tasks to be automated independently of any contextual features aside from the costs of automation. An important variant of managerial rationalism, structural analysis,[5] identifies critical contextural features of the organization or its environment that influence the utility and correct selection of the mode of automation [GALB77, COLT78]. Environmental uncertainties, slack resources, transaction volumes, communication channels, and standard operating procedures are among the common concepts employed by structuralists in characterizing the social world in which participants utilize technologies [THOM67, GALB77]. Human relations analysts [MUMF67, ARGY71] emphasize the role of technology in altering the quality of working life (see Table 1). While the human relations tradition developed in reaction to work practices based upon scientific management, that emphasized narrow concerns with technical efficiency [PERR79], this tradition has more in common with other variants of systems rationalism than with segmented institutionalism [MUMF78]. While human relations analysts often identify conflicts between workers and their managers, they assume that it is possible to organize the world of work so that all may be well off: satisfied workers will be productive [TAU77: 90–94].[6] While there may be conflict today over the role of computing developments in a given workplace, systems can be "properly designed and implemented" so that important common goals can be achieved [MUMF67, ARGY71, KLIN73, LUCA75a, KLIN77a].

Systems rationalists also differ on critical assumptions. For example, many systems rationalists imply that important social decisions can be made with one comprehensive, enduring rationality [DORF77, KANT77, BUFF79]. Others, structuralists like Simon [SIMO77], assume that the focal actors have fragmentary information and that goals may shift over time. Moreover, Simon has argued that for most important decisions, comprehensive knowledge about the costs and benefits of alternative lines of action is too costly and time-consuming to obtain, and decision makers must therefore select satisfactory but suboptimal choices. Systems rationalists also differ in their assessment of social conflict. Typically, management scientists ignore social conflicts by defining problems as if there were a commonly agreed-upon objective function whose optimization is collectively valued [BUFF79]. Some managerial rationalists attempt simply to resolve conflicts by appeals to administrative authority [DONN79]. Still other systems rationalists acknowledge the presence and persistence of social conflict but argue that conflict is "functional" for an identified social system [TURN78] by allowing a wider variety of perspectives to be incorporated in a plan of action and to release otherwise destructive social tensions. This is a key difference between even the conflict-oriented rationalist approaches and segmented institutionalism. Segmented institutionalists do not assume that the observed level of conflict in a social setting is necessarily "optimal," or even tends

---

[5] This is treated as a separate position in KLIN80c, ALLI71, and PERR79. Here it is integrated with other variants of systems rationalism to simplify the broader contrasts. See preceding note.

[6] See MUMF78 for an example. See SILV71 and PERR79 for sharp critiques of this position, and ARGY72 for an extended rejoinder.

towards some kind of "healthy equilibrium": most even reject the concepts of socially optimal and social equilibria.[7] Segmented institutionalists also differ among themselves on their assumptions about how to understand social life and the role of computing therein. Political analysts view social life as a continual contest for power by groups with conflicting interests and view computing as an instrument turned to aggrandizing power.[8]

In contrast, symbolic interactionists view social life as constructed from the interaction of people and groups as they create and respond to socially defined meanings. Conceptions of a "good system," for example, may depend critically upon whether the evaluator is a technical specialist interested in working with a state-of-the-art technology, a staff analyst interested in having an easily intelligible instrument, or a manager who is interested in reducing critical costs in his organizational unit [KLIN79a]. Interactionists view computing as an arena in which many participants with overlapping but conflicting interests—designers, vendors, service suppliers, users, consumers, consultants—are brought together [KLIN77b, KLIN78g, KLIN80e, SCAC80].

Systems rationalism and segmented institutionalism are two convenient and broad-brush labels. In practice, analysts take considerable license in appropriating concepts from either of these idealized perspectives. Thus, management scientists will, on occasion, deal with power, and political analysts will assume that there are technical systems that can simultaneously satisfy all parties. But analysts do usually adopt a primary perspective that is closely aligned with one of these sketched here.[9]

A Brief Example

These rather abstract considerations may best be grounded with a particular example before we embark on our complex tour through the empirical studies of computing in social life. Consider a hypothetical firm, Electroblast, which manufactures several lines of

---

[7] The conception of social systems of constrained conflict tending towards healthy equilibria is a common point of convergence among positions that are as diverse as the traditional market analysis of competitive capitalism [LOWI79], interest-group pluralism [LOWI69], structural functionalism [TURN78], "open-systems" theory [BAKE73, SWAN79], and cybernetic models of the social order [EMER69]. For criticisms of this assumption, see LOWI69, TURN78, and COLL75. Both major perspectives have rich traditions outside of computing. Systems rationalism has been closely aligned with structural functionalism in American sociology [TURN78, TAUS77], and segmented institutionalism with the conflict perspective [COLL75, RITZ77]. Their explanatory power has been the subject of considerable debate among sociologists, and the reader is encouraged to examine the broader accounts [COLL75, TURN78, CUFF79].

[8] Within this broadly construed political perspective, many more specific claims about the political order can be specified. Pluralists argue that many groups may organize and bargain for their interests, but that there is no ruling class or dominant elite which almost always wins. Those who argue for "reinforcement politics" claim that expensive and complex resources such as automated information systems are likely to be used by already powerful groups so that they can differentially accumulate further advantage over their competitors [KLIN78e, KRAE79a]. See DANZ80 for a careful analysis of four different political perspectives applied to the case of computing in organizations.

[9] Marxism (or class politics) is conspicuously missing from this set because it has not informed empirical studies of computing in social life. One exception is NOBL78; see BRAV74 for an interpretive essay. Interpretive studies of computing use in nominally Marxist societies such as the Soviet Union and China often rely upon other analytical perspectives [HOFF77, GOOD79, GORD79].

electronic products for commercial and consumer markets. Electroblast operates four different manufacturing plants, several hundred miles apart from each other and from corporate headquarters. Each plant produces several product lines and between 2,000 units per day and 2,000 units per month. Most of the consumer-oriented products are mass produced with no variations between lots, whereas some of the commercial items are extensively tailored to allow a dozen options which may be selected by the customer. Some of the manufacturing executives in the corporate headquarters have become concerned about relatively high levels of inventory that are carried by the plants and also about the commercial products being often delivered behind schedule. They believe that a "demand-dependent" material control system, which helps set inventory based upon the actual components that will be used in the items that are planned for production, will help reduce the level of ambient inventory and reduce unexpected delays in production schedules [BUFF79]. "Demand-dependent" material control systems typically require extensive amounts of data manipulation and are sensibly automated if they are to be employed in manufacturing plants [DONE79]. How should the design, development, deployment, use, and consequences of such a system for the staff of Electroblast be understood?

Analysts of different persuasions would demarcate the situation somewhat differently. The traditional management-science approach assumes that material control is largely a technical matter, and management scientists have developed an array of techniques to design the information flows of such a system. These depend primarily upon the particular material control discipline adopted, the ways in which subassemblies in each product fit together, and the lead times for their procurement or construction, etc. [BUFF79: 333–386; KANT77: 60–91]. These strategies provide sharp insights into design of systems that would be effective in an idealized world. But the practical concerns of the staff at Electroblast differ: what can *they* expect from the operation of computerized systems in *their* four plants? Demand-dependent material control systems might easily cost $500,000 per year to operate and require a $2 million investment in hardware [DONN79]. Thus, "successful" approaches to systems design, development, and deployment are of more than academic interest.

Human relations analysts would adopt a different strategy [ARGY71, KLIN73, LUCA75a, KLIN77a]. They note that many computerized information systems that have been "technically" well conceived have nevertheless failed to be accepted by a variety of organizational actors. They argue that in addition to "correct" technical designs, computerized systems must be well understood by different people who are expected to use them, and must meet their users' work-oriented needs. Human relations analysts would identify a wide array of organizational staff who interact with the proposed information agents, cost accountants, and production controllers). A new system is likely to intersect with each participant's work differently. Like other systems rationalists, human relations analysts accept the legitimacy of the traditional hierarchy of authority and believe that a workable system might be constructed that meets both the goals of central managers to improve the efficiency of manufacturing operations and the psychological needs of the variety of staff who will use it. However, rather than advocating the best "expert" designs, they emphasize strategies, such as participatory design, that would make the proposed system maximally acceptable to all parties.

Segmented institutionalists would approach the case of Electroblast very differently [BJOR77, MARK79, KLIN80e] (see Table 1). First they would treat any claim that Electroblast "wanted" a new material control system as a helpful fiction, at best. They would view the four manufacturing plants and central headquarters as a complex ecology of groups with overlapping and probably conflicting interests, particularly since there are several geographically dispersed organizational units that produce different products. Political analysts would emphasize the power relations between central headquarters and the four plants, and also power relations between different groups within each plant (e.g., production planners and plant managers)[BJOR77, MARK79].

They would expect the proposed system to fit into existing coalitions and conflicts, and perhaps to alter the alignments. But they would not expect even the *technically* most "optimal" system to be casually and easily accepted by all participants. Those groups who were at odds with promoters of the new system would be more likely to be uninterested in or even to oppose its use. They would also ask "Who works for the system (by entering data)?" and "Who benefits?" The staff at central headquarters would probably receive the greatest volume of usable information and enter the least amount of data. In contrast, production controllers or workers on the shop floors in each of the plants would be most likely to enter data about work-in-process and least likely to receive usable reports in return. Political analysts would be particularly sensitive to differentials such as these, because they identify groups that are most likely or least likely to support the new system, *ceteris paribus* (e.g., "good" technical design, accurate data). Systems rationalists imply that any manager or worker who should enter data will enter accurate and timely data; political analysts argue that staff are likely to enter data with care and speed depending upon the returns they perceive from the system.

Symbolic interactionists expand upon this political analysis by emphasizing the way that each participant *defines the situation* he or she works in (see Table 1). These subjective definitions can be drawn from any of the social worlds in which the person participates. In practice, orientations toward work and family, professional ideologies, career lines inside and outside the organization, and patterns of commitments along these same lines will influence orientations toward new computing developments. Even a clumsy system may be attractive to a material control manager if it helps him "get into" computing and increases his mobility inside and outside the firm [KLIN78g, KLIN80e]. In fact, a system that he believes to be state of the art (e.g., on a minicomputer, or "online," or "net change" rather than "regenerative") may be most attractive, independent of its economic or organizational payoffs to others in the firm. If production workers develop a sense of security in employment by seeing large stacks of work-in-process, a system that leads to overall efficiencies by decreasing those stacks to the minimum necessary to meet delivery schedules may make them jittery, despite any technical or economic advantages that it provides elsewhere. Both political and interactionist analysts view the actions of each participant as self-interested and situated in a complex web of ongoing activities. A new and expensive automated material control system that is deployed in a complex social arena can easily offer rich opportunities for some participants and new difficulties for others.

What will the introduction of a new material control system mean for the employees of Electroblast? Both systems rationalist and segmented institutionalist approaches emphasize different and even complementary elements of the computing world. Systems rationalists usually assume that participants are cooperative and consequently emphasize design techniques or strategies that optimize the technical system that is introduced. The segmented institutionalist approaches suggest that many participants may accurately perceive conflicting interests, act in accord with them, and prefer substantially different and thoroughly incompatible computing arrangements (or even none at all). To the extent that different parties can make their preferences stick, systems will be developed and installed that leave some staff grumbling, or systems costs and delays will increase beyond those estimated when a cooperative world was expected. Each of these different portraits has some face validity. A major thrust of this paper is to learn about their relative scientific and predictive value by examining empirical studies of computing use in organizations and in social life broadly.

Preview of Empirical Studies

In the following analyses, the terms *systems rationalism* and *segmental institutionalism* will be used where they fit and can generalize important observations without much inaccuracy. Where a line of investigation, style of analysis, or finding applies to a much more specialized approach (e.g., structuralist, organizational politics), then the specific, rather than the broader term, will be used.

Social analyses of computing serve both scientific and political roles. For example, advocates of decision-support systems [KEEN78] argue that they will improve their users' ability to make complex decisions. This descriptive and empirical statement is then used to justify the claim that managers should develop decision-support systems for their organizations [KEEN79, DONO77]. Other analysts argue that large automated data systems will be used in ways that diminish the personal privacy of citizens and hope that their arguments will influence decisions to initiate new computing developments [RULE74, RULE75]. Analyses such as these make normative and empirical claims about some observable world in which computing influences the lives of identified participants. The empirical claims can sometimes be investigated by examining the relevant aspects of current computing developments. More importantly, the underlying social and technical theories can be tested in empirical investigations.

·　　·　　·

On "The Computing Revolution"

Systems rationalists treat computing as a "force" or catalyst of social change, independent of the social world in which it is used [HILT78, SIMO77, CARN79]. However, recent studies examined here indicate that the social setting in which a technology is used can profoundly affect which aspects of it are developed, how it is used, and what the consequences of those uses will be. The programming of public access television provides a familiar and illustrative analogy. In the United States it is neither as aesthetically rich nor as dismal as it could be. Programming patterns are as strongly influenced by the dominance of three commercial networks that "counterprogram" to increase their ratings and advertising revenues as they are by the technical capabilities of television production and viewing equipment. Analyses of television programming that emphasize the technical capabilities of the medium and neglect the role of television business practices in influencing programming practices cannot provide serious guides for action. Although analyses of television written before 1945 could be excused for neglecting the effects of social milieu and business practices on programming, analyses of the 1970s cannot.

Computing is much like television; its programming is as strongly influenced by the social milieu in which it is used as by its technical capabilities alone. Generally, the development and uses of new technologies, like television and computers, are selected and shaped by institutional settings in which they have been adopted. During the last decade, there have been a number of careful studies of the social influences upon computer use and of the influences of computing on social life.

Several years ago it was fashionable to refer to an imminent "computing revolution." While computer-based systems have become commonplace in medium and large organizations and in public places through a spread of point-of-sale terminals, talk of "revolution" has diminished. Often the impacts of computing use are very diffuse and subtle. Decisions made by public officials are rarely dominated by computer-based systems, but occasionally automated data has a potent effect. Studies of computing in the workplace that measure not only the impacts of computing, but also their relative importance, also indicate that computing is noticeable, but subtle in its influences [KLIN78f]. Computer terminals are becoming more visible and widespread, but a "computer revolution" is still more of a publicist's phrase than a shrewd observation.

The current situation with computing is similar to that of automobiles at the turn of the century. The benefits to a few individuals seeking flexible transportation or social status were easily visible. Larger-scale effects were more difficult to discern. In Los Angeles there were few cars, and it was very difficult to predict what impacts the automobile would have simply by studying the uses to which automobiles were put or to study the major forms of social organization. The first time Los Angeles had smog was in 1940, 40 years after the automobile was developed in the United States. A new form of metropolitan organization in which the urban core was dwarfed by bedroom suburbs developed on a large scale well after World War II. The movement of families across the country, so that many people could live and work hundreds of miles from where they were born and raised, has been continuing during the last three decades. If one had wanted at the turn of the century to think ahead about what benefits cars would have or what social dilemmas certain styles of social organization around cars could produce, one would have had to be unusually prescient. There simply were neither enough cars nor a social system sufficiently saturated with them to really see the major effects. But an analyst who thought that automobiles were simply fun to drive, but portended nothing larger regardless of the scale on which they were to be used, would have been mistaken. By the time that major effects could be visible, often major investments were made that would be difficult to alter, even when troubles were obvious. By the time the smog had become so intense that the mountains surrounding Los Angeles were invisible most days, people had already become dependent not just on the car, but on forms of social life built around cars—nuclear families dwelling in suburban tracts without buses and living 10 to 30 miles from work, friends, shopping, and other posts of daily life. It is almost impossible to reverse these social elements in which the automobile is a central element.

There is no simple way to measure a "revolution." Saying that the average American family owns 1.8 cars does little to indicate how community life in the U.S. today differs from community life 100 years ago. Similarly, counting computers, computing expenditures, computing users, or other easily countable items only suggests a measure of social activity. Such numbers indicate little by themselves.

The social changes that can directly and unambiguously be attributed to computing are minor when compared with other dynamic elements of American social life: shifting lifestyles from cities to suburbs (and back again), women entering the workforce in large numbers, the increasing fragmentation of families, the spread of two-career families, and an aging population that is increasingly dependent upon energy-intensive technologies. In addition, capital and labor have become increasingly concentrated in several hundred large organizations, and public life is becoming more "privatized" [SILV71]. Not only are the effects of computing use subtle, but they are easily overshadowed by other ongoing social dynamics that cross-cut evaluations of their influence.

Many social observers and computer scientists have been fascinated by the potential potency of computing to alter social life profoundly. Technologies like computing do not "impact" life like "ships colliding at sea" [MOWS76], but rather are subtly woven into ongoing social patterns. One hopes that important technologies, such as computing, can be sufficiently well understood by many social groups early on, so that important decisions about whether, when, and how to utilize computer-based systems will be more socially benign than would otherwise be the case.

These observations have serious consequences for research designs. First, studies of computing are best conducted in settings where the technology is pervasive.[10] The pervasiveness of computing in large modern organizations makes them an especially attractive "laboratory" for learning about the roles of computing in social life. Second, analysts need to observe closely patterns of computer use and the sense that people make of computing in their lives. This argues for case studies and other qualitative field studies in which surveys serve primarily as a supplemental source of data. Third, analysts must be especially careful in extrapolating their results across social settings and time.

---

[10] Inferring influences of computing in settings where its use is weak is difficult at best and often misleading. Simon, for example, uses survey data from national surveys of job satisfaction to evaluate the influences of computing on worklife [SIMO77]. His attempt is laudable, given the paucity of data about computer use and its influences. But it is misleading. So few workers have had extended contact with computing that one should not expect surveys of workers sampled randomly from the U.S. population to show much, even if computing were extremely potent in the places where it was used. Even careful studies of computer use in relatively highly automated work settings show that its influences are subtle [KLIN78f]. Simon's use of national survey data opens important questions about the conditions under which one expects the influences of computing to be noticeable, how much they may be masked and coupled with the influences of other ongoing social patterns, over what time period one expects the influences of computing to become visible, etc. To raise these questions is not to answer them. Better analyses implicitly contrast the influences of computing on social life with other ongoing dynamics having similar or conflicting effects [LAUD74, RULE 74]. But it is easy even for sensitive analysts to confound the influences of computer use with other social patterns when they do not carefully account for them [WEIZ76].

References

ALLI71
   Allison, Graham. *The Essence of Decision: Explaining the Cuban Missile Crisis*, Little, Brown, and Co., Boston, Mass., 1971.
ARGY71
   Argyris, Chris. "Management Information Systems: The Challenge to Rationality and Emotionality," *Management Science 17*, pp. 275–292.
ARGY72
   Argyris, Chris. *The Applicability of Organizational Sociology.* Cambridge University Press, New York, 1972.
BAKE73
   Baker, Frank. *Organizational Systems: General Systems Approaches to Complex Organizations*, Richard D. Irwin, Homewood, Ill., 1973
BJOR77
   Bjorn-Anderson, Nils, and Poul Pederson. "Computer Systems as a Vehicle for Changes in the Management Structure," Working paper 77-3, Information Systems Research Group, University of Copenhagen, 1977.
BODE78
   Boden, Margaret. "Social Implications of Intelligent Machines," *Proceedings 1978 National ACM Conference* (December, 1978): 746–752,
BRAC78
   Bracchi, G., and P.C. Lockerman (eds.). *Information Systems Methodology*, Springer-Verlag, New York, 1978.
BRAV74
   Braverman, H. *Labor and Monopoly Capital: The Degradation of Work in the Twentieth Century*, Monthly Review Press, New York, 1974.
BUFF79
   Buffa, Elwood, and Jeffrey Miller. *Production-Inventory Systems: Planning and Control* (3rd ed), Richard D. Irwin, Homewood, Ill, 1979.
CARN79
   Carne, William. "The Wired Household," *IEEE Spectrum* (October 1979): 61–66.
CHAR71
   Chartrand, Robert. *Systems Technology Applied to Social and Community Problems*, Spartan Books, New York, 1971.
COLL75
   Collins, Randall. *Conflict Sociology: Towards an Explanatory Science*, Academic Press, New York, 1975.
COLT78
   Colton, K. (ed.). *Police Computer Technology*, Lexington Books, Lexington, Mass, (1978).
CUFF79
   Cuff, E.C., and G.C.F. Payne (eds.). *Perspectives in Sociology*, George Allen and Unwin, London, 1979.
DANZ80
   Danziger, James, William Dutton, Rob Kling, and Kenneth Kraemer. *Computers and Politics: High Technology in American Local Governments*, Columbia University Press, New York (forthcoming).
DONE79
   Donelson, William. "MRP—Who Needs It?" *Datamation*, 25(5)(May 1, 1979): 185–197.

DONO79
Donovan, John, and Stuart Madnick. "Institutional and Ad Hoc DSS and Their Effective Use," *Database*, 8(3)(Winter 1977): 79–88.
DORF77
Dorf, Richard. *Computers and Man* (2nd ed.), Boyd and Fraser, San Francisco, 1977.
EMER69
Emery, F. (ed.). *Systems Thinking*, Penguin Books, Baltimore, Md., 1969.
FLER77
Fleron, Federic. *Technology and Communist Culture: The Socio-cultural Impact of Technology Under Socialism*, Praeger, New York, 1977.
GALB77
Galbraith, Jay. *Organization Design*, Addison-Wesley, Reading, Mass, 1977.
GOOD79
Goodman, Seymour. "Software in the Soviet Union: Progress and Problems," in YOV179.
GORD79
Gordon, Andrew. "Computers and Politics in China," *Computers and Society*, 9(3/4)(Spring 1979): 18–30.
GOTL73
Gotlieb, C.C., and A. Borodin. *Social Issues in Computing*, Academic Press, New York, 1973.
HILT78
Hiltz, Roxanne Starr, and Murray Turoff. *The Network Nation*, Addison-Wesley, Reading, Mass, 1978.
HOFF77
Hoffman, Erik. "Technology, Values and Political Power in the Soviet Union: Do Computers Matter?" in FLER77.
KANT77
Kanter, J. *Management-oriented Information Systems* (2nd ed.), Prentice-Hall, Englewood Cliffs, N.J., 1977.
KEEN78
Keen, Peter, and M. Scott Morton. *Decision Support Systems: An Organizational Perspective*, Addison-Wesley, Reading, Mass., 1978.
KEEN79
Keen, Peter, and Gerald Wagner. "DSS: An Executive Mind-support System," *Datamation* 25(12)(November 1979): 117–122.
KERN79
Kerner, David. "Business Information Characterization Study," *Data Base*, 10(4)(Spring 1979): 10–17.
KILL72
Killough, Larry. "The Management System Viewed in Perspective," in LIU72.
KLIN73
Kling, Rob. "Toward a Person-Centered Computer Technology," *Proceedings of the 1973 ACM National Conference*, Atlanta, Ga.
KLIN77a
Kling, Rob. "The Organizational Context of User-Centered Software Design," *MIS Quarterly*, 1(4)(December 1977): 41–52.
KLIN77b
Kling, Rob, and Elihu Gerson. "The Social Dynamics of Technical Innovation in the Computing World," *Symbolic Interaction*, 1(1)(Fall 1977): 132–146.
KLIN78c
Kling, Rob. "Automated Welfare Client-tracking and Service Integration: The Political Economy of Computing," *Communications of the ACM*, 21(16)(June, 1978): 484–493.

KLIN78e

Kling, Rob. "Information Systems as Social Resources in Policymaking," *Proceedings of the 1978 ACM National Conference*, (December, 1978): 666–674.

KMLIN78f

Kling, Rob. "The Impacts of Computing on the Work of Managers, Data Analysts and Clerks," Working Paper, Public Policy Research Organization University of California—Irvine, Irvine, Cal., 1978.

KLIN78g

Kling, Rob, and Elihu Gerson. "Patterns of Segmentation and Intersection in the Computing World," *Symbolic Interaction*, 1(2)(Spring 1978): 24–43.

KLIN79a

Kling, Rob. "Alternative EFT Developments and Quality of Life," *Telecommunications Policy*, 3(1)(March 1979): 52–64.

KLIN80b

Kling, Rob. "Social Issues and Impacts of Computing: From Arena to Discipline," in MOSW80a.

KLIN80c

Kling, Rob, and Walt Scacchi. "Computing as Social Action: The Social Dynamics of Computing in Complex Organizations" in YOVI80.

KLIN80e

Kling, Rob. "The Social Dynamics of Computer Use with Technology of Large 'Social Scope': The Case of Material Requirements Planning," Technical Report, Department of Information and Computer Science, University of California—Irvine, Irvine, Cal., 1980.

KRAE79a

Kraemer, K.L., and W.H. Dutton. "The Interests Served by Technological Reform: The Case of Computing," *Administration and Society*, 11(1)(May 1979): 80–106.

KRAE79b

Kraemer, Kenneth, and John L. King. "Requiem for USAC," *Policy Analysis*, 5(3)(Summer 1979): 313–349.

KRAE80c

Kraemer, Kenneth. "Citizen Impacts from Information Technology in Public Administration," Working Paper, Public Policy Research Organization, University of California—Irvine, Irvine, Cal., 1980.

LAUD74

Laudon, Kenneth. *Computers and Bureaucratic Reform*, Wiley Interscience, New York, 1974.

LENK80

"Computer Use in Public Administration: Implications for the Citizen," in MOSW80a.

LICK78

Licklider, J.C.R., and Albert Vezza. "Applications of Information Networks," *Proc. IEEE*, 66(11)(November, 1978): 1330–1346.

LIU72

Liu, David. *Design and Management of Information Systems*, Science Research Associates, Palo Alto, Cal., 1972.

LOWI79

Lowi, Theodore J. *The End of Liberalism: The Second Republic*, W.W. Norton and Company, New York, 1979.

MARK79

Markus, M. Lynne. *Understanding Information Systems Use in Organizations: A Theoretical Explanation*, Ph.D. Thesis, Case Western Reserve University, Cleveland, Ohio, 1979.

MICH64

Michael, Donald. "Speculations on the Relation of the Computer to Individual Freedom and the Right to Privacy," *George Washington Law Review*, 33(October 1964): 270–286.

MOWS76

Mowshowitz, Abbe. *The Conquest of Will: Information Processing in Human Affairs*, Addison-Wesley, Reading, Mass., 1976.

MUMF67

Mumford, Enid, and Olive Banks. *The Computer and the Clerk*, Routledge and Keegan-Paul, London, 1967.

MUMF78

Mumford, Enid. "Values, Technology and Work," in BRAC78: 142–159.

NOBL78

Noble, David. "Social Choice in Machine Design: The Case of Automatically Controlled Machine Tools, and a Challenge for Labor," *Politics and Society*, 8(3–4): 313–47.

PERR79

Perrow, Charles. *Complex Organizations: A Critical Essay* (2nd. ed.), Scott, Forsman, and Co., Glenview, Ill., 1979.

PETT73

Pettigrew, Andrew. *The Politics of Organizational Decision-Making*, Tavistock, London, 1973.

RITZ77

Ritzer, George. *Working: Conflict and Change* (2nd ed.), Prentice-Hall, Englewood Cliffs, N.J., 1977.

RULE74

Rule, James. *Private Lives and Public Surveillance: Social Control in the Computer Age*, Schocken Books, New York, 1974.

RULE75

Rule, James. *Value Choices in Electronic Funds Transfer Policy*, Office of Telecommunications Policy, Executive Office of the President, Washington D.C., 1975.

SCAC80

Scacchi, Walt. *The Process of Innovation in Computing: A Study of the Social Dynamics of Computing*, Ph.D. Thesis, University of California—Irvine, 1980.

SCOT73

Scott, William G. "Organization Theory: An Overview and Appraisal," in BAKE73.

SCHI69

Schiller, Herbert. *Mass Communications and American Empire*, Beacon Press, Boston, Mass., 1969.

SILV71

Silverman, David. *The Theory of Organizations*, Basic Books, New York, 1971.

SIMO77

Simon, Herbert A. *The New Science of Management Decision-making*, Prentice Hall, Englewood Cliffs, N.J., 1977.

STER79

Sterling, T. "Consumer Difficulties with Computerized Transactions: An Empirical Investigation," *Communications of the ACM*, 22(5)(May 1979): 283–289.

SWAN79

Swanda, John. *Organizational Behavior: Systems and Applications*, Alfred Publishing Co., Sherman Oaks, Cal., 1979.

TAUS77

Tausky, Curt. *Work Organizations: Major Theoretical Perspectives* (2nd ed.), F.E. Peacock Publishers, Itasca, Ill., 1977.

THOM67

Thompson, Richard. *Organizations in Action*, McGraw-Hill, New York, 1967.

TURN78

  Turner, Jonathan. *The Structure of Sociological Theory* (rev. ed.), Dorsey Press, Homewood, Ill., 1978.

USGO77

  U.S. Government Department of Commerce. *Computers in the Federal Government: A Compilation of Statistics*, National Bureau of Standards Publication 500-7. U.S. Government Printing Office, Washington, D.C., 1977.

WEIZ76

  Weizenbaum, Joseph. *Computer Power and Human Reason*, Freeman and Co. San Francisco, Cal., 1976.

YOV179

  Yovits, Marshall (ed.). *Advances in Computers*, Vol. 18, Academic Press, New York, 1979.

P·A·R·T· II

7

Strategic Computing and Administrative Reform

Kenneth L. Kraemer

The recent literature on strategic information systems, strategic computing, and inform-ation systems as a competitive weapon have made remarkable claims about the potential of information technology in organizations. Although the specific claims are many and varied, they can be reduced to a single statement: Information technology has the potential for dramatically transforming organizations, but that potential is not being realized because managers fail to utilize the technology properly.

This article argues that, although information technology has long been viewed as capable of bringing about organizational change, it has never been shown to play this role in reality. Rather, information technology has tended to reinforce existing organizational arrangements and power distributions in organizations. Moreover, information tech-nology will have the same effects in the future because of fundamental relationships between the technology's use, control of the technology, and interests served by the technology. Stated simply, the relationships are as follows:

How the technology is used determines its effects and, indirectly, the interests served. Decisions about the technology's use are made by central managers or their subordinates. While they use the technology in the broader organizational interests, they also decide to use information technology for their own interests. And they have tended to use it to reinforce their position in organizations: to enlarge the information available to them; to enhance their choices through tight control of resources; to rationalize decisions to staff and their clients; to provide "visible deliverables" with the aid of technology; and to symbolize professionalism, modernity and rationality in the management of their organizations. Thus, managers see no need to change their ways. Quite the contrary. They have discovered that computing and other information technologies are a powerful way to reinforce them.

In order to explore this argument, this article does three things. First, it states four key propositions of the strategic computing thesis. (For simplicity, henceforth the phrase *strategic computing* is used to include the notions about strategic information systems and information systems as a competitive weapon.) Second, it assesses each proposition in light of existing research and experience. This research and experience has focused on computer use in public organizations, especially local governments in the United States, and to some extent, federal and state governments as well. Third, it concludes with what this assessment in public organizations might mean for business organizations as well, and it points to a fundamental weakness of the strategic computing thesis.

The analysis focuses on public organizations because computing has long been viewed as an instrument of administrative reform in American public administration. However, computing has never been shown to play this role (Laudon, 1974; Kraemer and King, 1979; Perry and Kraemer, 1979). Unlike the way they are characterized by the advocates of strategic computing, American public administrations have traditionally been eager to use information technology as each new wave of the technology has been introduced. And public managers at the national level have been leaders in stimulating others to adopt information technology. Although few public managers have fully understood the technology and what it can do, they have been bold in experimenting with information technology, in efforts both to bring about reform directly through information technology and to support other reforms such as reorganization. The American example is useful because the bureaucratic foot-dragging of the sort that exists in other countries (e.g., France, West Germany) is noticeably absent in many American cases.

Does this willingness and even enthusiasm to embrace information technology in American public administrations bear out the strategic computing view of what information technology can and should be used to do? If information technology is having the expected benefits, then the strategic computing advocates are right. If not, then we must reassess their thesis.

The Strategic Computing Thesis

The strategic computing thesis is not written in a single place. Rather, it permeates various writings on information technology and organizations in both business and public administration. Sometimes the thesis is explicit; almost always it is implicit. The strategic computing thesis in these writings can be reduced to four essential propositions as follows:

Proposition 1. Information technology has the potential to reform public administrations and their relations with their environments. For example, Gibson and Hammer (1985) claim that "today's applications of information technology can dramatically change and transform the way individuals, functional units, and whole organizations carry out their tasks."

Proposition 2. The potential of information technology for reform is rooted in its ability to change organization structures (Lenk, 1980; Reinerman, 1985, 1986). Information technology can directly impact the data structures of public administration by liberating them from past dependency on centralized, hierarchical forms. Thus, change in the data structures can trigger change in organization structures of public administration and, in turn, bring about a change of the roles of individual employees and of public administration as a whole.

Proposition 3. Properly used, information technology will be very beneficial for administrators, staff, citizens and public administration as a whole. Information technology has the potential to distribute computing broadly, decentralize administrations radically, reintegrate and enhance work life, open access to data within the government and with citizens outside, and rationalize decision making with data and models.

Proposition 4. Achievement of the potential benefits from information technology is frustrated by managers' lack of understanding of the technology and what it can do and their unwillingness to adopt the technology and to change their ways so that they can utilize the potential of the technology.

These four propositions argue for a reformation to bring about the necessary change in thinking and behavior of managers so that the benefits of information technology can be realized.

Information Technology and Administrative Reform: The American Experience

Taken together, these propositions are a contemporary and sophisticated summary of the traditional view that technology *per se* is a change agent. But is it? This article uses the experience with computing technology in American public administrations, where automation has continued unabated since first introduced in the early fifties, to answer this basic question. It views information technology to consist of computing, telecommunications, and management science technique (Whisler, 1976; Meyers, 1967). It focuses on computing technology rather than other information technologies because considerably more is known about the effects of computing in public administrations and because computing most frequently involves elements of the other information technologies and, therefore, provides the best single means of assessing propositions about information technology generally.

The extent of computerization in American public administrations is staggering. Federal agencies have more than 20,000 mainframes and minicomputers and 200,000 microcomputers installed, employ 100,000 data-processing (DP) people and spend more than $15 billion annually on computerization (GSA, 1985, 1986; OTA, 1981, 1985; Head, 1981). The 50 states have more than 1,000 mainframes and minicomputers and 20,000 microcomputers installed, employ 15,000 DP people, and spend over four billion dollars annually (NASIS, 1985, 1986).

The 2,000 governments of cities over 10,000 in population have 2,000 mainframes and minicomputers and 20,000 microcomputers, employ 20,000 DP people, and spend $4 billion annually for computerization (Kraemer et al., 1986). The uses of computers cover a wide range of applications, including sophisticated models for policy making, large database systems, office automation, teleprocessing, and traditional data processing. American public administrations cannot be described as reluctant to adopt and use the technology. On the contrary, they are enthusiastic about it. What has been the effect of this use?

Systematic, empirical research on the effects of computerization in public administrations has grown markedly over the last 15 years (Kraemer and King, 1986; Kraemer and King, 1987; Kling, 1980; Attewell and Rule, 1984). Although the empirical findings are fragmented and sometimes contradictory, they nevertheless point to certain overall conclusions. The research indicates that computing does have important benefits for public administration, but not of the kind predicted by the advocates of information technology and administrative reform. Four broad findings relate directly to the four propositions noted above. Each finding is reviewed next in relation to each proposition.

Finding 1

Proposition 1 states that information technology has the potential to reform public administrations and their relations with their environments. Yet most experiments with computer technology and administrative reform have shown that although the technology is a useful instrument of administrative reform, it does not *cause* reform. Some reforms such as reorganization, centralized accounting and budgeting, and services integration have survived in part because of computer technology, but its use has seldom survived when the broader reforms failed.

Two examples illustrate the futility of using computer technology to cause administrative reforms. The first is the federal USAC project to build integrated information systems in cities as a means of reforming local government management. Federal agencies wanted integrated information systems built because they felt such systems would improve intergovernmental information flows and increase local officials' use of information in policy making. Although integrated information systems were technically desirable, they were impractical to implement given the limits of the technology and the state of knowledge then extant. Moreover, local governments wanted computers to perform practical tasks like keep records, print bills, produce reports—all to speed up revenue collections and better monitor local spending. Local governments built the systems they wanted, and eventually the federal agencies abandoned the project when the larger vision collapsed. USAC failed both as a purely technical reform and as a management reform. The integrated information systems lacked the driving power to sustain themselves as technical reforms, let alone as broader management reform (Kramer and King, 1979).

Computer technology was also envisioned as an instrument of administrative reform in the projects of the U.S. Department of Health, Education and Welfare to create Inform-ation and Referral (I&R) systems for social service integration in the middle to late seventies. Social services integration at the local level was intended to consolidate the many public and private local agencies that served the larger urban areas. I&R systems were introduced to reinforce the consolidation efforts by sharing information about clients, needs, resources, and performance among all participating agencies. It was felt that the information systems would improve both service delivery to clients and the allocation of social service resources. It was even felt that the I&R systems would achieve admini-strative consolidation, central budgeting, and performance monitoring indirectly where reformers had failed to achieve them directly (Kling, 1974). Services integration itself failed because the local social service agencies were unconvinced of the benefits of integration, and especially the benefits to them as agencies. The I&R systems had no power to survive on their own, let alone bring about services integration indirectly, and they expired along with the whole reform effort.

Sometimes computer technology does help effect reform, however. Financial auto-mation in local governments fits perfectly with the desires of top managers to centralize budgeting and accounting systems. Computerization provides an important means of facilitating these reforms. Sometimes, implementation required replacement of recalcitrant finance directors and department heads, but top managers had the motive and the capability for bringing about the centralized reforms, and they persisted. Similarly, second-generation financial automation, with sophisticated capabilities for cost account-ing and billing on a fee-for-service basis, are now being implemented because local government managers seek new means of enhancing revenues in the face of fiscal limitations set by citizen referenda. The new computerized financial management systems help managers to overcome these fiscal limitations (Kraemer et al., 1986).

These foregoing examples illustrate the importance of management motive and implementation capability in administrative reform. They also illustrate that computer technology can be an instrument of broader administrative reform but cannot drive such reform. Thus, they challenge the validity of the first proposition underlying the strategic computing theses.

Finding 2

Proposition 2 states that the potential of information technology for reform is rooted in its ability to change organization structures. Yet computing has had relatively little effect on organization structures. The effect of computerization on organization structures has not yet been substantial, and probably will never have the effects implied by the second proposition.

A number of the strategic computing theses depend on the view that use of informa-tion technology can help bring about major changes in organizational structures, especi-ally relative centralization or decentralization of organizations. There is less accumulated evidence to assess this view than there is for whether use of information technology affects the fortunes of administrative reform efforts, as discussed above; but several conclusions can be drawn.

The effect of computing on organization structures is important to the overall theme of the strategic computing theses and deserves close examination of the experience to date in order to assess whether computerization has had any effect on organization structure.

The research indicates that where it has had an effect, the main impact of computing has been to reinforce existing structures of communication, authority, and power in organizations (Danziger et al., 1982; Dutton and Kraemer, 1977, 1978; King and Kraemer, 1985; King and Kraemer, 1986; Kraemer and King, 1986; Kraemer, 1980). This conclusion, which is in marked contrast to three common misconceptions about computerization, warrants further examination in light of those misconceptions.

The first misconception is that traditional mainframe-based computerization has resulted in greater centralization of organizational structures because of the tendency to centralize data along with the technology and expertise.

Because mainframe computers were expensive and technical expertise was limited, computers tended to be centralized when they were first introduced into organizations. Data tended to follow the computers and technical experts. This tendency has been called power-enhancing because it reflected the centralized and hierarchical nature of many organizations and, some thought, would result in even greater centralization of power and control.

Empirical research into the effects of computerization on the centralization/decentralization of organizations clearly indicates that information technology does not *cause* changes in organizational decision making and control structures. Most of the research indicates that computerization has not changed organization structure at all (Robey, 1981; Attewell and Rule, 1984; Kraemer and King, 1986, 1987). Rather, it has reinforced existing structures. For example, the URBIS Group found that computing reinforced existing distributions of power and control in local governments, regardless of the established structure.

Where computerization has changed structure, it has appeared to increase both centralization and decentralization. That is, it has allowed greater decision latitude to be exercised at lower levels of the organization while also allowing greater central control over those decisions through provision of performance records about decision outcomes. In reality, however, it has resulted in a general shift in control in the direction of more centralization. This is because what appears to be greater decentralization (exercise of greater decision latitude at lower levels) actually entails the delegation of more routine decisions whose outcomes are more closely controlled. Power and control over the premises for decision making are actually more concentrated than previously.

In summary, for the most part computing has had no discernible effect at all on organization structure. Where it has had a discernible effect, it has led to slightly greater centralization of already centralized organizations. Thus, computing has clearly reinforced existing organizational arrangements.[1]

---

[1] This finding has additional significance for the question of administrative reform through information technology because the research further indicates that several different organizational structures are compatible with computerization. Newer organizational forms like matrix organization and dual authority arrangements seem receptive as the more traditional bureaucracies to computer technology. Therefore one would expect that computerization in the context of these newer organizational forms would reinforce those structures also—it would not change them.

The second misconception is that the advent of microcomputers with their information-as-power-distributing bias is decentralizing computing within organizations and, with time, will decentralize organizations themselves.

Just as mainframe computing was thought to be power-enhancing because it centralized information, microcomputing is thought to be power-distributing because it potentially decentralizes both information and access to information. The problem with this view is that it is not supported by systematic, empirical research on computing—indeed, it is at odds with the current facts.

Recent research on microcomputing in American local governments shows that the actual use of microcomputing is still limited and that the distribution of microcomputing is not towards greater democratization but follows the past distribution of mainframe computing both vertically and horizontally. A 1985 survey of 102 cities that historically have been among the more extensive and more experienced users of computing (i.e., over 50,000 in population and over 10 years' experience) did not find a single site with extensive use of microcomputers, where "extensive" was operationally defined as more than 100 microcomputers in use. Not one of the 102 cities in the survey had even 50 microcomputers in use. The median number of micros in use was 10, and the median number of micros planned for use in the next year was also 10 (Kramer *et al.*, 1985).

These data corroborate data in another national survey, which found that less than 15% of municipal governments owned or leased even one microcomputer (Norris and Webb, 1983). In short, the actual systems in use in public administrations, and the impacts of those computing systems, are not dominated by microcomputing. They are dominated by mainframe computing and, as will be seen next, its pattern of resource distribution.[2]

Vertically, microcomputing has not been extended to all those who wish to take advantage of it. Microcomputers are distributed to the same role-types that have traditionally had mainframe resources. These tend to be staff professionals such as accountants, budget and personnel analysts, planners, and engineers—not policy makers, street-level workers (patrol officers, detectives, social workers, inspectors), or desk-top workers (with the exception of word-processing usage by secretarial/clerical staff).

Horizontally, microcomputing also has not been widely extended. The median number of city departments using microcomputing within the cities was 6.6. Departments that have traditionally been the most extensive users of mainframe- and mini-based computing are also the most extensive users of micros. Specifically, data processing, police, and finance are the most extensive users of micros (Kraemer *et al.*, 1985).

It is clear, therefore, that the new microcomputer technology is not currently bringing about computing democracy; nor is it bringing about organizational democracy. This finding, which is consistent with the findings about computing and organizational centralization, further supports the hypothesis that computing reinforces existing organizational arrangements rather than changes them.

---

[2] This research on local government is supported by similar research in business. A very large survey of organizational end users in the private sector supports the observation that microcomputer use is less than pervasive in many organizational settings. Of the 4,448 organizational end users in the survey, only 8% of the 4,448 primarily use minicomputers. Fully 92% of the users are primarily involved with mainframe computing systems (43%) and minicomputer networks (49%) in their work (Rushinek and Rushinek, 1985).

The third misconception is that today more than ever before in history there is no inherent organizational bias in computing technology. The technology removes limits of space and time. It can therefore be used to centralize organizations, decentralize them, or both.

It is not clear that computer technology no longer has a power-enhancing bias; indeed the potential power-distributing bias of the new microcomputer technology may simply be a new myth. Microcomputers lack the necessary power for large computing jobs; networking them to gain the power of a mainframe is impractical because it means everyone but the large-job-user must forego their jobs. Microcomputers also lack the storage capacity of mainframes. Therefore, they can be networked effectively to share data within a work group, but they can seldom be networked effectively to share data across major sub-units or a whole organization. As a consequence of the power and data sharing limitations of micros, one out of every three micros is linked to a mainframe today, and the ratio is expected to increase in the future. As a consequence, the growth of microcomputers will only further increase demand for central mainframes.

Microcomputer end users generally lack real computing expertise. While they might possess elementary computer literacy, they usually are unable to create their own programs. Most micro users are heavily dependent upon computer consultants for assistance with hardware, software and applications. After six years of experience with microcomputers in organizations, it is now clear that successful microcomputing depends very much upon the existence of a strong support group for technical consulting, training, procurement, and integration. And as a practical matter, that group is the data processing staff in most organizations. Thus, the net effect of microcomputing in most organizations has been to increase the demand for mainframe resources and to increase the power and influence of computer experts.

Regardless of whether computing no longer has a power-enhancing bias, organizations and managers do. Consequently, it is reasonable to expect that they will use the technology to reinforce managerial and political objectives. Most organizations are bureaucracies, which means that they are hierarchically organized with distributions of authority, resources and responsibility flowing to work units and information about organizational performance flowing back to the top as a means of control. Most managers want to keep organizations that way and to enhance their functioning.

In summary, since the second proposition of the strategic computing thesis appears to rest on three misconceptions, the proposition itself is invalid.

Finding 3

Proposition 3 states that, properly used, information technology will be very beneficial for administrators, staff, citizens and public administration as a whole. Yet, the benefits of computerization have not been evenly distributed within organizations. The primary beneficiaries of information technology have been the dominant political-administrative coalitions in public administrations, *not* the technical elites, middle managers, clerical staff, or ordinary citizens.

The benefits of computerization stem from computers' uses in public administration; and most use of computing is for traditional data processing, rather than management information systems, decision support systems, executive information systems, or end user computing. The traditional uses focus on the "institutional core" of public administration—that is, the day-to-day transaction-oriented information processing of administrative agencies concerned with producing bills, recording payments, paying vendors and employees, recording public documents, answering citizen inquiries, and so forth. These data-processing uses meet real needs of public agencies, and they represent substantial investments. They are not bold, innovative moves to transform public agencies; rather, they are useful adaptations of the technology mainly to increase administrative productivity.

Most empirical research confirms that computing has become a major source of productivity benefits for both individuals and organizations. The productivity gains from current applications of computing are greatest on more structured and repetitive tasks and most problematic on less structured tasks involving large-scale, complex information systems. Computing has particularly increased the information processing capabilities and the throughput/output for workers whose jobs have high information-processing content. In addition, most individuals who use computing perceive the direct impacts of computing to be mildly benign to the extent that any impact is perceived. Despite the imagery of the computer as a threatening and anxiety-producing technology, these attributes are quickly replaced in most individuals' assessments by a sense that computing can be controlled and that its use will result in net benefits for the individual (Danziger and Kraemer, 1985).

Other benefits from computing have been more subtle and indirect, but they are significant because they point to the primary beneficiaries from its application thus far. Computing in American cities has been primarily oriented toward improving governmental efficiency and the choices of top-level administrators rather than being oriented towards improving direct service delivery and enhancing the choices of citizens.

With respect to service delivery to citizens, computerized systems in government tend to be primarily used to (1) support basic government services such as police, fire, highways, and sanitation, rather than newer and more socially oriented services; (2) achieve efficiency payoffs rather than equity, effectiveness, or other possible benefits; and (3) enhance social control through inherently regulatory services such as law enforcement and various kinds of code enforcement. At a broad level, the wide variety of computerized systems in local governments do serve citizen interests, which scholars have characterized as the historically dominant interests of basic services, efficiency, and law enforcement. However, they do not serve the needs of special citizen groups such as the poor, the homeless, the aged, or the handicapped (Kraemer and Kling, 1985).

Within the government itself, computerized systems have been used to serve the interests of central administrators. Their values of efficiency, control and effectiveness of decision making have been served as a by-product of routine administrative automation in finance, general administration, and operating departments. Thus, even where computerized systems appear to have been broadly applied to a wide variety of government functions and departments, they have in fact been narrowly applied to generate efficiencies in large data-handling operations of the departments and to produce data that top managers can use for management and decision making. Computing developments have consistently reinforced the biases of central administrators (Kraemer and Kling, 1985).

This consistency stems from the fact that most key decisions about the uses of computing in a particular domain are directly made by those with power and control in that domain. At the city level, this is the city manager or mayor and members of their political coalition within the government. Alternatively, the key decisions about computing use are made by those who are subordinate to, and generally serve the interests of, these powerful people—the administrative staff and administrative departments who serve top management (Danziger et al., 1982; Dutton and Kraemer, 1977, 1978; Kraemer, 1980).

The finding that computer use in public adminstration has tended to reinforce the interests of central administrators and the dominant coalition they represent is not surprising. Those who control computing determine whose interests are served, and by and large, central administrators have controlled major decisions about computer use to their own ends. Thus, the proposition that computerization would result in the growing power of technical elites, especially computer specialists, or that computerization would be a democratizing tool since it can distribute information-as-power more widely, is erroneous.

Finding 4

Proposition 4 states that achievement of the potential benefits from information technology is frustrated by public managers' unwillingness to adopt the technology and to change their ways so that they utilize the potential of the technology. So-called reform governments such as city manager cities have adopted computers more rapidly and used them more extensively than nonreform governments, but they have used them in the same way as the nonreform governments—for political reinforcement. The factor that differentiates usage is the character of top departmental and data-processing managements, specifically their vision for computing in public administrations. The difference in application is basically the intensity and ingenuity with which these leaders of public administrations set out to exploit the potential of the technology for their own purposes. These purposes may be professional, organizational, political, or personal, but the specific motivation is less critical than the fact that the technology is being widely applied, not resisted.

Contrary to the fourth proposition, then, public managers are utilizing the potential of information technology. They are developing an understanding of the technology. They clearly see what it can do for them, and they are willing to adopt the technology for their own benefit. Public managers see no reason to change their ways, especially when computing represents a powerful means to reinforce them.

Assessment

American research and experience indicate that although benefits accrue from the use of information technology, they are not those predicted by the advocates of reform through information technology. The benefits are largely administrative and efficiency-oriented, although some job enlargement and enhancement also occurs at many organization levels. The benefits are not large-scale or even small-scale reform of administrative organization, practices, or behavior. Thus, the "reform through information technology" propositions of strategic computing are not supported.

What is wrong with the "reform through information technology propositions"? Two basic assumptions that underlie the propositions, and the broader strategic computing thesis, are faulty.

The first faulty assumption is that change is required. The strategic computing thesis assumes that change is required without specifying *why* the change is required. Moreover, the thesis contains an underlying bias wherein change required or enabled by the technology is inherently beneficial to the organization. The history of automation has demonstrated the folly of technology-dictated change. For example, batch automation took previously integrated clerical tasks and broke them into their respective DP and user components, and then made users hostage to DP's language, time schedule, and errors. This was using the potential of the technology as it was, and as it was understood, at the time. Yet the result was disastrous for both offices and office workers.

Another example is provided by the move towards integrated databases for organizations. These efforts to conceive of an organization-wide database in which to deposit all data and to organize public administrations around the care and feeding of these databases seems to be repeating the mistakes of batch processing automation. Such efforts might appeal to the Prussian sense of order and rationalization in organizations, but they are fraught with great problems. Currently, the data deposits in these databases far exceed the data withdrawals, raising a fundamental question about whether they were needed in the first place. Both of these examples suggest that just because the computer makes it possible to organize one way or the other, or appeals to ones' sense of order in the world, is insufficient reason to organize that way. It seems more prudent to rely upon other considerations first and then use information technology only if it supports those considerations.

The second faulty assumption underlying the strategic computing theses is that technology can *induce reform*. The implication of this assumption is that information technology is somehow revolutionary, having power to induce dramatic change. However, the empirical research clearly indicates that the short-run impacts of computing have been far less pervasive and dramatic than were frequently forecast. The introduction of computing into public administrations typically alters orientations, tasks, and interactions; but most affected individuals perceive short-term changes to be modest. And organizational analyses indicate that alterations in standard operating procedures and functions are usually limited. In most settings, computing is made to conform to existing behavior and practice in the short run, and immediate, major transformations of the type implied by the notion of "reform" rarely follow the introduction of computing.

Insight into cumulative and longer-term impacts is provided by two recent sets of case studies covering thirty years of computing in cities (Kraemer *et al.*, 1989) and federal agencies (Westin and Laudon, 1986, forthcoming). These studies clearly indicate that the cumulative impacts of the totality of computing uses and the longer-term impacts might constitute a reform, but it is mainly a reform of the information-processing aspects, not the broader aspects of the organization.

Thus, the clear indication from empirical research over the last 15 years is that there is no revolution occurring in organizations because of information technology. Rather there is a continuing evolution in the technology and its organizational impacts which has been occurring for nearly 30 years.

This second assumption incorrectly reasons that the indirect influence of information technology can accomplish the same level of genuine reform within the political-administrative system as can be accomplished through direct intervention. The notion that reform can be achieved through the implementation of information technology is shown by experience and research to be false and misleading. Although computing can in theory lead to new administrative structures, in practice, it doesn't, it can't, and it probably shouldn't. And every time such structures have been attempted in the past a disaster has resulted. The disasters will continue as long as the role of information technology in administrative reform is viewed from the perspective of managerial rationalism and the structural and behavioral realities of organizational power and politics are ignored.

Implications and Conclusion

It is possible that the corporate situation is different from the government situation, and therefore the foregoing analysis does not apply. However, this seems unlikely since the research clearly indicates that the structural impacts of information technology are negligible, and therefore variations in organizational structure are largely irrelevant.

In the end, the reason that technology-driven reforms will not happen is that proponents of this view have the whole equation backwards. Technology is not the driver; it is rarely even the catalyst; at most it is supportive of reform efforts decided on other grounds.

Reform depends upon political/administrative will and ability to implement. Although technology implementation is often rationalized on grounds of efficiency and effectiveness, most often it is driven by political and managerial considerations. For example, the early introduction of computers into government came at a time when top executives were trying to introduce centralized accounting and budgeting systems into government as a means of gaining greater control over department expenditures. Computing was introduced because it was thought to support these reforms: it would provide a technical rationale for centralization; it would allow financial data to be centralized in the finance department but distributed to the operating departments in the form of reports and terminal queries. Computing was not introduced because it had the power to bring about centralized accounting and budgeting systems. It supported and fit in with these broader administrative reforms.

Technology-related reform depends upon the congruence of proposed uses of information technology and the interests of the existing power structure. Use must reinforce the interests of the existing power structure, or the reform will not happen. This means that information technology is essentially conservative and helps to explain why the impacts from the computer technology have been so slight despite more than 30 years of continuing computerization.

This relationship between technology and administrative reform is not likely to change with different technologies. There is nothing about telecommunications and office automation technologies that suggests their history has been or will be any different than that of administrative computer technology.

References

Attewell, Paul, and James Rule (1984). Computing and Organizations: What We Know and What We Don't Know, *Communications of the ACM* 27 (December): 1184–1192.

Danziger, James N., William H. Dutton, Rob Kling, and Kenneth L. Kraemer (1982). *Computers and Politics*. Columbia University Press, New York.

Danziger, James N., and Kenneth L. Kraemer (1985). *People and Computers*. Columbia University Press, New York.

Dutton, William H., and Kenneth L. Kraemer (1977). Technology and Urban Management: The Power Payoffs of Computing. *Administration and Society* 9(3): 304–340.

Dutton, William H., and Kenneth L. Kraemer (1978). Management Utilization of Computers in American Local Governments, *Communications of the ACM* 21(3): 206–218.

General Services Administration (1985). *Automatic Data Processing Inventory*. Washington, DC: General Services Administration.

General Services Administration (1986). *Automatic Data Processing Inventory*. General Services Administration, Washington, DC.

Gibson, Cyrus, and Michael Hammer (1985). Information Technology and Organizational Change, *Indications*. Cambridge, MA: The Index Group.

Head, Robert (1981). Seeking a Path Through the Paperwork Jungle, *InfoSystems* 28 (April): 54–60.

King, John Leslie, and Kenneth L. Kraemer (1985). *The Dynamics of Computing*. Columbia University Press, New York.

King, John Leslie, and Kenneth L. Kraemer (1986). The Dynamics of Change in Computing Use: A Theoretical Framework, *Computers, Environment and Urban Systems* 11(1/2): 5–25.

Kling, Rob (1974). Automated Welfare Client Tracking and Service Integration, *Communications of the ACM* 21(6): 484–493.

Kling, Rob (1980). Social Analyses of Computing: Theoretical Perspectives in Recent Empirical Research, *Computing Surveys* 12(1): 61–110.

Kraemer, Kenneth L. (1980). Computers, Information and Power in Local Governments. In Abbe Mowshowitz, ed., *Human Choice and Computers, 2*, pp. 213–235. North-Holland Publishing Company, New York.

Kraemer, Kenneth L., and John Leslie King (1979). A Requiem for USAC, *Policy Analysis* 5(3): 313–349.

Kraemer, Kenneth L., and John Leslie King (1986). Computing and Public Organizations, *Public Administration Review* 46 (Special Issue): 488–496.

Kraemer, Kenneth L., and John Leslie King, 1987. Computers and the Constitution: a Helpful, Harmful, or Harmless Relationship? *Public Administration Review* 47(1): 93–105.

Kraemer, Kenneth L., and Rob Kling (1985). The Political Character of Computerization in Service Organizations: Citizen Interests or Bureaucratic Control, *Computers and the Social Sciences* 1(2): 77–89.

Kraemer, Kenneth L., and James L. Perry (1979). The Federal Push to Bring Computer Applications to Local Governments, *Public Administration Review* 39(3): 260–270.

Kraemer, Kenneth L., John Leslie King, Debora Dunkle, and Joseph P. Lane (1986). Trends in Municipal Information Systems, 1975–1985, *Baseline Data Reports* 18(2). Washington, DC: International Management Association.

Kraemer, Kenneth L., John Leslie King, Debora Dunkle, and Joseph P. Lane (1989). *Managing Information Systems: Change and Control in Organizational Computing.* San Francisco: Jossey-Bass.

Kraemer, Kenneth L., John Leslie King, Debora Dunkle, Joseph P. Lane, and Joey F. George (1986). *The Future of Information Systems in Local Governments.* Public Policy Research Organization, Irvine, CA.

Kraemer, Kenneth L., John Leslie King, Debora Dunkle, Joseph P. Lane, and Joey F. George (1985). Microcomputer Use and Policy, *Baseline Data Reports* 17(1). Washington, DC: International Management Association.

Laudon, Kenneth (1974). *Computers and Bureaucratic Reform.* John Wiley and Sons, New York.

Lenk, Klaus (1980). Computer Use in Public Administration: Implications for the Citizen. In Abbe Mowshowitz, ed., *Human Choice and Computers,* 2, pp. 193–212. North-Holland Publishing Company, New York.

Meyers, Charles A., ed. (1967). *The Impact of Computers on Management.* MIT Press, Cambridge, MA.

National Association for State Information Systems (1985). *Information Systems Technology in State Government.* Council of State Governments, Lexington KY.

National Association for State Information Systems (1986). *Information Systems Technology in State Government.* Council of State Governments, Lexington, KY.

Norris, Donald, and V. Webb (1983). *Microcomputers, Baseline Data Report.* International City Management Association, Washington D.C.

Office of Technology Assessment (1981). *Computer-Based National Information Systems.* U.S. Congress, Washington, DC.

Office of Technology Assessment (1985). *Automation of America's Offices.* U.S. Congress, Washington, DC.

Perry, James, L., and Kenneth L. Kraemer (1979). *Technological Innovation in American Local Governments.* Pergamon, New York.

Reinermann, Heinrich (1985). "Speyerer Thesen zu 'Verwaltung und Automation," *der ftaedtetag* 3 (March): 197–199.

Reinermann, Heinrich (1986). *Verwaltungsinnovation und Informationsmanagement: 92 Speyerer Thesen zur Bewaeltigung der Informationtechnischen Herausforberung.* No. 42, Heidelberger Forum. R.V. Decker and C.F. Muller, Heidelberg.

Robey, Daniel (1981). Computers, Information Systems and Organizational Structure. *Communications of the ACM* 24: 679–687.

Rushinek, A., and S. Rushinek (1985). The effects of sources of applications programs on user satisfaction: an empirical study of micro, mini, and mainframe computers. Paper presented at the ACM Conference on End User Computing, Management Information Systems Research Center, University of Minnesota, May 2–3.

Westin, Alan, and Kenneth Laudon (1986). Information Technology and the Social Security Administration: 1935–1990. Research Monograph completed for office of Technology Assessment, United States Congress. Panel on Information Technology and Democratic Government. Office of Technology Assessment, Washington, D.C.

Westin, Alan, and Kenneth Laudon, Forthcoming. *Information Technology and the Social Security Administration.* Harvard University Press, Cambridge, MA.

Whisler, Thomas L. (1976). The Impact of Information Technology on Organizational Control. In Charles A. Meyers, ed., *The Impact of Computers on Management,* pp. 16–40. MIT Press, Cambridge, MA.

P·A·R·T · III

Computerization and the Transformation of Work

P·A·R·T· III

Introduction

Computerization and the Transformation of Work

Charles Dunlop • *Rob Kling*

Work, Technology and Social Change

This section examines the extent to which computer-based systems are organized to enhance or degrade the quality of working life for clerks, administrative staff, professionals, and managers. We pay a lot of attention to computerization in work for three reasons. First, work is a major component of many people's lives. Wage income is the primary way that most people between the ages of 22 and 65 obtain money for food, housing, clothing, transportation, etc. The United States' population is about 250 million and well over 100 million work for a living. So, major changes in the nature of work —the number of jobs, the nature of jobs, career opportunities, job content, social relationships at work, working conditions of various kinds—can affect a significant segment of society.

Second, in the United States, most wage earners work 30–60 hours per week—a large fraction of their waking lives. And people's experiences at work, whether good or bad, can shape other aspects of their lives as well. Work pressures or work pleasures can be carried home to families. Better jobs give people some room to grow when they seek more responsible or complex positions, whereas stifled careers often breed boredom and resentment in comparably motivated people. Although people vary considerably in what kinds of experiences and opportunities they want from a job, few people would be thrilled with a monotonous and socially isolated job, even if it were to pay very well.

Third, computerization has touched more people more visibly in their work than in any other kind of setting—home, schools, churches, banking, and so on. Workplaces are good places to examine how the dreams and dilemmas of computerization really work out for large numbers of people under an immense variety of social and technical conditions.

When specialists discuss computerization and work, they often appeal to strong implicit images about the transformations of work in the last one hundred years and the role that technologies have played in some of those changes. In 19th-century North America, there was a major shift from farms to factories as the primary workplaces. Those shifts—often associated with the industrial revolution—continued well into the early 20th century. Industrial technologies such as the steam engine played a key role in the rise of industrialism. But ways of organizing work also altered significantly. The assembly line with relatively high-volume, low-cost production and standardized, fragmented jobs was a critical advance in the history of industrialization. During the last 100 years, farms also were increasingly mechanized, with motorized tractors, harvesters, and other powerful equipment replacing horse-drawn plows and hand-held tools. The farms also have been increasingly reorganized. Family farms run by small groups have been dying out, and have been bought up (or replaced by) huge corporate farms with battalions of managers, accountants, and hired hands.

Our 20th-century economy has been marked by the rise of human services in areas such as banking, insurance, travel, education, and health. And many of the earliest commercial computer systems were bought by large service organizations such as banks and insurance companies. (By some estimates, the finance industries bought about 30% of the computer hardware in the United States in the 1980s.) During the last three decades, computer use has spread to virtually every kind of workplace, although large firms are still the dominant investors in computer-based systems. Since offices are the predominant site of computerization, it is helpful to focus on offices in examining the role that these systems play in altering work.

Today, the management of farms and factories is frequently supported with computer systems in their offices. Furthermore, approximately 50% of the staff of high-tech manufacturing firms are white collar workers who make use of such systems—engineers, accountants, marketing specialists, etc. There is also some computerization in factory production lines through the introduction of numerically controlled machine tools and industrial robots. And certainly issues such as worklife quality and managerial control are just as real on the shop floor as in white-collar areas. (See Shaiken, 1986; Zuboff, 1988.) Although our selections examine white collar work, we invite the reader to consider the parallels between the computerization of blue-collar work and that of white-collar work. Many studies of the computerization of blue-collar work focus on factories (e.g., Noble, 1984; Shaiken, 1986; Weekley, 1983). Factories employ a significant fraction of blue-collar workers, but not a majority. Some of the major blue-collar occupations that are not factory jobs include bus and truck drivers, heavy equipment operators, construction workers, appliance repair personnel, automobile and airplane mechanics, gas station attendants, dockworkers, gardeners, and janitors. Factories have been the site of some major computerization projects, as in the use of robots for welding and painting and the use of numerically controlled machinery. But many other blue-collar jobs are being influenced by computerizations as well.

The Transformation of Office Work

Office work has always involved keeping records. We don't have many detailed accounts of the earliest offices—which date back before the Middle Ages. Today, offices with dozens of clerks carrying out similar tasks are commonplace. Before the 20th century, the majority of offices were small and were often the workplace of a single businessman or professional who kept informal records (Delgado, 1979). The shape of offices—the way work is organized, the role of women in their operation, career lines, and office technologies—has been radically transformed in the last 100 years.

Novelists like Charles Dickens have written some detailed descriptions of 19th-century English clerks. They were often viewed as a dull bunch of sickly men who had safe but tedious jobs. In the 19th century, information was recorded by clerks using pen and ink, and copies were also made by hand. There were no powerful technologies for assisting one's hand in writing, copying, or even doing calculations. Filing systems were relatively makeshift, and there weren't standardized sizes of forms such as 3 × 5" cards or letter-size paper. Clerical work was a man's job and was a common route for learning a business and becoming a potential owner.

In the early 20th century, the technologies and organization of office work underwent substantial change. Firms began to adopt telephones and typewriters, both of which had been recently invented. By the 1930s and 1940s, many manufacturers devised electromechanical machines to help manipulate, sort, and tally specialized paper records automatically. Some of the more expensive pieces of equipment, such as specialized card-accounting machines, were much more affordable and justifiable in organizations that centralized their key office activities.

Although new equipment was often adopted to enhance the efficiency of offices, its use was tied to more widespread changes in the shape of organizations: the shifts in control to central administrators, and an increase in the number of jobs that were mostly being filled by women. Women began to work in offices as typewriter operators and clerks, and were typically viewed as short-term job-holders, working between school and marriage during their early to mid-twenties. As larger firms hired professional managers, many aspiring professionals turned to graduate schools rather than apprenticeships to learn their craft. Increasingly, specialized colleges rather than on-the-job training became the key entry point for professional and managerial careers. And with these careers dominated by males, clerical work became the province of women who could not readily move into the upper cadres of professional or managerial life.

This sketch indicates some of the key themes that permeate discussions of computerization and the quality of worklife: how efficient and flexible work will be, who controls the work that is done and how it is organized, how work is divided by gender, and who shares in the benefits of technological and organizational change.

Businesses such as insurance companies and banks, along with public agencies, adopted computer-based information systems on a large scale in the 1960s. Many of the early digital computer systems replaced electromechanical paper-card systems. The earliest systems were designed for batch operation. Clerks filled in paper forms with information about a firm's clients, and the forms were then periodically sent to a special group of keypunchers to translate the data onto cardboard cards. These "Hollerith cards" each stored one line of data, up to 80 characters. They were punched with a series of holes for each character or number. Keypunch machines were clanky devices with a typewriter-style keyboard, a bin for storing blank cards, and a holder for the card being punched. There was no simple way for a keypunch operator to correct an error. Cards containing errors (e.g., a letter *s* instead of an *a*) had to be completely repunched. The punched cards were then taken to a data-processing department for a weekly or monthly "run," during which time records were updated and reports were produced. Errors often took a few cycles—sometimes weeks or months—to identify and correct. Using these early computerized systems required immense precision and care, since inaccuracies were detected and corrected very slowly. In addition, the data from one information system were usually formatted in a way that did not make them accessible to other systems. Professionals and managers often waited a few months for a new kind of report, and reports that required merging data from several separate systems were often viewed as prohibitively complex, time-consuming, and expensive to create. The earliest computer systems were speedier than the hand in processing large volumes of highly specialized transactions, but they were also rigid and cumbersome for many people who used them.

Furthermore, the transaction-processing and report-generating programs were usually written by specialized programmers who were organized into specialized data-processing departments. Often, the large specialized computer systems, their operators, and their programmers were all located in basement offices—isolating them from organizational life. During the last 20 years, most organizations have reorganized their computer-based information systems to be more responsive and flexible, and to support a richer array of organizational activities. Terminals connected to shared databases or microcomputers are commonplace in today's organizations. But have jobs improved in a way that is commensurate with the technical improvement in computer systems?

In our first selection, Vincent Giuliano examines the shift of office technologies from pen and paper through typewriters and mechanical devices, and again through interactive computer-based systems available on every desk. He argues that the social organization of office work is evolving through three stages: (a) an informal "preindustrial" office; (b) a highly regimented "industrial" office; and (c) a flexible "information-age" office in which operations are much more integrated than in the industrial office. There are major technical differences in Giuliano's illustrations of these archetypical offices. His preindustrial office relies on telephones, paper, and organized files. His industrial office relies on batch-run computerized information systems, as well as paper and telephones. And his information-age office relies on desktop computing linked to interactive databases on every desk. Giuliano characterizes the information-age office as one that "exploits new technology to preserve the best aspects of the preindustrial office and avoid their failings. At its best, it combines terminal-based work stations, a continuously updated database, and communications to attain high efficiency along with a return to people-centered work rather than machine-centered work. In the information-age office the machine is paced to the needs and abilities of the person who works with it. . . . The mechanization of office work is an essential element in the transformation of American society to one in which information work is the chief economic activity."

Giuliano's article paints a very optimistic portrait of technological and social change —one containing key elements of the *technological utopianism*, which we discussed in our introduction to Part I. Giuliano portrays information-age office work in utopian terms —flexible and efficient, cooperative and interesting. His argument illustrates technological utopianism because it assumes that better technologies necessarily create better jobs. This does not mean that Giuliano is completely "wrong." But it can lead the critical reader to ask whether advanced computer systems might not also be compatible with the informal preindustrial office or formalized and regimented industrial office organizations. Giuliano's article also illustrates the typical confusion between (a) information-oriented work and (b) the use of specific technologies. All of his illustrations refer to offices that are exclusively devoted to information-handling in some form. But there is no substantive rationale for labeling any of these office forms as "information-age" offices. The label glamorizes the kind of office technology that Giuliano would like to see widespread —interactive computer systems linked to integrated databases. Giuliano overlooks the fact that there was a substantial information work force in the United States by 1900, and it approached 30% of the work force by 1950—long before electronic computer systems of any kind were routine fixtures of white-collar work (see Kling, in press; Kling and Turner, 1991).

Some other analysts who examine computerization and work harbor viewpoints less utopian than Giuliano's. Discussions of women and computing often focus on clerical work because about one-third of the women in the work force are clerks. Conversely, about 80% of the 18 million clerks in the United States in 1988 were women. Women work in every occupation from janitors to ambassadors for the federal government, but they are not equally represented in the higher-status and better-paid professions. Less than 30% of the nation's one million programmers and systems analysts were women in 1988. But the nation's 14.6 million female clerks vastly outnumbered the nation's 300,000 female programmers and systems analysts in 1988. The typical female computer user today is a clerk who processes transactions—payroll, inventory, airline reservations, etc.

In our second selection, Iacono and Kling examine how the dramatic improvements in office technologies over the past 100 years have sometimes made many clerical jobs much more interesting, flexible, and skill-rich. But the authors also observe that these changes, especially those involving increased skill requirements, have not brought commensurate improvements in career opportunities, influence, or clerical salaries. They examine the actual changes in clerical work that have taken place over the last 100 years, from the introduction of the first typewriters through whole generations of office equipment— mechanical accounting machines, telephones, and photocopiers. Each generation of equipment has made certain tasks easier. At the same time, clerical work shifted from a predominantly male occupation, which provided an entry route to higher levels of management, to a predominantly female occupation that has been ghettoized. Iacono and Kling criticize Giuliano's utopianism by arguing that a new generation of integrated computer-based office systems will not automatically alter the pay, status, and careers of clerks without explicit attention.[1] Further, they argue that computerization is a continuous process which doesn't stop when a new kind of equipment is acquired (also see Kling, 1987; Kling and Iacono, 1989).

---

[1]See Iacono and Kling (1987) for a much more detailed version of this analysis.

Their observations take on more force when one remembers that the vast majority of working women are concentrated in a few occupations. Between 1950 and 1980, the fraction of women's jobs in clerical work rose from 27.4% to 33.8%. The fraction of women's jobs labelled "managerial" increased at a much more rapid rate, from 4.3% to 6.8%. In 1980, one working woman in three was a clerk, and one in 15 was a "manager."[2] Consequently, the way that clerical work is computerized affects a huge percentage of working women.

Control Over Work Processes

An important aspect of work life is the issue of who controls the way that work is organized, the way that people communicate, and workers' levels of skills. In the 1980s, many professionals became enamored with microcomputers. They became the new electronic typewriter for writers of all kinds. Engineers set aside their slide rules and electronic calculators for software that mechanized their calculations and produced graphic data displays. Accountants helped drive the demand for micros with their passion for computerized spreadsheets. And so on. Many professionals became hooked on the relative ease and speed of their computer tools and dreaded any return to manual ways of working. They often adopted computers and adapted them to their work in ways that enhanced their control. *Work still remained labor intensive,* since the working week did not diminish in length, but it sometimes became more fun, or at least less tedious. However, there is major controversy about the extent to which the romance between professionals and computing might be short-lived.

In Giuliano's account, managers organized "industrial-age" offices for efficiency, and they will organize "information-age" offices in a way that enhances the quality of jobs as well. But some observers argue that managers will not give up substantial control to their subordinates. Andrew Clement, for example, argues that the close monitoring of employee behavior represents the logical extension of a dominant management paradigm —pursuit of control over all aspects of the business enterprise. Indeed some believe that to manage is to control: "[M]anagement may be called 'the profession of control'" (Clement, 1984).

Some authors argue that the industrialization of clerical work sets the stage for the industrialization of professional work as well. In "The Social Dimensions of Office Automation," Abbe Mowshowitz summarizes his sharp vision in these concise terms:

> Our principal point is that the lessons of the factory are the guiding principles of office automation. In large offices, clerical work has already been transformed into factory-like

---

[2] Between 1950 and 1980, more women entered various professions. The change in professional employment rose from 12.2% of women's jobs in 1950 to 15.9% in 1980. About one working woman in seven was in a professional occupation, but women were most highly concentrated in nursing, social work, librarians and school teaching. Women have become much more visible in technical professions in the last 25 years. In 1966, about 0.4% of the B.S. engineering degrees were awarded to women, while in 1981 about 10% of engineering degrees were awarded to women. In 1981, about one third of the B.S. degrees in computer and information science were awarded to women. However, one should keep in mind that the clerical work force is about 15–20 times as large as the segment of the work force devoted to professional engineering and computer work.

production systems. The latest technology—office automation—is simply being used to consolidate and further a well-established trend. For most clerical workers, this spells an intensification of factory discipline. For many professionals and managers, it signals a gradual loss of autonomy, task fragmentation and closer supervision—courtesy of computerized monitoring. Communication and interaction will increasingly be mediated by computer. Work will become more abstract . . . and opportunities for direct social interaction will diminish. (Mowshowitz, 1986)

Andrew Clement follows up on Mowshowitz's theme in "Office Automation and the Technical Control of Information Workers." He examines the way that IBM has attempted to require mainframes as intermediaries for PC-to-PC communication via its Systems Network Architecture (SNA). He notes

If IBM can effectively assert its technical/organizational vision, then personal computers in large offices will evolve into powerful workstations strongly connected to corporate-wide computer systems. There will be local processing, but important software and data will be centrally managed. In other words, the prospect is that personal computing will be steadily absorbed into a subordinate role within the central hierarchy of corporate computing systems. . . . If this comes about, then the current wave of PCs can be seen as Trojan horses. Introduced under the guise of tools offering autonomy to users, they will be turned into extensions of the central computing systems and used as the means of extending managerial control. (Clement, 1988, p. 241).

One argument against stand-alone microcomputers is that they do not support electronic communication, whether by person-to-person mail or group bulletin boards.[3] Some analysts have hoped that new computer communication technologies, such as electronic mail, would enable workers to bypass rigid bureaucratic procedures (e.g., Hiltz and Turoff, 1978: 142). Some analysts have found that electronic mail can give groups more ability to develop their own culture (Finholt and Sproull, 1990). And some have hoped that electronic mail would reduce the barriers to communication between people at different levels of hierarchy in an organization. But the evidence is mixed. Zuboff (1988) reports an interesting case which can dim these unbridled enthusiasms and lead us to ask under what conditions they are most likely to occur. In a large drug company she studied, managers claimed that their communications to electronic groups were often treated as policy statements, even when they wanted to make informal observations or *ad hoc* decisions. Further, when a group of about 130 professional women formed a private conference that threatened male managers, participation was discouraged by upper managers and soon many participants dropped out (Zuboff, 1988: 382–383). We suspect that electronic communications systems are most likely to facilitate the formation of groups that upper managers deem to be safe, except in those special organizations —like universities and R&D labs—where there are strong norms against censorship. The controversy between technological utopians who see technologies as improving human and organizational behavior and those who see social systems as changing slowly in response to other kinds of social and economic forces will not be resolved by one or two case studies. But the cases are instructive to help focus the debate about what is possible and the conditions under which computer systems of specific kinds alter social life.

---

[3] We will examine computer-based communication in more detail in Section IV.

In our third selection, "Intellectual Assembly Lines," Judith Perrolle examines how managers can use expert systems and other advanced computer technologies to reduce the skill levels of professional jobs.[4] As an analyst of class politics, Perrolle divides the work world into two broad categories: owners and their managerial representatives on the one hand, and workers of various kinds on the other. Class politics analysts assume that these two groups are often in conflict: owners and managers seek to maximize their profits by reducing the costs of producing goods and services by many means, including reducing the costs of labor.

Perrolle draws on Harry Braverman's *Labor and Monopoly Capital,* which argues that owners and managers relentlessly try to enhance their control over workers to reduce labor costs.[5] One major managerial strategy is reducing the skills required for most jobs, thus enabling them to hire less expensive workers. Perrolle illustrates this theme through the example of computerized "application generators." Some of these facilities simplify the production of computer programs so they can be written by clerks paid $20,000 per year. A firm that delegates a lot of programming to clerks rather than to university-trained programmers who are paid $40,000 per year might reduce labor costs sub-stantially. But Perrolle argues that many expert systems will also be applied in ways that reduce the skill levels required for professional jobs. As skill levels of jobs are reduced, so is their pay, autonomy, status, and perhaps intrinsic interest.

The debates about up-skilling and de-skilling are complicated by the ways in which a de-skilled job can be up-skilled for a person who takes it after leaving a much less skilled job. For example, a law firm might organize some of its routine document production so that secretaries, rather than lawyers can do it. That set of tasks—put into a full-time job —might bore a skilled lawyer. But the same tasks might be fascinating for someone who was previously typing correspondence and who is eager to enter a new paralegal line of work.

Workers have often had no systematic voice in the direction of large computerization projects. Sometimes jobs appear to have been up-skilled when managers haven't paid direct attention to skill issues (Danziger and Kraemer, 1986). A few firms have attempted to involve workers in redesigning their own jobs as part of computerization projects (Levering, 1988; Jewett and Kling, 1990). But many organizations appear much more authoritarian or paternalistic. Unions have been the primary means by which workers have tried to counter the preferences of management with their own interests. But white-collar workers are relatively un-unionized. And professionals, the subject of Perolle's article, are particularly hostile to unions.

Authors like Clement, Giuliano, Mowshowitz, and Perrolle make powerful arguments

---

[4] An *expert system* is a computer system that (its designers claim) represents the knowledge of an expert or group of experts in a specific field by a set of symbolic rules. Some classic examples include MYCIN, a program that offers medical diagnosis and treatment plans, DENDRAL, which does spectrographic analysis, and XCON, used by the Digital Equipment Corporation in configuring computer installations. A less arcane example can be found at some local wine shops, where an expert system offers advice on wine selection. For further discussions of expert systems, see our excerpt from *The Fifth Generation* by Edward Feigenbaum and Pamela McCorduck in Part I.

[5] See Kuhn (1989) for a careful empirical examination of Braverman's thesis. See also Wood (1989: 10–11) for a discussion of the literature about Braverman's thesis.

that gain some of their force by identifying systematic conflicts between managers and their subordinates. But they treat organizations as if they are all alike with similar strategies of managerial control. Clear and fairly coherent stories sometimes don't match important patterns of computerization. For example, the information-age office is the only office type that Giuliano associates with computer terminals; in it, computer terminals are located on virtually every desk. It is also the only office that he depicts with plants in his diagrams. There is one photograph of a computerized office in Giuliano's article. It is an insurance claims office that combines an *industrial* work organization of a matrix of desks in an open area with the information-age element of a terminal on every desk . . . and plants! Oddly, Giuliano doesn't comment on the way that this glimpse of the world undermines his clean topology of three ideal types.

Similarly, Perrolle ignores some key aspects of the computerization of professional jobs in the United States. Spreadsheets, like Lotus 1-2-3 and Excel, have been one of the primary kinds of software that fueled the market for PCs in businesses in the mid-1980s. Although it is possible to regiment and de-skill jobs with spreadsheets, the majority of applications seemed to open up new ground for professionals and sometimes even for their clerical assistants. It is possible that professionals and managers, rather than clerks, may become the major users of application generators when they seek new information systems faster than local programmers can devise them. Many organizations and work groups standardize on software, such as word processors, databases, and spreadsheets; but this does not necessarily regiment the overall character of work.

Clement is correct in noting that central systems offer more possibilities for tightened technical standards and control over work; but they do not require it. In fact, electronic mail—one of the premier examples of computer systems that open new possibilities for communication—requires some kind of shared communication system. The coherence of utopian and anti-utopian stories like Giuliano's and Perrolle's gains rhetorical force by suggesting how only one "social logic" can be dominant. In the images of Mowshowitz, Clement, and Perrolle (which follow Braverman's argument), managers seek to tighten control at every turn. Moreover, these lines of analysis ignore the ways that managers sometimes seek to improve productivity through increasing responsibility, pay and morale, rather than tightening control and de-skilling (Jewett and Kling, 1990). And they ignore the way that workers sometimes undermine managerial control systems.[6]

Our fourth selection differs from their view by examining variations in the way that business firms and public agencies organize work and technology. Paul Attewell's article "Big Brother and the Sweatshop" examines the extent to which managers have used computer-based systems to increase their surveillance over workers. Attewell argues that managers have tremendous incentives in principle to learn about and control the work of their subordinates. But he observes that many practical conditions weigh against their using computer systems as instruments of surveillance in the vast majority of workplaces. Attewell's article is especially important because of the care with which he examines a variety of supervisory strategies and the ways that managers work with and without

---

[6] For an incisive analysis, which pre-dates the use of computers, of the ways that workers counteract work monitoring and incentive systems, see Whyte *et al.*, (1955). Part I should be read by anyone who is sure that managerial control systems can be easily perfected.

computerized monitoring systems. He observes that managers are concerned with controlling many resources, not just labor. For example, it's likely that the manager of a work group that manages multimillion-dollar investments will pay most attention to the quality of decisions being made rather than to a few thousand dollars in salary costs. In contrast, the manager of a work group where labor is the most costly resource and where judgmental errors are unlikely to be catastrophic may be very concerned to shave a few thousand dollars off the payroll by having people work to their maximum.

Control Over the Location of Work

It is possible for managers to work with several competing logics. They may be concerned with maintaining some control over their subordinates' time and pay, and also with allowing sufficient flexibility and self-direction to ensure good quality work and retain good employees. In fact, some organizations try to pay less by offering attractive working conditions. One of the interesting possibilities of computerized work—work at home—seems to have gotten stalled because of dilemmas of workplace control. Many self-employed people work at home. Futurists like Alvin Toffler have been especially excited by the possibilities that people who normally commute to a collective office could elect to work at home. In *The Third Wave*, Toffler portrayed homes with computer and communications equipment for work as "electronic cottages." There have been several studies of the pros and cons of firms' giving their employees computer equipment to use at home while communicating with their shared offices via electronic mail (Kraemer & King, 1982; Olson, 1983; Olson, 1989; Huws et al., 1990). Some analysts hoped that work at home will decrease urban congestion during computer hours, give parents more opportunity for contact with young children, and allow people to spend more time in their neighborhoods. However, people who work a substantial fraction of the time at home may be unavailable for meetings, may be less visible to their peers and (therefore) passed over for promotions, and may be difficult to supervise unless they work on a piece-rate system. And some employees may lack sufficient self-discipline for work at home.

Many popular accounts focus on the way that home can be a less distracting place to work than the collective office. We see home as a different kind of place to work—with its own privacies and distractions. Homeworkers report a different set of attractions and distractions at home: sociable neighbors may expect to be able to drop in any time; the refrigerator may beckon others too frequently, and so on. Some parents choose to work at home because they can spend time with their babies and pre-school children, but they often get much less done than at their collective offices.[7] Olson's (1989) study of full-time work at home by computer professionals exemplifies some of the empirical studies. She found reduced job satisfaction, reduced organizational commitment, and higher role conflict in her sample. She also wonders whether work-at-home practices can exacerbate workaholism. Forester (1989) recently critiqued the visions of full-time work at home via telecommuting as a romantic preference. After coming to appreciate the social isolation

---

[7] For an early enthusiastic account of work at home with computing, see Turoff and Hiltz (1983).

reported by several people who worked at home full time, he speculates that many analysts who most enthusiastically champion full-time work at home with computing have never done it themselves. It is still an open question whether many organizations will allow substantial fractions of their work force to work at home with computing part time (1–3 days a week), for reasons of personal flexibility or to facilitate regional transportation plans. We note that few homes are designated for significant home offices, and there are many important questions about the pros and cons of part-time work-at-home with computing (and fax) for those who prefer this option.[8]

A few firms have conducted pilot tests of the electronic cottage concept. And the members of a few occupations, such as journalists, professors, salesmen, and accountants, sometimes take laptop computers on the road when they travel. But the vast majority of firms keep their office-bound work force keystroking in the office rather than at home. Some workers are given computer equipment to use for unpaid overtime work. To date, however, no large firms have dispersed a large fraction of their full-time work force to their homes to work with computer systems. It seems that the desire to maintain control underlies many managers' fears of having their employees work full time at home. It is much easier for managers to be sure that people are putting in a fair day's work in an office from nine to five, than to work out elaborate contracts about the work to be done each week or month.

The Integration of Computing into Work

The vast majority of articles and books about computerization and work are written as if computer systems are highly reliable and graceful instruments. There are relatively few published studies of the ways that people actually use software systems in their work —which features they use, to what extent they encounter problems with systems or gaps in their own skills, how they resolve problems when difficulties arise, how the use of computerized systems alters the coherence and complexity of work.

There do not seem to be single simple answers to these questions. Some organizations computerize some jobs so as to make them as simple as possible. An extreme example is the way that fast food chains have computerized cash registers with special buttons for menu items like cheeseburgers and malts so that they can hire clerks with little math skill. Kraut, Dumais, and Koch (1989) report a case study of customer service representatives in which simplifying work was a major consequence of computerization.

But it is common for images of simplification to dominate talk about computerization, regardless of the complexity of systems. Clement (1990) reports a case of computerization for secretaries in which managers characterized new systems as "super typewriters" that didn't require special training; they were very mistaken. Many of the popular "full featured" PC software packages for text processing, spreadsheets, and databases include hundreds of features. Narratives that focus on the capabilities of systems usually suggest that people can readily have all the advantages that all the features offer; actual behavior

---

[8] Also, see Vitalari and Venkatesh (1987) for an assessment of in-home computing services that examines work-oriented technologies among other systems.

often differs from these expectations. Most people who use these powerful programs seem to learn only a small fraction of the available capabilities—enough to do their most immediate work. Moreover, it is increasingly common for many workers to use multiple computer systems, often with conflicting conventions, further complicating people's ability to "use computer systems to their fullest advantage." Some of these dilemmas can be resolved when organizations adopt relatively uncomplicated systems, train their staffs to use them, and provide consulting for people who have questions. However, many managers believe that supporting computer use with training and consulting is too expensive. Training is not cheap; an organization may pay $500 in labor time for a professional to learn to use a package that costs $150 to purchase.

One of the editors vividly remembers a research administrator of a major food processing firm who was using a popular and powerful spreadsheet to budget projects. He wanted to print out reports in different fonts, such as printing budget categories in larger bolder print. But he was perplexed. He knew that "it could be done" because he saw such a report in an advertisement. He treated his ignorance as a personal failing. He would have had to learn his spreadsheet's macro facility to produce this effect, and there was no clue in his manual about the appropriate strategy. In some organizations he might have turned to an information center with skilled consultants. But in his organization, the PC consultants were already overworked just installing new PCs and had no time to train users or consult on software use. This was not a critical problem for the manager. But it is indicative of the way that many organizations expect white-collar workers to learn to effectively use computer systems on their own, with little support besides limited manuals and advice from co-workers. Most computer systems do not work perfectly, further complicating what users have to learn and how they integrate systems into their work (see Kling and Scacchi, 1979; Gasser, 1986; Clement, 1990).

In our fifth selection, Christine Bullen and John Bennett examine the ways that people actually integrate computer systems to support collaborative work in groups (groupware) into their work. They report how several work groups have attempted to use some of today's best commercially available groupware systems with mixed results. Their informants often report that they value the electronic mail features of these systems as most important, even though each of these systems has many other advertised features. But many groups have found other features hard to use routinely, or simply not worth the effort. (Also see Grudin, 1989.)

More significantly, Bullen and Bennett report that many groups slowly learned that they would have to reorganize their work in order to take best advantage of their groupware. For example, the usage of electronic calendars to schedule meetings requires that all participants keep detailed calendars up to date on the computer system, even if they often spend much of their days out of the office. Many managers and professionals hope that they can computerize effectively by installing appropriate equipment, rather than by reorganizing work when they (re)computerize. Bullen and Bennett make a provocative attempt to characterize those groups that are high performers: they are not always the most computerized. They argue that group members and their managers have worked hard to create work environments that have "clear elevating goals," and that support and reward commitment. These groups have developed effective social systems with coherent goals and related rewards as well as adopting technologies that might help improve their performance.

There is considerable unpublished controversy about this kind of analysis, since many technologists and computer vendors try to convince computer-using organizations that appropriate new technologies alone will improve working styles and organizational effectiveness. During the 1990s interesting technologies such as expert systems, group-ware, and graphic interfaces will be written about by technologists and journalists as if they can significantly improve the ways that people work without requiring important changes in the way that groups organize their work. Careful studies, like Bullen and Bennett's, of work with new computing technologies suggest that new technologies alone are unlikely to be magic potions that can automatically improve work just by appearing in a workplace. (Also see Jewett and Kling, 1990.)

Social Design of Computerized Systems and Work Settings

One of the most exciting recent developments has been the efforts by a variety of computer scientists and social scientists to draw on the social sciences in designing computer systems or their social environments. In Part I on technological utopianism we discussed Grudin's critique of the social assumptions underlying typical uses of certain kinds of shared computer systems—e.g., the assumption that all users of a shared calendar system could access and update it readily as needed.

Our sixth selection, "The Art and Science of Designing Computer Artifacts," examines how the social sciences can inform designers in the planning and development of systems. The author, Pelle Ehn, argues that mathematics is appropriate for examining the efficiency of algorithms, but it is an inappropriate foundation for the design of "end-user" computer systems. He lays out the intellectual basis for the social science content of a curriculum for computer system designers.

In our final selection, "Understanding the Nature of the Office for the Design of Third Wave Office Systems," Jan Mouritsen and Niels Bjorn-Anderson examine the way that highly rationalistic conceptions of office work have undermined the ability of tech-nologists to design "successful" office systems. There are many criteria for assessing the "success" of a computerized office (Kling, 1984), e.g., whether the systems are used routinely, how much they reduce costs, the kinds of new services they provide, and the extent to which they improve work by making the content more interesting or the process more flexible. No computerized system is likely to effect substantial improvement in all of these aspects of organizations simultaneously. The choice of which criteria to emphasize depends upon whose values should be held preeminent in an organization, as well as the range of technical possibilities. Mouritsen and Bjorn-Anderson identify nine themes that would enrich the range of system designs and that would be more likely to lead to systems that are attractive to those whose work is most affected by them.

These last two selections are part of a larger literature about strategies for designing computerized systems so as to improve the work lives of those who work with them (for example, Briefs et al., 1983; Bikson et al., 1989).[9] In fact, many of these analysts argue that

---

[9] Also see the references contained in the selections by Pelle Ehn and by Jan Mouritsen and Niels Bjorn-Anderson.

the effective design of computer systems must go hand in hand with *redesigning the way that work is organized.*[10] They also argue that organizations will not reap important economic benefits from new computer systems without parallel changes in the structure of work responsibilities, relationships, and rewards. These strategies usually require that systems analysts and designers understand many of the work practices, schedules, resource constraints, and other contingencies seen by people who will use the new computerized systems. They also usually require that people who use systems have a substantial role in specifying their designs as well as the altered work practices. One reason that stand-alone microcomputers may have been so attractive for many people is that they gave them more control over the form of computerization and changes in work than did systems that ran on shared computer systems. In addition, the microcomputer users worked in ways that made them less dependent upon having access to busy full-time computer professionals to design and modify systems—thus making their arrangements more adaptable.

The main alternative approaches tend to rely on more formal conceptions of information flows and work (Ellis and Naffah, 1987; Mills *et al.*, 1986). Mouritsen and Bjorn-Anderson are criticizing office and information systems designed from that perspective—one that doesn't take the social nature of work and organizations seriously enough.

One way to ensure that systems are designed effectively for people who will use them is to include user representatives on design teams (Kling, 1984; Briefs *et al.*, 1983). This kind of user participation is particularly effective in the design of customized information systems. Although most computer systems professionals are likely to label themselves as "user oriented," only a fraction of organizations in the United States seem to integrate end-users effectively into system design projects. In Norway, participation has been institutionalized through laws requiring that unionized workers be informed of computerized systems early in their planning and design, and be given positions on design committees (Schneider and Ciborra, 1983). This approach gives workers much more voice than they often have in systems designs, but there are problems of integrating people with weak technical skills into design teams dominated by managers and technologists. It is easiest to involve people effectively in the design of information systems when the number of participants is small, perhaps fewer than 50, than when it is large. Some important computer systems, such as large airline reservations systems, police data systems, and social service payments systems, have thousands of users. In these cases, some participation is better than none, but it is not a panacea. In practice, there are no perfect systems or systems design strategies. But some of the most interesting design work aims to develop computerized systems that are organizationally effective and that also allow people who use them to have a significant voice in shaping their destinies. Design strategies that deny system users much voice seem paternalistic at best and oppressive at worst.

During the 1990s organizations will continue to computerize work—automating new activities and replacing earlier systems with newer technologies. Since organizations, workplaces, and appropriate technologies differ, we do not expect to see single patterns of computerization. The questions about how to change work with computer systems will

---

[10] See, for example, the case studies in Chapter 4 of Levering (1988) and Jewett and Kling (1990).

continue to have immense practical repercussions and will not be automatically resolved by some new kind of computer equipment. And the resulting choices will affect the lives of tens of millions of people. Fortunately, there is a significant body of good research to help make better choices.

Sources

Attewell, Paul (1987). "Big Brother and the Sweatshop: Computer Surveillance in the Automated Office," *Sociological Theory.* 5 (Spring), pp. 87–99.

Bullen, Christine, and John Bennett (1991). "Groupware in Practice: An Interpretation of Work Experience."

Ehn, Pelle (1989). "The Art and Science of Designing Computer Artifacts," *Scandinavian Journal of Information Systems.* 1 (August), pp. 21–42.

Giuliano, Vincent E. (1982). "The Mechanization of Work," *Scientific American.* 247 (September), pp. 148–164.

Kling, Rob, and Suzanne Iacono (1984). "Office Routine: The Automated Pink Collar," *IEEE Spectrum.* 21(6)(June), pp. 73–76.

Mouritsen, Jan, and Niels Bjorn-Anderson (1991). "Understanding Third Wave Information Systems."

Perrolle, Judith (1986). "Intellectual Assembly Lines: The Rationalization of Managerial, Professional and Technical Work," *Computers and the Social Sciences.* 2(3)(July–Sept.), pp. 111–122.

References

Bikson, Tora, J.D. Eveland and Barbara A. Gutek (1989). "Flexible Interactive Technologies for Multi-Person Tasks: Current Problems and Future Prospects," in Margrethe H. Olson (ed.), *Technological Support for Work Group Collaboration,* pp. 89–112, Lawrence Erlbaum Associates, Inc. Hillsdale, N.J.

Braverman, Harry (1974). *Labor and Monopoly Capital.* Monthly Review Press, New York.

Briefs, Ulrich, Claudio Ciborra, and Leslie Schneider (eds.)(1983). *Systems Design for, with, and by the Users.* Proceedings of the IFIP WG 9.1 Working Conference on Systems Design for, with, and by the Users, Riva del Sol, Italy, 20–24 September 1982. North-Holland Pub. Co., New York.

Clement, Andrew (1984). "Electronic Management: New Technology of Workplace Surveillance," *Proceedings, Canadian Information Processing Society Session 84,* Calgary, Alberta (May 9–11), pp. 259–266.

Clement, Andrew (1988). "Office Automation and the Technical Control of Information Workers," Chapter 11 in Vincent Mosko and Janet Wasco (eds.) *The Political Economy of Information.* University of Wisconsin Press, Madison, Wisc.

Clement, Andrew (1990). "Computer Support for Cooperative Work: A Social Perspective on Empowering End Users," *Proceedings of the Conference on Computer Supported Cooperative Work,* Los Angeles, Cal.

Danziger, James, and Kenneth Kraemer (1986). *Computers and People: The Impacts of Computing on End Users in Organizations.* Columbia University Press, New York.

Ehn, Pelle. *Work-Oriented Design of Computer Artifacts* (1989). Arbetslivcentrum, Stockholm. U.S. edition: Lawrence Erlbaum, Hillsdale, N.J. 1989.

Ellis, Clarence Arthur, and N. Naffah (1987). *Design of Office Information Systems.* Springer-Verlag, New York.

Finholt, Tom, and Lee Sproull (1990). "Electronic Groups at Work," *Organization Science* 1(1): 41–64.

Forester, Tom (1989). "The Myth of the Electronic Cottage," in Tom Forester (ed.), *Computers in the Human Context: Information Technology, Productivity, and People*. MIT Press, Cambridge, Ma.

Gasser, Les (1986). "The Integration of Computing and Routine Work," *ACM Transactions on Office Information Systems*. 4(3)(July), pp. 205–225.

Grudin, Jonathan (1989). "Why Groupware Applications Fail: Problems in Design and Evaluation," *Office: Technology and People*. 4(3), pp. 245–264.

Hiltz, Starr Roxanne, and Murray Turoff (1978). *The Network Nation: Human Communication via Computer*. Addison-Wesley Publishing Company, Inc., Reading, Mass.

Hirschheim, Rudi (1985). *Office Automation: A Social and Organizational Perspective*. John Wiley, New York.

Huws, Ursula, Werner Korte, and Simon Robinson (1990). *Telework: Towards the Elusive Office*. John Wiley, New York.

Iacono, Suzanne, and Rob Kling. "Changing Office Technologies and the Transformation of Clerical Jobs," Chapter 4 in Robert Kraut (ed.), *Technology and the Transformation of White Collar Work*. Lawrence Erlbaum and Associates, Hillsdale, NJ.

Jewett, Tom, and Rob Kling (1990). "The Work Group Manager's Role in Developing Computing Infrastructure," *Proceedings of the ACM Conference on Office Information Systems*, Boston, Mass.

Kling, Rob (1984). "Assimilating Social Values in Computer-based Technologies," *Telecommunications Policy*. (June), pp. 127–147.

Kling, Rob (in press). "More Information, Better Jobs? Occupational Stratification and Labor Market Segmentation in the United States' Information Labor Force." *The Information Society*.

Kling, Rob, and Walt Scacchi (1979). "Recurrent Dilemmas of Computer Use in Complex Organizations," *National Computer Conference Proceedings*, pp. 107–115.

Kling, Rob, and Clark Turner (1991). "The Information Labor Force," in Rob Kling, Spencer Olin, and Mark Poster (eds.), *Post-Suburban California*. University of California Press, Los Angeles, CA.

Kraemer, K.L., and J.L. King (1982). "Telecommunications-Transportation Substitution and Energy Productivity," *Telecommunications Policy*. Part I, 6(1), pp. 39–59; Part II, 6(2), pp. 87–99.

Kraut, Robert, Susan Dumais, and Susan Koch (1990). "Computerization, Productivity and Quality of Worklife," *Communications of the ACM*. 32(2)(February), pp. 220–238.

Kuhn, Sarah (1989). "The Limits to Industrialization: Computer Software Development in a Large Commercial Bank," in Stephen Wood (ed.), *The Transformation of Work: Skill, Flexibility and the Labour Process*. Unwin Hyman, London.

Levering, Robert (1988). *A Great Place to Work: What Makes Some Employers So Good (and Most So Bad)*. Random House, New York.

Mills, Harlan D., Richard C. Linger, and Alan R. Hevner (1986). *Principles of Information Systems Analysis and Design*. Academic Press, Orlando.

Noble, David F. (1984). *Forces of Production: A Social History of Industrial Automation*. Knopf, New York.

Olson, Margrethe H. (1983). "Remote Office Work: Changing Work Patterns in Space and Time," *Communications of the ACM*. 26(3)(March), pp. 182–187.

Olson, Margrethe H. (1989). "Work at Home for Computer Professionals: Current Attitudes and Future Prospects," *ACM Transaction on Information Systems*. 7(4)(October), pp. 317–338.

Schneider, Leslie, and Claudio Ciborra (1983). "Technology Bargaining in Norway," in U. Briefs, C. Ciborra, and L. Schneider (eds.), *Systems Design for, with, and by the Users*, Proceedings of the IFIP WG 9.1 Working Conference on Systems Design for, with, and by the Users, Riva del sol, Italy, 20–24 September 1982. North-Holland Pub. Co., New York.

Shaiken, Harley (1986). *Work Transformed: Automation and Labor in the Computer Age*. Lexington Books, Lexington, Mass.

Tracy, Diane (1990). "This State May be Penny-Wise, But it Sure Looks Pound Foolish," *Wall Street Journal*. April 9, p. B1.

Turoff, Murray, and Roxanne Hiltz (1983). "Working at Home or Living in the Office," in *Information Processing, 1983*, Proceedings of the IFIP 9th World Congress, Paris, France. September 1983, pp. 719–725. North Holland, New York.

Vitalari, Nicholas, and Alladi Venkatesh (1987). "In-home Computing Services and Information Services: A Twenty Year Analysis of the Technology and Its Impacts," *Telecommunications Policy*. (March), pp. 65–81.

Weekley, Thomas L. (1983). "Workers, Unions, and Industrial Robotics," *Annals, American Academy of Political and Social Sciences*. 470, pp. 146–151.

Whyte, William F., Melville Dalton, Donald Roy, Leonard Sayles, and Associates (1955). *Money and Motivation: An Analysis of Incentives in Industry*. Harper and Row, New York.

Winograd, Terry (1988). "A Language/Action Perspective on the Design of Cooperative Work," *Human-Computer Interaction*. 3(1)(1987–88), pp. 3–30. Reprinted in Irene Greif (1988). *Computer-Supported Cooperative Work: A Book of Readings*, Morgan-Kaufmann, San Mateo, California, pp. 623–653.

Wood, Stephen (1989). "The Transformation of Work," in Stephen Wood (ed.), *The Transformation of Work: Skill, Flexibility and the Labour Process*. Unwin Hyman, London.

Zuboff, Shoshana (1988). *In the Age of the Smart Machine: The Future of Work and Power*. Basic Books, New York.

Further Reading

Attewell, Paul (1987). The Deskilling Controversy, *Work and Occupations*. 14(3), pp. 323–346.

Bansler, Jorgen (1989). "Systems Development in Scandinavia: Three Theoretical Schools," *Office Technology and People*. 4(2).

Bikson, Tora K. (1987). "Understanding the Implementation of Office Technology," Chapter 9 in Robert Kraut (ed.), *Technology and the Transformation of White Collar Work*. Erlbaum, Hillsdale, N.J.

Checkland, Peter (1981). *Systems Thinking, Systems Practice*. John Wiley, New York.

Clement, Andrew, and C.C. Gotlieb (1987). "Evolution of an Organizational Interface: The New Business Department at a Large Insurance Firm," *ACM Transactions on Office Information Systems*. 5(4)(October), pp. 328–339.

Floyd, Christiane (1987). "Outline of a Paradigm Change in Software Engineering," in Gro Bjerknes, Pelle Ehn, and Morten Kyng (eds.), *Computers and Democracy: A Scandinavian Challenge*. Gower Pub. Co., Brookfield, Vt.

Galegher, Jolene, Robert Kraut, and Carmen Egido (eds.)(1990). *Intellectual Teamwork: Social and Technological Foundations of Cooperative Work*. Lawrence Erlbaum Associates, Hillsdale, N.J.

George, Joey, Rob Kling, and Suzanne Iacono (1990). "The Role of Training and Support in Desktop Computing," in Kate M. Kaiser and Hans J. Oppeland (eds.), *Desktop Information Technology: Organizational Worklife in the 1990s*. Elsevier/North Holland, Amsterdam.

Gerson, Elihu M. and Susan Leigh Star 1986). "Analyzing Due Process in the Workplace," *ACM Transactions on Office Information Systems*. 4(3)(July), pp. 257–270.

King, Morton, and Joan Greenbaum. *Design at Work: Cooperative Work of Computer Systems*. Lawrence Erlbaum, Hillsdale, N.J.

Kleiner, Art (ed.)(1985). The Health Hazards of Computers: A Guide to Worrying Intelligently," *Whole Earth Review*. 48 (Fall), pp. 80–93.

Kling, Rob (1987). "Computerization as an Ongoing Social and Political Process," in Gro Bjerknes, Pelle Ehn, and Morten Kyng (eds.), *Computers and Democracy: A Scandinavian Challenge*. Gower Pub. Co., Brookfield, Vt.

Kling, Rob (1987). "Defining the Boundaries of Computing Across Complex Organizations," in Richard Boland and Rudy Hirschheim (eds.), *Critical Issues in Information Systems*. John Wiley, London.

Kling, Rob, and Suzanne Iacono (1984). "Computing as an Occasion for Social Control," *Journal of Social Issues*. 40(3), pp. 77–96.

Kling, Rob, and Suzanne Iacono (1989). "Desktop Computerization and the Organization of Work," in Tom Forester (ed.), *Computers in the Human Context: Information Technology, Productivity, and People*. MIT Press.

Kraut, Robert E. (1987). "Predicting the Use of Technology: The Case of Telework," pp. 113–133 in Robert E. Kraut (ed.), *Technology & the Transformation of White Collar Work*. Erlbaum, Hillsdale, N.J.

Kraut, Robert E. (ed.)(1987). *Technology & the Transformation of White Collar Work*. Erlbaum, Hillsdale, N.J.

P·A·R·T·III

1

The Mechanization of Office Work

Vincent E. Giuliano

Mechanization was applied first to the processing of tangible goods: crops in agriculture, raw materials in mining, industrial products in manufacturing. The kind of work that is benefiting most from new technology today, however, is, above all, the processing of an intangible commodity: information. As machines based mainly on the digital computer and other microelectronic devices become less expensive and more powerful, they are being introduced for gathering, storing, manipulating and communicating information. At the same time, information-related activities are becoming ever more important in American society and the American economy; the majority of workers are already engaged in such activities, and the proportion of them is increasing. The changes can be expected to profoundly alter the nature of the primary locus of information work: the office.

An office is a place where people read, think, write and communicate; where proposals are considered and plans are made; where money is collected and spent; where businesses and other organizations are managed. The technology for doing all these things is changing with the accelerating introduction of new information-processing machines, programs for operating them and communications systems for interconnecting them. The transformation entails not only a shift from paper to electronics but also a fundamental change in the nature and organization of office work, in uses of information and communications and even in the meaning of the office as a particular place occupied during certain hours.

Office mechanization started in the second half of the 19th century. In 1850 the quill pen had not yet been fully replaced by the steel nib, and taking pen to paper was still

---

the main technology of office work. By 1900 a number of mechanical devices had established a place in the office, notably Morse's telegraph, Bell's telephone, Edison's dictating machine and the typewriter.

In 1850 there were at most a few dozen "writing machines" in existence, and each of them was a unique, handmade creation. Typewriters were among the high-technology items of the era; they could be made in large numbers and at a reasonable cost only with the adoption and further development of the techniques of precision manufacturing with interchangeable parts developed by Colt and Remington for the production of pistols and rifles during the Civil War. By the late 1890's dozens of companies were manufacturing typewriters of diverse designs, with a variety of layouts for the keyboard and with ingenious mechanical arrangements. (Some even had the type arrayed on a moving, cylindrical element and thus were 70 years ahead of their time.) By 1900 more than 100,000 typewriters had been sold and more than 20,000 new machines were being built each year. As precision in the casting, machining and assembly of metal parts improved and the cost of these processes was lowered, typewriters became generally affordable in offices and homes. The evolution of typewriter usage was comparable to what is now taking place—in only about a decade—in the usage of office computers and small personal computers.

With the typewriter came an increase in the size of offices and in their number, in the number of people employed in them and in the variety of their jobs. There were also changes in the social structure of the office. For example, office work had remained a male occupation even after some women had been recruited into factories. (Consider the staffing of Scrooge's office in Charles Dickens' "A Christmas Carol.") Office mechanization was a force powerful enough to overcome a longstanding reluctance to have women work in a male environment. Large numbers of women were employed in offices as a direct result of the introduction of the typewriter [see "The Mechanization of Women's Work," by Joan Wallach Scott, page 87].

The first half of the 20th century saw a further refinement of existing office technologies and the introduction of a number of new ones. Among the developments were the teletypewriter, automatic telephone switching, ticker tape, the electric typewriter, duplicating machines and copiers, adding machines and calculators, tape recorders for dictation, offset printing presses small enough for office use and data-processing equipment operated with punched paper cards. The new devices were accompanied by a rapid expansion in the volume of office communications and in the number of people engaged in white-collar work.

The first computers in offices were crude and very expensive by today's standards. By the mid-1960's most large businesses had turned to computers to facilitate such routine "back office" tasks as storing payroll data and issuing checks, controlling inventory and monitoring the payment of bills. With advances in solid-state circuit components and then with microelectronics the computer became much smaller and cheaper. Remote terminals, consisting of either a teletypewriter or a keyboard and a video display, began to appear, generally tapping the central processing and storage facilities of a mainframe computer. There was steady improvement in the cost-effectiveness of data-processing equipment.

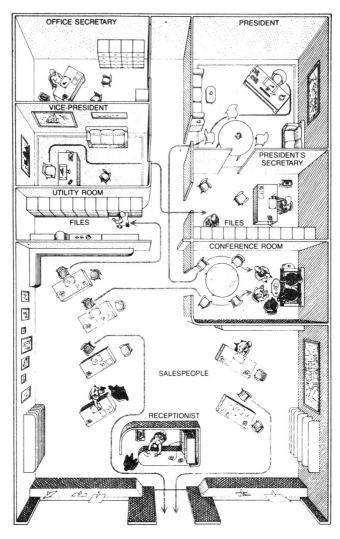

Figure 1. Three stages of office organization are defined by the author: preindustrial, industrial and information-age. Preindustrial organization dates back to the mid-19th century but is still
typical of most professional, small-business and even corporate-management offices today. It is
represented here by a hypothetical real-estate brokerage. There is little systematic organization.
Each person does his job more or less independently, moving about as necessary (*gray lines*) to
retrieve a file, to take a client to see a property or to attend a meeting where the sale of a house
is made final. Individuals can have different styles of work, and human relations are important. The
preindustrial model of office organization can still be effective for some small operations. Conversion to information-age methods is fairly easy.

All of this was reflected in a remarkable expansion of the computer industry. The late 1960's and the 1970's also saw the advent of inexpensive copiers, minicomputers, small and affordable private automated branch exchangers (electronic switchboards), the word processor (the typewriter's successor) and then, toward the end of the 1970's, the microcomputer.

An anthropologist visiting an office today would see much that he would have seen 25 years ago. He would see people reading, writing on paper, handling mail, talking with one another face to face and on the telephone, typing, operating calculators, dictating, filing and retrieving files from metal cabinets. He would observe some new behavior, too. He would see a surprising number of people working with devices that have a typewriter-like keyboard but also have a video screen or an automatic printing element. In 1955 the odds were overwhelming that someone working at an alphabetic keyboard device was female and either a typist or a key-punch operator. No longer. The keyboard workers are both female and male and the typewriter-like devices now accomplish an astonishing variety of tasks.

Some of the keyboard workers are indeed secretaries preparing or correcting conventional correspondence on word processors. Other workers are at similar keyboards that serve as computer terminals. In one office they are managers checking the latest information on production performance, which is stored in a corporate data base in the company's mainframe computer. Economists are doing econometric modeling, perhaps calling on programs and data in a commercial service bureau across the continent. Librarians are working at terminals connected to a national network that merges the catalogues of thousands of participating libraries. Attorneys and law clerks are at terminals linked to a company whose files can be searched to retrieve the full text of court decisions made anywhere in the country. Airline personnel and travel agents make reservations at terminals of a nationwide network. Some of the devices are self-contained personal computers that engineers and scientists, business executives and many other people depend on for computation, data analysis, scheduling and other tasks.

Many of the users of terminals and small computers can communicate with one another and with their home offices through one of the half-dozen "electronic mail" networks now in existence in the U.S. A surprising number of people are doing these things not only in the office but also at home, on the factory floor and while traveling. This article was written with a portable personal computer at home, in a hotel in Puerto Rico and at a cottage in New Hampshire. I have drawn on information from personal files in my company's mainframe computer and have also checked parts of the text with colleagues by electronic mail.

What all of this adds up to is a shift from traditional ways of doing office work based mainly on paper to reliance on a variety of keyboard-and-display devices, or personal work stations. A work station may or may not have its own internal computer, but it is ultimately linked to a computer (or to several of them) and to data bases, communications systems and any of thousands of support services. Today the work stations in widest service handle written and numerical information. In less than a decade machines will be generally available that also handle color graphics and store and transmit voice messages, as the most advanced work stations do today.

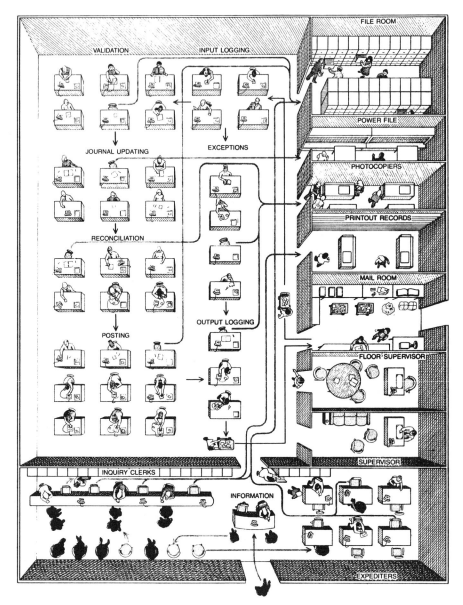

Figure 2. Industrial office, essentially a production line, has been favored for operations handling a large number of transactions, as in this claims-adjustment department of an insurance company. Tasks are fragmented and standardized. Documents are carried from the mail room to the beginning of the production line and eventually emerge at the other end. Successive groups of clerks carry out incremental steps in the processing of a claim; in general they leave their desks only to retrieve files or to examine computer printouts. If clients make inquiries, they are dealt with by clerks who may be able in time to answer a specific question but can seldom follow through to solve a problem. The work is usually dull. The flow of information is slow and service is poor.

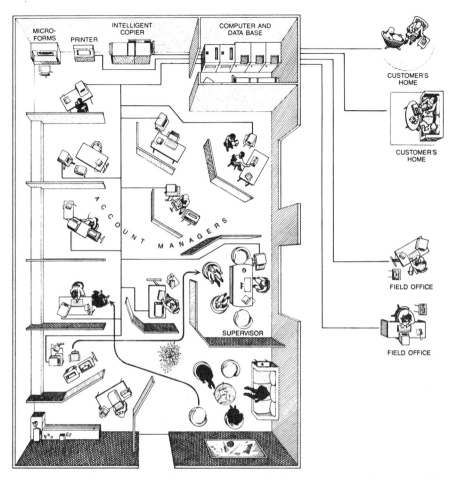

Figure 3. Information-age office exploits new technology to preserve the values of the preindustrial office while handling a large volume of complex information. The drawing shows an information-age claims-adjustment department. Each adjuster mans a work station, which is linked to a computer that maintains and continuously updates all client records. Each adjuster can therefore operate as an account manager, handling all operations for a few clients rather than one repetitive operation for a large number of clients. Necessary action can be taken immediately. Forms are updated and letters are written at the same work station that gives access to stored data, and the forms and letters can be printed automatically. The same facilities are available to adjusters visiting a client's home or working in one of the company's field offices (*right*). The work is more interesting, service to clients is improved and costs are reduced.

My colleagues and I at Arthur D. Little, Inc., expect that by 1990 between 40 and 50 percent of all American workers will be making daily use of electronic-terminal equipment. Some 38 million terminal-based work stations of various kinds are by then likely to be installed in offices, factories and schools. There may be 34 million home terminals (although most of them may not function as full work stations). In addition we expect there will be at least seven million portable terminals resembling today's hand-held calculators, most of them quite inexpensive.

Until recently most work stations and their supporting devices and data-base resources were designed to serve a single purpose: to prepare text, access stock-market data or make air-travel reservations, for example. The stockbroker's terminal started out as a replacement for the ticker tape, the word processor as a replacement for the typewriter. The first terminals therefore served as complete work stations only for people who were engaged in a more or less repetitive task.

Now the capabilities of the work station have been extended by developments in the technology of information processing, in communications and in enhancements of the "software," or programs, essential to the operation of any computer system. A variety of resources and functions have become accessible from a single work station. The stockbroker can not only check current prices with his terminal but also retrieve from his company's data base a customer's portfolio and retrieve from a distant data base information on stock-price trends over many years. Millions of current and historical news times can also be called up on the screen. He can issue orders to buy or sell stock, send messages to other brokers and generate charts and tables, which can then be incorporated into a newsletter addressed to customers. It is not only in large corporations that such tools are found. Low-cost personal computers and telecommunications-based services available to individuals make it possible for them to enjoy a highly mechanized work environment; indeed, many professionals and many office workers in small businesses have work station resources superior to those in large corporations where the pace of office mechanization has been slow.

By the year 2000 there will surely be new technology for information handling, some of which cannot now be foreseen. What can be predicted is that more capable machinery will be available at lower cost. Already a personal computer the size of a briefcase has the power and information-storage capacity of a mainframe computer of 1955. For a small computer an approximate measure of performance is the "width" of the data path, that is, the number of bits, or binary digits, processed at a time. Computational speed can be represented roughly by the frequency in megahertz of the electronic clock that synchronizes all operations in the central processor. Memory capacity is expressed in bytes; a byte is a group of eight bits. The customary unit is the kilobyte, which is not 1,000 bytes but rather 2^{10}, or 1,024. Only three years ago a powerful personal computer had 48 kilobytes of working memory and an eight-bit processor running at a rate of one megahertz.

Today about the same amount of money buys a machine with 256 kilobytes of working memory and a 16-bit processor chip that runs at four megahertz or more. Storage capacity and processing power will continue to increase—and their costs will continue to decrease—geometrically. By the year 2000 memory and processing power should be so cheap that they will no longer be limiting factors in the cost of information handling; they will be available as needed anywhere in an organization. The next 20 years will also see the continuing extension of high-capacity communications, of networks for the exchange of information between work stations and other computers and of centralized data banks. Together these developments will provide access to information, to processing capacity and to communications facilities no matter where the worker is or what time it is.

New technology inevitably affects the organization of work. One can define three evolutionary stages of office organization, which I shall designate preindustrial, industrial and information-age. Each state is characterized not only by its technology but also by its style of management, personnel policies, hierarchy of supervisory and managerial staff, standards of performance and human relations among office workers and between the workers and their clients or customers.

The first two stages correspond to the well-understood artisan and industrial models of production; the nature of the third stage is only now becoming clear. The operation of a preindustrial office depends largely on the performance of individuals, without much benefit from either systematic work organization or machines. The industrial office organizes people to serve the needs of a rigid production system and its machines. The information-age office has the potential of combining systems and machines to the benefit of both individual workers and their clients.

Most small-business, professional, general-management and executive offices are still at the preindustrial stage. In a preindustrial office little conscious attention if any is paid to such things as a systematic flow of work, the efficiency or productivity of work methods or modern information technologies. What information-handling devices are present (telephones, copiers and even word processors) may be central to the operation, but there is no deliberate effort to get the maximum advantage from them. Good human relations often develop among the employees; loyalty, understanding and mutual respect have major roles in holding the organization together. An employee is expected to learn his job, to do what is wanted and needed and to ask for help when it is necessary. Varied personal styles of work shape the style of the operation and contribute to its success.

Preindustrial office organization generally works well only as long as the operation remains small in scale and fairly simple. It is inefficient for handling either a large volume of transactions or complex procedures requiring the coordination of a variety of data sources. If the work load increases in such an office, or if business conditions get more complex, the typical response is to ask people to work harder and then to hire more employees. Such steps are likely to be of only temporary benefit, however. Without the help of additional systems or technology, effectiveness and morale may soon begin to break down.

One response to the limitations of preindustrial office organization has been to bring to bear in the office the principles of work simplification, specialization and time-and-motion efficiency articulated for factory work some 70 years ago by Frederick W. Taylor. The result is the industrial-stage office, which is essentially a production line. Work (in the form of paper documents or a folder of papers related to one customer) moves from desk to desk just as parts move from station to station along an assembly line. Each worker gets a sheaf of papers in an "in" box; his job is to perform one or two incremental steps in their processing and then to pass the paper through an "out" box to the next person, who performs the next steps. Jobs are simple, repetitive and unsatisfying. A worker may do no more than staple or file or copy, or perhaps check and confirm or correct one element of data. And of course everyone has to work together during the same hours in the same office to sustain the flow of paper.

The production-line approach has been considered particularly suitable for office activities in which the main job is handling a large volume of customer transactions, as in sending out bills or processing insurance claims. Many large production-line offices were instituted in the early days of computerization, when information had to be gathered into large batches before it could be processed by the computer; input to the machine then took the form of punched cards and output consisted of large books of printouts. Because early computers could do only a few steps of a complex process, the industrial office had to shape people's tasks to fit the needs of the machine. Computers and means of communicating with them have now been improved, but many large transaction-handing offices are still stuck at the industrial stage.

The industrial model of office organization is based on a deliberate endeavour to maximize efficiency and output. To create an assembly line the flow of work must be analyzed, discrete tasks must be isolated and work must be measured in some way. There is a need for standardization of jobs, transactions, technologies and even personal interactions. A fragmentation of responsibility goes hand in hand with bureaucratic organization and the proliferation of paperwork. Most of the workers have little sense of the overall task to which they are contributing their work or of how the system functions as a whole.

The industrial office has serious disadvantages. Many errors tend to arise in a production-line process. Because of the subdivision of tasks efforts to correct errors must often be made without access to all pertinent information, with the result that the errors are sometimes not corrected but compounded. Moreover, production-line operations can be surprisingly labor-intensive and costly. As more people are hired to cope with an error rate that increases faster than the volume of transactions, the cost per transaction increases and efficiency declines.

Effective people do not want to stay in boring jobs; people who do stay often lack interest in their work, which becomes apparent to the customer. Even if workers do their best, the system may defeat them, and customer service is likely to be poor. Because a given item can take weeks to flow through the pipeline it is often difficult to answer customer inquires about the current status of an account and even harder to take corrective action quickly. For example, a clerk may be able to check a sales slip and agree that a customer's bill is incorrect; in many instances, however, the clerk is able to change the account only by feeding a new input into the production line, with little assurance it will have the desired effect. As a result the billing error can be adjusted incorrectly or can be repeated for several months.

In the mid-1970's the recognition of these limitations, combined with the availability of new work station information systems, motivated a few progressive banks and other service organizations with a heavy load of transactions to take the next step: they converted certain departments to a mode of operation more appropriate to the information age. The information-age office exploits new technology to preserve the best aspects of the earlier stages and avoid their failings. At its best it combines terminal-based work stations, a continuously updated data base and communications to attain high

Figure 4. Computer terminals have a conspicuous place in an office of the Prudential Insurance Company of America in Parsippany, N.J., where claims are processed. Personnel who have identified themselves by entering a password at the keyboard of a terminal can retrieve information on an insured person's policy and claim, modify the information as necessary and add new information to the file. Tom Crane, Photographer. Reprinted courtesy of Daroff Design. *Note, 1991*: This photograph depicts a first generation computer workstation installation that has been upgraded at least three times since its early 1970s installation.

efficiency along with a return to people-centered work rather than machine-centered work. In the information-age office the machine is paced to the needs and abilities of the person who works with it. Instead of executing a small number of steps repetitively for a large number of accounts, one individual handles all customer-related activities for a much smaller number of accounts. Each worker has a terminal linked to a computer that maintains a data base of all customer-related records, which are updated as information is entered into the system. The worker becomes an account manager, works directly with the customer and is fully accountable to the customer.

Information is added incrementally to the master data base. The stored data are under the control of the worker, who can therefore be made responsible for correcting any errors that arise as well as for handling all transactions. Since information is updated as it becomes available there is no such thing as "work in process," with its attendant uncertainties. An inquiry or a change in status can be handled immediately over the telephone: the sales slip can be inspected, the customer's account can be adjusted and the bill that is about to be mailed can be corrected accordingly.

The design of effective systems and the measurement of productivity are still important in the information-age office with a large volume of transactions, but the context is different from that of the industrial office. Productivity is no longer measured by hours of work or number of items processed; it is judged by how well customers are served. Are they satisfied? Are they willing to bring their business back? Are they willing to pay a premium for a high level of service?

To the extent that the answers are yes the company gains an important competitive advantage. Even if cost cutting is not the only objective, the company can expect dramatic savings in personnel costs. Staff reductions of as much as 50 percent have been common in departments making the changeover to a work station system. Those employees who remain benefit from a marked improvement in the quality of their working life.

The benefits of the information-age office are not limited to the transaction-intensive office. A similar transformation can enhance productivity, effectiveness and job satisfaction in offices concerned with management, general administration and research. Most such offices are still in the preindustrial stage. They can be transformed to the information-age stage by the introduction of such person-centered technologies as the work station and electronic mail.

Once most of the activities of a job are centered on the work station the nature of the office can be transformed in still another way: there is no longer any need to assemble all workers at the same place and time. Portable terminals and computers, equipped with appropriate software and facilities for communication (including the telephone), create a "virtual" office, which is essentially anywhere the worker happens to be: at home, visiting a client or customer, in a hotel or even in an airplane. The remote work station can communicate electronically with the central office, and so it extends the range of places where written and numerical material can be generated, stored, retrieved, manipulated or communicated.

The effects of small-computer technology on the locale of work are analogous to those of the telephone. Because of the almost universal distribution of telephones it is not necessary to go to the office to call a customer or a co-worker, but until now it has been necessary to go there to write or dictate a letter, to read mail or to find something in a file. Now the work stations and ancillary electronic devices of an automated office can be linked to external terminals and personal computers. The job is no longer tied to the flow of paper across a designated desk; it is tied to the worker himself. The individual can therefore organize his own time and decide where and when he wants to do his work. Individuals who work best early in the morning or late at night can do so. A project team I have been working with for about a year has members in several East Coast and West Coast cities and rural areas, and we communicate regularly by electronic mail. The cost of the correspondence is about a tenth of the cost of regular mail per item, and it turns out that about half of the messages are generated outside of offices and outside of conventional working hours.

What will happen to the physical office? It has its virtues, after all. The office provides a home for organizations, a place for people to come together face to face and a work-oriented environment away from home. Many people need the structure of an office schedule; they like (or at least they are accustomed to) compartmentalization of the day and the week into time for work and time for other activities. Another role for the office is to house centralized forms of communications technology, such as facilities for video conferences, that are too expensive for the home. For these reasons and others I think the physical office will remain a part of working life, at least for as long as I am working. There will be continuing change, however, in how often some workers go to the office and in why they go there.

Many powerful factors are operating together to propel the transformation of office work. A complex set of feedback loops links economic and social change, new developments in information technology, the widespread adoption of the technology and the introduction of the new office organization the technology makes possible. The large number of information workers, for example, stimulates interest in enhancing their productivity. The concern for productivity serves to increase demand for technologies that can reduce the cost of handling information. Thus several trends reinforce one another to generate an ever stronger market for information products and services. The infiltration of the new devices into the workplace in turn creates an environment in which working electronically is the normal expectation of the worker.

Economics is a major factor. It is becoming far cheaper to communicate electronically than it is to communicate on paper. The transition to word processing from multidraft secretarial typing can reduce secretarial costs from more than $7 per letter to less than $2. Even more dramatic savings are associated with electronic mail, which can bring the cost of sending a message down to 30 cents or less. Electronic filing, in which a "document" is stored and indexed in a computer memory, brings further savings. (The highest-cost activities in manual correspondence are making multiple copies, filing them and retrieving them.) Such obvious reductions in cost are overshadowed by the savings in the time of managers and executives, the largest element by far in the cost of running an office.

The savings are becoming more significant each year as the cost of the electronic technology is reduced. For example, fast semiconductor memory is a tenth as expensive now as it was in 1975; the cost will drop by another factor of 10 by 1995. The result has been to bring into the individual consumer's price range information-handling capabilities that only a few years ago called for very expensive equipment.

As the market for mechanized work stations expands, more money is invested in research and development for communications, electronics, software, office-mechanization systems and the like. The time span between the development, introduction and obsolescence of a product becomes shorter. Each year brings a new generation of semiconductor devices; each generation makes possible a new set of applications. The dramatic improvement in products in turn builds demand for them and strengthens the trend toward office mechanization.

Whether a company's business is in farming, mining, manufacturing, transportation or retailing, its management, marketing, distribution and other operating controls are basically office-centered, information-handling activities. As the number of blue-collar workers decreases, the proportion of white-collar workers even in manufacturing organizations continues to increase. In virtually all commercial enterprises one finds executives, managers, clerks and secretaries; in most organizations there are also more specialized information workers, such as engineers and scientists, attorneys, salesmen, librarians, computer programmers and word processors. The people constitute the human-capital resources that can make an information-intensive economy viable.

Yet a tendency to think of white-collar workers in offices as support personnel, outside the economic mainstream, has tended to inhibit the transformation of office work. Physical activities that produce food, minerals and manufactured goods have been regarded as the only truly productive ones, whereas the handling of information has been considered necessary but essentially nonproductive. This way of looking at things (which may have been appropriate in an industrial society) persists today, even in the minds of economists who call for the "reindustrialization of America." It deeply affects the thinking of corporate management.

Even though most work in American society is information work and most such work is done in offices, the benefits of an increase in the productivity of office workers are not always within the field of view of managers. For those who retain a preindustrial view of office organization the very concept of productivity seems irrelevant or inappropriate in the context of offices or information work. Those who have an industrial-office orientation tend to focus on labor saving measurements; the installation of new technology and a system for exploiting it is evaluated only in the context of cutting visible office costs.

It is in offices that the basic decisions are made that determine the cost-effectiveness of an entire organization. The office is the place where the timelines of a decision or of a response can have immense consequences. If the office is ineffective, the organization must be ineffective. As it happens, moreover, a high degree of mechanization of the kind described in this article is much less expensive in the office than analogous mechanization is in the factory or on the farm.

The mechanization of office work is an essential element of the transformation of American society to one in which information work is the chief economic activity. If new information technology is properly employed, it can enable organizations to attain the following objectives: a reduction of information "float," that is, a decrease in the delay and uncertainty occasioned by the inaccessibility of information that is being typed, is in the mail, has been misfiled or is simply in an office that is closed for the weekend; the elimination of redundant work and unnecessary tasks such as retyping and laborious manual filing and retrieval; better utilization of human resources for tasks that require judgment, initiative and rapid communication; faster, better decision making that takes into account multiple, complex factors, and full exploitation of the virtual office through expansion of the workplace in space and time.

P·A·R·T· III

2

Computerization, Office Routines, and Changes in Clerical Work

Susan Iacono • Rob Kling

Electronic aids are changing work routines in offices, but not all changes may be for the better. Studies show that people's work lives must be considered in relation to the new equipment. Otherwise workers can become more disgruntled, even though their initial expectations for the new equipment may have been high.

In a similar vein, advanced electronic equipment is often sold to businesses with the promise of high gains in productivity. In practice, studies suggest, such gains may prove elusive.

Each new wave of technical development seems to be accompanied by high-spirited optimistic promotion. In the 1970s, one vision of the "office of the future" was based on IBM Corp.'s "word-processing plan." In its most rigid form, the plan projected that individual secretaries for managers would be eliminated in the office of 1985. Instead, several managers would share services from a secretarial pool. Few organizations adopted this vision literally, but IBM was able to articulate a persuasive image of professional office life with automatic text processing that excluded secretaries.

Present-day promotional language for office-automation systems tends to emphasize support for managerial and professional work rather than displacement of clerical employees. But care nevertheless must be taken in implementing the new support. The following example, reported by Enid Mumford in *Designing Secretaries* (Manchester Business School Press, 1983), illustrates some of the social complexities that can arise.

A department in a large British company, for example, bought two stand-alone word processors for a group of five secretaries to use. Space was limited, and the machines were placed in an isolated room. The secretaries had been used to typing reports and letters with occasional interruptions from telephone calls and other office staff. Now, with the word processors, they could work efficiently without interruption. But they hated the new arrangement. They had to work at a continuous tempo, moving their eyes from "paper to screen" for an hour or two, with few breaks in their relative isolation. In general, the secretary liked the flexibility of the new equipment, but they strongly disliked the new working conditions under which they used it.

In one sense, the word processors were the catalysts (and thus the "cause") for the change in the work arrangement. However, the technical capabilities of word processors were not the causal agents. These capabilities made them attractive to the director of the company, but cost—about $18,000 for each word processor—led him to insist that the machines be used efficiently. Because they were not sufficiently compact to replace a standard typewriter, they required additional space. The combination of space shortages in the department, the director's desire to have secretaries use expensive machines efficiently, and a social order that placed secretaries at the bottom resulted in work under pressure and in isolation—and a drop in office morale.

Technology Alters Jobs

In some cases, work place technologies have altered jobs. For example, telephone operators' jobs have changed considerably since the 1940s, when long-distance operators had to know routing patterns to direct cross-country calls. The jobs always tied operators to headphones and consoles. But as telephone switching became automated, the operators needed less skill. As a result the jobs became boring for many operators.

Before the advent of the automatic switchboard, a light would appear, but the operator had to plug in the cord to take the call. With the automatic switchboard, the calls are just there, whether the operator wants them or not or whether the operator needs a breather or not. Surreptitious monitoring—both of the number of calls taken and the rate at which they are handled and of the operator's demeanor—increases the tension.

In the book *Working* (Avon Books, 1972), Studs Terkel reported on a similar situation. Beryl Simpson, an airline reservations clerk said, "With Sabre [the computer system] being so valuable, you were allowed no more than three minutes on the telephone. You had 20 seconds to put the information into Sabre, then you had to be available for another phone call. It was almost like a production line; we adjusted to the machine. The casualness and informality that had been there previously were no longer there. The last three or four years on the job were horrible."

The obvious lesson is that workers may be highly pleased with the new technologies initially and simultaneously frustrated with the conditions under which they must use them. In a study of computers in the work life of traffic-ticket clerks in municipal courts, conducted at the University of California at Irvine in the mid-1970s, the authors found that most traffic-ticket clerks attributed job-enlarging characteristics, such as increased variety, to their use of automated equipment. Impacts of new technologies are varied. But "better" technologies do not guarantee a better work life.

Contemporary accounts of the "office of the future" focus primarily on computing technologies for flexible text processing, scheduling, and communication. Most analysts who write about such an office assume that the social dimensions of office life will mirror the flexibility provided by improved information technologies. Variations in the character of offices and life within them is largely ignored in these accounts. Most office workers have white-collar jobs, and there are usually a variety of jobs and roles in most offices. These activities often include planning, supervising, decision making, persuading, recording, typing, accounting, inventorying, and handling phone calls. Managers, and sometimes workers, organize who will be responsible for the execution of the various tasks through a division of labor. The hierarchy of roles identifies who will have the authority to implement certain decisions and decide schedules and who will abide by them.

Gains are Elusive as Equipment Advances

In 1800, office equipment consisted of pens, ink, and paper. At the turn of the century, a very primitive typewriter may have been deemed necessary for a clerk. Punched-card tabulating equipment began to be used in accounting offices, and the installation of telephones spread everywhere between the two world wars. After World War II, more office machines appeared on the market. Money counters, mechanical erasors, billing machines, and machines that can open envelopes and seal, stamp, and address them outfitted the automated offices of the day.

Today, most of these mechanical forms of office automation seem old-fashioned. All offices in the United States have telephones, most have access to photocopiers, and many have computer terminals or word processors. In 20 years, the advanced office systems of today, which feature integrated calendars, text processing, and electronic mail accessible through multiple windows on a 12-inch video data terminal, will also seem archaic. "Modern technologies" do not denote particular technologies; they are temporary pointers in a continuous cavalcade of technological devices.

When business computers first appeared, promotors promised that the machines would replace people who engaged in routine activites by simply mimicking their tasks. Computer applications would be more efficient than an office worker, and some said that office staffs could be reduced by 50 percent. Because clerical work is deemed the most repetitive and routine work done in an office, it was expected to be the easiest to automate.

Despite substantial investments in office automation in the 1970s, however, national estimates of productivity from 1968 to 1978 indicate only a 4 percent increase for office workers. While the office technologies of this period included such primitive machines as magnetic-tape and magnetic-card typewriters, they were sold as high-leverage advances. Aggregate national data cannot prove that new office technologies have had little impact, but they suggest caution in creating expectations or setting goals.

The abilities of information technologies to support real productivity gains in organizations is influenced by elements of work life beyond machine capabilities. Real gains can often be measured by focusing on one task under controlled conditions. However, in the "real" work place, these single-task gains do not translate directly into proportional gains in office productivity. Most office workers, aside from data-entry operators, perform several tasks. A secretary, for example, may answer phone calls, do photocopy work, type a document on a word processor, file, and communicate with the boss. Replacing one word processor with a "better" one may simplify formatting problems, for instance. But if the secretary spends 10 percent of the day formatting text and if the productivity gain is expected to be 50 percent, that only translates into a 5-percent gain in overall productivity.

Then there is the issue of overhead. In a major Southern California engineering firm, an advanced office system was installed. It was used by managers, engineers, and secretaries to write letters and documents, schedule rooms, arrange calendars, and communicate via electronic mail. The corporate managers expected this project to yield a 20-percent increase in productivity, but measuring the improvement has proved difficult. While many staff members like the new equipment, it is hard to show that they have actually gained any fixed fraction of their work time, because of the overhead for system use—learning time, the time it takes to turn from a task, log on to the system, and to check for electronic mail when perhaps there is none, and so on.

When real gains in productivity can be measured, people often find new tasks that exploit the gains. Photocopiers produce more copies, text-processing machines produce more versions of a manuscript, and computer-based accounting systems provide more detailed accounting data. Some of these additional uses help multiply organizational products; others add little. However, the process of exploiting these "labor saving" devices does not always reduce staff, as the work load may grow. The additional work is done by the system—a phantom, automated clerk. Consequently, extra working capacity does not necessarily translate into cost reduction or even improved overall effectiveness. When format changes are easier, document authors often request additional changes in a particular document. When the number of requested changes increase, these can reduce any time savings that might have accrued from using a new text formatter. Even so, many people like the feel of working with powerful tools.

The Phantom Efficiency

The efficiency standards that some companies set up—the monitoring and pacing of work that is made possible by new electronic equipment—can also be counterproductive, further eating away at the promised productivity gains. For example, some organizations monitor the number of keystrokes that a typist makes, and this information becomes a means of determining the pace of the work. There is some evidence that continual monitoring increases errors.

In an ongoing study of automated text processing, the authors have found that business organizations vary considerably in the way they organize clerical work. Some have centralized word-processing pools or data-entry departments in which clerical workers are isolated from the rest of the organization and have little opportunity to control the pace of their work. Others have decentralized office arrangements that can give clerical workers more opportunities for decision making.

A word-processing center can give employees several advantages not provided by a decentralized arrangement. One advantage is that the center offers a longer career path.

For example, in one organization that was studied, a woman started as a secretary and moved up to executive secretary, normally the top of the ladder in a decentralized organization. Then the company brought in a new word-processing system. The woman became active in the development of a word-processing center, soon was named supervisor to the center, and then was promoted to manager of administrative services, where she directed all of the company's secretarial functions.

Such career opportunities were available because a word-processing center is a complete support organization with its own hierarchical structure. In more conventional arrangements, a secretary is dependent on the boss for advancement: if the boss moves up, the secretary may also move up.

Clerical workers in a word-processing center have a second advantage: they develop a special expertise with their systems by working with them constantly. In addition, because of economies of scale, they tend to have the best equipment.

A centralized organization has disadvantages as well. The work is starkly routine and can be dull. There is less flexibility in determining the order of tasks. There is a reduced social contact with workers outside the word-processing center; operators become segregated, in touch only with a supervisor who collects work from the various departments and passes it along. The issue of monitoring job performance also arises more often than in a decentralized system.

On the other hand, clerical workers in a decentralized office arrangement, with individual managers having personal secretaries or several managers sharing one secretary, have considerable flexibility in determining their work schedule and the order of tasks. The situation can be more interesting than in a centralized arrangement, because the workers have more contact with other people in the company outside the secretarial class, and there is less likelihood of strict job performance monitoring.

Clerical workers in this arrangement, however, also have fewer opportunities for advancement and do not acquire the same level of technical expertise as workers in a word-processing center. From a political perspective, the individual secretary is also at a disadvantage. The clerical organization is fragmented, with secretaries having stronger ties to their bosses than to each other; therefore collective job action, such as forming a union, is more difficult.

Some organizations have both individual secretaries and a word-processing pool. The advantages of such a mixed arrangement are obvious for the managers: they have local support for immediate needs, and they can lean on the word-processing center for larger projects that would be difficult for one person to handle, but could be completed in a day if divided among five workers. For the clerical staff, the mixed arrangement also provides more options, but tension can result from the division of clerical workers into two types.

In one such organization that the authors studied, the word-processing workers saw themselves as much more professional than the traditional secretaries because of their higher level of technical expertise. The secretaries, because their jobs were more varied, did not have the opportunity to become so intimately familiar with the word-processing system. Also, secretaries were sometimes asked to do menial tasks, such as get coffee for the boss or buy a present for him to give to his wife, whereas no one in a word-processing center received such requests. In addition, the secretaries sometimes resented the people in the word-processing center because they were more likely to have the best equipment.

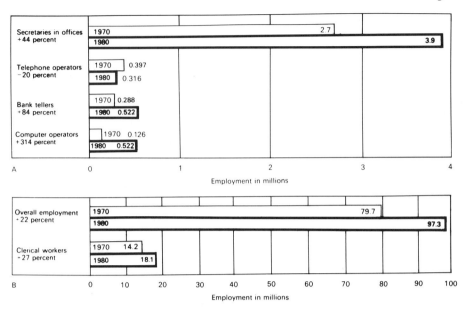

Figure 1. With the trend toward word-processing centers in large U.S. offices, there has been no trend toward fewer secretaries in the labor force. Rather, the number of secretaries has increased. On the other hand, automation of telephone switching devices has led to a decrease in the number of telephone operators. Automated teller machines theoretically allow banks to reduce the number of tellers, although this displacement has not yet arrived. Meanwhile, some clerical jobs have been created through computerization, such as those of computer and peripheral equipment operators (A). From 1970 to 1980, overall employment rose 22 percent, while the employment of clerical workers increased 27 percent (B). Source: U.S. Bureau of Labor Statistics.

Technology: No Guarantee of Improvement

The lesson is clear: technology alone cannot guarantee improved performance and higher morale in an office. The quality of people's work lives is equally involved. Gains come by a skillful blending of these two basic ingredients.

Many managers who work with information technologies come to this realization. They become fascinated with new equipment and point to the promised gains in office productivity to justify expensive purchases. Often they overestimate the actual gains, as the new equipment's use becomes routine and its limitations apparent. At a later time, the managers become aware of more advanced equipment in the marketplace; once again they succumb to vendor descriptions of increased productivity and decreased operating costs. The gains sought, however, may not be attained because human factors in the work place were not considered.

In the next 20 years it seems likely that offices will become even more automated. More clerical workers will sit in front of video display terminals (VDTs) as they handle inquiries from customers, prepare memos and reports, and communicate with certain co-workers. Most offices will not become "paperless." Rather, computer and tele-communications technologies will be more widely used to replace and to complement other information media. Office environments also should improve in general, as sensitivity to occupational hazards grows. Today, some employers may push their employees to work at VDTs, with fewer breaks than are healthy, or employers may not invest in proper lighting or office furnishings. These conditions should improve. However, change will not come uniformly, as offices vary in size and in what they produce. (The kind of work performed in the Oval Office of the White House is significantly different from work done in a typing-pool office.) Offices also differ in work organization, number of employees, diversity of tasks, physical arrangements, the kinds of technology in use, predominant control strategies, and so on.

A Woman's Place in the Office

The owner of the office, the one who does the actual business transactions, has one or two office workers working from him as apprentices. They are all sitting at very tall desks, some doing copy work, some running an accounting system, all using quill pens, which they dip in ink. They have an office boy who runs errands. All of course are male. The year is 1800.

For many men in the early 1800s, a clerkship was an entry point to learning a business and developing a career in it by working their way up from the bottom. Outside of medicine, professional schools were weak or undeveloped. As a consequence, advancement in most occupations, especially commercial ones, came through training on the job.

The advent of the typewriter in the late 1800s helped create the role of secretary in the office. Men who had previously started as clerks began to fill administrative positions, and the segregation of male and female office work began. By 1880, secretarial work had been split from administrative work, and most secretaries were women.

Even in the early twentieth century, most companies sought to hire 18-to-25-year-old women for secretary jobs. Since married women stayed at home, these jobs were usually organized on the assumption that secretaries would leave work, due to marriage, by their mid-twenties. These jobs could be dead-end by design and not be part of a world in which women "learned the business," because they were just temporary jobs. Moreover, entry into various professions was increasingly dependent upon some formal post-high-school education. While there was substantial variation across occupations, and even within them, clerical apprenticeships no longer led to a solid career.

According to Judy Gregory and Karen Nussbaum of 9 to 5, The Association of Working Women, this is one twentieth-century office, as described by a video-display-terminal operator.

"They have a new setup called the open office. There are panels 6 feet high around all the operators. We are divided into work groups—from four to six people per group—with a supervisor for each work group. In many cases we don't see another person all day, except for a 10-minute coffee break at lunchtime. All we see are the walls around us and sometimes the supervisor. The isolation is terrible."

In the last decade the skills in manipulating machines required for general secretarial work have been increasing. In 1970, most secretaries had to be able to use a typewriter. In 1984, some temporary placement agencies are requiring secretaries to be skilled on four or five machines. These new skills, in operating more complex photocopiers and word processors, primarily indicate the ways in which the technologies of office life have become more complex.

In today's office, clerks typically have limited contact with supervisors, except when they are being supervised. This is very different from early nineteenth-century offices, where there were opportunities for apprenticeship, learning the business, and moving up in the organization. As the trend toward feminization of the clerical work force continues, women who work in offices continue to find themselves isolated in dead-end jobs. It is important to ask whether clerical workers who use computer-based technologies can develop career lines that are more open-ended than traditional clerical work.

The office of the future thus holds little opportunity for career advancement for female clerical workers, if the segregated social relations of the office persist.

Researchers are less sanguine about changes in the structure of careers, pay, and job roles for clerical workers. The complexity of many clerical jobs will increase as offices adopt more complex arrays of computing and telecommunications equipment. But there will always be routine tasks, whether in preparing individual transactions for computer processing, scheduling meetings, or organizing files of data and memos on integrated office systems. Some of these jobs may become more interesting, but it is unlikely that the career lines for clerks will begin to parallel the careers and salaries of technicians. Discontent on the job will remain a major obstacle to gains in productivity.

One solution would be to reorganize routine clerical work so that the most monotonous jobs were truly automated, perhaps with optical data readers and similar technoligies. Clerical workers could then be used in less isolated work arrangements with greater opportunity for career development within the organization, if they desired. Such options hinge on a less stereotypical way of viewing clerical support work rather than on a new wave of office technologies.

P·A·R·T · I I I

3

Intellectual Assembly Lines: The Rationalization of Managerial, Professional, and Technical Work

Judith A. Perrolle

Developments in the computer field becoming known as knowledge engineering offer the technical means to create intellectual assembly lines for managerial, professional, and technical occupations. An intellectual assembly line is a division of labor in which the rationality of the bureaucratic organization acquires the mechanized efficiency of the factory, and in which mental labor is subjected to both the rationalization of its knowledge and the gradual automation of its productive activity. Technical, professional, and managerial work all involve the exercise of expert knowledge. Also involved in professional and managerial jobs are autonomous professional judgments based upon experience. Managerial activity in addition includes the evaluation and control of the work of others. To argue these mental activities can be organized in assembly line fashion presumes that computers can perform as technical experts, can acquire a kind of judgment based upon general principles and experience, and can make managerial decisions. These are precisely the claims of the research area known as artificial intelligence, which is part of the emerging field of knowledge engineering.

Knowledge engineering includes efforts to organize intellectual activity into a set of computer-coordinated tasks by means of data management and decision-support systems (Hayes-Roth, 1984). It also involves attempts to mechanize actual decision-making and knowledge production activities using expert systems and other types of artificial intelligence software (Coombs, 1984; Winston and Prendergast, 1984).

Reprinted with permission from Paradigm Press, Inc. "Intellectual Assembly Lines: The Rationalization of Managerial, Professional and Technical Work," Judith Perolle, *Computers and the Social Sciences* **2**(3) July–Sept. 1986, pp. 111–122.

While theoretical debates about the prospects for automating thought processes are found in a variety of disciplines, social theories of the effects of computing (for a review, see Kling, 1980—Chapter II.6 in this volume) generally neglect the issue of artificial intelligence. Although there are enormous discrepancies between optimistic claims that knowledge engineering can embody intellectual activity in computer systems and the actual performance of intelligent software, there are enough successes to demonstrate that machines can perform what were previously human mental activities (Pylyshyn, 1980). Although there are fewer than 200 commercial expert systems in operation (Frenkel, 1985), the rapid spread of robotics in industry and the growing business and military support for the "fifth generation" technology are indicators that, despite theoretical reservations of philosophers and cognitive scientists, artificial intelligence is becoming a social fact.

The Deskilling Debate

Debates about the effects of computerization on the labor process involve differing assumptions about both the nature of intellectual work and management strategies. Theorists who see a general trend toward the subordination of intellectual work predict deskilling (Cooley, 1980), white collar proletarianization (Wright and Singelmann, 1982; Salaman, 1982), and a declining middle class (Kuttner, 1983). They share the view presented in Braverman's *Labor and Monopoly Capitalism* (1974) that a devaluation of intellectual work to reduce the costs and power of labor is in the interests of business and industrial management. They also tend to agree that the structural consequences of such a devaluation will be to reduce the size, status, and power of the white collar middle-class occupations (Abercrombie and Urry, 1983; Goldthorpe, 1982).

Claims that professional, managerial, and technical work will be deskilled assume that the different experiences of highly skilled and less skilled mental labor with computerization so far are due to the lack of means to subordinate higher level work. These in turn rest on the assumption that Taylorism is the ideology behind the choice of technology under capitalism and that capital is ultimately extracted from subordinated labor. Under this set of assumptions, we could expect intellectual assembly lines to develop as the techniques of artificial intelligence improve upper management's ability to control the mental labor process. Artificial intelligence would be viewed as a labor-saving technology, performing professional and middle-level managerial tasks. The replacement of highly paid professionals by computer systems operated by less skilled labor would be considered an improvement in labor organization.

Different assumptions are made by those who argue that computers will enhance the quality and working conditions of intellectual labor, freeing humans *from* the drudgery of routine mental activity and freeing them *for* creative thought. The projected social consequences of this arrangement have been stated most optimistically by Daniel Bell (1980: 204–205), who envisions a growing egalitarianism as a large class of "knowledge elite" acquires computer-enhanced skills. The theoretical argument that intelligent software will enhance mental work assumes that creative intellectual activity is uniquely human, and can never be automated. Routine thought processes that are amenable to mechanization are considered mental drudgery; optimizing highly skilled human capital is believed to be the appropriate managerial strategy for dealing with intellectual labor. Under this set of assumptions, knowledge engineering applications should not reduce the wages, autonomy, or skill of employees in the professional, managerial, and higher level technical categories.

Available evidence on the deskilling debate is mixed and poorly supported by empirical research (Attewell and Rule, 1984). Deskilling claims are best supported for the lower levels of mental work—skilled blue collar, clerical and technician jobs (Ayres and Miller, 1983; Downing, 1980, Gottfried, 1982; Shaiken, 1984; Straw and Foged, 1983). For managerial, professional, and more highly skilled technical occupations, skill and autonomy enhancement (or at least the subjective impression of it) tend to be reported. Even among clerical workers, however, both skilling and deskilling evidence has been reported (Kling, 1985). Even when jobs are deskilled, the people performing those jobs may not be, as when unskilled workers enter low-skill computerized jobs, improving their relative position. It is clear that computer technology itself does not automatically have a single effect upon conditions of work. New means to rationalize intellectual activity and to embody technical skill, professional judgment, and decision-making logic in computers will not necessarily lead to intellectual assembly lines. They will, however, extend the deskilling debate to higher levels of the stratification system.

The Rationalization of Mental Labor

The idea of using computer technology as a means to rationalize intellectual labor dates back at least to the end of the seventeenth century, when Leibniz wrote: "It is unworthy of excellent men to lose hours like slaves in the labor of calculation which could be safely relegated to anyone else if machines were used" (1959: 156–164). Charles Babbage, whose 1833 design for the "analytical engine" was the prototype of the modern digital computer, developed factories organized around the principle that "Human labor is similar to capital, raw materials, etc. It is therefore subject, or ought to be subject, to similar input/output analyses, measurement, standards and controls" (Babbage, 1982). Although not a direct precursor of Frederick Taylor's work, Babbage was interested in the same sort of time and motion studies that became the hallmark of Scientific Management (Gideon, 1982: 114).

The substitution of machinery for labor was an early part of the industrialization process. Karl Marx (1973: 110–126) agreed with Babbage's definition of a machine as a division of labor in which a single engine links particular operations performed by a single instrument. Although Marx is often misquoted as having said that the hand mill produced feudalism and the steam mill produced capitalism, his theory was not one of simple technological determinism. Before new machinery could be introduced, he argued, those who have the power to redefine tasks and products must reorganize work to accommodate the equipment. While Marx applied his theory to the reorganization of manual labor under capitalism, the subject of rationalized intellectual labor was taken up by Max Weber and later theorists of bureaucratic organizations. Today, the automation of bureaucratically rationalized mental labor by computers is made possible by an extension of industrialization that Norbert Wiener called a "Second Industrial Revolution" in which "the sporadic design of individual automatic mechanisms" is replaced by "communication between machine and machine" (1967: 208).

Wiener's cybernetics is the study of communication and control in humans and machines. Based on the theoretical work of Willard Gibbs (whose research institute became a model for the contemporary division of labor in science), cybernetics made intellectual assembly lines theoretically possible, with coordination of rationalized mental tasks performed by communication and control technology. However, because computers can accommodate multiple tasks occurring at different tempos and sequences, intellectual assembly lines need not look like factories. Computers can be used to coordinate work performed by geographically dispersed individuals working at their own pace without direct human supervision. In theory, the rationalization of mental labor that characterizes the intellectual assembly line could integrate individual efforts into larger human projects as easily as it could subordinate their mental activity to alienating working situations. Thus, the way in which computerized work is rationalized depends more upon who is able to define whom as "excellent men" or "anybody else" than upon purely technological possibilities.

The Mechanization of Thought Processes

The field of computer science known as artificial intelligence involves the design of computer programs and automated equipment, such as industrial robots, with a limited capacity to behave in ways that at least resemble human thought processes (for a technical survey, see Barr and Feigenbaum, 1982; Hayes-Roth, 1983; or Coombs, 1984; for a sympathetic popular history, see McCorduck, 1979). Information from the outside world can be sought, interpreted, and used as the basis for "heuristic" decisions, which in humans would be called "best guesses." The program can, within the narrow range of the world to which they are applied, draw inferences, suggest solutions to previously unsolved problems, select relevant information according to their own internal criteria, and modify their own behavior as a result of the outcomes of their previous actions.

The theoretical possibility of representing human knowledge and decision-making processes in computer programs has been fiercely debated on both scientific and moral grounds, with the strongest objections coming from the philosopher Hubert Dreyfus in *What Computers Can't Do* (1972) and the artificial intelligence expert Joseph Weizenbaum in *Computer Power and Human Reason* (1976). One important issue is the degree to which human decision-making is believed to be rational and logical. Intelligent software has been most successful for those applications in which the knowledge of human experts is characterized by great rationality; to claim that such programs can perform in any area of human expertise is essentially to define all areas of human expertise as rationalizable. Such arguments are best received by industrial and professional managers interested in routine applications of knowledge and technique and by those who subscribe to the Taylorist principle that successful management involves maximum rationalization and control over labor.

Automated programming, industrial planning by machine, and mechanization of the professions were topics on the agenda of a 1958 international conference on the emerging field of artificial intelligence (National Physical Laboratory, 1959). In addition to Leibniz's goal of saving the labor of excellent men, managerial control and profitability were among the reasons advanced for supporting A.I. During the next twenty-five years, artificial intelligence was transformed from academic research projects to widely publicized commercial applications (see excerpts from Feigenbaum and McCorduck, 1983 in Chapter I.1 of this volume; Hayes-Roth, 1984). Expert system developers promise that their software will "capture" the knowledge of experts in programs that enable a less skilled person to achieve expert results:

> Knowledge is a scarce resource whose refinement and reproduction creates wealth. Traditionally the transmission of knowledge from human expert to trainee has required education and internship years long. Extracting knowledge from humans and putting it in compatible forms can greatly reduce the costs of knowledge reproduction and exploitation. . . . Skill means having the right knowledge and using it effectively. Knowledge engineering addresses the problem of building skilled computer systems, aimed first at extracting the expert's knowledge and then organizing it in an effective implementation. (Hayes-Roth, Waterman, and Lenat, 1983: 5, 13).

While the debate between those who argue that machines can think and those who argue that they can't is quite complex (for reviews, see Boden, 1977, and Haugeland, ed., 1981), the practical success of "intelligent" programs that play chess, infer chemical structures from molecular data, and diagnose illnesses indicates quite clearly that artificial intelligence is being "put to work" at industrial and professional tasks, despite the reservations of many theorists. The most ambitious practical proposals involving expert systems are those for the new fifth generation "supercomputers" (Feigenbaum and McCorduck, 1983 —Chapter I.1 in this volume). Promising higher industrial productivity and greater national security, the proposals call for many areas of military and civilian expert decision-making to be turned over to the faster, soon-to-be smarter machines. In his thoughtful critique of the fifth-generation idea, Joseph Weizenbaum questions Feigenbaum's assertion that computers will *produce* the future knowledge of the world, asking how are we to understand just what information a computer actually produces and how it does so (Weizenbaum, 1983). But if information itself is seen as a commodity produced for profit by the rational organization and mechanization of intellectual labor, then information can be produced by the computer in the same way that products were made by the factory machinery of the first industrial revolution—through the alienation of laborers from the production process (Perrolle, 1985).

The Transformation of Technical Skill: Rationalization and Mechanization in Software Production

In its short history, computer programming has been transformed from a manual task of wiring boards (performed by women clerical workers) to a romanticized craft popularly believed to be one of the major sources of future high-tech employment. Today, however, software production is being rapidly rationalized into routine work (Kraft, 1977; Kraft and Dubnoff, 1983). The word "computer" first described the jobs of women who performed calculations and wired hardware for the pioneering ENIAC, and only later came to mean the machines that replaced them. The manual and routine mental work of the women was taken over by machines; the creative component was transferred to male mathematicians who became known as programmers. This process simultaneously produced both skill enhancement and deskilling as the intellectual work was differentiated into design and execution tasks. The design phase was redefined as creative work; the routinized mental labor was devalued in symbolic and monetary terms and viewed as the appropriate target for automation.

From the compilers of the 1950s to contemporary structured programming, relational databases, application generators, and expert systems, technological developments in software production have all been applied to the routinization of programming, even though most were introduced to spare humans from mental drudgery. In 1958, Commander Grace Murray Hopper reported two consequences of her recently invented compiler: first, U.S. Naval officers found to their satisfaction that the new computer techniques gave project managers better control over the activities of programmers; second, experiments indicated that a new division of labor in programming, with highly skilled systems analysts producing flowcharts and clerically trained high school graduates producing code, was the optimal use of the new techniques. Programmers who at first opposed the change for fear of losing their jobs found that the new division of labor provided them with upward mobility while creating new low-level jobs for the coders (Hopper, 1959). Analyses of software production in the 1960s and 1970s have documented the emergence of a hierarchical division of labor similar to that in blue collar industries (Kraft, 1977; Kraft and Dubnoff, 1983).

Today, structured programming and its extensions offer new control mechanisms at a time when data security from high-tech crimes is a growing concern in economic institutions. It offers a way to replace temperamental programmer-craftsmen with better disciplined and less expensive technical laborers organized into intellectual assembly lines. Structured programming began with a 1967 paper by the Dutch computer scientist Edgar Dijkstra, who may become known as the Henry Ford of computer programming. He offered an elegant mathematical approach to the problem of program complexity and thus the hope of "bug-free" software (Olson, 1984). By rationalizing the process of software design and coding, structured programming offers firms a 10 percent to 20 percent increase in program productivity (McClure, 1984). However, there is at present no good empirical research supporting these claims (Vessey and Weber, 1984).

Structured programs are easy to understand, fix, modify and divide into separate parts. Well-defined tasks for programmers that can be integrated into larger programming projects are the software equivalent of interchangeable parts. According to the software engineer Frederick Brooks, Jr., the major impact of structured programming has been to introduce the concept of "control structures" into program design (1982: 144). But such control structures also control programmers by limiting the scope of their activity. An extension of the concept to database design has produced the "relational database," which maintains data in forms that can be used without being directly accessed (Codd, 1982). Although this introduces important technical improvements in data security, task coordination, and software reliability, the restructured working conditions restrict the autonomy and responsibility of programmers.

When combined with research on programmer knowledge (cf. Soloway and Ehrlich,

Table 1. Successful Expert Systems, by Occupational Area, 1984

Professional	Medical	15.9%
	Research	7.2%
	Engineering	3.7%
	Professional Services	3.6%
Technical	Computing	19.6%
	Electronics	6.5%
	Oil and Mineral Exploration	7.2%
Managerial	Financial Services	3.6%
Military		10.9%
Other		21.8%
		N = 138

Based on data from Tim Johnson, *The Commercial Application of Expert Systems Technology.* London, Ovum, 1984.

1984), structured programming techniques can be used in application generators. While application generators are not, strictly speaking, expert systems, they do enough "reasoning" to enable a relatively inexperienced programmer to produce software (Keller and Townsend, 1984). In a recent survey of one small company (50 programmers) that converted to application generators, productivity did increase markedly over a five-year period while real wages fell. Younger programmers were enthusiastic about them, reporting that their skills were enhanced. More experienced programmers, however, reported being "deskilled" (Perrolle, *et al.*, 1986).

Many artificial intelligence experts believe that software production will soon be largely performed by expert systems (Wenger, 1984; Frenkel, 1985). According to Bruce Buchanan (Shurkin, 1983: 77), a major problem in software production is the time it takes programmers to convert the acquired knowledge into programs. Implementation of "knowledge acquisition" systems connect the expert directly with the computer and save all that programmer labor. Programmer labor, however, is a significant part of those expanding high-tech jobs that proponents of the information revolution are promising.

Expert Systems in the Professions

Although business analysts report that "most of today's expert systems are limited in scope and quite costly" (Alexander, 1984: 118), specialists within the computer industry (Hayes-Roth, 1983; d'Agapeyeff, 1984; Basden, 1984) predict a steady growth in the replacement of humans with expert systems in narrowly defined areas of expertise. About a quarter of the "serious" expert systems in use in 1984 were in the professions, as shown in Table 1. Some knowledge engineers have begun to identify their potential for automating professional work as a problem. Feigenbaum recently pointed out that "Everyone worries about the fate of the blue-collar workers . . . it's the highly paid professionals we ought to start worrying about" (1984).

Although the use of expert systems presupposes, at least initially, that there are human experts to be consulted, in their industrial and professional applications expert systems use those experts as models for work settings in which people of much lower skills can achieve the same results. This implies that the "knowledge elite" is likely to be much smaller than usually predicted. Also, rather than being composed of our most creative thinkers, it is likely to be composed of those who have most successfully kept their knowledge to themselves.

At the 1958 international artificial intelligence conference, physician Francois Paycha outlined the logic of medical diagnosis and argued that mechanization could solve some of its difficulties. Legal expert Lucien Mehl proposed that "a machine for processing information can be an effective aid in searching for sources of legal information, in preparing the decision of the administrator or judge, and finally in checking the coherence of the solutions arrived at" (Mehl, 1959: 757). Although Paycha suggested that we could not anticipate the wider social consequences of mechanized medical diagnosis, Mehl echoed Leibniz's belief that the labor of excellent men would be saved for devotion "to research proper, to true scientific thought." He further argued that, although judicial machines would be suited to conducting legal argument, they could never replace human legal experts because they were incapable of formulating precepts.

In the next decades, medical and legal knowledge became the subject of intensive efforts to develop intelligent databases and software. While expert systems developers would claim that computers do have the technical capabilities to replace many of the functions of lawyers, the trends in computer usage indicate that they are being adopted in ways that facilitate the existing arrangements of legal practice. Although computer programs could be developed to render rational judgments for some sorts of cases, the human quality remains an almost sacred element in the administration of justice; we are thus unlikely to experience computerized judges. Most legal experts would agree with Joseph Weizenbaum (1976) that any conceivable intelligence on the part of a computer would lack the element of human wisdom. Even using computers as "informants" or providers of expert testimony is controversial (Marx and Richman, 1984; Jenkins, 1979).

What we can expect is accelerated use of computers to process court cases (now terribly backlogged in most jurisdictions) and to provide legal research services for attorneys. We may also expect computer law to become a professional specialization; by 1985 over 1000 lawyers belonged to national and regional computer law organizations (Connolly, 1985). The Lexis and Westlaw systems are examples of specialized database services for legal research (Bander and Sweetgall, 1983). Their use may lead to concentration of power in larger law firms, which are able to afford these services. Centralization tendencies could be avoided by making legal information services available inexpensively to individuals and small law firms.

In the medical profession as well, expert systems seem to be emerging as aids for human experts. While some skills, like using a scalpel, may be lost to laser surgery (Freifeld, 1984), techniques like computer-animated X-rays will give physicians more skill in diagnosing patients (Science86 March, 1986: 10). The serious threat to the status of doctors is from institutional pressures of hospital administrations and health care insurers (Anderson and Jay, 1985). Many government officials and health care administrators would like to rationalize the mental labor of physicians. But, despite the opinion among knowledge engineers that medical diagnosis is a relatively straightforward problem, no one has serious plans to automate doctors in the near future. In the long run, the impact of computers on the social organization of medicine may be as dramatic as the telephone's and automobile's contributions to shifting health care out of doctor's offices and into hospitals (Starr, 1983). But instead of becoming automated, physicians may use computer-based communications networks to move health care back out of hospitals.

The effects of computers on relatively powerful professions like law and medicine depend less upon technical possibilities for expert systems than upon political and economic issues of professional autonomy, credentials, regulation, and the role of para-professionals. Mental labor is most likely to be subject to rationalization, control, and eventual automation in professions that allow their work to be done by less skilled assistants. This is not a question of whether legal secretaries and nurses are capable of performing more skilled tasks, or even whether they in fact do so under a doctor or lawyer's direction. It is a question of whether the paraprofessional can be managed directly by institutions without the services of the supervisory professional. As in other instances of computerization, skill enhancement may occur for paraprofessionals as the professionals lose part of their privileged status.

Spokesmen for professional engineering have warned for decades that professional status is reduced by change that threatens expert knowledge:

> The engineer who at one time was the educated and elite leader in matching science to society is fast becoming just another member in the industrial labor force. (Forrester, 1967)

A review of the effects of computers on creativity in chemical engineering education (Drake and Perrolle, 1984) suggests that the employment of less expensive and more narrowly trained technical people may exacerbate the problem of obsolescence for more experienced engineers. In addition it appeared that the mental labor saved by the use of expert systems may be subjected to heavy pressures for higher productivity rather than freed for more interesting types of work. In actual implementations, however, intellectual assembly line arrangements sometimes prove unsatisfactory, even when initially chosen by management (Cass, 1985; Perrolle, et al., 1986). Engineering problem-solving often calls for broader understanding and more flexible thinking that can be embodied in even an extremely "intelligent" program. In the hands of experts, as in Digital Equipment Corporation's most recent chip design project (Bairstow, 1985), expert systems can save the labor of excellent people.

Computerized Decision-Making

In the 1950s, the application of computers to management decision-making was believed to be limited to the performance of routine clerical tasks and to objective decisions based solely on economic criteria. While admitting that management decisions ought to be objective wherever possible (and thus should be subject to automation), Merriman and Wass (1959) affirmed the subjective nature of managerial decisions as part of the spiritual nature of man. Like doctors and lawyers, managers claimed for themselves a special and creative role in human decision-making. In the next decades' debates over the possibility and desirability of mechanized thought processes, it was widely asserted that managers' functions simply could not be performed by machines.

Today, the capacities of expert systems include such domains as financial services currently performed by highly paid managerial employees (Sullivan, 1984). As Gio Wiederhold (1984) argues, the use of knowledge-based systems "can move well-understood human decision-making into the computer systems." This includes a wide range of middle managerial tasks. Even more important are developments in management information systems that allow a concentration of decision-making into the hands of fewer managers. Despite the optimism of Herbert Simon (1985), Kenneth Arrow (1980) and other economists who have examined the impact of information systems on business decision-making that centralization will not occur, they recognize the possibility.

In some areas, like modern petrochemical plants and the military, the new technological possibilities for centralized decision-making are already being realized. Embedded systems, combinations of hardware and software designed to function in integrated environments, are altering military and production technology. In chemical processing plants, integrated management information systems permit centralized control of everything from purchasing decisions on feedstocks to projected markets, pricing, process design and overall system optimization (Drake and Perrolle, 1984; "The New Cockpits of Industry," 1983). This industrial trend extends the work place routinization process to financial and other middle-level managers who formerly made independent evaluations and decisions in their own area of expertise.

The U.S. Defense Department's Ada project and Strategic Computing Initiative represent major efforts to rationalize, centralize, and automate military decision-making. Since almost all of the post–World War II developments in computer technology have been funded by the military (Atwater, 1982), Defense Department priorities will probably drive the development of intelligent software. The Ada project, intended to produce a huge standardized language for large-scale intelligent software applications, is a step toward promoting large, centralized control structures (for a description of the Ada language, see Barnes, 1982). Technical criticisms of the Ada project (Skelly, 1982; Ledgard and Singer, 1982; Winchman, 1984; and Hoare, 1981) include arguments that it is too large and too expensive to be implemented except by large organizations. Some critics suggest that it represents a stifling by military interests of other new programming ideas (Rosenberg, 1983; Begley, 1983).

The Strategic Computing Initiative (Office of Technology Assessment, 1986; Lin, 1985; Parnas, 1985—see Chapter VI.4 of this volume) is diverting expert systems research toward pilot's assistants, autonomous tanks, and battlefield management systems. Although there will undoubtedly be non-military spinoffs, the hierarchical nature of military decision-making may strongly promote decision-centralizing software as the industry standard. Also, as many opponents of militarized expert systems and structured programming fear, the belief that such systems can be made bug-free and reliable enhances the probability that military decision-making (especially in the area of nuclear strategy) will be embedded in these structures. Critics believe that the risk of an accidental computerized triggering of nuclear war is being significantly increased by the Pentagon's chosen directions in computer development.

The Devaluation of Mental Labor

In both an economic and a cultural sense, and regardless of the outcome of the deskilling debate, the spread of knowledge engineering will devalue some kinds of mental labor. In the economic sense, professional, technical and managerial employees who do the kind of thinking that machines do (or that inexpensive labor does with machines) will see a relative reduction in their wages and salaries unless they can acquire new tasks or protect their existing areas of expertise from automation.

As knowledge engineering rationalizes and automates some areas of mental labor, those who are less successful at finding creative new activities may shift the focus of job satisfaction from autonomy and real control over the labor process to symbolic gestures of social standing. Already the terminology of computer technology defines workers subjected to the control of management systems as computer "users." Job titles containing the words "manager," "designer," and "analyst" often do not correspond very well to wages and actual working conditions. Even computer equipment repairers (who often replace parts with little understanding of how the machinery works) wear business suits and carry their tools in briefcases. Among the middle class there is a growing concern for what Randall Collins (1979:72) calls a consciousness of formalism "directed away from the material realities of work experience and into the purely relative values of cultural currency."

In a culture concerned with self and status, the very meaning of work is changing. What one does in an instrumental sense is being replaced by what one displays in terms of symbolic status. So long as the illusion is maintained that employees on intellectual assembly lines are managing a system that enhances their intellectual skills, the symbolic token may be satisfactory. The contradiction in this arrangement is that if the computer software devalues labor in economic terms, the illusion will become increasingly difficult to maintain. In the long run, capitalist culture may teach that intellectual skills are not a source of human satisfaction; in the short run, downwardly mobile white-collar workers' demand for the material rewards "due" their middle-class status is predicted to create a crisis of distribution (Leontiff, 1980).

The mechanization of thought processes may be translated into a cultural devaluation of the rational, logical aspects of human knowledge and intelligence. Sherry Turkle (1983) finds young children exposed to computerized toys stressing "feelings" rather than "thinking" as the defining criteria of being alive and human. Critics of artificial intelligence and humanist critics of the social injustices of Western technological society (cf. Capra, 1982) tend to agree in condemning instrumental rationality as a form of tyranny over the human spirit. These combined assertions that the essence of human thought is "what machines can't do," and that it is feelings rather than logic which make humans human, somewhat paradoxically help to legitimate turning over instrumental decision-making processes to expert systems programs. The machines are only behaving in coldly instrumental ways which are not true expressions of our humanity. Unfortunately, instrumental decision-making is at the heart of democratic political institutions. A devaluation of decision-making logic may render the democratic process even more concerned with emotional symbols of group solidarity and less concerned with rational discussions of issues than it already is.

References

Abercrombie, Nicholas, and John Urry (1983). *Capital, Labor, and the Middle Classes.* George Allen and Unwin, London.

Alexander, Tom (1984). "Why Computers Can't Outthink the Experts," *Fortune,* August 20: 105–118.

Anderson, James G., and Stephen J. Jay (1985). "The Impact of Computers on the Practice of Medicine," presentation to the American Sociological Association, August. Washington, D.C.

Arrow, Kenneth (1980). "The Economics of Information," in Michael Dertouzos and Joel Moses (eds.), *The Computer Age: A Twenty-Year View.* MIT Press, Cambridge.

Attewell, Paul, and James Rule (1984). "Computing and Organizations: What We Know and What We Don't Know," *Communications of the ACM* 27, 12 (December): 1184–1192.

Atwater, Harry (1982). "Electronics and Computer Development: A Military History," *Technology and Responsibility* 1, 2 (Fall): 1–5.

Ayres, Robert, and Steven Miller (1983). "Robotic Realities: The Near-Term Prospects and Problems," *Annals of the American Academy of Political Science* 470 (November): 28–55.

Babbage, Charles (1982). Cited in Philip Kraft, Butler-Cox Foundation Lecture, Davos, Switzerland.

Bairstow, Jeffrey N. (1985). "Chip Design Made Easy: A New Generation of Tools Enables Nonexperts to Design Custom Integrated Circuits Cheaply and Easily," *High Technology* 5, 5 (June): 18–25.

Bander, Edward, and Susan Sweetgall (1983). "Westlaw and Lexis: A Comparison," pages 9–12 in *New Technology and the Law,* special issue of *The Advocate* 14, 2.

Barnes, J.G.P. (1982). *Programming in Ada.* Addison-Wesley, Reading, MA.

Barr, Avron, and Edward A. Feigenbaum (1982). *The Handbook of Artificial Intelligence.* Heuris Tech Press, Stanford.

Basden, A. (1984). "Application of Expert Systems," pages 59–75 in Coombs, *Developments in Expert Systems.*

Begley, Sharon (1983). "Can Ada Run the Pentagon?" *Newsweek* January 10: 71.

Bell, Daniel (1980). "The Social Framework of the Information Society," Michael Dertouzos and Joel Moses, *The Computer Age: A Twenty-Year View.* MIT Press, Cambridge.

Boden, Margaret (1977). *Artificial Intelligence and Natural Man.* Basic Books, New York.

Braverman, Harry (1974). *Labor and Monopoly Capitalism: The Degradation of Work in the Twentieth Century.* Monthly Review, New York.

Brooks, Frederick P., Jr. (1982). *The Mythical Man-Month: Essays on Software Engineering.* Addison-Wesley, Reading, MA.

Capra, Fritjof (1982). *The Turning Point: Science, Society, and the Rising Culture.* Bantam, New York.

Cass, Christopher (1985). "Linking Computer Technology with Plastic Modelling to Produce Quality-Assured Piping Drawings," paper presented to the American Engineering Model Society (May), Boston.

Codd, E.F. (1982). "Relational Database: A Practical Foundation for Productivity," *Communications of the ACM* 5, 2 (February): 109–117.

Collins, Randall (1979). *The Credential Society.* Academic Press, New York.

Connolly, James (1985). "Patent Disputes, Hacking Major DP Law Issues in '85," *Computerworld* (January 21): 14.

Cooley, Mike (1980). *Architect or Bee? The Human/Technology Relationship.* South End Press, Boston.

Coombs, J.J. (ed.)(1984). *Developments in Expert Systems.* Academic Press, New York.

d'Agapeyeff, Alex (1984). Quoted in *Computer* 17, 12 (December): 106.

Downing, Hazel (1980). "Word Processors and the Oppression of Women," pages 275–287 in Tom Forester, ed., *The Microelectronics Revolution.* MIT Press, Cambridge, MA.

Drake, Elisabeth, and Judith A. Perrolle (1984). "Computer-Aided Creativity." Presentation to the American Society of Chemical Engineers (March), Atlanta.

Dreyfus, Hubert L. (1972). *What Computers Can't Do*. Harper and Row, New York.

Feigenbaum, Edward (1984). Lecture at the Massachusetts Institute of Technology. October 31.

Feigenbaum, Edward, and Pamela McCorduck (1983). *The Fifth Generation: Artificial Intelligence and Japan's Computer Challenge to the World*. Addison-Wesley, Reading, MA.

Forrester, Jay (1967). Speech at the NAE Fall meeting, Washington, D.C., cited in Nigel Calder, *Technopolis: Social Control of the Uses of Science*, 1970: 152. Clarion Books, New York.

Freifeld, Karen (1984). "Obsoleting the Scalpel," *Fortune* (August 27): 130.

Frenkel, Karen A. (1985). "Toward Automating the Software-Development Cycle," *Communications of the ACM* 29, 6 (June): 578–589.

Gideon (1982). *Mechanization Takes Command*. Norton, New York.

Goldthrope, John (1982). "On the Service Class, Its Formation and Future," in Anthony Giddens and Gavin MacKenzie (eds.), *Social Class and the Division of Labor*, 162–185. Cambridge University Press, New York.

Gottfried, Heidi (1982). "Keeping the Workers in Line," *Science for the People* 14, 4 (July/August): 19–24.

Haugeland, John (ed.)(1981). *Mind Design*. MIT Press, Cambridge.

Hayes-Roth, Frederick (1984). "The Knowledge-Based Expert System: A Tutorial," *IEEE Computer* 17, 9 (September): 11–28.

Hayes-Roth, Frederick (1983). Roundtable discussion at Carnegie-Mellon (June 3) reported in *IEEE Spectrum* (November): 114–115.

Hayes-Roth, Frederick, Donald A. Waterman, and Douglas B. Lenat (eds.)(1983). *Building Expert Systems*. Addison-Wesley, Reading, MA.

Hoare, C.A.R. (1981). "The Emperor's Old Clothes," *Communications of the ACM* 24, 2 (February): 75–83.

Hopper, Grace (1959). "Automatic Programming: Present Status and Future Trends," in National Physical Laboratory, 155–194.

Jenkins, Martha M. (1979). "Computer-Generated Evidence Specially Prepared for Use at Trial," pages 283–295 in William E. Cwiklo (ed.), *Computers in Litigation Support*. Petrocelli, New York.

Keller, Robert, and Peter Townsend (1984). "Knowledge-Based System," *Computerworld Office Automation* 32.

Kling, Rob (1985). "The Impacts of Computing on the Work of Managers, Data Analysts, and Clerks," working paper 78–61. Department of Information and Computer Science, University of California, Irvine, CA.

Kling, Rob (1980). "Social Analyses of Computing: Theoretical Perspectives in Recent Empirical Research," *Computing Surveys* 12.1 (March): 61–110.

Kraft, Philip (1977). *The Sociology of Computer Programmers*. Springer-Verlag, New York.

Kraft, Philip, and Steven Dubnoff (1983). "The Division of Labor, Fragmentation, and Hierarchy in Computer Software Work," paper presented to the Society for the Study of Social Problems, Detroit, Michigan.

Kuttner, Robert (1983). "The Declining Middle," *The Atlantic Monthly* (July): 60–71.

Ledgard, Henry F., and Andrew Singer (1982). "Scaling Down Ada (Or Towards a Standard Ada)," *Communications of the ACM* 25, 2 (February): 121–125.

Leibniz (1959). In D.E. Smith (ed.), *A Sourcebook of Mathematics*, Vol. 1. Dover, New York.

Leontiff, W. (1980). "The Distribution of Work and Income," in Scientific American's *The Mechanization of Work*. W.H. Freeman, San Francisco.

Lin, Herbert (1985). "The Development of Software for Ballistic-Missile Defence," *Scientific American* 253, 6 (December): 46–53.

Marx, Gary T., and Nancy Richman (1984). "Routinizing the Discovery of Secrets: Computers as Informants," *American Behavioral Scientist* 27, 4 (March/April): 423–452.

Marx, Karl (1973). *The Poverty of Philosophy*. Progress Publishers, Moscow.

McCorduck, Pamela (1979). *Machines Who Think*. W.H. Freeman, San Francisco.

McClure, Carma (1984). Computer Applications Seminar in Structured Techniques for Fourth Generation Languages. April 2–4, Washington, D.C.

Mehl, L. (1958). "Automation in the Legal World," National Physical Laboratory, Vol. II. 1959: 755–780.

Merriman, J.H.H., and D.W.G. Wass (1958). "To What Extent Can Administration be Mechanizated?" National Physical Laboratory, Vol. II. 1959: 809–818.

"The New Cockpits of Industry" (1983). *Furtune* (November 28): 108–117.

National Physical Laboratory (1959). *Mechanisation of Thought Processes*, Proceedings of a Symposium November 24–27, 1958. Her Majesty's Stationery Office, London.

Office of Technology Assessment (1986). *Strategic Defenses*. Princeton University Press, Princeton, N.J.

Olson, Steve (1984). "Sage of Software," *Science84* (January/February): 74–80.

Parnas, David L. (1985). "Software Aspects of Strategic Defense Systems," *American Scientist* 73 (September–October): 432–440.

Paycha, Dr. F. (1958). "Medical Diagnosis and Cybernetics," in National Physical Laboratory, Vol. II, 1959: 635–660.

Perrolle, Judith A. (1985). "Computers and Capitalism," in Williamson, Evans, and Rustad (eds.), *Social Problems: The Contemporary Debates*. Little, Brown, Boston.

Perrolle, Judith A., *et al.* (1986). Preliminary case studies of Massachusetts firms introducing computer-aided design systems.

Pylyshyn, Zenon W. (1980). "Artificial Intelligence," Chapter 6 in Bruce Arden (ed.), *What Can Be Automated? The Computer Science and Engineering Research Study*. MIT Press, Cambridge, MA.

Rosenberg, Ronald (1983). "The Military Goes Great Guns for Ada," *The Boston Globe* (January 23): A1–A5.

Salaman, Graeme (1982). "Managing the Frontier of Control," in Anthony Giddens, Anthony, and Gavin Mackenzie (eds.), *Social Class and the Division of Labor*. Cambridge University Press, Cambridge.

Shaiken, Harley (1984). *Work Transformed: Automation and Labor in the Computer Age*. Holt, Rinehart, and Winston, New York.

Shurkin, Joel N (1983). "Expert Systems: The Practical Face of Artificial Intelligence," *Technology Review* (November/December): 72–78.

Simon, Herbert (1985). "The Consequences of Computers for Centralization and Decentralization," in Williamson, Evans, and Rustad (eds.), *Social Problems: The Contemporary Debates*. Little, Brown, Boston.

Soloway, Elliot, and Kate Ehrlich (1984). "Empirical Studies of Programming Knowledge." *IEEE Transactions on Software Engineering*, SE-10, 5 (September): 596–609.

Skelly, Patrick G. (for the ACM Standards Committee)(1982). "The ACM Position on Standardization of the Ada Language," *Communications of the ACM* 25, 2 (February): 118–120.

Starr, Paul (1983). *The Social Transformation of American Medicine*. Basic Books, New York.

Straw, Ronnie, and Lorel Foged (1983). "Technology and Employment in Telecommunications," *Annals of the American Academy of Political Science* 470 (November): 163–170.

Sullivan, Kathleen (1984). "Financial Industry Fertile Ground for Expert Systems," *Computerworld*, October 22: 29–31.

"Supercomputers: The High-Stakes Race To Build a Machine That Thinks," *newsweek* (July 4): 58–64.

Turkle, Sherry (1983). "The Psychological Machine: Computers and the Culture of Self-Reflection." Lecture at the New York Academy of Sciences Science Week Symposium (April 8).

Vessey, Iris, and Ron Weber (1984). "Research on Structured Programming: An Empiricist's Evaluation," *IEEE Transactions on Software Engineering* 10, 4 (July): 397–407.

Weizenbaum, Joseph (1983). "The Computer in Your Future," *New York Review* (October 27): 58–62.

Weizenbaum, Joseph (1976). *Computer Power and Human Reason: From Judgment to Calculation.* W.H. Freeman, San Francisco.

Wenger, Peter (1984). "Capital-Intensive Software Technology, Part 3: Knowledge Engineering," *IEEE Software* 1.3 (July): 33–37.

Wiederhold, Gio (1984). "Knowledge and Database Management," *IEEE Software* 1, 1 (january): 63–73.

Wiener, Norbert (1967). *The Human Use of Human Beings.* Avon Books, New York.

Winchman, Brian A. (1984). "Is Ada Too Big? A Designer Answers the Critics," *Communications of the ACM* 27, 2 (February): 98–103.

Winston, Patrick H., and Karen A. Prendergast (eds.)(1984). *The AI Business: The Commercial Uses of Artificial Intelligence.* MIT Press, Cambridge, MA.

Wright, Erik Olin, and Joachim Singlemann (1982)." Proletarianization in the Changing American Class Structure," *American Journal of Sociology* Vol. 88 Supplement: S176–S209.

Big Brother and the Sweatshop: Computer Surveillance in the Automated Office

Paul Attewell

Introduction

One of the most controversial aspects of the new information technologies concerns the capacity of new computerized office systems to count and continuously monitor white-collar employees' work. The surveillance capacity of electronic technology has disturbed a variety of academic and labor writers. Even such sober commentators as the Office of Technology Assessment, the US Bureau of Labor Statistics, and *The Wall Street Journal* have raised the prospect that computer surveillance may turn the automated office into a *sweatshop* (Austin and Drake, 1985; OTA, 1985; Wall Street Journal, 1985, 1986).[1]

Historically, the term sweatshop has a quite specific meaning,[2] but it is used by these writers to connote a system where computer surveillance is used to drive workers to work faster. In the most draconian of scenarios, computers track every move that workers make. Each visit to the bathroom, every pause or slackening of work pace, each error or oversight is silently tallied, to be used in assessing individual workers.

Microelectronics, viewed from this perspective, leads to a shift in the relative power of labor and management: as every activity of the worker is laid bare, so management is able to use this information to push for faster work, insisting on a relentless pace. Thus, far from opening up an age free from drudgery at work, as its admirers prophesied, microelectronics is said to usher in the age of electronically sweated labor.

At this point in time, we lack detailed studies of electronic sweatshops. A few short reports have appeared describing workplaces that sound like electronic sweatshops for telephone assistance operators, data entry clerks, airline booking agents, and claims payment staff. Unfortunately these accounts are so brief that one learns little about how the office works on a day to day basis, the use (or non-use) of surveillance information for pressure, punishment, and so on.

The purpose of this paper is to examine the idea that electronic sweatshops represent the future of clerical or white-collar work, from the vantage point of industrial sociology and managerial theory. Social scientists have charted the history and dynamics of control systems in industry. We know the conditions under which various measurement and control systems thrive, and the limits to such controls; the dynamics of payment by results, hourly wages, and quota systems; and the ways that surveillance works in non-computerized settings.

To the extent that we can build theoretical models of surveillance and control of workers, and identify factors contributing to and inhibiting speedups, we can make intelligent inferences about computer surveillance in the future. This paper is an initial exploration using this strategy.

The paper has three parts. First, I draw out five theoretical models from the managerial and sociological literature, each of which generates hypotheses about work monitoring. Then I briefly outline the history of work measurement in clerical occupations. Lastly, I present a case study of surveillance and control in one highly automated office in a large company, the purpose of which is to clarify and critique some of the models presented earlier.

Theoretical Approaches and Their Implications

Corporate Culture Theories

Corporate culture theorists emphasize that different firms have divergent or distinctive ways of behaving (Deal and Kennedy, 1984). From dress code, to managerial style, to concern with employee development, each company has its own unique philosophy and practice. Through historical accretion, these become institutionalized as traditions and as mindsets, into which new employees are socialized.

---

[1] See also Zuboff (1982); Howard (1985); Jacobson (1984); Reinecke (1984: 150–153); and Nine-to-Five (1986).

[2] In the early 19th century, sweating was associated with work done in the home. The sweater was a middleman who farmed out production from a manufacturer, and paid piece-rates to home-based workers (Marx, 1967:554). Gradually the term broadened to connote a certain kind of very low paid employment in shops and factories, under poor physical conditions. To earn even a meager living, one had to toil at high speed for long hours. The sweatshop has never been the norm for labor. Even in the grimmest period of 19th-century British industrialization, sweating was a term used pejoratively to describe a particularly debased situation, one where workers, unable to combine, and pressed upon by others seeking work, undercut one another's wages. Sweating was contrasted in popular speech with "the respectable portion of the trade" (Hollis, 1973: 61).

The corporate culture perspective can be applied to industrial relations or to technological change. Some firms have strong traditions of caring about the welfare, security, and aspirations of their work forces, while other companies have a corporate culture that emphasizes managerial prerogative above employee morale, views workers in a suspicious or adversarial light, and feels that "driving" workers is necessary in order to be profitable. There are, to borrow McGregor's terms, Theory X and Theory Y corporate cultures.

As applied to office automation, this corporate culture position hypothesizes substantial variation in the ways that new technologies are implemented—a spectrum from deskilling to job enrichment—and argues that a firm's past history of industrial relations will be the best predictor of how it uses office technology. Thus, Westin (1985) argues, based on a survey of 100 firms, that those firms that implemented office automation from top down, without concern for employee input, and that exploited the surveillance capacities of the new technology, were businesses with prior histories of adversarial labor relations. Conversely, firms with traditions of non-adversarial labor relations consulted employees prior to implementing the technologies, and did not use monitoring for speedups.

Neo-Marxist Theory

Neo-Marxist theories of the labor process provide a contrasting framework for conceptualizing issues of work discipline, surveillance, and work pace. According to Marx (1967), capitalists only purchase the labor power of their employees, their capacity to do work. It therefore falls to management to ensure that this labor power is turned into labor done and to maximize the labor done in order to generate profits.

For Braverman (1974), Tayloristic strategies of fragmenting skilled jobs into narrow tasks (deskilling) occur not only to cut costs, but also to enhance managerial control over labor. Technological innovation is therefore viewed, not as a neutral instrument to increase productivity, but as a deliberate tactic to enhance managerial power.

Howard (1985) applies this perspective to surveillance systems in office automation. For him, Taylorism is the pervasive perspective in American management. Computer surveillance of clerical workers enables managers to consolidate their power over labor, and to increase the pressure on employees to work fast. He and others give examples of the psychological pressures generated by computer surveillance, from buzzers that sound if a clerk doesn't enter data, to screens that ask "Were you at your workstation at 8:30 this morning? " to hidden monitoring that reveals whether a clerk slowed down her work pace during the day.

For the neo-Marxist perspective, computer surveillance is too important and useful for management to ignore, and is destined to become widespread, limited only by organized labor's opposition to it in contract negotiations, or by labor's ability to outlaw workplace surveillance via legislation.

Product or Technological Lifecycle Theories

Another, alternative approach to understanding the variations in computer surveillance, stems from recent theories of *product and technological lifecycles*. Leavitt (1965) used a lifecycle or stage theory to describe how product markets approach maturity over time, as measured by changes in sales volume. Abernathy and Utterback (1982) constructed a similar stage theory with respect to the rate of industrial innovation, and Sahal (1981) and Twiss (1979) have posited a "technological S curve" that charts the changing relationship between the performance capability of a technology and invested R&D.

What all of these theories have in common is an image of products or technologies reaching a stage of maturity, during which technological change is unable to enhance sales or profitability. Pressure therefore mounts in this mature stage to sustain profitability by cutting labor costs or intensifying work pressure. John Gosden (1986) has used a framework of this kind to analyze office automation at the Equitable company. He argues that as the insurance industry reached a state of product maturation after 1975, a shift occurred toward cost cutting, resulting in deskilling and increased pressure on work speed, in part via work measurement.

Developing a hypothesis from this, we would predict an intensification of surveillance in those industries in the mature phase of the product lifecycle. But we would not expect intensive use of surveillance for speedups in those industries at early stages of the product cycle or where technological innovations in production technologies are generating cost savings.

Contingency Theory

A related but somewhat different view of surveillance draws on the contingency approach to complex organizations (Woodward, 1965; Lawrence and Lorsch, 1967; Perrow, 1967; Hickson et al., 1969). This school posits a fit between various structural and environmental features of firms and seeks to explain the variation in any one element, such as surveillance practices, in terms of variations in other features. It expects to find systematic relationships between business strategy, technology, and organizational procedures, for example.

Applying it to office automation, one would predict a patterned variation in the way that OA is implemented. For example, in those clerical-intensive industries that operate in highly price-competitive environments, one would expect a tendency for OA to be used to reduce costs by eliminating clerical labor and to intensify the workplace of those that remain.

By contrast, in firms that are growing rapidly and in which clerical costs are a smaller proportion of costs, office automation is often viewed as the only way of hoarding or extending the skills of already-present staff, of enabling them to rapidly increase their volume of work to keep up with the growth of the firm. In such a context, work surveillance and driving are likely to be anathema: one desperately wants to keep hold of established trained staff, since they are holding the firm together. One searches for technologies that improve and enhance their work; one does not seek to deskill or eliminate them.

Yet another context occurs where clerical labor is a small percentage of costs and where the firm seeks to compete by differentiating itself from competitors. In such a situation, office automation may be viewed primarily as an opportunity to improve customer service, speed of response, or quality of product, rather than cost-saving. Here we are likely to find a proliferation of jobs that combine customer service/enquiry with clerical functions such as payables and receivables. Clerks become low-level account executives. The emphasis is not on surveillance and work speed, but on enhanced service.

These three examples represent cells in a contingency grid. One dimension of the grid is a highly-modified version of Porter's (1985) classification of business strategies: price-cutting, high growth, and product differentiation. The other dimension measures the importance of clerical costs as a factor in profitability. In terms of hypotheses regarding surveillance and sweating, this approach would *not* predict ubiquitous use of surveillance, but rather would predict that speedups would be limited to those firms in which routine clerical operations were central to profitability *and* where the competitive strategy was focused on price.

Industrial Sociology

There is no single theory of surveillance, work pace, and discipline in industrial sociology. However, there are many empirical studies from which we can cull various theoretical insights.

We should first note that there are two ways of enforcing a given work speed: piecework systems and ongoing surveillance. Far from being complementary, these two methods have in the past been *alternatives.* The purpose of paying by unit of output is to *remove* the burden of surveillance from the manager and to shift responsibility for directing the work onto the employee herself. The piece-rate, or production bonus, rather than the supervisor's gaze guarantees fast work.[3]

By contrast, where employees are paid salaries or by the hour, the responsibility for making sure that workers' hours are turned into useful work devolves upon management. This is usually accomplished by ongoing observation by first line supervisors, who check that employees are not absent from their desks and who intervene when talking or other activities seem to be slowing down production.

Both surveillance of hourly workers and piece-rate payment are aimed at a common problem: how to make employees work hard. Both depend on techniques of work measurement, but piece-rate systems measure output *after-the-fact*, to calculate payment or bonuses, whereas surveillance watches the work *as it is done*, primarily in order to know the work *not done.* It seeks to catch workers at rest ("wasted time") and to crack the whip.

From management's viewpoint there are difficult problems with using either piece-work or surveillance to speed up work.

Piece-rates can be used to intensify effort or output, by offering low rates per piece for some new task or by cutting existing rates for some product. Historically, such tactics have generated great worker resistance, *even among nonunionized workers* (Mathewson, 1931:136). Workers slow down and thereby refuse to work for rates they deem too low,

---

[3] The ecological niche of piece-payment has been shrinking in manufacturing as technological developments draw more and more firms away from depending on individual machine operatives who control their own pace of work. The ILO (1984) reports that, in the US, Payment by Results schemes peaked in the 1940s with 30% of manufacturing production workers, and was down to 18% by 1980.

and numerous strikes have been sparked by piece-rate disputes (Mathewson, 1931: 53–67; Edwards, 1979; cf. Aitken, 1960; Roy, 1952; Lupton, 1973).

Similarly, there have been periods in U.S. history when close surveillance was used to try to intensify work pace. The "Drive System" of the 1880s to the 1930s depended upon "close supervision, abuse, profanity, and threats of discharge. Workers were constantly urged to move faster and harder" (Jacoby, 1985:20).

But the drive system generated enormous conflict: an us versus them mentality. Unions fought it. Unorganized workers voted with their feet: quit rates soared, way above present levels. Union organizing drives flourished (cf. Gouldner, 1954 on attempted speedup via intensified surveillance in the 1950s).

Taken together, this means that although piece-rate and surveillance systems seem to be methods for *intensifying* and maximizing the effort of each individual worker, in practice they often erode into systems for maintaining an average acceptable level of effort, determined by formal or tacit agreements between management and labor (Baldamus, 1959; Mathewson, 1931; see also Hobsbawm, 1964; Edwards, 1976). When pressed into duty for speeding up work, both systems can generate conflict that is wounding to managerial goals. The desire to maximize production therefore has to be balanced against morale and other factors—a point to which we will return.

Nevertheless, one does find certain contexts in which a very fast work pace is sustained. The ecological niche of the sweatshop is quite specific. Sweating was and is characterized by piece-rates, rather than surveillance. The work involves unskilled routinized machine operation where the work pace is controlled by the operative. It applies to "pooled production," James Thompson's term for work in which each employee in essence works independently. Sweating (and piece-rates more generally) are not found where teamwork prevails, nor in automated process industries, where the speed of production is not directly dependent on the pace of workers (Carlson, 1982). Sweating is still found in some US firms in the garment industry (Jenson and Davidson, 1984).

Industries in which sweating plays a part also tend to be highly competitive, with many small firms. They are labor, rather than capital intensive—which is why pressuring workers to speed up is a crucial method of cutting unit costs.

Most importantly, sweatshops are associated with gluts of labor and high turnover. Sweating is an extreme form of work discipline, highly unattractive to employees and therefore possible only where there is a glut of labor, so limited in its opportunities and so desperate that it will accept very low wages for very long intensive work hours. In twentieth century western experience, immigrants (mostly women) isolated from better labor markets by language, lack of transport, lack of other industrial skills, or the need to work at home, have constituted the sweatshop work force in inner city ghettos from London's East End, to New York's China Town, to Hispanic East Los Angeles (Seidman, 1942: 52–74; Jenson and Davison, 1984).

If one tries to turn these historical lessons into a hypothesis regarding the contexts in which office work could be speeded up or sweated it would be as follows:

Speedups would be limited to routine repetitive paperwork jobs, those not involving discretion or teamwork, tasks where quantity rather than quality was of essence. Sweating would produce low morale, high turnover and labor conflict. It would therefore depend upon the existence of gluts of clerical labor.

Table 1. Theories and Hypotheses Regarding the Use of Surveillance or Work Measurement for Intensifying Work Pace

Theory		Hypothesis or Prognosis
Corporate Culture	#1.	Surveillance used to drive employees only in firms with prior histories of "Theory X" labor relations. Not used that way elsewhere.
Neo-Marxist	#2.	Surveillance widely used for speedups, limited only by union pressure or legislation.
Product or Technological Lifecycle	#3.	Surveillance used to drive employees only in firms with mature product markets, and mature technologies, where costs can only be cut by intensifying the work pace. Not used this way elsewhere.
Contingency Theory	#4.	Surveillance only used to intensity work pace where both (a) routine clerical jobs constitute a large percentage of costs, and (b) strategy is cost-competition, but not where differentiation or growth strategies occur or where clerical costs are not central to profitability.
Industrial Sociology	#5.	Surveillance generates organized resistance. Sweating can occur where (a) piece-payment predominates, (b) in highly-competitive labor-intensive markets with small firms, (c) pooled (individual) production, (d) high-turnover unskilled labor, (e) gluts of somewhat immobile labor, (f) work in the home. Workplaces with these characteristics seem to have been decreasing over time.

Table 1 summarizes the five theoretical approaches to surveillance and speedups and their differing prognoses. I should emphasize that the five are not all mutually exclusive, since they point in many cases to different variables.

I now turn to two sets of empirical materials. The first involves a historical treatment of work measurement in clerical occupations, the second a study of computer surveillance in a present-day automated office.

Clerical Work and Work Measurement

We can now pose the question of whether and how microelectronics has changed these two ancient strategies of control—surveillance and payment by results. Does computing enable managers to observe labor in ways that earlier techniques did not? Has it shifted the balance between piece-work and work paid by the hour?

The image of clerical workers in sociological classics such as Mill (1951), Lockwood (1958), and Crozier (1965) is one of *salaried* workers. Piece-work is not mentioned, nor are Modified Day Rate quotas. Supervision is described as involving varying degrees of tension, but work pace is not reported as an issue (Crozier, 1965: 107–133; Lockwood,

1958: 79). Kocka (1980: 179) mentions "occasional attempts" at using piece-rates in US office work during the 1920s but treats these as aberrations.[4]

Given this perception, it is not surprising that when journalists and others find work measurement, quotas, or piece-rates in today's computerized offices, they tend to ascribe this to the new technology and especially its powers of surveillance (Nine-to-Five, 1986; NY Times 1984, 1986; Howard, 1985; OTA, 1985:130).

However, it is easy to overstate the strictly technological advance embodied in computer work counting. It has been fairly easy to obtain work counts since the turn of the century. Mechanical keystroke counters ("cyclometers") were available for type-writers before 1913, and Taylorist texts offered a variety of schemes for measuring typing output, counting by area or by length, using sampling techniques to avoid having to count every piece (Schulze, 1913; Galloway, 1919).

Similarly the monitoring chart chosen by the OTA (1985:130) to illustrate com-puterized surveillance of telephone operators is much the same as the "Efficiency Blackboards for Typists" used in 1910 (Schulze, 1913). Howard (1985:28–35) expresses concern with the capacity of Management Information Systems to assign productivity ratings to clerical workers. But, the indices that he describes are very similar, if not identical, to those for use in non-computerized offices in Grillo and Berg (1959:140–180), and parallel those for stenographers and accounting clerks in Galloway (1919).

In insurance, long prior to computers, it was common to have claims payment personnel keep tallies of their own work, and it was relatively easy to detect false counts by balancing aggregate numbers of claims paid with individual reports. In banking, one could assess teller performance by auditing a random sample of each person's paperwork and by checking daily total transactions or balances. Indeed in almost all areas involving money, the need to control embezzlement and incompetence stimulated the development, decades ago, of various forms of *post hoc* auditing of individuals' work. Thus, counting a person's work, and assessing his/her performance without the knowledge of the employee ("hidden surveillance") are not recent inventions.

If contemporary commentators on office automation overstate the newness of these monitoring techniques, they also tend to ignore the historical role of quotas and work measurement in offices. In the heyday of scientific management in the office, from 1920–1930, work measurement schemes were devised and used for all manner of clerical tasks: stenography, typing, mailroom, payroll, and posting (Bills *et al.*, 1926; Clark, 1926; McAdams, 1927; Mitchell, 1928; Mitchell *et al.*, 1927; Rowland *et al.*, 1925). A 1925 mail survey of the membership of the American Management Association (mainly large corporations) found that 10% were measuring clerical output for some of their employees as a basis for payment (Bills *et al.*, 1926). Almost all of these schemes guaranteed a minimum wage and paid a bonus for production over a quota (Modified Day Rate). A similar survey indicated 8% of firms with payment by results schemes in 1929 and 12.5% in 1936 (Stivers *et al.*, 1936).[5] But these results should be treated with caution, since the AMA membership was more Taylorist than businesses in general.

---

[4] Braverman (1974) is the exception. He does document work measurement.
[5] I have followed Bills *et al.*'s unusual practice of counting non-responses as non-users of piece-rates, in citing their survey results.

Erikson's (1934) interview study of 314 offices in several cities is probably more representative. About 8% of firms had production bonus schemes for some of their clerical staff, but less than 2% of their clerical work force were covered by these schemes. She also found that many of those eligible never ever earned a bonus, suggesting that these schemes did not operate primarily as a system of payment by results, but instead had become unpaid quota systems. In such contexts work measurement has become a form of surveillance rather than an incentive payment. Management uses these work measurements to enforce work speed. Proponents of work measurement, however, are usually quick to disassociate work measurement from speedups: "It is not a speedup. The emphasis is on normal—what an average person can turn out under average work conditions" (Grillo and Berg, 1959: 28).

Clerical work measurement and payment schemes continued from the 1930s to the present. In 1959 a survey showed 15% of firms with schemes (Kenny, 1960). However, proponents repeatedly bemoaned the fact that most companies failed to adopt such systems (Rowland et al., 1936: 22–23; Grillo and Berg, 1959: 165).

It is not clear whether work measurement and payment schemes have increased or decreased with the recent advent of computers. A recent *Wall Street Journal* article was headlined "Back to Piecework," suggesting a sudden upsurge in payment by results. However, the article described firms that used performance data to determine annual bonuses and promotion prospects (or firing), rather than piece-payment. It also cited a 1985 survey of 600 firms that found that 11% of the firms presently use incentive payment systems (less than the 1959 rate cited above), and that one-third intend to adopt such systems (*Wall Street Journal*, 1985). Another recent survey contacted 685 firms, chosen because they were viewed as likely users of work measurement and productivity improvement programs, but it found a "surprisingly sparse number of businesses that are actually active in the field" and noted that productivity measurement typically consisted of output counts of "a lower-level group at work on a routine task, such as billing" (*World of Work Report*, 1983a).

Thus, despite decades of exhortations from Taylorists, work measurement and output incentives remain largely limited to highly routinized clerical labor in large firms—a minority of clerks even in those firms. One major constraint on the spread of work measurement has been that many managers believe that Taylorism is of no use in most clerical situations, where the work is unstandardized or too varied to benefit from these forms of industrial engineering (Strassman, 1985:18–19).

Several commentators have pointed to the phone company's ability to silently measure telephone operators' work performance as a prime example of the dangers of hidden or remote surveillance via computer (OTA, 1985; Howard, 1985: 63; Clement, 1985). Such systems are said to generate anxiety and stress. These are important concerns. However, the same problems have characterized telephone operators for decades. In 1946, operators' work was described as follows:

> Standards have been set for speed and performance on all kinds of work positions and calls. In carrying out the duties of her work . . . the operator's performance is being checked or inspected at every step by superiors and service observers.
>
> Telephone operating is exacting. A fagged-out feeling and tense nerves at the end of the day are common . . . working under close, hovering supervision. Close supervision and

remote observation by service observers add to the nervous tension of the job. (US Women's Bureau, 1946)

Hidden listening in and measuring operator's speed are of long standing: measures of time to complete a connection are available from as far back as 1922 (US Womens' Bureau, 1963).

It is true that computers lessen the effort needed for surveillance, and moreover, computers can count every instance of a person leaving their machine or slowing down work, whereas before a manager could usually only audit or observe a sample of each person's output. (In the operator's case, observation was continuous. See US Womens' Bureau, 1963:11.) But continuous or 100% monitoring may not be substantively important. Sampling theory suggests that if an employee works slowly, makes many errors, or is consistently late back from lunch, and surveillance systems are in place, that s/he will be noticed by a sampling form of surveillance, just as surely as by continuous monitoring via computer. It may take a little longer, but in standardized repetitive work, with thousands of transactions or units per month, trends emerge quite clearly.

We should therefore be skeptical of claims that computer surveillance will tell managers something totally new about each employee, things they never noticed before. Time clocks, paper and pencil work counts, and a sharp eye, have allowed clerical supervisors to know which of their workers are "high production" and which low, who is chronically late in the morning and who is regular as clockwork, whom supervisors judge to be wasting time talking and whom not, all without the assistance of interactive computing.

My point here is not to be cavalier about the dangers of surveillance and speedup in the workplace, but to stress that it has not been a *lack of technology* that has prevented surveillance or speedups in the past. Despite the availability of measurement and surveillance techniques in the past, they were only used on a small percentage of white-collar workers.

Control in an Automated Office

The office I studied was a regional office of one of the country's largest medical insurance companies. It specialized in claims evaluation and payment for group medical insurance. I carried out fieldwork in this office about two years after it was reorganized around state-of-the-art interactive computer workstations and claims payment software. I was allowed to interview managers and employees, observe the workplace over an extended period, and collect data on turnover, staffing, and productivity. The office consisted of about 100 persons (nonunionized), of whom the majority worked at computer consoles, entering claims data (data process and entry clerks), or evaluating medical claims and authorizing payment (claims examiners and adjusters).

Production levels were important to both management and workers: graphs of the office's aggregate production over time were posted prominently in the staff lunchroom, and statistics comparing this regional office with other regional offices on a variety of work measures were displayed at the entrance to the office. Workers were interested in both individual and group output. One employee referred to another employee as "high production," a term of respect. Many employees went to look at the cross-office statistics, soon after fresh statistics were posted. They joked about offices at the bottom of the league and discussed their own office's position.

Management were continuously aware of production levels. They prepared monthly reports that aggregated all the various kinds of claims paid, weighted each with a time norm, and calculated aggregate office productivity. Declines on this statistic over a course of months resulted in strong criticism from central office and spurred anxious local managers into diagnosing what was causing the slowdown.

Nevertheless, this sensitivity to productivity did not result in a draconian work regime or new uses of surveillance. Individual-level counts of work done were used in a relatively non-punitive way. Employees were evaluated annually using these data, and promotions were decided, in part, on these numbers. Each employee, when reviewed, was asked to strive for a goal expressed as a percentage increase over his/her previous year's perform-ance. Large disparities were tolerated between individuals' productivity levels: for example, the fastest examiners produced at twice the rate of the slowest workers. Yet, I found only one employee who was fired for slow work—a recently hired worker with health problems, whose medication slowed her production down so far below anyone else's that the person was the butt of jokes and commentary from other (non-managerial) employees.

I asked managers why work measurement was not used more forcefully to monitor and increase the work speed of individual employees. Their answers revealed several factors that resulted in the underutilization of these data, each of which has implications for the theories and hypotheses advanced earlier.

First, managers were concerned about office morale. The office functions as a unit, they argued. Pressuring one worker could undermine the commitment of that employee and that person's friends, and sour the happy, constructive attitude of the office as a whole. This was an expression of the managers' human relations ideology, which placed a strong emphasis on positive rather than negative incentives.

This managerial commitment to a human relations philosophy is worth stressing, because commentators such as Braverman (1974) and Howard (1985) write as if Taylorism is *the* perspective of management. They neglect the existence of an ideological battle that has been going on for the hearts and minds of managers over several decades. Gener-ations of managers have been schooled in the ideas of Maslow, McGregor, the Quality of Worklife and Job Enrichment movements. For example, both Citibank and Prudential Insurance have programs for redesigning "assembly-line" clerical jobs into more complex, varied, and skillful jobs. These programs are reported to have resulted in significant increases in productivity (*World of Work Report*, 1983b).

In terms of our earlier models, this suggests that the corporate culture model (hypo-thesis one) clearly has merit: some firms and/or managers refuse to equate increased productivity with close surveillance of individuals or speedups.

A second rationale was given for the circumscribed use of individual work measures. Managers said they preferred group measures to individual ones, because the office "worked as a team." Although partly a reflection of the same human relations ideology, this explanation was also grounded in real changes that took place in the division of labor following computerization.

Prior to the introduction of interactive computing, the office consisted of numerous individuals each doing their own separate work. Thus, each examiner assessed his/her particular allotment of claims, in most cases without the assistance of anyone else. Each file clerk pulled or returned files in isolation from other file clerks, examiners or other staff. The transfer of work from one step (or person) to the next was almost anonymous, involving movement of folders but not any coordination between individuals. James Thompson (1967) has called this kind of work situation, which requires minimum interaction with others, and no teamwork, "pooled production."

After the introduction of interactive computing, the degree of coordination and interdependence increased. Each examiner was paired with one or more data process and entry (DPE) clerks. Workflow patterns changed such that paperwork went to the examiner, then to the DPE, then back to the examiner. This led to increased coordination over workflow. Boundaries between these two jobs also began to blur: certain tasks "officially" part of the examiner's job were now sometimes done by the DPE. The work was becoming teamwork. Relationships between examiners also shifted: a lot of informal advising was going on.

This shift from individuated or pooled production to a team-oriented system with less rigid demarcation between jobs meant that individual work counts became less appropriate or useful. One examiner might look very productive on a work-count measure because his/her DPE clerk was carrying out certain of the examiner's tasks. Conversely, the DPE clerk looked slow on his/her own work statistics because s/he was doing that extra work but not being credited for it. Those workers who spent a lot of time advising or experimenting with new work techniques scored (i.e., unproductive) on the work counts, but in fact were very important for overall office productivity. In short, a work measurement system that was effective for pooled production was increasingly misleading as work became teamwork, as tasks migrated across job boundaries, and as coordination became an important activity, albeit an unmeasured one.

My observation that interactive computing increased the interdependence between workers has been noted elsewhere (Kling and Iaconno, 1984:87). It is of theoretical importance here because sweating, as mentioned in hypothesis five, has historically been found in pooled production situations—ones where each individual creates a product in a self-sufficient or isolated context. The rise of interdependencies means that each individual's performance increasingly depends on the actions of others outside his/her control. Using individual-level work measurements to pressure an individual consequently becomes less feasible. If this observation of increased interdependency in automated clerical work proves to be a widespread outcome, it would suggest that fields of clerical work are being removed from the (already limited) areas in which work measurement is effective (hypothesis 5).

Thirdly, managers pointed to a trade-off between speed and quality of work. Some examiners were slower but more meticulous, others faster but more error prone. Since managers themselves were unsure how to balance one goal against the other, they tolerated a range of combinations. Again put more abstractly, the tension between the qualitative/interpretive dimension of white-collar work and the routinized/quantitative dimension was manifesting itself in managerial reluctance to depend heavily on work-counts for assessing workers.

Fourthly, managers offered labor market explanations for not increasing pressure on the work force. It was not easy to find staff familiar with the particular data screen methods used by the company, and attrition among new trainee employees was high. Even during a period of high national unemployment, voluntary turnover rates in this office were 20% per annum. Given the effort put into training someone, one did not let him/her go lightly. And most importantly, managers didn't want to do anything that would increase turnover of *good* workers. As one manager put it: "as long as this is a nice place to work, we are able to hold onto people." Again, consonant with hypothesis five, managers had to balance increasing work speed against keeping turnover rates in the office down to manageable proportions.

Observation yielded several additional factors that made this non-aggressive management style rational. Productivity had increased as a result of the introduction of computers and was continuing to do so through the development of new work routines and workflow. To use Marx's terminology, local managers were increasing *relative surplus value* via computerization, rather than trying to squeeze out *absolute surplus value* via speedups. Or in a different formulation, they were working smarter, so they didn't have to work harder (cf. Kling and Iacono, 1984:89).

This finding that managers sought productivity increases via organizational innovations (which required the active commitment of employees) rather than by "cracking the whip" or speeding up is corroborated by the work of Strassman (1985). He argues, based on case studies, that speedups of office work rarely result in productivity increases, and that productivity gains claimed for the office automation of already routinized clerical tasks are often illusory (Strassman, 1985:18, 100–107, 238). By contrast, greater gains are obtained reorganizing work flow and by developing new jobs that group together tasks that were previously fragmented.

This may be conceptualized in terms of the earlier discussions of product and technological lifecycles. Group medical insurance is arguably a mature product. Competition between vendors is strong. According to Gosden (1986) this sets the stage for price competition, cost cutting, and pressure placed on employees. However, the introduction of office technology has caused the production technology (but not the product) to demature. Process innovations like OA mean that price competition can occur via technologically driven improvements in productivity, rather than pressure on workers to speed up. The very success of OA in increasing productivity by absorbing tasks helps buffer employees from surveillance pressures (cf. Hypothesis Three).

A fifth limitation on the use of surveillance measures for pressuring employees involves organizational constraints on intervention and punishment. There is a practical limit on the frequency of punishment possible without undermining employee morale. Consequently, managers prioritize problems and are reluctant to act in non-critical cases. There are venial and mortal sins in industry as elsewhere, and disciplinary action tends to be limited to the latter (cf. Gersuny, 1973; 1976).

The mortal sins, from management's point of view, were fraud, chronic lateness, absenteeism, and "fictional" sick days taken off (cf. Harman and Gibson, 1971). Excepting fraud, these are easy to observe, even without computers, but are difficult to control. The latter two are disruptive because managers get no advance warning of absences. Work has to be reassigned, backlogs develop, and important tasks are left undone where absentees cannot be replaced. In the case of sick days, the company also pays for the time off. In the firm studied, disciplinary actions were focused on chronic absenteeism or lateness, rather than on slower workers. When slackening business led to layoffs of a few workers, the fired employees were those with the worst records of absenteeism, as mandated by company policy. The seriousness of absenteeism in the firm studied seems typical. It is mirrored in complaints about absenteeism in the business press (Bureau of National Affairs, 1985) and explains in part why Edwards (1976; 1979) found that "dependability" is such a highly valued characteristic of workers in bureaucratic settings, one routinely stressed in evaluations and promotions.

By contrast, the kinds of offenses for which computer surveillance seems particularly suited (spotting individuals who clock in on time but then spend time chatting instead of working or "beeping" loudly when individuals daydream at a terminal and are not inputting data) are venial sins in the workplace, calling forth disapproving stares from a supervisor, or at most a caution, because the workers involved were valued. In sum, the kinds of information provided by computer surveillance do not aid managers in the most vexatious areas of workplace discipline. Problems of controlling workers often stem, not from lack of information, but from difficulties in dealing effectively with a known "culprit."

This does not mean that these forms of computer surveillance are not damaging. It is stressful to be greeted in the morning with a message on one's workstation saying "Were you here at 8:30 this morning?" (Reinecke, 1984: 150) or being beeped at whenever one leaves one's desk, or being reminded electronically that one is falling behind one's quota for the day. Electronic harassment is likely to generate the same kind of responses (stress, resentment, soldiering, worker solidarity) that Gouldner (1954) discovered for aggressive human supervision. Irving et al. (1986) document greater stress, lowered job satisfaction and a deterioration in relations with management among electronically monitored clerks in two firms. But monitoring is unlikely to solve the problems of workplace discipline; on the contrary, absenteeism and turnover are negatively associated with morale, as discussed below.

Yet another feature of clerical work militates against close surveillance, intensified production, and the adversarial labor relations which tend to follow in its wake. Many clericals either work with money, or with records about money, or with other information that is confidential. Embezzlement, collusion with clients to defraud one's employer, and leakage of confidential information to other workers, clients, or competitors are potentially grave consequences of alienated clerical labor. Managerial expectations of trust and loyalty from staff employees are therefore not just a fanciful ideological survival from Victorian days. They accurately express the vulnerability of a firm to vengeful staff with insider knowledge. Thus, firms continue, however factory-like clerical labor has become, to treat staff employees differently than blue-collar labor, to seek commitment and loyalty, and avoid polarization. (No doubt, fear of white-collar unionization bolsters this attitude.)

Finally, managerial desires to increase work speed are limited, in the most drastic case, by the dangers of sabotage. This was not a problem in the office studied, where morale was good and conflict muted. However, it was clear that the opportunities for sabotage are greatly increased in highly automated offices. Computer workstations are sensitive to paperclips, small magnets, and other detritus dropped into their innards. Despite the use of security access codes, workers knew how to access "secure" data files, using supervisors' codes. An angry employee could make alterations in computer records, which would take hundreds of hours to detect and correct. The data from the whole office fed through one multicable phone box, in an out-of-the-way corner. A malevolent individual with some wire snips could put a whole office out of commission for a day. Such acts of sabotage could be carried out without being caught, especially with the collusion of others.

Limitations on Managerial Power

The case study evidence presented above suggests that managers in automated offices face a variety of disincentives and constraints in using work measurement and surveillance to intensify the speed of work: morale and turnover; teamwork; the quality/quantity trade-off; working smarter rather than harder; the need to conserve punishments for severe offences; sabotage; and fear of provoking unionization.[6] Of these, turnover is clearly a central issue, and so is fear of unionization.

Studies of turnover demonstrate that low morale increases turnover. Turnover rates are also higher among women, among low-paid workers, and among those who perform routinized work—all characteristics of clerical labor. Finance and insurance, the two most bureaucratized settings for clerical labor, had the highest industry-wide turnover rates (about 25% to 35% per annum) in the U.S. economy, even *before* the widespread introduction of interactive computing (Price, 1977: 52; Mobley, 1982: 8).

High turnover is an expensive problem. Every time an employee quits, a company incurs direct costs for recruiting and training a replacement, as well as the indirect costs of lost production from the quitting employee. Estimates of the direct costs of turnover vary enormously, from about $2,000 per quitting employee up to $10,000 and more (Mobley, 1982).

Large private bureaucracies which lose a quarter or more of their staff every year therefore confront not only a financial and organizational burden, but also a significant limitation on managerial power. Even in the absence of unions, managers must balance their desire to increase production speed against the knowledge that major increases in speed brought about by intensified discipline or tougher quotas will lower morale and increase turnover, as employees seek more pleasant working conditions elsewhere (cf. Henry, 1983:114).

Conclusion

The foregoing analysis suggests that computers, *per se*, do not create sweatshop conditions in the office. Management has long had the tools necessary to tell who was, in its opinion, a good worker and who a bad worker, via observation, auditing, and related

---

[6] Worker manipulation of work measurement is another form of resistance. Computers can sometimes be fooled, both in terms of keystroke counts, numbers of claims paid, etc.

forms of surveillance of clerical workers. It has not had the capacity to notice each trip to the bathroom or every slow down, but such information, now made possible by computers, is often superfluous. Management needs only a ranking of its employees in terms of productivity for purposes of promotions, sanctions, or firings.

Clerical work has resisted being turned into a sweatshop for two centuries, not because of a lack of surveillance or work-count capacity, but because managers typically do not seek this kind of labor process. They usually do not fire swaths of slower workers, nor do they succeed in pushing the remaining employees into a frantic pace. The constraints that prevent them from doing so are numerous and complex. They may be summarized in a five part model that draws from the hypotheses developed above:

At the most macroscopic level, the *organizational environment* or context has causal force. We have identified several variables of importance: whether a firm operates in a mature or growing product market; whether its production technology is changing or is mature; its labor intensity—whether routine clerical costs constitute a major part of its operating budget.

On environmental variables, the major white-collar industries (e.g., banking and insurance) do not resemble those in which sweating has been prevalent in the past. They are not dominated by small competitive firms with low profit margins. Nor are they especially labor-intensive: capital investment per white-collar worker is now higher than capital per blue-collar production worker (Gay and Roach, 1986:13). Profits depend as much on interest rate spread (banking) and bond/stock market conditions (insurance) as on clerical worker productivity. Thus, the need to speed up or sweat labor should be less intense in these settings than in the traditional sweating industries.

In our model, environmental factors become translated into *business strategies*, each of which has different implications for the treatment of clerical work. One strategy *will* push toward intensification of clerical work: where clerical costs are central to profitability, and where product markets and technology are mature, firms may adopt a strategy of intense price competition, creating pressure on clerical employees to work faster.[7] But other environments lead to different strategies—differentiation via an emphasis on customer service; high-growth; and cost-cutting via technological innovation in production. Firms pursuing these latter strategies have "other fish to fry." Speeding up clerical work is not salient for them and might undermine their goals.

This perspective contradicts the neo-Marxist position, which views labor control and cost cutting as central to all sectors and kinds of businesses and which therefore hypothesizes a ubiquitous managerial strategy of work degradation.

Business strategies are, in turn, mediated by *corporate cultures and managerial philosophies*. Even among firms where clerical productivity has taken center stage, some managers believe that productivity is best increased by a human relations approach, job enrichment, and quality circles. Those businesses with a more Tayloristic or Theory X view of employees are likely to use surveillance to pressure workers.

However, even some of those firms that take the surveillance or speedup route will encounter *technical constraints* that may blunt the use of the computer data. OA may

---

[7] The *Wall Street Journal* (1983) gives examples where firms that have recently experienced losses or intensified competition turned to payment by results.

Table 2. Synthetic Model of Work Monitoring and Work Pace

Environment/Context	* Mature product market.
	Growing or de-mature product market.
	* Mature process technology.
	Immature/dynamic process technology generating productivity growth.
	* Routine clerical costs constitute a high % of total costs.
	Routine clerical costs not central factor in profitability.
Strategy	* Price competition via cost cutting.
	Differentiation via service/quality.
	Rapid Growth.
Culture/Managerial Philosophy	* Theory X or Taylorist.
	Theory Y or human relations.
Technical	* Emphasis on speed/quantity.
	Emphasis on quality/error rate.
	* Individual pooled production.
	Teamwork or interdependent work.
Employee Resistance	* Can manage with high turnover.
	High turnover a training/cost problem.
	* Unionization not a problem or threat.
	Unionization in place or immenent.
	* Abundant labor supply.
	Tight, competitive labor supply.

The asterisks mark the particular features which, in combination, are associated with the use of monitoring to intensify work pace. Those features that are unmarked would tend to militate against the use of monitoring for speedups.

transform the work process toward teamwork, and it may force a trade-off between speed and quality. For these and other reasons, computer monitoring may not prove useful in practice. For example, B.M. Johnson *et al.*, in a study of two hundred word processing centers "found that many organizations had stopped using computer-generated counts of production since they found them to be invalid, not cost effective, and degrading to employees" (Irving *et al.*, 1986:795).

Finally, even those who actively seek the work-monitoring option, and who face no technical problems, may face problems of *employee resistance*: higher turnover, unionization drives, perhaps even sabotage. We see evidence of these constraints in action in journalistic and other accounts that warn of computer sweatshops. Zuboff (1982), after describing the automation of a collections department, notes that turnover rates soared to 100% per year. The *Wall Street Journal* (1983), reporting on "Terminal Tedium" in computerized clerical work, gives four firms as examples. Employees of one firm subsequently unionized, and succeeded in changing the work monitoring process (*White Collar Report*, 1984), while employees at a second went on a prolonged strike, resulting in improvements in conditions.

This is a congruence or critical factors model. Only those firms with one particular combination of values on environment, strategy, and managerial culture, would be expected to push for speedups, and only in the absence of technical constraints and employee resistance would one expect to see clerical sweatshops in action. Table 2 gives a visual representation of the combination involved.

This does not mean that clerical work is not sometimes routinized, arduous, and fast-paced. It does mean that not all firms seek to develop clerical sweatshops, and that there are various brakes on the abuse of clerical labor. One of the most important of these has been the advantageous labor market position of clerical workers in recent decades. This market has been far more resistant to recessions than the market for blue-collar labor, and clerical work has expanded at about twice the rate of the overall work force since 1962 (Austin and Drake, 1985). An expanding market for clerical labor allows individuals to quit the most unpleasant of jobs and look for better ones; thus, it indirectly enforces an industry-wide effort bargain, or at least curtails extreme deviations from the norm.

Given this analysis, under what circumstances would we expect to find this changing; where and when would clerical sweatshops appear? First, where clerical employees work at home, piece-measurement or quotas will replace supervision or surveillance. And if these homeworkers are perceived as being unable to quit or to find work elsewhere, attempts at sweating may well occur. We see an early example in the case of eight home-based insurance claims workers who are presently suing their employer over "work quotas impossible to meet" and "sweatshop conditions" (*Wall Street Journal*, 1986).

Second, where localized gluts of clerical labor appear, we would expect some firms to try sweating methods. Labor markets in depressed and/or isolated areas (e.g., rural and small town), where alternative local opportunities for women's employment are scarce, and where people cannot easily commute to better jobs, would be logical candidates. Most, though not all, of the examples of computer-related sweating cited in the journalistic literature have been in smaller towns; part-time workers have also figured prominently (*Wall Street Journal*, 1983).

Finally, our analysis suggests that clerical sweating would become more widespread only if a dramatic imbalance develops between numbers of persons seeking this work, and available clerical jobs. This would presume a considerable shrinkage in the clerical sector, perhaps coinciding with a growth in the size of the labor-force seeking jobs. Some forecasts of technological displacement have predicted that computing technologies will cut the clerical work force by over 25% in the next two decades (Drennan, 1983; Roessner, 1985; Leontief and Duchin, 1986).

But these projections are discounted by others (Hunt and Hunt, 1986). The Bureau of Labor statistics has projected an expansion of clerical employment of 9.5% by 1995 (Silvestri and Luaksiewicz, 1985). At the same time the labor market is expected to tighten, as the number of young people entering the labor force shrinks. Under these latter conditions, one would not find the extreme imbalance between labor supply and demand that is a prerequisite for Big Brother to successfully franchise his electronically monitored clerical sweatshop.

References

Abernathy, William J. and James M. Utterback (1982). "Patterns of Industrial Innovation," in Tushman, Michael, and William Moore (eds.), *Readings in the Management of Innovation*, pp. 97–108. Pitman, Boston.

Aitken, Hugh (1960). *Taylorism at Watertown Arsenal.* Harvard, Cambridge, Mass.

Austin, William and Lawrence C. Drake, Jr. (1985). "Office Automation." *Occupational Outlook Quarterly.* Spring: 16–19.

Baldamus, William (1961). *Efficiency and Effort.* Tavistock, London.

Bills, Marion A., Wallace Clark, A.S. Donaldson, and E.G. Lies (1926). *Measuring Office Output.* Office Executives' Series No. 16. American Management Association, New York.

Bills, Marion A., A.C. Farrell, and H.B. Hill (1928). *Measuring Office Output.* Office Executives' Series No. 32. American Management Association, New York.

Braverman, Harry (1974). *Labor and Monopoly Capital.* Monthly Review, New York.

Burawoy, Michael (1979). *Manufacturing Consent.* University of Chicago Press, Chicago.

Bureau of National Affairs (1985). *Employee Discipline and Discharge.* Personnel Policy Forum Survey # 139. Washington, D.C.

Carlson, Norma (1982). "Time Rates Tighten Their Grip on Manufacturing." *Monthly Labor Review* May: 15–22.

Clark, Wallace (1926). *The Control of Output in Offices.* Office Executives' Series No. 9. American Management Association, New York.

Clement, Andrew (1985). "Electronic Management: The New Technology of Workplace Surveillance." Unpublished ms., Department of Computer Science, University of Toronto, Canada.

Crozier, Michel (1965). *The World of the Office Worker.* University of Chicago Press, Chicago.

Deal, Terrence, and Allan Kennedy (1984). *Corporate Cultures.* Addison Wesley, New York.

Drenna, Matthew P. (1983). *Implications of Computer and Communications Technology for Less Skilled Service Employment Opportunities.* Final Report prepared for the Employment and Training Administration, U.S. Department of Labor. Washington, D.C.

Edwards, Richard C. (1976). "Individual Traits and Organizational Incentives: What Makes a 'Good' Worker?" *Journal of Human Resources,* Winter.

Edwards, Richard C. (1979). *Contested Terrain.* Basic Books, New York.

Erikson, Ethyl (1934). "The Employment of Women in Offices." U.S. Women's Bureau *Bulletin* # 120. U.S. Government Printing Office, Washington, D.C.

Galloway, Lee (1919). *Office Management Its Principles and Practice.* Ronald Press Co., New York.

Gay, Robert, and Steven Roach (1986). "The Productivity Puzzle: Perils and Hopes." *Economic Perspectives.*

Gersuny, Carl (1973). *Punishment and Redress in a Modern Factory.* Lexington Books, Lexington, Mass.

Gersuny, Carl (1976). "A Devil In Petticoats and Just Cause: Patterns of Punishment in Two New England Textile Factories." *The Business History Review.* L: 131–152.

Gilinsky, Rhoda M. (1983). "Questioning Employment at Will: Right to Fire at Will Stirs Legal Controversy." *World of Work Report* 8: 1–62.

Gosden, John (1986). "Office Automation—The Impact of Work and Workers." Mimeo ms. New York University, Graduate School of Management, MIS Department.

Gouldner, Alvin (1954). *Patterns of Industrial Bureaucracy.* Free Press, Glencoe.

Grillo, Elmer V., and Charles J. Berg, Jr. (1959). *Work Measurement in the Office.* McGraw-Hill, New York.

Harman, Richard, and John Gibson (1971). "The Persistent Problem of Employee Absenteeism." *Personnel Journal* 50: 535–539.

Henry, Stuart (1983). *Private Justice.* Routledge & Kegan Paul, New York.

Hickson, David *et al.* (1969). "Operations Technology and Organizational Structure: An Empirical Appraisal." *Administrative Science Quarterly,* 13 378–397.

Hobsbawm, Eric J. (1964). *Laboring Men: Studies in the History of Labor.* London.

Hollis, Patricia (1973). *Class and Class Conflict in Nineteenth-Century England 1815–1850.* Routledge & Kegan Paul, London.

Howard, Robert (1985). *Brave New Workplace.* Viking Penguin, New York.

Hunt, H. Allen, and Timothy L. Hunt (1986). *Clerical Employment and Technological Change: A Review of Recent Trends and Projections.* Research Report Series 86-14. National Commission for Employment Policy, Washington, D.C.

International Labor Organization (ILO)(1984). *Payment by Results.* International Labour Office, Geneva.

Irving, R.H., C.A. Higgins, and F.R. Sasayeni (1986). "Computerized Performance Monitoring Systems: Use and Abuse." *Communications of the A.C.M.* Vol. 29, number 8, August: 794–801.

Jacobsen, Beverley (1984). "When machines monitor the work." *World of Work Report.* 9: 1–2.

Jacoby, Sanford M. (1985). *Employing Bureaucracy.* Columbia, New York.

Jensen, Joan, and Sue Davidson (1984). *A Needle, a Bobbin, a Strike.* Temple University Press, Philadelphia.

Kenny, Thomas (1960). "Office Productivity—New Path to Profits." *Dun's Review and Modern Industry.* September: 60.

Kling, Rob, and Suzanne Iacono (1984). "Computing as an Occasion for Social Control." *Journal of Social Issues* 40: 77–96.

Kocka, Jurgen (1980). *White Collar Workers in America: 1890–1940.* Sage Publications, Beverly Hills, CA.

Lawrence, Paul R., and Jay Lorsch (1967). *Organization and Environment.* Harvard Press, Cambridge.

Leontieff, Wassily, and Faye Duchin (1986). *The Impacts of Automation on Employment.* Oxford University Press, New York.

Levitt, Thomas (1965). "Exploit the Product Life-cycle." *Harvard Business Review* (November–December): 81–94.

Lockwood, David (1958). *The Blackcoated Worker.* Allen and Unwin, London.

Lupton, T. (1973). *On the Shop Floor: Two Studies of Workshop Organization and Efficiency.* Pergamon, Oxford.

McAdams, E.J. (1927). *Unit Costs as Measures of Office Output for the Control of Office Expense.* Office Executives' Series No. 26. American Management Association, New York.

Marschall, Daniel, and Judith Gregory (1983). *Office Automation: Jekyll or Hyde?* National Organization of Working Women, Cleveland.

Marx, Karl (1967). *Capital*, Vol. 1. International Publishers, New York.

Mathewson, Stanley (1931). *Restriction of Output Among Unorganized Workers.* Viking Press, New York.

Mills, C. Wright (1951). *White Collar.* Oxford University Press, Oxford.

Mitchell, John (1928). *Measuring Office Output: Summary of Studies.* Office Executives' Series No. 35. American Management Association, New York.

Mitchell, John, Gertrude Ballsieper, and R.M. Blakelock (1927). *Measuring Office Output.* Office Executives' Series No. 24. American Management Association, New York.

Mobley, William H. (1982). *Employee Turnover: Causes, Consequences, and Control.* Addison Wesley, Reading, MA.

New York Times (1984). "Electronic Office Conjuring Wonders, Loneliness, and Tedium." March 28: A16.

New York Times (1986). "Home-Based Work Grievance." May 26: 27.

Nine-to-Five (The National Association of Working Women)(1986). *Computer Monitoring and Other Dirty Tricks.* 9-to-5, Cleveland.

Office of Technology Assessment (TA) of the US Congress (1985). *Automation of America's Offices.* USGPO, Washington, D.C.

Perrow, Charles (1967). "A Framework for Comparative Analysis." *American Sociological Review* 32: 194–208.

Porter, Michael (1985). *Computer Advantage.* Free Press, New York.

Price, James L. (1977). *The Study of Turnover.* Iowa State University, Ames.

Reinecke, Ian (1984). *Electronic Illusions*. Penguin Books, New York.

Rogers, Robert, and Jack Stieber (1985). "Employee Discharge in the 20th Century." *Monthly Labor Review*. September: 35–41.

Roessner, J. David (1985). "Forecasting the Impact of Office Automation on Clerical Employment." *Technological Forecasting and Social Change*. 28: 203–216.

Roethlisberger, F.J., and W. Dickson (1939). *Management and the Worker*. Harvard, Cambridge, MA.

Rowland, F.L., W.J. Harper, and P.H. Myers (1925). *Extra Incentive Wage Plans*. Office Executives' Series No. 11. American Management Association, New York.

Rowland, F.L., R.E. McNeal, and L.H. Brigham (1936). *Progressive Management Policies*. Office Management Series No. 86. American Management Association, New York.

Roy, Donald (1952). "Quota Restriction and Goldbricking in a Machine Shop." *American Sociological Review* 60: 255–266.

Sahal, D. (1981). *Patterns of Industrial Innovation*. Addison Wesley, London.

Schulze, J. William (1913). *The American Office: Its Organization, Management, and Records*. Key Publishing Co., London.

Seidman, Joel (1942). *The Needle Trades*. Farrar and Rinehart, New York.

Selznick, Phillip (1969). *Society and Economic Justice*. Russell Sage Foundation, New York.

Silvestri, George T., and John Lukasiewicz (1985). "Occupational Employment Projections: 1984–1995." *Month Labor Review*. November: 42–56.

Slichter, Summer H. (1919). *The Turnover of Factory Labor*. New York.

Stivers, C.L., A.J. McCrickard, H. Hopf, C.E. Haines, and F.M. Knox (1936). *Revitalizing Office Practice*. Office Management Series No. 76. American Management Association, New York.

Strassman, Paul (1985). *Information Payoff*. Free Press, New York.

Thompson, James (1967). *Organizations in Action*. McGraw-Hill, New York.

Twiss, B. (1979). *Managing Technological Innovation*. Longman, London.

U.S. Women's Bureau (1946). "The Woman Telephone Worker." *Women's Bureau Bulletin* No. 207.

U.S. Women's Bureau (1963). "Women Telephone Operators and Changing Technology." *Women's Bureau Bulletin* No. 286.

Wall Street Journal (1983). "Terminal Tedium. As computers change the nature of work, some jobs lose savor." May 6: 1.

Wall Street Journal (1985). "Back to Piecework: Many companies now base worker's raises on productivity." November 15: 1.

Wall Street Journal (1986). "A Telecommuters' Suit Attacks Work Conditions for Some Home Employees." February 11: 1.

Westin, Alan (1986). *The Changing Workplace*. Knowledge Industries Press, Westchester, NY.

White Collar Report (1984). "District 925 of SEIU Ratifies First Contract with Equitable." 56: 593.

Woodward, Joan (1965). *Industrial Organization: Theory and Practice*. Oxford University Press, London.

World of Work Report (1983a). "A Steelcase Survey Finds: White-Collar Productivity Programs are Sparse and Poorly Planned. January: 4.

World of Work Report (1983b). "In the Financial Services: Productivity, Job Enrichment—Two Sides of the Same Coin." September: 5.

Zuboff, Shoshana (1982). "New Worlds of Computer-Mediated Work." *Harvard Business Review* (September–October): 142–152.

P·A·R·T · III

5

Groupware in Practice: An Interpretation of Work Experiences

Christine V. Bullen • John L. Bennett

Introduction

The fact that personal computer (PC) availability in the work place is growing at an astounding rate is being heralded from many corners:

> We're going from 11 million to 34 million PCs by 1994. PCs now make up about half the electronic keyboards in use but will account for 70% of the total in 1994. (Dalton, 1988)

> About 7 million PCs and 300,000 multiuser systems were installed in the United States by early 1985; and these numbers are still growing at about 15% annually. By 1985, there were terminals or microcomputers for at least 10 million people, or 20% of the United States' white collar work force. (Kling and Iacono, 1989)

The usual assumption, that the use of personal computers contributes to increased worker productivity, is turning into an open question: Loveman reports that at a national economy level, researchers have failed to establish a significant relationship between information technology investments and increased productivity (Loveman, 1988).

What aspects of PC use *could* contribute to measurable increased productivity? How do we get beyond the extravagant claims often associated with PCs to discover the reality of their value? Are changes in the organizational workplace or in the design of systems needed to bring the potential into actual realization? We believe that understanding how PCs are being used now can be important for understanding the value that PCs could potentially bring to the office environment.

One area where personal computers are being brought into use is to support work of business teams.

> Business teams are becoming a way of life in many organizations. . . . Business teams are seen by many as a wave of the future. (Bullen and Johansen, 1988)

> Traditional departments will serve as guardians of standards, as centers for training, and the assignment of specialists; they won't be where the work gets done. That will happen largely in task-focused teams. (Drucker 1988; see also Reich, 1987)

Our particular focus is on looking at people who work in teams and are networked through personal computer workstations. We seek to understand the value that the technology brings to the office environment. We believe the quality of the results of using information technology to support group work has the potential to far exceed what is achieved today through the use of PCs by relatively isolated individuals within organizations.

If indeed teamwork is an important form of office work now—and will be more so in the future—then investigating how teams of people work and studying the use of personal computer workstations in a team environment should be valuable for understanding how information technology is used and how this is affecting productivity in today's organizations. The MIT Commission on Industrial Productivity found the following:

> The third recurring weakness of the U.S. production system that emerged from our industry studies is a widespread failure of cooperation within and among companies. . . . Most thriving firms in the U.S. . . . have learned to integrate technology in their . . . strategies and to link [their strategies] to organizational changes that promote teamwork, training and continuous learning (Berger *et al.*, 1989).

The presence of PCs networked together in communication paths provides the physical infrastructure. But is a new kind of software needed to provide tools for team processes? A term that has become popular during the last few years is *groupware*, software that is intended to be used in support of interpersonal work within an organization:

> *Groupware* is a generic term for specialized computer aids that are designed for the use of collaborative work groups. Typically, these groups are small, project-oriented teams that have important tasks and tight deadlines. . . . Sometimes, groupware is used by permanent groups or departments. . . . Group interactions may be formal or informal, spontaneous or planned, structured or unstructured" (Johansen, 1988; see also Engelbart, 1963, 1968; Hiltz and Turoff, 1978; Stevens, 1981; Hiltz and Kerr, 1981; Kerr and Hiltz, 1982; Rice 1984).

Our questions about the use of PCs, the role of PCs when teams are linked through communications networks, the underlying issue of productivity, and the role of specialized software for use on PCs and workstations all served as background as we began this research project. We used a case study methodology to investigate the current status of group work in organizations and to observe how computer-based tools were being employed in the facilitation of group work. Our purposes in this research are to develop insight on factors that should be influencing software design and to report experiences that can help guide managers who put group support systems into practice.

Research Design

An interview framework (see Appendix I) served as a focus for data gathering. While the outline provided for initial distinctions we knew would be of interest, we let other distinctions emerge from our interviews. This work illustrates a research methodology often used by anthropologists and titled in a variety of ways, including *exploratory observation* (Malone, 1983) and *contextual inquiry* (Bennett *et al.*, 1990). This type of study is not intended to be a controlled experiment or a large sample survey. The technique focuses on interacting with people in their own contexts as they do actual work. The goal of data gathering is to obtain insights through observation, interviews, and interaction. The challenge of this methodology is that it relies on the skill of the observer to report and interpret accurately, while allowing unexpected phenomena to emerge from the examples studied. This approach often results in uncovering research questions that can be investigated through controlled experiments or additional contextual inquiry. Our conclusions present such opportunities for further research.

We spoke with 223 people in 25 organizations, represented at 31 sites (see Table 1 for details on companies, number of interviews, and groupware systems available in each). Each interview lasted a minimum of one hour, with the longest interview lasting two hours. In almost every case, the interviews were carried out in the individual's office or work area.

The 25 organizations represented a wide range of industries and size of companies. We chose organizations in which groupware systems were available, and those systems helped to define the set of groupware systems that we studied. Organization names are coded, as our agreement with those interviewed guaranteed confidentiality. We consulted with each organization to choose groups for our interviews that met the following criteria:

- cohesive business teams, facing challenging environmental conditions that would emphasize the importance of coordination for achieving their goals and objectives; and

- teams that had some form of information technology available to support the work of the group.

The size of our work groups ranged from 7 to 35 people. Those interviewed included individuals at all levels of management within the target work group and, where appropriate, support personnel (administrative assistants and secretaries). In most organizations, the managers to whom the work group reported were also included as part of the case study to help establish some of the contextual information.

We did not choose our groups for study on the basis of a statistically random sample. We contacted potential research sites on the basis of referrals and our own knowledge of their use of technology. However, the resulting sample is drawn from a wide variety of industries, and it includes a wide range of organizational sizes and geographic dispersion. Although these characteristics do not guarantee that the results can be generalized, they do suggest that we are not seeing isolated and unusual instances of groupware tool use.

Conducting a study of work groups raises some interesting questions about how to

Table 1. Companies Studied with Revenues,* Number of People Interviewed, and Groupware Systems Available

Company	Revenues in Billions	Number of People Interviewed	Groupware Systems
BigChem	$30.00	8	PROFS, Higgins, The Coordinator (V.I)
SoapCo	17.00	30	Other, Metaphor, ForComment
InsurCo	12.00	5	PROFS, Higgins
OilCo	11.00	5	PROFS
ExploreCo	10.00	3	Other
ConstrucCo	10.00	3	PROFS, Other
FoodCo	9.60	3	PROFS, The Coordinator (V.I), Higgins
TerminalCo	9.40	10	All-In-1
RBOC	8.00	10	PROFS, Higgins
HealthCo	8.00	20	All-In-1
BankCo	6.80	5	All-In-1
MedCons	6.00	3	PROFS, ForComment
LawCo	5.00	3	Higgins
ServBuro	4.40	13	The Coordinator (V.I)
SnackCo	2.00	35	The Coordinator (V.I), Other
BeerCo	1.40	6	Metaphor
SmallCons	1.40	10	Other
CableCo	1.00	15	The Coordinator (V.I)
SmallChem	1.00	5	The Coordinator (V.I)
PubServBuro	0.90	3	PROFS, Other
TransDist	0.18	10	The Coordinator (V.I)
SmallRes	**	3	Other
IndCons	**	2	The Coordinator (V.I)
StateBuro	n/a	3	PROFS, ForComment
BigU	n/a	10	PROFS, ForComment, Other

PROFS available in many places; studied in 2.
*Revenues approximate, 1988.
**Revenues less than $1 million.

define inclusion in a work group. What are its bounds? Work groups have been defined as "identifiable and bounded subsystems of a whole organization [with a] recognized purpose, which unifies the people and activities" (Trist, 1981); "collaborating groups of information workers" (Bikson et al., 1989); and "multiple individuals acting as a bounded whole in order to get something done" (Rousseau, 1983).

We found a variety of organizational forms constituting work groups and organizational conditions in which the work groups functioned. For example, at CableCo the work group coincides with the organizational department, although it is spread geographically across the continental United States. Four levels of management are included: corporate functional vice president, regional directors, geographic managers, and support staff. As a growing firm, this functional area is dealing with business pressure to support corporate client growth, a rapidly expanding customer group, hiring and training of new staff, and planning and managing new initiatives in international markets.

At SmallCons, the work group consists of the entire firm. As a very small organization, the work group handles a full range of organizational tasks. The following represent typical weekly topics: external issues like marketing and client management, internal issues like getting the work done, administrative issues like corporate planning and training. The work group includes everyone from the president and founder to the support staff.

At SoapCo, the work group is a flexible concept such that at times it involves an organizational entity at one location (e.g., the Boston marketing group), and at other times it consists of the worldwide instances of the organizational entity (e.g., all marketing groups), and under still other circumstances, the work group is a subset of entities (e.g., Boston, Chicago, and San Francisco marketing groups). Within each group, levels of management range from corporate vice president to support staff. The overriding functional responsibility focuses the work of each group on one primary area.

In the world of electronic communications, the composition of work groups is showing important changes from those observed in the past. Because of flexibility provided by communication technology of all kinds, it is becoming more difficult to identify a formal organizational unit as a work group. That is, some people co-located in an office area do not necessarily work together as a group, and people geographically separated may form a team focused on achieving a common work result. Through the power of electronic media, these groups are dynamic and fluid; this is true for both formal and information organizational units.

> The traditional concept of an 'organization' is no longer useful to managers or students of organizations. It is dominated by models of structure and physical identity at a time when telecommunications has eroded the boundaries between firms and changed the nature of coordination across geographic location (Keen, 1988).

Given our research interest in the factors important for software specifically designed for use by teams, we had to develop a working definition of what constitutes *groupware*. Early notions of groupware reflected a clear connection between the software tool and the group processes. However, current manifestations of groupware tools appear to focus on the technical qualities of functionality and may, in effect, ignore the dynamics of group use.

We have employed a broad definition in our research in order to accommodate the evolving nature of this field. In time, *groupware* will probably be narrowed to include only those tools specifically designed to support group work. However, at present, it is useful to include all tools being used to support group work, even if the tools represent user adaptation of an existing technology (e.g., group agreement to share files and calendars on a system designed to keep such functionality private). Therefore, our working definition of groupware is computer-based tools that can be used by work groups to facilitate the exchange and sharing of information.

A number of systems, with a large variety of functionality, fall under this groupware umbrella. Figure 1 illustrates a framework for organizing these systems using the dimensions of time and place to create four domains that describe circumstances of interpersonal work (Bullen and Johansen, 1988):

- same time, same place
- same time, different place
- different time, same place

	SAME TIME	DIFFERENT TIMES
SAME PLACE	Meeting Facilitation Group DSS Room	Presentation Project Management Team Room
DIFFERENT PLACES	Conference Calls Video Conf Screen Sharing Spontaneous Mtgs	Email Computer Conf Collab Write Conversational Struc

Figure 1. Categorizing systems with respect to time and place.

- different time, different place

Although each of these domains is important and the four are interdependent, for this study we decided to investigate those computer systems that can be used to facilitate work in the different time, different place domain. (The other domains are being extensively studied by a number of organizations, including the University of Arizona, the University of Michigan, IBM, GM, DEC, MCC, and others.)

Information Technology Tools Studied

In the course of the case studies, we focused on the use of eight different information technology systems at various times and various locations. The choice of the specific systems was influenced by their presence at the organizations that agreed to participate. Within the various systems a number of functions can be considered as tools that can be used for support of groups. In order to describe these systems broadly, we make the following generalizations. All of the systems studied provide the following functionality:

Construction/editing facilities. All systems provide at least a rudimentary text creation and editing facility. Some include elaborate editors and provide function to import graphics. One special-purpose system (ForComment) focuses on joint authorship and editing as an aspect of group work.

Electronic exchange of text. This includes electronic mail and/or conferencing, gateways to other systems (both internal and external, e.g., facsimile transfer), and document transfer. As a result of the text being captured in a computer-readable form, the content can be reused, edited, re-sent, etc. Capabilities with respect to exchange of graphics, images, and spreadsheet data differ in different tool environments. Some of the tools provide ways to manage the exchange of text through folders or through automatically linking related messages.

Directory. This functionality at a minimum provides a name and electronic address file to support data exchange by users of the system. Some of the tools provide a traditional "little black book" functionality, where extensive data on mailing addresses, multiple telephone numbers, and notes about individuals (e.g., secretary's name) can be stored.

Time marking and time keeping. All the tools except one (ForComment) provide a facility for recording events scheduled for a particular date. The capability ranges from this basic task to recording, for example, repetitive events, reminders, and "to do" lists, and linking these data to other system functions.

General tools. Some of the systems provide tools for the support of work in financial and budgeting areas, and because of the ways in which the tools can be used, support some project tracking capability.

Integration across the functionality provided is an interesting concept in groupware research for two specific reasons:

1. We found people hindered in the use of tools because of problems associated with the degree of integration.
2. This term is used imprecisely by both vendors and users as a measure of quality in describing groupware systems. Therefore it showed up often in our interviews and we feel there is value in defining integration and exploring its application to these systems.

The concept of *integration of function* needed for support of group work is a relative term. One aspect of integration can be measured by examining the process required for each user to move freely between functions, and by looking for the presence of system-dictated steps (e.g., log off from one function, log on to another function). Another aspect is the extent to which the software enables the user to move data from one function to another without requiring special transformations. Thus, integration, as we use the term, refers to the *flow of control* during work by an individual or by team members, and to the *flow of data* during the process of individual interaction with the software or during interaction among team members.

Integration within and across the functional categories listed above differed significantly among the various tools. As a result some of the systems resembled a group of functions rather than a cohesive package. Brief descriptions of the individual systems appear in Appendix II. Table 2 shows a list of the systems and gives the general categories of functionality provided in each. We do not provide here specific information on the details of operation for each tool. The range of capability is wide in terms of search mechanisms, ordering rules, etc.

Observations, Key Issues, and Conclusions

In this section we summarize the results of our study. It is important to understand that, because of the complexity of intervening factors, the observations we report here do not have simple explanations. Research by Iacono and Kling (1988) and Markus and Forman (1989) supports the notion that we need to take multiple perspectives in performing research in organizations. We have found the framework suggested by Iacono and Kling

Table 2. Tools Studied

	Construction/Editing Facilities	Electronic Exchange of Text	Directory	Time Marking/Time Keeping	General Tools
All-In-1	Yes	Yes	Yes	Yes	Some
ForComment	Yes	Specialized	Specialized	No	No
Higgins	Yes	Yes	Yes	Yes	Yes
In-House System 1	Yes	Yes	Specialized	No	Some
In-House System 2	Yes	Yes	No	No	No
Metaphor	Yes	Yes	Specialized	Some	Specialized
PROFS	Yes	Yes	Yes	Yes	Some
The Coordinator (V.I)	Yes	Yes	Specialized	Yes	Some

(shown in Table 3) to be particularly useful to us as we sorted out factors influencing the adoption of technology. From a tool perspective, technical solutions are offered as if the innovative benefits of the function would overshadow any historical, political, and social factors that might be present in the environment. Instead, Iacono and Kling find that the environments into which computer-based tools are introduced should be viewed as institutions. As institutions, the environments exhibit many barriers to adoption that have little or nothing to do with the technical merits of the innovative tools. Consideration of historical, political, and social factors can forewarn those developing tools and those introducing them into the environment where computer-based support is provided.

> We conceptualize these patterns as the social organization of computing. We define 'social organization of computing' as the choices about computing (both social and technical) which become embedded in work environments and which are experienced by the users as part of the social practices in their everyday work world (Iacono and Kling, 1988).

Other researchers have stressed the importance of understanding the balance between a technology perspective and an organizational one. Bikson *et al.* (1989) comment

> group members are interdependent not only on one another but also on the technology, and technical and organizational issues are closely interrelated. The more advanced the information-handling tools provided to the group, the more critical it becomes to give equivalent and concurrent attention to the social processes through which these tools are deployed, and to seek a mutual adaptation rather than maximization of either the social or technical system in isolation (p. 89). (See also Mumford and Ward, 1968.)

In making our observations and drawing conclusions we were struck by the importance of understanding the complex interplay of factors that influenced the specific organizations we studied. However, in order to simplify the presentation of our conclusions we have sorted them into two categories:

From a design perspective. In this category we discuss those conclusions that designers ought to consider when conceptualizing functionality for groupware systems. Our conclusions suggest that while designers must be concerned about the technical solutions, they need to go beyond the "tool perspective" to include an appreciation for organizational factors that may influence the use of groupware systems.

From an organizational perspective. In this category we discuss those conclusions that management ought to consider when planning for and implementing groupware systems. These conclusions suggest ways in which managers could anticipate organizational factors that might influence the groupware implementation process and subsequent use. However, managers must also be careful to not fall into a pure "institutional perspective" to the exclusion of concern about the quality of the technical solutions.

As with any categorization, this dichotomy of conclusions is an oversimplification that we make for analysis purposes. These groupings clearly overlap, and we believe designers will find useful information in the second grouping, and managers will benefit from the conclusions in the first category.

As interviewers, observers, and interpreters of these work experiences, we have been conscious of these perspectives. In the following dicussion of key issues and conclusions we support the ideas using observations and quotations from our field work. Some of the

Table 3. Iacono and Kling Framework

	Tool Perspective	Institution Perspective
Historical *past decisions that may limit future actions*	Assume freedom from past; focus on future technology per-fection; less attention to present; assume individuals free to move in new direction. Groups less a factor.	Interests served in past are present in current situation; those commitments constrain future choices; individuals assume current activities will persist; interdependence of groups.
Political *control over access to resources*	Local control and self-interest assumed paramount; potential conflicts rarely recognized; assume power of technology will overcome political barriers.	Shared control and shared interest groups recognized; specialization limits possible changes; organizational struc-ture (social-structure) may hinder adaptation and survival.
Social *staff skills, patterns of control and discipline*	Local and simple negotiating context without constraints from other sources.	Complex and overlapping negotiating contexts within and among groups.

researchable questions that emerged are suggested in each section. However, others can be formed from the work reported here.

From a Design Perspective

Electronic Message Communication is the Primary Tool

The functionality for sending and receiving electronic messages, available in all of the products we studied, was by far the function most heavily used and universally stated as valuable.

"I love this tool. I can reach people and they can reach me anytime, anyplace and discuss anything." (Senior Manager, SnackCo)

The desire to have support for communication within a work group was usually the primary motivation for acquiring the tool. People quickly learned the electronic messaging functions, and this contrasted with their failure to use many of the other functions available in these systems. The simple presence of function in a groupware tool does not in any way mean that it will be used. In each system we studied, several of the available functions were ignored by the using groups. However the electronic messaging capability, regardless of its user interface design, ease or difficulty, or level of sophistication, was used extensively. In several instances interface features were either ignored or adapted by the people to accomplish a simplified process of communicating electronically.

For example, the interface provided by The Coordinator (Version I) contains language related to the underlying theory of speech acts (Searle, 1969). This terminology is intended to lead the users to think about what they are doing and then to characterize particular communications as one of several choices, e.g., a request or promise, etc. While the software provides a choice for simple e-mail (called "free form"), we found people consistently sending each other "requests" regardless of the content of the message. Not surprisingly, "request" is the first menu choice and where the cursor falls by default. Many people we interviewed reported that they ignored the choices and just "hit enter" to send a message. However, they had high praise for the tool:

"The Coordinator gets the information out! . . . The Coordinator opens communication lines." (Senior Manager, CableCo)

"The Coordinator's major advantage: instant communication with a large audience." (Senior Manager, SnackCo)

In another example, the user interface for Higgins electronic mail walks the user through a series of steps to answer questions about how to assign key words, follow-up dates, etc. A person using Higgins to help manage information or for sharing messages in the groupware sense would answer these questions. However, the users we observed skipped through this menu leaving blanks in most categories. People reported that they understood the value of the categories, and knew that they "should" be filling the blanks, but that they were in a hurry and just wanted to get the message sent.

One possible response to this observation is that the message-flow needs of work groups are so great that they overshadow the other system-based activities. This immediately suggests that we need a definition for this kind of communication, which, on the basis of what we observed, could be termed sending and receiving messages. Any of a number of the tools provided as part of a groupware system can be also thought of as entering into "communication" in the sense that they can be used to support transfer of information in some way, for example:

- calendar entries
- expense reports
- reports of project status
- telephone directory
- spreadsheets
- budget reports
- tickler files/to do lists.

It is interesting to note that these particular functions tend to be separated from electronic messaging in the information technology tools themselves. We do not support this distinction as correct. However, as we observed and interviewed people, we found that they acted as if this separation of functionality was real for them, and they generally spoke in terms of "e-mail and the other things the system can do."

This raises the interesting point of how to distinguish between what people say they do (or want to do) with information technology tools versus what people think they should or should not do because they have been influenced by the tools at hand. We cannot answer this question definitively. We can, however, say that given the choices existing in information technology tools today, the people we studied used what we are calling "message functions" almost exclusively.

Our interviewees frequently stated that they chose groupware systems because of the mix of functionality offered. Given that, an important question is: Why do they *not* use most of the functions?

For example, users say they want groupware tools that provide calendaring functions. Yet in the majority of organizations we studied the calendar tools were not being used. People gave a variety of reasons; the net result is the fact that although the desired function was present, this did not in and of itself mean that it was used.

"We thought having the calendaring function available on PROFS would be useful in organizing meetings, but no one has taken the time to learn about it." (Manager, InsurCo)

"One of the reasons we chose Higgins was because of the wide range of functionality it provides. However, most people just use the e-mail." (Support Staff, RBOC)

If developers commit resources to provide function, it is important to understand what is seen by users as a barrier between "offered" (by the system) and "used" (by the people). Other factors, as we shall report, were important in determining whether a function was used.

Our field observations show that the tool people use the most is electronic messaging. The message flow needs of work groups appear to be so great that messaging over-shadows other system-based functions. If we can assume that these busy people would use just those system portions essential for their work, we may conclude that electronic messaging support is what is most needed. In the following sections, however, we discuss other factors that increase the complexity of forming this conclusion. A researchable question here revolves around gaining a better understanding of the value to the user of the electronic messaging function as compared to the value of other functionality. Another research topic raised by this conclusion is understanding the barriers to effective use of the functionality other than electronic messaging.

Message Linking is a Key Improvement Provided by Electronic Communications

One aspect of electronic message communication that stood out in our interviews was the ability to link messages concerned with one subject area or with a distribution list. This functionality is provided in two of the tools (Higgins and The Coordinator) and it is also inherent in the concept of computer conferencing, which is available in All-in-1 (VAX Notes) and in In-House System I.

Computer conferencing organizes all electronic messages according to topic areas. Therefore, when a message is composed and sent, it is addressed to a topic. The concept of a *topic* is not limited in any way, and can in fact represent a project, general discussion, software release, distribution list, individual, etc.

People reported in our interviews that they gained much value by being able to "look in one place for all discussion pertaining to project XYZ." In contrast to this observation, users of e-mail systems like PROFS and All-in-1 (without VAX Notes), complained about the difficulties of tracking down related messages and managing their mail folders (i.e., files for grouping messages by categories).

Message linking provides four primary values:

- collection of notes in one place
- chronological record
- ability for latecomers to view an entire record of interaction
- knowledge of the "right" place to put new messages.

In The Coordinator (Version I) this functionality is embodied in a concept basic to the underlying theory: the "conversation" is the primary unit of interaction. Because of this, each time someone replies to a message, the reply is automatically linked to all previous messages in the stream and becomes part of the "conversation."

"I use the traceback function a lot to find out how we arrived at a particular point in the conversation." (Senior Manager, SnackCo)

"If I receive an answer to my request that is not linked, I get annoyed because it messes up the ability to follow back through the conversation." (Manager, CableCo)

Users found this feature of The Coordinator one of the most valuable aspects of the tool.

Our interviews showed clearly that people value the ability to group and link messages that are related by subject. This "computer conferencing" capability has been available for more than 15 years in electronic communication systems (Johansen, 1988). However, general understanding of how it works and general availability to users has been limited. It remains interesting to us that this functionality should be singled out by many users as a key benefit of groupware.

Historically, knowledge workers have always sought ways to organize the volume of information they manage. The first major innovation to affect this process was the vertical file system (the file cabinet, in 1892), which facilitated the grouping of correspondence by subject:

> [Vertical files] had several advantages over [other forms of filing]. Most importantly, the folders allowed related papers to be grouped together and easily removed from the files for use. . . . The new equipment alone was not enough to make storage and retrieval efficient. In a textbook on filing published by the Library Bureau, vertical filing of correspondence was defined as including the *organization* of papers in the files, as well as the filing apparatus itself: "The definition of vertical filing as applied to correspondence is—the bringing together, in one place, all correspondence to, from or about an individual, firm, place or subject, filed on edge, usually in folders and behind guides, making for speed, accuracy and accessibility." (Yates, 1989)

In effect, nothing has changed: groupware message linking or conferencing allows people to carry out this task for electronic correspondence!

The need represented in our interviews (i.e., comments on the value of message linking) is one that should be carefully investigated by both designers and implementers of groupware. People use message linking to manage communications and documents, keep records, and develop "group memory." This conclusion may be telling us a great deal more than is at first obvious: rather than looking at "fancy," innovative functions for groupware systems, designers should be focusing on how to better solve the basic need of office workers, i.e., managing large volumes of information. There may well be ways other than those we see today for designers to address these needs and better serve the groupware user.

What Functionality is Included and How It Is Offered are Important Factors

It became very clear through our interviews that people did not use some of the functionality in groupware systems because of the design of the tool. There are two characteristics of design quality that we observed.

What functionality is included. One of the best examples of functionality requested by "the marketplace" but not used effectively is the calendaring function. The explanations we were given in our interviews focused on one fact: electronic calendars in their current form cannot replace traditional paper ones. The topic of electronic calendars would justify a separate paper, but we can summarize some of the key problems.

1. Traditional calendars are not simply places where you record times for events to take place on dates, though electronic calendars are usually limited to such a simple function. Traditional calendars have notes on them, contain telephone numbers, are often color coded, and have other papers attached (such as yellow sticky notes or paper-clipped memos, letters, etc.). The nonhomogeneity of traditional calendars is actually an asset for finding important information (there are parallels here with Malone's (1983) findings on desk organization).

   "I honestly tried to use the calendar in Higgins, but I found it frustrating to not have my familiar book with all its messy notes, colors, and papers clips." (Senior Manager, RBOC)

2. Electronic calendars are not portable, and paper copies of the information contained in the computer are inadequate substitutes. Notes made on the paper copies often do not get keyed back into the computer-based version.

"I need a portable calendar for traveling. My secretary makes me a copy of the computer one for trips, but it is ugly and hard to read. Then I have to make notes on it and do not put them in the computer, and everything gets out of sync for a while." (Manager, HealthCo)

3. The group calendaring value of electronic calendaring is lost unless everyone cooperates. People do not have an incentive to maintain their calendars in such a way that they support group use. In addition, people object to the notion that others (not their secretaries) may schedule their time.

"We tried to use it to schedule meetings and found that several guys weren't keeping their calendars up to date. So almost as many phone calls get made and it takes just as long." (Secretary, ConstrucCo)

4. The process of setting up meetings is not always a mechanical one. There are times when negotiation is required to secure the presence of all desired parties.

"When we set up meetings we have to go through lots of negotiation since the board is made up of members from many locations. Dates for regular meetings get established well in advance and put on everyone's calendar. But setting up special meetings requires lots of personal contact." (Administrative Assistant, TransDist)

5. Very often those who take time to input the information never gain the value of group calendaring because others (usually secretaries) do the group scheduling. Therefore people see a basic economic imbalance of input effort to output value (see also Grudin, 1988).

"It seems I do all the work and Harry's secretary gets all the benefits!" (Manager, BigU)

The calendar function has potential for supporting important group activities (keeping track of time commitments), but the current combination of software and hardware is seen by users as "not up to our needs."

How the functionality is offered. The second aspect of functionality relates to the way it is offered to users. Aside from the functional limitations mentioned above, calendaring was not used in several of the systems because people found the process of use awkward (e.g., no easy way to indicate recurring events). In other examples, people reported that they could not use a tool effectively because they could not remember how to access a particular function and could find no effective help on-line or in the written manuals.

Aspects of the user interface design were also important factors in the reaction people had to The Coordinator (Version I)(see also Bair and Gale, 1988). Although people in fact used the package, and stated that the product was valuable to them:

"It's great for communication breakdowns since you can backtrack the conversations and find out what went wrong." (Manager, SnackCo)

they also commented on the terminology of the interface:

"I am not enchanted with the verbiage." (Manager, ServBuro)

Two other products, ForComment and Higgins, were consistently praised for their interfaces, even though some other aspects of their designs were criticized.

"ForComment is a joy to use; it's so easy to understand the menu items without a manual or checking 'Help'." (Senior Manager, SoapCo)

"Higgins menus are self-evident, and the use of color is really nice." (Manager, RBOC)

It has long been recognized that user interface design is a critical element in the successful use of a software product (Martin, 1973). Therefore it is not surprising that it continues to be an important element in the case of groupware tools. However, it may be that because people in a work group use these tools, additional factors must be considered in interface design. For example, in a single-user product, like the spreadsheet, designers must be concerned about how each user interprets menus and takes action. In a groupware tool the designer must be concerned about the individual user and, in addition, must address the issue of how what that user does is interpreted by many others, individually and as a group. Additionally, the individual is acting as a representative of the group that may influence how the tool is used and interpreted.

> It is important to note that an intergroup transaction is not the same as an interpersonal one, although both take place between individuals. A group member involved in intergroup transactions acts as a representative of the group in accordance with the group's expectations. The member is not acting solely on an individual agenda (in Ancona, 1987).

For example, one person may choose to use an all-lower-case character style to indicate "informality" in notes. This style may be detrimental in communication if other users interpret this as not having enough concern to compose a note properly. The judgment of this user's behavior can then be made not only against that individual, but against the group as being, for example, unprofessional. Such issues introduce many more layers of complexity into the interface design process, and they emerge from a social analysis of our interview data rather than an analysis that looks purely at the technological merits of a design.

In conclusion, it is clear from our interviews that the quality of design, both in terms of functionality provided and access to that functionality, is an important factor in how and whether people use groupware tools. The researchable questions suggested by this conclusion focus on gaining a better understanding of 1) interface design in software that serves a team of users, and 2) the actual tasks carried out by individuals acting as members of groups.

Isolated Tools Hinder Productive Use of Groupware Systems

The tools are considered isolated with respect to the flow of user control during work and with respect to the flow of data among tools (as discussed earlier). In some cases the process of accessing the function of a second tool when using one tool (i.e., flow of control) requires an awkward sequence of user actions. Other cases require the transfer of data from one tool to another (i.e., flow of data). (See also Nielsen *et al.*, 1986.)

Transfer of user control. In several of the organizations we studied, it was necessary for the people to go through a series of steps in order to move from the groupware tool they were using for their business group/team to other tools they were required to use for tasks relating to the firm as a whole. For example, some groups used a personal computer e-mail system like those available on Higgins or The Coordinator within their departments, but they had to change to a mainframe-based tool like PROFS or All-In-1 for e-mail access to other parts of their companies. This was universally considered to be an aggravation and a waste of time, regardless of the ease or difficulty associated with the switch.

"I want to log on to The Coordinator and Excell at the same time because I need to bounce back and forth from moment to moment." (Manager, SmallChem)

"Because Forecasting uses Metaphor to analyze sales data from last year, pricing people are using HP3000's, and I have my analysis programs on a Compaq 386, I have a heck of a time moving between functions I need to access when we set up a promotional campaign." (Manager, BeerCo)

"It's such a pain. I actually have to crawl behind my desk and change plugs. Is this modern technology??!!" (Analyst, SnackCo)

Transfer of data. Tools that were not completely integrated required that the result from one task be consciously moved into the environment of another tool in order to perform additional tasks. Most users were annoyed by this step, irrespective of its ease or difficulty. From the examples given above to illustrate flow of control problems, it is clear that transfer of data is also a problem at some of the sites.

"I know it is hard to believe, but we actually have to print the output from the HP3000 programs and key the data in to the Compaq 386 because we haven't found a more cost-effective way to move the data across directly." (Analyst, BeerCo)

The ForComment system, highly praised in most respects, was singled out here with respect to data transfer. In order to use ForComment, the person must import text created elsewhere. Although this is a straightforward step, users consistently commented that they would prefer that the functionality provided by ForComment be available as part of the word processor they used to create the text.

"I love ForComment, but I wish it were part of our word processing package. I am always afraid something will get lost in the transfer, so I take the time to check the whole document." (Manager, BigU)

With respect to both flow of control and flow of data, the interviews showed very clearly that a lack of integration from either integration perspective was a barrier to the use of some groupware tools. In addition Ancona's (1987) research on boundary management (i.e., the management of the group's relations with environments and individuals external to the group) raises an interesting point with respect to flow of control. She found that teams equally matched on group process characteristics could be differentiated based on their boundary management capability. This implies that boundary management is a key aspect of team performance and, therefore, productivity. If teams are using groupware systems that interfere with their ability to perform boundary management (e.g., the team e-mail system is not easily connected to the organizational e-mail system), their productivity may be adversely affected. From this we conclude that productive use of groupware is reduced when the tools are isolated.

From an Organizational Perspective

People Report Most Value from Tools That Parallel Their Non-electronic Activities

Those we interviewed reported that use of e-mail, for example, was "easy" because it was analogous to, but better than, what they did without groupware tools. People saw computer messaging as an improvement over "the old way" because it was faster, traceable, geography- and time-independent, and accessible from almost any location (e.g., at home, while traveling). Therefore it was easy for people to see the benefits to them in learning how to communicate electronically.

Other functions provided by the systems either differed significantly from what people saw as needed (e.g., electronic calendars) or presented capabilities that they were not currently employing. In the latter category, functions such as project tracking, reminders, directories, and expense tracking all represent tasks that the people interviewed were not doing. Therefore, to use the electronic version of these tools would require them to expend resources for activities they did not normally carry out or carried out only infrequently.

We therefore conclude that the designers, developers, and installers of groupware tools are presented with an interesting challenge: How are people going to make a transition to the new practices that some of the functionality enables? Part of the answer lies in designing functionality that is easy to learn and to remember after long periods of non-use. However, another part of the answer is found in the organizational considerations related to examining current work processes.

Benefits Gained Need to Balance or Outweigh the Invested Resource

The benefits from some of the functionality (other than that provided for messaging) were neither clear nor balanced in our interviewees' minds. In fact users often perceived extra effort on their part for no corresponding gain. For example, people currently do not have an incentive to maintain an electronic calendar to support group use. They see the work involved as redundant (since most also wanted to have a portable calendar on paper in any case). Though they agreed that their managers and groups would benefit, the value to them personally was too far removed to motivate their behavior. They likened their maintaining calendars and project information to "keypunching" activities. Yet the group value of electronic calendaring is realized ony when everyone cooperates.

Messaging functions, however, had a beneficial impact on them directly. They experienced the satisfaction of "getting the message out," "putting the ball in the other guy's court," assigning tasks to group members, etc. On the receiving side, they had a record of what they were expected to do and, through being on copy lists, had a sense of being in touch with what was going on in the group. They had no need to conceptualize anything beyond a personal benefit.

Other functions as mentioned previously (e.g., project tracking, reminders, etc.) actually required additional effort on the part of the users to learn to do things in a different way, independent of the technology. Although the people we interviewed often said things like "I should do expense tracking," "I know it would be more efficient if I kept an electronic directory," "I could really benefit from the reminder function," invariably they were unwilling to adapt their behavior and invest the personal resources necessary to employ this kind of functionality. They had not identified benefits to using the technology that equalled or exceeded their resource investment.

Grudin explores "the disparity between who does the work and who gets the benefit" and raises some serious questions about whether groupware applications will ever succeed:

> Not all groupware introduces such a disparity—with electronic mail, for example, everyone generally shares the benefits and burdens equally. But electronic mail may turn out to be more the exception that proves the rule unless greater care is taken to distribute the benefit in other applications (Grudin, 1989).

Therefore, we can conclude that unless there is a balance between the effort required on the part of the user and the benefit delivered to that user, a person is not likely to employ the functionality present in a tool. Other forms of motivation (e.g., management directives, group agreement, education) can be important in influencing the perception of balance. Research to investigate motivation and change management as part of the implementation of groupware technology could be beneficial in understanding the dynamics here.

Groupware Implementation Is Simultaneously a Social and Technical Intervention

Our research observations support Kling and Iacono (1989): "computerization is simultaneously a social and technical intervention." One of the most important aspects of this complex intervention is that it is a "strategic intervention" (Kling and Iacono, 1989, p. 342). Whether the strategy of technology introduction is made explicit or kept implicit, it exists and can have a significant impact on the organization.

In our research we saw the effects of strategies on the individuals we interviewed. For example, when a groupware system was introduced as a way to streamline procedures by merely training new users in the mechanics of the tools, we saw people using a minimum of the functionality present in the systems. That is, people used what they were taught to use without any innovative thinking on their parts about either 1) how to employ other functionality present in the groupware systems, or 2) how to use what they had learned creatively to have an impact on the way they carried out their work. When instruction went beyond mechanical steps, however, to include, for example, a presentation on the concepts of groupware, or material on how to relate the groupware functionality to accomplishing their work tasks, then people made use of, and applied creative thinking to using, the functionality present in the tool.

When a groupware system was introduced as a new technology to experiment with, the people did not take it seriously and did not look for ways to augment their productivity. When decision makers held high expectations for productivity enhancement through groupware, yet gave no attention to examining the work process, people reported that they felt under pressure to perform better while learning a new tool and without a clear understanding of how the tool would make a difference. In many of these cases, the introduction of the groupware system had a negative effect on productivity.

Organizational factors in the following four general categories showed up as consistently important as we interviewed people in the 25 organizations.

Champions. Management support for the introduction of groupware tools varied significantly in our sample. In some organizations, support for the tool emanated from the top levels of the firm:

"When the president wanted us to use this e-mail package without even looking at any others, we thought it was strange, but had enough faith in [him] to try it." (Senior Manager, CableCo)

At others, like SnackCo, the management support was at the departmental level:

"We thought this tool was weird, but if WW asked us to try it, we knew it was worth doing." (Manager)

In some instances, the support came lower in the organization in the form of middle management individuals who felt they could engineer successful pilots and demonstrate the value of the tools to upper management:

"Through my own coaching and interpersonal skills I have been able to teach people and win them over to the value of using The Coordinator. Now management is paying attention." (Manager, ServBuro)

Though these instances of managerial support represent very different levels of power within each organization, they demonstrate the importance in general of a committed leader in the introduction of a new technology. Management literature for decades has discussed the value of leadership and champions for the successful implementation of an innovation. In the area of groupware tools, this common wisdom continues to be valid. However, as the previous observations have shown, and the next observations will suggest, managerial support by itself cannot guarantee successful implementation by itself.

Expectations. We observed two different work groups in one organization in which the same software had been introduced. In one of these groups (Group A) the tool was originally described as a new technology that the group members should familiarize themselves with and see what they could use it for. In the other group (Group B) the tool was described as an important new technology that was going to be used to improve communication throughout the organization. Five years later, when we conducted our interviews, the original attitudes were present in these two groups and were influencing the use of the software. As a result, in Group A the tool had never been taken seriously and was still considered "an experiment" and informal. In Group B the tool was described by people as "critical to their jobs."

It is clear from our studies and those of others "that the kinds of expectations with which an organization approaches new information technology do much to define the consequences that will be observed" (Carroll and Perin, 1988). Therefore the way in which new groupware tools are introduced into the work group will influence the ways in which they are used.

Training. Those interviewed generally described the training that they had received in the use of their software as directed toward building procedural or mechanical skills —basic instruction in what keys to push to accomplish specific tasks. This was true for all the tools we studied. However, in the case of The Coordinator, we did interview some users who had received training that included an introduction to the theory underlying this product. A subset of this group reported that the ideas were too sophisticated for them and their colleagues to assimilate:

"The linguistic concept went over most people's heads." (Manager, SnackCo)

"The training left me cold, but we pursued the value on our own." (Senior Manager, CableCo)

However, some reported that knowledge of the theory helped them to use the tool and to implement the communication practices that the tool supports:

"Knowledge of speech-act theory has really helped me use The Coordinator to be more effective in my daily communication." (Manager, ServBuro)

"The workshops were inspirational and make using The Coordinator vocabulary much easier." (Manager, SnackCo)

Given the previous observations that people are not using the functionality provided by these tools, the fact that they have received only basic, mechanical training would tend to indicate that the training is not adequate.

"Training was not very good, but we figured it out." (Manager, MedCons)

Evolution. After an initial introduction into the use of a groupware tool, the users we interviewed tended to "practice" only those procedures that they needed to accomplish their most urgent business tasks. As a result, much of what they were initially trained to do but did not continue to do regularly was forgotten.

"Two weeks after the training program I could barely remember how to get to my file directory." (Senior Manager, LawCo)

In the use of any system, people will encounter special case needs for functions from time to time in their work. Those interviewed did not regularly look up procedures in a manual when these situations arose. When online help was available, most who used it were unable to find what they needed. Instead, the typical form of help sought was to ask a colleague or subordinate.

"I refuse to read manuals and documentation; they aren't even written in English!" (Manager, BigChem)

"The only copy of the manual I could find was two years old and inappropriate to the version I am using." (Manager, SoapCo)

"On-line 'Help' is a bust. It never covers the exact problem I'm having and is written with lots of jargon." (Senior Manager, FoodCo)

"I always ask Joe for help. He can tell me in two seconds where I've gone wrong." (Support Staff, BigU)

"Sue explains my mistakes in the context of our work. That makes it easier for me to remember for next time." (Senior Manager, TerminalCo)

Some of the organizations provided a person or group to serve as the designated support source to which the users would turn for help. These organizations appeared to understand the evolutionary nature of a person's use of software, and they supported that evolution through a formal organizational entity. Other sites we studied assumed that once the initial training had taken place, no formal corporate role of an ongoing nature was needed. In these cases, de facto support grew up in the form of individuals in work groups who became "local gurus."

"Dick has become the guy we all go to for help. He's part of our department and understands our questions best." (Manager, TerminalCo)

"The Infocenter has been wonderful in supporting the use of this tool. They are always available and polite in telling you where you made your mistakes." (Senior Manager, OilCo)

We observed what might be called a "plateau of competence" in using a tool. Without a timely and user-appropriate incentive to move beyond self-standardized use, people tend to settle into standard operations (Rosson, 1985). We observed close group interaction serving as a constructive stimulus for individuals. In SnackCo a central person sent out a newsletter of hints and ideas that was found useful by some. However, the presence of new ideas was countered by pressure to "get the job done," so many people found little time to try new things. This suggests that such stimuli must be in the form of easily tried procedures with immediately visible value so that they fit into the practices carried out during a busy day.

In each of the categories—champions, expectations, training, evolution—we saw a need for sensitivity to organizational issues. In addition the degree and timing of organizational intervention must be planned. The risk of failure increases when the multiple organizational factors are not considered. In the case of groupware technology, there is very little experience in understanding these factors, which may be particularly complex because of the "group" aspects of the application.

Process Redesign May Be Required to Realize Productivity Improvement

We have just suggested that organizations should consider the perspectives of people at all levels when introducing technology. It is also interesting to consider the extent to which organizations need to alter their basic processes in order to achieve higher levels of coordination and productivity.

This process redesign may occur on a variety of levels. For example, traditional process redesign looks at formal processes that have been established in an organization in order to achieve its business goals and objectives. These processes are reevaluated for a variety of reasons, including changes in products or services, changes in the structure of industry, and the impacts of new technology on basic functions (e.g., manufacturing or distribution channels).

However, process redesign can be employed on a local level in an organization. For example, the process of work coordination in a department or the process of conducting meetings may be areas in which productivity gains could be achieved through rethinking and redesigning the traditional forms (e.g., Whiteside and Wixon, 1988). In our field work we observed instances of management expecting substantial productivity improvement to result from the simple act of putting a groupware system into place. In these instances our interviews did not uncover any significant change in how people approached their jobs. Some felt that the new technology created more work for them and therefore made them less productive.

Whenever we observed the implementation of groupware technology without a concurrent examination of how work procedures and coordination might change or evolve, we saw that these systems had very little impact on the perceived productivity of the groups. These observations lead us to the conclusion that in some cases when groupware systems are implemented, not enough attention is being placed on examining the basic processes of work and how technology may enhance these processes. Therefore, process redesign may be required to achieve productive benefits in using groupware technology.

Creating Productive Teams Is a Challenge

Managers in some of the organizations we studied had explicit goals of changing the way work was carried out, moving their groups to new planes of performance, creating "paradigm shifts":

"I am intrigued by the linguistic theory underlying The Coordinator and would like to see everyone undergo a paradigm shift and significantly change the way they interact." (Senior Manager, SnackCo)

Does the current generation of groupware systems facilitate this process? What is truly needed to create productive teams? In *TeamWork* (Larson and LaFasto, 1989), the authors present eight characteristics of high-performing teams, which they draw out of interviews with publicly acclaimed high-performing teams, including sports, science and technology, and industry. Most of these appear to reflect generally understood notions of good teamwork, and they are described at a somewhat abstract level, e.g., "clear elevating goal," "competent team members," "collaborative climate."

They also raise many questions in terms of *how* these characteristics are operationalized. In the context of our research, how can technology be applied to facilitate the creation of the key elements necessary to create productive teams?

The partnership of organizational process and technology is very clear. Management must carry out specific tasks to bring forth productive team characteristics. High-performing teams can be created without any technology. However, in the fast-paced, geographically dispersed environment of today's corporation, groupware technology could enhance the individual's ability to carry out the appropriate tasks.

Examining people's attitudes appears to be an important step in understanding barriers to productive teamwork. In our interviews we noted that when people saw the immediate value to themselves of using a function (e.g., messaging) they quickly adapted to its use. However when it was in the interests of the "higher good"—that is, the team, department, or organization would benefit—the incentive for the individual was missing. In these situations it took other motivators to cause people to use these tools. Some of the motivators included

- a charismatic leader
- orders from higher management
- workshops on organizational issues
- obtaining group agreement and individual permission.

In other words, the technology alone, regardless of its potential value, attractiveness, or ease of use, could not inspire people to use it. In addition, introducing new technology into a poorly operating work group is unlikely to improve its performance. In fact researchers have found that new technology may very well degrade performance because its introduction brings more complexity and a threat to the people on the team (Henderson and Cooprider, 1988).

The well-known concept of *unfreezing* in organizational change theory (Lewin, 1952) seems applicable here. The potential users of groupware systems need to *open up* or *unfreeze* to the possible value of learning to use the technology. Unfreezing is not a simple matter of mechanical training, but rather an organizational process that includes training, education, and rethinking the goals of the team and then considering how work results will be accomplished from the new perspective.

One of the lessons that comes out of *TeamWork* is that much of the success of teams depends on communication among team members on key issues. One of groupware's greatest values, according to our research, is the support it provides for electronic messaging. Our conclusion here is that if a groupware system can facilitate team interaction and information exchange, it has the potential to move group work into the realm of high-performance teams.

Summary

Is groupware to new to study conclusively? We have learned from innovation research (Rogers, 1983) that it takes time for new ideas to be assimilated by people. Although the technology for electronic mail and conferencing has been available for 15 years (Engelbart, 1964, Johansen, 1988), the concept of technology to support work groups has been discussed for only about four years. (Engelbart in the early 1960s developed pioneering technology especially designed to support high-performance teams, but this work was not well known outside the computer science community.) We may therefore be observing the use of these new tools when they are in their infancy and before people have learned to think about them as essential tools for effective office work.

Nonetheless, experiences gained from studying people as they learn to use new tools can benefit the designers of the next tool generation, thereby helping to accelerate the process of acceptance and use of these tools. We also believe that managers can learn to be sensitive to the complex balance that exists between the organization and the technology.

Our observations were consistent across a wide range of organizations. Work groups at the largest organization we studied, BigChem with $30 billion in revenues, experienced the same challenges in organizing work and using information technology as did those at the smallest organizations. Work groups at companies recognized as being "forward thinking," "networked," and participatory in management style did not differ in their problems or their attempted solutions from work groups in companies characterized as "conservative," hierarchical, and traditional in management style.

For example, CableCo ($1 billion in revenues) is a very young, quickly growing, highly successful company with a participatory management style. The work group consisted of nine people who had concerns related to effective communication and management of tasks in an accelerating, fast-paced environment that spanned several time zones. At SoapCo ($17 billion in revenues) one work group consisted of 15 people who expressed exactly the same concerns and were attempting to use information technology in the same way to support their work group. SoapCo is a very old company with a long tradition of hierarchical, conservative management, and with longstanding procedures for accomplishing tasks. A priori, we might have assumed the differing environments in these two organizations would have dictated different approaches to solving the coordination problems. We found this to be true neither here nor at other research sites. Apparently today's business environment of global, 24-hour marketplaces with the concurrent acceleration of information and coordination needs brings the same challenges in managing work groups to diverse organizations.

We have discussed major questions and conclusions about work groups and their use of information technology. We see an important interplay of factors in our major conclusions. For example, people seem to need training beyond the simple mechanical instruction that usually accompanies groupware tools. Because groupware is a relatively new technology, this may change in the future as the tools are more widely known and used. Their inherent value may become more obvious to people and they will adapt to their use more easily.

However, the organizational inhibitors that we observed cannot be dismissed. Recognizing the long-lasting constraints of history and the power of politics in the organization at the same time as considering the new possibilities for technology support may result in new insights. These contrast with insights suggested when using traditional requirements analysis, often focused on individual users to the exclusion of organizational factors. Understanding the interplay of

1. economic balances (i.e., input resources versus output value) inherent in the use of a tool,

2. the differential impacts on organizational roles (e.g., managerial impacts as compared with support staff impacts), and

3. the organizational readiness (i.e., management attention through planned change or intervention)

may lead management toward different technological paths than those discovered through simple analysis.

We have stated earlier that managing the volume of information has been traditionally, and still is, the major task facing knowledge workers. As we have interviewed, observed teams, and better understood the tasks they are undertaking, we have come to the conclusion that a groupware system like The Coordinator could have an effect on knowledge work by compressing it. That is, use of The Coordinator as its designers intended could reduce the volume and complexity of information so that managing the content and meaning of interaction would dominate managing volume.

Revolutionizing work may be an effective role for groupware systems in organizations. Most of today's groupware systems are not designed to do this. Instead they attempt to provide electronic support for the tasks people are believed to carry out in performing knowledge work in groups. If indeed the concept of work groups and business teams is the organizational concept of the future, it becomes critical to understand better the interaction of individuals in these groups and how information technology can support or even enhance the work of groups.

Acknowledgments

The authors acknowledge the many individuals who agreed to be interviewed, and who interacted with us in the course of this research. Without their cooperation and genuine interest in the topic, it would have been very difficult to learn about the experience of groupware use in organizations. We thank David L. Anderson who assisted us in the fieldwork and provided support for the ideas presented here. We also acknowledge the following for their valuable roles in reviewing drafts: John Henderson, J. Debra Hofman, Bob Johansen, Wendy Kellogg, Bob Mack, Tom Malone, Wanda Orlikowski, Judith A. Quillard, John Richards, and JoAnne Yates.

Appendix I

Case Study Interview Outline

General background information on the organization, the work group, and the individual being interviewed;

Detailed information on the work group or project:

- Members
- Description
- Mode of operation

meeting frequency
forms of communication (face-to-face, phone, electronic, video)
levels of stress
leadership
boundary management (relationship to world outside project);

Description of how tasks are accomplished;

Determination of information technology (IT) tools that are used to facilitate task accomplishment with detailed description of use;

Determination of general sense of satisfaction with existing mode of operation;

Suggestions for change;

Probing of interviewee's sense of the future:

- Types of group work that will take place;
- Changes anticipated for organization as a whole;
- Needs for different IT tools.

Appendix II

All-In-1™

All-In-1 is more accurately described as a family of tools or even an office tool environment. This system resides on a centralized computer, with PCs often serving as a means of access (both local and remote). It does not provide flow of data integration but does provide flow of control within its environment. The basic tool offers a variety of functions ranging from electronic mail to a spreadsheet package. An organization can customize All-In-1 by adding other commercial products under the general All-In-1 "umbrella." For example the popular word-processing software, Word Perfect, can be installed to operate under All-In-1. The extent to which the functionality provided under All-In-1 can be used as groupware depends on which functions are used and on what agreement the people in the organizational unit reach on how the functions will be used.

The logical groupware use of this tool involves employing the electronic mail function and VAX Notes (computer conferencing) for communication and the exchange of documents. A calendar function can be used for scheduling group meetings.

The basic All-In-1 functions described above are in use at three organizations in our study.

ForComment™

ForComment is a single-purpose system. It assists users in group authoring or editing of documents. This system is available in single PC and local area network configurations. ForComment "imports" text produced in most of the popular word processing environments or ASCII and allows multiple authors or reviewers to rewrite and/or comment on the document. Control over the final version of the document always remains with one individual, the designated primary author. Proposed rewrites and comments are noted through a symbol in the margin, and the actual text of the revision is displayed in a second window on the viewer's screen. Each entry is identified by reviewers' initials, color coding, and date of entry. The software automatically merges entries from multiple reviewers so that the primary author reviews a single, aggregated version. In this respect ForComment provides flow of data integration.

ForComment is used by four organizations in our sample. Each organization uses it unmodified as provided by the vendor.

Higgins™

Higgins is a personal computer system based on a local area network that provides a variety of functionality including electronic mail, personal information organization, project tracking, and project expense tracking. The electronic mail function links messages and their associated replies, allowing users to trace the history of communications leading to a current message. All of the functions are integrated on Higgins both with respect to flow of control and to flow of data. For example, a user can employ key words to find all entries dealing with specific categories. Therefore the name "project xyz" can be used to find electronic mail, "to do" entries, expense reports, calendar entries, etc., that relate to that project by its code name. In this way Higgins can be used both as a personal organization tool and as a groupware tool.

Higgins is used in five of the organizations in our sample, in each case in a stand alone local area network (LAN) mode as provided by the vendor.

In-House System I

One large organization in our sample developed its own global electronic mail, conferencing, and document exchange system. This system resides on a mainframe computer and is accessed by PCs acting as workstations (both locally and remote). Both integration in terms of flow of data and flow of control exist to varying degrees in this system. Development of increased integration in both areas is a current priority. This system has been in worldwide use by a very large number of people at this organization for more than 10 years.

In-House System II

One small organization in our sample developed its own relatively basic electronic messaging tool. This system resides on a centralized computer and is accessed by both local and remote PCs. The system is used primarily in the United States (although one European node is in place) and has been in use for approximately eight years.

Metaphor™

Metaphor provides high-end specialized, networked workstations and software to support professionals, managers, and executives in constructing complex queries against multiple databases. Users build queries by specifying data elements graphically and then by linking sequences of operations on that data. These queries can be saved in "capsules" for later use or for use by others. Data results can be passed to others on the specialized local area network in the form of spreadsheets, reports, and graphs. The graphic user interface is intended for easy and effective use by business professionals (such as marketing analysts) who need to review and aggregate data extracted from large databases. Flow of control and flow of data integration exist within the Metaphor environment.

Metaphor is in use at two sites in our sample. In one of those sites it is being used as a stand-alone system; in the other it is designed with a gateway into the corporate data network.

PROFS™

PROFS is a general purpose office system tool. This system resides on a centralized computer with PCs often serving as a means for access (both local and remote). PROFS includes functionality for electronic mail, calendaring, reminders, and folders for mail management. Other than the electronic mail component, the extent to which PROFS can be used as groupware depends upon the agreements people in an organization reach for allowing access to calendars and folders. Flow of control integration exists to a limited degree within the PROFS environment.

PROFS was studied at two of our sites.

The Coordinator System™ (Version I)

The Coordinator System (TCS) is a groupware system that was designed to support people in effective action during the course of their work in an organization. The system is generally available in two hardware configurations: either on a PC/local area network or via dial-up mode supported by the vendor. TCS differs from most of the other products we examined in that the software implementation is based on an underlying theory of human interaction. The theory suggests that the basic unit of interaction is a conversation, and that people use language (speech acts) to make requests, promise results, decline requests, declare commitments completed, etc. The software makes these distinctions visible and thereby is designed to encourage people to conduct their interactions in a way presumed (under the theory) to be more effective.

The Coordinator Version I is available in seven of the organizations in our sample. Technical details of the implementations differ (e.g., remote mail, local area network), but these differences do not play an important role in what the users see, or how they tend to employ the tool. The fact that Version I is the tool we studied is, however, important because the user interface of Version I differs significantly from that of Version II. Version II became available in 1989, and it is currently being marketed and used in a number of organizations.

The degree to which flow of control integration exists in a TCS implementation depends upon the nature of the implementation and bridges that have been established to other systems. Flow of data integration exists in some of the tools.

References

Ancona, Deborah Gladstein (1987). "Groups in Organizations," in Clyde Hendrick (ed.), *Group Processes and Intergroup Relations*. Sage Publications, Newbury Park, Cal., pp. 207–230.

Bair, James H, and Stephen Gale (1988). "An Investigation of the Coordinator as an Example of Computer Supported Cooperative Work," Extended Abstract, submitted to the Second Conference on Computer-Supported Cooperative Work, Portland, Oregon, September.

Bennett, J.L., K. Holtzblatt, S. Jones, and D. Wixon (1970). "Usability Engineering: Using Contextual Inquiry," tutorial at CHI '90, Empowering People (Seattle, WA, April 1–5), ACM, New York.

Berger, Suzanne, Michael Dertouzos, Richard K. Lester, Robert M. Solow, and Lester C. Thurow (1989). "Toward a New Industrial America," *Scientific American*. 260(6), pp. 39–47.

Bikson, Tora K., J.D. Eveland, and Barbara Gutek (1989). "Flexible Interactive Technologies for Multi-Person Tasks: Current Problems and Future Prospects," in Margrethe H. Olson (ed.), *Technological Support for Work Group Collaboration*. Lawrence Erlbaum Associates, Inc., Hillsdale, New Jersey, pp. 89–112.

Blomberg, Jeanette (1988). "The Variable Impact of Computer Technologies on the Organization of Work Activities," in Irene Greif (ed.), *Computer-Supported Cooperative Work: A Book of Readings*. Morgan Kaufmann Publishers, Inc., San Mateo, Cal.

Bullen, Christine V., and Robert R. Johansen (1988). "Groupware: A Key to Managing Business Teams?" CISR Work Paper # 169, Center for Information Systems Research, MIT, Cambridge, Mass.

Carroll, John S., and Constance Perin (1988). "How Expectations About Microcomputers Influence Their Organizational Consequences," Management in the 1990s Working Paper 80-044, Sloan School of Management, MIT, Cambridge, Mass.

Dalton, Richard (1988). *Open Systems*. (March), p. 7.

Drucker, Peter (1988). "The New Organization," *Harvard Business Review*. January–February.

Engelbart, Douglas C. (1963). "A Conceptual Framework for the Augmentation of Man's Intellect," in P. Howerton (ed.), *Vistas in Information Handling*. Spartan Books, Washington, D.C., pp. 1–29.

Engelbart, Douglas C., and William K. English (1988). "A Research Center for Augmenting Human Intellect," originally published in 1968 and reprinted in Irene Greif (ed.), *Computer-Supported Cooperative Work: A Book of Readings*. Morgan Kaufmann Publishers, Inc., San Mateo, Cal.

Grudin, Jonathan (1988). "Why CSCW Applications Fail: Problems in the Design and Evaluation of Organizational Interfaces," *Proceedings of the Conference on Computer-Supported Cooperative Work*, September 26–28, Portland, Oregon, pp. 85–93.

Grudin, Jonathan (1989). "Why Groupware Applications Fail: Problems in Design and Evaluation," *Office: Technology and People*. 4(3), pp. 245–264.

Henderson, J.C., and J. Cooprider (1988). "Dimensions of I/S Planning and Design Technology," Working Paper # 181, MIT Center for Information Systems Research, Cambridge, Mass.

Hiltz, S.R., and E.B. Kerr (1981). "Studies of Computer-Mediated Communication Systems: A Synthesis of the Findings," Final Report to the National Science Foundation.

Hiltz, S.R. and M. Turoff (1978). *The Network Nation: Human Communication via Computer*. Addison-Wesley Publishing Company, Inc., Reading, Mass.

Iacono, Suzanne, and Rob Kling (1988). "Computer Systems as Institutions: Social Dimensions of Computing in Organizations," *Proceedings of the Ninth International Conference on Information Systems*, 11/30–12/3, Minneappolis, Minn., pp. 101–110.

Johansen, Robert (1988). *Groupware: Computer Support for Business Teams*. The Free Press, New York.

Keen, Peter, G.W. (1988). "The 'Metabusiness' Evolution: Challenging the Status Quo," *ICIT Advance* (October), Washington, D.C.

Kerr, Elaine B., and Starr Roxanne Hiltz (1982). *Computer-Mediated Communication Systems: Status and Evaluation*. Academic Press, New York.

Kling, Rob, and Suzanne Iacono (1989). "Desktop Computerization & the Organization of Work," in Tom Forester *Computers in the Human Context*. MIT Press, Cambridge, Mass.

Larson, Carl E., and Frank M.J. LaFasto (1989). *TeamWork*. Sage Publications, Newbury Park, Cal.

Lewin, Kurt (1952). "Group Decision and Social Change," in G.E. Swanson, T.N. Newcome, and E.L. Hartley (eds.), *Readings in Social Psychology* (revised edition). Holt, New York.

Loveman, Gary W. (1988). "An Assessment of the Productivity Impact of Information Technologies," MIT Management in the 1990s Working Paper 88-504, Massachusetts Institute of Technology, Cambridge, Mass.

Malone, Thomas W. (1983). "How Do People Organize Their Desks? Implications for the Design of Office Information Systems," *ACM Transactions on Office Information Systems*. 1(1)(January), pp. 99–112.

Markus, M. Lynne, and Janis Forman (1989). "A Social Analysis of Group Technology Use," UCLA Information Systems Research Program Working Paper #2-90, July.

Martin, James (1973). *Design of Man-Computer Dialogues*. Prentice-Hall, Englewood Cliffs, New Jersey.

Mumford, E., and T.B. Ward (1968). *Computers: Planning for People*. Batsford, London.

Neilsen, J., R. Mack, K. Bergendorff, and N. Grischkowsky (1986). "Integrated Software Usage in the Professional Work Environment: Evidence from Questionnaires and Interviews," in *Proceedings of CHI'86 Human Factors in Computing Systems* (Boston, April 13–17). ACM, New York, pp. 162–167.

Reich, Robert B. (1987). "Entrepreneurship Reconsidered: The Team as Hero," *Harvard Business Review*. May–June, pp. 77–83.

Rice, Ronald, and Associates (1984). *The New Media*. Sage, Beverly Hills, Cal.

Rogers, Everett (1983). *The Diffusion of Innovation*. Free Press, New York.

Rosson, Mary Beth (1985). "The Role of Experience in Editing," *Proceedings of INTERACT'84*. Elsevier North-Holland, Amsterdam.

Rousseau, D.M. (1983). "Technology in Organizations: A Constructive Review and Analytic Framework," in Seashore, S.E., E.E. Lawler, P.H. Mirvis, and C. Caman (eds.), *Assessing Organizational Changes: A Guide to Methods, Measures and Practices*. Wiley & Sons, New York.

Searle, John R. (1969). *Speech Acts*. Cambridge University Press, Cambridge, England.

Stevens, Chandler Harrison (1981). "Many-to-Many Communications," Working Paper #72, MIT Center for Information Systems Research, Cambridge, Mass.

Trist, E.L. (1981). "The Sociotechnical Perspective," in Van de Ven, A.H., and W.F. Joyce (eds.), *Perspectives on Organization, Design and Behavior*. John Wiley & Sons, New York.

Whiteside, John, and Dennis Wixon (1988). "Contextualism as a World View for the Reformation of Meetings," in *Proceedings of the Conference on Computer-Supported Cooperative Work*. Association for Computing Machinery, New York.

Yates, JoAnne (1989). *Control Through Communication: The Rise of System in American Management*. Johns Hopkins University Press, Baltimore, Md.

P·A·R·T·III

6

The Art and Science of Designing Computer Artifacts

Pelle Ehn

Both art and design at last seem like meeting,
across the Cartesian split of mind from body,
to enable us to find a new genius collaboration
not in the making of
products and systems and bureaucracies
but in composing of contexts that include everyone,
designers too.
To be a part.
To find how to make all we do and think
relate to all we sense and know,
(not merely to attend to fragments
of ourselves and our situations).
It was a question of where to put your feet.
It became a matter of choosing the dance
Now its becoming
No full stop

J. Christopher Jones in *How My Thoughts About Design Methods Have Changed During the Years*

"The Art and Science of Designing Computer Artifacts," by Pelle Ehn, *Scandinavian Journal of Information Systems,* August 1989, pp. 21–42.

Introduction

Design of Computer Artifacts

This paper concerns activities that go under such names as system design, system development, systemeering, software engineering, etc. These activities are here referred to as *design of computer artifacts* in an attempt to avoid taking for granted some strongly embedded rationalistic presumptions of this activity.

I understand design of computer artifacts as a concerned social and historical activity in which artifacts and their use are envisioned, an activity and form of knowledge that is both planned and creative, and that deals with the contradiction between tradition and transcendence. The use of artifacts and the users themselves, not only the designer and the artifact in isolation, become constituent aspects of the design process (Ehn, 1988).

From this point of view I will investigate a very specific aspect of design of computer artifacts—*the academic organization for studies of design and the doctrines that are being taught.* This aspect of design and computers is here being referred to as *the art and science of designing computer artifacts*, in an attempt to avoid taking for granted the boundaries between art and science, and between natural, social and human sciences, manifested in the ruling paradigm of rationalistic natural science in computer studies.

1968—The Spell of Tradition

To me, 1968 stands out as a remarkable year in the history of the art and science of designing computer artifacts. Not because that was the year when I started my studies in Information and Computer Science at the University of Gothenborg. Three other events are far more interesting.

First of all, the years around 1968 was the time when *the first academic departments* for our discipline were established in Scandinavia. For an historic overview see Bansler (1987).

Secondly, 1968 was also the year when Nobel Prize winner Herbert A. Simon in a famous lecture at M.I.T. outlined *a program for rationalistic science of design*, and a curriculum for training of professional designers. He did this with engineering as an example, but he also argued that other fields were just as relevant, for instance, management science and computer science, fields from which he himself had experience (Simon, 1969). This was a program with far reaching consequences for the development of our art and science of designing computer artifacts.

Thirdly, 1968 was the year of the *student revolt* and the beginning of a process that aimed to democratize our academic institutions and to make scientific knowledge useful to ordinary people—a process that had strong influence on my life and more significantly the formation of the critical Scandinavian approach to systems development, an attempt to democratize design and use by the influence from trade unions and their members (Ehn and Kyng, 1987).

These events of 1968 were responses to different crises. Departments of mathematics, engineering or business administration were found to be insufficient platforms for the study of information and computer science. Hence, new departments. The engineering approach to design of the artificial was declared to be a tradition-bound craft not a real science. Hence, the rationalistic program for a real science of the artificial. The political rationality of science was considered counterproductive to the interests of democracy and emancipation. Hence, the student revolt and the "collective resource" approach.

In different ways these three events are still alive, influencing our academic life in Scandinavia. The early organization, with departments built around people with a natural science or mathematical background, focusing on the computer as such or on abstract information processing, still inform our activities. The same is the case with the rationalistic program for a science of design of the artificial that Simon informed us with. However, the "collective resource" approach to democratization has also survived.

A few years ago I started to write a doctoral dissertation about my 20 years of travels in the research landscape of information and computer studies in Scandinavia. My interest during these years are reflected in the title of the thesis: Work-Oriented Design of Computer Artifacts (Ehn 1988). The book is an investigation into the practical and theoretical possibilities of designing for democracy and skill. However, in the thesis work I also had to search for an academic "home" for design of computer artificats. So when the editors of the *Scandinavian Journal of Information Systems* generously asked me to contribute with a paper based on my thesis for the first issue of the journal I decided to focus on the more general home topic and the foundations that we have inherited from the late sixties, rather than on my own 1968-tradition and the "collective resource approach" to work-oriented design. Hence, the focus of the paper will be on the rationality of the academic organization of information and computer studies, and the doctrines that we teach.

Structure of the Paper

I start out with the critique of our *academic organization* of computer and information studies. I am not concerned with the names of academic departments conducting such studies, whether they should be called computer science, information science, information processing, informatics, datalogy or whatever, but on what we should be doing in research and in teaching in the art and science of designing computer artifacts. I argue that we must transcend the prevailing division of labor between our academic disciplines, focusing instead on the subject matter itself, reconstructing it so that we can grasp *use* as a fundamental aspect of design. In search for directions for reorganization I then turn to a discussion of the *a priori* anthropological everyday *knowledge interests* that guide programs and organization of our academic activities.

In the second part of the paper I draw the readers attention to our taken-for-granted background—the rationalistic tradition. Herbert Simon's program for the *rationalistic science for design of the artificial* will be used as example, but it is suggested that the early program for software engineering and the infological approach in Scandinavia are other examples of the same tradition. Against this background a reformulation of the subject matter is outlined, and I sketch a complementary program for an *art and science of designing computer artifacts*, and a curriculum for its study.

Academic Organization

Institutional Boundaries

Design of computer artifacts is not only studied at natural science departments, but also in social sciences and in the humanities. Nevertheless natural science based computer science departments are still often considered as the *real place for information and computer studies*. So, I will make computer science my point of reference. What is computer science? Not long ago this question was addressed by Paul Abrahams, president of the Association for Computing Machinery, in *Communications of the ACM* (Abrahams, 1987).

As a first conclusion he suggests that any definition whose scope strays too far from the pragmatic answer that computer science is what is taught by computer science departments is unlikely to meet much acceptance. I guess he is right. Nevertheless I agree with him that the question is worth discussing.

I also agree with Abrahams that computer science is not the study of Vaxes or Macintoshes, not even of Connection Machines or Turing Machines, though such studies may be part of it. However, I am afraid that this is where the agreement stops. At least when he suggests that most of the interesting questions in theory are special cases of two general types: what can we compute, and what resources do we need in order to compute it? I can imagine many other theoretically interesting questions for an art and science of designing computer artifacts. These questions concern designing computer artifacts for concerned human use. The disagreement may be due to a different emphasis, but I think it goes deeper.

It is not a disagreement on the belief that theory of computer science includes such specialities as algorithmic analysis, computational complexity, and formal language theory, but perhaps on the scope of what we are studying and what other theories we need. It is not a disagreement on the position that pragmatic computer science has a flavor of engineering (or is concerned with design of computer artifacts, as I would put it) but perhaps on the theoretical consequences of this position. Finally, it is not a disagreement on the position that the microstructure of computing is inherently mathematical, and that the macrostructure may not be, but maybe on what it may be.

I have neither competence nor reason to challenge the mathematical and natural science base of computer science when the subject matter is efficiency of algorithms, semantics of programming languages, computability, etc. However, I will have to consider it problematic as soon as any kind of human use of computers is involved, or when any social or organizational setting for its design ought to be taken into account. Here I am primarily thinking of systems development, but I also think matters become problematic in subject areas such as knowledge-based systems, human-computer interaction or design of programming environments.

In fact, the idea of mathematics and natural science as normal science (Kuhn, 1962) for a science of designing computer artifacts is due to history, tradition and coincidence, rather than fundamental reflections of the subject matter. Here, I have the history of our academic institutions in Scandinavia in mind (Bansler, 1987). When the first departments were established in the late sixties it was typically around people with a mathematics or natural science background. They had either participated in constructing computers or used computational power in their academic work. The focus on natural science and the neglect of other scientific perspectives may have been reasonable then. Today such a focus is too narrow, especially if systems development is to be part of what is studied at such departments. One obvious reason is the tremendous expansion in use of computers during the two decades when departments for computer or information science have existed in Scandinavia. Still, the natural science based tradition from 1968 seems hard to transcend. Why? What arguments towards change could be made? Personally, I have met two kind of arguments, and in my opinion neither holds.

The first argument is based on *the need for division of labor.* The argument is that computer science only deals with the natural science and mathematical aspects of computers, the rest being left to other disciplines in the human and social sciences.

I think that this argument holds insofar as the effects of using computers are studied by many other disciplines. However, there is, to my knowledge, no computer science department in Scandinavia that does not at least have something like knowledge-based systems, human-computer interaction, design of programming environments, or systems development in their curriculum for the students. Is the study of these subjects true natural science? I question the fruitfulness of such an assumption. I will also, at least in the case of systems development, argue against the fruitfulness of the prevailing division of labour between our academic disciplines. One of my arguments against this academic division of labour, an argument that can be raised as a critique from inside computer science, is that many researchers and teachers in the human and social sciences base their statements on too limited an understanding of computers. My other argument against the prevailing division of labour is more fundamental. Social and human sciences play an important role in the study of effects or long range social consequences of adaptation of computers in society. However, their role in *design* of computer artifacts is so far very limited and certainly constrained by the existing division of labour between the disciplines. When it comes to systems development I see this as a major obstacle.

Yes, we need division of labour in our academic field, but the existing division of labour is a dysfunctional, historic reminiscence. *An organizational change is needed.*

The other argument that I have met against change explicitly includes systems development in computer science at the same time as human and social science approaches are excluded. It is the idea of *a science of design of computer artifacts as engineering based on natural science theories and methods.* Historically I see this as the main approach to systems development. This approach seems stronger than ever today. A good example is the recent plea for real systems engineering by Janis Bubenko, a leading Scandinavian professor in our field. In a conference invitation recently he formulated the theme like this: "Information Systems Engineering represents an approach to information systems development that is based on an 'engineering' way of coming to grips with the different tasks to be solved in large systems development projects. (. . .) Information Systems Engineering represents work carried out by 'engineering' analysis and constructors in a rigorous, methodological way of coming to grips with every subproblem, no task in the systems development being solved by capricious approaches" (Bubenko, 1987, my translation).

Yes, we need a theoretically sound foundation for design of computer artifacts, but to solely base this on an engineering approach from the natural sciences is dysfunctional. *A change of basic doctrine is needed.* To explain why I take this position the notion of *knowledge interests* will be introduced.

Knowledge Interests

The notion of *knowledge interests* has been developed by the social philosopher Jürgen Habermas (Habermas, 1968a and 1968b). According to Habermas these *a priori* anthropological everyday procedures and interests of knowledge determine the conditions under which every science objectifies reality. He distinguishes between a *technical*, a *practical*, and an *emancipatory* knowledge interest.

The *technical control interest* focuses on observation, empirical analyses, and instrumental control, as in the technical and natural sciences. This is at the core of a science of design of computer artifacts concerned with the purposive rational design of systems and the technical functionality of these systems. This is the aspect of design where we as human beings encounter objects as things, events, and conditions which, in principle, can be manipulated.

The *practical interest in intersubjective communication* leads to focus on dialogues, participatory relations, and understanding, as in the social sciences and the humanities. If we accept that design and use of computer artifacts also are historical and social processes then we have to be concerned with this practical knowledge interest in intersubjective communication. For an art and science of designing computer artifacts this means a focus on interpretation, and human communication, and the establishment and expansion of action-oriented understanding.

The dilemma in determining the subject matter for an art and science of designing computer artifacts is that both the technical knowledge interest in instrumental control, and the practical knowledge interest in intersubjective communication seem equally fundamental. Furthermore, these double knowledge interests are fundamental both to *design* and to *use.* Design of computer artifacts is an activity of determining these artifacts so that they can be constructed and implemented. Hence, the technical interest in instrumental control. But it is also a dialogue and a participatory relation between those concerned about the computer artifact being designed. Hence the practical interest in intersubjective communication. Considering the use situation designed for, there is the same doubleness. Computer artifacts may be designed to support control of objects as well as to facilitate dialogues and intersubjective communication.

This doubleness I see as the fundamental condition under which design of computer artifacts must be objectified as a scientific subject matter. Hence, in studying this subject matter we must transcend the disciplinary boundaries between the natural sciences, the social sciences and the humanities to be able to deal with the different interests of knowledge that constitute the subject matter. The practical knowledge interest cannot be abandoned to *a posteriori* studies by the human sciences and social sciences, because *the design process is where the action is.* Critique may help change the conditions for design and use, but not until they are integrated into theory and methods of design can these interests have any real impact on how people design and use computer artifacts.

Finally, the *emancipatory interest* is a consciously incorporated interest in science that directs knowledge towards emancipation going beyond the other interests of knowledge.

As paradigms Habermas mentions the critique Marx developed as a theory of capitalism and Freud as a metapsychology. This is the interest in the process of critique as a means to reveal power relations embodied in our socio-cultural form of life as systematically distorted communication—the interest of liberation and a dialogue free from coercion through knowledge—hence the fundamental relations to political practice in Marxist theory and to therapy in Freudian theory. I am not proposing that the emancipatory interest of knowledge must be constituent to all aspects of the subject matter of designing computer artifacts, though the fundamental relation between such a science and changes in work and language is an obvious argument. However, for the "collective resource" approach I come from, this interest is cardinal.

In summary, the academic division of labour between natural science, social science and the humanities that we have inherited from the late sixties is a tradition that has not been able to adapt organization and theory to the drastically changed environment. Especially the dominating role of mathematically oriented natural science based computer science departments stands out as problematic. In rethinking the division of labour and the theoretical orientation Habermas notion of knowledge interests can be most useful. In an art and science of designing computer artifacts we need organization and theory that helps us deal *both* with the technical interest of instrumental control and the practical interest of intersubjective communication. Maybe even the interest of emancipation can be regarded as a legitimate research guiding interest once we transcend our rationalistic tradition in design of computer artifacts.

The Rationalistic Tradition

In the introduction I suggested that Herbert Simon's program for a rationalistic science of design of the artificial (Simon, 1969) may be the most important influence from 1968 on our tradition in the art and science of designing computer artifacts.

As students, we have, since the late sixties, met Simon's program or the rationalistic tradition in many guises.

Some of us have been confronted with the branch of rationalistic design formulated as the first program for software engineering (Naur and Randell, 1969). This was the idea of understanding computer programs as formal mathematical objects derived by formalized procedures from an abstract specification. The correctness of programs was guaranteed by methods for successive transitions from specification texts to computer-executable code. This development was very much a reaction to the software crisis of the late 1960s caused by the advent of powerful third generation computers with complex operating systems and numerous new sophisticated applications in many fields. The old methods and approaches were simply insufficient. However, this "new" product-oriented view leaves the relationship between programs and the living human world entirely open.

Others of us have met the rationalistic tradition in the form of "theoretical analysis of information systems" (Langefors, 1966). This was the idea of defining the elementary abstract information needs in an organization and then redesigning an optimal or at least satisfactory ("satisficing behaviour" as Simon puts it) information system. Based on this information systems analysis, specifications for implementation of computer-based information systems could be derived. This development was a reaction to the confusion of programming and data structures with information needs in organizations. However, this infological approach remained entirely within the rationalistic realm. The relation between people in an organization and their information needs was a question of objective facts to be discovered by the analyst.

In one or another of its different guises or disguises, the rationalistic tradition of 1968 really is *the* background for most of us educated at some department in Scandinavia, even if oppositional perspectives also have been suggested. To mention a few but significant examples see, e.g., the doctoral dissertations by Ivanov (1972), Mathiassen (1981), and Lyytinen (1986).

The Science of Design of the Artificial

In this paper I have chosen Simon's program for a science of design of the artificial as point of reference since it is such an explicit and elegant formulation of the rationalistic doctrine of design. Simon suggests that "the proper study of mankind is the science of design, not only as the professional component of a technical education but as a core discipline for every liberally educated man" (Simon, 1969, p. 83). He based this statement on his experiences from having lived close to the development of the modern computer and the growing communication among intellectual disciplines taking place around the computer. The ability to communicate across fields does not come from the computer as such, he argued, but from the need to "be explicit, as never before, about what is involved in creating a design and what takes place while the creation is going on" (Simon, 1969, p. 83).

He also observed that in order to gain academic respectability, e.g., "engineering schools have become schools of physics and mathematics; medical schools have become schools of biological science; business schools have become schools of finite mathematics. The use of adjectives like 'applied' conceals, but does not change, the fact" (Simon, 1969, p. 56). He did argue that this way of acquiring a scientific subject matter had moved the design disciplines away from their real subject—*the design of the artificial.*

On the one hand, Simon took the position that what was traditionally known about design was "intellectually soft, intuitive, informal, and cookbooky" (Simon, 1969, p. 57) and that this was scientifically unsatisfactory. At the same time he claimed that design of the artificial is really what most professions are about. Thus, it cannot be replaced by mathematics, physics, etc. This understanding of a fundamental dilemma for design sciences is an important observation by Simon.

The alternative that Simon suggested is a science of design of the artificial, a genuine science of its own. His elegant solution is to pose the problem of design of the artificial in such a way that we can apply methods of logic, mathematics, statistics, etc., just as we do in the natural sciences.

According to Simon's science of design of the artificial, computers are complex hierarchical systems, as are the users and the use organizations, and as is the design process—together they are subsystems of a bigger system, and we can define their various functionalities separately. In designing these systems we can use many scientific methods (based on theory in formal logic, mathematics and statistics) for evaluation of designs and in the search for alternatives.

About computer artifacts the science of design of the artificial informs us that computers are systems "of elementary functional components in which, to a high approximation, only the function performed by those components is relevant to the behaviour of the whole system" (Simon, 1969, p. 18).

Scientifically they can be studied both as abstract objects by mathematical theory and as objects in an empirical science of the behaviour of computers as complex systems. At the same time the computer artifact is also seen "as a tool for achieving a deeper understanding of human behaviour" (Simon, 1969, p. 22). This is, he argued, because of its similarity in organization of components with the "most interesting of all artificial systems, the human mind" (Simon, 1969, p. 22).

A science of design of the artificial did, according to Simon, already exist in the late sixties, "particularly through programs in computer science and 'systems engineering'" (Simon, 1969, p. 58). Management science was also included among the systems or design sciences that had started to develop "a body of intellectually tough, analytic, partly formalizable, partly empirical, teachable doctrine about the design process" (Simon, 1969, p. 58).

To Simon the natural sciences are concerned with how things are, whereas design is concerned with how things *ought to be*—we devise artifacts to attain goals. However, Simon saw no need for a new logic to deal with the normative character of design. The problem of design can be reduced to declarative logic. Hence, the teachable doctrine Simon suggested had the following seven topics (Simon, 1969, p. 62–79):

1. Utility theory and statistical decision theory—a logical framework for rational choice among given alternatives (. . .)
2. The body of techniques for actually deducing which of the available alternatives is the optimum (. . .)
3. Adaption of standard logic to the search for alternatives (. . .)
4. The exploitation of parallel, or near parallel, factorizations of differences (. . .)
5. The allocation of search resources to alternative partly explored action sequences (. . .)
6. The organization of complex structures and its implication for the organization of the design process (. . .)
7. Alternative representations for design problems.

It is beyond the scope of this paper to give an elaborate account and critique of the seven topics. Instead I will make a few summarizing comments.

To accept Simon's rationalistic program we have to assume that design is a process of *problem-solving by individual decision-makers among sets of possible worlds.* It may be that this transforms the question of design into the rationalistic scientific vein, but at the same time most essential aspects of design are lost. I am thinking of the creativity of professional designers and users that by its very nature defies to be reduced to formalized decision-making. I am also thinking of the social and historical character of the design process —the conflicting interests, the differences in skill, experiences and professional languages. Given such aspects, not much in the science of design of the artificial seems useful in organizing the design process and in designing in a social and historical setting.

From the Artificial to the Practical

The science of design of the artificial leads us in the direction of what we today know as the discipline of artificial intelligence. And even though computer artifacts are in the centre of most of Simon's examples of a science of design of the artificial, we are not told how to design computer artifacts that can be skillfully used by concerned users.

Simon's rationalistic science of design of the artificial may be an ever so "intellectually tough, analytic, partly formalizable, partly empirical, teachable [a] doctrine about the design process" (Simon, 1969, p. 58). Still we are forced to question his argument that since we have explicit knowledge of the design process in computer programs running optimizing algorithms, search procedures, etc., there is no need to retreat to "the cloak of 'judgment' or 'experience'" (Simon, 1969, p. 80). Practical understanding that shrinks when transformed by formalisms and put into the computer may well be the most essential experience and judgement in professional design.

In short, why should we accept that problem decomposition is more fundamental than problem identification, that descriptions should focus on redundancy rather than on uniqueness, that reduction of complexity by decomposition into simple subsystems is more relevant than to critically consider wholes, that subjectivity should be avoided rather than included in our understanding of objectivity? Why are, as Werner Ulrich has put it in a fictitious Simon-Churchman debate, "semantic precision of concepts, model building, explanation, mathematical analysis, empirical research, computer simulation, heuristic programming, scientific rigor and programmed decision making" more important to the designer than "reflection on the sources of knowledge and deception, ideas, experience, imagery, affectivity, faith, morality, interest, on-going debate and self-reflection in order to unfold problems and conflicts" (Ulrich, 1980, p. 38).

In my thesis (Ehn, 1988), I try to demonstrate the fruitfulness of an understanding of design of computer artifacts in a language that transcends the rationalistic natural science based language of systems, objects, information, and data. I also argue that with such an understanding of the subject matter, there already exist well elaborated and teachable theories and doctrines about what professional designers should do and know.

However, I do not argue for a reinvention of the wheel: the instrumental power of systems thinking for purposive rational action is beyond doubt, and many of the computer applications that function well today could not have been designed without rationalistic design methods. Instead I suggest a reinterpretation of design methods to take us beyond the so strongly embedded Cartesian mind-body dualism and the limits of formalization, towards an understanding that hopefully can support more creative designer ways of thinking and doing design as cooperative work, involving the skills of both users and designers.

The design approach that I outline is an attempt to include subjectivity in a double sense. I claim the importance of rethinking the design process to include structures through which ordinary people at their workplace more democratically can promote their own interests. I also claim the importance of rethinking the use of descriptions in design, and of developing new design methods that enable users of new or changed computer artifacts to envision their future use situation and to express all their practical competence and creativity in designing their future.

Based on this understanding I will below outline a curriculum for a disciplinary base in the studies of the art and science of designing computer artifacts.

The Art and Science of Designing Computer Artifacts

My arguments so far should hopefully have convinced the reader that we really need a complementary program in the art and science of designing computer artifacts. The good news is that there already exists well elaborated and teachable theories and doctrines to include in such a program. We do not have to start from scratch.

To paraphrase Simon, my thesis like his program suggests seven topics. They are

1. Social system design methods.
2. Theory of designing computer artifacts.
3. Process-oriented software engineering and prototyping.
4. History of design methodology.
5. Architectural and industrial design as paradigm.
6. Philosophy of design.
7. Practical design.

Below follows in summary my seven candidates for inclusion in a curriculum to be taught in disciplines dealing with the art and science of designing computer artifacts. For each of the topics I have included a list of suggested readings. Neither the choice of topics nor the lists of suggested readings are intended to be exclusive but should rather be understood as a possible start. Suggestions for improvements are more than welcome.

Social System Design Methods

This topic covers methods that include *the role of subjectivity* in the design of systems. Theoretically the different approaches to social systems design have their origin in rationalistic systems thinking but transcend this framework philosophically by including the subjectivity of the users. The different approaches are well developed and they are based on extensive practical experience. However, these approaches are fundamentally "pure" methodology. Hence a challenge will be to investigate how they can be integrated with, or supplemented by, substantial theory of the social situations in which they are to be used. Another challenge is how they can be refined to more specifically deal with design of computer artifacts and their use.

Suggested readings: Here I am especially thinking of three design researchers that have developed challenging alternatives to Simon's systems engineering. They are C. West Churchman, Russell L. Ackoff, and Peter Checkland. To Churchman, a designer is engaged in detached reflection over the possibilities for developing and implementing good systems. In this he is guided by the *systems approach*. This is a special development of ideas from American pragmatism, especially Churchman's philosophical mentor E.A. Singer. The systems approach is developed in (Churchman, 1968). The philosophical background is dealt with in (Churchman, 1971). Ackoff is another of Singer's disciples who has had a major influence on social systems thinking in operations research. See e.g. (Ackoff,

1974). As with Churchman, he includes subjectivity in objectivity. But whereas Churchman is basically interested in ideas, Ackoff argues the crucial role of *participation*. To him objectivity in design is the social product of the open interaction of a wide variety of individual subjectives. Ideally the design process involves as participants all those who can be directly affected by the system, its stakeholders. Ackoff's designer does not, like a doctor, identify or solve organizational messes by diagnoses or prescriptions. He is more like a teacher than a doctor. The designer is someone that through encouragement and facilitation, enables the participants and stakeholders to deal more effectively with their organizational messes—and have fun doing this. Checkland, like Ackoff and Churchman, started out in the tradition of rationalistic systems engineering. Like them he found that systems engineering simply was not appropriate for practical intervention in the complex and ambiguous *"soft" problem situations* in social practice. His systems methodology is focusing on the importance of the dialectics between the many and different world views involved. With Checkland a step is also take away from rationalistic systems thinking towards interpretation and phenomenology. See (Checkland, 1981).

Theory of Designing Computer Artifacts

This topic covers fundamental theory of what kind of phenomenon the design of computer artifacts actually is. It reframes the rationalistic understanding of computer artifacts. The point of departure is what people do with computers in concerned human activity within a tradition. This also means an emphasis on differences in kinds of knowledge between, on the one hand, human practical understanding and experiences and, on the other, knowledge representation in computers understood as "logic machines" or "inference engines."

In design, focus is on concerned involvement rather than on correct descriptions. Design becomes a process for anticipation of possible breakdowns for the users in future use situations with the computer artifacts being designed. This is anticipation both to avoid breakdowns and to recover from them.

As "founders" of this tradition two persons have been especially important, philosopher Hubert L. Dreyfus and computer scientist Terry Winograd. Dreyfus argues for the relevance and importance of skill and everyday practice in understanding the use of computers. His investigations are based on the philosophical positions of existential phenomenology in the tradition of philosophers like Heidegger and Merleau-Ponty, and the positions on ordinary language and language-games taken by Wittgenstein. Winograd has brought this view into computer science and the design of computer artifacts for human use. To Winograd it is in involved practical use and understanding, not in detached reflection, that we find the origin of design. Design is the interaction between understanding and creation.

Being a new and fundamentally ontological approach to design of computer artifacts, not much instrumental design methodology has as yet been developed. Neither has its relation to substantial social theory been extensively investigated. In both respects there are challenging possibilities.

Suggested readings: The two most important books by Dreyfus are (Dreyfus, 1972) and (Dreyfus and Dreyfus, 1986). Winograd's arguments have been put forward in the by now classical (Winograd and Flores, 1986). A good complement to those books is the ethnomethodological approach to plans and situated actions by anthropologist Lucy Suchman (Suchman, 1987).

Process-Oriented Software Engineering and Prototyping

This topic is a paradigmatic rethinking of the process of designing software much along the lines of the first two topics. The paradigmatic shift of primary point of view is from the design of software as formal mathematical objects derived by formalized procedures from abstract specifications towards a process-oriented view. In this new paradigm, the software engineering focus is on human learning and communication in the design process, and the *relevance, suitability and adequacy in practical use situations of the software being designed*, not just on the correctness and efficiency of the piece of code being produced.

The relevance of this view is also accentuated by the development in software engineering of powerful computer-based design artifacts for prototyping. So far this is a very open field including fourth generation tools (typically a database, a query language, a screen editor and a report generator) as well as more advanced exploratory programming environments (like Smalltalk or Lisp/Loops). Other aspects have to do with the kind of prototyping that is supported, e.g., horizontal prototyping (all functions, but with limited functionality) or vertical prototyping (few functions, but with full functionality). There is also the use of early non-computer-based design artifacts like mock-ups to consider.

However, the important point with all these design artifacts is the support for *involved envisionment*. This means a possibility for prospective users in cooperation with professional designers to *gain experience of future computer artifacts* by using these design artifacts as a basis for design requirements. A challenge is to develop programming environments for prototyping that can be integrated with full scenarios, role plays, etc., of future use situations, and to use these prototypes as design artifacts in playing language-games of design as games of involvement—and doing that defeat some of the limits of formal descriptions. Another challenge is to support the emergence of democratic environments for the utilization of this approach.

Suggested readings: This new orientation in software engineering, which so well matches the theoretical perspective in this outlined program, is suggested by people who were closely associated with the early software engineering program. See especially the paradigm shift paper by Chritiane Floyd (Floyd, 1987). In fact, Peter Naur, one of the founders of the software engineering tradition, has made comments in a similar direction (e.g., Naur, 1985). A good introduction to the prototyping field is found in (Floyd, 1984). For further references playing the language-games of design see (Ehn, 1988). For an introduction to the ideas of involved envisionment and design as cooperative work see (Bødker *et al.*, 1988; Ehn, 1988; Kyng, 1988 and Ehn, 1989).

History of Design Methodology

Another topic for the curriculum in design of computer artifacts is general reflections on design methodology. Computers are not the only artifacts that are designed. *How has design methodology developed in more mature design fields* such as architectural and industrial design? Why has there, e.g., been a shift from rationalistic, formal and mathematically oriented approaches toward both more participatory approaches and more design-like ways of thinking? Why have theoretically influential designers reacted so strongly against their own rationalistic approach "to fix the whole of life into a logical framework" (industrial designer Christopher Jones) that they now even advise us to "forget the whole thing" (architect Christopher Alexander) and start to experiment with art in the design process? It should be important to every well educated designer in our own field to reflect upon the relation between design methodology for computer artifacts and the experiences with different generations of design methodologies in other fields.

Suggested readings: A fine collection of major papers in the "design methodology movement" has been edited by architect and design researcher Nigel Cross (Cross, 1984). Since the early 1960's the movement has developed through three generations. The first rationalistic generation, up to the early 1970's, included important contributions like (Alexander, 1964; Simon, 1969; Jones, 1970). As a reaction to this expert role of the designer a participative second generation design methods developed in the 1970's (Rittel, 1984). In the 1980's focus has again shifted, and a third generation trying to understand what designers really do has emerged (Broadbent, 1984). The new transcending positions taken by early important members of the design methodology movement can be found in (Alexander, 1984; Jones, 1984).

Architectural and Industrial Design as Paradigm Examples

Still another relevant topic for our curriculum is *how design is carried out in other design disciplines* like architectural and industrial design. We can use design experiences from these disciplines as paradigm examples to reflect over theory, methods and practice in our own field. This includes reflections over the relations between science and art in design, on styles or "schools" in design, on the relation between science and styles in design, and on the social relations of designing in complex conflicting and pluralistic social settings.

Maybe these kinds of reflections are not relevant for a *science* of designing computer artifacts in a narrow sense, but certainly for extending it to, and incorporating in it, an *art* of designing computer artifacts, and for our understanding of what kind of enterprise design of computer artifacts is socially. Style might not be scientific, but it certainly plays an important role in design of computer artifacts, too. For example, today the "desktop metaphor" is à la mode in interface design, and "object orientation" is very popular in programming. What is style or art in this, and what is purely scientific? Ten years from now other styles may be in vogue. It should be worth reflecting about what was science and what was art in the ideas that Alan Kay, and before him Douglas Engelbart, had that today are manifested as Macintosh style workstations. Which ideas led Kristen Nygaard and Ole Johan Dahl to design SIMULA and basic concepts of what today is known as a school of object oriented programming? As I see it, these innovations are just as much artistic creations of new design styles as new scientific approaches, but that does not make them less important. On the contrary they show the importance of artistic competence in the field of designing computer artifacts.

Certainly an awareness of style, the history of schools and their programs, and experiences with different styles is important in a curriculum in design of computer artifacts. Style may not be scientific in a rigorous sense, but it is professionally important to be able to master different styles. Furthermore, to reflect about styles and schools in design of computer artifacts, as well as to investigate analogies to architectural and industrial design, is a most rational endeavour. After all, design styles and artistic ones live and die as scientific paradigms do. We had better be aware of both, both as tradition and for creative transcendence that can lead to better designs.

Design styles or schools like Bauhaus (as a proactive approach based on the insight that design of artifacts is design of future conditions of living, a vehicle for change) and Postmodernism (as the use of signs and metaphors that are joyful to play with) are good examples of such paradigm for reflections over the relations between science, art and society in design. The examples may also help us to focus on the styles used in design of computer artifacts, and they may themselves furnish some inspiration for design of computer artifacts.

Suggested readings: On Bauhaus see, e.g., the complete collection of documents in (Stein, 1969), and on Postmodern architecture (Jencks, 1984). In (Thachara, 1988) several articles argue that design of computer artifacts in the Postmodern era is becoming just as important a design field as architectural and industrial design. For several examples of the relevance of architectural reflections in our field see contributions in (Norman and Draper, 1986) and for further references (Ehn, 1988). (Norman, 1988) is a nice introduction to stories about industrial design. On professional designers' way of thinking and doing in other design fields, see especially (Schön, 1983).

Philosophy of Design

Philosophy, especially theory of knowledge, and its relation to design is a topic for a curriculum in design of computer artifacts that is inherent in many of the other topics, but that also should have a place of its own. A topic like this can be argued for any art and science, but it is crucial to design of computer artifacts, since this subject matter, as conceived here, is both interdisciplinary and concerned with basic conditions for knowledge production in practice.

Furthermore, we need philosophy to reflect on two different kinds of theories—*operational* and *substantial* theories (Bunge, 1967). Operational theory on how to do design is characteristic to the art and science of *design* as opposed to natural, social and human sciences in general. Such theories espouse design norms or rules to be followed and design artifacts to be used. But as in any other art or science we also need substantial theory about the phenomenon of design, about e.g., what kind of social, historical, scientific, artistic, and technical activity design is. Especially, we need approaches that allow us to integrate operational and substantial theories.

Suggested readings: Churchman's "interpretations" of philosophical ideas from Lebniz, Locke, Kant, Hegel and Singer in *Design of Inquiring Systems* is a great source to learn from (Churchman, 1981). In a modest but similar way, I have tried to "interpret" philosophical ideas from Marx, Wittgenstein, and Heidegger to make sense of an art and science of designing computer artifacts (Ehn, 1988). Like Churchman I argue the need for a more fundamental understanding of design than the one offered by the dominating rationalistic systems thinking based on the Cartesian dualism of the objective and the subjective of body and mind. This need concerns knowledge in the design process, as well as knowledge in doing design research, and knowledge in theories of design. The direction outlined for theory and practice is towards practical understanding of the games people play in design and use of computer artifacts. *Human practice and understanding in everyday life should be taken as the ontological and epistemological point of departure in inquiries into design and use of computer artifacts.*

However, the heritage from the rational Cartesian tradition in our field is overwhelming. Maybe the best way to contest this hegemony is by reading the two Wittgensteins —the young rational hero in *Tractatus Logico-Philosophiocus* (Wittgenstein, 1923) and the mature philosopher in *Philosophical Investigations,* who is trying to show us how he at first got philosophy wrong (Wittgenstein, 1953).

Practical Design

With the program outlined it is obvious that a reduction of a curriculum in design of computer artifacts to what can be taught and learned as detached theoretical reflections is contradictory. Both philosophical investigations and examples from architecture and industrial design point in the direction of the importance of practical understanding as knowledge by experience (Polanyi, 1957), by familiarity (Wittgenstein, 1953), and as reflection-in-action (Schön, 1983) in design. Hence practical design taught by professional designers of computer artifacts and their use, both as experimentation in a master-apprentice relation and as investigations into real cases, seems most fundamental to our curriculum.

This practical education should include examples of, and experimentation with, both a wide variety of application domains and a wide range of design artifacts and norms and rules for their use. Hence, application domains should not be restricted to traditional administrative systems but include new domains e.g., computer support for graphic arts, or cooperative work in small groups. Neither should design artifacts and methods be restricted to more or less formal system description techniques. A new focus should be on design artifacts that support involvement and experience, like the use of prototypes and mock-ups, exploratory programming environments, scenarios, maps, and even role playing.

The suggestions for practical design are certainly easier to proclaim than to implement. Not only do we lack economic resources for such a practical orientation. More serious is the fact that many of us teaching the art and science of designing computer artifacts probably lack the practical competence of professional design. That is perhaps the most threatening consequence of the proposal.

Suggested readings: For the importance of practice, and the master-apprentice relation in industrial design see (Mayall, 1979). At the annual *Information Systems Research Seminar in Scandinavia* there have also been some important practical suggestions for teaching the art and science of designing computer artifacts (Greenbaum and Mathiassen, 1987; Øgrim, 1988).

A Possible Transcendence?

I do not see the above listed topics of a curriculum in design of computer artifacts as a replacement of what is already taught in computer and information science. But any discipline that teaches and does research on the subject matter of design of computer artifacts is strongly encouraged to let it take its place by the side of what is already taught, because it covers some of the fundamental aspects of what design of computer artifacts is really about.

It has been my intention to provide arguments that any discipline that deals with the subject matter of design of computer artifacts should be able, theoretically and methodologically, to treat design as including aspects like interventions into practice, as communication between users and professional designers, as a creative process, and as a concerned human activity. And I have argued that any discipline dealing with such aspects of design will have to transcend a natural science foundation, regardless of whether the discipline is called computer science, information processing, informatics or information science.

The domain of the subject matter outlined is not primarily theory of physical events or logic inferences in a machine, but of concerned human activity within a background of tradition and conventions in designing and using these artifacts.

I find this subject matter truly interdisciplinary, with relations not only to aspects of traditional computer science, but also to theories and methods from social and human sciences such as sociology, psychology, anthropology, linguistics and business administration. Such relations have only marginally been touched upon in this paper, though the role of substantial theories and methods from these disciplines in a curriculum in design of computer artifacts is evident. Such relations, and central topics like computer graphics, ergonomics, theories of organizations and of social change will have to be discussed in another paper.

Furthermore, I have not discussed research methods for a science of design of computer artifacts, another obvious topic for our curriculum. However I think that many research situations bear a family resemblance with the design approaches discussed here. What I have in mind is participatory actions research, explorative experimentation, and case studies—not as a replacement for detached theoretical reflection in one or another theoretical context, but as their practical and empirical foundation.

Instead I have tried to focus on *a disciplinary base for the interdisciplinary subject matter of designing computer artifacts.* In doing this I have tried to benefit from developments in other more mature design disciplines, particularly using the theoretical and methodological discussions in architectural and industrial design as paradigm. However, recent developments in computer and information science have provided valuable contributions, as well.

There have also been indications that what professional designers really do is more art than science. This challenge to an art and science of designing computer artifacts particularly deserves further investigation. A first step could be to explore the traditional master-apprentice relation as one form for education in design of computer artifacts. A second is to consider the arts as paradigm cases for the design of computer artifacts.

However, the different contributions discussed in the outlined program indicate that we already have an intellectually sound and teachable disciplinary base for an art and science of design of computer artifacts. Much still remains to be developed, especially when it comes to methods. And in many respects we have to understand "the design process [as] hiding behind the cloak of 'judgment' and 'experience' " (Simon, 1969, p. 80), that Herbert Simon once started his rationalistic crusade against, and for which he has had so many followers. But this retreat to practical understanding is for theoretical reasons, not because of intellectual softness. Simon's rationalistic systems engineering approach may be an ever so elegant "intellectually tough, analytic, partly formalizable, partly empirical, teachable doctrine about the design process" (Simon, 1969, p. 58), but I see no reason for us to retreat to it as a paradigm for an art and a science of design of computer artifacts.

As compared with the rationalistic approach the outlined program may be a step backwards on the road towards operational theory and methodology, but by being more fundamental, this may also allow us to take two steps forward in designing powerful computer artifacts to augment the skill of users rather than replacing them by artificial intelligence.

By taking this road, we will certainly also need to make extensive use of many of the theoretical and methodological findings in the natural science based research tradition in the design of computer artifacts. By understanding computers as the material we use in design of computer artifacts, the importance of traditional computer science knowledge to design is obvious. An architect that has no understanding of building materials and techniques may design aesthetic and socially useful houses, but no one will be able to live in them if they cannot be physically constructed. The same holds for designers of computer artifacts.

The question is not whether the one kind of knowledge or the other is needed. Both the research-guiding interest in technical control and the interest in inter-subjective communication are fundamental to an art and science of designing computer artifacts. The problem is that the interest in inter-subjective communication has—hitherto to a great extent—been neglected in research and education of our subject matter. There are good theoretical and practical reasons for changing this.

Does this transcendence require a new 1968 and another "student revolt?" Will the emancipatory knowledge interest and the ethics and aesthetics of systems development then be an incorporated part of our art and science of designing computer artifacts? In another twenty years we may know.

References

Abrahams, P. (1987). What is Computer Science. In *Communications of the ACM*, 30(6).
Ackoff, R.L. (1974). *Redesigning the Future.* John Wiley.
Alexander, C. (1964). *Notes on Synthesis of Form.* Harvard University Press, Cambridge.

Alexander, C. (1984). The State of Art in Design Methods. In Cross, N. (ed.), *Developments in Design Methodology*. Wiley & Son Ltd, Bath.

Bansler, J. (1987). *Systemudvikling—teori og historie i skandinavisk perspektiv*. Studentlitteratur, Lund.

Broadbent, G. (1984). The Development of Design Methods. In Cross, N. (ed.), *Developments in Design Methodology*. John Wiley & Sons Ltd, Bath.

Bubenko, J. (1987). *Invitation to Conference in Åre*, April 6 8.

Bunge, M. (1967). *Scientific Research. The Search for System. The Search for Truth*. Springer Verlag.

Bødker, S., P. Ehn, J. Knudsen, M. Kyng, and K. Halskov-Madsen (1988). Computer Support for Cooperative Design. In *Proceedings of CSCW'88*, Portland.

Checkland, P. (1981). *Systems Thinking, Systems Practice*. John Wiley and Sons, Chichester.

Churchman, C.W. (1971). *The Design of Inquiring Systems Basic Concept of Systems and Organization*. Basic Book, New York.

Churchman, C.W. (1968). *The Systems Approach*. Delta, New York.

Cross, N. (ed.)(1984). *Developments in Design Methodology*. John Wiley & Sons Ltd, Bath.

Dreyfus, H.L., and S.D. Dreyfus (1986). *Mind Over Machine—The Power of Human Intuition and Expertise in the Era of the Computer*. Basil Blackwell, Glasgow.

Dreyfus, H.L. (1972). *What Computers Can't Do—A Critique of Artificial Reason*. Harper & Row, New York.

Ehn, P. (1988). *Work-Oriented Design of Computer Artifacts*. Arbeitslevscentrum, Falköping.

Ehn, P. (1989). Playing the Language Games of Design and Use. In *Proceedings of COIS '88*, Palo Alto, extended version in *Cypernetic* (in print).

Floyd, C. (1984). A Systematic Look at Prototyping in Budde, R., et al. (eds.), *Approaches to Prototyping*. Springer Verlag, Berlin.

Floyd, C. (1987). Outline of a Paradigm Change in Software Engineering. In Bjerknes, G., et al. (eds.), *Computers and Democracy—A Scandinavian Challenge*. Avebury, Aldershot.

Greenbaum, J., and L. Mathiassen (1987). Zen and the Art of Teaching Systems Development. In rvinen, P.J. (ed.), *The Report of the 10th IRIS Seminar*, University of Tampere, Tampere.

Habermas, J. (1968a). *Erkenntnis und Interesse*. Suhrkampf, Frankfurt.

Habermas, J. (1968b). *Technik und Wissenschaft als "Ideologie."* Suhrkampf, Frankfurt.

Ivanov, K. (1972). *Quality Control of Information*. Department of Information Processing, Royal Institute of Technology, Stockholm.

Jencks, C. (1984). *The Language of Postmodern Architecture*. Rizzoli, New York.

Jones, J.C. (1970). *Design Methods—Seeds of Human Futures*. Wiley, New York.

Jones, J.C. (1984). How My Thoughts about Design Methods have Changed During the Years. In Cross, N. (ed.), *Developments in Design Methodology*. John Wiley & Sons Ltd, Bath.

Kuhn, T.S. (1962). *The Structure of Scientific Revolution*. Chicago.

Kyng, M. (1988). Designing for a Dollar a Day. In *Proceedings of CSCW '88*, Portland.

Langefors, B. (1966). *Theoretical Analysis of Information Systems*. Studentlitteratur, Lund.

Lyttinen, K., (1986). *Information Systems Development as Social Action—Framework and Critical Implications*. Jyvaskyla Studies in Computer Science, Economics and Statistics, University of Jyvaskyla, Jyvaskyla.

Mathiassen, L. (1981). *Systemudvikling og Systemudviklingsmetode*. DAIMI PB-136, Department of Computer Science, University of Aarhus.

Mayall, W.H. (1979). *Principles in Design*. Design Council, London.

Naur, P., and B. Randell (eds.)(1969). *Software Engineering*. Report from a conference sponsored by the NATO Science Committee, Brussels.

Naur, P. (1985). Intuition and Software Development. In *Formal Methods and Software Development*, Lecture Notes in Computer Science No. 186, Springer Verlag.

Norman, D., and S. Draper (eds.)(1986). *User Centered System Design*. Lawrence Erlbaum, London.

Norman, D.A. (1988). *The Psychology of Everyday Things*. Basic Books, New York.

Polanyi, M. (1957). Second-generation Design Methods. In Cross, N. (ed.), *Developments in Design Methodology*. John Wiley & Sons Ltd, Bath.

Rittel, H. (1984) Second-generation Design Methods. In N. Cross, editor, *Developments in Design Methodology*. John Wiley & Sons Ltd, Bath.

Schön, D.A. (1983). *The Reflective Practitioner—How Professionals Think in Action*. Basic Books, New York.

Simon, H. (1969). *The Sciences of the Artificial*. The MIT Press, Cambridge.

Stein, J. (ed.)(1969). *Bauhaus*. MIT Press, Cambridge.

Suchman, L.A. (1987). *Plans and Situated Actions—The Problem of Human-Machine Communication*. Cambridge University Press, Wiltshire.

Thackara, J. (ed.)(1988). *Design After Modernism*. Thames and Hudson, New York.

Ulrich, W. (1980). The Metaphysics of Design: A Simon-Churchman "Debate." *Interfaces*, 10(2).

Winograd, T., and F. Lores (1986). *Understanding Computers and Cognition—A New Foundation for Design*. Ablex, Norwood.

Wittgenstein, L. (1923). *Tractatus Logico-Philosophicus*. Kegan Paul.

Wittegenstein, L. (1953). *Philosphical Investigations*. Basil Blackwell, Oxford.

Øgrim, L. (1988). Project Work in System Development Education. In Kasbøll, J. (ed.), *Report of the 11th IRIS*, University of Oslo.

P·A·R·T · III

7

Understanding Third Wave Information Systems

Jan Mouritsen • Niels Bjørn-Andersen

Introduction

In this chapter it is argued that it is necessary to incorporate questions of values, morality, and contradiction and their "resolution" into systems design. This is imperative if we want to develop office systems that are useful and relevant in organizational contexts (Lyytinen and Hirschheim, 1987). Often office systems seem to fail because of an overemphasis on the technological and economic aspects of systems development and a relative neglect of sociopolitical concerns (Kumar and Bjørn-Andersen, 1990). It is necessary, therefore, to develop another definition of systems work and its organizational and social significance (Hirschheim, 1985; Hoos, 1983; Iacono and Kling, 1988; Mowshowitz, 1976). Tools, methodologies, and social theory are separable only for analytical reasons. In practice they are mutually dependent in the sense that tools and methodologies are developed within a particular social system. These tools and methodologies in turn reproduce the characteristics of the social system in question through being used for solving the kinds of problems that arise within this social system. In short: tools, methodologies, and social theory are mutually constitutive.

The second, related concern deals with the relationship between humans and technology. Whereas for a number of years focus has been on the relationship between user and machine at the level of the individual, it appears important to start inquiring into the relationship between technological infrastructure and organization. The role of information technology in the overall constitution of organizational practices and in the regulation of human affairs needs to be addressed through broader social analysis. The role of information in modern societies is to establish a link between "control" or "government" and the regulatory aspirations of situated agents. Information technology is doubly significant. First, it portrays the world as amenable to having certain things done to it. The very idea of informing is to make a platform for changing the status quo. Secondly, it facilitates the concrete construction of visibility through surveillance and recording, on the basis of which interventions can be made (Foucault, 1979; Giddens, 1981; Miller and Rose, 1990).

These concerns provide the reasons why it is important to look at information technology and office systems in the context of organization. This approach means dealing with groups, collectivities, and organizations rather than with individuals (Bannon *et al.*, 1988; Sørgaard, 1987). Indeed, it is important to realize that organizational behavior involves practices that spread in time and space (Giddens, 1985). Throughout recent years much effort has been put into discussing the interface between user and machine. It is important also, we would argue, to take into consideration the relationships between groups and technology because of the possible synergetic and/or unintended consequences of organizational action. Rather than focus on areas such as man-machine interface and human-computer interaction, we give priority to what may be called group-systems interface and group-systems support.

In order to develop this point, in the next section we briefly discuss why systems analysis and design often appears to fail. Then we suggest some elements useful in the analysis of office systems in their organizational contexts. Next we discuss and compare three perspectives on office systems. Last, we discuss possible implications for systems design and analysis.

The Effectiveness of Information Systems

There are many accounts of successful systems implementation and use. Often they are found in various trade magazines. However, from these accounts it is often difficult to get an assessment of why the systems work beyond the description of what systems analysts and designers want to convey about their work: the image of success.

However, in much academic literature this conclusion is less clear. Defining failure as the "embodiment of a perceived situation," Lyytinen and Hirschheim suggest that about 50% of all systems are failures (1987, Lyytinen, 1988). Failure, according to this view, reflects an individual's subjective feelings about the degree to which a project has failed to produce an expected system. Failure is the perceived malfunctioning of a particular system. Lyytinen and Hirschheim suggest that it is possible to define four types of failures: the technical domain (physical means and technical know-how), the data-domain (nature, form and content of the data processed by the system), the user-domain (skills, competence, personality traits and motivational factors), and the organizational domain (behavior expectations, responsibility, authority, and task performance). They point out that we neither have sufficient knowledge about what stakeholders perceive to be reasons for failure, nor know what the most important reasons for failure are.

This account of reasons for failure, although it is an interesting and well-argued contribution to understanding failure, seems to adopt a narrow "psychologistic" understanding of failure. First, it adopts the view that failure/nonfailure can be explained

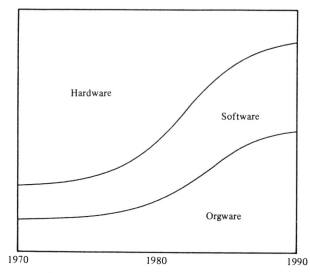

Figure 1. The distribution of total costs of an information systems project.

through an analysis of the perceptions of individuals from segregated segments of firms. These individuals supposedly experience only a limited range of the consequences of systems design and use. Little emphasis is on teasing out the overall systemic consequences of information technology. Second, this approach does not analyze the contextualization activities that people carry out to accommodate problems and mistakes. Such activities, for example, may involve manual rectification of problems of proper format of systems output, manual copying of data from one system to another, and the creation of informal, local systems to complement the information of the formal system. It may be that the very need for contextualization activities convinces users that the system is a failure, because such activities take time and may produce frustration. Contextualization activities sometimes imply that things are not as they should be. This very contextualization, however, may make the system work and therefore be a success in the eyes of management.

Therefore, there is a need to get away from merely stating and describing individuals' subjective evaluations. We have to start to inquire into the reasons for their evaluations. It is important to go beyond the segregated individual accounts in order to evaluate the overall systemic effects of information technology. Such effects may be neither fully comprehended by individuals nor necessarily intended (Giddens, 1984).

This is not to say that individual agents are unimportant. People do play a crucial role, as evident from the trivial fact that technological costs are increasingly a smaller part of total technology related costs. For example, the former vice-president of Xerox Corporation estimated that the first year costs of introducing a professional work station are approximately $10,000, almost half of which are organizational costs (support staff, start-up expense and training)(Strassman, 1985). Bjørn-Andersen (1988) illustrates this point as Figure 1. It shows the distribution of total costs of an information systems project and thus demonstrates how organizational costs take up an increasingly larger part of total costs.

Technological development may remedy some of the problems described above. In some situations technological innovation is indeed part of progress. For example the desktop metaphor used in some systems[1] is a progressive move since it reflects important familiar use-situations in offices ("desk archive," "wastebasket," etc.). The advantage of such forms of interface is that they are not just an upward extension of interface principles applied to the office using an information-processing system view of the office. They are a major step towards seeing the individual as something else than just an information processor.

However, these technological developments only solve a part of the problem. Even though this form of dialogue is extremely good in providing a good single user interface, it takes the individual user and his/her tasks for granted, as exogenously given and unchangeable. It provides a more efficient basis for performing existing forms of work, and it may thus inhibit our creativity to develop new forms of work organization and divisions of labour. Yet there is another and more crucial objection. The human-computer interface that focuses on the individual and on his/her machine is thought to contribute to the whole of the organization only through individual users. We would suggest that in order to understand organizational work it is necessary to develop ways of seeing and conceptualizing the office above and beyond an aggregation of individuals.

Understanding Organizational Practices

Many attempts have been made to define organization in an IT context (Hirschheim, 1988). This often involves statistical description of activities through registration of who does what, when, and how often. Typically, this research has addressed problems only in the context of routinized and structured work[2] (Schackel, 1985), and it is limited by its lack of capacity to interpret the results in convincing ways. Indeed, little seems to be gained in terms of understanding the motivation of different agents to participate in the reproduction of organizational practices; little seems to be said as to the significance and meaning of organizational work. These studies tell us the "how," and not the "why." If we want to understand human activities we must incorporate some kind of hermeneutic or phenomenological perspective to try to elicit the reasons participants have for engaging in organizational activities (Boland, 1985; Weber, 1962).[3]

A number of taxonomies have been suggested to study office work—for example, the tripartitions structured/semi-structured/unstructured and operational/tactical/strategic

---

[1] For example, Apple-MacIntosh, Xerox Star system, and HP's New Wave.

[2] We do not want to argue that routinized work is intrinsically easier to study than non-routinized work. The point is that often this seems to be a major assumption behind "activity-studies." In our view, routinized work is also a complex social situation (Hopper et al., 1989).

[3] Hermeneutics and phenomenology are philosophical traditions that assert that "reality" is accessible only through the significance that people attach to physical and social artifacts. Reality is not given independently of human cognition but is indeed mediated and constructed through human interpretation. Methodologically, this philosophical orientation "is based on the view that one can only understand the social world by obtaining firsthand knowledge of the subject under investigation. . . . (It) emphasizes the analysis of the subjective accounts which one generates by 'getting inside' situations and involving oneself in the everyday flow of life" (Burrell and Morgan, 1979, p. 6).

(for an overview, see Hirschheim, 1988).[4] These distinctions, however, merely reflect some analytical categories of what in practice are organized in very complicated and interdependent patterns of action. Some observers feel that "there is no underlying, enduring structure in the office that could be said to be useful for IT design" (Sheil, 1985). This lack of structure, we suggest, has something to do with the relative lack of concern to ground our understanding of office work theoretically.

We suggest that information systems design and use can be understood through sociological and organizational inquiry (Boland and Pondy, 1983). Rather than separating technical, conceptual, and theoretical concerns, we propose that they are understood in the context of each other. Tools and frameworks, for example, must be understood as giving priority to particular interpretations of organizational functioning. They themselves incorporate interpretations of how one can understand organizational practices. Therefore, understanding systems development and use involves understanding the relationships between organizational participants and groups. Very importantly, this involves understanding the micro-politics of any social system that is reproduced by differentially motivated agents (Crozier and Friedberg, 1980) and the broader social contradictions that will contextualize the forms of agreements that can be achieved (Elkjær et al., 1990). For example, if there are unresolvable contradictions between managers and employees, systems development will be involved in articulating and regulating potential conflicts. Although people may "accept" a particular solution, they may not necessarily actively promote it and make it work to its full potential (Hopper et al., 1986). This implies that systems will never succeed. If the yardstick is un-problematical use and total harmony about the meaning and significance of IT, success is impossible. It must be realized that in political, social systems there will always be some measure of counter-control (Giddens 1984) through which subordinates or other parties will exercise their margin of liberty to thwart or condition the functioning of the system according to their own local interests.

This orientation involves incorporating a series of *concerns* in analyses of information systems.

First, it is imperative to replace the concept of human factors with that of human actors/agents (Bannon, 1988; Bjørn-Andersen, 1988). This implies that humans are reflexively monitoring what goes on in a particular social system, that they are motivated by wants and aspirations, and that they have the power not to perform to the prescription laid down by systems designers (Giddens, 1984). Therefore, agents actively construct everyday interaction in accordance with their wants. Humans are not, as seems to be suggested by the idea of "human factor," merely an inactive although problematic part of a system, something that can be optimized through selection, education, and training.

Second, the content of the inquiry would focus on human orientations, organizational conditions, and technological interventions. Part of this involves realizing the importance of tacit (Polyani, 1958), practical (Giddens, 1984) knowledge. People know more about their lives than they can put into words. People do know how to handle practical affairs without being able to explain fully what they are really doing.

---

[4] It is noteworthy that these distinctions are not ontological. That is to say, e.g., through systems analysis systems designers often want to structure unstructured situations, and through information technology strategic situations are often translated into operational ones.

Third, although agents are capable and reflexive beings, their understanding is partial. There are always unacknowledged conditions for and unintended consequences of people's behavior. Systems reproduction may take on forms that are not intended by any agent. This among other things derives from the very proposition of agency. Any agent attempts to take into account the agency of the other agents, but each agent only has partial access to other agents' intentions and strategies (Giddens, 1984).

Fourth, information systems have an ambiguous position. They can be an aid to human emancipation, but they can potentially also be an important barrier to the resolution of human concerns. For example, in the area of expert systems, there are two trends: One is the type of expert system that deals with artificial intelligence. The key concept is knowledge extraction from human experts; the expert is being "squeezed" to elicit the knowledge, and when this process is completed she/he is scrapped. The expert is gradually made redundant. An alternative type of expert system is a system that is designed to make the expert a better expert. This type of system emphasizes the symbiosis between system and user. The objective is not to make the expert redundant, but to enable the expert to increase his/her understanding of the situation.

Fifth, it is important to recognize the character of shared knowledge and discourse systems in situations where professional groups compete to impose their definition of reality (Armstrong, 1985). Knowledge is relational and serves to make possible the articulated presentation of some points of view rather than other points of view (Miller and Rose, 1990).

Sixth, informal informing is an organizational fact (Preston, 1986). Formal information is always set in perspective by activities that reflect people's interrelationships. This exchange not only concerns the interpretation of existing forms of communication, but indeed also the production of new ways of informing. Therefore, it is necessary to understand how formal information is mediated through various more or less structured patterns of informing.

Seventh, it is important to attempt to interpret and develop the metaphors[5] (Morgan, 1986) of information systems products and artifacts.[6] It is important to consider information technology metaphorically in a series of contexts: for example, at the level of the individual (e.g., knowledge augmenter, expert system, intelligence amplifier) and at the group level (e.g., communication device, decision support system, argumentation facilitator). The development of new metaphors may make possible the development of new forms of insight. Indeed, the coining of new concepts about the social systems with which we are concerned may facilitate new forms of insights useful for constructing more relevant information systems.

Eighth, and finally, it is still necessary to underline that decisions are not always taken according to the model of a monolithic, rational organization. As Lindblom (1959) and March and Olsen (1976) have demonstrated, the rational model is not a viable way of

---

[5] We must be careful, however, not to confuse the metaphor for reality. A metaphor is a one-sided description of a social system, and it portrays only some of the system's characteristics. Reality is always more complicated. Therefore metaphors cannot be design-blueprints.

[6] For example, concepts like Work Perfect (Inc.), Decisionmate (NCR), Partner (RC), PET (Commodore), etc. convey a certain message about the purpose of the system. Of course, this intended message must not be equated with what actually happens in practice.

understanding the intricacies of modern business management. On the one hand it is questionable that decision makers cognitively are able to cope with the complexity and amount of information needed to make rational decisions, and on the other hand, it is probable that all sorts of political and social pressures are called upon in everyday management (Markus, 1983).

Perspectives on Information Systems

The analysis undertaken above suggests that it is important to extend contemporary understandings of information systems. It may be useful to distinguish three perspectives on information systems research and practice. Each of these perspectives suggests a unique understanding of the matter. Although each of them can be treated separately in theoretical discourse, in empirical and practical situations they are mutually constitutive.

The Tool Perspective. Within this perspective, office systems are seen to be technical phenomena that can be managed through structuring tasks, people and goals through a detached process of systems design (Lucas, 1982). The tool perspective not only treats office systems as abstract systems categories. It also incorporates idealized conceptions of people translated into nonpeople or people-substitutes. People are conceptualized as functions or variables rather than persons with personalities. Although the human relations movement—and through this the sociotechnical school—has coped with some of the problems of the user in systems design and use, it still seems to adopt a tool perspective. Its analytical separation of social and technical inquiry seems to indicate that it is possible—and in some situations quite appropriate—to look at the "human factor" and at the "technical factor" isolated from one another. The concern for the human is established in order to make implementation more efficient. Since it seems possible to "solve" the technical questions analytically, the sociotechnical methodology fails to consider fundamentally the socially constructed character of organizational problems and solutions. Sociotechnical design is in some sense a tool perspective with a view to resolve the problems of the "human factor" (Mumford, 1983).

The Communication Perspective. Within this perspective, information systems facilitate the transmission of meaning. The information system assists the flow of informing in the organizational setting. Often forms of language theory inform the grounding of these procedures (Winograd, 1987; Winograd and Flores, 1986). Indeed, it is recognized that the various aspects of language games are integrally part of formal systems. Often, the various explicit forms of knowledge that are represented through the formal systems are contextualized by their meaning in concrete language games (Lyytinen, 1985).

This perspective is oriented towards elucidating informing practices (Preston, 1986) in an organizational context. This means not only looking at the formal arrangements of informing but indeed having an eye on the informal arrangements of informing. As Preston suggests, informal informing is often more adequate than formal informing, but it depends on the capacity and motivation of each and every participant to become informed adequately and in a timely manner. This involves a moral commitment not to let one's associate down when it comes to informing properly. Nothing—apart from human concern—guarantees that this will actually be the case.

The Sociopolitical Perspective. Within this perspective, the information system has a part in the shaping of values and objectives of the organization, establishing consensus, creating commitment/trust, and directing the energies of various agents to purposes important for the organization (Iacono and Kling, 1988). Within this perspective, however, it is recognized that consensus is fragile since it is rooted in voluntary agreements between agents who may have diverse interests and goals. Indeed, the problems of organizational integration are taken seriously within this perspective in order to maintain some form of stability in spite of the centrifugal tendencies resulting from each agent's attempts to limit his/her interdependent relations with other parties involved in the reproduction of organizational practices (Crozier and Friedberg, 1980). Therefore, information systems need to be oriented towards regulating the diverse interests and wants of organizational participants. In a certain sense, this calls for an "ideal speech situation" that is nonetheless bounded by the degree to which one can remove "org-anizational barriers that prevent a discussion by all participants of values and norms" (Lyytinen and Klein, 1985, p. 228).

The question then becomes one of facilitating organizational practices as legitimate, morally justifiable, and socially acceptable. It involves mediating contradiction and conflict with a view to creating some form of consistency of behavior between partici-pants so that agreements can be trusted.[7] Often this is a delicate process where managers must have in mind not only the efficiency of organizational tasks but also the relationship between espoused theories of office practices ("culture") and theories-in-use in this context (Mouritsen, 1989). That is, it may be necessary to compromise and decide what kinds of "malpractices" are not to be remedied.

These comments suggest that within this perspective it is important to look at processes of contextualization. Often, taken-for-granted situations are reproduced as the only conceivable forms of organization (Iacono and Kling, 1988). Implicit, tacit, and practical knowledge (Polyani, 1958, Giddens, 1984) often leads to the reproduction of forms of work and behavior in a way that is blind to other potential forms of work organization. That is to say, values and ideology are reproduced through the contex-tualization of organizational practices. The pragmatic aspects of human life involve subjugating oneself to what may be seen as the obvious functioning of the social system at hand. "Organizational barriers," of which Lyytinen and Klein (1985) talk, are not easily resolved within a contradictory system of differentially motivated agents (Clegg and Dunkerly, 1980). Therefore, organizational practices are often anchored in delicate organizational processes, of which some are detrimental to organizational performance and others are not. Perhaps an organization functions not so much because of as in spite of its members (Crozier and Friedberg, 1980). The role of information technology may be to mediate conflict in an imperfect world. Whereas the tool perspective and to some degree the communication perspective take for granted that it is possible to create some form of optimal systems design, this present perspective rather implies a concern for the reduction of sub-optimality and inefficiency.

The archetypical differences among the three perspectives can be summarized as

---

[7] This raises the question of power. Power is a basic mechanism in the regulation of social practices (Clegg, 1989). Attempts have been made to apply it to the IT field (Bjørn-Andersen, 1987; Markus and Pfeffer, 1983).

Table 1.

Dimensions	Tool	Communication	Sociopolitical
IT-metaphor	tool	medium	system
Organizational process	individualistic	one—one, one—many	organizational and social
Semiotic dimension	syntactical rules	semantic	pragmatic implications
Focus	data/information	meaning-content language, meaning	values, conflict
IT-function	data processor	communication medium	conflict mediator

indicated by Table 1. This table characterizes the tool perspective as a formalistic exercise in abstract logic. It is orientated towards describing organizational practices in an idealized way on the basis of a detached, analytical process of inquiry. It is individualistic because an expert systems designer is supposed to be able to characterize the true interrelationships of the material system, which is modeled. The communication perspective is oriented towards the elucidation of meaning among a community of speakers who typically know each other. The creation of meaning is the outcome of a process of takes a broader organizational and social point of departure. Organizational practices are spread in time and space among people who are remote either geographically or professionally. This perspective is orientated towards integrating different world-views in a way that is not conflictual. It involves a delicate political process where claims and counter-claims are handled carefully in order not to compromise the delicate equilibrium of politicized social systems.

Implications for Systems Development

The three perspectives on office systems developed above reflect different research concerns in the IT community. In terms of the possible problems that face each of them, Table 2 illustrates current research efforts and possible future problem areas.

From a tool perspective, important research problems concern the development of better methodologies to analyze systems, and better ways in which to create artificial intelligence systems. Present methodologies could be extended to encompass ever more

Table 2.

Dimensions	Tool	Communication	Sociopolitical
Present/From	the structuring tasks	no. and types of contacts	technical/rational
Future/To	artificial intelligence; richer methodologies	meaning; interpretation of linguistic utterances	commitment/ trust; conflict resolution

complicated organizational practices in the processes of systems change, perhaps using forms of multiview systems analysis (Wood-Harper *et al.*, 1985).

From a communication perspective, the interest in measuring the quantity of information activities will probably be replaced by much more emphasis on meaning and the possibilities of reaching agreement among participants through the structuring of media of interaction. Meaning is not the property of any individual. Concern for meaning, therefore, implies studying the interrelated practices of situated agents in their reasoned accomplishment of social interaction.

The sociopolitical perspective involves understanding trust relations in political systems. It very much deals with the broader significance of information systems in their capacity as conflict regulators and government technologies (Miller and Rose, 1990). Within this perspective, the study of information systems takes on the task of analyzing why it is that organizations are not generally conflictual although they may be contradictory and political. One possible explanation is provided by Iacono and Kling (1988), who illustrate that information systems are often *stablizers* that cement and underline existing organizational practices and thus make them appear natural and unavoidable. Another possible explanation is that the individual "learns" a subjectivity that is in accordance with overall requirements and thus establishes a link between self and institution (Miller and Rose, 1990).

It probably is clear that the design imperatives of the different perspectives will have different characteristics. The relevance of the tool perspective is guaranteed by the fact of its consistency and Cartesian logic. To use one of Churchman's (1971) ideas, it is defined as relevant because of its character as Leibnitzean inquirer.[8]

The relevance of the communication perspective is derived from its implicit foundation in a Lockean inquirer with its focus on getting consensus on the basis of mutual agreement.[9] In this type of inquiring system it is suggested that there are no illegitimate bounds on the choices a person can make.

Finally, the sociopolitical perspective is guaranteed by its implicit reference to a Kantian or to a dialectical inquirer.[10] That is to say, it is acknowledged that it is impossible to understand a system in its totality. There will always be different interpretations of the character of the system one wants to plan for. Different theories will function as ammunition in this game (Miller and Rose, 1990). From this perspective, systems design is always partisan and loaded with values. The identification of socially relevant systems design is in important ways dependent on the social prejudice of a particular systems

---

[8] This inquirer starts from a set of elementary, primitive (i.e., undefined) explanatory variables, terms, or primitive truths. From these a Leibnitzean inquirer attempt to build up increasingly more general and universal formal truth nets through formal operations and transformations. This procedure is based on consistency, rigor, logical coherence, and little ambiguity over use of terms and over conditions of proof.

[9] This inquirer is an experimental, inductive and consensual system where truth is essentially an agreement between human beings.

[10] The Kantian inquirer presents at least two Leibnitzean models to the observer who selects the best one for his/her purpose. The dialectical inquirer, like the Kantian inquirer, assumes the existence of at least two Leibnitzean inquirers. These Leibnitzean inquirers must be in complete opposition to each other starting from the same set of Lockean data. The observer is subjected to different experts' interpretations of the situation. This inquirer attempts to point out the assumptions behind models, and it recognizes that more than one interpretation of the same set of data is possible.

model. If it is true that nobody has privileged access to understanding a particular social system, as may be the implication of Kantian and dialectical inquirers, systems designers will have to worry about the values they put into practice both in the narrow time-space setting of the office or of the organization and in the context of the wider—perhaps unintended—implications of social and material nature in society and in inter-societal arrangements (Elkjær et al., 1990).

In terms of possible concrete recommendations for design, the tool perspective seems to incorporate concerns for representation (e.g., flat panels for large interactive displays), for interaction (multiple access in storing), for quality indication on data (indication of originator), and for the possibility of allowing different world-views to be stored. The communication perspective probably would call upon the design of intelligent rather than finished systems that can be developed as the series of speech acts develops. The problem is to allow for new combinations of linguistic utterances. In terms of the ideology perspective, it may be warranted to explicate different world-views as an integral part of the mediation of contradictions between different groups of people. This will not be easy, because there are vested interests in the mere definition of which world-views are in fact to be considered appropriate.

Conclusion

With the hindsight of history it is possible to distinguish two major milestones in the development of office systems. The first one is the correction key on the IBM typewriter allowing the operator to correct wrong keystrokes. The next major step was the development of the desktop metaphor as it is seen, for instance, in Macintosh and Xerox Star systems. But what may be the third wave?

Probably the third milestone in office systems will be about sharing information among groups, departments, and organizations. This incorporates the explicit definition of information systems as shared. They will take place in the context of modern organization where participants are recognized as differentially motivated. The major problem is to establish systems and procedures that on the one hand reflect the interdependent practices of different groups, and on the other hand explicate the common interests of the parties involved. Perhaps, rather than focusing on designing optimal systems, the concern should be on minimizing sub-optimality. Managers and systems designers may need to compromise on their "professional" principles and beliefs in order not to destroy the delicate equilibrium of a political system.

Acknowledgments

We gratefully acknowledge the many helpful comments and suggestions provided by lektor Anne Loft, Copenhagen Business School, and by professor Rob Kling, University of California, Irvine.

References

Armstrong, P. (1985). "Changing Management Control Strategies: The Role of Competition Between Accountancy and Other Organizational Professions," *Accounting, Organizations and Society.*

Bannon, L. (1988). "From Human Factors to Human Actors: The Role of Psychology and Human-Computer Interaction Studies in Systems Design," in Greenbaum and Kyng, M. (eds.), *Design of Work.* Erlbaum, New York.

Bannon, L., N. Bjørn-Andersen, and B. Due-Thomsen (1988). "Computer Support for Cooperative Work: An Appraisal and Critique," in Bullinger, H-J., *et al.* (eds.), *Information Technology for Organizational Systems.* Elsevier, Amsterdam, North Holland.

Bjørn-Andersen, N. (1988). "Are 'Human Factors' Human?," *The Computer Journal.* 31(5), pp. 386–390.

Bjørn-Andersen, N., and P.H. Pedersen (1980). "Computer Facilitated Changes in the Management Power Structure," *Accounting, Organizations and Society*, pp. 203–216.

Boland, R.J. (1985). "Phenomenology. A Preferred Approach to Research on Information Systems," in Mumford, E., *et al.* (eds.), *Research Methods in Information Systems.* Elsevier, Amsterdam, North Holland.

Boland, R.J., and L.R. Pondy (1983). "Accounting in Organizations: a Union of Natural and Rational Perspectives," *Accounting, Organizations and Society*, pp. 223–234.

Burrell, G., and G. Morgan (1979). *Sociological Paradigms and Organizational Analysis.* Heinemann, London.

Churchman, C.W. (1971). *the Design of Inquiring Systems.* Basic Books, New York.

Clegg, S. (1989). *Framework of Power.* Sage, London.

Clegg, S., and D. Dunkerly (1980). *Organization, Class and Control.* Heinemann, London.

Crozier, M., and E. Friedberg (1980). *Actors and Systems. The Politics of Collective Action.* Chicago University Press.

Elkjær, B., P. Flensburg, J. Mourtisen, and H. Willmott (1990). "Systems Designers: Preoccupations, Knowledge and Power," working paper, Dept. of Informatics and Management Accounting, Copenhagen Business School.

Foucault, M. (1979). *Discipline and Punish.* Penguin Books, Hammondsworth.

Giddens, A.G. (1981). *A Contemporary Critique of Historical Materialism.* MacMillan. London.

Giddens, A.G. (1984). *The Constitution of Society.* Polity Press, Cambridge.

Giddens, A.G. (1985). "Time, Space and Regionalisation," in Gregory, D., and J. Urry (eds.), *Social Relations and Spatial Structures.* MacMillan, London.

Hirschheim, R. (1985). *Office Automation—A Social and Organizational Perspective.* Wiley. New York.

Hoos, I.R. (1983). "Systems Analysis in Public Policy—a critique," University of California Press, revised edition, London.

Hopper, T., D. Cooper, T. Lowe, T. Capps, and J. Mourtisen (1986). "Management Control and Worker Resistance in the National Coal Board: Financial Controls in the Labour Process," in Knights, D., and H. Willmott (eds.), *Managing the Labour Process.* Gower, Aldershot.

Iacono, S., and R. Kling (1988). "Computer Systems as Institutions: Social Dimensions of Computing in Organizations," in DeGroes, J.I., and M.H. Olson (eds.), *Proceedings of the Ninth International Conference on Information Systems*, November 30–December 3, Minneapolis, Minnesota.

Kumar, K., and N. Bjørn-Andersen (1990). "A Cross-Cultural Comparison of Information Systems Designer Values," *Communications of the ACM.* 33(5), pp. 528–538.

Lindblom, C.E. (1959). "The Science of Muddling Through," *Public Administration Review.* Spring.

Lucas, H.C., Jr. (1982). *Information Systems Concepts for Management.* McGraw Hill, New York.

Lyytinen, K. (1985). "Implications of Theories of Language for Information Systems," *MIS Quarterly*. March, pp. 61–73.

Lyytinen, K. (1988). "Expectation Failure Concept and Systems Analysts' View of Information Systems Failure: Results of an Exploratory Study," *Information & Management*. 14, pp. 45–56.

Lyytinen, K., and R. Hirschheim (1987). "Information Systems Failure—A Survey and Classification of Empirical Literature," *Oxford Surveys in Information Technology*. 4, pp. 257–309.

Lyytinen, K., and H.K. Klein (1985). "The Critical Theory of Jurgen Habermas As a Basis for a Theory of Information Systems," in Mumford, E., *et al.* (eds.), *Research Methods in Information Systems*. Elsevier, Amsterdam, North Holland.

March, J.G., and J.P. Olsen (1976). *Ambiguity and Choice in Organizations*. Universitetsforlaget, Oslo.

Markus, M.L. (1983). "Power, Politics and MIS Implementation," *Communications of the ACM*. 26(1), pp. 430–444.

Markus, M.L., and N. Bjørn-Andersen (1987). "Power over Users: Its Exercise by Systems Professionals," *Communications of ACM*. 30(6), pp. 498–504.

Markus, M.L., and J. Pfeffer (1983). "Power and the Design and Implementation of Accounting and Control Systems," *Accounting, Organizations and Society*, pp. 205–218.

Miller, P., and N. Rose (1990). "Governing Economic Life," *Economy and Society*. 19(1), pp. 1–31.

Morgan, G. (1986). *Images of Organizations*, Sage, Beverly Hills.

Mourtisen, J. (1989). "Accounting, Culture and Accounting-Culture," *Scandinavian Journal of Management Studies*, pp. 21–47.

Mowshowitz, A. (1976) *The Conquest of Will*, Addison Wesley, New York.

Mumford, E. (1983). *Designing Human Systems*. Manchester Business School. Manchester.

Polyani, M. (1958). *The Tacit Dimension*. Anchor Books, New York.

Preston, A. (1986). "Interactions and Arrangements in the Process of Informing," *Accounting, Organizations and Society*, pp. 521–540.

Schackel, B. (ed.)(1985). *Human-Computer Interaction*. Elsevier, Amsterdam, North Holland.

Sheil, B.A. (1986). "Coping with Complexity," *Office, Technology and People*. 1(4), pp. 295–320.

Sørgaard, P. (1987). "A Cooperative Work Perspective on Use and Development of Computer Artifacts," DAIMI PB–234, Aarhus University. Aarhus.

Strassman, P.A. (1985). *Information Payoff*. The Free Press, New York.

Weber, M. (1962). *Basic Concepts in Sociology*. The Citadel Press, New York.

Winograd, T. (1987). "A Language/Action Perspective on the Design of Cooperative Work," *Human-Computer Interaction*. 3(1), pp. 3–30. Elsevier, North Holland.

Winograd, T., and F. Flores (1986). *Understanding Computers and Cognition: A New Foundation for Design*. Ablex, Norwood, New Jersey.

Wood-Harper, A.T., L. Antill, and D.E. Avison (1985). *Information Systems Definition: The Multiview Approach*. Blackwell, Oxford.

P·A·R·T· IV

Social Relationships in Electronic Communities

P·A·R·T · IV

Introduction

Social Relationships in Electronic Communities

Charles Dunlop • Rob Kling

Personal Relationships and Electronic Communication

Electronic information exchanges—through electronic mail and other formats—create new social relationships and can transform existing relationships.[1] Intercontinental e-mail permits swift information transfer, indifferent to time zone variations that may inhibit telephone contact. Local Area Networks (LANs) in office buildings provide greater access to members of an organization, with fewer restrictions based upon one's position in the hierarchy. The "virtual office," unconstrained by geographical boundaries, is already a reality (see Giuliano's article in Part III of this volume). Faculty at different universities can use electronic mail to help manage the logistics of collaborative research. Professors and students can set up course-based conferencing to supplement—and occasionally supplant—face-to-face meetings. Special-interest groups and informal chat sessions abound on nationwide computer bulletin boards (BBS's) like CompuServe and The Source, where "electronic pen pal" friendships frequently develop. And in thousands of localities, individually operated BBS's permit all kinds of information sharing, from public domain software to information about computer systems, hobbies, medical care, etc.[2] In 1978 Roxanne Hiltz and Murray Turoff championed the spread of technologies like these with utopian enthusiasm in their book *Network Nation.*

Over the past dozen years, a small group of social researchers (including Hiltz and Turoff) have studied people's actual experiences with electronic mail and computerized bulletin boards. Users of computer-mediated communication often cite anonymity as one of its attractive features.[3] There is apparently a kind of freedom in conversing with someone who is known only through words on a video screen.[4] Research reported by Lee Sproull and Sara Kiesler (1986) supports this observation, noting however that side effects may include increased self-centeredness and anti-social behavior. In some circumstances, though, complete anonymity may prove helpful. For example, Jay Nunamaker and his collaborators at the University of Arizona studied electronic meetings between members of business organizations. They found that participants who know each other, and who are in relationships bound by status and hierarchy, are often much more open and innovative when key suggestions are anonymous.

Clearly, computer-mediated interaction is unique, being marked by the absence of various communicative cues, e.g., clothing, eye contact, body language, smell, voice inflections, vocalizations ("uh huh," "yeah"), and laughter. Some of these deficits also appear in other forms of communication, but computer-mediated telecommunications represents an extreme. At the same time, Perrolle (1987, p. 103) describes techniques for injecting emotional content into message systems and suggests that some signs of status and power may be conveyed there as well, e.g., by differential access privileges.[5]

Additional implications of social cue loss in computer-based communications systems are described in our first selection, by Kiesler, Siegel, and McGuire. In the absence of nonverbal contextual information, status signals, and well-defined etiquette conventions, electronic communications exhibit less self-regulation and self-awareness. Consequently, under some circumstances, there is a greater tendency for messages to embody hostility or aggressiveness. Furthermore, the leveling of status differences makes group consensus more difficult to achieve, although it may also promote consideration of minority views, and—as our selection by Perrolle observes—it may change the character of interactions between males and females. Applications of such findings to science, politics, business, and education easily come to mind. This is clearly an important area for further research.

It is ironic that the reduction in computerized BBS's of social cues that support "chat modes" sometimes foster special senses of personal trust and intimacy. That is, although they are less personal, they can also reduce social distance. In France, the government-operated Minitel system has developed a set of *messageries* that enable people to develop friendships, including romances, through simple terminals in their homes (see De Lacy,

---

[1] Increasingly, this point is being made in the mass media. See, for example, John Markoff, " 'Talking' on the Computer Redefines Human Contact," *New York Times* (front page), Sunday, May 13, 1990.

[2] In some exceptional cases hackers on "pirate" bulletin boards have posted charge-card numbers and instructions for breaking into computer systems.

[3] This, along with many other social aspects of electronic communities, has been investigated by Hiltz and Turoff, and by Kerr and Hiltz. Molotch and Boden describe some mechanisms for controlling conversation in face-to-face dialogue, although their analysis could perhaps be applied to electronic media as well. (See *Further Reading* for complete references.)

[4] The paper in this section by Kiesler, Siegel, and McGuire seems to suggest that anonymity in electronic message systems engenders depersonalization, since writers are inclined to think of their audience as the computer. To some degree, however, there is a "chicken-and-egg" question here, since highly introverted or socially isolated individuals may be encouraged by computer-mediated communication to break out of their shells.

[5] Finholt and Sproull (1990) report complementary findings, while noting some interesting differences between electronic communications that are *required* by an employer and those that are voluntary.

1987). The *messageries* have been popular—and controversial. Because they provide about 30% of the Minitel's revenues, the government has continued to allow them despite substantial controversy.

These systems are especially attractive to people who have trouble getting out of their homes to socialize—people who are handicapped, feel socially insecure, live alone with young children, work at unusual hours, etc. Such individuals are hardly the only, or even the primary, users of these systems. But for people with restricted social lives, electronic systems may provide truly important avenues to expand their social circles. "On-line" friendships may develop between people who never meet face-to-face ("FTF")—friendships that easily survive geographical relocation and that might not have begun had age, sex, race, etc. been evident from the start.

In our third selection, Lindsy Van Gelder's tale of "Alex" discusses the way in which some people have developed unusually intimate friendships on these electronic systems. Although the anonymity afforded by electronic communication can exhilarate and liberate, it also raises new possibilities for abuse. Van Gelder's tale serves as a reminder of this fact since "Alex" impersonated a disabled woman. Obviously, violations of trust are possible in many different arenas; however, the ease of computerized access to a special group of people, along with interactive yet voiceless dialogue, certainly aided Alex in perpetuating his fraud. Some readers may detect a slight moral ambiguity in this particular case, since Alex indisputably did some good as well as harm. Yet, not only were his intentions manipulative and largely self-serving, but some of his victims had a strong sense of "identity rape" as well. Didn't the harm outweigh whatever good was accomplished, and couldn't much of the good could have been achieved without deception?

Some Key Debates

As with other technologies, electronic communication does not come for free. Some of the costs may be hidden from immediate view and therefore may receive inadequate consideration; for instance, maintenance and support, along with extensive personnel training, are essential to ensure that new equipment is well utilized. And sometimes there are difficult social choices to be made, claims of "technological inevitability" notwithstanding.[6] Should an organization risk some erosion of managerial authority in order to secure the benefits of more participatory decision making? Should a college with limited resources install an electronic mail facility at the expense of new library acquisitions?

Kiesler (1986) quotes the president of one small college as saying that a new computer network would serve the same purpose as a student union. But this statement completely overlooks possible student preference for live conversation, music listening rooms, and billiards—as well as the palpable social presence of other people. As Perrolle's article convincingly argues (see her "coffeepot" example), there is an important difference between public information stores and public places where social interaction occurs.

---

[6] Good antidotes to such claims may be found in several articles reprinted in this book. See the selections by James B. Rule (Part V) and Joseph Weizenbaum (Part VII).

Professional and popular discussions of computer-based communication, like other discussions of computerization, often display a lamentable lack of nuance, sensitivity to social context, and appreciation for competing social values. Recently Roxanne Hiltz and Murray Turoff have proposed the use of computerized conferencing as "virtual class-rooms" for working students who take night classes. This kind of proposal has a certain appeal, since working people cannot always get to their night classes and remain alert after a long day's work. Being able to log into a computerized discussion later in the evening, on another evening, or on a weekend might facilitate access to certain kinds of classes that are logistically difficult for busy people to accommodate today. The teaching materials, teaching styles, and teaching load would differ from conventional classes in this hybrid between a traditional course and a correspondence course. It is a proposal worth exploring and carefully observing. Unfortunately, it is the kind of proposal that many journalists and casual observers are likely to trivialize by expanding it to encompass all higher education through "electronic universities."

The Control of Information

In Part V we discuss various issues arising from the fact that information can be used in social control. But the *control* of information also raises important problems. Information control (censorship), traditionally discussed in the context of print and broadcast media, has taken on an important new dimension in the age of the computer. Here the issue is freedom of information within the context of electronic communities.

Questions about who controls information in electronic networks have not been resolved. Universities, for example, usually try to maintain norms of openness, and are usually permissive in allowing information that is not illegal to be posted on publicly accessible bulletin boards. However, if a posting offends some groups, some people clamor to have it removed. Many political, religious, ethnic, and occupational jokes can offend the targets of humor. So the line between humor and libel, or between "fair humor" and cruelty, is not crisp.

In February 1988, the administration at Stanford University blocked access to an electronic bulletin board posting from Usenet.[7] The Stanford administration's action was stimulated by complaints about a racially insensitive joke that appeared on a Usenet bulletin board devoted to humor. Similar episodes have occurred at other universities. Administrators have responded to complaints about "offensive" bulletin board postings in various ways. Sometimes they have not attempted to remove postings that offend the complainants, while at other times they have tried to remove specific postings. Occasion-ally, they have closed access to specific boards and then usually restored access when others complained about censorship! At Stanford, the administrative action was highly selective, blocking access to the files containing jokes but reportedly not interfering with

---

[7] Usenet is an internationally distributed collections of over a thousand specialized electronic bulletin boards. The majority of Usenet boards cover technical topics, such as artificial intelligence, software engineering, and Unix. But it also includes some boards in which people discuss hobbies, such as audio systems and chamber music, as well as a few in which people discuss humor, marital life, singles life, and sexual relationships. It has a wide readership at over 7,500 universities and industrial laboratories.

an *un*moderated joke forum or with the multitude of other electronic forums (including some that allowed students to discuss sexual techniques and nude beaches).[8]

Access to this "offensive" humor board was later restored after Stanford's Computer Science Department Faculty voted unanimously to endorse a statement that supported the same kind of academic freedom of access to computerized newsgroups as access to books in the university libraries.[9]

In this section we present a debate over that episode with posters taken from another bulletin board—*RISKS-FORUM Digest*—a wide-ranging, moderated forum devoted to risks associated with computing. Les Earnest's submission argues that the Stanford administration's action was ineffective; the posting by John McCarthy argues that it violated academic freedom, whereas Jerry Hollombe maintains that the action was not one of censorship.

Fortunately, episodes such as the one at Stanford have been rare. But we foresee periodic debates about the nature of material that is appropriate for electronic bulletin boards, despite the judgmental and administrative quagmires that these debates open. The bulletin board ethos of open access and free exchange of ideas sets up the conditions where someone's humor or social mores will occasionally offend other parties, even if these parties do not normally read electronic boards. Further, social dogmatists are often irritated when they learn about "expensive computers" and "collective resources" fostering discussions of topics that they wish were taboo. The multitude of people who read Usenet and local boards are socially diverse and hold a wide variety of social values. Substantial conflicts of tastes and values are inevitable and sometimes lead to calls for censorship. When these debates take place in research universities that have a strong ethos of open inquiry and broad social tolerance, the value conflicts between expressive freedom and administrative censorship may be resolved more broad-mindedly than when the conflicts surface within less tolerant organizations. Although legal issues may shape the debates at some point, the controversies now appear to rest more on ethical choices than on legal restrictions. (For more on ethical controversies, see Part VII.)

Communication, Persuasion, and Influence in Scientific Communities

On March 23, 1989, chemists Martin Fleischmann and B. Stanley Pons announced that they had sustained a cold fusion nuclear reaction at the University of Utah, using relatively simple laboratory apparatus. Almost as noteworthy as their announcement was the way it was made. Rather than following the usual protocol of deferring public discussion until publication of experimental details in a scientific journal, Fleischmann and Pons called a news conference. Within hours scientists world-wide were apprised of the

---

[8] *RISKS-FORUM Digest*, **8**, (30) (February 24, 1989). This posting refers to an article by Tom Philip in the *San Jose Mercury News*, February 20, 1989.

[9] Stanford's Academic Council Committee on Libraries also approved a statement that read, in part, "The Preamble to the Statement on Academic Freedom (1974) states that 'Expression of the widest range of viewpoints should be encouraged, free from institutional orthodoxy and from internal or external coercion.' . . . this statement pertains to materials received on computer bulletin boards on campus."

Utah claim, and fax machines and electronic mail networks were soon abuzz with copies of a Fleischmann and Pons paper, which in turn generated hundreds of e-mail responses and discussions of details.[10]

Predictably, questions were raised about Fleischmann and Pons's decision to disseminate "science by fax," although opinion on this issue was by no means all negative.[11] In any case, it seems likely that the ease of electronic communication will increasingly encourage new forms of scholarly interchange, perhaps even undermining the time-honored tradition of formal conference presentations and publication in professional journals. What effects will this have on the practice of science?

Our short selection by Peter J. Denning envisions a new scientific paradigm arising from closer communication, which he sees as promoting collegial cooperation rather than conflict (also see the selection by Kiesler, Siegel, and McGuire). Denning was previously a president of the Association of Computing Machinery and is editor-in-chief of *Communications of the ACM*, the ACM's general journal, which is sent to more than 70,000 subscribers each month. He currently directs a major computer science research center for NASA. Consequently, he has had a major stake in helping to advance scientific communication. Unfortunately, Denning's proposal is only briefly sketched in his article. Some of the underlying technologies—such as the groupware that might facilitate collaboration—are still in early stages of development.[12] However, the scientific communities constrain their communications through key social processes and are not limited simply by available technologies.

Some of these other constraints are brought up in our selection by James R. Beniger. In contrast to Denning, Beniger argues that there are some pitfalls in the new openness wrought by electronic information transfer. Traditional forums, Beniger believes, provide an important control mechanism in the scientific community, conferring differential status on researchers according to the amount of recognition (collegial citation) that their work receives. Status in the global community translates into rewards (e.g., tenure, salary, promotion) at the local level. In one sense, this is the familiar point that nationally or internationally known faculty tend to fare better in their own universities and laboratories than do their less famous counterparts. But Beniger also observes that with continuing rewards from their own institutions, scientists are induced to engage in various forms of *non*remunerative global activity, e.g., reviewing books and grant proposals, refereeing articles for journals, and organizing and chairing professional meetings.

Suppose that at some point the traditional formats of publication and conference become supplanted by "telematic" discussions open to hundreds of participants. The usual routes to recognition and status would then tend to disappear.[13] Beniger worries that global science might be ill-served by such a development, although he acknowledges that the cost/benefit equation concerning greater openness cannot be solved definitively in

---

[10] Although the debate over cold fusion had quieted down considerably a year later, it has not yet been definitely resolved.

[11] "The Race for Fusion," *Newsweek*, May 8, 1989, pp. 49–54.

[12] Our introduction to Part I provides an extended analysis of one kind of groupware and comments on its underlying social assumptions.

[13] Other possible effects that also raise concerns are discussed by Solomon (1988).

advance. Several points should be added, however. First, Beniger's argument applies equally to *non*scientific academic research—e.g., work in the humanities. If he is correct, therefore, there will be serious ramifications for an enormous range of research. Second, despite the important role of traditional scholarship in fostering peer review, there is a negative side to the differential status mechanisms identified by Beniger, for they can make academic research unnecessarily cliquish. So a democratization of research may to some extent be welcomed. Third, it is not entirely clear that electronic communication will usher in the problem that Beniger foresees: computerized research dissemination and discussion might manage to preserve the relevant features of traditional scholarship. (See Beniger's footnote 30 and the surrounding text for further discussion of this point.)

Beniger anchors his argument in claims that computerization is part of a *control revolution* that began long before the invention of electronic digital computers—in the 19th century. But Beniger does not carefully link his account of that revolution to strategies employed by scholarly communities to control publication, influence, and status in the face of changing technologies.

While Beniger is cautionary about a greater openness fostered by the electronic communication of scientific work, Fred W. Weingarten and D. Linda Garcia explore an opposite concern. Their essay—our final selection—argues that the public dissemination of research that science requires and computer-based communication promotes is threatened both by the growing tendency to treat information as a commodity[14] and by the classification of research for national security purposes. For example, some universities, in order to secure new sources of large-scale research funding, are teaming up with private industry, which may receive proprietary research results in exchange. This means, however, that the research in question cannot be made available to the scientific community at large.[15] A parallel conclusion obviously holds concerning classified research. But although this classification in itself is nothing new, its significance is enhanced by the military's increasing reliance on technology that also has civilian applications. In the face of these pressures toward secrecy, Weingarten and Garcia question the extent to which the scientific communicaty "can avail itself of new opportunities that modern communication and computer technologies offer."

Together, our last three selections display quite different attitudes toward controls in the scientific world. Denning ignores control systems entirely. Beniger focuses on control systems within scholarly communities—enacted by scholars themselves—and argues that they cannot be elimiated. And Weingarten and Garcia examine business and the military as institutions whose control of scientific information can be self-serving and hurtful. These articles help articulate ongoing controversies about how to advance scholarly communication through computer-communications technologies, how to ensure that reliable knowledge is disseminated, and how to balance scholarly interests against other social interests.

---

[14] Additional social consequences of this theme are analyzed by Perrolle (1987), esp. Part Four.

[15] Roger C. Schank is sensitive to this problem in his discussion of the "entrepreneurial university," although his proposal that universities develop and manage profit-making corporations does not appear to solve it. See the epilogue to his book *The Cognitive Computer*, Addison-Wesley Publishing Company, Inc., Reading, Massachusetts (1984).

Sources

Beniger, James R. (1989). "Information Society and Global Science," *The Annals of The American Academy of Political and Social Science.* 495 (January), pp. 14–28.

Denning, Peter J. (1987). "A New Paradigm for Science," *American Scientist.* 75 (November–December), pp. 572–573.

Kiesler, Sara, Jane Siegel, and Timothy W. McGuire (1984). "Social Psychological Aspects of Computer-Mediated Communications," *American Psychologist.* 39 (10)(October), pp. 1123–1134.

Perrolle, Judith A. (1991). "Conversations and Trust in Computer Interfaces." (Original manuscript.) *RISKS-FORUM Digest* contributions by Les Earnest, John McCarthy, and Jerry Hollombe.

Van Gelder, Lindsy (1985). "The Strange Case of the Electronic Lover: A Real-Life Story of Deception, Seduction, and Technology," *Ms.* XIV(4)(October), pp. 94, 99, 101–104, 117, 123, 124.

Weingarten, Fred W., and D. Linda Garcia (1988). "Public Policy Concerning the Exchange and Distribution of Scientific Information," *The Annals of The American Academy of Political and Social Science*, 495 (January), pp. 61–72.

References

De Lacy, Justine (1987). "The Sexy Computer," *The Atlantic.* 20(1)(July), pp. 18–26.

Finholt, Tom, and Lee Sproull (1990). "Electronic Groups at Work." *Organization Science.* **1**(1): 41–64.

Kiesler, Sara (1986). "The Hidden Messages in Computer Networks," *Harvard Business Review.* (January–February), pp. 46–60.

Perrolle, Judith A. (1987). *Computers and Social Change: Information, Property, and Power.* Wadsworth, Inc., Belmont, California.

Sproull, Lee, and Sara Kiesler (1986). "Reducing Social Context Cues: Electronic Mail in Organizational Communication" *Management Science.* 32(11)(November), pp. 1492–1512.

Further Reading

Beniger, James R. (1986). *The Control Revolution.* Harvard University Press, Cambridge, Mass., and London.

Hiltz, Starr Roxanne, and Murray Turoff (1978). *The Network Nation: Human Communication via Computer.* Addison-Wesley Publishing Company, Inc., Reading, Massachusetts.

Kerr, Elaine B., and Starr Roxanne Hiltz (1982). *Computer-Mediated Communications.* Academic Press, New York and London.

Kiesler, Sara (1984). "Computer Mediation of Conversation," *American Psychologist.* 39, pp. 1123–1134.

Kraemer, K.L., and J.L. King (1982). "Telecommunications-transportation Substitution and Energy Productivity," *Telecommunications Policy.* Part I, 6(1), pp. 39–59; Part II, 6(2), pp. 87–99.

McGuire, Timothy W., Sara Kiesler, and Jane Siegel (1987). "Group and Computer-Mediated Discussion Effects in Risk Decision Making," *Journal of Personality and Social Psychology.* 32(5), pp. 917–930.

Molotch, Harvey L., and Deidre Boden (1985). "Talking Social Structure: Discourse, Domination and the Watergate Hearings," *American Sociological Review.* 50, pp. 273–288.

Solomon, Richard J. (1988). "Vanishing Intellectual Boundaries: Virtual Networking and the Loss of Sovereignty and Control," *The Annals of The American Academy of Political and Social Science.* 495 (January), pp. 40–48.

P·A·R·T·IV

1

Social Psychological Aspects of Computer-Mediated Communication

Sara Kiesler • *Jane Siegel* • *Timothy W. McGuire*

Computer technologies are improving so swiftly these days that few of us comprehend even a small part of the change. Computers are transforming work and, in some cases, lives. Whether eager for this or resistant, many people believe the organizational, social, and personal effects of computers will be deeply felt (De Sola Poole, 1977; Hiltz & Turoff, 1978; Kling, 1980—see Chapter II.6 of this volume).

Today, no one can predict in any detail the nature of the transformations that computers will bring, but one aspect of life that will certainly be affected is communication. The use of electronic mail and messages, long-distance blackboards, computer bulletin boards, instantaneously transferable data banks, and simultaneous computer conferences is reportedly advancing "like an avalanche" (Stockton, 1981; also see Kraemer, 1981). The U.S. federal judiciary, for example, is using electronic mail to speed the circulation of appellate opinion drafts among panels of judges (Weis, 1983). Computer conferences are being used for such legal proceedings as admission of evidence, trial scheduling, giving parties access to documents, and expert interrogation (Bentz & Potrykus, 1976; "Party-Line Plea," 1981). Other government agencies, such as the Department of Defense, as well as private firms, such as Westinghouse Corporation and Xerox Corporation, and some universities, use computer-mediated communication extensively for both routine transfer of data and nonroutine interpersonal communication and

"Social Psychological Aspects of Computer-Mediated Communication" by S. Kiesler, J. Siegel, and T.W. McGuire. *American Psychologist* (1984) **39**, (10) 1123–1134. Reprinted by permission of the American Psychological Association.

project work (e.g., Licklider & Vezza, 1978; U.S. Department of Commerce, 1977; Wang Corporation, 1982).

Computer-mediated communication was once confined to technical users and was considered somewhat arcane. This no longer holds true. Computer-mediated communication is a key component of the emerging technology of computer networks. In networks, people can exchange, store, edit, broadcast, and copy any written document. They can send data and messages instantaneously, easily, at low cost, and over long distances. Two or more people can look at a document and revise it together, consult with each other on critical matters without meeting together or setting up a telephone conference, or ask for and give assistance interactively (Hiltz & Turoff, 1978; Williams, 1977).

Networks, and hence computer-mediated communications, are proliferating at a tremendous rate. In addition to the older long-distance networks that connect thousands of scientists, professionals, and managers (e.g., the Department of Defense's ARPANET, GTE's TELENET), there are more and more local-area networks that link up computers within a region, city, or organization (e.g., Nestar System's CLUSTERBUS, Xerox's ETHERNET, Ford Aerospace's FLASHNET, and Wang Laboratories' WANGNET). Stimulating this growth are the decreasing costs and the advantages of networks over stand-alone systems, such as sharing high-speed printers and access to a common interface for otherwise incompatible equipment. The future of this technology cannot be foretold, but it is far from arcane.

The functions and impact of computer-mediated communication are still poorly understood. Critical information (such as who uses it for what purposes) is lacking, and the social psychological significance is controversial (see, e.g., Turoff, 1982). Computers could make communication easier, just as the canning of perishables and the development of can openers made food preparation easier, or they could have much more complex implications. For instance, access to electronic communication may change the flow of information within organizations, altering status relations and organizational hierarchy. When a manager can receive electronic mail from 10,000 employees, what happens to existing controls over participation and information? When people can publish and distribute their own electronic newspaper at no cost, does the distribution of power change too? When communication is rapid and purely textual, do working groups find it easier or harder to resolve conflict? These unanswered questions illustrate that, although the technology may be impressive, little systematic research exists on its psychological, social, and cultural significance. Given such conditions it seems sensible to try to understand the fundamental behavioral, social, and organizational processes that surround computer-mediated communication. We believe that ideas and approaches from social psychology and other areas of behavioral science can be applied to these questions.

This article is meant to describe some of the issues raised by electronic communication; to illustrate, from our own work, one empirical approach for investigating them; and to show why social psychological research might contribute to a deeper understanding of electronic communication specifically and of computers and technological change in society more generally. We begin by citing some existing research on computer-mediated communication. Most of this research addresses the technical capabilities of the electronic technologies. Next, we consider the possible social psychological impact, and we discuss some hypotheses and some possible implications for the outcomes of communication.

Finally, we describe some of our own experiments on social psychological aspects of computer-mediated communication, using these to indicate potential lines of future research.

Existing Research

With a few pioneering exceptions (Hiltz, Johnson, Aronovitch, & Turoff, 1980; Hiltz, Johnson, & Turoff, 1982; Kling, 1982; Short, Williams, & Christie, 1976), research on and analyses of computer communication technologies evaluate the efficiency of these technologies based on their cost and technical capabilities (Bikson, Gutek, & Mankin, 1981). Representative of this orientation are discussions of how computer communications can work in organizations such as libraries and engineering firms (e.g., Lancaster, 1978; Tapscott, 1982); surveys of the introduction of computer networks in organizations (e.g., Rice & Case, 1982; Sinaiko, 1963); and also experimental studies comparing the effects of various communication channels (Chapanis, 1972; Geller, 1981; Kite & Vitz, 1966; Krueger, 1976; Morley & Stephenson, 1969; Weeks & Chapanis, 1976; Williams, 1973a, 1973b, 1975a, 1976b). In general, research on the technical capabilities of computers has addressed questions about how particular technical, economic, or ergonomic characteristics of the technology are related to organizational efficiency and effectiveness. The instantaneous information exchange provided by electronic mail, for example, might allow people to work without regard for their geographic dispersion, their schedules, time zones, access to secretaries, and energy costs (Kraemer, 1981). If computer mail discourages chatting and off-task interaction (Weeks & Chapanis, 1976) or if people read more effectively than they listen (Hiltz & Turoff, 1978), then managers might be more efficient.

The approach based on technical capability is a common and convenient means of analyzing new technologies. However, in real life, technological functions do not exist in isolation. Each technical component may be part of a larger context or may trigger certain social psychological processes (Pye & Williams, 1977; Williams, 1977). Thus, for instance, a broadly accessible communication network might not only increase total communication rates but also stimulate communication up and down the organization. If supervisors find it easy to keep tabs on subordinates and subordinates "copy up" to superiors, centralization of control might increase even while communication becomes more participative.

The prospect of enhanced or changed flows of information among people raises many other social psychological issues. For example, managers who use computer conferences to look at and discuss on-line computerized forecasts and analyses (Dutton & Kraemer, 1980) might persuade each other too readily. On the other hand, there are various computer-aided decision-making techniques, such as Delphi, that are designed to increase decision quality by removing status and other social cues (Martino, 1972; Price, 1975). It is conceivable that by providing groups with more "hard" information, computers would reduce the probability of "groupthink" (Janis, 1972) or "tunnel vision" (Hedberg, Nystrom, & Starbuck, 1976) in group decision making (Krueger, 1976; Vallee, Johansen, Lipinski, & Wilson, 1977).

As these speculations suggest, a focused effort on the psychological and social aspects of computing environments revealed by technical capability studies (but not pursued in these studies) is needed. In the new research efforts, social psychologists and other social scientists would use the wealth of theory and previous research in their fields to generate hypotheses about computing and to evaluate these hypotheses empirically. This would mean studying the implications of the social features of computing, not just its technical characteristics. We expand on this notion next.

Social Psychological Aspects of Computer-Mediated Communication

Computer-mediated communication differs in many ways, both technically and culturally, from more traditional communication technologies. Technically, it has the speed (including simultaneity, if desired) and energy efficiency, but not the aural or visual feedback of telephoning and face-to-face communication. It has the adaptability of written text. Messages can be sent to groups of any size and can be programmed for such special functions as automatic copying to a prespecified distribution list. Culturally, computer-mediated communication is still undeveloped. Although computer professionals have used electronic communication for over two decades, and they make up a subculture whose norms influence computer users and electronic communication (Sproull, Kiesler, & Zubrow, in press), no strong etiquette as yet applies to how electronic communication should be used. A few user manuals devote a paragraph to appropriate uses of a computer network, but generally speaking, people do not receive either formal or informal instruction in an etiquette of electronic communication. These technical and cultural issues might be organized around the following questions.

Time and Information Processing Pressures

Does easy, rapid communication—messages exchanged literally at the touch of a key —change the quantity or the distribution or the timing of information exchanged? Availability of instantaneous electronic communication, for example, might lead people to expect immediate responses. (We have talked with a company president in Pittsburgh who sends computer mail at dinnertime asking his subordinates in Singapore for quarterly projections by breakfast.)

Absence of Regulating Feedback

Does communication through text alone reduce coordination of communication? In traditional forms of communication, head nods, smiles, eye contact, distance, tone of voice, and other nonverbal behavior give speakers and listeners information they can use to regulate, modify, and control exchanges. Electronic communication may be inefficient for resolving such coordination problems as telling another person you already have knowledge of something he or she is explaining (Kraut, Lewis, & Swezey, 1982).

Dramaturgical Weakness

Computer communication might weaken social influence by the absence of such non-verbal behavior as taking the head seat, speaking loudly, staring, touching, and gesturing (R. Kling, personal communication, May, 1983). The opportunity to hear someone's voice or to look him or her in the eye changes how bargains are negotiated or whether any real bargaining occurs (e.g., Carnevale, Pruitt, & Seilheimer, 1981; Krauss, Apple, Morencz, Wenzel, & Winton, 1981). When using computers to communicate, how will people compensate for the dramaturgical weakness of electronic media? For example, Hiltz and Turoff reported that computer conferees have developed ways of sending computerized screams, hugs, and kisses (in Pollack, 1982, p. D2).

Few Status and Position Cues

Software for electronic communication is blind with respect to the vertical hierarchy in social relationships and organizations. Once people have electronic access, their status, power, and prestige are communicated neither contextually (the way secretaries and meeting rooms and clothes communicate) nor dynamically (the way gaze, touch, and facial and paralinguistic behavior communicate; Edinger & Patterson, 1983). Thus, charismatic and high status people may have less influence, and group members may participate more equally in computer communication.

Social Anonymity

Is electronic communication depersonalizing? Because it uses printed text, without even the texture of paper to lend it individuality, electronic communication tends to seem impersonal. Communicators must imagine their audience, for at a terminal it almost seems as though the computer itself is the audience. Messages are depersonalized, inviting stronger or more uninhibited text and more assertiveness in return. It might be especially hard to communicate liking or intimacy without writing unusually positive text. (At our university, a computer manual warns, "Sometimes . . . users lose sight of the fact that they are really addressing other people, not the computer.")

Computing Norms and Immature Etiquette

Because electronic communication was developed and has been used by a distinctive subculture of computing professionals, its norms are infused with that culture's special language (i.e., people talk about "default" attitudes and "bogus" assertions) and its implicit rejection of organizational conventionality and eight-hour workdays. In our own university as well as other organizations (Sheil, personal communication, April 1982), people using electronic mail overstep conventional time boundaries dividing office and home; they mix work and personal communications; they use language appropriate for boardrooms and ballfields interchangeably; and they disregard normal conventions of privacy (for instance, by posting personal messages to general bulletin boards). This behavior is not counteracted by established conventions or etiquette for computer communication. There are few shared standards for salutations, for structuring formal versus informal messages, or for adapting content to achieve both impact and politeness. How do people develop a communication network social structure using a technology in cultural transition? Do they import norms from other technologies? Do they develop new norms?

From a social psychological perspective, this list of questions suggest that computer-mediated communication has at least two interesting characteristics: (a) a paucity of social context information and (b) few widely shared norms governing its use. These characteristics may affect communication via computer in at least three areas. First, the lack of social feedback and unpredictable style of messages might make it difficult to coordinate and comprehend messages (Kraut & Lewis, in press). Second, social influence among communicators might become more equal because so much hierarchical dominance and power information is hidden (Edinger & Patterson, 1983). Third, social standards will be less important and communication will be more impersonal and more free because the rapid exchange of text, the lack of social feedback, and the absence of norms governing the social interaction redirect attention away from others and toward the message itself. Indeed, computer-mediated communication seems to comprise some of the same conditions that are important for deindividuation—anonymity, reduced self-regulation, and reduced self-awareness (e.g., Diener, 1980; Festinger, Pepitone, & Newcomb, 1952; Forsyth, 1983, pp. 308–338).

This last point deserves some elaboration. Using traditional communication, norms, social standards, and inferences about individuals are made salient by observable social structural artifacts (such as prestige communicated through a person's dress or letterhead) and by communication itself, including nonverbal involvement (Edinger & Patterson, 1983; Patterson, 1982). However, terminals and electronic signals convey fewer historical, contextual, and nonverbal cues. Electronic media do not efficiently communicate nuances of meaning and frame of mind, organizational loyalties, symbolic procedural variations, and, especially, individuating details about people that might be embodied in their dress, location, demeanor, and expressiveness (e.g., Ekman, Friesen, O'Sullivan, & Scherer, 1980; Mehrabian, 1972). This situation, where personality and culture lack salience, might foster feelings of depersonalization. In addition, using the computer tends to be absorbing and conducive to quick response, which might reduce self-awareness and increase the feeling of being submerged in the machine. Thus, the overall weakening of self- or normative regulation might be similar to what happens when people become less self-aware and submerged in a group, that is, deindividuated (Diener, Lusk, DeFour, & Flax, 1980; Scheier, 1976; Scheier & Carver, 1977; Scheier, Carver, & Gibbons, 1981).

Outcomes of Technology Use

Most existing discussions of computers focus on the advantages of computer-mediated communication for work: fast and precise information exchange, increased participation in problem solving and decision making, and reduction of "irrelevant" status and prestige differences (Lancaster, 1978; Linstone & Turoff, 1975; Martino, 1972). This orientation is illustrated by the following:

> The scientific literature will become unified . . . . Scientists everywhere will have equal access . . . . The advantage of being in a famous center of research will be substantially

lessened. Scientists in obscure universities . . . will be able to participate in scientific discourse more readily. (Folk, 1977, p. 80)

Existing social psychological studies do not entirely contradict the forecasts that communicating by computer will increase participation, objectivity, and efficiency of groups and organizations. For example, any communication technology that reduces the importance of status and dominance could increase the likelihood that opinions in groups are sampled more widely. If people who are high in status usually talk most and dominate decision making (Hoffman, 1978), then computer-mediated communication that de-emphasizes the impact of status also might increase people's consideration of minority views. If minority opinions can enhance performance, then groups could be more effective when using computers to communicate.

On the other hand, equal participation, objectivity, and efficiency sometimes interfere with important group outcomes. To be effective, rather than encouraging equal participation, group members may need to organize themselves by discovering sources of information, deciding who can be depended on, distributing work to these people, and protecting their autonomy (e.g., Hackman & Morris, 1978). To be effective, rather than aiming at objectivity, groups may need affective bonds, a status distribution that helps sort out multiple objectives, and a hierarchy that determines influence, even if these behaviors interfere with "good" decisions (Kelley & Thibaut, 1978; March & Olsen, 1976; Salancik, 1977). For accomplishing these purposes, the social structure provided by roles, norms, and status and reinforced by trust and personal engagement with others is critical.

These ideas suggest that the use of computers for communication will be more complex than is typically envisioned in the computer technology literature. We have speculated that computer-mediated communication will influence group functions involving coordination of discussion, participation and influence of dominant individuals, and normative control. In technical problem solving, then, computer-mediated groups might be disorganized, democratic, unrestrained, and perhaps more creative than groups communicating more traditionally; they might have trouble reaching consensus if the "correct" answer is not obvious; they might not operate as cool, fast decision makers. What might be the outcome for real groups that have to deal with technical, political, and organizational tasks? Ultimately, it might depend on existing relationships. In computer-linked groups whose members are discontented and in conflict with one another, impersonal behavior might tend to polarize members, exacerbate aggressiveness and cause negative attributions to others (e.g., Gibbons & Wright, 1981; Goldstein, Davis, & Herman, 1975; McArthur & Solomon, 1978; Prentice-Dunn & Rogers, 1980). However, in computer-linked groups that are on friendly, cooperative terms, impersonal behavior might actually encourage joint approaches to decision making or negotiating (see Druckman, 1977; Pruitt & Lewis, 1975), and it could reduce self-consciousness and promote intimacy. Some of our colleagues, for example, notice that their students are more often willing to approach a professor for assistance with assignments or a potential date through electronic mail than in face-to-face encounters (Larkin, personal communication, July 1982; Welsch, 1982).

These speculations must be evaluated empirically. There are no experimental research studies published in scientific journals that focus directly on group behavior in modern computer-mediated communication, such as electronic mail. However, earlier studies of the teletypewriter lend support to the analyses we have presented. Sinaiko's (1963) experiments at the Institute for Defense Analyses indicated that "teletype quite dramatically depersonalizes negotiations . . . . Differences in initial positions held by negotiators converge more in a face-to-face situation, next by telephone and least when the teletypewriter is the medium of communication" (p. 18). Morley and Stephenson (1969, 1970) found that tasks requiring dependence on interpersonal or interparty considerations interacted strongly with media. Three studies that focused on group processes showed that role differentiation was diminished and more unstable in the computer-mediated cases. Moreover, frequency of participation was most equal in the teletypewriting mode, less equal with audio only, and least equal when subjects were face-to-face (Krueger, 1976; Strickland, Guild, Barefoot, & Patterson, 1975; Williams, 1975a). Communication by teletype was both "egalitarian" and "disorganized" (Williams, 1977).

The findings from research on earlier technologies indicate that computer-mediated communication raises some old issues. Technologies that lacked a distinctive etiquette (teletype, for instance) and/or the opportunity to exchange a full range of paralinguistic cues (such as freeze-frame videoconferencing) caused special problems for groups. In earlier advances of communication technology, people had to learn how to organize new and disparate pieces of information, and they had to learn how to behave toward one another.

Electronic communication differs from any other communication in time, space, speed, ease of use, fun, audience, and opportunity for feedback. For example, in one firm where someone posted a new product idea on the computer network, the proposition was sent in one minute to 300 colleagues in branches across the country, and, within two days, sufficient replies were received to launch a new long-distance joint project. We do not present this anecdote as though we know its precise significance, but we do mean to argue that computers are different from previous technologies. Research must discover how groups respond to the difference; how, given time, groups work out new communication traditions and rules; and what the requirements of the new communication culture will be. The answers to these questions ultimately will determine the nature of the social revolution embodied in modern communication technologies.

The rest of this article describes one approach to studying the social psychological dimensions of computer-mediated communication. In the following section, we summarize experiments on the effects on groups of simultaneous terminal-to-terminal teleconferencing and of electronic mail. Also, we have begun to study underlying processes and to explore questions of external generalizability. The final section summarizes the direction of this work.

Studies of Participation, Choice, and Interaction in Computer-Mediated Groups

The purpose of our initial studies (Siegel, Dubrovsky, Kiesler, & McGuire, 1983) has been to explore, experimentally, the impact of computer-mediated communication, as used in our own local computer network, on group interaction and decisions. To our knowledge, these are among the first controlled experiments using modern, fast terminals and flexible computer conference and mail software (see also Hiltz, Johnson, & Turoff, 1982). We emphasized control over generalizability in the first three experiments, choosing a small group size of three. The subjects were students who had used the computer network previously. Also, we used a group task about which there is considerable knowledge, that is, the Stoner (1961) choice–dilemma problems (see, e.g., Dion, Baron, & Miller, 1978; Kogan & Wallach, 1964, 1967; Lamm & Kogan, 1970; Vinokur & Burnstein, 1974; Zajonc, 1969). This research was carried out in offices and rooms where terminals were already in use so as to duplicate the actual setting where communication typically takes place.

The first experiment is prototypical of the rest. The study compared three-person groups who were asked to reached consensus on a choice–dilemma problem in three different contexts: once face-to-face, once using the computer anonymously (i.e., not knowing by name who within their group was talking), and once using the computer nonanonymously. In the computer-mediated discussions, each person was separated physically from the others, and each used a computer terminal to communicate. Each group member typed his or her remarks into the computer using a program called "Converse," which divides the screen into three or more parts and allows messages from different people to appear simultaneously and scroll independently.

The main dependent variables in all of the experiments were (a) communication efficiency, (b) participation, (c) interpersonal behavior, and (d) group choice. We derived hypotheses for the experiments both from our observations of the technology and from the social psychological literature. We tried to examine whether computer communication is depersonalizing and lacking in social structure, and we tried to test our hunches about the implications. Hence, in the first experiment we predicted that participation would be more equal in the computer-mediated communication conditions. We thought that coming to consensus would be more difficult. In carrying out pilot work, we had seen many instances of what appeared to be uninhibited behavior—subjects swearing, individuals shouting at their terminals, and groups refusing to make a group decision until a group member gave in—and as a result we systematically evaluated interpersonal interactions as revealed in the transcripts of both face-to-face and computer-mediated groups. We predicted more uninhibited behavior in computer-mediated groups. Also, we added an anonymous computer-mediated communication condition in order to explore whether not knowing specifically who was talking would increase depersonalization (e.g., Williams, Harkins, & Latane, 1981).

We hypothesized that choice shift would be greater when people used the computer, generally because norms are weaker and, hence, group members might be less likely to simply average initial opinions or obey the initial majority. According to social comparison theory (Brown, 1965; Goethals & Zanna, 1979; Sanders & Baron, 1977) and the persuasive arguments model (Vinokur & Burnstein, 1974, 1978), choice shift may occur in groups because people compare themselves to others with extreme or novel attitudes or because they are exposed to extreme arguments they would not otherwise hear (this assumes most people have moderate initial positions). If people in computer-mediated groups, as compared to face-to-face groups, are party to a broader distribution of opinions (because participation is spread more evenly across opinions) and extreme opinions are less likely to be withheld (because behavior is less inhibited), then we would predict more choice shift in computer-mediated groups.

Our data showed, in all three experiments, that computer-mediated communication, had marked effects on communication efficiency, participation, interpersonal behavior, and decision making.

Communication Efficiency

Three measures bear on communication efficiency: time to decision, number of remarks exchanged, and percentage of discussion remarks about the group choice rather than about extraneous topics (e.g., school work). We found that in spite of the fact that messages arrived instantaneously, using a keyboard took time. Computer-mediated groups took longer to reach consensus than did face-to-face groups, and they exchanged fewer remarks in the time allowed them. We think groups in the computer-communication conditions took more time to reach consensus for reasons beyond technical difficulties. They might have had greater difficulties reaching agreement, judging by the vehemence of their arguments. Also, when we asked people to type out remarks that subjects had made face-to-face, we found typing time could not account for all the time taken by computer-mediated groups to reach consensus.

We found that computer-mediated groups were as task oriented as face-to-face groups. This tends to rule out the idea that groups using the computer were inefficient because they were not paying attention to the task. In Figure 1, we summarize effects on equality of participation, group choice shift, and uninhibited interpersonal behavior.

Participation, Group Choice, and Interpersonal Behavior

Based on analyses of who talked and how much they talked (i.e., the distribution of remarks among group members), group members using the computer participated more equally than they did when they talked face to face. Although one person tended to dominate in both face-to-face and computer-mediated interaction, this dominance was less strong in computer-mediated groups.

Computer-mediated groups showed significantly higher choice shift. We do not fully understand this finding. Analyses of the group process (e.g., extreme positions taken, use of decision rules such as majority rule or simple averaging, or repeated stating of positions) did not reveal differences in these processes between face-to-face and computer-mediated groups. People in computer-mediated groups used a higher proportion of numeric arguments, but this tendency was uncorrelated with choice shift. Perhaps if communication using the computer was depersonalized, people felt more able to abandon their previous positions or to ignore social pressure to reach consensus.

People in computer-mediated groups were more uninhibited than they were in face-to-face groups as measured by uninhibited verbal behavior, defined as frequency of remarks containing swearing, insults, name calling, and hostile comments.

In addition to what is shown in Figure 1, each experiment incorporated different computer communication design features and samples. By varying technical features of the communication programs and changing subject samples, we hoped to address some

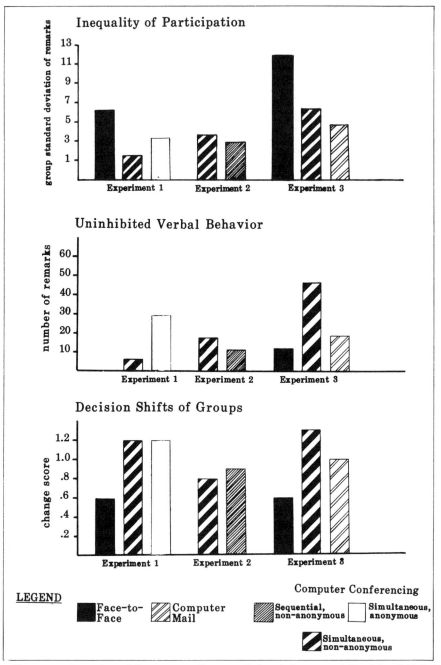

Figure 1. Inequality of Participation, Decision Shifts of Groups, and Uninhibited Verbal Behavior.
Note. These three experiments had varying conditions; a and f = face-to-face conferencing; b, d, and g = simultaneous computer conferencing; c = simultaneous computer conferencing with subjects speaking anonymously; e = sequential computer conferencing; and h = computer mail. Adapted from Siegel, Dubrovsky, Kiesler, and McGuire (1983).

plausible alternative explanations of our results. Based on these variations we did reach certain conclusions. First, from using trained and practiced subjects in Experiment 2 (and adult managers in our fourth and fifth experiments), we concluded that our findings are generalizable to adults and nonstudents as well as to undergraduate students. Second, from comparing experienced and inexperienced computer network users, we concluded that our results apply not just to novices but also to people who use computers often and for whom electronic mail and message systems as well as simultaneous discussion systems are familiar. Third, we also have compared strangers and friends and obtained similar results.

Is computer-mediated communication simply disorderly, perhaps because there is no constraint on interruptions and distracting remarks? In Experiment 2, Vitaly Dubrovsky (Dubrovsky, Kiesler, & Siegel, 1983) devised a technical variation of the simultaneous computer conversation program to see whether imposing procedural order through technical features of the communication medium would increase its similarity to face-to-face communication. He designed a sequential computer conference program that forced group members to take turns speaking and to indicate to other when they wished to interrupt. Hence, the new software allowed only one person to talk at a time, and we compared how groups used this method with how they used the regular simultaneous computer conference program. The most important outcomes of this study were to establish that software developed to control the sequence of interaction is disliked and that it does not necessarily coordinate or control discussions. The effects of the computer-mediated communication programs were equal to those of computer communication in the first experiment.

Experiment 3 was intended primarily to extend the study to electronic mail, which is used extensively in most computer networks. Although electronic mail has some of the same cultural and technical characteristics as simultaneous computer conferences, it does not require communication in real time. There is time for reflection, for composing one's thoughts, and for side discussions with only part of a group. Hence, we thought it possible that electronic mail would be relatively conflict free and would produce about the same decisions as face-to-face communication. In spite of our expectations, the findings of Experiment 3 were similar to those of the other experiments. However, uninhibited behavior was somewhat higher in the computer conference condition than in the computer mail condition.

How might we explain the results as a whole? There are at least three alternatives, having to do with (a) difficulties of coordination from lack of informational feedback, (b) absence of social influence cues for controlling discussion, and (c) depersonalization from lack of nonverbal involvement and absence of norms. We will consider each briefly. First, we can explain the greater time people took to reach consensus and the evenness of participation rates by pointing to the absence of informational feedback between speakers and listeners in the computer-mediated communication condition. That is, the usual forms of discussion control through back-channel communications (Kraut et al., 1982) could not be exerted. People did not know exactly when their arguments were understood or agreed to, and consequently everyone believed they had to exert more effort to be understood. This explanation, however, does not account for the findings of greater choice shift and uninhibited behavior, except indirectly. Perhaps it was frustrating for people to be discussing a problem inefficiently; they might have become angry and, hence, more extreme in decision making and more uninhibited.

A second explanation of our findings is that in computer communication there is less influence and control of a dominant person, moderator, or leader. Lack of leadership could have caused difficulties in reaching a group decision efficiently. Without leadership, a group might ignore social norms, standards, and precedents, causing both choice shift and uninhibited behavior.

A final explanation for our results is that electronic communication involves a process of depersonalization or a redirection of attention away from one's audience. Suppose computer-mediated communication prevented personal feedback and individuating information and at the same time lacked a shared etiquette and, further, was influenced by norms from the computer subculture. This could have made group members more responsive to immediate textual cues, more impulsive and assertive, and less bound by precedents set by societal norms of how groups should come to consensus. This explanation fits our data. However, we emphasize that our own data do not provide any evidence to distinguish among these tentative and somewhat limited potential explanations.

Another issue with which we must deal is external validity, that is, to what degree our results can be generalized across people and technologies. Based on our own research and anecdotal evidence from reports of computer network behavior, we are relatively sure that our findings apply to a wide sample of both novice and experienced computer users. For example, observers of computer networks have noticed uninhibited behavior for years. In the computer subculture, the word *flaming* refers to the practice of expressing oneself more strongly on the computer than one would in other communication settings. The Defense Communications Agency, which manages the 12-year-old ARPANET, has had to police use of the network bulletin boards by manually screening messages every few days to weed out those deemed in bad taste. Nor is flaming confined to government-sponsored networks. When IBM installed the personal computer in offices and created an internal message system, VNET, to link them, a "GRIPENET" emerged—organized complaints against management practices and policies whose form and substance deviate considerably from standard IBM culture (Emmett, 1981). Of course, whether this behavior was caused specifically by a lack of shared etiquette, by computer culture norms, or by the impersonal and text-only form of communication is not clear.

We are not so sure how our findings would apply to more sophisticated technologies, say those that include video or audio channels in electronic mail. We suspect that combining telephone with electronic mail in the same facility would decrease the differences between electronic communication and face-to-face communication, if only because the amount of feedback is increased. Based on current trends, text-only electronic communication systems will become more popular. In that case, we should study both their transient effects (those likely to disappear when the technologies are mature) and their more permanent and secondary effects. Judging from our own observations of existing networks, both kinds of change are important. For example, absence of computer etiquette is a transient problem, but it is one that raises significant policy debates over rights of computer users to privacy and freedom of exploration. A more permanent effect might be the extension of participation in group or organizational communication. This is important because it implies more shared information, more equality of influence, and, perhaps, a breakdown of social and organizational barriers.

Implications for Future Research

The conceptual framework for studies of computer-mediated communication will develop mainly from studies of social process. These studies will provide either detailed descriptions of behavior or tests of alternative theoretical ideas. In our own laboratory, we have just collected additional data on the process of computer-mediated communication. In one new experiment, we asked business managers and university administrators to use simultaneous computer conferences to reach decisions involving multiattribute risky choices (Payne & Laughhunn, in press; Tversky & Kahneman, 1981). Preliminary analyses of the decisions and the content of discussions indicate that when the managers used the computer to consider the issues, they were less effective in considering all the issues and coordinating their discussion. The findings suggest that if computer-mediated communication is used by managers to make group decisions, those decisions may differ qualitatively from decisions reached face-to-face.

In another study (Kiesler, Zubrow, Moses, & Geller, 1983), we tested whether using a computer to communicate is physiologically arousing or has other affective consequences. In a 2×2 design, we manipulated anxiety (anticipation of evaluation), and computer-mediated versus face-to-face communication in a study of how two people get to know each other. In this study, we measured physiological arousal (pore size and pulse), emotionality, interpersonal attraction, responsiveness to others, self-disclosure, and other aspects of interpersonal communication. Our results suggest that computer-mediated communication is not physiologically arousing. Once again we discovered more uninhibited behavior when people communicated using the computer. We also found that although people felt more embarrassed meeting one another face-to-face, they ended up liking each other better. Because other research suggests that gaze, smiling, and other nonverbal feedback is important to establish attraction (Scherer, 1974), our data do support our hypothesis that the lack of nonverbal involvement is a critical dimension of electronic communication.

Much more work on affective and cognitive dimensions of computer-mediated communication is needed to understand the issues we raised earlier. For example, further studies of affective responses may establish whether absorption in computer messages is arousing (see Zajonc, 1965), why users are sometimes aggressive (see Goldstein et al., 1975), whether attention is submerged in messages (see McArthur & Solomon, 1978), and under what conditions people will be uninhibited (see Zillman, Bryant, Cantor, & Day, 1975). The research could build on recent studies of affect in social cognition (e.g., Isen, Shalker, Clark, & Karp, 1978) that show how mood and emotion are connected to information processing, memory, and overt behavior using computers.

In addition to identifying behavioral dimensions of computer-mediated communications, research could reveal more about fundamental group processes, both inside and outside of computer-mediated settings. For example, social norms play a critical role in models of group decision making developed by Davis and his colleges (e.g., Davis,

1973). According to these models, changing the potential for normative influence, such as reducing face-to-face contact, changes the influence function (Stasser & Davis, 1981, p. 544). Because computers appear to alter the operation of normative influences, studies of computer-mediated decision making might contribute to our understanding of these and other models in social psychology that invoke group pressure, persuasion, and affectively relevant processes.

The potential for developing important organizational applications from social psychological studies of computer-mediated communication is also high. One avenue of development will be experimental research that suggests new ways to use computers in education (Lepper, 1982), public affairs, and mental health. It might be possible to turn computer networks into social support networks. Second, it might be possible, through experimental research, to establish the feasibility of using electronic communication for surveys, questionnaires, and interactive polling. A group at our university is carrying out what we believe are among the first controlled experiments on using the computer to collect survey data (Kiesler & Sproull, 1984).

Finally, quasi-experimental and field studies of networks will suggest applications for long-distance collaborative work and management. For example, geographically dispersed groups of scientists and their students are currently working to develop a common computer language (Common LISP) for artificial intelligence research. The groups have used electronic mail via ARPANET with everyone participating rather than forming committees and meeting face-to-face (Maddox, 1982). Reportedly, electronic mail was used during one year to discuss some 232 issues. About 150 of these issues were resolved before participants came to any face-to-face meeting. Most technical questions were resolved by someone in the group communicating a solution through the network. However, questions of style, for example, about programming conventions or systems architecture, evoked conflict and flaming on the computer. These matters had to be resolved by a mediator (appointed by the groups to organize the project) or in face-to-face meetings. Nonetheless, participants in the project report they have made more progress and acquired the active contribution of many more scientists by using the network. Their experience suggests that long-distance computer-mediated group problem solving could have many useful applications. Hiltz (1984) discussed many other instances of long-distance collaboration using the experimental Electronic Information Exchange System (EIES).

Although the social responses to computer-mediated communication described in this article occur in the situation in which the communication takes place, readers should not carry away the impression that all of the social implications are short term. Some effects, such as increased lateral communication in an organization or reduction in clerical staff, might develop over a long period through the actions and attitudes of many people (Hough & Panko, 1977). Others have examined organizational effects of computers generally (Boguslaw, 1981; Danziger, Dutton, Kling, & Kraemer, 1982; Whisler, 1970). Our aim has not been to delineate any particular social impact but to suggest, using our work as an example, the significance of understanding the broad range of social implications of computerization. Much of this work belongs in the field of social psychology, although the line between social psychology and other areas of psychology and social science is tenuous and arbitrary. Actually, studies of behavioral and social processes in computer-mediated communication (indeed of all computing) will be carried out best as an interdisciplinary effort.

Acknowledgments

The research described in this article was supported by grants from the Robotics Institute, Carnegie-Mellon University, and from the National Science Foundation (Grant No. IST-8210701) to the first author. We are grateful to colleagues who commented on the manuscript: Vitaly Dubrovsky, Rob Kling, Allen Newell, Drury Sherrod, and Lee Sproull. Also, we thank Arlene Simon and Mary Jo Dowling for their help in preparing the text.

Requests for reprints should be sent to Sara Kiesler, Department of Social Sciences, Carnegie-Mellon University, Schenley Park, Pittsburgh, Pennsylvania 15213.

References

Bentz, C. A., & Potrykus, T. M. (1976). *Visual communications in the Phoenix criminal justice system* (American Telephone and Telegraph Company Report No. 39-8-39-12). Morristown, NJ: American Telephone and Telegraph Company.

Bikson, T. K., Gutek, B. A., & Mankin, D. A. (1981). *Implementation of information technology in office settings: Review of relevant literature* (Report No. P-6691). Santa Monica, CA: Rand Corporation.

Boguslaw, R. (1981). *The new utopians: A study of system design and social change* (2nd ed.). New York: Irvington.

Brown, R. (1965). *Social psychology.* New York: Free Press.

Carnevale, P. J. E., Pruitt, D. G., & Seilheimer, S. D. (1981). Looking and competing: Accountability and visual access in integrative bargaining. *Journal of Personality and Social Psychology, 40,* 111–120.

Chapanis, A. (1972). Studies in interactive communication: The effects of four communication modes on the behavior of teams during cooperative problem-solving. *Human Factors, 14,* 487–509.

Danziger, J. N., Dutton, W. H., Kling, R., & Kraemer, K. L. (1982). *Computers and politics: High technology in American local governments.* New York: Columbia University Press.

Davis, J. H. (1973). Group decision and social interaction: A theory of social decision schemes. *Psychological Review, 80,* 97–125.

De Sola Poole, I. (1977). *The social impact of the telephone.* Cambridge, MA: MIT Press.

Diener, E. (1980). Deindividuation: The absence of self-awareness and self-regulation in group members. In P. Paulus (Ed.), *The psychology of group influence* (pp. 209–242). Hillsdale, NJ: Erlbaum.

Diener, E., Lusk, R., DeFour, D., & Flax, R. (1980). Deindividuation: Effects of group size, density, number of observers, and group member similarity on self-consciousness and disinhibited behavior. *Journal of Personality and Social Psychology, 39,* 449–459.

Dion, K. L., Baron, R. S., & Miller, N. (1978). Why do groups make riskier decisions than individuals? In L. Berkowitz (Ed.), *Group processes* (pp. 227–299). New York: Academic Press.

Druckman, D. (1977). *Negotiations: Social-psychological perspectives.* London: Sage.

Dubrovsky, V., Kiesler, S., & Siegel, J. (1983, October). *Human factors in computer-mediated communication.* Paper presented at the meeting of the Human Factors Society, Baltimore, MD.

Dutton, W. H., & Kraemer, K. L. (1980). Automating bias. *Society, 17,* 36–41.

Edinger, J. A., & Patterson, M. L. (1983). Nonverbal involvement and social control. *Psychological Bulletin, 93,* 30–56.

Ekman, P., Friesen, W. V., O'Sullivan, M., & Scherer, K. (1980). Relative importance of face, body, and speech in judgments of personality and affect. *Journal of Personality and Social Psychology, 38,* 270–277.

Emmett, R. (1981, November). VNET or GRIPENET? *Datamation,* pp. 48–58.

Festinger, L., Pepitone, A., & Newcomb, T. (1952). Some consequences of deindividuation in a group. *Journal of Abnormal and Social Psychology, 47,* 382–389.

Folk, H. (1977). The impact of computers on book and journal publication. In J. L. Divilbiss (Ed.), *The economics of library automation: Proceedings of the 1976 clinic on library applications of data processing* (pp. 72–82). Urbana, IL: University of Illinois Graduate School of Science.

Forsyth, D. R. (1983). *An introduction to group dynamics.* Monterey, CA: Brooks/Cole.

Geller, V. J. (1981, September). *Mediation of social presence: Communication modality effects on arousal and task performance.* Murray Hill, NJ: Bell Laboratories.

Gibbons, F. X., & Wright, R. A. (1981). Motivational biases in causal attributions of arousal. *Journal of Personality and Social Psychology, 40,* 588–600.

Goethals, G. R., & Zanna, M. P. (1979). The role of social comparison in choice shifts. *Journal of Personality and Social Psychology, 37,* 1469–1476.

Goldstein, J. H., Davis, R. W., & Herman, D. (1975). Escalation of aggression: Experimental studies. *Journal of Personality and Social Psychology, 31,* 162–170.

Hackman, J. R., & Morris, C. G. (1978). Group tasks, group interaction process, and group performance effectiveness: A review and proposed integration. In L. Berkowitz (Ed.), *Group processes* (pp. 1–55). New York: Academic Press.

Hedberg, B. L. T., Nyston, P. C., & Starbuck, W. H. (1976). Camping on seesaws: Prescriptions for a self-designing organization. *Administrative Science Quarterly, 21,* 41–65.

Hiltz, S. R. (1984). *Online scientific communities: A case study of the office of the future.* Norwood, NJ: Ablex Press.

Hiltz, S. R., Johnson, K., Aronovitch, C., & Turoff, M. (1980, August). *Face-to-face vs. computerized conferences: A controlled experiment: Vol. 1. Findings* (Report No. 12). Newark, NJ: New Jersey Institute of Technology.

Hiltz, S. R., Johnson, K., & Turoff, M. (1982). *The effects of formal human leadership and computer-generated decision aids on problem solving via computer: A controlled experiment* (Report No. 18). Newark, New Jersey Institute of Technology.

Hiltz, S. R., & Turoff, M. (1978). *The network nation: Human communication via computer.* Reading, MA: Addison-Wesley.

Hoffman, L. R. (1978). The group problem-solving process. In L. Berkowitz (Ed.), *Group processes* (pp. 101–112). New York: Academic Press.

Hough, R. W., & Panko, R. R. (1977). *Teleconferencing systems: A state-of-the-art survey and preliminary analysis* (National Science Foundation Report No. RA 770103, PB268455). Washington, DC: National Science Foundation.

Isen, A. M., Shalker, T. E., Clark, M., & Karp, L. (1978). Affect, accessibility of material in memory, and behavior. A cognitive loop? *Journal of Personality and Social Psychology, 36,* 1–12.

Janis, I. L. (1972). *Victims of groupthink.* Boston: Houghton Mifflin.

Kelley, H. H., & Thibaut, J. W. (1978). *Interpersonal relations.* New York: Wiley.

Kiesler, S., & Sproull, L. (1984). *Response effects in the electronic survey.* Unpublished manuscript, Carnegie-Mellon University, Pittsburgh, PA.

Kiesler, S., Zubrow, D., Moses, A., & Geller, V. (1983). *Affect in computer-mediated communication.* Manuscript submitted for publication.

Kite, W. R., & Vitz, P. C. (1966). *Teleconferencing: Effects of communication medium, network, and distribution of resources.* Arlington, VA: Institute for Defense Analyses.

Kling, R. (1980). Social analyses of computing: Theoretical perspectives in recent empirical research. *Computing Surveys, 12,* 61–110.

Kling, R. (1982). *Visible opportunities and hidden constraints: Engagements with computing on a social terrain.* Unpublished manuscript, University of California at Irvine.

Kogan, N., & Wallach, M. A. (1964). *Risk taking: A study in cognition and personality.* New York: Holt, Rinehart & Winston.

Kogan, N., & Wallach, M. A. (1967). Effects of physical separation of group decision-makers upon group risk taking. *Human Relations, 20,* 41–49.

Kraemer, K. L. (1981). *Telecommunications-transportation substitution and energy productivity: A re-examination.* Paris: Directorate of Science, Technology and Industry, Organization for Economic Cooperation and Development.

Krauss, R. M., Apple, W., Morencz, N., Wenzel, C., & Winton, W. (1981). Verbal, vocal, and visible factors in judgments of another's affect. *Journal of Personality and Social Psychology, 40,* 312–320.

Kraut, R. E., & Lewis, S. H. (in press). Some functions of feedback in conversation. In H. Applegate & J. Sypher (Eds.), *Understanding interpersonal communication: Social, cognitive, and strategic processes in children and adults.* Beverly Hills, CA: Sage.

Kraut, R. E., Lewis, S. H., & Swezey, L. W. (1982). Listener responsiveness and the coordination of conversation. *Journal of Personality and Social Psychology, 43,* 718–731.

Krueger, G. P. (1976). *Teleconferencing in the communication modes as a function of the number of conferees.* Unpublished doctoral dissertation, Johns Hopkins University, Baltimore, MD.

Lamm, H., & Kogan, N. (1970). Risk-taking in the context of intergroup negotiations. *Journal of Experimental Social Psychology, 6,* 351–363.

Lancaster, F. W. (1978). *Toward paperless information systems.* New York: Academic Press.

Lepper, M. R. (1982, August). *Microcomputers in education: Motivational and social issues.* Paper presented at the 90th annual convention of the American Psychological Association, Washington, DC.

Licklider, J. C. R., & Vezza, A. (1978). Applications of information networks. *Proceedings of the IEEE, 66,* 1330–1346.

Linstone, H. A., & Turoff, M. (Eds.). (1975). *The Delphi method: Techniques and applications.* Reading, MA: Addison-Wesley.

Maddox, W. (1982). *Computer communication in the Carnegie-Mellon University Spice Project.* Unpublished report, Carnegie-Mellon University, Pittsburgh, PA.

March, J. G., & Olsen, J. P. (1976). *Ambiguity and choice in organizations.* Bergen, Norway: Universitetsforiaget.

Martino, J. P. (1972). *Technological forecasting for decisionmaking.* New York: American Elsevier.

McArthur, L. Z., & Solomon, L. K. (1978). Perceptions of an aggressive encounter as a function of the victim's salience and the perceiver's arousal. *Journal of Personality and Social Psychology, 36,* 1278–1290.

Mehrabian, A. (1972). *Nonverbal communication.* Chicago: Aldine.

Morley, L. E., & Stephenson, G. M. (1969). Interpersonal and interparty exchange: A laboratory simulation of an industrial negotiation at the plane level. *British Journal of Psychology, 60,* 543–545.

Morley, L. E., & Stephenson, G. M. (1970). Formality in experimental negotiations: A validation study. *British Journal of Psychology, 61,* 383–384.

Party-line plea. (1981, January). *Time,* p. 49.

Patterson, M. L. (1982). A sequential functional model of nonverbal exchange. *Psychological Review, 89,* 231–249.

Payne, J. W., & Laughhunn, D. J. (in press). Multiattribute risky choice behavior: The editing of complex prospects. *Management Science.*

Pollack, A. (1982, May 27). Technology: Conference by computer. *New York Times*, p. D2.

Prentice-Dunn, S., & Rogers, R. W. (1980). Effects of deindividuating situational cues and aggressive models on subjective deindividuation and aggression. *Journal of Personality and Social Psychology, 39*, 104–113.

Price, C. R. (1975). Conferencing via computer: Cost effective communication for the era of forced choice. In H. A. Linstone & M. Turoff (Eds.), *The Delphi method: Techniques and applications* (pp. 497–516). Reading, MA: Addison-Wesley.

Pruitt, D. G., & Lewis, S. A. (1976). Development of integrative solutions in bilateral negotiations. *Journal of Personality and Social Psychology, 31*, 621–633.

Pye, R., & Williams, E. (1977). Teleconferencing: Is video valuable or is audio adequate? *Telecommunications Policy, 1*, 230–241.

Rice, R. E., & Case, D. (1982, May). Electronic messaging in the university organization. *Psychological Bulletin, 94*, 239–264.

Salancik, G. R. (1977). Commitment and the control of organizational behavior and belief. In B. M. Staw & G. R. Salancik (Eds.), *New directions in organizational behavior* (pp. 1–54). Chicago: St. Clair Press.

Sanders, G., & Baron, R. S. (1977). Is social comparison irrelevant for producing choice shifts? *Journal of Experimental Social Psychology, 13*, 303–314.

Scheier, M. F. (1976). Self-awareness, self-consciousness, and angry aggression. *Journal of Personality, 44*, 627–644.

Scheier, M. F., & Carver, C. S. (1977). Self-focused attention and the experience of emotion: Attraction, repulsion, elation, and depression. *Journal of Personality and Social Psychology, 35*, 625–636.

Scheier, M. F., Carver, C. S., & Gibbons, F. X. (1981). Self-focused attention and reactions to fear. *Journal of Research in Personality, 15*, 1–15.

Scherer, S. E. (1974). Influence of proximity and eye contact on impression formation. *Perceptual and Motor Skills, 38*, 538.

Short, J., Williams, E., & Christie, B. (1976). *The social psychology of telecommunications*. London: John Wiley & Sons.

Siegel, J., Dubrovsky, V., Kiesler, S., & McGuire, T. (1983). *Group processes in computer-mediated communications*. Manuscript submitted for publication.

Sinaiko, H. W. (1963). *Teleconferencing: Preliminary experiments* (Research Paper P-108). Arlington, VA: Institute for Defense Analyses.

Sproull, L., Kiesler, S., & Zubrow, D. (in press). Encountering the alien culture. *Social Issues*.

Stasser, G., & Davis, J. H. (1981). Group decision making and social influence: A social interaction sequence model. *Psychological Review, 88*, 523–551.

Stockton, W. (1981, June 28). The technology race. *New York Times Magazine*, p. 14.

Stoner, J. (1961). *A comparison of individual and group decisions including risk*. Unpublished master's thesis, School of Industrial Management, Massachusetts Institute of Technology.

Strickland, L. H., Guild, P. D., Barefoot, J. R., & Patterson, S. A. (1975). *Teleconferencing and leadership emergence*. Unpublished manuscript, Carleton University, Ottawa, Canada.

Tapscott, D. (1982, March). Investigating the electronic office. *Datamation*, pp. 130–138.

Turoff, M. (1982). Interface design in computerized conferencing systems. In *NYU Symposium on User Interfaces*. New York: New York University, Graduate School of Business Administration, Computer Applications and Information Systems. *Science, 211*, 453–458.

U.S. Department of Commerce. (1977). *Computers in the federal government: A compilation of statistics*. Washington, DC: U.S. Government Printing Office.

Vallee, J., Johansen, R., Lipinski, H., & Wilson, T. (1977). *Group communication through computers* (Vol. 4). Menlo Park, CA: Institute for the Future.

Vinokur, A., & Burnstein, E. (1974). The effects of partially shared persuasive arguments in group-induced shifts: A group problem-solving approach. *Journal of Personality and Social Psychology, 29*, 305–315.

Vinokur, A., & Burnstein, E. (1978). Novel argumentation and attitude change: The case of polarization following group discussion. *European Journal of Social Psychology, 8*, 335–348.

Wang Corporation. (1982). *Concepts*. Lowell, MA: Author.

Weeks, G. D., & Chapanis, A. (1976). Cooperative versus conflictive problem-solving in three telecommunication modes. *Perceptual and Motor Skills, 42*, 879–917.

Weis, J. F., Jr. (1983). Electronic mail. *Judges' Journal, 22*(3).

Welsch, L. A. (1982). Using electronic mail as a teaching tool. *Communications of the ACM, 23*, 105–108.

Whisler, T. L. (1970). *The impact of computers on organizations*. New York: Praeger.

Williams, E. (1973a). *Final report* (Reference No. P/73273/EL). (Available from Communications Studies Group, Wales House, 22 Gordon Street, London WC1H OQB, England).

Williams, E. (1973b). *The scope of person-to-person telecommunications in government and business* (Reference No. P/73272/EL). (Available from Communications Studies Group, Wates House, 22 Gordon Street, London WC1H OQB, England).

Williams, E. (1975a). *The effectiveness of person-to-person telecommunications systems research at the Communications Studies Group* (University College, Long Range Research Report 3, Reference No. LRRR 003/1TF). (Available from Communications Studies Group, Wates House, 22 Gordon Street, London WC1H OQB, England).

Williams, E. (1975b). Medium or message: Communications medium as a determinant of interpersonal evaluation. *Sociometry, 38*, 119–130.

Williams, E. (1977). Experimental comparisons of face-to-face and mediated communication: A review. *Psychological Bulletin, 84*, 963–976.

Williams, K., Harkins, S., & Latane, B. (1981). Identifiability as a deterrent to social loafing: Two cheering experiments. *Journal of Personality and Social Psychology, 40*, 310–311.

Zajonc, R. (1965). Social facilitation. *Science, 149*, 269–274.

Zajonc, R. (1969). Group and risk-taking in a two-choice situation: Replication, extension, and a model. *Journal of Experimental Social Psychology, 5*, 127–140.

Zillman, D., Bryant, J., Cantor, J. R., & Day, K. D. (1975). Irrelevance of mitigating circumstances in retaliatory behavior at high levels of excitation. *Journal of Research in Personality, 9*, 282–293.

P·A·R·T · IV

2

Conversations and Trust in Computer Interfaces

Judith A. Perrolle

Jurgen Habermas's theory of communicative action (Dews, 1986; Giddens, 1985; Habermas, 1979, 1984, & 1987; Postone, 1990) views conversation as a fundamental basis for society. In what Habermas calls the ideal speech situation, all participants have an equal opportunity to participate in nondistorted, rational discourse. In situations where some participants use their social status or their power and authority to inhibit the conversation of others, distorted communication occurs. Since computer interfaces remove individuals from the physical presence of others, the social context cues to status and power are obscured, reducing some of the means by which distorted communication occurs. Yet computer interfaces can embody unequal social relationships in their design, making power and authority appear as features of a world of objects. When this occurs, opportunities for computer-mediated ideal speech situations are limited.

Although nondistorted communication is an ideal, the vision of computers as supporting social interaction among equals in cooperative workplaces and in democratic public institutions has had a powerful appeal to the community of computer professionals. This article, by applying Habermas's theoretical conditions for ideal speech to the empirical literature on computer-mediated social interaction, identifies some important human factors in the design of computer interfaces intended to support communication among equals.

The Effects of Computer Interfaces on Communicative Action

In Habermas's theory, participants in communicative action must negotiate with one another to establish that what is being said is meaningful and true, that the speakers are sincere, and that the communication is socially appropriate. In doing this, participants must establish trust by successfully negotiating their claims to linguistic competence, truthfulness, sincerity, and appropriate behavior. From this theoretical perspective, one of the most important human factors in computer interface design is the impact that the interface has on users' abilities to negotiate these claims successfully.

Computer interfaces affect communicative action in two ways. First, *computer-mediated communication* (such as electronic mail or computer conferencing systems) changes the nature of conversations between people. Research indicates that computer-mediated communication alters the social norms governing conversation by removing elements of emotion and social control (Kiesler, 1984; Kiesler *et al.*, 1988; Kiesler and Sproull, 1986; McGuire *et al.*, 1987; Sheffield, 1989; Siegel *et al.*, 1986; Sproull and Kiesler, 1986). It also provides the possibility of more equal participation by obscuring the visual and verbal status distinctions that give higher-ranking or more aggressive people an advantage in face-to-face speech. In circumstances where opportunities for participation are enhanced and opportunities for one speaker to control another are reduced, the computer interface facilitates communicative action. Designs for cooperative work (Carasik and Grantham, 1988; Greif, 1988; Johnson *et al.*, 1986; Malone, 1987, 1988; Stevens, 1981; and Vaske, 1987) seek computer network support for precisely this sort of rational, nondistorted communication. But computer-mediated communication can embody inequalities in social relationships and can limit conversational participation, serving as a technology *for* distorted communication. Workplace surveillance (Attewell, 1987; Marx and Richman, 1984; U.S. Congress, 1987) is an extreme example of this. But computer system designers exercise more subtle power over users through their choice of designs (Marcus and Bjørn-Andersen, 1987). Computer interfaces, which are the result of choices made by designers, appear to many computer users as things to which they must adapt.

In *computer-human interaction*, when people perceive their interactions with a computer as "conversations" with a machine, communication becomes distorted in Habermas's sense. This is because, instead of claims to meaningfulness, truth, sincerity, and appropriateness being established by social interactions between people, such claims are preempted by the computer interface design. Social relationships of power and status are reified; they appear to be physical or logical characteristics of the machine rather than an outcome of human negotiation. In computer interfaces offering the illusion of conversation between person and machine, a problem of trust occurs that is fundamental to the nature of human conversation, and which cannot be considered merely a problem of individual psychology.

Validity Claims in Ideal Speech

Before communication can occur, participants must negotiate four kinds of validity claims:

- the comprehensibility of what is being said;

- the nature of external reality;
- the internal reality of the speaker's intentions; and
- the shared reality of the social norms governing conversation.

In order to approach the ideal speech situation of nondistorted communication, we must first trust that our conversational partners are speaking in linguistically meaningful ways. In other words, they must be making sense in a language that we understand. Linguistic incompetence by either of us will result in distorted communication. Second, we must trust our partners to refer to the same conversational domain, so that we may interrogate their claims to be making true statements about what exists there. This means that we are talking about the same thing and are prepared to trust the validity of what is being said to us. Third, we must trust that their intention is to have a rational conversation, rather than to intimidate or mislead us to their own advantage. If we mistrust a conversational partner's intent, distorted communication results. Finally, we must trust our partners to engage in socially appropriate conversation, rather than to offend or repulse us. This includes not only choice of acceptable vocabulary, but also adherence to interactional rules like turn taking.

Trust and Comprehensibility in Computer-Mediated Conversations

The first of Habermas's four validity claims involves the speaker's linguistic competence. For human speakers interacting through a computer interface, difficulties in typing or issuing appropriate commands for utilizing the communication network may be treated by others as indicators of incompetence. But this is not likely to be interpreted as a failure to be able to use language. Instead, the awkwardness of computer-mediated communication creates user incompetence and distorts communication. Siegel *et al.* (1986) estimate that, between their face-to-face experimental group and their computer-mediated one, about 40% of the difference in time to reach a decision was due to the fact that typing is slower than speaking. Computer interface innovators (Bolt, 1984; Brand, 1987) expect touch, voice, or even eye movements to replace the keyboard, enabling people to converse with one another more naturally. The physicist Stephen Hawking (1988: vi–vii) is a dramatic example of how such computer-mediated communication enhances the linguistic abilities of the physically disabled. Kobayashi (1986) predicts that computer interfaces will supply automatic translation from one language to another for international negotiators. If successful, this would reduce distorted communication across international boundaries. But such computer-mediated communication requires that computers themselves "understand" natural language.

Linguistic Competence in Natural Language Interfaces

If people must trust speakers' claims to linguistic competence in order to converse with them, and if natural language is not computable (as some language theorists beginning with Chomsky [1965] claim), then what does it mean to talk *to* a computer? Linguistic competence is at the heart of the debate over artificial intelligence. Turing (1950) made it a basic part of his test of whether a computer program could really think. Yet, while the argument goes on about whether artificial intelligence is possible (Goldkind, 1987; Newell, 1983; Gardner, 1987), natural-language interfaces are being developed in spite of theoretical reservations.

There are three directions of escape from the theoretical proposition that we cannot converse with computers because natural language cannot be computed. The first is simply to reject theoretical propositions about natural language noncomputability. A second route is to develop lanaguage processing software that uses heuristic rather than algorithmic strategies. Because these strategies are only accurate some of the time, they avoid theoretical objections by performing incompetently in some cases, such as under-standing the cultural context of

> Mary had a little lamb, then passed her plate and asked for more.

A complete understanding of this sentence requires knowledge of human biological experience, familiarity with English-language nursery rhymes, and comprehension of the cultural taboo on mentioning that we eat the same kinds of animals that we are emotionally attached to as pets. Also, the sentence's peculiar mix of revulsion and humor causes it to have an effect in a conversation that cannot be predicted from its grammar or from the specific meaning of each word. However, within specific, limited contexts appropriate to their applications, natural-language interfaces appear quite feasible. By giving up the claim of being able to make computer natural language "just like" human speech, interface designers can create some impressive "almost natural language" inter-faces.

A third route to linguistic competence in computer interfaces is based upon observ-ations of the human tendency to anthropomorphize objects, treating them as if they were living beings. As long as users will accept computer conversations as language, interface designers can ignore the fine points of linguistic theory. Weizenbaum (1976) found users of his ELIZA program deriving "interpersonal" satisfaction by "conversing" with an interface that only looked up responses in a small dictionary. To Turkle (1984), these conversations provide "the illusion of companionship without the demands of friend-ship." They represent a projection of the user's own personality onto the machine in a monologue mistaken for dialogue. In contrast, Bolt (1984) believes that computer interfaces of the future should become even more conversational. He thinks that computers should "know" where users are looking and accept speech and gestures as input, responding to the presence and normal behavior of the human. But Bolt's experi-mental interfaces that respond when you point or look at them are not conversations in the social sense.

Trust and the Nature of External Reality

Plato (Hamilton's translation 1973) distrusted writing because it was not possible to interact with a writer as one could with a speaker. Since Plato's time, we have developed ways of trusting the validity of the written word. Social norms about authorship, official editions, and authoritative versions define which written communications are valid

(Foucault, 1984). In ideal speech situations, speakers interrogate one another to establish claims about what is true. In writing we have developed letters to the editor, peer review, and other forms of validating dialogue. In computer-mediated communication participants can make immediate (in the case of real-time networks) or written (in the case of e-mail) inquiries.

Most computer interfaces are either not designed to allow the user to question data validity, or else designed so that data may be changed by anyone with a moderate level of technical skill. Until we have developed a new set of social norms for validating computer information, there will be some uneasiness about how much we can trust computer networks (Thompson, 1984). For example, new users of an electronic mail system go through a period in which they read everything because they haven't learned to trust electronic data storage (Hiltz and Turoff, 1985). A more extreme example is the current user uneasiness about computer viruses.

Computer graphics raises a new problem of trust. Research has shown that people trust pictures more than they do printed words, and that they are more likely to trust a television image than a newspaper article (Graber, 1984). Thus we could predict that computer graphics will increase our trust in computer-based information. But computer graphics allow us to manipulate images in realistic-looking ways. As it becomes harder to tell "real" pictures from "retouched" ones, we may eventually become reluctant to accept pictures as evidence of external reality (Brand et al., 1985).

Paradoxically, many inexperienced users attribute more validity to computer-based data than is warranted. Analyses of the effects of computer modeling on policy (Kraemer et al., 1987; Perrolle, 1987, 1988a, 1988b; Koh, 1984; Komsky, 1986) suggest that computer models serve to legitimate policy agendas of model users. The development of the "limits to growth" computer models of the 1970s (Meadows et al., 1972) and the decade of controversy they provoked (Humphrey and Buttel, 1982; Oltmans, 1974; Tinbergen et al., 1976) placed issues of world food shortages, population growth, pollution, and natural resource depletion on the policy agenda of many national and international bodies. In the 1980s a similar phenomenon occurred with the controversy surrounding the "nuclear winter" models (Turco et al., 1983; Ehrlich et al., 1984) that served to sensitize government and military policy makers to the possible ecological effects of nuclear war. Today, the global modeling efforts of atmospheric scientists (Richardson, 1984; Schneider, 1989a, 1989b) are being used as evidence of an urgent international policy issue (United States Environmental Protection Agency, 1989; Scientific American, 1989). In these cases, computer models seem to enhance the validity of scientific theories of global change (Perrolle et al., 1990).

Intentions in Computer-Mediated Communication

Research by Holstein (1988) in noncomputerized involuntary commitment hearings clearly shows the influence of intention on conversational interactions. Public defenders (who intend to get their clients acquitted) communicate very differently from district attorneys (who want to have those same clients declared mentally incompetent). In these courtroom settings, the testimony of powerless people trying to prove their competence is a classic study in distorted communication. Interruptions, ridicule, hostility, and disbelief are among the conversational behaviors of those trying to deny someone else's claim to communicative competence. It is more difficult to determine intention in more ordinary conversations. And, in computer-mediated communication, it is more difficult still. In the absence of social-context cues, it is even difficult to tell who is speaking, let alone what they intend.

This leads to the hypothesis that the use of computer-mediated conversation will increase our attention to validity claims about the nature of external reality—in other words, claims that the messages are "true." As it becomes more difficult for us to tell who is speaking, we may expand our willingness to trust the unseen stranger whose words we read, or we may place our trust in the computer itself as provider of messages. In the latter case, we may think of ourselves as engaged in conversation with an anonymous network and lose sight of the humans whose programs and messages we are using. Indeed, research on computer-mediated communication reports that a greater proportion of messages are substantive propositions about the topic being discussed. People focus more on the message and less on the person who sent it.

In situations where great differences in status or power distort face-to-face communication, this tendency to focus on statements of fact and not intentions can facilitate social interaction. Koh (1984) observed delegates to the International Law of the Sea Conference arriving at mutually agreeable solutions to the problem of how to divide the costs and benefits of seabed mining in international waters. By turning to a computer model to evaluate their individual proposals, delegates were able to distance themselves from feelings of national pride and suspicion of other nations' intentions.

Intentions in Computer/Human Interactions

Research on the perception of intention (Dasser *et al.*, 1989) indicates that people easily attribute intention to objects. It is not surprising that intentions are also rather easily attributed to computer interfaces. An example is the ANIMALS program distributed with the Apple IIe computer. A version of the game "Twenty Questions," the program begins by trying to "guess" the animal the user is thinking of. As the user supplies the program with information, it constructs a database. If used long enough, ANIMALS become a very simple expert system for guessing animals according to their traits. The educational function of the game (and presumably the intention of the programmer) is to teach a child that you can have fun while putting data and relationships of your choice into a computer. But in playing ANIMALS it is easy to feel that the computer "intends" to play a game with you.

One novice user (Brownstein, 1984) provided an entirely different interpretation of the conversational intentions of the ANIMALS program. Believing that computers neither know nor intend, he guessed that the programmer was making a joke. He missed the lesson about computer databases but hit upon the problem of whom we are speaking to when we converse with a computer. The answer from Richard Bolt is that we are engaged in a process of mutual self-disclosure: "The information base discloses itself to you as you disclose yourself to it (1984:87)". But conversational interfaces are not social activity. In place of the intentions of another speaker we have the external "reality" of the database.

This is an example of a reified social relationship. The relationship between the programmer and the program's user appears to be a relationship between the user and the program.

Reification distorts communication by making the intentions of those who design, implement, own, and manage computer interfaces appear as natural features of the environment. Instead of asking who is exerting what sort of control over the activities of whom through computer interfaces, analysts of reified social relationships frame their study in terms of relationships between persons and objects and focus on individual psychological issues of acceptance and adjustment.

Conversational Norms in Computer/Human Interfaces

Users report that response time (and problems with it) is the most important characteristic of computer interfaces (Rushinek and Rushinek, 1986). Designers frequently believe that faster response time is better (Lyman et al., 1985) without considering response time as part of a conversational pattern. Findings that user productivity is increased by increasing interface response times from two seconds to a few tenths of a second (Brady, 1986) ignore the fact that users tolerate longer delays for conversation-like tasks. The toleration of longer intervals for time for responses to queries or responses to user errors (Ericsson, 1984) can be interpreted as being governed by the norms for pauses in human conversation. Shorter response times are expected by users for such nonconversational tasks as displaying a new page or scrolling. This illustrates one of the drawbacks of users' treating computer interfaces as conversational partners—computer users tolerate a faster-paced interaction when objects (like pages) are being moved than they will for a "conversation."

Computer-Mediated Communication and Conversational Norms

Studies of interruption patterns in conversations show that, in the United States, women are interrupted by men more than 80% of the time. Women, who make less than 20% of conversational interruptions, are expected to allow themselves to be interrupted (Zimmerman and West, 1975). There are similar conversational norms allowing high-status people to interrupt low-status ones (Molotch and Boden, 1985). By interfering with our ability to tell if we are conversing with a man or a woman, most computer-mediated communication systems change the social norm of interruption of women by men. An alternative design less favorable to women and low-status people would be the establishment of social hierarchies in the access and priority designs of computer networks. Status differences can be preserved if our computer message systems tell us who is more important than whom.

The social history of the telephone gives reason for optimism in the prospects for equality in computerized communications. Early advertisements for the telephone depicted it as a device for giving orders to employees or servants; it became a means for two-way conversations between equals instead (Cherry, 1977). There is also reason for optimism in Reid's (1977) review of conflict and decision making in the absence of vision.

Although studies of computer-mediated communication generally report a reduction in cooperation and a lengthening of decision-making time, they also report an increase in participants' willingness to change their opinions. Emotionally based arguments, which often sway opinions in face-to-face situations, are less likely to influence the outcomes of computer-based discussions.

Kiesler et al. (1988) report the negative effect of removing emotion from discussion. Participants in her study were "out of control" and violated the rules of polite conversation. We use emotional expressions of approval or disapproval to exert normative power. With these ordinary mechanisms of social control missing, participants in computer-based discussions are free to develop new conversational rules and arrive at unconventional decisions.

These findings indicate that computer-aided decision making is more rational in terms of the information available to participants, but less strongly controlled by shared (or conflicting) emotional evaluations. For low-status participants, and in technical decisions where shared emotions are less relevant to the outcome than questions of fact, this should be an improvement. For decision-making *about human goals*, however, the absence of face-to-face contact can be a problem. The same nonverbal processes that reinforce feelings of interpersonal solidarity or antagonism also act to affirm shared values or to arrive at new ones (Druckman et al.; Baxter, 1982). Computer-mediated communication reduces the social solidarity in existing social groups, but it facilitates conversations among strangers.

Integration and Social Control in Electronic Communities

The negative effects of computer-based communication—loss of face-to-face contact, strains on trust, and a reduction in normative social control—are balanced by the possibilities for social integration in communities formed around electronic networks. Our traditional concept of a community has a geographical base, with people in regular face-to-face contact with one another. Yet widely scattered people have maintained their social ties through letters, phone calls, and periodic gatherings. The professional community of American sociologists gathers at the end of every summer to go through the ritual of delivering papers and seeing colleagues. During the year they communicate mainly by mail, telephone, and electronic mail.

One kind of computer network that facilitates solidarity within groups is the electronic bulletin board. Available at universities, as commercial information services, and as communications systems for special interest groups, bulletin boards support geographically scattered communities. Unlike most electronic mail systems, bulletin boards are designed to support conversations among many participants. Community bulletin boards like Berkeley, California's Community Memory Project, are experiments in social integration and democratic participation. Terminals in public places provide access for individuals who do not have computer terminals at home or work. Yet problems reported by bulletin-board operators include the exchange of pirated software, the use of inflammatory language, and vandalism by hackers. The social control that most communities exert over their members by persuasion has not been well established in electronic networks. Designing for normative social controls exerted by equals over one another (as opposed to control exercised by authorities) requires interfaces that support responsible participation in group discussion.

Organizational interfaces. Thomas Malone (1985) defines an organizational interface as the parts of a computer system that connect human users to one another. A text sharing system, for example, is an organizational interface. Other kinds of organizational interfaces are management tools for keeping track of resources and tasks (Fox *et al.*, 1983; Kedzierski, 1982; Sluizer and Cashman, 1985). The design choices for such interfaces incorporate choices about power and authority. If, like telephone conference calls, they are made for cooperative interaction, the organizational interfaces will integrate individual activities and facilitate the development of group goals. If, on the other hand, organizational interfaces are designed to monitor activities and allocate tasks to people, they become the instruments of managerial control. They will supervise and coordinate individual activities without providing the social interactions necessary for nondistorted group communication.

In a review of organizational interfaces allowing many-to-many communication, Chandler Harrison (1981) identified several attitudes that inhibit people from communicating with one another over computer networks:

- Feelings of isolation and powerlessness
- Inability to understand the information available on the network
- The belief that important decisions should be left to expert decision makers
- The expectation that information comes in pre-made packages, rather than being exchanged through social interaction
- The belief that competition is more advantageous than cooperation.

These attitudes are related to organizational interface design. If users are restricted to small subsets of system resources and given few choices, they will be isolated and powerless. If the interface is not easy to use, people will have difficulty understanding what is available to them from other people on the network. If the belief that only experts should make decisions is assumed by the designer, it may not be technically possible to use the system for any other form of decision making. If information comes in packages supplied by the system, the "nature of external reality" cannot be negotiated by those using it. Finally, if those who build organizational interfaces do not believe that cooperation is worthwhile, it may be difficult to use the interface for cooperative purposes.

Social control over public space. Even the best interface design for an organizational interface has its limitations. As Scragg (1985) points out by comparing his company's electronic mail system to Post-It notes, sometimes we want to put a message in a place, not send it to a person. If the message shown in Figure 1 were put in everyone's electronic mail box, it would not be as effective for group communication as a note on the door. The door is a public place; comments on it are group property. In most interface designs, there is no provision for public places or public commentary. And, without public social interaction, we cannot have communities (Sennett, 1974).

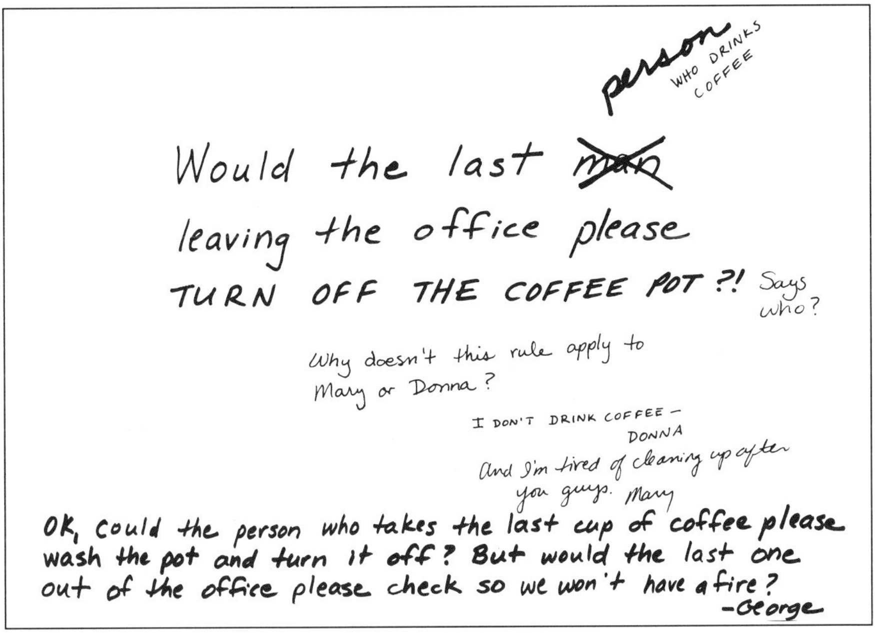

Figure 1.   Example of a Public Message.

It is not enough to have public places where common information is stored and retrieved. As Jane Jacobs pointed out in *The Life and Death of the Great American Cities*, social interaction in public spaces provides social control over what goes on in them. Without norms for public conversation, public messages collect graffiti—individual expressions of art, obscenity, philosophy, or protest. The message about the coffee pot is not just information to be stored and retrieved. It is a public discussion about organizational behavior and responsibility. It is this sort of discussion that distinguishes a social interface from an interface that only coordinates individual human/computer connections. An absence of public discussion about goals and behavior is characteristic of distorted communication. Organizational interfaces that restrict discussions to technical questions of how to accomplish predefined group tasks distort communication by embedding relationships of power and authority in the software itself.

Conclusion

In terms of Habermas's theory, some evidence from research on computer-mediated communication points towards an enhancement of nondistorted communication. The subversion of conversational norms seems to occur most sharply for norms that support symbolic expressions of status differentials and affectual sanctions. Discussions of what sort of norms should apply to computer-based conversation can be carried out through rational discourse—assuming that ideal speech situations are valued by the participants. This potential liberation from normative expressions of power and inequality in computer-mediated communication is in sharp contrast to the case where computer-human interfaces are substituted for human communicative action. There, unequal relations of power and authority become reified, removing them from the realm of rational discourse.

The implication of this is that we should conceive of the computer-human interface as occurring in a context of power and status relationships. In other words, we should consider it a social rather than a psychological or cognitive phenomena and should be sensitive to the problems of establishing nondistorted communication. In particular, we should remain aware that the nature of the world represented by computer software and databases is a socially negotiated one. If those who construct computer interfaces are committed to supporting conversations among equals and are willing to subject their own designs and data to negotiation, we may trust them to provide us with a technology for nondistorted communication. If not, we need a public discussion about social factors in computer interface design.

References

Attewell, Paul (1987). "Big Brother and the Sweatshop: Computer Surveillance in the Automated Office," *Sociological Theory.* 5, pp. 87–100.

Bolt, Richard A. (1984). *The Human Interface.* Wadsworth, Belmont, Cal.

Brady, James T. (1986). "A Theory of Creativity in the Creative Process," *IEEE Computer Graphics.* May, pp. 25–34.

Brand, Stewart (1987). *The Media Lab: Inventing the Future at MIT.* Viking Penguin, New York.

Brand, Stewart, Kevin Kelly, and Jay Kinney (1985). "Digital Retouching: The End of Photography as Evidence of Anything," *Whole Earth Review.* 47 (July), pp. 42–50.

Brownstein, Henry H. (1984). "How I Contacted a Human Form Through My Computer," *The Humanist Sociologist.* 9(4) (December), pp. 5–7.

Carasik, R. P., and C. E. Grantham (1988). "A Case Study of CSCW in a Dispersed Organization," pages 61–65 in Elliot Soloway, Douglas Frye, and Sylvia B. Sheppart, eds., *Human Factors in Computer Systems* (Special issue of *SIGCHI Bulletin*). Addison-Wesley, Reading, Mass.

Cherry, Colin (1977). "The Telephone System: Creator of Mobility and Social Change," in Ithiel de Sola Pool, ed., *The Social Impact of the Telephone.* MIT Press, Cambridge, Mass.

Chomsky, Noam (1965). *Aspects of the Theory of Syntax.* MIT Press, Cambridge, Mass.

Dasser, Verena, Ib Ulbaek, and David Premack (1989). "The Perception of Intention," *Science.* 243 (20 January), pp. 365–367.

Dews, Peter, ed. (1986). *Habermas: Autonomy and Solidarity.* Verso, London.

Druckman, Daniel, Richard M. Rozelle, and James C. Baxter (1982). *Nonverbal Communication: Survey, Theory, and Research.* Sage, Beverly Hills, Cal.

Ericsson Information Systems (1984). *Proceedings of the World Conference on Ergonomics in Computer Systems.* Ericsson, Garden Grove, Cal.

Ehrlich, Paul R., Carl Sagan, Donald Kennedy, and Walter Orr Roberts (1984). *The Cold and the Dark: The World after Nuclear War.* Norton, New York.

Foucault, Michel (1984). "What is an Author?," in Paul Rabinow, ed., *The Foucault Reader.* Pantheon, New York.

Fox, M., M. Greenberg, A. Sathi, J. Mattis, and M. Rychener (1983). "Callisto: An Intelligent Project Management System," Technical Report, Intelligent Systems Laboratory, Robotics Institute, Carnegie Mellon University, Pittsburgh: November.

Gardner, Howard (1987). *The Mind's New Science: A History of the Cognitive Revolution.* Basic Books, New York.

Giddens, Anthony (1985). "Reason without Revolution? Habermas' Theorie des kommunikafiven Handelns," Chapter 4 in Richard J. Bernstein, eds., *Habermas and Modernity.* MIT Press, Cambridge, Mass.

Goldkind, S. (1987). *Machines and Intelligence: A Critique of Arguments Against the Possibility of Artificial Intelligence.* Greenwood, Westport, Ct.

Graber, Doris A. (1984). *Processing the News: How People Tame the Information Tide.* Longman, New York.

Greif, Irene, ed. (1988). *Computer-Supported Cooperative Work.* Morgan Kaufmann, San Mateo, Cal.

Habermas, Jurgen (1979). *Communication and the Evolution of Society.* Beacon Press, Boston.

Habermas, Jurgen (1984). *The Theory of Communicative Action, Vol. 1. Reason and the Rationalization of Society.* Translated by Thomas McCarthy. Beacon Press, Boston.

Habermas, Jurgen (1987). *The Theory of Communicative Action, Vol. 2. Lifeworld and System: A Critique of Functionalist Reason.* Translated by Thomas McCarthy. Beacon Press, Boston.

Hawking, Stephen W. (1988). *A Brief History of Time.* Bantam Books, New York.

Hiltz, Starr Roxanne, and Murray Turoff (1985). "Structuring Computer-Mediated Communication Systems to avoid Information Overload," *Communications of the ACM.* 28(7) (July), pp. 680–689.

Holstein, James A. (1988). "Court Ordered Incompetence: Conversational Organization in Involuntary Commitment Hearings," *Social Problems.* 35(4) (October), pp. 458–73.

Humphrey, Craig, and Frederick Buttel (1982). "The Sociology of the 'Limits to Growth' Debate," pages 92–110 in *Energy, Environment, and Society.* Wadsworth, Belmont, Cal.

Jacobs, Jane (1961). *The Death and Life of the Great American Cities.* Vintage, New York.

Johnson, Bonnie, Margrethe Olson, and Geraldine Weaver (1986). "Using a Computer-Based Tool to Support Collaboration." MCC Conference on Computer-Supported Cooperative Work, Austin, Tex.

Kedzierski, B. (1982). "Communication and Management Support in System Development and Environments," *Proceedings, Conference on Human Factors in Computer Systems.* Gaithersburg, MD: March.

Kiesler, Sara (1984). "Computer Mediation of Conversation," *American Psychologist.* 39, pp. 1123–1134.

Kiesler, Sara, and Lee S. Sproull (1986). "Response Effects in the Electronic Survey," *Public Opinion Quarterly.* 50, pp. 402–413.

Kiesler, Sara, Jane Siegel, and Timothy W. McGuire (1988). "Social Psychological Aspects of Computer-Mediated Communication," pages 657–682 in Irene Greif, ed., *Computer-Supported Cooperative Work.* Morgan Kaufmann, San Mateo, Cal.

Kobayashi, Koji (1986). *Computers and Communications.* MIT Press, Cambridge, Mass.

Koh, T. T. B. (1984). "Computer-Assisted Negotiations: A Case History from the Law of the Sea Negotiations and Speculation Regarding Future Uses," in H. Pagels, ed., *Computer Culture: The Scientific, Intellectual, And Social Impact of the Computer.* New York Academy of Sciences, New York.

Komsky, Susan H. (1986). "Acceptance of Computer-Based Models in Local Government: Information Adequacy and Implementation," *Computers and the Social Sciences,* 2, pp. 209–220.

Kraemer, Kenneth L., Sigfried Dickhoven, Susan Fallows Tierney, and John Leslie King (1987). *Datawars: The Politics of Modeling in Federal Policymaking.* Columbia University Press, New York.

Lyman, H. Thaine, James Anderson, and Jeffrey Plewa (1985). "Are You Rushing Too Fast to Subsecond Response Time?" *Computerworld* (September 9): ID/5–14.

Malone, Thomas W. (1985). "Designing Organizational Interfaces," *Proceedings, Human Factors in*

Computing Systems. San Francisco: ACM Special Interest Group on Computer and Human Interaction (April 14–18), pp. 66–71.

Malone, Thomas W. (1987). "Computer Support for Organizations: Toward an Organizational Science," pages 294–324 in John M. Carroll, ed., *Interfacing Thought: Cognitive Aspects of Computer-Human Interaction*. MIT Press, Cambridge, Mass.

Malone, Thomas W. (1988). "Designing Organizational Interfaces," in Elliot Soloway, Douglas Frye, and Sylvia Sheppard, eds., *Human Factors in Computer Systems* (special issue of *SIGCHI Bulletin*). Addison-Wesley, Reading, Mass.

Marcus, M. Lynne, and Niels Bjørn-Andersen (1987). "Power over Users: Its Exercise by System Professionals," *Communications of the ACM*. 30(6), pp. 498–504.

Marx, Gary T., and Nancy Richman (1984). "Routinizing the Discovery of Secrets: Computers as Informants," *American Behavioral Scientist*, 27(4) (March/April), pp. 423–52.

McGuire, Timothy W., Sara Kiesler, and Jane Siegel (1987). "Group and Computer-Mediated Discussion Effects in Risk Decision Making," *Journal of Personality and Social Psychology*. 32(5), pp. 917–930.

Meadows, D. H., D. L. Meadows, J. Randers, and W. Behrens, III (1972). *The Limits to Growth*. Universe Books, New York.

Molotch, Harvey L., and Deirdre Boden. 1985. "Talking Social Structure: Discourse, Domination, and the Watergate Hearings," *American Sociological Review*. June, pp. 273–88.

Newell, Allen (1983). "Intellectual Issues in the History of Artificial Intelligence," pages 187–227 in Fritz Machlup and Una Mansfield, eds., *The Study of Information*. Wiley, New York.

Oltmans, Willem L., ed. (1974). *On Growth*. G. P. Putnam's Sons, New York.

Perrolle, Judith A. (1987). "Computer Models and Policy-Making," pages 223–229 in *Computers and Social Change: Information, Property, and Power*. Wadsworth, Belmonth, Cal.

Perrolle, Judith A. (1988a). "Computer Modelling and Environmental Protection," Oak Ridge National Laboratory, Oak Ridge, Tenn.

Perrolle, Judith A. (1988b). "Risk and Responsibility in a Computerized Environment," American Sociological Association, Atlanta, Ga.

Perrolle, Judith A., Nightingale Rukuba, Michele Eayrs, and A. Lee Gilbert (1990). "The Effects of Computer Models of Global Warming on Regional Environmental Policies in East Africa and Southeast Asia," Interdisciplinary Conference on the Environment: Global Problems—Local Solutions. Hofstra College.

Plato (1973). "The Inferiority of the Written to the Spoken Word," pages 95–103 in *Phaedrus* (Walter Hamilton, tr.), Penguin Books, London.

Postone, Moishe (1990). "History and Critical Social Theory," review of Jurgen Habermas's *The Theory of Communicative Action*, in *Contemporary Sociology*. 19(2) (March), pp. 170–76.

Reid, A. A. L. (1977). "Comparing Telephone with Face-to-Face Contact," in Ithiel de Sola Pool, ed., *The Social Impact of the Telephone*. MIT Press, Cambridge, Mass.

Richardson, John M. (1984). "Global Modeling in the 1980s," pages 115–129 in Jacques Richardson, ed., *Models of Reality: Shaping Thought and Action*. Lomond Publications, Mt. Airy, Md.

Rushinek, Avi, and Sara F. Rushinek (1986). "What Makes Users Happy?" *Communications of the ACM*. 29(7) (July), pp. 594–598.

Schneider, Stephen H. (1989a). *Global Warming*. Sierra Club Books, San Francisco.

Schneider, Stephen H. (1989b). "The Greenhouse Effect: Science and Policy," *Science*. 243, pp. 771–781.

Scientific American (1989). Special issue on Global Change. September.

Scragg, Greg W. (1985). "Some Thoughts on Paper Notes and Electronic Messages," *SIGCHI Bulletin*. 16(3) (January), pp. 41–44.

Sennett, Richard (1974).*The Fall of Public Man: On the Social Psychology of Capitalism.* Vintage, New York.

Sheffield, Jim (1989). "The Effects of Bargaining Orientation and Communication Medium on Negotiations in the Bilateral Monopoly Task: A Comparison of Decision Room and Computer Conferencing Communication Media," pages 43–48 in Ken Bice and Clayton Lewis, eds., *Human Factors in Computing Systems* (Special Issue of *SIGCHI Bulletin*). Addison-Wesley. Reading, Mass.

Siegel, Jane, Vitaly Dubrovsky, Sara Kiesler, and Timothy W. McGuire (1986). "Group Processes in Computer-Mediated Communication," *Organizational Behavior and Human Decision Processes.* 37, pp. 157–187.

Sluizer, S., and P. Cashman (1985). "XCP: An Experimental Tool for Managing Cooperative Activity," *Proceedings, ACM Computer Science Conference.* New Orleans: March.

Sproull, Lee, and Sara Kiesler (1986). "Reducing Social Context Cues: Electronic Mail in Organizational Communication," *Management Science.* 32(11), pp. 1492–1512.

Stevens, Chandler Harrison (1981). "Many-to-Many Communication," Center for Information Systems Research Working Paper No. 72. MIT Press, Cambridge, Mass.

Thompson, Ken (1984). "Reflections on Trusting Trust: Should We Trust the Program or Its Creator?" *Communications of the ACM.* August, pp. 758–760.

Tinbergen, Jan, Anthony J. Dolmen, and Jan van Ettinger (1976). *Reshaping the International Order: A Report to the Club of Rome.* E. P. Dutton and Company, New York.

Turco, Richard P., Owen B. Toon, Thomas P. Ackerman, James B. Pollack, and Carl Sagan (1983). "Nuclear Winter: Global Consequences of Multiple Nuclear Explosions," *Science.* 222, pp. 1283–92.

Turing, Alan M. (1950). "Computing Machinery and Intelligence," *Mind.* 59(236).

Turkle, Sherry (1984). Personal communication.

U.S. Congress, Office of Technology Assessment (1987). *The Electronic Supervisor: New Technology, New Tensions.* U.S. Government Printing Office, Washington, D.C.

U.S. Environmental Protection Agency, Office of Policy, Planning, and Evaluation (1989). *Policy Options for Stabilizing Global Climate.* U.S. Government Printing Office, Washington, D.C.

Vaske, J. J., and C. E. Grantham (1987). *Socializing the Human Computer Environment.* Ablex, Norwood, N.J.

Weizenbaum, Joseph (1976). *Computer Power and Human Reason: From Judgement to Calculation.* W. H. Freeman, San Francisco.

Zimmerman, Don, and Candace West (1975). "Sex Roles, Interruptions, and Silences in Conversation," in Barrie Thorne and Nancy Henley, eds., *Language and Sex: Difference and Domination.* Newbury House Publishers, Rowley, Mass.

3

The Strange Case of the Electronic Lover

Lindsy Van Gelder

I "met" Joan in the late spring of 1983, shortly after I first hooked my personal computer up to a modem and entered the strange new world of on-line communications. Like me, Joan was spending a great deal of time on the "CB" channel of the national network CompuServe, where one can encounter other modem owners in what amounts to a computer version of CB radio. I was writing an article for *Ms.* about modems and doing on-line interviews with CB regulars. Joan was already a sought-after celebrity among the hundreds of users who hung out on the channel—a telecommunications media star.

Her "handle" was "Talkin' Lady." According to the conventions of the medium, people have a (usually frivolous) handle when they're on "open" channels with many users; but when two people choose to enter a private talk mode, they'll often exchange real information about themselves. I soon learned that her real name was Joan Sue Greene, and that she was a New York neuropsychologist in her late twenties, who had been severely disfigured in a car accident that was the fault of a drunken driver. The accident had killed her boyfriend. Joan herself spent a year in the hospital, being treated for brain damage, which affected both her speech and her ability to walk. Mute, confined to a wheelchair, and frequently suffering intense back and leg pain, Joan had at first been so embittered about her disabilities that she literally didn't want to live.

Then her mentor, a former professor at Johns Hopkins, presented her with a computer, a modem, and a year's subscription to CompuServe to be used specifically doing what Joan was doing—making friends on-line. At first, her handle had been "Quiet Lady," in reference to her muteness. But Joan could type—which is, after all, how one "talks" on

Reprinted from "The Strange Case of the Electronic Lover," published in *Ms. Magazine*, October, 1985. Copyright © Lindsy Van Gelder, 1985.

a computer—and she had a sassy, bright, generous personality that blossomed in a medium where physicality doesn't count. Joan became enormously popular, and her new handle, "Talkin' Lady," was a reflection of her new sense of self. Over the next two years, she became a monumental on-line presence who served both as a support for other disabled women and as an inspiring stereotype-smasher to the able-bodied. Through her many intense friendships and (in some cases) her on-line romances, she changed the lives of dozens of women.

Thus it was a huge shock early this year when, through a complicated series of events, Joan was revealed as being not disabled at all. More to the point, Joan, in fact, was not a woman. She was really a man we'll call Alex—a prominent New York psychiatrist in his early fifties who was engaged in a bizarre, all-consuming experiment to see what it felt like to be female, and to experience the intimacy of female friendship.

Even those who barely knew Joan felt implicated—and somehow betrayed—by Alex's deception. Many of us on-line like to believe that we're a utopian community of the future, and Alex's experiment proved to us all that technology is no shield against deceit. We lost our innocence, if not our faith.

To some of Alex's victims—including a woman who had an affair with the real-life Alex, after being introduced to him by Joan—the experiment was a "mind rape," pure and simple. (Several people, in fact, have tentatively explored the possibility of bringing charges against Alex as a psychiatrist—although the case is without precedent, to put it mildly.) To some other victims, Alex was not so much an impostor as a seeker whose search went out of control. (Several of these are attempting to continue a friendship with Alex—and, as one woman put it, "to relate to the soul, not the sex of the person. The soul is the same as before.")

Either way, this is a peculiarly modern story about a man who used some of our most up-to-date technology to play out some of our oldest assumptions about gender roles.

More than most stories, it requires a bit of background. A modem, of course, is the device that connects a computer to the phone and from there to any other similarly equipped computer. CompuServe is the largest of a number of modem networks; it charges its subscribers an initial small fee to open an account with a special ID number and then charges hourly fees for access to its hundreds of services, from stock reports to airline information. In addition to its business services, the network also offers a number of "social" services (including numerous Special Interest Groups—SIGs—and the CB channels) where users can mingle.

The unfolding of an on-line relationship is unique, combining the thrill of ultrafuturistic technology with the veneration of the written word that informed 19th-century friendships and romances. Most people who haven't used the medium have trouble imagining what it's like to connect with other people whose words are wafting across your computer screen. For starters, it's dizzyingly egalitarian, since the most important thing about oneself isn't age, appearance, career success, health, race, gender, sexual preference, accent, or any of the other categories by which we normally judge each other, but one's *mind*. My personal experience has been that I often respond to the minds of people whom, because of my own prejudices (or theirs), I might otherwise not meet. (For example, my best friend on-line is from Appalachia, which I once thought was inhabited only by Li'l Abner and the Dukes of Hazzard. My friend, in turn, had never had a gay friend before.)

But such mind-to-mind encounters presume that the people at both keyboards are committed to getting past labels and into some new, truer way of relating. In the wake of the Alex/Joan scandal, some on-line habitués have soberly concluded that perhaps there's a thin line between getting out of one's skin and getting into a completely false identity—and that the medium may even encourage impersonation. (One network, for example, has a brochure showing a man dressed up as Indiana Jones, Michael Jackson, and an Olympic athlete; the copy reads, "Be anything you want on American PEOPLE/ LINK.") Still, when it works, it works. Disabled people are especially well represented on-line, and most of them say that it's a medium where they can make a first impression on their own terms.

Another positive consequence of the medium's mind-to-mind potential—and this is germane to Joan's story—is that it's powerfully conducive to intimacy. Thoughts and emotions are the coin of this realm, and people tend to share them sooner than they would in "real life" (what CBers refer to as "off-line"). Some people, in fact, become addicted to computer relationships, per se. But most use the modem merely as a way to start relationships that may, in time, continue off-line. After several on-line conversations with someone who seems especially compatible, people commonly arrange to speak on the telephone, to exchange photographs, and eventually, to meet in person, either by themselves or at one of the regular "CB parties" held around the country. (Several marriages have resulted from on-line meetings on CompuServe CB alone.) I've met four good computer friends in person, and found them all much the same off-line as on. For me, the only odd thing about these relationships has been their chronology. It's a little surreal to know intimate details about someone's childhood before you've ever been out to dinner together.

One of the reasons that Joan's real identity went undetected for so long was that her supposed disability prevented her from speaking on the phone. (Several people did communicate with Joan on the phone, in one case because Joan had said that she wanted to hear the sound of the other woman's voice. Joan in turn "would make horrible noises into the receiver—little yelps and moans.") There was also the matter of Joan's disfigure- ment; she supposedly drooled and had a "smashed up" face, untreatable by plastic surgery. She was, she said, embarrassed to meet her computer friends in person. Those who wanted to be sensitive to disabled concerns naturally didn't push. It was an ingenious cover.

Alex supposedly began his dual identity by mistake. One of the social realities of the computing world is that the majority of its inhabitants are male; women usually get a lot of attention from all the men on-line. (Women who don't want to be continually pestered by requests from strange males to go into private talk mode often use androgynous handles.) Female handles also get attention from other women, since many women on-line are pioneering females in their fields and feminists. Alex apparently came on-line sometime in late 1982 or early 1983 and adopted the handle "Shrink, Inc." His epiphany came one evening when he was in private talk mode with a woman who for some reason mistook him for a female shrink. "The person was open with him in a way that stunned him," according to one of the women—let's call her Laura—who has maintained a friendship with Alex. "What he really found as Joan was that most women opened up to him in a way he had never seen before in all his years of practice. And he realized he could help them."

"He later told me that his female patients had trouble relating to him—they always seemed to be leaving something out," said Janis Goodall, a Berkeley, California, software firm employee who also knew both Joan and Alex. "Now he could see what it was." (Despite their similar recollections, Goodall is in the opposite camp from Laura, and says: "For someone supposedly dedicated to helping people, I think he rampaged through all of our feelings with despicable disregard.") At some point after "Shrink, Inc.'s" inadvertent plunge into sisterhood, Joan was born.

According to both Goodall and Laura (both of whom are disabled themselves), Alex has a back condition, "arthritis of the spine or a calcium deposit of some kind," according to Goodall, " which causes him discomfort, and has the potential, but *not* the probability of putting him in a wheelchair someday." Goodall added that Alex later defended his choice of a disabled persona by claiming that he "wanted to find out how disabled people deal with it." Others on-line believe that Joan's handicaps were a way both to shroud her real identity and aggrandize her heroic stature.

If Joan began spontaneously, she soon became a far more conscious creation, complete with electronic mail drop, special telephone line, and almost novelistically detailed biography (although she sometimes told different versions to different people). She was, by my own recollection and by the accounts of everyone interviewed, an exquisitely wrought character. For starters, she had guts. (She had once, before the accident, driven alone across the interior of Iceland as a way to cure her agoraphobia.) She had travelled everywhere, thanks to money left to her by her family's textile mill fortune. She lived alone (although neighbours checked on her and helped her with errands) and was a model independent female. In fact, Joan was quite a feminist. It was she who suggested the formation of a women's issues group within CompuServe, and she actively recruited members. Several women had relationships with Joan in which they referred to each other as "sister."

Joan was earthy, too, and spoke easily about sex. One woman remembers hearing at length about Joan's abortion at age 16; another recalls having a long conversation about Joan's decision not to embark on a particular course of spinal surgery that might relieve her leg pain, but "would also affect her clitoral nerve, and she wouldn't do that." She was bisexual. Although her family had been religious (she told some people that her parents were ministers), she herself was an ardent atheist who liked to engage religious people in debate. She was also a grass-smoker who frequently confessed to being a little stoned if you encountered her late at night. Her usual greeting was a flashy, flamboyant "Hi!!!!!!!!!!!!"

Interestingly, the two people who knew Joan and also met Alex in person say that their surface personalities were opposite. Alex is Jewish. He almost never drinks or smokes pot although one of his medical specialties is pharmacology). He is a workaholic whose American Psychiatric Association biography reports wide publication in his field. "Joan was wild and zingy and flamboyant and would do anything you dared her to," notes Laura. "A part of Alex wanted to be like that, but he's actually quite intellectual and shy." Adds Janis Goodall: "Alex has a great deal of trouble expressing his emotions. There are long silences, and then he'll say, 'uh-huh, uh-huh'—just like a shrink."

Above all, Joan was a larger-than-life exemplary disabled person. At the time of her accident, she had been scheduled to teach a course at a major New York medical school (in fact, the teaching hospital that Alex is affiliated with as a psychiatrist). Ironically, Joan noted, the course dealt with many of the same neurological impairments that she herself now suffered. One of Joan's goals was eventually to resume her career as if the accident had never happened—and when I first knew her, she was embarked on an ambitious plan to employ a computer in the classroom to help her teach. The idea was that Joan would type her lecture into a computer, which would then be either magnified on a classroom screen or fed into student terminals. To all of us techno-fans and believers in better living through computers, it was a thrilling concept.

Joan was also a militant activist against the dangers of drunken drivers. Early in her convalescence, when she was frequently half out of her mind with anger, she had on several occasions wheeled herself out of her apartment and onto the streets of Manhattan, where she would shout at passing motorists. On one such occasion, police officers in her precinct, upon learning her story, suggested that she put her rage and her talent to more productive use. Joan then began to go out on patrol with a group of traffic cops whose job it was to catch drunken drivers. Joan's role in the project was twofold: (1) as a highly credentialed neuropsychologist, she was better trained than most to detect cars whose drivers had reflex problems caused by too much drinking, and (2) she was willing to serve as an example to drunken drivers of what could befall them if they didn't shape up.

On one of Joan's forays, she met a young police officer named Jack Carr. As he and Joan spent more time together, he came to appreciate her spirit in much the same way the rest of us had. They fell in love—much to the distress of Jack's mother, who thought he was throwing his life away. (Joan's on-line friends were heartened to learn much later that Mrs. Carr had softened after Joan bought her a lap-top computer, and the two of them learned to communicate in the on-line world where Joan shone so brightly.) Jack occasionally came on-line with Joan, although I remember him as being shy and far less verbal than Joan.

Shortly after I met Joan, she and Jack got married. Joan sent an elaborate and joyous announcement to all her CB pals via electronic mail, and the couple held an on-line reception, attended by more than 30 CompuServe regulars. (On-line parties are not unusual. People just type in all the festive sound effects, from the clink of champagne glasses to the tossing of confetti.) Joan and Jack honeymooned in Cyprus, which, according to Pamela Bowen, a Huntington, West Virginia, newspaper editor, Joan said "was one of the few places she'd never been." Bowen and many of Joan's other on-line friends received postcards from Cyprus. The following year Joan and Jack returned to Cyprus and sent out another batch of cards.

"I remember asking Joan how she would get around on her vacation," recalls Sheila Deitz, associate professor of law and psychology at the University of Virginia. "Joan simply replied that if need be, he'd carry her. He was the quintessential caring, nurturing, loving, sensitive human being"—a Mr. Right who, Deitz adds, exerted enormous pull on the imaginations of all Joan's on-line female friends. In hindsight, Deitz feels, "he was the man Alex would have loved to be"—but in fact could only be in the persona of a woman.

Joan was extraordinarily generous. On one occasion, when Laura was confined to her bed because of her disability and couldn't use her regular computer, Joan sent her a lap-top model—a gift worth hundreds of dollars. On another occasion, when Laura mentioned that no one had ever sent her roses, Joan had two dozen delivered. Marti Cloutier, a 42-year-old Massachusetts woman with grown children, claims that it was Joan who inspired her to start college. "She made me feel I could do it at my age." When it came time for Cloutier to write her first term paper, she was terrified, but Joan helped her through it, both in terms of moral support and in the practical sense of sending her a long list of sources. (Ironically, Cloutier's assignment was a psychology paper on multiple personalities. She got an "A" in the course.) On another occasion, Joan told Cloutier that she was going out to hear the "Messiah" performed. When Cloutier enviously mentioned that she loved the music, Joan mailed her the tape. On still another occasion, when Cloutier and her husband were having difficulties over the amount of time that she spent on-line, Joan volunteered to "talk" to him. Cloutier's husband is also a part-time police officer, as Jack ostensibly was, and he and Joan easily developed a rapport. According to Marti Cloutier, Joan was able to persuade him that if his wife had her own friends and interests, it would ultimately be good for their marriage. "She was always doing good things," Cloutier recalls, "and never asking anything in return."

My personal recollections are similar. Once, when Joan and I were chatting on-line late at night, I realized to my great disbelief that a bat had somehow gotten into my apartment and was flapping wildly about, with my cats in crazed pursuit. I got off the computer, managed to catch the bat and get it back out the window—but in the attendant confusion, the windowpane fell out of the window and onto my arm, slicing my wrist and palm. Needless to say, I ended up in the emergency room. Joan dropped me several extremely solicitous notes over the next few weeks, making sure that my stitches were healing properly and that I was over the scare of the accident. Even earlier, around the time I first met Joan, the child of two of my oldest friends was hit by a car and knocked into a coma that was to last for several weeks. Joan had a lot of thoughts about the physiology of comas, as well as about how to deal with hospital staffs, insurance companies, and one's own unraveling psyche in the midst of such a crisis. She offered to set up an on-line meeting with the child's mother. I later heard that Joan had also helped several women who had suicidal tendencies or problems with alcohol.

Still another way that Joan nurtured her friends—hilarious as it sounds in hindsight —was to try to keep CB free of impostors. Although Joan was probably the slickest and most long-lived impostor around, she was hardly the only one; they are a continuing phenomenon on CompuServe and on every other network. Some lie about their ages, others about their accomplishments. Some appropriate the handles of established CB personae and impersonate them. (Unlike ID numbers, handles can be whatever you hoose them to be.) There are also numerous other gender benders, some of them gay)r bisexual men who come on in female guise to straight men. Most aren't hard to spot. Joan herself told several friends she had been fooled by a man pretending to be a gay woman, and she was furious. "One of the first things she ever told me," recalls Janis Goodall, "was to be terribly careful of the people you meet on CB—that things were not always as they seemed."

Sheila Deitz remembers meeting a man on-line who said he was single, but turned out to be not only married in real life, but romancing numerous women on-line. Deitz met the man off-line and realized that his story was full of holes. "Joan was very sympathetic when I told her about it, and we agreed that we didn't want this guy to have the chance to pull this on other women." At some later point, according to Deitz, "Joan created a group called the Silent Circle. It was sort of an on-line vigilante group. She'd ferret out other impostors and confront them and tell them they'd better get their act together."

All of Joan's helping and nurturing and gift-giving, in Deitz's opinion, "goes beyond what any professional would want to do. Alex fostered dependency, really." But at the time, especially among those of us who are able-bodied, there was a certain feeling that here was a person who needed all the support we could give her. Numerous disabled women have since rightly pointed out that our Take-a-Negro-to-Lunch-like attitudes were in fact incredibly patronizing.

The truth is that there was always another side to Joan's need to be needed. She could be obnoxiously grabby of one's time. Because she and I both lived in New York, she once suggested that we talk directly, modem to modem, over our phone lines—thus paying only the cost of a local call instead of CompuServe's $6 an hour connect charges. But as soon as I gave Joan my phone number, I was sorry. She called constantly—the phone would ring, and there would be her modem tone—and she refused to take the hint that I might be busy with work, lover, or children. "Everybody else had the same experience," according to Bob Walter, a New York publisher who also runs CompuServe's Health SIG, where Joan (and later Alex, too) frequently hung out. "She would bombard people with calls." Finally, I had to get blunt—and I felt guilty about it, since Joan, after all, was a disabled woman whose aggressive personality was probably the best thing she had going for her. (My first somewhat sexist thought, when I found out that Joan was really a man, was *Of course! Who else would be so pushy?*)

Joan was sexually aggressive. Every woman I interviewed reported—and was troubled by—Joan's pressuring to have "compusex." This is on-line sex, similar to phone sex, in which people type out their hottest fantasies while they masturbate. (In the age of herpes and AIDS, it has become increasingly popular.) According to one woman, "one time she said she and Jack had been smoking pot and then he'd gone off to work, but she was still high. She told me she had sexual feelings toward me and asked if I felt the same." (Joan's husband, who was conveniently off on undercover detail most nights, supposedly knew about these experiments and wasn't threatened by them, since Joan's partners were "only" other women.) Her m.o., at least with friends, was to establish an intense nonsexual intimacy, and then to come on to them, usually with the argument that compusex was a natural extension of their friendship. In one case, cited by several sources, a woman became so involved as Joan's compusex lover that she was on the verge of leaving her husband.

Interestingly, Joan never came on to me—or, to my knowledge, to any bisexual or gay women. Sheila Deitz is of the opinion that Alex only wanted to have "lesbian" compusex with heterosexual women, those whom he might actually be attracted to in real life. Some straight women apparently cooperated sexually not out of physical desire, but out of supportiveness or even pity—and this too might have been part of Alex's game. But it would be misleading to overemphasize Joan's sexual relationships, since compusex in general tends to be a more casual enterprise on-line than affairs of the heart and mind. Deitz estimates that at least 15 people were "badly burned" by the revelation that Joan was Alex, and that only a few were compusex partners. Lovers or not, most were caught in Joan's emotional web.

Janis Goodall was in a category all her own. Now 37 and cheerfully describing herself as "a semiretired hippie from 'Berserkeley,' California," Goodall met Joan at a time in her life "when I was a real sick cookie—an open raw wound." Goodall was herself coping with the emotional and physical aftermath of an automobile accident. (Although she can walk, Goodall's legs are badly scarred and she suffers from both arthritis and problems of the sciatic nerve.) Beyond her injuries, Goodall was also dealing with a recent separation from her husband and her brother's death. "It was Joan who helped me to deal with those things and to make the transition into the life of a disabled person who accepts that she's disabled."

Joan and Goodall were "fixed up" by other CompuServe regulars after Goodall attended an on-line conference on pain management. When she and Joan arranged via electronic mail to meet in CB, "it was love at first sight. By the end of that first discussion, which lasted a couple of hours, we were honorary sisters. Later, I went around profusely thanking everyone who had told me to contact her."

The fact that Joan's disability was more severe than her own gave her an authority in Goodall's eyes, and her humor was especially therapeutic. "We used to make jokes about gimps who climb mountains. At the time, just to get through the day was a major accomplishment for me, and my attitude was screw the mountains, let me go to the grocery store." The two never became lovers, despite strenuous lobbying on Joan's part. ("I often found myself apologizing for being straight," said Goodall.) But they did become intense, close friends. "I loved her. She could finish my sentences and read my mind."

About a year ago, Joan began telling Goodall about "this great guy" who was also on-line. His name was Alex. He was a psychiatrist, very respected in his field, and an old friend of Joan's, an associate at the hospital. Largely on the strength of Joan's enthusiastic recommendation, Goodall responded with pleasure when Alex invited her into private talk mode. "During our second or third conversation, he began to get almost romantic. He clearly thought I was the greatest thing since sliced bread. I couldn't understand why an established Manhattan psychiatrist his age could be falling so quickly for a retired hippie—although of course I was very flattered. Hey, if a shrink thought I was okay, I was okay!"

Alex told Goodall that he was married, but that this marriage was in trouble. Last winter he invited her to come visit him in New York, and when she said she couldn't afford it, he sent her a round-trip ticket. "He treated me like a queen for the four days I was there," Goodall remembers. "He put me up at a Fifth Avenue hotel—the American Stanhope, right across the street from the Metropolitan Museum. He took me to the Russian Tea Room for dinner, the Carnegie Deli for breakfast, Serendipity for ice cream, museums, everywhere—he even introduced me to his daughters." The two became lovers, although, Goodall says, his back problems apparently affected his ability and their sex life was less than satisfactory. Still, it seems to have been a minor off note in a fabulously romantic weekend. There were also many gifts. Once, Goodall says, "he went out to the corner drugstore to get cigarettes and came back with caviar. I went to Berkeley on Cloud Nine."

Naturally, Goodall had also hoped that she might meet Joan during her New York holiday. None of Joan's other women friends had. Some of the able-bodied women, especially, were hurt that Joan still felt shame about her appearance after so many protestations of love and friendship. According to Sheila Deitz, several people were reported to have arranged rendezvous with Joan and were stood up at the last minute —"although you just know Alex had to be lurking about somewhere, checking them out." Joan would, in each case, claim to have gotten cold feet.

Marti Cloutier says that Joan told her that she had promised her husband that she would never meet any of her on-line friends, but "that *if* she ever changed her mind and decided to meet any of her on-line friends, I would be one of them." In fact, the only CB person who had ever seen Joan was her hospital colleague—Alex. Over the course of Goodall's four days in the city, she and Alex both tried to reach Joan by phone, but without success. Goodall had brought Joan a gift—a stylized, enameled mask of a smiling face. Alex promised to deliver it.

Back in Berkeley, Goodall resumed her on-line relationship with Joan, who had been out of town for the weekend. Joan, however, was anxious to hear every detail of Goodall's trip. Did she think she was in love with Alex? Was the sex good?

It was the disabled women on-line who figured it out first. "Some things about her condition were very farfetched," says one. Says another woman: "The husband, the accomplishments—it just didn't ring true from the beginning." But her own hunch wasn't that Joan was a male or able-bodied; she suspected that she was in fact a disabled woman who was pretending to have a life of dazzling romance and success.

Although such theories, however, ultimately ran up against the real postcards from Cyprus, people began to share their misgivings. "There were too many contradictions," says Bob Walter. "Here was this person who ran off to conferences and to vacations and did all these phenomenal things, but she wouldn't let her friends on-line even see her. After a while, it just didn't compute."

In hindsight, I wonder why I didn't question some of Joan's exploits more closely. As a journalist, I've dealt with the public relations representatives of both the New York City Police Department and the hospital where Joan supposedly taught—and it now seems strange to me that her exploits as drunk-spotter and handicapped professor weren't seized on and publicized. Pamela Bowen says she once proposed Joan's story to another editor, but urged him "to have somebody interview her in person because her story was too good to be true. So my instincts were right from the beginning, but I felt guilty about not believing a handicapped person. I mean, the story *could* have been true." It's possible that many of us able-bodied were playing out our own need to see members of minority groups as "exceptional." The more exceptional a person is, the less the person in the majority group has to confront fears of disability and pain.

Even with the contradictions, the game might have continued much longer if Joan hadn't brought Alex into the picture. According to both Goodall and Laura, Alex has, since his unmasking, said that he realized at some point that he had gotten in over his head and he concocted a plan to kill Joan off. But after seeing how upset people were on one occasion when Joan was off-line for several weeks, supposedly ill, he apparently couldn't go through with it. "It would have been a lot less risky for him to let Joan die," according to Laura, "but he knew it would be cruel." (Meanwhile, someone had called the hospital where Joan was thought to be a patient and been told that no such person was registered.)

What Alex seems to have done instead of commit compu-murder was to buy a new ID number and begin his dual *on-line* identity. Joan increasingly introduced people to her friend Alex, always with great fanfare. We may never know what Alex intended to do with Joan eventually, but there's certainly strong evidence that he was now trying to form attachments as Alex, both off-line (with Goodall) and on.

One might imagine that The Revelation came with a big bang and mass gasps, but this was not the case. According to Walter, months and months went by between the time that some of Joan's more casual acquaintances (he among them) put it together and the time that those of her victims whom they knew heeded their warnings. "People were so invested in their relationships with the female persona that they often just didn't want to know," Walter said. And Joan was also a brilliant manipulator who always had an explanation of why a particular person might be trashing her. "If you ever questioned her about anything," Goodall recalls, "she would get very defensive and turn the topic into an argument about whether you really loved her."

Goodall now acknowledges that she and others ignored plenty of clues, but, as she says, "Let's remember one thing—it was a *pro* doing this."

Deitz, whose off-line work sometimes involves counseling rape victims, agrees that Alex's victims were caught in an intolerable psychological bind. "Alex zeroed in on good people," she says, "although they were often good women at vulnerable stages of their lives." To admit that Joan was a phantom was, in many cases, also to assault the genuine support and self-esteem that they had derived from the relationship. In fact, with only two exceptions—pressuring for compusex and, in Goodall's case, using the Joan persona to pump "girl talk" confidences about Alex—there seems to have been absolutely nothing that Joan did to inspire anyone's rancor. What makes people angry is simply that Joan doesn't exist. "And a lot of what a lot of people were feeling," Deitz adds, "is mourning."

Laura ultimately confronted Joan on-line. She had already "cooled off" her relationship with Joan because of all the inconsistencies in her persona, but while she was suspicious, she had failed to suspect the enormity of the imposture. In February, however, she called another woman close to Joan, who told her she was convinced that Joan was a man. When Laura found Joan on-line later that night, she immediately asked Joan about the charge. Joan at first denied it. It was only after Laura made it clear that "I believed that we're all created after the image of God, and that I loved the person, not the sex, and would continue to do so" that Alex came out.

Laura, who is Catholic and says that her decision to stick with Alex is partially motivated by principles of Christian love, admits that it took her several weeks to "make the transition." Since then, however, she's met Alex in person and come to love him "as my adopted brother instead of my adopted sister."

Marti Cloutier to this day hasn't confronted Alex, although she has talked with him by CB and phone. "I just haven't the courage. Once, when we were talking, he mentioned something about going for a walk that day, and I wrote back that it would be a lovely day for Joan to go for a walk. I was instantly sorry." Cloutier adds: "Joan was a very special person and I loved Joan. I feel as if she died. I can't really say that I love Alex, although maybe I could, in time. Maybe I wouldn't have given him a chance if I'd known from the beginning he was a male. I've tried to sort out my feelings, but it's hard. I know I don't feel like a victim, and I don't understand why some of these other women have gone off the deep end. I don't think he was malicious. What I can't get out of my mind was that he's the same person I've spent hours and hours with."

Shiela Deitz had been introduced on-line to Alex by Joan, but found him "not all that interesting" and never became close to him. But as a visible on-line person known to many as a psychologist, she heard from many of the victims—some of whom formed their own circle of support, and in Goodall's words, "sort of held each other together with bubble gum." Some victims, according to Deitz, were so upset by the chain of events that they stopped using their modems temporarily.

Janis Goodall heard it first over the telephone, from Alex himself who mistakenly assumed that Goodall already knew. "I had just come home from the doctor, and was incredibly frustrated at having just spent $155 to have some asshole neurosurgeon tell me I would have to live with what was bothering me. The phone rang, and it was Alex. The first words out of his mouth were 'yep—it's me.' I didn't know what he was talking about. Then he said: 'Joan and I are the same person.' I went into shock. I mean, I really freaked out—I wanted to jump off a bridge."

Since then, she has communicated with Alex by letter but has refused to see him. She emphatically resents those on-line who have spent efforts trying to "understand" him. She agreed to speak for this interview in part because "although I think this is a wonderful medium, it's a dangerous one, and it poses more danger to women than men. Men in this society are more predisposed to pulling these kinds of con games, and women are predisposed to giving people the benefit of the doubt."

Laura thinks that CompuServe and other networks ought to post warnings to newcomers that they might, in fact, encounter impostors. Others believe that the fault doesn't lie with the medium or the network, but with human frailty. "Blaming CompuServe for impostors makes about as much sense as blaming the phone company for obscene calls," says Bob Walter. CompuServe itself has no official position on the subject, although CompuServe spokesman Richard Baker notes: "Our experience has been that electronic impersonators are found out about as quickly as are face-to-face impersonators. While face-to-face impersonators are found out due to appearance, on-line impersonators are found out due to the use of phrases, the way they turn words, and the uncharacteristic thought processes that go into conversing electronically. I also believe that people are angrier when they've been betrayed by an electronic impersonator."

It would have been nice to hear Alex's side of the story. The first time I called his office, I gave only my name (which Alex knows)—not my magazine affiliation or the information that I was working on an article about "our mutual friend Joan." The receptionist asked if I was a patient. Did I want to make an appointment? I had a giddy vision of impersonating one but decided against it. Although I telephoned twice more and identified myself as a journalist, Alex never returned my calls. He has continued his presence on-line, however, even telling Deitz that he planned to form a SIG—on another network—for psychologists and mental health professionals.

Meanwhile, in the aftermath of the Joan/Alex case, soul-searching has run rampant on CompuServe's CB and in certain SIGs. One common thread was that of Eden betrayed.

As one man wrote: "I guess I figured the folks here [on-line] were special . . . but this has certainly ruptured the 'pink cloud' of CompuServe." A woman wrote back: "The feelings remind me of the ending of my first love relationship. Before that, I didn't realize fully how much hurt could result from loving."

Some of the reactions were frankly conservative—people who were sickened simply by the notion of a man who wanted to feel like a woman. There was much talk of "latency." Others seemed completely threatened by the idea that they might ever have an "inappropriate" response to someone of the "wrong" gender on-line. One message left by a male gravely informed other users that he and his girlfriend had nearly been conned by a male pretending to be a swinging female—until the girlfriend was tipped off by the impersonator's "claiming to be wearing panty hose with jeans." The message prompted an indignant reply by someone who insisted: "I always wear heels with my jeans, and when I wear heels I wear panty hose, and I don't think that is odd, and I am all female!"

But Alex's story raises some other questions that have special resonance for feminists. Chief among them, for me, is why a man has to put on electronic drag to experience intimacy, trust, and sharing. Some women have suggested that the fault is partly ours as women—that if Alex had approached us as a male, with all of Joan's personality traits, we wouldn't have been open to him. I for one reject that notion—not only because I have several terrific male friends on-line but also because it presumes that men are too fragile to break down stereotypes about themselves. (After all, *we've* spent the last 15 years struggling to prove that we can be strong, independent, and capable.) On the other hand, in Alex's defense, I can't help but appreciate the temptation to experience life in the actual world from the point of view of the other sex. Think of "Tootsie" and "Yentl." Annie Lennox and Boy George. What Alex did was alien, taboo, weird . . . and yet the stuff of cosmic cultural fantasy. Haven't you ever wanted to be a fly on the locker room (or powder room) wall?

Sheila Deitz comments that some on-line transsexualism may be essentially harmless. Where she draws the line—and where I would also—is at the point that such experimentation starts impinging on other people's trust. Joan clearly stepped over that line years ago.

Maybe one of the things to be learned from Alex and Joan is that we have a way to go before gender stops being a major, volatile human organizing principle—even in a medium dedicated to the primacy of the spirit.

I personally applaud those souls on CB who, when asked "R u m or f?" [Are you male or female?], simply answer "yes."

P·A·R·T·IV

4

RISKS-FORUM
Digest Contributions

Les Earnest • John McCarthy • Jerry Hollombe

Date: 25 Feb 89 01:57:48 GMT
From: Les Earnest
Subject: Stanford board censorship

Public accounts of the Stanford bboard censorship case, including the San Jose Mercury News article that appeared in RISKS 8.30, give the impression that the administration's ban on newsgroup rec.humor.funny has been effective. Nothing could be farther from the truth—the "banned" jokes continue to be available on all computers where they were available before and are now more widely read than ever before.

Usenet newsgroups are stored on 9 primary distribution machines at Stanford but are accessed via ethernet from hundreds of computers and workstations on campus. Two of these distribution machines were affected by the administration's ban on rec.humor.funny. The rest of the system, which I organized several years ago, still carries all newsgroups.

Since the "ban" began, every message from rec.humor.funny has been cross-posted to another bboard at Stanford (su.etc) that goes to all machines, including those that are supposed to be censored. There has been no move so far by the administration to deal with this "civil disobedience."

Interestingly enough, the bureaucrats who decided to ban rec.humor.funny didn't have the technical expertise to carry out their intentions, so they came to the Computer Science

Department for help. This help was provided even though the individual involved disagreed with what they were doing.

The Usenet primary feed for Stanford is under the control of the Computer Science Department. There was a plan to turn control over to the administration but that plan has now been shelved. The Computer Science faculty voted this week to oppose newsgroup censorship.

Stanford's President Kennedy, who approved the original censorship decision, is now carefully dancing around the issue and has agreed that the Faculty Senate should review and decide on what the University's policy should be. It appears likely that the Senate will agree with the Computer Science Department.

Date: 26 Feb 89 1343 PST
From: John McCarthy
Subject: Stanford bboard censorship

The following statement was passed unanimously at a meeting of the Computer Science Department faculty on Tuesday, Feb 21, 1989.

Statement of Protest about the AIR Censorship of rec.humor.funny.

Computer scientists and computer users have been involved in making information resources widely available since the 1960s. Such resources are analogous to libraries. The newsgroups available on various networks are the computer analog of magazines and partial prototypes of future universal computer libraries. These libraries will make available the information resources of the whole world to anyone's terminal or personal computer.

Therefore, the criteria for including newsgroups in computer systems or removing them should be identical to those for including books in or removing books from libraries. For this reason, and since the resource requirements for keeping newsgroups available are very small, we consider it contrary to the function of a university to censor the presence of newsgroups in University computers. We regard it as analogous to removing a book from the library. To be able to read anything subject only to cost limitations is an essential part of academic freedom. Censorship is not an appropriate tool for preventing or dealing with offensive behavior.

We therefore think that AIR and SDC should rescind the purge of rec.humor.funny. The Computer Science Department has also decided not to censor Department Computers.

Date: 27 Feb 89 23:48:37 GMT
From: Gerald Hollombe[1]
Subject: Censorship

This is the same silly, emotional argument raised every time some form of public or semi-public media refuses to carry someone's pet hobby horse. If you throw out all the emotional baggage about "freedom of speech" and "censorship," Stanford's decision not to carry rec.humor.funny is no more illegal, unconstitutional or censorious then their (de facto) decision not to sell hard-core pornography in the Student's Store.

Only governments can commit censorship, by prohibiting all access to a set of facts. Rec.humor.funny still exists and is still accessible. Those at Stanford who wish to continue accessing it will simply have to sign up with a public access Unix site. (I believe the WELL is conveniently close, as are one or two free-access sites.) Stanford is well within its rights to refuse to spend campus resources to support it.

---

[1] Author's postscript, 1990: It's true only governments can commit censorship, and Stanford was within its rights to drop rec.humor.funny. However, whether that was appropriate behavior for an institution that exists for the dissemination of facts and information is open to debate. In my article, I object to the characterization of Stanford's actions as censorship, which is not meant to imply that I approve of those actions.

P·A·R·T·IV

5

A New Paradigm for Science

Peter J. Denning

Most of us think of science as a process for making inquiries about phenomena and for evaluating hypotheses generated by those inquiries. The results are organized bodies of knowledge in various disciplines. Besides its experimental side, the scientific process has an analytic side, which seeks to develop mathematical models of phenomena, and a computational side, which uses the models to make predictions for later experimental validation.

But science is not only the knowledge in various disciplines and the processes for producing that knowledge; it is groups of people working together in each discipline. They are the institutional memory, the selection mechanism, deciding what science is and is not. The knowledge of science and the expertise of science live in the people of science.

This larger view brings into focus an entity I will call the knowledge base of science, which is the sum total of all knowledge and know-how of all the disciplines. Here the term knowledge means something more dynamic than the organized body of facts and data about phenomena; it means "living information," the ability of people to draw inferences from facts and data and to invent new hypotheses. Similarly, the term know-how refers to more than processes and methods; it involves skills that can be developed only through experience and training. Only the facts, data, and algorithms of science can be recorded in books and other media; the rest of the knowledge and know-how lives in the people of science and in their conversations with one another. It is important to notice the distinction between the recorded part of the knowledge base and the newly created, living part.

How large is the science knowledge base? Its enormity can be estimated from the number of working scientists, the total funds expended on R&D, and the number of

Reprinted with permission of Sigma Xi: "A New Paradigm for Science," by P.J. Denning, *American Scientist* **75**, Nov/Dec. 1987, pp. 572–573.

scholarly publications. According to the National Science Foundation, there are about 825,000 R&D scientists and engineers in the United States (1). About 300,000 persons each year receive bachelor's or other first professional degrees in science and engineering. The corresponding figures worldwide are two or three times larger. There is an element of truth in the quip that half the scientists who ever lived are alive today.

As for expenditures, requests for R&D in the US government's budget for 1988 amount to almost $60 billion, and when industry's R&D is included, the total expenditure is approximately $120 billion. The competition for these funds has been keen, with the total number of scientists and the average request per scientist growing faster than the pot. And as for publications, David Walker estimates that in the United States there are approximately 1,500 journals that publish primary research (2).

Who can keep up with the rate at which information is produced? In every field, senior people say they cannot stay on top of their specialties, and junior people say there is no reward for learning anything outside a narrow area. The number of journals, reports, preprints, and conferences creates a demand for attention far in excess of the time that one can devote to them. Furthermore, it is very hard to locate information about projects related to one's own work. Competition among researchers seeking fame or fortune has bred secrecy rather than openness. Highly specialized subgroups form easily and take on lives of their own: a few hundred people with common interests can publish their own journal without outside contact. Don Swanson has even documented a case where two groups produced an extensive literature on the same medical phenomenon without knowledge of each other (3).

The conclusion is inescapable: production of scientific information is exceeding anyone's ability to assimilate and use it. The body of scientific information is so far beyond the grasp of individuals and small groups that it is becoming ever more fragmented and disorganized. What can be done?

To support the dissemination and use of recorded knowledge, several computing technologies can help. Databases can manage information bibliographies, access to facts and data, and cross-referencing. Algorithms can package procedures in forms that can be used reliably by those who do not know their details. Expert systems can store and apply rules for processes of inquiry. Local area networks can link databases, algorithms, and expert systems with other processors such as simulators, statistical analyzers, and equation solvers. Concurrent processing can support "agents" that automatically seek out information while their owners are occupied with other tasks. And finally, heuristic searches can help sift through databases looking for new patterns and correlations.

But this use of computing technology is not enough. It deals only with packaged and recorded knowledge, ignoring the information and expertise that live in people. A new paradigm is needed to support the entire science knowledge base.

The new paradigm will place people in a central role, supporting their conversations and collaborations. It will use networks of computers to nurture networks of people. Here the term network refers not merely to a data channel, but to all the individuals, institutions, and services that must communicate in pursuit of science. The network augments communication and sharing; it is both a learning device for novices and a tool kit for experts.

Computer networks that nurture networks of people are the culmination of a process

Recording and creating knowledge

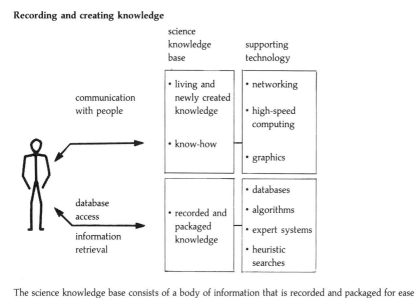

The science knowledge base consists of a body of information that is recorded and packaged for ease of retrieval and use, and a body of information constantly in the process of being brought forth in unpredictable ways from people's experience and knowledge. An individual gains access to the recorded and packaged part by accessing and retrieving information—from journals, libraries, or databases—and to the creative part by communicating with the people in whom it lives. Technological support for the recorded part is based on mass storage and fast algorithms for retrieving and processing. Technological support for the creative part is based on networking interpreted in the broad sense of interchange and collaboration among people, and also on high speed computation and graphics. The new paradigm for science will integrate computing technologies into the processes of scientific investigation. Indeed, these technologies are essential to surmount the growing glut of scientific information.

of evolution that can be said to have five stages: (1) file transfer, (2) remote connections, (3) distributed computation, (4) real-time collaboration, and (5) coherent function. At the first stage, a network is able to transfer files of information among computers, but without guaranteeing delivery time; this stage is sufficient to support electronic mail, bulletin boards, news services and jointly authored papers. At the second stage, the network enables a user to connect to remote resources, such as instruments, computers, or databases, and employ them in real time as if they were local. At the third stage, the network is able to support distributed computations that include computing processes and resources at widely separated nodes; an example is a user interface process on a workstation, connected to a numerical process on a supercomputer, connected in turn to a graphics display system. At the fourth stage, the network directly supports collaboration by permitting real-time conferences of users at different workstations, who can communicate as if they were gathered around one workstation—that is, they can tap into a "common universe" in which they can talk, point to and share objects, edit and run programs, and examine outputs. At the fifth stage, the network is a coherent system comprising people and the resources contributed by them; each person can look in at this world from his workstation. The network will provide services to help people locate, use, and contribute resources, and to translate between the terminologies of the disciplines.

Most personal computer networks today are at the file-transfer stage, offering only primitive remote connections. The ARPANET operates at the remote-connection stage and supports prototype subsystems for distributed computing and real-time conferences (4). No existing network is in the final stage of evolution, but government agencies are struggling at the beginning of it—an internet, a loose federation of community networks sharing common protocols and gateways. The internet establishes cooperation between communities, not a new centralized institution (5).

The evolution of networking toward a worldwide system will facilitate the transition to the new paradigm of science. Conversations, collaborations, and professional relationships will spring up among participants around the world. Search agents will scan knowledge bases around the network, looking for common patterns or new patterns, and report their findings to researchers. New ways to disseminate knowledge will come into existence, the definition of publication will change, intellectual property rights will be sharpened, and there may even be means to evaluate submitted "papers" before releasing them for distribution. The new paradigm will indeed permit us to stand on one another's shoulders rather than step on one another's toes.

Let me emphasize that the new paradigm is not merely a library function. Libraries are important repositories for recorded and packaged knowledge, but they do not support the critical function of networking. They will participate in the new paradigm but will not dominate it.

When computing technologies support both the recorded and living parts of the knowledge base, scientists will have new means of building, creating, storing, accessing, exchanging, assimilating, integrating, and using knowledge and know-how. Besides serving science, these technologies will promote closer communication among all peoples, supporting everything from business transactions to professional relationships. And any technology that puts people into closer communication cannot help but be a stabilizing influence in a jittery world.

We stand at the threshold of a new era of science. The glut of information is pushing us over that threshold, and information-processing technology is pulling us.

References

1. L. Lederman (1987). Science and technology policies and priorities: A comparative analysis. *Science* 237: 1125–33.
2. D. A. Walker (1987). Management of scholarly publications. *Scholarly Publishing* 18(3): 189–96.
3. D. R. Swanson (1987). Two medical literatures that are logically but not bibliographically connected. *J. ASIS* 38(4): 228–33.
4. P. J. Denning (1985). Computer networks. *Am. Sci.* 73: 127–29.
5. P. J. Denning (1985). Supernetworks. *Am. Sci.* 73: 225–27.

P·A·R·T · IV

6

Information Society and Global Science

James R. Beniger

To say that the advanced industrial world has become an information society has already become a cliché. In not only the United States but also Canada, Western Europe, and Japan, the bulk of the labor force now works primarily at informational tasks, including such readily identifiable ones as systems analysis and computer programming, while wealth comes increasingly from informational goods such as microprocessors and from informational services such as data processing.

Both the timing and direction of this great societal transformation can be measured using U.S. labor force statistics. In 1880, fewer than 7 percent of American workers produced informational goods and services, compared to the nearly 45 percent in agriculture. By far the fastest growth in information work came during the 1880s, when the sector nearly doubled to more than 12 percent of the work force. By 1930, the information sector had doubled again to occupy a quarter of all labor, compared to 35 percent in other industry and 20 percent each in other services and in agriculture.

Today, with many of those born in 1930 still in the labor force, America's information sector has doubled once again. Roughly half of us now earn our living from informational products, compared to less than 30 percent from other services, 20 percent from other industry, and scarcely 2 percent from agriculture.[1] The manufacture of noninformational goods—the so-called smokestack industries—once the backbone of the American economy, may employ fewer than 15 percent of our workers by the end of this decade, even as farm work all but disappears.

James R. Beniger, "Information Society and Global Science." *The Annals of the American Academy of Political and Social Science* **495** (January 1988), pp. 14–28. Copyright 1988 by Sage Publications. Reprinted by permission of Sage Publications, Inc.

An Emerging Global Sector

Parallel developments have transformed the economies of at least a dozen advanced industrial countries. A Japanese study finds that informational goods and services accounted for 35.4 percent of that nation's gross national product (GNP) in 1979, up from 21.3 percent in 1960; the information sector of Japan's work force increased to 37.7 from 21.3 percent over the same period.[2] Interpolating from comparable U.S. data,[3] information rose to 34.3 from 29.6 percent of GNP and to 53.1 from 42.1 percent of the American work force during the same years. At least by the metric of GNP—though not labor force composition—the Japanese data suggest that that nation passed the United States as the leading information society sometime in 1974 or 1975.

A study by the Organization for Economic Cooperation and Development of its member nations in 1978 and 1979 finds the information sector ranging from 14.8 percent of GNP in Australia to 24.8 percent in France and the United States.[4] These percentages include only the primary information sector, that is, only the informational goods and services sold directly to the market, excluding the roughly equal dollar amount produced and consumed internally by noninformation firms and by governments. This study also measures the spread of information work through the labor forces of advanced industrial countries, using data for individual years between 1970 and 1978: 27.5 percent in Finland, 29.6 in Japan, 32.1 in France, 32.2 in Austria, 33.2 in West Germany, 34.9 in Sweden, 35.6 in Great Britain, 39.9 in Canada, and 41.1 in the United States.

These and similar studies from three continents have identified a historic transformation of human society: the emergence of information as a major independent sector of the global economy. Unlike all other societies we know, in some 50,000 years of human history, a dozen or so nations now depend on informational goods and services more than on hunting and gathering, agriculture and mining, or noninformational manufacturing and commerce. The processing of matter and energy, it would seem, has begun to be overshadowed by the processing of information.

But why? Among the multitude of things that human beings value, why should it be information, embracing both goods and services, that has come to dominate the world's largest and most advanced economies? And why now? Information plays an important role in all human societies, after all—why in only this century should it emerge as a distinct and critical commodity?

---

[1] James R. Beniger, *The Control Revolution: Technological and Economic Origins of the Information Society* (Cambridge, MA: Harvard University Press, 1986), pp. 21–24.

[2] Seisuke Komatsuzaki *et al.*, *An Analysis of Information Economy in Japan from 1960 to 1980* (Tokyo: Research Institute of Telecommunications and Economics, n.d.).

[3] Michael Rogers Rubin and Mary Taylor Huber, *The Knowledge Industry in the United States, 1960–1980* (Princeton, NJ: Princeton University Press, 1986), pp. 19, 196.

[4] Organization for Economic Cooperation and Development, *Information Activities, Electronics and Telecommunications Activities, Impact on Employment, Growth, and Trade* (Paris: Organization for Economic Cooperation and Development, 1981).

The Control Revolution

Answers lie in what I call the Control Revolution,[5] a concentration of abrupt changes in the technological and economic arrangements by which information is collected, stored, processed, and communicated and through which formal or programmed decisions might effect societal control. From its origins in the later decades of the nineteenth century, the Control Revolution has continued to this day, sustained—in its more recent stages—by the appearance of business computers in the 1950s, microprocessors in the 1970s, and personal computers in the 1980s, as well as by countless other technological developments.

To glimpse the future course of this change, the technological counterpart to the transformation of the American labor force, it might be useful to reflect on its initial cause. The Control Revolution began as a response to rapid industrialization after 1830 and to the resulting crisis in control of the material economy.[6] Before the application of steam power, even the largest and most developed economies ran literally at a human pace, with processing speeds enhanced somewhat by draft animals and by wind and water power, but still well within the information-processing capabilities of individual human brains to control. System-level control could be maintained by relatively flat bureaucratic structures.

By far the greatest impact of industrialization, from the perspective of societal control, was to speed up the entire material economy, the system for the extraction, processing, and distribution of commodities from environmental input to final consumption. Almost overnight, with the harnessing of steam power, material flows could be moved ten to a hundred times faster, day and night and in virtually any weather. This brought widespread breakdowns of control: fatal train wrecks, misplacement of freight cars, loss of shipments, inability to maintain high rates of inventory turnover. What began as a crisis of safety on the railroads in the early 1840s spread to distribution—commission trading and wholesaling—by the 1850s, to production—rail mills and other metal-making and metalworking industries—in the late 1860s, and finally to the marketing of vast outputs of continuous-processing industries—flour, soap, cigarettes, matches, canned goods, and photographic film—in the early 1880s.

Even the word "revolution" seems barely adequate to describe what followed: the development, within the span of a single lifetime, of virtually every basic information-processing and communication technology still in use a century later. These included telegraphy and rotary power printing (1840s), postage stamps and a transatlantic cable (1850s), paper money and modern bureaucracy (1860s), the typewriter, telephone, and switching exchange (1870s), punchclock, cash register, and Linotype (1880s), motion pictures, magnetic tape recording, and four-function calculators (1890s), and electronic broadcasting (1900s). Just as the Industrial Revolution had marked a historical discontinuity in the ability to harness energy, the Control Revolution marked a similarly dramatic leap in the ability to exploit information.

But why does the Control Revolution continue to this day, a century and a half since

---

[5] Beniger, *Control Revolution*, esp. pt. 3.
[6] Ibid., chap. 6.

the onset of rapid industrialization? Several forces seem to sustain its momentum. Energy utilization, processing speeds, and control technologies have continued to coevolve in a positive spiral, advances in any one factor causing—or at least enabling—improvements in the other two. Additional energy has increased not only the speed of material processing and transportation but also their volume and predictability, which in turn have further increased both the demand for control and returns on new applications of information technology. Information processing and flows themselves need to be controlled, so that information technologies must continue to be applied at higher and higher layers of control—certainly an ironic twist to a Control Revolution.

Enter the Computer

Only through appreciation of the Control Revolution, I believe, can we hope to understand otherwise mysterious aspects of the history of the computer, such as why so many of the machine's major components had been anticipated by mid-nineteenth century. As early as 1833, Charles Babbage had designed his steam-powered Analytical Engine with the essential components of a digital computer: punch-card input and programming, internal memory ("store"), a central processing unit ("mil"), and output to be printed or set into type. Far from the ideas of a visionary mathematician, as they are often portrayed, Babbage's design followed by only six years his work on control of the British postal system and by one year the publication of his *On the Economy of Machinery and Manufactures*, a pioneering treatise on industrial control based on exhaustive empirical study—later reprinted as the first text on operations research. Six years after beginning work on his Analytical Engine, Babbage turned back to the crisis of industrial control in a series of studies of the great Western Railway.[7]

A century later in 1937, Howard Aiken, a former Westinghouse engineer teaching applied mathematics at Harvard, drafted a proposal arguing that scientists needed more powerful computing.[8] Inspired by Babbage's work on industrial control, Aiken included as an example the purposive monitoring and control of the material economy, what he termed the "science of mathematical economy"; his Harvard colleague, economist Wassily Leontief, had published a formal theory of input-output analysis toward the same goal earlier in the year, work that would culminate in a Nobel Prize in 1973. As an appendix to the proposal that, funded by IBM, would in six years yield the electromechanical Mark I, Aiken included a gloss of Babbage's 1833 design—proof enough of the intellectual continuity of the Control Revolution over the intervening century. Indeed, Mark I was in many ways inferior to Babbage's design: the new machine lacked a differentiated processing structure and any general-purpose central processing unit.

---

[7] Anthony Hyman, *Charles Babbage: Pioneer of the Computer* (Princeton, NJ: Princeton University Press, 1982).

[8] Howard H. Aiken, "Proposed Automatic Calculating Machine," in *Origins of Digital Computers: Selected Papers*, 3rd ed., ed. Brian Randell (New York: Springer-Verlag, 1982), pp. 195–201.

The Origins of Scientific Computing

The electronic numerical integrator and calculator (ENIAC), a fully functional electronic machine that ran its first program in November 1945 at the Moore School of Electrical Engineering, University of Pennsylvania, is often cited as the first scientific computer.[9] If we view computing as only one of several major developments in the emergence of the information society, however, ENIAC appeared closer to the midpoint than to the beginning. The machine ought to be seen as the culmination of work on generalized information-processing technology begun with the Control Revolution and interrupted by World War II.[10] Consider the intellectual as well as technological momentum the Control Revolution had gathered in the final prewar years. In 1936, Alonzo Church, Emil Post, and Alan Turing published separate papers equating decision and computability procedures; in Berlin, Konrad Zuse began to build a universal calculator that used binary numbers, floating decimal point calculation, and the programming rules of Boolean logic. In 1937, Claude Shannon published a paper equating logic and circuity; Aiken and John Atanasoff worked out separate designs for calculating machines; George Stibitz built the first binary relay adder. In 1938, the Foxboro Company devised an electronic analog computer; Zuse completed a mechanical prototype of his hardware. In 1939, three seminal machines—Atanasoff's electronic calculator, Zuse's binary relay computer, and Stibitz's AT&T Model I—were all completed; IBM agreed to build Aiken's Mark I.

Even cybernetics, usually considered a postwar development, was largely anticipated in a paper published in 1940 by a British scientist, W. Ross Ashby. By the end of 1940, Stibitz had successfully demonstrated telecomputing and Atanasoff had begun conversations with John Mauchly that would help to shape ENIAC. Even though it would not appear for another six years, ENIAC remained less modern—in some respects—than the prewar machines: it used decimal rather than binary numbers and hence could not exploit Boolean logic, lacked a general-purpose central processing unit, and only partially distinguished processing from memory.

Twenty years before the first tube glowed in ENIAC, America's top four information-processing companies, with total revenues—in 1928 dollars—exceeding $150 million, were Remington Rand, National Cash Register, Burroughs, and IBM—names still recognizable as forebears of three of today's top five.[11] The companies owe their origins to four distinct innovations in the information machines of the 1870s and 1880s: the Remington typewriter, the cash register, the printing adder of William Burroughs, and Herman Hollerith's punch-card tabulating equipment. We must look here, to the technological and economic innovations of 1870–1900, and not to ENIAC and other developments of the 1940s, to find the truly revolutionary origins of the information society and of computing in science.

---

[9] John G. Brainerd, "Genesis of the ENIAC," *Technology and Culture*, 17(3): 482–88 (1976).

[10] Beniger, *Control Revolution*, chap. 9.

[11] Stan Augarten, *Bit by Bit: An Illustrated History of Computers* (New York: Ticknor and Fields, 1984), p. 183.

Telematics and Science

Today the most revolutionary impact of computing on science comes with the continuing proliferation—since the early 1970s—of microprocessing technology. Perhaps most important, at least in terms of its impact on science as a social system, has been the progressive convergence of information-processing and communications technologies —including mass media, telecommunications, and computers—in a single infrastructure of control.

A 1978 report commissioned by the president of France—an instant bestseller in that country and abroad—likened the growing interconnection of information-processing, communications, and control technologies throughout the world to an alteration in "the entire nervous system of social organization."[12] The same report introduced the neologism "telematics" for this most recent stage of the information society, although similar words had been suggested earlier, such as "compunications"—from "computing" and "communications"—by Anthony Oettinger and his colleagues at Harvard's Program on Information Resources Policy.[13]

Development of telematics in science also stems from the consolidation of the Control Revolution in computing in the late 1930s. By October 1939, George Stibitz, a Bell Laboratories physicist, had completed his Model I, a 450-relay calculating machine that input and output via teletype. The following September, at the annual meeting of the American Mathematical Society at Dartmouth College, Stibitz installed several teletype terminals and linked them—via Bell's long-distance system—to the Model I in Manhattan, some 200 miles away. Conference participants used this system to solve the complex-number equations for which the Model I had been hardwired—the first use of remote computing via telephone that would characterize the emergent "telematic society" thirty years later.[14]

Crucial to modern telematics is increasing digitalization, the coding into discontinuous values—usually two-valued or binary—of information varying continuously in time, whether a telephone conversation, a radio broadcast, or a television picture. Because most modern computers process digital information, the progressive digitalization of mass media and telecommunications content begins to blur earlier distinctions between the communication of information and its processing—as implied by the term "communications"—as well as between people and machines. Digitalization makes communication from persons to machines, between machines, and even from machines to persons as easy as it is between persons. Also blurred are the distinctions between information types: numbers, words, pictures, and sounds, and eventually tastes, odors, and possibly even more complex sensations, all might one day be stored, processed, and communicated in the same digital form.

---

[12] Simon Nora and Alain Minc, *The Computerization of Society: A Report to the President of France* (Cambridge, MA: MIT Press, 1980), p. 3.

[13] Anthony G. Oettinger, "Compunications in the National Decision-Making Process," in *Computers, Communications, and the Public Interest*, ed. Martin Greenberger (Baltimore, MD: Johns Hopkins University Press, 1971), pp. 73–114.

[14] Evelyn Loveday, "George Stibitz and the Bells Labs Relay Computers." *Datamation*, 23(9): 80–85 (1977).

Through digitalization and telematics, currently scattered information—in diverse forms—will be progressively transformed into a generalized medium for processing and exchange by a global system, much as, centuries ago, the institution of common currencies and exchange rates began to transform local markets into a single world economy. We might expect the implications to be as profound for global science as the institution of money was for world trade. Indeed, digital electronic systems have already begun to replace money itself in many informational functions, only the most recent stage in a growing systemness of world society dating back at least to the Commercial Revolution of the fifteenth century.

Societal Choices: The Soviet Case

Analogies between the integrative functions of digitalization and money seem particularly appropriate in the case of the Soviet Union, which may be as suspicious of telematics in its own society as it has been ideologically opposed to market control of its economy. Despite the fact that the Soviet computing industry covers the full range of products and, at least in this aspect, ranks behind only the United States and Japan, the Soviet Union still has not successfully mass-produced most of its computer devices.[15] Although "the Soviets have every capability to be as intellectually advanced as we are in computing," according to William McHenry, a Georgetown University specialist in Soviet and East European computing,[16] the country's computing infrastructure has developed slowly compared to those of other information societies, as has the range of Soviet applications.

This lag in telematic development is particularly ironic in historical perspective.[17] Soon after the Bolshevik revolution, Soviet economists Krassin and Grinko had already begun to develop the scientific theory of central economic planning and control based on continuous data collection, processing, and analysis. By the time Joseph Stalin had fully consolidated his leadership in 1929, Russia had the third largest amount of data-processing equipment—Hollerith card punches, sorters, and tabulators—in the world, behind only the United States and Germany. The Soviet "Gosplan" or five-year plans, according to an IBM-sponsored history of computing, "implied a level of control that could hardly have been attempted without machines for the rapid assessment of statistics."[18] By 1938, the Soviet mathematician L. V. Kantorovich had begun to develop the linear programming theory that remains central to military and industrial planning and control by computer in all industrial nations to this day.

With this early lead, and with a secure position as producer of computer hardware, why does the Soviet Union lag behind other advanced industrial nations in telematic development? At least until the rise of Mikhail Gorbachev, with his policies of *glasnost*

[15] William McHenry, "Why Russian Computers Aren't Byting," *Times* (London), 28 July 1986.

[16] W. David Gardner, "To Russia with Love: The Intrigue behind the Soviets' Illegal IBM Installations," *Information WEEK*, 3 Feb. 1987, p. 41.

[17] Beniger, *Control Revolution*, pp. 416–22.

[18] Charles Eames and Ray Eames, *A Computer Perspective* (Cambridge, MA: Harvard University Press, 1973), p. 97.

("openness") and *perestoyka* ("restructuring"), most Western explanations centered on the Soviet leadership's reluctance to allow greater access to information, with the decentralization of control that would result. This overlooks the probability that state control of information might still be maintained simply by controlling a few basics: paper, photocopy machinery and supplies, computer printers, ribbons, and other printing supplies. At Moscow's huge Lenin Library, for example, photocopying is limited to 2000 sheets a day for the entire facility, portable computers are banned as "copying devices," and admission permits have been revoked for attempting to bring a Western newspaper clipping into the building.[19]

A more likely explanation of the Soviet Union's lag in telematics would appear to be its lack of a considerable spectrum of possible computer applications—including communications, entertainment, education, and consumer goods—that foster development of hardware and software in other advanced industrial countries. Even after a twenty-year drive to introduce computer-based information systems into Soviet management, 92 percent of the country's approximately 44,000 industrial enterprises still send their data out to a Central Statistical Administration for processing. Organizations that do have their own computers use them almost entirely for batch processing and the production of periodic statistical reports, thereby limiting possibilities that telematics might be integrated with day-to-day activities.[20]

It might seem that the Soviet Union's military and surveillance infrastructure alone would produce sufficient demand for telematic development. Although computer use by the Soviet military and intelligence communities is indeed great, Seymour Goodman of the University of Arizona, currently studying the prospects of a Soviet information society, finds that this demand cannot alone provide an adequate material base for the larger societal transformation.[21]

Perhaps new Soviet leadership initiatives, such as the Interbranch Scientific Technological, a kind of interministry research and development collective, or the State Committee for Informatics—a variant on "telematics"—and Computer Technology, with greater control over the country's computer industry, will help to promote the country's telematic development. They will not do so, however, without difficulties arising from the nature of control as a political as well as a technological problem. "Turning certain functions over to the computer presents a risk for the elite," McHenry writes of Soviet society, "the elite whose unique influence is based in part on controlling just a bit more information than subordinates do."[22]

The Soviet case shows that the information society does not spring spontaneously from advanced industrialization. Technological possibilities for control present societal choices, which are themselves subject to political control. It remains to be seen whether

---

[19] Nicholas A. Ulanov, "Soviet Fear of the Knowledge Revolution," *Wall Street Journal*, 13 May 1986, p. 32.

[20] William K. McHenry and Seymour E. Goodman, "MIS in Soviet Industrial Enterprises: The Limits of Reform from Above," *Communications of the ACM*, 29(11): 1034–43 (Nov. 1986).

[21] Seymour E. Goodman, *The Information Technologies in Soviet Society: Problems and Prospects* (Tucson: University of Arizona, Department of Management Information Systems, 1986).

[22] McHenry, "Why Russian Computers Aren't Byting."

the Soviet Union can compete as a world economic leader without the frenetic development of microprocessing, computing, and telematics that seems increasingly to energize
other information economies. It also remains to be seen whether Soviet scientists can
maintain their preeminence, outside of the telematics, as that technology increasingly
transforms science itself into one world system.

Control Problems in Science

How important is science in the information society? In the classification scheme developed by Marc Porat for the Office of Telecommunications, U.S. Department of
Commerce,[23] information workers are of three types: those whose output is an information product, constituting about 31 percent of U.S. information workers by compensation; those who process or move information within firms, constituting 64 percent; and
those who operate information technology, who constitute 5 percent. Virtually all
scientists can be found in the first category, which might be further divided into two
subcategories: knowledge producers—including scientists—and knowledge distributors
—educators, writers, editors, and the like.

Knowledge producers, about 19.0 percent of U.S. information workers by compensation, include scientific and technical workers—8.0 percent—and those who provide
private information services like counseling and advising—11.0 percent. The former
category includes not only workers in the sciences—2.4 percent—but also in engineering
—5.4 percent. When we use the term "science," therefore, we mean roughly 2.0 to 8.0
percent—exclusive to inclusive—of all information workers by compensation. The
importance to the information society of knowledge production—of which science and
engineering constitute 40 percent—is obviously much greater.

Before digitalization and telematics transform science into a global system, science
—much like the nineteenth-century railroads—will have to resolve certain problems of
control. Other authors in this volume discuss potential barriers to the global system-
atization of science, including different languages—scientific and computer as well as
natural—international politics, national information policies, laws concerning intellectual
property and privacy, incompatibility of systems, and the continuing so-called arms race
between code busters and encryptors.

As such barriers are overcome, science will face an even more challenging crisis of
control, one brought about—ironically enough—by the very efforts intended to ease
scientific communication. This crisis arises from the usually implicit assumption that
science primarily consists—as its most macro level—of a one-way informational flow:
knowledge is created, processed or refined, communicated and utilized, possibly to create
still more knowledge. Informed by this model, much computerization of information
systems slights the reciprocal or feedback signals by which scientific outputs are controlled. Such feedback, perhaps most familiar in the form of scientific citations but also
as reputations of journals, editorial decisions, and a wide range of other such signals, does

[23] Marc Uri Porat, *The Information Economy: Definition and Measurement* (Washington, DC: Department of
Commerce, Office of Telecommunications, 1977), chap. 7.

not represent knowledge produced but does confer status and authority differentially upon knowledge producers.

Exchange authority like that conferred by citation will be crucial to the control of any social system that has not been engineered. It will be crucial in any interorganizational network not under extraorganizational control, for example, but not within any of the constituent organizations, where other more formal lines of authority prevail. Global science, lacking centralized control, must depend on countless loosely knit and continuously shifting networks of individual researchers—most of whom resist outside intervention—in communication that crisscrosses the borders of well over a hundred sovereign nations. Because these scientists work in a wide variety of universities and colleges, technical and trade schools, government and corporate laboratories, public and private research centers and foundations, and other institutions, science must span many organizational and professional boundaries as well.

If this did not present difficulties enough for control of science, science must also transcend political and institutional boundaries in a more problematic sense: for science to exist beyond the contributions of independently wealthy or self-motivated amateur savants—as indeed it did not exist before the last century—the pecuniary rewards of local institutions must somehow be made to depend on contributions to the larger system. How else might science secure the labor of legions of workers, not only to publish and otherwise disseminate information, but also to referee papers and proposals, review books, organize and chair professional meetings, serve as discussants, respond to queries and correspondence, and engage in a host of other relationships with scientists in other organizations and countries? How else might so vast an amount of unpaid labor be obtained to power the global system of science, were not its workers convinced that rewards from their own institutions depend—at least indirectly and in part—on more universal contributions?

Still more problematic, it is not enough merely to energize the system; it must also be motivated at a higher level, that is, controlled toward collective goals. Not only must component organizations reward each worker according to his or her status in the larger scientific community, but such status must differentially accrue to individuals in a way that will serve the global system. Obviously, statuses that characterize more traditional societies—such as statuses based on family, gender, and age—will not be optimal for science. Nor will such ascribed statuses be as responsive to rapid change as will achieved statuses like specialty and rank. Exchange authority as represented by scientific citation, in contrast, cannot only respond to even the most rapid change, but communicates feedback about the value of each discrete output, from each of its potential users, for each of its potential applications, to the system as a whole. A computerization of science that fails to accommodate at least as finely tuned a control medium may experience system crisis—most acutely at the most global levels.

Generalized Media and Status Differentials

Scientific citation not only provides direct feedback about the value of each individual contribution—paper, article, book, piece of correspondence, and so forth—but also serves directly to control total production—the system-level goal—through differential rewards to individuals. Not only are salary, promotion, and other organizational rewards for scientists influenced by citation, but so are less tangible but more universal rewards like standing in the scientific community. Exchange authority as conferred through citation, serves to communicate status across institutional and cultural boundaries, where local organizational symbols—like formal titles and trappings of office—do not translate very well.

Thus citation serves science much as money—as noted by John Stuart Mill during the control crisis of the Industrial Revolution—can serve the political economy.[24] Both money and citation constitute symbolic systems that translate status across social contexts—the sense in which money is said to talk, or even to speak all languages. Like money, citation has several crucial characteristics of generalized symbolic media as first identified by Mill and elaborated by Talcott Parsons:[25] institutionalized function as a measure of value or status, no value in use but only in receipt or exchange, and non-zero-sum character in some contexts—just as money can be spent to create credit, citations can be made without loss to gain credit with those cited through norms of reciprocity.

Other social and control systems that span organizational and disciplinary or professional boundaries outside of science have been empirically shown to be integrated by generalized symbolic media of exchange. Among the educational, social service, legal, and health professions, for example, the concept of a professional referral is not only universally understood but plays a role analogous to that of citations in science.[26]

Higher-status scientists provide more information—they publish more and have wider networks—and receive more citations than do their lower-status colleagues. Analogously, in the four organizational sectors mentioned earlier, physicians and other professionals of higher status tend to supply specialized information in exchange for referrals, while their lower-status colleagues are more likely to serve as referral sources and information sinks in the same specialized system. In both the scientific and the other professional systems, in other words, movements of system information and referrals or citations communicate identical and opposite status relationships: information is better to give, while referrals or citations are better to receive, and these pairs of valued commodities tend to be exchanged directly between pairs of individuals.

Most critical for control of both systems is a seemingly anomalous finding: the pattern of exchange associated with higher status in the larger interorganizational systems— information source, citation or referral sink—is precisely opposite of the pattern having higher status within any of the constituent organizations—referral or acknowledgment source, information sink. Within a leading scientist's own organization, that is, the scientist expects to receive valuable information from his or her research assistants, whom

[24] John Stuart Mill, *Principles of Political Economy, with Some of Their Applications to Social Philosophy*, 2 vols. (Boston: Little, Brown, 1848).

[25] Talcott Parsons, "Social Structure and the Symbolic Media of Interchange," in *Approaches to the Study of Social Structure*, ed. Peter M. Blau (New York: Free Press, 1975), chap. 6, pp. 94–120.

[26] James R. Beniger, *Trafficking in Drug Users: Professional Exchange Networks in the Control of Deviance* (New York: Cambridge University Press, 1983).

the scientist may acknowledge in a footnote; outside of the organization, however, the scientist expects to provide valuable information to many other scientists, who the scientist hopes will acknowledge him or her by citing his or her work.

Herein lies a commonplace irony of professional life: the same individuals who cannot find time to diffuse information and who shun the intra-institutional equivalent of referrals —whether of students, patients, clients, or the like—within their own organizations may devote considerable time to establishing themselves as informational sources—to enjoy the higher status that accrues through referral or citation—for anonymous individuals scattered throughout the world. Such individuals share many of the characteristics that Robert Merton first identified with cosmopolitans, in contrast to the locals, who narrowly focus their interests on local affairs.[27]

Science as System: One Market, Many Organizations

Why do professionals divide into separate status groups with opposite patterns of exchange of system information and citations, acknowledgments, or referrals? This division, between what we might call organization-directed and system-directed scientists, following Riesman,[28] results from differences in the nature of control in formal or engineered systems, such as universities, research centers, and laboratories, versus free-market systems, such as global science in the ideal.

Formal organizational systems are designed—authority is distributed *a priori*—so that a few high-status individuals direct many others; they move the production of research or the processing of referrals and monitor organizational information for feedback to control these flows. To the extent that a market system lacks such design, by contrast, all producers control it in small measure. In science, researchers exploit information produced by others whose help they formally acknowledge in return, thereby distributing status and authority among a few leadership roles. Here the analogy between citations and money as market feedback to producers is straightforward.

Free-market patterns can obtain under all combinations of interpersonal or social network versus mass communication—in science, under all combinations of correspondence, draft, and preprint exchange versus formal publication. Whether in the networks of scientists called invisible colleges[29] or through a form of mass communication like an article in *Scientific American*, leading sources of system information will gain status and authority—or celebrity, in the case of mass entertainment systems—whether these are invested by sociometric centrality, citations, or audience ratings.

It might seem that such systems, far from being free, are in fact controlled by the informational sources who enjoy highest system status. System-directed elite do impact direction to their subfields, but at the whim of their audiences of publishing researchers.

---

[27] Robert K. Merton, *Social Theory and Social Structure*, enlarged ed. (New York: Free Press, 1968), chap. 12, pp. 441–74.

[28] David Riesman with Reuel Denny and Nathan Glazer, *The Lonely Crowd: A Study of the Changing American Character* (New Haven, CT: Yale University Press, 1950), chap. 1.

[29] Diana Crane, *Invisible Colleges: Diffusion of Knowledge in Scientific Communities* (Chicago: University of Chicago Press, 1972).

Ultimate control is not only distributed, if not diffused, but also renegotiated day to day; compared to organizational control, it is much less centralized and never tenured. Continual renegotiation makes markets—under the control of exchange authority—adaptive even to rapid change.

Considering the opposite status implications of system information and citation giving and receiving, inside versus outside of formal organizations, it is hardly surprising that scientists divide into separate status groups having opposite patterns of exchange. A leading research methodologist, for example, will not need to solve problems for students or colleagues in order to maintain status achieved through publication and correspondence. A scientist whose research draws few citations, by contrast, might still hope to achieve high local status by advancement through the formal hierarchy in his or her own institution, where he or she will tend to monitor rather than to disseminate system information and to make acknowledgments and referrals rather than to receive them.

Because local reputations are not generalized symbolic media in the larger system, however, they do not translate well across organizational boundaries, except in partially generalized and partly symbolic media like letters of recommendation, and then only to middle and lower organizational levels. Status in the inter-organizational or global system, by contrast, does translate well in most local contexts. This explains why organizational rewards tend to correspond to status on the global level, which has relatively few rewards of its own, Nobel Prizes providing a notable exception.

Translation from global system to organizational contexts remains imperfect, as, for example, when a scarce commodity like academic tenure is denied a talented scientist because she or he is a poor teacher or administrator. Fortunately for science, the generalized symbolic nature of global status assures that its failure to translate will occur less often than the reverse failure: when a poor scientist is promoted based on local contributions alone. Both types of failed translation bolster the view of science as a dual system, one in which the global goal to expand the universal body of scientific knowledge must continuously compete with more local but necessary functions ranging from teaching, fund raising, and administration to turning a profit and national defense. If the global goal were to cease to translate—via global status and authority—into organizational rewards, the system of science would deteriorate for lack of material incentives on the micro level and for want of control signals on the macro level.

Potential Crisis of Control

Telematics threatens global science—as distinct from all the other work scientists do within their own organizations—with just such a crisis of control. Many involved with the computerization of information system have predicted—some gleefully—a decline in the formal scientific paper, a blurring of the distinction between research notes and papers and between papers and the response to them by others, an increase in multiple authorship by scores or even hundreds who participate in a telematic discussion, and the decline of formal journals, editors, and the gatekeeping function more generally. Such developments, were they to occur, would destroy no less than the basic unit of research reporting, the paper; the organized system of communication, including conference presentations and journal publication; and the day-to-day feedback signals of exchange authority, like citation, that have served science since the Enlightenment.

Not everyone involved in the computerization of information systems intends to alter science so radically, of course. Starr Roxanne Hiltz and Murray Turoff, who pioneered the Electronic Information Exchange System for Scientific Research Communities (EIES) in the mid-1970s, describe their own approach:

> The design philosophy is to start with the existing communications forms and functions of a user group and to build a system that accommodates or replicates such communication patterns at an overall increase in speed or efficiency and decrease in cost; and then add communication and information processing capabilities not possible without the computer. The specific nature of any particular system optimized for human communication would vary somewhat from one organization and application to another.[30]

The difficulty here is in distinguishing those "communication forms and functions" that ought to be "accommodate[d] or replicate[d]" and those that ought to be speeded up, made more efficient or less expensive, or enhanced by computer, which might have unanticipated and possibly dysfunctional consequences like increasing volume, extending the user community, or weakening exchange authority. Who can know in advance whether speed, cost, efficiency, and other processing constraints—on a wide range of knowledge-creation, information-production, and communication activities—will be either crucial or incidental to any given social structure?

Even Hiltz and Turoff, based on their field trials of EIES, cite what they call "barriers and problems" in EIES's implementation in science. Reward systems are not currently constituted to measure and distribute credit for nonpublishing activities. Heavy capital investment in existing communication channels and delivery and distribution systems constitutes inertia inhibiting change. Competition for research funding undermines the sense of common interests necessary for free exchange. In subfields polarized by strong advocacy positions, many scientists do not want to confront each other except sporadically in print. Frequent communication among research sponsors, project leaders, and potential users may not benefit research.[31]

The Future

And what of the future? Most past attempts to forecast technological innovations or trends have proved worthless, at best, and certainly humbling. From the historical perspective outlined here, we might be tempted to conclude that—in at least broad outline—the Control Revolution will continue into the near future much as it has over the century just past. But even so cautious a forecast must be reconciled with perhaps the supreme dilemma of all control systems, including natural ecosystems: the greater the control, the more precarious, and the greater the potential for loss of control—with more disastrous consequences. The Chernobyl disaster and recent airline tragedies illustrate

---

[30] Starr Roxanne Hiltz and Murray Turoff, *The Network Nation: Human Communication via Computer* (Reading, MA: Addison-Wesley, 1978), p. 19.

[31] Ibid., pp. 249–50.

how much more precarious our control systems can make everyday life than it was in even the earliest days of industrialization.

Our information and control technologies continue to carry us, nevertheless, toward possible confrontations with the prospects of artificial intelligence, computer consciousness, even synthetic life. Intermediate forms already exist on both sides of life's boundaries: self-replicating polymers on the inorganic side, genetically engineered systems on the organic side. Considering the continued development and proliferation of nuclear weapons technology, under the control of worldwide and extraterrestrial systems of growing complexity, evolution's next stage might hinge on the question of which boundary we reach first: synthetic life, certainly one possible product of growing control, or the return of the planet to the inorganic level, another quite possible outcome—ironically enough—of the same revolution in control technology.

P·A·R·T·IV

7

Public Policy Concerning the Exchange and Distribution of Scientific Information

Fred W. Weingarten • D. Linda Garcia

Today, a wide variety of information and communications technologies are rapidly being developed that are profoundly altering the nation's and the world's communication systems. Included among them are storage technologies such as optical disks, computer networks for distributed information processing, fiber optic transmission systems, digital telephone switches, teletext and videotext systems and other forms of electronic publishing, and satellite distribution systems. These technologies not only permit the introduction and development of a wide variety of new information-based products and services; they also provide much greater flexibility in the processing, packaging, and distribution of information.

These rapid technological advances are bringing with them major social and economic changes. They are changing the way people work and conduct their business; how they interact and relate to one another; the way they learn, create, and process information; and their needs and expectations. In fact, these new technologies are altering the way that people view themselves and their places in the world.[1]

Together, the development and use of these new technologies are helping to usher in what some social observers characterize as a postindustrial or information society.[2] In this society, the creation, use, and communication of information plays a central role. Not only will the amount of information continue to increase, but people will also rely on it more

Fred W. Weingarten and D. Linda Garcia, "Public Policy Concerning the Exchange and Distribution of Scientific Information." *The Annals of The American Academy of Political and Social Science* **495** (January 1988), pp. 61–72. Copyright 1988 by Sage Publications. Reprinted by permission of Sage Publications, Inc.

and in different circumstances. The changes brought on by the new technologies will often generate new social, economic, and cultural opportunites and choices, which will bring with them the need for major policy decisions.

Given the capabilities of the new information and communications technologies and the enhanced role and value of information in all areas of life, disagreements have arisen over how, by whom, and for what purposes these technologies should be used. The creation of new opportunities for some often generates problems for others. For example, using new technologies to process and store socioeconomic data about individuals, public agencies can improve their efficiency and effectiveness; in doing so, however, they may create problems in the protection of individual rights to privacy.[3] Similarly, individuals can use the new technologies to access information more easily and inexpensively, but, in the process, they may undermine the existing system for protecting and enforcing intellectual property rights.[4]

One use of the new technologies that might cause considerable conflict is their use in science. The new technologies hold tremendous promise for both carrying out research and disseminating the results. As the following discussion points out, however, as we move further into an information age, with increasing competition for knowledge and information, the use of information and communication technologies for scientific purposes may conflict with and hamper their use for economic or military ends. Similarly, and perhaps more important, the way these technologies are used in the private sector and in defense may significantly alter the nature of scientific activity. To understand how such conflicts may occur, it is necessary to look first at what is meant by science.

The Nature of Scientific Activity and its Relationship to Society

Science can be defined as a social activity whereby people use rational thought to achieve empirical ends.[5] Viewed as such, it is clear that scientific activity is common to all societies, even to preliterate ones. For, as Bernard Barber has pointed out, "the germ of science in human society lies in man's aboriginal and unceasing attempt to understand and control the world in which he lives by the use of rational thought."[6]

NOTE: This article was written while the authors were employed by the government, and is in the public domain. The views expressed in this article are those of the authors and do not necessarily represent positions of the Office of Technology Assessment, the Technology Assessment Board, or the U.S. Congress.

[1] Sherri Turkle, *The Second Self: Computers and the Human Spirit* (New York: Simon & Schuster, 1984).

[2] For discussions and characterizations of the information society, see, for example, U.S., Congress, Office of Technology Assessment, *Computer-Based National Information Systems*, OTA-CIT-146 (Washington, DC: Government Printing Office, 1981); Susan Artandi, "Man, Information and Society: New Patterns of Interaction," *Journal for the American Society for Information Science* (Jan. 1979); Daniel Bell, *The Coming of Post-Industrial Society* (New York: Basic Books, 1973); James R. Beniger, "Information Society and Global Science," *The Annals* of the American Academy of Political and Social Science, Vol. 495 (January 1988).

[3] U.S., Congress, Office of Technology Assessment, *Federal Government Information Technology: Electronic Record Systems and Individual Privacy*, OTA-CIT-296 (Washington, DC: Government Printing Office, 1986).

[4] U.S., Congress, Office of Technology Assessment, *Intellectual Property Rights in an Age of Electronics and Information*, OTA-CIT-302 (Washington, DC: Government Printing Office, 1986).

[5] Bernard Barber, *Science and the Social Order* (New York: Free Press, 1952), pp. 7–8.

[6] Ibid., p. 7.

Although present in all societies and cultures, science has evolved and progressed —more slowly to begin with and then by leaps and bounds—throughout the course of human history. A dynamic activity that develops in response to continued, critical analysis, science has become increasingly conceptual and generalizable over time.[7] As part of its evolution, it has developed special investigative procedures and specialized roles.[8]

Science and society interact so that the nature and development of science at any particular time is strongly affected by the societal context in which it is operating.[9] The values and practices of some societies have been more conducive to scientific progress than others. The heavy emphasis on magic in preliterate cultures, for example, was incompatible with rational, empirical knowledge, and thus it inhibited its development.[10] Similarly, the Oriental conviction that the nature of the universe was unknowable long discouraged the practice of science.[11] Then, in contrast, during the Middle Ages, the writings of Saint Thomas Aquinas gave science a tremendous boost. The religious belief in the rationality of god, and hence in the rationality of nature, made the idea of science a real possibility.[12]

Science also benefited greatly from European developments during the sixteenth and seventeenth centuries: the birth of Cartesian philosophy, the invention of differential calculus, appreciation for the importance of theory, the development of new tools and procedures for observation and experimentation, mercantile capitalism, and the Protestant ethic.[13] More recently, the values of the liberal state—rationality, progress, freedom, and individualism—have strongly favored the growth of science.[14]

Although a reflection of society, science is also an activity unto itself, with its own moral purpose, structure, procedures, and norms.[15] Devoted above all to the advancement of knowledge, science typically prescribes the acceptable means and procedures for attaining it.[16] The scientific community, moreover, monitors itself, requiring its members to adhere strictly to four essential norms. These are (1) universalism, or the requirement that claims of truth be judged according to cognitive, and not personal, criteria; (2) disinterestedness, the requirement that scientists put the goals of science above the desire for personal gain; (3) organized skepticism, requiring scientists to evaluate all claims of truth in terms of empirical and logical criteria; and (4) communism, requiring that the findings of science be freely communicated and shared with the public.[17]

The publication and dissemination of scientific results are critical activities in the

---

[7] Ibid., pp. 45–46.

[8] Talcott Parsons, *The Social System* (New York: Free Press, 1951), p. 333.

[9] Ibid., pp. 332–33.

[10] Ibid., p. 333.

[11] Barber, *Science and the Social Order*, p. 46.

[12] Ibid.

[13] Ibid., pp. 50–52.

[14] Ibid., pp. 85–87.

[15] Ibid., p. 84.

[16] Robert K. Merton, *The Sociology of Science: Theoretical and Empirical Investigations* (Chicago: University of Chicago Press, 1973), p. 270.

[17] Ibid., pp. 270–78.

scientific process, if science is to function in accordance with these norms.[18] Publication and dissemination are necessary not only to meet the requirement of communism; they are also the means by which the criteria of disinterestedness and organized skepticism are fulfilled. Scientists are able to sublimate their need for pecuniary rewards because they gain fulfillment through the recognition that they receive from their colleagues for having contributed to the advancement of knowledge. Were their works to remain unpublished, they would have no reward.[19] So important is this kind of reward to the scientist that "once he has made his contribution, [he] no longer has exclusive rights of access to it. It becomes part of the public domain of science."[20]

Benjamin Franklin exemplified this ethic. Explaining why he turned down an offer from the governor of Pennsylvania to patent the Franklin stove, he wrote to a friend:

> I declined from a Principle which has weighed with me on such occasions, vis. That as we enjoy great Advantages from the Invention of others, we should be glad of an opportunity to serve others by an invention of ours, and this we should do freely and generously.[21]

Nor did scientists traditionally seek to market their discoveries. Louis Pasteur's attitude was typical. Although he himself estimated that the use of his method would save Fr100 million per year, he was not interested in profiting financially from his discoveries. As he explained to Napoleon III, "In France scientists would consider they lowered themselves by doing so."[22]

Without the publication and dissemination of scientific work, moreover, the scientific community would have no objective means by which to maintain the quality and validity of research. As Robert Merton has pointed out,

> Science is public and not private knowledge; and although the idea of "other persons" is not employed explicitly in science, it is always tacitly involved. In order to prove a generalization, which for the individual scientist, on the basis of his own private experience, may have attained the status of a valid law which requires no further confirmation, the investigator is compelled to set up critical experiments which will satisfy the other scientists engaged in the same cooperative activity. This pressure for so working out a problem that the solution will satisfy not only the scientist's own criteria of validity and adequacy, but also the criteria of the group with whom he is actually or symbolically in control, constitutes a powerful social impetus for cogent, rigorous investigation. The work of the scientist is at every point influenced by the intrinsic requirements of the phenomena with which he is

---

[18] The practice of publishing and disseminating scientific works was one of the developments that provided an impetus for science during the Renaissance. As Barber points out, "The [scientific] societies also became the channels not only of national but of international communication in the new knowledge. Each society had regular foreign correspondents charged with reporting events in his country; and reading letters of these correspondents was a feature of the meetings." Barber, *Science and the Social Order*, p. 54.

[19] Merton, *Sociology of Science*, p. 293. Describing the process, Merton says, "This way in which the norms of science help to produce this result seems clear enough. On every side the scientist is reminded that it is his role to advance knowledge and his happiest fulfillment of that role, to advance knowledge greatly. This is only to say, of course, that in the institution of science originality is at a premium." Ibid.

[20] Ibid., p. 294.

[21] As quoted in Bruce Willis Bugbee, *Genesis of American Patent and Copyright Law* (Washington, DC: Public Affairs Press, 1976), p. 72.

[22] As quoted in J. D. Bernal, *Science and Industry in the Nineteenth Century* (Boston: Routledge & Kegan Paul, 1953), p. 86.

dealing and perhaps just as directly by his reactions to the inferred critical attitudes or actual criticism of other scientists and by an adjustment of his behavior in accordance with these attitudes.[23]

The four scientific norms identified by Merton, which were long supported by society at large, have been quite successful in promoting the rapid advancement of science in the United States. Today, however—and in part, as a result of these scientific developments —society is undergoing a number of changes that may very well undermine these norms. In particular, given the greatly enhanced value of information in all aspects of life, pressure is mounting from many quarters, and for a variety of different purposes, to restrict the flow of scientific information by limiting access to it. Nowhere is this process better illustrated than in the following two cases, one involving the increased commoditization of knowledge and information and the other the restriction of the dissemination of scientific information for purposes of national security.

Increased Commoditization of Knowledge and Information

The new communication and information technologies will play a greatly enhanced role in all aspects of life. In fact, their availability and use may, in many cases, be the critical factor in personal and organizational success. The enhanced value of these technologies is reflected, first of all, in the growing number of people who, from whatever realm of life, are striving to integrate these technologies into their daily activities and operations. It is reflected, moreover, in the greatly increased market for information-based products and services and in the flourishing of new industries to provide for these burgeoning information needs.

Not all of these technological opportunities, however, will be exploited. In fact, taking advantage of some opportunities may preclude the development of others. The potential for conflict is likely to be most pronounced in areas, such as science, where the economic value of information is very high. For it is under such circumstances that the discrepancy between the need for exclusions and the need for distribution, sharing, and use is the most starkly drawn.

In contrast to the world of science, the value of information from the perspective of the economic realm is in its exclusivity—that is to say, in the ability of its owners to be able to exploit the difference between what they know and what other people do not know. In a horse race, for example, the value of an accurate assessment of the horse's chances increases directly with the exclusivity of that wisdom, and the value is obviously decreased by sharing. Similarly, an important factor in encouraging investment is the presumption that the investor is better informed than others about the outcome of the enterprise. To the degree that all investors have equal access to information, this potential for difference is reduced, along with the incentive for investment.[24]

---

[23] Robert Merton, *Science, Technology, and Society in Seventeenth Century England* (New York: Howard Fertig, 1938), p. 219, as quoted in Harriet Zuckerman, "Deviant Behavior and Social Control in Science," in *Deviance and Social Change*, ed. Edward Sagarin (Newbury Park, CA: Sage, 1977), pp. 88–89.

[24] Christopher Burns and Patricia Martin, *The Economics of Information*, Contractor report prepared for U.S. Congress, Office of Technology Assessment (Boston: Christopher Burns Inc., 1985).

The tension between the norms of business and the norms of science is clearly evident today in many institutions of higher education. Once the undisputed center of research efforts in the United States, American universities are today competing strenuously with one another and with business and governmental research institutes for money and resources. In the present economic climate, most universities are finding it difficult to compete. Equipment for advanced scientific research is extremely expensive to buy and to maintain. Faculty members, drawn by the superior research opportunities and financial benefits offered by private firms and government, are leaving the universities and taking their research teams with them.[25]

To make universities more competitive and more financially independent, many universities and colleges have established new relationships with the business community. Such arrangements generally involve some form of joint research. Probably the first such arrangement is the 10-year Harvard-Monsanto agreement signed in 1975, which provided that the chemical firm Monsanto would provide Harvard Medical School $23 million to support the research of two professors.[26] Many others have followed. Increasingly popular with both business and academia, these agreements are considered to be mutually beneficial. The universities receive money to finance research and to replace obsolete equipment, while the business communities obtain—often on a proprietary basis —access to basic, advanced technological research.[27]

Industry representatives are also actively courting the traditional scientist-scholar to leave academia for jobs in industry. As one professor of biological science at Harvard University explained, "At this point it is mind boggling. I'm courted every day. Yesterday, some guy offered me literally millions of dollars to go direct a research outfit on the west coast . . . . He said any price."[28] Such offers have caused much soul-searching among research scientists. While some respond favorably to these developments—even to the point of creating their own firms to exploit their discoveries for profit—others have opposed them as unsuitable for academic science. Trying to sort out what is appropriate behavior for academics and academia, a number of major universities have themselves begun working together to develop policy guidelines for university-industry relationships.[29]

Critics of new alliances between industry and academia are concerned lest these new partnerships serve to undermine the traditional norms of academic and scientific research. Above all, they fear that such agreements will be proprietary in nature and thus inhibit

---

[25] W. R. Lynn and F. A. Long, "University-Industrial Collaboration in Research," *Technology and Society*, 4: 199 (1982). The rapid obsolescence of laboratory and research tools, combined with the highly complex and sophisticated nature of the equipment now needed for advanced technology research, results in capital costs beyond the reach of most academic institutions. For example, in 1970 the cost of new instrumentation in U.S. universities' laboratories was estimated to be $200 million; in 1980, it was $1 billion. National Research Council, *Revitalizing Laboratory Instrumentation* (Washington, DC: National Academy Press, 1982).

[26] David Dickson, *The New Politics of Science* (New York: Pantheon, 1984), p. 66.

[27] Philip L. Bereano, "Making Knowledge a Commodity: Increased Corporate Influence on Universities," *IEEE Technology and Society Magazine*, pp. 8–9 (Dec. 1986).

[28] As quoted in Henry Etzkowitz, "Entrepreneurial Science and Entrepreneurial Universities in American Academic Science," *Minerva*, 21(2–3): 199 (Summer–Autumn 1985).

[29] "Academe and Industry Debate Partnership," *Science*, 219(4481): 150–51 (Jan. 1983).

the exchange of research. Regretfully noting such developments, Donald Kennedy, president of Stanford University, has said, for example,

> The commercial environment is characterized by many more constraints upon the openness and accessibility of scientific and technical information than is the university environment. Proprietary restraints on the free exchange of data have already begun to crop up . . . . There are at least three or four incidents during this past year (1980–81) at scientific meetings, at which the traditional evaluation of research had always been expected to prevail; there were communications in which a scientist actually refused on questioning to divulge some detail of technique, claiming that, in fact, it was a proprietary matter and that he was not free to communicate it.[30]

This problem is exacerbated by the fact that, as the market value of information increases, so does the pressure to treat information and knowledge as economic commodities. Not surprisingly, rivalry for ownership is becoming increasingly common at institutions of science and research where the potential for profits is very high. The claims and counterclaims of ownership are continually multiplying: claims of students against students, students against faculty members, faculty against faculty, and the university against students and faculty.[31] A particularly contentious issue is work for hire. Some university administrators now argue, for example, that just as companies automatically own the copyright on works done on company time and with company resources, so too universities should have the rights to everything created in conjunction with their facilities.[32] At Virginia Polytechnic Institute, this policy has been carried so far that lawyers at the university have recently concluded that students' assignments are the property of their professors.[33]

Conflicts such as these are likely to become more intense, more complicated, and more difficult to resolve as we move further into an information age. Only recently, for example, Harvard biologist Walter Gilbert announced his company's intention to copyright the sequence of human deoxyribonucleic acid.[34] Although most of the leading molecular biologists in the United States have some connections with industry, many of them view Gilbert's statement of intent with considerable alarm. They fear that if proprietary rights are granted to the mapping and sequencing of the human genome, the search for medically important genes will be greatly retarded. In addition, they themselves are asking whether there might not be certain kinds of information that, given their overwhelming importance to humankind, should never be owned by anyone or distributed through the marketplace.[35]

Notwithstanding such concerns, proprietary restrictions on the distribution and flow of information are likely to become commonplace in an economic environment that is

---

[30] L. Lindsay, "Troubled Conscience in Academe: Industry's Help Priced Too High," *Christian Science Monitor*, 29 Oct. 1982, as quoted in Bereano, "Making Knowledge a Commodity," p. 12.

[31] Dorothy Nelkin, *Science as Intellectual Property: Who Controls Scientific Research* (New York: Macmillan, 1984), pp. 1–8.

[32] Ivars Peterson, "Bits of Ownership: Growing Computer Software Sales Are Forcing Universities to Rethink Their Copyright and Patent Policies," *Science News*, 21 Sept. 1985, pp. 189–90.

[33] Ibid.

[34] "Who Owns the Human Genome?" *Science*, 237(4813): 358–61 (July 1987).

[35] Ibid.

increasingly fueled by information production and use. The repercussions of such developments will be felt not only by those who cannot afford the price of knowledge and information but also by the community of science as a whole. As Thorsten Veblen once said, "The outcome of any research can only be to make two questions grow where one question grew before."[36] Without the exchange of research, there can be no questioning, and without questioning there is no dynamic, no driving force, to science.

National Security and Scientific Information

For centuries, science and technology have been recognized for their contribution to the ability of societies to make war. Among his many and varied creative activities, Leonardo DaVinci invented military hardware. The invention of the stirrup transformed warfare in medieval Europe by establishing the technological basis for a horse-mounted armored fighter. More recently, in the United States, the National Academy of Sciences was formed during the Civil War to help the Union war effort, and the National Research Council was similarly a product of World War I.

Yet it was during World War II, with inventions such as radar and, of course, the atomic bomb, that the contribution of basic science to military power was fully recognized. For the bomb did not originate from weapons laboratories but from formulas on the chalkboards of theoretical physicists. It was then also, with the realization that science could make an immediate and profound contribution to war, that the modern conflict between national security concerns and the open exchange of scientific information was fully joined.

Legislative Control Over Information Flows

The Atomic Energy Act of 1946 defined a category of information called "Restricted Data" as information subject to government control. The act was written in such a way as to allow the inclusion of information not created by or in the direct control of the government. In certain cases, according to the definition, Restricted Data could be designated to be "Born Classified"—it could be confiscated and classified by government no matter who developed or held it. Thus was scientific publication in certain fields placed under threat of government restriction, even if it concerned basic research results and even if the research was conducted privately.

Subsequently, numerous other laws, executive orders, and regulations have established controls over the dissemination of scientific information. The Arms Export Control Act and its International Traffic in Arms Regulations, the Patent Secrecy Act, and the Arms Export Administration Act, as well as executive directives, have been used at times by the government to attempt to block the transfer of scientific communication. In the last two decades, government officials have invoked these and other rules to try, with varying success, to stop the publication of articles, the presentation of papers at conferences, the

---

[36] Thorsten Veblen, "The Evolution of the Scientific Point of View," in *The Place of Science in Modern Civilization and Other Essays* (New York: Viking, 1919), as cited in Barber, *Science and the Social Order*, p. 21.

participation by foreign graduate students in academic seminars, and access to government-supported research computing facilities.

The first such efforts to become widely known and followed in the press were attempts in the mid-1970s to control the publication and patenting of results from research projects funded by the National Science Foundation involving cryptography.[37] Since then, the controversy has ebbed and flowed, as compromises have been negotiated to avert criminal prosecution of offending scientists or court tests of constitutionality.[38] The most recent attempts at compromise centers on the concept of fundamental science as defined in National Security Decision Directive 189. In it, fundamental science, on which controls will not normally be imposed, is "basic and applied research in science and engineering, the results of which ordinarily are published and shared broadly within the scientific community, as distinguished from proprietary research."

The circularity of the definition, however, illustrates the difficulties in dealing with this issue. That is, fundamental research—research not subject to control—is defined as research not usually subject to control. Furthermore, given our earlier point that the line between appropriable and nonappropriable research in the commercial sector is blurring, the definition does not rest on a very robust distinction. In fact, the definition ties the two areas of conflict together in an interesting way. It suggests, plausibly, that once the research community gives up open communication of research on economic grounds, it loses force in its argument against national security controls.

Pressures Created by Military Needs

Despite recent compromises between researchers and government, government interest in controlling the flow of scientific information on national security grounds is bound to continue, for the conflict is rooted deeply in the evolution of the information society discussed in the beginning of this article.

In the first place, as the development of the atomic bomb suggests, the distinction between basic science and engineering and technological products of military interest is blurring. This convergence is true today not only in nuclear physics but in such diverse fields as biophysics, optics, geology, oceanography, mathematics, and computer science.

Second, the military dependency on so-called dual-use technologies—technologies with both civil and military applications—is also expanding. Armies have always needed boots and trucks, and navies have always needed navigational information similar or identical to that used by commercial sailors; the overlapping interest of military and civil sectors in certain technologies is not new. The overlap, however, seems to be expanding as the military becomes dependent on the same technological infrastructure that underlies civilian life. There seems to be little obvious dual-use technology underlying a bomb or rifle, but today the military uses many of the same microelectronics technologies that are used in consumer products, as well as aeronautical and nautical design and construction technologies that have civilian applications.

---

[37] Fred W. Weingarten, "Controlling Cryptographic Publication," *Computers & Security*, 2(1): 41–48 (1983).

[38] David A. Wilson, "Federal Control of Information in Academic Science," *Jurimetrics*, 27(3): 283–96 (Spring 1987).

Finally, the U.S. Defense Department is a major supporter of research in the nation's laboratories. In some fields, the Defense Department funds the majority of research pursued by civilian scientists, including research that is not explicitly for military purposes.[39] This direct involvement by the military serves to strengthen the presumption in some minds that there is a significant security interest in the results of the research. Furthermore, because the work is government funded, controls over the publication of results, if imposed, are seen more as the appropriate by-product of a contractual arrangement than as an abridgment of freedom of speech, because the sponsor has some proprietary rights over the disposition of the results. Yet when the Defense Department funds a significant majority of the research in a field, as it does in some cases, such rights, if exercised, can chill publication in an entire body of research.

It would be unfair to suggest that this debate is purely between the scientific community and defense interests. There have been times when the scientific community has worried deeply about the implications of research it was pursuing and wondered if publication, or even the research itself, should be suppressed. On the other side, a defense establishment that depends heavily on science and technology cannot afford to take actions that would stifle U.S. research. The conflict is much deeper—intrinsic to the information society. How can we continue to pursue science in the open, public international forum it requires while protecting secrets that are vital to our security?

The Promise and the Dilemma

The challenges faced by science due to the pressures our modern information society places on open communication are more far-reaching than the conflict between those asserting a right to control and those asserting academic freedom and First Amendment rights to publish. Certainly, this is a central issue. But another, possibly even more important, question is whether science, under such pressure, can avail itself of new opportunities that modern communication and computer technologies offer.

Just as the printing press shaped during the Renaissance what we know as modern scholarship, the electronic information tools emerging will most likely have, we think, a major transformational influence on scientific research. Such views are not idiosyncratic. The impact of information technology on research has been the subject of congressional hearings, study projects of the National Academy of Sciences, and reports to the National Science Foundation. The National Science Foundation's current program developments in supercomputers and networking reflect a growing awareness that information technology is becoming a fundamental instrumental infrastructure for the conduct of scientific research in many ways.[40] Among the predictions in this literature are the following:

---

[39] With respect to computer science support, see U.S. Congress, Office of Technology Assessment, *Information Technology R&D: Critical Trends and Issues*, OTA-CIT-268 (Washington, DC: Government Printing Office, 1985).

[40] For a particularly provocative bu informed picture of the future prospects, see John Seeley Brown, "The Impact of the Information Age on the Conduct and Communication of Science," *Information Hotline*, pp. 18–23 (June 1986). See also U.S. Congress, House, Committee on Science and Technology, *The Impact of Information Technology on Science: Science Policy Study Background Report No. 5*, 1986.

1. New generations of supercomputers, particularly the more affordable minisuper-computers, will provide large amounts of computational power for simulation and data analysis.

2. Optical disks and other technologies will provide inexpensive and transportable media for storing vast amounts of data.

3. Worldwide high-speed data communication networks will link researchers with each other and with specialized computers, data bases, and software.

4. High resolution, real-time color graphics will allow scientists to visualize the outcome of their theories and/or experiments in new, more intuitively suggestive ways.

5. Software based on artificial-intelligence techniques will help researchers screen enormous amounts of information for new patterns and ideas and bridge gaps between diverging specialties.

Taken together, these predictions suggest that scientific research in the next century will be as dependent on electronic information technology as it was in the past centuries on libraries and microscopes.

The technology also appears to facilitate scientific communication greatly, making control even more difficult. Controlling access to a supercomputer attached to an international communication network is no easy task. Compact optical disks small enough to fit in a shirt pocket can carry billions of bits of data. Data communication networks can transmit large software packages and data sets anywhere in the world in seconds. Hence information technology appears to support strongly the openness and international character of scientific research.

To control the flow of scientific information, then, may require controlling access to and even use of these modern research instruments. Such policies may seem feasible at first glance, for governments still have a great influence over communication policy. Furthermore, the cost of some of the technology will be great enough that only government will be able to underwrite it, and with the funds could come strings. At last word, the National Science Foundation was still in negotiation with its university-based supercomputer centers over access to the facilities by foreign students.

If access to modern information technology becomes synonymous with the ability to engage in scientific research, control of access to that technology, in the name of national security, economic advantage, or other social objectives, will determine who can participate, both within the U.S. research community and internationally. Furthermore, because the technology seems inherently to favor openness, attempts to control scientific information flow may require policies so draconian as to force science to forgo some of its most exciting opportunities in the next century.

The scientific community cannot hold itself aloof from the issues. It must play in the game. The decisions made in our information society will govern the flows of information within and across the borders of the United States and will affect scientific communication profoundly—perhaps even determining the future of U.S. science.

P·A·R·T·V

Social Control
and
Privacy

P·A·R·T · V

Introduction

Social Control and Privacy

Charles Dunlop • Rob Kling

Record Keeping in Mobile Societies

In any society, people and groups spend some effort in learning about and regulating each other's behavior. But the means differ, and social issues raised by different means also differ. In relatively small social units, such as families and villages, people learn about each other's behavior through direct observation, inference, and gossip. And the forms of social control—introduced to help ensure compliance with social expectations—can range from those that are gentle to those that are harsh and even brutal.

A distinctive feature of villages and small towns is that many business relationships are based on personal knowledge. For example, storekeepers and bankers know most of the people to whom they offer credit, and they also know the extent to which their customers are reliable. Yet even in small-town societies, people sometimes find it necessary to deal with large and distant organizations—e.g., government agencies such as tax collectors and the military.

During the last 100 years, there has been an astounding transformation in the ways that life in industrial (and postindustrial) societies is organized. New means of transportation—trains, buses, cars, and airplanes—have enabled people to become very mobile. In the early 19th century, most people who were born in the United States lived and died within 50 miles of their birthplaces. Today, in a highly mobile society, a huge fraction of the urban population moves from city to city, following better jobs and better places to live. Adolescents often leave their home towns to attend college, and may go even farther away for employment. This mobility means that many people will seek jobs, credit, housing, insurance, etc., from businesses whose proprietors and staff do not have much firsthand knowledge about them.

The last 100 years have also seen a substantial increase in the scale of businesses and the number of government agencies with huge clienteles. For example, in the 19th century, banking was a local affair. Today, banks can readily extend credit to people who come from anywhere in the country. And they can do so with relative safety because of large-scale credit record systems that track the credit history of over 100 million people. Other private firms, like credit agencies and insurance companies, also extend services to tens of thousands of people whom local agents do not—and could not—personally know. Furthermore, many new government agencies, responsible for accounting for the activities of millions of people, have been created in the 20th century: the Federal Bureau of Investigation (1908), the Internal Revenue Service (1913), and the Social Security Administration (1935), along with various state departments of motor vehicles, etc. The sheer scale of these services requires massive record systems for keeping track of some aspects of our lives.

In any era, organizations use the available technologies for keeping records; papyrus and paper were used for centuries. But in modern societies, where computers and telecommunications are a common medium for storing and accessing organizational records, the opportunites for social control, and the nature of potential problems, have changed a great deal.

Information, Value Systems, and Social Control

Discussions of computerization and privacy are embroiled in a major set of controversies with big stakes. On the one hand, some people fear that computer-based information systems are helping to erode personal privacy. They would like to see certain kinds of record systems regulated or limited in scope. And others fear that new ways of doing business—taken together with computer systems—have reduced people's control over their personal affairs. On the other hand, representatives of those private firms and government agencies that have an interest in expanding their computerized information systems frequently argue hard against legal limits or substantial accountability to people about whom records are kept. They deny that problems exist, or they argue that the reported problems are exaggerated in importance. They further argue that proposed regulations are either too vague or too burdensome and that new regulations about information systems would do more harm than good. The proponents of unregulated computerization have been wealthy, organized, and aligned with the anti-regulatory sentiments that have dominated U.S. federal politics during the last 15 years. Consequently, they have effectively blocked many attempts to preserve personal privacy through regulation.

Our first selection is Rob Kling's study of value conflicts in the organization of electronic funds transfer systems. Electronic Funds Transfer (EFT) systems encompass many different kinds of technologies that enable people to pay or receive funds electronically; these systems include automated teller machines, debit cards, direct check deposits, and electronic debiting of loans by banks. To help sort out central assumptions made by various groups who would be advantaged or harmed by different arrangements, Kling identifies several value positions that underlie the key debates. Many groups hold conflicting positions. For example, because of the ways that banking laws are structured, retail merchants like Sears are limited in the financial services they can provide. But there is a major debate between bankers and retail merchants about whether retail merchants can use EFT systems to provide quasi-banking services such as loans. In this example, both groups share the value of maximizing profitability through EFT systems, but there is a conflict over terrain.

Kling argues that other debates reveal conflicting values, not just conflicting interests. Many people who are especially sensitive to civil liberties maintain that most EFT systems provide much finer-grained information about people's lifestyles and where-abouts than is readily available in manual payments systems. Even if private firms have no special interest in using such data for social control, they are often required to provide it on demand to police agencies, which do act as agents of social control. Debates about whether certain EFT systems should be implemented typically reveal major conflicts between civil libertarians on the one hand, and those who value the preeminence of private enterprise or state efficiencies on the other. Kling argues that any particular EFT system is likely to advance some of these values at the expense of the others. His study of EFT systems serves as an exemplary illustration of the way that many socially complex information systems are enmeshed in a matrix of competing social values, and none is value free.

The collection of personal information carries with it the possibility of social control. Consider the following examples.

- A bank loans $10,000 to a new customer for a car purchase, after checking her credit history with a nationwide service and finding that she has routinely repaid previous loans and credit card bills on time for the last five years. The same bank denies a car loan of $6,000 to another potential customer who has a record of paying her credit cards three months late during the past two years.

- Employers can track the number of keystrokes at secretaries' terminals in order to measure "productivity," while computerized factories provide an analogous vehicle for monitoring blue collar workers.[1]

- The IRS matches individual taxpayers' returns against information provided by their banks and employers, and IRS computers assign each return a "Discriminant Function" number, used to assess the likelihood that auditing a given return will reveal further tax liabilities.

Such practices are certainly legal and may even be regarded with approbation. But there are other, more questionable uses of information as well. Fax machines receive junk mail sent by computers drawing from a database of fax telephone numbers. Police have seized personal computers containing electronic mail and private files, presumably rummaging through digital documents without any specific warrant. And insurance companies have "redlined" entire neighborhoods, leaving responsible homeowners without insurance simply because they reside within certain geographical boundaries.

---

[1] Electronic monitoring appears to be infrequent, although it can add substantial pressure when used. See Attewell (1987) and Shaiken (1986) for differing points of view on the prevalence of electronic monitoring.

Collectively, these examples suggest that computer-based information systems can be used in a myriad of ways that fit organizational practices. Many of these practices are legitimate; some may be questionable; and some may even be illegal.[2] Problems arise under a variety of circumstances, e.g., when the records about people are inaccurate and they are unfairly denied a loan, a job, or housing. In large-scale record systems (with millions of records), there are bound to be inaccuracies. But during the last 30 years, people have lost control over records about them, and they have few rights to inspect such records, except for credit histories. Increasingly, courts have ruled that records about a person belong to an organization, and the person to whom they apply cannot restrict their use. Consequently, inaccurate police records, medical records, employment histories, etc., can harm people without their explicit knowledge about why they are having trouble getting a job, a loan, etc.

Many of the issues of data ownership are complex and controversial in themselves. For example, today there are major controversies about whether people who test positive for AIDS should be able to keep that information completely private. In principle, the question has nothing to do with computer systems. The controversy focuses in part on the public good served by being able to identify AIDS carriers versus the concern that many people may avoid AIDS testing if they cannot be assured of the privacy of their test results. In practice, the ability of organizations to share files electronically makes it more likely that personal information can pass across organizational, state, and national boundaries, if it is shared at all.

Unfortunately, problems can also arise when the information is aggregated rather than individualized. One ominous case involved U.S. Census Bureau data, which assisted the Justice Department's roundup and incarceration of Japanese-Americans at the beginning of World War II by providing a description of areas with large Japanese populations. Since enterprises like this do not require the authorities to possess any individual names, their informational underpinnings may masquerade under the banner of privacy protection.

Information collection necessarily invades one's privacy but is usually considered fair exchange for a specific good or service. A bank, for example, has a legitimate interest in knowing a person's financial status and reliability before making a loan. And prospective borrowers routinely accept the legitimacy of that interest. This kind of example—an exchange of very specific information to a specific party in exchange for a service—is relatively clear-cut.

But many forms of information collection today are not so simple. With current technologies, information collected by one organization, such as a bank or insurance company, can easily be passed along to a company that specializes in brokering information. People are not usually informed as to when these companies get information or about the content of recipients of their records. TRW Credit Data Services, for example,

---

[2] Especially worrisome are the IRS audits that have been conducted at the directive of the CIA and FBI for the sole purpose of harassing political activists who held views with which key elected officials disagreed. For example, during Richard Nixon's presidency, the White House staff compiled a list of "enemies" whom they directed the FBI and IRS to harass. This example also illustrates how information collected for ostensibly benign ends may be pressed into the service of malevolent goals.

maintains financial records on more than 100 million people. The Medical Information Bureau tracks medical records of millions of people for the insurance industry. Although these organizations act as brokers, their primary clients are other businesses. They have no real accountability to the people about whom they maintain records.

The Fair Credit Reporting Act of 1970 (15 USC 1681) was the most comprehensive piece of federal legislation to give consumers legal protections from the difficulties of inaccurate credit records. The Act requires credit bureaus to have "reasonable procedures" for insuring that information that they collect and disseminate is accurate. It permits consumers to see any credit information that has been used to deny them a loan, and it also contains provisions for consumers to contest inaccurate information or to fill in incomplete information. But few people check their credit records with major data brokers like TRW until they have been denied a loan, and it can then take precious months to straighten out inaccurate records or problems of mistaken identity. As a U.S. government report aptly noted, "The fact that the Fair Credit Reporting Act will enable him to get errors in the record corrected can be small and bitter comfort to a traveler stranded in a strange city late at night because information about his credit-card account status was inaccurately reported to an independent authorization service."[3]

Many citizens have grown so accustomed to detailing their medical histories and handing over their social security numbers that they scarcely give the matter a second thought. Probably few of them realize the extent to which computerization provides a record of individual activities: an electronic trail of one's whereabouts is available in the records of Electronic Funds Transfers (EFTs), airline reservation systems, rental car agencies, telephone calls, and credit card purchases. In certain emergency situations, these records may be used for salutary purposes; the movements of accused killer Ramon Salcido were reportedly traced by monitoring his ATM transactions.[4] But in less extreme circumstances, certain aspects of one's life are arguably a private matter. Some video stores, for example, maintain an ongoing record of each customer's rentals, and the taste of a public official for X-rated videos was recently brought to light by this means. And given cheap long-term information storage, combined with interconnected data systems, it becomes progressively difficult for anyone to escape the record of an indiscretion long past. All of this information is subject to compromise and abuse any time that an unauthorized party gains access to it, and there is plenty of evidence that today's large-scale computer systems are not adequately secure. (Issues concerning the reliability and security of computer systems are discussed in Part VI of this volume.)

Some people do not find extensive record-keeping objectionable, arguing that "if you haven't done anything wrong, you have nothing to worry about." They think of

---

[3] From Chapter 1 of the Privacy Protection Study Commission report, excerpted in this section. Also see Chapter 2 of that report for one of the better statements of placing credit records in the context of an integrated information policy. For a recent harrowing example, see Riley (1990).

[4] It was also reported that authorities changed Salcido's credit ceiling to "unlimited," in order to forestall the possibility that he might become violent if denied ATM funds at some point. *RISKS-FORUM Digest*, Vol. 8, No. 62 (April 24, 1989).

record-keeping that fits the routine behavior of legitimate organizations—banks wanting to know credit histories, courts wanting to know prior criminal records, etc.

This approach has a certain clarity. But it is misleading as well. First, almost everyone recognizes *some* point at which one's personal activities are nobody else's business.[5] A person may wish only a specific party to know certain information—the bank to know the purpose of a loan, the doctor to know the reasons for a visit, etc. Second, as the White House "enemies" list and the Japanese-American incarceration sadly show, it cannot be assumed that (legally obtained) information will always be used for legal and ethical purposes. Last, in a society where so many records are not under the control of individual citizens, and are unavailable for people to review for accuracy, people may be denied key social goods—like employment, housing, or credit—when inaccurate information about them is passed through the files of businesses and public agencies without audit. Studies of existing records have revealed widespread inaccuracies and ambiguities, with some state criminal history systems having a majority of their records inaccurate or incomplete. Evelyn Richards's *Washington Post* article, reprinted in this section, vividly illustrates how inaccurate information can infringe on individual rights.

Government agencies are often charged with regulatory and policing activities—social control on a large scale. Information about the activities of potential or real lawbreakers is a critical resource for their operations. But privacy issues have taken on a new form and a new urgency with the advent of computer matching, a technique involving large databases with unrelated purposes that are cross-checked for consistency. For example, a state's automobile registration records might be matched against tax records, looking for individuals who own expensive cars but who declared only small incomes. Computer matching has been used to track down and withhold tax refunds from parents whose child support payments are in arrears; to ferret out young adult males who have failed to register for the draft; to detect ineligible welfare and/or food stamp recipients; and to locate former students with delinquent loan payments. Advocates of this approach, such as Richard Kusserow in our fourth selection, argue that it is simply a tool necessary to carry out institutional mandates—e.g., helping to ensure that fathers pay child support. Critics rarely object to the specific ends to which matching has been put so far. They would like to see fathers pay their required child support, to reduce welfare cheating, etc. At the same time, they see matching as Big Brother's encroachment on individual privacy. Today, the examples of computer matching are relatively benign—but there are no legal guarantees that the uses may not become more and more intrusive as we enter the 21st century.

Matching can assist in controlling various illegal activities, which is why the 1984 Deficit Reduction Act required all states to participate in matching programs. Our third selection, by John Shattuck, reviews various dangers, among them the idea that matching

---

[5] Just where that point lies doubtless reflects not only one's personal value system, but also one's conception of privacy. James Rule *et al.* (1980) distinguish between *aesthetic* privacy ("restriction of personal information as an end in itself") and *strategic* privacy ("restriction of personal information as a means to some other end"). The first notion is clearly wider in scope.

may involve a presumption of guilt.[6] Kusserow illustrates Kling's "statist" value position,[7] and Shattuck illustrates a civil libertarian argument. Our selection by Roger Clarke tries to balance both positions. But Clarke warns that serious inaccuracies can arise when data collected in one context are matched against data drawn from another. Related difficulties may be engendered by the arbitrary data categories that are often created for the convenience of programmers (see Les Earnest, 1989).

Regulatory Approaches to Protecting Privacy

The Privacy Act of 1974 established a Privacy Protection Study Commission, which in 1977 issued a substantial (600+ page) report on its findings and recommendations. Although computerization is not a focal point in the report, it is never far below the surface. Our fifth selection reprints excerpts from the first chapter of that document. It provides a very clear discussion of some key social issues arising out of information collection.

The commission made 155 recommendations to develop "fair information practices." Many of these recommendations gave people the right to know what records are kept about them, to inspect records for accuracy, to correct (or contest) inaccuracies, to be informed when records were transferred from one organization to another, etc. Less than a handful of these proposals were enacted into federal law. The commission was a creature of political compromises between civil libertarians on one hand and business and government agencies on the other.

Although the commission showed commendable sensitivity to a variety of social concerns, its attitude toward the problem of faulty record-keeping is worthy of special note. Rather than requiring corrected information to be forwarded to all recipients of incorrect data, the commission proposed "that record keepers need forward corrections and amendments only to past recipients designated by the individual and those to which the record-keeping organization regularly discloses the kind of information in question." In view of the ease with which computerized data can propagate from one system to another, this proposal is unlikely to lead to significantly improved records. As the commission itself pointed out in its discussion of the Tarver case, a woman's public assistance record that "was false, misleading, and prejudicial . . . would be available to other State social services agencies with whom she might subsequently have contact."

Moreover, in cases where incorrect information results in an individual's receiving an adverse decision from a private organization, the commission recommended no process of judicial appeal: "For private-sector organizations the adverse-decision requirements the

---

[6] This presumption may also appear in other forms of computerized data analysis, e.g., profiling techniques (described in Roger A. Clarke's contribution). Such a situation was poignantly portrayed in the 1988 film *Stand and Deliver*. This (true) story involves a group of Hispanic East Los Angeles high school students, whose scores on the Advance Placement Examination in calculus were challenged by the Educational Testing Service due to "unusual patterns" of answers. No other evidence of cheating was presented, and when the students ultimately elected to retake the examination, all of them passed.

[7] "The strength and efficiency of government institutions is the highest goal. Government needs access to personal data on citizens. The need for mechanisms to enforce obligations to the state will always prevail over other considerations."

Commission recommends will expose the records used in arriving at a decision to reject an applicant, but the Commission relies on the incentives of the marketplace to prompt reconsideration of a rejection if it turns out to have been made on the basis of inaccurate or otherwise defective information." A difficulty for this suggestion stems from the fact that many employers routinely check arrest records of job applicants. As Kenneth C. Laudon (1986) demonstrates, a person's arrest record almost always remains "in the system," regardless of the disposition of the case (false arrest, dismissal of charges, exoneration, etc.). All too often, the records show no disposition whatsoever. And many employers are unwilling to hire applicants with an arrest record, no matter how the case against them was eventually resolved. Laudon also found that employers and apartment house owners, not just police, were major users of criminal history systems.

The Growth of Personal Record Systems

What are the forces that underlie institutional information gathering? One view is that bureaucracies have a natural appetite for information, since information represents power.[8] Others see information collection as an inevitable consequence of technology, although this view often leads to an unwarranted feeling of impotence because it underemphasizes the role of social choice in the adoption of new technologies.[9] A third explanation is proposed in our selection by James B. Rule and his colleagues, who argue that much of the pressure for information gathering stems from public demand that org- anizations make "fine-grained" discriminations in determining eligibility for goods and services. If, for example, all citizens were entitled to free health care, the need to collect information about insurance and employment would disappear. If all car drivers paid similar rates—rather than receiving "good driver discounts" and paying higher rates for many driving offences—the demands for driver history information would be reduced.

All three viewpoints acknowledge the potential abuses of information gathering, but they divide over the appropriate remedies. The first two favor tight legal controls on data collection, while Rule's position points to the need for sweeping reform in social attitudes and social policy. Legal controls, unfortunately, provide no insurance against abuse.[10] John Shattuck's essay describes the progressive emasculation of the 1974 Privacy Act by the very federal agencies it was designed to control. And as Kling (1978) has observed, technologies that are developed in complex markets, and that serve unorganized popu- lations, are less susceptible to regulatory policy. Yet Rule's position is also not without its critics. For example, there may not be any clear relationship between how many discriminations an organization makes and how much information it collects. The 1986 U.S. Tax Reform Act, although greatly reducing the number of income brackets, does not

---

[8] When this attitude is coupled with a distorted sense of what constitutes national security, information collected on private citizens may go completely unchecked. Herbert Mitgang (1989) summarizes FBI files on some 35 artists and writers, including such "security risks" as E. B. White, William Faulkner, and Georgia O'Keeffe.

[9] See Section 5 of Kling (1978), as well as our Introduction to Part I of this book.

[10] For a comprehensive survey of abuses, see Burnham (1983).

appear to have resulted in a commensurate decrease in information collected by the IRS. Other arguments are developed in our selection containing Laudon's reply to Rule.[11]

A remedy intermediate to the two just outlined might sanction information collection, but place control of the accumulated data in the hands of individuals. Our final selection, by Roger C. Clarke, makes several proposals in this vein, including the use of digital "smart cards" issued by organizations to individuals, who would retain authority over the organization's dissemination of personal information. And Burnham (1989, p. 214) suggests that an individual's medical history might be contained on wallet sized microfiches, thereby obviating the need for computerized databases. But what if somebody loses his wallet? The microfiche would need to be reissued, which presupposes that the relevant information was stored elsewhere.

Conclusion

Debates about computerization and fair information practices will not go away—even though they catch public attention intermittently. For a variety of "sensible" social reasons, organizations expand their computerized record systems and their use of "dataveillance" techniques. As Roger Shattuck notes, it is difficult to document cases of real harm, because there are no agencies collecting such information. Consequently, those who see people losing control and organizations becoming less accountable hang a lot of weight on the relatively small number of well-documented problems. But, we wonder, is this an appropriate state of affairs? What social costs are we incurring as we wait for problems to become visible, or to mount until regulation—however late—becomes necessary?

In the meantime, computer professionals play key roles in expanding the variety and uses of personnel systems. But given that many such systems raise important ethical issues, the question arises as to why computer professionals often seem untroubled by their advocacy. Some may argue that they are unaware of any ethical repercussions; others maintain that computer science is a technical discipline, unconnected to value questions; and still others say, "If I don't do it, somebody else will anyway." We examine these and other ethical matters in Part VII.

Sources

Clarke, Roger C. (1988). "Information Technology and Dataveillance," *Communications of the ACM*, 31(5) (May), pp. 498–512.

Kling, Rob (1983). "Value Conflicts in EFT systems, excerpted from "Value Conflicts and Computing Developments: Developed and Developing Countries," *Telecommunications Policy*, 7(1) (March), pp. 12–34.

Kusserow, Richard P. (1984). "The Government Needs Computer Matching to Root Out Waste and Fraud," *Communications of the ACM*, 27(6) (June), pp. 542–545.

---

[11] It should be mentioned, however, that Laudon displays a considerably less sanguine attitude toward information collection in his thoroughgoing analysis of the FBI's proposed national computerized criminal history system—a system that Laudon describes as "clearly irresponsible." See Laudon (1986).

Laudon, Kenneth C. (1980). "Comment on 'Preserving Individual Autonomy in an Information-Oriented Society,'" in Lance J. Hoffman *et al.*, *Computer Privacy in the Next Decade*, Academic Press, New York, pp. 89–95.

Privacy Protection Study Commission (1977). *Personal Privacy in an Information Society*, U.S. Government Printing Office, pp. 3–37.

Richards, Evelyn (1989). "Proposed FBI Crime Computer System Raises Questions on Accuracy, Privacy . . .," *The Washington Post*, February 13. (Posted on *RISKS-FORUM Digest*, Vol. 8, No. 27 [February 16, 1989].)

Rule, James B., *et al.* (1980). "Preserving Individual Autonomy in an Information-Oriented Society," in Lance J. Hoffman *et al.*, *Computer Privacy in the Next Decade*, Academic Press, New York, pp. 65–87.

Shattuck, John (1984). "Computer Matching is a Serious Threat to Individual Rights," *Communications of the ACM*, 27(6) (June), pp. 538–541.

References

Attewell, Paul (1987). "Big Brother and the Sweatshop: Computer Surveillance in the Automated Office," *Sociological Theory*, 5 (Spring), pp. 87–99. (Reprinted in Part III of this book.)

Burnham, David (1983). *The Rise of the Computer State*. Random House, New York.

Earnest, Les (1989). "Can Computers Cope with Human Races?" *Communications of the ACM*, 32(2) (February), pp. 174–182.

Kling, Rob (1978). "Value Conflicts and Social Choice in Electronic Funds Transfer Systems," *Communications of the ACM*, 21(8) (August), pp. 642–657.

Mitgang, Herbert (1989). *Dangerous Dossiers*. Ballantine Books, New York.

Rule, James, Douglas McAdam, Linda Stearns, and David Uglow (1980). *The Politics of Privacy: Planning for Personal Data Systems as Powerful Technologies:*. Elsevier North-Holland, Inc., New York and Oxford; distributed by Greenwood Press, Westport, Conn.

Shaiken, Harley (1986). *Work Transformed: Automation and Labor in the Computer Age*, especially chapters 4–7. Lexington Books, Lexington, Mass.

Further Reading

Freedman, Warren (1987). *The Right of Privacy in the Computer Age*. Quorum Books, New York.

Kling, Rob, and Suzanne Iacono (1984). "Computing as an Occasion for Social Control." *Journal of Social Issues*, 40(3), pp. 77–96.

Laudon, Kenneth C. (1986). *Dossier Society: Value Choices in the Design of National Information Systems*. Columbia University Press, New York.

Marx, Gary (1985). "I'll Be Watching You: Reflections on the New Surveillance," *Dissent*, 32 (Winter), pp. 26–34.

Privacy Protection Study Commission (1977). *Personal Privacy in an Information Society*. U.S. Government Printing Office, Stock No. 052-003-00395-3.

Riley, Michael G. (1990). "Sorry Your Card Is No Good: A Nightmarish Tale from the Realm of Consumer Credit Ratings," *Time Magazine*, 135(15) (April 9), p. 62.

Rosenberg, Ronni (1987). "Selected and Annotated Bibliography on Computers and Privacy." Available at nominal charge from Computer Professionals for Social Responsibility, P.O. Box 717, Palo Alto, California 94301.

Rubin, Michael Rogers (1988). *Private Rights, Public Wrongs: The Computer and Personal Privacy.* Ablex Pub. Corp., Norwood, N.J.

Smith, Robert Ellis (1979). *Privacy, How to Protect What's Left of It.* Anchor Press, Garden City, N.Y.

1

Value Conflicts in the Design and Organization of EFT Systems

Rob Kling

Computing developments, like other social, economic, and technical developments, are not socially neutral. Different ways of organizing control over computing resources (such as data, machinery, communications, expertise, and administrative procedures) have an associated politics.[1] The political commitments that accompany computing developments are comprised by, in part, the way in which the equipment and support staff add to or subtract from other forms of social investment and foster dependencies on external vendors, technical labour markets, etc.[2] The political dimensions of computing development also hinge importantly on the kinds of social arrangements that accompany specific kinds of applications, e.g., the ways in which data subjects' privacy is affected by the collection of data about themselves,[3] the extent to which clients of computer data systems are buffered from input or programming errors,[4] and the extent to which the distribution of computing resources exacerbates social inequities.[5]

These political characteristics of computing are often subtle, particularly with respect to newer and more fragmented computer-based technologies. Systematic patterns are most visible when many cases are examined, and when interest groups have articulated their preferences. Thus, special insight can be gained by examining the deployment of the "moderately developed" computing technologies in which value conflicts are most dramatic. This observation may pose some problems for comparing computing developments cross-nationally, since the kind of computing development most often undertaken, as well as the depth of pertinent social conflict, may vary cross-nationally.

This article examines one political dimension of new computing developments—the

"Value Conflicts in Computing Developments: Developed and Developing Countries," by Rob Kling. *Telecommunications Policy*, March 1983, pp. 12–34.

value conflicts that they help catalyse. It examines conflicts of social values that are especially important in the deployment of electronic funds transfer (EFT) systems.

While many studies of international development call special attention to the social and political dimensions of technical development, most of the literature on "computing in developing countries" is apolitical[6] and value laden. In particular, most authors assume that rapid computing development is socially progressive, while ignoring large inequities in the distribution of wealth in developing countries. These analyses of computing developments or "policy options" addressed to problems of developing countries are consistent with the larger tradition of commentary about the social dimensions of computing in industrialized countries, commentary that also pays little attention to the politics of computing developments.

Commonly, such commentaries contain futuristic and naïve scenarios in which all (significant) members of a society have access to computer-based information services and "personal" computer systems.[7] Such views assume that there are no significantly scarce resources in the societies they describe—no poor, no infirm, no ill-educated, no socially stigmatized. These assumptions are unrealistic even for developed countries like the USA, Japan, and the countries of Western Europe. In short, much of the literature on new computing developments rests on an implicit utopian vision of ample social resources; all (industrialized) societies appear relatively underdeveloped in comparison with these "computopias." As a consequence, it is difficult to examine directly the political dimensions of the evolution of computing in developing countries by investigating the literature on future computing developments in general.

This article provides an alternative by focusing on value conflicts that are catalysed by current computing developjments in the USA. While values are inherently bound up with a particular cultural and historical period, the kinds of conflicts examined here help shed light on analogous conflicts in other developed and developing countries.

---

[1] James Danziger, William Dutton, Rob Kling and Kenneth Kraemer, *Computers and Politics: High Technology in American Local Government*, Columbia University Press, New York, 1982.

[2] Rob Kling and Elihu Gerson, "The social dynamics of technical innovation in the computing world," *Symbolic Interaction*, Vol. 1, No. 2, December 1977.

[3] James Rule, Douglas McAdams, Linda Stearns and David Uglov, *The Politics of Privacy*, New American Library, New York, 1980.

[4] Theodore Sterling, "Consumer difficulties with computerized transactions: an empirical investigation," *Communications of the ACM*, Vol. 22, No. 5, May 1979, pp. 283–289.

[5] John King, Rob Kling and Kenneth Kraemer, "Maintaining social equity in EFT developments," *Proceedings of the 3rd International Conference on Information Systems*, Ann Arbor, Michigan, 1982.

[6] Kalman provides a good example of the dominant apolitical literature (Robert Kalman, "Eight strategic issues for informatics," in J. M. Bennett and R. E. Kalman, *Computers in Developing Nations*, North Holland, New York, 1981). Prieto-Diaz and Wilson provide a politically sensitive alternative, rare in its examination both of the *costs* of computing support and of the *employment impacts* of computing (Ruben Prieto-Diaz and Stephen Wilson, "The impacts of computing on the Latin American countries," *Computers and Society*, Vol. 11, No. 2, Spring 1981, pp. 2–9).

[7] Christopher Evans, *The Micro Millenium*, Simon Schuster, New York, 1979; James Martin, *The Telemic Society*, Prentice Hall, New York, 1981.

Computers as Causal Agents

Before examining the ways in which computerized systems are catalysts for conflicts among social values, their roles as instruments of social action should be clarified. Computerized systems are usually portrayed as powerful actors at one extreme or as mere tools at the other. Large-scale computerized systems are probably better viewed as institutions with ecologies of social and political support that render them most responsive to particular elites and to the staff that develop, market, implement and operate them.[8] Even when seen as instruments, however, computer-based systems are complex relative to what the tool analogy leads one to expect.

Personal Knowledge of Computing

Our picture of computerized systems is predicated on and amplified by scattered news stories and gossip. We are led to entertain hastily formed beliefs concerning what computerized systems are good for, how they work, how and when they fail, and what interests they serve. Yet, although many people interact with computers frequently, few can claim direct experience with and knowledge of the full array of computing developments. There are so many different modalities of computing adapted to so many different social worlds that intimate knowledge of the complete world of computing is simply unobtainable even for computer experts.

Consider a technologist who specializes in electronic mail systems—one of several technologies that comprise contemporary office automation. He has accumulated detailed information about which mail systems have good facilities for saving and editing mail. He knows about the costs for preparing, sending and saving messages on various electronic mail systems. Developing this expertise takes attention and time. While he is a specialist in electronic mail he is often almost like a layman in understanding other computer-based technologies such as urban information systems,[9] artificial intelligence, military command and control systems, or EFT.[10] Each major class of computing applications rests on somewhat different technologies in different social and economic arrangements.

The modes of computing currently in use are extremely diverse. Furthermore, many computing technologies are not merely gadgets built of hardware and software and placed in social settings, but are the focus of technology-based social movements. These computer-based social movements include

- Computer assisted instruction.
- Personal computing.
- Office automation.
- Urban information systems.

---

[8] Rob Kling, "Defining the boundaries of computing in complex organizations," Working Paper, Public Policy Research Organization, University of California Irvine, Irvine, CA, 1982.

[9] Danziger *et al., op cit,* Ref 1.

[10] Rob Kling, "Value conflicts and social choice in electronic funds transfer system developments," *Communications of the ACM,* Vol. 21, No. 8, August 1978, pp. 642–657.

- Medical information systems.
- Simulation/gaming.
- Material requirements planning (manufacturing inventory control).
- Electronic funds transfer (EFT) systems.
- Artificial intelligence.

The preceding list of the uses of computer technologies hardly exhausts the different modes that are being developed and implemented today. There is no "automated payroll movement," but thousands of organizations have automated their payroll preparation. Other modes of computer use, such as complex statistical analyses in the social sciences or numerical analysis in the physical sciences, are simply part of a larger scientific movement, a movement that emphasizes quantification of research strategies and the use of computing when the number of samples and variables becomes large. Even the simplest labels, such as "personal computing" or "medical information systems," allude to whole families of computer applications. Each of these families, in turn, may have many specialized variants in use in many different organizations or social settings.

•   •   •

Computers as Actors and Instruments

Computers are often treated as powerful actors. Assertions such as "computers increase productivity," "computers dehumanize jobs," "computers make learning exciting," "computers improve decision making," and "computers are revolutionizing American society," make computer systems into powerful social actors. At best, these claims are shorthand codings for extremely complex sets of events. Computers are not active independent forces but are instrumentalities that have consequences under special and rather complex conditions.

The example of price scanners in North American supermarkets is illustrative. In some cases, the markets that adopt these computerized devices have laid off clerks or avoided hiring additional clerks in proportion as their business grew. But this is not a simple issue of "computers v. jobs" or "computers eliminate jobs." Such compact descriptions ignore the role of powerful actors, the supermarket owners and managers.

Storeowners hope to reduce costs by carefully replacing workers with capital equipment. Scanners do not show up unexpectedly in supermarkets like mushrooms sprouting on a lawn. Scanners are expensive and, hence, purposely planted. A pedestrian who is hit by a car doesn't say, "This is simply a case of technology versus people." He wants to know who was in the driver's seat. Compact slogans like "technology v. people" or "computers cut jobs" imply that there is no one in the driver's seat.

The development of supermarket scanners involves important social choices about the organization of work which are obscured by emphasizing "technology" and "jobs" and neglecting significant social choices. Supermarket owners can deploy scanners at the check-out stand and have checkers use them with or without abandoning item-pricing. Market owners often claim that they must abandon item-pricing to save sufficient labour costs to make the scanners economically efficient. If that were the case, they could introduced scanners and raise their prices or wait until scanners were cheaper.[11]

This example of supermarket scanners illustrates a common role played by computerized technologies as catalysts of social conflict. Market owners are said to be seeking ways to reduce costs. Computer systems might provide a useful means of doing so. When such systems are adopted, certain price-marking jobs will probably be eliminated. However, one by-product of eliminating these jobs is to reduce the job market for women and part-time workers. It also reduces the ability of consumers to audit their purchases at the checkstand to be sure they are not being overcharged.

In such cases, it is facile to attribute the outcomes such as the removal of item pricing to computers. The computer is a critical instrument that enables supermarket owners to consider the feasibility of both removing item prices and reducing their direct labour costs. But to neglect the role of the supermarket owners or managers would be mistaken. It leaves no one in the driver's seat.

This example also illustrates another critical aspect of computing. Most people do not interact in simple ways with computers or computer applications. We confront computerized technologies embedded in relatively complex social orders.[12] In the case of supermarket scanners, a customer deals with the price-marking policy of the store, with a database of prices that is kept up-to-date by clerical staff and with policies for having checkers rapidly scan the goods. The goods are managed by the floor supervisor, who can keep track of the productivity of each checker. A person who is at the receiving end of any of the socially important computer applications is inextricably bound up in the organizational world that it supports, whether the application by airline reservations, computer assisted instruction, long-distance dialing, the IRS tax auditing systems, or a police wants and warrants system. Dealing with computing entails dealing with the organizational arrangements that surround the technology.

·   ·   ·

Conflicts of Value and Interest in Computing

Computing developments cannot be assessed in isolation from the organizations or cultures that use them. Our example of price scanners also suggested that computers may catalyse conflicts between different groups that are impacted by their use.

Organizations can try to treat computer-based systems as instruments, and turn them to serve their interests. When groups conflict, one or more of them may find ways to exploit computerized technologies to their advantage. A group may exploit the symbolic dimensions of computerized data systems to gain legitimacy or to capture the substantive advantages of high speed communication and data manipulation.[13] In many cases where

---

[11] The arguments advanced by market owners are difficult to evaluate because good data about the costs and payoffs of scanners are scarce.

[12] Kling, *op cit*, Ref 8.

[13] Rob Kling, "Social analysis of computing: theoretical orientations in recent empirical research," *Computing Surveys*, Vol. 12, No. 1, March 1980, pp. 61–110; and Danziger *et al.*, *op cit*, Ref 1.

computer-based systems are exploited for relative advantage in inter-group conflict, there is conflict over resources and social terrain, but not over key social values. For example, if one department in an organization uses sophisticated breakdowns of its workload to argue for more staff during budget reviews, its managers need not differ significantly in value-orientation from those in other departments that are also competing for larger shares of the budgetary pie; all the managers may well want bigger and better-trained staffs.

On the other hand, some groups conflict in values, as well as in interests. The study of the dynamics of these kinds of groups is the subject of this inquiry. Value conflicts that are catalysed by computing developments in two domains of computer use, electronic funds transfer systems and instructional computing in secondary schools, are now examined. The specific values in each case derive from political debates within the USA. They will not apply in any straightforward way to developing countries. However, the ways in which groups that promote the deployment of new computing developments often serve some values at the expense of others is more universal. Also, many collateral social choices can be made in automating some activity. These include such matters as the particular form of technology employed, conditions under which different participants control data and associated computing resources, pricing policies, etc. Even when the equipment configurations are limited in variety, these collateral elements can vary significantly and support or undermine specific social values.

Value Conflicts in EFT Developments in the USA[14]

EFT systems are composed of an array of different technologies that transfer funds electronically between accounts. They include networks for automatically clearing cheques while debiting and crediting accounts, directly debiting and crediting individual bank accounts from point-of-sale terminals in retail stores, and providing cash on demand 24 hours a day.

EFT systems represent a particularly rich source of illustrations of value conflicts because they have now been in use for a significant period of time, because their adoption and promotion involve substantial commitments on the part of the financial institutions that use them, and because their diffusion has affected a broad cross-section of the public at large. Conflicting storylines about EFT systems are readily apparent in both popular and academic literatures.

At one extreme, some analysts identify emerging EFT systems with social progress. For example, Long claims that[15]

> EFTS is happening because it is a better way. All arguments about the sufficiency of the present paper system are meaningless. Television did not come about because the radio system was overloaded or was breaking down, nor did radio or the telephone develop because the mail was about to collapse. Neither were these systems built because the public

---

[14] This section and the next one draw upon more extensive analyses of EFT development (Kling, *op cit*, Ref 10).

[15] Robert Long, *EFT Systems, Banking and Regulation I*, American Bank Institute, 1974.

was crying for their development. They came about simply because they represented a "better way" of communication.

Such proponents of EFT systems point to their ability to reduce the cost of paper processing, reduce petty theft and support convenient add-on services such as automatic payroll deposits. They have visions of a chequeless and cashless society, in which integrated EFT systems transfer money instantaneously and efficiently. While Long's remarks were published over eight years ago, the storyline is common today.

At the other extreme, many analysts and policy makers have pointed to major and unresolved social and technical problems associated with EFT developments. Maintaining consumer sovereignty in markets within which EFT services are provided, the development of reliable systems, and the protection of individual privacy have been among the issues engendering controversy and debate.[16] In fact, the diffusion of EFT applications has not yet delivered anticipated benefits fully in many instances; and, while EFT systems are widespread, they are for the most part operated without large-scale integration.

The importance of these issues, and the sense one makes of them, is inextricably linked to the value orientation of the analyst.[17] At this point, EFT developments have matured sufficiently that at least five distinct value orientations, each resting on its own assumptions about which social goods should be maximized, can be identified in policy debates in the USA:

Private enterprise model: The pre-eminent consideration is profitability of financial systems, with the highest social good being the profitability of both the firms providing and the firms utilizing the systems. Other social goods such as consumers' privacy or the need of the government for data are secondary.

Statist model: The strength and efficiency of government institutions is the highest goal —government needs for access to personal data on citizens. The need for mechanisms to enforce citizens' obligations to the state will always prevail over other considerations.

Libertarian model: The civil liberties as specified by the US Bill of Rights are to be maximized in any social choice. Other social purposes such as profitability or welfare of the state would be sacrificed should they conflict with the prerogatives of the individual.

Neo-populist model: The practices of public agencies and private enterprises should be easily intelligible to ordinary citizens and be responsive to their needs. Societal institutions should emphasize serving the "ordinary person."

Systems model: Financial systems must be technically well organized, efficient, reliable, and aesthetically pleasing.

In different instances, policies and developments may support, conflict with, or be independent of these models. Each of them, except the Systems model, has a large number of supporters and a long tradition of support within the USA. Thus, EFT developments

---

[16] Mark Budnitz, "The impact of EFT on consumers: practical problems faced by consumers," *University of San Francisco Law Review*, Vol. 13, No. 2, Winter 1979, pp. 361–404; and Rule, *et al., op cit,* Ref 3.

[17] Kling, *op cit,* Ref 10. For a general introduction to the "value-conflict" approach, see Earl Rubington and Martin Weinberg, eds, *The Study of Social Problems: Five Perspectives,* Oxford University Press, New York, 1981, Chap 4.

that are congruent with any of these positions might be argued to be in "the public interest." These value positions are not all comparably developed in other countries, as we shall see in the discussion of computing development in a developing country, Brazil.

Perceptions of benefits and problems depend upon one's values and commitments. To illustrate this point, I will examine some of the meanings and conclusions each perspective generates when brought to bear on some specific areas of controversy: market arrangements, consumer protection, and the privacy of personal financial transactions.

Market Arrangements

According to advocates of *laissez-faire* markets, the class interests of consumers and suppliers are best served when goods and services are bought and sold under conditions of a perfectly competitive market: there are many buyers and sellers, none dominant, each of whom may easily enter or exit the marketplace and each of whom may easily alter his/her business associations; and, each party has complete information about a product or service through its price, since all costs are internalized.[18] According to the theory, the long-term interests of all parties are best served in perfectly competitive markets; the largest number of goods will be produced at the lowest overall price. Both neo-populist and private enterprise values would be jointly served by these arrangements.

As conditions in a particular market depart from this theoretical ideal, private enterprise and neo-populist values may increasingly conflict. If a market is dominated by a few suppliers, prices may be too high and the market will "inefficiently" produce too little. If all costs are not internalized in the price of a good, the market will price it too low, too much will be produced, and the real costs to consumers will be excessive. In that event, private enterprise criteria will dominate neo-populist values. (For example, the price of gasoline does not include the cost of cleaning up smog.)

Neo-populist critics of North American enterprise often equate size with market power. In their eyes, large organizations should not be trusted to act in the public interest: the major car manufacturers, "big oil," and "big government" all merit distrust. The US banking industry, with 19,000 banks of different kinds and sizes, might appear highly competitive. However, banking is highly concentrated in local markets and nationally in the USA. In many cities, a handful of banks have the majority of accounts. In 1973, the 100 largest banks, 0.5% of the banks, held 70% of the funds on deposit. Through bank mergers and acquisitions of bank holding companies, this industry has become more concentrated during the last decade. Since banks are authorized to operate in a given city or state, competition is currently focused on local rather than on national markets, which are also highly concentrated.

Some advocates of EFT services argue that banks should be allowed to extend their services via terminal networks into new markets. Banks are forbidden by federal law to operate in more than one state, and some states prohibit branch banking, although these limitations are being fought and removed. According to advocates of extended banking services, these laws are simply archaic. It should be possible, in this view, for the residents of Eugene, OR, to have easy access to the services of the Chase Manhattan Bank,

---

[18] Edwin Mansfield, *Microeconomics*, W. W. Norton, New York, 1981.

Citibank, Bank of America, Security Pacific, and the Chemical Bank of New York by allowing them to place teller machines in convenient locations nationwide. After all, no one objects to rows of candy machines or clusters of gas stations on the corners of intersections.

Representatives of smaller banks and of consumer groups believe that the expensive EFT costs can be more easily afforded by the larger banks. They fear that EFT developments will further accelerate the concentration of the banking industry. After all, it is more likely that large banks such as Citibank or Bank of America will extend teller machines to Eugene, OR, than that a small institution such as Laguna Federal Savings and Loan will. Those who fear a further increase in the concentration of the banking industry exacerbated by extended bank terminal systems argue that bank terminals should be mandatorily shared. In that way, if Citibank were to place a teller machine in Eugene, Laguna Federal Savings and Loan could also offer services to Eugene residents over the same terminal at a fair fee.[19]

In these debates, consumer groups utilize neo-populist criteria. Bankers utilize both neo-populist and private enterprise criteria in justifying their preferences.

Consumer Convenience and Protection

If a person uses an EFT system, what protections does he have if transfers are made without his authorization, if he wishes to stop payment or simply if there is an error? What kind of control does the individual have over his transactions? To what extent is the EFT provider liable? To what extent is the customer liable? In consumer protection, as in other market issues, the positions taken by various parties seem to hinge in large part on *a priori* value commitments. People who trust current market structures or who view the recent pro-consumer regulations as inimical to their own interest or to the broader public interest advocate reliance upon current market forces to select the best services. In their view, neopopulist and private enterprise values can be jointly served. Other analysts view the US economy as increasingly controlled by several hundred large corporations that are usually protected by the regulatory agencies that were originally supposed to oversee them. According to these analysts, reliance upon current market and regulatory arrangements would not serve the broad public interest. They point to the vigour with which specific industries have fought consumer reforms, such reforms as truth-in-advertising and fair credit reporting. Neo-populist advocates have been active, pressing for laws that limit the financial liability of consumers in case of errors in EFT systems, limit liability for unauthorized transfer, and increase consumer control by mandating stop-payment or reversible payment mechanisms.

In 1978, the US Congress enacted a special law, informally called the EFT Act (EFTA), which improved the kinds of protections for consumers using many kinds of EFT services.[20] It covers all transactions initiated through electronic terminals (e.g., telephone

---

[19] Some states in the USA, such as Iowa, have mandated sharing, while other states, such as California and Massachusetts, have not.

[20] Title XX of the Financial Institutions Regulatory Interest Rate and Control Act of 1978, Pub. L. No. 95–630 and 2001, 92 Stat. 3641 (1978) codified in 15 USC & 1692.

bill payment,[21] automated teller machines, and preauthorized debits and deposits), but not those initiated with paper instruments (e.g. truncated checking). EFTA mandates that financial institutions make disclosures in "readily understandable language" about the timing of transfers, charges, whom to notify in the event of unauthorized transfers, etc. The Act provides for consumer liability for unauthorized transfers on a sliding scale. While the law is ambiguous, a common reading suggests that consumers are absolved of financial responsibility if they report the loss of theft of an EFT card within two days, while they are strictly liable for unauthorized transfers if they wait over 60 days. Between these periods, they can be liable for up to $500.[22] The EFTA also specifies some procedures for resolving errors.

But the EFTA does not enable consumers to reverse or stop payments, nor does it prevent employers, creditors, or public agencies from requiring that a person use an EFT-based service to transact business. Also, many of the record-keeping, liability, and error-resolution procedures will work best for people who are sophisticated in their financial dealings, who keep good paper records, who are especially alert, and who are adept at resolving conflicts with bureaucratic organizations. Those people who are less "bureaucratically competent" will probably have some troubles.[23]

The EFTA is a compromise. It provides more protection to consumers than private enterprise advocates desired but far less protection than neo-populists advocated that Congress provide. As long as EFT systems are discretionary, they will most likely be used by those who can best cope with them. They do promise greater convenience for many routine transactions when they work well, yet they require substantial symbolic and organizational skills in order to detect and resolve problems when difficulties arise.

Privacy of Personal Transactions

In the popular conception, computers and concerns about privacy go hand-in-hand. Privacy connotes a complex array of issues. What information shall be collected about a person? How shall a person know about, complete, or correct a record (due process)? To whom and under what conditions shall personal records be made available (confidentiality)? A common view treats privacy as an elementary social exchange: people who desire a service relinquish certain information so that the provider may make a sound decision.

While this view locates privacy of personal data in the relationship of exchange between providers and clients of a service, it misses the ways in which much financial data collected by organizations in the late twentieth century is passed around to a wide array of third parties who in turn use it for a host of purposes that are well outside the control of the client.

Privacy issues in EFT can be illustrated with the example of automated cheque

---

[21] "Telephone bill payment" is a kind of service for paying bills such as rent or utilities via touchtone phone.

[22] Ellen Broadman, "Electronic Fund Transfer Act: is the consumer protected?" *University of San Francisco Law Review*, Vol. 13, No. 2, Winter 1979, p. 245–272.

[23] Budnitz, *op cit*, Ref 24; Kling *et al.*, *op cit*, Ref 5; and Bob Sipchen, "The creature that came out of the vaults," *Los Angeles*, Vol. 27, No. 12, December 1982, pp. 261–265, 430–435.

processing (ACP)[24] systems and bank records. ACP systems record to whom each person writes each cheque. This information, along with the date of the transaction, a cheque identifier, and the amount of transaction appears in the person's local bank record. A record of each payee is necessary in the event that a receipt is required and in order that the customer may audit his account. All this information is available now, since each bank microfilms every cheque cashed against one of its account holders and keeps it on file for six years, in accord with the Bank Secrecy Act of 1970.

Such records are a rich source of social data. US Supreme Court Justice Douglas once noted that

> In a sense, a person is defined by the checks he writes. By examining them, the agents get to know his doctors, lawyers, creditors, political allies, social connections, religious affiliation, educational interests, the papers and magazines he reads, and so on, ad infinitum.

In EFT systems, disclosure of information to third parties is the primary privacy issue. Typically, such data are sought by police and grand juries conducting legitimate investigations. But the data is sometimes sought by these same agencies acting against their political enemies. With manual records, the cost of finding out whether a particular individual wrote a cheque to a particular party or group is prohibitively expensive. With ACP systems, they would be neatly filed in machine readable form for six years, under the supervision of the Bank Secrecy Act of 1970.

The array of personally sensitive data made accessible is compounded in other EFT-related systems. Point-of-sale networks can be used to track the movements of particular individuals. Credit card or debit card files will also contain records of hotels stayed in, restaurants frequented, and other personal activities.

Libertarian criteria emphasize system designs, organization practices, and laws that minimize intrusiveness, maximize fairness, and maximize the control individuals have over the content and confidentiality of their records in the absence of competing concerns that outweigh the need for individual control. Advocates of statist and private enterprise positions emphasize the needs large organizations have for information, the costs of implementing due process procedures, and the infrequency of abuse.

In 1978, the US Congress passed the Financial Privacy Act, which extended an individual's rights regarding financial data kept about him by his bank, credit union, or similar organization. During the 1970s, several important court cases reduced the extent to which a person could have property rights over records about him (e.g., control their release to third parties). The 1978 Financial Privacy Act dictated that individuals' financial records were subject to property rights. These rights were declared to be partial, rather than complete. For example, the Act requires both that a bank inform its customers of the general conditions under which it discloses information to third parties (e.g., employers, public agencies, market research firms) and that it inform a customer if data about him has been subpoenaed by a court, but it does not require that the customer be informed

---

[24] Cheque truncation, a procedure in which a paper cheque is kept by the depository institution or the first bank to receive the cheque, is an example of an ACP system. An ACP system is operated by Bank One of Columbus, Ohio for clients of Merrill, Lynch, Pierce, Fenner and Smith's huge "CMA" money market fund.

whenever data about him has been released to a third party.[25] Nor does it require public agencies to obtain a court order before obtaining data about a customer. Nor does it limit the period of time that a depository institution should keep data about a customer.

This law, like the EFTA, is a compromise between parties with different values. In addition to advocates of libertarian and private enterprise values, advocates of statist values were major actors in the debate, arguing that public agencies should have unlimited access to financial data to pursue investigations and other mandated activities. In the net, libertarian values have suffered somewhat more than statist or private enterprise values by these legal developments related to EFT-based services.

Differing Incentives for EFT Developments

Making value stances explicit helps us interpret the meanings various interest groups have assigned to particular issues related to EFT systems. Focusing on value orientations also sharply illustrates an important aspect of computing's social impact. To the extent that value orientations conflict, it is impossible to develop policies that will optimize all parties' goals and interests simultaneously.

To understand how conflicts are resolved in the marketplace, it is important to recognize that even though EFT systems can foster some form of social progress, they are costly and will be developed by organizations with particular interests. While many EFT systems are to be used by the larger public, they are selected, financial and developed by financial institutions, retail firms and public agencies that embed them in their own operations. EFT systems have been most forcefully advocated and developed by groups that employ predominantly private enterprise or statist criteria for social choice. The following four examples of the interest that dictate use of EFT services include two that illustrate predominantly private enterprise interests and two that illustrate statist interests:

- Supermarkets and small businesses in USA often suffer large losses from bad cheques. Computer-based credit authorization services enable a merchant to reduce his losses.

- North American firms that advertise by mail often identify potential customers in terms of their demographic characteristics. Yet the knowledge that a person recently purchased a similar service is a better predictor of the likelihood that he will purchase a given service than is his membership in some demographically defined group. As financial transactions become automated, the pool of potential market data either for internal use by large retail firms or for sale by credit card firms could increase substantially and provide merchants with more effective mailing lists.

- The US Government's Federal Reserve Board (Fed) processes about 10 billion cheques annually for member banks, but is prohibited from passing its costs back to the banks. Banks have been steadily leaving the Federal Reserve System since the

---

[25] Office of Technology Assessment, Congress of the United States, *Selected Electronic Funds Transfer Issues: Privacy, Security and Equity*. U.S. Government Printing Office, Washington, DC, 1982.

second world war. The Fed provides special loans and market information in exchange for member banks' maintaining relatively high reserve funds on account without interest in the reserve system. If the Fed administered a national EFT infrastructure, it could increase the accuracy and timeliness of its data about transactions in the economy. If automated cheque processing systems could lower the cost of cheque handling, the Fed could lower its overheads. Improved information and reduced reserve requirements might entice banks to re-enter the Federal Reserve System and thereby help increase the Fed's effective control over monetary policy.

- By the end of 1981, more than 36 million people were receiving social security benefits. Automating the transfer of credit to social security recipients could save a large part of the costs of preparing and mailing monthly cheques. In addition, theft of cheques from post boxes would be eliminated.

To understand computing developments like these, it helps to distinguish benefits from incentives. An incentive is an expected good that induces a party to take action, while a benefit is any good derived from the action taken. Incentives precede benefits. It may benefit individuals to receive fewer unwanted advertisements, but the incentives for developing special-interest mailing lists would be the decreased costs of advertising borne by retailers and hence, by their customers. Some incentives, particularly those that emphasize competition for new customers, also promise benefits to consumers through convenient new services and faster credit through preauthorized payments. However, cost-savings to EFT-using institutions is more problematic. The little publicly available data with which we can assess the claims for cost savings indicates that most EFT systems become cost effective only with very high transaction volumes. The high capital costs of EFT systems and the high volumes of business that they require makes consumer acceptance vital.

Some incentives are more important than others to EFT-using organizations. It is unlikely that individual banks would save a substantial portion of the cost of paper handling with EFT systems. Rather, fear and hope drive many private organizations into developing EFT systems. A firm that develops EFT-related services may gain new customers; one that delays much longer than its competitors may lose out.

While private enterprise and statist interests encourage many organizations to develop specific EFT arrangements, some consumer convenience (a neo-populist goal) may result from them. However, no one argues that enhancing libertarian values are either a major incentive or a likely consequence of large-scale EFT developments. Last, systems advocates and those favouring consumer convenience may favour more integrated services (e.g., fewer cards and terminals).

The relatively few auspicious developments in the emergence of EFT for advocates of libertarian or neo-populist viewpoints may be underscored by reversing our analysis. EFT technologies may help solve some of the problems faced by profit-making firms or public agencies in carrying out their activities. But advocates of neo-populist criteria, who stress institutional and legislative reforms to render large organizations more accountable to the public, are unlikely to view EFT systems as important strategic instruments. Similarly, libertarian analysts, who are concerned about minimizing the intrusiveness of organizations into people's private lives, do not consider EFT technologies to be important means for protecting individual liberties.[26]

•   •   •

Value Conflicts in Different Computing Arenas in the USA

It is common to view technologies as potent forces that foster rapid social change,[27] but the most significant technologies are diffused through modern societies over several decades. Automobiles, telephones, electricity, central heating, television and birth control did not act as independent, powerful forces in the USA. They were shaped and fitted so that the larger social order was not radically uprooted. There is evidence that computerization develops similarly within public agencies.[28] It is also likely that EFT technologies and instructional computing will be similarly absorbed over several decades. We still have much to learn about the social dimensions of other computer technologies from these two cases.

In the short run, when these technologies substitute for less technically sophisticated alternatives, the values of key actors—developers, resource controllers, and users—play a critical role in setting the stage for later developments. Later on, new styles develop; e.g., automobiles do not function like horseless carriages and photocopiers do not function like automated carbon copiers.

In the short run, institutional styles dominate the use of new technologies. Hospitals that use computers heavily are much more like hospitals that are hardly automated than they are like some other kind of institution—a bank, a grade school or an architectural firm. Thus, one who asks how a technology shall be best used is also asking questions about the larger social context in which it is embedded. Identifying key values at issue in a given institutional area—here banking and schooling—may help to identify the kinds of interests that easily align with different modes of computerization.

It is not a bona fide issue whether or not computers are used in banks or schools or libraries or manufacturing firms. How they are used, what infrastructure or resources and legal arrangements accompany their use, and what interests the arrangements serve are the questions we need answers to. Much is written about the promise of computers in many spheres of US life. Despite the billions of dollars spent each year on different forms of computerization, we have little systematic data about the ways in which computing is being integrated into public life in the USA.[29] In the absence of systematic and high quality data, we must often rely upon scattered reports and *a priori* models.

The analyses presented here suggest that *laissez-faire* EFT developments best serve private enterprise and statist values. Furthermore, in schools, instructional computing best supports vocational matching. Conversely, EFT developments will not serve neo-populist

---

[26] Rule, *et al.*, *op cit*, Ref 3.
[27] Evans, *op cit*, Ref 7.
[28] Rob Kling and Kenneth Kraemer, "Computers and urban services," in Danziger *et al.*, *op cit*, Ref 1.
[29] Kling, *op cit*, Ref 21.

or libertarian interests without special legal and institutional supports. In short, *laissez-faire* computing best serves relatively powerful interests. At this time, both EFT developments are in their infancy in the USA. There are still many open social choices.

•   •   •

Conclusions

This article has examined the way in which new forms of computerization can be developed along different lines reflecting important social values. Key value issues differ somewhat in the case of different computer-based technologies. They also differ substantially in developed and developing countries. The value conflicts catalysed by new computing developments are sometimes subtle, and their political dimensions are often more important in the long run than in the short run. Many small decisions and commitments accumulate and alter the political economy of choice in many social arenas.

If the analyses developed here are valid for many other kinds of computing technologies, computing developments will often exacerbate social inequities unless disadvantaged groups are given special support. These inequities may be economic. They may be largely social and political as in the case of EFT developments. These inequities hinge as much upon access to collateral social resources—laws and practices to protect consumers in the case of EFT—as they do upon access to computing equipment. Socially sensitive proposals for computerization should take explicit account of the values sacrificed or compromised as well as those fostered by new forms of computerization.[30]

Acknowledgments

Portions of this article were prepared at the University of California, Irvine, under NSF Grant No. MCS 81-117719, and also at the Harvard University Program on Information Resources Policy. The views represented here are not necessarily those of either the National Science Foundation or the Harvard program.

The author appreciates the assistance of Plinio de Aguiar, Julio Leite, Gabriel Rozman and Diane Wilson in the preparation of this article. This article is based on a paper presented at "Informatica '82," Rio de Janeiro, Brazil, October 1982.

---

[30] For example, see Rob Kling, "Accounting for social impacts in the design and development of computer-based information systems," in Harry Otway and Malcom Peltu, eds, *New Office Technology*, Francis Pinter, London (in press); see also Kling *et al., op cit,* Ref 5.

P·A·R·T·V

2

Proposed FBI Crime Computer System Raises Questions on Accuracy, Privacy

Evelyn Richards

On a Saturday afternoon just before Christmas last year, U.S. Customs officials at Los Angeles International Airport scored a "hit."

Running the typical computer checks of passengers debarking a Trans World Airlines flight from London, they discovered Richard Lawrence Sklar, a fugitive wanted for his part in an Arizona real estate scam.

As their guidelines require, Customs confirmed all the particulars about Sklar with officials in Arizona—his birth date, height, weight, eye and hair color matched those of the wanted man.

Sklar's capture exemplified perfectly the power of computerized crime fighting. Authorities thousands of miles away from a crime scene can almost instantly identify and nab a wanted person.

There was only one problem with the Sklar case: He was the wrong man.

The 58-year-old passenger—who spent the next two days being strip-searched, herded from one holding pen to another and handcuffed to gang members and other violent offenders—was a political science professor at the University of California at Los Angeles.

After being fingered three times in the past dozen years for the financial trickeries of

Reprinted with permission of *The Washington Post.* "Proposed FBI Crime Computer System Raises Questions on Accuracy, Privacy," by Evelyn Richards, *The Washington Post*, February 13, 1989.

an impostor, Sklar is demanding that the FBI, whose computer scored the latest hit, set its electronic records straight.

"Until this person is caught, I am likely to be victimized by another warrant," Sklar said.

Nowhere are the benefits and drawbacks of computerization more apparent than at the FBI, which is concluding a six-year study on how to improve its National Crime Information Center, a vast computer network that already links 64,000 law enforcement agencies with data banks of 19 million crime-related records.

Although top FBI officials have not signed off on the proposal, the current version would let authorities transmit more detailed information and draw on a vastly expanded array of criminal records. It would enable, for example, storage and electronic transmission of fingerprints, photos, tattoos and other physical attributes that might prevent a mistaken arrest. Though controversial, FBI officials have recommended that it include a data bank containing names of suspects who have not been charged with a crime.

The proposed system, however, already has enraged computer scientists and privacy experts who warn in a report to be released today that the system would pose a "potentially serious risk to privacy and civil liberties." The report, prepared for the House subcommittee on civil and constitutional rights, also contends that the proposed $40 million overhaul would not correct accuracy problems or assure that records are secure.

Mostly because of such criticism, the FBI's revamped proposal for a new system, known as the NCIC 2000 plan, is a skeleton of the capabilities first suggested by law enforcement officials. Many of their ideas have been pared back, either for reasons of practicality or privacy.

"Technical possibility should not be the same thing as permissible policy," said Marc Rotenberg, an editor of the report and Washington liaison for Computer Professionals for Social Responsibility, a California organization.

The need to make that trade-off—to weigh the benefits of technological advances against the less obvious drawbacks—is becoming more apparent as nationwide computer links become the blood vessels of a high-tech society.

Keeping technology under control requires users to double-check the accuracy of the stored data and sometimes resort to old-fashioned paper records or face-to-face contact for confirmation. Errors have plagued the NCIC for many years, but an extensive effort to improve record-keeping has significantly reduced the problem, the FBI said.

Tapped by federal, state and local agencies, the existing FBI system juggles about 10 inquiries a second from people seeking records on wanted persons, stolen vehicles and property, and criminal histories, among other things. Using the current system, for example, a police officer making a traffic stop can find out within seconds whether the individual is wanted anywhere else in the United States, or an investigator culling through a list of suspects can peruse past records.

At one point, the FBI computer of the future was envisioned as having links to a raft of other data bases, including credit records and those kept by the Immigration and Naturalization Service, the Internal Revenue Service, the Social Security Administration and the Securities and Exchange Commission.

One by one, review panels have scaled back that plan.

"There's a lot of sensitive information in those data bases," said Lt. Stanley Michaleski, head of records for the Montgomery County police. "I'm not going to tell you that cops aren't going to misuse the information."

The most controversial portion of the planned system would be a major expansion to include information on criminal suspects—whose guilt has not yet been established.

The proposed system would include names of persons under investigation in murder, kidnapping or narcotics cases. It would include a so-called "silent hit" feature: An officer in Texas, for instance, would not know that the individual he stopped for speeding was a suspect for murder in Virginia. But when the Virginia investigators flipped on their computer the next morning, it would notify them of the Texas stop. To Michaleski, the proposal sounded like "a great idea. Information is the name of the game."

But the "tracking" ability has angered critics.

"That [data base] could be enlarged into all sorts of threats—suspected communists, suspected associates of homosexuals. There is no end once you start," said Rep. Don Edwards (D-Calif.), whose subcommittee called for the report on the FBI's system.

The FBI's chief of technical services, William Bayse, defends the proposed files, saying they would help catch criminals while containing only carefully screened names. "The rationale is these guys are subjects of investigations, and they met a certain guideline," he said.

So controversial is the suspect file that FBI Director William Sessions reportedly may not include it when he publicly presents his plan for a new system.

P·A·R·T·V

3

Computer Matching is a Serious
Threat to Individual Rights

John Shattuck

More and more frequently, government agencies have been employing a new investigative technique: the matching of unrelated computerized files of individuals to identify
suspected law violators. This technique—*computer matching*—provides a revolutionary
method of conducting investigations of fraud, abuse, and waste of government funds. It
permits the government to screen the records of whole categories of people, such as
federal employees, to determine who among them also falls into separate, supposedly
incompatible categories, such as welfare recipients.

Computer matching raises profound issues concerning individual privacy, due process
of law, and the presumption of innocence. It also poses serious questions about cost
effectiveness and the internal management of government programs.

Computer Matching versus Individual Rights

To understand the impact of computer matching on individual rights, it is first necessary
to grasp the difference between a computer-matching investigation and a traditional law
enforcement investigation.

A traditional investigation is triggered by some evidence that a person is engaged in
wrongdoing. This is true for cases of tax evasion, welfare fraud, bank robbery, or traffic
speeding. The limited resources of law enforcement usually make it impracticable to

---

"Computer Matching is a Serious Threat to Individual Rights," by J. Shattuck, *Communications of the ACM*, Association for
Computing Machinery, Inc. **27** (6) June 1984, pp. 538–541. Copyright 1984, Association for Computing Machinery, Inc.
Reprinted by permission.

conduct dragnet investigations. More importantly, our constitutional system bars the government from investigating persons it does not suspect of wrongdoing.

A computer match is not bound by these limitations. It is directed not at an individual, but at an entire category of persons. A computer match is initiated not because any person is suspected of misconduct, but because his or her category is of interest to the government. What makes computer matching fundamentally different from a traditional investigation is that its very purpose is to generate the evidence of wrongdoing required before an investigation can begin. That evidence is produced by "matching" two sets of personal records compiled for unrelated purposes.

There are four ways in which a computer match differs from a conventional law enforcement investigation in its impact on individual rights:

Fourth Amendment

The Fourth Amendment protects against unreasonable searches and seizures, the most blatant of which have been "fishing expeditions" directed against large numbers of people. From the "writs of assistance" used in the eighteenth century by royal revenue agents, to door-to-door searches for violations of the British tariff laws in the American Colonies, to the municipal code inspections of the twentieth century to enforce health and safety standards, the principle that generalized fishing expeditions violate the right to be free from unreasonable searches has held firm in American law.

That principle is violated by computer matching. The technique of matching unrelated computer tapes is designed as a general search. It is not based on any preexisting evidence to direct suspicion of wrongdoing to any particular person. Although systematic searches of personal records are not as intrusive as door-to-door searches, the result is the same: a massive dragnet into the private affairs of many people.

Presumption of Innocence

People in our society are not forced to bear a continuous burden of demonstrating to the government that they are innocent of wrongdoing. Although citizens are obliged to obey the law—and violate it at their peril—presumption of innocence is intended to protect people against having to prove that they are free from guilt whenever the government investigates them.

Computer matching can turn the presumption of innocence into a presumption of guilt. For instance, Massachusetts welfare recipients have been summarily removed from welfare rolls as the result of a computer match. These people fought for reinstatement based on information the state neglected to consider after their names appeared as "hits" in the match.

Another example of this "presumption of guilt" occurred three years ago in Florida. The state's attorney for a three-county area around Jacksonville obtained case files for all food stamp recipients in the area. He then launched fraud investigations against those receiving allotments of more than $125 a month. A federal court of appeals invalidated the file search and enjoined the investigation on the ground that the targeted food stamp recipients were put in the position of having to prove the allotment they had received was *not* based on fraud. Construing the Food Stamp Act, the Court held that "it did not allow the [state food stamp] agency to turn over files . . . for criminal investigation *without regard to whether a particular household has engaged in questionable behavior.*"

Once a computer match has taken place, any person whose name appears as a "raw hit" is presumed to be guilty. In part, this is because the technology of computer matching is so compelling and in part because its purpose—the detection of fraud and waste—is so commendable. The worst abuses of computer matching, such as summary termination of welfare benefits, have occurred when authorities have casually transformed this "presumption" into a conclusive proof of guilt.

Privacy Act

The most important principle governing collection and use of personal information by the government is that the individual has a right to control information about himself and to prevent its use without his consent for purposes wholly unrelated to those for which it was collected. This principle is imperfectly embodied in the Privacy Act of 1974.

The Privacy Act restricts disclosure by federal agencies of personally identifiable information—*unless* the subject consents. There are two major exceptions. The first involves a "routine use," defined as "the use of (a) record for a purpose which is compatible with the purpose for which it was collected." The second involves a "law enforcement" disclosure, which enables an agency to be responsive to a request by another agency for information relevant to the investigation of a specific violation of law.

When computer matching was in its infancy, the Privacy Act was correctly perceived by several federal agencies to be a major stumbling block. The Civil Service Commission initially balked in 1977 at the plans of Health, Education and Welfare (HEW) Secretary Joseph Califano to institute a match of federal employee records and state welfare rolls, on the ground that the use of employee records for such a purpose would violate the Privacy Act. The Commission's General Counsel, Carl F. Goodman, stated that the proposed match could not be considered a "routine use" of employee records, since the Commission's "information on employees was not collected with a view toward detecting welfare abuses." Similarly, it could not be considered a "law enforcement" use, continued Goodman, since "at the 'matching' stage there is no indication whatsoever that a violation or potential violation of law has occurred."

This reasonable interpretation of the Privacy Act soon gave way to a succession of strained readings. Since enforcement of the Privacy Act is left entirely to the agencies it regulates, it is hardly surprising that the agencies have bent the Act to their own purposes. They have now miraculously established that computer matching is a "routine use" of personal records. All that is required, they say, is to publish each new computer matching "routine use" in the *Federal Register*.

The Privacy Act has now been so thoroughly circumvented by executive action that it can no longer be seen as an effective safeguard. Nevertheless, the principle underlying the Act—that individuals should be able to exercise control over information about themselves that they provide to the government—is a bedrock principle of individual privacy. That principle is at war with the practice of computer matching.

Due Process of Law

Once a computer match has taken place, it will result in a series of hits. All those identified are in jeopardy of being found guilty of wrongdoing. To the extent that they are not given notice of their situation and an adequate opportunity to contest the results of the match, they are denied due process of law.

This is precisely what has happened in several matching programs. For example, the results of Secretary Califano's Operation Match were kept secret from federal employees whose records were matched with welfare rolls, because the Justice Department viewed the investigation "as a law enforcement program designed to detect suspected violations of various criminal statutes." The Justice Department ordered the Civil Service Commission not to notify any of the federal employees whose names showed up as hits, since "[t]he premature discussion of a specific criminal matter with a tentative defendant is in our view inimical to the building of a solid prosecutorial case." In Massachusetts, welfare authorities have terminated benefits of persons showing up as hits without even conducting an *internal* investigation.

This approach makes a mockery of due process. Due process is the right to confront one's accuser and introduce evidence to show that the accuser is wrong. When the accuser is a computer tape, the possibility of error is substantial. Keeping the subject of a raw hit in the dark increases the likelihood of an error's going undetected.

Some Comments on the Office of Management and Budget's (OMB's) Guidelines

Since 1979 computer matching at the federal level has been regulated by guidelines issued by the OMB. These guidelines, which were considerably looser in May 1982, are intended to "help agencies relate the procedural requirements of the Privacy Act to the operational requirements of computerized matching." Although Kusserow [following chapter] cites the guidelines as evidence of the federal government's concern about privacy protection, in fact, they constitute an effort to paper over the profound conflict between (1) the Privacy Act principle that personal records are to be used by federal agencies only for purposes compatible with those for which they were compiled and (2) the computer matching practice of joining personal records compiled for wholly unrelated purposes.

OMB's matching guidelines have rendered meaningless the central principle of the Privacy Act. In 1980, for instance, the Office of Personnel Management (OPM) published a notice in the *Federal Register* concerning its proposed use of personnel records for a matching program to help the Veterans' Administration (VA) verify the credentials of its hospital employees. The notice dutifully stated that the proposed match of OPM and VA records was a "routine use," which it explained as follows:

> An integral part of the reason that these records are maintained is *to protect the legitimate interests of the government* and, therefore, such a disclosure is compatible with the purposes for maintaining these records.

Under that broad justification any disclosure or matching of personal records would be permissible, since all federal records are purportedly maintained for the "legitimate interests of the government."

The guidelines, on which Kusserow so heavily relies, contain no requirements or limitations on the conduct of computer matching in these critical areas:

1. **The nature of the record systems to be matched**—There are no personal records, no matter how sensitive (e.g., medical files, security clearance records, intelligence records), that are beyond the reach of computer matching for any investigative purpose.
2. **The procedures to be followed in determining the validity of hits**—No particular procedures are required to ensure that the subjects of hits are afforded due process of law.
3. **The standards and procedures to be followed for securing OMB approval of a proposed match**—Since the first guidelines were promulgated in 1979, OMB has not disapproved a single computer match.
4. **The projected costs and benefits of a proposed match**—The 1982 guidelines have deleted all reference to cost-benefit analyses or reports on computer matches. It is entirely at an agency's discretion whether to undertake a proposed match or to report the costs and benefits of the match.

It is impossible not to conclude that computer matching at the federal level is a huge unregulated business, the only clear effect of which to date has been the undermining of individual privacy.

Some Examples of Computer Matching

In the seven years since the technique was first used, over 200 computer matches have been carried out. At the federal level there have been matches for a wide variety of investigative purposes, using a broad range of personal record systems of varying degrees of sensitivity.

These include matches of federal employee records maintained by the Civil Service Commission with files of persons receiving federal Aid to Families with Dependent Children, to investigate "fraud"; federal personnel records maintained by OPM with the files of VA hospital employees, to check "accreditation"; federal personnel records of Agriculture Department employees in Illinois with Illinois state files on licensed real estate brokers, to "ascertain potential conflicts of interest"; Internal Revenue Service (IRS) records of taxpayer addresses with lists of individuals born in 1963 supplied by the Selective Service System, to locate suspected violators of the draft registration law; and Labor Department files of persons entitled to receive Black Lung benefits with Health and Human Services (HHS) records of Medicare billings, to investigate double-billing medical fraud.

These matches are only a handful of the total conducted. Even with these, very little hard data are available, thanks to the extraordinarily weak oversight and reporting requirements of the OMB guidelines and to the lack of attention to this subject by Congress.

Conclusion

Computer matching is an attractive investigative technique. It appears to permit law enforcement officials to instantaneously root out all instances of a particular kind of wrongdoing in a particular segment of the population. It constitutes a general surveillance system that supposedly can detect and deter misconduct wherever it is used. It appeals to the view that "if you haven't done anything wrong, you don't have anything to worry about."

But there are heavy costs associated with computer matching, both in terms of individual rights and in terms of law enforcement expenditure. It is not at all clear that the benefits of the technique outweigh the costs.

The comparison of unrelated record systems is fraught with difficulty. Data on the computer tapes may be inaccurate or inaccurately recorded. It may present an incomplete picture. It is unlikely to be sufficient to "answer" difficult questions, such as whether a person is entitled to receive welfare or is engaged in a conflict of interest.

On the other hand, computer matching erodes individual rights: the Fourth Amendment right to be free from unreasonable search, the right to the presumption of innocence, the right to due process of law, and the right to limit the government's use of personal information to the purposes for which it was collected.

Moreover, the rapid and unchecked growth of computer matching leads inexorably to the creation of a *de facto* National Data System in which personal data are widely and routinely shared at all levels of government and in the private sector.

Recommendations

As a general framework for safeguarding individual rights, I propose the following:

1. The Privacy Act should be amended to clarify that computer matches are not *ipso facto* "routine uses" of personal record systems.
2. No further federal computer matches should be permitted without express congressional authorization.
3. Congress should not authorize computer matches of sensitive personal records systems (the confidentiality of which is otherwise protected by statute) such as taxpayer records maintained by the IRS, census records maintained by the Census Bureau, or bank records maintained by federally insured banking institutions.
4. No computer match should be authorized unless and until an analysis has been made of its projected costs and projected savings in the recoupment of funds owed to the government. The match should not be authorized unless the public benefit will far outweigh the cost—and unless individual rights will be protected. The results and full costs of any match should be published.
5. Procedural due process protections for the persons whose records are to be matched should be specified by statute, including the right to counsel, the right to a full hearing, and the right to confidentiality of the results of a match.

The thrust of my comments has been to raise some basic questions about computer matching. I recommend a moratorium on all further matching so Congress and the public can study the results of all computer-matching programs conducted to date and assess the long-term consequences.

In closing, I second the view of Justice William O. Douglas, when he said, "I am not ready to agree that America is so possessed with evil that we must level all constitutional barriers to give our civil authorities the tools to catch criminals."

The Government Needs Computer Matching to Root Out Waste and Fraud

Richard P. Kusserow

More information will be collected, stored, and retrieved in our lifetime than in all other generations combined. This information explosion, however, is creating new problems for the government manager.

Crucial issues revolve around the use of computer technology to ensure that taxpayers' money is being safeguarded and to manage personal data without sacrificing individuals' rights to privacy. Predictions about the dehumanizing effects of technology heat the issues.

Unfortunately, *computer matching*, charged with myth and misconception, has become fuel for this emotional debate. Critics depict mere man against massive computers and evoke the specter of the Orwellian 1984 and "Big Brother."

In reality, computer matching covers many processes used to detect payment errors, increase debt collection, and identify abusive grant or procurement practices. The Department of Education, for instance, uses computer matches to identify federal workers who default on student loans. The National Science Foundation screens research fund applicants against its employee and consultant lists to prevent any conflict of interest in grant awards.

My office in the federal Department of Health and Human Services (HHS) uses matches to unearth doctors who are double-billing Medicare and Medicaid for the same service.

Over 230 problem health providers were removed from participation in the Medicare program in the last fiscal year—a 253 percent increase over the previous year. We have also matched the Social Security benefit rolls against Medicare's record of deceased patients and discovered thousands of cases of administrative error and fraud. This project alone resulted in savings of over $25 million.

Without the computer, government could not fulfill many mandated missions. Forty million Social Security checks are issued each month—an impossible feat without automated data processing.

Computers are here to stay and will become even more pervasive. We are witnessing the virtual disappearance of hardcopy, a development of special importance to the government manager, auditor, and investigator. Without a paper trail, government workers must use innovative techniques to meet this new challenge.

Computer matching is an efficient and effective technique for coping with today's expensive, complex, and error-prone government programs. For instance, computer matching and other innovative techniques helped my office identify $1.4 billion in savings —about a 300 percent increase over the previous year.

The High Cost of Errors and Fraud

Over $350 billion is paid out every year through government entitlement programs to millions of recipients. Ineligibility and payment errors cost the taxpayers billions of dollars annually. Add to this the dollars lost through loan delinquencies, excessive procurement costs, and other abuses, and the losses become even more staggering. Perceptions of waste and cheating in government programs erode public support for the programs and respect for government itself.

Government managers cannot simply rely on chance discovery, voluntary compliance, or outdated manual procedures to detect errors. They have a responsibility to use innovative techniques to monitor the expenditures of program dollars, to detect fraud, to determine who is ineligible or being paid incorrectly, etc.

Computer Matching: Not a New Technique

Computer matching is not a new technique. The basic approach of matching one set of records to another has been used by both public and private sectors for years. Although matching predates the computer, the computer has made it quick and cost effective.

In 1977, Congress, recognizing the effectiveness of computer matching, passed Public Law 95-216. This law mandated that state welfare agencies use state wage information in determining eligibility for Aid to Families with Dependent Children (AFDC). Subsequent legislation also required similar wage matching for the Food Stamp program.

Computer matching can serve many objectives:

- assuring that ineligible applicants are not given costly program benefits;
- reducing or terminating benefits for recipients who are being paid erroneously;
- detecting fraudulent claims and deterring others from defrauding the program;

- collecting overpayments or defaulted loans more effectively;
- monitoring grant and contract award processes;
- improving program policy, procedures, and controls.

Simply defined, computer matching is a technique whereby information within two or more records or files is compared to identify situations that *could* indicate program ineligibility or payment errors.

The process, however, should not and does not stop there. The computer does *not* decide who is getting erroneous payments and does *not* automatically decide who should be terminated from the payment rolls. The computer merely provides a list of items that *could* indicate an erroneous or aberrant situation. The matched items must be investigated by program staff. Only then can an agency determine whether a payment should be adjusted or stopped, or the file record corrected.

Early computer matching efforts, which acted upon "raw hits" without proper follow-up, were justifiably criticized. Today, computer matching is far more effective, efficient, and less intrusive. A manual examiner had to search through *all* records in a file. A computer, however, picks out only those records that match and ignores all the others: it only scans for aberrations. In this sense, computer matching is far less of an invasion than 100 percent manual review.

President's Council on Integrity and Efficiency

In 1981, President Reagan formed the President's Council on Integrity and Efficiency (PCIE) to coordinate efforts to attack fraud and waste in expensive, government programs. One of its major activities is the Long-Term Computer Matching Project, which I cochair with the Inspector General of the Department of Labor.

Our overall objective is to expand the cost-effective use of computer matching techniques that prevent and detect fraud, abuse, and erroneous payments and, at the same time, to protect the rights and privacy of individuals. The Project does not run computer matches. Rather, through its membership of federal and state program administrators, the Project

- gathers and shares information about federal and state matching activities,
- analyzes and removes technical and administrative obstacles to computer matching, and
- fosters increased federal and state cooperation in computer-matching activities.

So far, the Project has inventoried federal and state matches, established a clearing-house and a newsletter, and launched an effort with eight states to test standardized data extraction formats for computer matching. The standardized formats will make matching "hits" more reliable, thereby reducing the need for manual review of client files.

One of the Project's first tasks was to revise the Office of Management and Budget's (OMB's) "Guidelines for Conducting Computer Matching Programs." The Guidelines were originally set forth in 1979 to implement the Privacy Act of 1974, in the context of federal computer matching efforts. The 1982 revision streamlined paper-work requirements and reiterated requirements for privacy and security of records.

The Guidelines call for public notice of proposed matches and strict safeguards concerning use, storage, and disclosure of information from matches. In his December 1982 testimony before Senator William S. Cohen's Subcommittee on Oversight of Government Management, David F. Linowes, former chairman of the Privacy Protection Study Commission, stated that the 1982 Guidelines make "sound provisions for protecting the privacy of the individual."

Fears of a National Database on Individuals Ungrounded

A major concern is that computer matching will ultimately result in the creation of a national database of computerized information on every individual. OMB Guidelines ensure that such would be impossible. Once a match is completed, Guidelines require that the files be returned to the custodian agency or destroyed.

To be effective, computer matching must be built into the administration of a government program—not just run as an *ad hoc* investigation. Also, matching should be performed *before* payments are made, as well as used in an ongoing monitoring effort. In this way, matching stops payment errors before they occur.

Prepayment screens using computer matching techniques not only detect errors, they also deter fraud and abuse in government programs. California, for instance, routinely checks public assistance claims against wage records, saving an estimated $1 million per month in overpayments.

Computer matching is racially, sexually, and ethnically blind. No person or group is targeted.

Some Existing Privacy Safeguards

A number of privacy safeguards have already been institutionalized. "The Computer Matching Reference Paper," published by the PCIE, sets forth "purpose" standards. An agency considering a match must first conduct a study to determine the match's scope and purpose, identify agencies and records involved, and ascertain the information and follow-up actions needed. A key aspect is the assessment of the estimated costs and benefits of a match.

Another safeguard is OMB's "Model Control System." This document suggests that government officials carefully analyze the hits from a computer match to verify the data with the source agency and determine whether the hit is the result of error or abuse. For large matches, officials would have to analyze only a sample of the hits to verify the matching process. After doing this, officials should take corrective measures, proceeding cautiously against any individual where doubt exists.

A third privacy safeguard is provided by a memorandum sent by the deputy director of OMB, Joseph A. Wright, Jr., to the heads of all government agencies on December 29, 1983.

That memorandum provides instructions for preparing a Computer Match Checklist, to be completed by each government agency involved in matching federal data records.

This checklist and the Model Control System help agencies to comply with the Privacy Act of 1974 and the OMB Computer Matching Guidelines of May 11, 1982.

Relevant government agencies must complete this checklist immediately following their announced intent (as indicated by publication in the *Federal Register*) to conduct a computer match. This checklist must be on file for review by OMB, Government Accounting Office (GAO), and others interested in ensuring that safeguards are being followed to protect personal data.

Still another privacy safeguard, the PCIE reference paper, calls upon government managers to do a cost-benefit analysis both before and after a computer-matching project. In some cases it will make sense to do a pilot match based on a sample. The results of this pilot study would provide a better idea of what could be achieved from a full-scale matching project. In any event, pilot matches are subject to Privacy Act safeguards.

Finally, the OMB Matching Guidelines require government managers to prepare a matching report at least 30 days prior to the start of the match project. It would be published in the *Federal Register* to give relevant parties an opportunity to comment.

Conclusion

Any computer match that does not consider privacy, fairness, and due process as among its major goals is not a good project. Well-designed computer matches are cost effective.

The government's need to ensure a program's integrity need not be incompatible with the individual's right to privacy and freedom from government intrusion. The point is to *balance* these competing interests. Government managers have a responsibility to ensure that program funds are spent as intended by Congress. At the same time, these managers must carry out those responsibilities within the requirements and spirit of the Privacy Act. Such a balance is both possible and essential.

Additional Comments

In addressing the concerns raised by John Shattuck [in the next chapter], I must first put federal computer-matching projects into perspective. A common misconception is that computer matching is primarily an investigative tool. In reality, matches are used primarily to assist in government audits to identify inappropriate data (e.g., mistakes or errors) in the records under review. Most of our computer-assisted audits use computer screens rather than tape-to-tape matches, which are usually performed on a one-time basis.

The goals of these matches are twofold: (1) to purify the databases, and (2) to build in routine front-end prevention procedures. ("Front-end matches" match data to an existing database before payments are made.) Shattuck's premise seems to be that computer-matching programs have enlarged the number of individuals subjected to government inquiry. This is not true. The criteria for identifying a "hit" are no different than the criteria for evaluating the need for further information received by other means. Computer matches have not created new areas of audit or investigation, but they have allowed agencies to improve their methods.

I fail to see the merit of requiring agencies to limit themselves to less effective audit activities. That argument is based on the unfounded belief that sophisticated proactive audit techniques are *per se* violative of individual rights.

Shattuck's comments demonstrate a lack of understanding of the procedures followed in federal computer matchings. The individuals whose records are included in a match are not really under investigation. The only records that can result in an inquiry are those that produce a hit. Such indicates a mistake, error, or possible fraud or abuse. In an Aid to Families with Dependent Children (AFDC) state-to-state match, for instance, records indicating a recipient receives AFDC benefits in several jurisdictions would be identified for further review. Since this clearly raises a question of eligibility, an eligibility review can hardly be characterized as a "fishing expedition."

The only real change from computer matches is the increased number of cases identified. Much of the alleged impact on individual rights discussed by Shattuck are issues separate and distinct from computer matching. Once hits are identified for further review, the reviews should be evaluated as any other reviews based on information from any source.

Examples cited by Shattuck of actions taken as a result of matches reflect his disagreement with the evidentiary criteria used by some agencies in pursuing an adverse action. They are in no way an indictment of computer matching for identifying cases for review. The two issues are separate.

The information produced by a matching program is no different from that produced by any other audit or law enforcement inquiry. Once that is recognized, the constitutional concerns raised by Shattuck can be put into perspective. I am unaware of any court decision even remotely indicating that computer-assisted audits of government records run afoul of the fourth amendment protections against unlawful search and seizure.

I also fail to see how a law enforcement inquiry based on a computer-matching hit has any impact on the presumption of innocence in a criminal proceeding. This presumption places the burden on the government to prove guilt in a criminal case. None of the examples cited by Shattuck have any bearing on this principle.

It is equally misleading to imply that computer matching has resulted in any weakening of due process. The right to confront an accuser has never applied to the purely investigative stages of a law enforcement inquiry. Shattuck apparently believes that individuals identified in a computer match should be afforded rights never afforded any investigative subject. Law enforcement inquiries can often be closed without a subject interview. This is equally true for inquiries triggered by a computer match. This in no way violates any legally recognized due process standards.

Criticisms made against computer matching are generally unfounded. I strongly oppose Shattuck's recommendations as being unnecessary and inappropriate. His intent is to greatly restrict, if not totally eliminate, the use of computer-matching projects by the federal government.

Requiring congressional authorization for each match and affording persons whose records are being matched rights far in excess of those available to the actual subjects of a law enforcement inquiry would not improve—but end—the use of matching. This is far too vital an audit technique to lose—especially in view of the fact that Shattuck has failed to provide even a *single* example of a federal computer match that violated an individual's legal rights.

The rights of individuals in federal criminal, civil, or administrative proceeding are already protected by constitutional and other legal constraints. I agree with Shattuck that matches should not be conducted prior to an analysis of their cost effectiveness. In fact, no federal agency has the resources to conduct such matches without careful consideration of costs versus benefits. Further restrictions are, therefore, unnecessary.

P·A·R·T·V

5

Excerpts from *Personal Privacy in an Information Society*

Privacy Protection Study Commission

Introduction

This report is about records and people. It looks toward a national policy to guide the way public and private organizations treat the records they keep about individuals. Its findings reflect the fact that in American society today records mediate relationships between individuals and organizations and thus affect an individual more easily, more broadly, and often more unfairly than was possible in the past. This is true in spite of almost a decade of effort to frame the objectives of a national policy to protect personal privacy in an information-dependent society. It will remain true unless steps are taken soon to strike a proper balance between the individual's personal privacy interests and society's information needs. In this report, the Privacy Protection Study Commission identifies the steps necessary to strike that balance and presents the Commission's specific recommendations for achieving it. This introductory chapter briefly describes the problem and focuses and defines the objectives of a national policy. It also weighs major competing values and interests and explains how the Commission believes its policy recommendations should be implemented.

•　　•　　•

The Framework for a National Policy

The imbalance in the relationship between individuals and record-keeping institutions today is pointedly illustrated by the experiences of Catherine Tarver, a "welfare mother" from the State of Washington, and Mitchell Miller, a businessman from Kathleen, Georgia.

In the late 1960's Mrs. Tarver became ill and was hospitalized. The Juvenile Court, after reviewing a report by her caseworker which contained "assertedly derogatory contents," including an allegation of child neglect, placed her children temporarily in the custody of the Department of Public Assistance. A few months later, the Juvenile Court, after another hearing, exonerated Mrs. Tarver and returned her children to her, but the caseworker's report remained in her file at the Department of Public Assistance.

Although Mrs. Tarver had her children back and was no longer on the welfare rolls, she still wanted to have the caseworker's report removed from her file on the grounds that it was false, misleading, and prejudicial and would be available to other State social services agencies with whom she might subsequently have contact. When she asked for a fair hearing to challenge the report, the Public Assistance Department rejected her request because the grievance was not directly related to eligibility for public assistance. She sued in a State court but lost, the court agreeing with the welfare agency that the fair hearing procedure was not meant to deal with collateral problems. The U.S. Supreme Court refused to review her case and the caseworker's report remained in her file.

Mitchell Miller's difficulties began on December 18, 1972, when a deputy sheriff from Houston County, Georgia, stopped a Pepsico truck purportedly owned by Miller and found it was transporting 150 five-gallon plastic jugs, two 100-pound bags of wheat shorts, cylinders of bottled gas, and a shotgun condenser. Less than a month later, while fighting a warehouse fire, the sheriff and fire department officials found a 7,500 gallon distillery and 175 gallons of untaxed whiskey. An agent from the U.S. Treasury Department's Bureau of Alcohol, Tobacco and Firearms suspected Miller of direct involvement in both events and two weeks later presented grand jury subpoenas to the two banks where Miller maintained accounts. Without notifying Miller, copies of his checks and bank statements were either shown or given to the Treasury agents as soon as they presented the subpoenas. The subpoenas did not require immediate disclosure, but the bank officers nonetheless responded at once.

After he had been indicted, Miller attempted to persuade the court that the grand jury subpoenas used by the Treasury Department were invalid and, thus, the evidence obtained with them could not be used against him. He pointed out that the subpoenas had not been issued by the grand jury itself, and further, that they were returnable on a day when the grand jury was not in session. Finally, Miller argued that the Bank Secrecy Act's requirement that banks maintain microfilm copies of checks for two years was an unconstitutional invasion of his Fourth Amendment rights. The trial court rejected Miller's arguments and he appealed.

The Fifth Circuit Court of Appeals also rejected Miller's claim that the Bank Secrecy Act was unconstitutional, an issue that had already been resolved by the U.S. Supreme Court in 1974. The Court of Appeals agreed, however, that Miller's rights, as well as the bank's, were threatened and that he should be accorded the right to legal process to challenge the validity of the grand jury subpoenas. The Court of Appeals saw Miller's interest in the bank's records as deriving from the Fourth Amendment protection against unreasonable searches and seizures, which protected him against "compulsory production of a man's private papers to establish a criminal charge against him."

On April 21, 1976, a fateful day for personal privacy, the U.S. Supreme Court decided that Mitchell Miller had no legitimate "expectation of privacy" in his bank records and thus no protectible interest for the Court to consider. The Court reasoned that because checks are an independent record of an individual's participation in the flow of commerce, they cannot be considered confidential communications. The account record, moreover, is the property of the bank, not of the individual account holder. Thus, according to the Court, Miller's expectation of privacy was neither legitimate, warranted, nor enforceable.

The *Tarver* and *Miller* decisions are the law of the land, and the Commission takes no issue with their legal correctness. Viewed from one perspective, these cases are very narrow and affect only a minute percentage of the population. *Tarver* might be seen as simply refusing an additional request from a welfare mother who had received the benefits she was entitled to under a program; *Miller* might be seen as a decision affecting only the technical procedural rights of a criminal defendant. Perhaps these two cases are not very compelling, but the Commission singles them out because each starkly underscores an individual's present defenselessness with respect to records maintained about him. Who is there to raise such issues if not people in trouble? They are the ones who reach for and test the limits of existing legal protections, and if the protections are not there for them, they will not be there for anyone.

In both cases, institutional policies and the legal system failed individuals in their efforts to limit the impact of records on their lives. The *Tarver* case warns that one may be able to do nothing about a damaging record, not even if it is false, until some adverse action is taken on the basis of it, that one has no way to prevent the damage such an action can do. The *Miller* decision goes even further, making records the property solely of the record keeper, so that the individual cannot assert any interest in them, although his interest would be assertible if he himself held the same records. Even worse, it warns that not only a "revenuer" but anyone, public or private, can gain access to an individual's bank records if the bank agrees to disclose them.

Each case illustrates systemic flaws in the existing means available to any individual who tries to protect himself against the untoward consequences of organizational record keeping. Together they strongly suggest that if Americans still value personal privacy, they must make certain changes in the way records about individuals are made, used, and disclosed.

Since so much of an individual's life is now shaped by his relationships with organizations, his interest in the records organizations keep about him is obvious and compelling. The above cases and the rest of this report show how poorly that interest is protected. If it is to be protected, public policy must focus on five systemic features of personal-data record keeping in America today.

First. While an organization makes and keeps records about individuals to facilitate relationships with them, it also makes and keeps records about individuals for other purposes, such as documenting the record-keeping organization's own actions and making it possible for other organizations—government agencies, for example—to monitor the actions of individuals.

Second. There is an accelerating trend, most obvious in the credit and financial areas, toward the accumulation in records of more and more personal details about an individual.

Third. More and more records about an individual are collected, maintained, and disclosed by organizations with which the individual has no direct relationship but whose records help to shape his life.

Fourth. Most record-keeping organizations consult the records of other organizations to verify the information they obtain from an individual and thus pay as much or more attention to what other organizations report about him than they pay to what he reports about himself; and

Fifth. Neither law nor technology now gives an individual the tools he needs to protect his legitimate interests in the records organizations keep about him.

•   •   •

The role that technology can play in determining whether a particular type of record or record-keeping operation is or is not within the scope of existing legal protections is comparatively new. It arises in the main from automation, which multiplies the uses that can be made of a record about an individual, and will grow in importance as new record-keeping applications of computer and telecommunications technology are developed. Computers and telecommunications serve the interests of institutions and can be best appreciated as extensions of those interests. The failure to recognize that relationship has deflected attention from the essential policy choices the new technologies offer. Nonetheless, without the new technologies, certain record-keeping practices and the organizational activities they support would not be possible.

The broad availability and low cost of computer and telecommunications technologies provides both the *impetus* and the *means* to perform new record-keeping functions. These functions can bring the individual substantial benefits, but there are also disadvantages for the individual. On one hand, they can give him easier access to services that make his life more comfortable or convenient. On the other, they also tempt others to demand, and make it easier for them to get access to, information about him for purposes he does not expect and would not agree to if he were asked.

It is also quite evident that record-keeping organizations exploiting these new technologies to facilitate their own operations now pay little heed to the ways they could use the same technologies to facilitate exercise of the individual's rights and prerogatives in records used to make important decisions about him. It is ironic but true that in a society as dependent as ours on computer and telecommunications technology, an individual may still have to make a personal visit to a credit bureau if he wants access to the information the bureau maintains about him, or to get an erroneous record corrected. Although an error in a record can now be propagated all over the country at the speed of light, many organizations have made no provision to propagate corrections through the same channels, and existing law seldom requires them to do so. As a general proposition, system designers by and large have not fully used their knowledge and capabilities to make record-keeping systems serve individual as well as organizational needs and interests.

This is not to lay the blame on system designers, who are people doing what they are asked to do by the record-keeping organizations that support or pay for their services. The fault lies in the lack of strong incentives for the organization to ask them to do what they know how to do in the individual's interest. One reason for the way systems are designed and have been operated in the past has been their high cost. Instead of costing more, however, increased technological capability is now costing less and less, making it easier than ever for record-keeping organizations to take account of the individual's interests as well as their own, if they have incentives to do so.

One of the most striking of the Commission's several findings with respect to the current state of record-keeping law and practice is how difficult it can be for an individual even to find out how records about him are developed and used. What makes the difficulty the more serious is that the limited rights he now has depend in the main on his taking the initiative to exercise them. The list of records kept about an individual of which he is not likely to be aware seems endless. Even when he knows a record is being compiled, he often does not know what his rights with respect to it are, much less how to exercise them effectively, nor is he likely to be aware at the time he enters a record-keeping relationship of the importance of finding out.

In most cases, the individual can only guess at what types of information or records will be marshaled by those making any particular decision about him; furthermore, the specific sources are likely to be concealed from him. The situation makes it all but impossible for him to identify errors, or if he does, to trace them to their source. It also makes it impossible for him to know whether organizations with which he believes he has a confidential relationship have disclosed records about him to others without his knowledge or consent.

The Objectives of a National Policy

Every member of a modern society acts out the major events and transitions of his life with organizations as attentive partners. Each of his countless transactions with them leaves its mark in the records they maintain about him. The uniqueness of this record-generating pressure cannot be overemphasized. Never before the twentieth century have organizations tried or been expected to deal with individuals in such an exacting fashion on such a scale. Never before have so many organizations had the facilities for keeping available the information that makes it possible for them to complete daily a multitude of transactions with a multitude of individuals and to have the relevant facts on each individual available as a basis for making subsequent decisions about him. Obviously the advent of computing technology has greatly contributed to these changes, but automated record-keeping has grown in concert with many other changes in administrative techniques and in public attitudes and expectations.

The Commission finds that as records continue to supplant face-to-face encounters in our society, there has been no compensating tendency to give the individual the kind of control over the collection, use, and disclosure of information about him that his face-to-face encounters normally entail.

What two people divulge about themselves when they meet for the first time depends on how much personal revelation they believe the situation warrants and how much confidence each has that the other will not misinterpret or misuse what is said. If they meet again, and particularly if they develop a relationship, their self-revelation may expand both in scope and detail. All the while, however, each is in a position to correct any misperception that may develop and to judge whether the other is likely to misuse the personal revelations or pass them on to others without asking permission. Should either suspect that the other has violated the trust on which the candor of their communication depends, he can sever the relationship altogether, or alter its terms, perhaps by refusing thereafter to discuss certain topics or to reveal certain details about himself. Face-to-face encounters of this type, and the human relationships that result from them, are the threads from which the fabric of society is woven. The situations in which they arise are inherently social, not private, in that the disclosure of information about oneself is expected.

An individual's relationship with a record-keeping organization has some of the features of his face-to-face relationships with other individuals. It, too, arises in an inherently social context, depends on the individual's willingness to divulge information about himself or to allow others to do so, and often carries some expectation as to its practical consequences. Beyond that, however, the resemblance quickly fades.

By and large it is the organization's sole prerogative to decide what information the individual shall divulge for its records or allow others to divulge about him and the pace at which he must divulge it. If the record-keeping organization is a private-sector one, the individual theoretically can take his business elsewhere if he objects to the divulgences required of him. Yet in a society in which time is often at a premium, in which organizations performing similar functions tend to ask similar questions, and in which organizational record-keeping practices and the differences among them are poorly perceived or understood, the individual often has little real opportunity to pick and choose. Moreover, if the record-keeping organization is a public-sector one, the individual may have no alternative but to yield whatever information is demanded of him.

Once an individual establishes a relationship with a record-keeping organization, he has even less practical control over what actually gets into a record about him, and almost none over how the record is subsequently used. In contrast to his face-to-face relationships with other individuals, he can seldom check on the accuracy of the information the organization develops about him, or discover and correct errors and misperceptions, or even find out how the information is used, much less participate in deciding to whom it may be disclosed. Nor, as a practical matter, can he sever or alter the terms of the relationship if he finds its informational demands unacceptable.

A society that increasingly relies on records to mediate relationships between individuals and organizations, and in which an individual's survival increasingly depends on his ability to maintain a variety of such relationships, must concern itself with such a situation. Ours has begun to do so, and the Commission's inquiry showed that the individual's ability to protect himself from obvious record-keeping abuses has improved somewhat in recent years. Nevertheless, most record-keeping relationships are still dangerously one-sided and likely to become even more so unless public policy makers create incentives for organizations to modify their record-keeping practices for the individual's protection, and give individuals rights to participate in record-keeping relationships commensurate with their interest in the records organizations create and keep about them.

Accordingly, the Commission has concldued that an effective privacy protection policy must have three concurrent objectives:

- to create a proper balance between what an individual is expected to divulge to a record-keeping organization and what he seeks in return (*to minimize intrusiveness*);
- to open up record-keeping operations in ways that will minimize the extent to which recorded information about an individual is itself a source of unfairness in any decision about him made on the basis of it (*to maximize fairness*); and
- to create and define obligations with respect to the uses and disclosures that will be made of recorded information about an individual (*to create legitimate, enforceable expectations of confidentiality*).

These three objectives both subsume and conceptually augment the principles of the Privacy Act of 1974 and the five fair information practice principles set forth in the 1973 report of the Department of Health, Education, and Welfare's Secretary's Advisory Committee on Automated Personal Data Systems. The second objective to maximize fairness, in a sense subsumes all of them, and many of the Commission's specific recommendations articulate them in detail. The Commission has gone about protecting personal privacy largely by giving an individual access to records that pertain to him. Taken together, however, the three proposed objectives go beyond the openness and fairness concerns by specifically recognizing the occasional need for *a priori* determinations prohibiting the use, or collection and use, of certain types of information, and by calling for legal definitions of the individual's interest in controlling the disclosure of certain types of records about him.

.   .   .

The Commission specifies what it considers to be the proper terms of the individual's enforceable expectation in relationships with credit grantors, depository institutions, insurers, medical-care providers, the Internal Revenue Service, and providers of long-distance telephone service. Once again the recommendations are tailored to the particulars of each kind of record-keeping relationship. In each case, the Commission recommends that a protectible legal interest for the individual be created by statute; specifies the voluntary disclosures it believes should be permissible without the individual's consent and the procedures for establishing them; and sets forth the rules for initiating and complying with government demands for access to records. In no instance, however, does the Commission advocate complete, unilateral control by the individual. In every case it has respected the record-keeping organization's legitimate interests when threatened by actions of the individual. In essence, the Commission has said that the individual's interest must be recognized; that there must be procedures to force conflicting claims into the open; and that within this framework established by public policy, value conflicts should be resolved on a case-by-case basis.

Competing Public-Policy Interests

A major theme of this report is that privacy, both as a societal value and as an individual interest, does not and cannot exist in a vacuum. Indeed, "privacy" is a poor label for many of the issues the Commission addresses because to many people the concept connotes isolation and secrecy, whereas the relationships the Commission is concerned with are inherently social. Because they are, moreover, the privacy protections afforded them must be balanced against other significant societal values and interests. The Commission has identified five such competing societal values that must be taken into account in formulating public policy to protect personal privacy: (1) First Amendment interests; (2) freedom of information interests; (3) the societal interest in law enforcement; (4) cost; and (5) Federal-State relations.

The First Amendment and Privacy

The legitimate expectation of confidentiality is a concept the Commission endorses for several of the record-keeping relationships examined in this report. The policy objective is that when the relationship is one involving confidentiality of records, the record keeper shall be constrained from disclosing information about an individual without his authorization, either voluntarily or in response to a demand for it. The Commission recognizes that recommending any restriction on the free flow of truthful information raises serious questions in a democratic society, and sought ways to avoid conflict with both the goals of the First Amendment to the Constitution, and with the policy of broad access to public information articulated in statutes like the Freedom of Information Act.

When the Commission recommends rules to govern a record keeper's voluntary disclosure of a record about an individual, it does not attempt to specify nor does it assign to either government or the individual the responsibility of determining which information in the record may or may not be disclosed. Neither does the Commission recommend any liability for third parties who merely receive information or records generated by a confidential relationship. The Commission's recommendations simply specify *to whom* information may be disclosed without the individual's consent. The role of government in the enforcement of a recommended expectation of confidentiality would be simply to act, through the courts, as referee in disputes between a record keeper and an individual about whether an expectation is legitimate and whether it has been violated. Government would have no independent interest to enforce, and would take no enforcement initiative, except where deception or misrepresentation is used to acquire medical records without the patient's consent. Only the individual would have an enforceable interest.

The Commission takes great care to avoid recommendations that would amount to regulating the content of records collected, maintained, or disclosed by private-sector organizations because of two related considerations, one abstract, the other concrete. The first consideration is that a democratic society must keep governmental intrusion into the flow of information to a minimum; the second is that the First Amendment sharply limits such government intrusion. Of importance here are the recent decisions of the U.S. Supreme Court that have found private commercial information flows as deserving of First Amendment protections as the personal exercise of the right of free speech.

·   ·   ·

Freedom of Information and Privacy

The second competing societal value the Commission identified is freedom of information. In enacting the Freedom of Information Act (FOIA) in 1966, and strengthening it eight years later, the Congress gave expression to society's strong interest in opening the records of Federal government agencies to public inspection. The FOIA, to be sure, allows for exceptions from the general openness rule which an agency may invoke for certain information pertaining to national defense and foreign policy, law enforcement, individuals, internal agency deliberations, trade secrets, and information specifically declared confidential by other statutes. The withholding of exempt records, however, is subject to administrative and judicial review. Most of the States have enacted their own FOIA statutes in one form or another. Other statutes, both Federal and State, open meetings of certain governmental bodies to the public. The legal actions brought to test these statutes have shown the courts to be generally sympathetic to broadening public access to government records and deliberations, and, of course, journalists are natural advocates of full access and disclosure. Altogether, the presumption against secrecy in decision making and record keeping by government agencies is now firmly established.

The Commission has recommended the continuation of restrictions on the disclosure of specific records about individuals maintained by government agencies. While this recommendation may seem to conflict with the principle of freedom of information and openness, the Commission firmly believes that it is compatible with those principles and, indeed, that they are complementary aspects of a coherent public policy concerning public records.

·   ·   ·

For government, the Commission believes that the policy of combining explicit legislation for particular types of records with a general standard to be applied in all other cases is an appropriate way to balance the freedom of information interests and confidentiality interests. As Chapter 13 explains,[1] the combination does not lead to resolution of difficult cases overnight, but it does create a framework within which the conflicts between the two competing though compatible interests can be resolved.

The general concept of freedom of information has no currency in the private sector. Issuers of regulated securities must publicly disclose particular items of information about the individuals who control or manage companies, but organizations in the private sector by and large have no affirmative obligation to disclose their records about individuals to the public. They may be required to disclose such records to government agencies for a variety of reasons, as described in Chapter 9, but in many cases government is prohibited from subsequently disclosing that information to the public. Thus, in the private sector there is no freedom of information policy to conflict with a confidentiality of records policy.

Indeed, the Commission believes that in most instances the persuasive power of an active press can be relied on to work out a proper adjustment between the right to privacy and the freedom of information principle as it applies to public disclosure of information in records about individuals maintained by private-sector organizations. However, the Commission also believes that the individual needs some limited control over the public disclosure of particular types of information about him. An individual should be able to limit the public disclosure of credit, insurance, medical, employment, and education record information about himself. In these areas, the Commission has recommended for the

---

[1] Editors' note: References to chapters in this selection pertain to the full-length *Report of the Privacy Protection Study Commission.*

individual an assertible interest so that he can have a role in determining whether information about him should be publicly released. In fact, as to certain identifying information referred to as *directory information,* the Commission's recommendations recognize the general practice of public disclosure in such areas as employment, medical care, and education. Thus, reporters should be able to continue to find out who is in what hospital, who is employed by what firm, and who is enrolled in what school.

The Commission's recommendations, with one exception, do not limit or affect the ability of the press to request or obtain information. The area of medical records is the one area where the Commission not only recommends a duty on the record keeper to respect an individual's expectation of confidentiality but also suggests that it be made a crime to seek such information through misrepresentation or deception. Specific abuses by persons seeking medical-record information for use in adversary situations have led the Commission to conclude that such a recommendation is necessary. In all other cases, the Commission's recommendations do not limit or affect the ability of the press to request or obtain information. These balances are difficult to strike and the Commission has attempted to establish mechanisms for doing so rather than recommend specific disclosure prohibitions.

Law Enforcement and Privacy

The third competing interest the Commission identified is the interest in preventing and prosecuting crime. Organizations do and should have the means of protecting themselves from suspected fraud in insurance claims, fraudulent use of credit cards, multiple welfare applications, and the like. Organizations, both private and public, exchange information among themselves and with law enforcement authorities to protect against such losses and to assist in the prosecution of crime. The Commission has not suggested that this organizational interest be curtailed. Rather, it recommends that individuals be apprised, at the time they establish a relationship involving confidential records, that information about them may be disclosed for investigative or enforcement purposes if the record keeper develops evidence that points to criminal behavior on their part.

Government requests or demands for recorded information about individuals for law enforcement purposes pose a special problem. As a result of the *Miller* decision discussed earlier, an individual has no constitutional protections against government demands for access to records third parties maintain about him. There are some statutory protections, such as those for census records, Federal income-tax returns, and records developed in connection with federally funded drug abuse research and treatment programs. The Commission believes, however, that the individual should have an assertible interest in other types of records about him, such as those maintained by financial institutions, insurance companies, medical-care providers, and providers of long-distance telephone service, as a matter of general policy.

Government agencies have testified that to enforce the law, they need full and complete access to records kept about individuals by third parties. They argue that to restrict their access, or more specifically to subject it to the assertion of an individual's interest, would unduly handicap their legitimate law enforcement activities. The Commission seriously considered these arguments and has developed a set of recommendations that allow for continued law enforcement access, but under stricter rules. These rules are in two parts. First, they require law enforcement agencies to use legal process of some form whenever they seek information about an individual from a third-party record keeper. Second, when they seek access to records in which the individual has a legitimate expectation of confidentiality, the Commission recommends that the individual involved be given notice and the legal capacity to contest the action. The Commission has not recommended prohibiting government access, but rather giving the individual an assertible interest in the process of government information gathering about him. The requirement for legal process in all instances has the further advantage that it creates the basis for meaningful accountability mechanisms.

The Cost of Privacy

The fourth competing interest the Commission identified is cost. In maximizing fairness, this is the most compelling competing interest. Whether an organization is public or private, to make changes in record-keeping practices can increase its cost of operation and thus make the product or service it provides either more expensive or less accessible, or both. When this happens, both the record-keeping organization and some if not all of its customers or clients suffer. Adoption of the Commission's recommendations means that a great many organizations will have to make some changes in their record keeping. The costs of compliance will be higher or lower depending on how well an organization's current practices reflect the recommended balance between organizational interests and the individual's interest. The Commission has tried to keep compliance costs to a minimum by not recommending that organizations be required to report periodically to Federal or State government agencies, and also by not recommending inflexible procedural requirements.

The Commission's recommendations are aimed at getting results. Thus, they try to take advantage of the shared interest of individuals and organizations in keeping records accurate, timely, and complete. As previously noted, one reason for giving an individual a right of access to records about him is that doing so affords an organization the free help of an expert—the individual himself—on the accuracy of the information the organization uses to make decisions about him. Organizations, however, need some assurance before they are willing to enlist such help that it will not turn out to be unduly or undeservedly expensive.

To open an insurance company's underwriting files to inspection by applicants and policyholders, for example, gives the company a powerful motive to record only accurate, pertinent information about them and to keep its records as timely and complete as necessary. To encourage applicants and policyholders to look for information in underwriting files that could serve as the basis for defamation actions and windfall recoveries, however, would be contrary to the Commission's cost-minimizing objective and also an impediment to systemic reform. *The Commission wants organizations to invest in improving their record-keeping practices, not to spend their money in costly litigation over past practices and honest mistakes.* Hence the Commission's recommendation is to limit the liability of a record keeper that responds to an individual's request for access to a record it maintains about him.

Organizations in the private sector have a strong interest in keeping their decisions about customers, clients, applicants, or employees free of unreasonable government interference. The Commission's recommendations recognize this interest by concentrating on the quality of the information an organization uses as the basis for making a decision about an individual, rather than on the decision itself. For private-sector organizations the adverse-decision requirements the Commission recommends will expose the records used in arriving at a decision to reject an applicant, but the Commission relies on the incentives of the marketplace to prompt reconsideration of a rejection if it turns out to have been made on the basis of inaccurate or otherwise defective information.

For public-sector organizations, the Commission recommends no affirmative requirement that they reverse an adverse decision made on the basis of faulty information. For educational institutions, where the procedures for correcting or amending records are likely to be divorced from decision-making procedures, and where the individual has no easily invokable due process protections, the Commission proposes an affirmative requirement to *reconsider* but not a requirement to *reverse*. The Commission strongly believes that to mix concern about the outcome of individual decisions with concern about the quality of the information used in arriving at them not only risks undesirable interference with organizational prerogatives but also invites confusion as to the nature and extent of the individual's privacy interest, possibly to its detriment in the long run.

Federal-State Relations and Privacy

A major interest that must be weighed in the balance of organizations' needs for information against the individual's interest in having his personal privacy protected is society's interest in maintaining the integrity of the Federal system. The division of responsibility and authority between the Federal government and States is a cornerstone of the American political system and the Commission has been particularly attentive to it in both the methods it recommends for establishing legal requirements and the regulatory mechanisms and sanctions for enforcing such requirements.

In areas of record-keeping where the States are prominent record-keepers, or where records are generated in carrying out State programs, the Commission pays particular attention to the reserved-powers principle enunciated in the Tenth Amendment to the Constitution, emulating the Supreme Court's care not to interfere with the conduct of essential State government functions. Thus, where Federal regulation seems necessary, the Commission recommends making the requirements a condition of Federal benefits, which leaves the States some degree of choice. The Commission recommends tempering such exercise of Federal spending power by leaving considerable latitude in how the States implement the policies, and by urging them to make the minimum Federal requirements part of their own State legislation and to assume most of the responsibility for enforcing them.

In the areas of private-sector record-keeping where the States share regulatory power with the Federal government, the Commission recommends maintaining the current balance. For example, in financial areas where the Federal government now does most of the regulating, the Commission relies heavily on current Federal mechanisms in the implementation of the measures it recommends, with the State playing a supplemental role. In the insurance area, where the States now do most of the regulating, the commission recognizes a need for some limited Federal intervention in order to provide the necessary uniformity, but relies on the State enforcement mechanisms that now have primary responsibility.

Each of the implementation measures the Commission recommends is designed to avoid disturbance of the current Federal-State political balance of power. Indeed, the structure of the Commission's recommendations as a whole should strengthen the Federal-State partnership and increase the State's role in protecting the interests of the individual.

Implementation Principles and Choices

Each policy recommendation in this report is supplemented by an implementation recommendation. Collectively, the Commission's implementation recommendations add up to a consistent strategy for the practical application of the policies and practices the Commission believes should be adopted. The Commission has not tried to draft any of its recommendations in final statutory language. The Commission does, however, suggest how and in what manner its recommendations should be adopted, since the impact and significance of policies can be adequately assessed only in light of how they are to be applied.

Implementation Principles

The Commission's findings clearly reveal an overwhelming imbalance in the record-keeping relationship between an individual and an organization, and its policy recommendations aim at strengthening the ability of the individual to participate in that relationship. This can be accomplished in three ways: by prohibiting or curtailing unjustifiably intrusive information collection practices; by granting the individual basic rights, such as the right to see, copy and correct records about himself, coupled with obligations or organizations to incorporate protections for personal privacy in their routine record-keeping operations; and by giving the individual control over the disclosure of records about him. In exploring ways to implement its policy recommendations, the Commission was guided by three principles: (1) that incentives for systemic reform should be created; (2) that existing regulatory and enforcement mechanisms should be used insofar as possible; and (3) that unnecessary cost should be avoided.

· · ·

The Commission's single deviation from these three principles is the approach it recommends to the problem of systematic or repeated violations. The Commission advocates rights for individuals and relies primarily on the individual to exercise and protect those rights with the help of the courts, but as many of the chapters point out, however, giving an individual better ways to protect himself can be an inadequate tool. Thus, when there is evidence of repeated or systematic violations, the measures recommended for particular record-keeping areas assign specific responsibility on behalf of the public for enforcing compliance to appropriate government agencies, such as the Federal Trade Commission or State insurance departments.

· · ·

Implementation Choices

The Commission had three basic alternatives for giving effect to its policy recommendations: (1) voluntary compliance; (2) statutory creation of rights, interests, or responsibilities enforceable through either individual or governmental action; and (3) establishment of ongoing governmental mechanisms to investigate, study, and report on privacy protection issues. Each of the Commission's policy recommendations specifies the alternative it believes is most appropriate for that particular measure.

In the areas of research and statistical activities, and education, for example, the Commission specifies legislation in the form of amendments to existing Federal statutes to define further the responsibilities and duties of those types of record-keepers. In the public assistance and social services area, the Commission specifies Federal action that would make State enactment of the recommended statutory rights and responsibilities a condition of Federal funding.

In the private sector, the Commission specifies voluntary compliance when the present need for the recommended change is not acute enough to justify mandatory legislation, or if the organizations in an industry have shown themselves willing to cooperate voluntarily. In its mailing list recommendations, for example, the Commission specifies that when an organization has a practice of renting, lending, or exchanging the names of its customers, members, or donors for use by others in a direct-mail marketing or solicitation, it should inform each of them that it does so and give each an opportunity to veto the practice with respect to his own name. The Commission does not call for legislation to enforce compliance with this recommendation because it has reason to believe the industry is willing to accept these restrictions voluntarily, and there are no legal impediments to stop it from doing so.

The Commission also relies mainly on voluntary compliance in the area of employment and personnel; though there are a few exceptions, the most notable being the recommendation dealing with the creation and use of investigative reports, where implementation by amendment of the Fair Credit Reporting Act is the Commission's choice. In this area, the Commission prefers to rely mainly on voluntary compliance because of the complexity of the relationship between employer and employee and the difficulty of classifying all the various records different employers maintain about their employees and the way they use these records in employment decision making. For the Commission to recommend otherwise would be to recommend uniformity where variation is not only widespread but inherent in the employee-employer relationship as our society now knows it.

Most of the Commission's recommendations, however, do specify mandatory measures. This is partly because the Commission believes that in most cases voluntary compliance would be too uneven to be dependable, but most importantly, many of the issues the Commission's recommendations address are legal ones and require legal remedies. In the *Miller* case described above, for example, if the bank had wholeheartedly tried to protect Miller's interest, it would have done him little or no good since under existing law, Miller would have no interest in the records to assert. If a Federal agency insists on having an individual's account record today, a bank cannot successfully refuse to make it available.

•   •   •

A primary objective of the Commission's implementation strategy is to make sure that the privacy issues stay in proper focus. This requires continuing attention from a broad public-policy perspective—a need that is not fulfilled today even within the scope of the Privacy Act. A means must be found to provide for continued public awareness of what is clearly a continuing and pivotal concern and to assure ongoing attention to develop and refine understanding of specific and emerging problems. Notwithstanding the broad scope of this report, a number of tasks remain. Significant record-keeping areas, such as licensing at the State and local level, remain unexplored, and several chapters of this report highlight other problem areas that need further analysis, including the issue of unreasonable intrusiveness as evidenced by the amount and type of information an individual is required to reveal about himself in return for a desired or needed service or benefit. As indicated earlier, the propriety question is an extremely delicate one and there is as yet no generally accepted method of arriving at answers to it in different contexts. The Commission's recommendations offer mechanisms to identify those kinds of questions so they can be debated in the context most likely to be constructive in determining public policy.

A further argument for combining all three alternatives is that experience with other public-policy issues of this sort suggests a continuing need to coordinate the policies that have been and will be adopted and to assist in identifying and resolving real or apparent conflicts between existing, modified, and new statutes and regulations.

There is also the consideration that decentralized enforcement spreads responsibility for enforcement among agencies, organizations and individuals, each of which has numerous other responsibilities, thus increasing the risk that privacy objectives and protections will be obscured. The Commission advocates rights for individuals and reliance primarily on the courts to assure exercise of those rights. As indicated in many chapters of this report, however, improving the capability of the individual to protect himself can be an adequate tool for resolving major systemic problems. The Commission sees a need for some influential "prodding" structure, some sustained oversight over the actual implementation of the protections it recommends. The Federal agency experience under the Privacy Act described in Chapter 13 attests to the need as it has arisen within the Federal government. The experience of the various Federal regulatory bodies that will have additional responsibilities if the Commission's recommendations are adopted—for example, the Federal Trade Commission, the Federal Reserve Board, and the compliance monitoring units of the Department of Health, Education and Welfare—further underscores it.

Finally, in all areas of the public sector the Commission has studied, the need for a mechanism to interpret both law and policy is clear. The difficulty of deciding which disclosures of records about individuals are routine within the meaning of the Privacy Act often raises conflicts of interest or interpretation between two or more Federal agencies. Similarly, as indicated in Chapter 13, Federal agencies often need an efficient means of arriving at common solutions to their common privacy protection problems, such as establishing procedures for the disposal of records, the propagation of corrections, and the maintenance of accountings of disclosures. State agencies frequently complain about being subjected to multiple, and sometimes incompatible, record-keeping rules as a consequence of participating in programs funded by different Federal agencies or by different components within a single agency. There must also be a way of bringing private-sector recommendations for voluntary action to the attention of all the relevant organizations. Many of these varied needs can best be met by the third implementation alternative.

Therefore the Commission recommends

That the President and the Congress establish an independent entity within the Federal government charged with the responsibility of performing the following functions:

(a) To monitor and evaluate the implementation of any statutes and regulations enacted pursuant to the recommendations of the Privacy Protection Study Commission, and have the authority to formally participate in any Federal administrative proceeding or process where the action being considered by another agency would have a material effect on the protection of personal privacy, either as the result of direct government action or as a result of government regulation of others.

(b) To continue to research, study, and investigate areas of privacy concern, and in particular, pursuant to the Commission's recommendations, if directed by Congress, to supplement other governmental mechanisms through which citizens could question the propriety of information collected and used by various segments of the public and private sector.

(c) To issue interpretative rules that must be followed by Federal agencies in implementing the Privacy Act of 1974 or revisions of this Act as suggested by this Commission. These rules may deal with procedural matters as well as the determination of what information must be available to individuals or the public at large, but in no instance shall it direct or suggest that information about an individual be withheld from individuals.

(d) To advise the President and the Congress, government agencies, and, upon request, States, regarding the privacy implications of proposed Federal or State statutes or regulations.

The entity the Commission recommends may be a Federal Privacy Board or some other independent unit. However, if a new entity is established, the only enforcement authority the Commission would recommend it be given would be in connection with the implementation by Federal agencies of the Privacy Act itself. Its oversight responsibility in all of the other areas covered by the Commission's recommendations would require it only to participate in the proceedings of other agencies when substantive privacy issues are involved. For example, if the Federal Reserve Board were to issue proposals to amend its Regulation Z pursuant to the Truth-in-Lending Act after the Commission's recommendations are adopted, the new entity could participate in the proceedings only to the extent of presenting testimony and other comments from a privacy protection point of view.

P · A · R · T · V

6

Preserving Individual Autonomy in an Information-Oriented Society

James B. Rule • Douglas McAdam
Linda Stearns • David Uglow

To locate our viewpoint among the variety of approaches to these issues, let us say that our emphasis has been less strictly technological and less optimistic. That is, we tend to see the most profound changes in relations between personal information and individual autonomy as effects of changes in social relationships, rather than as those of technological change. Furthermore, we see the social changes as so far-reaching as to defy easy resolution through the reform of personal data management. Thus stated, we realize, these characterizations amount to little more than a confession of bias. The implications of such biases for concrete analysis, however, should be amply apparent in what follows.

Some Sociological Background

Modern Americans inhabit a social environment virtually composed of formal organizations. The main source of the privacy controversies of the 1960s and 1970s has been the demands of formal organizations for information on the people with whom these organizations must deal. Each major life juncture seems to entail involvement of some formal organization. Birth, immunization, education, military service, marriage and divorce, the use of credit and insurance, homeownership, medical care, and, ultimately, death—these and countless other key life events require the participation of formal organizations. Such participation almost always seems to require intake of information on the persons concerned. Sometimes these intakes serve the purposes of certification of a key life transition such as a birth, immunization or treatment for a disease, or educational attainments. Elsewhere information helps the organization concerned to distinguish what treatment is to be accorded the individual concerned. In any event, the flow of personal information between organizations and individuals clearly affects the interests of the people concerned. The privacy issues of the 1960s and 1970s have amounted to conflicts over uses made by formal organizations of documentary information on the people with whom these organizations must deal.

Simply to characterize this new reality as reflecting the "appetite" of organizations for personal information would be accurate, but would miss much of the significance of these changes.[1] The growth of modern, bureaucratic personal data systems attests to the formation of new *relationships* between ordinary Americans and formal organizations. The organizations concerned hardly developed their present appetite for personal data as an end in itself. Rather, they did so in order to satisfy demands for authoritative action concerning the people depicted in the records. People expect certain organizations to deal intelligently with a heterogeneous array of people. These dealings are as multifarious in content as are the organizations themselves. In every case the organization is expected to render to each person his or her "due," that is, the "correct" form of bureaucratic action, in light of all relevant information on that person's past history and current statuses (see Rule, 1974, especially pp. 320–326). Clearly, such discriminating decision making can only take place by reliance on detailed recorded information on the persons concerned.

Income taxation, for example, entails assessment of precise liability for each taxpayer reckoned in terms of income, dependency status, assets and losses during the tax year, and a host of other circumstances. Given that the payment of taxes is a distasteful obligation, and that most persons strive to avoid paying any more than necessary, no system of enforcement could avoid collecting and using voluminous data on the persons concerned. Such data not only enable the organization concerned (the IRS, in this case) to assess the obligation to pay, but they also provide the basis on which to adjudicate disputes with taxpayers over their obligation and to locate those taxpayers judged delinquent or suspect.

The same observations could be offered for most other bureaucratic personal data systems that have sprung up since the last century. Consumer-credit data files, for example, enable credit-granting organizations to assess precisely how much credit should be extended to the person concerned. Insurance reporting systems afford insurance companies sophisticated bases for discriminating judgments about whether to insure people, and if so, at what rates. Law-enforcement records enable these organizations to distinguish their treatment of the literally millions of persons with whom they deal every year, according to the kinds of action which such people deserve.

Although one may not normally think of it this way, this organizational monitoring of persons is of a piece with broad ranges of other bureaucratic activity. Sociologists have

---

[1] For discussion of a number of these issues, see Edward Shils' (1975) remarks on the "cognitive passion" of government and related demands on privacy in "Privacy and Power" in his book of collected assays.

often characterized formal organizations as systems for coping with uncertainty in their environments (Perrow, 1972; Thompson, 1967). All organizations must keep track of more or less unpredictable aspects of their environments—making plans, adjustments, rearrangements, and the like, so as to achieve their desired results. If the critical goal is selling automobiles at a profit, then the organization must attend to variations in supplies of raw materials, costs of power, fluctuations in demand, availability of labor, and a host of other things in order to remain viable. If the goal is the administration of a church diocese, central management must monitor the attitudes of the clergy, the faithfulness of the communicants, the costs of maintaining the physical plant, the attitudes of the larger community toward the church, and many other potential sources of uncertainty. Formal organizations are not the only social forms that facilitate human action in the face of otherwise uncertain conditions. However, only formal organizations in the modern sense devote themselves so systematically and self-consciously to searching for unpredictable or disruptive elements in the environment and attempting to master them so as to achieve desired results.

For the organizational activities of interest here, the environment is people; the uncertainties to be mastered are ambiguities as to which people deserve what organizational responses. Modern income taxation systems are charged with enforcing an obligation according to complex principles, in the light of circumstances that differ in every case. Not only must such systems apply these principles to heterogeneous cases; they must also reckon with people's often strenuous efforts to withhold information. To confront this "blooming, buzzing confusion" of people's financial affairs and to enforce a modicum of compliance entails real mastery of uncertainty. The same holds true for other organizations that systematically demand and use personal information in dealing with very large publics. They can no more do without authoritative information on the people with whom they deal than can General Motors meet its goals without data about the costs of raw materials, the demand for finished automobiles, costs of transportation, and the thousands of uncertain circumstances that make formal organizations necessary in the first place.

Systems of detailed personal records do not appear *whenever* organizations deal with large numbers of people. Instead, they develop under conditions of complex obligations and extended mutual dependency between organizations and their publics. In *Private Lives and Public Surveillance*, Rules (1974) characterized these conditions as most propitious:

1. When an agency must regularly deal with a clientele too large and anonymous to be kept track of on a basis of face-to-face acquaintance;
2. When these dealings entail the enforcement of rules advantageous to the agency and potentially burdensome of the clientele;
3. When these enforcement activities involve decision-making about how to act towards the clientele . . . ;
4. When the decisions must be made discriminatingly, according to precise details of each person's past history or present situation;
5. When the agency must associate every client with what it considers the full details of his past history, especially so as to forestall people's evading the consequences of their past behavior [p. 29].

Thus, Yankee Stadium will require no detailed documentation on ticket purchasers, despite variation in ticket prices and seat assignment. When organizations enter into relationships enduring over time, whose outcomes must be geared to details of people's lives, the recourse to personal data systems as bases for action is very likely.

Thus the growth of vast, bureaucratic personal data systems, both computerized and conventional, often marks the development of characteristically modern forms of *social control*. By this we mean direct patterns of influence by organizations over the behaviors of individuals. Such influence may be benign, as in systems for administering medical care, or coercive, as in the development of dossiers on political enemies. The systematic collection and monitoring of personal information for purposes of social control we term *surveillance*—again, whether the purposes are friendly or not. The development of efficient systems of mass surveillance and control is one of the distinctive sociological features of advanced societies. Never before our own era have large organizations been able to remain in direct interaction with literally millions of persons, both keeping abreast of their affairs and reaching out with authoritative bureaucratic action in response to such monitoring.

The Extension of Surveillance

We believe that these rather abstract concepts earn their keep by helping us to formulate a question of fundamental interest: How far can we expect the development of modern surveillance and control to go? What forms of previously private information are most likely to come into demand as grist for the mills of bureaucratic surveillance? What forms of behavior are most likely to be subjected to centralized organizational control through the use of such information?

Much organizational interest in the details of people's private lives relates to the effort to curtail one or another form of deviant behavior. Credit systems serve largely to counteract disruptive effects from those unwilling or unable to pay; police record systems serve to aid in the control of crime and criminals. Thus, new forms of surveillance are especially likely when they promise to enable organizations to root out some troublesome form of misbehavior. Innovations in surveillance that promise to identify potential shoplifters to department stores, or terrorists to airlines, or illegal aliens to immigration authorities, then, are bound to attract intense interest from the organizations involved.

The nature of deviant activity, however, may be only indirectly related to the personal data sought for its control. This makes it especially difficult to foretell what forms of personal information are most likely to come into demand. When organizations take the record of past deviant behavior to predict future propensities for such behavior, the link is clear enough. No one is surprised that the police use criminal records from the past to anticipate and act against future criminality. But organizations also seek to predict the future behavior of those with whom they deal by studying nonintuitive statistical correlates of such behavior. Thus, if the IRS came to suspect that tax evasion was highly associated with venereal disease, that agency would probably seek the same sweeping power to delve through people's medical records that it now enjoys relative to their bank accounts. One ought not to smile too quickly at this seemingly far-fetched example. Social science research has turned up associations no less improbable than this one. Furthermore when a given form of deviant behavior offends particularly powerful interests, the efforts to seek out information on its possible correlates may become intense.

But the interest in understanding and thereby controlling deviant behavior is not the only occasion for the extension of bureaucratic surveillance. Many efforts to document details of persons' private lives arise in an attempt to document and define what one might term "fine-grained" bureaucratic obligations. The enormous amounts of personal documentation required for medical insurance and social security, for example, serve largely to establish eligibility for those services. The growing importance of these bureaucratically determined benefits is hardly less important in fueling the spread of surveillance than the effort to suppress deviance in the ordinary sense. The point is, both bureaucracies and the publics to which they respond expect exact distinctions to be drawn between the guilty and the innocent, between those likely to prove guilty and those not so likely, between the eligible and the ineligible, and among different forms and degrees of eligibility among the same people over time. When distinctions can be drawn in the treatments owing to different members of the public, one can expect efforts to document the bases for these distinctions and hence to render them grist for the mills of bureaucratic action.

In virtually all innovations in mass surveillance, the pressure of public demand plays an important part. One can point to few systems of collection and use of detailed personal information in America which were foisted on a wholly unwilling public simply for narrow bureaucratic purposes. On the contrary, people often want and even demand the fine-grained decision making afforded by personal data systems. Criminal record systems could not exist without the demands of the great majority of the public for keeping vigorous track of criminals. Credit systems would be impossible without the considerable public enthusiasm for the comforts of easy, convenient credit. People may feel that their privacy is threatened by the demands for personal information characteristic of the modern world; but they often seem willing enough to yield personal data in specific instances where desired services are at stake.

Indeed, available evidence suggests that people's desire to see "justice" done, in one way or another, accounts for much of the popular demand for extension of surveillance. People seek their own just desserts, in terms of the credit privileges, insurance rates, tax liability, passport use, or whatever, to which they feel themselves entitled. At the same time, the public also demands effective discriminations *against* welfare cheaters, poor credit risks, dangerous drivers, tax evaders, criminals, and the like. These discriminations in the treatment of persons by organizations can only be achieved by recourse to personal data keeping. The instinct of demanding justice in the allocation of scarce resources is of course as old as social life itself. However, the capabilities of modern organizations have made it possible for organizations to apply such principles in decision-making relations with literally millions of persons.

Often, it is difficult to say whether popular demands represent the cause or the effect of the growing sophistication of organization in surveillance and control. The result, in either event, is a secular trend toward increasingly effective bureaucratic attention to and demand for such information. Thus we confess real doubt about observations such as the following by Alan Westin (1967):

> A close survey of the positions adopted by leading ideological and civic groups toward issues of surveillance and privacy since 1945 indicates that there is now a general identification of privacy and liberty, and that concern over unlimited governmental or private surveillance runs the ideological spectrum from the Daughters of the American Revolution to the New Student Left, and from the *National Review* to the *Nation* . . . . The cry that "Big Brother is Watching" is now raised by any person or group protesting against what he or it considers unfair surveillance . . . . Anxious articles and editorials about restoring norms of privacy have appeared in business, labor, legal, and academic journals, and many civic groups have adopted policy resolutions deploring erosions of privacy [p. 378].

It all sounds good. No one, after all, is likely to come out *against* privacy. But a close look at the clamor for more of it suggests that its proponents do not all have the same thing in mind. The Daughters of the American Revolution may well deplore, let us say, government snooping into the tax-exempt status of conservative educational organizations, but they are likely to be the first to demand more vigorous invasion of the privacy of groups like the New Student Left. *The Nation* may well deplore invasions of the privacy, for example, of welfare mothers; but it would be quick to support FBI investigation of right-wing militant groups.

People do indeed protest what they consider "unfair surveillance," often in the same breath with which they demand more vigorous surveillance for purposes that they support. Nearly everyone can point to some form of surveillance with which they are unhappy, either because it strikes them as ineffective or because the form of control at which it aims seems undesirable in itself. The more fundamental public reflex, however, seems to be to insist that discrimination based on detailed personal data be made whenever the ends of such discrimination seems desirable. Public and private bureaucracies are usually only too willing to accommodate these demands, where indeed they have not encouraged them to begin with. The long-term effect can only be further pressure against individual privacy and autonomy, in the sense in which most people use these terms.

Given the forces fostering the growth of surveillance, we can identify no "natural limit" to the incorporation of personal information into the attentions of personal data systems. That is, we can conceive of no form of personal information that might not, under certain conditions, come to serve the purposes of bureaucracies aiming at some form of social control. Such forms of control may be brutal or humane; they may be instituted autocratically or with the widest popular participation. But so long as what we term the "efficiency criterion" continues to guide bureaucratic innovation in these respects, the potential for extension of surveillance to more and more areas of life is endless. The theoretical endpoint of such trends is a world in which every thought and action of everyone registers at once with a centralized monitoring agency. To note this extreme is scarcely to announce its imminent attainment; but the implications of this theoretical endpoint for present developments bear reflection nonetheless.

Certainly no area of human life is inherently too private to attract the application of bureaucratic surveillance. Indeed, the most sensitive and personal aspects of life are often most associated with the social uncertainties that make systematic monitoring and control attractive. People yield all sorts of embarrassing or otherwise sensitive information to medical personnel as one of the costs of modern medical care. Similarly, they provide documentary accounting of the disorders and treatments involved to insurance bureaucracies as a requirement for reimbursement for such treatment. As connections arise between forms of personal information and possibilities for urgently desired social control, demands for the data in question are sure to follow.

Thus, a fundamental trend in modern, highly developed societies is the progressive centralization of social control in large bureaucracies and the incorporation of more and more personal information in these bureaucratic systems to guide the workings of control. Other trends mitigate these effects to some extent. As the demands of centralized bureaucracies grow in these respects, those of local forms of surveillance and control —the family, the community, or the kinship system, for example—may subside (see Rule, 1974, pp. 331–332, 342–343). But no one can doubt that the growth of bureaucratic surveillance and control constrain individual autonomy and privacy in the sense in which most people use these terms. The value issues raised by the workings of a relative handful of mammoth systems of surveillance and control are bound to be weightier than those associated with the independent workings of many dispersed, local systems.

The Protection of Privacy and Its Limitations

In due course, the growing papers concentrated in bureaucratic systems of personal data management began to arouse considerable public anxiety. Who sets the purposes of bureaucratic surveillance? Can the systems be trusted?

The privacy issue, as it took shape in the late 1960s, represented a minefield for America's political and administrative elites. Dissatisfaction over organizational handling of personal data threatened to place important prerogatives up for grabs. On the one hand, ability to collect, store, and use personal information had become a major resource for key American bureaucracies, both public and private. On the other hand, some of the early objections to these practices sounded serious indeed. Given rising public mistrust of the official exercise of power, culminating, ultimately, in the Watergate affair, the nascent privacy protection movement of the late 1960s might have led to fundamental attacks upon established power positions. Whether this would occur depended on the meaning attributed to the protection of privacy in the emergent public understanding of that notion.

In fact, no frontal collision has occurred between an aroused public opinion and organizations engaged in what we term surveillance. The emergent official interpretation of privacy protection has forestalled any such confrontation. In this view, the noxious or dangerous feature of bureaucratic surveillance systems appear not as things inherent in their nature, but as failures to work "correctly"; and "correct," in this context, means consistent with the longer-term bureaucratic ends governing the systems. This convenient accommodation, from the standpoint of established forces, has made it possible to pursue the "reform" of these systems in ways that enhance, rather than threaten, their key interests. It would be difficult to overestimate the significance of this interpretation.

The domestication of the privacy issue has many parallels in the history of attempted regulation of noxious practices by powerful institutions in America.[2] In these instances, lost opportunities for thorough reshaping of the practices involved pass so subtly and quietly as to be virtually unnoticed. In the case of privacy, as with many other issues, the fateful turning points came out in the heat of public debate but at that subtle point where key assumptions are taken for granted.

Of enormous importance in these developments was the early penchant to focus on notorious abuses of personal data management. Congressional hearings, journalistic and popular writings, and scholarly treatments of the emergent issue all tended to dramatize certain categories of particularly ugly misuses of personal information. They publicized cases of credit bureaus causing damage by maintaining and reporting erroneous information, or they focused on instances of erroneous or misleading arrest data unjustly affecting a person's access, let us say, to employment, or they centered attention on cases of an early education record unfairly stigmatizing a child throughout his or her school career.

The more resourceful representatives of organizations engaged in surveillance basically accepted critics' objections to such abuses and the legitimacy of efforts to correct these. In so doing, however, they helped to shift the debate over privacy protection to one over elimination of particular sets of abusive practices. This was construed to mean making surveillance systems work *better*, on the assumption that both organizations and the individuals depicted in the systems shared an interest in achieving the ends for which the systems were created. By concentrating attention on abuses of personal record-keeping so extreme that they served neither individuals nor organizations, participants in this debate shut out examination of the larger desirability of the growing power of surveillance systems *in general.*

Perhaps even more important, by fostering an interpretation of privacy protection in these terms, both the critics and the defenders of surveillance practices could avoid the really difficult and painful questions: How much surveillance is a desirable thing? How far should the development or bureaucratic monitoring of otherwise private affairs be extended? Instead of engaging these enormously difficult and contentious questions, the privacy planners eventually evolved what we term the efficiency criterion. By this criterion, privacy is deemed protected if three conditions are met in managing personal data: (1) that the data be kept accurate, complete, up-to-date, and subject to review and correction by the persons concerned; (2) that the uses of filed data proceed according to rules of due process that data subjects can know and, if necessary, invoke; and (3) that the organizations collecting and using personal data do so only insofar as necessary to attain their appropriate organizational goals. Under these principles, organizations can claim to protect the privacy of the persons with whom they deal, even as they accumulate more and more data on those persons and greater and greater power over their lives. It would be difficult to imagine a more advantageous interpretation of privacy protection from the standpoint of surveillance organizations.

However, the terms of this emergent compromise neglect something very important.

---

[2] For those familiar with the work of Theodore Lowi, the similarity between this interpretation and his ideas will quickly be apparent. (See Lowi, 1971, especially the Prologue and Chapter 1.)

The growth of modern bureaucratic surveillance, we have argued, represents a social trend of enormous significance in itself. That significance extends far beyond the issues surrounding abuse of particular systems in their present form. It demands consideration of the directions of social change implicit in present practices and of the alternatives to increasing reliance on surveillance.

A hard look at these matters reveals many reasons for seeking limits to the extension of bureaucratic surveillance—not simply as a source of unfairness or inefficiency, but as a bad thing in itself. The simplest of these reasons is what we have termed "aesthetic" reactions against intensive surveillance. No one really wants to live in a world where every previously private moment becomes a subject of bureaucratic scrutiny. There is something inherently desirable, at least for most people, about maintaining realms where experiences are shared only by the parties to them (see Fried, 1968). Even when the ends of surveillance are impeccable and even when the agencies concerned carry out their monitoring with full rectitude and discretion, the monitoring of every moment would strike most people as unacceptable.

To be sure, present surveillance systems have hardly brought us to the point of total monitoring. But again, the logic of change in these systems suggests no natural limit to their further extension. So long as the efficiency criterion continues to guide the development of these systems, their attentions will continue to spread over larger and larger areas of what has been private experience. At some point, nearly everyone would acknowledge, such extension passes the point of moral or aesthetic acceptability. Where that point lies is not an objective matter. It can only be identified through earnest debate and thoughtful reflection on the values of privacy and autonomy versus those of efficiency. There are no grounds for assuming that such debate and reflection would yield consensus among all thoughtful parties, but this hardly justifies ignoring the incontestable fact that modern surveillance systems promise eventually to reach the limits of acceptability by everyone's standards. Where that point occurs is a matter that ought to be explored in any thoughtful treatment of the privacy issue. Yet the official response to these matters evades these difficult issues, rather than encouraging us to confront them.

Another reason for limiting the unrestricted growth of bureaucratic surveillance lies in the value of preserving what one might term a desirable "looseness" in social relations. Other differences notwithstanding, many, if not most, surveillance systems work to make people responsible for their pasts. Criminal records ensure that people to do not escape the repercussions of their criminal acts; insurance reporting works to link disreputable people to their community reputations; credit reporting helps credit grantors to hold people responsible for their past credit-using behavior.

Most Americans probably feel that these processes are legitimate and desirable, at least in some measure. However, most people probably also feel that there ought to be limits to the extent to which people's records are held against them. Statements like the following (House Committee on Government Operations, 1968) from a spokesman for the country's largest insurance and employment reporting firm do leave one a little uneasy:

> It is a fact that the interchange of business information and the availability of record
> information imposes a discipline on the American citizen. He becomes more responsible for

his performance whether as a driver of his car, as an employee in his job performance, or as a payor to his creditors. But this discipline is a necessary one if we are to enjoy the fruits of our economy and the present freedom of our private enterprise.

Is a system of soliciting and reporting accounts of people's lives from friends, neighbors, co-workers really essential to the enjoyment of freedom? More generally, is it desirable that people always be held fully responsible for all of what prospective employers, creditors, or insurors would consider their past shortcomings? (See Greenawalt, 1975.) It is true that the conventional wisdom in America endorses the notion that people must "reap as they sow," but popular sentiment also endorses the worth of "a fresh start" or "a clean slate." Systematic forgetting of a person's pasts, even when troublesome from the standpoint of bureaucratic efficiency, may reflect a social value of considerable importance. Whether the values of efficiency or those of "wiping the slate clean" ought to prevail in any particular setting is bound to be a contentious issue.

We hardly insist on any particular resolution of the issue; indeed, the nature of the choices seems to us to preclude any programmatic solution, apart from piecemeal compromises on a case-by-case basis. We do, however, insist that the issue be confronted directly, and that the interests of efficiency alone not serve as a satisfactory basis for such confrontation. Again, the official response to the privacy issue has most often obscured these agonizing choices precisely when they need to be dramatized.

A third compelling reason for limiting the growth of bureaucratic surveillance has to do with the effects of these systems on social power relations. The growth of modern surveillance inevitably brings about cumulative change in relations between what Shils (1975) would term "centers" of social power and the "peripheries." Surveillance makes it possible for those at the centers to monitor the activities of large populations and "reach out" with forceful actions to shape and control those behaviors. Often, of course, the purposes for which surveillance capacities are originally developed may be strictly mundane or indeed purely humanitarian. That is, the social control that the systems afford may entail nothing more objectionable than enforcing tax obligations or providing health care. However, once these surveillance capabilities are in place, there is always some risk of their appropriation for purposes of repression by centralized powers. Under these conditions, it may matter rather little what were the original intentions of those who created the system, or even whether the system is governmental or private. Changes in political climates, for example, may leave bank or credit card files more open to government snooping than even some government records. The results of increasing the power of centralized institutions over those who make up the peripheries cannot always be foreseen.

These powers need not always be exercised in order to have their undesirable effects. We must recall the chilling effect that stems from people's knowledge of the data-monitoring capabilities of centralized institutions (see Wessel, 1974). Events of the 1970s have certainly altered many American's views of what centralized institutions, especially government ones, are capable of in these respects. Now it is much more difficult than it once was to dismiss the possibility that one's phone is being tapped, or that one's tax returns may be used for unfriendly political purposes, or that one's life has become the subject of a CIA file. The realization that these activities *might* take place, whether they really do or not in any particular instance, has potentially destructive effects on the openness of social systems to innovation and dissent. Clearly, the best way to avoid these effects is to cut back the instrumentalities that convey such threats.

Virtually everyone would acknowledge some point at which surveillance by bureaucracies simply becomes too thoroughgoing, even when carried out with total discretion for seemingly unimpeachable purposes. What if, instead of electronic funds transfer (EFT) systems, someone were to propose a "wireless funds transfer" system, in which people were equipped with miniature radios, to be carried or worn at all times, capable of authorizing debits from their accounts. Such a system would obviously offer even greater convenience than EFT, since one would always have total access to one's resources. Most people, however, would begin to feel uneasy, we suspect, about any system that provided such intimate and potentially unerring contact between private persons and centralized powers. At some point, a measure of insulation between what Shils terms center and periphery becomes a highly desirable thing in itself.

Consider a medical surveillance system designed to provide timely intelligence on threats to people's physical or mental health. Suppose that a tiny radio transmitter could be implanted under one's skin, to send continuous signals to a central computer for recording and monitoring. The cumulative record of such things as heartbeat, blood sugar, electroencephalogram, and the like could provide a data base for predicting all sorts of dangerous conditions, ranging from heart attacks to psychopathic outbursts. Indeed, if participation in the monitoring were required of everyone, the expanded data base would afford insights to benefit the sick and the well alike. Furthermore, if the system embodied a way of pinpointing the location of each user, heart attack victims and others involved in emergencies could count on prompt help. Continuous monitoring and analysis of data, under a system like this, could make it possible to transmit timely warnings, perhaps through the radio transmitter itself, to people who, in light of their records, were in danger of ill health or antisocial behavior. From one point of view, a system like this would represent the ultimate in preventive health care.

No one, we imagine, would find fault with the ultimate ends of such an undertaking —improving the quality of health care, and providing such care in the widest and most timely way. Nor would most people deny that public institutions have an authentic interest in establishing control over the uncertainties of public health. After all, the burdens of ill-health invariably fall in one way or another on society as a whole. There would be no insuperable difficulty in ensuring privacy in the conventional sense in a system like this. Procedural guarantees could well ensure such things as confidentiality, access rights, and due process in the use of data.

We suspect, however, that none of these redeeming possibilities would suffice to make such an arrangement acceptable to most people. Even if administered with the most scrupulous guarantees on behalf of impeccable ends, a system like this would strike most of us as excessive. Such examples cause us to smile, or, if we take them seriously, to shudder, because these arrangements simply go too far in breaking down barriers that insulate individuals from larger institutions. Aesethetically, such arrangements, revolt us because they would destroy the sense of aloneness and autonomy that most people count essential ingredients of life. Strategically, the powers that such systems would confer on an overbearing regime are so sweeping that the risks implicit in their existence are simply better not taken. Even without repressive intent, the administration of such a system could hardly remain indefinitely free of pressures to share its capabilities for surveillance and control with other systems. The accretion of extraneous social control functions in the case of Social Security would be trivial compared to the demands made on systems like the ones imagined here.

Spokesmen for programs of privacy protection through due process in personal data management have generally characterized their intent as that of "restoring the balance" between individuals and data-keeping institutions (for further discussion see Westin, 1967; Miller, 1971; PPSC, 1977). Although the details are never very clearly specified, the idea seems to be that procedural guarantees like those discussed above eliminate dangers potentially arising from misuse of personal data systems. But in the light of larger patterns of social change, the notion of "balancing" the prerogatives of data-keeping organizations and those of individuals, or of weighing the demands of privacy against the need for information, seems superficial. Procedural reforms may indeed provide an arena where individuals can assert their interests in the uses of their personal documentation; but these safeguards are matters of social convention. They endure only as long as the political and social climate in which they arise. In a more profound sense, the balance between individuals and centralized organizations is permanently altered once such systems are in place. Certainly one would always prefer procedural safeguards to their absence wherever personal data systems exist. However, it is misleading to argue that such safeguards somehow return the balance of social power to its status before the establishment of centralized institutions.

Let us remember that bureaucratic structures have no *purposes* of their own. Formal organizations develop capabilities to do certain kinds of things and of mastering given forms of uncertainty, but the ends that these skills serve are not dictated by the tools. A list of names and addresses, an array of pertinent information, or a bureaucratic mechanism for collecting and ordering such data, once in place, exists for the benefit of whoever controls them at any given time. The purposes leading to the founding of such a system need not necessarily shape their continued working. Creating pluralistic rules of the game by which individuals are accorded some influence over treatment of their data is desirable in itself, but it has no effect beyond the point where participants stop playing by the rules.

Again, there need be no question of the sincerity of the intentions of the founders of these systems, or of the seriousness with which procedural safeguards are originally instated. The point is simply that political and social climates change and that the inherent capabilities of organizational forms typically outlive the frame of mind of those who bring them into existence. David J. Seipp (1978) has found a remarkable quote from a spokesman for the FBI back in 1931. Asked whether the Bureau would consider resorting to wiretapping, he replied,

> No sir. We have a very definite rule in the bureau that any employee engaging in wiretapping will be dismissed from the service of the bureau . . . . While it may not be illegal, I think it is unethical, and it is not permitted under the regulations by the Attorney General [p. 108].

The speaker was a young J. Edgar Hoover, replying to a query in a Congressional committee on Expenditures hearing.

What constitutes "acceptable practice" does change, then, and the tempting availability of sophisticated personal-data-monitoring techniques may bring about recourse to practices previously foresworn. This makes it risky to place too much confidence in the self-restraint of any institution. Consider the following quote (Westin, 1967) from the middle 1960s:

> The history of police-force use of eavesdropping is sufficiently stained with misconduct throughout the nation that use of physical surveillance devices at the state level should be strictly limited to district attorney's offices and state attorney generals' offices, and at the federal level to the FBI and military agencies [p. 376].

Obviously, any attempt to safeguard individual privacy and autonomy while leaving the powers of personal-data collection intact must identify some institution as a trustworthy repository of such powers. In light of events since the 1960s, however, the choice of the FBI and the military for this role can only be described as quaint.

The Alternative: A Looser, More Private World

We suspect that most people, confronted with the foregoing concerns, would hardly remain indifferent. No one really likes the idea of endless growth of bureaucratic surveillance, but what alternative can there be?

The fact that it may be difficult to conceive of realistic alternatives reflects the important gaps in most discussions of the privacy issue. A key assumption in these interpretations is that of organizations' needs for personal data. The underlying logic in this approach seems to go something like this:

1. The needs of organizations for personal data are relentlessly rising.
2. The continued satisfaction of these needs is a condition for a more bountiful, more efficient, more "advanced" social world.
3. The only policy is to satisfy such needs while making organizational demands for data as fair and as palatable to the public as possible.

Obviously, we share the view that modern formal organizations have characteristic reasons for relying on personal documentation, but the lock-step argument noted above caricatures the thoughtful analysis of this reliance which the issue requires. The message seems to be that we can choose only between increasing loss of personal information to bureaucratic surveillance and a return to some sort of organizational "Stone Age." Yet a searching look at the needs of organizations for personal information suggests that they hardly represent a *sine qua non* of organizational life. In fact, one can identify a range of alternatives to increasingly intense use of personal data in organizational decision-making; these alternatives have not received the attention that they deserve.

Organizations collect personal information largely in order to sustain discriminating decision-making processes concerning the persons depicted by the data. In an effort to produce just the proper treatment of each individual, and hence to forestall squandering resources on improper treatments, organizations seek more and more pertinent data to afford closer and closer discrimination among cases. However, what represents an improper application of resources is not eternally given; it is a social convention that might well be reconsidered in the interests of protecting privacy and autonomy. If organizations were not expected to make such fine discriminations in their treatments of persons, the need for rigorous data-collection would be greatly eased. The alternative to endless erosion of personal privacy and autonomy through increased surveillance lies in lessening discriminations among people in the application of organizational resources.

Today organizations, both governmental and private, invest enormous resources in pursuing what has been termed fine-grained discrimination. What we are proposing is a reallocation of resources to develop and underwrite less discriminatory, and hence less information-intensive, ways of dealing with people. What we face here is not simply a choice between meeting the information needs of organizations and seeing these organizations grind to a halt. Instead, the choice lies between meeting the costs of discriminating and paying the costs of relaxing such discrimination. For every degree of intimacy of surveillance relinquished by organizations, benefits accrue in privacy and autonomy.

Pursuit of less information-intensive alternatives would entail a fundamental change in expectations about the treatments that organizations owe to their publics. It would mean minimizing differences in how people are treated in light of their records, and hence minimizing the necessity for developing such records. Instead of sharpening their discriminations, organizations would be expected to provide a baseline of adequate resources for all, with minimal differences according to cases.

Again, the alternatives here are not binary choices, but choices among many possible degrees of discrimination and the commensurately rising demands on privacy. Such tradeoffs are easily noted, for example, in income taxation. From its relatively simple beginnings, the U.S. income tax system has become a giant consumer of personal data. The rise in the range and frequency of data intake, of course, corresponds directly to the growing multiplicity of personal circumstances which tax laws take into account in assessing liability. A major impetus for such growth, one supposes, is public demand for "just consideration" of various extenuating circumstances. Simpler tax laws might well aim at limiting the range of circumstances bearing on tax obligations. If discriminations were made less complicated, then demands for personal information would drop commensurately. Planners for tax reform could make an enormous contribution to privacy protection by cutting back the range of personal data that bears on tax liability.

A relatively easy avenue for seeking less information-intensive forms of bureaucratic action lies in those areas where the use of personal information is least cost-effective. One of the most intrusive bureaucratic demands now widespread in America is that associated with security clearances. Millions of people must routinely undergo such investigations as conditions of their employment. Yet to our knowledge, compelling statistical associations between the results of these investigations and, let us say, unauthorized leaks of security-related information have never been demonstrated. We suspect that the information needs attributed to our security apparatus in these respects simply would not withstand close examination. Such an examination would more likely show that whatever benefits such procedures yield do not nearly warrant the costs in loss of privacy and the chilling effects of dissent and diversity in American life.

Attacking demands on personal privacy that do not really pay off in terms of organization gain, however, is easy. Indeed, nearly all writers on the subject have exploited this argument. The difficult cases concern organizational use of personal information that is both useful by the standards presently prevailing in organizations and destructive of privacy and autonomy.

Here we feel that serious consideration of the arguments put forward above demands foreswearing bureautically attractive uses of personal data. This would mean setting policies in which organizations would relax or abandon the single-minded pursuit of efficient discrimination among persons in favor of other considerations.

No doubt the easiest settings in which to begin applying this thinking are in the planning for bureaucratic systems that do not yet exist. The prospect of national health insurance, for example, is receiving increasingly serious discussion at the time of this writing. The degree of discrimination built into a system of this kind is obviously full of implications for personal privacy. Systems that embody complicated eligibility requirements and other forms of discrimination governing access to treatment are driven to make very intensive demands on personal data. The most appealing alternative is a system that offers its services to all, as in Britain's National Health Service. Since every Briton is eligible, the system need not develop the detailed inquiries into the backgrounds of its clients which would otherwise be the case. Thus, the system actually entails relatively loose central record-keeping. What there is serves mainly to keep track of the numbers of patients for whom individual physicians are responsible. Case histories and other personal background information are stored locally, much as they are in countries where medicine is private.

One can also envisage ways to enhance privacy by restricting surveillance where it is already well established, although resistance would be greater here. Consider the case of consumer credit. The first consumer-credit reporting operations were basically simple listings of bad debts held in common among several firms, to enable each to avoid giving credit to persons who had defaulted elsewhere. Today, by contrast, credit surveillance entails use of a very wide variety of information pooled among many different sources. The sophistication of modern credit systems depends on the use of these rich informational resources to predict which credit applicants should be trusted and to what extent. The interests of privacy would be well served by deliberately blunting some of these discriminations.

This possibility has not gone altogether unnoticed among writers on privacy. Kent Greenawalt (1975), in his thoughtful study of the status of privacy in American law, has commented,

> If information about credit standing is easily available on a national basis, it is virtually impossible to avoid one's low credit rating. This information allows credit-granting agencies to make more intelligent decisions about risk, but is it socially desirable that persons who admittedly pose a high risk be unable to get credit? Perhaps it would be socially preferable if credit were more freely available, even if good credit risks ended up paying the tab (e.g., in increased prices) so that poor credit risks could get credit [p. 92].

Nonetheless, Greenawalt's remarks here are exceptional; most writers have taken the sacredness of organizational efficiency for granted in these matters. We share Greenawalt's view. The effectiveness of discriminations between good and poor credit risks is hardly the only social value that ought to be considered in this important relationship. Competing values here are those of a looser social world, one with less potential for serving the needs of oppressive centralized powers and more capacity for extending opportunities to those who, in light of "all the facts," may appear to be poor risks. We favor a commitment of resources to pursuit of these latter values over and against those of pure efficiency in discriminating as to who will be the most profitable credit customers.

Any number of concrete measures, more or less sweeping, might serve to put this principle into effect. One might restrict the retention of derogatory credit information to, let us say, 2 years. This would have the effect of wiping the slate clean after a relatively short period for those who have been unwilling or unable to pay in the past. Or one might do away with centralized credit reporting altogether, so that every firm extending credit would have to develop its own bases for deciding whether to open an account with a given applicant.[3] This would surely countervail against the thoroughgoing and intrusive character of modern credit investigations. Our point is not to argue for any particular measure, but rather to emphasize alternatives to the single-minded pursuit of efficient discrimination that characterizes current credit policy. Whether the resulting policies are sweeping or cautious matters less than recognizing that protection of privacy requires compromises in bureaucratic efficiency.

Similar less information-intensive alternatives can be envisaged for many other social settings now marked by growing reliance on surveillance. In all of these cases, gains for privacy and autonomy can be purchased at incremental costs in the relinquishment of fine discriminations among persons in the application of bureaucratic resources. Whether such costs are warranted in any particular instance is not a question to be answered *a priori* for all settings at all times. Indeed, it is misleading to suggest that such questions have objective solutions, independent of the values of any particular thinker. We scarcely mean to insist, then, on anything so heavy-handed as curtailment of surveillance in all cases as a matter of principle; but we do insist that values of bureaucratic efficiency are not the only ones that ought to inform policy in personal data systems.

Conclusion

One might view very modern, "advanced" societies as characterized by reliance on especially powerful technologies. These include not only technologies in the usual sense, but also what one might term social technologies—techniques for mobilizing the actions of large numbers of people. These techniques afford relative handfuls of decision makers the means, for example, to activate party faithful in politics; or to direct the movement of investment capital; or to orchestrate the movement of armies in military campaigns; or to determine what people will read or hear or see via mass communications. Surveillance systems, of course, represent simply another refinement in social technologies. They enable elites to monitor the individual behavior of very many people at a time and to use the data so acquired to shape people's behavior in return.

---

[3] To the consternation of the credit-reporting industry, certain large credit grantors, mostly petroleum companies, are developing systems to evaluate applicant credit worthiness without recourse to centralized credit files. Moreover, they are refusing to disclose information about existing accounts to credit bureaus.

The growth of such powerful technologies—surveillance very much included here —raises the *stakes* of social planning. When the technologies of small-scale, simple social systems go wrong, the numbers of persons to be affected will at least not be too great. But when the powerful technologies of large-scale modern societies meet with destructive uses, the results may take the form of nuclear warfare or totalitarianism. Individually, there may not be a great deal to choose between victimization in a witch hunt in a small seventeenth-century New England town and persecution in a modern totalitarian regime. Collectively, the scope of human tragedy in the second case must surely be counted far greater.

The dawning realization of the potential evils of powerful technologies gone wrong has injected into contemporary culture a remarkable ambivalence about science and its status in society. Throughout most of the nineteenth century, the idea grew that enhanced scientific understanding of both the natural and social worlds would lead to a richer, more materially bountiful and less socially conflict-ridden existence for everyone. "Know, in order to foretell; foretell, in order to control," thus one might translate Comte's optimistic dictum on the spirit of science. Certainly the growth both of scientific understanding and of the resulting scope of human control have, if anything, overfulfilled Comte's predictions. The expanding sphere of human control has not been an unmixed blessing, however. For members of advanced, affluent societies, life has become more comfortable in countless ways. Yet the unintended effects of the technologies that afford such affluence give rise to the possibility of all sorts of man-made disasters on a scale never before possible. The use in warfare of sophisticated technologies for mobilizing energy for the first time raises the possibility of the extinction of the species. The applications of other sophisticated natural science technologies raises serious possibilities of environmental disaster. And the growth of social technologies, including but by no means limited to surveillance, raises the possibility of totalitarianism. The growth of human control, it would seem, offers the drawbacks of its successes.

These realizations cast an ironic light on the original, almost unbounded optimism concerning the social effects of science, an optimism that social science has until very recently helped to promote.[4] In many of the earlier evolutionary interpretations of social development, the enhancement of human control was seen as a virtually unambiguous gain in the *security* of social life. After all, the growth of more powerful technologies promised to preserve human life from the uncertainties of disease, scarcity, superstition and the like. These uncertainty-reducing features of social organization thus seemed to offer a more secure role of humankind on the planet. A number of social scientists have contended, even very recently, that growing understanding of social processes will make social systems more rational. Now we must face the fact that modern natural technologies have created highly *un*steady states (Granovetter, 1979). Though we may live in many ways a more bountiful material life, say, than the indigenous North American peoples, we know that present patterns of technology and energy use, drawing as they do on zero-sum resources and pushing against limited environments, cannot continue in-

---

[4] The durability of such reflexive optimism in the face of all sorts of danger signs is truly remarkable. See, for example, Pool *et al.* (1971).

definitely. Thus our relations with our natural environments are *less* stable over the longer run than those of less-developed peoples. Similarly, the development of surveillance and the countless other sophisticated social arrangements of bureaucratic civilization offer all sorts of enriching comforts and conveniences. No one, however, can be certain when we may come to regret the longer-term effects of the application of such powerful systems.

In 1969, we suspect, these arguments would have struck nearly everyone as hopelessly utopian. Today, perhaps, this is slightly less the case. We have lately been witnessing, in America and other highly developed societies, a remarkable disenchantment with powerful technologies, at least as they relate to the nonhuman world. These attitudes are perhaps most evident with regard to environmental and energy policy. As everyone knows who has been attentive to public debates on these matters, antagonism toward powerful, centralized approaches to these issues goes very deep among many people. These are of course the same people who prefer soft energy technologies such as wind and water power, technologies that disperse both social and natural power into as many relatively autonomous elements as possible.

In our view, some elements of radical environmentalism have their own irrational tinge, but many of the concerns of the technological skeptics, as we have called them, seem to us to embody certain unassailably valid principles. Very powerful technologies, both social and natural, entail the risks of putting all of one's eggs in a single basket; any disaster is apt to be a very large-scale disaster indeed. By contrast, the failures of soft, dispersed technologies at least limit the scope of the resulting damage. No one who thinks carefully about it can really like the idea of a world in which man-made concentrations of power grow larger endlessly. Yet only self-conscious efforts to enlarge the array of alternatives considered in planning for these things can reverse the trend in this direction.

If we are right, the current erosion in the once seemingly boundless faith in the prospects of growing human control represents a trend of major significance. At a gut level, people are growing skeptical of more and more powerful technologies as solutions to the problems of highly developed societies. These changes in public attitudes cry out for a redefinition of rationality in these respects. Thoughtful, scientifically reputable people must be prepared to affirm that preference for smaller, more modest forms of control need not be superstitious or irrational. On the contrary, people need to hear it said that limitations on the scope of human intervention need not be antiscientific, but may simply reflect the humility due to planning for situations where the stakes may grow very great indeed. Such humility, it seems to us, is particularly fitting where the damage inflicted by misapplied human powers affects far more people than the planners themselves. In short, we need a program for rational limits to the extension of rational human control.

Happily, a number of thoughtful commentators have begun to play this role. Regarding the risks of nuclear power production, for example, Amitai Etzioni (1974) has written,

> To say that reactors have a 1 out of 10,000 chance to blow each year (or 1 out of 1,000,000 per community), which makes them about as safe as flying, does not take into account the number of persons to be killed in a nuclear disaster . . . . Most persons who would accept a $10.00 bet at odds of 99 to 1 in their favor, would hesitate if the bet was $1000 at the *same* odds, and refuse a $100,000 bet at *identical* odds. Why? Only because the disutility changed.

Moreover, as Etzioni would undoubtedly also emphasize, calculations regarding nuclear power must be calculations of *cumulative* probability. That is, one's concern must be with the probability of such systems' *ever* going seriously wrong; these probabilities of course rise steadily over the time span under consideration. And we hold that planning for powerful technologies in general, either natural or social, must rely on this form of thinking. One wishes to be as certain as possible that a surveillance system *never* becomes a vehicle for repressive control. Given the uncertainty that seems to mark the changing political and social climates in which such systems exist, such assurances are difficult to come by.

In another context, Kenneth Boulding (1977) has written,

> One of the major principles of the universe as a general system is that over a long enough period of time very improbable events will have happened. It is easy to show that an event with a probability of $1/n$ in a year has a probability of happening equal to 0.9995 at sometime in a period of $10n$ years. Thus, a 100-year flood is virtually certain to happen sometime within 1000 years. Within the ten-billion-year history of the universe it is virtually certain that some event with a probability of one billionth per annum will have come off [p. 301].

Of course, it is comforting to assume that events that we regard as unlikely are really such remote possibilities as to be discountable. However, Boulding's observation should remind us of the cumulative increase of unwanted risks over time. In developing social and technological powers that have the potential to shape both our world and that of succeeding generations, prudence in dealing with risks of very serious occurrences is surely warranted.

Acknowledgments

Portions of this contribution are from *The Politics of Privacy* by James Rule, Douglas McAdam, Linda Stearns, and David Uglow, ©1980 by James B. Rule; reprinted by arrangement with the New American Library, Inc., New York, New York. Our collaboration on the book grew out of our work together on a study of ordinary Americans' experiences with and understandings of personal data systems, supported by the National Science Foundation, Division of Mathematical and Computer Sciences.

References

Boulding, K. (1977). The universe as a general system. Fourth annual Ludwig von Bertalanffy Memorial Lecture, *Behavioral Science*, 22.

Etzioni, A. (1974). Letter to the editor, *New York Times Magazine*, (March 24).

Fred, C. (1968). Privacy, *Yale Law Journal*, 77.

Granovetter, M. (1979). The idea of "advancement" in theories of social evolution and development, *American Journal of Sociol.*, 85.

Greenawalt, K. (1975). *Legal protections of privacy*. Washington, D.C.: Office of Telecommunications Policy.

House Committee on Government Operations. 90th Congress, 2nd Session. Testimony of May 16, 1968. Washington, D.C.: U.S. Government Printing Office, 1968.

Lowi, T. (1971). *The politics of disorder*. New York: Basic Books.

Miller, A. (1971). *Assault on privacy*. Ann Arbor: University of Michigan Press.

Perrow, C. (1972). *Complex organizations: A critical essay*. Glenview, Ill.: Scott Foresman and Co.

Pool, I., McIntosh, S., and Griffel, D. (1971). Information systems and social knowledge. In A. Westin (Ed.), *Information technology in a democracy*. Cambridge, Mass.: Harvard University Press.

Privacy Protection Study Committee. *Personal privacy in an information society*. Washington, D.C.: U.S. Government Printing Office, 1977.

Rule, J. (1974). *Private lives and public surveillance*. New York: Schocken Books.

Rule, J., McAdam, D., Stearns, L., and Uglow, D. (1980). *The politics of privacy: Planning for personal data systems as powerful technologies*. New York: Elsevier.

Seipp, D. J. (1978). *The right to privacy in American history*. Cambridge, Mass.: Harvard University Program on Information Resources Policy.

Shils, E. (1975). Privacy and power. In E. Shils (Ed.), *Center and periphery: Essays in macrosociology*. Chicago: University of Chicago Press.

Thompson, J. (1967). *Organizations in action*. New York: McGraw-Hill.

Wessel, M. (1974). *Freedom's edge: The computer threat to Society*. Reading, Mass.: Addison-Wesley.

Westin, A. (1967). *Privacy and freedom*. New York: Atheneum.

P·A·R·T·V

7

Comment on "Preserving Individual Autonomy in an Information-Oriented Society"

Kenneth C. Laudon

I was very pleased when Lance Hoffman asked me to comment on James Rule's paper, and when I received the draft I was not disappointed. Rule's paper is provocative because it questions some of the fundamental values upon which modern American society is based. The paper forces us to evaluate some of the value choices we have made with respect to personal information systems.

To avoid creating a straw man to argue with, let me review some of the arguments in Rule's paper. The place to start is in the conclusion, for here one finds some of the judgments that inform much of the paper. Rule points out that human control—the effort in Western societies to employ science and technology to shape the world according to human designs—has some drawbacks. Systems of human control can fail, and they do fail; big systems of human control informed by big science and big technology can fail in big ways, create disasters, and create unsteady states of human existence.

These observations are important for understanding Rule's treatment of large, personal data banks, which are a kind of social technology. As Rule points out, formal organizations play an increasing role in the life of citizens, as these organizations respond to public demands that citizens be treated as individuals, in accordance with the uniqueness of their circumstances. In response to these public demands for new organizational

Reprinted with permission from Academic Press. Laudon, Kenneth C., "Comment on 'Preserving Individual Autonomy in an Information-Oriented Society," in *Computers and Privacy in the Next Decade*, edited by Lance Hoffman, pp. 89–96, 1980.

relationships and greater individual consideration, organizations develop personal information systems in order to make the "fine-grained" decisions demanded, and this marks the growth of uniquely modern forms of social control, or what Rule chooses to call surveillance systems.

Rule claims that the growth of bureaucratic surveillance has resulted in (although he does not say over what time period) more and more personal information in record systems, a long-term decline in privacy and autonomy, centralization of social control, a concomitant weakening of other forms of social control such as families, communities, and the like. So long as the value of efficiency is supreme, there is no natural limit on this degradation of the human condition, and the logical endpoint, Rule believes, is a centralized monitoring agency where no area of personal life would exist beyond bureaucratic scrutiny.

Rule dismisses the privacy debate and legislation of the 1970s for having failed to attack established power positions in society (presumably, large organizations), as having been preoccupied with making large personal information systems simply more hygienic, and as having allowed these systems to accrue more information and power.

We should resist these developments, Rule argues, on aesthetic grounds, in order to preserve "looseness" (treating people irrespective of their uniqueness) and because the same tools that bring us efficiency in housing programs, welfare, and social security, could just as well lead to totalitarian regimes.

The alternative, Rule suggests, is not to go back to an organizational "Stone Age," but to become less discriminating, less information intensive, and if necessary, to eliminate especially obnoxious national, personal information systems and replace them with local systems, even if the costs to all are higher.

If I have correctly characterized the arguments, then I raise the following issues. An oft-repeated word in this paper is "surveillance," and it calls up some very nasty literary and historical images. Those who survived Sociology 101 in a conscious state will remember that surveillance—the collection of information for the purposes of social control—is a fundamental requirement of any form of social life whatsoever, from the family, community, city, to the state. Only at Walden Pond is there no surveillance. Those familiar with the revisionist history of the family and community will probably agree that for those of us who live in families and communities, there is nothing particularly benign about this "local" surveillance. It is incredibly intrusive. Within a few months of moving to a new community or suburb, it is pretty easy to invade the privacy of your neighbors, and vice versa, to the point where you know the state of their marriages, their occupations, religions, shopping habits, travel, indeed endless details of their personal lives, including how they avoid paying taxes; likewise with family life.

I think bureaucracies would give a year's budget to develop this kind of surveillance capacity. The implication of Rule's paper at various points—that bureaucratic surveillance is particularly onerous, intrusive, and threatening to human freedom, dignity, and autonomy, and therefore ought to be replaced by local systems of control—is, I think, wrong.

I believe, too, that Rule's opposition to the notion of fine-grained decision making is wrong. I think organizations would all like to make fine-grained decisions, and some may be able to when compared to other bureaucracies. Yet when compared to small, local surveillance systems, a great deal of bureaucratic decision making can only be compared to a meat cleaver in the hands of an amateur. The redlining of entire zip-code areas by mortgage banks, the withdrawing of insurance coverage from teenagers, the seeking of real human pluralism in universities and businesses (by adding a black, a Jew, a Mid-westerner, a female), is not the sophisticated use of statistical techniques to attain fine-grained decision making. The differences between groups on almost any important characteristic are far smaller than the differences between individuals within a group. Briefly, not taking into account the characteristics of individuals, instead deciding about individuals on the basis of their group membership, leads to all sorts of absurdities but clearly not to fine-grained decision making.

The place to find fine-grained decision making is, of course, in the small, local systems of social control. The banker in a small community who lets a resident know that the bank still owns the car he or she bought on their credit, and therefore it had better be kept clean; the grocer who grants credit because he "knows" a person; the cop who detains someone because he does not "know" him or her; the judge who gives someone the stiff sentence because he "knows" that person's family: These are the fine-grained decision makers, and they often are not benign, fair, or even analyzable.

Now, in theory, it may be that organizations are necessarily driven to collect more and more information to achieve fine-grained decision making, but in reality, Rule's state-ments about more and more information in personal data banks is a knotty issue to untangle.

If we restrict our vision to the period 1960–1980, we find some contradictory empirical evidence. As Westin and I looked at local and state public systems in the mid 1960s, we found some organizations converting from manual to automated systems and, in the process, throwing out a lot of information items in individual records, and throwing out a lot of entire records that had been lying around in manual files for no good reason, for example, criminal record systems. In some instances we found personal record systems being created which had not existed in manual form (for example, centralized social service systems). Then, Westin and Baker looked at private and public systems in the early 1970s and found the amount of information in individual records actually declining with automation (in part because of economic constraints such as memory cost). For the last two years I have worked with the Office of Technology Assessment (U.S. Congress) and other groups looking at three system-development projects in which third-generation designs are being replaced with fourth-generation designs suitable for operation in the 1980s. In looking at truly mammoth systems, such as the FBI Criminal History Message Switching proposal, the IRS Tax Administration System, and the proposed Social Security Future Process System, it would seem that with a few minor exceptions, it is *not the case* that more and more information is being collected in individual records.

On the other hand, from a total system of information perspective, while individual records may be more streamlined and actually smaller, telecommunications advances combined with distributed fourth-generation architecture result in more information being available to more decision makers on more individuals than ever before. Current distributed designs considerably enlarge the security and trust perimeters, strain existing control and accountability mechanisms, and vitiate the force of privacy legislation adopted in the 1970s.

Briefly, the "more and more information" thesis of Rule is rather complicated as an empirical matter. Much would seem to depend on the historical period under consideration, the theoretical perspective (a record versus system perspective), and the cost of computer memory, which is declining rapidly.

Yet another image that Rule invokes is that of totalitarianism, and the notion that development of personal information systems has no logical limit. Rule argues that developing large information systems will, or at least may, result in centralized monitoring agencies. Well, many things have no logical endpoint, like love, but there are empirical constraints. In any event, the image of totalitarianism invoked by Rule is largely literary in origin: the notion that a political decision maker one day will throw a switch, and in an orderly yet rapid transition, democracy ends and totalitarianism begins.

When we look at the history of real totalitarian regimes, we see that they did not originate through an orderly transition from bureaucratic efficiency to bureaucratic despotism. Rather, they seem to originate in the collapse of bureaucratic efficiency, social, and civic order. Totalitarian regimes, in fact, did not require (as necessary or sufficient conditions of coming to power) the existence of large personal data banks of any sort. And totalitarian regimes did not, and today do not, require large personal data banks in order to stay in power. The truly frightening aspect of totalitarian regimes is not their rational bureaucratic character, their reliance on huge personal record files, but just the opposite, that is, reliance on small local systems of social control.

Totalitarian regimes are not so incompetent as to think they can really control people using the frail, gross, and soft decision making powers of bureaucratics. Until recently, in China it was the small; local study group, *hsüeh-hsi*, at the block or factory level, or the use of forced biographies recorded by a neighborhood party team, in which people were forced to give complete accounts of themselves and their neighbors. The records were analyzed on a local level, and candidates were selected for "reform" by local leaders (Whyte, 1974; Price, 1976). Likewise with the Soviet purges of the 1930s: It was the local party cell operating in neighborhoods and the Army who carried out the orders of Stalin to supply victims (Fainsod, 1965). As in most totalitarian regimes, the selection process is not bureaucratically "rational" in character but just the opposite: merciless settling of local scores combined often with random selection to fulfill quotas.

The key personnel of totalitarian regimes are not bureaucrats. They are the Gauleiter; the block worker; the party member, who is the mechanic or high school teacher; or the secret police goon, who may be a neighbor. When you have these kinds of people in a society—devoted members of the party willing to inform and murder for whatever reason—who needs a cumbersome bureaucracy? Perhaps because totalitarian regimes have far more effective means of social control, namely local systems, we find that computerized personal data banks, say in the Soviet Union, the Eastern Bloc, China, Argentina, and Brazil, are not very well developed at all. It may be that large, bureaucratic personal data banks are a sufficient, adequate means of social control only in relatively free, voluntaristic, consensual societies because they rely so much upon individual compliance.

A good argument could be made that totalitarian regimes are inherently antibureaucratic, and vice versa. It is probably no accident that the totalitarian leaders of the past all distrusted their bureaucracies. Note, for example, the appearance with totalitarian leaders of Black Shirts to circumvent the regular police, the Red Guards to discipline the bureaucrats, the cadre worker to watch the colonels. It is no accident that former President Nixon profoundly distrusted his bureaucracy and found it necessary to create a White House group personally loyal to him. True, Nixon did abuse some large personal record systems, but he did encounter resistance in this effort, he was usually dissatisfied with the results, and I believe it was not his main threat to American democracy.

It may be that the literary image of totalitarianism called forth by Rule will one day be history; but, based on past experience, the best defense against the insanity of local totalitarian control may be centralized, efficient, rule-governed, and humane bureaucracies relying on personal record systems. From the point of view of accountability and oversight, from the view of public surveillance over public decision making, I would much rather oversee a few mammoth centralized systems than thousands of local systems.

Now let me reverse directions for a moment and try to escape Dr. Pangloss's corner, into which some may wish to paint me. I support most of Rule's concerns, which he raised so forcefully and clearly in his paper, even though I disagree with some of the conclusions. Rule seems to me absolutely correct when he suggests that the growth and redevelopment of large personal record systems is moving us toward a "tighter" society, one I would call a "dossier society." Here, most all of the important and not so important events in the lives of individuals are recorded and increasingly influence public and private decision making about one's future. I believe the pursuit of total efficiency in, say, criminal history record-keeping, probably does and will conflict with the pursuit of other critical values such as the integration of urban blacks into a complex economy, or for that matter, any former offender. I believe the technical capability presented by computerized record systems for, say, backing politically unpopular groups, really does influence the political process which has in fact come to authorize such tracking, for example, the recent Locator System of Department of Health, Education and Welfare, and numerous "matching" programs. At the same time, the technical capability of large systems can dull the blade of positive reform and social change as, for instance, it becomes possible to efficiently operate antiquated tax, welfare, and criminal justice programs designed generations ago. As it turns out, large personal record systems quite naturally reflect the extant social and political faces of their time. In some instances they do indeed magnify underlying inequities and mask over irrationality.

At a broader level, I believe Rule, along with others, only some of whom are present at the workshop, are members of a younger generation of scholars, policy analysts, and commentators who take a more critical view of the social impact of personal data banks than previous writers. This "second generation" of writers in the field of social impact of computing and personal data banks must now be starting to coalesce and to have some impact on public and private policy regarding personal data banks. Although I cannot speak for all of this generation, I can speak for myself and a few others whose views I know well.

Many of us believe that we are operating large personal data banks today at both local and national levels whose broad social consequences and whose impact on decision making we do not understand. For instance, I think it is a little ridiculous that a major State Criminal Justice Information System is generating a criminal history file used by police, district attorneys, judges, and God knows who else, and in which only 27% of the underlying records were found to be complete and accurate. The Department of Justice wants to link with state files so that by 1985 we will have a National Criminal History File influencing about 19 million criminal justice decisions per annum. My curiosity and fear is heightened by knowledge of the fact that in a system like Social Security, which distributes $7 billion to 37 million individuals every month, there are errors in a minimum of 20% of case files. There are more examples about which I have written (Laudon, 1974, 1979a, b), but at a minimum, it is clear to me the implications of large personal data banks for privacy—in the broadest sense of that word—due process, equity, and the balance of power between citizen and state, are not fully understood and have not been extensively investigated. It may be that we have systems designed by geniuses and run by idiots, but then we should plan for that eventuality. Or, it may be that we are operating systems designed by idiots and run by geniuses, the ordinary human cop or caseworker, who interprets system output before it has a negative impact on citizens. I wonder what happens then as the pursuit of efficiency causes us to eliminate these lower level decision makers and replace many of them with on-line, realtime, decision-making designs.

I believe, second, that we are operating large personal data bank systems whose full complexity is not understood, and which, therefore, are difficult to control and to hold accountable. If programming is an art, then imagine what descriptions of programs are like. As it turns out, we have no really good methodology to explain or describe programs. The first words out of a programmer's mouth when explaining his artful creation is liable to be, "Well, it's kind of complicated but it works this way." Pretty soon, the conference table starts to look like an arterial road map of the United States.

The implications of these remarks are as follows. If we start building systems like the proposed Social Security Future Process system involving 30,000 terminals in a partially distributed design, then what kinds of additional oversight and control mechanisms are required to assure its proper operation? Put another way, if the objective complexity of a system increases tenfold, what increase in management oversight and control capacity is required (none, 1%, 10%)? In the past, we have tended to find out the answers through a seat-of-the-pants, trial-and-error method. I do not think that it's good enough anymore. I think Congress, in the appropriations and oversight process, is starting to address the practical side of these questions which is: Are the existing institutional mechanisms sufficient to provide adequate control and oversight for some of these mammoth public systems?

This takes us to the area of future and past legislation, an area of which Rule was especially critical. If you look at the kinds of requests that the Office of Technology Assessment (U.S. Congress) receives from congressional committees, if you talk with certain congressmen and their staffs, there is a growing belief that, whereas existing privacy legislation may provide important legal remedies to individuals to correct failures of personal data systems, the laws do not provide positive institutional mechanisms to monitor, oversee, and gauge the full social, legal, political, and economic impacts of these systems. Many congressmen felt this way in 1974—the year the Privacy Act was passed —but in disagreement with Rule, I do not believe there was sufficient political horse-power to support stronger legislation. I do not believe there was a chance in the early 1970's that privacy could be used as the issue to attack fundamental positions of power in the United States.

Nevertheless, I do believe stronger legislation is on the way, reflecting a growing congressional uneasiness. The political momentum in Congress for such legislation is in part provided by Executive agencies who come to Congress with very complex and mammoth system-development projects whose social impact and whose privacy impact they really had not even considered in the design process. The haughty attitude of IRS —which came to Congress with its proposed Tax Administration System saying, in essence, we really do not know and have not studied the potential social impact questions, but it should be approved because we say it is more efficient—just will not work anymore. The FBI and Social Security system-development projects have taken this experience into account, and I think are more mindful of social-impact questions as a result. However, as more sophisticated projects keep coming to Congress, there is a feeling that some institutional vehicle is needed to provide coherent knowledge, information, and judgments about the social impact of operating and proposed systems. No doubt, as with other technologies, it may take a few disasters and some near misses before we actually establish such institutions.

All of these remarks put me in the position of calling for better system design, more critical knowledge and thinking about the relation between systems and society, and stronger oversight mechanisms to assure accountability as we move into the 1980s. The challenge is to envision efficient and humane systems operating within constitutional limits and under strong statutory control. These systems will require a broader base of public participation; they will be more expensive to build, more difficult to manage well, and will be of somewhat reduced efficiency than technologically feasible. The alternative appears to be fewer services delivered in a manner neither efficient or humane. Frankly, I do not believe this last alternative has much political support.

References

Fainsod, M. (1965). *How Russia is ruled*. Cambridge, Mass.: Harvard University Press.

Laudon, K. C. (1974). *Computers and bureaucratic reform*. New York: Wiley.

Laudon, K. C. (1979a). Complexity in large federal databanks. *Society/Transaction*, May.

Laudon, K. C. (1979b). Problems of accountability in federal databanks, *Proceedings of the American Association for the Advancement of Science*, January.

Price, J. L. (1976). *Cadres, commanders, and commissars*. Boulder, Col.: Westview Press.

Whyte, M. K. (1974). *Small groups and political rituals in China*. Berkeley: University of California Press.

P·A·R·T · V

8

Information Technology and Dataveillance

Roger A. Clarke

Concern about freedom from tyranny is a trademark of democracy. Between 1920 and 1950, the anti-utopian novels of Zamyatin [78], Kafka, Huxley [21], and Orwell [45] unleashed a visionary, yet paranoic "literature of alarm" (see, e.g., [5], [12], [15], [19], [32], [36], [49], [53], and [62]).

Surveillance is one of the elements of tyranny. The word conjures up unpleasant visions of spies, repression of individuals, and suppression of ideas. Nevertheless, some classes of people, at least when they undertake some classes of activity, are deemed by society to warrant surveillance. Few would contest that people reasonably suspected of terrorism and organized, violent crime are candidates for surveillance. Meanwhile, the growth in crimes against property has resulted in the widely acclaimed "neighborhood watch" movement.

The computer has been accused of harboring a potential for increased surveillance of the citizen by the state, and the consumer by the corporation. Most accusations have been vague, asserting that harm will result, rather than showing the mechanisms by which it will come about. Some have even claimed that the potential is already realized: "It is possible . . . to imagine what one might call a "central clearing house" for mass surveillance and control, without straining the limits of present-day [i.e., 1974] technology and organisational skills . . . . [A]ll major agencies would render unlimited assistance to one another. Information generated in the relationship between a client and any one system would automatically be available to any other system . . . . [T]he client's contact with one

"Information Technology and Datavallience," by R.C. Clarke, *Communications of the ACM*, Association for Computing Machinery, Inc. **31** (5) May 1989, pp. 498–512. Copyright 1989, Association for Computing Machinery, Inc. Reprinted by permission.

would have the effect of contact with all . . . . [N]o favourable decision from any agency would be implemented while there remained a dispute between the client and another agency" [55, p. 319].

Apart from research by Kling [23, 24] and Laudon [27–31], there has been little discussion in the computing literature. Most of the important contributions have been by observers rather than practitioners of computing, particularly Rule [55–59], Marx [33, 34], and Reichman and Marx [35, 50]. See also [2, 11, 52].

The purpose of this article is to make the work of such authors more readily accessible to computing practitioners and academics, to extend it somewhat, and to propose a framework for policy. It commences by clarifying the concept of *dataveillance*, and then describes the manner in which information technology (IT) is stimulating its development. Popular publications have tended to deal with the topic in colorful, at times even hysterical, fashion (see, e.g., [1], [4], [6], [7], [12], [13], [64], [70], and [73]). To enable the problems to be appreciated and responded to rationally, I will attempt to deal with the topic in a more neutral and dispassionate manner. In particular, I explicitly reject the notion that surveillance is, of itself, evil or undesirable; its nature must be understood, and society must decide the circumstances in which it should be used, and the safeguards that should be applied to it.

Surveillance

The *Oxford Dictionary* explained surveillances as "watch or guard kept over a person, etc., esp. over a suspected person, a prisoner, or the like; often spying, supervision; less commonly, supervision for the purpose of direction or control, superintendence" [46]. The oldest usage noted was in the "Committee of Surveillance" immediately after the French Revolution. *Webster's 3rd Edition* defines it as "1. close watch kept over one or more persons: continuous observation of a person or area (as to detect developments, movements or activities); 2. close and continuous observation for the purpose of direction, supervision or control" [71].

Rule uses the term for "any form of systematic attention to whether rules are obeyed, to who obeys and who does not, and how those who deviate can be located and sanctioned" [55, p. 40], and later as "the systematic collection and monitoring of personal data for the purpose of social control" [59, p. 47] (see also [20, p. 90]). In this article the following definition is used:

Surveillance is the systematic investigation or monitoring of the actions or communications of one or more persons. Its primary purpose is generally to collect information about them, their activities, or their associates. There may be a secondary intention to deter a whole population from undertaking some kinds of activity.

The basic form, physical surveillance, comprises watching and listening (visual and aural surveillance). Monitoring may be undertaken remotely in space, with the aid of image-amplification devices like field glasses, infrared binoculars, light amplifiers, and satellite cameras, and sound-amplification devices like directional microphones; and remotely in time, with the aid of image and sound-recording devices. Several kinds of communications surveillance are practiced, including mail covers and telephone interception. The popular term *electronic surveillance* refers to both augmentations to physical surveillance (such as directional microphones and audio bugs) and to communications surveillance, particularly telephone taps.

These forms of direct surveillance are commonly augmented by the collection of data from interviews with informants (such as neighbors, employers, workmates, and bank managers). As the volume of information collected and maintained has increased, the record collections (or personal data systems) of organizations have become an increasingly important source.

Dataveillance is the systematic use of personal data systems in the investigation or monitoring of the actions or communications of one or more persons.

The terms *personal surveillance* and *mass surveillance* are commonly used, but seldom defined. In this article the following definitions are used:

Personal surveillance is the surveillance of an identified person. In general, a specific reason exists for the investigation or monitoring.

Mass surveillance is the surveillance of groups of people, usually large groups. In general, the reason for investigation or monitoring is to identify individuals who belong to some particular class of interest to the surveillance organization.

Personal surveillance is an important weapon in the fight against such social evils as terrorism and organized crime. It is used to collect evidence in civil cases. It is also a means of learning sufficiently embarrassing facts about a person to assist in discrediting him or her in the eyes of some other person or group, or buying his or her silence or agreement. At its most secret, it can deny the subject natural justice, and at its most open, it can be tantamount to coercion or blackmail.

Personal-surveillance activities are undertaken by "private investigators" for corporate and personal clients. The majority of these activities, however, are undertaken by staff employed by government agencies, including police, national security, customs, and telecommunications officials.

Mass surveillance is difficult to discuss dispassionately because of the impact on our culture of the anti-utopian novels, particularly *1984* [45]. Its primitive forms include guards on raised walkways and observation turrets. More recently, closed-circuit television has offered a characteristic that significantly enhances the effectiveness of surveillance: The subjects, even if they know they are subject to monitoring, cannot know precisely when the observer is actually watching.

"Modern techniques have made possible a new intensity of governmental control, and this possibility has been exploited very fully in totalitarian states . . . . [E]mphasis upon the value of the individual is even more necessary now than at any former time" [60, p. 35]. Such a sentiment could be expected from the contemporary civil libertarian lobby. In fact, the words predate the use of computers even in information management, let alone personal data management, having been written in 1949 by Bertrand Russell. Ubiquitous two-way television à la *1984* has not arrived, even though it is readily deliverable. It is unnecessary because dataveillance is technically and economically superior.

- Magnetic data-storage capabilities have improved immensely between 1965 and 1985, and optical storage is expected to have a significant impact in at least some application areas.

- A rich assortment of input and output technologies has been developed to support the capture and dissemination of data.

- Textual and conventional "structurable" data have been dealt with successfully for some years by DBMS technology. The management of image and voice data is improving, and integrated data management and conversion between the various forms are now being addressed.

- Inroads have been made into natural languge understanding, at least in respect of the more formal usages of language by humans.

- The hitherto numerical bias of computing technology is being augmented by symbolic manipulative capabilities. Many kinds of complex deterministic problems can now be tackled, and progress is being made in modeling probabilistic, "fuzzy," and stochastic processes.

- Significant improvements in telecommunications continue, particularly in speed, cost, reliability, robustness, security, and standardization.

Figure 1.   Relevant Components of IT Development.

Relevant IT Trends

Computers were originally developed for their high-speed computational capabilities. They subsequently spawned or stimulated a wide variety of related technologies and have been married with telecommunications. Data can now be captured, stored, processed, and accessed readily and economically, even when the facilities and their users are physically dispersed. Figure 1 identifies some particularly pertinent aspects of current developments in IT.

Apparently distinct technologies have drawn together very quickly, as in electronic funds transfer systems (EFTS) and their nephew EFT/POS (point of sale). Change is being wrought less by computers themselves than by amalgams of many interacting and mutually supporting technologies. Optical-storage technology may portend a new surge in such compound high-technology ventures.

IT crystal-ball gazing is fraught with danger. Nevertheless, discernible trends include the integration with EFTS of air-travel systems and telephone charging; road-traffic monitoring, including vehicle identification, closely integrated with ownership and driver's-license records; computerization and integration of court records, criminal records, fingerprint records, and criminal-investigation systems; integration of structured and textual data to support criminal investigation and national-security applications; computerization and integration of birth, death, and marriage records; and homes wired for reasons of employment, security, entertainment, and consumerism.

As a consequence of the centralizing tendency of early IT, a "data imperative" arose, with government agencies and private companies alike collecting ever more data. Rule interpreted this as commitment to the "efficiency criterion," whereby privacy concerns should be recognized, but not at the cost of administrative efficiency. IT led to increasingly information-intensive practices and increasingly fine-grained decision making [55, 59].

With the repeal of Grosch's law during the 1970s, economies of scale no longer apply to processing power. Other factors that are militating against the old centralist notions are the systems software overheads of large-scale centralized processing; risks associated with single-site activities; standardization of local and site networking standards; fast-growing capabilities of network workstations and servers; decreasing cost and increasing portability and robustness of dense storage, as in the so-called "smart card"; established techniques of distributed DBMS; and emerging techniques of distributed operating systems. The once-obvious tendency of computers to centralize information, and hence power, is quickly giving way to the looser concepts of networking and dispersion.

The National Data Center Issue

In the mid-1960s the U.S. government considered creating a national data center. The prime motivation was stated to be the need for more coherent data management to support economic and sociological research. Such a data collection, however, had clear potential for supporting administrative decision making. A few people recognized the vital role of data dispersion: "One of the most practical of our present safeguards of privacy is the fragmented nature of present information. It is scattered in little bits and pieces across the geography and years of our life. Retrieval is impractical and often impossible. A central data bank removes completely this safeguard" (Representative Frank Horton, 1966–67 hearings on a proposed national data center, quoted in [59, p. 56]). Concerns such as these resulted in the proposal not proceeding.

Centralized storage, however, is no longer a precondition of the dossier society that Horton feared. For dataveillance purposes a single centralized data bank is unnecessary, provided that three conditions are fulfilled:

1. A range of personal data systems must exist, each processing data for specific purposes.
2. Some, preferably all, personal data systems must be connected via one or more telecommunications networks.
3. The data must be identified consistently.

A recent report of the Office of Technology Assessment (O.T.A.) of the U.S. Congress discussed the manner in which use of IT is quickly leading to a de facto national identification system [43, pp. 3, 68–74]. There are also reports suggesting that both the NCIC (National Crime Information Center) and NSA (National Security Agency) are providing foci for such a system (e.g., [54, pp. 185–186]).

Beyond assisting in the investigation of people's pasts, IT is also dramatically improving the monitoring of people's ongoing activities and present location. A person's most recent financial (or indeed any other kind of) transaction indicates where the person can currently be found. If that location is communicated to surveillance staff immediately, they can literally be on their way to the scene before the person leaves the checkout counter. A recent Australian report commenced with the sentence "EFTPOS is not a

Greek island" [3]. The comment had a poignancy that its authors may not have appreciated. People go to Greek islands to escape from it all. EFT/POS constitutes a real-time locator service: You cannot escape from it at all. This was recognized at least as long ago as 1971, when it was suggested as an appropriate surveillance tool for the KGB (Armer, quoted in [59, p. 115]).

Physical and even communications surveillance are labor-intensive activities, which have so far proved difficult to automate. Dataveillance is essentially computer based, with the "watch and report" responsibility delegated to a reliable, ever-wakeful servant. It is increasingly cost-effective for organizations to place people under surveillance via their records and transactions, and traditional methods are being relegated to the role of complementary techniques. Furthermore, because dataveillance is cheaper than traditional methods, there is a tendency for more organizations to monitor more people: Both personal and mass surveillance are becoming routinized [35, 51].

The Central Role of Identification Schemes

Of the three requirements for a dispersed national data center identified earlier, the first two are already fulfilled. The third has not as yet been achieved, because of the difficulties of reliably identifying surveillance subjects, in associating stored data with individuals, and in associating new data with old.

The vast majority of personal data systems use schemes based on documentary evidence, possession of tokens, and personal knowledge. None of these can provide a satisfactory basis for a high-integrity system [9]. Many organizations that need to recognize identities in successive transactions assign their data subjects a more-or-less arbitrary unique identifying code. Some organizations prefer to (or have to) identify individuals by their names, usually supplemented by additional data such as date of birth. This approach involves a great deal of ambiguity, and name-matching routines have been developed to apply algorithms to such data in order to display synonyms "most-likely-first."

These various schemes may be of a reasonable level of integrity where data subjects have an interest in their accuracy, but are otherwise of, at best, only moderate integrity. Organized crime finds such low-integrity schemes as a social-security number a positive boon in its aims to legitimize false identities.

A high-integrity identification scheme is only possible if some physiological attribute is used that the person cannot alienate, and that the organization can capture, recognize, and store with its records. During 1987 the New South Wales (N.S.W.) Police Department implemented a fingerprint-record system based on Japanese technology. Although some U.S. state and local government law-enforcement agencies have installed such systems, the N.S.W. initiative is quite significant, since its bureau operates on behalf of all police departments throughout Australia, and it appears to have been the first national system to enter operation anywhere in the world. Apart from criminal records, and limited applications in building security arrangements, fingerprint identification has not been socially acceptable. It can confidently be expected that there will be considerable efforts to make it so.

Historically, organizations have developed their identification schemes independently of one another, and large, multifunction organizations have run multiple schemes. However, organizations are increasingly using a single code for multiple purposes. For example, since at least the early 1970s, financial institutions have been moving toward "client-oriented" data management, whereby all of a client's data carry the same identifying code. The Australian Department of Social Security has committed itself to a common identification scheme for recipients of all classes of benefits by 1990.

Some identifiers were designed to be used for multiple purposes, whether by a single organization or by several. For example, in European countries it is normal for the same number to be used for the national superannuation fund as for taxation. Despite successive reports recommending the contrary (e.g., [48, 68]), the United States is continuing its trend toward using the (originally single-purpose) social security number as a de facto national identification code. For example, in 1985 a database called ESVARS was established, explicitly to enable any organization (federal, state, or private sector) to verify social-security numbers [43, p. 73].

General-purpose schemes, for use by all organizations for all purposes, have been attempted in a number of countries during wartime, including the United Kingdom and Australia, when the "inducement of rationing" has made them workable [55, p. 314]. The few countries that have considered such a scheme in peacetime have rejected the idea. The United States did so in the mid-1970s [68]. The Australian government proposed such a scheme in 1985, although the proposal was subsequently amended to a multipurpose scheme for three main agencies, and finally withdrawn in the third quarter of 1987 when serious public concern arose about its implications [9]. As the scope of use of an identification scheme moves from single-use via multiple-use toward general-purpose use, the ease with which dataveillance can be undertaken increases significantly.

Techniques of Dataveillance

This section discusses the techniques used in personal dataveillance, mass dataveillance, and facilitative mechanisms. Figure 2 provides a summary.

Personal Dataveillance Techniques

Organizations maintain records about individuals they are concerned with (their *data subjects*). In most cases data subjects are clients of the organization, because they have a known and fairly explicit relationship with them. This relationship may be direct (as with financial institutions and the Internal Revenue Service (IRS) or indirect (as is sometimes the case with superannuation funds). With some record-keeping organizations, there may be no overt relationship (e.g., counterintelligence agencies, private investigators, and credit bureaus).

Subjects of personal dataveillance have attracted attention for some reason. The reason may be benign, for example, because they have applied for employment or a service. An investigation will usually have the intention of disqualifying the person from the employment or service they seek, but sometimes the organization may be considering whether the person may qualify for extra assistance, say, because of aboriginal ancestry.

Personal dataveillance of identified individuals who have attracted attention:

- *Integration of data* hitherto stored in various locations within the organization.
- *Screening or authentication of transactions*, against internal norms.
- *Front-end verification of transactions* that appear to be exceptional, against data relevant to the matter at hand and sought from other internal databases or from third parties.
- *Front-end audit of individuals* who appear to be exceptional, against data related to *other* matters and sought from other internal databases or from third parties.
- *Cross-system enforcement against individuals*, where a third party reports that the individual has committed a transgression in his or her relationship with the third party.

Mass dataveillance of groups of people, with the intention of finding individuals in need of attention:

- *Screening or authentication of all transactions*, irrespective of whether or not they appear to be exceptional, against internal norms.
- *Front-end verification of all transactions*, irrespective of whether or not they appear to be exceptional, against data relevant to the matter at hand and sought from other internal databases or from third parties.
- *Front-end audit of individuals*, irrespective of whether or not they appear to be exceptional, against data related to *other* matters and sought from other internal databases or from third parties.
- *Single-factor file analysis of all data held or able to be acquired*, irrespective of whether or not they appear to be exceptional—variously involving transaction data compared against a norm, against a legal or other *a priori* norm, and against a norm inferred from a population a posteriori; transaction data compared against permanent data; and transaction data compared against other transaction data.
- *Profiling*, or multifactor file analysis, *of all data held or able to be acquired*, irrespective of whether or not they appear to be exceptional—variously involving singular profiling of data held at a point in time, and aggregative profiling of transaction trails over time.

Facilitative mechanisms:

- *Matching*—expropriation and merger of data held in separate data systems, whether operated by the same organization or by third parties.
- *Data concentration*—by organizational merger or by the operation of data-interchange networks and hub systems.

Figure 2.   Techniques of Dataveillance.

Another class of reasons for investigation is suspicion that the person has committed a crime or misdemeanor. A transaction may have taken place that appears inconsistent with existing records, or potentially incriminating information may have been received from outside the organization.

Dataveillance depends on data that identify people. Despite the increase in information intensity in recent years, there remain many economic relationships in which the parties do not necessarily identify themselves. These include barter and cash transactions ranging from hunting and fishing licenses, through gambling, and bus, train, and ferry tickets to quite large consumer items, including expensive cars and boats. Authorities throughout the world, concerned about the ease with which organized crime "washes" its illegally gained cash, have set, or are considering setting, maximum limits on unidentified cash transactions.

Given that identified records exist, a variety of dataveillance techniques are available. The most primitive technique, *record integration*, brings together all of the data an organization holds about each person. For many organizations this is not the trivial exercise it appears. Data may be dispersed in many ways, such as geographically across different offices and files, or under different codes or names (e.g., where the person has changed name; operates under multiple identities, including married and maiden names, and business and company names; operates joint accounts, sometimes with another party's name first; uses various combinations of given names; or has a name that is subject to spelling variants). In addition, during the early years of administrative and commercial applications of computing, it has been cost-effective and even necessary to store transaction data separately from permanent data, and transaction data for each period of time in distinct files. Financial institutions have undergone the transition to client-oriented data storage, the insurance industry is going through it, and airlines have commenced the changeover.

An approach adopted by most organizations is to monitor new transactions. Each transaction an organization receives (e.g., an application for employment, a loan, or a government benefit) is processed according to standard rules to determine whether the transaction is valid and acceptable. Additional rules may be applied, expressly designed to detect both inaccuracies and attempts to cheat the decision criteria. Exceptional cases are generally submitted to a more senior authority for more careful, nonroutine consideration.

Where the processing rules depend only on data already available to the organization, these practices are generally referred to as screening or authentication. Some commercial and administrative activity is impractical without such basic data processing, and in many cases the law requires it, as, for example, in the processing of applications for government benefits. Moreover, the stewardship responsibilities to which any organization is subject generally require that controls be built into transaction processing, subject to cost-effectiveness constraints.

Front-end verification of transactions represents a further development beyond screening [25; 43, pp. 67–83]. It involves the collection of data from other personal-data systems in order to facilitate the processing of a transaction. The source of the data may be elsewhere in the same organization; for example, a driver's-licensing authority might consult its traffic-offenses database when renewing licenses. More commonly, however, front-end verification involves communication between two or more distinct organizations, either on an ad hoc basis or under a standing data-interchange arrangement.

Front-end verification is a personal-dataveillance technique when the transaction has been identified as exceptional, and the purpose of collecting the additional data is to establish whether there is any inconsistency between the various sources of data. An inconsistency may disqualify the transaction or be evidence of some wrongdoing such as providing misleading information. The data-interchange arrangements necessary to support front-end verification are not well documented in the literature. Rule provides one good reason: "No topic evoked less candour . . . or gave rise to more vivid displeasure when I insisted on pursuing it" [55, p. 308].

Front-end verification tests transactions. A broader form of personal dataveillance is what might be termed *front-end audit*. This uses the occasion of the detection of an exceptional transaction as an opportunity to further investigate other matters relating to the individual. For example, when a driver is stopped for a traffic offense, it is becoming standard practice for the police officer to initiate on-line inquiries. These typically concern the vehicle (whether it is currently registered and whether it has been reported stolen), the vehicle's registered owner, and the driver (whether the driver is being sought for questioning or has an outstanding arrest warrant). The first transaction generally arises because there are reasonable grounds for believing that an offense has been committed. The justification for the subsequent transactions is less clear.

Intersystem and interorganizational arrangements can be pursued a step further by means of *cross-system enforcement*. This technique makes an individual's relationship with one organization dependent on his or her performance in relation to another. For example, there have been proposals in some U.S. states whereby renewal of a driver's license or entry to a turnpike would be precluded until the person has paid all outstanding parking fines. Steps have been taken in this direction (e.g., to preclude the sale of books of turnpike tickets), but to date their effectiveness appears to be doubtful.

In those cases the systems to be used for cross-enforcement are different, but to some extent related. There have been suggestions in New York City that even the issuing of a marriage license might be made dependent on payment of outstanding parking fines. In this case the link between the two systems is rather tenuous—it is merely that the same organization has responsibility for both functions. Such a mechanism was included in the Australian government's proposed national identification scheme: The individual's rights under Medicare to free treatment or a refund of medical expenses would have been suspended until that person's obligation to have a national identity card was fulfilled [9].

Mass Dataveillance Techniques

Personal dataveillance is concerned with identified individuals about whom some kind of concern or suspicion has arisen. On the other hand, mass dataveillance is concerned with groups of people and involves a generalized suspicion that some (as yet unidentified) members of the group may be of interest. Its purposes are to identify individuals who may be worth subjecting to personal surveillance, and to constrain the group's behavior.

Screening or authentication of transactions, discussed earlier, is arguably a form of mass surveillance to the extent that it is routinely or automatically applied to every transaction, whether or not it appears to be exceptional. Similarly, when data are routinely sought from other internal databases or third parties in order to undertake front-end verification of all transactions, mass dataveillance is being undertaken. This is a recent development in which IT's role has been criticized: "In the past, such verification was done manually on a random basis or when the accuracy of information provided was suspect. Today . . . computerized databases and on-line networking make it possible to carry out such verification routinely" [43, p. 67]. Similarly, front-end audit is a mass-surveillance technique if the investigation of multiple aspects of a person's performance arises without any explicit cause, rather than as a result of some exceptional transaction.

The application of such techniques to existing records, rather than to new transactions, is referred to here as *file analysis*: "The files are most useful where they enable the system quickly and unerringly to single out the minority of their clients who warrant some measure of social control" (Rule, quoted in [67]). File analysis can be effective in searching out what Marx and Reichman refer to as "low-visibility offenses" [35]. In a recent instance in the United Kingdom, government investigators applied file-analysis techniques to detect and prosecute multiple applications for shares in "privatized" government enterprises such as Telecom and British Petroleum.

Screening, front-end verification, front-end audit, and file analysis may all be undertaken with varying degrees of sophistication. Transaction data may be compared against a formal standard or other norm, for example, highlighting those tax returns that include deductions above a certain value or show more than, say, eight dependents. The norms against which the data are compared may be either legal or other a priori norms that have been set down in advance by some authority, possibly for good reasons, possibly quite arbitrarily. Alternatively, they may be a posteriori norms that were inferred from analysis of the collection of records.

Alternatively, transaction data may be compared against permanent data, for example, highlighting tax returns where the spouse's name does not match that on file. Or transaction data may be compared against other transaction data, for example, highlighting people whose successive tax returns show varying numbers of dependents.

The previous examples are each based on a single factor. Judgments of any complexity must be based on multiple factors, rather than just one. *Profiling*, as it is commonly known, may be done on the basis of either a priori arbitrary or pragmatic norms, or on a posteriori norms based on empirical evidence. Rule noted in 1974 that the IRS used an a posteriori technique for predicting the "audit potential" of different returns. It did this by inferring unknown characteristics from known characteristics by applying discriminant analysis to a small random sample of returns [55, p. 282]. Marx and Reichman's description of this technique is "correlating a number of distinct data items in order to assess how close a person comes to a predetermined characterization or model of infraction" [35, p. 429]. These authors further distinguish "singular profiling" from "aggregative profiling," which involves analyzing transaction trails over a period of time.

Sophisticated profiling techniques are claimed to hold great promise because they can detect hidden cases amid large populations. Benefits could be readily foreseen from profiles of young people with proclivities toward particular artistic and sporting skills; propensity for diseases, disorders, delinquency, or drug addiction; or suicidal or homicidal tendencies. A recent O.T.A. report noted that most U.S. federal agencies have applied the technique to develop a wide variety of profiles including drug dealers, taxpayers who underreport their income, likely violent offenders, arsonists, rapists, child molesters, and sexually exploited children [43, pp. 87–95].

Facilitative Mechanisms

Mass-dataveillance techniques may be successfully applied within a single personal-data system, but their power can be enhanced if they are applied to data from several. These systems might all be operated by the organization concerned or by a number of distinct organizations. In such cases a preliminary step may be undertaken:

Computer matching is the expropriation of data maintained by two or more personal-data systems, in order to merge previously separate data about large numbers of individuals.

Matching has become technically and economically feasible only during the last decade, as a result of developments in IT. The first large program reported was Project Match, undertaken by the U.S. Department of Health, Education and Welfare (HEW), now known as Health and Human Services (HHS). By 1982 it was estimated that about 500 programs were carried out routinely in the U.S. state and federal agencies [69], and O.T.A. estimated a tripling in use between 1980 and 1984 [43, p. 37]. Moreover, a succession of federal laws, culminating in the 1984 Budget Deficit Reduction Act, imposed matching on state administrations as a condition of receiving federal social-welfare funding. (For references descriptive of and supportive of matching, see [25], [39]–[41], [65], and [66]. Cautionary and critical comments are to be found in [22], [23], [26], [35], [43], [50], and [61]).

Matching makes more data available about each person and also enables comparison between apparently similar data items as they are known to different organizations. Rather than relating to a single specified person for a specific reason, matching achieves indiscriminate data cross-referencing about a large number of people for no better reason than a generalized suspicion: "Computer matches are inherently mass or class investigations, as they are conducted on a category of people rather than on specific individuals . . . in practice, welfare recipients and Federal employees are most often the targets" [43, p. 40].

Matching may be based on some common identifier that occurs in both files, in which case the error rate (measured by the proportion of undetected matches and spurious matches) will tend to be fairly low. There are few opportunities for such matching, however, and instead it is usually necessary to correlate several items of information. Intuitively, name, birth date, and sex seem appropriate, but it appears that greater success has been achieved by using some component of address as a primary matching criterion.

Individuals may be judged to be interesting because of

- the existence of a match where none should exist,
- the failure to find a match where one was expected,
- inequality between apparently common data items (e.g., different numbers of dependents), or
- logical inconsistency among the data on the two files (e.g., the drawing of social-welfare benefits during a period of employment).

Curiously, the current U.S. government matching guidelines [40] define matching only in terms of the first of these criteria.

An additional facilitative mechanism for both personal and mass dataveillance is referred to here as *data concentration*. The conventional approach is to merge existing organizations in search of economies of scale in administration. If the capabilities of large-scale data-processing equipment were to continue to increase, the merger of social-welfare and internal-revenue agencies could be anticipated enabling welfare to be administered as "reverse taxation."

Organizational merger is an old-fashioned "centralized" solution. The modern, dispersed approach to data concentration is to establish systems that can function as the hub of a data-interchange network. For example, the U.S. government has developed new systems to facilitate routine front-end verification. These initiatives, in the name of waste reduction, involve both federal government sources (including IRS and criminal records) and private-sector credit bureaus, and their use not only extends across many federal government agencies, but is also imposed on state welfare administration agencies [14; 42, pp. 68–74]. The Australian government's proposal for a national identification scheme involved just such a coordinating database [9].

Dataveillance's Benefits and Dangers

In this section the advantages dataveillance techniques offer are briefly discussed. Greater space is then devoted to the threats dataveillance represents. Figure 3 summarizes these dangers.

Benefits

Significant benefits can result from dataveillance. The physical security of people and property may be protected, and financial benefits may accrue from the detection and prevention of various forms of error, abuse, and fraud. Benefits can be foreseen both in government activity (e.g., tax and social welfare) and in the private sector (e.g., finance and insurance). (For the limited literature on the benefits of matching, see [16], [25], [43, pp. 50–52], [65], and [66]. Literature on the benefits of other dataveillance techniques is very difficult to find).

Some proponents claim that the deterrent effect of public knowledge that such techniques are applied is significant, perhaps even more significant than direct gains from their actual use. There may be symbolic or moral value in dataveillance, irrespective of its technical effectiveness.

Few people would contest the morality of an organization applying the more basic techniques, for example, record integration and screening. Some would go so far as to regard organizations that did not apply modern IT in such ways as failing to fulfill their responsibilities to taxpayers and shareholders. Nevertheless, dataveillance is, by its very nature, intrusive and threatening. It therefore seems reasonable that organizations should have to justify its use, rather than merely assuming its appropriateness.

Dangers of Personal Dataveillance

Because so few contemporary identification schemes use a physiological identifier, they are, at best, of moderate integrity. Rather than individuals themselves, what is monitored is data that purport to relate to them. As a result there is a significant likelihood of wrong identification.

The vast majority of data systems operators are quite casual about the quality of most of their data; for example, the O.T.A. reported that few federal government agencies have

Dangers of personal dataveillance

- Wrong identification
- Low data quality
- Acontextual use of data
- Low-quality decisions
- Lack of subject knowledge of data flows
- Lack of subject consent to data flows
- Blacklisting
- Denial of redemption

Dangers of mass dataveillance

(1) To the individual

- Arbitrariness
- Acontextual data merger
- Complexity and incomprehensibility of data
- Witch hunts
- Ex ante discrimination and guilt prediction
- Selective advertising
- Inversion of the onus of proof
- Covert operations
- Unknown accusations and accusers
- Denial of due process

(2) *To society*

- Prevailing climate of suspicion
- Adversarial relationships
- Focus of law enforcement on easily detectable and provable offenses
- Inequitable application of the law
- Decreased respect for the law
- Reduction in the meaningfulness of individual actions
- Reduction in self-reliance and self-determination
- Stultification of originality
- Increased tendency to opt out of the official level of society
- Weakening of society's moral fiber and cohesion
- Destabilization of the strategic balance of power
- Repressive potential for a totalitarian government

Figure 3. Real and Potential Dangers of Dataveillance.

conducted audits of data quality [43, p. 26]. For many organizations it is cost-effective to ensure high levels of accuracy only of particular items (such as invoice amounts), with broad internal controls designed to ensure a reasonable chance of detecting errors in less vital data. Some errors are intentional on the part of the data subject, but many are accidental, and some are a result of design deficiencies such as inadequate coding schemes. Similar problems arise with other elements of data quality such as the timeliness and completeness of data. Even in systems where a high level of integrity is important, empirical studies have raised serious doubts [30; 43, pp. 52–53]. Data quality is generally not high, and while externally imposed controls remain very limited, it seems likely that the low standards will persist.

People and matters relating to them are complicated, and organizations generally have difficulty dealing with atypical, idiosyncratic cases or extenuating circumstances [35, p. 436]. A full understanding of the circumstances generally requires additional data that would have seemed too trivial and/or expensive to collect, but also depends on common sense, and abstract ideas like received wisdom, public opinion, and morality [54]. When the data are used in their original context, data quality may be sufficient to support effective and fair decision making, but when data are used outside their original context, the probability of misinterpreting them increases greatly. This is the reason why information privacy principles place such importance on relating data to the purpose for which they are collected or used [44], and why sociologists express concern about the "acontextual" nature of many administrative decision processes [35].

Much front-end verification is undertaken without the subject's knowledge. Even where an organization publicizes that it seeks data from third parties, the implications of the notice are often unclear to the data subject. International conventions stipulate that data should not be used for purposes other than the original purpose of collection, except with the authority of law or the consent of the data subject (e.g., [44]). Where consent is sought, the wording is often such that the person has no appreciation of the import of the consent that is being given, or the bargaining position is so disproportionately weighted in favor of the organization that the data subject has no real option but to comply. Effective subject knowledge and consent mechanisms are necessary, both as a means of improving data quality, and to avoid unnecessary distrust between individuals and organizations.

Front-end audit and cross-system enforcement give rise to additional concerns. Their moral justification is not obvious, and they create the danger of individuals being effectively blacklisted across a variety of organizations. Credit-bureau operations are extending in some countries into insurance, employment, and tenancy. Acute unfairness can arise, for example, when organizations blacklist a person over a matter that is still in dispute. It is particularly problematic where the person is unaware that the (possibly erroneous, incomplete, or out-of-date) data have been disseminated. Finally, even where individuals have brought the problems upon themselves, blacklisting tends to deny them the ability to redeem themselves for past misdemeanors.

Dangers of Mass Dataveillance to the Individual

Mass dataveillance embodies far greater threats. In respect of each individual, mass surveillance is clearly an arbitrary action, because no prior suspicion existed. The analogy may be drawn with the powers of police officers to interfere with the individual's quiet enjoyment. If a police officer has grounds for suspecting that a person has committed, or even is likely to commit, an offense, then the police officer generally has the power to intercept and perhaps detain that person. Otherwise, with rare and, in a democratic state, well justified exceptions, such as national security emergencies and, in many jurisdictions, random breath testing, even a police office does not have the power to arbitrarily interfere with a person.

With mass dataveillance, the fundamental problems of wrong identification, unclear, inconsistent, and context-dependent meaning of data, and low data quality are more intense than with personal dataveillance. Data arising from computer matching are especially problematic. Where there is no common identifier, the proportion of spurious matches (type (1) errors) and undetected matches (type (2) errors) can be very high. The causes include low quality of the data upon which computer matching depends (variants, misspellings, and other inaccuracies, and incompleteness), inappropriate matching criteria, widely different (or subtly but significantly different) meanings of apparently equivalent data items, or records with differing dates of applicability. Marx and Reichman report a New York State program in which half of the matches were spurious due to timing problems alone [35, p. 435]. In addition, the meaning of the record as a whole must be properly understood. Although it might seem improper for a person to be both in employment and in receipt of a social-welfare benefit, many pensions and allowances are, in law, either independent of, or only partially dependent on, income from other sources.

Data on the error rates of matching programs are difficult to find: They are mostly conducted away from the glare of public, or indeed any other kind of supervision. In an incident in Australia in 1986, the federal agency responsible for the Medicare scheme calmly, and without apparent legal authority, expropriated and merged data from several federal government agencies, relating to all inhabitants of the small island state of Tasmania. The agency reported the 70 percent hit rate across the databases as a good result, confirming its belief that a national identification scheme could be based on such a procedure. They ignored the implication that across the national population the records of nearly five million persons would remain unmatched, and failed to apply any tests to establish what proportion of the 70 percent were spurious matches and what proportion of the 30 percent nonmatches were failures of the algorithm used. Australians embrace a popular mythology that everyone in Tasmania is related to everyone else. For this reason alone, the agency might have been expected to recognize the need for such testing.

The complexities of each system (particularly a country's major data systems such as taxation and social welfare) are such that few specialists are able to comprehend any one of them fully. It is arguably beyond the bounds of human capability to appreciate the incompatibilities between data from different systems and to deal with the merged data with appropriate care. Computer matching, therefore, should never be undertaken without the greatest caution and skepticism.

Profiling makes a judgment "about a particular individual based on the past behavior of other individuals who appear statistically similar" [43, p. 88]. Statistical techniques such as multivariate correlation and discriminant analysis have limited domains of applicability that are often poorly understood or ignored. Even if the statistical procedures are properly applied, a profile needs to be justified by systemic reasoning. In the hands of the inadequately trained, insufficiently professional, or excessively enthusiastic or pressured, profiling has all the hallmarks of a modern witch-hunting tool.

Profiling is not restricted to retrospective investigation. It purports to offer the possibility of detecting undesirable classes of people before they commit an offense. O.T.A. documents a "predelinquency" profile developed for the U.S. Law Enforcement Assistance Administration [43, p. 90]. Even if the technique is perceived to be successful, its use seems to run counter to some fundamental tenets of contemporary society. It is unclear on what moral and, indeed, legal grounds profiling may be used to reach administrative determinations about individuals or discriminate between individuals. Such vague constraints may not be sufficient to stultify an attractive growth industry. With computer displays and printouts lending their (largely spurious) authority to such accusations, how will the tolerance needed in complex social environments be maintained?

Not only in government, but also in the private sector, dangers arise from both the effectiveness and ineffectiveness of profiling. The combination of consumer profiles with cheap desktop publishing is dramatically altering the cost-effectiveness of customized "mail shots." Applied to cable television, the technique will enable the operator to selectively transmit "commercials" to those subscribers who seem most likely to be susceptible to the client's product (or perhaps just the advertisement). Whereas Vance Packard could only prophesy the development of such technology [47], the components can now be identified, and the economics described.

Conventional justice is expensive and slow. Some procedures are now being structured, particularly in such areas as taxation, such that a government agency makes a determination, and individuals who disagree must contest the decision [61]. This inversion of the onus of proof exacerbates the problems of misinterpretation resulting from data merger, and uncertainty arising from correlative profiling. It is further compounded by the imbalance of power between organization and individual. Marx and Reichman provide an example in which individuals were confronted by a complex of difficulties: A remote examination authority statistically analyzed answer sheets, and threatened students who had sat in the same room and given similar (incorrect) answers with cancellation of their results unless they provided additional information to prove they did not cheat [35, p. 432].

Some dataveillance is undertaken with dubious legal authority or in the absence of either authority or prohibition. To avoid being subjected to public abuse and perhaps being denied the right to undertake the activity, it is natural for organizations to prefer to undertake some operations covertly. There are also cases where the benefits of surveillance may be lost if it is not undertaken surreptitiously (e.g., because of the likelihood of the person temporarily suspending, rather than stopping, undesirable activities; or of "skips" on consumer credit transactions).

To protect the mechanism or the source, an individual may not be told that dataveillance has been undertaken, the source of the accusation, the information on which the accusation is based or even what the accusation is. Such situations are repugnant to the concept of due process long embodied in British law and in legal systems derived from it. Dataveillance tends to compromise the individual's capacity to defend him or herself or to prosecute his or her innocence. In its most extreme form, one Kafka could not anticipate, the accuser could be a poorly understood computer program or a profile embodied in one.

Social Dangers of Mass Dataveillance

At the social level, additional problems arise. With personal dataveillance, investigation and monitoring normally take place after reasonable grounds for suspicion have arisen. Mass surveillance dispenses with that constraint because the investigation is routinely performed and the suspicion arises from it. The organization therefore commences with a presumption of guilt on the part of at least some of the data subjects, although at the beginning of the exercise it is unknown which ones. The result is a prevailing climate of suspicion.

The organizational functionary who communicates with the data subject often only partially understands the rationale underlying the decision, prefers not to admit that lack of understanding, and is often more concerned with case resolution than with public relations. Hence, there is an increased tendency for organizations and data subjects to develop adversarial relationships. Moreover, since organizations generally have the information, the size and the longevity, the bargaining positions are usually unequal.

Some of the "atypical, idiosyncratic, and extenuating cases" that are uncovered by mass dataveillance are precisely the deviants who are being sought. But others are just genuinely different, and such people tend to have difficulties convincing bureaucrats that their idiosyncrasies should be tolerated. Dataveillance encourages investigators to focus on minor offenses that can be dealt with efficiently, rather than more important crimes that are more difficult to solve. Law enforcers risk gaining a reputation for placing higher priority on pursuing amateur and occasional violators (particularly those whose records are readily accessible, like government employees and welfare recipients), rather than systematic, repetitive, and skilled professional criminals. The less equitably the law is perceived to be enforced, the greater the threat to the rule of law.

An administrative apparatus that has data available to it from a wide variety of sources tends to make decisions on the person's behalf. Hence, a further, more abstract, yet scarcely less real impact of dataveillance is reduction in the meaningfulness of individual actions, and hence in self-reliance and self-responsibility. Although this may be efficient and even fair, it involves a change in mankind's image of itself, and risks sullen acceptance by the masses and stultification of the independent spirit needed to meet the challenges of the future.

Some people already opt out of official society, preferring bureaucratic anonymity even at the costs of foregoing monetary and other benefits, and, consequently, attracting harassment by officialdom. There may already be a tendency toward two-tiered societies, in which the official documentary level of government facts and statistics bears only an approximate relationship to the real world of economic and social activity. If uncontrolled dataveillance were to cause the citizens of advanced Western nations to lose confidence in the fairness with which their societies are governed, it would be likely to exacerbate that trend.

An increase in the proportion of economic activity outside mainstream society would prompt, and be used to justify, a further increase in the use of mass surveillance. Assuming that world politics continues to be polarized into an East-West confrontation. It would be very easy to justify tighter social controls since any sign of serious weakening in the moral fiber and integrity of the West would be destabilizing. Since "mastery of both mass communications and mass surveillance is necessary for an elite to maintain control" [57, p. 176], IT will be a major weapon whereby ruling groups seek to exercise control over the population.

Finally, it is necessary to mention (but not overdramatize) the risk of dataveillance tools supporting repressive actions by a future invader, or by the "dirty-tricks department" of some democratically elected government gone, as Hitler's did, somewhat off the rails: "Orwell foresaw—and made unforgettable—a world in which ruthless political interests mobilized intrusive technologies for totalitarian ends. What he did not consider was the possibility that the development of the intrusive technologies would occur *on its own, without the spur of totalitarian intent.* This, in fact, is what is now happening" [57, p. 179].

In general, mass dataveillance tends to subvert individualism and the meaningfulness of human decisions and actions, and asserts the primacy of the state.

Safeguards

Intrinsic Controls over Dataveillance

Some natural controls exist that tend to limit the amount of dataveillance undertaken. The most apparent of these is its expense. There have been claims of dramatic success for matching schemes, but these have generally been made by the agencies that conducted them, and independent audits are hard to come by. The U.S. government's original (1979) guidelines on matching required that cost/benefit analyses be undertaken prior to the program being commenced [39]. However, there are many difficulties in undertaking a cost/benefit analysis of such a program. Many benefits are vague and unquantifiable, and many expenses are hidden or already "sunk." As a result, the requirement was rescinded in 1982 and has not been reimposed [40]. Moreover, there is seldom any other legal or even professional requirement that a cost/benefit analysis be performed [61, p. 540]. In 1986 O.T.A. concluded that few U.S. government programs are subjected to prior cost/benefit assessment [43, pp. 50–52].

Although reliable audits are difficult to find, anecdotal evidence throws doubts on the efficacy of matching. In the original Project Match, HEW ran its welfare files against its own payroll files. The 33,000 raw hits that were revealed required a year's investigation before they could be narrowed to 638 cases, but only 55 of these were ever prosecuted. Of a sample of 15 cases investigated by the National Council for Civil Liberties after HEW released the names of the people involved, 5 were dismissed, 4 pleaded guilty to misdemeanors (theft under $50), and only 6 were convicted of felonies. No prison sentences resulted, and the fines totaled under $2,000 [14, 49]. A 1983 match between Massachusetts welfare and bank files found 6,500 hits in five million records, resulting in 420 terminations of benefits, but also much confusion and recrimination [50]. Recent U.S. government reports have also raised doubts about the economic worth of many matching programs. A more positive report on several local government systems is to be found in [16].

There is very little evidence concerning the economics of other dataveillance techniques. Effective cost/benefit assessment, however, appears to be very rare (e.g., [43, pp. 80–81]). Unless credible cost/benefit analyses are undertaken, at least retrospectively, and preferably in advance, the potential economic safeguard against excessive use of dataveillance cannot be realized.

Economic controls, even if they were effective, may not be sufficient to protect individual freedoms. In the early years of personal-data systems, the dominant school of thought, associated with Westin, was that business and government economics would ensure that IT did not result in excessive privacy invasion [74–76]. This view has been seriously undermined by Rule's work, which has demonstrated that, rather than supporting individual freedoms, administrative efficiency conflicts with it. Organizations have perceived their interests to dictate the collection, maintenance, and dissemination of ever more data, ever more finely grained. This is in direct contradiction to the interests of individuals in protecting personal data [55–59]. Meanwhile, the onward march of IT continues to decrease the costs of dataveillance.

Another natural control is that surveillance activities can incur the active displeasure of the data subject or the general public. Given the imbalance of power between organizations and individuals, it is unrealistic to expect this factor to have any relevance outside occasional matters that attract media attention. Another, probably more significant control is that an organization's activities may incur the displeasure of some other organization, perhaps a watchdog agency, consumer group, or competitor.

In any case, these natural controls cannot be effective where the surveillance activities are undertaken in a covert manner. Intelligence agencies in particular are subject to few and generally ineffective controls. Also, many controls, such as the power to authorize telephone interception, may not be subject to superordinate control. Intrinsic controls over dataveillance are insufficient to ensure that the desirable balance is found.

Extrinsic Controls over Dataveillance

The establishment of extrinsic controls over dataveillance cannot even be embarked upon until comprehensive information privacy laws are in place. Proper protection of privacy-invasive data handling was stillborn in the United States in the early 1970s by the limited official response associated with Westin [74–76], the Privacy Act of 1974, and the PPSC report [48]. Westin found no problems with extensive surveillance systems as such, only with the procedures involved, and the PPSC's aim was to make surveillance as publicly acceptable as possible, consistent with its expansion and efficiency [59, pp. 75, 110].

The U.S. Privacy Act was very easily subverted. Publication of uses in the Federal Register has proved to be an exercise in bureaucracy rather than control. The "routine use" loophole in the act was used to legitimize virtually any use within each agency (by declaring the efficient operation of the agency to be a routine use) and then virtually any dissemination to any other federal agency (by declaring as a routine use the efficient operation of the federal government) (see [35, p. 449; 43, pp. 16–21; 48]).

Rule's thesis [55–59]—that privacy legislation arose out of a concern to ensure that the efficiency of business and government was not hindered—has been confirmed by developments in international organizations and on both sides of the Atlantic. The OECD's 1980 Guidelines for the Protection of Privacy were quite explicitly motivated by the economic need for freedom of transborder data flows [44]. In the United States, the President's Council for Integrity and Efficiency (PCIE) and Office of Management and

Budget (OMB) have worked not to limit matching, but to legitimize it [25]. In the United Kingdom, the Data Protection Act of 1984 was enacted explicitly to ensure that U.K. companies were not disadvantaged with respect to their European competitors.

There have been almost no personal-data systems, or even uses of systems, that have been banned outright. Shattuck [61, p. 540] reported that, during the first five years, the OMB's cavalier interpretation of the Privacy Act had resulted in not a single matching program being disapproved. Few sets of Information Privacy Principles appear to even contemplate such an extreme action as disallowing some applications of IT because of their excessively privacy-invasive nature. Exceptions include those of the New South Wales Privacy Committee [38], which are not legally enforceable, and, with qualifications, Sweden. This contrasts starkly with the conclusions of observers: "At some point . . . the repressive *potential* of even the most humane systems must make them unacceptable" [59, p. 120]; and "We need to recognize that the potential for harm from certain surveillance systems may be so great that the risks outweigh their benefits" [33, p. 48].

Some countries, such as Australia, have no information privacy legislation, and only incidental protections exist, such as breach of confidence, telephonic interception, trespass, and official secrecy [18]. In jurisdictions where information privacy safeguards do exist, they are piecemeal, restricted in scope, and difficult to enforce. In particular, many countries restrict the protections to government data or computer-based systems, or make no provision for such conventional safeguards as detailed codes of practice, oversight by an adequately resourced and legally competent authority, or the right to sue for damages.

Moreover, technological developments have rendered some information privacy protections ineffective. For example, the O.T.A. concluded that "the Privacy Act . . . offers little protection to individuals who are subjects of computer matching" [43, p. 38] (see also [17] and [63]).

Avenues of Change

Only once the principles of fair information practices have been engrained into our institutions and our ways of thought will it be possible to address the more complex, subtle, and pervasive threats inherent in contemporary IT.

In some countries the courts have absolved themselves of responsibility to change the law for policy reasons, unequivocally asserting not just Parliament's primacy in, but its exclusive responsibility for, law reform. In the United States, although the Bill of Rights does not mention a right to privacy, the courts have progressively established such a right based on elements of several of the amendments. The likely present view of the U.S. Supreme Court, however, might be indicated by this quotation: "I think it quite likely that self-discipline on the part of the executive branch will provide an answer to virtually all of the legitimate complaints against excesses of information-gathering" (Rehnquist, 1971, then a spokesperson for the Justice Department, now Chief Justice, quoted in [59, p. 147]). Moreover, courts throughout the world have difficulty with cases involving recent developments in technology [10, 72]. Accordingly, they prefer to await statutory guidance from parliaments, with their generally better-financed and less-fettered access to technological know-how.

However, parliaments also tend toward inaction on difficult technological matters, particularly when they are proclaimed to be the salvation of the domestic economy or are tangled up with moral issues, such as "dole cheating" and "welfare fraud." Consumer-protection laws in many countries still have yet to be adapted to cater for the now well-developed EFTS. Although the early literature on EFTS omits mention of its social impact, testimony was given before U.S. Senate subcommittees at least as early as 1975 on the repressive potentials of computerized payment systems [59, p. 115] (see also [24] and [55]). The call for protection was still necessary in 1984 in the United States [77] and in 1986 in Australia [3]. Parliaments in some countries such as Australia look less like sober lawmaking institutions than gladiatorial arenas. There are serious difficulties in convincing such legislatures to constrain the development of new "wonder technologies."

The conclusion is inescapable that the populations of at least some of the advanced Western nations are severely threatened by unbridled, IT-driven dataveillance.

Policy Proposals

New and Improved Safeguards

Since its brief period in the sun in the early 1970s, privacy has become unfashionable among lawmakers, and the momentum that the fair information practices/data protection/ information privacy moment once had, has been lost. The PPSC concluded that "the real danger is the gradual erosion of individual liberties through the automation, integration and interconnection of many small, separate record-keeping systems, each of which alone may seem innocuous, even benevolent, and wholly justifiable" [48, p. 533]. Its recommendations were ignored and are now in serious need of resuscitation, not just in the United States, but also in other countries whose information privacy protection regime has not kept pace with developments in IT.

In some countries an effective foundation for dealing with information privacy problems was established during the 1970s. In others, such as the United States, the first attempt failed to establish an adequate basis. Still others have not taken the first step. That necessary foundation can be roughly equated with the OECD's 1980 guidelines [44].

Additional steps must now be taken. It is clear today that the dictates of administrative efficiency are at odds with individual freedoms, and the power of dataveillance techniques is far greater than a decade and more ago. It is now essential that governments consider each dataveillance technique and decide whether it should be permitted under any circumstances at all; if so, what those circumstances are and how each proposal should be assessed in order to judge its compliance with those criteria; what code of practice should apply to its use; and what control mechanisms will ensure that each of these safeguards operates effectively and efficiently.

Further, it must be recognized that IT continues to develop, and mechanisms are needed to ensure that legislators in particular, and the public in general, are kept up-to-date with the salient features of new applications.

- Society demands many different services, and many different organizations exist to provide them. Each of these organizations designs its information systems to support the functions it performs.

- For each system the data definition, the level of integrity of identification, and the degree of data quality are chosen to ensure cost-effectiveness. The definition, identification mechanism, and data quality features of each system are therefore qualitatively different from those of every other system.

- Hence, a single information system cannot economically serve the interests of all organizations. Clusters of organizations may be supported by a single information system, but only at the risk of compromising the effectiveness of each of them. Economies of scale will only be achieved when the functions and priorities of the organizations are closely aligned.

Figure 4. The Law of Requisite Variety in Information Systems.

The Responsibilities of IT Professionals

It would be inappropriate for the purveyors of any technology to be responsible for decisions regarding its application. The technologist has an unavoidable interest in the outcome, and cannot appreciate and take into consideration the interests of the many different social groups who may consider themselves to be affected.

However, this necessary neutrality must not be interpreted as an excuse for inaction. IT professionals and academics alike have a moral responsibility to appreciate the power of the technology in which they play a part. Academe should commit some amount of research effort to the testing of the contentions in this paper as well as originate and evaluate proposals for technical safeguards. Both groups must publicize the nature and implications of their work, both for classes of affected individuals and for society as a whole. This applies as much to the negative consequences as it does to the potential benefits.

Finally, where there are acknowledged shortfalls in the regulatory environment in which IT is being applied, the IT practitioner has a responsibility to lobby for effective and efficient safeguards. This article has argued that existing safeguards are entirely inadequate. This implies a responsibility to approach lawmakers about the urgent need for developments in information privacy law. Although the actions of individual practitioners can be significant, coordinated policy efforts by professional bodies, such as the British and Australian Computer Societies, and by common-interest groups, such as ACM and the IEEE Computer Society, are likely to have greater effect.

IT as an Antidote to Information Concentration

If society is to control its fate, it must recognize a new Law of Requisite Variety in Information Systems (see Figure 4). Dispersion of authority and power, and, hence, of information, has long been regarded as vital to the survival of individualism and democracy. This law goes further, by recognizing that dispersion of data is also economic. Contrary to conventional wisdom, it is *not* administratively wasteful to treat the organs of executive government as distinct agencies, but rather administratively sensible.

Society may be better served by an alternative to centralization and its concomitant notions of rigidity and risklessness. If looseness, diversity, tolerance, initiative, enterprise, experimentation, and risk management were adopted as the bases for social and economic organization, then society could develop the adaptiveness needed to cope with technology-induced change. In the words of one philosopher, "The problem is . . . to combine that degree of security which is essential to the species, with forms of adventure and danger and contest which are compatible with the civilised way of life" [60, p. 21].

Some elements will be critical to a human-oriented IT. For example, the alternative approach to identification proposed by Chaum [8] proposes that the capabilities of "smart cards" be used not only for the benefit of organizations, but also of individuals. Each organization would know each individual by a different "digital pseudonym," which would be the joint property of both parties. Each individual could deny organizations the ability to link their data about him or her without consent. Both parties would have their interests protected. By such approaches, contemporary, decentralizing IT can support the evolution of human-oriented society, rather than hasten the demise of the age of individualism.

Conclusion

Dataveillance applications of IT have serious implications for individualism and society. The limited improvements in information practices that were achieved during the last decade have been outpaced by technological developments. Yet until and unless comprehensive information privacy protection is in place, effective controls over the new and emerging techniques of dataveillance will not be possible.

This article does *not* argue that personal and mass dataveillance are intrinsically evil and should be proscribed. However, their serious implications must be traded off against their benefits in each and every instance. Moreover, those benefits must not be assumed, but carefully assessed. We must appreciate the implications of the new technological capabilities, and create safeguards such that some applications are proscribed and the remainder controlled. We need to harness the new, decentralizing potential of IT as a means of achieving a looser, more tolerant, diverse, robust, and adaptive society.

Acknowledgments

This article arises from collaborative research undertaken with Graham Greenleaf, of the Faculty of Law at the University of New South Wales. Assistance is also gratefully acknowledged from research assistants Louise Macauley and Chris Keogh, and Jim Nolan, executive member of the New South Wales Privacy Committee. The constructive criticism of referees and the area editor was also very helpful.

Financial assistance for this research has been granted from the Faculties' Research Fund of the Australian National University, Canberra.

References

1. Ackroyd, C., Margolis, K., Rosenhead, J., and Shallice, T. (1977). *The Technology of Political Control*. Penguin Books, New York.

2. Askin, F. (1972). Surveillance: The social science perspective. *Columbia Hum. Rights Law Rev.* 4, 1 (Winter), (see also the remainder of the issue).

3. Australian Science and Technology Council, (1986). *Towards a Cashless Society*, ASTEC, Canberra Australia, (May).

4. Bramford, J. (1983). *The Puzzle Palace*. Penguin Books, New York.

5. Brenton, M. (1964). *The Privacy Invaders*. Coward-McCann.

6. Burnham, D. (1983). *The Rise of the Computer State*. Random House/Weidenfeld and Nicolson.

7. Campbell, D., and Connor, S. (1986). *On the Record*. Michael Joseph.

8. Chaum, D. (1985). Security without identification: Transaction systems to make Big Brother obsolete. *Commun. ACM 28*, 10 (October), 1030–1044.

9. Clarke, R. A. (1987). Just another piece of plastic for your wallet: The Australia card scheme. *Prometheus 5*, 1 (June), 29–45.

10. Clarke, R. A. (1988). Judicial understanding of information technology. *Comput. J. 31*, 1 (February).

11. Cowen, Z. (1969). *The Private Man*. Australian Broadcasting Commission.

12. Crispin, A. (1981). *Who's Watching You*. Penguin Books, New York.

13. Donner, F. J. (1980). *The Age of Surveillance*. Knopf, New York.

14. Early, P. (1986). Big Brother makes a date. *San Francisco Exam.* (October 12).

15. Ellul, J. (1964). *The Technological Society*. Knopf, New York.

16. Greenberg, D. H., and Wolf, D. A. (1985). Is wage matching worth all the trouble? *Public Welfare* (Winger), 13–20.

17. Greenleaf, G. W., and Clarke, R. A. (1984). Database retrieval technology and subject access principles. *Aust. Comput. J. 16*, 1 (February), 27–32.

18. Greenleaf, G. W., and Clarke, R. A. (1986). Aspects of the Australian Law Reform Commission's information privacy proposals. *J. Law and Inf. Sci. 2*, 1 (August), 83–110.

19. Gross, M. L. (1963). *The Brain Watchers. Signet*.

20. Hoffman, L. J., Ed. (1980). *Computers and Privacy in the Next Decade*. Academic Press, New York.

21. Huxley, A. (1975). *Brave New World*. Penguin Books, New York (originally published in 1932).

22. Kircher, J. (1981). A history of computer matching in federal government programs. *Computerworld* (December 14).

23. Kling, R. (1978). Automated welfare client-tracking and service integration: The political economy of computing. *Commun. ACM 21*, 6 (June), 484–493.

24. Kling, R. (1978). Value conflicts and social choice in electronic funds transfer system developments. *Commun. ACM 21*, 8 (August), 642–657.

25. Kusserow, R. P. (1984). The government needs computer matching to root out waste and fraud. *Commun. ACM 27*, 6 (June), 542–545.

26. Langan, K. J. (1979). Computer matching programs: A threat to privacy? *Columbia J. Law Soc. Probl. 15*, 2.

27. Laudon, K. C. (1974). *Computers and Bureaucratic Reform*. Wiley, New York.

28. Laudon, K. C. (1979). Complexity in large federal databanks. *Soc./Trans.* (May).

29. Laudon, K. C. (1979). Problems of accountability in federal databanks. In *Proceedings of the American Association for the Advancement of Science* (May). American Association for the Advancement of Science.

30. Laudon, K. C. (1986). Data quality and due process in large interorganizational record systems. *Commun. ACM 29*, 1 (January), 4–11.

31. Laudon, K. C. (1986). *Dossier Society, Value Choices in the Design of National Information Systems*. Columbia University Press, New York.

32. Long, E. V. (1967). *The Intruders*. Praeger, New York.

33. Marx, G. T. (1985). The new surveillance. *Technol. Rev.* (May–June).
34. Marx, G. T. (1985). I'll be watching you: Reflections on the new surveillance. *Dissent* (Winter).
35. Marx, G. T., and Reichman, N. (1984). Routinising the discovery of secrets. *Am. Behav. Sci.* 27, 4 (March–April), 423–452.
36. Miller, A. R. (1972). *The Assault on Privacy.* Mentor.
37. Neier, A. (1974). *Dossier.* Stein and Day.
38. New South Wales Privacy Committee (1977). *Guidelines for the Operation of Personal Data Systems.* NSWPC, Sydney, Australia.
39. Office of Management and Budget (1979). *Guidelines to Agencies on Conducting Automated Matching Programs.* OMB, (March).
40. Office of Management and Budget (1982). *Computer Matching Guidelines.* OMB, (May).
41. Office of Management and Budget President's Commission for Integrity and Efficiency (1983). *Model Control System for Conducting Computer Matching Projects Involving Individual Privacy Data.* OMB/PCIE.
42. Office of Technology Assessment (1985). Federal government informatior technology: Electronic surveillance and civil liberties. OTA-CIT-293. U.S. Congress, Washington, D.C., (October).
43. Office of Technology Assessment (1986). Federal government information technology: Electronic record systems and individual privacy. OTA-CIT-296, U.S. Congress, Washington, D.C., (June).
44. Organisation for Economic Cooperation and Development (1980). *Guidelines for the Protection of Privacy and Transborder Flows of Personal Data.* OECD, Paris, France.
45. Orwell, G. (1984). Penguin Books, New York, 1972 (originally published in 1948).
46. *Oxford Dictionary* (1983). Vol. X, p. 248.
47. Packard, V. (1964). *The Naked Society.* McKay, New York.
48. Privacy Protection Study Commission (1977). *Personal Privacy in an Information Society.* U.S. Government Printing Office, Washington, D.C., (July).
49. Raines, J. C. (1974). *Attack on Privacy.* Judson Press.
50. Reichman, N., and Marx, G. T. (1985). Generating organisational disputes: The impact of computerization. In *Proceedings of the Law and Society Association Conference* (San Diego, Calif., June 5–9). Law and Society Association.
51. Rodota, S. (1976). Privacy and data surveillance: Growing public concern. Inf. Stud. 10, OECD, Paris, France.
52. Rosenberg, J. M. (1969). *The Death of Privacy.* Random House.
53. Rosenberg, R. S. (1986). *Computers and the Information Society.* Wiley, New York.
54. Roszak, T. (1986). *The Cult of Information.* Pantheon.
55. Rule, J. B. (1974). *Private Lives and Public Surveillance: Social Control in the Computer Age.* Schocken Books.
56. Rule, J. B. (1975). *Value Choices in E.F.T.S.* Office of Telecommunications Policy. Washington, D.C.
57. Rule, J. B. (1984). The ingredients of totalitarianism. In *1984 Revisited—Totalitarianism in Our Century.* Harper and Row, New York, 1983, pp. 166–179.
58. Rule, J. B. (1983). Documentary identification and mass surveillance in the United States. *Soc. Probl. 31,* 222.
59. Rule, J. B., McAdam, D., Stearns, L., and Uglow, D. (1980). *The Politics of Privacy.* New American Library.
60. Russell, B. (1949). *Authority and the Individual.* George Allen and Unwin.
61. Shattuck, J. (1984). Computer matching is a serious threat to individual rights. *Commun. ACM 27,* 6 (June), 538–541.

62. Stone, M. G. (1968). *Computer Privacy*. Anbar.

63. Thom, J., and Thorne, P. (1983). Privacy legislation and the right of access. *Aust. Comput. J.* 15, 4 (November), 145–150.

64. Thompson, A. A. (1970). *A Big Brother in Britain Today*. Michael Joseph.

65. U.S. Dept. of Health and Human Services (1983). *Computer Matching in State Administered Benefit Programs: A Manager's Guide to Decision-Making*. HEW, Washington, D.C.

66. U.S. Dept. of Health and Human Services (1984). *Computer Matching in State Administered Benefit Programs*. HEW, Washington, D.C., (June).

67. U.S. Dept. of Health, Education and Welfare (1973). Secretary's Advisory Committee on Automated Personal Data Systems. *Records, Computers and the Rights of Citizens*. MIT Press, Cambridge, Mass.

68. U.S. Federal Advisory Committee on False Identification (1976). *The Criminal Use of False Identification*. FACFI, Washington, D.C.

69. U.S. Senate (1982). *Oversight of Computer Matching to Detect Fraud and Mismanagement in Government Programs*. U.S. Senate, Washington, D.C.

70. Warner, M., and Stone, M. (1976). *The Data Bank Society: Organisations, Computers and Social Freedom*. George Allen and Unwin.

71. *Webster's 3rd Edition* (1976). p. 2302.

72. Weeramantry, C. G. (1983). *The Slumbering Sentinels: Law and Human Rights in the Wake of Technology*. Penguin Books, New York.

73. Wessell, M. R. (1974). *Freedom's Edge: The Computer Threat to Society*. Addison-Wesley, Reading, Mass.

74. Westin, A. F. (1967). *Privacy and Freedom*. Atheneum, New York.

75. Westin, A. F., Ed. (1971). *Information Technology in a Democracy*. Harvard University Press, Cambridge, Mass.

76. Westin, A. F., and Baker, M. (1974). *Databanks in a Free Society*. Quadrangle, New York.

77. Yestingsmeier, J. (1984). Electronic funds transfer systems: The continuing need for privacy legislation. *Comput. Soc. 13*, 4 (Winter), 5–9.

78. Zamyatin, Y. (1983). *We*. Penguin Books, New York (originally published in Russian, 1920).

P·A·R·T· VI

Security
and
Reliability

P·A·R·T·VI

Introduction

Security and Reliability

Charles Dunlop • Rob Kling

Computer System Security

In the 1960s and 1970s, the public viewed computer systems as occasionally unreliable, but usually secure. Recent events publicized in the mass media, as well as Hollywood films, have radically changed that image. The 1983 film *Wargames* depicted a teenage computer-hobbyist whose intrusion into a U.S. military computer system brought the world to the brink of nuclear war. Although the film's premise—that an unauthorized user could gain access to NORAD's strategic computer systems—is extremely dubious, many other military-related computer systems do have very serious security problems (see Daniel Ford, 1985). In February, 1989, eighteen-year-old Chicagoan Herbert Zinn, Jr., was sentenced to nine months' imprisonment plus a $10,000 fine for breaking into U.S. military computers and AT&T computers, and stealing 55 programs.[1]

Clifford Stoll, an astronomer at the University of California's Lawrence Berkeley Laboratory, started investigating a "hacker" who gained unauthorized access to an account, and who was able to use the Berkeley system as a springboard to other (primarily military) computer systems. Over a period of months Stoll followed the hacker, who entered over 430 computers connected by several networks in the United States and Western Europe. Our selection by Stoll provides a facscinating account of the arduous work that may be required to locate an intruder's entry point and eventually identify the intruder—who in this case turned out to be located in West Germany.[2] As a result of Stoll's detective work, three West German programmers were eventually arrested and

---

charged with espionage for the Soviet KGB; reportedly, they gained access to computerized information in NASA headquarters, Los Alamos and Fermilab, along with various U.S. Army computers and military-related computers in Europe.[3]

These examples are particularly serious because they compromise national security, and involve computer systems designed to be open only to a relatively small group of authorized users. Moreover, intrusions may be difficult to detect (and even more difficult to trace) because of a multitude of interconnections among electronic networks.

Of course, not all breaches of computer security involve tightly restricted military systems, and not all are marked by malicious intent. In a widely reported episode during November 1988, Cornell University graduate student Robert T. Morris, Jr. planted a "worm"[4] that soon spread worldwide across several thousand computers linked to a large research computer network (Internet).[5] A small programming miscalculation caused the worm to replicate much faster than the programmer had intended, necessitating the temporary shutdown of many Internet computers while a "fix" was devised. Aside from this considerable inconvenience, which cost thousands of hours of technical time to detect and correct, no other damage was done.

But the Internet worm stimulated considerable controversy (see Eisenberg et al., 1989). Although a few people argued that Morris's experiment helped call attention to an important computer security weakness, Morris's critics argued that specialists knew that Internet was not totally secure. In fact, its gaps were a bit like unlocked house doors in a village. In the critics' view, someone who wandered through unlocked houses and left some annoying signs of intrusion—like tracking mud across carpets, opening dresser drawers, and leaving notes on beds—was not giving people real news about their vulnerability. In any case, the surrounding media publicity served to heighten public awareness of computer security issues.[6]

Balancing Security and Usability

Security, however, is not the only priority in computer systems: accessibility and ease of use are often competing requirements. As the Cornell Commission pointed out in its comments on the Morris episode, "A community of scholars should not have to build

---

[1] *RISKS-FORUM Digest*, Vol 8, No. 29 (February 22, 1989). The Government information in this case was described as unclassified, but "highly sensitive."

[2] Stoll's (1989) book-length account of the saga explains how he tried to enlist the help of the FBI and CIA with only minor success.

[3] *RISKS-FORUM Digest*, Vol. 8, No. 35 (March 6, 1989).

[4] A worm is a piece of stand-alone code capable of replicating itself and propagating through a series of interconnected computer systems. It may or may not be intentionally destructive, but in either case it can consume significant system resources to the point where a computer system is rendered essentially inoperative.

[5] The June, 1989, issue of *Communications of the ACM* contains a special section devoted to the character of Morris's worm, its pattern of destruction, and the strategies that system operators used to detect and correct it. See the articles by Spafford (1989), Rochlis Eichen (1989), Donn Seeley (1989).

[6] See, for example, the Sunday *New York Times*, November 13, 1988, front page article, plus a related story in Section E, p. 7. Denning (1989) provides a useful description and assessment of the Internet worm's significance. Morris was convicted of federal computer tampering charges, placed on three years' probation, fined $10,000, and sentenced to 400 hours of community service.

walls as high as the sky to protect a reasonable expectation of privacy, particularly when such walls will equally impede the free flow of information" (Eisenberg *et al.*, 1989, p. 707).

A system such as Internet, which provides electronic mail links and data exchange among thousands of researchers around the globe, can be made virtually worthless if security procedures make its operation so cumbersome that people become reluctant or unable to use it.[7] The same tradeoff confronts millions of microcomputer users, who want easy access to electronic bulletin boards from which they may download software for personal use. Increasingly, they must deal with the possibility that a downloaded program may contain a virus that is designed maliciously to lock up their system or erase all the files on their hard disk.[8]

The most emphasized aspect of system security has been the protection of information by prohibiting unauthorized access. Given a sufficient commitment and sufficient precautions (passwords, data encryption, call-back systems, restrictions on levels of access, or even physical identification of users and elimination of dial-in access), a reasonably high level of security can be achieved. It should be emphasized, though, that like many computer-related issues, "security" has both social and technical dimensions. This further complicates matters, since, as Peter J. Denning's contribution observes, no consensus has emerged concerning the accountability of people for their actions on computer systems.

Computer System Reliability

Security is just one step in building dependable computer systems, since the trustworthiness and reliability of systems themselves—both hardware and legitimate software—

---

[7] One way that computer networks are intruded upon is for a person (or program) to guess passwords that are similar to an account name or to the account holder's name. Users can reduce the risk of intrusion by choosing very obscure passwords. In addition, system administrators could enforce rules that require users to change their password frequently or to answer a set of personal questions before actually gaining access to a system. But security measures requiring people to remember complex passwords and pass "security tests" involve substantial effort. The problem is that as access procedures become increasingly complex, some people will be less inclined to use computer systems frequently, and those who do use them will find their work onerous and less productive. In either case, the systems become less valuable as a communication medium.

[8] A computer virus is a piece of program code that exists within an otherwise normal program. When this program is run, the viral code seeks out other programs within the computer and modifies them. The other programs can be anywhere in a computer system and can even be the operating system itself. This alteration of program code can grow geometrically depending on the number and different types of programs that are run (1 program modifies 2, which modify 4, which modify 8, etc.). At a given point in time or based on some other external trigger (such as the number of times the program was run or the amount of remaining free disk space), the viral code goes to work. Some viruses are designed as nuisances and simply leave cute messages on a computer screen. But many viruses are designed to lock up systems and erase files. They are very costly to those who lose important work when their systems are attacked. See Cohen (1987) and Duff (1988) for sample virus code, and McIlroy (1988) for descriptions of experiences with viruses on UNIX systems.

Several vendors have released software packages designed to prevent this kind of harm, but at least one (public domain) version itself turned out to be a culprit program. By late 1989, there were almost 50 known kinds of viruses that had "infected" IBM PCs, and many more kinds that had been designed to infect Apple Macintoshes and other kinds of computers. Fortunately, the number of computer systems attacked by any specific virus has usually been relatively small—from a handful to a few hundred.

must also be addressed.[9] As might be expected, some very difficult problems surface at this point. In thinking about system reliability, consider the wide range of computer-based systems whose reliable functioning is indispensable for human health, safety, and general well-being. These include transportation (air, rail, automobile, ship), national defense, communication, payrolls, medicine, law enforcement, nuclear power, elections, elevators, chemical plants, space exploration, mining, the food industry, and record-keeping associated with many social and governmental services.

Serious computer hardware failures are certainly not unknown: a component malfunction was the underlying cause of the 1980 ARPANET collapse (see Rosen, 1981). Our third selection, by Alan Borning, documents a famous 46-cent chip failure in a military computer that falsely signaled a Soviet missile attack. Even so, hardware failure does not constitute the most serious problem in building reliable computer systems. Quality control, component redundancy,[10] and parity error-checking (absent in the case discussed by Borning) can all contribute to the improved hardware reliability.

Far more common and vexing, however, are problems with *software*—a fact that will come as no surprise even to casual computer users. Millions of Americans encountered a frustrating example on January 15, 1990, when AT & T's long-distance telephone service seriously degraded for about nine hours. The problem was ultimately traced to a flaw in a software update that had been introduced just one month earlier. The new software, of course, had been extensively tested, and it is interesting to note also that the volume of long-distance telephone calls passing through AT & T on January 15 was not abnormal. But an unanticipated sequence of events caused the system to fail, providing a graphic demonstration of how advanced testing cannot guarantee successful operation in actual use.[11]

Our fourth selection, by David Parnas, catalogues a number of reasons for software unreliability.[12] Although Parnas focuses on the Strategic Defense Initiative, his comments clearly apply beyond that particular project. Parnas, who once served on a panel convened by the SDI Organization, eventually resigned, concluding that "no knowledgeable person would have much faith in the system." A key point made in this selection is that the SDI system software could never be tested under conditions of realistic nuclear attacks despite the fact that field-testing is an indispensable feature of successful software

---

[9] The term *trustworthiness* and *reliability* often carry a specialized meaning: "Whereas reliability is a measure of the probability of a problem occurring while the system is in service, trustworthiness is a measure of the probability of a serious flaw remaining after testing and review." Parnas *et al.* (1990), p. 639.

[10] Obviously, however, if the component in question involves a *design* flaw—e.g., incorrect micro-code embedded in hardware—redundancy will only replicate the failure. See Severo Ornstein's discussion in Bellin and Chapman (1987), esp. pp. 17–19.

[11] See *RISKS-FORUM Digest*, Vol. 9, No. 63, for a technical description and related discussion. Also compare Note 14 below.

[12] A variety of comments on Parnas's paper may be found in *Communications of the ACM*, Vol. 29, No. 4 (April, 1986), pp. 262–265. Harold Brown (1986, esp. Sections V, VII, and VIII) defends SDI research, viewing it as a confederation of technologies with differing timetables for successful development. Brown does acknowledge various problems that SDI software developers must face; however, he suggests that those problems can be addressed by artificial intelligence, automated programming, and program verification technology.

development. Other computer-based defense systems, though less exotic than SDI, are vulnerable to the very same critique, and the documented false alerts that they have already produced do not inspire great confidence. In a "worst case" scenario, they raise the specter of accidental nuclear war.[13]

Although many defense-related computer systems are unique insofar as their very nature precludes realistic testing, other points made by Parnas apply to *all* large-scale software projects, raising reliability questions about them as well. For example, *exhaustive* testing may be ruled out by an impossibly large number of possible program states; unforeseen timing problems may occur with multiple processors running in parallel (Borning's description of the first space shuttle, where the problem itself arose as the result of a previous "cure"); or a program may satisfy the conditions of a specification that is itself incorrect (a theme elaborated in Brian Smith's essay). And in cases involving human operators, unanticipated interactions may occur between the software and the operator (Jonathan Jacky's contribution provides a chilling description of this kind of error in a medical setting), or in unplanned sequences of "normal" events.[14]

Strategies for Achieving Reliability

Despite the many difficulties catalogued so far, it is apparent from existing systems (space exploration, airline transportation, etc.) that high-quality software is not always an impossible dream. Software engineering methods incorporate various error-reducing strategies, including systematic testing strategies.[15] Some writers have called for the licensing of professional programmers (see Jacky's discussion). The topic of software design has also received recent emphasis (see Winograd and Flores, 1987). And formal verification techniques, still in their infancy, may help to uncover discrepancies between a program's specification and the actual program. Even so, vendors' claims should be met with a cautious eye when they contain reassuring terms like "software engineering" and "program verification," particularly in contexts where mistakes may be irreversible and catastrophic.

---

[13] Although Alan Borning believes that isolated false alerts have not brought the United States close to starting World War III, he worries about the dangerous "possibility of a *combination* of such events as international crises, mutually reinforcing alerts, computer system misdesign, computer failure, or human error." (Compare Note 14 below.) Discussions of this subject, unfortunately, often lose sight of the full range of horrors that such a holocaust might engender. For a graphic description of the details, see Jonathan Schell's book *The Fate of the Earth* (in Further Reading). Despite the views of some technological utopians, it seems clear that the solutions to international problems are more social and political than technological.

[14] Ornstein notes (*op. cit.*, p. 26) that "the 'unforeseen events' that cause trouble are less often unforeseen external events than perverse combinations of perfectly normal events." An analogous theme is developed in Perrow (1984), which documents how multiple failures in a high-technology system can produce disasters by interacting in unexpected ways. As Perrow's study shows, this point may apply whether or not computers are essentially involved.

[15] For a provocative discussion of two different approaches to software engineering, see Christiane Floyd, "Outline of a Paradigm Change in Software Engineering," in Gro Bjerknes, Pelle Ehn, and Morten Kyng (eds.), *Computers and Democracy*, Brookfield, Vermont: Gower Publishing Company (1987), pp. 191–210. Floyd's contrast between a "product-oriented" view (programs as abstract objects) and a "process-oriented" view (programs as tools for humans) also bears directly on some of the program verification issues discussed below.

Discussions of program verification often tend to bog down because of unclarity over what "verification" actually involves. Jacky describes the VIPER microprocessor that was "proven" free of certain design errors, although advertising claims unfortunately went on to exaggerate the import of this accomplishment.[16] There is certainly room for informed debate on the meaning and significance of formal verification. Brian Smith's paper—our sixth selection—provides one lucid interpretation, explaining that a verification ("formal proof of correctness") only establishes *relative consistency* between a program specification and program code. Smith goes on to observe, however, that if the specification itself reflects a world model that is deficient in some relevant respect, the deficiency will carry over to the program, thus remaining undetected by any formal consistency proof. This point is crucial, for it implies that a computer system with perfectly functioning hardware, and software that adheres accurately to a set of written requirements, may still result in serious failures. The indispensability of robust testing should be apparent in the face of this argument.[17] Still, some software engineers argue that formal methods help improve programs by encouraging people to think hard about their designs and to develop simpler systems which are easier to verify.[18]

Given the infusion of computer technology into everyday affairs, it is only to be expected that malfunctions may result in inconvenience, serious harm, or even threats to life, in an ever-widening spectrum. This section concludes with a series of cases described on *RISKS-FORUM Digest*, an electronic newsletter moderated by Peter Neumann of SRI International, with support from the Association for Computing Machinery (ACM). These selections sample a wide range of contexts in which computer-related difficulties may arise. The first describes a "Trojan Horse" program, masquerading as an information disk on AIDS, but in fact designed to damage the system of anyone who installed the disk. This is followed by Clifford Johnson's posting, which expresses concern over the increased use of computer-based testing, especially in situations where the tests are both unreliable and inappropriate. Next, Fernando Corbato's discussion shows how problems can arise through "natural" extensions of software beyond its original conception. Computer-driven "voice-mail" provides yet another source of concern, as the amusing entry by R. Aminzade indicates. Finally, two short entries illustrate how a lack of foresight can result in questionable or dangerous consequences. These particular cases involved the very elderly, but analogous mistakes apply elsewhere. For example, the hole in the ozone layer over the Antarctic went undetected for a number of years because computers had been instructed to ignore data outside of specified range. The assumption was that such data *would just have to be* spurious. Of course, they were not.

One sign in health in the computing profession lies in the fact that many of the contributors to Neumann's newsletter are themselves working computer scientists. Their

---

[16] John Dobson and Brian Randell, "Program Verification: Public Image and Private Reality," *Communications of the ACM*, Vol. 32, No. 4 (April 1989), pp. 420–422. Discussion of the VIPER microprocessor is on p. 422.

[17] Much-discussed papers by DeMillo, Lipton, and Perlis (1979) and by Fetzer (1988) contain different arguments with complementary conclusions. A recent paper by Parnas *et al.* (1990) discusses the issue in the context of safety-critical computing. For an excellent and balanced discussion of formal verification in the context of software safety, see Leveson (1986).

[18] Nancy Leveson, personal communication, November 7, 1989.

concern over computer-related risks is obvious. Unfortuntely, however, only a tiny fraction of practicing computer specialists are knowledgeable about the kinds of issues and debates examined in *RISKS-FORUM Digest*. Techniques for ensuring that computer systems are safe and reliable—topics within "software engineering"—are not yet a routine part of computer science curricula at many colleges and universities.

Controversies over System Reliability

It is difficult to find professionals and managers who explicitly advocate the sale and use of unreliable systems that place human lives in jeopardy. Consequently, there is no open controversy between advocates of reliable systems and countervailing advocates of unreliable systems! The debates, rather, are of different kinds. One set of relatively technical arguments focuses on whether certain types of programming techniques will substantially improve the reliability of computer systems.[19] Here the issue hinges on the extent to which programs written with devices like distributed interrupts and recursion are likely to be harder for reviewers to validate. Much of this controversy is framed in terms of what can be done—or not done—in principle.

A second set of debates focuses on the extent to which reliable practices can be effectively listed and embodied in procedures for building safe systems. This controversy is of a different sort, since the issue is whether an organization can specify a simple list of rules for ensuring that software contractors produce reliable systems. The virtue of simple rules is that they allow relatively routine checking by relatively unskilled people; but they can hamper good technological solutions as well.

A third set of debates focuses on the extent to which industrial firms can and will follow the best possible practices for building reliable systems. Some computer professionals note that commercial firms face severe shortages of skilled programmers who are well trained to use modern system development techniques skillfully. Usually, these techniques require that people have good technical training in computer science. However, many organizations try to cut costs by hiring people with limited computer science backgrounds. Professional engineers are licensed by states, but there is really no equivalent and effective form of licensing for programmers.

Sources

Borning, Alan (1987). "Computer System Reliability and Nuclear War," *Communications of the ACM*, 30(2) (February), pp. 112–131.

---

[19]Some of the technical proposals to help insure that programs are more reliable (and that their reliability can be assessed) include avoiding the use of certain programming constructs and design features and using mathematical methods to "prove" that programs are correct. For a running debate about the workability of guidelines like these, see *RISKS-FORUM Digest*, Vol. 9, No. 1 (July 1, 1989); *RISKS-FORUM Digest*, Vol. 9, No. 2 (July 10, 1989); *RISKS-FORUM Digest*, Vol. 9, No. 3 (July 11, 1989); *RISKS-FORUM Digest*, Vol. 9, No. 5 (July 15, 1989); *RISKS-FORUM Digest*, Vol. 9, No. 6 (July 17, 1989); and *RISKS-FORUM Digest*, Vol. 9, No. 8 (July 28, 1989).

Denning, Peter J. (1987). "Computer Viruses," *American Scientist*, 76 (May–June), pp. 236–238.

Jacky, Jonathan (1991). "Safety-Critical Computing: Hazards, Practices, Standards and Regulation" (original manuscript).

Parnas, David Lorge (1985). "Software Aspects of Strategic Defense Systems." Originally published in *American Scientist*, 73(5), pp. 432–440. Reprinted in *CACM*, 28(12) (December), pp. 1326–1335.

RISKS-FORUM Digest. Contributions from John McAffee, Clifford Johnson, Fernando J. Corbato, R. Aminzade, David Sherman, and David B. Benson.

Smith, Brian Cantwell (1985). "The Limits of Correctness." Report No. CSLI-85-35, Center for the Study of Language and Information (Stanford University).

Stoll, Clifford (1988). "Stalking the Wily Hacker," *Communications of the ACM*, 31(5) (May), pp. 484–497.

References

Brown, Harold (1986). "Is SDI Technically Feasible," *Foreign Affairs*, 64(3), pp. 435–454.

Cohen, Fred (1987). "Computer Viruses: Theory and Experiments," *Computers and Security*, Vol. 6, pp. 22–35.

DeMillo, Richard, A., Richard J. Lipton, and Alan J. Perlis (1979). "Social Processes and Proofs of Theorems and Programs," *Communications of the ACM*, 22(5) (May), pp. 271–280. See also various replies published in the same journal, Vol. 22, No. 11 (November 1979), pp. 621–630.

Denning, Peter J. (1989). "The Science of Computing," *American Scientist*, 77(2) (March–April), pp. 126–128.

Duff, Tom (1989). "Experiences with Viruses on UNIX Systems," *Computing Systems*, 2(2) (Spring), pp. 155–172.

Eisenberg, Ted, David Gries, Juris Hartmanis, Don Holcomb, M. Stuart Lynn, and Thomas Santoro (1989). "The Cornell Commission: On Morris and the Worm," *Communications of the ACM*, 32(6), pp. 706–709.

Fetzer, James H. (1988). "Program Verification: The Very Idea," *Communications of the ACM*, 31(9) (September), pp. 1048–1063. See also replies in the same journal, Vol. 32, No. 3 (March 1989), pp. 287–290; 374–381, and Vol. 32, No. 4 (April 1989), pp. 420–422; 506–512.

Ford, Daniel (1985). *The Button*. Simon and Schuster, New York.

Forester, Tom and Perry Morrison (1990). "Computer Unreliability and Social Vulnerability," *Futures*. pp. 462–474.

Leveson, Nancy G. (1986). "Software Safety: Why, What, and How," *Computing Surveys*, 18(2) (June), pp. 125–163.

McIlroy, M. Douglas (1989). "Virology 101," *Computing Systems*, 2(2) (Spring), pp. 173–182.

Ornstein, Severo (1987). Chapter in David Bellin and Gary Chapman (eds.), *Computers in Battle: Will They Work?* Harcourt Brace Jovanovich Inc. Boston, Mass., pp. 1–43.

Parnas, David L., A. John van Schouwen, and Shu Po Kwan (1990). "Evaluation of Safety-Critical Software," *Communications of the ACM*, 33(6), pp. 636–648.

Perrow, Charles (1984). *Normal Accidents*. Basic Books, New York.

Rochlis, Jon, and Mark W. Eichen (1989). "With Microscope and Tweezers: The Worm from MIT's Perspective," *Communications of the ACM*, 32(6), pp. 689–699.

Rosen, Eric C. (1981). "Vulnerabilities of Network Control Protocols: An Example," ACM SIGSOFT *Software Engineering Notes*, 5(1) (January), pp. 6–8.

Seeley, Donn (1989). "Password Cracking: A Game of Wits," *Communications of the ACM*, 32(6), pp. 700–705.

Spafford, Eugene (1989). "The Internet Worm: Crisis and Aftermath," *Communications of the ACM*, 32(6), pp. 678–688.

Stoll, Clifford (1989). *The Cuckoo's Egg: Tracking a Spy Through the Maze of Computer Espionage.* Doubleday, New York.

Winograd, Terry, and Fernando Flores (1987). *Understanding Computers and Cognition.* Addison-Wesley Publishing Company, Inc., Reading, Mass., esp. Part III.

Further Reading

ACM SIGSOFT *Software Engineering Notes.* A monthly ACM periodical that regularly documents computer failures along with other articles, such as the design of programming environments.

Bellin, David, and Gary Chapman (eds.) (1987). *Computers in Battle: Will They Work?* Harcourt Brace Jovanovich, Boston, Mass.

The CPSR Newsletter. Published by Computer Scientists for Social Responsibility, P.O. Box 717, Palo Alto, California 94301.

Moulton, Rolf T. (1986). *Computer Security Handbook: Strategies and Techniques for Preventing Data Loss or Theft.* Prentice-Hall, Englewood Cliffs, N.J.

RISKS-FORUM Digest. Distributed electronically by Peter Neumann at SRI International, and available through the computer systems of many universities.

Schell, Jonathan (1982). *The Fate of the Earth.* Alfred A. Knopf, New York.

P · A · R · T · VI

1

Stalking the Wily Hacker

Clifford Stoll

In August 1986 a persistent computer intruder attacked the Lawrence Berkeley Laboratory (LBL). Instead of trying to keep the intruder out, we took the novel approach of
allowing him access while we printed out his activities and traced him to his source. This
trace back was harder than we expected, requiring nearly a year of work and the
cooperation of many organizations. This article tells the story of the break-ins and the
trace, and sums up what we learned.

We approached the problem as a short, scientific exercise in discovery, intending to
determine who was breaking into our system and document the exploited weaknesses.
It became apparent, however, that rather than innocuously playing around, the intruder
was using our computer as a hub to reach many others. His main interest was in
computers operated by the military and by defense contractors. Targets and keywords
suggested that he was attempting espionage by remotely entering sensitive computers
and stealing data; at least he exhibited an unusual interest in a few, specifically military
topics. Although most attacked computers were at military and defense contractor sites,
some were at universities and research organizations. Over the next 10 months, we
watched this individual attack about 450 computers and successfully enter more than 30.

LBL is a research institute with few military contracts and no classified research (unlike
our sister laboratory, Lawrence Livermore National Laboratory, which has several classified projects). Our computing environment is typical of a university: widely distributed,
heterogeneous, and fairly open. Despite this lack of classified computing, LBL's management decided to take the intrusion seriously and devoted considerable resources to it, in
hopes of gaining understanding and a solution.

The intruder conjured up no new methods for breaking operating systems; rather he repeatedly applied techniques documented elsewhere. Whenever possible he used known security holes and subtle bugs in different operating systems, including UNIX,[1] VMS,[2] VM-TSO,[3] EMBOS,[4] and SAIL-WAITS. Yet it is a mistake to assume that one operating system is more secure than another: Most of these break-ins were possible because the intruder exploited common blunders by vendors, users, and system managers.

Throughout these intrusions we kept our study a closely held secret. We deliberately remained open to attacks, despite knowing the intruder held system-manager privileges on our computers. Except for alerting management at threatened installations, we communicated with only a few trusted sites, knowing this intruder often read network messages and even accessed computers at several computer security companies. We remained in close touch with law-enforcement officials, who maintained a parallel investigation. As this article goes to press, the U.S. FBI and its German equivalent, the *Bundeskriminalamt* (BKA), continue their investigations. Certain details are therefore necessarily omitted from this article.

Recently, a spate of publicity surrounded computer break-ins around the world [23, 33, 37]. With a few notable exceptions (e.g., [24, 36]), most were incompletely reported anecdotes [7] or were little more than rumors. For lack of substantive documentation, system designers and managers have not addressed important problems in securing computers. Some efforts to tighten security on common systems may even be misdirected. We hope that lessons learned from our research will help in the design and management of more secure systems.

How should a site respond to an attack? Is it possible to trace the connections of someone trying to evade detection? What can be learned by following such an intruder? Which security holes were taken advantage of? How responsive was the law-enforcement community? This article addresses these issues, and avoids such questions as whether there is anything intrisically wrong with browsing through other people's files or with attempting to enter someone else's computer, or why someone would wish to read military databases. Nonetheless, the author holds strong opinions on these subjects.[5]

Detection

We first suspected a break-in when one of LBL's computers reported an accounting error. A new account had been created without a corresponding billing address. Our locally developed accounting program could not balance its books, since someone had incorrectly added the account. Soon afterwards, a message from the National Computer Security Center arrived, reporting that someone from our laboratory had attempted to break into one of their computers through a MILNET connection.

We removed the errant account, but the problem remained. We detected someone

---

[1] UNIX is a registered trademark of AT&T Bell Laboratories.

[2] VMS is a registered trademark of Digital Equipment Corporation.

[3] VM-TSO is a registered trademark of International Business Machines Corporation.

[4] EMBOS is a registered trademark of ELXSI.

[5] Friendly reader, if you have forgotten Thompson's article "Reflections on Trusting Trust" [44], drop this article and run to your nearest library. Consider his moral alongside the dry case study presented here.

acting as a system manager, attempting to modify accounting records. Realizing that there was an intruder in the system, we installed line printers and recorders on all incoming ports, and printed out the traffic. Within a few days, the intruder showed up again. We captured all of his keystrokes on a printer and saw how he used a subtle bug in the Gnu-Emacs text editor [40] to obtain system-manager privileges. At first we suspected that the culprit was a student prankster at the nearby University of California. We decided to catch him in the act, if possible. Accordingly, whenever the intruder was present, we began tracing the line, printing out all of his activity in real time.

Organizing Our Efforts

Early on, we began keeping a detailed logbook, summarizing the intruder's traffic, the traces, our suspicions, and interactions with law-enforcement people. Like a laboratory notebook, our logbook reflected both confusion and progress, but eventually pointed the way to the solution. Months later, when we reviewed old logbook notes, buried clues to the intruder's origin rose to the surface.

Having decided to keep our efforts invisible to the intruder, we needed to hide our records and eliminate our electronic messages about his activity. Although we did not know the source of our problems, we trusted our own staff and wished to inform whoever needed to know. We held meetings to reduce rumors, since our work would be lost if word leaked out. Knowing the sensitivity of this matter, our staff kept it out of digital networks, bulletin boards, and, especially, electronic mail. Since the intruder searched our electronic mail, we exchanged messages about security by telephone. Several false electronic-mail messages made the intruder feel more secure when he illicitly read them.

Monitors, Alarms, and Traffic Analysis

We needed alarms to instantly notify us when the intruder entered our system. At first, not knowing from which port our system was being hit, we set printers on all lines leading to the attacked computer. After finding that the intruder entered via X.25 ports, we recorded bidirectional traffic through that set of lines. These printouts proved essential to our understanding of events; we had records of his every keystroke, giving his targets, keywords, chosen passwords, and methodologies. The recording was complete in that virtually all of these sessions were captured, either by printer or on the floppy disk of a nearby computer. These monitors also uncovered several other attempted intrusions, unrelated to those of the individual we were following.

Off-line monitors have several advantages over monitors embedded in an operating system. They are invisible even to an intruder with system privileges. Moreover, they gave printouts of the intruder's activities on our local area network (LAN), letting us see his attempts to enter other closely linked computers. A monitor that records keystrokes within an operating system consumes computing resources and may slow down other processes. In addition, such a monitor must use highly privileged software and may introduce new security holes into the system. Besides taking up resources, on-line

---

What Is a Hacker?

The term hacker has acquired many meanings, including, a creative programmer, one who illicitly breaks into computers, a novice golfer who digs up the course, a taxicab driver, and ditch-digger. Confusion between the first two interpretations results in the perception that one need be brilliant or creative to break into computers. This may not be true. Indeed, the person we followed was patient and plodding, but hardly showed creative brilliance in discovering new security flaws.

To point out the ambiguity of the word hacker, this paper uses the term in the title, yet avoids it in the text.

Alternatives for describing someone who breaks into computers are: the English word "Cracker," and the Dutch term "Computerredebrenk" [14], (literally, computer peace disturber). The author's choices include "varmint," "reprobate," "swine," and several unprintable words.

---

monitors would have warned the intruder that he was being tracked. Since printers and personal computers are ubiquitous, and because RS-232 serial lines can easily be sent to multiple receivers, we used this type of off-line monitor and avoided tampering with our operating systems.

The alarms themselves were crude, yet effective in protecting our system as well as others under attack. We knew of researchers developing expert systems that watch for abnormal activity [4, 35], but we found our methods simpler, cheaper, and perhaps more reliable. Backing up these alarms, a computer loosely coupled into our LAN periodically looked at every process. Since we knew from the printouts which accounts had been compromised, we only had to watch for the use of these stolen accounts. We chose to place alarms on the incoming lines, where serial line analyzers and personal computers watched all traffic for the use of stolen account names. If triggered, a sequence of events culminated in a modem calling the operator's pocket pager. The operator watched the intruder on the monitors. If the intruder began to delete files or damage a system, he could be immediately disconnected, or the command could be disabled. When he appeared to be entering sensitive computers or downloading sensitive files, line noise, which appeared to be network glitches, could be inserted into the communications link.

In general, we contacted the system managers of the attacked computers, though in some cases the FBI or military authorities made the contact. Occasionally, they co-operated by leaving their systems open. More often, they immediately disabled the intruder or denied him access. From the intruder's viewpoint, almost everyone except LBL detected his activity. In reality, almost nobody except LBL detected him.

Throughout this time, the printouts showed his interests, techniques, successes, and failures. Initially, we were interested in how the intruder obtained system-manager privileges. Within a few weeks, we noticed him exploring our network connections— using ARPANET and MILNET quite handily, but frequently needing help with lesser known networks. Later, the monitors showed him leapfrogging through our computers, connecting to several military bases in the United States and abroad. Eventually, we observed him attacking many sites over Internet, guessing passwords and account names.

By studying the printouts, we developed an understanding of what the intruder was looking for. We also compared activity on different dates in order to watch him learn a new system, and inferred sites he entered through pathways we could not monitor. We observed the intruder's familiarity with various operating systems and became familiar with his programming style. Buried in this chatter were clues to the intruder's location and persona, but we needed to temper inferences based on traffic analysis. Only a complete trace back would identify the culprit.

Trace Backs

Tracing the activity was challenging because the intruder crossed many networks, seldom connected for more than a few minutes at a time, and might be active at any time. We needed fast trace backs on several systems, so we automated much of the process. Within seconds of a connection, our alarms notified system managers and network control centers automatically, using pocket pagers dialed by a local modem [42]. Simultaneously, technicians started tracing the networks.[6]

Since, the intruder's traffic arrived from an X.25 port, it could have come from anywhere in the world. We initially traced it to a nearby dial-up Tymnet port, in Oakland, California. With a court order and the telephone company's cooperation, we then traced the dial-up calls to a dial-out modem belonging to a defense contractor in McLean, Virginia. In essence, their LAN allowed any user to dial out from their modem pool and even provided a last-number-redial capability for those who did not know access codes for remote systems.

Analyzing the defense contractor's long-distance telephone records allowed us to determine the extent of these activities. By cross-correlating them with audit trails at other sites, we determined additional dates, times, and targets. A histogram of the times when the intruder was active showed most activity occurring at around noon, Pacific time. These records also demonstrated the attacks had started many months before detection at LBL.

Curiously, the defense contractor's telephone bills listed hundreds of short telephone calls all around the United States. The intruder had collected lists of modem telephone numbers and then called them over these modems. Once connected, he attempted to log in using common account names and passwords. These attempts were usually directed at military bases; several had detected intruders coming in over telephone lines, but had not bothered to trace them. When we alerted the defense contractor officials to their problem, they tightened access to their outbound modems and there were no more short connections.

After losing access to the defense contractor's modems, the still undeterred intruder connected to us over different links. Through the outstanding efforts of Tymnet, the full X.25 calling addresses were obtained within seconds of an attack. These addresses pointed to sources in Germany: universities in Bremen and Karlsruhe, and a public dial-up modem in another German city. When the intruder attacked the university in Bremen, he acquired

---

[6] The monitoring and trace-back efforts mixed frustration with excitement. If the computer was hit at 4:00 A.M., by 4:02, the author was out of bed, logged into several computers, and talking with the FBI. Telephone technicians in Germany, as well as network controllers in Europe and stateside, awaited the signal, so we had to eliminate false alarms, yet spread the word immediately. Several intimate evenings were spoiled by the intruder setting off the alarms, and a Halloween party was delayed while unwinding a particular convoluted connection.

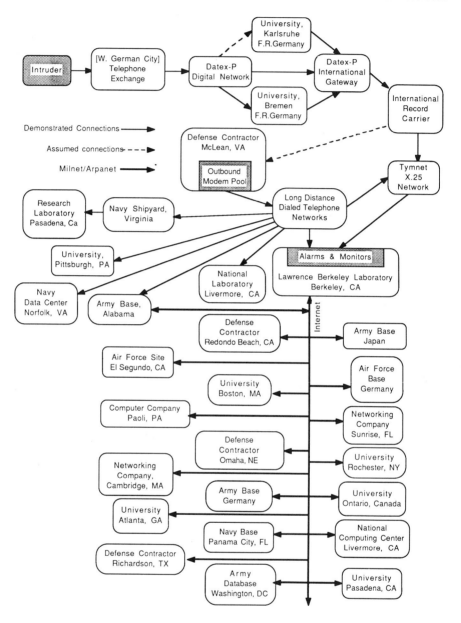

Figure 1. Simplified Connectivity and Partial List of Penetrated Sites.

system-manager privileges, disabled accounting, and used their X.25 links to connect around the world. Upon recognizing this problem, the university traced the connections to the other German city. This, in turn, spurred more tracing efforts, coordinating LBL, Tymnet, the university, and the German Bundespost.

Most connections were purposely convoluted. Figure 1 summarizes the main pathways that were traced, but the intruder used other connections as well. The rich connectivity and redundant circuits demonstrate the intruder's attempts to cover his tracks, or at least his search for new networks to exploit.

Besides physical network traces, there were several other indications of a foreign origin. When the intruder transferred files, we timed round-trip packet acknowledgments over the network links. Later, we measured the empirical delay times to a variety of different sites and estimated average network delay times as a function of distance. This measurement pointed to an overseas origin. In addition, the intruder knew his way around UNIX, using AT&T rather than Berkeley UNIX commands. When stealing accounts, he sometimes used German passwords. In retrospect, all were clues to his origin, yet each was baffling given our mind-set that "it must be some student from Berkeley campus."

A Stinger to Complete the Trace

The intruder's brief connections prevented telephone technicians from determining his location more precisely than to a particular German city. To narrow the search to an individual telephone, the technicians needed a relatively long connection. We baited the intruder by creating several files of fictitious text in an obscure LBL computer. These files appeared to be memos about how computers were to support research for the Strategic Defense Initiative (SDI). All the information was invented and steeped in governmental jargon. The files also contained a mailing list and several form letters talking about "additional documents available by mail" from a nonexistent LBL secretary. We protected these bogus files so that no one except the owner and system manager could read them, and set alarms so that we would know who read them.

While scavenging our files one day, the intruder detected these bogus files and then spent more than an hour reading them. During that time the telephone technicians completed the trace. We celebrated with milk shakes made with homegrown Berkeley strawberries, but the celebration proved premature. A few months later, a letter arrived from someone in the United States, addressed to the nonexistent secretary. The writer asked to be added to the fictitious SDI mailing list. As it requested certain "classified information," the letter alone suggested espionage. Moreover, realizing that the information had traveled from someone in Germany to a contact in the United States, we concluded we were witnessing attempted espionage. Other than cheap novels, we have no experience in this arena and so left this part of the investigation to the FBI.

Break-in Methods and Exploited Weaknesses

Printout of the intruder's activity showed that he used our computers as a way station; although he could become system manager here, he usually used LBL as a path to connect to the ARPANET/MILNET. In addition, we watched him use several other networks, including the Magnetic Fusion Energy network, the High Energy Physics network, and several LANs at invaded sites.

While connected to MILNET, this intruder attempted to enter about 450 computers, trying to log in using common account names like *root, guest, system,* or *field.* He also tried default and common passwords, and often found valid account names by querying each system for currently logged-in accounts, using *who* or *finger.* Although this type of attack is the most primitive, it was dismayingly successful: In about 5 percent of the machines attempted, default account names and passwords permitted access, sometimes giving system-manager privileges as well.

When he succeeded in logging into a system, he used standard methods to leverage his privileges to become system manager. Taking advantage of well-publicized problems in several operating systems, he was often able to obtain root or system-manager privileges. In any case, he searched file structures for keywords like "nuclear," "sdi," "kh-11," and "norad." After exhaustively searching for such information, he scanned for plain-text passwords into other systems. This proved remarkably effective: Users often leave passwords in files [2]. Electronic mail describing log-in sequences with account names and passwords is commonly saved at foreign nodes, allowing a file browser to obtain access into a distant system. In this manner he was able to obtain both passwords and access mechanisms into a Cray supercomputer.

Typical of the security holes he exploited was a bug in the Gnu-Emacs program. This popular, versatile text editor includes its own mail system, allowing a user to forward a file to another user [40]. As distributed, the program uses the UNIX Set-User-ID-to-Root feature; that is, a section of the program runs with system-manager privileges. This movemail facility allows the user to change file ownership and move files into another's directory. Unfortunately, the program did not prevent someone from moving a file into the systems area. Aware of this hole, the intruder created a shell script that, when executed at root level, would grant him system privileges. He used the movemail facility to rename his script to masquerade as a utility periodically run by the system. When the script was executed by the system, he gained system-manager privileges.

This intruder was impressively persistent and patient. For example, on one obscure gateway computer, he created an account with system privileges that remained untouched until six months later, when he began using it to enter other networked computers. On another occasion, he created several programs that gave him system-manager privileges and hid them in system software libraries. Returning almost a year later, he used the programs to become system manager, even though the original operating-system hole had been patched in the meantime.

This intruder cracked encrypted passwords. The UNIX operating system stores passwords in publicly readable, but encrypted form [26]. We observed him downloading encrypted password files from compromised systems into his own computer. Within a week he reconnected to the same computers, logging into new accounts with correct passwords. The passwords he guessed were English words, common names, or place-names. We realized that he was decrypting password files on his local computer by successively encrypting dictionary words and comparing the results to password file entries. By noting the length of time and the decrypted passwords, we could estimate the size of his dictionary and his computer's speed.

The intruder understood what he was doing and thought that he was not damaging anything. This, alas, was not entirely true. Prior to being detected, he entered a computer used in the real-time control of a medical experiment. Had we not caught him in time, a patient might have been severely injured.

Throughout this time the intruder tried not to destroy or change user data, although he did destroy several tasks and unknowingly caused the loss of data to a physics experiment. Whenever possible, he disabled accounting and audit trails, so there would be no trace of his presence. He planted Trojan horses to passively capture passwords and occasionally created new accounts to guarantee his access into computers. Apparently he thought detection less likely if he did not create new accounts, for he seemed to prefer stealing existing, unused accounts.

Intruder's Intentions

Was the intruder actually spying? With thousands of military computers attached, MILNET might seem inviting to spies. After all, espionage over networks can be cost-efficient, offer nearly immediate results, and target specific locations. Further, it would seem to be insulated from risks of internationally embarrassing incidents. Certainly Western countries are at much greater risk than nations without well-developed computer infrastructures.

Some may argue that it is ludicrous to hunt for classified information over MILNET because there is none. Regulations [21] prohibit classified computers from access via MILNET, and any data stored in MILNET systems must be unclassified. On the other hand, since these computers are not regularly checked, it is possible that some classified information resides on them. At least some data stored in these computers can be considered sensitive,[7] especially when aggregated. Print-outs of this intruder's activities seem to confirm this. Despite his efforts, he uncovered little information not already in the public domain, but that included abstracts of U.S. Army plans for nuclear, biological, and chemical warfare for central Europe. These abstracts were not classified, nor was their database.

The intruder was extraordinarily careful to watch for anyone watching him. He always checked who was logged onto a system, and if a system manager was on, he quickly disconnected. He regularly scanned electronic mail for any hints that he had been discovered, looking for mention of his activities or stolen log-in names (often, by scanning for those words). He often changed his connection pathways and used a variety of different network user identifiers. Although arrogant from his successes, he was nevertheless careful to cover his tracks.

Judging by the intruder's habits and knowledge, he is an experienced programmer who understands system administration. But he is by no means a "brilliant wizard," as might be popularly imagined. We did not see him plant viruses [18] or modify kernel code, nor did he find all existing security weaknesses in our system. He tried, however, to exploit problems in the UNIX/*usr/spool/at* [36], as well as a hole in the *vi* editor. These problems had been patched at our site long before, but they still exist in many other installations.

---

[7] An attempt by the National Security Council [34] to classify certain public databases as "sensitive" met with widespread objections [11].

Did the intruder cause damage? To his credit, he tried not to erase files and killed only a few processes. If we only count measurable losses and time as damage, he was fairly benign [41]. He only wasted systems staff time, computing resources, and network connection time, and racked up long-distance telephone tolls and international network charges. His liability under California law [6], for the costs of the computing and network time, and of tracking him, is over $100,000.

But this is a narrow view of the damage. If we include intangible losses, the harm he caused was serious and deliberate. At the least, he was trespassing, invading others' property and privacy; at worst, he was conducting espionage. He broke into dozens of computers, extracted confidential information, read personal mail, and modified system software. He risked injuring a medical patient and violated the trust of our network community. Money and time can be paid back. Once trust is broken, the open, co-operative character of our networks may be lost forever.

Aftermath: Picking Up the Pieces

Following successful traces, the FBI assured us the intruder would not try to enter our system again. We began picking up the pieces and tightening our system. The only way to guarantee a clean system was to rebuild all systems from source code, change all passwords overnight, and recertify each user. With over a thousand users and dozens of computers, this was impractical, especially since we strive to supply our users with uninterrupted computing services. On the other hand, simply patching known holes or instituting a quick fix for stolen passwords [27] was not enough.

We settled on instituting password expiration, deleting all expired accounts, eliminating shared accounts, continued monitoring of incoming traffic, setting alarms in certain places, and educating our users. Where necessary, system utilities were compared to fresh versions, and new utilities built. We changed network-access passwords and educated users about choosing nondictionary passwords. We did not institute random password assignment, having seen that users often store such passwords in command files or write them on their terminals.

To further test the security of our system, we hired a summer student to probe it [2]. He discovered several elusive, site-specific security holes, as well as demonstrated more general problems, such as file scavenging. We would like to imagine that intruder problems have ended for us; sadly, they have not, forcing us to continue our watch.

Remaining Open to an Intruder

Should we have remained open? A reasonable response to the detection of this attack might have been to disable the security hole and change all passwords. This would presumably have insulated us from the intruder and prevented him from using our computers to attack other internet sites. By remaining open, were we not a party to his attacks elsewhere, possibly incurring legal responsibility for damage?

Had we closed up shop, we would not have risked embarrassment and could have resumed our usual activities. Closing up and keeping silent might have reduced adverse publicity, but would have done nothing to counter the serious problem of suspicious (and possibly malicious) offenders. Although many view the trace back and prosecution of intruders as a community service to network neighbors, this view is not universal [22].

Finally, had we closed up, how could we have been certain that we had eliminated the intruder? With hundreds of networked computers at LBL, it is nearly impossible to change all passwords on all computers. Perhaps he had planted subtle bugs or logic bombs in places we did not know about. Eliminating him from LBL would hardly have cut his access to MILNET. And, by disabling his access into our system, we would close our eyes to his activities: we could neither monitor him nor trace his connections in real-time. Tracing, catching, and prosecuting intruders are, unfortunately, necessary to discourage these vandals.

Legal Responses

Several laws explicitly prohibit unauthorized entry into computers. Few states lack specific codes, but occasionally the crimes are too broadly defined to permit conviction [38]. Federal and California laws have tight criminal statutes covering such entries, even if no damage is done [47]. In addition, civil law permits recovery not only of damages, but also of the costs to trace the culprit [6]. In practice, we found police agencies relatively uninterested until monetary loss could be quantified and damages demonstrated. Although not a substitute for competent legal advice, spending several days in law libraries researching both the statutes and precedents set in case law proved helpful.

Since this case was international in scope, it was necessary to work closely with law-enforcement organizations in California, the FBI in the United States, and the BKA in Germany. Cooperation between system managers, communications technicians, and network operators was excellent. It proved more difficult to get bureaucratic organizations to communicate with one another as effectively. With many organizational boundaries crossed, including state, national, commercial, university, and military, there was confusion as to responsibility: Most organizations recognized the seriousness of these break-ins, yet no one agency had clear responsibility to solve it. A common response was, "That's an interesting problem, but it's not our bailiwick."

Overcoming this bureaucratic indifference was a continual problem. Our laboratory notebook proved useful in motivating organizations: When individuals saw the extent of the break-ins, they were able to explain them to their colleagues and take action. In addition, new criminal laws were enacted that more tightly defined what constituted a prosecutable offense [6, 38, 47]. As these new laws took effect, the FBI became much more interested in this case, finding statutory grounds for prosecution.

The FBI and BKA maintained active investigations. Some subjects have been apprehended, but as yet the author does not know the extent to which they have been prosecuted. With recent laws and more skilled personnel, we can expect faster and more effective responses from law-enforcement agencies.

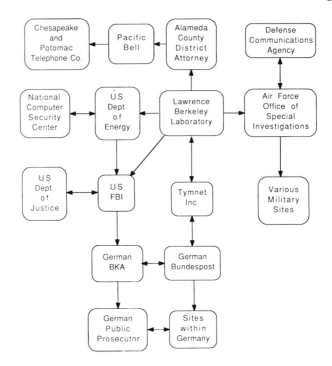

Figure 2. Simplified Communications Paths between Organizations.

Errors and Problems

In retrospect, we can point to many errors we made before and during these intrusions. Like other academic organizations, we had given little thought to securing our system, believing that standard vendor provisions were sufficient because nobody would be interested in us. Our scientists' research is entirely in the public domain, and many felt that security measures would only hinder their productivity. With increased connectivity, we had not examined our networks for cross-links where an intruder might hide. These problems were exacerbated on our UNIX systems, which are used almost exclusively for mail and text processing, rather than for heavy computation.

Password security under Berkeley UNIX is not optimal; it lacks password aging, expiration, and exclusion of passwords found in dictionaries. Moreover, UNIX password integrity depends solely on encryption; the password file is publicly readable. Other operating systems protect the password file with encryption, access controls, and alarms.

We had not paid much attention to choosing good passwords (fully 20 percent of our users' passwords fell to a dictionary-based password cracker). Indeed, we had allowed our Tymnet password to become public, foolishly believing that the system log-in password should be our only line of defense.

Once we detected the intruder, the first few days were confused, since nobody knew what our response ought to be. Our accounting files were misleading since the system clocks had been allowed to drift several minutes. Although our LAN's connections had

---

The Intruder versus the Tracker

Skills and techniques to break into systems are quite different from those to detect and trace an intruder. The intruder may not even realize the route chosen; the tracker, however, must understand this route thoroughly. Although both must be aware of weaknesses in systems and networks, the former may work alone, whereas the latter must forge links with technical and law-enforcement people. The intruder is likely to ignore concepts of privacy and trust during a criminal trespass; in contrast, the tracker must know and respect delicate legal and ethical restrictions.

Despite occasional reports to the contrary [19], rumors of intruders building careers in computer security are exaggerated. Apart from the different skills required, it is a rare company that trusts someone with such ethics and personal conduct. Banks, for example, do not hire embezzlers as consultants. Donn Parker, of SRI International, reports (personal communication, September 1987) that job applications of several intruders have been rejected due to suspicions of their character and trustworthiness. On March 16th, the *Washington Post* reported the arrest of a member of the German Chaos computer club, prior to his giving a talk on computer security in Paris. Others who have broken into computers have met with physical violence [33] and have been ostracized from network activities [3]. A discipline that relies on trust and responsibility has no place for someone technically competent yet devoid of ethics.

---

been saved, nobody knew the file format, and it was frustrating to find that its clock had drifted by several hours. In short, we were unprepared to trace our LAN and had to learn quickly.

We did not know who to contact in the law-enforcement community. At first, assuming that the intruder was local, our district attorney obtained the necessary warrants. Later, as we learned that the intruder was out of state, we experienced frustration in getting federal law-enforcement support. Finally, after tracing the intruder abroad, we encountered a whole new set of ill-defined interfaces between organizations. The investigation stretched out far beyond our expectations. Naively expecting the problem to be solved by a series of phone traces, we were disappointed when the pathway proved to be a tangle of digital and analog connections. Without funding to carry out an investigation of this length, we were constantly tempted to drop it entirely.

A number of minor problems bubbled up, which we were able to handle along the way. For a while this intruder's activity appeared similar to that of someone breaking into Stanford University; this confused our investigation for a short time. Keeping our work out of the news was difficult, especially because our staff is active in the computing world. Fortunately, it was possible to recover from the few leaks that occurred. At first, we were confused by not realizing the depth or extent of the penetrations. Our initial confusion gave way to an organized response as we made the proper contacts and began tracing the intruder. As pointed out by others [25, 36], advance preparations make all the difference.

Lessons

As a case study, this investigation demonstrates several well-known points that lead to some knotty questions. Throughout this we are reminded that security is a human problem that cannot be solved by technical solutions alone [48].

The almost obsessive persistence of serious penetrators is astonishing. Once networked, our computers can be accessed via a tangle of connections from places we had never thought of. An intruder, limited only by patience, can attack from a variety of directions, searching for the weakest entry point. How can we analyze our systems' vulnerability in this environment? Who is responsible for network security? The network builder? The managers of the end nodes? The network users?

The security weaknesses of both systems and networks, particularly the needless vulnerability due to sloppy systems management and administration, results in a surprising succes rate for unsophisticated attacks. How are we to educate our users, system managers, and administrators?

Social, ethical, and legal problems abound. How do we measure the harm done by these penetrators? By files deleted or by time wasted? By information copied? If no files are corrupted, but information is copied, what damage has been done? What constitutes unreasonable behavior on a network? Attempting to illicitly log in to a foreign computer? Inquiring who is currently logged in there? Exporting a file mistakenly made world readable? Exploiting an unpatched hole in another's system?

Closing out an intruder upon discovery may be a premature reflex. Determining the extent of the damage and cooperating with investigations argue for leaving the system open. How do we balance the possible benefits of tracking an intruder against the risks of damage or embarrassment?

Our technique of catching an intruder by providing bait and then watching what got nibbled is little more than catching flies with honey. It can be easily expanded to determine intruders' interests by presenting them with a variety of possible subjects (games, financial data, academic gossip, military news). Setting up disarmed files is straightforward, so this mechanism offers a method to both detect and classify intruders. It should not be used indiscriminately, however.

Files with plaintext passwords are common in remote sub-entry computers, yet these systems often are not protected since they have little computational capability. Such systems are usually widely networked, allowing entry from many sources. These computers are fertile grounds for password theft through file scavenging since the passwords are left in easily read command procedures. These files also contain instructions to make the network connection. Random character passwords make this problem worse, since users not wishing to memorize them are more likely to write such passwords into files. How can we make secure remote procedures calls and remote batch job submissions?

Passwords are at the heart of computer security. Requirements for a quality password are few: Passwords must be nonguessable, not in a dictionary, changed every few months, and easily remembered. User-generated passwords usually fail to meet the first three criteria, and machine-generated passwords fail the last. Several compromises exist: forcing "pass phrases" or any password that contains a special character. There are many other possibilities, but none are implemented widely. The Department of Defense recommends pronounceable machine-generated words or pass phrases [5]. Despite such obvious rules, we (and the intruder) found that poor-quality passwords pervaded our networked communities. How can we make users choose good passwords? Should we?

Vendors usually distribute weakly protected systems software, relying on the installer

---

Legal Constraints and Ethics

As communities grow, social and legal structures follow. In our networked community, there is frustration and confusion over what constitutes a crime and what is acceptable behavior. Legal constraints exist, but some do not recognize their applicability. Richard D'Ippolito laments:

> Our view of computer crimes has not yet merged with society's view of other property crimes: while we have laws against breaking and entering, they aren't widely applied to computer crimes. The property owner does not have to provide "perfect" security, nor does anything have to be taken to secure a conviction of unauthorized entry. Also, unauthorized use of CPU resources (a demonstrably saleable product) amounts to theft. There still seems to be the presumption that computer property, unlike other property, is fair game . . . . We deserve the same legal persumption that our imperfectly protected systems and work are private property subject to trespass and conversion protection [12].

The "ACM Code of Professional Conduct" also leaves little doubt:

> An ACM member shall act at all times with integrity . . . shall always consider the principle of the individual's privacy and to minimize the data collected, limit authorized access, [and] provide proper security for the data . . . [1]

---

to enable protections and disable default accounts. Installers often do not care, and system managers inherit these weak systems. Today, the majority of computer users are naive; they install systems the way the manufacturer suggests or simply unpackage systems without checking. Vendors distribute systems with default accounts and backdoor entryways left over from software development. Since many customers buy computers based on capability rather than security, vendors seldom distribute secure software. It is easy to write procedures that warn of obvious insecurities, yet vendors are not supplying them. Capable, aware system managers with plenty of time do not need these tools —the tools are for novices who are likely to overlook obvious holes. When vendors do not see security as a selling point, how can we encourage them to distribute more secure systems?

Patches to operating-system security holes are poorly publicized and spottily distributed. This seems to be due to the paranoia surrounding these discoveries, the thousands of systems without systems administrators, and the lack of channels to spread the news. Also, many security problems are specific to a single version of an operating system or require systems experience to understand. Together, these promote ignorance of problems, threats, and solutions. We need a central clearinghouse to receive reports of problems, analyze their importance, and disseminate trustworthy solutions. How can we inform people wearing white hats about security problems, while preventing evil people from learning or exploiting these holes? Perhaps zero-knowledge proofs [20] can play a part in this.

Operating systems can record unsuccessful log ins. Of the hundreds of attempted log ins into computers attached to Internet, only five sites (or 1–2 percent) contacted us when they detected an attempted break-in. Clearly, system managers are not watching for intruders, who might appear as neighbors, trying to sneak into their computers. Our networks are like communities or neighborhoods, and so we are surprised when we find unneighborly behavior.

Does security interfere with operational demands? Some security measures, like random passwords or strict isolation, are indeed onerous and can be self-defeating. But many measures neither interfere with legitimate users nor reduce the system's capabilities. For example, expiring unused accounts hurts no one and is likely to free up disk space. Well thought out management techniques and effective security measures do not bother ordinary users, yet they shut out or detect intruders.

Internet Security

The intruder's successes and failures provide a reasonable snapshot of overall security in the more than 20,000 computers connected to Internet. A more detailed analysis of these attacks is to be published in the *Proceedings of the 11th National Computer Security Conference* [43]. Of the 450 attacked computers, half were unavailable when the intruder tried to connect to them. He tried to log into the 220 available computers with obvious account names and trivial passwords. Of these 220 attempted log ins, listed in increasing importance,

- 5 percent were refused by a distant computer (set to reject LBL connects),
- 82 percent failed on incorrect user name/passwords,
- 8 percent gave information about the system status (who, sysstat, etc.),
- 1 percent achieved limited access to databases or electronic-mail shells,
- 2 percent yielded normal user privileges and a programming environment, and
- 2 percent reached system-manager privileges.

Most attempts were into MILNET computers (Defense Data Network address groups 26.i.j.k). Assuming the population is representative of nonmilitary computers and the last three categories represent successful penetrations, we find that about 5 percent of Internet computers are grossly insecure against trivial attacks. This figure is only a lower limit of vulnerability, since military computers may be expected to be more secure than civilian systems. Further, cleverer tactics for entering computers could well lead to many more break-ins.

Whereas the commercial sector is more concerned with data integrity, the military worries about control of disclosure [8]. With this in mind, we expect greater success for the browser or data thief in the commercial world.

In a different set of penetrations [37], NASA experienced about 130 break-ins into its

---

Should This Have Been Published?

The very act of publishing this article raises questions. Surely it creates a new set of problems by exposing widely distributed holes to some amoral readers. Worse, it describes ways to track such individuals and so suggests avoidance techniques, possibly making other intrusions more difficult to track and prosecute.

In favor of publishing, Maj. Gen. John Paul Hyde of the U.S. Joint Chiefs of Staff informed the author that "to stimulate awareness of the vulnerabilities of networks, along with the complexities of tracking a distant intruder, papers such as this should be widely distributed. It's obvious that inattention to established security practices contributed to the success of this intruder; systems with vigilant security programs detected and rejected unauthorized accesses."

nonclassified, academic computers on the SPAN networks. Both the NASA break-in and our set of intrusions originated in West Germany, using similar communications links and searching for "secret" information. Pending completion of law enforcement and prosecution, the author does not make conjectures as to the relationshps between these different break-ins.

Between 700 and 3000 computers are reachable on the SPAN network (exact figures depend on whether LANs are counted). In that incident the break-in success rate was between 4 and 20 percent. Considering the SPAN break-ins with the present study, we find that, depending on the methods chosen, break-in success rates of 3–20 percent may be expected in typical network environments.

Conclusions and Comments

Perhaps no computer or network can be totally secure. This study suggests that any operating system will be insecure when obvious security rules are ignored. From the intruder's widespread success, it appears that users, managers, and vendors routinely fail to use sound security practices. These problems are not limited to our site or the few dozen systems that we saw penetrated, but are networkwide. Lax system management makes patching utility software or tightening a few systems ineffective.

We found this intruder to be a competent, patient programmer, experienced in several operating systems. Alas, some system managers violate their positions of trust and confidence. Our worldwide community of digital networks requires a sense of responsibility. Unfortunately, this is missing in some technically competent people.

Some speak of a "hacker ethic" of not changing data [37]. It is astounding that intruders blithely tamper with someone else's operating system, never thinking they may destroy months of work by systems people, or may cause unforeseen system instabilities or crashes. Sadly, few realize the delicacy of the systems they fool with or the amount of systems staff time they waste.

The foreign origin of the source, the military computers entered, and the keywords searched *suggest* international espionage. This author does not speculate as to whether this actually was espionage, but does not doubt that someone took the opportunity to try.

Break-ins from abroad seem to be increasing. Probably this individual's intrusions are different from others only in that his efforts were noticed, monitored, and documented. LBL has detected other attempted intrusions from several European countries, as well as from the Orient. Individuals in Germany [37] have claimed responsibility for breaking into foreign computers. Such braggadocio may impress an unenlightened public; it has a different effect on administrators trying to maintain and expand networks. Indeed funding agencies have already eliminated some international links due to these concerns. Break-ins ultimately destroy the network connectivity they exploit. If this is the object of such groups as the German Chaos Club, Data Travellers, Network Rangers, or various contributors to *2600 Magazine*, it reflects the self-destructive folly of their apparent cleverness.

Tracking down espionage attempts over the digital networks may be the most dramatic aspect of this work. But it is more useful to realize that analytic research methods can be fruitfully applied to problems as bizarre as computer break-ins.

Computer Security Resources

Much has been published on how to make a secure operating system, but there is little literature about frontline encounters with intruders. Computer security problems are often aired over Internet, especially the "UNIX-wizards," "info-vax," and "security" conferences. A lively, moderated discussion appears in the *Risks Forum* [12] addressing social issues relating to computer system risks. Private security conferences also exist; their "invitation only" membership is evidence of the paranoia surrounding the field. There are also private, anonymous, and pirate bulletin boards. These seldom have much useful information—their puerile contents apparently reflect the mind-sets of their contributors, but they do indicate what one segment of the population is thinking.

Perhaps the best review of problems, technology, and policy is represented in "Defending Secrets, Sharing Data" [32]. Whitten provides an excellent introduction to systems problems in "Computer Insecurity, Infiltrating Open Systems" [48]. Although slightly dated, the January 1983 issue of *Computer* [16] is devoted to secure computer systems, with a half-dozen good articles on the subject. See the especially cogent review article on secure operating systems [15]. Recent work concentrates on secure networks; an entire issue of *Network* is devoted to it [17]. Also see D. Denning's *Cryptography and Data Security* [9], and *Computer Security: An Introduction*, by R. Kemmerer at U.C. Santa Barbara.

Journals of interest include *Computer Security Journal, Computer Fraud and Security Bulletin, ACM SIGPLAN Notices, Computer Security Newsletter, Computer Law Journal*, and, of course, *Communications of the ACM*. Several semiunderground journals are devoted to illicitly entering systems; these are often short lived. The best known is *2600 Magazine*, named after a frequency used to steal long-distance telephone services.

Current research in computer security covers information theory, cryptology, graph theory, topology, and database methods. An ongoing debate rages over whether cryptographic protection or access controls are the best choice. Since it is tough to prove an operating system is secure, a new field of research has sprung up examining ways to formally verify a system's security.

The standard for secure operating systems is the Orange Book, "DoD Trusted Computer System Evaluation Criteria" [29], from the NCSC. This document sets levels of security, ranging from class D (minimal protection) through C (discretionary protection), B (mandatory access controls), and A (formally verified security controls). Since the Orange Book is not easy to comprehend, the NCSC has published an explanatory document [30]. There is also a document giving the technical rationale behind the explanatory document [28]. Some networks link classified computers, and these systems' security is being studied and standardized (see [31]).

UNIX security is covered by Grampp and Morris in [13] and by Wood and Kochan in [49]. Wood and Kochan's book is a good guide for system managers and users, although much of the book is spent on program listings. More recently, *Unix Review* presented several articles on securing UNIX [45]. In that issue Smith's article is especially appropriate, as he describes in detail how secure systems are weakened by poor system administration [39]. Carole Hogan also examines Unix problems in her report, *Protection Imperfect*, available from Lawrence Livermore Labs, L-60; Livermore, CA.

Operating systems verified to Orange Book security ratings include security documentation. For an example of a well-written manual, see [10] the DEC VMS System security manual. Building a secure operating system is challenging and M. Gasser has written a book with just that title, available from Van Nostrand and Reinhold.

Should you have computer security worries, you may wish to contact either the National Bureau of Standards (NBS) Institute for Computer Science and Technology (Mail Stop Tech-A216, Washington, DC 20234) or the NCSC (Mail Stop C4, 9800 Savage Road, Ft. Meade, MD 20755). Both set standards and certify secure computers, as well as conduct research in secure networks. Jointly, NBS and NCSC sponsor the annual "National Computer Security Conference." Recently, Federal Law 100-235 has shifted civilian computer security research from the NCSC to the NBS, apparently wishing to separate military and civilian policy.

With luck, you will never be confronted by a break-in. If you are, you can contact your local police, the FBI, or the U.S. Secret Service. Within the U.S. Air Force, computer security problems are handled by the Air Force Office of Special Investigations, at Bolling AFB, Washington, D.C. Within our military branches, such problems go to the respective investigative services. MILNET and ARPANET problems should be reported to the Security Office of the Defense Communications Agency, which will contact the Network Operations Center at BBN Communications. You do not need a court order to trace a call on your own line [46]. Most telephone companies have security departments that operate trace backs. For a variety of ways to respond to a break-in, see "What do you Feed a Trojan Horse" [42].

It seems that everyone wants to hear stories about someone else's troubles, but few are willing to write about their own. We hope that in publishing this report we will encourage sound administrative practices. Vandals and other criminals reading this article will find a way to rationalize breaking into computers. This article cannot teach these people ethics; we can only hope to reach those who are unaware of these miscreants.

An enterprising programmer can enter many computers, just as a capable burglar can break into many homes. It is an understandable response to lock the door, sever connections, and put up elaborate barriers. Perhaps this is necessary, but it saddens the author, who would rather see future networks and computer communities built on honesty and trust.

Acknowledgements

A dozen diverse organizations cooperated in solving this problem. Superb technical support from the German Bundespost and Tymnet allowed this project to reach fruition; both showed phenomenal dedication and competence throughout months of tracing. LBL's staff and management were especially supportive—systems people and the real-time systems group provided technical wizardry when everything seemed mysterious. The U.S. FBI and the German BKA demonstrated creative approaches to novel problems and logged many long hours. The Bremen Public Prosecutor's office, U.S. Department of Justice, and Alameda County District Attorney handled the prosecution and legal efforts. Additional help came from the NCSC, the Defense Communications Agency, the Air Force Office of Special Investigations, the University of Bremen, Pacific Bell, and the Chesapeake and Potomac Telephone Company. None of this work could have taken place without the support from the good folks of the U.S. Department of Energy. To the people in these organizations, I extend my heartfelt thanks.

Many others helped in this project, including Ken Adelman, Dot Akins, Marv Atchley, Bruce Bauer, Paul Boedges, Eric Beals, Leon Breault, Darren Busing, Rick Carr, Jack Case, Bill Chandler, Jim Christie, Dave Cleveland, Dana Conant, Joanne Crafton, Ken Crepea, Steve Dougherty, *Dave Farnham*, Ann Funk, Mike Gibbons, Wayne Graves, Tom Hitch-cock, Roy Kerth, Dan Kolkowitz, Steve Kougoures, Diane Johnson, Dave Jones, Dan Lane, *Chris McDonald*, Chuck McNatt, *Martha Matthews*, Sandy Merola, Gene Miya, Maggie Morley, Bob Morris, Paul Murray, Jeff Olivetto, Joeseph Rogan, Steve Rudd, Barbara Schaefer, Steve Shumaker, *Phil Sibert*, *Dave Stevens*, Dan Van Zile, Ron Vivier, Regina Wiggen, Steve White, and Hellmuth Wolf. I am deeply indebted to each of these folks. For critical reviews of this article, thanks go to the folks accented in italic, as well as Dean Chacon, Dorothy Denning, John Paul Hyde, Jeff Kuhn, Peter Neumann, Serge Polevitzky, Howard Weiss, and two anonymous reviewers.

This work was supported in part by the U.S. Department of Energy, under Contract DE-AC03-76SF00098.

References

1. ACM. ACM code of professional conduct. Bylaw 19, Cannon 1–5, ACM, New York.
2. Beals, E., Busing, D., Graves, W., and Stoll, C. (1987). Improving VMS security: Overlooked

ways to tighten your system. In *Session Notes, DECUS Fall Meeting* Anaheim, Calif., Dec. 7–11). Digital Equipment User's Society, Boston, Mass.

3. Bednarek, M. (1987). Re: Important notice [distrust software from people breaking into computers]. *Internet Info-Vax Conference* (August 4).

4. Boing, W., and Kirchberg, B. (1988). L'utilisation de systemes experts dans l'audit informatique. In *Congress Programme, Securicom 88*, 6th World Congress on Computer Security (Paris, France, March 17).

5. Brand, S., and Makey, J. (1985). J. Dept. of Defense password management guideline. CSC-STD-002-85, NCSC, Ft. Meade. Md., (April).

6. California State Legislature (1986). Computer crime law. California Penal Code S. 502, (revised 1987).

7. Carpenter, B. (1986). Malicious hackers. *CERN Comput. Newsl. ser. 185* (September), 4.

8. Clark, D., and Wilson, D. (1987). A comparison of commercial and military computer security policies. In *Proceedings of the IEEE Symposium on Security and Privacy* (Oakland, Calif., April 27–29). IEEE Press, New York, pp. 184–194.

9. Denning, D. (1982). *Cryptography and Data Security*. Addison-Wesley, Reading, Mass.

10. Digital Equipment Corporation (1985). Guide to VAX/VMS system security. AA-Y510A-TE. DEC, (July).

11. Dilworth, D. (1987). "Sensitive but unclassified" information: The controversy. *Bull. Am. Soc. Inf. Sci. 13* (April).

12. D'Ippolito, R. S. (1987). AT&T computers penetrated. *Internet Risks Forum 5.* 41 (September 30).

13. Grampp, F. T., and Morris, R. H. (1984). Unix operating system security. *AT&T Bell Laboratories Tech. J. 63*, 8 (October), pt. 2, 1649–1672.

14. Hartman, W. (1988). The privacy dilemma. Paper presented at the "International Conference on Computers and Law" (Santa Monica, Calif., February). Available from Erasamus Universiteit, Rotterdam.

15. IEEE (1983). The best techniques for computer security. *Computer 16*, 7 (January), 86.

16. IEEE (1983). *Computer 16*, 7 (January).

17. IEEE (1987). *Network 1*, 2 (April).

18. Israel, H. (1987). Computer viruses: Myth or reality. In *Proceedings of the 10th National Computer Security Conference* (Baltimore, Md., September 21–24).

19. Kneale, D. (1987). It takes a hacker. *Wall Street J.* (November 3).

20. Landau, S. (1988). Zero knowledge and the Department of Defense. *Not. Am. Math. Soc. 35*, 1 (January), 5–12.

21. Latham, D. (1985). Guidance and program direction applicable to the Defense Data Network. In *DDN Protocol Handbook*, NIC 50004, vol. 1, Defense Data Network, Washington, D.C., (December), pp. 1–51.

22. Lehmann, F. (1987). Computer break-ins, *Commun. ACM 30*, 7 (July), 584–585.

23. Markoff, J. (1986). Computer sleuths hunt a brilliant hacker. *San Francisco Examiner* (October 3).

24. McDonald, C. (1987). Computer security blunders. In *Proceedings of the DOE 10th Computer Security Group Conference* (Albuquerque, N.M., May 5–7), Dept. of Energy, Washington, D.C., pp. 35–46.

25. Metz, S. J. (1987). Computer break-ins. *Commun. ACM 30*, 7 (July), 584.

26. Morris, R. H., and Thompson, K. (1984). Password security: A case history. In *Unix Programmer's Manual*. AT&T Bell Laboratories, sec. 2.

27. Morshedian, D. (1986). How to fight password pirates. *Computer 19*, 1 (January).

28. National Computer Security Center (1985). CSC-STD-004-85. NCSC, Ft. Meade, Md.

29. National Computer Security Center (1983). DoD trusted computer system evaluation criteria. CSC-STD-001-83. NCSC, Ft. Meade, Md.

30. National Computer Security Center (1985). Guidance for applying the Orange Book. CSC-STD-003-85. NCSC, Ft. Meade, Md.

31. National Computer Security Center (1987). Trusted network interpretation of the trusted computer system evaluation criteria. DoD 5200.28-STD. NCSC, Ft. Meade, Md.

32. Office of Technology Assessment (1987). U.S. Congress, Defending secrets, sharing data: New locks and keys for electronic information. OTA-CIT-310. U.S. Government Printing Office, Washington, D.C., (October).

33. Omond, G. (1987). Important notice [on widespread attacks into VMS systems]. In *Internet Info-Vax Conference*, (July 31).

34. Poindexter, J. (1984). National security decision directive. NSDD-145. National Security Council, Washington, D.C., (September 17).

35. *Proceedings of the Intrusion Detection Expert Systems Conference* (1987). (November 17).

36. Reid, B. (1987). Reflections on some recent widespread computer break-ins. *Commun. ACM 30*, 2 (February), 103–105.

37. Schmemann, S. (1987). West German computer hobbyists rummaged NASA's files. *New York Times*, (September 16).

38. Slind-Flor, V. (1988). Hackers access tough new penalties. *The Recorder Bay Area Legal Newsp.*, (January 6).

39. Smith, K. (1988). *Unix Rev. 6*, 2 (February).

40. Stallman, R. *Gnu-Emacs Text Editor Source Code.*

41. Stevens, D. (1987). Who goes there? A dialog of questions and answers about benign hacking. In *Proceedings of the Computer Measurement Group* (December). Computer Measurement Group.

42. Stoll, C. (1987). What do you feed a Trojan horse? In *Proceedings of the 10th National Computer Security Conference* (Baltimore, Md., September 21–24).

43. Stoll, C. How secure are computers in the US? In *Proceedings of the 11th National Computer Security Conference* (Baltimore, Md., October 17). To be published.

44. Thompson, K. (1984). Reflections on trusting trust. *Commun. ACM 27*, 8 (August), 761–763.

45. *Unix Review. 6.* (1988). 2 (February).

46. U.S. Congress (1986). Exception to general prohibition on trap and trace device use. 18 U.S.C.A. 3121, secs. (b)(1) and (b)(3), U.S. Congress, Washington, D.C.

47. U.S. Congress (1986). The federal computer crime statute. 18 U.S.C.A. 1030, U.S. Congress, Washington, D.C.

48. Whitten, I. H. (1987). Computer (in)security: Infiltrating open systems. *Abacus* (Summer 1987).

49. Wood and Kochan (1985). *Unix System Security.* Sams, Indianapolis, Ind.

P·A·R·T·VI

2

Computer Viruses

Peter J. Denning

Sometime in the middle 1970s, the network of computers at a Silicon Valley research center was taken over by a program that loaded itself into an idle workstation, disabled the keyboard, drew random pictures on the screen, and monitored the network for other idle workstations to invade. The entire network and all the workstations had to be shut down to restore normal operation.

In early September 1986, a talented intruder broke into a large number of computer systems in the San Francisco area, including 9 universities, 15 Silicon Valley companies, 9 ARPANET sites, and 3 government laboratories. The intruder left behind recompiled login programs to simplify his return. His goal was apparently to achieve a high score on the number of computers cracked; no damage was done [1].

In December 1987, a Christmas message that originated in West Germany propagated into the Bitnet network of IBM machines in the United States. The message contained a program that displayed an image of a Christmas tree and sent copies of itself to everyone in the mail distribution list of the user for whom it was running. This prolific program rapidly clogged the network with a geometrically growing number of copies of itself. Finally the network had to be shut down until all copies could be located and expurgated.

For two months in the fall of 1987, a program quietly incorporated copies of itself into programs on personal computers at the Hebrew University. It was discovered and dismantled by a student, Yuval Rakavy, who noticed that certain library programs were growing longer for no apparent reason. He isolated the errant code and discovered that on certain Fridays the thirteenth a computer running it would slow down by 80%, and on Friday, 13 May 1988, it would erase all files. That date will be the fortieth anniversary of the last day Palestine was recognized as a separate political entity. Rakavy designed

Reprinted with permission of Sigma Xi, "Computer Viruses," by P.J. Denning, *American Scientist* 76, June 1988, pp. 236–238.

another program that detected and erased all copies of the errant program it could find. Even so, he could not be completely sure he had eradicated it.

These four incidents illustrate the major types of programs that attack other programs in a computer's memory. The first type is a worm, a program that invades a workstation and disables it. The second is a Trojan horse, a program that performs some apparently useful function, such as login, while containing hidden code that performs an unwanted, usually malicious function. This name is inspired by the legendary wooden horse built by the Greek army, ostensibly as an offering to Athena, which in the dark of night disgorged its bellyful of murderous soldiers into the sleeping streets of Troy. The third type is a bacterium, a program that replicates itself and feeds off the host system by preempting processor and memory capacity. The fourth is a virus, a program that incorporates copies of itself into the machine codes of other programs and, when those programs are invoked, wreaks havoc in the manner of a Trojan horse.

I can cite numerous other incidents in which information stored in computers has been attacked by hostile programs. An eastern medical center lost nearly 40% of its records to a malicious program in its system. Students at Lehigh University lost homework and other data when a virus erased diskettes inserted into campus personal computers. Some programs available publicly from electronic bulletin boards have destroyed information on the disks of computers into which they were read. A recent *New York Times* article [2] describes many examples and documents the rising concern among computer network managers, software dealers, and personal computer users about these forms of electronic vandalism. In an effort to alert concerned computer scientists to the onslaught, the Association for Computing Machinery sponsors the Computer *Risks Forum*, an electronic newsletter moderated by Peter G. Neumann of SRI International, which regularly posts notices and analyses of the dangers.

The recent rash of viral attacks has drawn everyone's attention to the more general problem of computer security, a subject of great complexity which has fascinated researchers since the early 1960s [3]. The possibility of pernicious programs propagating through a file system has been known for at least twenty-five years. In his May 1985 Computer Recreations column in *Scientific American*, Kee Dewdney documented a whole menagerie of beastly threats to information stored in computer memories, especially those of personal computers [4], where an infected diskette can transmit a virus to the main memory of the computer, and thence to any other diskette (or to hard disk). Ken Thompson, a principal designer of UNIX™, and Ian Witten have documented some of the more subtle threats to computers that have come to light in the 1980s [5, 6].

It is important to keep in mind that worms, Trojan horses, bacteria, and viruses are all programs designed by human beings. Although a discussion of these menaces brings up many intriguing technical issues, we should not forget that at the root of the problem are programmers performing disruptive acts under the cloak of anonymity conveniently provided by many computer systems.

I will focus on viruses, the most pernicious of the attacks against information in computers. A virus is a code segment that has been incorporated into the body of another program, "infecting" it. When the virus code is executed, it locates a few other uninfected programs and infects them; in due course, the number of infected programs can grow quite large. Viruses can spread with remarkable speed: in experimental work performed

How a virus works

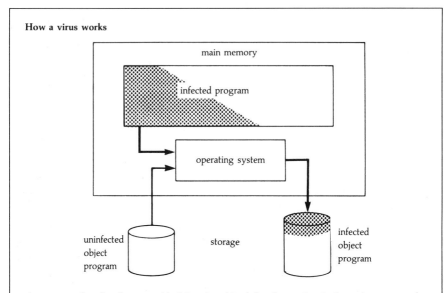

A program infected with a virus (*shaded area*) and loaded and executing in the main memory of a computer can infect another executable (object) program in the computer's operating system to append a copy of the virus code to the object program, usually at the start. The infection makes the object program slightly longer.

When the newly infected program is itself loaded into memory and invoked, the virus in it takes control and performs hidden functions, such as infecting yet other object programs. The virus may also perform destructive functions before transferring control to the original entry point. The virus code contains a marker so that the virus won't attempt to infect a program already infected by its own kind: multiple infections would cause an object file to grow ever larger, leading to easy detection.

The same principle works in personal computers, where floppy disks play the role of object programs in the description above. In this case, the virus usually attacks the copy of the operating system contained on the floppy disk so that the virus is automatically invoked whenever the disk's operating system is started. Since the operating system then resides in the PC's main memory, it can infect any diskettes inserted into the PC.

in 1983 and 1984, Fred Cohen of the University of Cincinnati demonstrated that a simple virus program can propagate to nearly every part of a normally operating computer system within a matter of hours. Most viruses contain a marker that allows them to recognize copies of themselves; this enables them to avoid discovery, because otherwise some programs would get noticeably longer under multiple infections. The destructive acts themselves come later: any copy of the virus that runs after an appointed date will perform such an unwanted function.

A Trojan horse program is the most common means of introducing a virus into a system. It is possible to rig a compiler with an invisible Trojan horse that implants another Trojan horse into any selected program during compilation.

A virus that takes the form of statements inserted into the high-level language version of a program—that is, into the source file—can possibly be detected by an expert who reads the program, but finding such an infected program in a large system can be extremely difficult. Many viruses are designed to evade detection completely by attaching themselves to object files, the machine-coded images of high-level program sources that are produced by compilation. These viruses cannot be detected from a reading of source programs.

The first serious discussions of Trojan horses took place in the 1960s. Various hardware features were developed to reduce the chances of attack [3], including virtual memory, which restricts a program to a limited region of memory, its "address space" [7]. All these features are based on the principle of least privilege, which reduces the set of accessible objects to the minimum a program needs in order to perform its function. Because a suspect program can be run in a strictly confined mode, any Trojan horse it contains will be unable to do much damage.

How effective is virtual memory against viruses? Memory protection hardware can significantly reduce the risk, but a virus can still propagate to legitimately accessible programs, including portions of the operating system. The rate of propagation may be slowed by virtual memory, but propagation is not stopped. Most PCs are especially vulnerable because they have no memory protection hardware at all; an executing program has free access to anything in memory or on disk. A network of PCs is even more vulnerable, because any PC can propagate an infected copy of a program to any other PC, no questions asked.

What can be done to protect against viruses in a computer or workstation without memory protection hardware or controls on access to files? One common proposal is to retrofit the operating system with a write query check that asks the user for permission to allow a program to modify a file. This gives the user an opportunity to determine that the program is attempting to gain access to unauthorized files. It is, unfortunately, hardly workable even for experienced programmers because of the difficulty of discovering which files a running program must legitimately modify. A design that suppresses write queries for files named in an authorization list associated with a program can be subverted by a virus that adds the name of an unauthorized file to the list before attacking it.

A more powerful immunization scheme is based on digital signatures of object files. When a program is installed in a system, an authenticator is created by producing a checksum that depends on all the bits in the file, which is then signed with the secret key of the person who stored the file [8]. The authenticator can be unlocked by applying the public key of that person. A user can confirm that a file is an exact copy of what was stored by computing its checksum and comparing that with the unlocked authenticator. A program infected by a virus would fail this test. Without access to the secret key, the designer of the virus could not produce a valid authenticator for the infected program. This scheme also works for programs obtained from trusted sources over a network: each program comes with an authenticator sealed by the trusted producer.

One way to implement this scheme is to equip the operating system with a background process that randomly checks files against their authenticators. If a virus has entered the system, this process will eventually discover an infected file and raise the alarm. Another way to implement the scheme is to "inoculate" an object program by placing an authentication subroutine at its entry point. This implementation is slow, however, and

A Trojan horse in a compiler

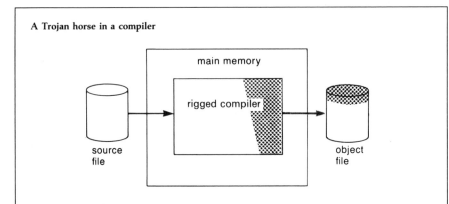

A Trojan horse is a useful program containing hidden code (*shaded area*) that performs an unwanted, mischievous function. It might copy an invoker's private files into an area of memory belonging to its own designer, thereby circumventing the invoker's file protection. It might obtain access to a subsystem normally inaccessible to the designer. A Trojan horse that destroys or erases files is also called a logic bomb.

It is sometimes suggested that Trojan horses can be detected by scanning a program's source file for statements that perform operations outside the program's specifications. Ken Thompson, one of the principal designers of UNIX™, has pointed out that this approach is fundamentally incomplete, demonstrating how to rig a compiler to introduce a Trojan horse into the object file of any other selected program, for example a login program [5]. Whenever the login program is recompiled, the rigged compiler always inserts a segment of code that allows login when a special password (known only to the Trojan horse's designer) is given. The login program's Trojan horse cannot be detected by reading its source file.

Now, it might seem that a careful reading of the rigged compiler's own source file would reveal the Trojan horse that inserts the login Trojan horse. But this is not so. The rigged compiler is itself an object file, and can thereby contain its own Trojan horse without a record in its source file. Thompson has demonstrated a scheme to rig a compiler in this way [5, 6].

can be defeated by a virus that invades entry points: by the time the authenticator gets control, the virus will already have acted.

The authenticator scheme relies on the protection of the secret key, which cannot be complete unless the key is kept outside the system. It also rests on the integrity of the system itself: for example, a sophisticated attack against the program that reports whether a file has been infected could disable this scheme.

A program called an antibody can offer limited remedies should a virus penetrate a system. Such a program examines an object file to determine whether a known virus has been incorporated. It may also remove the virus from the infected program. This limited form of protection can be very effective against known viruses, but it cannot identify new ones.

As we have seen, each of the major technical mechanisms—memory protection hardware, authenticators, and antibodies—offers limited protection against viruses (and Trojan horses). Can the operating procedures followed by those who use a computer system lower the risk further?

Yes! An additional measure of protection can be obtained by care in the way one uses a computer. Analogies with food and drug safety are helpful. Just as one would not consider purchasing food or capsules in unsealed containers or from untrusted sources, one can refuse to use any unsealed software or software from untrusted sources. Never insert a diskette that has no manufacturer's seal into your PC. Never use a program borrowed from someone who does not practice digital hygiene to your own standards. Beware of software obtained from public bulletin boards. Purchase programs that check other programs for known viruses. Be wary of public domain software (including virus eradicators!). Monitor the last-modified dates of programs and files. Don't execute programs sent in electronic mail—even your friends may have inadvertently forwarded a virus. Don't let employees bring software from home.

The problem of viruses is difficult, both technically and operationally, and no solution oriented entirely along technical and operational lines can be complete. There is a third, social dimension to the problem: we don't know how to hold people fully accountable for the actions of their programs in a networked system of computers. A complete solution must involve all three dimensions.

Computer scientists are divided over whether it serves the field to publish accounts of viral attacks in full technical detail. (This article, being superficial, does not count.) Some hold that revelations of technical detail—as in Dewdney [4] or Witten [6]—are reprehensible because they give the few would-be perpetrators a blueprint for actions that can make life exceedingly difficult for the many innocent users, and because there are few successful defenses against the attacks. Others hold that the main hope for a long-term solution is to mobilize the "good guys" by setting forth the problems in detail; the short-term risk, according to this view, is offset by the long-term gain. Most computer scientists favor this way of mobilizing forces to oppose computer sabotage.

References

1. Reid, B. (1987). Reflections on some recent widespread computer break-ins. *Commun. ACM*, 30(2): 103–5.
2. McLellan, V. (1988). Computer systems under siege. *New York Times*, 31 January, sect. 3.
3. Denning, D. E. (1982). *Cryptography and Data Security*. Addison-Wesley.
4. Dewdney, A. K. (1985). A Core War bestiary of viruses, worms and other threats to computer memories. *Sci. Am.* 252(3): 14–23.
5. Thompson, K. (1984). Computer (in)security: Infiltrating open systems. *Abacus* 4(4): 7–25.
6. Witten, I. H. (1987). Computer (in)security: Infiltrating open systems. *Abacus* 4(4): 7–25.
7. Denning, P. J. (1986). Virtual memory. *Am. Sci.* 74: 227–29.
8. Denning, P. J. (1987). Security of data in networks. *Am. Sci.* 75: 12–14.

P · A · R · T · VI

3

Computer System Reliability and Nuclear War

Alan Borning

How dependent should society be on computer systems and computer decision making? What are the cost-benefit trade-offs between the advantages of computerization (greater efficiency, speed, precision, and so forth), and the jeopardy we are in when critical computer systems break down or otherwise fail to meet our intentions? These questions arise most compellingly in the use of computers in command and control systems for nuclear weapons, and it is on such uses that this article will concentrate. In this context the problem of defining "reliability" is clearly at issue. Obviously the concept extends beyond merely keeping a system running and invades the realm of system intention or even of *what we* should *have intended—had we only known.* To what extent are we able to state and codify our intentions in computer systems so that *all* circumstances are covered? Such questions have profound implications for the entire field of computer science; they also have important practical implications about how and where it is appropriate for us to use computers in critical systems.

Computers are used extensively in military applications: for managing data on friendly and enemy forces, simulating possible battles, and aiding in the design of weapons systems, as well as for such mundane tasks as keeping track of personnel, inventories, and payrolls. Nuclear forces in particular depend heavily on computer systems to guide missiles, analyze sensor data and warn of possible attack, and control communications systems. In fact, it would be quite impossible at present to do without computers in these systems. The short warning times required by current nuclear strategies, for example, necessitate the use of computers for data anlaysis and control of communications systems. Computers also play an essential role in the monitoring systems used to verify arms control agreements and could serve an important role in the future crisis control center. Several aspects of nuclear weapons systems and strategy that interact in significant ways with computer system reliability are discussed here.

False Alerts

On several occasions, the North American Aerospace Defense Command Center (NORAD) early warning system has mistakenly indicated that Soviet missiles were headed for the United States. These incidents raise certain questions: Could a computer failure, in either the U.S. or the Soviet warning systems, start an accidental nuclear war? What risks are associated with placing the nuclear forces of one or both powers on alert? Would it be responsible for a country to adopt a policy of launch-on-warning, in which missiles would be fired based on warnings that an attack was imminent? Only the nuclear forces of the United States and the USSR are examined here, but the warning systems and nuclear forces of other countries clearly add to the problems described.

Missile Attack Warning Systems

Both the United States and the Soviet Union maintain elaborate systems for the detection of attack by enemy missiles presumed to be carrying nuclear weapons. The primary sensors include satellites that can detect the infrared signature of a burning missile engine seconds after launch, and a variety of radar systems that can detect missiles in flight. Raw sensor data from the satellites must be processed by computer; processed data are available within minutes. Intercontinental ballistic missiles (ICBMs) have a flight time of about 30 minutes from the USSR to the United States; the U.S. ballistic missile early warning radars in Alaska, Greenland, and Britain can detect such missiles within 15 minutes, about halfway into their flight. Similar times apply to missiles launched from the United States toward the Soviet Union. There are shorter flight times for missiles launched from submarines off the coast for the enemy country, or for missiles launched from Western Europe toward the Soviet Union or vice versa [70, 120].

In the United States, the command post for the missile attack warning system is at NORAD, located 1200 feet under the solid granite of Cheyenne Mountain, Colorado. Other ground stations are located elsewhere in the United States and abroad. In the Soviet Union, the Air Defense Forces are responsible for early warning of nuclear attack and for attack assessment. A central underground Air Defense command center, similar to NORAD, is reportedly located about 50 kilometers from Moscow; there is also an extensive network of satellites, missile early warning radars, and communications facilities. (See [7] and [10] for more detailed descriptions of these systems.)

June 1980

On Tuesday, June 3, 1980, at 1:26 A.M., the display system at the command post of the Strategic Air Command (SAC) at Offutt Air Force Base near Omaha, Nebraska, indicated that two submarine-launched ballistic missiles (SLBMs) were headed toward the United States. Eighteen seconds later, the system showed an increased number of SLBM launches. SAC personnel called NORAD, who stated that they had no indication of SLBM launches. After a brief period, the SAC screens cleared. Shortly thereafter, the warning display at SAC indicated that Soviet ICBMs had been launched toward the United States. Then the display at the National Military Command Center (NMCC) in the Pentagon indicated that SLBMs had been launched. The SAC duty controller directed all alert crews to move to their B-52 bombers and to start their engines, so that the planes could take off quickly and not be destroyed on the ground by a nuclear attack. Land-based missile crews were put on a higher state of alert, and battle-control aircraft prepared for flight. In Hawaii, the airborne command post of the Pacific Command took off, ready to pass messages to U.S. warships if necessary. In the meantime, a Threat Assessment Conference was convened among the top duty officers at NORAD, SAC, and NMCC.[1] For the next three minutes, there was discussion among the three officers. There were a number of factors that made them doubt that an actual attack was under way: NORAD itself had no indications of an attack, the indications on the displays at SAC and NMCC did not follow any logical pattern, and the different command posts were receiving different information. Three minutes and 12 seconds into the alert, it was canceled. It was a false alert.

NORAD left the system in the same configuration in hopes that the error would repeat itself. The mistake recurred three days later, on June 6 at 3:38 P.M., with SAC again receiving indications of an ICBM attack. Again, SAC crews were sent to their aircraft and ordered to start their engines.

The cause of these incidents was eventually traced to the failure of a 74175 integrated circuit chip in a Data General computer used as a communications multiplexer. This machine took the results of analysis of sensor data and was part of the system that transmitted it from NORAD to SAC, NMCC, and Canadian Headquarters in Ottawa. The communications links were constantly tested by means of sending filler messages. At the time of the false alerts, these filler messages had the same form as attack messages, but with a zero filled in for the number of missiles detected. The system did not use any of the standard error correction or detection schemes for these messages. When the chip failed, the system started filling in the "missiles detected" field with random digits.

These false alerts received considerable press attention at the time [3, 29, 60, 139]. As a result of the publicity, on June 20, Senators Gary Hart and Barry Goldwater were asked to investigate the incidents by Senator John Stennis, chairman of the Senate Committee on Armed Services. They prepared both classified and unclassified versions of a report; the unclassified report [64] was the principal source of information for the above account of the incident. Other relevant U.S. government documents include [26], [34], and [132].

---

[1] This is a formal step in the alert process. The successive levels of formal conferences are the Missile Display Conference, a relatively routine event; the Threat Assessment Conference, which is more serious; and the Missile Attack Conference, in which the president and all other senior personnel are brought in.

Other Incidents

The incidents of June 3 and 6, 1980, illustrate one sort of error—a hardware failure coupled with bad design—that can cause a false alert. Another incident illustrates a different realm of error: human operator error. On November 9, 1979, a test tape containing simulated attack data, used to test the missile warning system, was fed into a NORAD computer, which through human error was connected to the operational missile alert system. During the course of the ensuing six-minute alert, 10 tactical fighter aircraft were launched from bases in the northern United States and Canada, and as in the June 3 incident, a Threat Assessment Conference was convened [59, 64, 90]. (For information on other Threat Assessment Conferences during the period January 1977–May 1983 see [64] and the letter written by Col. J. H. Rix, director of adminstration at NORAD, to David C. Morrison, Center for Defense Information, Washington, D.C., November 4, 1983.)

Unsettling as the false alerts in November 1979 and June 1980 were, in the opinion of most reviewers of the incidents, including myself, the United States was nowhere near to launching its missiles and starting World War III. Most importantly, human judgment played an essential role in the procedures followed in the event of an alert, and these procedures provided enough time for the people involved to notice that a computer system was operating incorrectly. Also, NORAD procedures call for confirmation of the attack by an independent system—radar systems that observe the attacking missiles in flight, for example—and the chance of simultaneous false alerts from both systems under normal circumstances is very small.

What about similar failures in the Soviet warning systems? I have been unable to ascertain whether or not such failures have occurred, and it is unlikely that the Soviet government would choose to reveal them if they existed. For example, a recent paper on accidental nuclear war [46] by a member of the Soviet Academy of Sciences and former chairman of the State Committee for Atomic Energy of the USSR discusses U.S. warning system failures, without mentioning whether corresponding failures have occurred in the USSR. (Hints of the U.S. warning system failures were leaked to the press; the Pentagon stated that they would otherwise not have been made public [60].) At a news conference shortly after the June 1980 incident, Assistant Secretary of Defense Thomas Ross would not say whether the United States knew about similar false alerts in the USSR [60]. However, the Korean Airlines Flight 007 incident, in which a civilian aircraft was shot down by the USSR over two hours after it had entered Soviet airspace and just before it was back over international waters, would seem to indicate that the Soviet command and control system has problems. We do know that the state of the art in Soviet computer science lags several years behind that in the United States [37, 56, 124]. However, the NORAD computers are very old by computing-industry standards,[2] whereas Soviet military computers are on the leading edge of their technology [127, p. 75].

---

[2] One 1982 congressional report termed the NORAD computers "dangerously obsolete" [26]. There have been upgrades since that report: nevertheless, the five largest on-line computers at NORAD are currently Honeywell 6080s (personal communication by D. W. Kindschi, chief of the Media Relations Division of NORAD, August 23, 1984). The machines in the Honeywell 6000 series were designed in the mid 1960s primarily for batch processing [126, p. 1]. Current plans call for replacing the Honeywell machines with IBM 3083 computers in 1988 [58, p. 86–87].

Tightly Coupled Nuclear Forces

In looking at the false alert of June 3, 1980, one is struck by the widespread effects of the failure of a single integrated circuit chip: Some 100 B-52 bomber crews were directed to start their engines, a battle-control aircraft took off in Hawaii, land-based missile crews were put on a higher state of alert, and submarines were notified. It is quite possible that some of these preparations were observed by the Soviet Union. After the incident, it was feared that such Soviet observations could in turn lead them to move their forces to a higher state of readiness, causing an escalating series of alerts and moving the two powers dangerously close to war.

Pentagon officials stated that in the case of the June 3 incident there was no discernible rise in the level of Soviet readiness in response to the U.S. alert. At a news conference shortly afterwards, however, when Assistant Secretary of Defense Ross was asked about this danger of escalating responses, his reply was, "I'm going to duck that question" [60]. Similarly, at a subsequent press conference, neither Assistant Secretary of Defense Gerald Dinneen nor other officials could assure that such a chain reaction would not be caused by another false alert [91]. The start of World War I following the assassination of the archduke in Sarajevo, in which the alerts and mobilizations of the European powers interacted in just this way, is a historical precedent for this possibility [21, 93, 137].

In response to the very short time in which a nuclear war could begin, the command and control systems of both the United States and the USSR have become highly reactive; given the possibilities of interacting alerts, we can view the nuclear weapons and control systems of both countries as a *single* interacting system. (This point is discussed at length in [21] and from a more mathematical viewpoint in [15].)

During times of relative international calm, the combined U.S.–Soviet system probably has enough human checks—more abstractly, enough stability or hysteresis—to cope with a single mechanical or operator error, or perhaps even a few such errors. The situation would be different during a time of great tension or conventional war. Under such circumstances the officers monitoring the systems would be less ready to dismiss a warning as being the result of a computer error, and the danger of escalating alerts on each side would be much greater. Again taking the single-system view, in times of tension and higher states of alert, the nuclear forces of the opposing sides become more tightly coupled.

A further danger comes from the possibility of compound stimuli to the system, perhaps from ambiguous or incomplete intelligence information. Bracken [21, pp. 65–66] describes one such example that occurred in 1956, at the time of the Suez Crisis and Hungarian uprising. On the night of November 5, the following four coincidental events occurred: First, U.S. military command headquarters in Europe received an urgent message that unidentified jet aircraft were flying over Turkey. Second, there were additional reports of 100 Soviet MiG-15 fighters over Syria. Third, there was a report that a British bomber had been shot down over Syria (presumably by the MiGs). Fourth, were reports that a Russian naval fleet was moving through the Dardanelles, perhaps to leave the Black Sea in preparation for hostilities. General Andrew Goodpaster was reportedly afraid that the events "might trigger off all the NATO operations plan," which at the time called for a single massive nuclear attack on the Soviet Union.

As it turned out, all four reports were incorrect or misinterpretations of more innocent activities: The jets over Turkey turned out to be a flock of swans, the MiGs over Syria were part of an official escort for the Syrian president, the British bomber was downed by mechanical difficulties, and the Russian fleet was on a scheduled exercise. In Bracken's words, "The detection and misinterpretation of these events, against the context of world tensions from Hungary and Suez, was the first major example of how the size and complexity of worldwide electronic warning systems could, at certain critical times, create a crisis momentum of its own."

The worldwide electronic warning and communications systems of today are immensely more complex and reactive than those of 1956. As in the 1956 incident, events that are in actuality unrelated may seem to be part of a larger pattern. Once the nuclear forces are placed on alert, further human or mechanical errors may occur. After the June 3, 1980, incident, the Hart–Goldwater report notes that, "Even though the command post controller prevented any undue reaction to the false and erroneous data, there seemed to be an air of confusion following the determination that the data were erroneous." It is likely that the "air of confusion" would be much worse if it were suspected that the indications of attack might be real.

An additional complication is the growing use of computer systems for "data fusion." One defense industry manager writes, "The most challenging information problem in modern command, control, communications and intelligence (C^3I) systems is the merging of diverse data into a single, coherent representation of the tactical, operational, or strategic situation. As C^3I systems have increased in complexity and scope, manual methods of merging data are no longer adequate, resulting in the need for fully automated methods, variously referred to as data fusion, multisource correlation or multisensor integration" [138, p. 217]. The motivation for this computerization is clear. The dangers are clear as well. As the amount of data increases and the time requirements become more stringent, less and less time is available for humans to check the outputs of the computer systems. Computer systems (including current artificial intelligence systems) are notoriously lacking in common sense: The system itself will typically not indicate that something has gone amiss and that the limits of its capabilities have been exceeded. This is an important aspect of automatic systems and one to which we will return.

To be at all confident about the reliability of complex systems, there must be a period of testing under conditions of actual use. As far as is publicly known, the command and control systems of the United States and the USSR have never been "tested" under conditions of simultaneous high alert: in fact, the highest level of conference in the U.S. missile warning system, the Missile Attack Conference, has never been called [64, p. 5]. Further, in a crisis situation, the very short times available for military personnel and national leaders to react and make decisions will undoubtedly lead to poorer judgment than under more usual circumstances, increasing the chances of misinterpretation of data and of error in operation of systems [18, 50]. The combination of the untestability of the warning and control systems under highly stressed conditions and the short times available for making decisions is grounds for considerable concern.

Launch-on-Warning

Launch-on-warning is a strategy for retaliation to a nuclear attack, under which retaliatory missiles are launched in response to sensor indication that enemy missiles are on the way, before the warheads on the attacking missiles have detonated [52, 94, 109]. This strategy stands in contrast to "riding out the attack," a strategy in which a nation would absorb a nuclear strike and would retaliate only after positive verification had been obtained that an attack has taken place.[3]

Launch-on-warning makes stringent demands on a nation's nuclear weapons command and control systems. Warning data from sensors must be processed quickly, and it must be possible to relay launch orders through the command system quickly enough that missiles can be launched before the enemy missiles strike. Most importantly, the warning system must be exceedingly reliable, lest a retaliatory strike be triggered not by an enemy attack, but by computer or other error. (In recognition of this, if launch-on-warning were adopted as a strategy, it almost certainly would be activated only in times of crisis, rather than continuously [21, pp. 43–44]. Note that a policy of activation on this basis is an admission of distrust in the complete reliability of the warning systems and would result in a questionable system being activated at precisely the moment when the greatest caution was required.)

Given this danger of unintentional nuclear war, why would we consider adopting launch-on-warning? The reason is that the land-based missiles of both the United States and the Soviet Union have been growing more accurate over the years.[4] This increased missile accuracy puts at risk all fixed targets, such as land-based missile silos and command centers, even highly hardened ones. Although it is not at all certain that this vulnerability of fixed targets implies that a first strike could be successfully launched [28], strategic planners in both the United States and the USSR have nevertheless been concerned for decades with the problem. One way of dealing with it is launch-on-warning: If one side believes that an enemy attack is coming, retaliatory missiles can be launched and on their way, leaving the attacking warheads to explode on empty missile silos.

Although weapons based on submarines at sea and on aircraft are not threatened by this increasing accuracy, the present U.S. doctrine calls for all three "legs of the strategic triad" to be capable of inflicting retaliation. The risks to deterrence are more acute for the

---

[3] There are of course other strategies as well. In a launch-on-impact strategy, missiles are launched after indications have been received that at least one detonation has occurred. Launch-under-attack is defined differently by different authors: Sometimes it is used interchangeably with launch-on-warning, and sometimes to refer to a strategy that requires a high confidence confirmation that an attack is under way. This higher confidence could be based either on reports of actual detonations (see [63]), making it the same as launch-on-impact, or on information from redundant sensors (as in [52]).

[4] For example, the U.S. Minuteman III Mk 12 missile has a reported accuracy of 280 m circular error probable, whereas the older Titan II missile has an accuracy of 1300 m. Similarly, the Soviet SS-18 Mod 3 missile has an accuracy of 350 m; the older SS-11 Mod 1 an accuracy of 1400 m [70, pp. 118–119]. The Pershing II missile is even more accurate. It uses a new guidance technology in which live radar images of the landscape surrounding the target area are compared during its descent with internally stored map information, so that course corrections can be made before impact. Its accuracy is reportedly 30 m [70, p. 118]. Missiles with similarly high accuracies are scheduled for deployment on nuclear submarines as well, for example, the D-5 missile due to be deployed on the U.S. Trident II submarines starting in 1989 [122, p. 54].

Soviet Union, which has a higher proportion of its strategic nuclear weapons on land-based missiles.

Launch-on-Warning Proposals in the United States

In April 1983, the President's Commission on Strategic Forces (often referred to as the Scowcroft Commission, after its chairman, retired Air Force Lt. Gen. Brent Scowcroft) issued its report on basing alternatives for the MX missile [109]. Acting on the committee's recommendation, the Reagan administration abandoned the goal of alternate basing modes and instead proposed that MX missiles be placed in existing Minuteman silos. This of course would leave them as vulnerable to Soviet attack as the Minuteman missiles.

In May 1983, in testimony before the Senate Appropriations Committee, Secretary of Defense Caspar Weinberger and the chairman of the Joint Chiefs of Staff, Gen. John Vessey, Jr., repeatedly told the committee that MX missiles deployed in existing silos would be vulnerable to a Soviet first strike "only if we ride out the attack" without launching a retaliatory strike. Vessey also said at one point, "The Soviets have no assurance that we will ride out the attack" [63]. However, on further questioning by senators, Weinberger and Vessey refused to say whether or not the United States are moving toward a launch-under-attack strategy.

Dr. Richard Garwin, a distinguished physicist and well-known defense consultant, has advocated the implementation of a system that can reliably support a launch-under-attack capability. The system would be enabled if it were determined that the U.S. submarine force had become vulnerable. In [52] Garwin advocates a system in which a limited number (50 or so) of Minutemen III missiles would be launched if an attack were detected. These missiles could be launched unarmed, subject to an encrypted command to arm them in flight. The decision process would be entirely predetermined, with the role of the U.S. National Command Authority (NCA) limited to assessing that a massive attack was indeed under way. Garwin also discusses alternatives, such as missiles launched armed but subject to a disarm command, or missiles launched irrevocably armed. In Garwin's proposal, an attack would be determined to be under way based on information from redundant infrared satellite sensors, not from reports of impacts or even radar data.

Launch-on-Warning Proposals in the Soviet Union

The Soviet Union has considered launch-on-warning as well, in particular as a threatened response to the Pershing II missile deployment by the NATO countries in Europe [41, 42, 140]. However, in a March 1983 statement, former Soviet Defense Minister Dmitri Ustinov categorically denied that the Soviets were adopting launch-on-warning [53]. While the political motivation behind these statements is clear, there appear to be real military issues as well. The Soviets would have 12 minutes or less from the time Pershing II missiles were launched until they hit [123, p. 46]. (Whether the current Pershing IIs could reach the command and control centers around Moscow is a matter of debate [122, p. 8].) The problem of short missile flight times is not new—missiles from Polaris submarines in the Arctic Ocean have been able to strike the Soviet Union since the 1960s —but the coupling of such short flight times with great accuracy is new.

More recently, Ustinov stated that the Soviet Union had increased the number of its nuclear-armed submarines off the U.S. coasts, to threaten the United States with more missiles with short flight times [110]. Although not the threatened response of launch-on-warning, in light of the previous discussion of tightly coupled forces, this action clearly has its dangers as well.

Discussion of Launch-on-Warning

Because of public perception of the risk of disaster due to computer or other error, the formal adoption of a launch-on-warning policy has always been controversial. Those authors who do advocate it do not appear to pay a great deal of attention to these dangers, particularly to the problems of very complex systems, short reaction times, and unanticipated events. For example, consider Garwin's discussion of accidental launch [52, pp. 124–125]:

> Launch under attack seems to present no more hazard of unauthorized or accidental launch than does the present system . . . .
>
> [The problem of an unauthorized launch] may be addressed by the use of PAL (permissive action links) in the silo and in the warhead. There are cryptographic safeguards which could be borrowed from modern message-security systems, which are adequate for the transmission of millions of characters per day with assurance against being "read" (deciphered) even if all the message traffic is intercepted by an enemy. These same systems could be used to encipher a short (20-digit) "go-code," receipt of which would cause the warhead to arm, while receipt of another go-code of similar length would fire the missile, having opened the silo door, and so on. The probability of accidental launch can be calculated as the number of candidate signals per year, times the likelihood that any one will be interpreted as a real go-code. Presumably very few putative go-codes would be received per year (the expected number is less than one per year, caused by lightning, electrical noise, or the like). If 1000 per minute were received, the pure-chance firing of the missiles would shorten the average human life by less than 0.1 seconds, even if only a single 20-digit code sufficed (and not 2, as assumed). For some cosmic-scale troublemaker to steal the actual go-code and so mimic the NCA launch order to the ICBM force, or bypass the wiring in the missile silos, is little different from what could be done now without a launch-under-attack system.
>
> . . . Only a limited number (say, 50) of Minutemen need or should be launched— unarmed, subject to command-arm in flight. One hopes that launch under attack will never occur inappropriately, in response to false indication of sensors, or other cause. Should such an unwarranted launch occur, however, we would prefer not to have armed the missiles, nor would we want to disarm ourselves by having launched the entire ICBM force, which would thus be lost to our future capability.

Some would argue that there are a number of important omissions in Garwin's analysis. The calculation of the probability of a randomly generated valid go-code, while correct in a narrow sense, is most misleading, as it ignores the host of other things that might go wrong. In Garwin's proposal, for example, the doctrine of dual phenomenology would be abandoned, so that a retaliatory strike would be launched based only on data from one kind of sensor, rather than two as at present. The discussion of launching missiles unarmed, subject to a command to arm them in flight, does not treat the real danger that the Soviet Union would observe the 50 missiles headed toward their territory and launch a retaliatory strike.

As mentioned previously, the formal adoption of a launch-on-warning policy—a declaration that launch-on-warning is the preferred response in a crisis—has always been controversial. Nevertheless, it appears that it is and has been regarded as an option by both the United States and the USSR. According to testimony by General Ellis of the U.S. Strategic Air Command [135, p. 3834],

> launch on warning is an option we have and must maintain. It remains a useful option because the enemy cannot be certain it will not be used or know the conditions under which it would be used . . . and therefore, he must always make it a part of his planning deliberations.

This is corroborated by recent testimony by General Herres, commander in chief, NORAD [134, p. 72]. A recent book on the U.S. Single Integrated Operating Plan (SIOP) for waging nuclear war states that launch-on-warning has *always* been an option in the SIOP [102, pp. 187–188]. More alarmingly, Bruce Blair, a former launch control officer and DoD official, has testified [134, pp. 32–34]

> declatory doctrine is a poor guide to actual employment doctrine. At present, we are operationally geared for launch on warning, a reflection of the low confidence we have in our ability to absorb the brunt of an attack before retaliating . . . . I restress the fact that the United States relies heavily on launch on warning for positive control, for force coordination and for retaliation. Fortunately, our tactical warning system on which launch on warning depends is fairly fault tolerant. But again, it is not as tolerant as it should be to justify U.S. reliance on it.

Launch-on-warning is the subject of a current lawsuit,[5] in which the plaintiff complains that the secretary of defense is presently operating a launch-on-warning capability. This operation, according to the suit, unconstitutionally unsurps the power of Congress to declare war, and unlawfully delegates presidential powers to subordinates, since the very short times involved would not allow time for a decision by the president.

Regarding the Soviet Union, a DoD publication [129, p. 20] states

> launch-under-attack circumstances would place the greatest stress on attack warning systems and launch coordination. To meet this demand, the Soviets have established a satellite-based ICBM launch detection system, built an over-the-horizon radar missile launch detection system to back up the satellites and have large phased-array radars ringing the U.S.S.R. These warning devices could give the Soviet leadership time to launch their forces after an enemy strike had been launched. To prepare for this possibility, the Soviets practice launching weapons under stringent time constraints.

Because of the very short times involved, there is doubt that launch-on-warning is a practical policy [120], since it would be difficult to maintain an acceptable level of control on the nuclear forces of the country that adopted it. From a broader viewpoint, launch-on-warning can be seen as one point on a spectrum of policies for retaliation, the dimension of the spectrum being how long a country waits to respond when it believes that an attack is imminent or under way. Taking this broader view, pressures toward launch-on-warning are actually a symptom of underlying problems. Among these problems are (1) the

---

[5] Johnson v. Secretary of Defense, U.S. District Court, San Francisco, Calif., case C86 3334.

strategic doctrine that holds that military assets at known, fixed locations (land-based ICBMs and command posts) are an essential part of a nation's nuclear forces, (2) the perception that the vulnerability of these fixed targets is a pressing problem, (3) new weapons systems that make them more vulnerable, and (4) the consequent decrease in time available to make decisions in nuclear crises. (See [120] for a longer treatment of this viewpoint.)

The Reliability of Complex Systems

Would it be responsible for either the USSR or the United States to adopt weapons systems and policies that assume that computer systems, such as missile warning systems, can function without failure? I argue that it is not. I will not attempt to prove that failures will occur in complex military systems, but rather I will attempt to show that there is considerable doubt that adequate reliability can be achieved. The standard of reliability required of a military system that can potentially help precipitate a thermonuclear war if it fails must be higher than that of *any* other computer system, since the magnitude of disaster is so great.

Techniques for Building Reliable Systems

Much research and development effort has been devoted to the construction of reliable computer systems, and some impressive results have been achieved. As a comprehensive treatment of this topic is well beyond the scope of this article, an outline of some well-known techniques for achieving reliability is presented, along with references to the literature, with particular emphasis on military computer systems.

Hardware. At the hardware level, one obvious technique is to use very reliable components. Here the large body of knowledge about quality control for other kinds of manufacturing can be applied, including quality control of raw materials, testing and tracking each component produced, destructively testing a certain percentage of the devices, and keeping records of the reliability of components produced by a particular line to spot variations in reliability. The MIL-SPEC program codifies standards for many kinds of devices that the military procures. In addition, the DoD has funded much work on building models of component reliability, such as the widely used MIL-HDBK-217C reliability model for estimating the failure rate for various kinds of integrated circuit chips [125]. Above the chip level, techniques for building reliable devices include component burn-in, careful signal routing, shielding, cabinet grounding, environmental controls, power supply regulation, and other conservative, well-established design practices.

Regardless of the methods used, in a very large system it is unreasonable to expect that every component will be totally reliable. For this reason, a body of techniques has been accumulated that allow a system to continue functioning even when individual components fail. These techniques all involve redundancy, and include n-modular redundancy with voting, error-correcting codes, and dynamically reconfigurable systems.

Complementing this work on the construction of reliable hardware has been development of modeling techniques; useful measures include mean time to failure, mean time to detection, mean time to repair, and availability. More information on hardware reliability, along with an extensive bibliography, may be found in [111]; [31] is a review of techniques for achieving hardware fault tolerance.

Software. For large computer systems, the cost and complexity of the software typically dominate that of the hardware. To construct a very complex system at all, let alone to make it reliable, a disciplined approach is necessary. An extensive set of sources discussing the software development process is available. Texts on software engineering include [19, [47], [71], and [115]; these have references to many other sources, including seminal papers on software engineering in the literature.

It is generally accepted that reliability cannot be "tested into" a software system: it is necessary to plan for reliability at all points in the development process. As with hardware, the DoD has codified standards for how its software is to be specified, designed, written, and tested. One such standard is *DOD-STD-2167: Military Standard Defense System Software Development* [131], for the development of mission-critical software. It specifies such things as software requirements analysis standards, coding standards, and the information that must be gathered on software trouble reports. In addition, other administrative requirements may be imposed, such as formal requirements for a contractor's Quality Assurance Program (MIL-STD-1535) and requirements for configuration control (DOD-STD-480). Formal reviews of the software development process are required at each stage by DoD directives. As enumerated in [2, p. 186], these are

- a *Systems Requirements Review,*
- a *System Design Review,*
- a *Preliminary Design Review,*
- a *Critical Design Review,*
- a *Functional Configuration Audit,*
- a *Physical Configuration Audit,* and
- a *Formal Qualification Review.*

The DoD will typically contract with a company (other than the software contractor) to assist it with some of these reviews.

Testing is not simply performed at the end of coding, but rather must be planned and developed in parallel with the software system itself. A typical contractual requirement would be that, for every item in the system specification, a corresponding test be performed to check that the software meets each specification. Even after the system is installed, the set of tests should be kept and updated as well, so that, as the system is modified during maintenance, previous tests can be rerun to check that the system still meets them (regression testing). More information on software reliability, safety, quality assurance, testing, and validation may be found in [2], [5], [40], [68], [77], [81], and [82].

Quantifying software reliability. Two kinds of software quality measures are in general use: estimates of the number of errors remaining in a program, and estimates of the mean time to failure (MTTF) of a system. Angus [6] describes the application of six models of the first sort to a major C^3I system, with poor results. Regarding estimates of MTTF, Currit, Dyer, and Mills [36] describe a procedure for producing a certified estimate of the MTTF of a system, using statistical testing.

Any estimate of the errors remaining in a program requires a complete specification against which the program can be compared. The testing regimes assume either that the testers know what kinds of inputs the system will be subjected to, or that the system can be extensively tested under conditions of actual use. (Even then, a problem with statistical testing is that it takes prohibitively long to obtain high confidence that the errors found are manifested only rarely.) The importance of these limitations will be discussed later in this article.

Sources of System Failure

The sources of computer system failure include incorrect or incomplete system specifications, hardware failure, hardware design errors, software coding errors, software design errors, and human error (such as incorrect equipment operation or maintenance). Particularly with complex, normally highly reliable systems, a failure may be caused by some unusual *combination* of problems from several of these categories.

Hardware failures are perhaps the most familiar cause of system failures, as in the NORAD failures of June 1980. As noted previously, individual components can be made very reliable by strict quality control and testing, but in a large system it is unreasonable to expect that no component will ever fail, and other techniques that allow for individual component failures must be used. However, when one builds very complex systems —and a command and control system in its entirety is certainly an example of a complex system—one becomes less certain that one has anticipated all the possible failure modes, that all the assumptions about independence are correct. A serious complicating factor is that the redundancy techniques that allow for individual component failures themselves add additional complexity and possible sources of error to the system.

Another potential cause of failure is a hardware design error. Again, the main source of problems is not the operation of the system under the usual, expected sets of events, but its operation when *unexpected* events occur. For example, timing problems due to an unanticipated set of asynchronous parallel events that seldom occurs are particularly hard to find.

It is in the nature of computer systems that much of the system design is embodied in the computer's software. Errors may be introduced at any of the steps in its production: requirements specification, design, implementation, testing and debugging, or maintenance.

Errors in the system requirements specification are perhaps the most pernicious. It is at this level that the system's connection with the outside world is expressed; we must therefore anticipate *all* the circumstances under which the system might be used and describe in the requirements specification what action it should take under those circumstances. For a very complex system, it is unrealistic to imagine that one can foresee all of these circumstances. We can have confidence in such systems only after they have been tested for a considerable time under conditions of actual use.

Errors may also be introduced when the requirements are translated into a system design, as well as when the design is translated into an actual computer program. Again, the sheer complexity of the system is itself a basic cause of problems. Anyone who has worked on a large computer system knows how difficult it is to manage the development process; usually, there is *nobody* who understands the entire system completely. Given a complete requirements document, however, many of the errors at these levels can be prevented by using strategies such as modular design, information hiding, and the like; also, a wider range of automated tools is available to help us detect which parts of the program affect which other parts. Nevertheless, it is widely acknowledged that the process is not completely satisfactory.

The cost of maintenance usually dominates the other costs of military software development. Program maintenance, either to fix bugs or to satisfy new system requirements, is itself a frequent source of errors. Meyers [81, p. 252], for instance, states that "experience has shown that fixes have a high probability (usually from 20 to 50 percent) of introducing a *new* error into the program."

Another source of failure is human operator error. People do make mistakes, despite elaborate training and precautions, especially in time of stress and crisis. Dumas [44] cites some worrying statistics about alcohol, drug abuse, and aberrant behavior among military personnel with access to nuclear weapons. Alcoholism is a major health problem in the Soviet Union and may be a problem among such personnel in the Soviet military as well [32].

Some Instructive Failures

There have been some impressive failures of computer (and other) systems designed to be reliable, and it is instructive to look at a few of these. I have attempted to categorize these failures using the sources of failure listed in the previous section; however, as will be seen, these failures often arise from a combination of errors.

Examples of failures due to hardware errors include the NORAD false alerts described earlier. (However, it could also be said that these false alerts are illustrations of hardware design errors instead, in that it is a grave oversight that such critical data should have been sent without using parity, cyclic redundancy, or other checks.) From a technical point of view, a more interesting and complex failure was the total collapse of a U.S. computer communications network (the ARPANET) in October 1980 due to an unusual hardware malfunction that caused a high-priority process to run wild and devour resources needed by other processes [107]. The ARPANET was designed to be highly available—the intent of the software design was that it should prevent a single hardware malfunction from being able to bring down the whole network. It was only after several years of operation that this problem manifested itself.

The launch of the first space shuttle was delayed at the last minute by a software problem. For reliability, the shuttle used four redundant primary avionics computers, each running the same software, along with a fifth backup computer running a different system. In the incident, a patch to correct a previous timing bug opened a 1 in 67 probability window that, when the system was turned on, the computers would not be properly synchronized. There are a number of noteworthy features of this incident: First, despite great attention to reliability in the shuttle avionics, there was still a software failure;

second, this particular problem arose from the additional complexity introduced by the redundant systems designed to achieve reliability; and third, the bug was introduced during maintenance to fix a previous problem. Garman [51] gives a detailed account of the incident, along with some pithy observations on the problems of complex software systems in the real world.

There are many examples of errors arising from incorrect or incomplete specifications. One such example is a false alert in the early days of the nuclear age [16, 69, 89], when on October 5, 1960, the warning system at NORAD indicated that the United States was under massive attack by Soviet missiles with a certainty of 99.9 percent. It turned out that the Ballistic Missile Early Warning System (BMEWS) radar in Thule, Greenland, had spotted the *rising moon*. Nobody had thought about the moon when specifying how the system should act.

Gemini V splashed down 100 miles from its intended landing point because a programmer had implicitly ignored the motion of the earth around the sun—in other words, had used an incorrect model [49, pp. 187–188]. In 1979 five nuclear reactors were shut down after the discovery of an error in the program used to predict how well the reactors would survive in earthquakes [87]. One subroutine, instead of taking the sum of the absolute values of a set of numbers, took their arithmetic sum instead.[6] In 1983 severe flooding along the lower Colorado River killed six persons and caused millions of dollars in damage. The governor of Nevada stated that this was caused by a "monumental mistake" in federal computer projections of snow melt-off flow, so that too much water was kept dammed prior to spring thaws [92].

ACM SIGSOFT Software Engineering Notes is a good place to find descriptions of real-world computer problems, catastrophic and otherwise (e.g., see [88]). See also [102] for a listing of some other incidents.

In hindsight, the blame for each of the above incidents can be assigned to individual component failures, faulty design, or specific human errors, as is almost always the case with such incidents. In designing automatic systems, we must anticipate all possible eventualities and specify what should happen in all cases. The real culprit is simply the complexity of the systems, and our inability to anticipate and plan for all of the things that can go wrong.

Outside of the realm of computer systems, incidents such as the tragic explosion of the space shuttle *Challenger* in 1986, the accidents at the nuclear power plants at Chernobyl in 1986 and Three Mile Island (TMI) in 1979, and the 1965 northeast power blackout are sobering reminders of the limitations of technology.

At Chernobyl, operators deliberately disabled warning and safety mechanisms so that they could conduct an experiment, with the catastrophic result of two explosions at the plant and the release of enormous amounts of radioactive material. The TMI accident began with an equipment failure (of a pressurizer relief valve), but its severity was

---

[6] It is not clear whether this should be classified as an error in the specification or in the program—probably there *was* no separate formal specification or model, so that the program itself became the model.

compounded by subsequent operator error [106].[7] In another nuclear reactor accident, at Browns Ferry in Alabama in 1975, a single failure—a fire in an electrical cable tray—disabled a large number of redundant systems designed to ensure safety at the plant. This incident demonstrates that one should look with a skeptical eye at calculations indicating extremely low probabilities for failure due to independent systems.

Prospects for Military Computer System Reliability

What are the prospects for the reliability of military computer systems in the future?

Clearly, substantial improvements in the reliability of systems like NORAD are possible simply by using state-of-the-art hardware and software engineering techniques: A system that uses 1960s vintage computers or that as recently as 1980 transmitted critical data with no parity checks is not state-of-the-art. Nor are these isolated incidents. The World-Wide Military Command and Control System (WWMCCS) has been plagued with problems of inadequate performance, cost overruns, and poor management [22]. In the 1977 PRIME TARGET exercises, for example, only 38 percent of the attempts to use the system were successful [33, p. 51]. There are also problems with personnel training and preparation. A recent book by Daniel Ford [48, p. 21] describes an incident in which Ford asked Gen. Paul Wagoner, at the time in charge of NORAD combat operations, to demonstrate the special black telephone that provides a direct link to the NMCC. This telephone would be used, for instance, for a Missile Attack Conference. Wagoner picked up the phone—and nothing happened. His subsequent explanation was that, "I didn't know that I had to dial '0' to get the operator." (See [17] for further discussion of the deficiencies of the current U.S. command and control system. Kling [75] discusses computer system, points out the inadequacies of describing such systems in isolation, and advocates the use of "web models" as an appropriate tool for describing such systems.)

This is not to say that there have been *no* improvements in these systems—a good example of a positive step has been the installation of Permissive Action Links (PALs) on all U.S. nuclear weapons except SLBMs [83, p. 52]. The PAL system requires that a code be received from a higher authority before a nuclear weapon can be armed, thus reducing the probability of unauthorized use.

Nevertheless, substantial improvements are possibly using existing state-of-the-art technology. What are the practical and theoretical limits of reliability, now and in the next decade?

In regard to the practical limits of reliability, most professional programmers today do not use such software engineering techniques as structured programming, modularity and information hiding, cooperating sequential processes, or formal program semantics [96]. The DoD is engaged in several efforts to develop new technology for software production and to make it widely available to military contractors [78]. The STARS (Software Technology for Adaptable, Reliable Systems) program [43, 128] and the Software Engineering Institute at Carnegie-Mellon University are examples. Large organizations

---

[7] See also [100] and [101] for a discussion of the TMI incident as a "normal accident"—an unanticipated accident in a complex, tightly coupled system. This "normal accident" viewpoint is also applicable to other complex systems such as nuclear weapons command and control systems.

move slowly, and it will be some years (at least) before these newer software engineering techniques are generally adopted. Use of these techniques should decrease, but not eliminate, errors in moving from the specification to the program.

Program maintenance, as noted previously, is itself a frequent source of errors. This problem is further aggravated by the fact that program maintenance is presently regarded as one of the least desirable programming jobs and is often assigned to junior or less-skilled employees. Programming support environments that keep track of versions, note the effects of changes, and the like are becoming available [12, 66]. Eventually, the use of these tools should help decrease the number of errors introduced during maintenance.

In the long term, formal techniques such as proofs of program correctness (program verification), automatic programming, and proofs of design consistency have been advocated as tools for improving computer system reliability. In a proof of program correctness, either a human or a computer proves mathematically that a program meets a formal specification of what it should do. In automatic programming, the program is written automatically from the specification. In a proof of design consistency, the proof must show that a formal specification satisfies a set of requirements, for example, for security or fault tolerance. (The difference between requirements and specifications in this case is generally that the former tend to be simply stated global properties, whereas the latter tend to be detailed sets of constraints defined functionally on state transitions or algebraically on inputs and outputs.)

In theory, these techniques could produce programs or designs guaranteed to meet their specifications. Some practical use is being made of design proof techniques, primarily in proving security properties of system designs, although such proofs are still nontrivial. Thus, one might prove that, within the computer, information cannot flow in the wrong direction in a multilevel security system.[8] Proofs about program correctness, however, are very much in the research stage. For example, simple compilers have been proved correct, but programs of the complexity of the real-time satellite data analysis programs are well beyond the state-of-the-art. Automatic programming is even less advanced. A useful reference discussing program verification is [20]; for an up-to-date collection of papers on verification, see [8]. The current state of automatic programming is discussed in [99]; discussions of future applications of automatic programming to software engineering may be found in [11] and [13]. In [97] Parnas critiques the possible roles that automatic programming and program verification could play in the production of software for ballistic missile defense.

The hardest and most intractable problem in the construction of software for complex tasks, such as command and control systems, is specifying what the system should do. *How does one know that the specification itself is correct, that is, that it describes what one intends?* Are there events that may occur that were simply not anticipated when the specification was written? Program verification and automatic programming techniques can offer no help here. A proof of correctness, for example, simply shows that one formal

---

[8] Design proofs have been done successfully in the SCOMP kernel [112], while other relevant properties have been proved about the trusted code that runs on top of the kernel [14].

description (the specification) is equivalent to another formal description (the program). It does not say that the specification meets the perhaps unarticulated desires of the user, nor does it say anything about how well the system will perform in situations never imagined when the specification was written. For example, in the 1960 false alert, proving that the system met its specifications would not help if nobody thought about the rising moon when writing the specifications. (The term *proof of correctness* is thus a misnomer —a better term might be *proof of relative consistency*. This point is discussed at length in [113].)

Both the practical and theoretical limits of reliability bump up against this problem of specification. It constitutes the major long-term practical barrier to constructing reliable complex systems. From a theoretical point of view, depending on the language used to express the specification, it may be possible to prove that it has certain properties, for example, that it is self-consistent or that, given a set of possible inputs, the action to be taken for each of these inputs is specified. However, the answers to such critical questions as, "Will the system do what we reasonably expect it to do?" or "Are there external events that we just didn't think of?" lie inherently outside the realm of formal systems.

On Testing

To be at all confident of the reliability of complex systems, there must be a period of testing under conditions of actual use. Simulations, analyses of possible modes of failure, and the like can each expose some problems, but all such tests are limited by the fact that the designers test for exactly those circumstances that they anticipate may occur.[9] It is the *unexpected* circumstances and interactions that cause the most severe problems.

Some problems, like spotting the rising moon, will be uncovered quickly when the system is in routine operation. However, the conditions under which command and control systems for nuclear forces are expected to function include not just peacetime, but also times of international tension and high alert. It is these latter situations that are of the most concern. Short of having many periods of great tension and high alert—clearly an unacceptably dangerous proposition—the nuclear weapons command and control systems simply cannot be tested completely. The most extreme situation in which, under current doctrine, these systems are expected to function is that of limited or protracted nuclear war; this topic is discussed in the next section.

A final issue is that systems in flux are more prone to problems than those that have remained stable for some time. As noted above, program maintenance is a frequent source of errors. Better programming environments will help eliminate some of these errors, but such errors also arise from changing specifications, in which some loophole or problem in the specification is introduced by other changes. If the arms race continues unabated, due to the changing nature of the weapons and their deployment, the specifications for the command and control systems for nuclear forces will necessarily be changing as well.

---

[9] See [121] for an interesting although dated discussion of how the NORAD system was tested, including simulated battle exercises.

Limited or Protracted Nuclear War

In this section a number of issues concerning limited or protracted nuclear war are examined. Many of the technical issues that arise concern the physical survival of computers and communications lines; there are also implications for the software that must run in such an environment.

Nuclear Strategy

Deterrance theory states that, to prevent nuclear war, each opponent must have nuclear weapons systems, strategies for using them, and the perceived will to retaliate in the event that deterrence fails [85]. One policy to implement deterrance is "mutual assured destruction" (MAD): An attack by one side would result in massive retaliation by the other, essentially resulting in mutual suicide.

Many strategists have long been dissatisfied with MAD. A fundamental problem is that, if the Soviet Union commits a very aggressive act that is short of an all-out attack, the president's only options are to do nothing or to launch an all-out attack (which would doubtless lead the Soviets to do the same). For this reason, there has been an evolution toward plans that include more flexible options (selective targeting of enemy nuclear forces, conventional forces, military and political leadership, communications facilities, industrial targets, and cities), and capabilities to fight limited or protracted nuclear wars. For example, directives issued under the Carter administration (such as Presidential Directive 59) called for provision of a wide variety of responses following a nuclear attack; a major change was the requirement to support fighting a protracted nuclear war, lasting perhaps months rather than days [7, pp. 459–460]. A more recent document from the Reagan administration, "Fiscal Year 1984–1988 Defense Guidance," which was leaked to the press in May 1982 [61], goes beyond PD-59 in recommendations for preparing for a protracted nuclear war. The document states that "the United States nuclear capabilities must prevail even under the conditions of a prolonged nuclear war" and that U.S. nuclear forces "must prevail and be able to force the Soviet Union to seek earliest termination of hostilities on terms favorable to the United States" [62].

According to a basic Soviet text, *Soviet Military Strategy* by Marshal V. D. Sokolovskiy [114, p. 279], "Apparently, in a nuclear war a victory can be counted upon only if the basic power is used in the shortest possible period . . . . At the same time, the possibility of a relatively protracted nuclear war cannot be excluded." Similarly, a DoD publication [129, p. 20] states that "the Soviets appear to believe that nuclear war might last for weeks, even months, and have factored this into their force development." Testimony before the Armed Services Committee, U.S. Senate [136, p. 2491], supports the view that both the United States and the USSR are building systems to support fighting a limited nuclear war.

These moves toward a capability to fight limited or protracted nuclear wars have been controversial. As described above, some strategists argue that, to maintain an effective deterrent, we must plan for nuclear conflict at any level of violence, and that we must plan for ways to control such a conflict if it breaks out at a level below an all-out attack [84, pp. 94–97]. Others maintain that, although some flexibility in response is essential, the sorts of carefully controlled responses now being planned deceive us into believing that nuclear war *can* be successfully controlled [84, pp. 130–131]. Taking this latter viewpoint, if leaders believe that nuclear war can be controlled, then, for example, in a severe crisis they may be less reluctant to launch a small tactical strike, thus making nuclear war more likely. More extensive discussions of deterrence and nuclear war strategies—and a variety of viewpoints—can be found in [54], [57], [67], [72], [73], [74], and [85].

Command, Control, and Communications System Requirements

Different strategies make different demands on a nation's command, control, and communications (C^3) system. Listed below are some basic attributes of a C^3 system that are governed by the choice of strategy:

- the length of time the system needs to survive during and after nuclear attacks of various scales,
- the amount of information that needs to be transmitted from the NCA to the nuclear forces.
- the amount of information that needs to be transmitted from the field back to the NCA, and
- the facilities for communicating with the enemy during and after the war.

How long does the C^3 system need to survive during and after nuclear attacks of various scales? The problem of C^3 vulnerability, analogous to the problem of land-based missile vulnerability, has begun to be widely discussed. One extreme position would be that the C^3 does not need to survive an attack at all: Retaliatory missiles would be launched on warning, obviating the need for both survivable missiles and communications systems. As previously discussed, such a policy would be quite dangerous. Blair [17, pp. 289–295] proposes as a long-term goal for the United States a quite different policy: "no immediate second use." Under such a policy, authority to conduct offensive operations would be withheld for 24 hours after a Soviet attack. Such a policy would lead to much greater stability in a crisis: the obvious question is whether the U.S. C^3 system could survive that long to permit an order to retaliate to be issued. (Survival of the weapons themselves is less of a problem, since submarine-based missiles have the desired characteristics.)

Another issue is how much information needs to be transmitted from the NCA to the nuclear forces, and how much information needs to be gathered from military installations and possible civilian targets and transmitted back to the NCA. Under a policy of MAD, a minimal amount of information needs to be transmitted from the NCA to the nuclear forces: 1 bit, along with authentication codes. No information need be transmitted in the other direction.

However, under policies that include flexible responses to various kinds of attacks, greater communications bandwidth from the NCA to the fighting units is required; further, information must move in the other direction as well, so that the NCA can receive damage reports, current warning information, and intelligence reports to use in deciding further responses. Preparing to fight a protracted nuclear war makes even greater demands on C^3 systems, which would have to survive for days or months through a nuclear war. The "Fiscal Year 1984–1988 Defense Guidance" document, for example, calls for C^3 systems that "provide the capability to execute ad hoc plans, even subsequent to repeated attacks . . . in particular, these systems should support the reconstitution and execution of strategic reserve forces, specifically full communications with our strategic submarines." A recent report by the U.S. secretary of defense to the Congress [141, p. 195] tends to confirm these plans:

> Our C^3 systems must be able to provide our leaders the information they need to assess the size and scope of an attack, determine an appropriate response, and issue initial retaliatory orders. These systems also must be able to ensure that our forces would receive those orders, called emergency action messages (EAMs), and remain responsive to national authority both during and after an attack.
>
> Strategic C^3 systems must be able to operate reliably under the extremely stressful conditions of a nuclear conflict . . . . The FY 1985–89 program will improve our strategic C^3 systems—sensors, command centers, and communications—by upgrading and augmenting their capabilities, increasing their mobility, protecting essential equipment against nuclear effects, and providing alternate and redundant methods of communication.

The nature of the facilities for communicating with the enemy during and after the war is also at issue. If a limited nuclear war strategy is to be pursued, a means to communicate with the enemy to call a cease-fire or to terminate the conflict is important. Theorists of nuclear war have described scenarios in which there would be a kind of communication by attacking or holding back attacks on given targets, but it is not clear that the signals would be interpreted correctly, or that in the emotion and tension of the war, the leaders of each country would react with the calm rationality assumed by these scenarios. Further, such theories require that the facilities for receiving damage reports and sending out new commands to the fighting units work extremely reliably during the conflict.

Prospects for C^3 System Reliability during a Nuclear War

Both the strategies of delayed and of flexible response require C^3 systems that can survive for some period in a nuclear conflict. Even if C^3 systems were built as well as we knew how, this requirement would be difficult to meet. Blasts destroy control centers and communications apparatus. Particularly when detonated high in the atmosphere, thermonuclear warheads can create an electromagnetic pulse (EMP), a strong electric field (up to 50,000 volts per meter) that can cripple computer equipment, communications and power lines, and other electrical and electronic apparatus [17, 23–25, 55, 118]. For example, after a 1962 test in the South Pacific, 800 miles away in Hawaii streetlights failed, burglar alarms started ringing, and circuit breakers opened. Modern integrated circuits are much more sensitive to these effects than are door bells and circuit breakers. Since the 1963 Limited Test Ban Treaty, which stopped atmospheric testing, data on EMP has been derived from EMP simulators, computer simulations, and underground weapons tests (obvious a different environment from a high-altitude airburst). Also, the electronic devices of today have changed greatly since 1963.

It is possible to harden electronic apparatus against EMP using a variety of techniques [39, 104, 105], for example, by enclosing it in a Faraday cage (a metal shield). (The wires to the outside world, which must pierce the cage, are a harder problem.) Another and less attractive technique is to use less sophisticated technologies, which are in general more resistant to EMP effects—for example, vacuum tubes rather than integrated circuits. Some systems, such as long transmission lines or the large antennas needed for the very low frequency transmissions used to communicate with submarines, are inherently vulnerable, although one can add circuitry to isolate them from other components in the system. Further, in the current U.S. C^3 system there are many components that are not hardened; it would be prohibitively expensive to harden the entire system. There is clearly no way of testing the entire system short of an actual battle to find out how much of it would survive.

The status of the C^3 systems of the Soviet Union in regard to EMP hardening is debated among defense strategists [23]. However, EMP is at some level a threat to the Soviet systems as well, with its vast array of computers, communications lines, antennas, power stations, and so forth.

In addition to EMP, there are other effects of radiation on integrated circuits, including total dose effects that can cause some integrated circuits to break down on exposure to 500 rads, and transient effects that can wipe out computer memories or cause semiconductor components to go into an abnormal conducting state [76]. Again, there are techniques to mitigate these effects, for example, by using technologies that are inherently harder, such as integrated circuits based on gallium arsenide rather than silicon. However, as with EMP effects, there is clearly no way of realistically testing the entire system short of actual warfare.

A number of authorities have stated that the current U.S. C^3 system is deficient in regard to survivability (see, e.g., [17, 30, 48, 142]); some authors have gone further and stated that the current system is so vulnerable that a Soviet strike on communications facilities could wipe out the ability for the NCA to issue an order to retaliate.[10]

Limited nuclear war strategies put a greater burden on C^3 systems than do delayed retaliation strategies. Whether or not *any* C^3 system could support fighting a limited and centrally controlled nuclear war is a question hotly debated by experts in the field. Some experts assert that, although difficult, this is a goal worth pursuing: To maintain an effective deterrant, we must plan for nuclear conflict at any level of violence, and we must plan for ways to control such a conflict if it breaks out at a level below an all-out attack. For example, Charles Zraket, an executive vice-president of MITRE Corporation, writes, "The United States can achieve reliable deterrence only if it can ensure that it can retaliate discriminately and end a nuclear war as quickly as possible. Without this, deterrence is at the mercy of provocative rhetoric, threats of mutually assured destruction (MAD), or suicidal attacks" [142, p. 1306]. On the other hand, other experts, such as Desmond Ball,

---

[10] It does not necessarily follow, however, that there would be no retaliation: in a crisis, forces might be put in a "fail-deadly" mode: If there was no communication for some period of time, retaliatory missiles would be launched. Such plans, if they exist, are highly classified. Some discussion of what such plans might be like may be found in Bracken [21]. On the same topic, former Secretary of Defense Harold Brown writes, "But a submarine-based missile could wipe out Washington with no more than ten minutes' warning, perahps less. It is inappropriate to go into the details of the arrangements that have been made for such contingencies and thus suggest to the Soviets how to get around those arrangements. But one criterion for such arrangements ought properly to be that a decapitating attack should have the effect of making the response an all-out, unrestrained one" [27, p. 79].

believe that the construction of a C^3 system to support fighting a limited nuclear war is not a reasonable option and should not be pursued [9, p. 38]. Supposing these latter experts are correct, then if a superpower attempts to fight a limited nuclear war, a likely outcome would be disconnected forces—each relying on its own damage assessments in deciding what to do next [21, pp. 98–128]. Under such conditions, it could be virtually impossible for an NCA to limit or stop the war, since even one of the isolated forces could continue it by launching another attack.

As discussed previously, means of communicating with the enemy would be important in trying to limit the scope of a nuclear war. Currently, the Hot Line linking Washington and Moscow terminates in the Pentagon and the Kremlin, neither of which is hardened against nuclear attack [80]. Various proposals have been made to add more redundancy to the Hot Line, perhaps with direct connections to the U.S. National Emergency Airborne Command Post[11] and its Soviet counterpart. Of course, nuclear war would have at least as severe an effect on U.S.–Soviet communications as on communications internal to the forces of one country.

An additional problem with limited nuclear war strategies is that, from a military point of view, one of the most efficient kinds of attack in a nuclear war is decapitation: attacks on political and military leadership and on command and control systems [119]. The "Fiscal Year 1984–1988 Defense Guidence" document cited previously states that U.S. nuclear war strategy is to be based on decapitation [61]. However, controlled nuclear war presumes that there is an NCA with which one can communicate. In the words of retired Air Force Lt. Gen. Brent Scowcroft [108, p. 95].

> there's a real dilemma here that we haven't sorted out. The kinds of controlled nuclear options to which we're moving presume communication with the Soviet Union; and yet, from a military point of view, one of the most efficient kinds of attack is against leadership and command and control systems. It's much easier than trying to take out each and every bit of the enemy's offensive forces. This is a dilemma that, I think, we still have not completely come to grips with.

It appears that Soviet military doctrine also calls for attacks on command and control systems at the outset of any strategic nuclear exchange to disrupt the enemy's forces and political and administrative control [9, p. 32].

It is beyond the scope of this article to evaluate closely the technical arguments regarding the hardening of C^3 systems, and in any event much of the information is classified. What *is* within the scope of this article is to observe that these C^3 systems are enormously complex and inherently untestable. In light of the previous discussions, there is thus considerable room for doubt that they would operate as planned in the event of a war.

---

[11] According to plan, this airborne command post would be in charge of the nation's nuclear forces if the land-based command posts were destroyed.

Future Computer-Controlled Military Systems

If the arms race continues unabated, we will see increasing use of computer-controlled weapons systems that include little or no possibility of human intervention. Two specific projects are discussed here: the Strategic Defense Initiative (SDI), and the Strategic Computing Initiative (SCI).

The Strategic Defense Initiative

In his now-famous speech of March 23, 1983, President Reagan presented a vision of the future: a technological means to escape the trap of MAD by the construction of a ballistic missile defense system that would render nuclear weapons "impotent and obsolete." That vision is now being pursued under the Stategic Defense Initiative Organization.

The SDI envisions a multilayer defense against nuclear ballistic missiles. The computer software to run such a defense would be the most complex ever built: A report by the Defensive Technologies Study Team, commissioned by the DoD to study the feasibility of such a system, estimates a system with 6–10 million lines of code [130, p. 45]. Enemy missiles would first be attacked in their boost phase, requiring action within 90 seconds or so of a detected launch. This time interval is so short that the human role in the system could be minimal at best, with virtually no possibility of decision making by national leaders. Although pieces of the system could be tested and simulation tests performed, it would be impossible to test the entire system under actual battle conditions short of fighting a nuclear war. It has been the universal experience in large computer systems that there is no substitute for testing under actual conditions of use. The SDI is the most extreme example so far of an untestable system. How could there be confidence that it would perform as intended? There are many other complicating factors, such as the constant need to update the software in response to new Soviet threats, and the difficulties of making updates to an operational space-based system. If the system is not trustworthy, it would seem unwise for the United States to abandon deterrence and nuclear missiles. How then could the SDI meet the goal of rendering nuclear weapons "impotent and obsolete?"

A more recent report by the Eastport Study Group [45], also commissioned by the DoD, stated that software considerations were the paramount problem in the SDI, and recommended a decentralized system rather than one requiring tight coordination. Nevertheless, the problems listed above hold whether a centralized or a decentralized architecture is used [98]. First, a battle station that is loosely coupled to the rest of the system must perform the functions of the whole system. The original arguments regarding complexity and untestability still apply. Second, individual battle stations would continue to interact. Some communication between stations would be needed for accurate tracking and for discrimination of warheads from decoys in the presence of noise. There would also be interactions through the weapons of one station and the sensors of another, for example, through the effect of noise generated by the destruction of a warhead. Again, we can have confidence that such interactions are well understood only by testing under realistic battle conditions.

If the SDI is deployed, there are two significant failure modes: failure of the system to stop a Soviet attack, and activation of the system due to a false alarm. Failure under attack would of course mean that a Soviet attack would *not* be stopped; if some plan is executed in which it is assumed that Soviet missiles have been rendered useless, the consequences would be devastating. Activation due to a false alarm would in itself not be as serious as inadvertently firing a missile. (However, some of the defensive systems being examined include nuclear weapons themselves, such as nuclear-pumped X-ray lasers. Further, it could be hard to distinguish quickly some defensive systems from offensive ones, such as those involving pop-up systems deployed on submarine-launched missiles.) The real danger is that the SDI would be integrated with the national strategic forces as a whole. An accidental SDI activation could trigger other responses, perhaps leading to a series of coupled escalating alerts on both sides or to other offensive actions. To lessen the chances of accidental activation in peacetime, Lieutenant General Abrahamson, the director of the Strategic Defense Initiative Organization, has suggested in testimony to Congress [133, pp. 704–705] that important parts of the system be placed under automatic control only during a crisis—but this is the worst possible time for an accidental activation to occur. There is a great deal more to be said on this topic, and the reader is referred to [79], [86], [97], and [98]. For two general overviews of SDI systems, see [1] and [4].

The Strategic Computing Initiative

In 1983 the Defense Advanced Research Projects Agency (DARPA) of the DoD proposed the SCI, a five-year $600,000,000 effort to develop new computer-based military systems, emphasizing research in microelectronics and artificial intelligence [38]. Specific military applications to be built under the program are an autonomous robot vehicle capable of far-ranging reconnaissance and attack missions, an automated pilot's associate to aid fighter aircraft pilots, and a battle management system that can monitor incoming information, generate potential courses of action, disseminate orders, and compare actual events with those anticipated.

The integration of these weapons with nuclear war-fighting capabilities is planned: For example, the SCI states, "For certain space, air, and sea vehicles, the constraints and requirements will be even higher and will include the capability to operate in high-radiation environments" [38, p. 23].

Whether or not artificial intelligence techniques are used (e.g., rule-based expert systems [65, 117] as is proposed in the SCI), the basic limitations discussed previously still hold. A battle-management systems, for example, would in all probability give useful responses only in those situations for which rules were available—in other words, situations that had been anticipated by the experts who developed the rules. Again, as with any other computer system, we cannot be confident of its reliability until it has been extensively tested under conditions of actual use.

A more detailed analysis of the SCI may be found in an assessment by Computer Professionals for Social Responsibility [95]; a reply from the director of DARPA is in [35]. Another, more favorable assessment of the SCI was recently published by Mark Stefik [116].

Conclusions

How much reliance is it safe to place on life-critical computer systems, in particular, on nuclear weapons command and control systems? At present, a nuclear war caused by an isolated computer or operator error is probably not a primary risk, at least in comparison with other dangers. The most significant risk of nuclear war at present seems to come from the possibility of a *combination* of such events as international crises, mutually reinforcing alerts, computer system misdesign, computer failure, or human error.

A continuing trend in the arms race has been the deployment of missiles with greater and greater accuracies. This trend is creating increasing pressure to consider a launch-on-warning strategy. Such a strategy would, however, leave very little time to evaluate the warning and determine whether it were real or due to a computer or human error—we would be forced to put still greater reliance on the correct operation of the warning and command systems of the United States and the USSR. Deployment of very accurate missiles close to enemy territory exacerbates the problem.

C^3 systems should be such that leaders in both the United States and the USSR will not be forced into a "use it or lose it" situation, in which they feel they must launch a strike quickly lest their ability to retaliate is destroyed. Current war plans are more elaborate and include an array of options for flexible, limited nuclear responses. However, if a nuclear war should start, it is not at all clear that it would unfold according to these plans. We should always bear in mind that untested systems in a strange and hostile environment are not likely to perform reliably and as expected. In particular, it is impossible to determine exactly which components of a strategic command and control system would still work correctly after hostilities have commenced. This rules out strategies that depend on finely graded or complexly coordinated activites after the initial attack.

The construction of a ballistic missile defense system has been proposed. However, there could be no confidence that it would work as expected; in addition, its accidental activation during a crisis might trigger other hostilities. In the longer term, weapons systems equipped with extremely fast computers and using artificial intelligence techniques may result in battles (including nuclear ones) that must be largely controlled by computer.

Where then does that leave us? There is clearly room for technical improvements in nuclear weapons computer systems. I have argued, however, that adding more and more such improvements cannot ensure that they will always function correctly. The fundamental problems are due to untestability, limits of human decision making during high tension and crisis, and our inability to think through all the things that might happen in a complex and unfamiliar situation. We must recognize the limits of technology. The threat of nuclear war is a political problem, and it is in the political, human realm that solutions must be sought.

Acknowledgments

Many people have helped me in gathering information and in developing the ideas described here. Some of the original research was done in connection with a graduate seminar on Computer Reliability and Nuclear War held in the University of Washington Computer Science Department in Autumn 1982, and I thank the other participants in the seminar. Subsequently, a number of members of Computer Professionals for Social Responsibility have been generous with their help; I would particularly like to thank Guy Almes, Andrew Black, Gary Chapman, Calvin Gotlieb, Laura Gould, William Havens, Robert Henry, Jonathan Jacky, Cliff Johnson, Ira Kalet, Ed Lazowska, Peter Neumann, Severo Ornstein, David Parnas, Scott Rose, and Philip Wadler. Thanks also to Milton Leitenberg and Herbert Lin for expert advice on arms and arms control, and to Rob Kling for useful recommendations and suggestions in his role as area editor for this article.

Portions of a preliminary version of this article were presented at the Fourth Congress of the International Physicians for the Prevention of Nuclear War and appeared in the *IPPNW Report*, volume 2, number 3, October 1984.

References

1. Adams, J. A., and Fischetti, M. A. (1985). "STAR WARS"—SDI: The grand experiment, *IEEE Spectrum 22*, 9 (September), 34–64.
2. Adrion, W. R., Branstad, M. A., Cherniavsky, J. C. (1982). Validation, verification, and testing of computer software. *ACM Comput. Surv. 14*, 2 (June), 159–192.
3. Albright, J. (1980). False missile alert required 3 minute to cancel. *San Jose Mercury* (June 15), 1 H.
4. American Academy of Arts and Sciences (1985). Weapons in space. Vol. I: Concepts and technologies. *Daedalus 114*, 2 (Spring), 9–189.
5. Anderson, T., and Randell, B. Eds. (1979). *Computing Systems Reliability: An Advanced Course.* Cambridge University Press, Cambridge, Mass.
6. Angus, J. E. (1984). The application of software reliability models to a major C^3I system. In *Proceedings of the Annual Reliability and Maintainability Symposium* (San Francisco, Calif., January 24–26). IEEE Press, New York, pp. 268–274.
7. Arkin, W. M. (1984). Nuclear weapon command, control, and communications. In *World Armaments and Disarmament: SIPRI Yearbook 1984*, F. Blackaby, Ed. Taylor and Francis, London, pp. 455–516.
8. Association for Computing Machinery (1985). Proceedings of VERkshop III—A formal verification workshop. *Softw. Eng. Notes 10*, 4.
9. Ball, D. (1981). Can nuclear war be controlled? Adelphi Pap. 169. International Institute for Strategic Studies, London.
10. Ball, D. (1986). The Soviet strategic C^3I system. In C^3I *Handbook*. EW Communications. Palo Alto, Calif., pp. 206–216.
11. Balzer, R., Cheatham, T. E., and Green, C. (1983). Software technology in the 1990's: Using a new paradigm. *Computer 16*, 11 (November), 39–45.
12. Barstow, D. R., Shrobe, H. E., and Sandewall, E., Eds. (1984). *Interactive Programming Environments.* McGraw-Hill, New York.
13. Barstow, D. R. (1985). Domain-specific automatic programming. *IEEE Trans. Softw. Eng. SE-11*, 11 (November), 1321–1336.
14. Benzel, T. C. V., and Tavilla, D. A. (1985). Trusted software verification: A case study. In *Proceedings of the 1985 Symposium on Security and Privacy* (Oakland, Calif., Apr. 22–24). IEEE Press, New York, pp. 14–31.

15. Bereanu, B. (1983). Self-activation of the world nuclear weapons system. *J. Peace Res. 20*, 1, 49–57.
16. Berkeley, E. C. (1962). *The Computer Revolution*. Doubleday, New York.
17. Blair, B. G. (1985). *Strategic Command and Control*. Brookings Institution, Washington, D.C.
18. Bloomfield, L. P. (1985). Nuclear crisis and human frailty. *Bull. At. Sci. 41*, 9 (October), 26–30.
19. Boehm, B. W. (1981). *Software Engineering Economics*. Prentice-Hall, Englewood Cliffs, N.J.
20. Boyer, R. S., and Moore, J. S., Eds. (1981). *The Correctness Problem in Computer Science*. Academic Press, New York.
21. Bracken, P. (1983). *The Command and Control of Nuclear Forces*. Yale University Press, New Haven, Conn.
22. Broad, W. J. (1980). Computers and the U.S. military don't mix. *Science 207*, 4436 (March 14), 1183–1187.
23. Broad, W. J. (1981). Nuclear pulse (I): Awakening to the chaos factor. *Science 212*, 4498 (May 29), 1009–1012.
24. Broad, W. J. (1981). Nuclear pulse (II): Ensuring delivery of the doomsday signal. *Science 212*, 4499 (June 5), 1116–1120.
25. Broad, W. J. (1981). Nuclear pulse (III): Playing a wild card. *Science 212*, 4500 (June 12), 1248–1251.
26. Brooks, J. (1982). NORAD computer systems are dangerously obsolete. House Rep. 97-449. Committee on Government Operations, United States House of Representatives. Washington, D.C., (March 8).
27. Brown, H. (1983). *Thinking about National Security: Defense and Foreign Policy in a Dangerous World*. Westview Press, Boulder, Colo.
28. Bunn, M., and Tsipis, K. (1983). The uncertainties of a preemptive nuclear attack. *Sci. Am. 249*, 5 (November), 38–47.
29. Burt, R. (1980). False nuclear alarms spur urgent effort to find faults. *New York Times* (June 13), A16.
30. Carter, A. B. (1985). The command and control of nuclear war. *Sci. Am. 252*, 1 (January), 32–39.
31. Carter, W. C. (1979). Hardware fault tolerance. In *Computing Systems Reliability: An Advanced Course*, T. Anderson and B. Randell, Eds. Cambridge University Press, Cambridge, Mass., Chap. 6, pp. 211–263.
32. Cockburn, A. (1983). *The Threat: Inside the Soviet Military Machine*. Random House, New York.
33. Comptroller General of the United States (1979). The world wide military command and control system—Major changes needed in its automated data processing management and direction. Rep. LCD-80-22, Comptroller General of the United States, Washington, D.C., (December 14).
34. Comptroller General of the United States (1981). *NORAD's Missile Warning System: What Went Wrong?* United States General Accounting Office. Washington, D.C., (May 15).
35. Cooper, R. S. (1985). Letter to the editor. *Bull At. Sci. 41*, 1 (January), 54–55
36. Currit, P. A., Dyer, M., and Mills, H. D. (1986). Certifying the reliability of software. *IEEE Trans. Softw. Eng. SE-12*, 1 (January), 3–11.
37. Davis, N. C., and Goodman, S. E. (1978). The Soviet bloc's unified system of computers. *ACM Comput. Surv. 10*, 2 (June), 93–122.
38. Defense Advanced Research Projects Agency. *Strategic Computing—New-Generation Computing Technology: A Strategic Plan for its Development and Application to Critical Problems in Defense*. U.S. Department of Defense, Arlington, Va., (October 28).
39. Defense Nuclear Agency (1971). *EMP Awareness Handbook*. Defense Nuclear Agency. Washington, D.C.

40. Deutsch, M. S. (1982). *Software Verification and Validation: Realistic Project Approaches*. Prentice-Hall, Englewood Cliffs, N.J.

41. Doder, D. (1982). Soviets said to consider faster nuclear missile launch in crisis. *Washington Post* (April 11), A5.

42. Doder, D. (1982). Kremlin defense official warns of policy shift to quicken nuclear response. *Washington Post* (July 13), A1a.

43. Druffel, L. E., Redwine, S. T., and Riddle, W. E. (1983). The STARS program: Overview and rationale. *Computer 16*, 11 (November), 21–29.

44. Dumas, L. J. (1980). Human fallibility and weapons. *Bull. At. Sci. 36*, 9 (November), 15–20.

45. Eastport Study Group (1985). *Summer Study 1985: A Report to the Director, Strategic Defense Initiative Organization*. Strategic Defense Initiative Organization, (December).

46. Emelyanov, V. S. (1984). The possibility of an accidental nuclear war. In *The Arms Race at a Time of Decision*, J. Rotblat and A. Pascolini, Eds. Macmillan, New York, Chap 9, pp. 73–79.

47. Fairley, R. E. (1985). *Software Engineering Concepts*. McGraw-Hill, New York.

48. Ford, D. (1985). *The Button*. Simon and Schuster, New York.

49. Fox, R. (1982). *Software and Its Development*. Prentice-Hall, Englewood Cliffs, N.J.

50. Frei, D. (1983). *Risks of Unintentional Nuclear War*. Allanheld, Osmun and Co., Totowa, N.J.

51. Garman, J. R. (1981). The "bug" heard round the world. *Softw. Eng. Notes 6*, 5 (October), 3–10.

52. Garwin, R. (1979). Launch under attack to redress minuteman vulnerability? *Int. Secur. 4*, 3 (Winter), 117–139.

53. Gelb, L. H. (1983). Soviet marshal warns the U.S. on its missiles. *New York Times* (March 17), A1.

54. George, A., and Smoke, R. (1974). *Deterrence in American Foreign Policy*. Columbia University Press, New York.

55. Glasstone, S., and Dolan, P. J. (1977). *The Effects of Nuclear Weapons*. U.S. Department of Defense, Washington, D.C.

56. Goodman, S. E. (1979). Computing and the development of the Soviet economy. A Compendium of Papers Submitted to the Joint Economic Committee of the Congress of the United States. Washington, D.C. (October 10).

57. Gray, C. S., and Payne, K. (1980). Victory is possible. *Foreign Policy 39* (Summer), 14–27.

58. Gumble, B. (1985). Air Force upgrading defenses at NORAD. *Def. Electron. 17*, 8 (August), 86–108.

59. Halloran, R. (1979). U.S. aides recount moments of false missile alert. *New York Times* (December 16), 25.

60. Halloran, R. (1980). Computer error falsely indicates a Soviet attack. *New York Times* (June 6), 14.

61. Halloran, R. (1982). Pentagon draws up first strategy for fighting a long nuclear war. *New York Times* (May 30), 1: 1.

62. Halloran, R. (1982). Weinberger confirms new strategy on atom war. *New York Times* (June 4), A10.

63. Halloran, R. (1983). Shift of strategy on missile attack hinted by Weinberger and Vessey. *New York Times* (May 6), 1: 1.

64. Hart, G., and Goldwater, B. (1980). *Recent False Alerts from the Nation's Missile Attack Warning System*. United States Senate, Committee on Armed Services, Washington, D.C.

65. Hayes-Roth, F., Waterman, D., and Lenat, D. (1983). *Building Expert Systems*. Addison-Wesley, Reading, Mass.

66. Henderson, P., Ed. (1984). *Proceedings of the ACM SIGSOFT/SIGPLAN Software Engineering Symposium on Practical Software Development Environments*. ACM, New York.

67. Howard, M. (1981). On fighting a nuclear war. *Int. Secur. 5*, 4 (Spring), 3–17.

68. Howden, W. E. (1982). Validation of scientific programs. *ACM Comput. Surv. 14*, 2 (June), 193–227.

69. Hubbell, J. C. (1961). You are under attack! The strange incident of October 5. *Reader's Dig. 78*, 468 (April), 37–41.

70. International Institute for Strategic Studies. (1983). *The Military Balance 1983–1984.* International Institute for Strategic Studies, London.

71. Jensen, R. W., and Tonies, C. C. (1979). *Software Engineering.* Prentice-Hall, Englewood Cliffs, N.J.

72. Kahn, H. (1960). *On Thermonuclear War.* Princeton University Press, Princeton, N.J.

73. Kaplan, F. (1983). *The Wizards of Armageddon.* Simon and Schuster, New York.

74. Kissinger, H. A. (1957). *Nuclear Weapons and Foreign Policy.* Harper, New York.

75. Kling, R. (1987). Defining the boundaries of computing across complex organization. In *Critical Issues in Information Systems Research*, R. Boland and R. Hirschheim, Eds. Wiley, New York.

76. Lerner, E. J. (1982). Electronics and the nuclear battlefield. *IEEE Spectrum 19*, 10 (October), 64–65.

77. Leveson, N. G. (1986). Software safety: Why, what, and how. Rep. 86-04, Dept. of Information and Computer Science, Univ. of California, Irvine, (February).

78. Lieblein, E. (1986). The Department of Defense Software Initiative—A status report. *Commun. ACM 29*, 8 (August), 734–744.

79. Lin, H. (1985). Software for ballistic missile defense. Rep. C/85-2, Center for International Studies, MIT, Cambridge, Mass., (June).

80. Martin, R. (1982). Stopping the unthinkable: C^3I dimensions of terminating a "limited" nuclear war. Rep. P-82-3. Center for Information Policy Research. Harvard Univ., Cambridge, Mass., (April).

81. Meyers, G. J. (1976). *Software Reliability: Principles and Practices.* Wiley, New York.

82. Meyers, G. J. (1979). *The Art of Software Testing.* Wiley, New York.

83. Miller, G. E. (1979). Existing systems of command and control. In *The Dangers of Nuclear War*, Griffiths, Franklyn, and Polanyi, Eds. University of Toronto Press, Toronto, Ontario, pp. 50–66.

84. MITRE Corp. (1982). National security issues symposium: Strategic nuclear policies, weapons, and the C^3 connection. Doc. M82-30, MITRE Corp., Bedford, Mass.

85. Morgan, P. M. (1983). *Deterrence: A Conceptual Analysis.* 2nd ed. Sage, Beverley Hills, Calif.

86. Nelson, G., and Redell, D. (1986). The Star Wars computer systems. *Abacus 3*, 2 (Winter), 8–20.

87. Neumann, P. G. (1979). An editorial on software correctness and the social process. *Softw. Eng. Notes 4*, 2 (April), 3–4.

88. Neumann, P. G. (1985). Letter from the editor. *Softw. Eng. Notes 10*, 1 (January), 3–11.

89. *New York Times* (1960). Moon stirs scare of missile attack. *New York Times* (December 8), 71: 2.

90. *New York Times* (1979). False alarm on attack sends fighters into sky. *New York Times* (November 10), 21.

91. *New York Times* (1980). Missile alerts traced to 46 cent item. *New York Times* (June 18), 16.

92. *New York Times* (1983). Nevada governor says errors led to flooding. *New York Times* (July 4), 1–10.

93. Nye, J. S., Allison, G. T., and Carnesale, A. (1985). Analytic conclusions: Hawks, doves, and owls. In *Hawks, Doves, and Owls*, G. T. Allison, A. Carnesale, and J. S. Nye, Eds. Norton, New York, Chap. 8, pp. 206–222.

94. Office of Technology Assessment (1981). MX missile basing—Launch under attack. Office of Technology Assessment, Washington, D.C.

95. Ornstein, S., Smith, B. C., and Suchman, L. (1984). Strategic computing: An assessment. *Bull. At. Sci. 40*, 10 (December), 11–15.

96. Parnas, D. L., Clements, P. C., and Weiss, D. M. (1984). The modular structure of complex systems. In *Proceedings of the 7th International Conference on Software Engineering* (Orlando, Fla., March 26–29), IEEE Press, New York, pp. 408–417.

97. Parnas, D. L. (1985). Software aspects of strategic defense systems. *Am. Sci. 73*, 5 (September–October), 432–440.

98. Parnas, D. L. (1987). SDI: A violation of professional responsibility. *Abacus 4*, 2 (Winter), 46–52.

99. Partsch, H., and Steinbruggen, R. (1983). Program transformation systems. *ACM Comput. Surv. 15*, 3 (September), 199–236.

100. Perrow, C. (1981). Normal accident at Three Mile Island. *Society 18*, 5 (July–August), 17–26.

101. Perrow, C. (1984). *Normal Accidents: Living with High-Risk Technologies*. Basic Books, New York.

102. Pollack, A. (1983). Trust in computers raising risk of errors and sabotage. *New York Times* (August 22), 1.

103. Pringle, P., and Arkin, W. (1983). *S.I.O.P.: The Secret U.S. Plan for Nuclear War*. Norton, New York.

104. Ricketts, L. W. (1972). *Fundamentals of Nuclear Hardening of Electronic Equipment*. Wiley, New York.

105. Ricketts, L. W., Bridges, J. E., and Miletta, J. (1976). *EMP Radiation and Protective Techniques*. Wiley, New York.

106. Rogovin, M., and Frampton, G. T. (1980).*Three Mile Island: A Report to the Commissioners and to the Public*. Nuclear Regulatory Commission Special Inquiry Group, U.S. Nuclear Regulatory Commission, Washington, D.C.

107. Rosen, E. (1981). Vulnerabilities of network control protocols: An example. *Softw. Eng. Notes 6*, 1 (January), 6–8.

108. Scowcroft, B. (1982). C^3 systems for the president and military commanders. In *National Security Issues Symposium: Strategic Nuclear Policies, Weapons, and the C^3 Connection*, D. M. Ace, Ed. MITRE Corp., Bedford, Mass., pp. 93–97.

109. Scowcroft, B. (1983). *Report of the President's Commission on Strategic Forces*. U.S. Department of Defense. Washington, D.C., (April).

110. *Seattle Post-Intelligence* (1984). Russia puts more N-arms off U.S. Coast. *Seattle Post-Intelligence* (May 21), A2.

111. Siewiorek, D. P., and Swarz, R. S. (1982). *The Theory and Practice of Reliable System Design*. Digital Press, Bedford, Mass.

112. Silverman, J. M. (1983). Reflections on the verification of the security of an operating system. In *Proceedings of the 9th ACM Sympsoium on Operating Systems Principles* (October), ACM, New York, pp. 143–154.

113. Smith, B. C. (1985). The limits of correctness. *ACM SIGCAS Newsl. 14*, 4 and *15*, 1–3 (Winter–Fall), 18–26.

114. Sokolovskiy, V. D. (1975). *Soviet Military Strategy*. Edited, with an analysis and commentary, by H. Fast Scott, Crane, Russak and Co., New York.

115. Sommerville, I. (1982). *Software Engineering*. Addison-Wesley, Reading, Mass.

116. Stefik, M. (1985). Strategic computing at DARPA: Overview and assessment. *Commun. ACM 28*, 7 (July), 690–704.

117. Stefik, M., Aikins, J., Balzer, R., Benoit, J., Birnbaum, L., Hayes-Roth, F., and Sacerdoti, E. (1982). The organization of expert systems, a tutorial. *Artif. Intell. 18*, 2 (March), 135–173.

118. Stein, D. L. (1983). Electromagnetic pulse—The uncertain certainty. *Bull. At. Sci. 39*, 3 (March), 52–56.

119. Steinbruner, J. D. (1981–1982). Nuclear decapitation. *Foreign Policy 45* (Winter), 16–28.

120. Steinbruner, J. D. (1984). Launch under attack. *Sci. Am. 250*, 1 (January), 37–47.

121. Stevens, R. T. (1968). Testing the NORAD command and control system. *IEEE Trans. Syst. Sci. Cybern. SSC-4*, 1 (March), 47–51.

122. Stockholm International Peace Research Institute (1983). *World Armaments and Disarmament: SIPRI Yearbook 1983*. Taylor and Francis, London.

123. Stockholm International Peace Research Institute (1984). *World Armaments and Disarmament: SIPRI Yearbook 1984*. Taylor and Francis, London.

124. Tasky, K. (1979). Soviet technology gap and dependence on the west: The case of computers. A Compendium of Papers Submitted to the Joint Economic Committee of the Congress of the United States. Washington, D.C., (October 10).

125. U.S. Department of Defense (1980). *Military Standardization Handbook: Reliability Prediction of Electronic Equipment. MIL-STD-HDBK-217C*. Notice 1 ed. U.S. Department of Defense. Washington, D.C.

126. U.S. Department of Defense (1982). *Modernization of the WWMCCS Information System (WIS)*. The Assistant Secretary of Defense (CCCI) with the assistance of the WWMCCS System Engineer (DCA). U.S. Department of Defense. Washington, D.C., (July 31).

127. U.S. Department of Defense. (1983). *Soviet Military Power*. 2nd ed. U.S. Government Printing Office. Washington D.C.

128. U.S. Department of Defense (1983). Software technology for adaptable, reliable systems. *Softw. Eng. Notes 8*, 2 (April), 55–84.

129. U.S. Department of Defense (1984). *Soviet Military Power*, 3rd ed. U.S. Government Printing Office. Washington, D.C.

130. U.S. Department of Defense (1984). *Report of the Study on Eliminating the Threat Posed by Nuclear Ballistic Missiles*. Vol. 5, *Battle Management, Communications, and Data Processing*, U.S. Department of Defense. Washington, D.C., (February).

131. U.S. Department of Defense (1985). *DOD-STD-2167: Military Standard Defense System Software Development*. U.S. Department of Defense, Washington, D.C.

132. U.S. House of Representatives (1981). *Failures of the North American Aerospace Defense Command's (NORAD) Attack Warning System*. Hearings before a Subcommittee of the Committee on Government Operations, U.S. House of Representatives, 97th Congress, 1st session, May 19 and 20.

133. U.S. House of Representatives (1984). *Hearings, Department of Defense Appropriations for 1985*. Committee on Appropriations, Subcommittee on the Department of Defense. U.S. Government Priting Office, Washington, D.C.

134. U.S. House of Representatives (1985). *Our Nation's Nuclear Warming System: Will It Work If We Need It?* Hearings before a Subcommittee of the Committee on Government Operations. U.S. House of Representatives, 99th Congress, 1st session, (September 26).

135. U.S. Senate Committee on Armed Services (1981). *Hearings, Department of Defense Authorization for Appropriations for FY 1982, Part 7*. U.S. Government Printing Office, Washington, D.C.

136. U.S. Senate Committee on Armed Services (1983). *Hearings, Department of Defense Authorization for Appropriations for FY 1984, Part 5*. U.S. Government Printing Office. Washington, D.C.

137. Van Evera, S. (1984). The cult of the offensive and the origins of the First World War. *Int. Secur. 9*, 1 (Summer), 58–107.

138. Waltz, E. L. (1986). Data fusion for C³I systems. In *C³I Handbook*. EW Communications. Palo Alto, Calif., pp. 217–226.

139. *Washington Post* (1980). Computer again gives signal of false Soviet attack. *Washington Post* (June 8), A7.

140. *Washington Post* (1983). Soviet warns of automatic retaliation against new U.S. missiles. *Washington Post* (May 18), A12.

141. Weinberger, C. W. (1984). *Report of the Secretary of Defense to the Congress on the FY 1985 Budget, FY 1986 Authorization Request and FY 1985–89 Defense Programs*. U.S. Government Printing Office. Washington, D.C.

142. Zraket, C. A. (1984). Strategic command, control, communications, and intelligence. *Science* 224, 4655 (June 22), 1306–1311.

4

Software Aspects of Strategic Defense Systems

David Lorge Parnas

This report comprises eight short papers that were completed while I was a member of the Panel on Computing in Support of Battle Management, convened by the Strategic Defense Initiative Organization (SDIO). SDIO is part of the Office of the U.S. Secretary of Defense. The panel was asked to identify the computer science problems that would have to be solved before an effective antiballistic missile (ABM) system could be deployed. It is clear to everyone that computers must play a critical role in the systems that SDIO is considering. The essays that constitute this report were written to organize my thoughts on these topics and were submitted to SDIO with my resignation from the panel.

My conclusions are not based on political or policy judgments. Unlike many other academic critics of the SDI effort, I have not, in the past, objected to defense efforts or defense-sponsored research. I have been deeply involved in such research and have consulted extensively on defense projects. My conclusions are based on more than 20 years of research on software engineering, including more than 8 years of work on real-time software used in the military aircraft. They are based on familiarity with both operational military software and computer science research. My conclusions are based on characteristics peculiar to this particular effort, not objections to weapons development in general.

I am publishing the papers that accompanied my letter of resignation so that interested people can understand why many computer scientists believe that systems of the sort being considered by the SDIO cannot be built. These essays address the software

Reprinted with permission of Sigma Xi, "Software Aspects of Strategic Defense Systems," D.L. Parnas, *American Scientist* **73** (5) pp. 432–440.

engineering aspects of SDIO and the organization of engineering research. They avoid political issues; those have been widely discussed elsewhere, and I have nothing to add.

In these essays I have attempted to avoid technical jargon, and readers need not be computer programmers to understand them. They may be read in any order.[1]

The individual essays explain:

1. The fundamental technological differences between software engineering and other areas of engineering and why software is unreliable;
2. The properties of the proposed SDI software that make it unattainable;
3. Why the techniques commonly used to build military software are inadequate for this job;
4. The nature of research in software engineering, and why the improvements that it can effect will not be sufficient to allow construction of a truly reliable strategic defense system;
5. Why I do not expect research in artificial intelligence to help in building reliable military software;
6. Why I do not expect research in automatic programming to bring about the substantial improvements that are needed;
7. Why program verification (mathematical proofs of correctness) cannot give us a reliable strategic defense battle-management system;
8. Why military funding of research in software and other aspects of computing science is inefficient and ineffective. This essay responds to the proposal that SDIO should be funded even if the ABM system cannot be produced, because the program will produce good research.

Why Software is Unreliable

Introduction

People familiar with both software engineering and older engineering disciplines observe that the state-of-the-art in software is significantly behind that in other areas of engineering. When most engineering products have been completed, tested, and sold, it is reasonable to expect that the product design is correct and that it will work reliably. With software products, it is usual to find that the software has major "bugs" and does not work reliably for some users. These problems may persist for several versions and sometimes worsen as the software is "improved." While most products come with an express or implied warranty, software products often carry a specific disclaimer of warranty. The lay public, familiar with only a few incidents of software failure, may regard them as exceptions caused by inept programmers. Those of us who are software professionals

---

[1] Edmund Berkeley, *The Computer Revolution*, Doubleday, 1962, pp. 175–177, citing newspaper stories in the *Manchester Guardian Weekly* of Dec. 1, 1960, a UPI dispatch published in the *Boston Traveller* of Dec. 13, 1960, and an AP dispatch published in the *New York Times* on Dec 23, 1960.

know better; the most competent programmers in the world cannot avoid such problems. This section discusses one reason for this situation.

System Types

Engineering products can be classified as discrete state systems, analog systems, or hybrid systems.

Discrete state or digital systems are made from components with a finite number of stable states. They are designed in such a way that the behavior of the system when not in a stable state is not significant.

Continuous or analog systems are made from components that, within a broad operating range, have an infinite number of stable states and whose behavior can be adequately described by continuous functions.

Hybrid systems are mixtures of the two types of components. For example, we may have an electrical circuit containing, in addition to analog components, a few components whose descriptive equations have discontinuities (e.g., diodes). Each of these components has a small number of discrete operating states. Within these states its behavior can be described by continuous functions.

Mathematical Tools

Analog systems form the core of the traditional areas of engineering. The mathematics of continuous functions is well understood. When we say that a system is described by continuous functions we are saying that it can contain no hidden surprises. Small changes in inputs will always cause correspondingly small changes in outputs. An engineer who ensures, through careful design, that the system components are always operating within their normal operating range can use a mathematical analysis to ensure that there are no surprises. When combined with testing to ensure that the components are within their operating range, this leads to reliable systems.

Before the advent of digital computers, when discrete state systems were built, the number of states in such systems was relatively small. With a small number of states, exhaustive testing was possible. Such testing compensated for the lack of mathematical

---

The Requirements of a Strategic Defense System

In March 1983, President Reagan said, "I call upon the scientific community, who gave us nuclear weapons, to turn their great talents to the cause of mankind and world peaces; to give us the means of rendering these nuclear weapons impotent and obsolete."

To satisfy this request the software must perform the following functions:

- Rapid and reliable warning of attack
- Determination of the source of the attack
- Determination of the likely targets of the attack
- Determination of the missile trajectories
- Coordinated interception of the missiles or warheads during boost, midcourse, and terminal phases, including assignment of responsibility for targets to individual sensors or weapons
- Discrimination between decoys and warheads
- Detailed control of individual weapons
- Evaluation of the effectiveness of each attempt to destroy a target.

tools corresponding to those used in analog systems design. The engineers of such systems still had systematic methods that allowed them to obtain a complete understanding of their system's behavior.

The design of many hybrid systems can be verified by a combination of the two methods. We can then identify a finite number of operating states for the components with discrete behavior. Within those states, the system's behavior can be described by continuous functions. Usually the number of states that must be distinguished is small. For each of those states, the tools of continuous mathematics can be applied to analyze the behavior of the system.

With the advent of digital computers, we found the first discrete state systems with very large numbers of states. However, to manufacture such systems it was necessary to construct them using many copies of very small digital subsystems. Each of those small subsystems could be analyzed and tested exhaustively. Because of the repetitive structure, exhaustive testing was not necessary to obtain correct and reliable hardware. Although design errors are found in computer hardware, they are considered exceptional. They usually occur in those parts of the computer that are not repetitive structures.

Software systems are discrete state systems that do not have the repetitive structure found in computer circuitry. There is seldom a good reason to construct software as highly repetitive structures. The number of states in software systems is orders of magnitude larger than the number of states in the nonrepetitive parts of computers. The mathematical functions that describe the behavior of these systems are not continuous functions, and traditional engineering mathematics does not help in their verification. This difference clearly contributes to the relative unreliability of software systems and the apparent lack of competence of software engineers. It is a fundamental difference that will not disappear with improved technology.

How Can We Understand Software?

To ameliorate the problems caused by this fundamental difference in technology two techniques are available: (1) the building of software as highly organized collections of small programs and (2) the use of mathematical logic to replace continuous mathematics.

Dividing software into modules and building each module of so-called "structured" programs clearly helps. When properly done, each component deals with a small number of cases and can be completely analyzed. However, real software systems have many such components, and there is no repetitive structure to simplify the analysis. Even in highly structured systems, surprises and unreliability occur because the human mind is not able to fully comprehend the many conditions that can arise because of the interaction of these components. Moreover, finding the right structure has proved to be very difficult. Well-structured real software systems are still rare.

Logic is a branch of mathematics that can deal with functions that are not continuous. Many researchers believe that it can play the role in software engineering that continuous mathematics plays in mechanical and electrical engineering. Unfortunately, this has not yet been verified in practice. The large number of states and lack of regularity in the software result in extremely complex mathematical expressions. Disciplined use of these expressions is beyond the computational capacity of both the human programmer and current computer systems. There is progress in this area, but it is very slow, and we are far from being able to handle even small software systems. With current techniques the mathematical expressions describing a program are often notably harder to understand than the program itself.

The Education of Programmers

Worsening the differences between software and other areas of technology is a personnel problem. Most designers in traditional engineering disciplines have been educated to understand the mathematical tools that are available to them. Most programmers cannot even begin to use the meager tools that are available to software engineers.

Why the SDI Software System Will be Untrustworthy

Introduction

In March 1983, the President called for an intensive and comprehensive effort to define a long-term research program with the ultimate goal of eliminating the threat posed by nuclear ballistic missiles. He asked us, as members of the scientific community, to provide the means of rendering these nuclear weapons impotent and obsolete. To accomplish this goal we would need a software system so well-developed that we could have extremely high confidence that the system would work correctly when called upon. In this section, I will present some of the characteristics of the required battle-management software and then discuss their implications on the feasibility of achieving that confidence.

Characteristics of the Proposed Battle-Management Software System

1. The system will be required to identify, track, and direct weapons toward targets whose ballistic characteristics cannot be known with certainty before the moment of battle. It must distinguish these targets from decoys whose characteristics are also unknown.
2. The computing will be done by a network of computers connected to sensors, weapons, and each other, by channels whose behavior, at the time the system is invoked, cannot be predicted because of possible countermeasures by an attacker. The actual subset of system components that will be available at the time that the system is put into service, and throughout the period of service, cannot be predicted for the same reason.
3. It will be impossible to test the system under realistic conditions prior to its actual use.
4. The service period of the system will be so short that there will be little possibility of human intervention and no possibility of debugging and modification of the program during that period of service.
5. Like many other military programs, there are absolute real-time deadlines for the computation. The computation will consist primarily of periodic processes, but the number of those processes that will be required, and the computational requirements of each process, cannot be predicted in advance because they depend on target

characteristics. The resources available for computation cannot be predicted in advance. We cannot even predict the "worse case" with any confidence.

6. The weapon system will include a large variety of sensors and weapons, most of which will themselves require a large and complex software system. The suite of weapons and sensors is likely to grow during development and after deployment. The characteristics of weapons and sensors are not yet known and are likely to remain fluid for many years after deployment. The result is that the overall battle-management software system will have to integrate a software system significantly larger than has ever been attempted before. The components of that system will be subject to independent modification.

Implications of these Problem Characteristics

Each of these characteristics has clear implications on the feasibility of building battle-management software that will meet the President's requirements.

1. Fire-control software cannot be written without making assumptions about the characteristics of enemy weapons and targets. This information is used in determining the recognition algorithms, the sampling periods, and the noise-filtering techniques. If the system is developed without the knowledge of these characteristics, or with the knowledge that the enemy can change some of them on the day of battle, there are likely to be subtle but fatal errors in the software.

2. Although there has been some real progress in the area of "fail-soft" computer software, I have seen no success except in situations where (a) the likely failures can be predicted on the basis of past history, (b) the component failures are unlikely and are statistically independent, (c) the system has excess capacity, (d) the real-time deadlines, if any, are soft, i.e., they can be missed without long-term effects. None of these is true for the required battle-management software.

3. No large-scale software system has ever been installed without extensive testing under realistic conditions. For example, in operational software for military aircraft, even minor modifications require extensive ground testing followed by flight testing in which battle conditions can be closely approximated. Even with these tests, bugs can and do show up in battle conditions. The inability to test a strategic defense system under field conditions before we actually need it will mean that no knowledgeable person would have much faith in the system.

4. It is not unusual for software modifications to be made in the field. Programmers are transported by helicopter to Navy ships; debugging notes can be found on the walls of trucks carrying computers that were used in Vietnam. It is only through such modifications that software becomes reliable. Such opportunities will not be available in the 30–90 minute war to be fought by a strategic defense battle-management system.

5. Programs of this type must meet hard real-time deadlines reliably. In theory, this can be done either by scheduling at runtime or by preruntime scheduling. In practice, efficiency and predictability require some preruntime scheduling. Schedules for the worst-case load are often built into the program. Unless one can work out

worst-case real-time schedules in advance, one can have no confidence that the system will meet its deadlines when its service is required.

6. All of our experience indicates that the difficulties in building software increase with the size of the system, with the number of independently modifiable subsystems, and with the number of interfaces that must be defined. Problems worsen when interfaces may change. The consequent modifications increase the complexity of the software and the difficulty of making a change correctly.

Conclusion

All of the cost estimates indicate that this will be the most massive software project ever attempted. The system has numerous technical characteristics that will make it more difficult than previous systems, independent of size. Because of the extreme demands on the system and our inability to test it, we will never be able to believe, with any confidence, that we have succeeded. Nuclear weapons will remain a potent threat.

Why Conventional Software Development Does Not Produce Reliable Programs

What is the Conventional Method?

The easiest way to describe the programming method used in most projects today was given to me by a teacher who was explaining how he teaches programming. "Think like a computer," he said. He instructed his students to begin by thinking about what the computer had to do first and to write that down. They would then think about what the computer had to do next and continue in that way until they had described the last thing the computer would do. This, in fact, is the way I was taught to program. Most of today's textbooks demonstrate the same method, although it has been improved by allowing us to describe the computer's "thoughts" in larger steps and later to refine those large steps to a sequence of smaller steps.

Why this Method Leads to Confusion

This intuitively appealing method works well—on problems too small to matter. We think that it works because it worked for the first program that we wrote. One can follow the method with programs that have neither branches nor loops. As soon as our thinking reaches a point where the action of the computer must depend on conditions that are not known until the program is running, we must deviate from the method by labeling one or more of the actions and remembering how we would get there. As soon as we introduce loops into the program, there are many ways of getting to some of the points and we must remember all of those ways. As we progress through the algorithm, we recognize the need for information about earlier events and add variables to our data structure. We now have to start remembering what data mean and under what circumstances data are meaningful.

As we continue in our attempt to "think like a computer," the amount we have to remember grows and grows. The simple rules defining how we got to certain points in a program become more complex as we branch there from other points. The simple rules defining what the data mean become more complex as we find other uses for existing variables and add new variables. Eventually, we make an error. Sometimes we note that error; sometimes it is not found until we test. Sometimes the error is not very important; it happens only on rare or unforeseen occasions. In that case, we find it when the program is in use. Often, because one needs to remember so much about the meaning of each label and each variable, new problems are created when old problems are corrected.

What is the Effect of Concurrency on this Method?

In many of our computer systems there are several sources of information and several outputs that must be controlled. This leads to a computer that might be thought of as doing many things at once. If the sequence of external events cannot be predicted in advance, the sequence of actions taken by the computer is also not predictable. The computer may be doing only one thing at a time, but as one attempts to "think like a computer," one finds many more points where the action must be conditional on what happened in the past. Any attempt to design these programs by thinking things through in the order that the computer will execute them leads to confusion and results in systems that nobody can understand completely.

What is the Effect of Multiprocessing?

When there is more than one computer in a system, the software not only appears to be doing more than one thing at a time, it really is doing many things at once. There is no sequential program that one can study. Any attempt to "think like the computer system" is obviously hopeless. There are so many possibilities to consider that only extensive testing can begin to sort things out. Even after such testing, we have incidents such as one that happened on a space shuttle flight several years ago. The wrong combination of sequences occurred and prevented the flight from starting.

Do Professional Programmers Really Use This Approach?

Yes. I have had occasion to study lots of practical software and to discuss programs with lots of professional programmers. In recent years many programmers have tried to improve their working methods using a variety of software design approaches. However, when they get down to writing executable programs, they revert to the conventional way of thinking. I have yet to find a substantial program in practical use whose structure was not based on the expected execution sequence. I would be happy to be shown some.

Other methods are discussed in advanced courses, a few good textbooks, and scientific meetings, but most programmers continue to use the basic approach of thinking things out in the order that the computer will execute them. This is most noticeable in the maintenance (deficiency correction) phase of programming.

How Do We Get Away with This Inadequate Approach?

It should be clear that writing and understanding very large real-time programs by "thinking like a computer" will be beyond our intellectual capabilities. How can it be that we have so much software that is reliable enough for us to use it? The answer is simple; programming is a trial and error craft. People write programs without any expectation that they will be right the first time. They spend at least as much time testing and correcting errors as they spent writing the initial program. Large concerns have separate groups of testers to do quality assurance. Programmers cannot be trusted to test their own programs adequately. Software is released for use, not when it is known to be correct, but when the rate of discovering new errors slows down to one that management considers acceptable. Users learn to expect errors and are often told how to avoid the bugs until the program is improved.

Conclusion

The military software that we depend on every day is not likely to be correct. The methods that are in use in the industry today are not adequate for building large real-time software systems that must be reliable when first used. A drastic change in methods is needed.

The Limits of Software Engineering Methods

What is Software Engineering Research?

We have known for 25 years that our programming methods are inadequate for large projects. Research in software engineering, programming methodology, software design, etc., looks for better tools and methods. The common thrust of results in these fields is to reduce the amount that a programmer must remember when checking and changing a program.

Two main lines of research are (1) structured programming and the use of formal program semantics and (2) the use of formally specified abstract interfaces to hide information about one module (work assignment) from the programmers who are working on other parts. A third idea, less well understood but no less important, is the use of cooperating sequential processes to help deal with the complexities arising from concurrency and multiprogramming. By the late 1970s the basic ideas in software engineering were considered "motherhood" in the academic community. Nonetheless, examinations of real programs revealed that actual programming practice, especially for military systems, had not been changed much by the publication of the academic proposals.

The gap between theory and practice was large and growing. Those espousing structured approaches to software were certain that it would be easy to apply their ideas to the problems that they faced in their daily work. They doubted that programs organized according to the principles espoused by academics could ever meet the performance constraints on "real" systems. Even those who claimed to believe in these principles were not able to apply them consistently.

In 1977 the management of the Naval Research Laboratory in Washington, D.C., and the Naval Weapons Center in China Lake, California, decided that something should be done to close the gap. They asked one of the academics who had faith in the new approach (myself) to demonstrate the applicability of those methods by building, for the sake of comparison, a second version of a Navy real-time program. The project, now known as the Software Cost Reduction project (SCR), was expected to take two to four years. It is still going on.

The project has made two things clear: (1) much of what the academics proposed can be done; (2) good software engineering is far from easy. The methods reduce, but do not eliminate, errors. They reduce, but do not eliminate, the need for testing.

What Should We Do and What Can We Do?

The SCR work has been based on the following precepts.

1. The software requirements should be nailed down with a complete, black-box requirements document before software design is begun.
2. The system should be divided into modules using information-hiding (abstraction) before writing the program begins.
3. Each module should have a precise, black-box, formal specification before writing the program begins.
4. Formal methods should be used to give precise documentation.
5. Real-time systems should be built as a set of cooperating sequential processes, each with a specified period and deadline.
6. Programs should be written using the ideas of structured programming as taught by Harlan Mills.

We have demonstrated that the first four of these percepts can be applied to military software by doing it. The documents that we have written have served as models for others. We have evidence that the models provide a most effective means of technology transfer.

We have not yet proved that these methods lead to reliable code that meets the space and time constraints. We have found that every one of these precepts is easier to pronounce them to carry out. Those who think that software design will become easy, and that errors will disappear, have not attacked substantial problems.

What Makes Software Engineering Hard?

We can write software requirements documents that are complete and precise. We understand the mathematical model behind such documents and can follow a systematic procedure to document all necessary requirements decisions. Unfortunately, it is hard to make the decisions that must be made to write such a document. We often do not know how to make those decisions until we can play with the system. Only when we have built a similar system before is it easy to determine the requirements in advance. It is worth doing, but it is not easy.

We know how to decompose complex systems into modules when we know the set of design decisions that must be made in the implementation. Each of these must be assigned to a single module. We can do that when we are building a system that resembles a system we built before. When we are solving a totally new problem, we will overlook difficult design decisions. The result will be a structure that does not fully separate concerns and minimize complexity.

We know how to specify abstract interfaces for modules. We have a set of standard notations for use in that task. Unfortunately, it is very hard to find the right interface. The interface should be an abstraction of the set of all alternative designs. We can find that abstraction only when we understand the alternative designs. For example, it has proved unexpectedly hard to design an abstract interface that hides the mathematical model of the earth's shape. We have no previous experience with such models and no one has designed such an abstraction before.

The common thread in all these observations is that, even with sound software design principles, we need broad experience with similar systems to design good, reliable software.

Will New Programming Languages Make Much Difference?

Because of the very large improvements in productivity that were noted when compiler languages were introduced, many continue to look for another improvement by introducing better languages. Better notation always helps, but we cannot expect new languages to provide the same magnitude of improvement that we got from the first introduction of such languages. Our experience in SCR has not shown the lack of a language to be a major problem.

Programming languages are now sufficiently flexible that we can use almost any of them for almost any task. We should seek simplifications in programming languages, but we cannot expect that this will make a big difference.

What about Programming Environments?

The success of UNIX™ as a programming development tool has made it clear that the environment in which we work does make a difference. The flexibility of UNIX™ has allowed us to eliminate many of the time-consuming housekeeping tasks involved in producing large programs. Consequently, there is extensive research in programming environments. Here, too, I expect small improvements can be made by basing tools on improved notations but no big breakthroughs. Problems with our programming environment have not been a major impediment in our SCR work.

Why Software Engineering Research Will Not Make the SDI Goals Attainable

Although I believe that further research on software engineering methods can lead to substantial improvements in our ability to build large real-time software systems, this work will not overcome the difficulties inherent in the plans for battle-management computing for SDI. Software engineering methods do not eliminate errors. They do not eliminate the basic differences between software technology and other areas of engineering. They do not eliminate the need for extensive testing under field conditions or the need for opportunities to review the system while it is in use. Most important, we have learned that the successful application of these methods depends on experience accumulated while building and maintaining similar systems. There is no body of experience for SDI battle management.

Conclusion

I am not a modest man. I believe that I have as sound and broad an understanding of the problems of software engineering as anyone that I know. If you gave me the job of building the system, and all the resources that I wanted, I could not do it. I don't expect the next 20 years of research to change that fact.

Artificial Intelligence and the Strategic Defense Initiative

Introduction

One of the technologies being considered for use in the SDI battle-management software is artificial intelligence (AI). Researches in AI have often made big claims, and it is natural to believe that one should use this technology for a problem as difficult as SDI battle management. In this section, I argue that one cannot expect much help from AI in building reliable battle-management software.

What is Artificial Intelligence?

Two quite different definitions of AI are in common use today.

AI-1: The use of computers to solve problems that previously could be solved only by applying human intelligence.

AI-2: The use of a specific set of programming techniques known as heuristic or rule-based programming. In this approach human experts are studied to determine what heuristics or rules of thumb they use in solving problems. Usually they are asked for their rules. These rules are then encoded as input to a program that attempts to behave in accordance with them. In other words, the program is designed to solve a problem the way that humans seem to solve it.

It should be noted that the first definition defines AI as a set of problems, the second defines AI as a set of techniques. The first definition has a sliding meaning. In the Middle Ages, it was thought that arithmetic required intelligence. Now we recognize it as a mechanical act. Something can fit the definition of AI-1 today, but, once we see how the program works and understand the problem, we will not think of it as AI anymore.

It is quite possible for a program to meet one definition and not the other. If we build a speech-recognition program that uses Bayesian mathematics rather than heuristics, it is AI-1 but not AI-2. If we write a rule-based program to generate parsers for precedence grammars using heuristics, it will be AI-2 but not AI-1 because the problem has a known algorithmic solution.

Although it is possible for work to satisfy both definitions, the best AI-1 work that I have seen does not use heuristic or rule-based methods. Workers in AI-1 often use traditional engineering and scientific approaches. They study the problem, its physical and logical constraints, and write a program that makes no attempt to mimic the way that people say they solve the problem.

What Can We Learn from AI that will help us Build the Battle-Management Computer Software?

I have seen some outstanding AI-1 work. Unfortunately, I cannot identify a body of techniques or technology that is unique to this field. When one studies these AI-1 programs one finds that they use sound scientific approaches, approaches that are also used in work that is not called AI. Most of the work is problem specific, and some abstraction and creativity are required to see how to transfer it. People speak of AI as if it were some magic body of new ideas. There is good work in AI-1 but nothing so magic it will allow the solution of the SDI battle-management problem.

I find the approaches taken in AI-2 to be dangerous and much of the work misleading. The rules that one obtains by studying people turn out to be inconsistent, incomplete, and inaccurate. Heuristic programs are developed by a trial and error process in which a new rule is added whenever one finds a case that is not handled by the old rules. This approach usually yields a program whose behavior is poorly understood and hard to predict. AI-2 researchers accept this evolutionary approach to programming as normal and proper. I trust such programs even less than I trust unstructured conventional programs. One never knows when the program will fail.

On occasion I have had to examine closely the claims of a worker in AI-2. I have always been disappointed. On close examination the heuristics turned out to handle a small number of obvious cases but failed to work in general. The author was able to demonstrate spectacular behavior on the cases that the program handled correctly. He marked the other cases as extensions for future researchers. In fact, the techniques being used often do not generalize and the improved program never appears.

What about Expert Systems?

Lately we have heard a great deal about the success of a particular class of rule-based systems known as expert systems. Every discussion cites one example of such a system that is being used to solve real problems by people other than its developer. That example is always the same—a program designed to find configurations for VAX computers. To many of us, that does not sound like a difficult problem; it sounds like the kind of problem that is amenable to algorithmic solution because VAX systems are constructed from well-understood, well-designed components. Recently I read a paper that reported that this program had become a maintenance nightmare. It was poorly understood, badly structured, and hence hard to change. I have good reason to believe that it could be replaced by a better program written using good software engineering technique instead of heuristic techniques.

SDI presents a problem that may be more difficult than those being tackled in AI-1 and expert systems. Workers in those areas attack problems that now require human expertise. Some of the problems in SDI are in areas where we now have no human experts. Do we now have humans who can, with high reliability and confidence, look at missiles in ballistic flight and distinguish warheads from decoys?

Conclusion

Artificial intelligence has the same relation to intelligence as artificial flowers have to flowers. From a distance they may appear much alike, but when closely examined they are quite different. I don't think we can learn much about one by studying the other. AI offers no magic technology to solve our problem. Heuristic techniques do not yield systems that one can trust.

Can Automatic Programming Solve the SDI Software Problem?

Introduction

Throughout my career in computing I have heard people claim that the solution to the software problem is automatic programming. All that one has to do is write the specifications for the software, and the computer will find a program. Can we expect such technology to produce reliable programs for SDI?

Some Perspective on Automatic Programming

The oldest paper known to me that discusses automatic programming was written in the 1940s by Saul Gorn when he was working at the Aberdeen Proving Ground. This paper, entitled "Is Automatic Programming Feasible?" was classified for a while. It answered the question positively.

At that time, programs were fed into computers on paper tapes. The programmer worked the punch directly and actually looked at the holes in the tape. I have seen programmers "patch" programs by literally patching the paper tape.

The automatic programming system considered by Gorn in that paper was an assembler in today's terminology. All that one would have to do with his automatic programming system would be to write a code such as CLA, and the computer would automatically punch the proper holes in the tape. In this way, the programmer's task would be performed automatically by the computer.

In later years the phrase was used to refer to program generation from languages such as IT, FORTRAN, and ALGOL. In each case, the programmer entered a specification of what he wanted, and the computer produced the program in the language of the machine.

In short, automatic programming always has been a euphemism for programming with a higher-level language than was then available to the programmer. Research in automatic programming is simply research in the implementation of higher-level programming languages.

Is Automatic Programming Feasible? What Does That Mean?

Of course automatic programming is feasible. We have known for years that we can implement higher-level programming languages. The only real question was the efficiency of the resulting programs. Usually, if the input "specification" is not a description of an algorithm, the resulting program is woefully inefficient. I do not believe that the use of nonalgorithmic specifications as a programming language will prove practical for systems with limited computer capacity and hard realtime deadlines. When the input specification is a description of an algorithm, writing the specification is really writing a program. There will be no substantial change from our present capability.

Will Automatic Programming Lead to More Reliable Programs?

The use of improved languages has led to a reduction in the amount of detail that a programmer must handle and hence to an improvement in reliability. However, extant programming languages, while far from perfect, are not that bad. Unless we move to nonalgorithmic specifications as an input to these systems, I do not expect a drastic improvement to result from this research.

On the other hand, our experience in writing non-algorithmic specifications has shown that people make mistakes in writing them just as they do in writing algorithms. The effect of such work on reliability is not yet clear.

Will Automatic Programming Lead to a Reliable SDI Battle-Management System?

I believe that the claims that have been made for automatic programming systems are greatly exaggerated. Automatic programming in a way that is substantially different from what we do today is not likely to become a practical tool for real-time systems like the SDI battle-management system. Moreover, one of the basic problems with SDI is that we do not have the information to write specifications that we can trust. In such a situation, automatic programming is no help at all.

Can Program Verification Make the SDI Software Reliable?

Introduction

Programs are mathematical objects. They have meanings that are mathematical objects. Program specifications are mathematical objects. Should it not be possible to prove that a program will meet its specification? This has been a topic of research now for at least 25 years. If we can prove programs correct, could we not prove the SDI software correct? If it was proved correct, could we not rely on it to defend us in time of need?

What Can We Prove?

We can prove that certain small programs in special programming languages meet a specification. The word *small* is a relative one. Those working in verification would consider a 500-line program to be large. In discussing SDI software, we would consider a 500-line program to be small. The programs whose proofs I have seen have been well under 500 lines. They have performed easily defined mathematical tasks. They have been written without use of side effects, an important tool in practical programs.

Proofs for programs such as a model of the earth's gravity field do not have these properties. Such programs are larger; their specifications are not as neat or mathematically formalizable. They are often written in programming languages whose semantics are difficult to formalize. I have seen no proof of such a program.

Not only are manual proofs limited to programs of small size with mathematical specifications; machine theorem provers and verifiers are also strictly limited in the size of the program that they can handle. The size of programs that they can handle is several orders of magnitude different from the size of the programs that would constitute the SDI battle-management system.

Do We Have the Specifications?

In the case of SDI we do not have the specifications against which a proof could be applied. Even if size were not a problem, the lack of specifications would make the notion of a formal proof meaningless. If we wrote a formal specification for the software, we would have no way of proving that a program that satisfied the specification would actually do what we expected it to do. The specification itself might be wrong or incomplete.

Can We Have Faith in Proofs?

Proofs increase our confidence in a program, but we have no basis for complete confidence. Even in pure mathematics there are many cases of proofs that were published with errors. Proofs tend to be reliable when they are small, well polished, and carefully read. They are not reliable when they are large, complex, and not read by anyone but their author. That is what would happen with any attempt to prove even a portion of the SDI software correct.

What About Concurrency?

The proof techniques that are most practical are restricted to sequential programs. Recent work on proofs of systems of concurrent processes has focused on message-passing protocols rather than processes that cooperate using shared memory. There are some techniques that can be applied with shared memory, but they are more difficult than proofs for sequential programs or proofs for programs that are restricted to communication over message channels.

What About Programs that are Supposed to be Robust?

One of the major problems with the SDI software is that it should function with part of its equipment destroyed or disabled by enemy action. In 20 years of watching attempts to prove programs correct, I have seen only one attempt at proving that a program would get the correct answer in the event of a hardware failure. That proof made extremely unrealistic assumptions. We have no techniques for proving the correctness of programs in the presence of unknown hardware failures and errors in input data.

Conclusion

It is inconceivable to me that one could provide a convincing proof of correctness of even a small portion of the SDI software. Given our inability to specify the requirements of the software. I do not know what such a proof would mean if I had it.

Is SDIO an Efficient Way to Fund Worthwhile Research?

The subject of this section is not computer science. Instead, it discusses an issue of concern to all modern scientists: the mechanism that determines what research will be done. These remarks are based on nearly 20 years of experience with DoD funding as well as experience with other funding mechanisms in several countries.

The Proposal

In several discussions of this problem, I have found people telling me they knew the SDIO software could not be built but felt the project should continue because it might fund some good research. In this section I want to discuss that point of view.

The Moral Issue

There is an obvious moral issue raised by this position. The American people and their representatives have been willing to spend huge amounts of money on this project because of the hope that has been offered. Is it honest to take the attitude expressed above? Is it wise to have our policyholders make decisions on the assumption that such a system might be possible? I am not an expert on moral or political issues and offer no answers to these questions.

Is DoD Sponsoring of Software Research Effective?

I can raise another problem with this position. Is the SDIO an effective way to get good research done? Throughout many years of association with DoD I have been astounded at the amount of money that has been wasted in ineffective research projects. In my first contact with the U.S. Navy, I watched millions of dollars spent on a wild computer design that had absolutely no technical merit. It was abandoned many years after its lack of merit became clear. As a consultant for both the Navy and a number of contractors, I have seen expensive software research that produces very large reports with very little content. I have seen those large, expensive reports put on shelves and never used. I have seen many almost identical efforts carried out independently and redundantly. I have seen talented professionals take approaches that they considered unwise because their "customers" asked for it. I have seen their customers take positions they do not understand because they thought that the contractors believed in them.

In computer software, the DoD contracting and funding scheme is remarkably ineffective because the bureaucrats who run it do not understand what they are buying.

Who Can Judge Research?

The most difficult and crucial step in research is identifying and defining the problem. Successful researchers are usually those who have the insight to find a problem that is both solvable and important.

For applied research, additional judgment is needed. A problem may be an important one in theory, but there may be restrictions that prevent the use of its solution in practice. Only people closely familiar with the practical aspects of the problem can judge whether or not they could use the results of a research project.

Applied research must be judged by teams that include both successful researchers and experienced system engineers. They must have ample opportunity to meet, be fully informed, and have clearly defined responsibilities.

Who Judges Research in DoD?

Although there are a few notable exceptions within DoD, the majority of those who manage its applied research program are neither successful researchers nor people with extensive system-building experience. There are outstanding researchers who work for DoD, but most of them work in laboratories, not in the funding agencies. There are many accomplished system builders who work for DoD, but their managers often consider them too valuable to allow them to spend their time reviewing research proposals. The people who end up making funding decisions in DoD are very often unsuccessful researchers, unsuccessful system builders, and people who enter bureaucracy immediately after their education. We call them technocrats.

Technocrats are bombarded with weighty volumes of highly detailed proposals that they are ill prepared to judge. They do not have the time to study and think; they are forced to rely on the advice of others. When they look for advice, they look for people that they know well, whether or not they are people whose areas of expertise are appropriate, and whether or not they have unbiased positions on the subject.

Most technocrats are honest and hard-working, but they are not capable of doing what is needed. The result is a very inefficient research program. I am convinced that there is now much more money being spent on software research than can be usefully spent. Very little of the work that is sponsored leads to results that are useful. Many useful results go unnoticed because the good work is buried in the rest.

The SDIO

The SDIO is a typical organization of technocrats. It is so involved in the advocacy of the program that it cannot judge the quality of the research involved.

The SDIO panel on battle-management computing contains not one person who has built actual battle-management software. It contains no experts on trajectory computations, pattern recognition, or other areas critical to this problem. All of its members stand to profit from continuation of the program.

Alternatives

If there is good research being funded by SDIO, that research has an applicability that is far broader than the SDI itself. It should be managed by teams of scientists and engineers as part of a well-organized research program. There is no need to create a special organization to judge this research. To do so is counterproductive. It can only make the program less efficient.

Conclusion

There is no justification for continuing with the pretense that the SDI battle-management software can be built just to obtain funding for otherwise worthwhile programs. DoD's overall approach to research management requires a thorough evaluation and review by people outside the DoD.

P·A·R·T·VI

5

Safety-Critical Computing: Hazards, Practices, Standards, and Regulation

Jonathan Jacky

A Horror Story

On March 21, 1986, oilfield worker Ray Cox visited a clinic in Tyler, Texas, to receive his radiation treatment. Cox knew from his previous visits that the procedure should be painless—but that day, he felt a jolt of searing heat. Outside the shielded treatment room, the therapy technologist was puzzled. The computer terminal used to operate the radiation machine displayed the cryptic message, "Malfunction 54," indicating the incorrect dose had been delivered. Clinic staff were unable to find anything wrong with the machine, so they sent Cox home and continued treating other patients.

But Cox's condition worsened. Spitting blood, he checked into a hospital emergency room. Clinic staff suspected Cox had received an electrical shock, but specialists were unable to locate any hazard. Less than a month later, malfunction 54 occurred again —this time striking Verdon Kidd, a 66-year-old bus driver. Kidd died in May, reportedly the first fatality ever caused by an overdose during a radiation treatment. Meanwhile, Cox became paralyzed and lapsed into a coma. He died in a Dallas hospital in September 1986.

As news of the Tyler incidents spread, reports of other accidents surfaced. A patient in Canada and another in Georgia had received mutilating injuries in 1985. Another overdose occurred in Washington state in January 1987. All victims had been treated with the Therac-25, a computer-controlled radiation machine called a *linear accelerator* manufactured by Atomic Energy of Canada, Ltd (AECL). Physicist Fritz Hager and therapy technologists at the Tyler clinic discovered that the accidents were caused by errors in

This article is reprinted by permission of *The Sciences* and is from the September/October 1989 issue.

the computer programs that controlled the Therac-25. Cox and Kidd had been killed by software [1, 2, 3, 4, 5].

The Therac accidents were reported in the national press [6, 7, 5] and featured in the television news program *20/20* [8]. Journalist Edward Joyce discovered that different problems with the Therac-25 and its predecessor, the Therac-20, had been turning up for years prior to the Tyler accidents but were not widely known [9, 10, 2, 11]. Injured patients had been largely ignored and machines kept in use. Fixes requested by the Canadian government in the wake of one accident had never been installed [2]. After the Tyler clinic staff explained the cause of the problems, Therac-25s were not withdrawn from service; instead, warnings were circulated and a makeshift temporary fix was recommended [12]—which proved unable to prevent another accident [3].

After the fifth accident, clinics using the Therac-25 were advised—but not ordered —to discontinue routine use until a set of fixes approved by the Food and Drug Administration (FDA) was installed. The major effect of these fixes was to provide traditional safety features that would function independently of the computer [13]. By that time, the Tyler clinic had vowed never to use the Therac-25 again and was attempting to obtain a refund from AECL [10]. AECL stopped selling therapy machines in 1985, citing competitive pressure and poor sales [1].

The accidents showed that computer-controlled equipment could be *less* safe than the old-fashioned equipment it was intended to replace. Hospitals and patients had assumed that manufacturers developed new products carefully, and that any remaining defects would be spotted by the FDA. The Therac incidents revealed that computer system safety had been overlooked by vendors and regulators alike. Software that controlled devices critical to human safety was being developed in a haphazard, unsystematic fashion, and receiving little meaningful review from regulatory agencies—who had little experience with the new equipment and meager resources to deal with it in any case. The never-ending "software crisis" [14, 15]—the unexpected difficulty and expense of creating high-quality software—had finally caught up with the medical equipment industry. But here, instead of merely causing frustration or financial loss, errors could *kill*.

Using computers to control hazardous machinery raises difficult questions. Some are specific to computing: Why use computers at all, if satisfactory techniques already exist? Do computers introduce new kinds of problems unlike those encountered in traditional control systems? What techniques exist now for creating safe and reliable computer-controlled systems, and could they be improved? Other questions are perennial for society at large but are only now beginning to be considered in the computing field: How are we to decide whether a product is safe enough to place on the market? How can we ensure that product developers and service providers are competent and that poor practices are discouraged? Who is held responsible when systems fail and people get killed?

How Did It Happen?

It is useful to explain how the Therac accidents happened, to show how seemingly trivial mistakes can have terrible consequences.

When the accidents occurred, radiation therapy had become a routine, safe and frequently effective procedure, used on almost 450,000 patients each year in over 1,100 clinics in the United States [16]. Much of the success was due to the convenience and therapeutic properties of linear accelerators, which began to replace cobalt units in the 1960s [17, 18]. The million-dollar Therac-25, introduced in 1982 [2, 9], was thought to be among the best available and was one of the first of a new generation of computer-controlled machines. The traditional operator's control panel, festooned with switches, buttons and lamps, was replaced by a computer video display terminal, and much of the internal control electronics was replaced by a computer. This was intended to make operation more convenient, improve the accuracy of treatments, and decrease the time needed to treat each patient [18]. A particular innovation of the Therac-25 was to use the computer to perform many of the safety functions traditionally allocated to independent, or *hard-wired*, electromechanical circuits called *interlocks* [9].

Control systems have traditionally used physical forces transmitted by the motions of wheels, levers, cables, fluids or electric current to transmit the will of a human operator to the controlled devices. Through a more or less indirect chain, the operator's hands and feet were physically connected to the machinery that did the work.

The computer changed all that. Today, it is necessary to transmit only information, not force. Instead of designing a complex control system that depends on meshing cogs, fluid flow or electric current to transform the operator's commands, the designer can plug in a standard computer—perhaps a microprocessor costing only a few dollars. The operator's commands are mediated by software—lists of instructions that tell the computer what to do.

The proper operation of a traditional control system largely depended on the *physical* soundness of the control mechanism. When it failed, it was usually because some part broke or wore out: teeth broke off gears, tubes burned out, hydraulic fluid leaked away. These failures were usually caused by manufacturing defects or wear and could be prevented by inspecting the product and replacing defective parts.

Computer hardware can also break or wear out, but many computer failures are not so easy to understand. They are *design* failures, caused by *logical* unsoundness in the control mechanism. There is no material defect that can be discovered by inspection. As one aircraft accident investigator ruefully noted, "Malfunctioning electrons will not be found in the wreckage" [19].

Some design failures are in the hardware—the computer chips themselves. A design error caused parts from early production runs of the popular Intel 80386 microprocessor, introduced in August 1986, to compute the wrong answer when multiplying certain combinations of numbers. The flaw was not discovered until over 100,000 units had been sold [20]. But design errors in mass-produced computer hardware are unusual. More frequently, design errors occur in the software: the instructions provided to the computer are wrong.

A software error killed Cox and Kidd. It involved the apparently straightforward operation of switching the machine between two operating modes. Linear accelerators, including the Therac-25, can produce two kinds of radiation beams: electron beams and X-rays. Patients are treated with both kinds. First, an electron beam is generated. It may irradiate the patient directly; alternatively, an X-ray beam can be created by placing a metal target into the electron beam: as electrons are absorbed in the target, X-rays emerge from the other side. However, the efficiency of this X-ray-producing process is very poor, so the intensity of the electron beam has to be massively increased when the target is in place. The electron beam intensity in X-ray mode can be over 100 times as great as during an electron beam treatment.

There is great danger that the electron beam might attain its higher intensity with the X-ray target absent, and be driven directly into a patient. This hazard has been well understood for more than twenty years. Three patients were overdosed in one day at Hammersmith Hospital in London in 1966, when the (noncomputer) controls in one of the earliest linear accelerators failed [21, 22].

In most of today's accelerators, hard-wired electromechanical interlocks ensure that high electron beam intensity cannot be attained unless the X-ray target is in place. In the Therac-25, however, both target position and beam intensity were controlled solely by the computer. When the operator switched the machine from X-ray to electron mode, the computer was supposed to withdraw the target and set the beam to low intensity.

Usually it worked that way. At Tyler, more than 500 patients had been treated without mishap in the two years preceding the accidents [1]. However, if the operator selected X-rays by mistake, realized her error, and then selected electrons—all within 8 seconds [12]—the target was withdrawn but the full-intensity beam was turned on. This error —trivial to commit—killed Cox and Kidd. Measurements at Tyler by physicist Fritz Hager, in which he reproduced the accident using a model of a patient called a "phantom," indicated that Kidd received a dose of about 25,000 rads—more than 100 times the prescribed dose [1, 4].

After the Tyler staff explained the mechanism of the accident, AECL recommended a makeshift fix: to make it difficult for the technologist to change the beam type from X-rays to electrons, remove the keycap from the "up-arrow" key and cover it with electrical tape [4]. The FDA concurred that "the interim disabling of the edit mode, in combination with user adherence to operating instructions, will prevent similar mishaps" [12].

But the FDA was mistaken. Another accident occurred in Yakima in Washington state in 1987, caused by a *different* error that also involved the X-ray target [3].

Why Did It Happen?

How was it possible that these accidents could occur—not once, but at least five times? Much of the blame lies with the product and the vendor, but the hazard was exacerbated by problems with the customers.

Other Problems with the Product

The problems with the X-ray target were the immediate cause of the accidents. But those were exacerbated by a poor "user interface" that encouraged technologists to operate the machine in a hazardous fashion. According to a therapist at the site of the Georgia accident, the Therac-25 often issued up to 40 error messages a day. Most of these messages simply indicated that the beam intensity was slightly less than expected, due to the machine being "out of tune." It was possible to cancel the message and proceed with treatments by pressing the "P" key, and operators quickly learned to respond this way to almost any error message—which were hard to tell apart, since they were numerical codes rather than English text.

Unfortunately, it was also possible to proceed in the same casual way after serious faults with safety implications. After an accident in Ontario in 1985, a report by Gordon Symonds of the Canadian Bureau of Radiation and Medical devices criticized this feature. However, the changes it requested—which would have required a more elaborate recovery procedure after safety-related errors—were never made. The consequences were grave. In Tyler, the only indication of trouble that the operators saw was the cryptic message, "Malfunction 54." They repeatedly pushed "P" and turned the beam on again and again, dosing Ray Cox three times [2] (investigators concluded that the first dose alone was fatal).

Problems with the Vendor

AECL allowed a very hazardous product to reach the market. The central problem was *not* that some individual made a couple of mistakes while writing the computer code that handled the X-ray target. That was inevitable; the best programmers make lots of mistakes. The real problem was that AECL failed *as an organization*; it was unable to protect its customers from the errors of one of its staff.

Producing safe products requires a systematic approach to the whole development process. It has to involve several stages of review and evaluation by different people, backed by attention and commitment from those in authority. At AECL, this process must have broken down. It is to be expected that a few errors will slip through any review process (as we shall see, quite a few slip through most software quality assurance programs). However, a history of problems with the Therac series foreshadowed the fatal accidents and should have prompted a thorough reevaluation of its design.

In June 1985 a massive assembly rotated spontaneously on the Therac-25 at the Albert Einstein Medical Center in Philadelphia. Had a patient been present at the time, he might have been crushed. The cause was a hardware failure: a diode had blown out on a circuit board. AECL redesigned the circuit so that failure of the diode could not, by itself, caused unintended movement [11]. Then in July 1985 a patient in Hamilton, Ontario was seriously overdosed. At that time the error was thought to derive from a hardware circuit; at the request of the Canadian government, AECL redesigned the circuit [2]. After he learned of the Tyler accidents in June 1986, physicist Frank Borger at the Michael Reese/University of Chicago Joint Center for Radiation Therapy discovered a similar problem with the X-ray target in the Therac-20. Consequences in the Therac-20 were much less serious; fuses were blown, but hard-wired protective circuits prevented the beam from turning on [9]. In August 1986 technicians at a Mobile, Alabama clinic discovered a similar Therac-20 problem that could result in moderate overdoses. AECL had actually discovered the problem three years earlier and provided a fix (another microswitch), but somehow the retrofit had never been applied to some machines in the field [10].

This history suggests that AECL had no effective mechanism—which amounts to having no effective people in positions of real authority—responsible for ensuring the safety of the Therac product line.

Problems with the Customers

AECL sold a hazardous machine, but their customers also contributed to the accidents. Clinic staff discounted injured patients' complaints and kept using the machines. Tyler continued treating after Cox's injuries were apparent, and Kidd was killed in the next month. In June 1985 Katy Yarbrough was badly injured by the Therac-25 at a clinic in Marietta, Georgia. After the treatment, crying and trembling, she told the treatment technologist, "You burned me." "I'm sorry," the woman replied, "but that's not possible, it's just not possible."

No signs of injury are apparent immediately after an overdose, but within days Yarbrough had a visible burn and was in excruciating pain. Her oncologist believed she was suffering muscle spasms and continued administering treatments. Eventually Yarbrough refused any more. She survived, but lost her breast and the use of one arm. The clinic continued treating others and did not report any problem to AECL or the FDA. They didn't realize what had happened to Yarbrough until news of the Tyler accidents reached them nearly a year later [5].

This misplaced faith in the technology could be the product of years of mishap-free experience with other machines. Moreover, the *physical* design of the Therac-25 beam-production apparatus was considered superb; referring to its dosimetric properties, physicist Alan Baker of Albert Einstein Medical Center in Philadephia, said "It's a wonderful machine, a physicist's delight" [11]. AECL even published a paper in a technical journal describing its radiation protection features—which concentrated exclusively on shielding against low-level hazards and did not even consider the X-ray target or the control system [23]. Furthermore, customers' intuition may have left them unprepared for a particularly diabolical characteristic of software errors: systems that perform most tasks correctly can fail catastrophically when attempting apparently similar tasks. Finally, there was unwarranted confidence in the kludgey keycap fix recommended by AECL—as if there were only one error to be guarded against. Programmers have learned that errors often come in clusters, and units with a history of buggy behavior continue to reveal new faults even as old ones are fixed [24].

There is a less innocent reason why clinics continued to use their machines after injuries and deaths occurred: they were driven by what accident researcher Charles Perrow calls *production pressures*. In his classic study of high-technology mishaps [25], Perrow describes how plant operators, under pressure to keep production lines running, will sometimes tolerate unsafe conditions—until an accident occurs. Today's cancer clinic is hardly less driven by economics than a power plant or chemical refinery; an idle clinic must still pay for the million-dollar machines and the staff that tend them. Pressures may be the most acutely felt in the for-profit "free-standing" clinics that only provide radiation therapy, which have burgeoned in recent years and are actively competing with hospitals and with each other [16]. The FDA is sensitive to the clinics' plight. Asked after the fifth accident whether the FDA was considering a total ban, Edwin Miller of the Office of Compliance in the agency's Division of Radiological Products replied, "No such action is planned at this time. A complete ban would require an extensive study of risk assessment" [3].

Production pressures bear most heavily on the therapy technologists who actually administer the daily treatments (usually in the absence of a physician). The working world is largely divided between people whose job it is to track down problems and others who are supposed to get on with production. Technologists find themselves in the latter category, and can become inured to 40 dose rate errors a day, routinely pressing the "P" key rather than interrupting treatments for the hours or days required to get the machine back in tune. When Cox was hurt at Tyler, he was at first unable to communicate with the technologist outside the heavily shielded treatment room because the intercom and closed-circuit TV were not working that day [1, 4]. The tangled culpabilities are still being unravelled in court [26, 4].

Some clinics resist the pressure. The Hamilton, Ontario, clinic kept its machine out of service for months following their accident, until the fault was positively identified and repaired [2]. Recently, a prominent radiation therapy journal felt it necessary to remind readers, "Remove the patient from the treatment room as a first step when uncertainty in normal treatment unit operation occurs; err on the side of safety rather than staying on schedule" [27].

Other Safety-Critical Applications in Medicine

Fortunately, only 11 Therac-25s had been installed when the hazards became known [1]. But the incidents raised concerns about computer-controlled therapy machines about to be introduced by several manufacturers, as well as other types of computer-controlled medical devices. The FDA anticipates that by 1990, virtually all devices produced by the $11-billion-per-year medical electronics industry will include an embedded micro- or minicomputer [28]. The Therac accidents were only the worst examples of a trend that the FDA had been tracking for several years: computer-related problems in medical devices were on the increase.

The evidence was in the FDA's "recall" database. The medical equipment industry recalls about 400 products a year. Not all recalls involve life-threatening problems, but each implies that the product has serious problems inherent in its design. Twice as many computer-related recalls occurred in 1984 as in 1982 or any prior year. Most computer-related recalls were caused by software errors [28]. There were 84 software-related recalls from 1983 through 1987 [29]. Recalled devices included ultrasound units, patient monitors, blood analyzers, pacemakers, ventilators, and infusion pumps. A blood analyzer displayed incorrect values because addition, rather than subtraction, had been programmed into a calibration formula. A multiple-patient monitoring system mixed up patients' names with the wrong data. An infusion pump would continually infuse insulin if the operator entered "0" as the maximum value to be infused. Another pump would ignore settings of less than 1.0 milliliter per hour and deliver instead whatever the previous setting was, up to 700 milliliters per hour. If a certain command sequence was entered into one pacemaker programmer, the pacemaker would enter a random unpredictable state. In one ventilator, the patient disconnect alarm could fail to sound when

when needed, and the gas concentrations (like oxygen) could decrease without activation of an alarm or indication on the display. In many of these applications, as in the Therac incidents, failure of the control system could cause people to be killed.

Other Safety-Critical Applications

Because of their low cost and versatility, computers are replacing traditional controls in all kinds of products. The Airbus Industries A320 airline attracted great press attention when it debuted in 1988 because it was the first commercial airliner to feature "fly-by-wire" controls—in which computers, rather than cables and hydraulics, connect the pilot's control stick to the elevator and other control surfaces [30, 31]. It was not so widely noted that other computers onboard the A320 are needed to turn on the cabin lights and even flush the toilets [32]! In today's new cars, computers control the fuel injection and spark timing and may control the suspension and an anti-lock braking mechanism [33, 34]. GM is already experimenting with "drive-by-wire" automobiles in which there is no physical connection (other than the computer) from the steering wheel to the tires [35]. In railroads, computers control the switches that are supposed to prevent trains from colliding [36]. Computers are used extensively to control processes in factories and power plants. Some of the emergency shutdown systems that are supposed to "scram" nuclear reactors are computer controlled—including ones built by AECL [37]. In weapons systems, computers warn of imminent attack, identify and track targets, aim guns and steer missiles, and arm and detonate explosives [38].

Software Errors Are a Serious Problem

All safety-critical applications depend on software, but software is among the most *imperfect* of the products of modern technology. Pundits debate whether computers will develop superhuman intelligence or conduct automated wars in space, but back here on planet Earth, after more than 30 years of commercial data processing, folks are still receiving $20 million tax bills [39] and dunning letters for $0.00 [40]. Ensuring that simple results are reliably achieved strains the limits of the typical programmer's art. In the last few years, industry giants IBM, Digital Equipment Corporation, Lotus, and Microsoft have all sold programs containing errors that could destroy users' data [41–45]. A repository of problem reports maintained by Peter Neumann at SRI International under the co-sponsorship of the Association for Computing Machinery (ACM), a professional organization, currently lists more than 400 incidents in which computer problems caused or threatened injury or significant financial loss [46, 47].

These are not isolated incidents. They follow from typical practices that, in educator Maurice Naftalin's words, "encourage programmers to produce, as quickly as possible, large programs which they know will contain serious errors" [48].

How Programs Are Written

When manufacturers began installing computers in medical equipment, they introduced a new kind of problem, never encountered in simpler devices: programming errors, or, as programmers say, "bugs." Mechanical and electrical design and assembly are only a part of the effort involved in constructing a computer-controlled device. The behavior of the machinery is determined by lists of instructions called programs, or *software*. Programs are not manufactured in any traditional sense; they are written in a notation called a programming language. To understand why bugs are such a problem, it is necessary to know a little about how a program is built.

Ideally, a program is developed in several stages. First, it is *specified*: designers try to anticipate every situation that the machine might encounter, and then describe exactly how it should respond to each one. One of the most important jobs designers have is providing programmers with a complete and unambiguous specification. Features that are not clearly specified will be handled by default or at the whim of some programmer —who may not be familiar with important practical details of the machine's operations. It is possible that the designers and programmers of the Therac-25 forgot to consider that the operator might switch from X-rays to electrons at the last minute, so that contingency was handled badly.

The program is then *designed*: a sort of rough outline is drawn up, in which different program subdivisions, or *modules*, are distinguished. At this stage, specific behaviors are assigned to each module. It is the designers' responsibility to ensure that when the finished modules are collected, or *linked*, into a working program, the specified system behavior emerges. Usually, modules are delegated to different programmers, who work independently. Large programs are often composed of modules produced over several years by programmers who never meet.

Finally, the program is *coded*: programmers compose each module by writing lists of programming language statements that they believe will accomplish the behaviors assigned in the design. At this stage, programmers typically compose by typing the program text into a video terminal or personal computer. This part of the activity very much resembles writing letters on a word processor, except that the text produced resembles no human language. When the program text is complete, it must be translated to machine code. Usually, the computer cannot follow the instructions that the programmer writes. Instead, the programmer's text must be converted to a much more elemental set of instructions that the computer can execute. The translation is performed by another program called a *compiler* or *assembler*. The Therac-25 was programmed in *assembly language*, a notoriously obscure and error-prone notation that is quite close to the machine code.

A program's size is measured by counting the number of programming language statements, or *lines of code*, it contains. Simple appliances like microwave ovens may contain a few hundred or a few thousand lines. Typical commercial products like word processors contain tens of thousands of lines, and large systems like aircraft flight control programs contain hundreds of thousands of lines.

Producing quality software is largely a *design* and *management* problem, not a coding problem. Individual programmers usually comprehend their creations at the level of modules that are at most a few hundred lines long. Most programmers' training concentrates on this level. Building large programs that are tens of thousands of lines long requires a different set of skills, emphasizing communication and organization, in order to extract useful specifications, divide the project into modules that are reasonable work assignments, ensure continuity and consistency among the programmers and their individual products, and make sure that meaningful testing is performed. Without this guidance, skilled coders flounder.

Unfortunately, the programming culture has tended to glorify instead the lone "hacker" who energetically but unsystematically improvises huge programs. (This usage of "hacker" is much older than its recent connotations of computer crime, and derives from the original meaning, "to cut irregularly, without skill or definite purpose.") The consequences are aptly described by Marvin Minsky, dean of American artificial intelligence researchers: "When a program grows in power by an evolution of partially understood patches and fixes, the programmer begins to lose track of internal details, loses his ability to predict what will happen, begins to hope instead of to know, and watches the results as though the program were an individual whose range of behavior is uncertain" [49].

The all-too-frequent result is programs that *seem* to work, but then fail unexpectedly. The persistence of lurking defects in products released on the market is one of the main things that distinguishes software from hardware. Software engineer John Shore says, "It's extremely hard to build a large computer program that works correctly under all required conditions, but it's easy to build one that works 90 percent of the time. It's also hard to build reliable airplanes, but it's not particularly easy to build an airplane that flies 90 percent of the time" [14].

How Errors Are Detected

Most programmers are not able to demonstrate that their creations will compute the intended results, except by running tests. It is *literally* a trial-and-error process. It is not terribly confidence-inspiring because the number of possible situations that a program must deal with is usually much too large to test, and a case that was left out of the test set may cause the program to fail. As a result, errors are left in products when they reach the market, to be discovered and corrected over time as the system is used. The term *maintenance* is used in the computer field to describe this continuous error-removal process.

How many errors are left in typical programs? A lot. Typical commercial programs contain between 10,000 and 100,000 lines of code. One measure of program quality is the number of errors per thousand lines of code. Typical programmers leave around 50 errors per thousand lines in the code they write [50, 51]; these must be weeded out during testing or actual use. One report on "the American data processing industry" says that vendors find less than 75% of the programming errors, leaving customers to stumble over the remaining 25% [52]. One reviewer concludes that conscientious vendors try to test until only one or two errors per thousand lines remain in the products they place on the market [53]. Errors reported in newly delivered products range from less than one per thousand lines to around ten per thousand [50, 54], with "good" products clustering around one to five errors per thousand lines. This means that a typical "good" program may contain hundreds of errors.

Usually, software errors do not have serious consequences because people can repair the damage—at some cost in time and aggravation. The state sends you a $20 million tax bill? Clear it up with a phone call—or several. The telephone switching computer cut off your call? Hang up and dial again. The word processor at the office deleted your letter? Type it in again, and this time be sure to make a backup copy to store offline—just as you were warned to do. Experienced computer users develop a defensive style, a whole repertoire of workarounds. It is this human ability to adapt to problems that makes it possible to base a computerized society on imperfect products.

But some products do not provide much opportunity for people to correct errors. When a computer controls a linear accelerator or an airplane, the results of an error cannot be discarded or ignored. If the patient dies or the airplane crashes, the computation cannot be done over. Applying typical programming practices to critical systems like these can result in tragedy.

Building Better Computer-Controlled Systems

Safety-critical products demand a different, more rigorous approach than most other computer applications. They require several disciplines that are still unfamiliar to many programmers and programming managers: *Safety engineering* teaches how to design systems that remain safe even when hardware or software fails. *Software engineering* provides methods for developing complex programs systematically. *Formal methods* are mathematically based techniques for increasing product reliability that overcome some of the limitations of trial-and-error testing. In addition, *certification* and *regulation* may help ensure that products are produced using the best techniques available, by people who understand how to use them. *Liability* must fall upon vendors who fail.

All of this is expensive. Computer system safety expert Nancy Leveson says, "I do not know how to develop safety-critical software cheaply" [55].

Safety Engineering

Safety engineering emerged from the missile projects of the late 1950s and early 1960s. A series of spectacular explosions demonstrated that the complexity and risk of modern technologies demand a systematic approach to controlling hazards [56, 57, 19]. In a famous 1962 incident, the Mariner I Venus probe had to be destroyed when it went off-course because of a single-character transcription error in the equations used as specifications for its control program [58].

The most important lesson of safety engineering is that safety is an important system requirement in its own right and must be designed into a product, not added on as an afterthought. Safety requirements often conflict with other system requirements and may suggest a quite different design than would be obtained if cost and performance were the only considerations. Resolving such conflicts in a consistent and intelligent manner (rather than by default or at the whim of the individual) demands that safety requirements be explicitly separated out and that responsibility for meeting them be assigned to someone with authority.

Safety is not the same thing as reliability. Reliability is a measure of how well the system does exactly what it is intended to do. A safe system protects from hazards whether its intended function is performed correctly or not. In fact, safety is most concerned with what happens when the system does not work as expected. Safety engineers assume that systems will fail—and then they work through the consequences.

Computers—by providing convenient controls, well-designed displays, and more comprehensive diagnostics and error logging—can increase safety. But naive application of computers can increase hazards. It is possible to replace a complex control mechanism with a single computer; the Therac-25 was very close to that idea. But this simplification violates the first rule of safety engineering—that failure of a single component should never, by itself, be capable of causing an accident. This principle rules out designs in which safety depends entirely upon correct operation of a single computer, unprotected by hardwired interlocks.

Some designers of computer-based systems seem unaware of the principles of safety engineering. Part of the problem may be lack of instruction. Builders of hard-wired radiation therapy machines can refer to very detailed guides that explain how to design and test safety circuits [59]. Nothing like this exists for computer-controlled machines. A new specialty called *software safety* is beginning to adapt the principles of safety engineering to software-controlled systems [60].

Software Engineering

Software engineering takes its name from a conference convened by NATO in 1968, when the incipient "software crisis" [15] began to make it clear that building software demands a systematic, disciplined approach rather than ad-hoc tinkering.

The central idea of software engineering is that programming projects have to be performed in stages, with an identifiable end product at each stage. The final product is the program itself, but there are several, or many, intermediate stages of design as well. The visible products of most of these intermediate stages are documents *about* the program. Typically, these include a *specification* describing what the product is supposed to do, a *design guide* describing how the program is organized, a *test plan* describing a series of tests that are supposed to show that the program works as promised in the specification, and a *test report* that presents the test results and explains how any problems were resolved.

Requiring the programmers to obtain approval of each document before proceeding to the next stage enforces an orderly development process, makes progress visible to management, and enables products to be reviewed by experts other than their creators [61]. Auditing these documents is the primary means of quality assurance in engineered projects. The auditors join the programmers in sharing responsibility for the product. It is analogous to civil engineering, where engineers must produce detailed designs that are subjected to analysis and review before anyone starts pouring concrete. This process is contrary to the stereotype of the eccentric genius programmer, but, as programming expert Tony Hoare notes, "The principle that the work of an engineer should be inspected and signed off by another more experienced and competent engineer lies at the heart of the codes of safe practice in all branches of engineering" [62].

Programmers work much differently on engineered software projects. They find about half their effort is devoted to planning and design, and much of the rest goes for testing and quality assurance. Only 15% to 20% is actually spent coding statements in a programming language—what most people think of as programming [63]. The paradox of software engineering is that the least amount of effort is devoted to the one component that can be sold to the customer. Of course, the effort devoted to the other stages is supposed to ensure the quality of the delivered code, and some studies have found that fixing an error discovered by customers costs as much as 100 times as much as catching it early in development [63].

Software Engineering "Standards"

The whole purpose of staged development is to ensure that the necessary planning and design is performed, but regulatory agencies tend to focus on the visible products of the effort: the documents. There exist many so-called *software standards* that are actually *documentation* standards that describe the format of the documents in considerable detail. The fact that the standards define only what the reports must look like but not what programmers must do explains the disappointment that most programmers feel when they first read them. Conscientious programming teams usually develop their own documentation style, which is well-matched to their product and their favored design methods.

The document-driven approach in its most hypertrophied form is practiced by the United States Department of Defense (DoD) and its contractors, who must observe a standard called DOD-STD-2167A that requires 16 separate documents [64]. The DoD standard is oriented towards huge projects costing hundreds of millions of dollars, employing thousands of staff generating millions of lines of code, and practically defines a separate programming culture. They have their own programming language, Ada, which is just now becoming usable after more than 10 years of development and is not widely used outside the defense contract world [65]. They built a $100 million Software Engineering Institute attached to Carnegie-Mellon University to teach and promulgate their techniques [66, 67]. There are firms that specialize in auditing other contractors' projects, a practice called *independent validation and verification*, or *IV&V* [68].

Despite these efforts, software developed to DoD standards still reaches the field with serious errors. Several software-related accidents accompanied the introduction of "fly-by-wire" aircraft into the United States' combat forces. A computer-controlled wing-mounted launcher retained its grip after its missile was ignited, creating what someone described as "the world's largest pinwheel" when the aircraft went violently out of control. An F-14 drove off the deck of an aircraft carrier on command from its computer-controlled throttle. Another jet crashed when its flight control program was confronted with an unanticipated mechanical problem [19]. The widow of the pilot who died in a software-related F-16 crash has brought a lawsuit [69].

The expense of the DoD approach precludes its use on civil projects, except those built on the same gigantic scale by the same contractors, like the space station and the FAA's new air traffic control system. Little guidance is offered to "small" projects—described as those costing "no more than several million dollars a year" [70]. The IEEE, a professional society, recommends a relatively lightweight standard (only six documents [64]) but even this is considered to be too expensive for projects comprising fewer than 10 person-years of effort [71]. An IEEE survey finds this standard is rarely used. One disappointed standards writer says, "Perhaps software standards are successfully applied only when they are mandatory" [72].

When the FDA began moving to regulate software in 1987, it appeared to favor an approach similar to the IEEE recommendations [73]. Some medical equipment vendors opposed the additional documentation effort. At a 1988 medical equipment manufacturer's meeting, James Howard of GE Medical Systems criticized the IEEE-based approach [73] as "an effective, costly and time-consuming strategy based on documentation of many specific steps during software development" [74]. The FDA's Frank Houston found that "a significant amount of software for life-critical systems comes from small firms . . . some of which operate literally in basements and garages . . . so there is little perceived incentive on the part of small, commercial sector businesses to read or heed the lessons learned by large companies in the defense industry [75]."

Formal Methods

Formal methods are software engineering techniques that apply mathematical logic to programming. People who have heard that computers are logical machines are surprised to learn that this is a radical innovation. In fact, most programs today evolve in a rather ad-hoc fashion and are evaluated empirically, by trial-and-error testing. Some formal techniques concentrate on special notations that completely and unambiguously describe software requirements and designs. These are analogous to the notations that other engineers use, like circuit diagrams or architectural prints. These notations describe abstract models whose behavior can be analyzed mathematically prove the product is actually constructed. Some formal techniques attempt to *prove* that programs are correct, in much the same sense that theorems in geometry can be proved correct [62, 76, 77]. Advocates believe that these methods can provide a powerful supplement to testing and subjective documentation reviews.

Computer scientists have been pursuing formal methods for more than 20 years, but they are almost never used in practice. In 1986, advocate Tony Hoare was unable to find a single safety-critical program that had ever been checked by the available mathematical techniques, and he learned that many programmers working on safety-critical projects had never heard of them [62]. Some scientists argue that the techniques are so difficult and cumbersome that it will never be practical to apply them to useful programs [78, 68]. Other caution that the expression *proved correct* promises too much to laypeople, since formal proof does not guarantee that a program is perfect and cannot assure that the mathematical properties that can be proved actually capture the behavior that the customer wants.

Testing and subjective documentation reviews are so inefficient that formal methods need not be perfect to be cost-effective. Formal methods can uncover errors that were missed by the other techniques. Recently the British Royal Signals and Radar Establishment (RSRE), the central electronics research laboratory of the UK Ministry of Defence

(MOD), applied formal analysis to a sample of program fragments drawn from the NATO military software inventory. Of these, 1 in 10 were found to contain errors, and of those, 1 in 20 (or 1 in 200 overall) had errors serious enough to result in loss of the vehicle or plant—for example, an actuator could be driven in the direction opposite from the intended one. Some of these modules had passed extensive tests on multimillion-dollar test rigs [68, 79].

It remains to be seen how effective formal methods will be in practice, but the Europeans are betting heavily on them. In the largest formal effort to date, a British team proved that the hardware of a new microprocessor called the VIPER was free of certain kinds of design errors. The proof included more than a million steps and was partly generated and checked by computer [68, 79, 69, 80, 81]. New regulations from the British MOD will *require* formal methods for some safety-critical products [68, 79], and a government-sponsored report strongly encourages their use in civil products as well [82]. Nothing like this is planned in the United States. Some observers suggest that cultural differences play a role: Europe places greater emphasis on formal, scholastic ideas, and its engineering education emphasizes mathematical rigor; Americans purchase more computer power and like to do a lot of hands-on testing [83].

Certification and Regulation

We regulate products that have safety implications: buildings, bridges, airplanes, drugs. The government establishes standards that these products must meet and conducts inspections to make sure products comply. We also regulate people that provide safety-critical services: they must satisfy educational requirements and pass examinations. Designers can also be regulated: states usually require that bridges and large buildings be signed off by a licensed *professional engineer* who assumes responsibility for the structure's safety on behalf of the contractor.

Software is still largely unregulated. Until recently, aviation and nuclear power were the only applications in which software purchased or operated by private enterprise was subject to approval by the government. In September 1987 the FDA announced its intention to regulate software in some classes of medical devices [84].

Programmers and programming managers are entirely unregulated. The programming profession includes a great range of education and abilities, and many curricula do not provide instruction in topics relevant to building safe systems. Studies of employed programmers have found that the best can be more than 25 times as able as the worst, and some teams outproduce others by factors of four or five [63]. Nor is incompetence and ignorance limited to junior programmers; numerous runaway computing projects in which millions of dollars are wasted are evidence that many managers also have a poor grip on their responsibilities [85, 86].

Some are calling for more regulation. John Shore says, "We require certification for doctors, lawyers, architects, civil engineers, aircraft pilots, automobile drivers, and even hair stylists! Why not software engineers?" [87]. Referring to the Therac accidents, software safety expert Nancy Leveson says, "This is appalling. There needs to be some kind of certification of software professionals working on safety-critical projects or much stricter government controls." Others disagree, fearing government interference and increased costs. "I'll fight them to the death," says Robert Ulrickson, president of Logical Services Inc., a Santa Clara company that designs computerized instruments. "I don't want to be part of an economy that's run by the government. The way to get quality is not to regulate, but to manage" [88]. But Tony Hoare says, "No industry and no profession has ever voluntarily and spontaneously developed or adopted an effective and relevant code for safe practice. Even voluntary codes are established only in the face of some kind of external pressure or threat, arising from public disquiet, fostered by journals and newspapers and taken up by politicians" [62].

Liability

When systems fail, victims or their survivors may sue vendors and service providers for compensation. An important (if abstruse) legal issue turns on whether software is considered a *service* (in which case providers will be found liable if it can be shown they were *negligent*), or a *product* (in which case *strict liability* holds—it is only necessary to show that the plaintiff was injured). It is usually easier for plaintiffs to recover damages under strict liability than under negligence (which requires that they investigate the defendant's conduct), so it is usually to the plaintiff's advantage if software is regarded as a product [4].

A New Leaf?

Meanwhile, the medical community is attempting to respond to the problems revealed by the Therac accidents. In September, 1987, the FDA announced its intent to regulate some computer software as medical devices [84] and began to work out guidelines for its investigators [73, 89]. A staff member from the House Science and Technology Committee has begun investigating industry software quality assurance practices on behalf of Congress [88, 68]. Medical equipment manufacturing associations and professional societies are instructing their members in software quality assurance and acceptance testing [90, 68, 91, 92], and organizing to prevent the FDA regulations from becoming too onerous or intrusive (from their point of view) [93]. Manufacturers are sending their staff to courses on computer system safety and devoting unusually thorough quality assurance efforts toward their new machines [94, 95]. Some have contracted with outside firms to perform independent tests and evaluations [96, 68].

It remains to be seen how effective all of this will be. Considerable improvement seems certain, if only because the baseline is so low. Eventually a much better level of practice should emerge. In the meantime, a lot of new products will be released. Today, and for years to come, our safety largely depends on the skill and conscientiousness of individual engineers, programmers, and managers.

References

1. Joyce, Edward J. (1986). "Malfunction 54: Unraveling Deadly Medical Mystery of Computerized Accelerator Gone Awry," *American Medical News*, October 3, pp. 1, 13–17.

2. Joyce, Edward J. (1989). "Software Flaw Known before Radiation Killed Two," *American Medical News*, January 16, p. 3, 42–45.

3. Joyce, Edward J. (1987). "Accelerator Linked to Fifth Radiation Overdose," *American Medical News*, February 6, p. 1, 49, 50.

4. Joyce, Edward J. (1987). "Software Bugs: A Matter of Life and Liability," *Datamation*, May 15, pp. 88–92.

5. Breu, Giovanna, and William Plumber (19??). A Computer Glitch Turns Miracle Machine into Monster for Three Cancer Patients," *People*.

6. *New York Times* (1986). "Computer Error is Cited in Radiation Death." June 21, p. 8.

7. Saltos, Richard (1986). "Man Killed by Accident with Medical Radiation," *Boston Globe*, June 20, p. 1.

8. Wizenberg, M. D. Morris (1987). Letter to American Society for Therapeutic Radiology and Oncology members (June 26).

9. Joyce, Edward J. (1986). "Software 'Bug' Discovered in Second Linear Accelerator," *American Medical News*, November 7, p. 20–21.

10. Joyce, Edward J. (1986). "Firm Warns of Another Therac 20 Problem," *American Medical News*, November 7, p. 20, 21.

11. *American Medical News* (1987). "Failure Not the First Time." January 16, p. 43.

12. *Radiological Health Bulletin* (1986). FDA Monitoring Correction of Therac Radiation Therapy Units." 20(8), (December), pp. 1–2.

13. *Radiological Health Bulletin* (1987). Therac-25 Accelerator Purchasers Advised to Discontinue Routine Use." 21(3), (March), pp. 1–2.

14. Shore, John (1985). *The Sachertorte Algorithm and Other Antidotes to Computer Anxiety*. Viking, New York.

15. Randell, Brian (1979). Software Engineering in 1968," in *Proceedings of the Fourth International Conference on Software Engineering*, IEEE Computer Society, p. 1–10.

16. Diamond, James J., Gerald E. Hanks, and Simon Kramer (1988). "The Structure of Radiation Oncology Practices in the United States". *International Journal of Radiation Oncology, Biology and Physics*, 14(3), (March), pp. 547–548.

17. Hanks, Gerald E., James J. Diamond, and Simon Kramer (1985). "The Need for Complex Technology in Radiation Oncology: Correlations of Facility Characteristics and Structure with Outcome," *Cancer*, 55, pp. 2198–2201.

18. Karzmark, C. J., and Neil C. Pering (1973). "Electron Linear Accelerators for Radiation Therapy: History, Principles and Contemporary Developments," *Physics in Medicine and Biology*, 18(3), (May), pp. 321–354.

19. Frola, F. R., and C. O. Miller (1984). *System Safety in Aircraft Acquisition*. Logistics Management Institute, Washington, D.C.

20. *IEEE Spectrum* (1987). "Faults and Failures: Multiplying Mistakes." 24(8), p. 17.

21. *British Medical Journal* (1966). "Radiation Accident at Hammersmith." Number 5507 23 July, p. 233.

22. Karzmark, C. J. (1967). "Some Aspects of Radiation Safety for Electron Accelerators Used for Both X-ray and Electron Therapy," *British Journal of Radiology*, 40, pp. 697–703.

23. O'Brien, P., H. B. Michaels, B. Gillies, J. E. Aldrich, and J. W. Andrew (1985). "Radiation Protection Aspects of a New High-Energy Linear Accelerator," *Medical Physics*, 12(1), (January/February), pp. 101–107.

24. Dunsmore, H. E. (1988). "Evidence Supports Some Truisms, Belies Others," *IEEE Software*, 5(3), (May), pp. 96, 99.

25. Perrow, Charles (1984). *Normal Accidents: Living with High-Risk Technologies*. Basic Books, New York.

26. *American Medical News* (1987). "Suits Filed Over Deaths Linked to Therac 25." January 16, p. 44.

27. Karzmark, C. J. (1987). "Procedural and Operator Error Aspects of Radiation Accidents in Radiotherapy," *International Journal of Radiation Oncology, Biology and Physics*, 13(10), (October), pp. 1599–1602.

28. Bassen, H., J. Silberberg, F. Houston, W. Knight, C. Christman, and M. Greberman (1985). "Computerized Medical Devices: Usage Trends, Problems, and Safety Technology," in James C. Lin and Barry N. Feinberg, editors, *Frontiers of Engineering and Computing in Health Care: Proceedings of the Seventh Annual Conference of the IEEE/Engineering in Medicine and Biology Society*, p. 180–185.

29. Jorgens, Joseph (1991). "Purposes of Software Quality Assurance: A Means to an End," in Richard Fries, editor, *Developing, Purchasing, and Using Safe, Effective, and Reliable Medical Software*, Association for the Advancement of Medical Instrumentation, Arlington, Virginia.

30. Spitzer, Cary R. (1986). "All-digital Jets Are Taking Off," *IEEE Spectrum*, September, pp. 51–56.

31. Rouquet, J. C., and P. J. Traverse (1986). "Safe and Reliable Computing on Board the Airbus and ATR Aircraft," in W. J. Quirk, editor, *Proceedings of Safecomp '86: Safety of Computer Control Systems*, Pergamon Press, Oxford, England.

32. *Flight International.* September 3, 1988.

33. Jurgen, Ronald K. (1987). Detroit '88: Driver-friendly Innovations," *IEEE Spectrum*, December, pp. 53–57.

34. Voelcker, John (1988). Electronics Puts Its Foot on the Gas," *IEEE Spectrum*, May, pp. 53–57.

35. Stambler, Irwin (1988). "Fly-by-Wire Techniques Are Being Adapted for Automobile Controls," *Research and Development*, March, p. 41.

36. Murphy, Erin E. (1988). "All Abroad for Solid State," *IEEE Spectrum*, 25(13), December, pp. 42–45.

37. Gilbert, R. S. (1985). "Control and Safety Computers in CANDU Power Stations," *IAEA Bulletin*, Autumn, pp. 7–12.

38. Bellin, David, and Gary Chapman, editors (1987). *Computers in Battle: Will They Work?* Harcourt, Brace Jovanovich, Boston.

39. McBride, Steven (1988). "State Taxes on a New Computer System," *RISKS-FORUM Digest*, 6(6), (April 13), (cites March 15, 1988, Ogden Standard Examiner).

40. Saltzer, Jerome H. (1988). "Zero-balance Dunning Letter," *RISKS-FORUM Digest*, 7(36), (August 17).

41. Rogers, Michael (1986). "Software Makers Battle the Bugs," *Fortune*, February 17, p. 83.

42. Ruby, Daniel, and Shan Chan (1986). "Who's Responsible for the Bugs?" *PC Week*, May 27, pp. 51–54.

43. Kneale, Dennis (1985). "Buyer Beware: Software Plagued by Poor Quality and Poor Service," *Wall Street Journal*, October 2.

44. Digital Equipment Corporation (1986). "Problem in VAX/VMS Data Encryption Facility," *VAX/VMS Systems Dispatch*, March, p. 21.

45. Jones, Stephen (1988). "Microsoft Scrambles to Head Off Runaway Mouse with Word Rewrite," *Computerworld*, 39, 42, September 5, pp. 39–42.

46. Neumann, Peter G. (1987). "Index for Computer-related Risks in SEN," *ACM Software Engineering Notes*, 12(1), (January), pp. 22–28.

47. Neumann, Peter G. (1988). "Illustrative Risks to the Public in the Use of Computer Systems and Related Technology," SRI International. Menlo Park, California, 5 April.

48. Naftalin, Maurice (1988). "Correctness for Beginners," in R. Bloomfield, L. Marshall, and R. Jones, editors, *VDM '88: VDM—The Way Ahead (Lecture Notes in Computer Science No. 328),*

Proceedings of the 2nd VDM-Europe Symposium, Dublin, Ireland, Springer-Verlag, Berlin.

49. Minsky, Marvin (1967). "Why Programming Is a Good Medium for Expressing Poorly Understood and Sloppily Formulated Ideas," in *Design and Planning II*, Hastings House, New York. (Quoted by J. Weizenbaum in *Computer Power and Human Reason*, pps. 234–235).

50. Beizer, Boris (1984). *Software System Testing and Quality Assurance*. Van Nostrand Reinhold, New York.

51. Perry, W. E. (1987). "Software Is Still Arriving with Those Annoying Bugs," *Government Computer New*, October 27, pp. 43–47.

52. Jones, C. (1988). "Building a Better Metric," *Computerworld Extra* (a supplement to *Computerworld*), June 20, pp. 38–39.

53. Petschenik, N. H. (1985). "Practical Priorities in System Testing," *IEEE Software*, 2(5), pp. 18–23.

54. Musa, J. D., A. Iannino, and K. Okumoto (1987). *Software Reliability: Measurement, Prediction, Application*. McGraw-Hill, New York.

55. Leveson, Nancy (1987). "A Scary Tale—Sperry Avionics Module Testing Bites the Dust!" *ACM Software Engineering Notes*, 12(2), (April), pp. 23–25.

56. Rodgers, W. P. (1971). *Introduction to System Safety Engineering*. Wiley, New York.

57. Miller, C. O. (1971). "Why System Safety?" *Technology Review*, 73(4), (February), pp. 28–33.

58. Ceruzzi, Paul E. (1989). Beyond the Limits: Flight Enters the Computer Age. MIT Press, Cambridge, Mass. pp. 202–203.

59. Post, R. J. (1971). "Some Considerations of Interlocking and Safety Circuits for Radiotherapy Apparatus," *International Journal of Radiation Engineering*, 1(2), pp. 169–191.

60. Leveson, Nancy G. (1986). "Software Safety: What, Why and How," *ACM Computing Surveys*, 18(2), (June), pp. 125–163.

61. Parnas, David Lorge, and Paul C. Clements (1986). "A Rational Design Process: How and Why to Fake It," *IEEE Transactions on Software Engineering*, SE-12(2), (February), pp. 251–257.

62. Hoare, Tony (1986). "Maths Adds Safety to Computer Programs," *New Scientist*, 18 September, pp. 53–56.

63. Boehm, Barry (1987). "Industrial Software Metrics Top Ten List," *IEEE Software*, 4(5), (September), pp. 84–85.

64. Tice, George (1988). "Documentation: How Much Is Enough?" *IEEE Software*, May, p. 95.

65. Jacky, Jonathan (1987). "Ada's Troubled Debut," *The Sciences*, 27(1), (January/February), pp. 20–29.

66. Barbacci, Marlo R., A. Nico Habermann, and Mary Shaw (1985). "The Software Engineering Institute: Bridging Practice and Potential," *IEEE Software*, November.

67. Joyce, Edward J. (1986). "SEI: The Software Battleground," *Datamation*, September 15, pp. 109–116.

68. Jacky, Jonathan (1988). "COMPASS '88 Trip Report," *ACM Software Engineering Notes*, 13(4), (October), pp. 21–27.

69. Woolnough, Roger (1988). "The VIPER: Developers Pushed by a Sense of Danger," *Electronic Engineering Times*, March 14, pp. 53, 55, 59, 60.

70. Bryan, W., and S. Siegel (1984). "Making Software Visible, Operational, and Maintainable in a Small Project Environment," *IEEE Transactions on Software Engineering*, SE-10(1), pp. 59–67.

71. Poston, Robert M. (1985). "IEEE 730: A Guide for Writing Successful SQA Plans," *IEEE Software*, March, pp. 86–88.

72. Tice, George (1988). "Are Software Standards Wasted Efforts?" *IEEE Software*, 5(5), (September), pp. 88–89.

73. Food and Drug Administration (1987). Technical Reference on Software Development Activities (draft).

74. Howard II, J. M. (1988). "A Hazard Oriented Approach to Computer System Safety," in

Proceedings, AAMI 23rd Annual Meeting and Exposition, Association for the Advancement of Medical Instrumentation, Arlington, Virginia, p. 48.

75. Houston, M. Frank (1987). "What Do the Simple Folk Do? Software Safety in the Cottage Industry," in *Proceedings of the COMPASS '87 Computer Assurance Conference (Supplement)*, pages S-20–S-25.

76. Hoare, C. A. R. (1987). "An Overview of Some Formal Methods for Program Design, *Computer*, 20(9), (September), pp. 85–91.

77. Carre, B. A. (1980). "Software Validation," *Microprocessors and Microsystems*, 4(10), (December), pp. 395–406.

78. DeMillo, Richard A., Richard J. Lipton, and Alan J. Perlis (1979). "Social Processes and Proofs of Theorems and Programs," *Communications of the ACM*, 22(5), (May), pp. 271–280.

79. Cullyer, W. J. (1988). "High Integrity Computing," in M. Joseph, editor, *Formal Techniques in Real-Time and Fault-Tolerant Systems (Lecture Notes in Computer Science No. 331)*, Springer-Verlag, Berlin, p. 1–35.

80. Cullyer, W. J. (1988). "Implementing Safety-critical Systems: The VIPER Microprocessor," in Graham Birtwistle and P. A. Subrahmanyam, editors, *VLSI Specification, Verification, and Synthesis*, Kluwer Academic Publishers, Boston, p. 1–25.

81. Cohn, Avra (1988). "A Proof of Correctness of the VIPER Microprocessor: The First Level," in Graham Birtwistle and P. A. Subrahmanyam, editors, *VLSI Specification, Verification, and Synthesis*, Kluwer Academic Publishers, Boston, pp. 27–71.

82. Her Majesty's Stationary Office (1986). Software, Vital Key to UK Competitiveness. Report of Cabinet Office Advisory Council for Applied Research and Development (ACARD).

83. Gerhart, Susan, Harlan Mills *et al.* (1988). "Methods, Educated Managers' Key to Good Design," *IEEE Software*, 5(5), (September), pp. 96–97.

84. Food and Drug Administration (1987). "Draft FDA Policy for the Regulation of Computer Products," *Federal Register*. September 25.

85. *Business Week* (1988). "It's Late, Costly, Incompetent—But Try Firing a Computer System." November 7.

86. Carroll, Paul B. (1988). "Computer Glitch: Patching up Software Occupies Programmers and Disables Systems," *Wall Street Journal*, January 22, pp. 1, 12.

87. Shore, John (1988). "Why I never met a programmer I could trust," *Communications of the ACM*, 31(4), (April), pp. 372–375.

88. Carey, Peter (1987). "Programmers May be Facing Regulation," *San Jose Mercury News*, December 1, back page.

89. Food and Drug Administration (1988). Reviewer Guidance for Computer-controlled Medical Devices (draft).

90. Jacky, Jonathan (1988). "Quality Assurance in Medical Computer Systems," *American Association of Physicists in Medicine Newsletter*, 13(1), (January/February), pp. 5–6.

91. Fries, Richard, editor (1989). *AAMI TIR No. ?: Developing, Purchasing, and Using Safe, Effective, and Reliable Medical Software*. Association for the Advancement of Medical Instrumentation, Arlington, Virginia.

92. Health Industry Manufacturers Association (1987). *FDA Regulation of Medical Software*, Washington, D.C., (HIMA Report 88-4).

93. Medical Device Industry Computer Software Committee (1988). Final reports. Health Industry Manufacturers Association.

94. Ting, J. (1987). "Software Validation and Acceptance Testing for Computer-controlled Medical Linear Accelerators," 14, p. 483 (abstract), *Medical Physics*.

95. Weinhous, M., J. Purdy, and C. Granda (1988). "Experience in the Acceptance Testing and Use of a Computer-controlled Therapy Linear Accelerator," *Physics in Medicine and Biology*, 33, p. 50 (Supplement 1).

96. Zachary, G. Pascal (1988). "Designers Take Aim at Software Bugs," *San Jose Mercury News*, Monday, September 5, 1C, 7C.

P·A·R·T·VI

6

Limits of Correctness in Computers

Brian Cantwell Smith

Introduction

On October 5, 1960, the American Ballistic Missile Early-Warning System station at Thule, Greenland, indicated a large contingent of Soviet missiles headed towards the United States.[1] Fortunately, common sense prevailed at the informal threat-assessment conference that was immediately convened: international tensions weren't particularly high at the time, the system had only recently been installed, Kruschev was in New York, and all in all a massive Soviet attack seemed very unlikely. As a result no devastating counter-attack was launched. What was the problem? The moon had risen, and was reflecting radar signals back to earth. Needless to say, this lunar reflection hadn't been predicted by the system's designers.

Over the last ten years, the Defense Department has spent many millions of dollars on a new computer technology called "program verification"—a branch of computer science whose business, in its own terms, is to "prove programs correct." Program verification has been studied in theoretical computer science departments since a few seminal papers in the 1960s,[2] but it has only recently started to gain in public visibility, and to be applied to real world problems. General Electric, to consider just one example, has initiated verification projects in their own laboratories: they would like to prove that the programs used in their latest computer-controlled washing machines won't have any "bugs" (even one serious one can destroy their profit margin).[3] Although it used to be that only the simplest programs could be "proven correct"—programs to put simple lists into order, to compute simple arithmetic functions—slow but steady progress has been made in extending the range of verification techniques. Recent papers have reported

Reprinted with permission of the Center for the Study of Language and Information; Smith, Brian Cantwell, "The Limits of Correctness," Center for the Study of Language and Information, Stanford University, Report Number CSLI-85-35 (1985).

correctness proofs for somewhat more complex programs, including small operating systems, compilers, and other material of modern system design.[4]

What, we do well to ask, does this new technology mean? How good are we at it? For example, if the 1960 warning system had been proven correct (which it was not), could we have avoided the problem with the moon? If it were possible to prove that the programs being written to control automatic launch-on-warning systems were correct, would that mean there could be a catastrophic accident? In systems now being propsed computers will make launching decisions in a matter of seconds, with no time for any human intervention (let alone for musings about Kruschev's being in New York). Do the techniques of program verification hold enough promise so that, if these new systems could all be proven correct, we could all sleep more easily at night? These are the questions I want to look at in this paper. And my answer, to give away the punch-line, is no. For fundamental reasons—reasons that anyone can understand—there are inherent limitations to what can be proven about computers and computer programs. Although program verification is an important new technology, useful, like so many other things, in its particular time and place, it should definitely not be called verification. Just because a program is "proven correct," in other words, you cannot be sure that it will do what you intend.

First some background.

General Issues in Program Verification

Computation is by now the most important enabling technology of nuclear weapons systems: it underlies virtually every aspect of the defense system, for the early warning systems, battle management and simulation systems, and systems for communication and control, to the intricate guidance systems that direct the missiles to their targets. It is difficult, in assessing the chances of an accidental nuclear war, to imagine a more important question to ask than whether these pervasive computer systems will or do work correctly.

Because the subject is so large, however, I want to focus on just one aspect of computers relevant to their correctness: the use of *models* in the construction, use, and analysis of computer systems. I have chosen to look at modelling because I think it exerts the most profound and, in the end, most important influence on the systems we build. But it is only one of an enormous number of important questions. First, therefore—in

---

[1] Edmund Berkeley, *The Computer Revolution*, Doubleday, 1962, pp. 175–177, citing newspaper stories in the *Manchester Guardian Weekly* of Dec. 1, 1960, a UPI dispatch published in the *Boston Traveller* of Dec. 13, 1960, and an AP dispatch published in the *New York Times* on Dec 23, 1960.

[2] McCarthy, John, "A Basic for a Mathematical Theory of Computation," 1963, in P. Braffort and D. Hirschberg, eds. *Computer Programming and Formal Systems*, Amsterdam: North-Holland, 1967, pp. 33–70. Floyd, Robert, "Assigning Meaning to Programs," Proceedings of Symposia in Applied Mathematics 19, 1967 (also in F. T. Schwartz, ed. *Mathematical Aspects of Computer Science*, Providence: American Mathematical Society, 1967). Naur, P, "Proof of Algorithms by General Snapshots," *BIT* Vol. 6, No. 4, pp. 310–316. 1966.

[3] Al Stevens, BBN Inc., personal communication.

[4] See for example R. S. Boyer, and Moore, J. S., eds., *The Correctness Problem in Computer Science*, London: Academic Press, 1981.

order to unsettle you a little—let me just hint at some of the equally important issues I will not address:

1. *Complexity:* At the current state of the art, only very simple programs can be proven correct. Although it is terribly misleading to assume that either the complexity or power of a computer program is a linear function of length, some rough numbers are illustrative. The simplest possible arithmetic programs are measured in tens of lines; the current state of the verification art extends only to programs of up to several hundred. It is estimated that the systems proposed in the Strategic Defense Initiative (Stars Wars), in contrast, will require at least 10,000,000 lines of code.[5] By analogy, compare the difference between resolving a two-person dispute and settling the political problems of the Middle East. There's no a priori reason to believe that strategies successful at one level will scale to the other.

2. *Human Interaction:* Not much can be "proven," let alone specified formally, about actual human behaviour. The sorts of programs that have so far been proven correct, therefore, do not include much substantial human interaction. On the other hand, as the moon-rise example indicates, it is often crucial to allow enough human intervention to enable people to over-ride system mistakes. System designers, therefore, are faced with a very real dilemma: should they rule out substantive human intervention, in order to develop more confidence in how their systems will perform, or should they include it, so that costly errors can be avoided or at least repaired? The Three-Mile Island incident is a trenchant example of just how serious this trade-off can get: the system design provided for considerable human intervention, but then the operators failed to act "appropriately." Which strategy leads to the more important kind of correctness?

A standard way out of this dilemma is to specify the behaviour of the system *relative to the actions of its operators.* But this, as we will see below, pressures the designers to specify the system totally in terms of internal actions, not external effects. So you end up proving only that the system will *behave in the way that it will behave* (i.e., it will raise this line level 3 volts), not *do what you want it to do* (i.e., launch a missile only if the attack is real). Unfortunately, the latter is clearly what is important. Systems comprising computers and people must function properly as integrated systems; nothing is gained by showing that one cog in a misshapen wheel is a very nice cog indeed.

Furthermore, large computer systems are dynamic, constantly changing, embedded in complex social settings. Another famous "mistake" in the American defense system happened when a human operator mistakenly mounted a training tape, containing a simulation of a full-scale Soviet attack, onto a computer that, just by chance, was automatically pulled into service when the primary machine ran into a problem. For some

---

[5] Fletcher, James, study chairman, and McMillan, Brockway, panel chairman, *Report of the Study on Eliminating the Threat Posed by Nuclear Ballistic Missiles (U),* Vol. 5, *Battle Management, Communications, and Data Processing (U),* U.S. Department of Defense, February 1984.

tense moments the simulation data were taken to be the real thing.[6] What does it mean to install a "correct" module into a complex social flux?

3. *Levels of Failure*: Complex computer systems must work at many different levels. It follows that they can fail at many different levels too. By analogy, consider the many different ways a hospital could fail. First, the beams used to frame it might collapse. Or they might perform flawlessly, but the operating room door might be too small to let in a hospital bed (in which case you would blame the architects, not the lumber or steel company). Or the operating room might be fine, but the hospital might be located in the middle of the woods, where no one could get to it (in which case you would blame the planners). Or, to take a different example, consider how a letter could fail. It might be so torn or soiled that it could not be read. Or it might look beautiful, but be full of spelling mistakes. Or it might have perfect grammar, but disastrous contents.

Computer systems are the same: they can be "correct" at one level—say, in terms of hardware—but fail at another (i.e., the systems built on top of the hardware can do the wrong thing even if the chips are fine). Sometimes, when people talk about computers failing, they seem to think only the hardware needs to work. And hardware does from time to time fail, causing the machine to come to a halt, or yielding errant behaviour (as for example when a faulty chip in another American early warning system sputtered random digits into a signal of how many Soviet missiles had been sighted, again causing a false alert[7]). And the connections between the computers and the world can break: when the moon-rise problem was first recognized, an attempt to override it failed because an iceberg had accidentally cut an undersea telephone cable.[8] But the more important point is that, in order to be reliable, a system has to be correct *at every relevant level*: the hardware is just the starting place) (and by far the easiest, at that). Unfortunately, however, we don't even know what all the relevant levels are. So-called "fault-tolerant" computers, for example, are particularly good at coping with hardware failures, but the software that runs on them is not thereby improved.[9]

4. *Correctness and Intention*: What does *correct* mean, anyway? Suppose the people want peace, and the president thinks that means having a strong defense, and the defense department thinks that means having nuclear weapons systems, and the weapons designers request control systems to monitor radar signals, and the computer companies are asked to respond to six particular kinds of radar pattern, and the engineers are told to build signal amplifiers with certain circuit characteristics, and the technician is told to write a program to respond to the difference between a two-volt and a four-volt signal on a particular incoming wire. If being correct means *doing what was intended*, whose intent

---

[6] See, for example, the Hart-Goldwater report to the Committee on Armed Services of the U.S. Senate: "Recent False Alerts from the Nation's Missile Attack Warning System" (Washington, D.C.: U.S. Government Printing Office, Oct. 9, 1980); Physicians for Social Responsibility, *Newsletter*, "Accidental Nuclear War," (Winter, 1982), p. 1.

[7] Ibid.

[8] Berkeley, op. cit. See also Daniel Ford's two-part article "The Button," *New Yorker*, April 1, 1985, p. 43, and April 8, 1985, p. 49, excerpted from Ford, Daniel, *The Button*, New York: Simon and Schuster, 1985.

[9] Developing software for fault-tolerant systems is in fact an extremely tricky business.

matters? The technician's? Or what, with twenty years of historical detachment, we would say *should have been intended?*

With a little thought any of you could extend this list yourself. And none of these issues even touch on the intricate technical problems that arise in actually building the mathematical models of software and systems used in the so-called "correctness" proofs. But, as I said, I want to focus on what I take to be the most important issue underlying all of these concerns: the pervasive use of models. Models are ubiquitous not only in computer science but also in human thinking and language; their very familiarity makes them hard to appreciate. So we'll start simply, looking at modelling on its own, and come back to correctness in a moment.

The Permeating Use of Models

When you design and build a computer system, you first formulate a model of the problem you want it to solve, and then construct the computer program in its terms. For example, if you were to design a medical system to administer drug therapy, you would need to model a variety of things: the patient, the drug, the absorption rate, the desired balance between therapy and toxicity, and so on and so forth. The absorption rate might be modelled as a number proportional to the patient's weight, or proportional to body surface area, or as some more complex function of weight, age, and sex.

Similarly, computers that control traffic lights are based on some model of traffic—of how long it takes to drive across the intersection, of how much metal cars contain (the signal change mechanisms are triggered by metal-detectors buried under each street). Bicyclists, as it happens, often have problems with automatic traffic lights, because bicycles don't exactly fit the model: they don't contain enough iron to trigger the metal-detectors. I also once saw a tractor get into trouble because it couldn't move as fast as the system "thought" it would: the cross-light went green when the tractor was only half-way through the intersection.

To build a model is to conceive of the world in a certain delimited way. To some extent you must build models before building any artifact at all, including televisions and toasters, but computers have a special dependence on these models: *you write an explicit description of the model down inside the computer,* in the form of a set of rules or what are called *representations*—essentially linguistic formulae encoding, in the terms of the model, the facts and data thought to be relevant to the system's behaviour. It is with respect to these representations that computer systems work. In fact that's really what computers are (and how they differ from other machines): they run by manipulating representations, and representations are always formulated in terms of models. This can all be summarized in a slogan: no computation without representation.

The models, on which the representations are based, come in all shapes and sizes. Balsa models of cars and airplanes, for example, are used to study air friction and lift. Blueprints can be viewed as models of buildings; musical scores as models of a symphony. But models can also be abstract. Mathematical models, in particular, are so widely used that it is hard to think of anything that they haven't been used for: from whole social and economic systems, to personality traits in teen-agers, to genetic structures, to the mass and charge of sub-atomic particles. These models, furthermore, permeate all discussion and communication. Every expression of language can be viewed as resting implicitly on some model of the world.

What is important, for our purposes, is that every model deals with its subject matter *at some particular level of abstraction*, paying attention to certain details, throwing away others, grouping together similar aspects into common categories, and so forth. So the drug model mentioned above would probably pay attention to the patients' weights, but ignore their tastes in music. Mathematical models of traffic typically ignore the temperaments of taxi drivers. Sometimes what is ignored is at too "low" a level; sometimes too "high": it depends on the purposes for which the model is being used. So a hospital blueprint would pay attention to the structure and connection of its beams, but not to the arrangements of proteins in the wood the beams are made of, nor to the efficacy of the resulting operating room.

Models *have* to ignore things exactly because they view the world at a level of abstraction ("abstraction" is from the Latin *abstrahere*, "to pull or draw away"). And it is good that they do: otherwise they would drown in the infinite richness of the embedding world. Though this isn't the place for metaphysics, it would not be too much to say that every act of conceptualization, analysis, categorization, does a certain amount of violence to its subject matter, in order to get at the underlying regularities that group things together. If you don't commit that act of violence—don't ignore some of what's going on—you would become so hypersensitive and so overcome with complexity that you would be unable to act.

To capture all this in a word, we will say that models are inherently *partial*. All thinking, and all computation, are similarly partial. Furthermore—and this is the important point—thinking and computation *have* to be partial: that's how they are able to work.

Full-blooded Action

Something that is not partial, however, is action. When you reach out your hand and grasp a plow, it is the real field you are digging up, not your model of it. Models, in other words, may be abstract, and thinking may be abstract, and some aspects of computation may be abstract, but action is not. To actually build a hospital, to clench the steering wheel and drive through the intersection, or to inject a drug into a person's body, is to act in the full-blooded world, not in a partial or distilled model of it.

This difference between action and modelling is extraordinarily important. Even if your every thought is formulated in the terms of some model, to act is to take leave of the model and participate in the whole, rich, infinitely variegated world. For this reason, among others, action plays a crucial role, especially in the human case, in grounding the more abstract processes of modelling or conceptualization. One form that grounding can take, which computer systems can already take advantage of, is to provide feedback on how well the modelling is going. For example, if an industrial robot develops an internal three-dimensional representation of a wheel assembly passing by on a conveyor belt, and then guides its arm towards that object and tries to pick it up, it can use video systems or force sensors to see how well the model corresponded to what was actually the case.

The world doesn't care about the model: the claws will settle on the wheel just in case the actualities mesh.

Feedback is a special case of a very general phenomenon: you often learn, when you do act, just how good or bad your conceptual model was. You learn, that is, if you have adequate sensory apparatus, the capacity to assess the sensed experience, the inner resources to revise and reconceptualize, and the luxury of recovering from minor mistakes and failures.

Computers and Models

What does all this have to do with computers, and with correctness? The point is that computers, like us, participate in the real world: they take real actions. One of the most important facts about computers, to put this another way, is that we plug them in. They are not, as some theoreticians seem to suppose, pure mathematical abstractions, living in a pure detached heaven. They land real planes at real airports; administer real drugs; and —as you know all too well—control real radars, missiles, and command systems. Like us, in other words, although they base their actions on models, they have consequence in a world that inevitably transcends the partiality of those enabling models. Like us, in other words, and unlike the objects of mathematics, they are challenged by the inexorable conflict between the partial but tractable model, and the actual but infinite world.

And, to make the only too obvious point: we in general have no guarantee that the models are right—indeed we have no *guarantee* about much of anything about the relationship between model and world. As we will see, current notions of "correctness" don't even address this fundamental question.

In philosophy and logic, as it happens, there is a very precise mathematical theory called "model theory." You might think that it would be a theory about what models are, what they are good for, how they correspond to the worlds they are models of, and so forth. You might even hope this was true, for the following reason: a great deal of theoretical computer science, and all of the work in program verification and correctness, historically derives from this model-theoretic tradition, and depends on its techniques. Unfortunately, however, model theory doesn't address the model-world relationship at all. Rather, what model theory does is to tell you how your descriptions, representations, and programs *correspond to your model*.

The situation, in other words, is roughly as depicted in Figure 1. You are to imagine a description, program, computer system (or even a thought—they are all similar in this regard) in the left hand box, and the very real world in the right. Mediating between the two is the inevitable model, serving as an idealized or preconceptualized simulacrum of the world, in terms of which the description or program or whatever can be understood. One way to understand the model is as the glasses through which the program or computer looks at the world: it is the world, that is, as the system sees it (though not, of course, as it necessarily is).

The technical subject of "model theory," as I have already said, is a study of the relationship on the left. What about the relationship on the right? The answer, and one of the main points I hope you will take away from this discussion, is that, at this point in intellectual history, we have no theory of this right-hand side relationship.

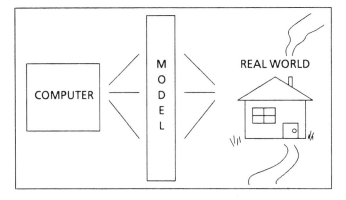

Figure 1. Computers, Models, and the Embedding World.

There are lots of reasons for this, some very complex. For one thing, most of our currently accepted formal techniques were developed, during the first half of this century, to deal with mathematics and physics. Mathematics is unique, with respect to models, because (at least to a first level of approximation) its subject matter *is* the world of models and abstract structures, and therefore the model–world relationship is relatively unproblematic. The situation in physics is more complex, of course, as is the relationship between mathematics and physics. How apparently pure mathematical structures could be used to model the material substrate of the universe is a question that has exercised physical scientists for centuries. But the point is that, whether or not one believes that the best physical models do more justice and therefore less violence to the world than do models in so-called "higher-level" disciplines like sociology or economics, formal techniques don't themselves address the question of adequacy.

Another reason we don't have a theory of the right-hand side is that there is very little agreement on what such a theory would look like. In fact all kinds of questions arise, when one studies the model–world relationship explicitly, about whether it can be treated formally at all, about whether it can be treated rigorously, even if not formally (and what the relationship is between those two), about whether any theory will be more than usually infected with prejudices and preconceptions of the theorist, and so forth. The investigation quickly leads to foundational questions in mathematics, philosophy, and language, as well as computer science. But none of what one learns in any way lessens its ultimate importance. In the end, any adequate theory of action, and, consequently, any adequate theory of correctness, will have to take the model–world relationship into account.

Correctness and Relative Consistency

Let's get back, then, to computers, and to correctness. As I mentioned earlier, the word "correct" is already problematic, especially as it relates to underlying intention. Is a program correct when it does what we have instructed it to do? or what we wanted it to do? or what history would dispassionately say it should have done? Analysing what correctness *should* mean is too complex a topic to take up directly. What I want to do, in the time remaining, is to describe what sorts of correctness we are presently capable of analysing.

In order to understand this, we need to understand one more thing about building computer systems. I have already said, when you design a computer system, that you first develop a model of the world, as indicated in the diagram. But you don't, in general, ever get to hold the model in your hand: computer systems, in general, are based on models that are purely abstract. Rather, if you are interested in proving your program "correct," you develop two concrete things, structured in terms of the abstract underlying model (although these are listed here in logical order, the program is very often written first):

1. A *specification*: a formal description in some standard formal language, specified in terms of the model, in which the desired behaviour is described; and
2. The *program*: a set of instructions and representations, also formulated in the terms of the model, which the computer uses as the basis for its actions.

How do these two differ? In various ways, of which one is particularly important. The program has to say *how the behaviour is to be achieved*, typically in a step by step fashion (and often in excruciating detail). The specification, however, is less constrained: all it has to do is to specify *what proper behaviour would be*, independent of how it is accomplished. For example, a specification for a milk-delivery system might simply be: "Make one milk delivery at each store, driving the shortest possible distance in total." That's just a description of what has to happen. The program, on the other hand, would have the much more difficult job of saying how this was to be accomplished. It might be phrased as follows: "drive four blocks north, turn right, stop at Gregory's Grocery Store on the corner, drop off the milk, then drive 17 blocks north-east, . . ." Specifications, to use some of the jargon of the field, are essentially *declarative*; they are like indicative sentences or claims. Programs, on the other hand, are *procedural*: they must contain instructions that lead to a determinate sequence of actions.

What, then, is a proof of correctness? It is a proof that any system that *obeys the program* will *satisfy the specification*.

There are, as is probably quite evident, two kinds of problems here. The first, often acknowledged, is that the correctness proof is in reality only a proof that two characterizations of something are compatible. When the two differ—i.e., when you try to prove correctness and fail—there is no more reason to believe that the first (the specification) is any more correct than the second (the program). As a matter of technical practice, specifications tend to be extraordinarily complex formal descriptions, just as subject to bugs and design errors and so forth as programs. In fact they are very much like programs, as this introduction should suggest. So what almost always happens, when you write a specification and a program, and try to show that they are compatible, is that you have to adjust both of them in order to get them to converge.

For example, suppose you write a program to factor a number C, producing two answers A and B. Your specification might be

Given a number C, produce numbers A and B such that $A \times B = C$.

This is a specification, not a program, because it doesn't tell you *how* to come up with

A and *B*. All it tells you is what properties *A* and *B* should have. In particular, suppose I say: ok, *C* is 5,332,114; what are *A* and *B*? Staring at the specification just given won't help you to come up with an answer. Suppose, on the other hand, given this specification, that you then write a program—say, by successively trying pairs of numbers until you find two that work. Suppose further that you then set out to prove that your program meets your specification. And, finally, suppose that this proof can be constructed (I won't go into details here; I hope you can imagine that such a proof could be constructed). With all three things in hand—program, specification, and proof—you might think you were done.

In fact, however, things are rarely that simple, as even this simple example can show. In particular, suppose, after doing all this work, that you try your program out, confident that it must work because you have a proof of its correctness. You randomly give it 14 as an input, expecting 2 and 7. But in fact it gives you the answers $A = 1$ and $B = 14$. In fact, you realise upon further examination, it will *always* give back $A = 1$ and $B = C$. It does this, *even though you have a proof of its being correct*, because you didn't make your specification meet your intentions. You wanted both *A* and *B* to be *different* from *C* (and also different from 1), but you forgot to say that. In this case you have to modify both the program and the specification. A plausible new version of the latter would be

Given a number *C*, produce numbers *A* and *B* such that $A \neq 1$ and $B \neq 1$ and $A \times B = C$.

And so on and so forth: the point, I take it, is obvious. If the next version of the program, given 14, produces $A = -1$ and $B = -14$, you would similarly have met your new specification, but still failed to meet your intention. Writing "good" specifications— which is to say, writing specifications that capture your intention—is hard.

It should be apparent, nonetheless, that developing even straightforward proofs of "correctness" is nonetheless very useful. It typically forces you to delineate, very explicitly and completely, the model on which both program and specification are based. A great many of the simple bugs that occur in programs, of which the problem of producing 1 and 14 was an example, arise from sloppiness and unclarity about the model. Such bugs are not identified by the proof, but they are often unearthed in the attempt to prove. And of course there is nothing wrong with this practice; anything that helps to erradicate errors and increase confidence is to be applauded. The point, rather, is to show exactly what these proofs consist of.

In particular, as the discussion has shown, when you show that a program meets its specifications all you have done is to show that two formal descriptions, slightly different in character, are compatible. This is why I think it is somewhere between misleading and immoral for computer scientists to call this "correctness." What is called a proof of correctness is really a proof of the compatibility or consistency between two formal objects of an extremely similar sort: program and specification. As a community, we computer scientists should call this *relative consistency*, and drop the word *"correctness"* completely.

What proofs of relative consistency ignore is the second problem intimated earlier. Nothing in the so-called program verification process per se deals with the right-hand side relationship: the relationship between the model and the world. But, as is clear, it is over inadequacies on the right-hand side—inadequacies, that is, in the models in terms of which the programs and specifications are written—that systems so commonly fail.

The problem with the moon-rise, for example, was a problem of this second sort. The difficulty was not that the program failed, in terms of the model. The problem, rather, was that the model was overly simplistic; *it didn't correspond to what was the case in the world*. Or, to put it more carefully, since all models fail to correspond to the world in indefinitely many ways, as we have already said, it didn't correspond to what was the case *in a crucial and relevant way*. In other words, to answer one of our original questions, even if a formal specification had been written for the 1960 warning system, and a proof of correctness generated, there is no reason to believe that potential difficulties with the moon would have emerged.

You might think that the designers were sloppy; that they would have thought of the moon if they had been more careful. But it turns out to be extremely difficult to develop realistic models of any but the most artificial situations, and to assess how adequate these models are. To see just how hard it can be, think back on the case of General Electric, and imagine writing appliance specifications, this time for a refrigerator. To give the example some force, imagine that you are contracting the refrigerator out to be built by an independent supplier, and that you want to put a specification into the contract that is sufficiently precise to guarantee that you will be happy with anything that the supplier delivers that meets the contract.

Your first version might be quite simple—say, that it should maintain an internal temperature of between 3 and 6 degrees Centigrade; not use more than 200 Watts of electricity; cost less than $100 to manufacture; have an internal volume of half a cubic meter; and so on and so forth. But of course there are hundreds of other properties that you implicitly rely on: it should, presumably, be structurally sound: you wouldn't be happy with a deliciously cool plastic bag. It shouldn't weigh more than a ton, or emit loud noises. And it shouldn't fling projectiles out at high speed when the door is opened. In general, it is impossible, when writing specifications, to include *everything* that you want: legal contracts, and other humanly interpretable specifications, are always stated within a background of common sense, to cover the myriad unstated and unstable assumptions assumed to hold in force. (Current computer programs, alas, have no common sense, as the cartoonists know so well.)

So it is hard to make sure that everything that meets your specification will really be a refrigerator; it is also hard to make sure that your requirements don't rule out perfectly good refrigerators. Suppose for example a customer plugs a toaster in, puts it inside the refrigerator, and complains that the object he received doesn't meet the temperature specification and must therefore not be a refrigerator. Or suppose he tries to run it upside down. Or complains that it doesn't work in outer space, even though you didn't explicitly specify that it would only work within the earth's atmosphere. Or spins it at 10,000 rpm. Or even just unplugs it. In each case you would say that the problem lies not with the refrigerator but with the use. But how is *use* to be specified? The point is that, as well as modelling the artifact itself, you have to model the relevant part of the world in which it will be embedded. It follows that the model of a refrigerator as a device that *always* maintains an internal temperature of between 3 and 6 degrees is too strict to cover all possible situations. One could try to model what appropriate use would be, though specifications don't, ordinarily, even try to identify all the relevant circumstantial factors. As well as there being a background set of constraints with respect to which a model is formulated, in other words, there is also a background set of assumptions on which a specification is allowed at any point to rely.

The Limits of Correctness

It's time to summarize what we've said so far. The first challenge to developing a perfectly "correct" computer system stems from the sheer complexity of real-world tasks. We mentioned at the outset various factors that contribute to this complexity: human interaction, unpredictable factors of setting, hardware problems, difficulties in identifying salient levels of abstraction, etc. Nor is this complexity of only theoretical concern. A December 1984 report of the American Defense Science Board Task Force on "Military Applications of New-Generation Computing Technologies" identifies the following gap between current laboratory demonstrations and what will be required for successful military applications—applications they call "Real World; Life or Death." In their estimation the military now needs (and, so far as one can tell, expects to produce) an increase in the power of computer systems of nine orders of magnitude, accounting for both speed and amount of information to be processed. That is a 1,000,000,000-fold increase over current research systems, equivalent to the difference between a full century of the entire New York metropolitan area, compared to one day in the life of a hamlet of hundred people. And remember that even current systems are already several orders of magnitude more complex than those for which we can currently develop proofs of relative consistency.

But sheer complexity has not been our primary subject matter. The second challenge to computational correctness, more serious, comes from the problem of formulating or specifying an appropriate model. Except in the most highly artificial or constrained domains, modelling the embedding situation is an approximate, not a complete, endeavour. It has the best hopes of even partial success in what Winograd has called "systematic domains": areas where the relevant stock of objects, properties, and relationships are most clearly and regularly pre-defined. Thus bacteremia, or warehouse inventories, or even flight paths of airplanes coming into airports, are relatively systematic domains, at least compared to conflict negotiations, any situations involving intentional human agency, learning and instruction, and so forth. The systems that land airplanes are hybrids—combinations of computers and people—exactly because the unforeseeable happens, and because what happens is in part the result of human action, requiring human interpretation. Although it is impressive how well the phone companies can model telephone connections, lines, and even develop statistical models of telephone use, at a certain level of abstraction, it would nevertheless be impossible to model the content of the telephone conversations themselves.

Third, and finally, is the question of what one does about these first two facts. It is because of the answer to this last question that I have talked, so far, somewhat interchangeably about people and computers. With respect to the ultimate limits of models and conceptualization, both people and computers are restrained by the same truths. If the world is infinitely rich and variegated, no prior conceptualization of it, nor any abstraction, will ever do it full justice. That's ok—or at least we might as well say that it's ok, since that's the world we've got. What matters is that we not forget about that richness—that we not think, with misplaced optimism, that machines might magically have access to a kind of "correctness" to which people cannot even aspire.

It is time, to put this another way, that we change the traditional terms of the debate. The question is not whether machines can do things, as if, in the background, lies the implicit assumption that the object of comparison is people. Plans to build automated systems capable of making a "decision," in a matter of seconds, to annihilate Europe, say, should make you uneasy; requiring a person to make the same decision in a matter of the same few seconds should make you uneasy too, and for very similar reasons. The problem is that there is simply no way that reasoning of any sort can do justice to the inevitable complexity of the situation, because of what reasoning is. Reasoning is based on partial models. Which means it cannot be guaranteed to be correct. Which means, to suggest just one possible strategy for action, that we might try, in our treaty negotiations, to find mechanisms to slow our weapons systems down.

It is striking to realise, once the comparison between machines and people is raised explicitly, that we don't typically expect "correctness" for people in anything like the form that we presume it for computers. In fact quite the opposite, and in a revealing way. Imagine, in some by-gone era, sending a soldier off to war, and giving him (it would surely have been a "him") final instructions. "Obey your commander, help your fellow-soldier," you might say, "and above all do your country honour." What is striking about this is that it is considered not just a weakness, but a punishable weakness—a breach of morality—to obey instructions *blindly* (in fact, and for relevant reasons, you generally *can't* follow instructions blindly; they have to be interpreted to the situation at hand). You are subject to court-martial, for example, if you violate fundamental moral principles, such as murdering women and children, even if following strict orders.

In the human case, in other words, our social and moral systems seem to have built in an acceptance of the uncertainties and limitations inherent in the model-world relationship. We *know* that the assumptions and preconceptions built into instructions will sometimes fail, and we know that instructions are always incomplete; we exactly rely on judgment, responsibility, consciousness, and so forth, to carry someone through those situations—all situations, in fact—where model and world part company. In fact we never talk about people, in terms of their overall personality, being *correct*; we talk about people being *reliable*, a much more substantive term. It is individual actions, fully situated in a particular setting, that are correct or incorrect, not people in general, or systems. What leads to the highest number of correct human actions is a person's being reliable, experienced, capable of good judgment, etc.

There are two possible morals here, for computers. The first has to do with the notion of experience. In point of fact, program verification is not the only, or even the most common, method of obtaining assurance that a computer system will do the right thing. Programs are usually judged acceptable, and are typically accepted into use, not because we prove them "correct," but because they have shown themselves relatively reliable in their destined situations for some substantial period of time. And, as part of this experience, we expect them to fail: there always has to be room for failure. Certainly no one would ever accept a program without this *in situ* testing: a proof of correctness is at best added insurance, not a replacement, for real life experience. Unfortunately, for the ten million lines of code that is supposed to control and coordinate the Star Wars Defense System, there will never, God willing, be an *in situ* test.

One answer, of course, if genuine testing is impossible, is to run a *simulation* of the real situation. But simulation, as our diagram should make clear, *tests only the left-hand side relationship*. Simulations are defined in terms of models; they don't test the relationship between the model and the world. That is exactly why simulations and tests can never replace embedding a program in the real world. All the war-games we hear about, and hypothetical military scenarios, and electronic battlefield simulators and so forth, are all based on exactly the kinds of models we have been talking about all along. In fact the subject of simulation, worthy of a whole analysis on its own, is really just our whole subject welling up all over again.

I said earlier that there were two morals to be drawn, for the computer, from the fact that we ask people to be reliable, not correct. The second moral is for those who, when confronted with the fact that genuine or adequate experience cannot be had, would say, "oh, well, let's build responsibility and morality into the computers—if people can have it, there's no reason why machines can't have it too." Now I will not argue that this is inherently impossible, in a metaphysical or ultimate philosophical sense, but a few short comments are in order. First, from the fact that humans sometimes *are* responsible, it does not follow that we know what responsibility is: from tacit skills no explicit model is necessarily forthcoming. We simply do not know what aspects of the human condition underlie the modest levels of responsibility to which we sometimes rise. And second, with respect to the goal of building computers with even human levels of full reliability and responsibility, I can state with surety that the present state of artificial intelligence is about as far from this as mosquitos are from flying to the moon.

But there are deeper morals even than these. The point is that even if we could make computers reliable, they still wouldn't necessarily always do the correct thing. *People* aren't provably "correct," either: that's why we hope they are responsible, and it is surely one of the major ethical facts is that correctness and responsibility don't coincide. Even if, in another 1,000 years, someone were to devise a genuinely responsible computer system, there is no reason to suppose that it would achieve "perfect correctness" either, in the sense of never doing anything wrong. This isn't a failure, in the sense of a performance limitation; it stems from the deeper fact that models must abstract, in order to be useful. The lesson to be learned from the violence inherent in the model-world relationship, in other words, is that there is an *inherent* conflict between the power of analysis and conceptualization, on the one hand, and sensitivity to the infinite richness, on the other.

But perhaps this is an overly abstract way to put it. Perhaps, instead, we should just remember that there will always be another moon-rise.

Acknowledgments

The preparation and publication of this report have been made possible in part through the support of Xerox Corporation and in part through an award from the System Development foundation.

P · A · R · T · VI

7

RISKS-FORUM Digest Contributions

John McAfee • Clifford Johnson
Fernando J. Corbato • R. Amizade
David Sherman • David B. Benson

Date: **Tue, 12 Dec 89 11:26:29 PST**
From: **John McAfee**[1]
Subject: **Major Trojan Warning**

A distribution diskette from a corporation calling itself PC Cyborg has been widely distributed to major corporations and PC user groups around the world and the diskette contains a highly destructive trojan. The Chase Manhattan Bank and ICL Computers were the first to report problems with the software. All systems that ran the enclosed programs had all data on the hard disks destroyed. Hundreds of systems were affected. Other reports have come in from user groups, small businesses and individuals with similar problems. The professionally prepared documentation that comes with the diskette purports that the software provides a data base of AIDS information. The flyer heading reads "AIDS Information—An Introductory Diskette." The license agreement on the back of the same flyer reads:

"In case of breach of license, PC Cyborg Corporation reserves the right to use program mechanisms to ensure termination of the use of these programs. These program mechanisms will adversely affect other program applications on microcomputers. You are hereby advised of the most serious consequences of your failure to abide by the terms of this license agreement."

Further in the license is the sentence: "Warning: Do not use these programs unless you are prepared to pay for them".

If the software is installed using the included INSTALL program, the first thing that the program does is print out an invoice for the software. Then, whenever the system is re-booted, or powered down and then re-booted from the hard disk, the system self destructs.

Whoever has perpetrated this monstrosity has gone to a great deal of time, and more expense, and they have clearly perpetrated the largest single targeting of destructive code yet reported. The mailings are professionally done, and the style of the mailing labels indicate the lists were purchased from professional mailing organizations. The estimated costs for printing, diskette, label and mailing is over $3.00 per package. The volume of reports imply that many thousands may have been mailed. In addition, the British magazine "PC Business World" has included a copy of the diskette with its most recent publication—another expensive avenue of distribution. The only indication of who the perpetrator(s) may be is the address on the invoice to which they ask that $378.00 be mailed:

PC Cyborg Corporation
P.O. Box 871744
Panama 7, Panama

Needless to say, a check for a registered PC Cyborg Corporation in Panama turned up negative.

An additional note of interest in the license section reads: "PC Cyborg Corporation does not authorize you to distribute or use these programs in the United States of America. If you have any doubt about your willingness or ability to meet the terms of this license agreement or if you are not prepared to pay all amounts due to PC Cyborg Corporation, then do not use these programs".

Date: Tue, 19 Dec 89 15:58:44 PST
From: Clifford Johnson
Subject: California Supreme Court Endorses Computerized Horoscopes

Excerpted from the S.F. Chronicle, 19 Dec 1989:[2]

The California Supreme Court cleared the way yesterday for the use of standardized psychological tests in criminal trials to prove that a defendent does not fit the personality type likely to have committed the charged crime. In a 5-2 ruling, the court rejected a comparison that likened personality tests to lie detectors or voiceprints, which are excluded from trials because their reliability is not commonly accepted by the scientific community. The court majority said introduction of standardized psychological tests in

---

[1] Reprinted with permission from McAfee Associates.
[2] Article by William Carlsen. ©San Francisco Chronicle. Reprinted by permission.

trials is not a revolutionary development and the tests reliability can be challenged by prosecutors.

"We see no reason to subject (these tests) to the special restrictions governing admission of new, novel or experimental scientific techniques not previously accepted by the courts," wrote Justice David Eagleson for the majority.

Chief Justice Malcolm Lucas dissented, saying the decision opened the way for new "mini-trials" focusing not on a defendant's guilt or innocence but on his personality profile and whether it conforms to "the profile displayed by the average child molester, robber, arsonist, or whomever." He acknowledged that personality tests have been admitted by some courts to show a defendant's mental state at the time of the crime. But that is "far different than using them to exclude the defendant from the relevant class of defenders in much the same manner as a blood test or voice print," Lucas wrote.

With the vote, the court reversed the child molestation convictions of a Kern County couple found guilty of committing lewd acts with four young boys in 1983 and 1984. During the trial of Margie Grafton and Timothy Palomo, they attempted to call as an expert witness a psychologist who had given them two commonly used tests—the Minnesota Multiphasic Personality Inventory and the Millon Clinical Multiaxial Inventory. The psychologist, Roger Mitchell of Bakersfield, was prepared to testify on the basis of the test results and his interview with Grafton and Palomo that they showed no indications of deviance and were unlikely to be involved with the charged crimes.

Out of the presence of the jury, Mitchell told the trial court judge that the 566-question Minnesota test, copyrighted in 1943, had a reliability rating of over 70% [sic!!!] in diagnosing the illness of some patients and included hidden questions that detected lies by the person taking the exam.

Many experts believed that the test makes it impossible [sic!!!] to conceal an abnormal personality profile, Mitchell told the judge.

But the trial judge ruled that Mitchell could not testify because the defense had failed to prove the tests met the legal standard of general acceptance in the scientific community.

The court yesterday overturned that ruling, saying the judge should have allowed Mitchell to testify. The majority also found that if his testimony had been allowed, it may have changed the outcome of the case.

What has this to do with comp. risks? The tests at issue are all wholly computerized. Moreover, as if common sense were not enough, it is well established (the tests were statistically debunked in the 1960s) that the maximum accuracy of diagnosis, in most unrealistically favorable circumstances, is of the order of 20%—hardly an improvement over a guess. Besides, the test is readily foolable, so much so that it is generally regarded as per se invalid the second time it's taken by the same person. Moreover, the "reliability" pertains only to the crudest mental types of disability (schitzophrenia, paranoia, and five other yes/no nasties), whereas the computer tests are generally preprogrammed to spew out pages of rambling mumbo-jumbo analogous to daily horoscopes, except that long psychiatric words are used. Such print-outs more often than not contradict themselves in details.

I was once compelled to take such a test, by a California judge. The examiner, who actually gave classes in psychology to high-power groups of attorneys and judges, without blush permitted me to answer difficult questions by tossing a coin, because I said that was my "natural response" to the test. Still, the computer nevertheless reported that the test was "valid." On one page it reported that I had a compelling aversion to publicity, on another that I avidly desired publicity. One amusing diagnosis was the computer's finding that I lacked a sense of humor!

I think this is worth the long posting, because these computerized tests are administered almost universally now, and decide everything from employability to the suitability of a mother to be a mother.

Date: Mon, 8 Jan 1990 18:02:43 EST
From: Fernando J. Corbato
Subject: Re: Password Security: A Case History

Peter's note recalling the colossal time-sharing mishap of the interchange of the message-of-the-day with the password file which occurred on CTSS in the early 1960's made me go look up the article and see what was said about the cause. The article says, "due to a software design error, the temporary editor files of the two users were inter-changed . . . ," but it was deeper than that.

To simplify the organization of the initial CTSS system, a design decision had been made to have each user at a terminal associated with his own directory of files. Moreover the system itself was organized as a kind of quasi user with its own directory which included a large number of supporting applications and files including the message-of-the-day and the password file. So far, so good. Normally a single system programmer could login to the system directory and make any necessary changes. But the number of system programmers had grown to about a dozen in number, and, further, the system by then was being operated almost continuously so that the need to do live maintenance of the system files became essential. Not surprisingly, the system programmers saw the one-user-to-a-directory restriction as a big bottleneck for them. They thereupon proceeded to cajole me into letting the system directory be an exception "since system programmers would be careful to not make mistakes."

But of course a mistake was made. Overlooked was that a software design decision had been made in the standard system text editor that it would only be used by one user at a time working in one directory so that a temporary file could have the same name for all instantiations of the editor. And with two system programmers editing at the same time in the system directory, the disaster of the swapped temporary files finally occurred.

The tale has at least two morals: First, design bugs are often subtle and occur by evolution with early assumptions being forgotten as new features or uses are added to systems;

Second, even system programmers make mistakes so that prudent system management must be based on expecting errors and not on perfection.

Date: Thu, 18 Jan 90 08:24:18 EST
From: R. Aminzade
Subject: Risks of Voicemail Systems That Expect a Human at the Other End

Last night my car had a dead battery (I left the lights on—something that a very simple piece of digital circuitry could have prevented, but I digress), so I called AAA road service. I noted that they had installed a new digital routing system for phone calls. "If you are cancelling a service call Press 1, if this is an inquiry about an existing service call, Press 2, if this is a new service call, Press 3." All well and good, except that when I finally reached a real operator, she informed me that the towtruck would arrive "within 90 minutes." In less than the proposed hour and a half I managed to beg jumper cables off of an innocent passerby and get the car started, so I decided to call AAA and cancel the service call.

I dialed, pressed 1 as instructed, and waited. The reader should realize that my car was illegally parked (this is Boston), running (I wasn't going to get stuck with a dead battery again!), and had the keys in the ignition. I was not patient. I waited about four minutes, then tried again. Same result. I was now out of dimes, but I noticed that the AAA machine began its message with "we will accept your collect call . . ." so I decided to call collect.

Surprise! I discovered that New England Telephone had just installed its digital system for collect calls. It is quite sophisticated, using some kind of voice recognition circuit. The caller dials the usual 0—(phone number), and then is asked "If you wish to make a collect call, press 1 . . . If you wish to . . ." Then the recording asks "please say your name." The intended recipient of the collect call then gets a call that begins "Will you accept a collect call from ⟨recording of caller stating his name⟩."

I knew what was coming, but I didn't want to miss this experience. I gave my name as something like "Russell, Goddammit!," and NETs machine began asking AAAs machine if it would accept a collect call (which it had already, plain to the human ear, said it would accept) from "Russell Goddammitt!" Ms. NET (why are these always female voices?) kept telling Ms. AAA "I'm sorry, I don't understand you, please answer yes or no," but Ms. AAA went blithely on with her shpiel, instructing Ms. NET which buttons to push.

I stood at the phone (car still running . . . machines nattering away at each other) wondering who could do this episode justice. Kafka? Orwell? Groucho? I was sure that one machine or the other would eventually give up and turn things over to a human being, but, I finally decided to dial a human operator, and subject the poor woman to a stream of abuse. She connected me to AAA, where I punched 3 (rather than the appropriate but obviously malfunctioning 1), and subjected yet another underpaid clerk to my wrath.

Date: Mon, 26 Feb 90 07:55:31 EST
From: David Sherman
Subject: 100-year-old Can Drive Four Years Without Test

Toronto Star, February 26, 1990:[3]

"I think it's stupid—the whole damn thing," grumbled Charles Narraway. The Nepean, Ont. [suburb of Ottawa—DS] resident will be 100 years old in March, and that seems to have turned up a bug in the transportation ministry's computer. For 20 years, Narraway has had to take an annual road test to get his driver's license renewed. And for 20 years he passed it the first time, every time. But this year he got a license, good for four years, without a test. Narraway's driver's license shows his date of birth as 90-03-04, and he figures the computers have tacked the wrong century on to the front . . .

Date: Sun, 4 Mar 90 14:13:34 PST
From: David B. Benson
Subject: Another 100-year Computer Saga

Chemical & Engineering News, February 26, 1990, 68(9), p. 168:

Physician Beatrice Golomb tells of a 99-year-old man who turned up in the emergency room (JAMA, Dec. 8, 1989, 262(22), page 3132[4]). His white blood cell count, although far out of line, was reported by the computer to be within normal limits. The computer, it turned out, was reporting values for the newborn, having figured that year of birth, plugged in as '89 was 1989, not 1889. Golomb's comment: "The normal ranges provided by hospital computers are not always to be credited."

---

[3] Reprinted from The Toronto Star.
[4] Copyright 1989, American Medical Association.

P·A·R·T· VII

Ethical Perspectives and Professional Responsibilities

P·A·R·T· VII

Introduction

Ethical Perspectives and Professional Responsibilities

Charles Dunlop • Rob Kling

Values In Technology

Ethical issues permeate many of the discussions about computing technology elsewhere in this volume. To cite just a few examples: What is the appropriate response to someone who unilaterally decides to experiment on a large-scale communications network, causing a shutdown of numerous system components? Who should be blamed when medical software contains bugs that result in the deaths of several patients? Assuming that computerization of schools is desirable, what is society's responsibility to ensure equal access across socioeconomic boundaries? When an imposter on a BBS creates significant violations of trust, is his behavior mitigated by the fact that some therapeutic good was also achieved?

The pervasive computerization of various segments of society (education, military, business, communications) can have far-reaching impacts on people's lives—for good or ill—as can the decision *not* to computerize. Choosing to pursue one research project than another reflects a perception that the first is more valuable. Those who work in technical disciplines, although they may not directly decide which project is allocated to research and development groups, are at the very least instruments of decisions made by others. Deferring to managerial authority is itself a normative decision, and several essays in this section argue that deferential silence is not always golden. There is, of course, a common belief that technology is somehow neutral or "value free." Yet it seems highly artificial to separate the existence of various technologies from the uses to which they will almost certainly be put. When a worker maintains that he is responsible only for the technical capabilities of nerve gas—not for its deployment—is he really offering anything more than a rationalization for his line of work? Would he say the same thing if involved in the design of automobile seatbelts and home smoke alarms, or would he take some pride in his contribution to devices that save lives?

Responsibility, Values, and Abuse in Organizational Settings

Opponents of legislation to regulate handguns often claim that "guns don't kill people; people kill people." This sort of argument could be extended to claim that other, potentially dangerous technologies are also ethically neutral: automobiles, nuclear weapons systems, automated battlefields, computer-controlled medical devices, etc. In our first selection, John Ladd argues that technological neutrality is a myth, perpetuated in part by what he calls the "transparency" of technology: "Thus, we are hardly ever conscious of the part that an automobile or a telephone system plays in determining what we do when we use them or of how they impose patterns of their own on our actions and their outcomes."[1]

If this point is correct then, in actions involving (non-defective) technological inter-mediaries, one might expect to find a fairly *immediate* link of responsibility between agents and their actions.[2] And in some cases this is true—e.g., harassment by telephone or deaths due to negligent driving. Here, the technology is viewed primarily as an extension of the human voice or limbs, and it remains essentially invisible in our assessments of moral responsibility. The issue becomes appreciably more complex, however, when computers are assigned roles formerly reserved for human judgment (e.g., computers that land airplanes or control nuclear power plants). An additional compli-cation stems from the large numbers of people that can be involved in system design and implementation. When things go wrong, it is tempting to blame the computer and to argue that human responsibility is spread so thin that it is essentially nonexistent. But Ladd argues this response is simply a moral cop-out. He develops a conception of responsibility that—even for these difficult cases—(a) applies to *people*, not to machines or to organizations *per se*, and (b) provides a vehicle for assigning responsibility to individuals even within a complex social system that includes sophisticated technology "in charge" of important operations. As Ladd sees it, responsibility may be diffused, but not eliminated.

Our second selection, by Rob Kling, explores the notion of *computer abuse* as an umbrella term covering both illegal and unethical practices (notoriously, the latter concepts do not coincide). Unlike many other studies, this one identifies organizations as perpetrators as well as victims of abusive behavior. Kling wrote his article long before computer viruses and software piracy became publicly visible. But his analysis suggests

---

[1] Excellent further discussions of this issue are contained in Teich (1972); the essay by Paul Goodman is especially valuable. Goodman suggests that technology is a branch of moral philosophy. See our discussion of Goodman's viewpoint in our introduction to Section I of this book.

[2] When the technology is defective, further complications arise. For one example, see Jonathan Jacky's paper, reprinted in Part VI.

that these kinds of abuses fit a conventional formula in which the perpetrators are individuals and the victims are often organizations. He identifies several kinds of practices in which organizations may abuse their clients—both individuals and other organizations —in the course of "routine business." He also notes that responsible computer specialists often have trouble standing up for their clients' rights when organizations are perpetrators. Kling also reports the interesting view that an organization's opportunistic and exploitative ethos may return to haunt it, since its employees may adopt that very value system and end up turning it against their employer. Assuming this view to be correct, ethics seminars and explicit codes of conduct for employees may do little good when unsavory organizational behavior is the norm.

Ethical Codes

Many professional organizations, the Association for Computing Machinery (ACM) included, have adopted codes of conduct for their members; the ACM's is reproduced here as our third selection. Virtually none of the ACM's code is connected specifically with computing, except those portions that pertain to maintaining the privacy of data. Most can be derived from self-evident ethical injunctions, e.g., "Tell the truth"; "Don't violate trust." Moreover, most of the guidelines protect the interests of employers of ACM members rather than the clients of the employing organizations.

We have also included a draft of an ethical code developed by a committee of the International Federation of Information Processing Societies (IFIP). This proposed IFIP code is substantially more stringent than the ACM's code of ethics, and many of its provisions are much more specific to information technology. Like the ACM code, many of the provisions of the IFIP code can also be derived from self-evident ethical injunctions. Even so, the IFIP code spells out the meaning of such injunctions for computer specialists much more fully than does the ACM code. Moreover, some of the provisions apply to organizations, not just to individuals (see section 2 of the IFIP code). This IFIP Code of Ethics illustrates some of the newer codes of ethics that are being proposed for computing specialists.

As examples from earlier sections suggest, however, computer specialists and other people in positions of responsibility sometimes don't follow "self-evident" ethical guidelines. One set of controversies concerns the extent to which professional codes can influence the behavior of people who may not be oriented toward ethical behavior— either because of character flaws or because of fear of losing their jobs.[3] We find the role of professional codes in law and medicine instructive. They set guidelines for professionally specific behavior that are not simply part of common sense. And although only a small fraction of actual abuses by doctors and lawyers may be penalized by their

---

[3] There is an ongoing debate as to whether (and how) professional ethics can be taught. A narrow view would focus simply on a code of behavior. But value judgments cannot be valuable in a factual vacuum. Professionals should be encouraged to look beyond the technical aspects of their work in order to visualize and assess its implications for society and the world at large. This has implications for computer science curricula (see our selection by Carl Barus) and also argues for an understanding of other disciplines, including the humanities and social sciences.

professional societies, we feel more confident with these standards weakly enforced than with no codes or professional enforcement at all. Despite the controversy among computer specialists about the value of professional codes, the ACM's code has a very limited reach. It provides for sanctions against offenders, but we know of no instances where this provision has been invoked. Moreover, it focuses on the conduct of individuals and does not address the issues of organizational responsibility.[4] Punishment and reward for corporations is quite unlike that for individuals. And those individuals who make key organizational decisions may very well not even be members of the ACM.

Career-minded professionals often find it difficult to make moral considerations paramount in the workplace.[5] Whistle-blowers are at least as likely to be penalized as rewarded (see the "Byterite" case in our selection by Kling for one illustration). We are struck by the extent to which commercial software products are frequently oversold. But computer specialists who know the products best are often mute about their limitations or flaws. A strong professional code might give computer specialists some basis for insisting that products be fairly advertised, or that they be developed and tested and with high-quality tools and techniques. But any attempt to develop a strong code that would strengthen professional standards or provide protections for whistle-blowers is certain to be embroiled in bitter controversy.

Although we endorse strong codes of professional conduct, there is the interesting question whether such codes are correctly characterized as codes of *ethics*. It is natural to regard ethical codes as embodying values that are autonomously chosen. But professional codes, with quasi-legal force, are not held out to professionals as value systems to be autonomously accepted or rejected; on the contrary, they typically provide for sanctions against those who fail to abide by them (see Ladd, in Johnson and Snapper, under Further Reading).

The Military's Role In The Funding of Computer Research and Development

The military has played a major and controversial role in the development of computer technology. Some of the earliest digital computers were developed with military sponsorship. In addition, the Advanced Research Projects Agency of DoD-funded research led to the development of important computer technologies: timesharing, the Lisp programming language, and computer networking. Today, some fields of computer science, such as artificial intelligence and software engineering, get the lion's share of their funding directly from the military. Computer scientists who develop research careers in these areas can effectively develop significant employment relationships with the military— even when they are university professors.

Not everybody finds these relationships with the military attractive. Some, in fact, view the military as a problematic institution in American society (see, for example,

---

[4] For an exploration of differences between corporate and individual responsibility, see Ladd (1984).

[5] See Jackall (1988) for some detailed accounts of the ways in which managers often place loyalty to their superiors above ethical commitments to their clients, co-workers, and subordinates.

Melman, 1970, 1985). It is a major part of the federal budget. And the military seems to take an institutional stance that more weapons and more "defense" are always necessary. The most important controversies do not focus on whether or not there should be a military. Rather, they focus on whether the military's institutional style is helping to develop a safer world; whether the aerospace firms sell overly complex weapons systems that may not be adequately reliable in battle; whether the military absorbs a large fraction of such scarce resources as the federal budget and the nation's scientific and technical manpower.[6] Sometimes Pentagon officials have threatened to withdraw scientific funding from professors who criticized the military's role in domestic or foreign policy. Not long ago, for example, the U.S. undersecretary of defense for research and development made the following comments: "I am not enthusiastic about the idea of using defense forces to subsidize the work of people who are outspoken critics of our national defense goals or policies . . . . If they want to get out and use their roles as professors to make statements, that's fine, it's a free country. [But] freedom works both ways. They're free to keep their mouths shut . . . . I'm also free not to give money."[7]

A large military presence can have a chilling effect when the research community is blackmailed into political submission, by being channeled into particular areas of science in order to keep its work funded.[8] But when the military dominates certain areas of computer science, career-minded professors may find great difficulty in choosing how much or how little they can afford to work inside the military's affluent research cocoon.

An assistant professor of computer science in pursuit of tenure may feel that he or she can ill afford to pass up military funding, even if the project at hand conflicts with the individual's personal values. Terry Winograd, an associate professor of Computer Science at Stanford University and a president of Computer Professionals for Social Responsibility during the late 1980s, rejects *all* military research funding. But he observers that major computer science departments depend upon large amounts of military funding for their research. Their faculties are unlikely to give up military funds if they can't readily find comparable research funds elsewhere.[9] At the very least, however, this sort of decision should be squarely confronted.

In our fourth selection, Winograd describes a study undertaken at Stanford, where researchers' descriptions of their projects were compared with descriptions of the same projects put out by the Department of Defense. Major discrepancies turned up in some cases: "For example, one professor had a contract for research on 'High-power broadly tunable laser action in the ultraviolet spectrum,' which he justified to the campus in terms of medicine. The DoD title was 'Weaponry—lasers for increased damage effectiveness.'

---

[6] See for example, Fallows (1981). This issue has become even more acute in the light of recent, dramatic political changes in the Soviet Union and Eastern Europe. Debates include the extent to which the private sector can absorb large cuts in military manpower, and what nonmilitary uses to make of the "peace dividend."

[7] *Toronto Globe and Mail*, August 12, 1986, p. A7. Quoted by Vincent Mosco in "Star Wars Is Already Working," *Science as Culture*, Pilot Issue (May 1987), pp. 12–34. The quotation appears on p. 23.

[8] A perhaps less chilling, but still powerful, effect comes when the research of university computer science departments is over-responsive to the demands of private corporations that give them grant money. For a discussion of this issue, see the epilogue to Schank (1984).

[9] "Minor" computer science departments have a different, though related, funding problem, since the big military-funded research grants have gone primarily to a few elite universities.

Another project on 'Dynamic behavior and stability of solids and structures' was described in the work unit summary as relevant to 'weapon delivery and reconnaissance...knowledge of landing fields and silo interaction with missiles.' " Such discordant project descriptions raise the possibility that some researchers may end up deceiving themselves and their students (as well as others) if they refuse to acknowledge the real implications of their work. Were the researchers in this case trying to conceal the real nature of their projects from the university community, or were they attempting to make "benign" research appear to have military significance in order to qualify for DoD funding? Either way, deception is involved.

Winograd also points out another source of concern about large-scale military funding of university research. There has been a trend among some universities toward permitting —and even encouraging—classified research. But the secrecy that classified research entails is at odds with the traditional academic ideal of intellectual openness. Already, some ominous cases are on record (see p. 711 of Winograd's essay for examples).

There is yet a further issue here. The Strategic Defense Initiative has been a rich source of funding for computer science departments in the United States. Some researchers believe that a reliable Star Wars system cannot be built, but they continue to accept SDI funding because (a) it is there, and (b) "After all, *someone* is going to take it." Winograd has criticized this view as deriving from what he calls "the fixed effect fallacy":

> Consider an analogy. Imagine that everyone in my neighborhood burns their garbage, resulting in noxious pollution. I say that I am going to quit burning my garbage. In some sense it is a symbolic act. N-1 people burning the garbage will produce essentially the same level of pollution, and I will end up having to pay for a trash hauler. But of course, if we all quit burning it we would all breathe better, and that's where the collective effect comes in. If I take the view that the rest of the world is a "fixed effect" then indeed anything I do is useless. The issue is to ask what it is that we are all doing together, and what we all might do differently, then to look at ways in which individuals can make changes. (Winograd, 1984, pp. 1–2)

A complementary position is taken by David Parnas, who has been an outspoken critic of the argument under discussion:

> I believe that it's quite appropriate for professionals to devote their energies to making the people of their land more secure. In contrast, it is not professional to accept employment doing "military" things that do not advance the legitimate defense interests of that country. If the project would not be effective, or if, in one's opinion, it goes beyond the legitimate defense needs of the country, a professional should not participate. Too many do not ask such questions. They ask only how they can get another contract. (Parnas, 1987, p. 52)

Parnas's remarks are particularly noteworthy inasmuch as they do not represent a wholesale condemnation of military research; in fact, Parnas has served regularly as a consultant to the defense department over the past 20 years.

Ethical and Social Issues in Computer Science Curricula

Funding sources can affect not only an individual's or university's research directions, but also the content of coursework. Our fifth selection, by Carl Barus, analyzes this phenomenon in the electrical engineering curriculum, although much of his view could be applied to computer science curricula as well. For example, some computer science departments conduct their programming labs in Ada, a language used primarily by the military, rather than in Pascal or C, because key faculty with military grants shape that part of the curriculum. Graduates who leave such programs with Ada skills rather than C skills are then much more attractive to aerospace firms—which must use Ada—than to civilian software houses, which are much more likely to use C.

Fundamental to Barus's discussion is the question, "What should be the task of any 'higher' education?" There is no single answer to this question, of course, but Barus is deeply concerned that undue military influence on a university's engineering curriculum will bypass the essential goal of creating "the informed, thoughtful, critical citizenry necessary for democracy to survive and flourish." Barus's article makes the important point that a total curriculum subtly embodies a value system, and implies that the task of producing an "informed, thoughtful, critical citizenry" falls to the sciences as much as to the humanities.

How well do contemporary visions of the computer science curriculum meet this responsibility? Some computer science departments offer courses on the social issues of computing and professional ethics for their students. A few even require such courses. But most departments, especially those in the most prestigious research universities, don't offer such courses regularly. We suspect that the academic politics regarding the "scientific status" of computer science have led some academics to distance themselves from the kind of professional education they provide for the vast majority of their undergraduate students. At some major technical universities, the social sciences play a decidedly diminished role, and academics in those fields are sometimes called "fuzzies" by colleagues anxious to distinguish "hard science" from "soft science."

A recent report of the Task Force on the Core of Computer Science takes an unusually narrow view of the discipline at the very time at which its social significance is expanding. Here is its fundamental conception of the dicipline:

> Computer science and engineering is the systematic study of algorithmic processes—their theory, analysis, design, efficiency, implementation, and application—that describe and transform information. The fundamental question underlying all of computing is, What can be (efficiently) automated. This discipline was born in the early 1940s with the joining together of algorithm theory, mathematical logic, and the invention of the stored-program electronic computer.
>
> The roots of computing extend deeply into mathematics and engineering. Mathematics imparts analysis to the field; engineering imparts design. The discipline embraces its own theory, experimental method, and engineering, in contrast with most physical sciences, that apply their findings (e.g., chemistry and chemical engineering principles). The science and engineering are inseparable because of the fundamental interplay between the scientific and engineering paradigms within the discipline. (Denning *et al.*, 1989, p. 16.)

•   •   •

> Theory includes the processes for developing the underlying mathematics of the subarea. These processes are supported by theory from other areas. For example, the subarea of algorithms and data structures contains complexity theory and is supported by graph theory. Abstraction deals with modeling potential implementations. These models suppress

detail while retaining essential features; they are amenable to analysis and provide means for calculating predictions of the modeled system's behavior. Design deals with the process of specifying a problem, transforming the problem statement into a design specification, and repeatedly inventing and investigating alternative solutions until a reliable, maintainable, documented, and tested design that meets cost criteria is achieved. (*Ibid.*, p. 12.)

Not only do the concerns expressed by Barus go unmet here; nowhere in this description is there any reference to the social milieu in which computers function, or the risks and responsibilities that go with designing certain kinds of systems. Of course, mathematical analysis does play a fundamental role in the history of computing, and in some kinds of systems analysis. But there are areas of the discipline that also owe much to philosophy, linguistics, sociology and psychology—for example, artificial intelligence, human factors in design, social impacts of computing, and software engineering. Some academics' desire to establish computer science as *science* rather than as a lower-status collection of "computer studies" should not be allowed to obscure the importance of these contributions.

Our final selection, Joseph Weizenbaum's "Against the Imperialism of Instrumental Reason," was described by one commentator as a "cry from the heart."[10] It is indeed a strong personal statement, but one exhorting readers to define high (if different) standards for themselves as well. The reference to "instrumental reason" in Weizenbaum's title recalls Aristotle's distinction between "intrinsic" goods—chosen for their own sake—and "instrumental" goods, chosen because they lead beyond themselves to some desired end. Seen in this light, Weizenbaum's essay cautions against focusing on means at the expense of ends. It also emphasizes how value judgments inevitably underlie one's choice of a research project, although Winograd's remarks on Department of Defense "guidance" of research directions may indicate that choices here are more tightly circumscribed than Weizenbaum allows.

Despite his explicit claims to the contrary, Weizenbaum is sometimes (mis)read as making pronouncements on specific research agendas that no one ought to pursue. In fact, however, his writing invites discussion and critical reflection. Some of Weizenbaum's examples of immoral research surely are one-sided. For instance, automatic speech recognition systems probably stand a better chance of aiding disabled computer uses than of assisting our government in mass surveillance of citizens' telephone calls. And coupling an animal's visual system to computers could conceivably assist in the development of prosthetic vision for the blind. But these criticisms should not be permitted to detract from Weizenbaum's important thesis that social choice rather than technological inevitability is the real key to progress in our world.

Further Studies of Professional Ethics

Of necessity, much of the material presented in this section relies on an intuitive understanding of ethical concepts. While most readers may feel that they know what is

---

[10] McCorduck (1979), p. 323. This book is a readable though evangelical defense of AI research, and it is critical of many authors, Weizenbaum included, who have become skeptical.

right and what is wrong, few will have worked out a systematic ethical theory. What is the basis of ethical principles—what society says, the Christian Bible, the Koran, Confucian teaching, or one's intuitive sense of justice? Are ethical rules absolute? If not, what kinds of conditions justify murder, theft, or deception? When there are ethical conflicts between what is good for your family and what is good for your clients, how do you resolve them? People who think that they can readily agree that theft and deception are (usually) wrong may nevertheless disagree in answering all of the preceding questions. The tough cases are those where there are real ethical conflicts, and there our intuitive ideas are often weakest in guiding us to deal with ethical conflicts in a coherent way.

Anyone seriously concerned about moral issues is urged to consult the philosophical literature. For an entry point see Rachels (1986), Bayles and Henley (1983), or Johnson (1984); additional suggestions are listed under Further Reading. Although the philosophical tradition does not provide ready-made answers, it does provide careful analysis and clarification of key moral theories, and often illuminates the application of theories to everyday moral judgments. Studying this literature can help deepen one's understanding of what is really at stake in various ethical dilemmas. It can also help develop a finer appreciation of what constitutes a moral point of view, and hone some analytical tools that are helpful for evaluating alternative courses of action.

Sources

Ladd, John (1989). "Computers and Moral Responsibility: A Framework for Ethical Analysis," Chapter 11 in Carol Gould (ed), *The Information Web: Ethical and Social Implications of Computer Networking.* Westview Press, Boulder Colo., pp. 207–227.

Kling, Rob (1980). "Computer Abuse and Computer Crime as Organizational Activities," *Computer/Law Journal,* II(2) (Spring), pp. 403–427. Reprinted in *Computers and Society,* 12 (1982), pp. 12–24.

"ACM Code of Professional Conduct" (1985). Constitution of the Association for Computing Machinery.

Winograd, Terry A. (1987). "Strategic Computing Research and the Universities," Stanford University, Department of Computer Science, Report No. STAN-CS-87-1160 (March).

Barus, Carl (1987). "Military Influence on the Electrical Engineering Curriculum Since World War II," *IEEE Technology and Society Magazine,* 6(2) (June), pp. 3–9.

Weizenbaum, Joseph (1976). *Computer Power and Human Reason,* Chapter 10. W. H. Freeman and Company, San Francisco, pp. 258–280 + Notes to Chapter 10, pp. 286–287.

References

Bayles, Michael D., and Kenneth Henley (eds.) (1983). *Right Conduct: Theories and Applications.* Random House, New York.

Denning, Peter J., Douglas E. Comer, David Gries, Michael C. Mulder, Allen Tucker, A. Joe Turner, and Paul R. Young (1989). "Computing as a Discipline," *Communications of the ACM,* 32(1) (January), pp. 9–23.

Fallows, James (1981). *National Defense.* Random House, New York.

Jackall, Robert (1988). *Moral Mazes: The World of Corporate Managers*. Oxford University Press, New York.

Johnson, Oliver (1984). *Ethics* (Fifth Edition). Holt, Rinehalt, Winston, New York.

Ladd, John (1984). "Corporate Mythology and Individual Responsibility," *The International Journal of Applied Philosophy*, 2(1) (Spring), pp. 1–21.

McCorduck, Pamela (1979). *Machines Who Think*. W. H. Freeman and Company, San Francisco.

Melman, Seymour (1970). *Pentagon Capitalism: The Political Economy of War* [1st ed.]. McGraw-Hill, New York.

Melman, Seymour (1985). *The Permanent War Economy: American Capitalism in Decline*. Revised and updated. Simon & Schuster, New York.

Parnas, David Lorge (1987). "SDI: A Violation of Professional Responsibility," *Abacus*, 4(2), pp. 46–52.

Rachels, James (1986). *The Elements of Moral Philosophy*. Random House, New York.

Schank, Roger C. (1984). *The Cognitive Computer*. Addison-Wesley Publishing Company, Reading, Mass.

Teich, Albert H. (ed.) (1972). *Technology and Man's Future*. St. Martin's Press, New York.

Winograd, Terry (1984). "Some Thoughts on Military Funding," *The CPSR Newsletter*, 2(2) (Spring), pp. 1–3.

Further Reading

Bayles, Michael D. (1981). *Professional Ethics*. Wadsworth Pub. Co., Belmont, Calif.

Beauchamp, Tom L. (1982). *Philosophical Ethics*. McGraw-Hill, New York.

The CPSR Newsletter. Published by Computer Scientists for Social Responsibility, P.O. Box 717, Palo Alto, California 94301.

Feldman, Fred (1978). *Introductory Ethics*. Prentice-Hall, Englewood Cliffs, N.J.

Goldman, Alan H. (1980). *The Moral Foundations of Professional Ethics*. Rowman and Littlefield, Totowa, N.J.

Johnson, Deborah G., and John W. Snapper (eds.) (1985). *Ethical Issues in the Use of Computers*. Wadsworth Publishing Company, Belmont, Calif.

Johnson, Deborah G. (1985). *Computer Ethics*. Prentice-Hall, Englewood Cliffs, N.J.

Martin, Mike W., and Roland Schinzinger (1983). *Ethics in Engineering*. McGraw-Hill, New York.

Robison, Wade L., Michael S. Pritchard, and Joseph Ellin (1983). *Profits and Professions: Essays in Business and Professional Ethics*. Humana Press, Clifton, N.J.

Pojman, Louis P. (1989). *Ethical Theory*. Wadsworth Publishing Company, Belmont, Calif.

Werhane, Patricia, and Kendall D'Andrade (eds.) (1985). *Profit and Responsibility: Issues in Business and Professional Ethics*. E. Mellen Press, New York.

P·A·R·T· VII

1

Computers and Moral Responsibility: A Framework for an Ethical Analysis

John Ladd

The Need for New Ethical Concepts

This chapter will deal with an issue that is as much a problem for moral philosophy as it is for the computer world. My basic theme is that high technology, and computer technology in particular, raises ethical problems of a new sort that require considerable restructuring of our traditional ethical categories. It follows that our job as philosophers is not, as it is often thought to be, simply to apply ready-made categories to new situations; rather, it is to find new categories, or new ways of interpreting old categories, in order to accommodate the challenges presented by new technologies.

Although I shall not directly address privacy issues here, they do provide a good illustration of the way that our traditional cateogories, such as the category of rights, are unable to provide needed direction in dealing with new realities. The traditional concept of privacy itself, involving, say, control over information about oneself of the sort that formerly was secured by pulling down curtains and locking drawers, has no application in the modern world of computer technology, where detrimental information about individuals can be easily collected without violating physical barriers. In view of new developments, the very definition of privacy needs to be revamped. In addition to problems of definition, there is the further problem of what might be called *complicity*

"Computers and Moral Responsibility: A Framework for Ethical Analysis," by John Ladd, from *The Information Web: Ethical and Social Implications of Computer Networking*, edited by Carol Gould, Westview Press, Boulder, Colorado, 1989, pp. 207–227.

—on the part of everyone with the system itself—through the use of inherently privacy-invading mechanisms such as credit cards. The concept of rights begins to lose its bite when we freely abandon the claim to privacy without a second thought whenever it is personally convenient for us to do so. The lapse into this kind of inconsistency deprives our complaints of their credibility and leaves us in a kind of ethical no-man's land.

Much of the same sort of predicament about basic ethical categories is encountered in other issues coming under the rubric of computer ethics—issues relating to intrusion, piracy, and others that this chapter explores. Having used the concept of privacy to make a simple point, I leave that subject to others who are better equipped than I to deal with it and turn directly to my subject: computers and moral responsibility.

As its title indicates, my main concern in this chapter, is what I call *moral responsibility*, in particular, with moral responsibility for evil outcomes—disasters past, present, and future—such as calamitous computer mistakes and errors. I shall explain presently in more detail the concept of responsibility involved here and how it applies to the computer world. In the meantime, we may take the basic question to be about the ethics of what people unintentionally do to harm other people through the use of computers.

My procedure is as follows: First, I discuss how the problem arises and how it is generally handled. Second, I outline a revamped and relatively sophisticated conception of moral responsibility, which I put forward as a useful conceptual tool for understanding and dealing with a number of basic ethical issues connected with computers. Third, I introduce the concept of intermediaries as a complicating factor when responsibility is connected with technology, computers, and bureaucracies. Fourth, I compare and contrast human and computer control over intermediaries in order to bring out further facets of responsibility. I conclude the essay with two examples of how the concept of moral responsibility can be applied to concrete cases.

Responsibility in the World of Technology

The general area of concern in this chapter is a well-known problem connected with high technology in general, although more especially with computer technology; namely, How is it possible for particular individuals to have any moral responsibility at all for evil outcomes that are the compound product of complicated interacting processes that themselves apparently bypass human agency altogether? The question could be put in metaphorical terms by saying that there is such a long distance between the inputs of particular individuals and their significant outcomes, and there are so many different kinds of input from so many different sources (designers, operators, managers, and consumers), that as far as establishing human responsibility is concerned, we find ourselves adrift in a vast sea of anonymity where responsibility has become so diffused as to evaporate into nothingness.

The difficulty in relating responsibility to technology is due not only to technological and social complexity but also to the fact that multipurpose technology such as computers can be used both for good and for ill. Consequently, telephones, automobiles, and now computers must be ostensibly judged as good or bad by reference to the specific purposes for which they are used. When particular uses of computers are bad, we say that they have been misused or abused. The underlying assumption behind the use of terms like "misuse" or "abuse" is that computers, like telephones and automobiles, are essentially good and are evil only in exceptional cases that can easily be recognized.

The reliance on purpose and uses, good and bad, open and hidden, social and antisocial, as the primary standard for the moral evaluation of a particular technology or of a particular use of it becomes problematic as soon as we take into consideration, as we must, the unanticipated outcomes of the use of technology, such as accidents. Consider, for example, a nuclear accident, an airplane crash, or a police misidentification. Computers also crash—sometimes with disastrous results. In these cases, our focus shifts from purposes—what a computer is used for—to what it in fact *does*, the consequences of its operations. This aspect of computers is what I shall be concerned with in this chapter; the comprehensive concept of responsibility is designed to deal with problems of this type.

The Myth of Technological Neutrality

Underlying the problem of the moral evaluation of technologies—which in the present context involves such things as computer hardware, computer software, networks and their uses—is the generally unquestioned assumption that technology per se is *ethically neutral*. Examples abound: "Guns don't kill, only outlaws kill"; "Nuclear weapons aren't evil, only when used by evil people like the Russians are they evil"; or, closer to home, " 'Matching' and 'Profiling' are not evil, only those who use them are evil" (e.g., the secret police). In other words, the moral acceptability or unacceptability of a particular technology depends on what it is used for and who uses it. Ethics and value questions are, as it were, external to computer technology. Doctrines like this, I shall argue, are an ethical cop-out.

The neutralist thesis, on analysis, is not as self-evident as it might at first seem to be. To begin with, it is quite obvious that technology changes our lives and therewith our ethics. A new technology makes certain modes of conduct easier and others more difficult; Saturday Night Specials facilitate, perhaps even encourage and invite, hold-ups. We are sucked in by new technologies, sometimes quite against our will and better judgment. It is clear that, like the Saturday Night Specials, computers facilitate, encourage, and invite new practices, such as matching and profiling, and along with them new types of surveillance. Thus, like other new technologies, computer technology has created new modes of conduct and new social institutions, new vices and new virtues, new ways of helping and new ways of abusing other people.

Ethical neutralism with regard to technology rests on a doctrinaire separation of means and ends, of tools and human well-being. I shall argue throughout this chapter that this separation is not only unrealistic but is also ethically mischievous; I shall try to show in particular that it leads to a serious misunderstanding of the nature of moral responsibility in relation to computers. Human agents are responsible not only for the outcomes of their actions and for their uses of technology but also for how the technology itself shapes our conduct, our attitudes, and our institutions. But the argument is complicated. It can only be understood by reference to a comprehensive conception of responsibility, which I shall now try to sketch.

A Comprehensive Concept of Moral Responsibility

My purpose in introducing what I call a "comprehensive concept of moral responsibility" is to provide a more satisfactory conceptual tool for analyzing problems in computer ethics than other generally recognized concepts, such as rights or utility, can provide. At the outset, however, I should point out that the conception of responsibility that I have in mind departs in essential respects from the received notion discussed by philosophers under the heading of free will and determinism. Philosophical discussions of the latter are generally more concerned with defining the conditions of nonresponsibility (e.g., excusing conditions) than with giving an account of responsibility in a positive full-blown moral sense. Lawyers, for somewhat different reasons, are also concerned primarily with conditions of nonresponsibility; that is, conditions that exempt a person from criminal or civil liability.[1] In contrast to these notions, which I shall call "negative conceptions of responsibility," there is a broader, positive conception of moral responsibility that refers, for example, to a person's duties to others with whom he or she has a relationship, such as children, employees, or associates, and to a person's duty to have due regard for the consequences of his or her actions for the safety and welfare of others.

This positive sense of responsibility is partly captured by general terms like "social responsibility" and by other more specific terms like "family responsibility." It is also reflected in the use of "responsible" to stand for a virtue—that is, a character trait that persons ought to have and actions that ought to be done. In this sense, responsibility is contrasted with irresponsibility, and not being responsible means simply being irresponsible.[2]

It should be clear by now that the concept of responsibility involved here breaks the traditional ties between responsibility and liability (e.g., having to pay for damages) and between responsibility and punishability or blameworthiness. These other concepts can still be linked to the comprehensive concept of responsibility but only indirectly. The comprehensive concept focuses on what ought or ought not to be done, rather than on the responses that third parties, such as spectators and judges, are permitted to adopt in the form of disapproving, blaming, or punishing those who are on the giving or receiving end of transactions.

The positive conception of moral responsibility differs from the negative conceptions usually discussed by philosophers and lawyers in two basic respects: First, positive responsibility is nonexclusive. One person's being responsible does not entail that other persons are not also responsible; hence, it is possible for a lot of people to be coresponsible for something, although perhaps in varying degrees. Second, responsibility need not always be direct and proximate; it may be and more commonly is indirect and remote. Unlike negative responsibility, which is characteristically a black-and-white issue, positive moral responsibility has no clear-cut borders and, like a magnetic field, varies from point to point in degrees of strength and stringency. The advantage of the open-texture quality of positive moral responsibility is that it makes it possible to use sophisticated, complex,

---

[1] See the classic discussion by H. L. A. Hart, *Punishment and Responsibility* (New York: Oxford University Press, 1968).

[2] G. Haydon, "On Being Responsible," *The Philosophical Quarterly* 28 (1979), pp. 46–57.

and multiple causal analyses in detailing the moral responsibilities of individual human agents in relation to particular untoward outcomes.[3]

In the comprehensive moral sense, responsibility expresses a certain kind of moral and social relationship between persons. It builds on the fact that human agents and other human beings are affected by the outcomes that are the consequences of the agents' actions or omissions. (The persons affected might be called "victims" or "recipients.") The interpersonal relationship involved in responsibility has two sides: (1) a subjective (or mental) attitude, present or absent in the agent(s), such as a concern (or lack of concern) for the safety or welfare of another person; (2) an objective side, namely, a causal connection between the agents' actions (or omissions) and the unfortunate outcome for the victim(s).[4] The first side, the subjective attitude, can be illustrated by reference to the tort of negligence, where the agent may be reckless, careless, unconcerned, or plain thoughtless about the consequences of his or her actions (or nonactions) for the safety or welfare of others (victims).[5]

The comprehensive concept of responsibility is intended to cover both retrospective and prospective responsibility and so applies both to past and to future actions and outcomes. Accordingly, it lays down moral requirements about what people ought to have done and about what people ought to do in the future. For example, a reckless driver who causes the death of another is retrospectively responsible for the outcome (liable) because he caused it by being reckless, and other drivers are prospectively responsible for preventing such outcomes and for being neither reckless nor a cause. The same thing, of course, could be said of a thoughtless programmer whose program has led or might lead to an accident. Because, as I have already pointed out, positive responsibility is non-exclusive, other people besides the driver or the programmer might also be either directly or indirectly responsible for preventing (or not having prevented) the accident.

Philosophically, one of the merits of the proposed comprehensive concept of moral responsibility is that, in current jargon, it is both "consequentialist" and "agent-relative." As such, it reflects the basic insights of the traditional concept of responsibility, which focuses on the moral linkage between outcomes, human agents, and human victims.[6] I shall now apply this notion to some of the ethical problems of responsibility that are connected with computers.

---

[3] I have explained the present conception of responsibility in a number of other writings: "The Ethical Dimensions of the Concept of Action," *Journal of Philosophy* (4 November 1965), where I argue that responsibility applies to states of affairs rather than to actions; "The Ethics of Participation," in *NOMOS XVI: Participation in Politics*, R. Pennock and J. Chapman eds. (New York: Atherton-Lieber, 1975), which contains arguments for a nonexclusive concept of responsibility; "Philosophical Remarks on Professional Responsibility in Organizations," *Applied Philosophy*, 1, no. 2 (Fall 1982); "Morality and the Ideal of Rationality in Formal Organizations," *Monist* (October 1970), where I argue that formal organizations as such cannot have moral responsibilities; and as a followup to the above, "Corporate Mythology and Individual Responsibility," *Applied Philosophy* 2, no. 1 (Fall 1984).

[4] The comprehensive conception of responsibility also covers cases analogous to strict liability and vicarious liability, but I omit the discussion of them here.

[5] William L. Prosser, *The Law of Torts*, 4th ed. (St. Paul, MN: West Publishing Co., 1971).

[6] Thomas Nagel, "The Limits of Objectivity," in *The Tanner Lectures on Human Values*, vol 1, Sterling M. McMurrin, ed. (Cambridge: Cambridge University Press, 1980); Amartya Sen, "Rights and Agency," *Philosophy and Public Affairs* 2, no. 1 (Winter 1982), pp. 3–39.

Intermediaries

Technology adds another element to the analysis of responsibility just outlined, namely, *an intermediary*. An intermediary provides the causal mechanism or causal structure that mediates between the actions of human agents and significant outcomes. In the case of the reckless driver, the technological intermediary is the automobile; in the case of the careless programmer, it is the technological process of running the program and tying it up with other parts of the system.

It is obvious that where complex technology is involved, the interposition of intermediaries of various sorts tends to make the assignment of responsibility for particular outcomes to particular agents difficult and ambiguous, simply because the causal nexus is so complicated. To this difficulty must be added the further difficulty that we have a natural tendency to ignore the role of intermediaries in determining responsibility relations, because the technological infrastructure that acts as intermediary is almost always phenomenologically transparent. Thus, we are hardly ever conscious of the part that an automobile or a telephone system plays in determining what we do when we use them or of how they impose patterns of their own on our actions and their outcomes.

By the same token, we tend to take for granted the "ethical neutrality" of intermediaries, as I have already mentioned. Occasionally, of course, we do take the properties of a technological intermediary into account; for example, as far as automobiles are concerned, experience has taught us not only to drive carefully but also to check on the condition of the machine, brakes, tires, and so on. As far as other technologies are concerned, we often have no way of assessing how and in what way they shape our actions and structure the outcomes. Presumably, with computers, the complicated (and hidden) nature of the technology reinforces our propensity to ignore our responsibility for the outcomes of computer operations.

Needless to say, there are serious moral objections to ignoring responsibility relations with respect to intermediary systems, even where they are quite complicated. One reason why we feel justified in doing so is that we assume, falsely I have argued, that moral responsibility must always be direct and proximate. This assumption has its roots in an oversimplified linear notion of causality, which is fostered perhaps by the law, inasmuch as law needs a standardized conception of causal relations for the purposes of establishing legal guilt and legal liability.[7]

Another consideration contributes to the disavowal of responsibility: Where complex technological systems are involved, the causal contribution of any particular individual agent to bringing about a disastrous outcome may not be decisive and is usually neither necessary nor sufficient. In fact, of course, the precise causal nature of the contribution may not be know. Charles Perrow has described in detail some of the disastrous accidents that have taken place in complex technological systems. He called them "normal

---

[7] In the law, the accepted principle is *novus actus interveniens*, which means that the causal chain can be broken by an intervening action. See H. L. A. Hart and A. M. Honore, *Causation in the Law* (Oxford: Clarendon Press, 1959), pp. 69 ff. My position, which is moral and not legal, rejects this notion. I am not alone in finding moral objections to it.

accidents."[8] In his detailed descriptions of such accidents, he argued persuasively for the conclusion that it is more plausible to attribute these industrial disasters to the complexities of the systems than to the failures of human operators.

Nevertheless, the comprehensive conception of moral responsibility outlined above implies that human agents are, in the final analysis, responsible for the systems themselves —that is, for the way that intermediaries function—and that human responsibility for disasters (past and potential) is not limited to the direct input of particular individuals, such as operators. Responsibility in the full moral sense covers indirect and remote causal relations, partial and contributory causes, as well as direct and proximate ones; even though individual persons are only indirectly or remotely connected with the outcome, they are not freed from the requirements of responsibility. However difficult it may be to determine, there is always some sort of human responsibility for the outcome of even the most complicated intervening technology.

The kind of indirect and diffused responsibility involved here is sometimes called "collective responsibility." However, I find this concept more confusing than helpful because it diverts attention from the crucial question about responsibility; namely, Which people in particular are responsible? To answer this question requires tracing the causal connections and responsibility relations for outcomes to particular individuals and to their individual failures stemming from such things as self-centered projects, narrow and single-minded interests, unconcerns, and moral mindlessness.

So far I have addressed the role of an intermediary between agents and outcomes only in relation to technology and mechanical processes, but now I wish to extend the notion to apply to structured human processes, such as those found in formal organizations or bureaucracies. For, like machines, the latter act as a sort of conduit for individual human actions and decision-making. They are, in this sense, also intermediaries.

There is obviously an intimate connection between structured social processes and technology. It is usually difficult to separate them from each other; the relationship may be said to be "symbiotic." Consider, for example, the use of automated bank tellers, which employ new computer technology to execute financial transactions that themselves are defined through a complex set of social structures, processes, and practices.

The structured processes themselves, as adopted and employed in formal organizations, perform the role of intermediaries in a way that is comparable to the role of technological systems. Like machines, they are purported to be immune to imputations of responsibility on the grounds that they are ethically neutral. The imputation of responsibility to particular individuals in such systems is often difficult and almost always complicated. And, just as with machines, the social mechanism itself—in the cashing of checks, for instance—becomes phenomenologically transparent. The actions that we perform as "autonomous individuals" appear to be our own, although in fact their form, structure, and meaning are shaped by the social systems in which they take place, that is, by intermediaries.

In both types of intermediaries, however, individual human agents are not let off the hook as far as responsibility is concerned. The comprehensive conception of responsibility

---

[8] Charles Perrow, *Normal Accidents* (New York: Basic Books, 1984).

makes room for indefinitely large numbers of people to be morally responsible for an outcome, although their various contributions are at different levels and vary considerably in amounts and degrees.

As far as formal organizations (or bureaucracies) are concerned, I have argued at length elsewhere that it is both a conceptual mistake and a moral error to attribute moral responsibility to formal organizations as such, as is done in most of the literature on corporate responsibility.[9] To hold organizations as such morally responsible for untoward outcomes may be compared to holding a machine—for example, a robot that kills a person—morally responsible for homicide.[10] It is a bit of anthropomorphic nonsense to ascribe moral responsibility to systems, whether they be technological or social, in addition to or instead of to the individuals that make and use them. Questions about who was responsible for the Nazi holocaust are not simply answered by reference to the technological machinery involved or to the bureaucratic system that carried it out; rather, responsibility must be attributed to indefinitely large numbers of individuals who in one way or another contributed quite indirectly and remotely to the outcome.[11]

Individuals, whoever they are and however minor their contribution, cannot escape either their retrospective or their prospective moral responsibilities in an organization by appeal to the doctrine of *respondeat superior*.[12] For the same reason, computer professionals, users, operators, programmers, and managers cannot escape their responsibilities for ties for outcomes by appeal to a doctrine of *respondeat computer*!

Computers as Metamachines

We come at last to the computer, which is typically a very special sort of machine: a *metamachine*. For, unlike other machines, computers are usually second-level machines that are used to control other machines. More generally, computer technology provides systems for controlling other systems, namely, those that I have called "intermediaries." Computers are, as it were, superintermediaries. The intermediaries that are controlled by computers may be either mechanical systems or organizational systems; the latter are controlled largely through networking.

In precomputer days, the intermediaries and processes that are now controlled by computers were and could only be controlled by human beings. Now, computers have begun to replace human beings in their capacity as controllers, which is precisely the capacity that makes human beings morally responsible for outcomes. To put the point more picturesquely, just as other machines (and tools) have in the past been used to replace hands (and bodies), so computers, the metamachines, are now being used to

[9] John Ladd, "Morality and the Ideal of Rationality in Formal Organizations," *Monist* 54, no. 4 (October 1970), pp. 488–516.

[10] See "In the Lion's Cage," *Forbes* 136, no. 9 (7 October 1985), pp. 142–143.

[11] Although it is not directly material to the present subject, one should remember that there is a subjective component to responsibility as well as the objective component we have been discussing. In the cases mentioned, there was a large amount of "unconcern" on the part of the general public—and not only in Germany—about what was going on in the concentration camps.

[12] Hannah Arendt, *Eichmann in Jerusalem* (New York: Viking Press, 1963).

replace brains. The special responsibility problems raised by computers are due, then, to the fact that they are used to replace minds, or brains, which, as I have said, are the source of human responsibility.

It can be readily seen that the introduction of computers to replace human controllers of first level intermediaries complicates an already complicated picture of moral responsibility. It sometimes appears to be the case that we have "delegated" or "abdicated" our decision-making powers to computers and have made computers responsible for outcomes for which human beings used to be responsible. That is why it has become popular to "blame" the computer for mistakes that were previously blamed on human beings. In earlier days, if one received a bill with an error in it, one blamed a person; nowadays, one blames the computer. Even though blaming a computer is silly, the excuse for doing so is that computers now do the sort of thing that human beings used to do and for which human beings used to be responsible, such as carrying out financial transactions, making reservations, and landing aircraft. But being dumb machines, when confronted with their mistakes, computers do not answer with a polite, "I am sorry" (unless they are programmed to do so). And one soon concludes that it is not a violation of the rules of politeness to turn them off when they do not behave; for, after all, it is impossible to insult a computer.

Disregarding such anthropomorphic responses to computers, let us return to ethics, which is and must be grounded on realities rather than on fairy stories and mythologies. What happens then when computers take over peculiarly human functions? What ethical consequences does the replacement of human controllers by computer controllers have for the original responsibility functions of human beings? In other words, where a human being is replaced by a computer, what happens to the responsibility that the human being used to have?

The obvious answer to the question about responsibility is that, as with other intermediaries, human control and moral responsibility move to a third level. At that level, we have a new kind of control—control over computers—which itself is an example of indirect and less easily assigned responsibility. This move, however, leads to a whole new set of questions, issues, and problems relating to responsibility; namely, it leads to questions about the formerly human functions performed by computers and how computers perform them in specific instances. Do they perform them well or badly? And what kind of controls should be exercised over computers in order to obtain morally responsible outputs?

Responsibility and the Shift from Human Control to Computer Control

The new set of issues raises questions about the ethically significant differences between human and computer control and about the effect of the shift from one kind of control to the other on the assignments of responsibility, especially as it relates to intermediaries at the first level. The shift to computers might be exemplified by controlled aircraft landing and computerized banking. Both of these innovations have brought many benefits along with new hazards and, indeed, a number of disasters. In order to bring out the ethically significant aspects of this shift in control, we must examine more closely the similarities and differences between the two kinds of control.

There are, to begin with, certain obvious similarities between the jobs normally performed by human beings in controlling intermediaries and those performed by computers. As in human decision-making, computers make decisions based on the use of information processing. The decision-making process is structured through means-ends relationships of one sort or another. For computers, the ordering of means and ends is accomplished through the use of algorithms. In the cases under consideration here, the means consist of operations of intermediary systems, either mechanical or organizational.

The resemblance between the two types of decision-making or control may be seen by comparing, for example, a computer-directed operation with a human-directed operation such as the landing of an aircraft. As control centers, they both receive information and process it for the purposes of controlling the system, the intermediary, so that the latter will satisfactorily serve the purpose for which it is designed—in this case, flying and making a safe landing.

Inasmuch as computers, like human operators, operate at a second level—that is, they operate on other systems (intermediaries)—the final evaluation of their second-level operations is a function of how well or poorly the first-level controlled system performs. A good aircraft control system, whether human or computer, is one that flies and lands the airplane effectively and properly. What is important here is that neither human controllers nor computers produce their effects directly, whether good or bad, but only indirectly through the systems that they control. Hence, computers cannot be dangerous or safe in themselves but only on account of the inherent features of the systems (machines) they control. A computer-controlled nuclear power plant is dangerous because it involves nuclear processes, not because it involves computers. By itself, a computer is harmless or useless. As the value of computers—their programs and operations, both positive and negative—depends on the systems they are used to control, they could be said to be *parasites* from the value point of view. In the final analysis, as far as values are concerned, the outcome is what counts.

To pursue these similarities further, computers and human controllers are almost always superior to purely mechanical controls. They are more flexible, and they are responsive to different environments and varying sorts of data and information processing.[13] Such controls "monitor" changes in the environment and direct the systems they control (intermediaries) accordingly.

But here we begin to see differences between human and computer controls. On one hand, computers are in many respects clearly better than human beings are at controlling some systems because they have larger memories and can process information faster and more accurately, perhaps also more economically. They do not have to sleep or take coffee breaks. For these reasons, computer controllers are frequently and justly preferred to human controllers.

On the other hand, computerized controls are for certain purposes of limited value, either because they are ineffectual or because they are liable to error. They are limited

---

[13] Nancy Leveson, "Software Safety: Why, Where, What?" (unpublished manuscript).

for a number of reasons having to do with the peculiar properties of computers and how computer systems are coupled to other systems. Thus, computers are unable to deal with certain kinds of surprises and accidents. Their proneness to new and unexpected kinds of error may lead to disastrous results. It is unnecessary to repeat the horror stories.[324]

It is clear, therefore, that we need to ask which sort of control, computer or human, is best for a particular purpose and for a particular kind of intermediary, or more generally, we need to ask: What do computers do best and what do human beings do best? As we are concerned here with responsibility for avoiding disastrous outcomes, our answers must be framed with such outcomes in mind.

As a general principle the following seems most plausible: In situations where satisfactory controls require dealing only with closed systems of factors, data, or tasks, computers are probably superior; when the systems required are open-ended and fluid, human controllers are generally preferable. In an old-fashioned terminology, human beings are better than computers where "judgment" is required. Granting all this, however, we still have to answer crucial and controversial questions concerning which kinds of problems belong to each of these categories; more exactly, we must ask which *parts* of a problem belong in which of these categories.[325]

Given the difficulties created by the computer revolution, even after this general principle is accepted in the abstract, problems that properly belong to the open fluid category are likely to be handled as if they belonged to the other category. Thus, jobs were still be given to computers that they are intrinsically incapable of handling. Mismatching of this kind raises a new consideration: When, for some reason or other (such as incomplete or incorrect data or a rigid, inflexible program), the computer decision-making is defective, we need to have some way "to get out" and to revert to human controls. In order to do this, there needs to be a loose coupling between the computers and the systems they are controlling and between the latter and the production of outcomes. This kind of safety mechanism is especially necessary where there is a possibility that a computer error might lead to disastrous consequences.[326]

So there are at least two kinds of things that we, as responsible human beings, need to watch out for: first, not giving the computer control over jobs that it is unequipped to handle, and second, providing some way to decouple from the computer if things go wrong. Two examples will illustrate these points.

Lessons in Irresponsibility: Two Cases

There are a number of well-attested cases of police misidentification based on computer-based information (or disinformation) about the identity of individual criminals being searched for. These cases generally take the same form; namely, from available databanks, using matching and profiling techniques, the inference is made that the wanted person

---

[14] See newsletters of Computer Professionals for Social Responsibility and other CPSR material on computer unreliability (CPSR, P.O. Box 717, Palo Alto, CA 94301).

[15] The following is an example provided by Richard van Slyke at the conference for which this essay was written.

[16] Perrow, *Normal Accidents*.

has certain identifying characteristics. An individual is then found who by coincidence happens to have a few or even most of the characteristics in question. He or she is then apprehended and perhaps falsely arrested and in at least one case, even shot to death.[17] The disastrous outcome in these cases is the result of too tight coupling between the computer-generated profile, bureaucratic procedures (police protocols), and actions directly affecting individual victims. (Often the information in the databank is incorrect.[18]) This tight coupling might be said to be the cause of the disaster, as in some of the normal accidents described by Perrow.[19]

A second example is the tie-up of the Bank of New York in November 1985 when a computer foul-up prevented the bank from delivering securities to buyers and making payments to sellers. The system was down for twenty-eight hours, and the bank had to borrow $20 billion at an interest expense of about $4 million. A number of other financial losses were incurred. A seemingly minor computer error led to a near financial disaster.[20] Again, we have a case of over-tight coupling between the computer system and the intermediary, the Bank of New York and the Wall Street financial system.

These two examples of overdependence on computers may serve as illustrations of how the framework or moral responsibility set forth in this chapter could be applied to real situations. In particular, they show us how, as human agents, we must take moral responsibility for preventing the disastrous outcomes that computer operations can have for the safety, health, welfare, and moral integrity of innocent victims. Unless as citizens and responsible human beings we assume prospective responsibility of this kind—for example, for errors that might happen in the computer system that controls our nuclear arsenal—we may end up being retrospectively responsible for a nuclear holocaust and the end of civilization as we know it.[21] In view of the disastrous outcomes that may result in such cases, responsibility should be something to take seriously.

---

[17] The goriest case can be found in Jacques Vallee, *The Network Revolution* (Berkeley: And/Or Press, 1982), where the innocent victims were shot to death by the French police acting on a computer report.

[18] An FBI audit of the National Crime Information Center showed that "the NCIC computer's responses include at least 12,000 invalid or inaccurate personal records each day." Ross Gelbspan, "Technological Surveillance: 1985 in the U.S.A.," *Computers and People* (March–April 1986), pp. 18–20.

[19] Gary Marx, "Routinizing the Discovery of Secrets: Computers as Informants," *Software Law Journal* 1 (Fall 1985).

[20] Phillip L. Zweig and Allanna Sullivan, "A Computer Snafu Snarls the Handling of Treasury Issues," *Wall Street Journal* (25 November 1985), p. 58.

[21] Paul Bracken, *The Command and Control of Nuclear Forces* (New Haven: Yale University Press, 1983); See also, *Computers in Battle*, D. Bellin and G. Chapman, eds. (Boston, MA: Harcourt Brace Jovanovich, 1987).

P·A·R·T·VII

2

When Organizations Are Perpetrators: Assumptions about Computer Abuse and Computer Crime

Rob Kling

Introduction[1]

"Computer abuse," "computer crime," and "computer fraud" are sensitizing concepts; they suggest that unsavory practices differ in important ways from "usual" when a computer is employed as a critical instrument. For example: individual thefts may more easily be hundreds of thousands or even millions of dollars because of the amount of money that can be accessible in computerized accounts.[2]

Frauds may be more difficult to uncover since computerized files are often substantially more complex and difficult to audit than their manual precursors.[3] Overcharging supermarket customers may become more common with product scanners and the disappearance of individually marked prices on each item, since customers will be less easily able to audit their charges. Outside auditors may be unduly impressed or "snowed" by the operations of an organization which are extensively automated with particularly sophisticated, complex systems.[4] Analysts of computer abuse are quick to point out that activities such as these fall under conventional labels (e.g., theft, fraud). They also argue that employing a computer as a critical instrument alters their character: they are particularly subtle and difficult to detect routinely.

Reprinted with permission of the Center for Computer Law. "Computer Abuse and Computer Crime as Organizational Activities," by Rob Kling, *Computer/Law Journal*, Center for Computer Law, vol. II (2), Spring 1980.

While most analysts of computer abuse devote some attention to the nature of computers that make these episodes special, few carefully examine their conceptions of "abuse" or "crime," and the social conditions when they are most likely to occur. Authors develop implicit images when they select and interpret illustrative cases. Usually these are frauds or thefts in which isolated individuals abuse organizations, rather than cases in which organizations abuse their clients in the course of doing relatively routine business. Typically, authors develop their concepts of computer crime or abuse through the case examples, rather than conceptually. Partly to persuade readers that computer abuses are significant, and partly to maintain interest, the cases selected for explication are typically those where losses are immense or the activities are exotic, rather than those where the losses are small.[5]

There is growing literature about computer abuse and computer crime which includes short stories in the news media as well as detailed specialized publications for auditors,[6] criminal prosecutors,[7] computer specialists,[8] consumer advocates,[9] and federal policy makers.[10] Each audience has special needs and interests. It is difficult to find studies of

---

[1] This article is excerpted from "Computer Abuse and Computer Crime as Organizational Activities" *Computers and Law Journal*, II(2) (Spring 1980): 403–427. See the original article for elaborations of some arguments and additional sources and citations.

[2] Most analysts of computer crime emphasize the extent to which automated data system are vulnerable to large scale thefts. See for example, "The Embezzler's Guide to Computer Systems" Brandt Allen, *Harvard Business Review*, 53 (July–Aug 1975): 75–89; "Value Conflicts and Social Choice in Electronic Funds Transfer Systems Developments," Rob Kling, *Communications of the ACM*, 21(8) (August 1978): 642–657; *Crime by Computer*, Donn Parker, Charles Scribners and Sons, New York, 1976; "Vulnerabilities of EFTs to Intentionally Caused Losses," Donn Parker, *Communications of the ACM*, 22(12) (December 1979): 654–660; *Computer Capers: Tales of Electronic Thievery, Embezzlement, and Fraud*, Thomas Whiteside, Thomas Y. Crowell and Company, New York, 1978. However, there is some good evidence that the "typical" reported computer crime entails losses of several thousand dollars rather than several hundred thousand dollars. See "A Survey of Computer Crime Studies," John Taber, *The Computer-Law Journal* (1980).

[3] See *Computer Fraud and Countermeasures*, Leonard I. Krauss and Aileen MacGahan, Prentice Hall, Englewood-Cliffs, N.J., 1979.

[4] See the Equity Funding case reported in Parker, 1976, and Whiteside, 1978, footnote 2.

[5] Many authors casually extend their examples to make their points. Stanley Rifkin's theft of $10.2 million from the Security Pacific Bank in 1978 is often treated as a computer crime and used to illustrate the magnitude of funds that can be stolen from electronic funds transfer systems. While his theft was accomplished through wire transfers and no computer system was directly employed, it is often used to indicate the way in which electronic funds transfer systems are particularly vulnerable to massive thefts.

[6] See Krauss and MacGahan, footnote 3.

[7] See *Computer Crime: Criminal Justice Resource Manual*, SRI International, U.S. Government Printing Office, Washington, D.C., 1979.

[8] See "Consumer Difficulties With Computerized Transactions: An Empirical Investigation," Theodor D. Sterling, *Communications of the ACM*, 22(5) (May 1979): 283–289.

[9] See Mark Budnitz, "The Problems of Proof When There's A Computer Goof: Consumers Versus ATMs" *Computer Law Journal*, 49 (1980); Mark Budnitz, "The Impact of EFT upon Consumers: Practical Problems Faced by Consumers," *University of San Francisco Law Review*, 13(2) (Winter 1979): 361–404; Ellen Broadman, "Electronic Fund Transfer Act: Is the Consumer Protected?" *University of San Francisco Law Review*, 13(2) (Winter 1979): 245–272; and Theordor D. Sterling, "Computer Ombudsman," *Society*, 17(2) (January/February 1980): 31–35.

[10] See, for example, Kenneth Laudon, *Dossier Society: Value Choices in the Design of National Information Systems*. New York: Columbia University Press, 1986.

computer abuse or computer crime which self-consciously make important assumptions explicit. Much hinges on matters such as (a) whether one emphasizes "abuses," "crimes," or "frauds" that are married to computing; (b) the conceptions of "abuses," "crimes," or "frauds" that are adopted; and (c) the particular role that computing plays in these events. Despite the many choices about these matters which can be made in principle, there is substantial consensus over the social location of perpetrators and victims and the "conventional" stories of these events. First, most of the cases examined are those in which businesses are victims; the perpetrators are individuals or small groups acting in relative isolation and pursuing idiosyncratic criminal ventures. In contrast, cases in which computer systems are instruments of businesses acting against their clients (e.g., consumer fraud) are largely ignored. Second, these events are also typically lifted out of the social worlds in which they occur and simply labelled as "abuses" or "crimes" (e.g., "invasion of privacy," fraud). Consequently, some stories will treat students who play unauthorized games on university run computers as having "stolen" thousands of dollars. These distinctions are not merely academic matters, since "computer crime" is increasingly becoming subject to special legislation. Special "computer crime" bills have been enacted into law in several states and as Federal law.

Some of the cases described in the computer crime literature are legally "crimes" since they violate existing statutes. However, the "criminal" label cannot be taken for granted when existing laws must be modified for the acts in question to be officially defined as "crimes." For example, the use of "spare" computer time for private recreational purposes by a computer programmer may be viewed as "theft" of private property or as a job perquisite akin to using a company telephone for limited private calls. People often differ about whether such acts should be labelled as "abuses" and furthermore, even if labelled as abuses, whether they should further be sanctioned by law. (However, if "unauthorized use of computer resources" are legislated as criminal offenses, some informal but acceptable work practices would be illegal.) Similarly, there is considerable debate about which procedures for handling personally sensitive data should be treated as fair business practices, and which are so unfair and intrusive that they abuse individual rights to privacy and should be made illegal. The literature about "computer abuse" and "computer crime" is skewed by emphasizing white collar crimes in which businesses are the primary victims in thefts and abuses of trust such as embezzlement. Business crimes and abuses such as consumer fraud, invasions of personal privacy, and contractual violations in the computer industry are routinely neglected. Moreover, the labels "abuse" and "crime" are usually taken for granted as objective properties of the acts in question rather than as the signposts of conflicts over rights and obligations.

A major thrust of this article is to expand the prevailing conceptions of computer abuse to include the wider class of activities in which organizations are sometimes perpetrators, as well as victims. A second focus of this paper is to better understand the causes of computer abuses. Should they be viewed as the idiosyncratic acts of individuals or as routinized occurrences in "criminogenic" environments? The current literature emphasizes individual characteristics and character profiles of "computer abuse perpetrators." This paper examines the social contexts in which computer abuses are likely to occur. The following discussion emphasizes computer abuses and computer crimes which may be viewed as organizational actions, insofar as organizations which employ the "perpetrators" also profit from their actions.

Computer Abuse and Computer Crime

"Computer abuse" connotes a wide range of unsavory practices which can be married to computing (e.g., fraud, theft, invasions of privacy). Selecting "computer abuse" as a sensitizing concept in contrast with "computer crime" or "computer fraud" offers two advantages. First, it allows a larger variety of problematic practices to be addressed since the "criminal" status of many "computer crimes" is sometimes problematic. Some of these activities, such as "invasions of privacy" or "swamping consumers with individually addressed junk mail" may not violate existing statutes. But much is gained by providing a covering term by which they might be examined. Other activities, such as copying proprietary computer programs, can arguably be treated as major or minor thefts. Second, since the term "computer abuse" is more transparently a label whose appropriateness and use is not "given" but negotiated, it is easier to examine a wider array of actors who participate in and "define" computer abuses and computer crimes in addition simply to "perpetrator" and "victim." These additional actors also include "moral entrepreneurs" who define particular acts as abusive or criminal, security specialists, auditors, and law enforcers.[11]

Most analysts rely upon implicit conceptions of computer crime or computer abuse. Parker has been most explicit by defining computer abuse as "any incident associated with computer technology in which a victim suffered or could have suffered loss and a perpetrator by intention made or could have made a gain."[12] This definition allows too broad a connection between computing and some abusive act, and also emphasizes loss too strictly.

First, computer-based systems must be a critical handmaiden to the loss or abuse. If computers are merely "used" incidentally, little is gained by drawing special attention to "computer" abuses. If an extortion attempt is made by long distance telephone, a computer is "associated with" the act since direct-long-distance dialing is automated. But nothing is gained by treating a long-distance extortion aided by telephone as a "computer crime." A second kind of "association" between computer technology and abuse can occur when computerized products or services are deceptively represented or contracted. Because of the complexity of computer based products (e.g., mainframes, systems software), data analyses (e.g., simulation models), and services (e.g., payment systems), a loss may be induced by simply misrepresenting a product to a "reasonable," but inexpert agent (e.g., customer, auditor).

"Computer abuse" is a sensitizing concept which is difficult to define sharply. But it helps focus attention on the ways in which computerized technologies may be problematic for computer-using organizations or the public. If one wonders whether electronic funds transfer systems will be more subject to theft, large or small, then their manual precursors, "computer abuse" may be a useful point of departure.

---

[11] See *Outsiders: Studies in the Sociology of Deviance*, Howard S. Becker, Free Press of Glencoe, New York, 1963.

[12] See Parker 1976, footnote 2, page 12.

The Construction of "Computer Abuses"

Analysts of computer abuse often illustrate important principles through example cases: to steal from a computerized record system, one might need only to manipulate normal transaction cards and need not understand the software; a computer theft may be executed by employing a data entry clerk as an accomplice; computer frauds can persist through standard audits and are often found only through accidental occurrences.[13] Patterns like these are worth knowing to those who seek to diminish the volume and frequency of loss by designing different computer systems, altering organizational procedures, and enacting and enforcing laws. The literature about computer abuse has been largely developed to draw attention to the peculiar properties of computer systems that make them more complex and special instruments. Many analysts of computer crime view themselves as demythologizing or debunking "conventional" images which attribute extensive security to automated systems or which treat crimes with computer as no different in kind from crimes without a computer.

Presumably, the illustrative cases reported would span the range of actual and potential abuses; actually, they form a peculiarly biased sample. The lion's share of attention is turned to episodes of theft or fraud where the victim is a computer using organization and the identified perpetrator is an individual or small group engaging in clearly illegal acts. These cases (or "capers") are briefly presented and are similar to formula detective stories sans detective.[14] Much of the attention hinges on the scheme used by the perpetrators, and possibly on the organizational practices which allow them to continue undetected. Typically, these are large frauds or embezzlements in which the losses to the victimized business are hundreds of thousands or millions of dollars. The sheer scale of these frauds and or thefts helps the analyst dramatize their importance.

In understanding the social or technical conditions under which different kinds of acts are likely to be defined as computer abuse and are likely to occur, it helps to have a set of categories to situate the major actors and their relations to one another. In the special case of white collar crime, Edelhertz suggests a useful classification for situating "perpetrators" and "victims":

1. "Crimes by persons operating on an individual, *ad hoc* basis, for personal gain in a non-business context (hereinafter referred to as *personal crimes*).
2. Crimes in the course of their occupations by those operating inside businesses,

---

[13] The more serious compendia each include over a dozen cases. See, Allen 1978, Parker 1976, and Whiteside 1978, footnote 2, Krauss and MacGahan, footnote 3.

[14] One might suspect that computer abuses would more aptly conform to the formulas of crime novels than detective novels since the attention hinges on the deceptions employed by the perpetrator and the logical sequence of events rather than on the forensic powers of the investigators. In fact, since many computer abuses are discovered by accident or when a perpetrator confesses on his own initiative, the absence of "detection" is even more characteristic of many cases of computer abuse. Symon contrasts "crime novels" with "detective novels" and argues that detective novels emphasize a plot based upon deception while crime novels depict relatively straightforward crimes and focus on the circumstances and interactions of the characters. See *Mortal Consequences: A History—from the Detective Story to the Crime Novel*, Julian Symons, Harper and Row, New York, 1972. Also, *Adventure, Mystery and Romance: Formula Stories as Art and Popular Culture*, John G. Cawelti, University of Chicago Press, Chicago, 1976.

Government, or other establishments, or in a professional capacity, in violation of their duty of loyalty and fidelity to employer or client (hereinafter referred to as *abuses of trust.*)

3. Crimes incidental to and in furtherance of business operations, but not the central purpose of such business operations (hereinafter referred to as *business crimes*).
4. White collar crimes as a business, or as the central activity of the business (hereinafter referred to as *con games*)."[15]

While organizations may be victims of white collar crimes in any of these categories, individual clients are most likely to be victimized by business crimes and con games.[16] While technically, any of these crimes are perpetrated by "individuals," as one moves from personal crimes to con games, the social scale of the collusion helpful for success increases. In Edelhertz's terms, most of the cases of computer crime which appear in the literature illustrate personal crimes and abuses of trust. Business crimes are typically excluded from attention, although they are perhaps the most important category which would cover a variety of consumer frauds.[17] And one con game, the Equity Funding Case, is often cited in any of the accounts of computer crime.[18]

Much of our attention will be directed to business crimes in this paper. The concept has been best defined by Shover who employed the label "organizational crime" to denote

> criminal acts committed by individuals or groups of individuals, thus including conspiracies, during the normal course of their work as employees of organizations, which they intend to contribute to the achievement of goals or other objectives thought to be important for the organization as a whole, some subunit within the organization, or their own particular job duties.[19]

Business crimes (or organizational crimes) include price-fixing, false advertising, and consumer fraud. When restricted to the cases where computing technology is instrumental, "business computer crimes" are most likely to be consumer fraud and contractual fraud. When we extend these conceptions to include "computer abuse" as defined above, "business computer abuses" include invasions of privacy, misleading sales practices in the

---

[15] From *The Nature, Impact and Prosecution of White Collar Crime,* Herbert Edelhertz, U.S. Government Printing Office, 1970. Quoted in *Crime and Criminology,* p. 223, Sue Titus Reid, The Dryden Press, Hinsdale, Ill., 1976.

[16] Individuals can be victimized by abuses of trust and businesses victimized by others engaging in business crimes. These are relatively gross generalizations. Books written for auditors either assume that the computer using organization is acting ethically or argue that it should be.

[17] In this respect, the literature of computer crime parallels much of the crime literature which neglects organizational and occupational crimes. See, *Crime at the Top: Deviance in Business and the Professions,* John Johnson and Jack Douglas, J. B. Lippincott and Co., New York, 1978.

[18] See footnote 4.

[19] See "Defining Organizational Crime" by Neal Shover in *Corporate and Governmental Deviance: Problems of Organizational Behavior in Contemporary Society* (ed. by) M. David Ermann and Richard Lundman, Oxford University Press, New York, 1978. When the criminal activities are common to an occupation, not just to an organization (e.g., kickbacks from laboratories to doctors), the term "occupational crime" is a useful designation. See, "The Study of White Collar Crime: Toward a Reorientation in Theory and Research," Richard Quinney in *White Collar Crime Offenses in Business, Politics, and the Professions* (revised ed.) (ed. by) Gilbert Geis and Robert Meier, The Free Press, New York, 1977.

computer industry and deceptive presentations of computerized data analysis. Both individuals and organizations may be the "victims" of these practices.

Individuals as Victims of Business Computer Abuse

As computerized information systems spread throughout the economy, the opportunities for computer-related abuses and crimes are likely to increase proportionally. These may occur in any of several ways. Customers of organizations using electronic billing, funds transfer, or calculating aids (e.g., supermarket scanners) may simply be defrauded. As the data collected in these systems increases in richness, they are likely to be turned to other purposes (e.g., identifying "good customers," locating debtors) which invade the privacy of the individual customer. If individuals who elect to use computerized financial services are misled in understanding their risks and liabilities by service providers, they will suffer unexpected and unfair losses. This is a broad collection of activities—consumer fraud, "invasions of personal privacy," and false advertising. Activities such as these range from practices that some parties feel to be abusive, but are well within the bounds of legal business practices, to those that violate current laws.

Civil libertarians argue that certain routine organizational practices unduly invade personal privacy. For example, computer using organizations have been willing to turn their files to new purposes such as market surveys, matching payroll against welfare files to identify "cheaters," and the use of business records for the Parent Locator System.[20] Advocates of these practices emphasize their efficiency in helping an organization conduct its business or a public agency carry out its legislated obligations. In contrast, civil libertarians advocate maximizing individual liberty as a competing value which should not be easily compromised.[21] Guttman, for example, asserts,

> As valuable to the business and scientific communities as such research might prove, the use of data acquired and maintained by an electronic fund transfer system for any purpose other than transfer of money *would be to misuse the system, to abuse it, to betray a reasonable anticipation of privacy* to which the consumer is entitled (emphasis added).[22]

An analyst of computer abuse with civil libertarian sympathies would focus on a different set of episodes than one who accepts prevailing "legitimate" organizational record-handling practices as *unabusive by definition*.[23]

---

[20] See Privacy Protection Study Commission, *Personal Privacy in an Information Society*, U.S. Government Printing Office, Washington, D.C., July 1977.

[21] See Kling, 1978, footnote 2, and Rob Kling, "Value Conflicts in Organizing Computerized Systems," excerpted in Part V of this book.

[22] From "Observations of a Civil Libertarian on Electronic Funds Transfer," Jeremiah Guttman (May 1979): 2 (unpublished ms.) Some uses of financial record systems for other purposes, such as the Parent Locator System are mandated by law.

Advertising and complex contracts that mislead or confuse consumers about the nature of computerized financial services is a second example of business computer abuse where individuals may be victimized. Evidence about these matters is scanty and usually anecdotal. For example, Budnitz carefully examined the case of one "pay by phone" service whose advertising misleads customers about its convenience and liabilities.[24] Usually, legal remedies are employed to ameliorate problems like these. While laws such as the EFT Act[25] and the New York consumer contracts law[26] require that contracts "be written in a clear and coherent manner using words with common and everyday meanings,"[27] business practices may not be in compliance. There is scanty evidence about the extent to which actual contracts for EFT services comply with these criteria. One survey of EFT contracts and advertising 15 New York State chartered banks suggests serious discrepancies between the intent of these laws and routine practice.[28]

> Some banks took greater care to insure that their contracts were able to be easily read and understood . . . . However, even when customer contracts of the more conscientious banks are compared to promotional contracts used by all the banks to entice new EFT customers, the shortcomings of the contracts are clear and the potential for readable contracts becomes obvious. The banks artfully designed the promotional materials . . . . When compared with the contracts, the promotional materials were printed in more simplified language and with more effective use of large and bold print . . . . Furthermore, none of the promotional materials we reviewed described all the terms and conditions written into the customer contracts. The most important omission from the promotional materials was the provision on the customer's liability for the unauthorized use of his debit card."[29]

These practices certainly leave substantial room for abuse in the provision of computer-based services. Stronger regulations for fair and complete advertising as well as simple contracts may ease these difficulties. As Budnitz notes,

---

[23] The abusiveness of a practice and its legality are independent. One may hope that laws will not permit or mandate "abusive" practices. But legality is no insurance that a practice is not harmful. Laws are often the product of legislative compromises between conflicting interests which may even hold conflicting values; consequently, laws sometimes violate the values cherished by legitimate groups. In order to contrast what is legal from what should be legal, one needs a way to discuss the character and consequences of proposed statutes in which attributes such as the "interests they serve," their "constitutionality," their "efficacy," their "enforceability," and their "abusiveness" can be analyzed. In the case of data collected for one purpose being turned to other purposes, one must weigh the value of personal privacy against values such as the efficiency of state investigations, and the abilities of a private organization to make a profit. See Kling, footnote 2, the Privacy Protection Study Commission, footnote 20 and Rob Kling, "Value Conflicts in Organizing Computerized Systems," excerpted in Part V of this book.

[24] See Budnitz 1979, footnote 9.

[25] The Electronic Funds Transfer Act is title XX of the Financial Institutions Regulatory and Interest Rate Control Act of 1978, Pub. Law. No. 95-630, (2001), 92. Stat 3641 (to be codified at 15 U.S.C. 1962).

[26] See Harold Abrahamson and Jay Martin, "The Impact of the Federal EFT Act on Consumer Contracts in New York State," *University of San Francisco Law Review*, 13(2) (Winter 1979): 467–483.

[27] From Abrahamson and Martin, footnote 26.

[28] From Abrahamson and Martin, footnote 26.

[29] From Abrahamson and Martin, footnote 26.

It is unrealistic to expect financial institutions voluntarily to describe what may go wrong if they (consumers) use EFT, or to provide more complete disclosures than the law requires. However, it is equally unrealistic to pretend that consumers who lack this information truly understand the consequences of agreeing to use EFT."[30]

Unfortunately, the ease of disclosure is made difficult by complex or ambiguous laws such as the EFTA where the very conditions of liability are ambiguous and incomplete. For example, Broadman observes that the EFTA is ambiguous and may be interpreted as limiting consumers' liability to $0, $50 or $500 when they inform a bank of a lost debit card within two days depending different legitimate readings of the text.[31]

The third class of abusive activities, computer-related consumer frauds, are also poorly treated in the literature on computer crime. Reports of "consumer difficulties" with computerized billing and payment systems are easy to find, although episodic. While the transitions from "consumer difficulties" to "consumer abuse" to "consumer fraud" are neither direct nor simple, evidence of systematic consumer difficulties is the most likely indicator of fraud. Many people have had difficulties with errors in computerized systems and in correcting errors once found. A priori, there is no reason to suspect that such errors are necessarily "intentional," rather than "accidental."

Even the better quality automated record systems are not entirely free of data or software errors. Since imperfection is the rule, the practical questions hinge on the quality of data and software, and the extent to which an organization is adequately attentive to correcting data and software errors. While the boundaries between "accident," "negligence," and "criminal negligence" may be clear in principle, they are difficult to specify in practice in automated data systems.

All computer systems of any scale are likely to suffer from system design flaws and data entry errors. Thus, the presence of errors detected in say, disputed billings, only suggests the possibility of abuse or crime rather than "commonly accepted" and "acceptable" difficulties. Much depends upon the rate of errors found in specific systems, the extent to which design flaws are corrected over time, and the ease that consumers have in bringing errors to the attention of organizational staff and having them resolved. Despite the widespread and increasing use of computerized systems in business transactions, little systematic data is publicly available regarding these matters.

However, there are indications that consumers have systematic difficulties in correcting computerized errors. Consumer-oriented centers which are set up to investigate consumer complaints attributable to computer errors also shed some light on the presence of consumer difficulties. Sterling reported on a variety of cases of computer "billing errors" that were referred to in a "Computer Ombudsman Office" which was administered by a society of computer specialists.[32] In the 1970s, one trade newspaper, *Computerworld*, routinely reported computer errors which were brought to the attention of a special contributor, Alan Taylor, by individual complainants. While only several episodes were

---

[30] See Budnitz (1979), footnote 9.

[31] See, Ellen Broadman, p 256, footnote 9.

[32] The office was sponsored by the Vancouver Chapter of the Canadian Information Processing Society. See Theordor D. Sterling, "Computer Ombudsman," *Society*, 17(2) (Jan/Feb 1980): 31–35.

published each year, these were relatively "hard cases" since they were brought by complainants who usually worked hard to correct an error without success.[33]

Victimization surveys could shed systematic light about the occurrence of untoward errors and abuses, if not consumer crimes, which are associated with computerized information systems. In 1978 Ted Sterling published the results of a mail survey of 500 households in British Columbia about their experiences with errors in computerized record systems.[34] Approximately 40% of the sample reported at least one error in the preceding year, and about 15% reported two or more errors. 105 households reported specific problems and errors with computerized transactions; each of these was followed up with an intensive telephone interview. Of those people with errors, 74% were able to resolve them, although satisfactory resolution required several contacts with the computer-using organization. Some respondents found correcting errors to be time-consuming (20% spent more than 20 hours attempting to resolve a single error!). Moreover, some respondents suffered additional costs since they were unable to have interest charges on disputed amounts removed, even when they were reimbursed or credited for the disputed amounts. 7% of the respondents gave up trying to resolve their difficulties. (Of the remaining households, 8% never tried to resolve their computer errors and 11% were engaged in ongoing, but unresolved attempts to resolve their problems at the time of the study.) In addition, 36% of the households with errors had interest charged on the disputed amount. In 19% of the cases, the interest was removed at the time the charges error was corrected. Another 11% of the households with computer errors had to take yet additional action to have interest on the disputed amount removed. 6% of the households paid interest on the disputed amount. Sterling's study indicates that correcting computerized errors can be very troublesome for many people. Moreover, it was quite clear to many respondents that their identification of errors and attempts to correct them were not appreciated by the staff with which they dealt. "In 16% of cases, respondents reported that they were coerced in some way to pay a disputed amount, and in approximately 9% of the cases they were specifically urged to pay the disputed amount to protect their 'good credit rating.' "[35] Sterling's study illustrates how computerized transaction systems can be embroiled in conflicts between the public and computer-using organizations.

These studies do not directly address the question of whether individuals are subject to intentionally abusive billing practices which employ computerized systems. But at the very least, they indicate that many people may experience errors with computerized billing systems and that some of these errors prove so difficult to correct that people would rather pay the amount due than continue to fight their cases. In none of the cases published in "The Taylor Report" or reported by Sterling could criminal intent be proved. It was simply not investigated since the complaint bureaus aim to investigate, negotiate,

---

[33] See, for example, Alan Taylor, "New Approach Combats Deceptive Trade Practices," *Computerworld*, XIII(32) (August 6, 1979): 21–22; and Alan Taylor, "Two Problems Crop Up in Bankcard Procedures," *Computerworld* XIII(34) (August 20, 1979): 15–16. The second of these illustrates a particular consumer complaint investigated by Taylor.

[34] See Sterling, footnote 8.

[35] Quoted from pp. 286–287, Sterling, 1979, footnote 8.

and rectify the complaints of individuals. In these negotiations, the ombudsman adopts a strategy which allows the organizational staff the greatest opportunity to rectify an error without losing face. Consequently, he is more likely to avoid blaming "errors" on "intentional" actions and tightly pin down blame and motive as would an investigator seeking evidence of criminal activity. And a telephone survey of consumers could not provide data about the "intent" or organizational procedures. One possible exception is the extent to which consumers are "coerced" into paying disputed bills. Nonetheless, it is difficult to review Sterling's report and the occasional cases published in *Computerworld* and escape the suspicion that some businesses are systematically abusing some of their customers.[36]

As consumer-oriented computer systems such as electronic funds transfer systems and supermarket scanners become more common, it is likely that the incidence of losses related to computer errors will rise. Whether these are accidental, the results of negligence, or intentional can only be resolved empirically. But special attention need be given to consumer difficulties if they be investigated at all, since they are unlikely to be reported in the press or brought to the attention of lawyers or prosecutors without special support. Individual losses are likely to be small, even if they are large when aggregated over thousands of customers and transactions. It is most likely that individuals will simply seek to recover their own losses, and it is difficult to prove "intent" in many cases.

We have examined three different kinds of computer-related activities which civil libertarians or consumers would be likely to label as "abusive": turning financial record keeping systems into instruments of surveillance or research; completeness and clarity of advertising and contracts of computerized services; and procedures for correcting errors in computerized billing systems. Each of these activities illustrates the ways in which "computer abuse" is a socially defined label, since the legitimacy of each practice is subject to debate. There is little evidence about incidence or seriousness of each of these kinds of activities. But they typically are ignored by analysts of "computer abuse" even though they may constitute a large fraction of abuses for those who do not accept them.

Organizations as Victims of Business Computer Abuse

Increasingly, computerized systems serve as instruments in the transactions between organizations: sales and payments are recorded, computer equipment and software is bought and sold, and organizational participants display their work to clients and auditors in other organizations using computer-based data analyses for insight and persuasion. Certainly, organizations can be victims of con games that employ computerized systems. For example, if a firm is sending bogus bills to "randomly" selected organizations for

---

[36] There is some evidence that consumer abuses are infrequently reported to consumer protection agencies. While other forms of consumer abuse such as home repair swindles and bait and switch sales practices may form the majority of larger consumer abuses, there is simply a paucity of evidence to draw strong conclusions about the incidence and importance of computer-related consumer abuses. See Mary V. McGuire and Herbert Edelhertz, "Consumer Abuse of Older Americans: Victimization and Remedial Action in Two Metropolitan Areas," in *White Collar Crime: Theory and Research*, Gilbert Geis and Ezra Stotland (eds.), Sage Publications, Beverley Hills, Ca., 1980.

services that were never rendered (e.g., newspaper advertisements), businesses may be likely to pay the bills as if they were routine expenses that were properly incurred. If the bogus bills are produced by a computer system (to increase their legitimacy and also to operate on a larger scale), this would illustrate a computer fraud. Similarly, businesses are the identified victims in a variety of other computer crimes such as fraud[37] and embezzlement.

There are "routine" business practices which may be examples of computer abuse or computer crime, but which are ignored in most stories of computer crime or abuse. There are three commonplace occupational activities involving computer technology which can range from those that are clearly legitimate to some that are questionable, and still others that are deemed abusive, unethical, and possibly criminal:

1. Selling computing equipment and services;
2. "Delivering" software which meets contractual specifications;
3. Employing complex or sophisticated computer technologies to persuade a client that a given line of action is appropriate.

All of these activities entail legitimate practices. Salesmen are expected to place their wares in the best possible light. Software developers will produce products that resemble their contractual specifications. Analysts, such as engineers, actuaries, and urban planners, are expected to utilize sophisticated means, including computer based systems, when they provide better insight or "analytic penetration" into a complex problem.

But staff acting for the computer-using or computer-selling organization can also rely upon stratagems to advance the interests of their own organization, subunit, or job, and which "cause losses" to the client organization. Sales staff will certainly inform prospective buyers of software developed for their machine which meets their client's needs. But sometimes the promised software differs substantially from what the client seeks. Early delivery deadlines may be set to "beat the competition," even though they are unrealistic and turn out later to be unmet. Similarly, vendors sometimes sell undersized mainframes and minicomputes since the lower price may beat the competition, and once the equipment is acquired, the customer is locked in to upgrading from the same vendor.[38] Some misrepresentations are unintentional. But others which clearly serve the vendor's interest are likely to be negligent or intentional. Sales staff vary in the integrity with which they promise, and their own sophistication in accurately assessing their own product lines and

---

[37] See, for example, Diane Vaughan "Crime Between Organizations: Implications for Victimology" in *White Collar Crime: Theory and Research*, Gilbert Geis and Ezra Stotland (eds.), Sage Publications, Beverley Hills, Ca., 1980.

[38] Undersizing computer systems may also serve the interests of computer users. The author is familiar with a large multi-division organization which has firm policies about the level of scrutiny given to computer system acquisitions of different sizes. (The organization has an annual operating revenue of approximately one billion dollars and several thousand employees spread over several geographically dispersed divisions.) Systems or components which cost less than $100,000 may be authorized by Division directors without evaluations which integrate the acquisition into the organization-wide computing plan. The staff of an operating department in one division wished to acquire a computer system which would cost almost $175,000. With the support of the Division director, they proposed an inadequate $95,000 system. The system could be approved at the Division level, and its users fully expected to expand it to its proper size after the second year.

likely delivery schedules. Consequently, it is difficult to clearly demonstrate that un-reliable sales promises were intentionally misleading, except in the most blatant cases.

Some sales practices, in turn, are related to slips between the (usually vague) contractual specifications of software, and the relatively concrete package that is actually provided to a customer. "Missing features" are common in contractually developed software. Estimating the costs of complex software developments is more art than science, and a poorly developed art for many. Thus, there are not terribly strong professional standards by which to compare software costing or scheduling strategies. Consequently, it may be difficult to distinguish a good professional judgement which results in a poor outcome, from a poor professional judgement, and furthermore to distinguish either of these from rank deception except in the most blatant cases.

However, even sharply defined contracts may not be sufficient. An illustrative example concerns a major computer manufacturer, Byterite, which provides a FORTRAN on its SUMMA machine series, which is supposed to meet ANSI[39] FORTRAN Standards. A programmer was assigned to maintain Byterite's SUMMA FORTRAN by implementing enhancements, repairing errors, and issuing memos about new developments. Some of the error reports she received from installations using SUMMA FORTRAN indicated subtle but important discrepancies between SUMMA FORTRAN and ANSI FORTRAN. FORTRAN programmers who believed that SUMMA FORTRAN was compatible with the ANSI standard wrote programs which did not run "properly." SUMMA's pro-grammer prepared a variance report which she planned to send to all sites which had adopted SUMMA FORTRAN. Her supervisor objected and argued that Byterite could not acknowledge any discrepancy between SUMMA FORTRAN and ANSI FORTRAN since it was contractually obligated to provide an ANSI-compatible FORTRAN. She persisted, since she knew of the difficulties that the unexpected discrepancy between published specifications and actual behavior of SUMMA FORTRAN was causing in the field. Her supervisor threatened to fire her, she relented, and did not publish a report of the discrepancy.[40] This is the sort of situation where a strong professional association and professional ethos could assist a computer specialist in standing up for truth in advertising and fairness to clients. Unfortunately, the Association for Computing Machinery does not provide that kind of support for computer specialists today. Unfortunately, principled professionals are often treated as foolish troublemakers when organizations are per-petrators.

The use of computers to favorably impress clients or auditors is commonplace. Remarkably, the literature of computer crime and computer abuse chronicle few other cases where computerized information systems are used as instruments of impression

---

[39] The American National Standards Institute (ANSI), develops standards for various programming languages. These are voluntary in principle, but often compulsory in practice since Federal agencies usually specify software to meet ANSI Standards. (FORTRAN was the first language to be standardized, in 1966.)

[40] The programmer was demoralized, and later left her job. Data about matters such as these is scanty and anecdotal. Programmers usually resolve conflicts such as these privately by compliance or departure. Those who complain loudly, or "whistle blow" are likely to be penalized in their "efficiency reviews" or by being fired. For a case of engineering design with similar dynamics, see Kermit Vandivier, "Why Should My Conscience Bother Me?" in *Life in Organizations: Workplaces as People Experience Them*, Rosabeth Moss Kanter and Barry Stein (eds.), Basic Books, New York, 1979.

management. Such cases, however, are reported by social analysts who examine computer use in organizations. Rob Kling reports the case of a welfare agency which used an automated client tracking system to favorably impress Federal auditors[41] and the case of an engineering firm which turned to complex data analyses to snow auditors who were hired by their client to review a slow moving project.[42] The practical success of the Polaris nuclear missile and launch platform project, the U.S. first underwater missile, was often attributed (in part) to the use of PERT (Program Evaluation and Review Technique). PERT is a flashy graphical project scheduling method which was developed to help manage Polaris' construction and has subsequently been used on many other large construction projects. However, Sapolsky[43] persuasively argues that PERT was not used to manage Polaris' schedule and costs. The Admiral in charge of Polaris development was not concerned how PERT was used, only that its presence be visible. PERT served to sufficiently enhance the image of the Navy teams that were managing Polaris' development so that they were relatively unburdened by the scrutiny and intrusive demands of external review boards. On other projects, PERT might well serve as an instrument of managerial control. But in its first, and most publicized use, it served primarily as an instrument of deception. I have described three kinds of activities where organizational participants sometimes use computerized systems in abusive ways in the course of routine work. The activities—selling computerized equipment, delivering software to contractual specifications, and the use of computerized systems for management control—illustrate how legitimate organizations can be perpetrators of computer abuse.

The Causes of Computer Abuse

Most analysts of computer abuse or computer crime explain the causes of these activities by emphasizing individual motivations and life circumstances. Parker, for example, has identified profiles of "computer abuse perpetrators" based on interviews with people who engaged in personal crimes or abuses of trust. Mowshowitz criticizes this approach for neglecting the ethos of the organization which employs the "computer abuse perpetrator."[44] He believes that Parker's data support the hypothesis that "computer abuse perpetrators" are acting in accord with the ethos of their employer, but have turned their behavior against the employer rather than on his behalf. Thus, a workplace principle that "customers can be deceived if they won't bear visible losses" can be modified to legitimize embezzling sums that are not "visible" to the organization.[45] Mowshowitz's analysis shifts

---

[41] See "Automated Welfare Client-tracking and Service Integration: The Political Economy of Computing," Rob Kling *Communications of the ACM,* 21(6) (June 1978): 484–493.

[42] See "Social Analyses of Computing: Theoretical Perspectives in Recent Empirical Research," Rob Kling, *Computing Surveys,* 12(1) (March 1980): 61–110.

[43] See *The Polaris System Development,* Harvey Sapolsky, Harvard University Press, Cambridge, Mass., 1972.

[44] See "Computers and Ethical Judgement in Organizations," Mowshowitz, Abbe, *Proceedings 1978 National ACM Conference,* (December 1978): 675–683.

[45] A Security Pacific Bank official reported that Stanley Rifkin's theft of $10.2 million was unlikely to have been missed or felt as a profound loss. While Rifkin was not an employee, and the theft was technically a wire fraud rather than a computer theft, it is sufficiently close to illustrate the principle.

shifts attention from characteristics of the individual—his background, motives, financial needs and opportunities—to the social context in which computer abuses take place.[46]

In the business computer abuses examined in this paper, abusive sales practices, contractual fraud, or deceptive impression management techniques constitute the corrupt ethos which Mowshowitz employs as an explanation. In the case of many business computer abuses or computer crimes, practices which entail computing may be similar to other work practices which are less related to computing. Of these activities, impression management strategies which are common in entrepreneurial and bureaucratic organizations may be common, with or without computing.[47]

However, difficult abusive practices may be the by-product of different social processes. One promising line of inquiry examines the social arrangements under which systematic abuses are most likely. Recent analyses of industries in which illegal practices are common have led sociologists to develop the conception of "criminogenic markets" and "conditioned" or "coerced" crime. Leonard and Weber, for example, examined abusive and illegal practices adopted by automobile dealers including "forcing accessories," "service gouging," "high finance (charges)," "parts pushing," and "the warranty sham."[48] While these activities are carried out by the sales and service personnel of a new car dealerships, Leonard and Weber argue that they are "conditioned by" policies of the major automakers. The "criminogenic" policies, which regulate the relations between the automakers and their dealers, reward them for new car sales and implicitly penalize good service. They also provide dealers with meager markups for selling "stripped down" versions of new cars. Faberman explicitly defines a "criminogenic market" as "the deliberate and lawful enactment of policies by those who manage economically concentrated and vertically integrated corporations and/or industries which coerce lower level (dependent) participants into unlawful acts.[49] He also notes that "those who set the conditions which cause others to commit unlawful acts remain non-culpable."

If the sales staff of a contract software firm set contract dates without consulting with the technical staff, or "lowball" the estimates to "beat the competition," the technical staff are unlikely to be able to deliver on the contract.[50] These arrangements would be criminogenic, and the technical staff is placed in the position of covering up the areas where the product fails to meet specifications. Unfortunately, there is little systematic data about arrangements such as these even though they are known to participants in the software industry, and a source of dissatisfaction amongst software specialists.

---

[46] See "The Social Meanings of Employee Theft," David Altheide, Patricia Adler, Peter Adler, and Duane Altheide in Johnson and Douglas, 1978, footnote 17.

[47] See Richard Gabriel and Paul Savage, *Crisis in Command: Mismanagement in the Army*, Wang and Hill, New York, 1978. Peter Blau, *The Dynamics of Bureaucracy*, University of Chicago Press, Chicago, Ill., 1955. Robert Jackall, *Moral Mazes: The World of Corporate Managers*, New York, Oxford University Press, 1988.

[48] See "Automakers and Dealers: A Study of Criminogenic Market Forces" by William Leonard and Marvin Weber in Geiss and Meier, 1977, footnote 19.

[49] See, "A Criminogenic Market Structure: The Automobile Industry," Harvey Farberman, *Sociological Quarterly 16* (Autumn 1975): 438–457.

[50] Sometimes, the technical staff and marketing staff each anticipate the other's actions. Technical staff will increase their deadlines or budgets by, say, 100%, and the marketing staff will, in turn, reduce their estimates by half.

It is difficult to understand the causes of business crimes and abuses by reference to a profile of "abuse perpetrators" since business abuses are often "normal" occupational activities. To the extent that is the case, perpetrators will be identical to other participants in the same organization or occupation. An alternative perspective shifts attention from the proclivities of individuals to the structuring of organizational worlds which make abusive or untoward activities more likely. Contractual frauds in the delivery of computer software may be a byproduct of "criminogenic" organizational arrangements. This is a tenative explanation, and does not necessarily fit all forms of business computer abuse. But it provides a promising starting point for serious investigation.[51]

Conclusions

Computer uses are increasing in variety, and a larger fraction of socially and economically sensitive data are maintained on automated data systems. Questions of their vulnerability to abuse or utility as abusive instruments are correspondingly important. The audiences for investigations include computer specialists, technology assessors, auditors, law enforcement agents, prosecutors, lawyers, legislators, and consumer advocates. However, these groups have somewhat different orientations and interest in different forms of computer abuse or computer crime.

Much of the literature on computer abuse and crime is sensitizing, and is written to attract attention to the peculiar problems of computerization. Unfortunately, it also sensationalizes computer crimes and computer abuse to help attract attention. The labels "computer crime" or "computer abuse" have been overgeneralized. In this paper, we have examined a broad range activities which can be identified as computer abuse or computer crime. But, in practice these terms have denoted personal crimes and abuses of trust. Spectacular wire frauds and embezzlements make interesting reading and capture the popular imagination, but they probably illustrate but a small class of important computer abuses and computer crimes. Occupational crimes are usually ignored, except insofar as they are abuses of trust. As a consequence, the computer crime and abuse literature emphasizes the protection of computer-using organizations, rather than the public.

Fortuntely, there are relatively few instances of verified computer abuses or computer crimes. Thus most analyses draw strong conclusions from small collections of cases. These include claims about the nature and causes of computer abuses, the nature of perpetrators and victims, the conditions under which they occur, and their social significance. That is to be expected at this time. But it is important to expand the common conceptions of computer abuse and computer activities to include business and occupational activities.

It may not be prudent for all forms of abuse to be prohibited or remedied by legal actions. But if one is interested in reducing the frequency of "computer abuses," a serious approach cannot merely emphasize the "deviant acts" of ne'er-do-wells who engage in personal crimes or abuses of trust. To the extent that computer-related abuses and crimes are business or occupational activities, strategies for abatement will have to be altered.

---

[51] For one investigation, which uses the characteristics of organizational victims and interorganizational relations as a point of departure, see Vaughan, footnote 37.

That means that programs to minimize computer abuse would emphasize matters others than the detection and prosecution of clever computer manipulations. They would attempt to inhibit contractual abuses of computer systems by providing some protection for "whistle blowers." Such programs aimed at minimizing computer-related consumer abuse would include a variety of measures. These would range from laws such as the EFT Act which provide consumers with minimal protections in case of errors, to legal requirements for clear contracts spelling out the responsibilities and obligations of consumers, through the establishment of consumer action agencies.

Lawyers and lawmakers are particularly concerned about activities such as "computer abuse" or "computer crime" insofar as they alter the lawful relationships between parties or merit changes of law. But clear conceptions of the kinds of abuses or crimes in which computerized technologies may be significant media are useful for other purposes as well. In particular, they help policy makers, managers, consumers, legislators as reviewers of administrative activity, and computer specialists understand the opportunities and difficulties of different modes of computing development and use, and the appropriateness of different strategies for resolving difficulties.

The main point of this article has been to expand the prevailing conceptions of the nature of computer abuse and the conditions under which abuses are likely. It identifies the kinds of abusive activities in which organizations may be "perpetrators" as well as "victims." It also suggests some ways in which abusive practices in the development, sale, and provision of computer-based systems and services should not be viewed simply as individual "regrettable" events which are simply the acts of a few misguided individuals. Rather, they should be viewed as routine organizational practices which are likely to occur under specifiable conditions. The vast majority of activities practiced in the development, sale, or use of computing are neither abusive nor criminal. But the prevailing conceptions of computer abuse are simply too narrow. Consequently, computer crime bills are based on narrow conceptions of computer abuse and computer crime. They fail to identify common forms of computer abuse where organizations are likely to be perpetrators. They also fail to address the conditions under which computing may be most abusive for organizations or the broader public.

P·A·R·T·VII

3

ACM Code of Professional Conduct and Procedures for the Enforcement of the ACM Code of Professional Conduct

Association for Computing Machinery

Preamble

Recognition of professional status by the public depends not only on skill and dedication but also on adherence to a recognized code of Professional Conduct. The following Code sets forth the general principles (Canons), professional ideals (Ethical Considerations), and mandatory rules (Disciplinary Rules) applicable to each ACM Member.

The verbs "shall" (imperative) and "should" (encouragement) are used purposefully in the Code. The Canons and Ethical Considerations are not, however, binding rules. Each Disciplinary Rule is binding on each individual Member of ACM. Failure to observe the Disciplinary Rules subjects the Member to admonition, suspension or expulsion from the Association as provided by the Procedures for the Enforcement of the ACM Code of Professional Conduct, which are specified in the ACM Policy and Procedures Guidelines. The term "member(s)" is used in the Code. The Disciplinary Rules of the Code apply, however, only to the classes of membership specified in Article 3, Section 4, of the Constitution of the ACM.

Bylaw 19. ACM Code of Professional Conduct from Constitution of the Association for Computing Machinery. Courtesy ACM.

Canon 1

An ACM member shall act at all times with integrity.

Ethical Considerations

EC1.1 An ACM member shall properly qualify himself when expressing an opinion outside his areas of competence. A member is encouraged to express his opinion on subjects within his area of competence.

EC1.2 An ACM member shall preface any partisan statements about information processing by indicating clearly on whose behalf they are made.

EC1.3 An ACM member shall act faithfully on behalf of his employers or clients.

Disciplinary Rules

DR1.1.1 An ACM member shall not intentionally misrepresent his qualifications or credentials to present or prospective employers or clients.

DR1.1.2 An ACM member shall not make deliberately false or deceptive statements as to the present or expected state of affairs in any aspect of the capability, delivery, or use of information processing systems.

DR1.2.1 An ACM member shall not intentionally conceal or misrepresent on whose behalf any partisan statements are made.

DR1.3.1 An ACM member acting or employed as a consultant shall, prior to accepting information from a prospective client, inform the client of all factors of which the member is aware which may affect the proper performance of the task.

DR1.3.2 An ACM member shall disclose any interest of which he is aware which does or may conflict with his duty to a present or prospective employer or client.

DR1.3.3 An ACM member shall not use any confidential information from any employer or client, past or present, without prior permission.

Canon 2

An ACM member should strive to increase his competence and the competence and prestige of the profession.

Ethical Considerations

EC2.1 An ACM member is encouraged to extend public knowledge, understanding, and appreciation of information processing, and to oppose any false or deceptive statements relating to information processing of which he is aware.

EC2.2 An ACM member shall not use his professional credentials to misrepresent his competence.

EC2.3 An ACM member shall undertake only those professional assignments and commitments for which he is qualified.

EC2.4 An ACM member shall strive to design and develop systems that adequately perform the intended functions and that satisfy his employer's or client's operational needs.

EC2.5 An ACM member should maintain and increase his competence through a program of continuing education encompassing the techniques, technical standards, and practices in his fields of professional activity.

EC2.6 An ACM member should provide opportunity and encouragement for professional development and advancement of both professionals and those aspiring to become professionals.

Disciplinary Rules

DR1.1.1 An ACM member shall not intentionally misrepresent his qualifications or credentials to present or prospective employers or clients.

DR2.2.1 An ACM member shall not use his professional credentials to misrepresent his competence.

DR2.3.1 An ACM member shall not undertake professional assignments without adequate preparation in the circumstances.

DR2.3.2 An ACM member shall not undertake professional assignments for which he knows or should know he is not competent or cannot become adequately competent without acquiring the assistance of a professional who is competent to perform the assignment.

DR2.4.1 An ACM member shall not represent that a product of his work will perform its function adequately and will meet the receiver's operational needs when he knows or should know that the product is deficient.

Canon 3

An ACM member shall accept responsibility for his work.

Ethical Considerations

EC3.1 An ACM member shall accept only those assignments for which there is reasonable expectancy of meeting requirements or specifications, and shall perform his assignments in a professional manner.

Disciplinary Rules

DR3.1.1 An ACM member shall not neglect any professional assignment which he has accepted.

DR3.1.2 An ACM member shall keep his employer or client properly informed of the progress of his assignments.

DR3.1.3 An ACM member shall not attempt to exonerate himself from, or to limit his liability to clients for his personal malpractice.

DR3.1.4 An ACM member shall indicate to his employer or client the consequences to be expected if his professional judgment is overruled.

Canon 4

An ACM member shall act with professional responsibility.

Ethical Considerations

EC4.1 An ACM member shall not use his membership in ACM improperly for professional advantage or to misrepresent the authority of his statements.

EC4.2 An ACM member shall conduct professional activities on a high plane.

EC4.3 An ACM member is encouraged to uphold and improve the professional standards of the Association through participation in their formulation, establishment, and enforcement.

Disciplinary Rules

DR4.1.1 An ACM member shall not speak on behalf of the Association or any of its subgroups without proper authority.

DR4.1.2 An ACM member shall not knowingly misrepresent the policies and views of the Association or any of its subgroups.

DR4.1.3 An ACM member shall preface partisan statements about information procedure by indicating clearly on whose behalf they are made.

DR4.2.1 An ACM member shall not maliciously injure the professional reputation of another person.

DR4.2.2 An ACM member shall not use the services of his membership in the Association to gain unfair advantage.

DR4.2.3 An ACM member shall take care that credit for work is given to whom credit is properly due.

Canon 5

An ACM member should use his special knowledge and skills for the advancement of human welfare.

Ethical Considerations

EC5.1 An ACM member should consider the health, privacy, and general welfare of the public in the performance of his work.

EC5.2 An ACM member, whenever dealing with data concerning individuals, shall always consider the principle of the individual's privacy and seek the following: To minimize the data collected.

To limit authorized access to the data.

To provide proper security for the data.

To determine the required retention period of the data.

To ensure proper disposal of the data.

Disciplinary Rules

DR5.2.1 An ACM member shall express his professional opinion to his employers or clients regarding any adverse consequences to the public which might result from work proposed to him.

P·A·R·T·VII

A Prototype IFIP Code of Ethics Based on Participative International Consensus

Hal Sackman

Abstract

The International Federation of Information Processing (IFIP) approved a project proposal at their 1988 General Assembly to administer an exploratory ethics survey questionnaire mailed to representatives of approximately 80 national computer societies, IFIP officers and international affiliate organizations worldwide. The goal was to assess the level of international consensus for developing a prototype IFIP Code of Ethics.

The exploratory questionnaire design involved some 70 structured and open-end items based on a four-fold ethical construct domain linked to leading edge developments in information technology. This domain covers 1) individual professional ethics; 2) multinational organizational ethics; 3) international legal informatics; and 4) international public policy.

Statistical analyses of the data from 24 respondents to the questionnaire demonstrated psychometric reliability and validity of the survey instrument, including reliability of differential levels of consensus over the four-fold ethical construct domain. Only the most favored ethical items from these IFIP respondents were selected as the basis for an initial illustrative prototype code of ethics. This preliminary code was reviewed by the 1989 Technical Assembly and General Assembly at San Francisco, and approved for further revision and refinement, based on worldwide feedback from IFIP newsletter readers. A short questionnaire was sent out with the revised preliminary code to IFIP Newsletter readers in December, 1989.

Thirty-three letter and questionnaire responses were received from the Newsletter readership. The respondents represent all continents, including developing nations. Some are eminent leaders in the worldwide information technology community, including two presidents of national professional societies, a vice-president of a major multinational organization, and several informatics scholars with international reputations.

The overall results of this small sample revealed generally favorable support for the preliminary code, with an average overall rating approximately mid-way between "Very Good" and "Good" for all ethical areas, which is consistent with similar findings using the same rating scale in the initial survey. The preliminary code was substantially revised to reflect extensive feedback and detailed editorial recommendations from the Newsletter respondents. This revision has resulted in a shortened, simplified and more understandable version for expected worldwide dissemination. It is hoped that these participative and open efforts over a two year period will provide the basis for acceptable convergence toward an initial IFIP Code of Ethics, subject to continuing IFIP oversight and periodic improvements.

Revision of the Preliminary IFIP Code of Ethics

Preamble

The IFIP Code of Ethics has been constructed not only for individual Information Technology (IT) professionals, but also for multinational IT organizations, and the extended IT community concerned with international legal informatics and related public policy. This Code provides guidelines for the individuals, international organizations, national societies, and those influencing international public policy. The guidelines are global and multi-cultural, and are not intended to reflect any particular ideology or creed. It is hoped that the evolving Code will contribute to the constructive development and application of Information Technology throughout the world.

Individual Professional Ethics

Social Responsibility

IT professionals strive to use their technical expertise to advance international human welfare and the quality of life for citizens of all nations. They accept the ethical obligation to assess social consequences and help ensure safe and beneficial use of IT applications.

Protection of Privacy

IT professionals respect the privacy and integrity of individuals, groups, and organizations. They believe that computerized invasion of privacy, without informed authorization or consent, is a continuing threat for individuals and groups. Public trust in informatics is based on vigilant protection of established ethical standards of information privacy.

Individual Integrity

IT professionals maintain high standards of personal integrity which are basic for the harmonious integration of organizations and society. Individual integrity encompasses desirable traits such as honesty, probity, objectivity, sensitivity to others, and trustworthiness in human relations. IT professionals respect and defend the free inquiry of their associates. They do not misrepresent capabilities of information processing systems for their personal gain.

Professional Competence

IT professionals continually maintain and upgrade their competence in the swiftly changing world of computer-based information systems. They understand the capabilities and limitations of their specialized expertise, and the general field of information processing.

Personal Accountability

IT professionals accept personal responsibility for agreed expectations concerning their role and work. They accept assignments only when there are reasonable and informed expectations of successfully meeting requirements. They attempt to keep all involved parties—co-workers, management, clients and users—properly informed on the progress and status of their tasks. IT professionals objectively test and evaluate information system effectiveness to certify beneficial applications.

International Organizational Ethics

High Performance Standards

Multinational organizations are aware of their social responsibilities to provide quality goods and services from computer-based information systems and networks. The pursuit of performance excellence, particularly in system reliability and tested system effectiveness, is indispensible for quality information system services.

International Standards and Regulations

International IT organizations foster international progress by actively contributing to the development of acceptable international IT standards, and in following established regulatory standards. IT multinational organizations are aware that successful globalization of computer-communications networks and beneficial international information services requires the good-will and voluntary concurrence of host governments, competitors, professional informatics societies, and other stakeholders, especially end-users.

International Legal Protection

In pursuing constructive ethical objectives, multinational IT organizations require legal protection. Such protection includes general legal safeguards such as protection against unfair competition. It also includes protection against computer crime, and intellectual property protection. Multinational organizations conform to the laws of their host countries and established international law pertaining to their operations.

Employee Productivity and Quality of Working Life

IT organizations strive to improve information systems to enhance the quality of working life for employees. Such enhancements facilitate individual and organizational productivity. These improvements aim at morally desirable goals such as personal development, physical safety, personal dignity and human fulfillment in the computerized workplace. IT employees recognize their obligations to foster ethical management/labor relations based on constructive cooperation and shared trust.

User Participation and Feedback

International IT organizations encourage harmonious user participation in computer-based information system design and development. The user is an integral part of the total information system, and is the ultimate beneficiary or victim. Integration of user attitudes, training, experience, interests, and needs, should be linked with effective human feedback throughout the entire system development cycle. Cooperative and constructive human feedback is a fundamental guarantor of IT social responsiveness.

Ethics for International Legal Informatics

Intellectual Property Law

The IT community values the creative energy that generates new scientific and technological discoveries for worldwide benefits. This creativity often requires international legal protection for intellectual property in hardware, software, telecommunications and related goods and services. Without such protection, desirable long-term investments in IT research and development would be severely constrained to the detriment of the entire world community. Intellectual property protection should be balanced against the free flow of open scientific knowledge in the international public domain.

International Public Law

The IT community strives to meet the social obligations of international public law. Such laws pertain to interrelations among host countries, government institutions, multinational corporations, workers, suppliers, vendors, competitors, international professional organizations, and affected public groups. In legal informatics, these concerns include privacy law, antitrust law, health and welfare law, and regulatory law, including protection from harmful environmental pollution linked to IT industrial operations.

International Telecommunications Law

The IT community is mindful of expanding legal consequences of worldwide computer-based telecommunication networks and associated information services. Numerous legal issues arise from international telecommunication agreements and protocols for future networks. These networks anticipate virtually unlimited bandwidth capacities for multimedia communications, with major social impacts. The facilitation of open and equitable global communications through computerized telecommunications can accelerate international trade, understanding, cooperation, and friendship. The development of international legal informatics serving these worldwide goals is a long-range ethical objective of the IT community.

International Criminal Law

The proliferation of international computer-based networks has led to the emergence of transnational computer crime, raising new challenges for international legal informatics. These crimes have assumed diverse forms, including computerized international money laundering, racketeering, fraud, information piracy, theft, embezzlement, computer program and data contamination, and sabotage. The IT community unequivocally opposes international criminal use of computers, and endorses vigorous international cooperation and legal countermeasures, consistent with due process, to protect the international public interest.

International Public Policy Ethics

Freedom of Communication

The IT community, aware of the rapid growth of international communications and networking, appreciates the social responsibilities of international freedom of communication. Such international freedoms include open access to computer-based information in the public domain, freedom to hold and express personal and group opinions, and, as indicated in the United Nations Charter on Human Rights, the "freedom to communicate through any media regardless of frontiers."

Privacy and Dignity of Individuals

The international IT community endorses the fundamental human rights of privacy and dignity for all individuals using computer-based information systems. These ethical imperatives stem from a strong concern that such systems should never be deliberately or inadvertently harnessed to demean or enslave individuals or groups. The IT community believes that the key safeguard is ethically oriented system design, such that explicit protection or privacy, and enhancement of personal dignity are major system objectives. The worldwide informatics community aspires to prevent oppressive computerized control and degradation of human behavior.

Humanized Information Systems

The international IT community recognizes the primacy of serving social needs. It also recognizes that rapid computerization has consistently outraced humanization of information services. In particular, poorly designed person/machine interfaces may lead to physical disabilities, psychological disturbances, and psychophysical stress syndromes. IT professionals and organizations affirm their obligation to continually humanize computer information systems through internationally accepted techniques and standards. These include ergonomic test, evaluation, and certification of information system hardware, software, communications and user services.

International Computer Literacy

IT professionals and organizations appreciate the need to promote global computer literacy. The fruits of IT are ultimately only as good as the informed and knowledgeable social use to which they are applied. International educational advances in computer literacy may be the most cost-effective general approach to optimize worldwide computer benefits. The professional IT community encourages global excellence in introductory and continuing education in informatics in schools, universities, the home, and the workplace.

Equitable Opportunity for Information Services

The IT community is concerned about the growing global gap between the information rich and the information poor, which contributes to worldwide social instability, particularly between developing and industrialized nations. IT professionals and organizations are dismayed by international trends toward inequitable distribution of computer-based information systems, which reinforces this growing information gap. This problem primarily originates from complex international economic forces which are beyond the scope of this Code of Ethics. Nevertheless, the IT community believes it should conscientiously contribute toward helping to establish a more just and equitable socioeconomic international solution.

Cultural Quality of Life and Human Choice

The IT community notes the penetration of computer-based information services into virtually all walks of life. It is concerned with the powerful social consequences of international computerization on cultural styles and values. It appreciates the priceless human heritage of pluralistic, worldwide cultures. The IT community affirms its dedication to harmonize technological change with the distinctive ethos and quality of life associated with each culture. The IT Community supports the basic right of all individuals to participate in shaping the computerization of their culture and society.

P·A·R·T · VII

5

Strategic Computing Research and the Universities

Terry A. Winograd

Introduction

The Strategic Computing Initiative offers the potential of new research funds for university computer science departments. As with all funds, they bring benefits and can have unwanted strings attached. In the case of military funding, the web of attached strings can be subtle and confusing. The goal of this paper is to delineate some of these entanglements and perhaps provide some guidance for loosening and eliminating them.

The issues are not peculiar to the Strategic Computing Initiative, and it will be useful to point out other examples that illustrate them, especially as they have emerged in the SCI's successor, the Strategic Defense Initiative. In fact, military research funding is so commonplace in major universities in the United States that it appears to be a basic, permanent fact of academic life. I will focus on the funding of computer science research, but a similar pattern holds in many areas of both science and engineering. In computer science, the SCI represents a particularly noticeable step in a progression towards more direct military involvement by scientists in universities.

History

We can gain some useful perspective by looking at the history of military support for science. Although technology has been developed for military ends throughout history,

Reprinted with permission of T. Winograd. From "Strategic Computing Research and the Universities," Stanford University, Department of Computer Science, Report No. STAN-CS-87-1160 (March).

the modern form of research funding developed during the years leading up to World War II. The first R&D contract was with Westinghouse in 1937,[1] and the universities developed substantial research programs during the war years (such as MIT's work on radar and navigation). After WWII, the technology demands of the Cold War put the relationship on a permanent footing, and introduced it on a massive scale.[2]

The American reaction to the launching of Sputnik in 1957 led to a substantial increase in government funding for scientific research. One impact was the creation by the Department of Defense of an Advanced Research Projects Agency (ARPA, later re-christened as DARPA). ARPA was chartered to do the most basic and visionary research in a number of areas, including materials sciences and behavioral sciences, but its most visible impact in the academic community has come from early and substantial support of the fledgling field of computer science. During the sixties and seventies, ARPA sponsored a broad spectrum of high-quality basic research, often put forward as a positive example of what can be done with "enlightened" military funding.

During the Vietnam War, general campus resistance to the war effort was reflected in attacks on military-sponsored research. In some cases, laboratories doing large amounts of such research (such as the Stanford Research Institute and MIT's Draper Lab) were reorganized into quasi-independent institutes that were no longer considered an official part of the university. Also during that period, the Mansfield Amendment to the 1969 military funding authorization stipulated that "none of the funds authorized by this act may be used to carry out any research project or study unless such a project or study has a direct and apparent relationship to a specific military function or operation." The intent of this requirement was to get the military out of the business of funding the general work of the universities—to limit its range of activities.

Although the goal was to move the military out of non-military areas, the effect was more complex. In the absence of equivalent alternative sources of funding, researchers were pressed to make their work fall under the umbrella of relevance. At times this could be done in a very general way. For example, computer research could be justified as increasing the cost-effectiveness of computing in the military services. In other cases there was conscious or unconscious duplicity in the portrayal of research projects.

In 1971, a group of students and faculty at Stanford, under the auspices of the Stanford Workshop on Political and Social Issues (SWOPSI), examined the "Work Unit Summaries" that the DoD published as justification for research projects. They compared them to statements that researchers made about their own work on campus and asked researchers to comment on them. In some cases there were serious discrepancies. For example, one professor had a contract for research on "High-power broadly tunable laser action in the ultraviolet spectrum," which he justified to the campus in terms of medicine. The DoD title was "Weaponry—lasers for increased damage effectiveness." Another project on "Dynamic behavior and stability of solids and structures" was described in the

[1] H. A. Zahl, "The Invention of the R&D Contract," *Signal*, February, 1970, pp. 34–37.

[2] Bernard Roth, "The Impact of the Arms Race on the Creation and Utilization of Knowledge," presented at the Symposium on the Optimum Utilization of Knowledge, Amherst, Massachusetts, Nov. 5–8, 1981.

work unit summary as relevant to "weapon delivery and reconnaissance . . . knowledge of landing fields and silo interaction with missiles."[3]

During the 1970s, military funding continued at a relatively stable level in most areas of science. More recently, there has been a renewed growth in support, at a time when financing from other agencies that were mainstays of scientific research in the 1970s —the Department of Energy, the National Aeronautics and Space Administration, and the Department of Agriculture—has leveled off or declined. Pentagon spending on campuses grew to $930 million in the 1985 fiscal year, an 89% increase over the $495 million spent in 1980, while Health and Human Services' increase over that period was 34%. Counting approximately $230 million spent off-campus at MIT's Lincoln Laboratories, DoD University research funding now exceeds that of the National Science Foundation.[4]

Computer science in particular has always been heavily dependent on military support, especially through DARPA and the ONR (Office of Naval Research), but here too the amount is increasing. The DoD proportion of federal funds for basic research in the academic computer science climbed from 28% in 1977 to almost 60% in 1983, while the NSF portion declined from 69% to under 40%. As of 1984, the DoD supplied about 40 percent of all computer-related R&D funds in the nation, and this is likely to increase with the massive computer-related spending on SDI.[5]

To put this in perspective, we must realize that university basic science research funding is a tiny drop in the bucket compared to the overall DoD budget or even to its R&D expenses alone (proposed as $42 *billion* in the 1986 budget). While a program like SCI offers lucrative possibilities to individual departments, it is but a fraction of the funds allocated to research and development on computing.

It is relatively unimportant, therefore, to focus on whether the money is well-spent or wasted in simple economic terms. If it were all a total waste, it would still pale before the much larger items in the Pentagon budget. But the effects of military spending in academe are more subtle and more significant. There is a "leverage" effect, in which the money serves to influence the conduct of the university and to promote the public attitudes that are required for the continuation of military spending. The remainder of this paper will examine those effects more closely.

The Problems for the University

The first question is why university involvement with the military is a problem at all. My own understanding rests on a global assessment that national security will not be gained

---

[3] Stanton A. Glantz and Norm V. Albers, "Department of Defense R&D in the University," *Science* 186, Nov. 22, 1974, pp. 703–711; Deborah Shapley, "Defense Research: the Names Are Changed to Protect the Innocent," *Science* 175, February 1972, pp. 866–868.

[4] David Sanger, "Campuses' Role in Arms Debated as 'Star Wars' Funds are Sought," *New York Times*, Monday, July 22, 1985.

[5] Clark Thompson, "Military Direction of Academic CS Research," *Communications of the ACM* 29: 7 (July 1986), pp. 583–85. Also see Kenneth Flamm, "Federal Support for Computer Research: A Brief History," in Paul N. Edwards and Richard Gordon, eds., *Strategic Computing: Defense Research and High Technology* (New York: Columbia University Press, forthcoming).

by creating more weapons technology, and that the current policies of the DoD lead to unrealistic expectations that political problems can be solved through military means.

Programs like the SCI (and even more so, the SDI) represent a general trend towards proposing high-tech systems to solve military and political problems. Constructive alternatives are often sidetracked by promises that the technology will make diplomatic or political solutions unnecessary, while the long development times and shifting goals of the high-tech programs make it difficult to give clear demonstrations of their ultimate futility. Along with this goes a general "militarization" of the society, in which the methods and values of the military are in ascendance over the more open and non-authoritarian values traditional to the university. As an employer, a purchaser, a lobbying group, a trainer of people, and in its many other capacities, the military has a strong influence on attitudes and practices. Although, of course, not everyone would agree with this perspective, it is clear that the majority of academic researchers (in computer science and in other fields as well) are reluctant to do weapons-related work unless they can justify it on other grounds. They go to some lengths to characterize their work as "basic research" which, although it may have military applications, will have a wide range of potentially beneficial applications as well.

Some of the problems described below only appear as problems from this overall perspective. Others, such as the imposition of secrecy on research results, are recognized as problematic even by those who support the overall objectives of the military. The goal of presenting them is not to argue for one side or the other, but to point out and clarify the possibilities.

Direction of Research Content

The most direct impact of funding is on the direction of the research work itself. The proverb that says "he who pays the piper picks the tune" is just as true here as elsewhere, but it is often denied in the context of computer science research support. There are some standard forms of denial, as illustrated in the response of one of my colleagues to an appeal to sign a pledge refusing funding from the SDI Office. He said, "I think you are barking up the wrong tree. Discussions I have had with SDIO folks let me believe that

1. They are interested in funding the sort of research that NSF funds, in the areas of their interests.
2. They are interested in some really interesting problems of a general nature, e.g. implementation of very high-level languages and parallel languages.
3. The work they propose to support is going to be done anyway."

The thrust of the argument is that it does not matter who funds it, since the work itself remains the same. This belief is based on two unstated assumptions:

(a) The researchers come up with the proposals, so it is they, not the funders, who choose the topics.

(b) Most of the support is for basic research, not militarily-oriented projects, so it is not biased by its military sources.

The first of these contentions is either deceptive or naive. It simply ignores the realities of human decision-making. DoD sponsors are fully aware of how the overall research direction in a field can be "guided" by selective choice of what to support. It is not necessary to tell someone what to work on. One has only to make known which kinds of work will find funding. There is nothing inherently wrong or devious about this, when it is open and acknowledged. For example, the document describing "Office of Naval Research Selected Research Opportunities (SRO IV)" for fiscal year 1985 states the purpose of the program as the promotion of ". . . increased involvement of the U.S. academic research community in selected fundamental research areas and, by fostering stronger linkages between this community and the Navy, . . . to attract new investigators to Naval research programs."[6] The document on the DoD-University Research Instrumentation Program FY 84/85 lists over 300 areas of interest, some as specific as "Armor materials" and "Synthesis of advanced propellant and explosive materials" and others as general as "Better fundamental insight into phenomena of known or potential practical utility" (listed under Chemistry).[7]

One might take the attitude that researchers will only accept such funding if they decide on independent grounds that the proposed programs are the best direction for research. But again this is unrealistic, given the exigencies of modern university financing. At Stanford, for example, all engineering school faculty have for many years been expected to raise at least 20% of their salary from research contracts. This situation places pressure on researchers to obtain funding for their research—even those who could otherwise manage their research quite well with no outside funding. It causes a skewing of research towards fundable topics, and therefore towards the defense establishment. In addition, universities have developed a pattern of charging various parts of their normal expenses to research overhead and also to direct research costs wherever possible. For example, graduate students are supported on research assistantships rather than university funds, and are expected to use research-supported computer facilities for the bulk of their computing needs. Thus when schools lose research funding, other sectors of the institution are jeopardized.

There is also a multiplier effect. Money provided to a few researchers at elite institutions can have a powerful impact on the field as a whole, leading to conferences in new areas, shifts in emphasis in selection of journal articles, channeling of the best new students into particular research subareas, and so on. For example, the field of artificial intelligence developed almost entirely under the guidance of ARPA-supported researchers at three elite universities (MIT, Stanford, and Carnegie-Mellon). In addition to supporting the research itself, APRA provided the funds that made conferences possible in this new area, and held annual "contractors' meetings" at which the principal investigators came together to discuss overall research directions.

---

[6] Office of Naval Research, Selected Research Opportunities (SRO IV), FY 1985, Washington, D.C., 1984.

[7] Army Research Office, Office of Naval Research, Air Force Office of Scientific Research, Announcement: "DoD-University Research Instrumentation Program FY 1984/FY 1985," Washington, D.C. 1983.

The second argument—that most of the support is for basic research—is more believable in computer science than in many other disciplines, but still leaves many questions. First, as mentioned above, basic research can be "steered" even without pushing it into specific applications. Second, there has been a continuing shift away from the former policy of support for basic research. Since 1983, DARPA has begun to shift from a wide dispersal of basic research funding towards more narrowly focused projects, such as the SCI. Much of its support for artificial intelligence has been resassigned from category 6.1 (the most basic) to 6.2 (more applied), with corresponding shifts in the requirements imposed on researchers. In the plans for the SCI, there was a good deal of explicit concern with "pulling" the technology in accord with specific near-term application goals. The plan states, "We are initially concerned with the development of appropriate military applications that will pull the technology base."[8] The result has been to shift the emphasis from basic research towards specific military applications. Once a dependency on military funding has been established, it is difficult for researchers to resist its pressures.

In a highly publicized incident at the California Institute of Technology in 1984, President Marvin Goldberger was called to task by the faculty for his role in establishing a classified "think tank," called the Arroyo Center, for the Army. A few years earlier, after seeing its money from the National Aeronautics and Space Administration begin to dry up, the Jet Propulsion Laboratory (a major research wing of Caltech) had asked Caltech for authority to get up to 30% of its budget from the Department of Defense. The faculty was told at the time that this was the only way to keep together the unique teams that had been assembled at the lab and to continue its basic research on aeronautics and astronautics. When the Arroyo Center was created as a major new part of JPL, its organizers had abandoned this justification and argued instead that a new role and mission in military policy analysis was necessary in order to maintain funding for the laboratory. When pressed by the faculty, Goldberger admitted ". . . serious concern about the appropriateness of JPL as a part of Caltech operating an Army analysis program. It is not consistent with the high-technology and systems engineering capabilities of the laboratory." Although the faculty overwhelmingly passed a resolution that "Caltech divest itself of the Arroyo Center expeditiously and in a responsible fashion at the earliest possible time," contracts had been signed and it was impossible to back out. Vague commitments were made to phase the center out over a period of years.[9]

Shifting the Focus of the University

The university is much more than a producer of specific research results. As the center of higher education, what goes on there shapes the society in direct and subtle ways. Military funding affects the balance of activities and priorities within the university in a way that can have a deep impact outside specific research areas.

---

[8] Defense Advanced Research Projects Agency, "Strategic Computing: New Generation Computing Technology: A Strategic Plan for Its Development and Application to Critical Problems in Defense," October, 1983, p. 59.
[9] Lee Dembart, "Army Think Tank Plan Stirs Caltech," *Los Angeles Times*, January 30, 1984.

Within a scientific discipline, it can distort the distribution of funds, people, and educational opportunities. A number of prominent university leaders have raised this issue in conjunction with the SDI. President Donald Kennedy of Stanford said that SDI funding "throws the balance of science research all out of whack." Marvin L. Goldberger, president of the California Institute of Technology, held that "the infusion of such a large amount of money can distort activities within the university. It can draw people into research areas they might not otherwise pursue."[10] Similar objections have been raised about the effect of projects such as the SCI on computer science research.

The DoD-University Research Instrumentation Program (FY 1984/85) offered $150 million to universities to "acquire research equipment at universities to address DoD basic research needs," stating,

> The goal of this program is to improve the capability of universities to perform research in support of national defense. Specifically, it is a program to provide funding for the acquisition of research equipment at universities for the stimulation and support of basic research which supports the technology goals of the Department of Defense . . . . Instrumentation requested must be for use in research in areas of priority concern to the military services.[11]

In a separate program, called the University Research Initiative Program, DoD states

> The . . . programs are designed to increase the number of science and engineering graduate students; to increase the investment in major pieces of research equipment at universities; to increase the investment in higher risk basic scientific research in support of critical Navy and DoD technologies; and to provide more opportunities for contracts between universities, industry, and Navy and other DoD laboratories.[12]

These program goals are broader than specific military applications. They are part of a larger pattern of the past few years, in which for the first time since the Vietnam War, the DoD is proposing to fund a variety of programs designed more to enhance the health of the universities than to meet short-term defense needs. But the political significance of the new initiative is that it sends a strong message that the Pentagon now considers broad support of university programs a legitimate part of its mission. As in the past, research-justified equipment will end up playing a large role in the university, beyond the specific research projects. It is commonplace for such equipment to be used unofficially for a wide variety of academic and instructional purposes, and in many cases such sources are the only way to fund new general-use facilities.

The net effect will be to strengthen certain departments (those that "support the technology goals of the Department of Defense") at the expense of others. Those that bring in new equipment will be in a better position to acquire new faculty slots, to attract bright students, and in general to compete in the world of academic resources. One

---

[10] Sanger, op. cit.

[11] Army Research Office, Office of Naval Research, Air Force Office of Scientific Research, Announcement: "DoD-University Research Instrumentation Program FY 1984/FY 1985," Washington, D.C. 1983, p. 1.

[12] Office of Naval Research and Defense Advanced Research Projects Agency, Broad Agency Announcement: "University Research Initiative Program," Washington D.C., January 1986, p. 4.

obvious impact is the further strengthening of the "hard sciences" and engineering (including computer science), at the expense of the social sciences and humanities.

Another is an increase in the advantage of the elite universities (the grants come in chunks of up to $20 million). In fact, the creation of this advantage has been a significant effect of military computer science funding in general over the last thirty years. It has resulted in a highly unequal situation in which a few schools have received almost all the resources. Although this may have led to more effective research in the short run, it has also been a factor contributing to the significant long-term shortage of trained computer researchers.

The issue here is not whether any of these policy decisions are right or wrong. Debates about the balance betwen science and the humanities, for example, are central to the ongoing life of the university. The problem is that they are being decided not on the basis of what will constitute a good educational system for our nation, but on the basis of what will most effectively satisfy military research goals.

Restrictions on the Exchange of Ideas

Independent of the actual research topics, there are hidden costs associated with military funding. One major area of concern has to do with the fundamentally divergent attitudes of the two institutions toward the public dissemination of knowledge. The university has a long tradition as a forum for the open exchange of ideas. One of its highest values is openness to sharing, criticism, and transmission of knowledge. For the military, knowledge is power in a very direct sense, and its elaborate system of classification and secrecy is designed to prevent others from finding out what our side knows.

This has long been a bone of contention, and for many years (since the Vietnam war) a large number of universities have had a policy of prohibiting classified research. On this view, all work done in a university should be open to scrutiny. But this attitude is shifting, as pressure has been applied to allow classified research in order to obtain general defense funding. For example, the Georgia Tech Research Institute, on the campus of the Georgia Institute of Technology, carried out about $60 million in sponsored research in 1985, 80 percent of it government-financed. The flow of Defense Department research funds to the campus has increased ninefold since 1976, spurred greatly by the Institute's willingness to take on classified work. Unlike most universities, it allows students to obtain security clearance to participate in the work. The university takes few foreign students—in part, officials say, so that its classified work will not be jeopardized.[13] Other universities (such as Brown) have recently reversed previous anti-secrecy policies, in order to compete for funds.[14]

However, even without accepting classified research, a University can find itself at odds with DoD secrecy policies. A 1982 memo from the Stanford administration to the faculty stated

---

[13] Sanger, op. cit.

[14] NARMIC Project, "Uncle Sam Goes to School: Colleges and Universities Enlist in the Arms Race," Philadelphia, American Friends Service Committee, January 1986.

Although both ITAR [International Traffic in Arms Regulation] and EAR [Export Administration Regulations] have been in effect for some time, the government has only recently
attempted to apply them to unclassified university research activities. The potential effect
of these new interpretations on universities is far-reaching: not only would certain research
results be subject to government approval prior to publication, but laboratories and
classrooms would have to be "closed" and monitored to prohibit research participation by
certain foreign scholars. Indeed, an export license could be required for a Stanford faculty
member to deliver a scientific paper at a conference at another American university.[15]

In January 1984, Jeffrey T. Richelson, a political scientist at American University in
Washington, D.C., was threatened by Air Force officials as he prepared to give a speech
on satellite systems for verifying arms control agreements. They did not deny his
statement that everything in the talk was gathered from public sources, but argued that
it was possible for unclassified material to be put together into a classified whole. The
Los Angeles Times reported that "for its part, the Air Force says it did not mean to prevent
Richelson from speaking; it only wanted to advise him that his paper might be classified
and that he might be in serious trouble if he delivered it."[16]

In March 1985, the DoD blocked the presentation of 43 out of 219 technical papers
just before they were to be delivered at the annual symposium of the Society of
Photo-Optical Instrumentation Engineers. Although only 13 were deemed to contain
classified information, the rest were judged to be "militarily sensitive." At an earlier
meeting in 1982, some 100 papers scheduled to be presented at a conference by the
society in San Diego were withdrawn at the last moment, following Defense Department
objections.[17]

Although occurrences like these are not commonplace and there has been a good deal
of resistance by university officials, it is likely that the general pattern will increase. The
1985 contract with the Air Force establishing the Software Engineering Institute at
Carnegie-Mellon University specifies that "distribution will not be made of technical
data" that either the contractor or the government finds "to have classified or potentially
classified military end-item applications." In case of doubt, Carnegie-Mellon must obtain
Pentagon permission for publication.[18] Even outside of such agreements, the fact that
secrecy clampdowns are possible will lead to increased self-censorship by researchers
eager not to attract the DoD's ire.

Secrecy concerns go beyond publication, to issues such as the selection of students. In
the summer of 1985, the DoD announced plans to prohibit certain foreign students from
access to four university supercomputer facilities specifically intended for nonclassified
research. Georgia Tech may not be the only school that finds it convenient to shift
admissions policies in order to forestall potential problems.

Finally, more subtle but potentially more dangerous is the effect of military funding
on the open political activity of students and faculty within the universities. University
administrators know that an atmosphere of student antimilitary activism may well lead

---

[15] Gerald Lieberman, Memo to Stanford Faculty on Federal Export Regulations, July 1, 1982.

[16] Lee Dembart, "AF Bid to Prevent Talk at UCLA Called Illegal," Los Angeles Times, January 30, 1984.

[17] Colin Norman, "Security Problems Plague Scientific Meeting," Science, April 26, 1985, pp. 471–472.

[18] Sanger, op. cit.

military sponsors to fear the disruption of research activities, or at least to see the university as a less congenial environment for the research. Although direct pressure is rarely applied against student activities, it would be naive to think that university administrators were immune to such important financial considerations.

At the individual faculty level, such pressure has been more overt. In his Senate confirmation hearings in 1985, Undersecretary of Defense Donald Hicks (the head of research for the Pentagon) sharply criticized opponents of the Strategic Defense Initiative and stated: "I am not particularly interested in seeing department money going someplace where an individual is outspoken in his rejection of department aims, even for basic research." Hicks was later quoted in *Science* as saying, "Those who want to accept the money to help us with programs we need, we want to have. But I don't particularly view it as appropriate when somebody says we don't like the way you're running the department, but we sure like your money." He said later that he was principally upset by computer scientists who depend in part on DoD support, but voice skepticism about the feasibility of the software demanded by a comprehensive missile defense. "If they want to get out and use their roles as professors to make statements, that's find, it's a free country," Hicks said. "But freedom works both ways. They're free to keep their mouths shut . . . [and] I'm also free not to give them money . . . . I have a tough time with disloyalty."[19]

The Problems for Society

The previous section focused on problems within the university. Now, taking a less parochial standpoint, we can ask how military funding in the universities can have an adverse impact on the larger society.

Legitimization of Projects

Once dependent on military support, the university can be used to justify and legitimate military projects. Scientists enjoy a high degree of public respect, and their reputations can be enlisted to support military objectives both with the public and in Congress. The most blatant example of this strategy has been the attempt to use the promise of research funding as a way of marshalling support for SDI. Even before Congress began serious deliberations on the budget, project officials were already seeking proposals from scientists, reversing the usual sequence of events. SDIO Director James Ionson stated, "It's probably something that's never been done, but this office is trying to sell something to Congress. If we can say that this fellow at MIT will get money to do such and such research, it's something real to sell. That in and of itself is innovative."[20]

In announcing the first university consortiums, the Defense Department listed a host of "participating institutions," although only one or two researchers were involved in many campuses. Paul E. Gray, president of the Massachusetts Institute of Technology,

[19] R. Jeffrey Smith, "Hicks Attacks SDI Critics," *Science* 232, April 25, 1986, p. 444.
[20] Sanger, op. cit.

charged that the involvement of MIT professors in the research, though limited, was being cited by the Administration in a "manipulative effort to garner implicit institutional endorsement" of the project.[21] The success of this tactic is illustrated by the comment of Congressman Ed Zschau (whose district included Stanford University and much of Silicon Valley): "If all this money were going to the Lockheeds of the world, I wouldn't feel as good about it as I do about a program that's going to the universities."[22]

Some researchers were enlisted in this hard sell without their knowledge, or under duress. One computer scientist at the University of Washington was called by a reporter regarding his participation in SDI research. He denied having SDI funding, and only later discovered that his previous grant from the Office of Naval Research had been shifted without his knowledge to the SDI Organization. In that shift it had also been listed as a more applied project than in the original grant. One Stanford researcher described his decision to convert his DARPA funding to the SDI as necessary "in order to avoid a 40% Gramm-Rudman cut in the funds."

More direct support for military projects can be encouraged through funding as well. When David Parnas resigned from the panel of scientists investigating the feasibility of the SDI computing requirements, he noted the fact that all of the panelists stood to benefit from large research contracts if the project were well funded. Given such conflicts of interest, one can question the objectivity with which the "scientific experts" advise the public.

Legitimization of Military Control

Above and beyond any particular program, the DoD seeks public support for its overall function and for the levels and types of resources it desires. University funding can contribute to a general picture of what role the military should take in society as a whole. Everyone would agree that the DoD has responsibility for direct defense activities, but there is much less agreement about whether it should play an active role in determining the relative numbers of scientists being trained, the fields in which they are trained, or how they are educated. All military funding of research, regardless of particular projects, contributes to an increased military voice in educational policy and practice.

In computer science one often hears assertions that DARPA funding has been much better and more effective than the funding provided by civilian agencies such as the NSF. Although DARPA-sponsored research has produced many valuable results in a relatively cost-effective way, this argument needs to be examined more closely.

It is true that obtaining funding through NSF can be a frustrating and time-consuming process, and that the choice of scientific goals is influenced by many more political considerations. This is due to the nature of the peer review process (both slow and political) and the sensitivity to Congressional scrutiny (which includes special interests and pressures for geographical distribution of funding). The compensations lie along two dimensions. First, NSF has to be responsive to a broader set of concerns. One example mentioned above was that the concentration of military funding in elite schools has

---

[21] Ibid.

[22] Willie Schatz and John W. Verity, "DARPA's Big Push in AI," *Datamation*, February, 1984, pp. 48–50.

served to inhibit the development of educational programs on a broader base. NSF has put more resources into providing facilities at a larger number of universities. This may pay off not in immediate research, but by building the body of researchers that will make future advances. In a similar vein, the heavy military funding of Very High Speed Integrated Circuits (VHSIC) may have produced useful results for military hardware, but there is a serious possibility that it could actually hurt U.S. chances for commercial success in the semiconductor markets of the future.[23]

A further benefit is the democratic nature of the peer-review process. Like all democratic processes, it can be slow and frustrating, but that same inertia can also prevent abuses. To some extent DARPA was for many years a relatively benevolent dictator in its funding of basic computer science research. Recent trends (such as the direct military applications "pulling" the SCI research, and the shift of funds to more applied categories) indicate that this policy is changing. Once the dependency on military funds is established, it will not be easy to reverse it.

Responses

The issues raised above have been noted and discussed by researchers at a large number of institutions. They have responded in a variety of ways.

The most direct action that individual researchers or institutions take is to refuse military funding (either in general, from particular sources, or for particular projects). Many universities have a policy of refusing classified research, and some research institutes do not, on principle, accept funding for applied military research, although they will accept it for what they consider basic research. There are individuals, including myself and Professor Joseph Weizenbaum of MIT,[24] who reject all military funding. For the reasons discussed above, the cost of refusing funding (to both the individual researcher and his or her institution) can be high, and often it is not feasible without dropping out of the research area altogether. In many cases there are no alternate sources of support, and in others nonmilitary sources cannot provide the amount or kind of resources necessary. In order to make this strategy a viable alternative, pressure needs to be brought to bear on a larger scale—to change the overall pattern of how government research spending is managed.

As a step in this direction, criticism of military research funding has been taken up by larger groups. The Stanford SWOPSI report, mentioned above, was an attempt by a group of students and faculty to raise the issue of research funding on a larger scale and to affect public opinion. More recently, there has been a growing campaign among researchers around the country (and the world) seeking pledges that they will not accept SDI funding. As of summer 1986, over 3,800 university faculty members (mostly in physics and computer science) had signed this pledge, representing majorities in 110

---

[23] See Leslie Brueckner and Michael Borrus, "The Commercial Impact of the VHSIC Program," in Edwards and Gordon, op. cit. Also see Charles H. Ferguson, "The Microelectronics Industry in Distress," *Technology Review*, August/September, 1983.

[24] Joseph Weizenbaum, "Facing Reality: Computer Scientists Aid War Efforts," *Technology Review*, January, 1987, pp. 22–23.

research departments. They are concerned with the direct effects of the funding on campus (especially the skewing of research priorities and the potential for imposition of secrecy) and also with opposing the SDI project on the grounds that it is not feasible or effective in increasing national security.

In the case of the Strategic Defense Initiative, this refusal has had a visible impact on the program. In discussing the decision by many scientists not to work on SDI research, Lt. Col. David Audley (head of the battle management and command, control, and communications program for the SDI) told of some code used in an astronomy project that "had just what we needed, but the guy who owned the code restricted it so it couldn't be applied for SDI . . . It hurts. We need all the talent that we have."[25]

Other groups have taken public education about military research goals as a primary activity. For example, Computer Professionals for Social Responsibility has issued informational papers on several issues, including the SCI and the SDI.[26] It has also worked with universities to sponsor public debates on the technical merits of the SDI, in order to give the public a more balanced view in which computer science experts argue both sides. As an organization of computer professionals, CPSR provides expert testimony to counteract the "enlistment" through funding of university scientists into the debate over projects and strategies.

Those of us doing computer science research in the universities must acknowledge the fact that computer technology plays a major role in modern military development. We have the obligation to ourselves and to our students to seriously examine the consequences of our actions, in all of the domains I have discussed, and to make informed and responsible decisions about our work and the ways in which it is supported.

Acknowledgments

I have made extensive use of material from several other papers on military research funding, especially those of Bernie Roth, Clark Thompson, and Richard Wallstein. I thank them for their written work and for the useful discussions I have had with them.

[25] Galen Gruman, "Architecture, Simulation Key to SDI Success," IEEE Software 3:6, November, 1986, pp. 82–3.
[26] See, for example, Severo Ornstein, Brian Smith, and Lucy Suchman, "Strategic Computing," Bulletin of the Atomic Scientists, December 1984, pp. 11–15; Greg Nelson and David Redell, "The Star Wars Computer System," Abacus, Winter 1986; and the special issue on "Growing Concern About the Militarization of Artificial Intelligence," CPSR Newsletter 4:4, Fall 1986, available from CPSR, PO Box 717, Palo Alto, CA 94301.

6

Military Influence on the Electrical Engineering Curriculum since World War II

Carl Barus

Introduction

An "intriguing bond . . . exists between military enterprise, with its emphasis on uniformity, and other dominant institutions in American, indeed Western, civilization: science, engineering, business, government, religion, and education." So says Merritt Roe Smith, Professor of History of Technology at MIT and editor of *Military Enterprise and Technological Change* [1]. Smith makes it clear that this bond has a long history. We might expect, then, to find nothing new about military influence in engineering education since World War II.

However, another theme in Smith's book is the traditional reluctance of the military to adopt new technologies. Thus, the Navy resisted radio until shortly before World War I, although it was available well before that [2]. In the same way, as a battleship radar officer (I know from experience), the Navy at first restricted the use of radar in World War II. But by the end of the war, radar had proved its worth to the military (the same might be said of the atom bomb), and military mistrust of "science" had turned to awe. The stage was set for continuing post-war military support of science in the universities. The war caused a nearly discontinuous jump in military influence.

It did not go unnoticed that both radar and the atom bomb had been developed mainly by physicists acting as engineers [3]. The implication was that university engineering, especially electrical engineering, needed beefing up. For these reasons and others, military thinking and military needs soon found expression in the accredited undergraduate electrical engineering curriculum. This trend was of course accelerated by the launching of the Soviet *Sputnik* in 1957 [4].

Electrical engineering (EE) education did indeed need beefing up in the 1940s. Before the war, such topics as radio (the term "electronics" was seldom heard) were rare in undergraduate curricula. Faculties, like the Navy, resisted change. After the war, new junior faculty members, many fresh from war-time R&D or military service, were eager to introduce their special, weapons-related knowledge into the curriculum. So were those senior faculty members who had held important advisory or administrative positions in the war-time R&D establishment.

I shall argue that military perspectives have dominated the EE undergraduate curriculum since World War II.

Engineering Education

What should be the task of engineering education, or of any "higher" education? At least three goals have been frequently put forth:

a) Train people for the technical and managerial needs of industry and the state.
b) Help create the informed, thoughtful, critical citizenry necessary for democracy to survive and flourish.
c) Help and encourage each individual student to realize his or her unique potentialities.

Goal a) is politically safest for educational administrators concerned with raising money, whether in the form of alumni contributions or of grants and contracts. Administrators who give excessive priority to goals b) and c) risk falling behind in competition with those who bill their institutions as providers of "the nation's manpower needs."

On the other hand, official university rhetoric has often told us that the university's ultimate goal is the quest for truth. Clearly goal a)—meeting the needs of industry and the state—has more to do with *policies* than with truth. Commitment to goal a) tacitly grants the premises on which those policies are based—premises which truth-seekers could well find questionable. A university commitment to U.S. military policies under goal a) or through sponsored research subverts the noble educational ideals which university spokesmen proclaim in their rhetorical moments.

The continuing dominant presence of military-sponsored research on campus cannot but lead to an atmosphere of pervasive normalcy: this is the way the university *is*; this is the way the world is. In this hostile world we must have a strong "defense," and the best brains in the country should devote themselves first of all to that purpose. These propositions may sound very much like the truth to undergraduate engineers. Worse they are often accepted as "givens" by the best brains themselves.

But is it not the business of university faculties to question such a set of premises, which belong at bottom to a hard-line U.S. foreign and military policy? What is the educational effect on undergraduate minds of the subservience of their mentors to political-military money? To what extent is military activity in the university part of a self-fulfilling prophecy, an unstable feedback loop accelerating the arms race?

Academic Research after World War II

To understand the evolution of the undergraduate EE curriculum, one must look at the activities of the faculties and administrators who shaped that evolution. During the war, much academic research in science and engineering was devoted to wartime needs—notably in radar and gunfire control, not to mention atomic energy. This work was largely coordinated by the civilian-run Office of Scientific Research & Development (OSRD), a federal agency headed by Vannevar Bush, who was an MIT electrical engineer. This arrangement proved highly successful in the minds of both academics and the military.

However, it did not escape the notice of those involved that this satisfactory and productive military-academic cooperation might fade at the end of the war unless something were done. Bush and others, including Karl T. Compton of MIT and James B. Conant of Harvard sought to keep federal support for academic research continuing at least at wartime levels, but there was some disagreement among scientists, industrialists, senators and government officials as to who should set the course of research: scientist-engineers themselves, the military, the public acting through Congress, or a new federal agency [5].

Industry, too, found wartime relations with government and with academic researchers both profitable and patriotic. Thus, in 1944 Charles Wilson, president of General Electric, proposed a "permanent war economy"—that is, a permanent set of relations between business and the military [6]. Wilson's hopes appear to have been well fulfilled [7].

As for academic research support, OSRD was disbanded in 1945, and the Office of Naval Research (ONR) became the major source of funds. For the first few years, ONR was eager to support basic research having no immediate useful outcome, but by 1950 it was forced by military-political considerations to turn to more direct naval interests [4]. In the meantime the National Academy of Sciences (NAS) and the National Science Foundation (NSF) had been created. The first director of NSF had been chief scientist at ONR, and the early ONR principle of having scientific proposals evaluated by scientists (not by the public through Congress) continued at NSF [8]. Soon other branches of the Department of Defense (DoD)—and later NASA—began major funding of academic research. Compared to DoD's, NSF's funding remained minor [9].

Much DoD-funded research since the 1950s appears non-weapons-related and "basic" while in fact proposals are judged carefully according to projected military needs. DoD descriptions of a funded project may emphasize military applications, often to the surprise of the principal investigator. DoD officials have been quoted: "The extent to which a project aids the educational function of the university is not important in the decision to grant a contract" [4], [10].

What have been the dominant subjects of university EE research since World War II? In some cases, institutions have continued direct weapons R&D (often in special labs) in WWII style [1]. Aside from that work, I mention briefly some areas of key interest to the military. At first, much remained to be done in carrying further and exploiting directly the wartime advances that made radar systems possible: microwave techniques, circuit theory, electronics, feedback control, communication theory, etc. This work has led to complex electronic warfare systems, inertial navigation and missile guidance systems, among others. Solid-state electronics grew out of the need to miniaturize military systems; the development of that field is a good example of military-industrial-academic cooperation [12].

The entire field of electronic computers has been military-inspired beginning at least as far back as the ENIAC, developed at the University of Pennsylvania in WWII [13]. The field has of course become a major one for university research as well as commercial exploitation. The federal government, especially the military, has been the largest supporter of computer research and by far the largest user. Its applications, present and anticipated, include weapons control, battle management, "C^3I", cryptology, and of course Star Wars control.

Finally, the space program, which has had military motivation from the outset, has been a continuing source of academic research sponsorship [9]. "Space has been an integral part of the superpower arms race for over 25 years" [14]. The Star Wars program makes clear the military nature of government support of space research; it appears that the administration is planning to shift certain ongoing space and defense R&D to Star Wars sponsorship in an effort to spread academic commitment to the program.

Weapons-development programs have not experienced uniformly smooth sailing in the universities. Critics, both inside and outside the university community have questioned the propriety of such activity from time to time, especially during the Vietnam war. In a 1967 Senate-floor speech, Senator J. W. Fulbright, then Chairman of the Foreign Relations Committee, deplored the fact that

> more and more of our economy, our Government and our universities are adapting themselves to the requirements of continuing war—total war, limited war and cold war . . .

The universities might have insisted, he said,

> on the traditional values of our democracy, but . . . they have lent their power and influence to the monolith by welcoming contracts and consultantships from the military establishment.

Moreover, they have neglected their "fundamental reason for existence . . . the advancement of man's search for truth and happiness" [15].

On March 4, 1969, a nationwide movement among academic scientists, originating at MIT, discussed renouncing military research. A major outcome of this occasion was the formation of the Union of Concerned Scientists (UCS), still a growing public-interest group [16].

During the Vietnam war, student (and faculty) protests were effective in driving weapons R&D contracts off the campuses of many institutions—or at least having them moved to affiliated off-campus laboratories [17]. But in 1980, we read a *New York Times* headline: "Pentagon Renews Ties with Colleges: Sharp Rise in Funds for Campus Research" [18]. And in 1985, *Science* announced, "Pentagon Seeks to Build Bridges to Academe" and "Star Wars Grants Attract Universities" [19].

But the sheer incredibility of Star Wars may be causing another backlash. By mid-May

1986, 6500 academic scientists and engineers had signed a pledge not to participate in Star Wars R&D, and the list is growing [20]. At MIT, the faculty has set up an "Ad Hoc Committee on the Military Presence at MIT" at a time when MIT's DoD funding is increasing. This event was reported by *Science* under the heading: "MIT's Faustian Bargain: Signs of Malaise" [21].

The Undergraduate Engineering Curriculum

Professors teach what they know. They write textbooks about what they teach. What they know that is new comes mainly from their own research. It is hardly surprising, then, that military research in the university leads to military-centered undergraduate curricula.

To be fair to young professors enthusiastic from their WWII experiences, it must be noted that most looked to new civilian applications of such fields as electronics, microwaves, and of course nuclear energy. Indeed, we know that many such applications did occur, bringing great benefits—as well as some serious problems—to modern society. This phenomenon has been called "spinoff," a topic to be dealt with below.

One might ask them, *What else is there to teach if not the natural sequels to the great progress of war-time developments?* This seems a difficult question, but it is the wrong one [22]. To see why, let's examine the loaded words *natural, sequel* and *progress*. At the outset it is fair to observe that our present form of technological society was not inevitable in 1945.

The word *natural* in the paragraph above suggests inevitability in the absence of purposeful counteraction. In fact though, there has been continuing military input to the curriculum since World War II; "*natural* sequel" would apply only if that input had ceased abruptly after the war. One can hardly claim that the input that has occurred has been either "natural" or irrelevant to curricular development.

The work *sequel* seems somehow to include "natural," but it does more. It suggests there is only one way to go from where you are, as if you were crossing a stream on stepping stones or following a blazed trail through a forest. But who put the stones or blaze-marks there? Science and engineering are not like that. There are many possible next steps. The ones actually taken are determined by those in positions of power [23].

The word *progress* is heavily value-laden. "Progress for what?" asks Noble [24]. Progress *toward* what? Suppose electrotechnology had taken a quite different path—with emphasis on non-centralized renewable energy systems, for example. Would that have put us in a better position today than our actual position? Which would represent the greatest progress? Clearly "progress" has many directions, some more desirable than others. It is a matter of value judgment to pick a preferred direction.

It is a common belief that technology is "neutral," that any technological advance is potentially good for society—and potentially harmful as well. "Society," in this view, decides whether to use it for good or evil (consider nuclear energy, for example) [25]. This view is consistent with that of the "natural next step" of progress, which I am criticizing here. Even if there *is* a choice among several possible next steps, then the choice doesn't matter as long as it leads to "progress." Thus it doesn't matter whether the choice is motivated by military, commercial, or altruistic interests, the improved technology can be applied to any of these purposes as "society's" pleasure.

What this view holds, in effect, is that R&D *policies* make no difference. Only "society's" decision on how to use the results counts. Hence, military R&D motivation. Educators need have no qualms: they are contributing to the advance of "neutral" technology when their research (hence teaching) is given direction by the military. There is no such thing as military technology. There is only *technology*, progressing "naturally" like biological evolution.

In contrast, I am claiming that the underlying motivation for research *does* make a difference in the way technology evolves—in the direction of technological "progress" (that is, change). Under military sponsorship, the evolving technology will be suitable for military purposes and not necessarily for certain others. The nonmilitary consumer must be content with "spinoff." The technology is not neutral, for "society" has made the decision in advance as to how to use it. The curriculum, so influenced, is not neutral either.

What has been variously called "fallout," "spillover," and "spinoff" is the application of developments in military technology to civilian consumer goods or industrial use. A classic example of spinoff is the Teflon frying pan. Teflon was developed as a microwave dielectric material during World War II; it was later discovered to have properties suitable for cooking utensils. But if a non-stick frying pan is a worthy goal, why not pursue it directly?

NASA, since 1961 a sponsor of large-scale university research, purposely encouraged spinoff. "This area of technology utilization . . . was a primary aspect of NASA's mission as mandated in the Space Act of 1958 . . . and permeated NASA's concerns and hopes in the 1960s" [9].

Spinoff is frequently mentioned as a justification for military R&D in the university, and the notion is certainly good for relations with congress and the public. Worst of all, the notion of spinoff surely helps justify a military-oriented education in the minds of engineering undergraduates. It also reinforces the fallacious idea of the necessary next step in the evolution of a basically neutral technology. But it cannot in fact claim a significant fraction of the technological results of vast U.S. military and space outlays.

Evolution of the EE Curriculum

During the war, educators who had participated in wartime developments became sharply aware that the traditional undergraduate EE curriculum had proved inadequate. Physicists, not engineers, did most of the electronic engineering to develop radar and allied devices and systems. Thus began a trend toward what was later called *engineering science* as basic to the curriculum. At leading schools which aggressively pursued DOD research [26], new courses in electromagnetic theory, electronics, servomechanisms and advanced circuit theory were introduced, though at first mostly at the graduate level. However, it took years before this scientific approach (as opposed to the older emphasis on practice) became generally accepted in undergraduate EE curricula.

A number of classic EE textbooks and monographs appeared before, during and shortly after the war years, which helped to set the trend of the postwar curriculum. Among them were Terman's *Radio Engineering*, Ramo and Whinnery's *Fields and Waves in Modern Radio*, Guillemin's *Communication Networks*, Brown and Campbell's *Principle of Servomechanisms*,

Gardner and Barnes' *Transients in Linear Systems*, and of course the multivolume MIT *Radiation Laboratory Series*. These books, most of them products of war-era R&D, outlined what was to become the subject matter of the new EE curriculum. Many textbooks published since and many still appearing to the present day follow the material presented in these classics.

A number of committees of educators were established after the war (following an older tradition) to recommend curricular changes. As early as 1944, a committee of the then Society for Promotion of Engineering Education SPEE—later renamed American Society for Engineering Education (ASEE)—produced a report urging more scientific content in the undergraduate program [27]. The better-known ASEE Grinter report of 1955 introduced the term *engineering science* and went so far as to spell out engineering science core for all undergraduates [28]. Although the Grinter report caused much controversy at the time, it succeeded in establishing the engineering sciences—discovered, as it were, in World War II—as part of the curriculum.

This success was consolidated at the 1957 EE Curriculum Workshop held at MIT. Although this well-attended event brought together speakers and an audience of EE faculty members from all over the country, its chief function was to present MIT's new undergraduate curriculum. Under EE Chairman Gordon Brown, the Department had abandoned emphasis on electric power systems and had moved much material from graduate courses to the undergraduate curriculum.

Senior professors, who had been devoting most of their time to research and graduate teaching were enlisted to develop new undergraduate courses, including laboratories, and to write a new series of textbooks [29]. As Gordon Brown was at pains to point out, the new courses were "heavily influenced" by current faculty research—much of which was military-supported. The occasion was a time of enthusiastic revival for forward-looking EE educators. There is no doubt that it had tremendous influence on EE departments, textbook writers, and the Engineers' Council for Professional Development (ECPD), which then accredited undergraduate curricula.

In 1968 another committee of ASEE published its Final Report on the *Goals of Engineering Education* ("*Goals*" (30)). *Goals* devotes less attention to goals in the sense of what we are trying to do than to what and how we should teach. However, in Part C it asserts three "responsibilities of basic engineering education": (1) to the individual, (2) to society, and (3) to the engineering profession. These can be compared with the three possible goals I listed at the outset: (a) to meet the needs of industry and the state, (b) to produce a critical, informed citizenry, and (c) to help the individual realize his or her potential.

Goals properly puts the individual first (my goal (c)), but it treats the individual more as career than as a person. Numbers (2) and (3) of *Goals* amount together to my goal (a): to serve the needs of industry and the state, which I consider the least worthy of the three for educators. As an educational goal it implies an intent to produce a breed of subservient engineers rather than responsible a professionals. There is nothing corresponding to my goal (b).

Elsewhere in *Goals* it is made clear that the tacit purpose of engineering education is to meet industrial and military needs (often the same). Part B, The Engineer in Future Society, begins by summarizing 1964 RAND Corporation forecasts of the world in 1984 and in 2000. (The 1984 forecast is not far off the mark). Both forecasts give strong emphasis to military technology. *Goals* interprets the forecasts as follows:

These forecasts suggest that (1) large scale systems will be created for the development, control, and use of our natural resources, and (2) that development will continue (a) of automated manufacturing . . . , (b) of synthetic foods . . . , (c) of rapid transportation systems . . . , (d) of space programs and design of more efficient and humane [*sic*] military defense systems, and (e) biosocial systems . . . (p. 379).

The report then claims that "within this context" *Goals* "has attempted to point the way toward the development of engineering education in the decades ahead." Thus forecasts by an essentially military organization (RAND), forecasts which themselves were highly military-centered, were used by *Goals* to tell us where we *should* be going, a classic case of self-fulfilling prophecy.

The *Goals* committee, like the subservient engineers it would produce, failed to recognize that it had the power and influence to "point the way" to a far more harmonious technological future than that envisioned by RAND. Instead, the committee concerned itself chiefly with the needs of employers and "society." In a list of six supplemental goals to those articulated by an earlier committee in 1940, for example, the first item is "To prepare the student, *ideologically* [my emphasis], for constructive participation in the competive, profit-motivated economy" (p. 387).

While *Goals* thus eschews leadership in determining the shape of future technology, it does make a strong plea for broadening and improving the engineer's education. It strongly endorses the engineering-science basis of the curriculum, then widely in effect as a consequence of the Grinter report, and it elaborates on the content of engineering science. It calls for increased social-humanistic material in the curriculum and for a five-years-to-master's degree "basic engineering education." It notes the rising important of computer education. Always however, it returns to the "needs of society" (largely military) to justify its exhortations. These needs themselves are not examined but are treated as givens, nor is there any attempt to differentiate among society's numerous constituencies [31].

Most recently, engineering science may be falling into decline. Perhaps the traditional engineering sciences have temporarily been milked dry. Solid state theory seems almost irrelevant now that chip fabrication has become a standard industrial technique. Fourier transforms and correlation functions are done by computer, and the engineer can work on applications (often military) of these mathematical tools without understanding the basic theorems involved; this material has been thinned in recent textbooks (although discrete transforms and digital operations have gained). Electromagnetic theory (except at such as the fiber-optics level) no longer seems urgent, for microwave components are standardized. As with electric motors and electronic circuits, the design "learning curve" has leveled off. Only at the advanced cutting edge is engineering *science* needed now in industry. It is fast reducing to formulas and computer programs. The lofty claims of "scientific" engineering are giving way again to practical knowledge of formulas, simulation techniques and vendors.

In short, I suggest that much of the science that our military society has needed has been displaced by technical and managerial skills. Engineering *practice*, as in the 1920s and

1930s [32], but of course on a different scale, is now perceived as needed. And again physicists are taking the lead in advanced weapons work at Lawrence Livermore Lab and in the "Star Wars" program.

As *engineering science*—at least as a prestige term—declines in the undergraduate curriculum, what is taking its place? In recent years the rallying cry has been *"engineering design."* The Accreditation Board for Engineering and Technology (ABET) now requires substantial curricular content in engineering design, and it looks at individual courses as to design vs. science subject matter. Design may be more than the current term for the old "practice," but clearly it is what military-industrial employers want in the curriculum today. The subjects of EE design-oriented courses include electronic, communication and control systems; automation and robotics; design of computer systems; and computer-aided design (CAD). The latter few topics lead logically to techniques of computer-aided manufacturing (CAM). David Noble argues that modern "efficient" manufacturing methods, derived for example from Frederick W. Taylor's turn-of-the-century "scientific management," and especially automated methods such as numerical control of machine tools (developed under Air Force sponsorship) embody *per se* a military mind-set [24, 33].

I am not trying to argue here the relative merits of engineering science and engineering design in the EE curiculum, but rather that the shifts in emphasis since World War II have followed perceived military needs as expressed through the "military-industrial-academic complex."

What is wrong if the curriculum bends to the wishes of the largest group of employers of electrical engineers? After all, a majority of EEs do go into military-related work. Should not engineering schools teach what major employers want new engineers to know? To put the question another way, what voice should employers (whether or not military contractors) have in setting the undergraduate curriculum as against the voice of the community of educators? If the task of educators is to "meet the needs of society," then who is "society"? Corporations? Politicians? The military and their contractors? It seems the general public has little say. Why are not engineering educators, self-charged with meeting the "needs," foremost among those groups who *articulate* the needs? I have already suggested that too many engineering educators take a subservient position in matters of educational policy, not to mention matters of national policy. What is the responsibility of professional educators, of engineering schools and of universities in *assessing* "society's needs" as well as "meeting" them?

The phrase "military-industrial-academic complex" is not a flattering one to most educators. It suggests prostitution of traditional academic values. Should not the universities in "searching for truth" try to articulate the needs of the vast majority of the populace which has little influence on technological policy? Or should the universities act as servants to power groups by carrying out their designs?

The self-perpetuating arms race can be seen as an unstable positive-feedback system, involving on each side political, military, industrial and academic elements. This academic element today, like the others, has a vested interest in the continuing arms race; yet it is the one most able to understand the mechanisms by which the arms race escalates and the most ethically obligated to break the unstable loop.

The academic community is especially obligated to give undergraduates an understanding that nuclear destruction is not inevitable and that engineers can make a difference by their choice of work and by asserting professional, ethical values.

Conclusions

I have argued that the standard, accredited EE undergraduate curriculum since World War II has been largely determined by military needs expressed through a "military-industrial-academic complex." I have claimed that military sponsorship has not only *hastened* postwar progress, as generally agreed, but has also *shaped* it.

There are many roads that a developing technology could follow. Educators in U.S.A. have chosen the military road, and we point with pride to the "spinoffs"—from microwave ovens to jet airliners to robotized manufacturing—that have supposedly improved our world.

But suppose we had taken a different road in the first place, directly aimed at improving our world—aimed at harmonizing technology with all of society, with our ecological environment, and with third world development. That choice would have led to a *different* curriculum, but not necessarily one less rigorous, less intellectual, less scientific, less design-centered than what we have now. But the expressed goal of harmony could inspire students in a way that today's suppressed goal of military gain cannot. In particular, it could inspire a vision of a world at peace. That is what our present curriculum cannot do.

References

1. Smith, M. R. (Ed.) (1985). *Military Enterprise and Technological Change*. Cambridge, MA: MIT Press, p. 20.
2. Douglas, S. J. "The navy adopts radio," in [1].
3. McMahon, Michal A. (1984). *The Making of a Profession: A Century of Electrical Engineering in America*. New York: IEEE Press, pp. 232–233.
4. Sapolsky, H. M. (1986). "The office of no return?: the office of naval research and the issue of relevance." Presented at the Workshop of Military and Post-War Academic Science, The Johns Hopkins University, Department of History of Science, (April).
5. Reingold, N. "Vannevar Bush's new deal for research," JHU Workshop in [4]; also prepared for Amer. Acad. Arts and Sci., *Study of Knowledge in American Society*.
6. Barnet, R. (1969). *The Economy of Death*. New York: Atheneum, p. 116.
7. Melman, S. (1974). *The Permanent War Economy*. New York: Simon and Schuster.
8. D. Noble (1983). "Academia incorporated," *Science for the People*, (January/Feburary).
9. McMahon, A. M. "Big science technology and the universities: NASA and MIT in the 1960's," JHU Workshop in [4].
10. Glantz, S. A. and Albers, N. V. (1974). "Department of Defense R&D in the university," *Science*, vol. 186, (November 22), pp. 706–711.
11. For example, weapons R&D took place at Research Laboratory of Electronics and Lincoln Laboratory of MIT, Jet Propulsion Laboratory of Caltech, Applied Physics Laboratory of Johns Hopkins, and Stanford Electronics Research Laboratory.
12. Misa, T. J. "Military needs, commercial realities, and the development of the transistor," in [1].

13. McMahon, A. M. [3], p. 229.

14. Stares, P. B. (1986). *The Militarization of Space,* as reviewed and quoted by Keith L. Nelson in *Science,* vol. 233, (August 1).

15. *The New York Times,* December 14, 1967, p. 6.

16. "MIT's March 4: scientists discuss renouncing military research" (1969). *Science,* vol. 163, (News and Comment), (March 14).

17. For example, at the University of Pennsylvania, a biological warfare project ("Spicerack") was finally terminated due to protest (1967). See "University of Pennsylvania: it's hard to kick the habit," *Science,* (January 13), (News and comment).

18. *The New York Times,* (Science Times), May 13, 1980.

19. *Science,* vol. 228, (News and Comment), April 19, 1985.

20. *The Washington Post* May 14, 1986, p. A3.

21. *Science,* vol. 233, (News and Comment), July 25, 1986.

22. This question may have a familiar ring to educators who remember the surprisingly smooth transition from warbased to peacetime academic pursuits. A better question at the war's end would have been: how can academic engineering now move so as best to bring technology into line with the needs and hopes of humanity at large?

23. See, for example, A. Lovins (1977). "Energy strategy: the road not taken?," Chap. 2 in his *Soft Energy Paths.* New York: Ballinger.

24. D. Noble, "Command Performance," in [1].

25. For a critique, see N. Balabanian, "Presumed neutrality of technology," *Society,* March/April 1980; rpt. in J. H. Schaub and S. K. Dickison (eds.), *Engineering and Humanities.* New York: Wiley, 1982.

26. See, for example, Stuart W. Leslie, "Redefining post-war science and engineering at Stanford," JHU Workshop, [4]. See also, McMahon, [3].

27. McMahon, [3], p. 234.

28. Grinter, L. E., (ed.) (1955). "Report on evaluation of engineering education," *Journal of Engineering Education,* (September). See also, [3], p. 235 ff.

29. Examples of this series include: Guillemin's *Introductory Circuit Theory,* two volumes on electronics by Zimmerman and Mason, two on electromagnetic fields and waves by Fano, Chu and Adler, and one by White and Woodson on electromechanical energy conversion.

30. Walker, E. A. *et al.* (1968). "Goals of engineering education," *Journal of Engineering Education,* (January), pp. 369–446.

31. For a more extensive critique of the *Goals* report, see N. Balabanian, "The essential focus of engineering education—the individual student," *IEEE Trans. on Education,* vol. E-12, (March), p. 1–3.

32. McMahon, A. M., [3], p. 233.

33. Smith, M. R. [1], p. 12 ff.

7

Against the Imperialism of Instrumental Reason

Joseph Weizenbaum

That man has aggregated to himself enormous power by means of his science and technology is so grossly banal a platitude that, paradoxically, although it is as widely believed as ever, it is less and less often repeated in serious conversation. The paradox arises because a platitude that ceases to be commonplace ceases to be perceived as a platitude. Some circles may even, after it has not been heard for a while, perceive it as its very opposite, that is, as a deep truth. There is a parable in that, too: the power man has acquired through his science and technology has itself been converted into impotence.

The common people surely feel this. Studs Terkel, in a monumental study of daily work in America, writes,

> "For the many there is hardly concealed discontent . . . . 'I'm a machine,' says the spot welder. 'I'm caged,' says the bank teller, and echoes the hotel clerk. 'I'm a mule,' says the steel worker.' A monkey can do what I do,' says the receptionist. 'I'm less than a farm implement,' says the migrant worker. 'I'm an object,' says the high fashion model. Blue collar and white call upon the identical phrase: 'I'm a robot.' "[1]

Perhaps the common people believe that, although they are powerless, there is power, namely, that exercised by their leaders. But we have seen that the American Secretary of State believes that events simply "befall" us, and that the American Chief of the Joint Chiefs of Staff confesses to having become a slave of computers. Our leaders cannot find the power either.

Even physicians, formerly a culture's very symbol of power, are powerless as they

---

increasingly become mere conduits between their patients and the major drug manufacturers. Patients, in turn, are more and more merely passive objects on whom cures are
wrought and to whom things are done. Their own inner healing resources, their capacities
for self-reintegration, whether psychic or physical, are more and more regarded as
irrelevant in a medicine that can hardly distinguish a human patient from a manufactured
object. The now ascendant biofeedback movement may be the penultimate act in the
drama separating man from nature; man no longer even senses himself, his body, directly,
but only through pointer readings, flashing lights, and buzzing sounds produced by
instruments attached to him as speedometers are attached to automobiles. The ultimate
act of the drama is, of course, the final holocaust that wipes life out altogether.

Technological inevitability can thus be seen to be a mere element of a much larger
syndrome. Science promised man power. But, as so often happens when people are
seduced by promises of power, the price exacted in advance and all along the path, and
the price actually paid, is servitude and impotence. Power is nothing if it is not the power
to choose. Instrumental reason can make decisions, but there is all the difference between
deciding and choosing.

The people Studs Terkel is talking about make decisions all day long, every day. But
they appear not to make choices. They are, as they themselves testify, like Winograd's
robot. One asks it "Why did you do that?" and it answers "Because this or that decision
branch in my program happened to come out that way." And one asks "Why did you
get to that branch?" and it again answers in the same way. But its final answer is "Because
you told me to." Perhaps every human act involves a chain of calculations at what a
systems engineer would call decision nodes. But the difference between a mechanical act
and an authentically human one is that the latter terminates at a node whose decisive
parameter is not "Because you told me to," but "Because I chose to." At that point
calculations and explanations are displaced by truth. Here, too, is revealed the poverty
of Simon's hypothesis that

> "The whole man, like the ant, viewed as a behaving system, is quite simple. The apparent
> complexity of his behavior over time is largely a reflection of the complexity of the
> environment in which he finds himself."

For that hypothesis to be true, it would also have to be true that man's capacity for
choosing is as limited as is the ant's, that man has no more will or purpose, and, perhaps
most importantly, no more a self-transcendent sense of obligation to himself as part of
the continuum of nature, than does the ant. Again, it is a mystery why anyone would
want to believe this to be the true condition of man.

But now and then a small light appears to penetrate the murky fog that obscures man's
authentic capacities. Recently, for example, a group of eminent biologists urged their
colleagues to discontinue certain experiments in which new types of biologically functional bacterial plasmids are created.[2] They express "serious concern that some of these
artificial recombinant DNA molecules could prove biologically hazardous." Their concern
is, so they write, "for the possible unfortunate consequences of the indiscriminate

---

[1] S. Terkel *Working* (New York: Pantheon, 1974), p. xi.
[2] P. Berg *et al., Letter to Science,* July 26, 1974.

application of these techniques." Theirs is certainly a step in the right direction, and their initiative is to be applauded. Still, one may ask, why do they feel they have to give a reason for what they recommend at all? Is not the overriding obligation on men, including men of science, to exempt life itself from the madness of treating everything as an object, a sufficient reason, and one that does not even have to be spoken? Why does it have to be explained? It would appear that even the noblest acts of the most well-meaning people are poisoned by the corrosive climate of values of our time.

An easy explanation of this, and perhaps it contains truth, is that well-meaningness has supplanted nobility altogether. But there is a more subtle one. Our time prides itself on having finally achieved the freedom from censorship for which libertarians in all ages have struggled. Sexual matters can now be discussed more freely than ever before, women are beginning to find their rightful place in society, and, in general, ideas that could be only whispered until a decade or so ago may now circulate without restriction. The credit for these great achievements is claimed by the new spirit of rationalism, a rationalism that, it is argued, has finally been able to tear from man's eyes the shrouds imposed by mystical thought, religion, and such powerful illusions as freedom and dignity. Science has given to us this great victory over ignorance. But, on closer examination, this victory too can be seen as an Orwellian triumph of an even higher ignorance: what we have gained is a new conformism, which permits us to say anything that can be said in the functional languages of instrumental reason, but forbids us to allude to what Ionesco called the living truth. Just as our television screens may show us unbridled violence in "living color" but not scenes of authentic intimate love—the former by an itself-obscene reversal of values is said to be "real," whereas the latter is called obscene—so we may discuss the very manufacture of life and its "objective" manipulation, but we may not mention God, grace, or morality. Perhaps the biologists who urge their colleagues to do the right thing, but for the wrong reasons, are in fact motivated by their own deep reverence for life and by their own authentic humanity, only they dare not say so. In any case, such arguments would not be "effective," that is to say, instrumental.

If that is so, then those who censor their own speech do so, to use an outmoded expression, at the peril of their souls.

There is still another way to justify a scientist's renunciation of a particular line of research—and it is one from which all of us may derive lessons pertinent to our own lives. It begins from the principle that the range of one's responsibilities must be commensurate with the range of the effects of one's actions. In earlier times this principle led to a system of ethics that concerned itself chiefly with how persons conducted themselves toward one another. The biblical commandments, for example, speak mainly of what an individual's duties are toward his family and his neighbors. In biblical times few people could do anything that was likely to affect others beyond the boundaries of their own living spaces. Man's science and technology have altered this circumstance drastically. Not only can modern man's actions affect the whole planet that is his habitat, but they can determine the future of the entire human species. It follows therefore that man, particularly man the scientist and engineer, has responsibilities that transcend his immediate situation, that in fact extend directly to future generations. These responsibilities are especially grave since future generations cannot advocate their own cause now. We are all their trustees.[3]

The biologists' overt renunciation, however they themselves justify it, is an example which it behooves all scientists to emulate. Is this to suggest that scientists should close their minds to certain kinds of "immoral" hypotheses? Not at all. A scientific hypothesis is, at least from a scientific point of view, either true or false. This applies, for example, to Simon's hypotheses that man is "quite simple" and that he can be entirely simulated by a machine, as well as to McCarthy's hypothesis that there exists a logical calculus in terms of which all of reality can be formalized. It would be a silly error of logic to label such (or any other) hypotheses either moral or immoral or, for that matter, responsible or irresponsible.

But, although a scientific hypothesis can itself have no moral or ethical dimensions, an individual's decision to adopt it even tentatively, let alone to announce his faith in it to the general public, most certainly involves value judgments and does therefore have such dimensions. As the Harvard economist Marc J. Roberts recently wrote,

"Suppose we must choose between two hypotheses. No matter which we select, there is always the possibility that the other is correct. Obviously the relative likelihood of making a mistake when we select one or the other matters—but so too do the costs of alternative mistakes, the costs of assuming A is true when in fact B is true or vice versa. We might well choose to risk a more likely small cost than a less likely large one. Yet the magnitude of the cost of being wrong in each case cannot be determined except on the basis of our values.

"Consider an extreme example: the view that there are genetic differences in the mental functioning of different races. Suppose society were to accept this view, and it proved false. I believe that very great evil would have been done. On the other hand, suppose society adopted the view that there are no difference, and that turned out to be incorrect. I would expect much less harm to result. Given these costs, I would want evidence which made the hypothesis of interracial similarity very unlikely indeed before I would reject it. My scientific choice depends on my values, not because I am uncritical or would like to believe that there are no such differences, but because consistent choices under uncertainty can only be made by looking at the cost of making alternative kinds of errors. In contrast, a would-be 'value-neutral scientist' would presumably be willing to operate on the assumption that such differences exist as soon as evidence made it even slightly more likely than the reverse assumption.

"These questions do not arise routinely in scientific work because traditional statistical methods typically subsume them under the choice of test criteria or of the particular technique to be used in estimating some magnitude. That choice is then made on conventional or traditional grounds, usually without discussion, justification, or even acknowledgement that value choices have been made."[4]

Roberts chose to illustrate that scientific hypotheses are not "value free" by citing that values enter into the scientist's choice to tolerate or not to tolerate the potential cost of

---

[3] The point of this paragraph is argued at much greater length and very persuasively by Hans Jonas in his paper "Technology and Responsibility: Reflections on the New Tasks of Ethics," which appeared in *Social Research*, vol. 40, no. 1 (Spring 1973), pp. 31–54. I am grateful to Prof. Langdon Winner of M.I.T. for calling that paper to my attention.

[4] Marc J. Roberts, "Nature and Condition of Social Science," in *Daedalus*, Summer, 1974, pp. 54–55.

being wrong. Values, as I will try to show, enter into choices made by scientists in other (and I believe even more important) ways as well. For the moment, however, I mean only to assert that it is entirely proper to say "bravo" to the biologists whose example we have cited, and to say "shame" to the scientists who recently wrote that "a machine-animal symbiont with an animal visual system and brain to augment mecahnical functions" will be technically "feasible" within the next fifteen years.[5]

The introduction of words like "ethics" and "ought" into conversations about science seems almost always to engender a tension not unlike, I would say, the strain one can sense rising whenever, in conversation with elderly German university professors, one happens to allude to the career of one of their colleagues who prospered during the Hitler years. In the latter situation, the lowering of the social temperature betrays the fear that something "unfortunate" might be said, especially that the colleague's past inability to renounce his personal ambitions for the sake of morality might be mentioned. There is a recognition, then, of course, that the conduct not only of the colleague, but of all German academicians of the time, is in question. In the former situation, the tension betrays a similar concern, for ethics, at bottom, deals with nothing so much as renunci- ation. The tension betrays the fear that something will be said about what science, that is, scientists, ought and ought not to do. And there is a recognition that what might be talked about doesn't apply merely to science generally or to some abstract population known as scientists, but to the very people present.

Some scientists, though by no means all, maintain that the domain of science is universal, that there can be nothing which, as a consequence of some "higher" principle, ought not to be studied. And from this premise the conclusion is usually drawn that any talk of ethical "oughts" which apply to science is inherently subversive and anti-scientific, even anti-intellectual.

Whatever the merits of this argument as abstract logic may be, it is muddleheaded when applied to concrete situations, for there are infinitely many questions open to scientific investigation, but only finite resources at the command of science. Man must therefore choose which questions to attack and which to leave aside. We don't know, for example, whether the number of pores on an individual's skin is in any way correlated with the number of neurons in his brain. There is no interest in that question, and therefore no controversy about whether or not science ought to study it. The Chinese have practiced acupuncture for many centuries without arousing the interest of Western science. Now, suddenly, Western scientists have become interested. These examples illustrate that scientific "progress" does not move along some path determined by nature itself, but that it mirrors human interests and concerns.

Surely finely honed human intelligence is among the scarcest of resources available to modern society. And clearly some problems amenable to scientific investigation are more important than others. Human society is therefore inevitably faced with the task of wisely distributing the scarce resource that is its scientific talent. There simply is a responsibility

---

[5] O. Firschein, M. A. Fischler, L. S. Coles, and Tenenbaum, J. M. "Intelligent Machines Are on the Way," *IEEE Spectrum*, July 1974, p. 43. The opinion I have quoted here appears to be the consensus of "41 artificial intelligence experts—including members of the International Joint Artificial Intelligence Council." The paper makes clear that the opinion is shared by the paper's authors.

—it cannot be wished away—to decide which problems are more important or interesting or whatever than others. Every specific society must constantly find ways to meet responsibility. The question here is *how*, in an open society, these ways are to be found; are they to be dictated by, say, the military establishment, or are they to be open to debate among citizens and scientists? If they are to be debated, then why are ethics to be excluded from the discussion? And, finally, how can anything sensible emerge unless all first agree that, contrary to what John von Neuman asserted, technological possibilities are not irresistible to man? "Can" does not imply "ought."

Unfortunately, the new conformism that permits us to speak of everything except the few simple truths that are written in our hearts and in the holy books of each of man's many religions renders all arguments based on these truths—no matter how well thought out or eloquently constructed—laughable in the eyes of the scientists and technicians to whom they may be addressed. This in itself is probably the most tragic example of how an idea, badly used, turns into its own opposite. Scientists who continue to prattle on about "knowledge for its own sake" in order to exploit that slogan for their self-serving ends have detached science and knowledge from any contact with the real world. A central question of knowledge, once won, is its validation; but what we now see in almost all fields, especially in the branches of computer science we have been discussing, is that the validation of scientific knowledge has been reduced to the display of technological wonders. This can be interpreted in one of only two ways: either the nature to which science is attached consists entirely of raw material to be molded and manipulated as an object; or the knowledge that science has purchased for man is entirely irrelevant to man himself. Science cannot agree that the latter is true, for if it were, science would lose its license to practice. That loss would, of course, entail practical consequence (involving money and all that) which scientists would resist with all their might. If the former is true, then man himself has become an object. There is abundant evidence that this is, in fact, what has happened. But then knowledge too has lost the purity of which scientists boast so much; it has then become an enterprise no more or less important and no more inherently significant than, say, the knowledge of how to lay out an automobile assembly line. Who would want to know that "for its own sake"?

This development is tragic, in that it robs science of even the possibility of being guided by any authentically human standards, while it in no way restricts science's potential to deliver ever-increasing power to men. And here too we find the root of the much-talked-about dehumanization of man. An individual is dehumanized whenever he is treated as less than a whole person. The various forms of human and social engineering we have discussed here do just that, in that they circumvent all human contexts, especially those that give real meaning to human language.

The fact that arguments which appeal to higher principles—say, to an individual's obligations to his children, or to nature itself—are not acknowledged as legitimate poses a serious dilemma for anyone who wishes to persuade his colleagues to cooperate in imposing some limits on their research. If he makes such arguments anyway, perhaps hoping to induce a kind of conversion experience in his colleagues, then he risks being totally ineffective and even being excommunicated as a sort of comic fool. If he argues for restraint on the grounds that irreversible consequences may follow unrestrained research, then he participates in and helps to legitimate the abuse of instrumental reason (say, in the guise of cost-benefit analyses) against which he intends to struggle.

As is true of so many other dilemmas, the solution to this one lies in rejecting the rules of the game that gave rise to it. For the present dilemma, the operative rule is that the salvation of the world—and that *is* what I am talking about—depends on converting others to sound ideas. That rule is false. The salvation of the world depends only on the individual whose world it is. At least, every individual must act as if the whole future of the world, of humanity itself, depends on him. Anything less is a shirking of responsibility and is itself a dehumanizing force, for anything less encourages the individual to look upon himself as a mere actor in a drama written by anonymous agents, as less than a whole person, and that is the beginning of passivity and aimlessness.

This is not an argument for solipsism, nor is it a counsel for every man to live only for himself. But it does argue that every man must live for himself first. For only by experiencing his own intrinsic worth, a worth utterly independent of his "use" as an instrument, can he come to know those self-transcendent ends that ultimately confer on him his identity and that are the only ultimate validators of human knowledge.

But the fact that each individual is responsible for the whole world, and that the discharge of that responsibility involves first of all each individual's responsibility to himself, does not deny that all of us have duties to one another. Chief among these is that we instruct one another as best we can. And the principal and most effective form of instruction we can practice is the example our own conduct provides to those who are touched by it. Teachers and writers have an especially heavy responsibility, precisely because they have taken positions from which their example reaches more than the few people in their immediate circle.

This spirit dictates that I must exhibit some of my own decisions about what I may and may not do in computer science. I do so with some misgivings, for I have learned that people are constantly asking one another what they must do, whereas the only really important question is what they must be. The physicist Steven Weinberg, in commenting on recent criticisms of science, writes, for example,

> "I have tried to understand these critics by looking through some of their writings, and have found a good deal that is pertinent, and even moving. I especially share their distrust of those, from David Ricardo to the Club of Rome, who too confidently apply the methods of the natural sciences to human affairs. But in the end I am puzzled. What is it they want *me* to do?"[6]

My fear is that I will be understood to be answering a question of the kind Weinberg asks. That is not my intention. But the risk that I will be misunderstood cannot excuse me from my duty.

There is, in my view, no project in computer science as such that is morally repugnant and that I would advise students or colleagues to avoid. The projects I have been discussing, and others I will mention, are not properly part of computer science. Computers are not central to the work of Forrester and Skinner. The others are not computer science, because they are for the most part not science at all. They are, as I have

---

[6] Steven Weinberg, "Reflections of a Working Scientist," in *Daedalus*, Summer 1974, p. 41.

already suggested, clever aggregations of techniques aimed at getting something done. Perhaps because of the accidents of history that caused academic departments whose concerns are with computers to be called "computer science" departments, all work done in such departments is indiscriminately called "science," even if only part of it deserves that honorable appellation. Tinkerers with techniques (gadget worshippers, Norbert Wiener called them) sometimes find it hard to resist the temptation to associate themselves with science and to siphon legitimacy from the reservoir it has accumulated. But not everyone who calls himself a singer has a voice.

Not all projects, by very far, that are frankly performance-oriented are dangerous or morally repugnant. Many really do help man to carry on his daily work more safely and more effectively. Computer-controlled navigation and collision-avoidance devices, for example, enable ships and planes to function under hitherto disabling conditions. The list of ways in which the computer has proved helpful is undoubtedly long. There are, however, two kinds of computer applications that either ought not be undertaken at all, or, if they are contemplated, should be approached with utmost caution.

The first kind I would call simply obscene. These are ones whose very contemplation ought to give rise to feelings of disgust in every civilized person. The proposal I have mentioned, that an animal's visual system and brain be coupled to computers, is an example. It represents an attack on life itself. One must wonder what must have happened to the proposers' perception of life, hence to their perceptions of themselves as part of the continuum of life, that they can even think of such a thing, let alone advocate it. On a much lesser level, one must wonder what conceivable need of man could be fulfilled by such a "device" at all, let alone by only such a device.

I would put all projects that propose to substitute a computer system for a human function that involves interpersonal respect, understanding, and love in the same category. I therefore reject Colby's proposal that computers be installed as psychotherapists, not on the grounds that such a project might be technically infeasible, but on the grounds that it is immoral. I have heard the defense that a person may get some psychological help from conversing with a computer even if the computer admittedly does not "understand" the person. One example given me was of a computer system designed to accept natural-language text via its typewriter console, and to respond to it with a randomized series of "yes" and "no." A troubled patient "conversed" with this system, and was allegedly led by it to think more deeply about his problems and to arrive at certain allegedly helpful conclusions. Until then he had just drifted in aimless worry. In principle, a set of Chinese fortune cookies or a deck of cards could have done the same job. The computer, however, controlled a certain aura—derived, of course, from science —that permitted the "patient" to believe in it where he might have dismissed fortune cookies and playing cards as instruments of superstition. The question then arises, and it answers itself, do we wish to encourage people to lead their lives on the basis of patent fraud, charlatanism, and unreality? And, more importantly, do we really believe that it helps people living in our already overly machine-like world to prefer the therapy administered by machines to that given by other people? I have heard this latter question answered with the assertion that my position is nothing more than "let them eat cake." It is said to ignore the shortage of good human psychotherapists, and to deny to troubled people what little help computers can now give them merely because presently available computers don't yet measure up to, say, the best psychoanalysis. But that objection misses the point entirely. The point is (Simon and Colby to the contrary notwithstanding) that there are some human functions for which computers *ought* not to be substituted. It has nothing to do with what computers can or cannot be made to do. Respect, understanding, and love are not technical problems.

The second kind of computer application that ought to be avoided, or at least not undertaken without very careful forethought, is that which can easily be seen to have irreversible and not entirely foreseeable side effects. If, in addition, such an application cannot be shown to meet a pressing human need that cannot readily be met in any other way, then it ought not to be pursued. The latter stricture follows directly from the argument I have already presented about the scarcity of human intelligence.

The example I wish to cite here is that of the automatic recognition of human speech. There are now three or four major projects in the United States devoted to enabling computers to understand human speech, that is, to programming them in such a way that verbal speech directed at them can be converted into the same internal representations that would result if what had been said to them had been typed into their consoles.

The problem, as can readily be seen, is very much more complicated than that of natural-language understanding as such, for in order to understand a stream of coherent speech, the language in which that speech is rendered must be understood in the first place. The solution of the "speech-understanding problem" therefore presupposes the solution of the "natural-language-understanding problem." And we have seen that, for the latter, we have only "the tiniest bit of relevant knowledge." But I am not here concerned with the technical feasibility of the task, nor with any estimate of just how little or greatly optimistic we might be about its completion.

Why should we want to undertake this task at all? I have asked this question of many enthusiasts for the project. The most cheerful answer I have been able to get is that it will help physicians record their medical notes and then translate these notes into action more efficiently. Of course, anything that has any ostensible connection to medicine is automatically considered good. But here we have to remember that the problem is so enormous that only the largest possible computers will ever be able to manage it. In other words, even if the desired system were successfully designed, it would probably require a computer so large and therefore so expensive that only the largest and best-endowed hospitals could possibly afford it—but in fact the whole system might be so prohibitively expensive that even they could not afford it. The question then becomes, is this really what medicine needs most at this time? Would not the talent, not to mention the money and the resources it represents, be better spent on projects that attack more urgent and more fundamental problems of health care?

But then, this alleged justification of speech-recognition "research" is merely a rationalization anyway. (I put the word "research" in quotation marks because the work I am here discussing is mere tinkering. I have no objection to serious scientists studying the psycho-physiology of human speech recognition.) If one asks such questions of the principal sponsor of this work, the Advanced Research Projects Agency (ARPA) of the United States Department of Defense, as was recently done at an open meeting, the answer given is that the Navy hopes to control its ships, and the other services, their weapons, by voice commands. This project then represents, in the eyes of its chief sponsor, a long step toward a fully automated battlefield. I see no reason to advise my students to lend their talents to that aim.

I have urged my students and colleagues to ask still another question about this project: Granted that a speech-recognition machine is bound to be enormously expensive, and that only governments and possibly a very few very large corporations will therefore be able to afford it, what will they use it for? What can it possibly be used for? There is no question in my mind that there is no pressing human problem that will more easily be solved because such machines exist. But such listening machines, could they be made, will make monitoring of voice communication very much easier than it now is. Perhaps the only reason that there is very little government surveillance of telephone conversations in many countries of the world is that such surveillance takes so much manpower. Each conversation on a tapped phone must eventually be listened to by a human agent. But speech-recognizing machines could delete all "uninteresting" conversations and present transcripts of only the remaining ones to their masters. I do not for a moment believe that we will achieve this capability within the future so clearly visible to Newell and Simon. But I do ask, why should a talented computer technologist lend his support to such a project? As a citizen I ask, why should my government spend approximately 2.5 million dollars a year (as it now does) on this project?

Surely such questions presented themselves to thoughtful people in earlier stages of science and technology. But until recently society could always meet the unwanted and dangerous effects of its new inventions by, in a sense, reorganizing itself to undo or to minimize these effects. The density of cities could be reduced by geographically expanding the city. An individual could avoid the terrible effects of the industrial revolution in England by moving to America. And America could escape many of the consequences of the increasing power of military weapons by retreating behind its two oceanic moats. But those days are gone. The scientist and the technologist can no longer avoid the responsibility for what he does by appealing to the finite powers of society to transform itself in response to new realities and to heal the wounds he inflicts on it. Certain limits have been reached. The transformations the new technologies may call for may be impossible to achieve, and the failure to achieve them may mean the annihilation of all life. No one has the right to impose such a choice on mankind.

I have spoken here of what ought and ought not to be done, of what is morally repugnant, and of what is dangerous. I am, of course, aware of the fact that these judgments of mine have themselves no moral force except on myself. Nor, as I have already said, do I have any intention of telling other people what tasks they should and should not undertake. I urge them only to consider the consequences of what they do do. And here I mean not only, not even primarily, the direct consequences of their actions on the world about them. I mean rather the consequences on themselves, as they construct their rationalizations, as they repress the truths that urge them to different courses, and as they chip away at their own autonomy. That so many people so often ask what they must do is a sign that the order of being and doing has become inverted. Those who know who and what they are do not need to ask what they should do. And those who must ask will not be able to stop asking until they begin to look inside themselves. But it is everyone's task to show by example what questions one can ask of oneself, and to show that one can live with what few answers there are.

But just as I have no license to dictate the actions of others, neither do the constructors of the world in which I must live have a right to unconditionally impose their visions on me. Scientists and technologists have, because of their power, an especially heavy responsibility, one that is not to be sluffed off behind a facade of slogans such as that of technological inevitably. In a world in which man increasingly meets only himself, and then only in the form of the products he has made, the makers and designers of these products—the buildings, airplanes, foodstuffs, bombs, and so on—need to have the most profound awareness that their products are, after all, the results of human choices. Men could instead choose to have truly safe automobiles, decent television, decent housing for everyone, or comfortable, safe, and widely distributed mass transportation. The fact that these things do not exist, in a country that has the resources to produce them, is a consequence, not of technological inevitability, not of the fact that there is no longer anyone who makes choices, but of the fact that people have chosen to make and to have just exactly the things we have made and do have.

It is hard, when one sees a particularly offensive television commercial, to imagine that adult human beings sometime and somewhere sat around a table and decided to construct exactly that commercial and to have it broadcast hundreds of times. But that is what happens. These things are not products of anonymous forces. They are the products of groups of men who have agreed among themselves that this pollution of the consciousness of the people serves their purposes.

But, as has been true since the beginning of recorded history, decisions having the most evil consequences are often made in the service of some overriding good. For example, in the summer of 1966 there was considerable agitation in the United States over America's intensive bombing of North Viet Nam. (The destruction rained on South Viet Nam by American bombers was less of an issue in the public debate, because the public was still persuaded that America was "helping" that unfortunate land.) Approximately forty American scientists who were high in the scientific estate decided to help stop the bombing by convening a summer study group under the auspices of the Institute of Defense Analyses, a prestigious consulting firm for the Department of Defense. They intended to demonstrate that the bombing was in fact ineffective.[7]

They made their demonstration using the best scientific tools, operations research and systems analysis and all that. But they felt they would not be heard by the Secretary of Defense unless they suggested an alternative to the bombing. They proposed that an "electronic fence" be placed in the so-called demilitarized zone separating South from North Viet Nam. This barrier was supposed to stop infiltrators from the North. It was to consist of, among other devices, small mines seeded into the earth, and specifically designed to blow off porters' feet to be insensitive to truck passing over them. Other devices were to interdict truck traffic. The various electronic sensors, their monitors, and so on, eventually became part of the so-called McNamara line. This was the beginning of what has since developed into the concept of the electronic battlefield.

The intention of most of these men was not to invent or recommend a new technology that would make warfare more terrible and, by the way, less costly to highly industrialized

---

[7] See the Gravel Edition of *The Pentagon Papers* (Boston, Mass.: Beacon Press, 1971), volume IV, especially p. 115.

nations at the expense of "underdeveloped" ones. Their intention was to stop the bombing. In this they were wholly on the side of the peace groups and of well-meaning citizens generally. And they actually accomplished their objective; the bombing of North Viet Nam was stopped for a time and the McNamara fence was installed. However, these enormously visible and influential people could have instead simply announced that they believed the bombing, indeed the whole American Viet Nam adventure, to be wrong, and that they would no longer "help." I know that at least some of the participants believed that the war was wrong; perhaps all of them did. But, as some of them explained to me later, they felt that if they made such an announcement, they would not be listened to, then or ever again. Yet, who can tell what effect it would have had if forty of America's leading scientists had, in the summer of 1966, joined the peace groups in coming out flatly against the war on moral grounds? Apart from the positive effect such a move might have had on world events, what negative effect did their compromise have on themselves and on their colleagues and students for whom they served as examples?

There are several lessons to be learned from this episode. The first is that it was not technological inevitability that invented the electronic battlefield, nor was it a set of anonymous forces. Men just like the ones who design television commercials sat around a table and chose. Yet the outcome of the debates of the 1966 Summer Study were in a sense foreordained. The range of answers one gets is determined by the domain of questions one asks. As soon as it was settled that the Summer Study was to concern itself with only technical questions, the solution to the problem of stopping the bombing of the North became essentially a matter of calculation. When the side condition was added that the group must at all costs maintain its credibility with its sponsors, that it must not imperil the participants' "insider" status, then all degrees of freedom that its members might have had initially were effectively lost. Many of the participants have, I know, defended academic freedom, their own as well as that of colleagues whose careers were in jeopardy for political reasons. These men did not perceive themselves to be risking their scholarly or academic freedoms when they engaged in the kind of consulting characterized by the Summer Study. But the sacrifice of the degrees of freedom they might have had if they had not so thoroughly abandoned themselves to their sponsors, whether they made that sacrifice unwittingly or not, was a more potent form of censorship than any that could possibly have been imposed by officials of the state. This kind of intellectual self-mutilation, precisely because it is largely unconscious, is a principal source of the feeling of powerlessness experienced by so many people who appear, superficially at least, to occupy seats of power.

A second lesson is this. These men were able to give the counsel they gave because they were operating at an enormous psychological distance from the people who would be maimed and killed by the weapons systems that would result from the ideas they communicated to their sponsors. The lesson, therefore, is that the scientist and technologist must, by acts of will and of the imagination, actively strive to reduce such psychological distances, to counter the forces that tend to remove him from the consequences of his actions. He must—it is as simple as this—think of what he is actually doing. He must learn to listen to his own inner voice. He must learn to say "No!"

Finally, it is the act itself that matters. When instrumental reason is the sole guide to action, the acts it justifies are robbed of their inherent meanings and thus exist in an ethical vacuum. I recently heard an officer of a great university publicly defend an important policy decision he had made, one that many of the university's students and faculty opposed on moral grounds, with the words: "We could have taken a moral stand, but what good would that have done?" But the good of a moral act inheres in the act itself. That is why an act can itself ennoble or corrupt the person who performs it. The victory of instrumental reason in our time has brought about the virtual disappearance of this insight and thus perforce the delegitimation of the very idea of nobility.

I am aware, of course, that hardly anyone who reads these lines will feel himself addressed by them—so deep has the conviction that we are all governed by anonymous forces beyond our control penetrated into the shared consciousness of our time. And accompanying this conviction is a debasement of the idea of civil courage.

It is a widely held but a grievously mistaken belief that civil courage finds exercise only in the context of world-shaking events. To the contrary, its most arduous exercise is often in those small contexts in which the challenge is to overcome the fears induced by petty concerns over career, over our relationships to those who appear to have power over us, over whatever may disturb the tranquility of our mundane existence.

If this book is to be seen as advocating anything, then let it be a call to this simple kind of courage. And, because this book is, after all, about computers, let that call be heard mainly by teachers of computer science.

I want them to have heard me affirm that the computer is a powerful new metaphor for helping us to understand many aspects of the world, but that it enslaves the mind that has no other metaphors and few other resources to call on. The world is many things, and no single framework is large enough to contain them all, neither that of man's science nor that of his poetry, neither that of calculating reason nor that of pure intuition. And just as a love of music does not suffice to enable one to play the violin—one must also master the craft of the instrument and of music itself—so is it not enough to love humanity in order to help it survive. The teacher's calling to teach his craft is therefore an honorable one. But he must do more than that: he must teach more than one metaphor, and he must teach more by the example of his conduct than by what he writes on the blackboard. He must teach the limitations of his tools as well as their power.

It happens that programming is a relatively easy craft to learn. Almost anyone with a reasonably orderly mind can become a fairly good programmer with just a little instruction and practice. And because programming is almost immediately rewarding, that is, because a computer very quickly begins to behave somewhat in the way the programmer intends it to, programming is very seductive, especially for beginners. Moreover, it appeals most to precisely those who do not yet have sufficient maturity to tolerate long delays between an effort to achieve something and the appearance of concrete evidence of success. Immature students are therefore easily misled into believing that they have truly mastered a craft of immense power and of great importance when, in fact, they have learned only its rudiments and nothing substantive at all. A student's quick climb from a state of complete ignorance about computers to what appears to be a mastery of programming, but is in reality only a very minor plateau, may leave him with a euphoric sense of achievement and a conviction that he has discovered his true calling. The teacher, of course, also tends to feel rewarded by such students' obvious enthusiasm, and therefore continues to encourage it, perhaps unconsciously and against his better judgment. But for the student this may well be a trap. He may so thoroughly commit himself to what he naively perceives to be computer science, that is, to the mere polishing of his programming skills, that he may effectively preclude studying anything substantive.

Unfortunately, many universities have "computer science" programs at the undergraduate level that permit and even encourage students to take this course. When such students have completed their studies, they are rather like people who have somehow become eloquent in some foreign language, but who, when they attempt to write something in that language, find they have literally nothing of their own to say.

The lesson in this is that, although the learning of a craft is important, it cannot be everything.

The function of a university cannot be to simply offer prospective students a catalogue of "skills" from which to choose. For, were that its function, then the university would have to assume that the students who come to it have already become whatever it is they are to become. The university would then be quite correct in seeing the student as a sort of market basket, to be filled with goods from among the university's intellectual inventory. It would be correct, in other words, in seeing the student as an object very much like a computer whose storage banks are forever hungry for more "data." But surely that cannot be a proper characterization of what a university is or ought to be all about. Surely the university should look upon each of its citizens, students and faculty alike, first of all as human beings in search of —what else to call it?—truth, and hence in search of themselves. Something should constantly be happening to every citizen of the university; each should leave its halls having become someone other than he who entered in the morning. The mere teaching of craft cannot fulfill this high function of the university.

Just because so much of a computer-science curriculum is concerned with the craft of computation, it is perhaps easy for the teacher of computer science to fall into the habit of merely training. But, were he to do that, he would surely diminish himself and his profession. He would also detach himself from the rest of the intellectual and moral life of the university. The university should hold, before each of its citizens, and before the world at large as well, a vision of what it is possible for a man or a woman to become. It does this by giving ever-fresh life to the ideas of men and women who, by virtue of their own achievements, have contributed to the house we live in. And it does this, for better or for worse, by means of the example each of the university's citizens is for every other. The teacher of computer science, no more nor less than any other faculty member, is in effect constantly inviting his students to become what he himself is. If he views himself as a mere trainer, as a mere applier of "methods" for achieving ends determined by others, then he does his students two disservices. First, he invites them to become less than fully autonomous persons. He invites them to become mere followers of other people's orders, and finally no better than the machines that might someday replace them in that function. Second, he robs them of the glimpse of the ideas that alone purchase for computer science a place in the university's curriculum at all. And in doing that, he blinds them to the examples that computer scientists as creative human beings might have provided for them, hence of their very best chance to become truly good computer scientists themselves.[8]

Finally, the teacher of computer science is himself subject to the enormous temptation to be arrogant because his knowledge is somehow "harder" than that of his humanist colleagues. But the hardness of the knowledge available to him is of no advantage at all. His knowledge is merely less ambiguous and therefore, like his computer language, less expressive of reality. The humanities particularly

> "have a greater familarity with an ambiguous, intractable, sometimes unreachable [moral] world that won't reduce itself to any correspondence with the symbols by means of which one might try to measure it. There is a world that stands apart from all efforts of historians to reduce [it] to the laws of history, a world which defies all efforts of artists to understand its basic laws of beauty. [Man's] practice should involve itself with softer than scientific knowledge . . . that is not a retreat but an advance."[9]

The teacher of computer science must have the courage to resist the temptation to arrogance and to teach, again mainly by his own example, the validity and the legitimacy of softer knowledge. Why courage in this connection? For two reasons. The first and least important is that the more he succeeds in so teaching, the more he risks the censure of colleagues who, with less courage than his own, have succumbed to the simplistic worldviews inherent in granting imperial rights to science. The second is that, if he is to teach these things by his own example, he must have the courage to acknowledge, in Jerome Bruner's words, the products of his subjectivity.

Earlier I likened the unconscious to a turbulent sea, and the border dividing the conscious, logical mind from the unconscious to a stormy coastline. That analogy is useful here too. For the courage required to explore a dangerous coast is like the courage one must muster in order to probe one's unconscious, to take into one's heart and mind what it washes up on the shore of consciousness, and to examine it in spite of one's fears. For the unconscious washes up not only the material of creativity, not only pearls that need only be polished before being strung into structures of which one may then proudly speak, but also the darkest truths about one's self. These too must be examined, understood, and somehow incorporated into one's life.

If the teacher, if anyone, is to be an example of a whole person to others, he must first strive to be a whole person. Without the courage to confront one's inner as well as one's outer worlds, such wholeness is impossible to achieve. Instrumental reason alone cannot lead to it. And there precisely is a crucial difference between man and machine: Man, in order to become whole, must be forever an explorer of both his inner and his outer realities. His life is full of risks, but risks he has the courage to accept, because, like the explorer, he learns to trust his own capacities to endure, to overcome. What could it mean to speak of risk, courage, trust, endurance, and overcoming when one speaks of machines?

---

[8] Almost immediately after writing the last few paragraphs, I received a paper entitled "Methodology and the Study of Religion, Some Misgivings" from Wilfred Cantwell Smith, McCulloch Professor of Religion at Dalhousie University, Halifax, Nova Scotia. His paper expresses, among many other important ideas, many of the same points I have mentioned here. Since I had read some earlier papers by Prof. Smith, I cannot help but believe that I owe some of the ideas expressed here to him.

[9] C. Oglesby, "A Juanist Way of Knowledge," lecture given to the M.I.T. Technology and Culture Seminar, October 26, 1971. Copies are available from the Rev. John Crocker, Jr., 312 Memorial Drive, Cambridge, MA 02139.

·Index·